MADAMA BUTTERFLY

Giacomo Puccini

1 8 5 8 – 1 9 2 4

Madama Butterfly . . . . Renata Scotto
Suzuki . . . . Anna Di Stasio
Kate Pinkerton . . . . Silvana Padoan
B. F. Pinkerton . . . . Carlo Bergonzi
Sharpless . . . . Rolando Panerai
Goro . . . . Piero De Palma
Prince Yamadori . . . . Giuseppe Morresi
Il Bonzo . . . . Paolo Montarsolo
Il Commissario . . . . Mario Rinaudo

Conducted by Sir John Barbirolli C. H.
Orchestra e Coro del Teatro dell'Opera di Roma
Chorus Master: Gianni Lazzari

MADAMA BUTTERFLY

MADAMA BUTTERFLY

Giacomo Puccini

TEXT BY DANIEL S. BRINK

Additional commentary by William Berger

BLACK DOG
& LEVENTHAL
PUBLISHERS
NEW YORK

Published by
Black Dog & Leventhal Publishers, Inc.
151 West 19th Street
New York, NY 10011

Distributed by
Workman Publishing Company
708 Broadway
New York, NY 10003

Manufactured in China

Cover and interior design by Liz Driesbach.

Cover image © Archivo Iconografico, S.A./Corbis

ISBN-10 : 1-57912-510-7
ISBN-13 : 978-1-57912-510-3

h g f e d c b

Library of Congress Cataloging-in-Publication Data available on file.

Madama Butterfly is a tragic story of love, misunder-standing, cultural mismatching, honor, and dishonor, all woven together. A seemingly simple tale about a young Japanese girl and her love for an American soldier who is careless with her devotion, *Butterfly* is brought to life—and eventually to her death—by Puccini's powerfully heartbreaking music. He touches on so many aspects of the human experience—overwhelming love, unbearable loss, rejection, motherhood, and clashing cultural ideals—with tenderness, honesty, and poignance.

Explore the pages of this book: learn about the origins of the operas, the lives of the composers, and the world of opera singers and conductors. Listen to the complete opera on the two CD's included in the inside front and back covers of this book, while following along with the complete libretto. You will find both an English and an Italian version, complete with annotations by the author.

Enjoy this book and enjoy the music.

ABOUT THE AUTHOR

$\mathcal{D}$aniel S. Brink is the Artistic Advisor and Principal Coach/Accompanist for the Colorado Opera Festival, Artistic Director for the Company Singers, a development program for young operatic hopefuls and Artistic Director/Conductor of the Colorado Springs Choral Society small ensemble, MOSI-AC. Mr. Brink is a lecturer in Music and principal accompanist at The Colorado College, and has performed extensively in the United States and Europe. He is a highly regarded director, recitalist, teacher, adjudicator, and writer.

ACKNOWLEDGEMENTS

I would like to thank Annette Megneys of the Colorado College Music Library and Jan Boothroyd, Executive Director of the Colorado Opera Festival for their invaluable assistance in researching this project. I would also like to thank my editor, Jessica MacMurray, whose influence afforded me the opportunity to write about these beloved works.

MADAMA BUTTERFLY

$\mathcal{A}$t the beginning of the twentieth century, Giacomo Puccini had already established himself as the heir apparent to Giuseppe Verdi—the leading Italian opera composer for the better part of the 1800s. In keeping with the nineteenth-century ideal of the suffering artist, Puccini had had his share of struggles in achieving this standing.

Giacomo Puccini was born on December 22, 1858, in the small provincial capital of Lucca, in Tuscany. He was the seventh of eight children (six of whom were elder sisters) born to Michele and Albina-Magi Puccini. For five generations, Puccini men had studied at the conservatory in Naples. There they acquired the requisite skills to maintain the honored position of Maestro Di Capella Palatina at the Cathedral of San

Giacomo Puccini (1858-1924) in a portrait by Arturo Rietti.

Martino in Lucca. The Puccini family had manned this post since 1739, and it was expected that the young Giacomo would also assume the family's musical duties at the cathedral in due course.

However, it was not to be. In January of 1864, when Giacomo was five years old, his father died unexpectedly. It was decided that his widow's brother, Fortunato Magi, would assume the musical leadership at the Cathedral until the young Giacomo was old enough and sufficiently trained to take over his late father's position. Although his intention to follow in his father's footsteps was never realized, he would, in fact, become the last and most famous of the composing Puccinis—but in a far different artistic arena.

Noël Eadie as Butterfly, 1928.

Giacomo's childhood was undistinguished. He did not do well in school and had the reputation of being lazy, expending his creative energies on various pranks, rather than on his studies. He was a tall and handsome young man with a winning smile whose charm always kept him just out of the reach of real trouble. His initial musical studies were undertaken with his uncle, Fortunato Magi, whose severe and even abusive tutorial style engendered little love for the art in his student. Magi believed that Giacomo showed no particular talent in music and frequently despaired that the boy had no potential as a professional.

The great light in the early part of Puccini's life was his mother, whose unfailing belief in him would clear the path for all his early successes. After his graduation from the local seminary school, where he repeated his final year of study, his mother enrolled him at the Pacini Institute, Lucca's music conservatory. It was there, under the sympathetic tutelage of Carlo Angeloni, that Puccini's musical route began to come into focus. Angeloni had been a student of Puccini's father, Michele, and had since distinguished himself as a composer of opera and choral works. He befriended young Giacomo, engaging him not only in the classroom, where he introduced Puccini to the genius of Verdi's scores, but also as a hunting partner in the countryside surrounding Lucca. Angeloni instilled in him a fascination with and love for music that his stern uncle never could.

Puccini's skills began to flourish, and he was soon able to contribute to the fiscal stability of his mother's household by working as an organist in local churches. It was also during this time that the adolescent Puccini developed his unfortunate passion for cigarettes, a habit which would eventually lead to his premature death from throat cancer in 1924. Ever the prankster, it is said that Puccini stole pipes from the various organs on which he performed and sold them for scrap metal to support his smoking habit. He also earned money by playing in a small dance orchestra. By the age of sixteen, he had so distinguished himself at the Pacini Institute that he received the first prize in 1875 for organ performance.

Puccini's vision for Act 1, in a painting dated 1904.

Madama Butterfly Atto I

Early in 1876, Puccini had his first taste of professional opera at the Teatro Nuovo (now the Teatro Verdi) in Pisa. It was a production of Verdi's *Aïda*, which had enjoyed unparalleled success since its premiere in Cairo in 1871. Giacomo and two friends walked seven hours to Pisa and, lacking the funds to buy tickets, hid in the empty gallery of the theater for three hours awaiting the performance. Some years later, Puccini said of that performance, "When I heard *Aïda* in Pisa, I felt that a musical window had opened for me."

Despite this small tribute to Verdi, Puccini's art is cut from a much different cloth. Indeed, the style of his operas owes much to Richard Wagner. The majority of Verdi's operas are written as a series of set numbers, in what had been the Italian tradition. In contrast, Puccini's operas are "through composed"—a continuous outpouring of melody unified by the use of musical motives which represent specific characters, emotions, and situations. Puccini's ability to cleverly and subtly manipulate these motives is one of the factors which sets him above his contemporaries working in the same style.

After graduation from the Pacini Institute, it became clear that Puccini's musical ambitions deserved to reach beyond the confines of the artistic life of Lucca. It was decided that he would go to study at the Conservatory in Milan, the center of Italian musical life and the home of La Scala—Italy's greatest opera house. But the Puccini family was not financially able to accomplish this feat. Nonetheless, Giacomo's mother was determined to see her son's potential realized. She petitioned the queen for a scholarship, which was granted. Support was also secured from her late husband's cousin, Dr. Nicolai Ceru, who had become interested in Giacomo's progress in the latter part of his studies at the Institute. The young Puccini would attend the Milan Conservatory.

Puccini arrived in Milan in the fall of 1880. At twenty-two years of age, he was past the normal acceptance age by several years, but the excellence of his entrance exams assured him a place at the Conservatory. There, as at the Pacini Institute, he was befriended by a sympathetic mentor. Amilcare Ponchielli was a fine composer and professor whose opera, *La Gioconda*, set the direction for Italian opera in the latter part of the nineteenth century and remains in the repertoire today.

Yasuko Hayashi as Butterfly.

Puccini's three years at the Milan Conservatory were characterized by extreme financial hardship on the one hand and great artistic joy, development and discovery on the other. In late June of 1883, he completed his final examinations more than satisfactorily and began work on his final composition project, an orchestral work entitled *Capriccio Sinfonico*. It would have an obligatory first performance under the baton of a leading conductor from La Scala, and if successful, it would open doors for Puccini at Italy's leading publishing houses. *Capriccio Sinfonico* premiered on July 14, 1883, and won Puccini critical praise. He graduated from the Milan Conservatory with the Bronze Medal, the school's highest honor.

During the six years following his graduation, Puccini produced his first two operatic efforts, *Le Villi* and *Edgar*, both with librettos by Fernando Fontana. *Le Villi* enjoyed a modicum of success and served to establish Puccini with Giulio Ricordi, the leading publisher of Italian opera at the time. Ricordi was the great Verdi's publisher as well, and he saw Puccini as the rightful successor to Verdi. Puccini's second opera, *Edgar*, however, was a failure. Both works showed the promise of great things to come, but they suffered from weak librettos not well suited to Puccini's specific talents.

Personal problems also plagued Puccini during this period. Not long after the premiere of *Le Villi*, Puccini's mother died. The loss was devastating to the young composer, coming as it did just when he was beginning to prove himself worthy

The Royal Opera House at Covent Garden, London.

Puccini at a rehearsal for Madama Butterfly.

of her unfailing belief in him. After his mother's death, Puccini's return to work was slow and fitful, and he would never fully recover from the loss.

Puccini's private life at this time was tumultuous. He had always had an eye for the ladies, and he became involved with Elvira Bonturi Gemignani, the wife of a prominent business-man in Lucca. Their affair caused her to leave her husband, taking her small daughter with her and leaving a younger son with her husband. Several months later, on December 23, 1886, Elvira bore Puccini's only child, Antonio. The people of Puccini's hometown were outraged, and he would never live there again. Elvira stayed with Puccini, eventually marrying him after the death of her husband, but the passion which brought them together would wane in the ensuing years. Puccini's entire adult life was punctuated by various sexual scandals—both real and imagined—which scuttled any hope of domestic bliss with Elvira.

It was not only in Puccini's personal life that a fascination with women held sway. Eight of his twelve operas are named for their heroines, and eight of his major female characters die, their tragic deaths invariably linked in some way to their unwavering love for a naive or unscrupulous man.

In 1889, following the failure of *Edgar* and under increased pressure from his publishers to see a return on their investment—they had been supporting him since 1884—Puccini began making plans for his next opera, *Manon Lescaut.* This subject, based on a novel by Abbé Prévost, had already been successfully set by Jules Massenet, a fact that only seemed to fire Giacomo's desire to tackle it. Here the young composer began to trust his own dramatic instincts and doggedly hounded his librettists until he got what he wanted. As a result, the libretto of *Manon Lescaut* can be attributed to no fewer than seven poets, including Ruggiero Leoncavallo, Marco Praga, Giuseppe Giacosa and Luigi Illica (with whom Puccini would have a long and fruitful collaboration), as well as Puccini's publisher, Giulio Ricordi, and even Puccini himself!

Until the premiere of *Manon Lescaut* on February 1, 1893, there had been no clear successor to Verdi's Italian operatic throne. Leoncavallo had successfully produced his famous *I Pagliacci*, Pietro Mascagni had achieved renown for *Cavalleria Rusticana* and Alfredo Catalani's *La Wally* had been highly acclaimed. Now Puccini hoped to join their ranks, and both the composer and his publisher were nervous, but hopeful.

Their hopefulness was rewarded. *Manon Lescaut* was a complete triumph, both with the public and with the critics. In fact, it would be the only completely unqualified success of Puccini's career. Now, not only Ricordi, but the press hailed Puccini as the successor to the esteemed Verdi. In only a few years, *Manon* was performed throughout Europe and in South America. Puccini's future was secure, and his financial struggles were forever ended.

The rest, as they say, is history. Exactly three years after the premiere of *Manon*, on February 1, 1896, *La Bohème*, with libretto by Illica and Giacosa, was unveiled. Based on Henri Murger's *La Vie de Bohème*, the story of the poverty-stricken young Parisian artists was not uniformly praised by critics, but it was enthusiastically embraced by the public and quickly became a mainstay of the operatic repertoire. On January 14, 1900, amid rumored bomb threats and various other intrigues, Puccini's *Tosca* premiered. Reviews found fault with the subject and libretto, but

Sylvia Sydney and Cary Grant in a 1933 movie version of *Butterfly*.

24

agreed on the quality of the music. And though the opening-night audience was not overwhelmingly appreciative, the opera continued to play to sold-out houses. The team of Puccini, Illica, Giacosa and Ricordi appeared to be unbeatable.

Puccini divided his time between traveling to oversee productions of his operas in the capitals of Europe and enjoying the sanctuary of his villa in the sleepy village of Torre del Lago. There he could indulge his passion for hunting and fishing and compose in peace and quiet. Puccini was feted wherever he went, and he spent the rest of his life alternately buoyed by the adulation of the public and subdued by his basically shy and unassuming nature.

The summer of 1900 found Puccini in London to oversee the Covent Garden premiere of *Tosca*. At the suggestion of friends, he attended a performance of *Madame Butterfly*, a one-act melodrama by the successful American playwright and producer, David Belasco. Belasco's play was based on a novella by an American writer-journalist, John Luther Long, which had appeared in *Century Magazine* in January 1898. Puccini was deeply moved by the tragic story of the little geisha, and despite the fact that he understood no English, he was able to follow the plot. He was especially taken with Cio-Cio-San's night-long vigil awaiting Pinkerton's return and with the scene's accompanying lighting effects. In the Belasco version, this particular scene was completely wordless, but lasted fourteen minutes.

David Belasco, author of the original *Madame Butterfly*.

When he saw Belasco's *Madame Butterfly*, Puccini had been seeking a source for his next opera for several months. The process of choosing a new subject was always a restless time for him, and he relentlessly drove his collaborators until a story was chosen and a libretto was in his hands. Since the failure of *Edgar*, Puccini had been very careful to choose plots and characters that touched and convinced him personally. He had already entertained several possible stories for his next opera and found them all wanting, but he saw in this exotic tale the qualities that would inspire him again.

Immediately following the play's performance, Puccini supposedly approached Belasco asking permission for the rights to set *Madame Butterfly* as an opera. Verbal permission was granted, although it took many months for the official permission to come through. In the meantime, Illica and Giacosa were able to acquire Long's story and translate it into Italian in order to begin work.

Puccini was excited about the project, and the creative process went smoothly compared to the heated deliberations characteristic of the development of previous works. But injury and illness delayed the completion of *Butterfly*. Puccini had a passion for cars; he loved their speed and was among the first Italian composers to own one. On a foggy evening in February 1903, he was returning home from Lucca with Elvira and their son, Tonio, when their chauffeur rounded a slippery curve and went off the road. The vehicle landed fifteen feet down an embankment. Elvira and Tonio were able to walk away from the accident, but the driver's thigh was broken, and

Puccini was trapped under the car, unconscious and with a severe fracture of his right tibia. Fortunately, a doctor living nearby had heard the crash and came to Puccini's aid, taking the composer to his home for the night.

The leg didn't mend properly and had to be rebroken and reset. The healing process was inexplicably slow, and his doctors discovered that Puccini had diabetes. Bedridden and unable to work, the despondent composer wrote to Illica, "Farewell to everything, farewell to *Butterfly*, farewell to my life. How can I endure the terrible summer months? What will I do? My God, this is enough to age a newborn child." But by June there were signs of improvement, and when the completed libretto was delivered, Puccini devised a way to sit at the piano and work.

Slowly regaining his strength, and happy to be at work again, Puccini completed the score on December 27, 1903. He wrote to a friend, "It's not bad. We'll see."

The premiere was set for February 14, 1904, at La Scala in Milan. Because of Puccini's unaccustomed confidence in the quality of the work, a veil of secrecy surrounded the rehearsal period, with no previews of the libretto in the press and none of the customary invitations to the final rehearsal for the local intelligentsia. The scores were not even allowed to leave the theatre, so the singers had to study their roles on site.

Originally conceived as a prologue and two acts, then as three acts—one of which was to take place at the American Consulate as in Long's story—Puccini decided finally to set the work in two acts. The first act was the wedding and lasted an hour; the second act began three years after Pinkerton's departure and lasted almost an hour and a half. Illica, Giacosa and Ricordi were certain that the public, accustomed to acts lasting no more than forty minutes, would not stand for scenes of this length. They suggested that the second act be divided in two at the close of the vigil. The composer, however, was adamant and would not consider the alteration.

Puccini was pleased with his cast, especially Rosina Storchio as Cio-Cio-San, to whom he wrote before the opening, "My good wishes are superfluous! So true, so delicate, so moving is your great art that the public must succumb to it! … Tonight then, with sure confidence and much affection, dear child!"

The stage was set for a triumphant premiere. Puccini was confident, the music and the singers were ready to thrill the public, and the critics were poised to be amazed. But, despite (or because of) all the anticipation, the premiere was one of the greatest disasters in operatic history. The audience, at first apathetic, soon became hostile. The performance was continually interrupted by laughter, shouts, catcalls, animal noises and accusations that Puccini had stolen from himself and from other composers. At one point, Storchio's kimono was caught by a breeze and billowed up causing someone to shout, "Butterfly's pregnant … Toscanini's baby!" (The soprano and Arturo Toscanini were embroiled in a rather well-publicized affair at the time.) With the final curtain, stony silence.

Although it was clear to the press and to many in attendance that the hostility was borne out of envy of Puccini's

A painting of Butterfly
done in 1904 for the
opera's premiere.

unparalleled standing, he was devastated. He withdrew the opera and returned the advance which he had been paid. The work was not completely flawed, but both the opera and Puccini had fallen victim to a well-organized attempt to sabotage his extraordinary career.

Within a week, Puccini, still convinced that *Butterfly* was his best work to date, began work with his librettists on revisions, which were surprisingly few. The wedding scene in the first act was tightened up, deleting unnecessary details; an intermission was added to the second act, as Puccini's collaborators had requested; Pinkerton's aria, *Addio, fiorito asil,* was added—this had been a bone of contention with Giacosa, whose lines were now restored; and the final encounter with Pinkerton's American wife, Kate, was reworked.

On May 28, 1904, the revised opera was given at the smaller provincial house at Brescia, although the house was again filled with critics and interested parties from Milan. It was a complete triumph, with thirty-two curtain calls and seven encores. Puccini's faith in his little Butterfly was vindicated, and the opera officially began its journey toward continuing international fame and success.

Puccini's faith in his work was well-founded. Though he was accused of rehashing ideas already heard in *La Bohème*, nothing could have been further from the truth. He had gone to great pains to incorporate oriental flavors into his score. A number of the melodies he used are authentic Japanese folk

Puccini with his librettists, Giuseppe Giacosa and Luigi Illica.

songs which he learned in interviews with the wife of the Japanese Ambassador to Italy and through other research. He also constructed original tunes based on the pentatonic scale—a five-note scale used extensively in Japanese music. Yet, these oriental colors never seem like self-conscious interpolations into the score. They are always fully integrated into Puccini's own style.

This score also marks Puccini's first extensive use of the whole-tone scale and the harmonies derived from it. This ambiguous sound is thought of as an "impressionistic" musical tool, most closely identified with the work of Claude Debussy, a French contemporary of Puccini's whom he greatly admired. In his next opera, *La Fanciulla del West* (The Girl of the Golden West), Puccini used this technique even more lavishly, having been exposed to Debussy's opera, *Pelléas et Mélisande.*

Since the early days of his career, Puccini had always been lauded for his colorful orchestrations, and *Butterfly* represented his richest score to date. The percussion section is employed liberally and includes the unusual sounds of Japanese bells and Japanese tam-tam or gong. As morning breaks following Butterfly's vigil awaiting Pinkerton's arrival, the score even requires bird calls. He also employs an unusual technique in the famous *Humming Chorus* heard during Butterfly's vigil, using voices as instruments, an innovation he would repeat in later scores.

Arturo Toscanini (1867–1957).

In short, Puccini was not a composer willing to rest on his laurels. He constantly challenged himself to expand the palette of musical colors and textures from which he produced his art.

How is it that this opera survives while the story and play on which it is based have fallen into oblivion? At the turn of the twentieth century, the countries of the Far East had been open to the west for some forty years, and there was widespread interest among westerners in oriental culture. Eastern settings were popular in the Western theatre and in literature, but while the delicacy and balance of Eastern art was highly appreciated, the people of the Far East were perceived as backward. Western nations sought to "improve" the culture of the Far East with the infiltration of western, Christian ideals.

The condescending Western view of the Japanese people is all too clear in the work of Long and Belasco. Cho-Cho-San's (her name is spelled differently in the Belasco version) pidgin English is an embarrassing parody, not unlike the treatment of African-American speech in the popular Minstrel shows of the same era. These works would never hold the stage today.

Puccini's appreciation of, and perspective on, the international picture is debatable. Unlike Verdi, whose intricate plots frequently reflected some social or political injustice, Puccini chose to focus his art on the intimate setting of human emotions. While Pinkerton is certainly a cad to Puccini, he is at least partially redeemed by his remorseful acknowledgment of what his actions have caused. And Butterfly, while naive, is still afforded the dignity of beautiful and poetic Italian dialogue. Thus, Puccini's protagonists, regardless of their setting, are characters who are focused, essentially, on the human experience, and to whom the world will always relate.

Act 1

The curtain opens on a beautiful Japanese scene: a small, delicate Japanese house on a hill overlooking the harbor and city of Nagasaki. An American Naval Officer, Benjamin Franklin Pinkerton, is being given a tour of the house he is to rent with his new bride, Cio-Cio-San (who he has never seen), by Goro, the marriage broker. The young American is delighted with the movable walls and their functional flexibility, and he makes a point to ask the location of the bedroom.

With a clap of his hands, Goro summons the servants. Among them is Suzuki, Cio-Cio-San's longtime personal maid and confidante. She proceeds to recite a litany of compliments to her new American employer, but is interrupted by Pinkerton who inquires about the guest list for the wedding. Goro enumerates the many friends, relatives and officials who will be in attendance.

Sharpless, the American Consul, breathlessly enters after his climb up the hill. As Sharpless admires the house and the view, Pinkerton explains that he has leased the property for nine hundred ninety-nine years, an agreement which can be canceled in any month he chooses. To the opening phrase of "The Star Spangled Banner," Pinkerton rhapsodizes about the life of a young naval officer, going where he chooses, facing adventures of every sort, and having a love in every port. Sharpless comments about the irresponsibility of the young man's vision, but his opinion goes unnoticed. They toast to "America forever!"

Pinkerton asks Goro if his young bride is beautiful. Goro responds with poetic descriptions of the young geisha and then is suddenly sent away to see if she's coming.

Sharpless inquires as to whether Pinkerton's intentions in this marriage are honorable. Pinkerton replies that he is only living for the moment and, for the moment, he must possess Butterfly. Sharpless confesses that the girl had visited his office and that she seemed to take the marriage quite seriously. He warns the officer not to break her heart, but his warning goes unheeded, and Pinkerton proposes a toast to the happy day when he will have a real marriage to an American girl.

Suddenly, Goro reenters, and women's voices can be heard in the distance. Butterfly and her friends are about to arrive. As they climb the hill, the girls remark about the beauty of the sea and sky, and Butterfly's voice soars above them, declaring

Renata Scotto in a 1986 production at the Metropolitan Opera in New York.

that in all the world there is no happier girl than she, for love is to greet her at the top of the hill. Upon their arrival, she asks her companions to bow to Pinkerton.

Pinkerton is charmed by Butterfly's innocence and beauty. Sharpless asks if she is from Nagasaki. Butterfly replies she is, and from a once wealthy family, but now they are poor and must work as geishas to keep the wolf from the door. The Americans are amused by her candor. When asked about her family, Butterfly replies that she has no siblings, only her poverty-stricken mother. Sharpless inquires about her father, and she curtly responds, "Dead." The gentlemen then engage in a guessing game regarding her age. She finally confesses that she is fifteen, rather old. The Americans respond in shocked delight—she is only a child.

Other guests are arriving, and Goro announces the presence of the Imperial Commissioner, the Registrar and Cio-Cio-San's family. The family members mill around, gossiping negatively about Pinkerton, Butterfly and the whole affair. Pinkerton, in turn, finds the family amusing. Goro tries to quiet them, and Sharpless comments how lucky Pinkerton is to have found such a lovely creature. But he warns Pinkerton again that Butterfly's love is in earnest and therefore he should be careful.

As the family goes into the garden, Pinkerton shows Butterfly the house. She takes the opportunity to show Pinkerton

Preceding Spread: Butterfly, waiting for Pinkerton's return, sings of her frustration and loneliness, Act II.

44

some of the things she has brought with her, asking his permission to keep them. She has brought some silk kerchiefs, a belt, a pipe, a mirror, a fan, and various other personal items. When Pinkerton reacts with amusement to a jar of makeup, she quickly discards it. She holds up a long narrow box, and Pinkerton asks her what it holds. She replies that it is something sacred, and he may see it when there are not so many people around. In an aside, Goro explains to Pinkerton that it is the knife the Mikado had sent to her father, with the order to kill himself, which he did. Butterfly has also brought her *Ottoke*, small statues representing the spirits of her ancestors.

Taking Pinkerton aside, Butterfly confides that early that morning she went to the Mission, and for love of him, had abandoned her religion to embrace his American God. She confesses that she would abandon family, friends—everything— for love of him.

Goro calls for silence, and the brief marriage ceremony takes place, involving only the reading and signing of a document. Congratulations are offered all around, and the officials and Sharpless prepare to leave. As he goes, Sharpless warns Pinkerton one last time to be prudent.

Pinkerton proposes a toast to their marriage, but as they are about to drink, the festive mood is interrupted by the arrival of Butterfly's uncle, the Bonze. In angry tones, he informs the guests that Butterfly had gone to the mission and betrayed her family and her religion, for which he reviles her. Pinkerton responds angrily, ordering him to leave. The Bonze and the family comply, but not before they vehemently renounce Butterfly. Their outraged cries continue as they leave.

Pinkerton tenderly turns to comfort Butterfly, saying that all the Bonzes in Japan are not worth one tear from her lovely eyes. She feels better and kisses his hand, saying she's been told it is a sign of great respect in his culture. They are interrupted by a voice from the house. Butterfly tells Pinkerton it is only Suzuki saying her evening prayers.

They observe that night is falling, and Suzuki is asked to close the house and bring Butterfly's robe. Butterfly goes in to change and comes out in the radiant white robe of a bride. Pinkerton is smitten. They join in a rapturous love duet, and Pinkerton asks her to confess her love. She declares her joy at their marriage, and in tender phrases she asks Pinkerton to love her only a little, as he would love a baby, purely and humbly. His ardor increases, but she is hesitant, having heard that in America, when butterflies are caught, they are impaled and imprisoned in a glass case. He admits that this is true, but that it is only done so the butterflies may not fly away. Gradually she succumbs to the lure of the night and his advances, and they go inside.

Act 2

PART ONE

The curtain opens on Suzuki and Butterfly in a semi-darkened
room of the house. It has been three years since Pinkerton's
departure. Suzuki prays in a sorrowful monotone to the Japanese household gods. Butterfly, no longer the innocent girl,
stands immobile and declares that the Japanese gods are fat
and lazy. She is sure her American god would answer their
prayers more quickly, but he probably doesn't know where
they are.

   Butterfly asks how long it will be before they run out of
money and starve, waiting for her American husband's return.
Suzuki shows her a few coins, saying that if Pinkerton does-
n't return soon they will have nothing but trouble. Butterfly
insists he will come. Suzuki is dubious. In an increasingly heated exchange, Butterfly tries to convince Suzuki of his return.
He had promised, after all, to return when the robins nest.

47

Butterfly insists Suzuki admit he will return. Suzuki finally does, but then breaks into sobs.

Butterfly's angry insistence abates, and in comforting tones she describes his return. One fine day, a ship will enter the harbor—his ship—and they will see him begin to climb the hill. She will not respond to his call at first, partly to tease him, partly so she won't die from joy and excitement at their first encounter. All this will come to pass, she assures Suzuki, and she will wait for him with certain faith.

Goro and Sharpless arrive, and Butterfly welcomes the American Consul to her "American" household with enthusiasm. She is the perfect hostess until Sharpless informs her that he has brought a letter from Pinkerton. This news only enhances her joy. She inquires as to the nesting habits of robins in America, whereupon she hears Goro laughing (he has remained outside) and sends him away. Sharpless feigns ignorance regarding the difference in nesting patterns between Japanese and American robins.

Butterfly tells him that Goro insists that she marry a wealthy local prince. Yamadori. She no sooner finishes, but Goro reenters, telling Sharpless that Butterfly is in dire straits because her family has disowned her. Suddenly, Yamadori enters in a flurry of princely grandeur to woo Butterfly. She greets him with polite amusement, but tells him that she is already married. Goro and Yamadori assert that her marriage to Pinkerton is at an end and that she has been abandoned.

Puccini, four years before his death, in a 1920 portrait.

She responds dramatically that in America, wives are not so easily divorced. An American husband who tried to leave his wife would be dealt with by the courts. She concludes her speech offhandedly and sends Suzuki for tea. The suitor and his agent ask Sharpless to try to make Butterfly listen to reason: Her husband no longer wants her, but they've heard Pinkerton's ship is due. Sharpless interrupts, telling them

that Pinkerton doesn't want to see her, and he has been sent to deliver the bad news. Yamadori once again offers Butterfly his heart and hand, but she politely refuses, and she is left alone with Sharpless.

They sit together so that Sharpless can read Pinkerton's letter to her, but the reading is continually interrupted by her rhapsodic reflections upon hearing his words. Sharpless

Butterfly, confident that her husband will return, denies Yamadori's proposal, Act II.

stops short when the bad news is about to be read, and asks her what she would do if Pinkerton were not to return. Butterfly is wounded by the suggestion. In halting phrases, she responds that she could go back to being a geisha, or better, she could die. Sharpless gently suggests she consider Yamadori's offer. Even more deeply wounded by this thought, Butterfly asks Suzuki to see Sharpless to the door. Apologetically, he turns to go, but turns back to her again when she suddenly feels faint.

In a defiant tone, Butterfly asks, "He forgot me?" She turns and leaves the room as a triumphant theme surges in the orchestra. She returns carrying the child who is the result of her marriage to Pinkerton, and she asks if he, too, will be forgotten. Sharpless, shocked, inquires if Pinkerton knows of the child's existence. She replies that he doesn't, but surely if he knew a son awaited him, he would return. Addressing the child, who is too young to understand, Butterfly marvels that Sharpless would send her into the streets again to entertain as a geisha, begging for the support of the public for her and her child. She reaffirms that she would rather die. Moved by her plight, Sharpless assures her that Pinkerton will be informed about his son. He asks the child's name, and Butterfly directs the child to tell Sharpless that his name is Sorrow, but upon his father's return, his name will be Joy. Sharpless departs.

A sharp cry is heard from Suzuki. She has found Goro lurking outside and has learned that he has been spreading the rumor that the child is illegitimate. In a rage, Butterfly grabs the knife with which her father committed *hara-kiri* and swoops toward Goro. As he narrowly escapes, Butterfly turns to the child and hysterically assures him of his father's return. Suddenly, a gunboat thunders in the harbor.

Butterfly and Suzuki take a small telescope from the table and rush to the terrace. Butterfly strains to identify the incoming ship. It is the *Abraham Lincoln*—Pinkerton's ship! Butterfly's faith in his return is vindicated. The women proceed to fill the house and its entrance with flowers to welcome Pinkerton. Butterfly then asks Suzuki's help in dressing herself for his arrival. Looking in the mirror, she notices that her long wait has aged her face, and she decides to mask the toll of her sorrow with a small application of color. She also colors the cheeks of her little son. Cutting three small holes in the paper wall of the little house, Butterfly, her son and her servant take their places to wait and watch for Pinkerton's arrival. Night falls to the accompaniment of the off-stage *Humming Chorus.* The child gradually falls asleep and Suzuki rests, but Butterfly steadfastly stares out at the city below.

Act 2

As the curtain opens we hear sailors calling to one another in the harbor. Day is dawning and Butterfly has not moved. Suzuki rouses from her sleep and convinces Butterfly to take the child and get some rest, assuring her that she will awaken her when Pinkerton arrives.

No sooner have Butterfly and the child retired then there is a knock at the door. It is Sharpless and Pinkerton, who immediately silence Suzuki's excitement, telling her not to rouse Butterfly. Suzuki tells them of their preparations for Pinkerton's arrival and of Butterfly's all-night vigil. She then notices a woman in Victorian dress standing in the garden. She nervously inquires about the lady's identity, and Sharpless finally tells her it is Kate, Pinkerton's American wife. Suzuki bursts into sobs of despair. Sharpless explains that they arrived early to enlist her aid in asking Butterfly to give up the child to Pinkerton and Kate. A moving trio ensues in which Sharpless tries to persuade Suzuki to intercede for them with Butterfly, Pinkerton reflects on the flood of memories that surround him in the little house, and Suzuki reflects on the hopelessness of Butterfly's situation.

Pinkerton is overcome with remorse and says he must leave. Sharpless pointedly reminds him that he was warned of the potential for this disaster before his wedding. In an emotional outpouring, Pinkerton bids farewell to his flowered haven and the happiness he had known there. Admitting that he is the vile cause of all of Butterfly's sorrows, he flees the scene.

Suzuki then promises Kate she will tell Butterfly of Pinkerton's wish to take their son, but she demands that she must be allowed to break the news in private. At that moment we hear Butterfly call to Suzuki from the other room. Suzuki's efforts to keep Butterfly from entering are in vain—she knows Pinkerton has arrived! She searches the room excitedly, but he is nowhere to be found. She sees Sharpless, then notices Kate in the garden and asks who she is and what she wants. Sharpless replies that Kate is the innocent cause of all Butterfly's sorrows and asks forgiveness for her. Butterfly realizes the truth. She will be asked to surrender her son. After a moment of desperate disbelief, she resigns herself and says she will obey Pinkerton's wishes. Kate asks Butterfly if she will ever be able to forgive her. In a magnanimous gesture, Butterfly wishes Kate happiness and tells her that Pinkerton may return in half an hour to get the child. Sharpless and Kate depart.

Butterfly collapses, weeping. She tells Suzuki to close up the room—there is too much light and too much springtime. Suzuki complies. Butterfly asks where the child is. Suzuki tells her he is playing and offers to bring him to her, but Butterfly tells her to let him play and to go and be with him. Suzuki objects, but Butterfly sternly orders her to go, and she tearfully complies.

Alone, Butterfly kneels before the image of Buddha. She then takes the knife with which her father had killed himself, kisses it and reads the inscription on the blade aloud: "Let him die with honor who can no longer live with honor." She lifts the blade to plunge it into her throat, when suddenly Suzuki pushes the child into the room. He runs toward her with outstretched arms.

Yasuko Hayashi as Butterfly.

Butterfly drops the knife, embraces the child, and in a poignant aria bids farewell to her son, begging him to look well at her features and always to remember her. She then tells him to go and play. She hands him a doll and an American flag, gently blindfolds him and faces him away from her. She takes up the knife, goes behind a screen and stabs herself. We hear the knife drop, and Butterfly begins to crawl from behind the screen to hold her child one last time. In the distance, we hear Pinkerton call her name, but as he and Sharpless arrive she falls dead beside her son. Pinkerton falls on his knees beside her lifeless body, and Sharpless, sobbing, embraces her orphaned child.

MADAMA BUTTERFLY

Giacomo Puccini

1858 - 1924

Madama Butterfly . . . . Renata Scotto
Suzuki . . . . Anna Di Stasio
Kate Pinkerton . . . . Silvana Padoan
B. F. Pinkerton . . . . Carlo Bergonzi
Sharpless . . . . Rolando Panerai
Goro . . . . Piero De Palma
Prince Yamadori . . . . Giuseppe Morresi
Il Bonzo . . . . Paolo Montarsolo
Il Commissario . . . . Mario Rinaudo

Conducted by Sir John Barbirolli C. H.
Orchestra e Coro del Teatro dell'Opera di Roma
Chorus Master: Gianni Lazzari

THE PERFORMERS

RENATA SCOTTO (Cio-Cio-San) was born in Savona, Italy. She began her vocal studies at age 14 as a mezzo-soprano, but after two years of study moved to Milan, where, under the guidance of Mercedes Llopart, she became a soprano. After winning a competition, Scotto was afforded the opportunity to make her debut in 1952 in her home town as the tragic Violetta in Verdi's *La Traviata*. In 1953 she repeated the role at Milan's Teatro Nuovo, and the following year, just barely in her twenties, she made her debut at La Scala. There, she sang the secondary role of Walter in Catalani's *La Wally*, but she soon left the famous house for the opportunity to sing leading roles in smaller provincial houses. Appearances in Rome and Venice soon followed, and by 1957 Scotto made her London debut as Mimì in Puccini's *La Bohème*. That same year, she got the "big break" that changed her professional life forever. On three days notice, she assumed the difficult role of Amina in Bellini's *La Sonnambula* at the Edinburgh Festival, replacing an ailing Maria Callas. Triumphant, Scotto returned to La Scala as a star, and her career was launched in all the major opera houses on both sides of the Atlantic and in Japan, where she was the first interpreter of the title role in Donizetti's *Lucia di Lammermoor*.

Scotto's American debut took place in 1960, again as Mimì, at the Chicago Lyric Opera. She debuted at New York's Metropolitan Opera in 1965 as Cio-Cio-San, the role heard here. Her early career included the bel canto roles of Lucia, Amina, Adina in Donizetti's *L'Elisir d'Amore*, and Bellini's *Norma*, as well as various Verdi and Puccini heroines. In the decades that followed she added to her repetoire such roles as Marguerite in Gounod's Faust, Berthe in Meyerbeer's *Le Prophete*, the heavier Verdi heroines, and verismo gems like the title role in Cilea's *Adriana Lecouvreur* and Maddalena in Giordano's *Andrea Chénier*. She was the first to sing all three heroines in Puccini's *Il Trittico* (three one-act operas) in one evening at the Met. Also at the Met, Scotto was the first performer ever to sing both Mimì and Musetta in *La Bohème* in a single season.

In recent years Scotto has moved into the German repertoire, singing the Marschalin in Strauss's *Der Rosenkavalier* and a number of Wagner roles as well. In 1987, she made her directing debut with a production of *Madame Butterfly* at the Met, a production in which she, among others, also sang the title role. She now divides her time between singing, directing and concert work.

Scotto, with over twenty-five complete opera recordings to her credit, has always been known for her vocal beauty and agility and her unfailing dramatic instincts. She is the quintessential singing actress, and this recording finds her at the

height of her powers. This *Butterfly* is the first of two complete recordings she did of the work, and she portrays the geisha's innocence and tender charm with unequaled perception and clarity.

CARLO BERGONZI (Lieutenant Benjamin Franklin Pinkerton) was born in Polisene, Italy—near Parma—in 1924. His initial studies were undertaken at the Boito Conservatory in Parma, but were interrupted by World War II, during which he was, for a time, a prisoner of the Nazis. After the war, he resumed his studies and made his debut in 1948 as a baritone in the role of Figaro in Rossini's *Il Barbiere di Siviglia* at Lecce. After a period of study, he debuted as a tenor in 1951 at Bari in the title role of Giordano's *Andrea Chénier*.

Renata Scotto, 1986.

Bergonzi's La Scala debut took place in 1953 when he created the title role in Napoli's *Masaniello*, and he continued to appear there until the early 1970s. He made his London debut at the Stoll Theatre in 1953 as Don Alvaro in Verdi's *La Forza del Destino*, and he repeated the role at his Covent Garden debut in 1962. He appeared at Covent Garden regularly until 1985. His final role there was as Edgardo in Donizetti's *Lucia di Lammermoor*.

American audiences first heard Bergonzi in 1955, when he debuted at the Chicago Lyric Opera in a double bill, singing Luigi in Puccini's *Il Tabarro* and Turiddu in Mascagni's *Cavalleria Rusticana* in the same evening. In 1956, he debuted at the Metropolitan Opera as Radames in Verdi's *Aïda*. He sang at the Met for over thirty years, making his final appearance there in 1988 in the role of Rodolpho in Verdi's *Luisa Miller*.

Bergonzi had a beautiful lyrico-spinto voice and was prized for his seamless line and his capacity to sing soft phrases with ease and control. These talents stood him in good stead with the lighter Italian repertoire, including Alfredo in Verdi's *La Traviata* and Nemorino in Donizetti's *L'Elisir d'Amore*. Yet his voice had the power to soar over the orchestral texture, making his portrayals of the heavier repertoire, such as Verdi's Radames, equally attractive. His favorite role was that of Riccardo in Verdi's *Un Ballo in Maschera*.

In recent years Begonzi has made a series of farewell performances at the various houses graced by his talents through his 45-year career. He appeared in concert singing Neopolitan songs with The Opera Orchestra of New York as recently as April 1996. Today he makes occasional concert appearances, but spends much of his time at the Inn he owns and runs called *I Due Foscari* in Verdi's hometown of Busseto, Italy.

Bergonzi recorded over twenty complete operas, most of which are Verdi roles, but he recorded Pinkerton twice, first with Renata Tebaldi under Tullio Serafin in 1958, then in the recording heard here in 1966. At forty-two years of age, he portrays the American officer with a youthful vigor and an idealistic naivete that makes it difficult to paint him as a complete villain. This recording affords the listener an opportunity to hear Bergonzi at his very best.

ROLANDO PANERAI (Sharpless) was born in the small town of Campi Bisenzio, near Florence. He pursued his vocal studies in Florence and Milan and made his debut in 1946 in Florence as Enrico Ashton in Donizetti's *Lucia di Lammermoor.* Over the following two years he appeared regularly in Naples, where he had debuted as Pharaoh in Rossini's *Mosé in Egitto,* and in 1951 he made his La Scala debut as the High Priest in Saint-Saëns's *Samson et Dalila.* He appeared there regularly for a number of years, singing such diverse roles as Apollo in Gluck's *Alceste* and the husband in Menotti's comedy, *Amelia al Ballo.* In 1957 he sang the title role in the Italian premiere of Hindemith's *Mathis der Maler* at La Scala, and in 1962 he created the title role in Turchi's *Il Buon Soldato Svejk* there.

Panerai's international career began in 1955 when he created the role of Ruprecht in Prokofiev's *The Fiery Angel* in Aix-en-Provence. There he also portrayed Mozart's Figaro. He debuted in Salzburg in 1957 as Ford in Verdi's *Falstaff*, and his American debut was with the San Francisco Opera in 1958, where he sang both the Rossini and Mozart Figaros and Marcello in Puccini's *La Bohème*. His career has included all the major houses in Italy, Great Britain, France, Germany and the United States, including the Metropolitan in New York. He remains active today, emphasizing two of his latest specialties: the title roles in Verdi's *Falstaff* and Puccini's *Gianni Schicchi*.

Panerai's extensive discography includes over twenty complete operas, ranging from Mozart to Wagner in the German repertoire and from Rossini to Puccini in the Italian repertoire. This is his only recording of Sharpless, but it is one of his most effective audio portrayals. Known for his dark, vibrant sound and superb acting, Panerai's Sharpless is characterized by a warmth and beauty of tone and a tenderness of delivery. At the same time, it is never weak or ineffectual, as Sharpless is so often portrayed. Panerai contributes fully to what is a dream cast for this subtle and intricate opera.

SIR JOHN BARBIROLLI (the conductor) was born in London in 1899 of Italian-French descent. He was a scholarship student at Trinity College of Music and the Royal Academy of Music, and at age seventeen, he became the youngest member of the Queen's Hall Orchestra. Barbirolli's first conducting experiences were with an all-volunteer orchestra while serving in the army. His work there led to an invitation in 1928 to conduct

Sir John Barbirolli (1899–1970).

the British National Opera Company on tour. From 1929 to 1933 he served as guest conductor with Covent Garden, conducting their international and English seasons. In 1934 he conducted at the Sadler's Wells Opera Company, returning to Covent Garden in 1937.

What appeared to be a career focused in opera took a turn when Barbirolli accepted the musical leadership of the New York Philharmonic. Later he conducted the Halle Orchestra in Germany. He returned to opera only intermittently for the remainder of his career, most notably as guest conductor at Covent Garden for three seasons, between 1951 and 1954. Toward the end of his life he recorded this *Madama Butterfly* and Verdi's *Otello,* and conducted Verdi's *Aïda* in Rome in 1969.

Barbirolli was knighted in 1949, made Companion of Honour in 1969 and died in London in 1970. He recorded only the two complete operas mentioned above, but he left an extensive discography of the orchestral repertoire which is uniformly admired. He was especially fond of late romantic literature, and his skill is apparent in this recording. Puccini's lush orchestrations and soaring vocal lines frequently persuade conductors to take slower tempi, much to the dismay of many a singer and to Puccini himself, who frequently complained of lugubrious tempi in the performances of his operas. By contrast, Barbirolli here achieves an ideal balance of movement and restraint, demonstrating a thorough understanding of Puccini and the little geisha he immortalized.

The Libretto

Act 1

DISC NO. 1/TRACK 1

The act opens with a vigorous motive beginning in the violins, then taken up in turn by the violas, cellos and basses in fugal style. Then Puccini introduces a sprightly little oriental theme (00:31), after which the curtain opens and the winds take up the first theme again. Both of these motives are used throughout the opera. The "scurrying" music depicts Goro's fussing, but also reflects Pinkerton's impatient nature.

A hill near Nagasaki. A Japanese house, with terraced garden. At back, below, the harbour and the city. Goro is showing the house to Pinkerton, who goes from one surprise to another.

PINKERTON
E soffitto…e pareti…

PINKERTON
And ceiling and walls…

GORO
Vanno e vengono a prova
a norma che vi giova
nello stesso locale
alternar nuovi aspetti ai consueti.

GORO
Go back and forth at will,
so that you can enjoy
from the same spot
different views to the usual ones.

PINKERTON
Il nido nuziale
dov'è?

PINKERTON
Where is
the nuptial nest?

GORO
Qui, o là…secondo…

GORO
Here, or there…depending…

PINKERTON
Anch'esso a doppio fondo!
La sala?

PINKERTON
It has false ends,, too!
And the living room?

GORO *(mostrando la terrazza)*
Ecco!

PINKERTON
All'aperto?

GORO
Un fianco scorre…

PINKERTON
Capisco! Capisco!
Un altro…

GORO
scivola!

PINKERTON
È la dimora frivola…

GORO
Salda come una torre,
da terra fino al tetto.

PINKERTON
È una casa a soffietto.

GORO

GORO *(indicating the terrace)*
There it is!

PINKERTON
In the open air?

GORO
One side slides along…

PINKERTON
I understand!
Another one…

GORO
…glides along!

PINKERTON
And this ridiculous little place…

GORO
Solid as a tower,
from floor to ceiling.

PINKERTON
…is a concertina house.

GORO

(claps his hands and two men and a woman enter and kneel before Pinkerton.)

Questa è la cameriera
che della vostra sposa
fu già serva amorosa.
Il cuoco. Il servitor. Sono confusi
del grande onore.

This is the maid
who was your bride's
faithful servant before.
The cook. The manservant. They are
embarrassed by the great honour.

71

PINKERTON	PINKERTON
I nomi?	Their names?

GORO	GORO
"Miss Nuvola leggera."	"Miss Light Cloud."
"Raggio di sol nascente."	"Ray of the Rising Sun."
"Esala aromi."	"The Aromatic One."

SUZUKI	SUZUKI
Sorride Vostro Onore?	Your Honour is smiling?
Il riso è frutto e fiore.	Laughter is fruit and flower.
Disse il savio Ocunama:	The wise Ocunama has said:
"Dei crucci la trama	"A smile breaks through
smaglia il sorriso.	a web of trouble.
Schiude alla perla il guscio,	It opens the shell for the pearl,
apre all'uom l'uscio	to man it opens the gates
del Paradiso.	of Paradise.
Profumo degli dei…	Perfume of the gods…
fontana della vita…"	fountain of life…"
Disse il savio Ocunama:	The wise Ocunama has said:
"Dei crucci la trama smaglia il sorriso."	"A smile breaks through a web of troubles."

(Goro realizes that Pinkerton is bored. He claps his hands. The three servants run back into the house.)

DISC NO. 1/TRACK 2

Although both Goro and Pinkerton are sung by tenors, Goro sings lighter music in hurried phrases with small intervals (spaces between notes), while Pinkerton's music is louder and in larger intervals. The different expressions of their clashing cultures are already apparent in the score of this expository passage.

PINKERTON	PINKERTON
A chiacchiere costei	By her chattering

mi par cosmopolita.
Che guardi?

GORO
Se non giunge ancor la sposa.

PINKERTON
Tutto è pronto?

GORO
Ogni cosa.

PINKERTON
Gran perla di sensale!

GORO
Qui verran:
l'Ufficiale del Registro,
I parenti, il vostro Console,
la fidanzata.
Qui si firma l'atto
e il matrimonio è fatto.

PINKERTON
E son molti i parenti?

GORO
La suocera, la nonna,
lo zio Bonzo (che non
ci degnerà di sua presenza)
e cugini, e le cugine!
Mettiam fra gli ascendenti
ed i collaterali un due dozzine.
Quanto alla discendenza…
provvederanno assai
Vostra Grazia e la bella Butterfly.

she seems just like all woman the world
over. What are you looking at?

GORO
To see if the bride's coming yet.

PINKERTON
Is everything ready?

GORO
Everything.

PINKERTON
Priceless pearl of a marriage-broker!

GORO
The Registrar,
the relations,
your Consul and the bride
will all come here.
You'll sign the documents here,
and you'll be married.

PINKERTON
And are there many relations?

GORO
The mother-in-law, the grandmother,
her uncle the Bonze (who won't
honour us with his presence),
and her male and female cousins…
Let's say, with ancestors
and contemporaries, about two dozen.
As for descendants…
Your Grace and the pretty Butterfly
will take good care of that.

PINKERTON
Gran perla di sensale!

VOCE DI SHARPLESS
E suda e arrampica!
Sbuffa, inciampica!

GORO
Il Consol sale.

SHARPLESS *(apparendo sbuffando)*
Ah! quei ciottoli
mi hanno sfiaccato!

PINKERTON
Bene arrivato!

GORO
Bene arrivato!

SHARPLESS
Ouff!

PINKERTON
Presto, Goro -
qualche ristoro.

SHARPLESS
Alto.

PINKERTON
Ma bello.

SHARPLESS
Nagasaki, il mare, il porto…

PINKERTON
You priceless pearl of a marriage-broker!

VOICE OF SHARPLESS
You sweat and climb,
puff and stumble!

GORO
The Consul's coming up.

SHARPLESS *(appearing, out of breath)*
Those stones
have reduced me to a jelly!

PINKERTON
Welcome!

GORO
Welcome!

SHARPLESS
Uff!

PINKERTON
Quick, Goro,
some refreshments.

SHARPLESS
It's high up, here!

PINKERTON
But, it's beautiful!

SHARPLESS
Nagasaki, the sea, the harbour…

PINKERTON	PINKERTON
…e una casetta	And a little house
che obbedisce a bacchetta.	that works by magic.

SHARPLESS	SHARPLESS
Vostra?	Is it yours?

PINKERTON	PINKERTON
La comperai per novecento	I've bought it for nine hundred
novantanove anni,	and ninety-nine years,
con facoltà, ogni mese,	with the right, every month,
di rescindere i patti.	to cancel the agreement.
Sono in questo paese	In this country
elastici del par,	houses and contracts
case e contratti.	are equally elastic.

SHARPLESS	SHARPLESS
E l'uomo esperto ne profitta.	And the clever man makes the most of it.

PINKERTON	PINKERTON
Certo.	Certainly.

(Goro hurries from the house, followed by two servants bearing glasses, bottles, plates, cutlery and two wicker chairs. They lay two places at a little table, and return to the house.)

DISC NO. 1/TRACK 3

***Dovunque al mondo*, Pinkerton's ode to American entitlement, appropriately opens with a quote from "The Star Spangled Banner". Pinkerton's blustery nature is revealed to the audience and his fellow countryman, but not to the heroine, in this solo.**

Dovunque al mondo	Everywhere in the world
lo Yankee vagabondo	the roving Yankee
si gode e traffica	takes his pleasure and his profit,
sprezzando rischi.	indifferent to all risks.

Affonda l'àncora	He drops anchor
alla ventura…	at random…

(He breaks off to offer a drink to Sharpless.)

Milk-punch, o wisky?	Milk punch or whisky?
Affonda l'àncora	…He drops anchor
alla ventura	at random
finché una raffica scompigli	till a sudden squall wrecks
nave e ormeggi, alberatura…	the ship, hawsers rigging and all…
La vita ei non appaga	He's not satisfied with life
se non fa suo tesor	unless he makes his own
i fiori d'ogni plaga…	the flowers of every shore…

SHARPLESS	**SHARPLESS**
È un facile vangelo…	It's an easy-going creed.

PINKERTON	**PINKERTON**
d'ogni bella gli amor.	…the love of every pretty girl.

SHARPLESS	**SHARPLESS**
…è un facile vangelo	…an easy-going creed
che fa la vita vaga	that makes life delightful
ma che intristisce il cor.	but saddens the heart.

PINKERTON	**PINKERTON**
Vinto si tuffa,	If beaten,
la sorte riacciuffa.	he tries his luck again.
Il suo talento	He follows his bent
fa in ogni dove.	wherever he may be.
Così mi sposo	So I'm marrying
all'uso giapponese	in Japanese fashion
per novecento	for nine hundred and
novantanove anni. Salvo	ninety-nine years. With the right
a prosciogliermi ogni mese.	to be freed every month!

SHARPLESS
È un facile vangelo.

PINKERTON
"America for ever!"

SHARPLESS
"America for ever!"
Ed è bella la sposa?

GORO *(udendo, si avanza.)*
Una ghirlanda di fiori freschi,
una stella dai raggi d'oro.
E per nulla: sol cento yen.
Se Vostra Grazia mi comanda
ce n'ho un assortimento…

PINKERTON
Va, conducila Goro.

SHARPLESS
Quale smania vi prende!
Sareste addirittura
cotto?

SHARPLESS
It's an easy-going creed.

PINKERTON
"America for ever!"

SHARPLESS
"America for ever!"
And is the bride pretty?

GORO *(overhearing, comes forward.)*
A garland of fresh flowers,
a star with golden rays…
And for next to nothing: only a hundred
yen. If your Grace wishes
I have a good selection.

PINKERTON
Go and fetch her, Goro.

SHARPLESS
What madness has got hold of you!
Are you completely
infatuated?

DISC NO. 1/TRACK 4

Amore o grillo: **Pinkerton's lyrical music is at odds with his insensitive words, and provide a hint to how we should interpret his expressions of love in the later love duet.**

PINKERTON
Non so! non so! Dipende
dal grado di cottura!
Amore o grillo -
dir non saprei.

PINKERTON
I don't know! It depends
on the degree of infatuation!
Love or passing fancy -
I couldn't say.

Certo costei m'ha colle ingenue
arti invescato.
Lieve qual tenue vetro soffiato
alla statura, al portamento
sembra figura da paravento.
Ma dal suo lucido fondo di lacca
come con subito moto
si stacca; qual farfalletta
svolazza e posa
con tal grazietta silenziosa,
che di rincorrerla
furor m'assale -
se pure infrangerne
dovessi l'ale.

SHARPLESS

Ier l'altro, il Consolato
sen' venne a visitar!
Io non la vidi,
ma l'udii parlar.
Di sua voce il mistero
l'anima mi colpì.
Certo quando è sincer
l'amor parla così.
Sarebbe gran peccato
le lievi ali strappar
e desolar forse un credulo cor.
Quella divina mite vocina
non dovrebbe dar note di dolor.

PINKERTON

Console mio garbato,
quietatevi! si sa:
la vostra età è di flebile umor.
Non c'è gran male

She's certainly bewitched me
with her innocent arts.
Delicate and fragile as blown glass,
in stature, in bearing
she resembles some figure on a painted
screen, but as, from her background of
glossy lacquer, with a sudden movement
she frees herself; like a butterfly
she flutters and settles
with such quiet grace
that a madness seizes me
to pursue her,
even though I might
damage her wings.

SHARPLESS

The day before yesterday she came
to visit the Consulate.
I didn't see her myself
but I heard her speak.
The mystery of her voice
touched me to the heart.
True love surely
speaks like that.
It would be a great sin
to strip off those delicate wings
and perhaps plunge a trusting heart into
despair. That heavenly, meek, pretty, little
voice shouldn't utter a note of sadness!

PINKERTON

My dear Consul,
don't worry! It's usual
at your age to take a pessimistic view.
There's no great harm done

s'io vo' quell'ale	if I want those wings
drizzare ai dolci voli dell'amor!	to be spread in love's tender flight!
Whisky?	Whisky?

SHARPLESS

SHARPLESS

| Un'altro bicchiere. | Another little glassful. |
| Bevo alla vostra famiglia lontana. | Here's to your family at home. |

PINKERTON

PINKERTON

E al giorno in cui mi sposerò	And to the day when I shall get married
con vere nozze	in real earnest
a una vera sposa americana.	to a real American bride.

GORO *(riappare correndo)*

GORO *(re-enters at a run)*

Ecco! Son giunte	Here they come! They've reached
al sommo del pendìo.	the top of the hill.
Già del femmineo sciame	You can already hear the swarm
qual di vento in fogliame	of women rustling like
s'ode il brusìo.	leaves in the wind!

DISC NO. 1/TRACK 5

O quanto cielo, quanto mar. **Butterfly's entrance begins with shimmering high strings, then as she climbs the hill to meet her husband, the harmonies climb through several modulations. Puccini includes the "whole-tone scale" – a technique now familiar from countless film scores – to depict the emergence of a mysterious new world. When Puccini finished this part, early in the creative process, he wrote to a friend, "I am pleased with it"–and rightfully so.**

VOCE DI RAGAZZE

GIRLS' VOICES

Ah! ah!	Ah! Ah!
Quanto cielo!	What an expanse of sky!
Quanto mar!	What an expanse of sea!

VOCE DI BUTTERFLY

VOICE OF BUTTERFLY

| Ancora un passo or via. | Just one more step now… |

VOCE DI RAGAZZE
Come sei tarda.

VOCE DI BUTTERFLY
Aspetta.

VOCI DI RAGAZZE
Ecco la vetta.
Guarda, guarda quanti fior!

VOCE DI BUTTERFLY
Spira sul mare e sulla terra
un primaveril soffio giocondo.

SHARPLESS
O allegro cinquettar di gioventù.

VOCE DI BUTTERFLY
Io sono la fanciulla
più lieta del Giappone,
anzi del mondo.
Amiche, son venuta
al richiamo d'amor…
D'amor venni alle soglie
ove s'accoglie il bene
di chi vive e di chi muor.

VOCI DI RAGAZZE
Gioia a te sia, doilce amica,
ma pria di varcar
la soglia che t'attira
volgiti e mira
quanto cielo, quanti fiori,
quanto mar; mira
le cose tutte che ti son sì care.

GIRLS' VOICES
How slow you are!

VOICE OF BUTTERFLY
Wait.

GIRLS' VOICES
Here we are at the summit!
Look, just look at all the flowers!

VOICE OF BUTTERFLY
Over land and sea there floats
a joyous breath of spring.

SHARPLESS
Oh, the gay chatter of youth!

VOICE OF BUTTERFLY
I am the happiest
girl in Japan,
or rather, in the whole world.
Friends, I have come
at the call of love…
I have come to the portals of love
where is gathered the happiness
of all who live and die.

GIRLS' VOICES
Joy to you, sweet friend,
but before crossing
the threshold which draws you,
turn and look at
the things which you hold dear,
look at all that sky,
all those flowers and all that sea!

BUTTERFLY	**BUTTERFLY**
Siam giunte.	We have arrived.

(She sees the group of men and recognises Pinkerton. She closes her parasol smartly, and points Pinkerton out to her friends.)

B. F. Pinkerton. Giù.	B. F. Pinkerton. Down.

LE AMICHE	**GIRL FRIENDS**
Giù.	Down.

DISC NO. 1/TRACK 6

The bride and groom exchange pleasantries. When asked about her father, she responds "Dead," and we first hear the motive connected with the dagger (02:55) that took his life and will also, in the end, take Butterfly's.

BUTTERFLY	**BUTTERFLY**
Gran ventura.	Good luck attend you.

LE AMICHE	**GIRL FRIENDS**
Riverenza.	Our respects.

PINKERTON	**PINKERTON**
È un po' dura	The climb is
la scalata?	rather difficult?

BUTTERFLY	**BUTTERFLY**
A una sposa costumata	To a court bride
più penosa è l'impazienza.	impatience is more trying.

PINKERTON	**PINKERTON**
Molto raro complimento.	A very rare complement.

BUTTERFLY	**BUTTERFLY**
Dei più belli ancor ne so.	I know some even prettier ones.

PINKERTON
Dei gioielli!

PINKERTON
Real gems!

BUTTERFLY
Se vi è caro sul momento…

BUTTERFLY
If you like, this very instant…

PINKERTON
Grazie…no.

PINKERTON
Thank you…no.

SHARPLESS
Miss Butterfly…Bel nome,
vi sta a meraviglia.
Siete di Nagasaki?

SHARPLESS
Miss Butterfly. A pretty name -
it suits you to perfection.
Do you come from Nagasaki?

BUTTERFLY
Signor, sì. Di famiglia
assai prospera un tempo.

BUTTERFLY
Yes, sir. From a family
which at one time was quite well-to-do.

(to her friends)

Verità?

Isn't that so?

LE AMICHE
Verità.

GIRL FRIENDS
It is!

BUTTERFLY
Nessuno si confessa mai
nato in povertà.
Non c'è vagabondo
che a sentirlo non sia
di gran prosapia. Eppur
conobbi la ricchezza.
Ma il turbine rovescia
le quercie più robuste
e abbiam fatto la ghescia
per sostentarci.

BUTTERFLY
No one ever admits
he was born in poverty.
There's not a beggar
who, to hear him, doesn't
come of high lineage. All the same,
I have known riches.
But storms uproot
the sturdiest oaks…
and we became geishas
to support ourselves.

(to her friends)

Vero?	That's so, isn't it?

LE AMICHE
Vero!

GIRL FRIENDS
It is!

BUTTERFLY
Non lo nascondo,
né m'adonto.
Ridete? Perché?
Cose del mondo…

BUTTERFLY
I don't hide it,
neither do I feel hard done by.
Why do you laugh?
It's the way of the world.

PINKERTON
Con quel fare di bambola
quando parla m'infiamma.

PINKERTON
With those childlike ways,
when she talks she sets my blood on fire.

SHARPLESS
Ed avete sorelle?

SHARPLESS
And have you any sisters?

BUTTERFLY
No, signore. Ho la mamma.

BUTTERFLY
No, sir. I have my mother.

GORO
Una nobile dama.

GORO
A noble lady.

BUTTERFLY
Ma senza farle torto,
povera molto anch'essa.

BUTTERFLY
But without wronging her,
very poor, too.

SHARPLESS
E vostro padre?

SHARPLESS
And your father?

BUTTERFLY *(bruscamente)*
Morto.

BUTTERFLY *(abruptly)*
Dead.

SHARPLESS	**SHARPLESS**
Quant'anni avete?	How old are you?
BUTTERFLY	**BUTTERFLY**
Indovinate.	Guess.
SHARPLESS	**SHARPLESS**
Dieci.	Ten.
BUTTERFLY	**BUTTERFLY**
Crescete.	Make it more.
SHARPLESS	**SHARPLESS**
Venti.	Twenty.
BUTTERFLY	**BUTTERFLY**
Calate.	Make it less.
Quindici netti, netti.	Just exactly fifteen;
Sono vecchia diggià.	I'm already old.
SHARPLESS	**SHARPLESS**
Quindici anni.	Fifteen!
PINKERTON	**PINKERTON**
Quindici anni!	Fifteen!
SHARPLESS	**SHARPLESS**
L'età dei giuochi…	The age for games…
PINKERTON	**PINKERTON**
E dei confetti.	…and wedding cake.

DISC NO. 1/TRACK 7

The mundane chatter of the relatives is in great contrast to Butterfly's dreamy lines. Already, her perception of the situation is dangerously separated from anyone else's.

GORO	**GORO**
L'Imperial Commissario,	The Imperial Commissioner,
l'Ufficiale del Registro,	the Registrar,
i congiunti.	the bride's family.
PINKERTON	**PINKERTON**
Fate presto.	Get on with it quickly.

(Goro runs into the house. Pinkerton talks apart to the Consul.)

Che burletta la sfilata	What a farce, this parade
della nuova parentela!	of my new relations,
CUGINI E PARENTI	**COUSIN AND RELATIONS**
Bello non è, in verità.	He's not handsome, truly.
Bello non è.	He's not handsome.
BUTTERFLY	**BUTTERFLY**
Bello è così	He's so handsome
che non si può sognar di più.	one just couldn't imagine anything better!
MADRE ED AMICHE	**MOTHER AND FRIENDS**
Mi pare un re!	He seems like a king to me.
Vale un Perù!	He's worth a fortune.
CUGINA *(a Butterfly)*	**COUSIN** *(to Butterfly)*
Goro l'offrì pur anco a me,	Goro offered him to me too,
ma s'ebbe un no!	but he has got no for an answer!
BUTTERFLY	**BUTTERFLY**
Sì, giusto tu!	Of course, you would!
PARENTI *(a Cugina)*	**RELATIONS** *(to cousin)*
La sua beltà già disfiori.	Her looks have already faded.
Divorzierà.	He'll divorce her.

CUGINA E PARENTI
Spero di sì.

LO ZIO YAKUSIDÉ
Vino ce n'è?
Guardiamo un po'.
Ne vidi già
color di thé e chermisì.

GORO
Per carità, tacete un po'!
Sch! Sch! Sch!

SHARPLESS
O amico fortunato!
O fortunato Pinkerton,
che in sorte v'è toccato
un fior pur or sbocciato.

PINKERTON
Sì, è vero, è un fiore, un fiore!
L'esotico suo odore
m'ha il cervello sconvolto.

CUGINA E PARENTI
Ei l'offrì pur anco a me,
ma risposi non lo vo'!

MADRE ED AMICHE
Egli è bel, mi pare un re!
Non avrei risposto no,
non direi mai no!

SHARPLESS
Non più bella e d'assai fanciulla

COUSIN AND RELATIONS
I hope so.

UNCLE YAKUSIDE
Is there any wine here?
Let's have a look.
I've just seen some the colour of tea,
and some red!

GORO
For goodness sake, keep quiet!
Sh! Sh! Sh!

SHARPLESS
My lucky young friend!
Lucky Pinkerton,
on whom Fate has bestowed
this newly opened flower!

PINKERTON
Yes, it's true, she's a flower, a flower!
Her exotic fragrance
has turned my head.

COUSIN AND RELATIONS
He offered him to me too,
but I answered I don't want him!

MOTHER AND FRIENDS
He's too handsome, he seems like a king to
me! I wouldn't have answered no,
I would never have said no!

SHARPLESS
No lovelier girl have I ever seen

io vidi mai di questa Butterfly!
E se a voi sembran scede
il patto e la sua fede…

CUGINA E PARENTI
Senza tanto ricercar
io ne trovo dei miglior
e gli dirò un bel no.

MADRE ED AMICHE
No, mie care, non mi par,
è davvero un gran signor,
nè gli direi di no!

BUTTERFLY
Badate, attenti a me!

PINKERTON
Sì, è vero, è un fiore, un fiore,
e in fede mia l'ho colto!

SHARPLESS
Badate! Ella ci crede!

BUTTERFLY
Mamma, vien qua.
Badate a me:
attenti, orsù,
uno, due, tre,
e tutti giù.

than this Butterfly.
And if you don't take this contract
and her trust seriously…

COUSIN AND RELATIONS
Without looking too hard
I've found better,
and I shall roundly tell him no!

MOTHER AND FRIENDS
No, my dears, I didn't think so,
he's a real gentleman,
and I would not say no!

BUTTERFLY
Attention, listen to me.

PINKERTON
Yes, it's true, she's a flower, a flower,
and, upon my honour, I've plucked her!

SHARPLESS
…Beware! She believes in them!

BUTTERFLY
Mother, come here.
Listen to me:
attention, come now,
one, two, three,
and everybody down.

(They all bow low in front of Pinkerton and Sharpless. Pinkerton takes Butterfly's hand.)

DISC NO. 1/TRACK 8

As Butterfly shows her few belongings to Pinkerton, Puccini uses a Japanese melody familiar to most Americans, "Sakura" (01:10). Again, we hear the dagger theme (02:04) when Goro explains her father's suicide to Pinkerton.

PINKERTON
Vieni, amor mio!
Ti piace la casetta?

PINKERTON
Come, my love,
do you like our little house?

BUTTERFLY
Signor B. F. Pinkerton, perdono…
Io vorrei…pochi oggetti da donna…

BUTTERFLY
Mr. B. F. Pinkerton, excuse me…
I would like…a few woman's possessions…

PINKERTON
Dove sono?

PINKERTON
Where are they?

BUTTERFLY
Sono qui…vi dispiace?

BUTTERFLY
They're here…you don't mind?

(She produces various small objects from the capacious sleeves of her kimono.)

PINKERTON
O perché mai, mia bella Butterfly?

PINKERTON
Why ever should I, my pretty Butterfly?

BUTTERFLY
Fazzoletti. La pipa.
Una cintura. Un piccolo fermaglio.
Uno specchio. Un ventaglio.

BUTTERFLY
Handkerchiefs. Pipe.
A sash. A little clasp.
A mirror. A fan.

PINKERTON
Quel barattolo?

PINKERTON
What's that pot?

BUTTERFLY
Un vaso di tintura.

BUTTERFLY
A jar of rouge.

PINKERTON
Ohibò.

PINKERTON
Oh dear!

BUTTERFLY
Vi spiace?

BUTTERFLY
Don't you like it?

(She throws it away.)

Via.

Away with it!

PINKERTON
E quello?

PINKERTON
And that?

BUTTERFLY
Cosa sacra e mia.

BUTTERFLY
My most sacred possession.

PINKERTON
E non si può vedere?

PINKERTON
And mayn't one see it?

BUTTERFLY
C'è troppa gente.
Perdonate.

BUTTERFLY
There are too many people.
Forgive me.

GORO *(sottovoce a Pinkerton)*
È un presente del Mikado
a suo padre…coll'invito…

GORO *(whispering to Pinkerton)*
It's a present from the Mikado
to her father…inviting him to…

(He imitates the gesture of hara-kiri.)

PINKERTON
E…suo padre?

PINKERTON
And her father?

GORO
Ha obbedito.

GORO
Obeyed.

BUTTERFLY	BUTTERFLY

(taking some statuettes from her sleeve)

Gli Ottokè.	My Ottoke.

PINKERTON	**PINKERTON**
Quei pupazzi? Avete detto?	These puppets? You said?

BUTTERFLY	**BUTTERFLY**
Son l'anime degli avi.	They are the spirits of my ancestors.

PINKERTON	**PINKERTON**
Ah! il mio rispetto.	Oh! My respects.

DISC NO. 1/TRACK 9

Ieri son salita tutta sola, Butterfly's solo, describing her trip to the Mission, is doubled by the orchestra's strings, indicating her full sincerity. At the end, however, we hear suggestions of the "dagger theme," a subtle foreshadowing of events. The subsequent ceremony is restrained and formal, with hints of Japanese motifs.

BUTTERFLY	**BUTTERFLY**
Ieri son salita tutta sola	Yesterday I went, alone
in segreto alla Missione.	and in secret, to the Mission.
Colla nuova mia vita	With my new life
posso adottare nuova religione.	I can adopt a new religion.
Lo zio Bonzo nol sa,	My uncle, the Bonze, doesn't know,
né i miei lo sanno.	neither do my people.
Io seguo il mio destino	I follow my destiny
e piena d'umiltà	and, filled with humility,
al Dio del signor Pinkerton	I kneel before
m'inchino.	Mr. Pinkerton's God.
È mio destino;	It is my fate.

nella stessa chiesetta
in ginocchio con voi
pregherò lo stesso Dio.
E per farvi contento potrò forse
obliar la gente mia.
Amore mio!

In the same little church,
beside you on my knees,
I will pray to the same God,
and to please you I may perhaps be able
to forget my own people.
My dearest love!

GORO
Tutti zitti!

GORO
Quiet, everybody!

IL COMMISSARIO
È concesso al nominato
Benjamin Franklin Pinkerton,
Luogotenente della cannoniera
"Lincoln",
marina degli Stati Uniti,
America del Nord,
ed alla damigella Butterfly,
del quartiere d'Omara, Nagasaki,
d'unirsi in matrimonio,
per dritto il primo
della propria volontà,
ed ella per consenso dei parenti
qui testimoni all'atto…

COMMISSIONER
It is permitted to the herein named
Benjamin Franklin Pinkerton,
Lieutenant in the warship
Lincoln,
United States Navy,
North America,
and to Miss Butterfly
of the Omara district of Nagasaki,
to be united in matrimony,
the first by right
of his own wish
and she by consent of her relations
here witness to the contract.

GORO *(con cerimonia)*
Lo sposo.
Poi la sposa.
E tutto è fatto.

GORO *(with ceremony)*
The bridegroom.
Then the bride.
And everything's concluded.

LE AMICHE
Madama Butterfly.

FRIENDS
Madam Butterfly!

BUTTERFLY
Madama B. F. Pinkerton.

BUTTERFLY
Madam B. F. Pinkerton.

IL COMMISSARIO	COMMISSIONER
Auguri molti.	My best wishes.

PINKERTON	PINKERTON
I miei ringraziamenti.	Many thanks.

IL COMMISSARIO	COMMISSIONER
Il Signor Console scende?	Are you going, sir?

SHARPLESS	SHARPLESS
L'accompagno.	I'll go along with you.

(to Pinkerton)

Ci vedrem domani.	See you tomorrow.

PINKERTON	PINKERTON
A meraviglia.	Capital.

UFFICIALE DEL REGISTRO	OFFICIAL REGISTRAR
Posterità.	May you have many descendants.

PINKERTON	PINKERTON
Mi proverò.	I'll try.

SHARPLESS *(partendo, a Pinkerton)*	SHARPLESS *(going, to Pinkerton)*
Giudizio!	Have a care!

(Sharpless, the Rigstrar and the Commissioner leave.)

DISC NO. 1/TRACK 10

The brief role of the Bonze bursts in upon the niceties [0:53] like a vengeful deity. The startling cries of the relatives as they denounce Butterfly [1:44] are almost like sharp pangs of guilt from within Butterfly.

PINKERTON *(a parte)*
Ed eccoci in famiglia.
Sbrighiamoci al più presto
in modo onesto.

(He raises his glass.)

Hip! Hip!

PARENTI
O Kami! O Kami!

PINKERTON
Beviamo ai novissimi legami.

(Suddenly a terrifying character appears. It is the Bonze, who comes forward in a rage; holding his hand out towards Butterfly, he threatens her.)

IL BONZO
Cio-Cio-San! Abominazione!

BUTTERFLY E PARENTI
Lo zio bonzo!

GORO
Un corno al guastafeste!
Chi ci leva d'intorno
le persone moleste?

IL BONZO
Cio-Cio-San! Che hai tu fatto
alla Missione?

TUTTI
Rispondi, Cio-Cio-San!

PINKERTON *(to himself)*
And here we are in the family circle!
Let's get rid of all these people
as soon as we decently can.

Hip! Hip!

RELATIONS
O Kami! O Kami!

PINKERTON
Let's drink to the new ties.

BONZE
Cho-Cho-San! Abomination!

BUTTERFLY AND RELATIONS
Our uncle the Bonze!

GORO
Confound the spoilsport!
Who will rid us
of such nuisances?

BONZE
Cho-Cho-San! What were you up to
at the Mission?

ALL
Answer, Cho-Cho-San!

PINKERTON
Che mi strilla quel matto?

IL BONZO
Rispondi, che hai tu fatto?
Come, hai tu gli occhi asciutti?
Son dunque questi i frutti?
Ci ha rinnegato tutti.

TUTTI
Hou! Cio-Cio-San!

IL BONZO
Rinnegato vi dico…
il culto antico.

TUTTI
Hou! Cio-Cio-San!

IL BONZO
Kami sarundasico!
All'anima tua guasta
qual supplizio sovrasta!

PINKERTON
Ehi, dico, basta, basta!

IL BONZO
Venite tutti.
Andiamo!
Ci hai rinnegato e noi
ti rinneghiamo!

PINKERTON
Sbarazzate all'istante.

PINKERTON
What's that madman shouting about?

BONZE
Answer, what were you about?
What, can your eyes be dry!
So then, these are the fruits?
She has renounced us all.

ALL
Oh, Cho-Cho-San!

BONZE
I tell you she has renounced
our ancient faith.

ALL
Oh! Cho-Cho-San!

BONZE
Kami sarundasico!
What torments
threaten your lost soul!

PINKERTON
Hey, that's enough, I say!

BONZE
Come, everybody!
Let us go!
You have renounced us and we
renounce you!

PINKERTON
Get out of here at once.

In casa mia niente baccano
e niente bonzeria.

TUTTI (*partendo*)
Hou! Cio-Cio-San! Kami sarundasico.
Hou! Cio-Cio-San! Ti rinneghiamo!

PINKERTON
Bimba, bimba, non piangere
per gracchiar di ranocchi.

PARENTI (*lontani*)
Hou! Cio-Cio-San!

BUTTERFLY
Urlano ancor!

PINKERTON
Tutta la tua tribù
e i Bonzi tutti del Giappon
non valgono il pianto
di quegli occhi cari e belli.

BUTTERFLY
Davver? non piango più.
E quasi del ripudio
non mi duole
per le vostre parole
che mi suonan così dolci nel cor.

(She kisses his hand.)

PINKERTON
Che fai? La man?

I'll have no shindy in my house
and none of this bonzing!

ALL (*leaving*)
Hou! Cho-Cho-San! Kami sarundasico.
Oh! Cho-Cho-San! We renounce you!

PINKERTON
Dear child, don't cry
over that croaking of frogs.

RELATIONS (far off)
Oh! Cho-Cho-San!

BUTTERFLY
They're still howling!

PINKERTON
The whole tribe of them
and all the bonzes in Japan
aren't worth a tear
from your sweet, pretty eyes!

BUTTERFLY
Really? Then I won't cry any more.
And I scarcely mind
their repudiation
because of your words
which echo so sweetly in my heart.

PINKERTON
What are you doing? My hand?

BUTTERFLY	BUTTERFLY
M'han detto che laggiù	I've been told that over there
fra la gente costumata	among well-bred people
è questo il segno	it's a sign
del maggior rispetto.	of the greatest respect.

SUZUKI *(dentro la casa)*	SUZUKI *(from inside the house)*
E Izaghi ed Izanami sarundasico,	Izaghi, Izanami sarundasico,
e Kami, e Izaghi,	Kami, Izaghi,
ed Izanami sarundasico, e Kami.	Izanami sarundasico, Kami.

PINKERTON	PINKERTON
Chi brontola lassù?	Who's that muttering in there?

BUTTERFLY	BUTTERFLY
È Suzuki che fa	It's Suzuki saying
la sua preghiera seral.	her evening prayers.

DISC NO. 1/TRACK 11 & 12

Vieni la sera. Here begins one of the most famous love duets in all opera. The music surges with Pinkerton's passion until at last he possesses Butterfly. Although Pinkerton and Butterfly often sing the same musical lines, their meanings diverge through their different voices, expressions, and from what we (if not they) know of their contrasting motivations. More than just a pretty duet, this section is a marvelously apt dramatic representation of two people who are at cross-purposes while superficially in agreement.

PINKERTON	PINKERTON
Viene la sera.	Night is falling.

BUTTERFLY	BUTTERFLY
E l'ombra e la quiete.	And darkness and peace.

PINKERTON	PINKERTON
E sei qui sola.	And you are here alone.

BUTTERFLY
Sola e rinnegata!
Rinnegata…e felice!

BUTTERFLY
Alone and renounced!
Renounced and happy!

PINKERTON

PINKERTON

(claps; the servants run out.)

A voi, chiudete.

Come here and close up the house.

BUTTERFLY
Sì, sì, noi tutti soli…
E fuori il mondo…

BUTTERFLY
Yes, yes, we are all alone…
and the world shut outside…

PINKERTON
E il Bonzo furibondo!

PINKERTON
And the furious Bonze.

BUTTERFLY
Suzuki, le mie vesti.

BUTTERFLY
Suzuki, my clothes.

(Suzuki goes to a chest and gives Butterfly her night clothes.)

SUZUKI
Buona notte.

SUZUKI
Good night.

BUTTERFLY
Quest'obi pomposa
di scioglier mi tarda…
Si vesta la sposa
di puro candor.
Tra moti sommessi
sorride e mi guarda.
Celarmi potessi!
Ne ho tanto rossor!
E ancor l'irata voce

BUTTERFLY
I long to take off
this ceremonial sash,
let the bride be dressed
in pure white.
Whispering to himself
he smiles and watches me.
If I could only hide!
It makes me blush so!
And still the angry voice

mi maledice…
Butterfly rinnegata,
rinnegata…e felice.

PINKERTON
Con moti di scoiattolo,
i nodi allenta e scioglie!
Pensar che quel giocattolo
è mia moglie! Mia moglie!
Ma tal grazia dispiega
ch'io mi struggo
per la febbre
d'un subito desìo.

(Pinkerton approaches Butterfly, who has finished dressing.)

Bimba dagli occhi pieni di malia
ora sei tutta mia.
Sei tutta vestita di giglio.
Mi piace la treccia tua bruna
fra candidi veli.

BUTTERFLY
Somiglio la dea della luna,
la piccola dea della luna
che scende la notte
dal ponte del ciel.

PINKERTON
E affascina i cuori…

BUTTERFLY
E li prende, e li avvolge
in un bianco mantel.
E via se li reca
negli alti reami.

is cursing me…
Butterfly renounced,
renounced… and happy.

PINKERTON
With squirrel-like movements
she shakes the knots loose and undoes
them!
To think that this little toy
is my wife! My wife!
But she displays such grace
that I am consumed
by a fever of sudden desire!

Dear child, with eyes full of witchery,
now you are all mine.
You're dressed all in lily-white.
I love your dark tresses
amid the white of your veils.

BUTTERFLY
I am like the moon-goddess,
the little goddess of the moon,
who comes down at night
from the bridge of heaven.

PINKERTON
And captivates all hearts…

BUTTERFLY
…and takes them and folds them
in a white cloak.
And carries them away
to the higher regions.

PINKERTON

Ma intanto finor non m'hai detto,
ancor non m'hai detto che m'ami.
Le sa quella dea le parole
che appagan gli ardenti desir?

BUTTERFLY

Le sa. Forse dirle non vuole
per tema d'averne a morir,
per tema d'averne a morir!

PINKERTON

Stolta paura,
l'amor non uccide,
ma dà vita, e sorride
per gioie celestiali
come ora fa
nei tuoi lunghi occhi ovali.

PINKERTON

But meanwhile, you haven't told me yet,
you haven't told me you love me.
Does that goddess know the words
that satisfy burning desire?

BUTTERFLY

She does. Maybe she's unwilling
to say them for fear of dying of it,
for fear of dying of it!

PINKERTON

Foolish fear -
love does not kill,
but gives life and smiles
for heavenly joy,
as it does now
in your almond eyes.

DISC NO. 1/TRACK 13

Vogliatemi bene. **"Love me well," Butterfly says to the gentle accompaniment of a solo violin. This melody is repeated several times, modulating upward with increasing instrumentation and tension. At last she is ready to succumb, and we hear again the music of her entrance (04:20), slowly climbing in passion just as she had slowly climbed the hill. Again, the strokes of the whole-tone chord suggest the emergence of a mysterious new world.**

BUTTERFLY

Adesso voi siete per me
l'occhio del firmamento.
E mi piaceste dal primo momento
che vi ho veduto.
Siete alto, forte.
Ridete con modi sì palesi!
E dite cose

BUTTERFLY

For me you are now
the eye of heaven.
And I liked you from the first moment
I set eyes on you.
You are tall and strong.
You laugh out so heartily.
And you say things

che mai non intesi.
Or son contenta. Or son contenta.
Vogliatemi bene, un bene piccolino,
un bene da bambino
quale a me si conviene.
Noi siamo gente avvezza
alle piccole cose,
umili e silenziose,
ad una tenerezza
sfiorante e pur profonda
come il ciel, come l'onda del mare.

I've never heard in my life before.
I'm happy now, so happy.
Love me with a little love,
a child-like love,
the kind that suits me.
Love me, please…
We are a people used to small,
modest, quiet things,
to a tenderness gently caressing,
yet vast as the sky
and as the waves of the sea.

PINKERTON
Dammi ch'io baci
le tue mani care,
mia Butterfly!
Come t'han ben nomata
tenue farfalla…

PINKERTON
Give me your dear hands
and let me kiss them!
My Butterfly!
How aptly you were named,
fragile butterfly!

BUTTERFLY
Dicon ch'oltre mare
se cade in man dell'uom
ogni farfalla d'uno spillo
è trafitta
ed in tavola infitta!

BUTTERFLY
They say that overseas
if it should fall into the hands of man
a butterfly is stuck through
with a pin
and fixed to a board!

PINKERTON
Un po' di vero c'è:
e tu lo sai perché?
Perché non fugga più.
Io t'ho ghermita…
Ti serro palpitante.
Sei mia.

PINKERTON
There's some truth in that;
and do you know why?
So that it shouldn't fly away again.
I've caught you…
Quivering, I press you to me.
You're mine.

BUTTERFLY
Sì, per la vita.

BUTTERFLY
Yes, for life.

PINKERTON

Vieni, vieni…
Via dall'anima in pena
l'angoscia paurosa.
È notte serena! Guarda:
dorme ogni cosa!
Sei mia! Ah! vien!

BUTTERFLY

Ah! dolce notte! quante stelle!
Non le vidi mai sì belle!
Trema, brilla ogni favilla
col baglior d'una pupilla.
Oh! quanti occhi fisi, attenti,
d'ogni parte a riguardar!
pei firmamenti, via pei lidi,
via pel mare…ride il ciel!
Ah! dolce notte!
Tutto estatico d'amor,
ride il ciel!

PINKERTON

Come along, come…
Cast all sad fears
out of your heart!
The night is clear! See,
all things sleep!
You are mine! Oh, come!

BUTTERFLY

Oh, lovely night! What a lot of stars!
Never have I seen them so beautiful!
Every spark twinkles and shines
with the brilliance of an eye.
Oh! What a lot of eyes fixed and staring,
looking at us from all sides!
In the sky, along the shore,
out to sea…the sky is smiling!
Oh, lovely night!
In a ecstasy of love
the sky is smiling!

Act 2

INSIDE BUTTERFLY'S HOUSE

DISC NO. 1/TRACK 14

Act II begins with an impatient motive in the solo flute, taken over first by high strings, then low strings. Two clarinets then lead us up to a tragic motive (00:43) before Suzuki, tired of the trials they have endured for three years, dutifully says her prayers to a plodding string accompaniment. A second tragic motive is heard at the close of her prayer (01:56)

(Suzuki is praying in front of a statue of Buddha, occasionally ringing the prayer-bell. Butterfly is standing, erect and immobile, by a screen.)

SUZUKI	**SUZUKI**
E Izaghi e Izanami	Izaghi, Izanami,
sarundasico e Kami…	sarundasico Kami…
Oh! la mia testa!	Oh, my head!
E tu, Ten-Sjoo-daj!	And thou, Ten-Sjoo-daj,
Fate che Butterfly	don't let Butterfly
non pianga più, mai più.	cry any more, any more.
BUTTERFLY	**BUTTERFLY**
Pigri ed obesi	Fat and lazy
son gli dei giapponesi!	are the gods of Japan.
L'americano Iddio,	The American God,
son persuasa,	I'm sure,
ben più presto risponde	is much quicker in answering
a chi l'implori.	those who pray to him.
Ma temo ch'egli ignori	But I'm afraid he may not know
che noi stiam qui di casa.	we have our home here.

Suzuki…
è lungi la miseria?

Suzuki… how long will it be before we run
out of money?

(Suzuki opens a little table, takes out a few coins and shows them to Butterfly.)

SUZUKI
Questo è l'ultimo fondo.

SUZUKI
This is all we have left.

BUTTERFLY
Questo? Oh! troppe spese!

BUTTERFLY
This? Oh! We've been too extravagant!

SUZUKI
S'egli non torna e presto,
siamo male in arnese.

SUZUKI
If he doesn't come back, and soon,
we shall be in a bad way.

BUTTERFLY
Ma torna.

BUTTERFLY
But he will come back!

SUZUKI
Tornerà?

SUZUKI
He will come back?

BUTTERFLY
Perché dispone che il Console
provveda alla pigione,
rispondi, su!
Perché con tante cure
la casa rifornì di serrature,
s'ei non volesse ritornar mai più?

BUTTERFLY
Why does he arrange for the Consul
to look after the rent?
Tell me, quick!
Why did he take such care to have
the house fitted with locks
if he didn't mean to come back again?

SUZUKI
Non lo so.

SUZUKI
I don't know.

BUTTERFLY
Non lo sai?
Io te lo dico

BUTTERFLY
You don't know?
I'll tell you then:

per tener ben fuori le zanzare,
i parenti ed i dolori,
e dentro, con gelosa custodia,
la sua sposa -
la sua sposa che son io, Butterfly!

in order to keep mosquitos,
relations and troubles outside,
and inside, jealously guarded,
his bride -
his bride - me - Butterfly!

SUZUKI
Ma non s'è udito
di straniero marito
che sia tornato al suo nido.

SUZUKI
No one has ever heard
of a foreign husband
returning to his home.

BUTTERFLY
Ah! taci, o t'uccido.
Quell'ultima mattina:
"Tornerete signor?"
gli domandai.
Egli, col cuore grosso,
per celarmi la pena
sorridendo rispose:
"O Butterfly,
piccina mogliettina,
tornerò colle rose
alla stagion serena
quando fa la nidiata
il pettirosso."
Tornerà.

BUTTERFLY
Be quiet, or I'll kill you!
On that last morning,
"Are you coming back, sir?"
I asked him.
With a heavy heart,
trying to hide his unhappiness from me,
smiling he replied:
"Oh, Butterfly,
my dear sweet little wife,
I'll return with the roses
in that happy season
when the robin
builds his nest."
He'll come back.

SUZUKI
Speriam.

SUZUKI
Let us hope so.

BUTTERFLY
Dillo con me:
tornerà.

BUTTERFLY
Say it with me.
He'll come back.

SUZUKI
Tornerà.

SUZUKI
He'll come back.

Un bel dì vedremo is one of the mainstays of any soprano's repertoire. Butterfly describes the day of Pinkerton's return as she imagines it, and the aria covers the gamut of human emotions and demands every vocal resource a soprano can manage.

BUTTERFLY	BUTTERFLY
Piangi? Perché? Perché?	You're crying? Whatever for?
Ah, la fede ti manca!	Oh, you are lacking in faith!
Senti;	Listen.
Un bel dì vedremo	One fine day we'll see
levarsi un fil di fumo	a wisp of smoke arising
sull'estremo confin del mare.	over the extreme verge of the sea's horizon,
E poi la nave appare -	and afterwards the ship will appear.
poi la nave bianca	Then the white ship
entra nel porto, romba	will enter the harbour, will thunder
il suo saluto. Vedi?	a salute. You see?
È venuto!	He's arrived!
Io non gli scendo incontro.	I shan't go down to meet him.
Io no. Mi metto là	No, I shall stand there
sul ciglio del colle e aspetto,	on the brow of the hill and wait,
e aspetto gran tempo	and wait a long time,
e non mi pesa	and I shan't find
la lunga attesa.	the long wait wearisome.
E uscito dalla folla cittadina	And from the midst of the city crowd
un uom, un picciol punto	a man - a tiny speck -
s'avvia per la collina.	will make his way up the hill.
Chi sarà? chi sarà?	Who can it be?
E come sarà giunto -	And when he arrives -
Che dirà? che dirà?	what, what will he say?
Chiamerà "Butterfly!"	He'll call, "Butterfly!"
dalla lontana.	from the distance.
Io senza dar risposta	Not answering, I'll
me ne starò nascosta,	remain hidden,
un po' per celia	partly to tease,
e un po' per non morir	and partly so as not to die
al primo incontro,	at the first meeting.

ed egli alquanto in pena	And, a trifle worried,
chiamerà, chiamerà:	he'll call, he'll call
"Piccina mogliettina,	"My dear little wife,
olezzo di verbena!" -	fragrance of verbena!" -
i nomi che mi dava	the names he used to call me
al suo venire.	when he came here.
Tutto questo avverrà,	And this will happen,
te lo prometto.	I promise you.
Tieni la tua paura,	Keep your fears;
io con sicura fede l'aspetto.	with unalterable faith I shall wait for him.

(She dismisses Suzuki, who leaves. Sharpless and Goro can be seen entering the garden.)

DISC NO. 1/TRACK 16

The following exchanges between Butterfly and Sharpless are in short, interrupted phrases. In contrast to the previous aria, this scene is a study in what cannot be said.

GORO	**GORO**
C'è. Entrate.	She's there. Go in.
SHARPLESS	**SHARPLESS**
Chiedo scusa…Madama Butterfly…	Excuse me…Madam Butterfly…
BUTTERFLY	**BUTTERFLY**
Madama Pinkerton, prego.	Madam Pinkerton, please.

(She turns round.)

Oh! il mio signor Console,	Oh! My dear consul,
signor Console!	my dear sir!
SHARPLESS	**SHARPLESS**
Mi ravvisate?	You remember me?
BUTTERFLY	**BUTTERFLY**
Ben venuto in casa americana.	Welcome to an American house.

SHARPLESS

Grazie.

BUTTERFLY

Avi, antenati - tutti bene?

SHARPLESS

Ma, spero.

BUTTERFLY

Fumate?

(She beckons to Suzuki to prepare the pipe.)

SHARPLESS

Grazie. Ho qui…

BUTTERFLY

Signore, io vedo il cielo azzurro.

SHARPLESS

Grazie. Ho…

BUTTERFLY

Preferite forse le sigarette
americane?

SHARPLESS

Grazie. Ho da mostrarvi…

BUTTERFLY

(porgendo un fiammifero acceso)
A voi.

SHARPLESS

Thank you.

BUTTERFLY

Your grandparents and ancestors are quite
well?

SHARPLESS

I sincerely hope so.

BUTTERFLY

Will you smoke?

SHARPLESS

Thank you. I have here…

BUTTERFLY

Sir, I see the skies are blue.

SHARPLESS

No thank you. I have…

BUTTERFLY

Perhaps you would prefer American cigarettes?

SHARPLESS

Thank you. I have to show you…

BUTTERFLY

(offering Sharpless a light)
Here you are.

107

SHARPLESS
Mi scrisse Benjamin Franklin
Pinkerton.

SHARPLESS
Benjamin Franklin Pinkerton has written
to me…

BUTTERFLY
Davvero! È in salute?

BUTTERFLY
Really! Is he quite well?

SHARPLESS
Perfetta.

SHARPLESS
Perfectly.

BUTTERFLY
Io son la donna più lieta del Giappone.
Potrei farvi una domanda?

BUTTERFLY
I am the happiest woman in Japan.
May I ask you a question?

SHARPLESS
Certo.

SHARPLESS
Certainly.

BUTTERFLY
Quando fanno il lor nido
in America i pettirossi?

BUTTERFLY
When do the robins make their nests
in America?

SHARPLESS
Come dite?

SHARPLESS
What did you say?

BUTTERFLY
Sì…prima o dopo di qui?

BUTTERFLY
Yes…before or after they do here?

SHARPLESS
Ma…perché?

SHARPLESS
But…why?

BUTTERFLY
Mio marito m'ha promesso
di ritornar nella stagion beata
che il pettirosso rifà la nidiata.
Qui l'ha rifatta

BUTTERFLY
My husband promised
to return in that happy season
when the robin builds his nest again.
Here, it has done so

per ben tre volte, ma può darsi	three times already, but it may be
che di là usi nidiar men spesso.	that over there it doesn't nest so often.
Chi ride?	Who's that laughing?
Oh, c'è il nakodo.	Oh, it's the marriage-broker.
Un uom cattivo.	A bad man.

GORO
Godo…

GORO
I am enjoying…

BUTTERFLY
Zitto.

BUTTERFLY
Be quiet.

(to Sharpless)

Egli osò…No,	He dared…No,
prima rispondete alla domanda mia.	first answer my question.

SHARPLESS
Mi rincresce, ma ignoro…
non ho studiato ornitologia.

SHARPLESS
I'm sorry, but I don't know.
I haven't studied ornithology.

BUTTERFLY
Orni…

BUTTERFLY
Orni…

SHARPLESS
tologia.

SHARPLESS
…thology.

BUTTERFLY
Non lo sapete insomma.

BUTTERFLY
So you don't know, then.

DISC NO. 1/TRACK 17

Now we first hear the music associated with Butterfly's suitor, Yamadori (00:48). His upbeat, Japanese melody is contrasted with Butterfly's soaring and mocking response to his offer of marriage. She may be detaching from the reality of her situation, but her emotional sincerity is clearly greater than those around her (01:02).

SHARPLESS
No. Dicevamo…

BUTTERFLY
Ah sì, Goro, appena
B. F. Pinkerton fu in mare,
mi venne ad assediare
con ciarle e con presenti
per ridarmi ora questo,
or quel marito.
Or promette tesori
per uno scimunito…

GORO
Il ricco Yamadori.
Ella è povera in canna.
I suoi parenti
l'han tutti rinnegata.

SHARPLESS
No. We were saying…

BUTTERFLY
Ah, yes… Goro, as soon as
B. F. Pinkerton was at sea,
he came annoying me
with gossip and presents,
offering me first this one,
then that one in second marriage.
Now he's promising me riches
from a silly idiot.

GORO
The rich Yamadori.
She hasn't a penny.
Her relations
have all renounced her.

(Beyond the terrace Yamadori can be seen approaching on a palanquin, surrounded by servants.)

BUTTERFLY
Eccolo. Attenti.
Yamadori…
Ancor le pene dell'amor
non v'han deluso?
Vi tagliate ancor le vene
se il mio bacio vi ricuso?

YAMADORI
Tra le cose più moleste
è inutil sospirar.

BUTTERFLY
Tante mogli omai toglieste,
vi doveste abituar.

BUTTERFLY
There he is. Look.
Yamadori…
aren't you disillusioned
with love's pains yet?
Do you still intend to cut your veins
if I refuse you a kiss?

YAMADORI
One of the most annoying things
is hopeless sighing.

BUTTERFLY
You've had so many wives by now
you must be used to it.

YAMADORI	YAMADORI
L'ho sposate tutte quante	I married them, one and all,
e il divorzio mi francò.	and divorce has set me free.

BUTTERFLY	BUTTERFLY
Obbligata.	Most obliged.

DISC. NO. 2/TRACK 1

Butterfly declares her independence from Japanese law to the strains of "The Star Spangled Banner" (00:46), and after refusing Yamadori's advances, she serves tea to the accompaniment of a decidedly Western-sounding waltz (02:00)

YAMADORI	YAMADORI
A voi però giurerei	But to you I would vow
fede costante.	to be faithful.

SHARPLESS	SHARPLESS
Il messaggio, ho gran paura,	I'm afraid I shan't succeed
a trasmetter non riesco.	in delivering the message…

GORO	GORO
Ville, servi, oro, ad Omara	Villas, servants, gold, and at Omara
un palazzo principesco.	a princely palace!

BUTTERFLY	BUTTERFLY
Già legata è la mia fede.	My troth is plighted already.

GORO E YAMADORI *(a Sharpless)*	**GORO AND YAMADORI** *(to Sharpless)*
Maritata ancor si crede.	She thinks she's married.

BUTTERFLY	BUTTERFLY
Non mi credo. Sono, sono.	I don't think so - I am. I am.

GORO	GORO
Ma la legge…	But the law…

BUTTERFLY
Io non la so.

GORO
Per la moglie, l'abbandono
al divorzio equiparò...

BUTTERFLY
La legge giapponese...
non già del mio paese.

GORO
Quale?

BUTTERFLY
Gli Stati Uniti.

SHARPLESS
Oh, l'infelice!

BUTTERFLY
Si sa che aprir la porta
e la moglie cacciar
per la più corta
qui divorziar si dice.
Ma in America questo non si può -

(to Sharpless)

Vero?

SHARPLESS
Vero...Però...

BUTTERFLY
Là un bravo giudice serio,

BUTTERFLY
I don't know anything about that.

GORO
...for the wife has made desertion
equivalent to divorce.

BUTTERFLY
The Japanese law...
not that of my country now.

GORO
Which country?

BUTTERFLY
The United States.

SHARPLESS
Poor thing!

BUTTERFLY
We're quite aware that to open the door
and chase out the wife
with no further ado
is called divorce here.
But in America you can't do that.

Can you?

SHARPLESS
No. But...

BUTTERFLY
There, a good judge, grave

impettito dice al marito:
"Lei vuol andarsene?
Sentiam perché?"
"Sono seccato
del coniugato."
E il magistrato:
"Ah, mascalzone,
presto in prigione."
Suzuki, il thè.

and upright, says to the husband:
"You want to go away?
Let us hear why?"
"I'm bored
with married life!"
And the magistrate:
"You rascal,
into prison with you, quick!"
Tea, Suzuki.

YAMADORI
Udiste?

YAMADORI
You heard?

SHARPLESS
Mi rattrista
una sì piena cecità.

SHARPLESS
Such utter
blindness grieves me deeply.

GORO
Segnalata è già
la nave di Pinkerton.

GORO
Pinkerton's ship
is already signalled.

YAMADORI
Quand'essa lo riveda…

YAMADORI
When she sees him again…

SHARPLESS
Egli non vuol mostrarsi.
Io venni appunto
per levarla d'inganno…

SHARPLESS
He doesn't wish to show himself.
I have come expressly
to relieve her of any illusions on that score.

BUTTERFLY
Vostra Grazia permette…
che persone moleste!

BUTTERFLY
If your Grace will allow…
What tiresome people!

YAMADORI
Addio. Vi lascio

YAMADORI
Farewell. I leave you

il cuor pien di cordoglio:	with my heart full of grief,
ma spero ancor…	but I still hope…

BUTTERFLY   **BUTTERFLY**
Padrone.   Please yourself.

YAMADORI   **YAMADORI**
Ah, se voleste…   Oh, if only you would…

BUTTERFLY   **BUTTERFLY**
Il guaio è che non voglio…   The trouble is, I don't want to.

(Yamadori leaves. Goro follows him.)

DISC NO. 2/TRACK 2

Finally, Sharpless gets the chance to read Pinkerton's letter to Butterfly, and the moment is accompanied by our first hearing of the music of the Humming Chorus (01:01), which will accompany her patient vigil at the close of the scene. Struck by Sharpless's suggestion that Pinkerton may not return, Butterfly sings in short, separated phrases, exploring her options (03:34). Concluding that she would prefer death, the truncated phrases become a funeral march.

SHARPLESS   **SHARPLESS**
Ora a noi.   Our turn now.
Sedete qui.   Sit down here.
Legger con me   Will you read
volete questa lettera?   this letter with me?

BUTTERFLY   **BUTTERFLY**
Date.   Give it to me.

(She takes it and kisses it, then gives it back to the Consul.)

Sulla bocca, sul cuore…	To my lips, on my heart…
Siete l'uomo migliore del mondo.	You're the kindest man in the whole world.
Incominciate.	Please begin.

SHARPLESS

"Amico, cercherete
quel bel fiore di fanciulla…"

BUTTERFLY

Dice proprio così?

SHARPLESS

Sì, così dice,
ma se ad ogni momento…

BUTTERFLY

Taccio, taccio,
più nulla…

SHARPLESS

"Da quel tempo felice
tre anni son passati…"

BUTTERFLY

Anche lui li ha contati!

SHARPLESS

"E forse Butterfly
non mi rammenta più."

BUTTERFLY

Non lo rammento?
Suzuki, dillo tu.
"Non mi rammenta più."

SHARPLESS

Pazienza!
"Se mi vuol bene ancor,
se m'aspetta…"

SHARPLESS

"My dear friend, will you go and see
that pretty flower of a girl…"

BUTTERFLY

Does he really say that?

SHARPLESS

Yes, he does,
but if every moment…

BUTTERFLY

I'll keep quiet, I'll keep quiet.
I won't interrupt any more.

SHARPLESS

"Since that happy time
three years have gone by…"

BUTTERFLY

He's counted them, too!

SHARPLESS

"And perhaps Butterfly
does not remember me any more."

BUTTERFLY

Not remember him?
- Suzuki, tell him.
"Does not remember me any more…"

SHARPLESS

Patience!
"If she still loves me,
if she expects me…"

BUTTERFLY
Oh, le dolci parole!
Tu, benedetta!

SHARPLESS
"A voi mi raccomando perché vogliate
con circospezione prepararla…"

BUTTERFLY
Ritorna…

SHARPLESS
"…Al colpo."

BUTTERFLY
Quando? Presto! Presto!

SHARPLESS (fre sé)
Benone.
Qui troncarla conviene.
Quel diavolo d'un Pinkerton!

(to Butterfly)

Ebbene, che fareste,
Madama Butterfly,
s'ei non dovesse ritornar
più mai?

BUTTERFLY
Due cose potrei far:
tornar a divertir la gente
col cantar…oppur…
meglio, morire.

BUTTERFLY
Oh, what sweet words!
You blessed, blessed letter!

SHARPLESS
"I beg you to be so good as,
with tact, to prepare her gently…"

BUTTERFLY
He's coming.

SHARPLESS
"… for the blow."

BUTTERFLY
When? Quick! Quick!

SHARPLESS (to himself)
This is fine, I must say!
I must break it to her without more ado.
That devil of a Pinkerton!

Well now, what would you do,
Madam Butterfly,
if he were never
to return?

BUTTERFLY
I could do one of two things:
go back to entertaining people
with my songs;
or better, die.

SHARPLESS

Di strapparvi assai mi costa
dai miraggi ingannatori.
Accogliete la proposta
di quel ricco Yamadori.

BUTTERFLY

Voi, signor, mi dite questo! Voi!

SHARPLESS

Santo Dio, come si fa?

BUTTERFLY

Qui, Suzuki, presto, presto,
che Sua Grazia se ne va.

SHARPLESS

Mi scacciate?

BUTTERFLY

Ve ne prego,
già l'insistere non vale.

SHARPLESS

Fui brutale,
non lo nego.

BUTTERFLY

Oh, mi fate tanto male,
tanto male, tanto, tanto!
Niente, niente! Ho creduto morir…
Ma passa presto come passan
le nuvole sul mare…
Ah! m'ha scordata?

SHARPLESS

It grieves me deeply to rob you
of your illusions.
Accept the proposal
of the wealthy Yamadori.

BUTTERFLY

You! You, sir, tell me this! You!

SHARPLESS

Great God, what am I to do?

BUTTERFLY

Come here quickly, Suzuki.
His Grace is going.

SHARPLESS

Are you turning me out?

BUTTERFLY

Please,
forget what I said.

SHARPLESS

I was brutal,
I don't deny it.

BUTTERFLY

Oh, you hurt me so much,
so much, so very much!
It's nothing, nothing! I thought I was going
to die,
but it soon passes like
clouds over the sea…
Has he forgotten me, then?

(Going into the inner room, she returns with a child in her arms.)

DISC NO. 2/TRACK 3

The child is introduced, appropriately, with a reminiscence of "The Star-Spangled Banner" combined with a Japanese-derived theme, which will subsequently be associated with the child. Butterfly's vocal exclamation over this theme is an explosion of true emotion entirely at odds with her usual formality around Sharpless.

E questo? E questo?
E questo egli potrà pure scordare?

And this? And this?
Can he forget this as well?

SHARPLESS
Egli è suo?

SHARPLESS
It is his?

BUTTERFLY
Chi vide mai a bimbo
di Giappon occhi azzurrini?
E il labbro?
E i ricciolini d'oro schietto?

BUTTERFLY
Whoever saw a
Japanese child with blue eyes?
And his mouth?
And his curls of pure gold?

SHARPLESS
È palese. E Pinkerton lo sa?

SHARPLESS
It's obvious. And does Pinkerton know?

DISC NO. 2/TRACK 4

Che tua madre. **Butterfly addresses this aria to her child, and we hear the "geisha" theme (00:37) as she describes what their lives would be like if she returned to her former livelihood.**

BUTTERFLY
No. No. È nato
quand'egli stava in quel
suo gran paese. Ma voi…
gli scriverete.
Che l'aspetta un figlio
senza pari!

BUTTERFLY
No, no. The child was born
after he'd gone back
to that great country of his. But you
will write him
that a son without equal
is waiting for him here!

E mi saprete dir	And then you'll see
s'ei non s'affretta	if he doesn't come hurrying
per le terre e pei mari!	over the land and sea!
Sai cos'ebbe cuore	Do you know what that gentleman
di pensar quel signore?	had the heart to think?
Che tua madre dovrà	That your mother would have
prenderti in braccio	to take you in her arms
ed alla pioggia e al vento	and in all weathers
andar per la città	walk the city streets
a guadagnarti	to earn you
il pane e il vestimento.	food and clothing,
Ed alle impietosite genti	and to the pitying crowd
la man tremante stenderà	stretch out a trembling hand,
gridando, "Udite, udite	crying, "Listen, listen
la triste mia canzon.	to my sad tale.
A un'infelice madre	Charity for an unhappy mother!
la carità, muovetevi a pietà."	Have pity!"
E Butterfly, orribile destino,	And Butterfly - oh, horrible fate -
danzerà per te!	will dance for you!
E come fece già	And as she used to do,
la ghescia canterà.	the geisha will sing!
E la canzon giuliva e lieta	And the gay and merry song
in un singhiozzo finirà.	will end in a sob!
Ah, no! no! questo mai!	Oh no, no, never!
Questo mestier	Not that profession
che al disonore porta!	which leads to dishonour!
Morta! morta! Mai più danzar!	Rather let me die! To dance no more!
Piuttosto la mia vita vo' troncar!	I will cut my life short rather!
Ah! morta!	Oh, let me die!

DISC NO. 2/TRACK 5

Sharpless can barely speak after witnessing Butterfly's solo. Butterfly's words to her child quote "Un bel dì" when she mentions "the day of his return" [0:58] and then climax immediately after on the word "Gioia!" She is speaking of her own hoped-for transformation as much as the child's name.

SHARPLESS *(fra sé)*
Quanta pietà.

(to Butterfly)

Io scendo al piano.
Mi perdonate?

BUTTERFLY
A te, dagli la mano.

SHARPLESS
I bei capelli biondi!
Caro, come ti chiamano?

BUTTERFLY
Rispondi:
Oggi il mio nome è Dolore.
Però, dite al babbo,
scrivendogli,
che il giorno del suo ritorno
Gioia, Gioia mi chiamerò.

SHARPLESS
Tuo padre lo saprà, te lo prometto.

(He leaves hurriedly.)

SHARPLESS *(to himself)*
How pitiful!

I must go back now.
Will you forgive me?

BUTTERFLY
You… give him your hand.

SHARPLESS
What pretty fair curls!
What is your name, darling?

BUTTERFLY
Answer:
My name is Sorrow now.
But when you write
to Daddy tell him
that the day he comes back
I shall be called Joy, Joy!

SHARPLESS
Your father shall know it. I promise you.

DISC NO. 2/TRACK 6

Butterfly's reverie is interrupted by the marvelously sneaky music of Goro, who seems to be always within earshot.

SUZUKI *(gridando da fuori)*
Vespa! Rospo maledetto!

SUZUKI *(shouting outside)*
Serpent! Accursed toad!

(She comes in, dragging Goro by the ear.)

BUTTERFLY

Che fu?

SUZUKI

Ci ronza intorno
il vampiro! e ogni giorno
ai quattro venti spargendo va
che niuno sa chi padre
al bimbo sia!

GORO

Dicevo...solo...
che là in America
quando un figliuolo è nato maledetto
trarrà sempre reietto
la vita fra le genti!

BUTTERFLY

Ah! tu menti! menti!
Dillo ancora e t'uccido!

SUZUKI

No!

BUTTERFLY

Va via!
Vedrai, piccolo amor,
mia pena e mio conforto,
mio piccolo amor,
Ah! vedrai che il tuo vendicator
ci porterà lontano, lontan,
nella sua terra...lontan ci porterà.

(A cannon is heard.)

BUTTERFLY

What's happened?

SUZUKI

He buzzes round us,
the vampire! And every day
to the four winds he spreads abroad
that nobody knows
who the baby's father is!

GORO

I only said
that over there in America
when a child is born so unfortunate
he will always be an outcast
among people!

BUTTERFLY

Ah! you lie! you lie! you lie!
Say it again and I'll kill you!

SUZUKI

No!

BUTTERFLY

Get out!
You'll see, my little love,
my sorrow and my comfort,
my little love,
oh, you will see, your avenger will
take us far, far away
to his own country...he'll take us far away.

As we hear the aria "Un bel dì" again in the orchestra, Butterfly scans the horizon for Pinkerton's ship. She is breathless, hardly daring to believe it, until she reads the ship's name Abramo Lincoln [0:57]. The vindication of her love against the entire world climaxes spectacularly and almost in madness when she declares "He loves me!" [1:35]

SUZUKI
Il cannone del porto!
Una nave da guerra…

SUZUKI
The harbour gun!
A warship!

BUTTERFLY
Bianca…bianca…il vessillo
americano delle stelle…
Or governa per ancorare.

BUTTERFLY
It's white… white… the American flag!
with the stars…
Now it's manoeuvring to drop anchor.

(She takes the telescope.)

Reggimi la mano
ch'io discerna il nome,
il nome, il nome…
Eccolo: Abramo Lincoln!
Tutti han mentito!
Sol io lo sapevo,
sol io che l'amo.
Vedi lo scimunito tuo dubbio?
È giunto! è giunto!
Proprio nel punto
che ognun diceva:
piangi e dispera.
Trionfa il mio amor! il mio amor!
La mia fè trionfa intera.
Ei torna e m'ama!
Scuoti quella fronda di ciliegio
e m'innonda di fior.

Steady my hand
so that I can see the name…
the name, the name…
There it is: Abraham Lincoln!
They all lied! The lot of them!
I alone knew…
Only I who love him.
Do you see how foolish your doubts were?
He's come! He's come! He's come!
Just at the very moment
when everybody said:
weep and despair!
My love triumphs, yes, triumphs!
My faith is completely vindicated!
He has come back and he loves me!
Shake that branch of the cherry tree
and rain down

Io vò tuffar
nella pioggia odorosa
l'arsa fronte.

blooms on me.
I want to plunge
my burning brow in its fragrant rain.

DISC NO. 2/TRACK 8

Butterfly and Suzuki decorate the house for Pinkerton's arrival. Puccini was accused of using a Viennese operetta style in this piece. Even if he did, the lesser style in the hands of such a master created one of opera's most endearing moments, as the swirling music accompanies the women dancing in circles and strewing flowers through the house.

SUZUKI
Signora, quietatevi…quel pianto.

SUZUKI
Madam, calm yourself…those tears…

BUTTERFLY
No, rido, rido!
Quanto lo dovremo aspettar?
Che pensi? Un'ora?

BUTTERFLY
No, no, I'm laughing!
How long shall we have to wait for him?
What do you think? An hour?

SUZUKI
Di più.

SUZUKI
Longer.

BUTTERFLY
Due ore forse.
Tutto…tutto…
sia pien di fior, come
la notte è di faville.
Va pei fior.

BUTTERFLY
Two hours, maybe.
Everywhere
must be full of flowers,
as the night is of stars.
Go and pick the flowers!

SUZUKI
Tutti i fior?

SUZUKI
All of them?

BUTTERFLY
Tutti i fior, tutti, tutti.
Pesco, viola, gelsomin,

BUTTERFLY
All of them, all, all.
Peach blossom, violets, jasmine -

quanto di cespo, o d'erba,
o d'albero fiorì.

SUZUKI
Uno squallor d'inverno
sarà tutto il giardin.

BUTTERFLY
Tutta la primavera
voglio che olezzi qui.

SUZUKI
Uno squallor d'inverno
sarà tutto il giardin.
A voi, signora.

BUTTERFLY
Cogline ancora.

SUZUKI
Sovente a questa siepe
veniste a riguardare lungi,
piangendo nella deserta immensità.

BUTTERFLY
Giunse l'atteso,
nulla più chiedo al mare;
diedi pianto alla zolla,
essa i suoi fior mi dà.

SUZUKI
Spoglio è l'orto.

BUTTERFLY
Spoglio è l'orto?
Vien, m'aiuta.

every bush, plant
and tree that's in flower!

SUZUKI
The whole garden will be
as desolate as winter.

BUTTERFLY
I want all the perfume
of spring in here.

SUZUKI
The whole garden will be
as desolate as winter.
Here you are, Madam.

BUTTERFLY
Pick some more.

SUZUKI
You used to come to this hedge
so often to gaze in tears,
far out over the empty expanse.

BUTTERFLY
The long-awaited one has come,
I ask nothing more of the sea,
I gave tears to the soil,
it gives its flowers to me!

SUZUKI
The garden's bare.

BUTTERFLY
Is it? Then come
and help me.

SUZUKI	**SUZUKI**
Rose al varco della soglia.	Roses at the entrance to the threshold.
BUTTERFLY	**BUTTERFLY**
Tutta la primavera	I want all the perfume of spring
voglio che olezzi qui.	in here.
BUTTERFLY E SUZUKI	**BUTTERFLY AND SUZUKI**
Seminiamo intorno april.	Let us sow April all about us.
SUZUKI	**SUZUKI**
Gigli? viole?	Lilies? Violets?
BUTTERFLY	**BUTTERFLY**
Intorno spandi…	Scatter lilies and violets all about us!
Il suo sedil s'inghirlandi	His chair let us twine
di convolvi, gigli e rose.	with flower garlands!
BUTTERFLY E SUZUKI	**BUTTERFLY AND SUZUKI**
Gettiamo a mani piene	By the handful let's scatter
mammole e tuberose,	violets and tuberoses,
corolle di verbene,	blossoms of verbena,
petali d'ogni fior!	petals of every flower!

DISC NO. 2/TRACK 9

The score becomes quiet and introspective as Butterfly regards herself in the mirror.

BUTTERFLY	**BUTTERFLY**
Or vienmi ad adornar.	Now, come and dress me.
No, pria portami il bimbo.	But no! First bring me the baby.
Non son più quella!	I'm no longer what I was.
Troppi sospiri la bocca mandò…	These lips have breathed too many sighs…
E l'occhio riguardò	and these eyes have gazed
nel lontan troppo fiso.	too hard into the distance.
Dammi sul viso	Give my face
un tocco di carminio…	a touch of rouge…

Ed anche a te, piccino,
perché la veglia
non ti faccia vôte
per pallore le gote.

SUZUKI
Non vi movete
che v'ho a ravviare i capelli.

BUTTERFLY
Che ne diranno!
E lo zio Bonzo?
Già del mio danno
tutti contenti!
E Yamadori coi suoi languori!
Beffati, scornati,
spennati gli ingrati!

SUZUKI
È fatto.

BUTTERFLY
L'obi che vestii da sposa.
Qua, ch'io lo vesta.
Vo' che mi veda indosso
il vel del primo dì.
E un papavero rosso
nei capelli…Così.
nello shosi or farem tre forellini
per riguardar,
e starem zitti come topolini
ad aspettar.

and you too, little one,
so that the long wait
won't leave your cheeks
pale and hollow.

SUZUKI
Keep still,
I have to do your hair.

BUTTERFLY
What will they say now?
And my uncle, the Bonze?
All of them so glad
at my sad plight!
And Yamadori, with his languishing!
Ridiculed, disgraced,
shown up, the unkind creatures!

SUZUKI
I've finished.

BUTTERFLY
The sash I wore as a bride.
Bring it here for me to put on.
I want him to see me dressed
as I was that first day.
And a red poppy
in my hair… like that.
Now we'll make three little holes
in the paper screen to look through,
and we'll stay quiet as mice,
waiting.

(Butterfly leads the baby to the soshi and makes three holes in it; Suzuki sits on her haunches and looks out. Butterfly places herself in front of the biggest hole, and looking outside remains motionless and rigid as a statue. The baby is between his mother and Suzuki, and looks out-

side curiously. Night has fallen. Moon beams light up the soshi from outside. From far away voices can be heard humming.)

DISC NO. 2/TRACK 10

"The Humming Chorus" is one of the most prized of the operatic choruses. The wordless melody, reflecting the sleeping town below but also possibly suggesting the voices of the spirit world, is heartrending in its plaintive simplicity.

Coro a bocca chiusa   Humming chorus

It is dawn. Butterfly still stands watching, motionless. The baby and Susuki are asleep. Sailor's voices are heard from the harbour below.

DISC NO. 2/TRACK 11

The second scene of act II begins with an extended orchestral Intermezzo in which we seem to follow Butterfly's thoughts during her long vigil. It begins with a fortissimo statement of one of the themes associated with ill-fortune. This is followed by the melody from the act I when Butterfly kisses Pinkerton's hand (00:56). It gives way to a new, beautiful and aching melody which seems to reflect Butterfly's longing for her husband's return (01:28). This melody grows and modulates, culminating in a triumphant quote from the act I love duet and a whole series of quoted themes from earlier in the opera. As the music calms, we hear the sailors calling to one another in the harbor (04:44), and finally the orchestration reflects the sun rising over the water (05:46)

VOCI DEI MARINAI *(da lontano)*   **SAILORS VOICES** *(from afar)*
Oh eh! Oh eh! Oh eh!   Oh eh! Oh eh! Oh eh!

DISC NO. 2/TRACK 12

The triumphant theme we heard when the child, Sorrow, was first introduced now becomes a lullaby as Butterfly puts him to bed (00:23)

SUZUKI   **SUZUKI**
Già il sole!   The sun's up already!
Cio-Cio-San…   Cho-Cho-San!

BUTTERFLY
Verrà…verrà col pieno sole.

SUZUKI
Salite a riposare, affranta siete.
Al suo venire vi chiamerò.

BUTTERFLY
Dormi, amor mio,
dormi sul mio cor.
Tu sei con Dio,
ed io col mio dolor.
A te i rai
degli astri d'or,
bimbo mio, dormi.

BUTTERFLY
He'll come… he'll come, you'll see.

SUZUKI
Go and rest, you're tired out…
When he arrives I'll call you.

BUTTERFLY
Sleep, my love,
sleep on my heart.
You are with God,
and I'm with my sorrow.
On you shine the rays
of the golden stars…
Sleep, my child.

DISC NO. 2/TRACK 13

Pinkerton's actual return is quiet and understated, in contrast to Butterfly's fantasies of his return.

SUZUKI
Povera Butterfly!

BUTTERFLY
Dormi, amor mio,
dormi sul mio cor.
Tu sei con Dio,
ed io col mio dolor.

SUZUKI
Povera Butterfly!
Chi sia?
Oh!

SUZUKI
Poor Butterfly!

BUTTERFLY
Sleep, my love,
sleep on my heart.
You are with god,
and I'm with my sorrow.

SUZUKI
Poor Butterfly!
Who can that be?
Oh!

(Pinkerton and Sharpless enter.)

PINKERTON
Zitta! Zitta! Non la destare.

SUZUKI
Era stanca, sì tanto!
Vi stette ad aspettare
tutta la notte col bimbo.

PINKERTON
Come sapea…?

SUZUKI
Non giunge da tre anni
una nave nel porto
che da lunge Butterfly
non ne scruti il color, la bandiera.

SHARPLESS *(a Pinkerton)*
Ve lo dissi?

SUZUKI
La chiamo…

PINKERTON
No, non ancor.

SUZUKI
Lo vedete, ier sera,
la stanza volle sparger
di fiori.

SHARPLESS
Ve lo dissi?

PINKERTON
Hush! Hush! Don't wake her.

SUZUKI
She was quite worn out!
She has been standing waiting for you
all night long with the baby.

PINKERTON
How did she know?

SUZUKI
For three years now
no ship has put into the harbour
without Butterfly scrutinising
its colour and flag from afar.

SHARPLESS *(to Pinkerton)*
I told you, didn't I?

SUZUKI
I'll call her…

PINKERTON
No, not yet.

SUZUKI
You see, last night
she insisted on strewing
flowers all over the room.

SHARPLESS
I told you, didn't I?

PINKERTON
Che pena!

SUZUKI
Chi c'è là fuori nel giardino?

PINKERTON
Zitta!

SUZUKI
Chi è? Chi è?

SHARPLESS
Meglio dirle ogni cosa.

SUZUKI
Chi è? Chi è?

PINKERTON
È venuta con me.

SUZUKI
Chi è? Chi è?

SHARPLESS
È sua moglie.

SUZUKI
Anime sante degli avi!
Alla piccina
s'è spento il sol!

SHARPLESS
Scegliemmo quest'ora mattutina
per ritrovarti sola, Suzuki,

PINKERTON
This is dreadful!

SUZUKI
Who's that out there in the garden?
It's a woman!

PINKERTON
Hush!

SUZUKI
Who is it? Who is it?

SHARPLESS
Best tell her everything.

SUZUKI
Who is it? Who is it?

PINKERTON
She has come with me.

SUZUKI
Who is it? Who is it?

SHARPLESS
His wife.

SUZUKI
Holy spirits of my ancestors!
For the little one
the sun has gone out!

SHARPLESS
We chose this early hour
in order to find you alone, Suzuki,

e alla gran prova	and in this hour of trial
un aiuto, un sostegno	to seek some means of consolation
cercar con te.	and support with you.

SUZUKI

Che giova? Che giova?

SUZUKI

What's the use? What's the use?

DISC NO. 2/TRACK 14

Io so che alle sue pene. In this gorgeous trio, Puccini allows each of his characters to pour out their despair. The plodding motive in the low strings reflects the various shades of sadness – guilt, pity, dread – of all three.

SHARPLESS

Io so che alle sue pene
non ci sono conforti.
Ma del bimbo conviene
assicurar le sorti.

SHARPLESS

I know that for her deep distress
there is no consolation.
But it is necessary to provide
for the child's future.

PINKERTON

Oh! l'amara fragranza
di questi fior
velenosa al cor mi va;
immutata è la stanza
dei nostri amor…

PINKERTON

Oh, the bitter perfume
of these flowers
is poison to the heart!
The room where we loved
is unchanged…

SHARPLESS

La pietosa
che entrar non osa
materna cura
del bimbo avrà.

SHARPLESS

That kind woman
who dares not enter
will care like a mother
for the child.

SUZUKI

Oh, me trista!
E volete ch'io chieda
ad una madre…

SUZUKI

Oh, I'm so miserable!
And you want me
to ask a mother…

SHARPLESS

Suvvia, parla con quella pia
e conducila qui…
S'anche la veda Butterfly,
non importa…anzi
meglio se accorta del vero
si facesse alla sua vista.
Vien, Suzuki, vien…

PINKERTON

Ma un gel di morte vi sta.
Il mio ritratto…
Tre anni son passati,
e noverati n'ha i giorni
e l'ore!
Non posso rimaner…
Sharpless, v'aspetto
per via…

SHARPLESS

Non ve l'avevo detto?

PINKERTON

Datele voi qualche soccorso…
Mi struggo dal rimorso.

SHARPLESS

Vel dissi? vi ricorda?
Badate, ella ci crede.
E fui profeta allor!
Sorda ai consigli,
sorda ai dubbi, vilipesa,
nell'ostinata attesa
raccolse il cor…

SHARPLESS

Come, speak to that kind lady
and bring her in here.
Even if Butterfly should see her,
no matter… On the contrary,
better if she should realize
the truth through seeing her.
Come, Suzuki, come…

PINKERTON

But the coldness of death is in here.
My picture!…
Three years have passed,
and she has counted the days
and the hours!
I can't stay here…
Sharpless, I'll wait for you
on the way back…

SHARPLESS

Didn't I tell you so?

PINKERTON

You give her some help…
I am completely crushed by remorse.

SHARPLESS

I told you! Do you remember?
When she gave you her hand,
"Beware!" I said, "she believes in all this!"
and my words were prophetic then!
Deaf to advice, deaf to all doubts, a victim
of scorn, obstinately waiting,
she fortified her heart.

PINKERTON

Sì, tutto in un istante
io vede il fallo mio
e sento che di questo tormento
tregua mai non avrò.
No!

SHARPLESS

Andate.
Il triste vero
da sola apprenderà.

PINKERTON

Yes, all in an instant
I see how I have sinned
and realise I shall never
find respite from this torture.
Never!

SHARPLESS

Go.
The sad truth
she'll learn alone.

DISC NO. 2/TRACK 15

Addio, fiorito asil. This aria was added to the score after the disastrous premiere, in order to balance the length of the final scene with the preceding scene, which are now separated by an intermission. Some critics feel it softens Pinkerton's question-able character, while others find him only more self-pitying, but most agree the addition of this beautiful tenor solo greatly improves the structure of the act.

PINKERTON

Addio, fiorito asil
di letizia e d'amor…
Sempre il mite suo sembiante
con strazio atroce vedrò.

SHARPLESS

Ma or quel cor sincero
presago è già… Vel dissi, ecc.

PINKERTON

Addio, fiorito asil…
Non reggo al tuo squallor…
Fuggo, fuggo…son vil!

PINKERTON

Farewell, flowery refuge
of happiness and love…
Her sweet face will haunt me ever,
torturing me agonizingly.

SHARPLESS

But by now the faithful heart
maybe half suspects. I told you, etc.

PINKERTON

Farewell, flowery refuge…
I can't bear your desolation…
I must fly! I'm beneath contempt!

SHARPLESS

Andate, il triste vero apprenderà.

SHARPLESS

Go, she will learn the sad truth.

(Pinkerton hurries away as Kate and Suzuki come in from the garden.)

DISC NO. 2/TRACK 16

Kate originally sang in the previous ensemble, but in the revised version she does not have a coherent musical identity in the opera. While sympathetic, she remains more of an idea to augment, rather than distract from, the all-encompassing emotional journey of Butterfly.

KATE

Glielo dirai?

KATE

Will you tell her that?

SUZUKI

Prometto.

SUZUKI

I promise.

KATE

E le darai consiglio
d'affidarmi…

KATE

And you'll advise her
to trust me?

SUZUKI

Prometto.

SUZUKI

Yes.

KATE

Lo terrò come un figlio.

KATE

I'll care for him like my own son.

SUZUKI

Vi credo. Ma bisogna
ch'io le sia sola accanto…
nella grande ora…sola!
Piangerà tanto, tanto!

SUZUKI

I believe you. But I must
be quite alone with her…
quite alone in this hour of crisis!
She'll cry so bitterly!

BUTTERFLY

Suzuki, Suzuki! Dove sei? Suzuki!
Suzuki, Suzuki! Dove sei?

BUTTERFLY

Suzuki! Suzuki! Where are you?
Suzuki!

SUZUKI

Son qui…
Pregavo e rimettevo
a posto…No…no…no…
Non scendete…no…no…

SUZUKI

Here I am…
I was praying tidying up…
No… no… no…
Don't come in… no… no…

DISC NO. 2/TRACK 17

In halting phrases, Butterfly slowly realizes the truth and gradually becomes resigned to the surrender of her child. In long stately phrases she wishes her rival, Kate, all the happiness she deserves (04:00), and when asked how the child will be turned over, Butterfly quotes from her own happy vision, "Un bel di," saying Pinkerton should ascend the hill in half an hour to take the child (05:08)

BUTTERFLY

È qui…è qui…
dove è nascosto?
È qui…è qui…
ecco il Console…
e…dove? dove?
Non c'è.
Quella donna!
Che vuol da me?
Niuno parla!
Perché piangete?
Non, non ditemi nulla…nulla…
Forse potrei cader morta sull'attimo…
Tu, Suzuki, che sei tanto buona,
non piangere!
E mi vuoi tanto bene -
un Sì, un No, di' piano:
vive?

BUTTERFLY

He's here, he's here…
where's he hidden?
He's here… he's here…
There's the Consul…
and where?… where?
He isn't here!
That woman?
What does she want at my house?
Nobody speaks!
Why are you crying?
No, don't tell me anything…
I might fall dead on the spot.
You, Suzuki, who are so good,
don't cry!
You love me so much -
yes or no - whisper…
Is he alive?

SUZUKI

Sì.

SUZUKI

Yes.

BUTTERFLY
Ma non viene più.
Te l'han detto!
Vespa! voglio che tu risponda.

SUZUKI
Mai più.

BUTTERFLY
Ma è giunto ieri?

SUZUKI
Sì.

BUTTERFLY
Ah! quella donna
mi fa tanta paura!
tanta paura!

SHARPLESS
È la causa innocente
d'ogni vostra sciagura.
Perdonatele.

BUTTERFLY
Ah! è sua moglie!
Tutto è morto per me!
Tutto è finito!

SHARPLESS
Coraggio!

BUTTERFLY
Voglion prendermi tutto!
Il figlio mio!

BUTTERFLY
But he won't come back any more.
They've told you?
Serpent! Will you answer me?

SUZUKI
Never again.

BUTTERFLY
But he arrived yesterday?

SUZUKI
Yes.

BUTTERFLY
Oh, that woman makes
me feel so afraid,
so afraid!

SHARPLESS
She is the innocent cause
of all your misfortunes.
Forgive her.

BUTTERFLY
Ah! she's his wife!
Everything is finished for me!
Everything is over! Oh!

SHARPLESS
Be brave.

BUTTERFLY
They want to take everything
away from me! My son!

SHARPLESS

Fatelo pel suo bene il sacrifizio.

BUTTERFLY

Ah! triste madre!
Abbandonar mio figlio!
E sia.
A lui devo obbedir!

KATE

Potete perdonarmi, Butterfly?

BUTTERFLY

Sotto il gran ponte del cielo
non v'è donna di voi più felice.
Siatelo sempre…
Non v'attristate per me…

KATE

Povera piccina!

SHARPLESS

È un'immensa pietà.

KATE

E il figlio lo darà?

BUTTERFLY

A lui lo potrò dare,
se lo verrà a cercare.
Fra mezz'ora
salite la collina.

SHARPLESS

Make the sacrifice for his sake.

BUTTERFLY

Oh, unhappy mother!
To be obliged to give up my son!
Very well then!
I must obey him in everything.

KATE

Can you ever forgive me, Butterfly?

BUTTERFLY

Under the great dome of heaven,
there isn't a happier woman than you.
May you always be so…
Don't upset yourself about me…

KATE

Poor little thing!

SHARPLESS

It's a terrible shame!

KATE

And will she give up the child?

BUTTERFLY

I'll be able to give up the child to him,
if he'll come and fetch him.
Return up the hill
in half-an-hour's time.

DISC NO. 2/TRACK 18

Butterfly's real thoughts are expressed by the orchestra in these guarded exchanges with Suzuki. The woodwinds quietly quote her child's theme when she asks where he is [1:13], like an idea forming in her mind. When she dismisses Suzuki, her bursting emotions are represented by insistent beats on the tympani [1:40], growing louder, then soft and ominous, and finally loud again, never changing rhythm. Few composers have been able to say so much with such economy of means.

SUZUKI	**SUZUKI**
Come una mosca prigioniera	Like the wings of a captive fly
l'ali batte il piccolo cuor!	her little heart is beating!
BUTTERFLY	**BUTTERFLY**
Troppa luce è di fuor,	There's too much light outside,
e troppo primavera.	and too much spring.
Chiudi.	Close the screens to.
Il bimbo ove sia?	Where's the baby?
SUZUKI	**SUZUKI**
Giuoca...Lo chiamo?	He's playing...Shall I call him?
BUTTERFLY	**BUTTERFLY**
Lascialo giocar...	Let him play...
Va a fargli compagnia.	Go and keep him company.
SUZUKI	**SUZUKI**
Resto con voi.	I'll stay with you.
BUTTERFLY	**BUTTERFLY**
Va, va. Te lo comando.	Go along, I order you to.

(Suzuki goes out, crying. Butterfly lights a taper in front of the sanctuary, and bows. Then she takes her father's knife from the wall, kisses it, and slowly reads the inscription on the blade.)

Again we hear the dagger theme as Butterfly takes it up and reads the inscription.
The theme is thundered in the orchestra this time, as if the reality of Butterfly's true
Japanese identity and situation is finally blasting away her American illusions. Suddenly, Suzuki pushes the child into the room (00:48) and Butterfly sings her farewell,
"Tu, Tu piccolo Iddio!" (You, Little Idol), accompanied by an upwardly surging
motive (01:52) which dissolves in the end into a funeral march (03:06). She stabs herself, and we hear Pinkerton's voice calling her in the distance. When he arrives on
the scene, the full orchestra reiterates the "geisha" theme in B minor, ending the
opera on a jarring G-major chord.

"Con onor muore	"He dies with honour
chi non può serbar vita con onore."	who cannot live with honour."

(As she places the blade against her throat, the door opens and Suzuki's arm pushes the child
towards his mother. Butterfly drops the knife and rushes to the child, which she seizes up and
kisses passionately.)

Tu? tu? tu? tu?	You? You? You?
Piccolo iddio!	Little idol of my heart.
Amore, amore mio.	My Love, my love,
Fior di giglio e di rosa.	flower of the lily and rose.
Non saperlo mai…per te,	Never know that, for you,
pei tuoi puri occhi	for your innocent eyes,
muore Butterfly…	Butterfly is about to die…
Perché tu possa andar	so that you may go
di là dal mare	away beyond the sea
senza che ti rimorda	without being subject to remorse
ai dì maturi	in later years
il materno abbandono.	for your mother's desertion.
O a me, sceso dal trono	Oh, you who have come down to me
dell'alto Paradiso,	from high heaven,
guarda ben fiso, fiso,	look well, well
di tua madre la faccia!	on your mother's face,
Che ten' resti una traccia,	that you may keep a faint memory of it,

guarda ben!	look well!
Amore, addio, addio!	Little love, farewell!
Piccolo amor!	Farewell, my little love!
Va, gioca, gioca.	Go and play.

(She picks up the child and sets him down on a mat; she gives him an American flag and a doll to play with and gently blindfolds his eyes. Picking up the knife she goes behind the screen. Then appearing from behind the screen with the white veil clasped round her throat, Butterfly staggers across the room towards the baby, and collapses beside him.)

VOCE DI PINKERTON	**VOICE OF PINKERTON**
Butterfly! Butterfly! Butterfly!	Butterfly! Butterfly! Butterfly!

(Pinkerton and Sharpless burst into the room, and run to her side. With a weak gesture Butterfly points to her child and dies. Pinkerton kneels down beside her, while Sharpless goes to pick up the child.)

FINE	**END**

PHOTO CREDITS

MADAMA BUTTERFLY

Giacomo Puccini

COMPACT DISC ONE   72:07:00

ATTO PRIMO/ACT ONE

1	E soffitto…epareti… *Pinkerton/Goro*	2:17
2	Questa ä la cameriera *Goro/Pinkerton/Suzuki/Sharpless*	4:36
3	Dovunque al mundo *Pinkerton/Sharpless/Goro*	4:08
4	Quale smania vi prende *Pinkerton/Sharpless/Coro/Goro*	4:11
5	Quanto cielo!…Ancora un passo or via *Coro/Butterfly/Sharpless*	3:36
6	Gran Ventura *Coro/Butterfly/Pinkerton/Goro/Sharpless*	3:48
7	L'Imperial Commissario *Coro/Butterfly/Pinkerton/Goro/Sharpless/* *Cugino/La Madre/Yakuside/Zio*	3:22
8	Vieni, amor mio! *Pinkerton/Butterfly/Goro*	2:46
9	Ieri son salita tutta sola *Coro/Butterfly/Pinkerton/Goro/Sharpless/* *Il Commissario/Ufficiale del Registro*	4:42

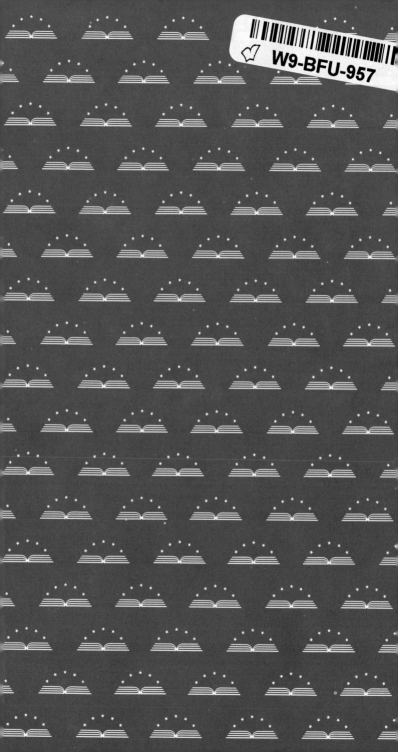

Complete Stories of Henry James

HENRY JAMES

HENRY JAMES

COMPLETE STORIES
1874–1884

THE LIBRARY OF AMERICA

The paper used in this publication meets the
minimum requirements of the American National Standard for
Information Sciences—Permanence of Paper for Printed
Library Materials, ANSI z39.48—1984.

Distributed to the trade in the United States
by Penguin Putnam Inc.
and in Canada by Penguin Books Canada Ltd.

Library of Congress Catalog Number: 98–19252
For cataloging information, see end of Notes.
ISBN 1–883011–63–9
—————
First Printing
The Library of America—106

Manufactured in the United States of America

WILLIAM L. VANCE
WROTE THE NOTES FOR THIS VOLUME

Contents

Professor Fargo

T HE LITTLE TOWN of P—— is off the railway, and reached
by a coach drive of twenty-five miles, which the primitive
condition of the road makes a trial to the flesh, and the dulness of the landscape a weariness to the spirit. It was therefore
not balm to my bruises, physical or intellectual, to find, on
my arrival, that the gentleman for whose sake I had undertaken the journey had just posted off in a light buggy for a
three days' holiday. After venting my disappointment in a variety of profitless expletives, I decided that the only course
worthy of the elastic philosophy of a commercial traveller was
to take a room at the local tavern and await his return.
P—— was obviously not an exhilarating place of residence, but
I had outweathered darker hours, and I reflected that having,
as the phrase is, a bone to pick with my correspondent, a little
accumulated irritation would arm me for the combat. Moreover, I had been rattling about for three months by rail; I was
mortally tired, and the prospect of spending a few days beyond earshot of the steam whistle was not unwelcome. A certain audible, rural hush seemed to hang over the little town,
and there was nothing apparently to prevent my giving it the
whole of my attention. I lounged awhile in the tavern porch,
but my presence seemed only to deepen the spell of silence
on that customary group of jaundiced ruminants who were
tilting their chairs hard by. I measured thrice, in its length,
the dusty plank sidewalk of the main street, counted the holly-
hocks in the front yards, and read the names on the little glass
door plates; and finally, in despair, I visited the cemetery. Although we were at the end of September, the day was hot,
and this youthful institution boasted but a scanty growth of
funereal umbrage. No weeping willow, no dusky cypress offered a friendly shelter to the meditative visitor. The yellow
grass and the white tombstones glared in the hot light, and
though I felt very little merrier than a graveyard ghost, I staid
hardly longer than one who should have mistaken his hour.
But I am fond of reading country epitaphs, and I promised
myself to come back when the sun was lower. On my way

back to the inn I found myself, on a lately opened cross street,
face to face with the town hall, and pausing approached its
threshold with hopes of entertainment scarcely less ardent
than those which, during a journey abroad, had guided my
steps toward some old civic palace of France or Italy. There
was, of course, no liveried minion to check my advance, and
I made my way unchallenged into the large, bare room which
occupied the body of the edifice. It was the accustomed theatre of town meetings, caucuses, and other solemn services,
but it seemed just now to have been claimed for profaner uses.
An itinerant lecturer, of a boisterous type, was unpacking his
budget and preparing his *mise en scène*. This seemed to consist
simply of a small table and three chairs in a row, and of a
dingy specimen of our national standard, to whose awkward
festoons, suspended against the blank wall at the rear of the
platform, the orator in person was endeavoring to impart a
more artistic grace. Another personage on the floor was engaged in scrawling the date of the performance, in red chalk,
upon a number of printed handbills. He silently thrust one of
these documents at me as I passed, and I saw with some elation that I had a resource for my evening. The latter half of
the page consisted of extracts from village newspapers, setting
forth the merits of the entertainments. The headings alone,
as I remember them, ran somewhat in this fashion:

A MESSAGE FROM THE SPIRIT WORLD.
THE HIGHER MATHEMATICS MADE EASY TO LADIES AND CHILDREN.
A NEW REVELATION! A NEW SCIENCE!
GREAT MORAL AND SCIENTIFIC COMBINATION.
PROFESSOR FARGO, THE INFALLIBLE WAKING MEDIUM AND
MAGICIAN, CLAIRVOYANT, PROPHET, AND SEER!
COLONEL GIFFORD, THE FAMOUS LIGHTNING
CALCULATOR AND MATHEMATICAL REFORMER!

This was the substance of the programme, but there were
a great many incidental *fioriture* which I have forgotten. By
the time I had mastered them, however, for the occasion, the
individual who was repairing the tattered flag, turned round,
perceived me, and showed me a countenance which could
belong only to an "infallible waking medium." It was not,
indeed, that Professor Fargo had the abstracted and emaciated

aspect which tradition attributes to prophets and visionaries. On the contrary, the fleshy element in his composition seemed, superficially, to enjoy a luxurious preponderance over the spiritual. He was tall and corpulent, and wore an air of aggressive robustness. A mass of reddish hair was tossed back from his forehead in a leonine fashion, and a lustrous auburn beard diffused itself complacently over an expansive but by no means immaculate shirt front. He was dressed in a black evening suit, of a tarnished elegance, and it was in keeping with the festal pattern of his garments, that on the right forefinger of a large, fat hand, he should wear an immense turquoise ring. His intimate connection with the conjuring class was stamped upon his whole person; but to a superficial glance he might have seemed a representative of its grosser accomplishments. You could have fancied him, in spangled fleshings, looking down the lion's mouth, or cracking the ring-master's whip at the circus, while Mlle. Josephine jumped through the hoops. It was his eyes, when you fairly met them, that proved him an artist on a higher line. They were eyes which had peeped into stranger places than even lions' mouths. Their pretension, I know, was to pierce the veil of futurity; but if this was founded, I could only say that the vision of Ezekiel and Jeremiah was but another name for consummate Yankee shrewdness. They were, in a single word, the most impudent pair of eyes I ever beheld, and it was the especial sign of their impudence that they seemed somehow to undertake to persuade you of their disinterested benevolence. Being of a fine reddish brown color, it was probable that several young women that evening would pronounce them magnificent. Perceiving, apparently, that I had not the rustic physiognomy of a citizen of P——, Professor Fargo deemed my patronage worth securing. He advanced to the cope of the platform with his hands in his pockets, and gave me a familiar nod.

"Mind you come to-night, young man!" he said, jocosely imperious.

"Very likely I shall," I answered. "Anything in the world to help me through an evening at P——."

"Oh, you won't want your money back," the Professor rejoined. "Mine is a first-class entertainment; none of your shuffling break-downs. We are perfect, my friends and I, in our respective parts. If you are fond of a good, stiff, intellectual problem, we'll give you something to think about." The Professor spoke very slowly and benignantly, and his full, sonorous voice rolled away through the empty hall. He evidently liked to hear it himself; he balanced himself on his toes and surveyed the scene of his impending exploits. "I don't blow my own trumpet," he went on; "I'm a modest man; you'll see for yourself what I can do. But I should like to direct your attention to my friend the Colonel. *He's* a rare old gentleman to find in a travelling show! The most remarkable old gentleman, perhaps, that ever addressed a promiscuous audience. You needn't be afraid of the higher mathematics; it's all made as pretty as a game of billiards. It's his own daughter does the sums. We don't put her down in the bills, for motives of delicacy; but I'll tell you for your private satisfaction that she is an exquisite young creature of seventeen."

It was not every day that I found myself in familiar conversation with a prophet, and the opportunity for obtaining a glimpse of the inner mechanism of the profession was too precious to be neglected. I questioned the Professor about his travels, his expenses, his profits, and the mingled emotions of the itinerant showman's lot; and then, taking the bull by the horns, I asked him whether, between ourselves, an accomplished medium had not to be also a tolerable conjurer? He leaned his head on one side and stood stroking his beard, and looking at me between lids shrewdly half closed. Then he gave a little dry chuckle, which expressed, at my choice, compassion either for my disbelief in his miracles or for my faith in his urbanity.

"I confess frankly," I said, "that I'm a skeptic. I don't believe in messages from the spirit world. I don't believe that even the depressing prospect of immortality is capable of converting people who talked plain sense here on earth into the authors of the inflated platitudes which people of your profession pretend to transmit from them. I don't believe people who have expressed themselves for a lifetime in excellent English can ever be content with conversation by raps on the dinner table. I don't believe that you know anything more about the future world than you do about the penal code of China. My impression is that you don't believe so yourself. I can hardly expect you, of course, to take the wind out of your own sails. What I should vastly like you to do is, to tell me *viva voce*, in so many words, that your intentions are pure and your miracles genuine."

The Professor remained silent, still caressing his prophetic beard. At last, in a benevolent drawl, "Have you got any dear friend in the spirit land?" he asked.

"I don't know what you call the spirit land," I answered. "Several of my friends have died."

"Would you like to see 'em?" the Professor promptly demanded.

"No, I confess I shouldn't!"

The Professor shook his head.

"You've not a rich nature," he rejoined blandly.

"It depends on what you call rich. I possess on some points a wealth of curiosity. It would gratify me peculiarly to have you say outright, standing there on your own platform, that you're an honest man."

It seemed to give him pleasure to trifle with my longing for this sensation. "I'll give you leave," he said, for all answer, "to tie my hands into the tightest knot you can invent—and then I'll make your great-grandfather come in and stop the clock. You know I couldn't stop a clock, perched up on a mantel shelf five feet high, with my heels."

"I don't know," said I. "I fancy you're very clever."

"Cleverness has nothing to do with it. I've great magnetism."

"You'd magnetize my great-grandfather down from heaven?"

"Yes, sir, if I could establish communication. You'll see to-night what I can do. I'll satisfy you. If I don't, I shall be happy to give you a private sitting. I'm also a healing medium. You don't happen to have a toothache? I'd set you down there and pull it right out, as I'd pull off your boot."

In compliment to this possibility, I could only make him my bow. His, at least, was a "rich nature." I bade him farewell, with the assurance that, skeptic as I was, I would applaud him impartially in the evening. I had reached the top of the hall, on my way out, when I heard him give a low, mellifluous whistle. I turned round, and he beckoned to me to return. I

walked back, and he leaned forward from the platform, up-
lifting his stout forefinger. "I simply desire to remark," he
said, "that I'm an honest man!"

On my return to the hotel I found that my impatience for
the Professor's further elucidation of his honesty made the
interval look long. Fortune, however, assisted me to traverse
it at an elastic pace. Rummaging idly on a bookshelf in the
tavern parlor, I found, amid a pile of farmers' almanacs and
Methodist tracts, a tattered volume of "Don Quixote." I repaired to my room, tilted back my chair, and communed deliciously with the ingenious hidalgo. Here was "magnetism"
superior even to that of Professor Fargo. It proved so effective
that I lost all note of time, and, at last on looking at my watch,
perceived that dinner must have been over for an hour. Of
"service" at this unsophisticated hostelry there was but a rigidly democratic measure, and if I chose to cultivate a too elegant absence of eagerness for beefsteak pie and huckleberry
pudding, the young lady in long, tight ringlets and short
sleeves, who administered these delicacies in the dining-room,
was altogether too haughty a spirit to urge them on my attention. So I sat alone and ate them cold. After dinner I
returned for an hour to La Mancha, and then strolled forth,
according to my morning's vow, to see the headstones in the
cemetery cast longer shadows. I was disappointed in the epitaphs; they were posterior to the age of theological *naïveté*.
The cemetery covered the two opposed sides of a hill, and on
walking up to the ridge and looking over it, I discovered that
I was not the only visitor. Two persons had chosen the spot
for a quiet talk. One of them was a young girl, dressed in
black, and seated on a headstone, with her face turned toward
me. In spite of her attitude, however, she seemed not to perceive me, wrapt as she was in attention to her companion—a
tall, stout fellow, standing before her, with his back to me.
They were at too great a distance for me to hear their talk,
and indeed in a few minutes I began to fancy they were not
speaking. Nevertheless, the young girl's eyes remained fixed
on the man's face; he was holding her spellbound by an influence best known to himself. She was very pretty. Her hat was
off, and she was holding it in her lap; her lips were parted,
and her eyes fixed intently on her companion's face. Suddenly

she gave a bright, quick smile, made a rapid gesture in the air, and laid her forefinger on her lips. The movement, and the manner of it, told her story. She was deaf and dumb, and the man had been talking to her with his fingers. I would willingly have looked at her longer, but I turned away in delicacy, and walked in another direction. As I was leaving the cemetery, however, I saw her advancing with her companion to take the path which led to the gate. The man's face was now turned to me, and I straightway recognized it, in spite of the high peaked white hat which surmounted it. It was natural enough, I suppose, to find Professor Fargo in a graveyard; as the simplest expedient for ascertaining what goes on beyond the tomb might seem to be to get as close as possible to the hither cope of it. Besides, if he was to treat the townsfolk to messages from their buried relatives, it was not amiss to "get up" a few names and dates by the perusal of the local epitaphs. As he passed me, however, and flourished his hand in the air by way of salutation, there was a fine absence in his glance of any admission that he had been caught cheating. This, too, was natural enough; what surprised me was that such a vulgar fellow should be mated with so charming a companion. She gave me as she passed the trustfully unshrinking glance of those poor mortals who are obliged to listen, as one may say, with their eyes. Her dress was scanty and simple, but there was delicacy in her mobile features. Who was she, and how had *he* got hold of her? After all, it was none of my business; but as they passed on, walking rather briskly, and I strolled after them, watching the Professor's ponderous tread and the gliding footfall of the young girl, I began to wonder whether he might not be right—might not, in truth, have that about him which would induce the most venerable of my ancestors to revert from eternity and stop the clock.

II.

His handbills had done their office, and the Town Hall, when I entered it that evening, was filled with a solemnly expectant auditory. P—— was evidently for the evening a cluster of empty houses. While my companions scanned the stage for the shadow of coming events, I found ample pastime in perusing the social physiognomy of the town. A shadow presently appeared in the person of a stout young countryman, armed with an accordion, from which he extracted an ingenious variety of lamentable sounds. Soon after this mysterious prelude, the Professor marshalled out his forces. They consisted, first and foremost, of himself, his leonine *chevelure*, his black dress suit, and his turquoise ring, and then of an old gentleman who walked in gravely and stiffly, without the Professor's portentous salaam to the audience, bearing on his arm a young girl in black. The Professor managed somehow, by pushing about the chairs, turning up the lamps, and giving a twist to the patriotic drapery in the background, to make his audience feel his presence very intimately. His assistants rested themselves tranquilly against the wall. It took me but a short time to discover that the young girl was none other than the companion of the Professor's tour of inspection in the cemetery, and then I remembered that he had spoken in the morning of the gentleman who performed the mathematical miracles being assisted by his daughter. The young girl's infirmity, and her pretty face, promised to impart a picturesque interest to this portion of the exhibition; but meanwhile I inferred from certain ill-suppressed murmurs, and a good deal of vigorous pantomime among the female spectators, that she was found wanting in the more immediate picturesqueness demanded of a young lady attached to a show. Her plain black dress found no favor; the admission fee had justified the expectation of a good deal of trimming and several bracelets. She, however, poor girl, sat indifferent in her place, leaning her head back rather wearily against the wall, and looking as if, were she disposed, she might count without trouble all the queer bonnets among her judges. Her father sat upright beside her, with a cane between his knees and his two hands crossed on the knob. He was a man of sixty-five—tall, lean, pale, and serious. The lamp hanging above his head deepened the shadows on his face, and transformed it into a sort of pictorial mask. He was very bald, and his forehead, which was high and handsome, wore in the lamplight the gleam of old ivory. The sockets of his eyes were in deep shadow, and out of them his pupils gazed straight before him, with the glow of smouldering fire. His high-arched nose cast a long shadow over his mouth and chin, and two intensified wrinkles, beside his moustache, made him look strangely tragic. With his tragic look, moreover, he seemed strangely familiar. His daughter and the Professor I regarded as old friends; but where had I met this striking specimen of antique melancholy? Though his gaze seemed fixed, I imagined it was covertly wandering over the audience. At last it appeared to me that it met mine, and that its sombre glow emitted a spark of recognition of my extra-provincial and inferentially more discriminating character. The next moment I identified him—he was Don Quixote in the flesh; Don Quixote, with his sallow Spanish coloring, his high-browed, gentlemanly visage, his wrinkles, his moustache, and his sadness.

Professor Fargo's lecture was very bad. I had expected he would talk a good deal of nonsense, but I had imagined it would be cleverer nonsense. Very possibly there was a deeper cleverness in it than I perceived, and that, in his extreme shrewdness, he was giving his audience exactly what they preferred. It is an ascertained fact, I believe, that rural assemblies have a relish for the respectably ponderous, and an honest pride in the fact that they cannot be bored. The Professor, I suppose, felt the pulse of his listeners, and detected treasures of latent sympathy in their solemn, irresponsive silence. I should have said the performance was falling dead, but the Professor probably would have claimed that this was the rapture of attention and awe. He certainly kept very meagrely the promise of his grandiloquent programme, and gave us a pound of precept to a grain of example. His miracles were exclusively miracles of rhetoric. He discoursed upon the earth life and the summer land, and related surprising anecdotes of his intimacy with the inhabitants of the latter region; but to my disappointment, the evening passed away without his really bringing us face to face with a ghost. A number of "prominent citizens" were induced to step upon the platform and be magnetized, but the sturdy agricultural temperament of P—— showed no great pliancy under the Professor's manual blandishments. The attempt was generally a failure—the only brilliant feature being the fine impudence with which the operator lodged the responsibility of the *fiasco* upon what he called his victim's low development. With three or four young girls the thing was a trifle better. One of them closed her eyes and shivered; another had a fearful access of nervous giggling; another burst into tears, and was restored to her companions with an admonitory wink. As every one knew every one else and every one else's family history, some sensation was probably produced by half a dozen happy guesses as to the Christian names and last maladies of certain defunct town worthies. Another deputation of the prominent citizens ascended the platform and wrote the names of departed friends on small bits of paper, which they threw into a hat. The Professor then folded his arms and clutched his beard, as if he were invoking inspiration. At last he approached the young girl, who sat in the background, took her hand, and led her forward. She picked the papers out of the hat and held them up one by one, for the Professor to look at. "There is no possible collusion," he said with a flourish, as he presented her to the audience. "The young lady is a deaf mute!" On a gesture of her companion she passed the paper to one of the contemplative gray heads who represented the scientific curiosity of P——, and he verified the Professor's guess. The Professor risked an "Abijah" or a "Melinda," and it turned out generally to be an Ezekiel or a Hepzibah. Three several times, however, the performer's genius triumphed; whereupon, the audience not being up to the mark, he gave himself a vigorous round of applause. He concluded with the admission that the spirits were shy before such a crowd, but that he would do much better for the ladies and gentlemen individually, if they would call on him at the hotel.

It was all terribly vulgar rubbish, and I was glad when it was over. While it lasted, the old gentleman behind continued to sit motionless, seeming neither to see, to hear, nor to understand. I wondered what he thought of it, and just what it cost his self-respect to give it the sanction of his presence. It seemed, indeed, as if mentally he were not present; as if by an intense effort he had succeeded in making consciousness a blank, and was awaiting his own turn in a kind of trance. Once only he moved—when the Professor came and took his daughter by the hand. He gave an imperceptible start, controlled himself, then, dropping his hand a little, closed his eyes and kept them closed until she returned to his side. There was

an intermission, during which the Professor walked about the
platform, shaking his mane and wiping his forehead, and surveying the audience with an air of lofty benevolence, as if,
having sown the seed, he was expecting to see it germinate
on the spot. At last he rapped on the table and introduced
the old gentleman—Colonel Gifford, the Great Mathematical
Magician and Lightning Calculator; after which he retreated
in turn to the background—if a gentleman with tossing mane
and flowing beard, that turquoise ring, and generally expansive and importunate presence, could be said to be, under any
circumstances, in the background. The old gentleman came
forward and made his bow, and the young girl placed herself
beside him, simply, unaffectedly, with her hands hanging and
crossed in front of her—with all the childish grace and serenity
of Mignon in "Wilhelm Meister," as we see her grouped with
the old harper. Colonel Gifford's performance gave me an
exquisite pleasure, which I am bound to confess was quite
independent of its intrinsic merits. These, I am afraid, were at
once too numerous and too scanty to have made it a popular
success. It was a very ingenious piece of scientific contrivance,
but it was meagrely adapted to tickle the ears of the ground-
lings. If one had read it—the substance of it—in a handsomely
printed pamphlet, under the lamp, of a wet evening when no
one was likely to call, one would have been charmed at once
with the quaint vivacity of the author's mode of statement,
and with the unexpected agility of one's own intellect. But in
spite of an obvious effort to commend himself to understand-
ings more familiar with the rule of thumb than with the dif-
ferential calculus, Colonel Gifford remained benignantly but
formidably unintelligible. He had devised—so far as I understood it—an extension of the multiplication table to enormous
factors, by which he expected to effect a revolution in the
whole science of accounts. There was the theory, which rather
lost itself, thanks to his discursive fervor in the mists of the
higher mathematics, and there was the practice, which, thanks
to his daughter's coöperation, was much more gracefully concrete. The interesting thing to me was the speaker's personality, not his system. Although evidently a very positive old
man, he had a singularly simple, unpretentious tone. His intensity of faith in the supreme importance of his doctrine gave

his manner a sort of reverential hush. The echoes of Professor Fargo's windy verbiage increased the charms of his mild sincerity. He spoke in a feeble, tremulous voice, which every now and then quavered upward with excitement, and then subsided into a weary, plaintive cadence. He was an old gentleman of a single idea, but his one idea was a religion. It was impossible not to feel a kindness for him, and imagine that he excited among his auditors something of the vague good will—half pity and half reverence—that uncorrupted souls entertain for those neat, keen-eyed, elderly people who are rumored to have strange ways and say strange things—to be "cracked," in short, like a fine bit of porcelain which will hold together only so long as you don't push it about. But it was upon the young girl, when once she had given them a taste of her capacity, that they bestowed their frankest admiration. Now that she stood forward in the bright light, I could observe the character of her prettiness. It was no brilliant beauty, but a sort of meagre, attenuated, angular grace, the delicacy and fragility of the characteristic American type. Her chest was flat, her neck extremely thin, her visage narrow, and her forehead high and prominent. But her fair hair encircled her head in such fleecy tresses, her cheeks had such a pale pink flush, her eyes such an appealing innocence, her attitude such a quaint unconscious felicity, that one watched her with a kind of upstart belief that to such a stainless little spirit the working of miracles might be really possible. A couple of blackboards were hung against the wall, on one of which the old man rapidly chalked a problem—choosing one, of course, on the level of the brighter minds in the audience. The young girl glanced at it, and before we could count ten dashed off a great bold answer on the other tablet. The brighter minds were then invited to verify, and the young lady was invariably found to have hit the mark. She was in fact a little arithmetical fairy, and her father made her perform a series of gymnastics among numbers as brilliant in their way as the vocal flourishes and roulades of an accomplished singer. Communicating with her altogether by the blackboard, he drew from her a host of examples of the beauty of his system of transcendent multiplication. A person present was requested to furnish two enormous numbers, one to multiply the other. The old man wrote them out. After standing an instant meditative and just touching her forehead with her forefinger, she chalked down the prodigious result. Her father then performed rapidly, on the blackboard, the operation according to his own system (which she had employed mentally), and finally satisfied every one by repeating it in the roundabout fashion actually in use. This was all Colonel Gifford's witchcraft. It sounds very ponderous, but it was really very charming, and I had an agreeable sense of titillation in the finer parts of my intellectual mechanism. I felt more like a thinking creature. I had never supposed I was coming to P—— to take a lesson in culture.

It seemed on the morrow as if, at any rate, I was to take a lesson in patience. It was a Sunday, and I awoke to hear the rain pattering against my window panes. A rainy Sunday at P—— was a prospect to depress the most elastic mind. But as I stepped into my slippers, I bethought myself of my unfinished volume of "Don Quixote," and promised myself to borrow from Sancho Panza a philosophic proverb or so applicable to my situation. "Don Quixote" consoled me, as it turned out, in an unexpected fashion. On descending to the dining-room of the inn, while I mentally balanced the contending claims of muddy coffee and sour green tea, I found that my last evening's friends were also enjoying the hospitality of the establishment. It was the only inn in the place, and it would already have occurred to a more investigating mind that we were fellow-lodgers. The Professor, happily, was absent; and it seemed only reasonable that a ghost-seer should lie in bed late of a morning. The melancholy old mathematician was seated at the breakfast table cutting his dry toast into geometrical figures. He gave me a formal bow as I entered, and proceeded to dip his sodden polygons into his tea. The young girl was at the window, leaning her forehead against the pane, and looking out into the sea of yellow mud in the village street. I had not been in the room a couple of minutes when, seeming in spite of her deafness to feel that I was near, she turned straight round and looked at me. She wore no trace of fatigue from her public labors, but was the same clear-eyed, noiseless little sprite as before. I observed that, by daylight, her black dress was very shabby, and her father's frock coat, buttoned with military precision up to his chin, had long since exchanged its original lustre for the melancholy brilliancy imparted by desperate brushing. I was afraid that Professor Fargo was either a niggardly *impresario*, or that the great "moral and scientific combination" was not always as remunerative as it seemed to have been at P——. While I was making these reflections the Professor entered, with an exhilaration of manner which I conceived to be a tribute to unwonted success.

"Well, sir," he cried, as his eyes fell upon me, "what do you say to it now? I hope we did things handsomely, eh? I hope you call that a solid entertainment. This young man, you must know, is one of the scoffers," he went on, turning to the Colonel. "He came yesterday and bearded the lion in his den. He snaps his fingers at spirits, suspects me of foul play, and would like me to admit, in my private character, that you and I are a couple of sharpers. I hope we satisfied you!"

The Colonel went on dipping his toast into his tea, looking grave and saying nothing. "Poor man!" I said to myself; "he despises his colleague—and so do I. I beg your pardon," I cried with warmth; "I would like nothing of the kind. I was extremely interested in this gentleman's exhibition;" and I made the Colonel a bow. "It seemed to me remarkable for its perfect good faith and truthfulness."

"Many thanks for the compliment," said the Professor. "As much as to say the Colonel's an apostle, and I'm a rascal. Have it as you please; if so, I'm a hardened one!" he declared with a great slap on his pocket; "and anyhow, you know, it's all one concern," and the Professor betook himself to the window where Miss Gifford was standing. She had not looked round at him on his entrance, as she had done at me. The Colonel, in response to my compliment, looked across at me with mild benignity, and I assured him afresh of my admiration. He listened silently, stirring his tea; his face betrayed an odd mixture of confidence and deprecation; as if he thought it just possible that I might be laughing at him, but that if I was not, it was extremely delightful. I continued to insist on its being distinctively *his* half of the performance that had pleased me; so that, gradually convinced of my respectful sympathy, he seemed tacitly to intimate that, if we were only alone and he knew me a little better, it would do him a world of

good to talk it all over. I determined to give him a chance at
the earliest moment. The Professor, meanwhile, waiting for
his breakfast, remained at the window experimenting in the
deaf and dumb alphabet with the young girl. It took him, as
an amateur, a long time to form his sentences, but he went
on bravely, brandishing his large, plump knuckles before her
face. She seemed very patient of his slowness, and stood
watching his gestures with the same intense earnestness I had
caught a glimpse of in the cemetery. Most of my female
friends enjoy an unimpeded use of their tongues, and I was
unable from experience to appreciate his situation; but I could
easily fancy what a delightful sense of intimacy there must be
in this noiseless exchange of long looks with a pretty creature
toward whom all *tendresse* of attitude might be conveniently
attributed to compassion. Before long the Colonel pushed
away his cup, turned about, folded his arms, and fixed his eyes
with a frown on the Professor. It seemed to me that I read in
his glance a complete revelation of moral torture. The stress
of fortune had made them associates, but the Colonel jealously guarded the limits of their private intimacy. The Professor, with all his audacity, suffered himself to be reminded of
them. He suddenly pulled out his watch and clamored for his
coffee, and was soon seated at a repast which indicated that
the prophetic temperament requires a generous diet. The
young girl roamed about the room, looking idly at this and
that, as if she were used to doing nothing. When she met my
eye, she smiled brightly, after a moment's gravity, as if she
were also used to saying to people, mentally, "Yes, I know
I'm a strange little creature, but you must not be afraid of
me." The Professor had hardly got that array of innumerable
little dishes, of the form and dimensions of soap-trays, with
which one is served in the rural hostelries of New England,
well under contribution, before a young lady was introduced
who had come to request him to raise a ghost—a resolute
young lady, with several ringlets and a huge ancestral umbrella, whose matutinal appetite for the supernatural had not
been quenched by the raw autumnal storm. She produced
very frankly a "tin-type" of a florid young man, actually
deceased, and demanded to be confronted with his ghost.
The day was beginning well for the Professor. He gallantly

requested her to be seated, and promised her every satisfaction. While he was hastily despatching his breakfast, the Colonel's daughter made acquaintance with her bereaved sister. She drew the young man's portrait gently out of her hand, examined it, and then shook her head with a little grimace of displeasure. The young woman laughed good-naturedly, and screamed into her ear that she didn't believe she was a bit deaf and dumb. At the announcement the Colonel, who, after eyeing her while she stated her credulous errand with solemn compassion, had turned away to the window, as if to spare himself the spectacle of his colleague's unblushing pretensions, turned back again and eyed her coldly from head to foot. "I recommend you, madam," he said sternly, "to reserve your suspicions for an occasion in which they may be more pertinent."

Later in the morning I found him still in the dining-room with his daughter. Professor Fargo, he said, was in the parlor, raising ghosts by the dozen; and after a little pause he gave an angry laugh, as if his suppressed irritation were causing him more than usual discomfort. He was walking up and down, with slow, restless steps, and smoking a frugal pipe. I took the liberty of offering him a good cigar, and while he puffed it gratefully, the need to justify himself for his odd partnership slowly gathered force. "It would be a satisfaction for me to tell you, sir," he said at last, looking at me with eyes that fairly glittered with the pleasure of hearing himself speak the words, "that my connection with Professor Fargo implies no—no—" and he paused for a moment—"no intellectual approval of his extraordinary pretensions. This, of course, is between ourselves. You're a stranger to me, and it's doubtless the height of indiscretion in me to take you into my confidence. My subsistence depends on my not quarrelling with my companion. If you were to repeat to him that I went about undermining the faith, the extremely retributive faith, as you see" (and he nodded toward the parlor door), "of his audiences, he would of course dissolve our partnership and I should be adrift again, trying to get my heavy boat in tow. I should perhaps feel like an honest man again, but meanwhile, probably, I should starve. Misfortune," he added bitterly, "makes strange bedfellows; and I have been unfortunate!"

There was so much melancholy meaning in this declaration that I asked him frankly who and what he was. He puffed his cigar vigorously for some moments without replying, and at last turned his fine old furrowed visage upon me through a cloud of smoke. "I'm a fanatic. I feed on illusions and cherish ambitions which will never butter my bread. Don't be afraid; I won't buttonhole *you*; but I have a head full of schemes which I believe the world would be the happier for giving a little quiet attention to. I'm an inventor; and like all inventors whose devices are of value, I believe that my particular contrivance would be the salvation of a misguided world. I have looked a good deal into many things, but my latest hobby is the system of computation of which I tried to give a sketch last night. I'm afraid you didn't understand a word of it, but I assure you it's a very beautiful thing. If it could only get a fair hearing and be thoroughly propagated and adopted, it would save our toiling human race a prodigious deal of ungrateful labor. In America alone, I have calculated, it would save the business community about 23,000 hours in the course of ten years. If time is money, they are worth saving. But there I go! You oughtn't to ask me to talk about myself. Myself is my ideas!"

A little judicious questioning, however, drew from him a number of facts of a more immediately personal kind. His colonelship, he intimated, was held by the inglorious tenure of militia service, and was only put forward to help him to make a figure on Professor Fargo's platform. It was part of the general humbuggery of the attempt to *bribe* people to listen to wholesome truths—truths the neglect of which was its own chastisement. "I have always had a passion for scientific research, and I have squandered my substance in experiments which the world called fruitless. They were curious, they were beautiful, they were divine! But they wouldn't turn any one's mill or grind any one's corn, and I was treated like a mediæval alchemist, astray in the modern world. Chemistry, physics, mathematics, philology, medicine—I've dug deep in them all. Each, in turn, has been a passion to which I've given my days and my nights. But apparently I haven't the art of finding favor for my ideas—of sweetening the draught so that people will drink it. So here I am, after all my vigils and ventures, an obscure old man, ruined in fortune, broken down in health and sadly diminished in hope, trying hard to keep afloat by rowing in the same boat as a gentleman who turns tables and raises ghosts. I'm a proud man, sir, and a devotee of the exact sciences. You may imagine what I suffer. I little fancied ten years ago that I was ever going to make capital, on a mountebank's booth, of the pathetic infirmity of my daughter."

The young girl, while her father talked, sat gazing at him in wistful surprise. I inferred from it that this expansive mood was rare; she wondered what long story he was telling. As he mentioned her, I gave her a sudden glance. Perceiving it, she blushed slightly and turned away. The movement seemed at variance with what I had supposed to be her characteristic indifference to observation. "I have a good reason," he said, "for treating her with more than the tenderness which such an infirmity usually commands. At the time of my marriage, and for some time after, I was performing a series of curious chemical researches. My wife was a wonderfully pretty little creature. She used to come tripping and rustling about my laboratory, asking questions of the most comical ignorance, peeping and rummaging everywhere, raising the lids of jars, and making faces at the bad smells. One day while she was in the room I stepped out on the balcony to examine something which I had placed to dry in the sun. Suddenly I heard a terrific explosion; it smashed the window-glass into atoms. Rushing in, I found my wife in a swoon on the floor. A compound which I had placed to heat on a furnace had been left too long; I had underestimated its activity. My wife was not visibly injured, but when she came to her senses again, she found she had lost her hearing. It never returned. Shortly afterwards my daughter was born—born the poor deaf creature you see. I lost my wife and I gave up chemistry. As I advanced in life, I became convinced that my ruling passion was mathematics. I've gone into them very deeply; I consider them the noblest acquisition of the human mind, and I don't hesitate to say that I have profound and original views on the subject. If you have a head for such things, I could open great vistas to you. But I'm afraid you haven't! Ay, it's a desperately weak-witted generation. The world has a horror of concen-

trated thought; it wants the pill to be sugared; it wants everything to be made easy; it prefers the brazen foolery that you
and I sat through last night to the divine harmonies of the
infinite science of numbers. That's why I'm a beggar, droning
out my dreary petition and pushing forth my little girl to catch
the coppers. That's why I've had to strike a partnership with
a vulgar charlatan. I was a long time coming to it, but I'm
well in for it now. I won't tell you how, from rebuff to rebuff,
from failure to failure, through hope deferred and justice denied, I have finally come to this. It would overtax both your
sympathy and your credulity. You wouldn't believe the stories
I could relate of the impenetrable stupidity of mankind, of the
leaden empire of Routine. I squandered my property, I confess
it, but not in the vulgar way. It was a carnival of high research,
a long debauch of experiment. When I had melted down my
last cent in the consuming crucible, I thought the world
might be willing to pay me something for my results. The
world had better uses for its money than the purchase of sov-
ereign truth! I became a solicitor; I went from door to door,
offering people a choice of twenty superb formulated schemes,
the paltriest of which contained the germs of a peaceful revolution. The poor unpatented visions are at this hour all in a
bundle up stairs in my trunk. In the midst of my troubles I
had the ineffable pleasure of finding that my little girl was a
genius. I don't know why it should have been a pleasure; her
poor father's genius stood there before me as a warning. But
it was a delight to find that her little imprisoned, soundless
mind was not a blank. She had inherited my passion for numbers. My folly had taken a precious faculty from her; it was
but just I should give her another. She was in good hands for
becoming perfect. Her gift is a rare one among women, but
she is not of the common feminine stuff. She's very simple—strangely simple in some ways. She has never been talked
to by women about petticoats, nor by men about love. She
doesn't reason; her skill at figures is a kind of intuition. One
day it came into my head that I might lecture for a livelihood.
I had listened to windy orators, in crowded halls, who had
less to say than I. So I lectured, sometimes to twenty people,
sometimes to five, once to no one at all. One morning, some
six months ago, I was waited upon by my friend there. He

told me frankly that he had a show which didn't draw as powerfully as it deserved, and proposed that, as I also seemed
unable to catch the public ear, we should combine our forces
and carry popularity by storm. His entertainment, alone, was
rather thin; mine also seemed to lack the desirable consistency;
but a mixture of the two might produce an effective compound. I had but five dollars in my pocket. I disliked the man,
and I believe in spiritualism about as much as I believe that
the sun goes round the earth. But we must live, and I made
a bargain. It was a very poor bargain, but it keeps us alive. I
took a few hints from the Professor, and brightened up my
lucky formulas a little. Still, we had terribly thin houses. I
couldn't play the mountebank; it's a faculty I lack. At last the
Professor bethought himself that I possessed the golden
goose. From the mountebank's point of view a pretty little
deaf and dumb daughter, who could work miracles on the
blackboard, was a treasure to a practical mind. The idea of
dragging my poor child and her pathetic idiosyncrasies before
the world was extremely repulsive to me; but the Professor
laid the case before the little maid herself, and at the end of
a fortnight she informed him that she was ready to make her
curtsey on the platform as a 'lightning calculator.' I consented
to let her try, and you see that she succeeded. She draws, not
powerfully, but sufficiently, and we manage to keep afloat."

Half an hour later the Professor returned from his morning's labors—flushed, dishevelled, rubbing his hands, evidently in high good humor. The Colonel immediately became
silent and grave, asked no questions, and, when dinner was
served shortly afterwards, refused everything and sat with a
melancholy frown and his eyes fixed on his plate. His comrade
was plainly a terrible thorn in his side. I was curious, on the
other hand, to know how the Colonel affected the Professor,
and I soon discovered that the latter was by no means his
exuberant impudent self within the radius of his colleague's
pregnant silence. If there was little love lost between them,
the ranting charlatan was at least held in check by an indefinable respect for his companion's probity. He was a fool,
doubtless, with his careful statements and his incapacity to
take a humorous view of human credulity; but, somehow, he
was a venerable fool, and the Professor, as a social personage,

without the inspiration of a lecture-room more or less irritat-ingly interspaced, and with that pale, grave old mathematician sitting by like a marble monument to Veracity, lacked the courage to ventilate his peculiar pretensions. On this occasion, however, he swallowed the Colonel's tacit protest with a wry face. I don't know what he had brought to pass in the dark-ened parlor; whatever it was, it had agreeably stimulated his confidence in his resources. We had been joined, moreover, at dinner by half a dozen travellers of less oppressively skep-tical mould than the Colonel, and under these circumstances it was peculiarly trying to have to veil one's brighter genius. There was undischarged thunder in the air.

The rain ceased in the afternoon, and the sun leaped out and set the thousand puddles of the village street a-flashing. I found the Colonel sitting under the tavern porch with a village urchin between his knees, to whom he seemed to be imparting the rudiments of mathematical science. The little boy had a bulging forehead, a prodigious number of freckles, and the general aspect of a juvenile Newton. Being present at the Colonel's lecture, he had been fired with a laudable cu-riosity to know more, and learning that Professor Fargo im-parted information *à domicile*, had ventured to believe that his colleague did likewise. The child's father, a great, gaunt, brown-faced farmer, with a yellow tuft on his chin, stood by, blushing at the audacity of his son and heir, but grinning de-lightedly at his brightness. The poor Colonel, whose meed of recognition had as yet been so meagre, was vastly tickled by this expression of infantine sympathy, and discoursed to the little prodigy with the most condescending benevolence. Cer-tainly, as the boy grows up, the most vivid of his childish memories will be that of the old man with glowing eyes and a softened voice coming from under his white moustache— the voice which held him stock-still for a whole half hour, and assured him afterwards that he was a little Trojan. When the lesson was over, I proposed a walk to the Colonel, and we wandered away out of the village. The afternoon, as it waned, became glorious; the heavy clouds, broken and dispersed, sailed through the glowing sky like high-prowed galleys, draped in purple and silver. I, on my side, shall never forget the Colonel's excited talk, nor how at last, as we sat on a rocky ridge looking off to the sunset, he fairly unburdened his conscience.

"Yes, sir!" he said; "it's a base concession to the ignoble need of keeping body and soul together. Sometimes I feel as if I couldn't stand it another hour—as if it were better to break with the impudent rascal and sink or swim as fate decrees, than get a hearing for the truth at such a cost. It's all very well holding my tongue and insisting that I, at least, make no claims for the man's vile frauds; my connection with him is itself a sanction, and my presence at his damnable mummeries an outrage to the purity of truth. You see I have the misfortune to believe in something, to *know* something, and to think it makes a difference whether people feed, intellectually, on poisoned garbage or on the ripe, sweet fruit of true science! I shut my eyes every night, and lock my jaws, and clench my teeth, but I can't help hearing the man's windy rubbish. It's a tissue of scandalous lies, from beginning to end. I know them all by heart by this time, and I verily believe I could stand up and rattle them off myself. They ring in my ears all day, and I have horrible dreams at night of crouching under a table with a long cloth, and tapping on the top of it. The Professor stands outside swearing to the audience that it's the ghost of Archimedes. Then I begin to suffocate, and overturn the table, and appear before a thousand people as the accomplice of the impostor. There are times when the value of my own unheeded message to mankind seems so vast, so immeasurable, that I am ready to believe that any means are lawful which may enable me to utter it; that if one's ship is to set sail for the golden islands, even a flaunting buccaneer may tow it into the open sea. In such moods, when I sit there against the wall, in the shade, closing my eyes and trying not to hear—I really *don't* hear! My mind is a myriad miles away—floating, soaring on the wings of invention. But all of a sudden the odiousness of my position comes over me, and I can't believe my senses that it's verily I who sit there—I to whom a grain of scientific truth is more precious than a mountain of gold!"

He was silent a long time, and I myself hardly knew what consolation to offer him. The most friendly part was simply to let him expend his bitterness to the last drop. "But that's

not the worst," he resumed after a while. "The worst is that
I hate the greasy rascal to come near my daughter, and that,
living and travelling together as we do, he's never far off. At
first he used to engage a small child beforehand to hold up
his little folded papers for him; but a few weeks ago it came
into his head that it would give the affair an even greater air
of innocence, if he could make use of my poor girl. It does,
I believe, and it tells, and I've been brought so low that I sit
by night after night and endure it. She, on her side, dreams
of no harm, and takes the Professor for an oracle and his lecture for a masterpiece. I have never undeceived her, for I have
no desire to teach her that there are such things as falsity and
impurity. Except that our perpetual railway journeys give her
bad headaches, she supposes that we lead a life of pure felicity.
But some fine day our enterprising friend will be wanting to
put her into a pink dress and a garland of artificial flowers,
and then, with God's help, we shall part company!"

My silence, in reply to this last burst of confidence, implied
the most deferential assent; but I was privately wondering
whether "the little maid" was so perfectly ignorant of evil as
the old man supposed. I remembered the episode at the cemetery the day before, and doubted greatly whether her father
had countenanced it. With his sentiments touching the Professor, this was most unlikely. The young girl, then, had a
secret, and it gave me real discomfort to think this coarse
fellow should keep the key of it. I feared that the poor Colonel
was yoked to his colleague more cruelly than he knew. On
our return to the inn this impression was vividly confirmed.
Dusk had fallen when we entered the public room, and in the
gray light which pervaded it two figures at one of the windows
escaped immediate recognition. But in a moment one of them
advanced, and in the sonorous accents of Professor Fargo
hoped that we had enjoyed our expedition. The Colonel
started and stared, and left me to answer. He sat down heavily
on the sofa; in a moment his daughter came over and sat
beside him, placing her hand gently on his knee. But he let it
lie, and remained motionless, resting his hot head on his cane.
The Professor withdrew promptly, but with a swagger which
suggested to my sense that he could now afford to treat his
vanity to a dose of revenge for the old man's contempt.

Late in the evening I came down stairs again, and as I passed along the hall heard Professor Fargo perorating vigorously in the bar-room. Evidently he had an audience, and the scene was probably curious. Drawing near, I found this gifted man erect on the floor, addressing an assemblage of the convivial spirits of P——. In an extended hand he brandished a glass of smoking whiskey and water; with the other he caressed his rounded periods. He had evidently been drinking freely, and I perceived that even the prophetic vision was liable to obfuscation. It had been a brilliant day for him; fortune smiled, and he felt strong. A dozen rustic loafers, of various degrees of inveteracy, were listening to him with a speechless solemnity, which may have been partly faith, but was certainly partly rum. In a corner, out of the way, sat the Colonel, with an unfinished glass before him. The Professor waved his hand as I appeared, with magnificent hospitality, and resumed his discourse.

"Let me say, gentlemen," he cried, "that it's not my peculiar influence with the departed that I chiefly value; for, after all, you know, a ghost is but a ghost. It can't do much any way. You can't touch it, half the time you can't see it. If it happens to be the spirit of a pretty girl, you know, this makes you kind of mad. The great thing now is to be able to exercise a mysterious influence over living organisms. You can do it with your eye, you can do it with your voice, you can do it with certain motions of your hand—as thus, you perceive; you can do it with nothing at all by just setting your mind on it. That is, of course, some people can do it; not very many— certain rich, powerful, sympathetic natures that you now and then come across. It's called magnetism. Various works have been written on the subject, and various explanations offered, but they don't amount to much. All you can say is that it's just magnetism, and that you've either got it or you haven't got it. Now the Lord has seen fit to bestow it on me. It's a great responsibility, but I try to make a noble use of it. I can do all sorts of things. I can find out things. I can make people confess. I can make 'em sick and I can make 'em well. I can make 'em in love—what do you say to that? I can take 'em out of love again, and make 'em swear they wouldn't marry the loved object, not if they were paid for it. How it is I do it I confess I can't tell you. I just say to myself, 'Come now, Professor, we'll fix this one or that one.' It's a free gift. It's magnetism, in short. Some folks call it animal magnetism, but I call it spiritual magnetism.'"

There was a profound silence; the air seemed charged with that whimsical retention of speech which is such a common form of American sociability. I looked askance at the Colonel; it seemed to me that he was paler than usual, and that his eyes were really fierce. Professor Fargo turned about to the bar to replenish his glass, and the old man slowly rose and came out into the middle of the room. He looked round at the company; he evidently meant to say something. He stood silent for some moments, and I saw that he was in a tremor of excitement. "You've listened to what this gentleman has been saying?" he began. "I won't say, Have you understood it? It's not to be understood. Some of you, perhaps, saw me last night sitting on the platform while Professor Fargo said his say. You know that we are partners—that for convenience' sake we work together. I wish to say that you are not therefore to believe that I assent to the doctrines he has just promulgated. 'Doctrines' is a flattering name for them. I speak in the name of science. Science recognizes no such thing as 'spiritual magnetism'; no such thing as mysterious fascinations; no such thing as spirit-rappings and ghost-raisings. I owe it to my conscience to say so. I can't remain there and see you all sit mum when this gentleman concludes such a monstrous piece of talk. I have it on my conscience to assure you that no intelligent man, woman, or child need fear to be made to do anything against his own will by the supernatural operation of the will of Professor Fargo."

If there had been silence on the conclusion of Professor Fargo's harangue, what shall I say of the audible absence of commentary which followed the Colonel's remarks? There was an intense curiosity—I felt it myself—to see what a clever fellow like the Professor would do. The Colonel stood there wiping his forehead, as if, having thrown down the gauntlet, he were prepared to defend it. The Professor looked at him with his head on one side, and a smile which was an excellent imitation of genial tolerance. "My dear sir," he cried, "I'm glad you've eased your mind. I knew you wanted to; I hope

you feel better. With your leave, we won't go into the philosophy of the dispute. It was George Washington, I believe,
who said that people should wash their dirty linen at home.
You don't endorse my views—you're welcome. If you weren't
a very polite old gentleman, I know you'd like to say that, in
a single word, they're the views of a quack. Now, in a single
word, I deny it. You deny the existence of the magnetic
power; I reply that I personally possess it, and that if you'll
give me a little more time, I'll force you to say that there's
something in it. I'll force you to say I can do something.
These gentlemen here can't witness the consummation, but
at least they can hear my promise. I promise you evidence.
You go by facts: I'll give you facts. I'd like just to have you
remark before our friends here, that you'll take account of
them!"

The Colonel stood still, wiping his forehead. He had even
less prevision than I of the character of the Professor's projected facts, but of course he could make but one answer. He
bowed gravely to the Professor and to the company. "I shall
never refuse," he said, "to examine serious evidence. Whatever," he added, after a moment, "it might cost my prejudices."

III.

The Colonel's incorruptible conservatism had done me good
mentally, and his personal situation had deeply interested me.
As I bade him farewell the next day—the "Combination" had
been heralded in a neighboring town—I wished him heartily
that what was so painfully crooked in the latter might be
straightened out in time. He shook his head sadly, and answered that his time was up.

He was often in my thoughts for the next six weeks, but I
got no tidings of him. Meanwhile I too was leading an am-
bulant life, and travelling from town to town in a cause which
demanded a good deal of ready-made eloquence. I didn't exactly pretend that the regeneration of society depended on its
acceptance of my wares, but I devoted a good deal of fellow
feeling to the Colonel's experience as an uncredited soliciter.
At the beginning of the winter I found myself in New York.

One evening, as I wandered along a certain avenue, undedi-
cated to gentility, I perceived, in the flare of a gas-lamp, on a
placard beside a doorway, the name and attributes of Professor
Fargo. I immediately stopped and read the manifesto. It was
even more grandiloquent than the yellow hand-bill at P——;
for to overtop concurrence in the metropolis one must mount
upon very high stilts indeed. The "Combination" still sub-
sisted, and Colonel Gifford brought up the rear. I observed
with interest that his daughter now figured in an independent
and extremely ornamental paragraph. Above the door was a
blue lamp, and beneath the lamp the inscription "Excelsior
Hall." No one was going in, but as I stood there a young
man in a white overcoat, with his hat on his nose, came out
and planted himself viciously, with a tell-tale yawn, in the
doorway. The poor Colonel had lost an auditor; I was determined he should have a substitute. Paying my fee and making
my way into the room, I found that the situation was indeed
one in which units rated high. There were not more than
twenty people present, and the appearance of this meagre
group was not in striking harmony with the statement on the
placard without, that Professor Fargo's entertainment was
thronged with the intellect and fashion of the metropolis.
The Professor was on the platform, unfolding his budget of
miracles; behind him, as at P——, sat the Colonel and his
daughter. The Professor was evidently depressed by the preponderance of empty benches, and carried off his revelations
with an indifferent grace. Disappointment made him brutal.
He was heavy, vulgar, slipshod; he stumbled in his periods,
and bungled more than once in his guesses when the folded
papers with the names were put into the hat. His brow wore
a vicious, sullen look, which seemed to deepen the expression
of melancholy patience in his companions. I trembled for my
friends. The Colonel had told me that his bargain with his
impresario was a poor one, and I was sure that if, when the
"Combination" was in a run of luck, as it had been at P——,
his dividend was scanty, he was paying a heavy share of the
penalty for the present eclipse of fortune. I sat down near the
door, where the hall was shrouded in a thrifty dimness, so that
I had no fear of being recognized. The Professor evidently
was reckless—a fact which rather puzzled me in so shrewd a

man. When he had brought his own performance to an un-applauded close, instead of making his customary speech on behalf of his coadjutor, he dropped into a chair and gaped in the face of his audience. But the Colonel, after a pause, threw himself into the breach—or rather lowered himself into it with stately gravity—and addressed his humble listeners (half of whom were asleep) as if they had been the flower of the Intellect and Fashion. But if his manner was the old one, his discourse was new. He had too many ideas to repeat himself, and, although those which he now attempted to expound were still above the level of my frivolous apprehension, this unbargained abundance of inspiration half convinced me that his claim to original genius was just. If there had been something grotesquely sad in his appeal to the irresponsive intellect of P——, it was almost intolerably dismal to sit there and see him grappling with the dusky void of Excelsior Hall. The sleepers waked up, or turned over, at least, when Miss Gifford came forward. She wore, as yet, neither a pink dress nor an artificial garland, but it seemed to me that I detected here and there an embryonic hint of these ornaments—a ruffle round her neck, a colored sash over her black dress, a curl or two more in her hair. But her manner was as childish, as simple and serene as ever; the empty benches had no weary meaning for her.

I confess that in spite of my personal interest in my friend, the entertainment seemed wofully long; more than once I was on the point of departing, and awaiting the conclusion in the street. But I had not the heart to inflict upon the poor Colonel the sight of a retreating spectator. When at last my twenty companions had shuffled away, I made my way to the platform and renewed acquaintance with the trio. The Professor nodded with uncompromising familiarity, the Colonel seemed cordially glad to see me, and his daughter, as I made her my bow, gazed at me with even more than usual of her clear-eyed frankness. She seemed to wonder what my reappearance meant for them. It meant, to begin with, that I went the next day to see the Colonel at his lodging. It was a terribly modest little lodging, but he did me the honors with a grace which showed that he had an old habit of hospitality. He admitted frankly that the "Combination" had lately been doing a very

poor business, but he made the admission with a gloomy sto-
icism which showed me that he had been looking the event
full in the face, and had assented to it helplessly. They had
gone their round in the country, with varying success. They
had the misfortune to have a circus keeping just in advance
of them, and beside the gorgeous pictorial placards of this
establishment, their own superior promises, even when swim-
ming in a deluge of exclamation points, seemed pitifully
vague. "What are my daughter and I," said the Colonel, "after the educated elephant and the female trapezist? What even
is the Professor, after the great American clown?" Their profits, however, had been kept fairly above the minimum, and
victory would still have hovered about their banners if they
had been content to invoke her in the smaller towns. The
Professor, however, in spite of remonstrance, had suddenly
steered for New York, and what New York was doing for them
I had seen the night before. The last half dozen performances
had not paid for the room and the gas. The Colonel told me
that he was bound by contract for five more lectures, but that
when these were delivered he would dissolve the partnership.
The Professor, in insisting on coming to the city, had shown
a signal want of shrewdness; and when his shrewdness failed
him, what had you left? What to attempt himself, the Colonel
couldn't imagine. "At the worst," he said, "my daughter can
go into an asylum, and I can go into the poor-house." On
my asking him whether his colleague had yet established, according to his vow, the verities of "spiritual magnetism," he
stared in surprise and seemed quite to have forgotten the Professor's engagement to convert him. "Oh, I've let him off,"
he said, shaking his head. "He was tipsy when he made the
promise, and I expect to hear no more about it."

I was very busy, and the pensive old man was gloomy company; but his characters and his fortunes had such a melancholy interest that I found time to pay him several visits. He
evidently was thankful to be diverted from his sombre self-
consciousness and his paternal anxiety, and, when once he was
aroused from the dogged resignation in which he seemed
plunged, enjoyed vastly the chance to expatiate on his multitudinous and irrealizable theories. Most of the time his
meaning was a cloud bank to me, but I listened, assented,

applauded; I felt the charm of pure intellectual passion. I incline to believe that he had excogitated some extremely valuable ideas. We took long walks through the crowded streets. The Colonel was indefatigable, in spite of his leanness and pallor. He strode along with great steps, talking so loud, half the time, in his high, quavering voice, that even the eager pedestrians in the lower latitudes of Broadway slackened pace to glance back at him. He declared that the crowded streets gave him a strange exhilaration, and the mighty human hum of the great city quickened his heart-beats almost to pain. More than once he stopped short on the edge of a curbstone or in the middle of a crossing, and laying his hand on my arm, with a deeper glow beneath his white eyebrows, broke into a kind of rhapsody of transcendental thought. "It's for all these millions I would work, if they would let me!" he cried. "It's to the life of great cities my schemes are addressed. It's to make millions wiser and better that I stand pleading my cause so long after I have earned my rest." One day he seemed taciturn and preoccupied. He talked much less than usual, noticed nothing, and walked with his eyes on the pavement. I imagined that, in a phrase with which he had made me familiar, he had caught the tail of an idea and was holding it fast, in spite of its slippery contortions. As we neared his lodging at the end of our walk, he stopped abruptly in the middle of the street, and I had to give him a violent pull to rescue him from a rattling butcher's cart. When we reached the pavement he stopped again, grasped me by the hand, and fixed his eyes on me with a very extraordinary exaltation. We were at the top of the shabby cross-street in which he had found a shelter. A row of squalid tenements faced us, and half a dozen little Irish ragamuffins were sprawling beneath our feet, between their doorways and the gutter. "Eureka! Eureka!" he cried. "I've found it—I've found it!" And on my asking him what he had found, "Something science has groped for, for ages—the solution of the incalculable! Perhaps, too, my fortune; certainly my immortality! Quick, quick! Before it vanishes I must get at my pen." And he hurried me along to his dingy little dwelling. On the doorstep he paused. "I can't tell you now," he cried. "I must fling it down in black and white. But for heaven's sake, come to-night to the lecture, and in the first flush of apprehension I think I can knock off a statement!" To the lecture I promised to come. At the same moment I raised my eyes and beheld in the window of the Colonel's apartment the ominous visage of Professor Fargo. I had been kindled by the Colonel's ardor, but somehow I was suddenly chilled by the presence of the Professor. I feared that, be the brilliancy of my friend's sudden illumination what it might, the shock of meeting his unloved *confrère* under his own roof would loosen his grasp of his idea. I found a pretext for keeping him standing a moment, and observed that the Professor disappeared. The next moment the door opened and he stepped forth. He had put on his hat, I suppose, hastily; it was cocked toward one side with a jauntiness which seemed the climax of his habitual swagger. He was evidently in better spirits than when I listened to him at Excelsior Hall; but neither the Professor's smiles nor his frowns were those of an honest man. He bestowed on my companion and me one of the most expansive of the former, gave his hat a cock in the opposite direction, and was about to pass on. But suddenly bethinking himself, he paused and drew from his pocket a small yellow ticket, which he presented to me. It was admission to Excelsior Hall.

"If you can use this to-night," he said, "I think you'll see something out of the common." This intimation, accompanied with a wink of extreme suggestiveness, seemed to indicate that the Professor also, by a singular coincidence, had had a flash of artistic inspiration. But giving me no further clue, he rapidly went his way. As I shook hands in farewell with the Colonel, I saw that the light of the old man's new inspiration had gone out in angry wonderment over the Professor's errand with his daughter.

I can hardly define the vague apprehensiveness which led me to make that evening a peculiarly prompt appearance at Excelsior Hall. There was no one there when I arrived, and for half an hour the solitude remained unbroken. At last a shabby little man came in and sat down on the last bench, in the shade. We remained a while staring at the white wall behind the three empty chairs of the performers and listening to the gas-burners, which were hissing with an expressiveness which, under the circumstances, was most distressing. At last my companion left his place and strolled down the aisle. He stopped before the platform, turned about, surveyed the capacity of the room, and muttered something between a groan and an imprecation. Then he came back toward me and stopped. He had a dirty shirt-front, a scrubby beard, a small, wrathful black eye, and a nose unmistakably Judaic.

"If you don't want to sit and be lectured at all alone," he said, "I guess you'd better go."

I expressed a hope that some one would turn up yet, and said that I preferred to remain, in any event, as I had a particular interest in the performance.

"A particular interest?" he cried; "that's about what I've got. I've got the rent of my room to collect. This thing has been going on here for three weeks now, and I haven't seen the first dollar of *my* profits. It's been going down hill steady, and I think the Professor, and the Colonel, and the deaf and dumb young woman had better shut up shop. They ain't appreciated; they'd better try some other line. There's mighty little to this thing, anyway; it ain't what I call an attractive exhibition. I've got an offer for the premises for a month from the Canadian Giantess, and I mean to ask the present company to pay me down and vacate."

It looked, certainly, as if the "Combination" would have some difficulty in meeting its engagements. The Professor's head emerged inquiringly from a door behind the stage and disappeared, after a brief communion with the vacuity of the scene. In a few minutes, however, the customary trio came forth and seated itself gravely on the platform. The Professor thrust his thumbs into his waistcoat and drummed on the floor with his toes, as if it cost his shrewdness a painful effort to play any longer at expectation. The Colonel sat stiff and solemn, with his eyes on the ground. The young girl gazed forth upon the ungrateful void with her characteristically irresponsible tranquillity. For myself, after listening some ten minutes more for an advancing tread, I leaned my elbows on the back of the bench before me and buried my head; I couldn't bear any longer to look at the Colonel. At last I heard a scramble behind me, and looking round, saw my little Jew erecting himself on his feet on a bench.

"Gentlemen!" he cried out, "I don't address the young woman; I'm told she can't hear. I suppose the man with the biggest audience has a right to speak. The amount of money in this hall to-night is just thirty cents—unless, indeed, my friend here is on the free list. Now it stands to reason that you can't pay your night's expenses out of thirty cents. I think we might as well turn down some of this gas; we can still see to settle our little account. To have it paid will gratify me considerably more than anything you can do there. I don't judge your entertainment; I've no doubt it's a very smart thing. But it's very evident it don't suit this city. It's too intellectual. I've got something else in view—I don't mind telling you it's the Canadian Giantess. It is going to open to-morrow with a matinée, and I want to put some props under that platform. So you'd better pay this young man his money back, and go home to supper. But before you leave, I'll trouble you for the sum of ninety-three dollars and eighty-seven cents."

The Professor stroked his beard; the Colonel didn't move. The little Jew descended from his perch and approached the platform with his bill in his hand. In a moment I followed him.

"We're a failure," said the Professor, at last. "Very well! I'm not discouraged; I'm a practical man. I've got an idea in my head by which, six months hence, I expect to fill the Academy of Music." Then, after a pause, turning to his companion, "Colonel, do you happen to have ninety-three dollars and eighty-seven cents?"

The Colonel slowly raised his eyes and looked at him; I shall never forget the look.

"Seriously speaking," the Professor went on, daunted but for an instant, "you're liable for half the debt. But I'll assume your share on a certain condition. I have in my head the plan of another entertainment. Our friend here is right; we have been too intellectual. Very good!" and he nodded at the empty benches. "I've learned the lesson. Henceforth I'm going to be sensational. My great sensation"—and he paused a moment to engage again the eye of the Colonel, who presently looked vaguely up at him—"is this young lady!" and he thrust out a hand toward Miss Gifford. "Allow me to exhibit your daughter for a month, in my own way and according to my own notions, and I assume your debt."

The young girl dropped her eyes on the ground, but kept her place. She had evidently been schooled. The Colonel slowly got up, glaring and trembling with indignation. I wished to cut the knot, and I interrupted his answer. "Your inducement is null," I said to the Professor. "I assume the Colonel's debt. It shall be paid this moment."

Professor Fargo gave an honestly gleeful grin; this was better even than the Colonel's assent. "You refuse your consent then," he demanded of the old man, "to your daughter's appearance under my exclusive management."

"Utterly!" cried the Colonel.

"You are aware, I suppose, that she's of age?"

The Colonel stared at me with a groan, "What under heaven is the fellow coming to?"

"To this!" responded the Professor; and he fixed his eye for a moment on the young girl. She immediately looked up at him, rose, advanced, and stood before him. Her face betrayed no painful consciousness of what she was doing, and I have often wondered how far, in her strangely simple mood and nature, her consciousness on this occasion was a guilty one. I never ascertained. This was the most unerring stroke I had seen the Professor perform. The poor child fixed her charming eyes on his gross, flushed face, and awaited his commands. She was fascinated; she had no will of her own. "You'll be so good as to choose," the Professor went on, addressing her in spite of her deafness, "between your father and me. He says we're to part. I say you're to follow me. What do you say?"

For all answer, after caressing him a moment with her gentle gaze, she dropped before him on her knees. The Colonel sprang toward her with a sort of howl of rage and grief, but she jumped up, retreated, and tripped down the steps of the platform into the room. She rapidly made her way to the door. There she paused and looked back at us. Her father stood staring after her in helpless bewilderment. The Professor disappeared into the little ante-room behind the stage, and came back in a moment jamming his hat over his eyes and carrying the young girl's shawl. He reached the edge of the platform, and then, stopping, shook the forefinger with the turquoise ring at the Colonel.

"What do you say now?" he cried. "Is spiritual magnetism a humbug?"

The little Jew rushed after him, shrieking and brandishing the unpaid bill; but the Professor cleared at half a dozen strides the interval which divided him from the door, caught the young girl round the waist, and made a triumphant escape. Half an hour later the Colonel and I left the little Jew staring distractedly at his unretributed gas-burners.

I walked home with the old man, and, having led him into his shabby refuge, suffered him to make his way alone, with groans, and tears, and imprecations, into his daughter's empty room. At last he came tottering out again; it seemed as if he were going mad. I brought him away by force, and he passed the night in my own quarters. He had spoken shortly before of the prospect of an asylum for his daughter, but it became evident that the asylum would have to be for him.

I sometimes go to see him. He spends his days covering little square sheets of paper with algebraic signs, but I am assured by his superintendent, who understands the matter, that they represent no coherent mathematical operation. I never treated myself to the "sensation" of attending Professor Fargo's new entertainment.

Eugene Pickering

IT WAS at Homburg, several years ago, before the gaming had been suppressed. The evening was very warm, and all the world was gathered on the terrace of the Kursaal and the esplanade below it, to listen to the excellent orchestra; or half the world, rather, for the crowd was equally dense in the gaming-rooms, around the tables. Everywhere the crowd was great. The night was perfect, the season was at its height, the open windows of the Kursaal sent long shafts of unnatural light into the dusky woods, and now and then, in the intervals of the music, one might almost hear the clink of the napoleons and the metallic call of the croupiers rise above the watching silence of the saloons. I had been strolling with a friend, and we at last prepared to sit down. Chairs, however, were scarce. I had captured one, but it seemed no easy matter to find a mate for it. I was on the point of giving up in despair and proposing an adjournment to the silken ottomans of the Kursaal, when I observed a young man lounging back on one of the objects of my quest, with his feet supported on the rounds of another. This was more than his share of luxury, and I promptly approached him. He evidently belonged to the race which has the credit of knowing best, at home and abroad, how to make itself comfortable; but something in his appearance suggested that his present attitude was the result of inadvertence rather than of egotism. He was staring at the conductor of the orchestra and listening intently to the music. His hands were locked round his long legs, and his mouth was half open, with rather a foolish air. "There are so few chairs," I said, "that I must beg you to surrender this second one." He started, stared, blushed, pushed the chair away with awkward alacrity, and murmured something about not having noticed that he had it.

"What an odd-looking youth!" said my companion, who had watched me, as I seated myself beside her.

"Yes, he is odd-looking; but what is odder still is that I have seen him before, that his face is familiar to me, and yet that I can't place him." The orchestra was playing the Prayer

36

from *Der Freischütz*, but Weber's lovely music only deepened the blank of memory. Who the deuce was he? where, when, how, had I known him? It seemed extraordinary that a face should be at once so familiar and so strange. We had our backs turned to him, so that I could not look at him again. When the music ceased we left our places, and I went to consign my friend to her mamma on the terrace. In passing, I saw that my young man had departed; I concluded that he only strikingly resembled some one I knew. But who in the world was it he resembled? The ladies went off to their lodgings, which were near by, and I turned into the gaming-rooms and hovered about the circle at roulette. Gradually, I filtered through to the inner edge, near the table and, looking round, saw my puzzling friend stationed opposite to me. He was watching the game, with his hands in his pockets; but singularly enough, now that I observed him at my leisure, the look of familiarity quite faded from his face. What had made us call his appearance odd was his great length and leanness of limb, his long, white neck, his blue, prominent eyes, and his ingenuous, unconscious absorption in the scene before him. He was not handsome, certainly, but he looked peculiarly amiable; and if his overt wonderment savoured a trifle of rurality, it was an agreeable contrast to the hard, inexpressive masks about him. He was the verdant offshoot, I said to myself, of some ancient, rigid stem; he had been brought up in the quietest of homes, and he was having his first glimpse of life. I was curious to see whether he would put anything on the table; he evidently felt the temptation, but he seemed paralysed by chronic embarrassment. He stood gazing at the chinking complexity of losses and gains, shaking his loose gold in his pocket, and every now and then passing his hand nervously over his eyes.

Most of the spectators were too attentive to the play to have many thoughts for each other; but before long I noticed a lady who evidently had an eye for her neighbours as well as for the table. She was seated about half way between my friend and me, and I presently observed that she was trying to catch his eye. Though at Homburg, as people said, "one could never be sure," I yet doubted whether this lady were one of those whose especial vocation it was to catch a gentleman's

eye. She was youthful rather than elderly, and pretty rather
than plain; indeed, a few minutes later, when I saw her smile,
I thought her wonderfully pretty. She had a charming grey
eye and a good deal of yellow hair disposed in picturesque
disorder; and though her features were meagre and her complexion faded, she gave one a sense of sentimental, artificial
gracefulness. She was dressed in white muslin very much
puffed and frilled, but a trifle the worse for wear, relieved here
and there by a pale blue ribbon. I used to flatter myself on
guessing at people's nationality by their faces, and, as a rule,
I guessed aright. This faded, crumpled, vaporous beauty, I
conceived, was a German—such a German, somehow, as I had
seen imagined in literature. Was she not a friend of poets, a
correspondent of philosophers, a muse, a priestess of æsthet-
ics—something in the way of a Bettina, a Rahel? My conjectures, however, were speedily merged in wonderment as to
what my diffident friend was making of her. She caught his
eye at last, and raising an ungloved hand, covered altogether
with blue-gemmed rings—turquoises, sapphires, and lapis—
she beckoned him to come to her. The gesture was executed
with a sort of practised coolness and accompanied with an
appealing smile. He stared a moment, rather blankly, unable
to suppose that the invitation was addressed to him; then, as
it was immediately repeated with a good deal of intensity, he
blushed to the roots of his hair, wavered awkwardly, and at
last made his way to the lady's chair. By the time he reached
it he was crimson, and wiping his forehead with his pocket-
handkerchief. She tilted back, looked up at him with the same
smile, laid two fingers on his sleeve, and said something,
interrogatively, to which he replied by a shake of the head.
She was asking him, evidently, if he had ever played, and he
was saying no. Old players have a fancy that when luck has
turned her back on them, they can put her into good-humour
again by having their stakes placed by a novice. Our young
man's physiognomy had seemed to his new acquaintance to
express the perfection of inexperience, and, like a practical
woman, she had determined to make him serve her turn. Unlike most of her neighbours, she had no little pile of gold
before her, but she drew from her pocket a double napoleon,
put it into his hand and bade him place it on a number of his

own choosing. He was evidently filled with a sort of delightful trouble; he enjoyed the adventure, but he shrank from the hazard. I would have staked the coin on its being his companion's last; for, although she still smiled intently as she watched his hesitation, there was anything but indifference in her pale, pretty face. Suddenly, in desperation, he reached over and laid the piece on the table. My attention was diverted at this moment by my having to make way for a lady with a great many flounces, before me, to give up her chair to a rustling friend to whom she had promised it; when I again looked across at the lady in white muslin, she was drawing in a very goodly pile of gold with her little blue-gemmed claw. Good luck and bad, at the Homburg tables, were equally undemonstrative, and this happy adventuress rewarded her young friend for the sacrifice of his innocence with a single, rapid, upward smile. He had innocence enough left, however, to look round the table with a gleeful, conscious laugh, in the midst of which his eyes encountered my own. Then, suddenly the familiar look which had vanished from his face flickered up unmistakably; it was the boyish laugh of a boyhood's friend. Stupid fellow that I was, I had been looking at Eugene Pickering!

Though I lingered on for some time longer, he failed to recognise me. Recognition, I think, had kindled a smile in my own face; but, less fortunate than he, I suppose my smile had ceased to be boyish. Now that luck had faced about again, his companion played for herself—played and won, hand over hand. At last she seemed disposed to rest on her gains, and proceeded to bury them in the folds of her muslin. Pickering had staked nothing for himself, but as he saw her prepare to withdraw, he offered her a double napoleon and begged her to place it. She shook her head with great decision, and seemed to bid him put it up again; but he, still blushing a good deal, pressed her with awkward ardour, and she at last took it from him, looked at him a moment fixedly, and laid it on a number. A moment later the croupier was raking it in. She gave the young man a little nod which seemed to say, "I told you so"; he glanced round the table again and laughed; she left her chair, and he made a way for her through the crowd. Before going home I took a turn on the terrace and

looked down on the esplanade. The lamps were out, but the
warm starlight vaguely illumined a dozen figures scattered in
couples. One of these figures, I thought, was a lady in a white
dress.

I had no intention of letting Pickering go without reminding him of our old acquaintance. He had been a very singular
boy, and I was curious to see what had become of his singu-
larity. I looked for him the next morning at two or three of
the hotels, and at last I discovered his whereabouts. But he
was out, the waiter said; he had gone to walk an hour before.
I went my way confident that I should meet him in the evening. It was the rule with the Homburg world to spend its
evenings at the Kursaal, and Pickering, apparently, had already
discovered a good reason for not being an exception. One of
the charms of Homburg is the fact that of a hot day you may
walk about for a whole afternoon in unbroken shade. The
umbrageous gardens of the Kursaal mingle with the charming
Hardtwald, which in turn melts away into the wooded slopes
of the Taunus Mountains. To the Hardtwald I bent my steps,
and strolled for an hour through mossy glades and the still,
perpendicular gloom of the fir-woods. Suddenly, on the grassy
margin of a by-path, I came upon a young man stretched at
his length in the sun-checkered shade and kicking his heels
towards a patch of blue sky. My step was so noiseless on the
turf, that before he saw me, I had time to recognise Pickering
again. He looked as if he had been lounging there for some
time; his hair was tossed about as if he had been sleeping; on
the grass near him, beside his hat and stick, lay a sealed letter.
When he perceived me he jerked himself forward, and I stood
looking at him without introducing myself—purposely, to give
him a chance to recognise me. He put on his glasses, being
awkwardly near-sighted, and stared up at me with an air of
general trustfulness, but without a sign of knowing me. So at
last I introduced myself. Then he jumped up and grasped my
hands and stared and blushed and laughed and began a dozen
random questions, ending with a demand as to how in the
world I had known him.

"Why, you are not changed so utterly," I said; "and after
all, it's but fifteen years since you used to do my Latin exercises for me."

"Not changed, eh?" he answered, still smiling, and yet speaking with a sort of ingenuous dismay.

Then I remembered that poor Pickering had been in those Latin days a victim of juvenile irony. He used to bring a bottle of medicine to school and take a dose in a glass of water before lunch; and every day at two o'clock, half an hour before the rest of us were liberated, an old nurse with bushy eyebrows came and fetched him away in a carriage. His extremely fair complexion, his nurse, and his bottle of medicine, which suggested a vague analogy with the sleeping-potion in the tragedy, caused him to be called Juliet. Certainly, Romeo's sweetheart hardly suffered more; she was not, at least, a standing joke in Verona. Remembering these things, I hastened to say to Pickering that I hoped he was still the same good fellow who used to do my Latin for me. "We were capital friends, you know," I went on, "then and afterwards."

"Yes, we were very good friends," he said, "and that makes it the stranger I shouldn't have known you. For you know as a boy I never had many friends, nor as a man either. You see," he added, passing his hand over his eyes, "I am rather dazed, rather bewildered at finding myself for the first time—alone." And he jerked back his shoulders nervously and threw up his head, as if to settle himself in an unwonted position. I wondered whether the old nurse with the bushy eyebrows had remained attached to his person up to a recent period, and discovered presently that, virtually at least, she had. We had the whole summer day before us, and we sat down on the grass together and overhauled our old memories. It was as if we had stumbled upon an ancient cupboard in some dusky corner, and rummaged out a heap of childish playthings—tin soldiers and torn story-books, jack-knives and Chinese puzzles. This is what we remembered between us.

He had made but a short stay at school—not because he was tormented, for he thought it so fine to be at school at all that he held his tongue at home about the sufferings incurred through the medicine-bottle; but because his father thought he was learning bad manners. This he imparted to me in confidence at the time, and I remember how it increased my oppressive awe of Mr. Pickering, who had appeared to me in glimpses as a sort of high-priest of the proprieties. Mr.

Pickering was a widower—a fact which seemed to produce in him a sort of preternatural concentration of parental dignity. He was a majestic man, with a hooked nose, a keen, dark eye, very large whiskers, and notions of his own as to how a boy— or his boy, at any rate—should be brought up. First and foremost, he was to be a "gentleman"; which seemed to mean, chiefly, that he was always to wear a muffler and gloves, and be sent to bed, after a supper of bread and milk, at eight o'clock. School-life, on experiment, seemed hostile to these observances, and Eugene was taken home again, to be moulded into urbanity beneath the parental eye. A tutor was provided for him, and a single select companion was prescribed. The choice, mysteriously, fell on me, born as I was under quite another star; my parents were appealed to, and I was allowed for a few months to have my lessons with Eugene. The tutor, I think, must have been rather a snob, for Eugene was treated like a prince, while I got all the questions and the raps with the ruler. And yet I remember never being jealous of my happier comrade, and striking up, for the time, one of those friendships of childhood. He had a watch and a pony and a great store of picture-books, but my envy of these luxuries was tempered by a vague compassion which left me free to be generous. I could go out to play alone, I could button my jacket myself, and sit up till I was sleepy. Poor Pickering could never take a step without asking leave, or spend half an hour in the garden without a formal report of it when he came in. My parents, who had no desire to see me inoculated with importunate virtues, sent me back to school at the end of six months. After that I never saw Eugene. His father went to live in the country, to protect the lad's morals, and Eugene faded, in reminiscence, into a pale image of the depressing effects of education. I think I vaguely supposed that he would melt into thin air, and indeed began gradually to doubt of his existence and to regard him as one of the foolish things one ceased to believe in as one grew older. It seemed natural that I should have no more news of him. Our present meeting was my first assurance that he had really survived all that muffling and coddling.

I observed him now with a good deal of interest, for he was a rare phenomenon—the fruit of a system persistently and uninterruptedly applied. He struck me, in a fashion, as certain young monks I had seen in Italy; he had the same candid, unsophisticated cloister-face. His education had been really almost monastic. It had found him evidently a very compliant, yielding subject; his gentle, affectionate spirit was not one of those that need to be broken. It had bequeathed him, now that he stood on the threshold of the great world, an extraordinary freshness of impression and alertness of desire, and I confess that, as I looked at him and met his transparent blue eye, I trembled for the unwarned innocence of such a soul. I became aware, gradually, that the world had already wrought a certain work upon him and roused him to a restless, troubled self-consciousness. Everything about him pointed to an experience from which he had been debarred; his whole organism trembled with a dawning sense of unsuspected possibilities of feeling. This appealing tremor was indeed outwardly visible. He kept shifting himself about on the grass, thrusting his hands through his hair, wiping a light perspiration from his forehead, breaking out to say something and rushing off to something else. Our sudden meeting had greatly excited him, and I saw that I was likely to profit by a certain overflow of sentimental fermentation. I could do so with a good conscience, for all this trepidation filled me with a great friendliness.

"It's nearly fifteen years, as you say," he began, "since you used to call me 'butter-fingers' for always missing the ball. That's a long time to give an account of, and yet they have been, for me, such eventless, monotonous years, that I could almost tell their history in ten words. You, I suppose, have had all kinds of adventures and travelled over half the world. I remember you had a turn for deeds of daring; I used to think you a little Captain Cook in roundabouts, for climbing the garden fence to get the ball, when I had let it fly over. I climbed no fences then or since. You remember my father, I suppose, and the great care he took of me? I lost him some five months ago. From those boyish days up to his death we were always together. I don't think that in fifteen years we spent half-a-dozen hours apart. We lived in the country, winter and summer, seeing but three or four people. I had a succession of tutors, and a library to browse about in; I assure

you I am a tremendous scholar. It was a dull life for a growing
boy, and a duller life for a young man grown, but I never
knew it. I was perfectly happy." He spoke of his father at some
length, and with a respect which I privately declined to em-
ulate. Mr. Pickering had been, to my sense, a frigid egotist,
unable to conceive of any larger vocation for his son than to
strive to reproduce so irreproachable a model. "I know I have
been strangely brought up," said my friend, "and that the
result is something grotesque; but my education, piece by
piece, in detail, became one of my father's personal habits, as
it were. He took a fancy to it at first through his intense affection for my mother and the sort of worship he paid her
memory. She died at my birth, and as I grew up, it seems that
I bore an extraordinary likeness to her. Besides, my father had
a great many theories; he prided himself on his conservative
opinions; he thought the usual American *laisser-aller* in education was a very vulgar practice, and that children were not
to grow up like dusty thorns by the wayside. So you see,"
Pickering went on, smiling and blushing, and yet with something of the irony of vain regret, "I am a regular garden plant.
I have been watched and watered and pruned, and if there is
any virtue in tending I ought to take the prize at a flower-
show. Some three years ago my father's health broke down,
and he was kept very much within doors. So, although I was
a man grown, I lived altogether at home. If I was out of his
sight for a quarter of an hour he sent some one after me. He
had severe attacks of neuralgia, and he used to sit at his window, basking in the sun. He kept an opera-glass at hand, and
when I was out in the garden he used to watch me with it. A
few days before his death, I was twenty-seven years old, and
the most innocent youth, I suppose, on the continent. After
he died I missed him greatly," Pickering continued, evidently
with no intention of making an epigram. "I stayed at home,
in a sort of dull stupor. It seemed as if life offered itself to me
for the first time, and yet as if I didn't know how to take hold
of it."

He uttered all this with a frank eagerness which increased
as he talked, and there was a singular contrast between the
meagre experience he described and a certain radiant intelligence which I seemed to perceive in his glance and tone. Ev-

idently he was a clever fellow, and his natural faculties were excellent. I imagined he had read a great deal, and recovered, in some degree, in restless intellectual conjecture, the freedom he was condemned to ignore in practice. Opportunity was now offering a meaning to the empty forms with which his imagination was stored, but it appeared to him dimly, through the veil of his personal diffidence.

"I have not sailed round the world, as you suppose," I said, "but I confess I envy you the novelties you are going to behold. Coming to Homburg you have plunged *in medias res.*"

He glanced at me to see if my remark contained an allusion, and hesitated a moment. "Yes, I know it. I came to Bremen in the steamer with a very friendly German, who undertook to initiate me into the glories and mysteries of the fatherland. At this season, he said, I must begin with Homburg. I landed but a fortnight ago, and here I am." Again he hesitated, as if he were going to add something about the scene at the Kursaal; but suddenly, nervously, he took up the letter which was lying beside him, looked hard at the seal with a troubled frown, and then flung it back on the grass with a sigh.

"How long do you expect to be in Europe?" I asked.

"Six months, I supposed when I came. But not so long— now!" And he let his eyes wander to the letter again.

"And where shall you go—what shall you do?"

"Everywhere, everything, I should have said yesterday. But now it is different."

I glanced at the letter interrogatively, and he gravely picked it up and put it into his pocket. We talked for a while longer, but I saw that he had suddenly become preoccupied; that he was apparently weighing an impulse to break some last barrier of reserve. At last he suddenly laid his hand on my arm, looked at me a moment appealingly, and cried, "Upon my word I should like to tell you everything!"

"Tell me everything, by all means," I answered, smiling. "I desire nothing better than to lie here in the shade and hear everything."

"Ah, but the question is, will you understand it? No matter; you think me a queer fellow already. It's not easy, either, to tell you what I feel—not easy for so queer a fellow as I to tell you in how many ways he is queer!" He got up and walked away a moment, passing his hand over his eyes, then came back rapidly and flung himself on the grass again. "I said just now I always supposed I was happy; it's true; but now that my eyes are open, I see I was only stultified. I was like a poodle-dog that is led about by a blue ribbon, and scoured and combed and fed on slops. It was not life; life is learning to know one's self, and in that sense I have lived more in the past six weeks than in all the years that preceded them. I am filled with this feverish sense of liberation; it keeps rising to my head like the fumes of strong wine. I find I am an active, sentient, intelligent creature, with desires, with passions, with possible convictions—even with what I never dreamed of, a possible will of my own! I find there is a world to know, a life to lead, men and women to form a thousand relations with. It all lies there like a great surging sea, where we must plunge and dive and feel the breeze and breast the waves. I stand shivering here on the brink, staring, longing, wondering, charmed by the smell of the brine and yet afraid of the water. The world beckons and smiles and calls, but a nameless influence from the past, that I can neither wholly obey nor wholly resist, seems to hold me back. I am full of impulses, but, somehow, I am not full of strength. Life seems inspiring at certain moments, but it seems terrible and unsafe; and I ask myself why I should wantonly measure myself with merciless forces, when I have learned so well how to stand aside and let them pass. Why shouldn't I turn my back upon it all and go home to—what awaits me?—to that sightless, soundless country life, and long days spent among old books? But if a man *is* weak, he doesn't want to assent beforehand to his weakness; he wants to taste whatever sweetness there may be in paying for the knowledge. So it is that it comes back—this irresistible impulse to take my plunge—to let myself swing, to go where liberty leads me." He paused a moment, fixing me with his excited eyes, and perhaps perceived in my own an irrepressible smile at his perplexity. " 'Swing ahead, in Heaven's name,' you want to say, 'and much good may it do you.' I don't know whether you are laughing at my scruples or at what possibly strikes you as my depravity. I doubt," he went on gravely, "whether I have an inclination toward wrong-doing; if I have, I am sure I shall not prosper in it. I

honestly believe I may safely take out a licence to amuse myself. But it isn't that I think of, any more than I dream of,
playing with suffering. Pleasure and pain are empty words to
me; what I long for is knowledge—some other knowledge
than comes to us in formal, colourless, impersonal precept.
You would understand all this better if you could breathe for
an hour the musty in-door atmosphere in which I have always
lived. To break a window and let in light and air—I feel as if
at last I must *act!*"

"Act, by all means, now and always, when you have a
chance," I answered. "But don't take things too hard, now
or ever. Your long confinement makes you think the world
better worth knowing than you are likely to find it. A man
with as good a head and heart as yours has a very ample world
within himself, and I am no believer in art for art, nor in
what's called 'life' for life's sake. Nevertheless, take your
plunge, and come and tell me whether you have found the
pearl of wisdom." He frowned a little, as if he thought my
sympathy a trifle meagre. I shook him by the hand and
laughed. "The pearl of wisdom," I cried, "is love; honest love
in the most convenient concentration of experience! I advise
you to fall in love." He gave me no smile in response, but
drew from his pocket the letter of which I have spoken, held
it up, and shook it solemnly. "What is it?" I asked.

"It is my sentence!"

"Not of death, I hope!"

"Of marriage."

"With whom?"

"With a person I don't love."

This was serious. I stopped smiling and begged him to
explain.

"It is the singular part of my story," he said at last. "It will
remind you of an old-fashioned romance. Such as I sit here,
talking in this wild way, and tossing off provocations to destiny, my destiny is settled and sealed. I am engaged, I am given
in marriage. It's a bequest of the past—the past I had no hand
in! The marriage was arranged by my father, years ago, when
I was a boy. The young girl's father was his particular friend;
he was also a widower, and was bringing up his daughter, on
his side, in the same severe seclusion in which I was spending

my days. To this day I am unacquainted with the origin of
the bond of union between our respective progenitors. Mr.
Vernor was largely engaged in business, and I imagine that
once upon a time he found himself in a financial strait and
was helped through it by my father's coming forward with a
heavy loan, on which, in his situation, he could offer no security but his word. Of this my father was quite capable. He
was a man of dogmas, and he was sure to have a rule of
life—as clear as if it had been written out in his beautiful copper plate hand—adapted to the conduct of a gentleman
toward a friend in pecuniary embarrassment. What is more,
he was sure to adhere to it. Mr. Vernor, I believe, got on his
feet, paid his debt, and vowed my father an eternal gratitude.
His little daughter was the apple of his eye, and he pledged
himself to bring her up to be the wife of his benefactor's son.
So our fate was fixed, parentally, and we have been educated
for each other. I have not seen my betrothed since she was a
very plain-faced little girl in a sticky pinafore, hugging a
one-armed doll—of the male sex, I believe—as big as herself.
Mr. Vernor is in what is called the Eastern trade, and has been
living these many years at Smyrna. Isabel has grown up there
in a white-walled garden, in an orange grove, between her
father and her governess. She is a good deal my junior; six
months ago she was seventeen; when she is eighteen we are
to marry!"

He related all this calmly enough, without the accent of
complaint, dryly rather and doggedly, as if he were weary of
thinking of it. "It's a romance, indeed, for these dull days,"
I said, "and I heartily congratulate you. It's not every young
man who finds, on reaching the marrying age, a wife kept in
a box of rose-leaves for him. A thousand to one Miss Vernor
is charming; I wonder you don't post off to Smyrna."

"You are joking," he answered, with a wounded air, "and
I am terribly serious. Let me tell you the rest. I never suspected this superior conspiracy till something less than a year
ago. My father, wishing to provide against his death, informed
me of it very solemnly. I was neither elated nor depressed; I
received it, as I remember, with a sort of emotion which varied
only in degree from that with which I could have hailed the
announcement that he had ordered me a set of new shirts. I

supposed that was the way that all marriages were made; I had heard of their being made in heaven, and what was my father but a divinity? Novels and poems indeed talked about falling in love; but novels and poems were one thing and life was another. A short time afterwards he introduced me to a photograph of my predestined, who has a pretty, but an extremely inanimate, face. After this his health failed rapidly. One night I was sitting, as I habitually sat for hours, in his dimly lighted room, near his bed, to which he had been confined for a week. He had not spoken for some time, and I supposed he was asleep; but happening to look at him I saw his eyes wide open, and fixed on me strangely. He was smiling benignantly, intensely, and in a moment he beckoned to me. Then, on my going to him—'I feel that I shall not last long,' he said; 'but I am willing to die when I think how comfortably I have arranged your future.' He was talking of death, and anything but grief at that moment was doubtless impious and monstrous; but there came into my heart for the first time a throbbing sense of being over-governed. I said nothing, and he thought my silence was all sorrow. 'I shall not live to see you married,' he went on, 'but since the foundation is laid, that little signifies; it would be a selfish pleasure, and I have never thought of myself but in you. To foresee your future, in its main outline, to know to a certainty that you will be safely domiciled here, with a wife approved by my judgment, cultivating the moral fruit of which I have sown the seed—this will content me. But, my son, I wish to clear this bright vision from the shadow of a doubt. I believe in your docility; I believe I may trust the salutary force of your respect for my memory. But I must remember that when I am removed, you will stand here alone, face to face with a hundred nameless temptations to perversity. The fumes of unrighteous pride may rise into your brain and tempt you, in the interest of a vulgar theory which it will call your independence, to shatter the edifice I have so laboriously constructed. So I must ask you for a promise—the solemn promise you owe my condition.' And he grasped my hand. 'You will follow the path I have marked; you will be faithful to the young girl whom an influence as devoted as that which has governed your own young life has moulded into everything amiable; you will marry

Isabel Vernor.' This was pretty 'steep' as we used to say at school. I was frightened; I drew away my hand and asked to be trusted without any such terrible vow. My reluctance startled my father into a suspicion that the vulgar theory of independence had already been whispering to me. He sat up in his bed and looked at me with eyes which seemed to foresee a lifetime of odious ingratitude. I felt the reproach; I feel it now. I promised! And even now I don't regret my promise nor complain of my father's tenacity. I feel, somehow, as if the seeds of ultimate repose had been sown in those unsuspecting years—as if after many days I might gather the mellow fruit. But after many days! I will keep my promise, I will obey; but I want to *live* first!"

"My dear fellow, you are living now. All this passionate consciousness of your situation is a very ardent life. I wish I could say as much for my own."

"I want to forget my situation. I want to spend three months without thinking of the past or the future, grasping whatever the present offers me. Yesterday, I thought I was in a fair way to sail with the tide. But this morning comes this memento!" And he held up his letter again.

"What is it?"

"A letter from Smyrna."

"I see you have not yet broken the seal."

"No, nor do I mean to, for the present. It contains bad news."

"What do you call bad news?"

"News that I am expected in Smyrna in three weeks. News that Mr. Vernor disapproves of my roving about the world. News that his daughter is standing expectant at the altar."

"Is not this pure conjecture?"

"Conjecture, possibly, but safe conjecture. As soon as I looked at the letter, something smote me at the heart. Look at the device on the seal, and I am sure you will find it's *Tarry not!*" And he flung the letter on the grass.

"Upon my word, you had better open it," I said.

"If I were to open it and read my summons, do you know what I should do? I should march home and ask the Ober-kellner how one gets to Smyrna, pack my trunk, take my ticket, and not stop till I arrived. I know I should; it would be the fascination of habit. The only way, therefore, to wander to my rope's end is to leave the letter unread."

"In your place," I said, "curiosity would make me open it."

He shook his head. "I have no curiosity! For a long time now the idea of my marriage has ceased to be a novelty, and I have contemplated it mentally in every possible light. I fear nothing from that side, but I do fear something from conscience. I want my hands tied. Will you do me a favour? Pick up the letter, put it into your pocket, and keep it till I ask you for it. When I do, you may know that I am at my rope's end."

I took the letter, smiling. "And how long is your rope to be? The Homburg season doesn't last for ever."

"Does it last a month? Let that be my season! A month hence you will give it back to me."

"To-morrow, if you say so. Meanwhile, let it rest in peace!" And I consigned it to the most sacred interstice of my pocket-book. To say that I was disposed to humour the poor fellow would seem to be saying that I thought his request fantastic. It was his situation, by no fault of his own, that was fantastic, and he was only trying to be natural. He watched me put away the letter, and when it had disappeared gave a soft sigh of relief. The sigh was natural, and yet it set me thinking. His general recoil from an immediate responsibility imposed by others might be wholesome enough; but if there was an old grievance on one side, was there not possibly a new-born delusion on the other? It would be unkind to withhold a reflection that might serve as a warning; so I told him, abruptly, that I had been an undiscovered spectator, the night before, of his exploits at roulette.

He blushed deeply, but he met my eyes with the same clear good-humour.

"Ah, then you saw that wonderful lady?"

"Wonderful she was indeed. I saw her afterwards, too, sitting on the terrace in the starlight. I imagine she was not alone."

"No, indeed, I was with her—for nearly an hour. Then I walked home with her."

"Ah! And did you go in?"

"No, she said it was too late to ask me; though she remarked that in a general way she did not stand upon ceremony."

"She did herself injustice. When it came to losing your money for you, she made you insist."

"Ah, you noticed that too?" cried Pickering, still quite unconfused. "I felt as if the whole table were staring at me; but her manner was so gracious and reassuring that I supposed she was doing nothing unusual. She confessed, however, afterwards, that she is very eccentric. The world began to call her so, she said, before she ever dreamed of it, and at last finding that she had the reputation, in spite of herself, she resolved to enjoy its privileges. Now, she does what she chooses."

"In other words, she is a lady with no reputation to lose!"

Pickering seemed puzzled; he smiled a little. "Is not that what you say of bad women?"

"Of some—of those who are found out."

"Well," he said, still smiling, "I have not yet found out Madame Blumenthal."

"If that's her name, I suppose she's German."

"Yes; but she speaks English so well that you wouldn't know it. She is very clever. Her husband is dead."

I laughed involuntarily at the conjunction of these facts, and Pickering's clear glance seemed to question my mirth. "You have been so bluntly frank with me," I said, "that I too must be frank. Tell me, if you can, whether this clever Madame Blumenthal, whose husband is dead, has given a point to your desire for a suspension of communication with Smyrna."

He seemed to ponder my question, unshrinkingly. "I think not," he said, at last. "I have had the desire for three months; I have known Madame Blumenthal for less than twenty-four hours."

"Very true. But when you found this letter of yours on your plate at breakfast, did you seem for a moment to see Madame Blumenthal sitting opposite?"

"Opposite?"

"Opposite, my dear fellow, or anywhere in the neighbourhood. In a word, does she interest you?"

"Very much!" he cried, joyously.

"Amen!" I answered, jumping up with a laugh. "And now, if we are to see the world in a month, there is no time to lose. Let us begin with the Hardtwald."

Pickering rose, and we strolled away into the forest, talking of lighter things. At last we reached the edge of the wood, sat down on a fallen log, and looked out across an interval of meadow at the long wooded waves of the Taunus. What my friend was thinking of, I can't say; I was meditating on his queer biography and letting my wonderment wander away to Smyrna. Suddenly I remembered that he possessed a portrait of the young girl who was waiting for him there in a white-walled garden. I asked him if he had it with him. He said nothing, but gravely took out his pocket-book and drew forth a small photograph. It represented, as the poet says, a simple maiden in her flower—a slight young girl, with a certain child-ish roundness of contour. There was no ease in her posture; she was standing, stiffly and shyly, for her likeness; she wore a short-waisted white dress; her arms hung at her sides and her hands were clasped in front; her head was bent downward a little, and her dark eyes fixed. But her awkwardness was as pretty as that of some angular seraph in a mediæval carving, and in her timid gaze there seemed to lurk the questioning gleam of childhood. "What is this for?" her charming eyes appeared to ask; "why have I been dressed up for this cere-mony in a white frock and amber beads?"

"Gracious powers!" I said to myself; "what an enchanting thing is innocence!"

"That portrait was taken a year and a half ago," said Pick-ering, as if with an effort to be perfectly just. "By this time, I suppose, she looks a little wiser."

"Not much, I hope," I said, as I gave it back. "She is very sweet!"

"Yes, poor girl, she is very sweet—no doubt!" And he put the thing away without looking at it.

We were silent for some moments. At last, abruptly—"My dear fellow," I said, "I should take some satisfaction in seeing you immediately leave Homburg."

"Immediately?"

"To-day—as soon as you can get ready."

He looked at me, surprised, and little by little he blushed. "There is something I have not told you," he said; "some-thing that your saying that Madame Blumenthal has no rep-utation to lose has made me half afraid to tell you."

"I think I can guess it. Madame Blumenthal has asked you
to come and play her game for her again."

"Not at all!" cried Pickering, with a smile of triumph. "She
says that she means to play no more for the present. She has
asked me to come and take tea with her this evening."

"Ah, then," I said, very gravely, "of course you can't leave
Homburg."

He answered nothing, but looked askance at me, as if he
were expecting me to laugh. "Urge it strongly," he said in a
moment. "Say it's my duty—that I *must*."

I didn't quite understand him, but, feathering the shaft with
a harmless expletive, I told him that unless he followed my
advice I would never speak to him again.

He got up, stood before me, and struck the ground with
his stick. "Good!" he cried, "I wanted an occasion to break
a rule—to leap a barrier. Here it is! I stay!"

I made him a mock bow for his energy. "That's very fine,"
I said; "but now to put you in a proper mood for Madame
Blumenthal's tea, we will go and listen to the band play Schu-
bert under the lindens." And we walked back through the
woods.

I went to see Pickering the next day, at his inn, and on
knocking, as directed, at his door, was surprised to hear the
sound of a loud voice within. My knock remained unnoticed,
so I presently introduced myself. I found no company, but I
discovered my friend walking up and down the room and apparently declaiming to himself from a little volume bound in
white vellum. He greeted me heartily, threw his book on the
table, and said that he was taking a German lesson.

"And who is your teacher?" I asked, glancing at the book.

He rather avoided meeting my eye, as he answered, after
an instant's delay, "Madame Blumenthal."

"Indeed! Has she written a grammar?"

"It's not a grammar; it's a tragedy." And he handed me the
book.

I opened it, and beheld, in delicate type, with a very large
margin, an *Historisches Trauerspiel* in five acts, entitled "Cleopatra." There were a great many marginal corrections and
annotations, apparently from the author's hand; the speeches
were very long, and there was an inordinate number of solil-

oquies by the heroine. One of them, I remember, towards the end of the play, began in this fashion—

"What, after all, is life but sensation, and sensation but deception?—reality that pales before the light of one's dreams, as Octavia's dull beauty fades beside mine? But let me believe in some intenser bliss and seek it in the arms of death!"

"It seems decidedly passionate," I said. "Has the tragedy ever been acted?"

"Never in public; but Madame Blumenthal tells me that she had it played at her own house in Berlin, and that she herself undertook the part of the heroine."

Pickering's unworldly life had not been of a sort to sharpen his perception of the ridiculous, but it seemed to me an unmistakable sign of his being under the charm, that this information was very soberly offered. He was preoccupied, he was irresponsive to my experimental observations on vulgar topics —the hot weather, the inn, the advent of Adelina Patti. At last, uttering his thoughts, he announced that Madame Blumenthal had proved to be an extraordinarily interesting woman. He seemed to have quite forgotten our long talk in the Hardtwald, and betrayed no sense of this being a confession that he had taken his plunge and was floating with the current. He only remembered that I had spoken slightingly of the lady, and he now hinted that it behoved me to amend my opinion. I had received the day before so strong an impression of a sort of spiritual fastidiousness in my friend's nature, that on hearing now the striking of a new hour, as it were, in his consciousness, and observing how the echoes of the past were immediately quenched in its music, I said to myself that it had certainly taken a delicate hand to wind up that fine machine. No doubt Madame Blumenthal was a clever woman. It is a good German custom, at Homburg to spend the hour preceding dinner in listening to the orchestra in the Kurgarten; Mozart and Beethoven, for organisms in which the interfusion of soul and sense is peculiarly mysterious, are a vigorous stimulus to the appetite. Pickering and I conformed, as we had done the day before, to the fashion, and when we were seated under the trees, he began to expatiate on his friend's merits.

"I don't know whether she is eccentric or not," he said; "to me every one seems eccentric, and it's not for me, yet a while, to measure people by my narrow precedents. I never saw a gaming-table in my life before, and supposed that a gambler was of necessity some dusky villain with an evil eye. In Germany, says Madame Blumenthal, people play at roulette as they play at billiards, and her own venerable mother originally taught her the rules of the game. It is a recognised source of subsistence for decent people with small means. But I confess Madame Blumenthal might do worse things than play at roulette, and yet make them harmonious and beautiful. I have never been in the habit of thinking positive beauty the most excellent thing in a woman. I have always said to myself that if my heart were ever to be captured it would be by a sort of general grace—a sweetness of motion and tone—on which one could count for soothing impressions, as one counts on a musical instrument that is perfectly in tune. Madame Blumenthal has it—this grace that soothes and satisfies; and it seems the more perfect that it keeps order and harmony in a character really passionately ardent and active. With her eager nature and her innumerable accomplishments, nothing would be easier than that she should seem restless and aggressive. You will know her, and I leave you to judge whether she does seem so! She has every gift, and culture has done everything for each. What goes on in her mind, I of course can't say; what reaches the observer—the admirer—is simply a sort of fragrant emanation of intelligence and sympathy."

"Madame Blumenthal," I said, smiling, "might be the loveliest woman in the world, and you the object of her choicest favours, and yet what I should most envy you would be, not your peerless friend, but your beautiful imagination."

"That's a polite way of calling me a fool," said Pickering. "You are a sceptic, a cynic, a satirist! I hope I shall be a long time coming to that."

"You will make the journey fast if you travel by express trains. But pray tell me, have you ventured to intimate to Madame Blumenthal your high opinion of her?"

"I don't know what I may have said. She listens even better than she talks, and I think it possible I may have made her listen to a great deal of nonsense. For after the first few words I exchanged with her I was conscious of an extraordinary evaporation of all my old diffidence. I have, in truth, I suppose," he added, in a moment, "owing to my peculiar circumstances, a great accumulated fund of unuttered things of all sorts to get rid of. Last evening, sitting there before that charming woman, they came swarming to my lips. Very likely I poured them all out. I have a sense of having enshrouded myself in a sort of mist of talk, and of seeing her lovely eyes shining through it opposite to me, like fog-lamps at sea." And here, if I remember rightly, Pickering broke off into an ardent parenthesis, and declared that Madame Blumenthal's eyes had something in them that he had never seen in any others. "It was a jumble of crudities, and inanities," he went on; "they must have seemed to her great rubbish; but I felt the wiser and the stronger, somehow, for having fired off all my guns—they could hurt nobody now if they hit—and I imagine I might have gone far without finding another woman in whom such an exhibition would have provoked so little of mere cold amusement."

"Madame Blumenthal, on the contrary," I surmised, "entered into your situation with warmth."

"Exactly so—the greatest! She has felt and suffered, and now she understands!"

"She told you, I imagine, that she understood you as if she had made you, and she offered to be your guide, philosopher and friend."

"She spoke to me," Pickering answered, after a pause, "as I had never been spoken to before, and she offered me formally all the offices of a woman's friendship."

"Which you as formally accepted?"

"To you the scene sounds absurd, I suppose, but allow me to say I don't care!" Pickering spoke with an air of genial defiance which was the most inoffensive thing in the world. "I was very much moved; I was in fact, very much excited. I tried to say something, but I couldn't; I had had plenty to say before, but now I stammered and bungled, and at last I bolted out of the room."

"Meanwhile she had dropped her tragedy into your pocket!"

"Not at all. I had seen it on the table before she came in. Afterwards she kindly offered to read German aloud with me, for the accent, two or three times a week. 'What shall we

begin with?' she asked. 'With this!' I said, and held up the
book. And she let me take it to look it over.'"

I was neither a cynic nor a satirist, but even if I had been,
I might have been disarmed by Pickering's assurance, before
we parted, that Madame Blumenthal wished to know me and
expected him to introduce me. Among the foolish things
which, according to his own account, he had uttered, were
some generous words in my praise, to which she had civilly
replied. I confess I was curious to see her, but I begged that
the introduction should not be immediate, for I wished to let
Pickering work out his destiny alone. For some days I saw
little of him, though we met at the Kursaal and strolled occasionally in the park. I watched, in spite of my desire to let
him alone, for the signs and portents of the world's action
upon him—of that portion of the world, in especial, of which
Madame Blumenthal had constituted herself the agent. He
seemed very happy, and gave me in a dozen ways an impression of increased self-confidence and maturity. His mind was
admirably active, and always, after a quarter of an hour's talk
with him, I asked myself what experience could really do, that
innocence had not done, to make it bright and fine. I was
struck with his deep enjoyment of the whole spectacle of foreign life—its novelty, its picturesqueness, its light and shade
—and with the infinite freedom with which he felt he could
go and come and rove and linger and observe it all. It was an
expansion, an awakening, a coming to moral manhood. Each
time I met him he spoke a little less of Madame Blumenthal;
but he let me know generally that he saw her often, and continued to admire her. I was forced to admit to myself, in spite
of preconceptions, that if she were really the ruling star of this
happy season, she must be a very superior woman. Pickering
had the air of an ingenuous young philosopher sitting at the
feet of an austere muse, and not of a sentimental spendthrift
dangling about some supreme incarnation of levity.

II.

Madame Blumenthal seemed, for the time, to have abjured
the Kursaal, and I never caught a glimpse of her. Her young

friend, apparently, was an interesting study, and the studious
mind prefers seclusion.

She reappeared, however, at last, one evening at the opera,
where from my chair I perceived her in a box, looking extremely pretty. Adelina Patti was singing, and after the rising
of the curtain I was occupied with the stage; but on looking
round when it fell for the *entr'acte*, I saw that the authoress
of "Cleopatra" had been joined by her young admirer. He
was sitting a little behind her, leaning forward, looking over
her shoulder and listening, while she, slowly moving her fan
to and fro and letting her eye wander over the house, was
apparently talking of this person and that. No doubt she was
saying sharp things; but Pickering was not laughing; his eyes
were following her covert indications; his mouth was half
open, as it always was when he was interested; he looked intensely serious. I was glad that, having her back to him, she
was unable to see how he looked. It seemed the proper moment to present myself and make her my bow; but just as I
was about to leave my place, a gentleman, whom in a moment
I perceived to be an old acquaintance, came to occupy the
next chair. Recognition and mutual greetings followed, and I
was forced to postpone my visit to Madame Blumenthal. I
was not sorry, for it very soon occurred to me that Niedermeyer would be just the man to give me a fair prose version
of Pickering's lyric tributes to his friend. He was an Austrian
by birth, and had formerly lived about Europe a great deal in
a series of small diplomatic posts. England especially he had
often visited, and he spoke the language almost without accent. I had once spent three rainy days with him in the house
of an English friend in the country. He was a sharp observer
and a good deal of a gossip; he knew a little something about
every one, and about some people everything. His knowledge
on social matters generally had the quality of all German science; it was copious, minute, exhaustive.

"Do tell me," I said, as we stood looking round the house,
"who and what is the lady in white, with the young man
sitting behind her."

"Who?" he answered, dropping his glass. "Madame
Blumenthal! What? It would take long to say. Be introduced;

it's easily done; you will find her charming. Then, after a week, you will tell me what she is."

"Perhaps I should not. My friend there has known her a week, and I don't think he is yet able to give a coherent account of her."

He raised his glass again and after looking a while, "I am afraid your friend is a little—what do you call it?—a little 'soft.' Poor fellow! he's not the first. I have never known this lady that she has not had some eligible youth hovering about in some such attitude as that, undergoing the softening process. She looks wonderfully well, from here. It's extraordinary how those women last!"

"You don't mean, I take it, when you talk about 'those women,' that Madame Blumenthal is not embalmed, for duration, in a certain infusion of respectability?"

"Yes and no. The atmosphere that surrounds her is entirely of her own making. There is no reason in her antecedents that people should drop their voice when they speak of her. But some women are never at their ease till they have given some damnable twist or other to their position before the world. The attitude of upright virtue is unbecoming, like sitting too straight in a fauteuil. Don't ask me for opinions, however; content yourself with a few facts and with an anecdote. Madame Blumenthal is Prussian, and very well born. I remember her mother, an old Westphalian Gräfin, with principles marshalled out like Frederick the Great's grenadiers. She was poor, however, and her principles were an insufficient dowry for Anastasia, who was married very young to a vicious Jew, twice her own age. He was supposed to have money, but I am afraid he had less than was nominated in the bond, or else that his pretty young wife spent it very fast. She has been a widow these six or eight years, and has lived I imagine, in rather a hand-to-mouth fashion. I suppose she is some six or eight-and-thirty years of age. In winter one hears of her in Berlin, giving little suppers to the artistic rabble there; in summer one often sees her across the green table at Ems and Wiesbaden. She's very clever, and her cleverness has spoiled her. A year after her marriage she published a novel, with her views on matrimony, in the George Sand manner—beating the drum to Madame Sand's trumpet. No doubt she was very unhappy; Blumenthal was an old beast. Since then she has published a lot of literature—novels and poems and pamphlets on every conceivable theme, from the conversion of Lola Montez, to the Hegelian philosophy. Her talk is much better than her writing. Her *conjugophobia*—I can't call it by any other name—made people think lightly of her at a time when her rebellion against marriage was probably only theoretic. She had a taste for spinning fine phrases, she drove her shuttle, and when she came to the end of her yarn, she found that society had turned its back. She tossed her head, declared that at last she could breathe the sacred air of freedom, and formally announced that she had embraced an 'intellectual' life. This meant unlimited *camaraderie* with scribblers and daubers, Hegelian philosophers and Hungarian pianists. But she has been admired also by a great many really clever men; there was a time, in fact, when she turned a head as well set on its shoulders as this one!" And Niedermeyer tapped his forehead. "She has a great charm, and, literally, I know no harm of her. Yet for all that, I am not going to speak to her; I am not going near her box. I am going to leave her to say, if she does me the honour to observe the omission, that I too have gone over to the Philistines. It's not that; it is that there is something sinister about the woman. I am too old for it to frighten me, but I am good-natured enough for it to pain me. Her quarrel with society has brought her no happiness, and her outward charm is only the mask of a dangerous discontent. Her imagination is lodged where her heart should be! So long as you amuse it, well and good; she's radiant. But the moment you let it flag, she is capable of dropping you without a pang. If you land on your feet, you are so much the wiser, simply; but there have been two or three, I believe, who have almost broken their necks in the fall."

"You are reversing your promise," I said, "and giving me an opinion, but not an anecdote."

"This is my anecdote. A year ago a friend of mine made her aquaintance in Berlin, and though he was no longer a young man, and had never been what is called a susceptible one, he took a great fancy to Madame Blumenthal. He's a major in the Prussian artillery—grizzled, grave, a trifle severe, a man every way firm in the faith of his fathers. It's a proof of Anastasia's charm that such a man should have got into the habit of going to see her every day of his life. But the major was in love, or next door to it! Every day that he called he found her scribbling away at a little ormolu table on a lot of half-sheets of note-paper. She used to bid him sit down and hold his tongue for a quarter of an hour, till she had finished her chapter; she was writing a novel, and it was promised to a publisher. Clorinda, she confided to him, was the name of the injured heroine. The major, I imagine, had never read a work of fiction in his life, but he knew by hearsay that Madame Blumenthal's literature, when put forth in pink covers, was subversive of several respectable institutions. Besides, he didn't believe in women knowing how to write at all, and it irritated him to see this inky goddess correcting proof-sheets under his nose—irritated him the more that, as I say, he was in love with her and that he ventured to believe she had a kindness for his years and his honours. And yet she was not such a woman as he could easily ask to marry him. The result of all this was that he fell into the way of railing at her intellectual pursuits and saying he should like to run his sword through her pile of papers. A woman was clever enough when she could guess her husband's wishes, and learned enough when she could read him the newspapers. At last, one day, Madame Blumenthal flung down her pen and announced in triumph that she had finished her novel. Clorinda had expired in the arms of—some one else than her husband. The major, by way of congratulating her, declared that her novel was immoral rubbish, and that her love of vicious paradoxes was only a peculiarly depraved form of coquetry. He added, however, that he loved her in spite of her follies, and that if she would formally abjure them he would as formally offer her his hand. They say that women like to be snubbed by military men. I don't know, I'm sure; I don't know how much pleasure, on this occasion, was mingled with Anastasia's wrath. But her wrath was very quiet, and the major assured me it made her look uncommonly pretty. 'I have told you before,' she says, 'that I write from an inner need. I write to unburden my heart, to satisfy my conscience. You call my poor efforts coquetry, vanity, the desire to produce a sensation. I can prove to you that it is the quiet labour itself I care for, and not the world's more or less flattering attention to it!' And seizing the history of Clorinda she thrust it into the fire. The major stands staring, and the first thing he knows she is sweeping him a great curtsey and bidding him farewell for ever. Left alone and recovering his wits, he fishes out Clorinda from the embers and then proceeds to thump vigorously at the lady's door. But it never opened, and from that day to the day three months ago when he told me the tale, he had not beheld her again."

"By Jove, it's a striking story," I said. "But the question is, what does it prove?"

"Several things. First (what I was careful not to tell my friend), that Madame Blumenthal cared for him a trifle more than he supposed; second, that he cares for her more than ever; third, that the performance was a master-stroke, and that her allowing him to force an interview upon her again is only a question of time."

"And last?" I asked.

"This is another anecdote. The other day, Unter den Linden, I saw on a bookseller's counter a little pink-covered romance—"Sophronia," by Madame Blumenthal. Glancing through it, I observed an extraordinary abuse of asterisks; every two or three pages the narrative was adorned with a portentous blank, crossed with a row of stars."

"Well, but poor Clorinda?" I objected, as Niedermeyer paused.

"Sophronia, my dear fellow, is simply Clorinda re-named by the baptism of fire. The fair author came back, of course, and found Clorinda tumbled upon the floor, a good deal scorched, but on the whole more frightened than hurt. She picks her up, brushes her off and sends her to the printer. Wherever the flames had burnt a hole, she swings a constellation! But if the major is prepared to drop a penitent tear over the ashes of Clorinda, I shall not whisper to him that the urn is empty."

Even Adelina Patti's singing, for the next half-hour, but half availed to divert me from my quickened curiosity to behold Madame Blumenthal face to face. As soon as the curtain had fallen again, I repaired to her box and was ushered in by Pickering with zealous hospitality. His glowing smile seemed to say to me "Ay, look for yourself, and adore!" Nothing could have been more gracious than the lady's greeting, and, I found, somewhat to my surprise, that her prettiness lost nothing on a nearer view. Her eyes indeed were the finest I have ever seen—the softest, the deepest, the most intensely responsive. In spite of something faded and jaded in her physiognomy, her movements, her smile, and the tone of her voice, especially when she laughed, had an almost girlish frankness and spontaneity. She looked at you very hard with her radiant gray eyes, and she indulged while she talked in a superabundance of restless, rather affected little gestures, as if to make you take her meaning in a certain very particular and superfine sense. I wondered whether after a while this might not fatigue one's attention; then meeting her charming eyes, I said, Not for a long time. She was very clever, and, as Pickering had said, she spoke English admirably. I told her, as I took my seat beside her, of the fine things I had heard about her from my friend, and she listened, letting me go on some time, and exaggerate a little, with her fine eyes fixed full upon me. "Really?" she suddenly said, turning short round upon Pickering, who stood behind us, and looking at him in the same way. "Is that the way you talk about me?"

He blushed to his eyes, and I repented. She suddenly began to laugh; it was then I observed how sweet her voice was in laughter. We talked after this of various matters, and in a little while I complimented her on her excellent English, and asked if she had learnt it in England.

"Heaven forbid!" she cried. "I have never been there and wish never to go. I should never get on with the—" I wondered what she was going to say; the fogs, the smoke, or whist with sixpenny stakes?—"I should never get on," she said, "with the aristocracy! I am a fierce democrat—I am not ashamed of it. I hold opinions which would make my ancestors turn in their graves. I was born in the lap of feudalism. I am a daughter of the crusaders. But I am a revolutionist! I have a passion for freedom—my idea of happiness is to die on a great barricade! It's to your great country I should like to go. I should like to see the wonderful spectacle of a great people free to do everything it chooses, and yet never doing anything wrong!"

I replied, modestly, that, after all, both our freedom and

our good conduct had their limits, and she turned quickly about and shook her fan with a dramatic gesture at Pickering. "No matter, no matter!" she cried, "I should like to see the country which produced that wonderful young man. I think of it as a sort of Arcadia—a land of the golden age. He's so delightfully innocent! In this stupid old Germany, if a young man is innocent he's a fool; he has no brains; he's not a bit interesting. But Mr. Pickering says the freshest things, and after I have laughed five minutes at their freshness it suddenly occurs to me that they are very wise, and I think them over for a week. True!" she went on, nodding at him. "I call them inspired solecisms, and I treasure them up. Remember that when I next laugh at you!"

Glancing at Pickering, I was prompted to believe that he was in a state of beatific exaltation which weighed Madame Blumenthal's smiles and frowns in an equal balance. They were equally hers; they were links alike in the golden chain. He looked at me with eyes that seemed to say, "Did you ever hear such wit? Did you ever see such grace?" It seemed to me that he was but vaguely conscious of the meaning of her words; her gestures, her voice and glance, made an absorbing harmony. There is something painful in the spectacle of absolute enthralment, even to an excellent cause. I gave no response to Pickering's challenge, but made some remark upon the charm of Adelina Patti's singing. Madame Blumenthal, as became a "revolutionist," was obliged to confess that she could see no charm in it; it was meagre, it was trivial, it lacked soul. "You must know that in music, too," she said, "I think for myself!" And she began with a great many flourishes of her fan to explain what it was she thought. Remarkable things, doubtless; but I cannot answer for it, for in the midst of the explanation the curtain rose again. "You can't be a great artist without a great passion!" Madame Blumenthal was affirming. Before I had time to assent, Madame Patti's voice rose wheeling like a skylark, and rained down its silver notes. "Ah, give me that art," I whispered, "and I will leave you your passion!" And I departed for my own place in the orchestra. I wondered afterwards whether the speech had seemed rude, and inferred that it had not, on receiving a friendly nod from the lady, in the lobby, as the theatre was emptying itself. She was on

Pickering's arm, and he was taking her to her carriage. Distances are short in Homburg, but the night was rainy, and Madame Blumenthal exhibited a very pretty satin-shod foot as a reason why, though but a penniless widow, she should not walk home. Pickering left us together a moment while he went to hail the vehicle, and my companion seized the opportunity, as she said, to beg me to be so very kind as to come and see her. It was for a particular reason! It was reason enough for me, of course I answered, that she had given me leave. She looked at me a moment with that extraordinary gaze of hers, which seemed so absolutely audacious in its candour, and rejoined that I paid more compliments than our young friend there, but that she was sure I was not half so sincere. "But it's about him I want to talk," she said. "I want to ask you many things; I want you to tell me all about him. He interests me; but you see my sympathies are so intense, my imagination is so lively, that I don't trust my own impressions. They have misled me more than once!" And she gave a little tragic shudder.

I promised to come and compare notes with her, and we bade her farewell at her carriage door. Pickering and I remained a while, walking up and down the long glazed gallery of the Kursaal. I had not taken many steps before I became aware that I was beside a man in the very extremity of love. "Isn't she wonderful?" he asked, with an implicit confidence in my sympathy which it cost me some ingenuity to elude. If he were really in love, well and good! For although, now that I had seen her, I stood ready to confess to large possibilities of fascination on Madame Blumenthal's part, and even to certain possibilities of sincerity of which my appreciation was vague, yet it seemed to me less ominous that he should be simply smitten than that his admiration should pique itself on being discriminating. It was on his fundamental simplicity that I counted for a happy termination of his experiment, and the former of these alternatives seemed to me the simpler. I resolved to hold my tongue and let him run his course. He had a great deal to say about his happiness, about the days passing like hours, the hours like minutes, and about Madame Blumenthal being a "revelation." "She was nothing to-night," he said; "nothing to what she sometimes is in the way of brilliancy—in the way of repartee. If you could only hear her when she tells her adventures!"

"Adventures?" I inquired. "Has she had adventures?"

"Of the most wonderful sort!" cried Pickering, with rapture. "She hasn't vegetated, like me! She has lived in the tumult of life. When I listen to her reminiscences, it's like hearing the opening tumult of one of Beethoven's symphonies, as it loses itself in a triumphant harmony of beauty and faith!"

I could only lift my eyebrows, but I desired to know before we separated what he had done with that troublesome conscience of his. "I suppose you know, my dear fellow," I said, "that you are simply in love. That's what they happen to call your state of mind."

He replied with a brightening eye, as if he were delighted to hear it—"So Madame Blumenthal told me only this morning!" And seeing, I suppose, that I was slightly puzzled, "I went to drive with her," he continued; "we drove to König-stein, to see the old castle. We scrambled up into the heart of the ruin and sat for an hour in one of the crumbling old courts. Something in the solemn stillness of the place un-loosed my tongue; and while she sat on an ivied stone, on the edge of the plunging wall, I stood there and made a speech. She listened to me, looking at me, breaking off little bits of stone and letting them drop down into the valley. At last she got up and nodded at me two or three times silently, with a smile, as if she were applauding me for a solo on the violin. 'You are in love,' she said. 'It's a perfect case!' And for some time she said nothing more. But before we left the place she told me that she owed me an answer to my speech. She thanked me heartily, but she was afraid that if she took me at my word she would be taking advantage of my inexperience. I had known few women; I was too easily pleased; I thought her better than she really was. She had great faults; I must know her longer and find them out; I must compare her with other women—women younger, simpler, more innocent, more ignorant; and then if I still did her the honour to think well of her, she would listen to me again. I told her that I was not afraid of preferring any woman in the world to her, and then she repeated, 'Happy man, happy man! you are in love, you are in love!' "

I called upon Madame Blumenthal a couple of days later, in some agitation of thought. It has been proved that there are, here and there, in the world, such people as sincere impostors; certain characters who cultivate fictitious emotions in perfect good faith. Even if this clever lady enjoyed poor Pickering's bedazzlement, it was conceivable that, taking vanity and charity together, she should care more for his welfare than for her own entertainment; and her offer to abide by the result of hazardous comparison with other women was a finer stroke than her reputation had led me to expect. She received me in a shabby little sitting-room, littered with uncut books and newspapers, many of which I saw at a glance were French. One side of it was occupied by an open piano, surmounted by a jar full of white roses. They perfumed the air; they seemed to me to exhale the pure aroma of Pickering's devotion. Buried in an arm-chair, the object of this devotion was reading the *Revue des Deux Mondes*. The purpose of my visit was not to admire Madame Blumenthal on my own account, but to ascertain how far I might safely leave her to work her will upon my friend. She had impugned my sincerity the evening of the opera, and I was careful on this occasion to abstain from compliments and not to place her on her guard against my penetration. It is needless to narrate our interview in detail; indeed, to tell the perfect truth, I was punished for my rash attempt to surprise her, by a temporary eclipse of my own perspicacity. She sat there so questioning, so perceptive, so genial, so generous, and so pretty withal, that I was quite ready at the end of half an hour to subscribe to the most comprehensive of Pickering's rhapsodies. She was certainly a wonderful woman. I have never liked to linger, in memory, on that half-hour. The result of it was to prove that there were many more things in the composition of a woman who, as Niedermeyer said, had lodged her imagination in the place of her heart, than were dreamt of in my philosophy. Yet, as I sat here stroking my hat and balancing the account between nature and art in my affable hostess, I felt like a very competent philosopher. She had said she wished me to tell her everything about our friend, and she questioned me as to his family, his fortune, his antecedents and his character. All this was natural in a woman who had received a passionate declaration of love, and it was expressed with an air of charmed solicitude, a radiant confidence that there was really no mistake about his being a most distinguished young man, and that if I chose to be explicit, I might deepen her conviction to disinterested ecstasy, which might have almost provoked me to invent a good opinion, if I had not had one ready made. I told her that she really knew Pickering better than I did and that until we met at Homburg I had not seen him since he was a boy.

"But he talks to you freely," she answered; "I know you are his confidant. He has told me certainly a great many things, but I always feel as if he were keeping something back; as if he were holding something behind him, and showing me only one hand at once. He seems often to be hovering on the edge of a secret. I have had several friendships in my life— thank Heaven! but I have had none more dear to me than this one. Yet in the midst of it I have the painful sense of my friend being half afraid of me; of his thinking me terrible, strange, perhaps a trifle out of my wits. Poor me! If he only knew what a plain good soul I am, and how I only want to know him and befriend him!"

These words were full of a plaintive magnanimity which made mistrust seem cruel. How much better I might play providence over Pickering's experiments with life, if I could engage the fine instincts of this charming woman on the providential side! Pickering's secret was, of course, his engagement to Miss Vernor; it was natural enough that he should have been unable to bring himself to talk of it to Madame Blumenthal. The simple sweetness of this young girl's face had not faded from my memory; I could not rid myself of the suspicion that in going further Pickering might fare much worse. Madame Blumenthal's professions seemed a virtual promise to agree with me, and after some hesitation I said that my friend had, in fact, a substantial secret, and that perhaps I might do him a good turn by putting her in possession of it. In as few words as possible I told her that Pickering stood pledged by filial piety to marry a young lady at Smyrna. She listened intently to my story; when I had finished it there was a faint flush of excitement in each of her cheeks. She broke out into a dozen exclamations of admiration and compassion. "What a wonderful tale—what a romantic situation! No wonder poor Mr. Pickering seemed restless and unsatisfied; no wonder he wished to put off the day of submission. And the poor little girl at Smyrna, waiting there for the young Western prince like the heroine of an Eastern tale! She would give the world to see her photograph; did I think Mr. Pickering would show it to her? But never fear; she would ask nothing indiscreet! Yes, it was a marvellous story, and if she had invented it herself, people would have said it was absurdly improbable." She left her seat and took several turns about the room, smiling to herself and uttering little German cries of wonderment. Suddenly she stopped before the piano and broke into a little laugh; the next moment she buried her face in the great boquet of roses. It was time I should go, but I was indisposed to leave her without obtaining some definite assurance that, as far as pity was concerned, she pitied the young girl at Smyrna more than the young man at Homburg.

"Of course you know what I wished in telling you this," I said, rising. "She is evidently a charming creature, and the best thing he can do is to marry her. I wished to interest you in that view of it."

She had taken one of the roses from the vase and was arranging it in the front of her dress. Suddenly, looking up, "Leave it to me, leave it to me!" she cried. "I am interested!" And with her little blue-gemmed hand she tapped her forehead. "I am deeply interested!"

And with this I had to content myself. But more than once, the next day, I repented of my zeal, and wondered whether a providence with a white rose in her bosom might not turn out a trifle too human. In the evening, at the Kursaal, I looked for Pickering, but he was not visible, and I reflected that my revelation had not as yet, at any rate, seemed to Madame Blumenthal a reason for prescribing a cooling-term to his passion. Very late, as I was turning away, I saw him arrive—with no small satisfaction, for I had determined to let him know immediately in what way I had attempted to serve him. But he straightway passed his arm through my own and led me off towards the gardens. I saw that he was too excited to allow me to speak first.

"I have burnt my ships!" he cried, when we were out of earshot of the crowd. "I have told her everything. I have insisted that it's simple torture for me to wait with this idle view of loving her less. It's well enough for her to ask it, but I feel strong enough now to override her reluctance. I have cast off the millstone from round my neck. I care for nothing, I know nothing, but that I love her with every pulse of my being— and that everything else has been a hideous dream, from which she may wake me into blissful morning with a single word!''

I held him off at arm's-length and looked at him gravely. ''You have told her, you mean, of your engagement to Miss Vernor?''

''The whole story! I have given it up—I have thrown it to the winds. I have broken utterly with the past. It may rise in its grave and give me its curse, but it can't frighten me now. I have a right to be happy, I have a right to be free, I have a right not to bury myself alive. It was not *I* who promised—I was not born then. I myself, my soul, my mind, my option —all this is but a month old! Ah,'' he went on, ''if you knew the difference it makes—this having chosen and broken and spoken! I am twice the man I was yesterday! Yesterday I was afraid of her; there was a kind of mocking mystery of knowledge and cleverness about her, which oppressed me in the midst of my love. But now I am afraid of nothing but of being too happy!''

I stood silent, to let him spend his eloquence. But he paused a moment, and took off his hat and fanned himself. ''Let me perfectly understand,'' I said at last. ''You have asked Madame Blumenthal to be your wife?''

''The wife of my intelligent choice!''

''And does she consent?''

''She asks three days to decide.''

''Call it four! She has known your secret since this morning. I am bound to let you know I told her.''

''So much the better!'' cried Pickering, without apparent resentment or surprise. ''It's not a brilliant offer for such a woman, and in spite of what I have at stake I feel that it would be brutal to press her.''

''What does she say to your breaking your promise?'' I asked in a moment.

Pickering was too much in love for false shame. ''She tells me that she loves me too much to find courage to condemn

me. She agrees with me that I have a right to be happy. I ask
no exemption from the common law. What I claim is simply
freedom to try to be!"

Of course I was puzzled; it was not in that fashion that I
had expected Madame Blumenthal to make use of my information. But the matter now was quite out of my hands, and
all I could do was to bid my companion not work himself into
a fever over either fortune.

The next day I had a visit from Niedermeyer, on whom,
after our talk at the opera, I had left a card. We gossiped a
while, and at last he said suddenly, "By the way, I have a
sequel to the history of Clorinda. The major is at Homburg!"

"Indeed!" said I. "Since when?"

"These three days."

"And what is he doing?"

"He seems," said Niedermeyer with a laugh, "to be chiefly
occupied in sending flowers to Madame Blumenthal. That is,
I went with him the morning of his arrival to choose a nosegay, and nothing would suit him but a small haystack of white
roses. I hope it was received."

"I can assure you it was," I cried. "I saw the lady fairly
nestling her head in it. But I advise the major not to build
upon that. He has a rival."

"Do you mean the soft young man of the other night?"

"Pickering is soft, if you will, but his softness seems to have
served him. He has offered her everything, and she has not
yet refused it." I had handed my visitor a cigar and he was
puffing it in silence. At last he abruptly asked if I had been
introduced to Madame Blumenthal, and, on my affirmative,
inquired what I thought of her. "I will not tell you," I said,
"or you'll call *me* soft."

He knocked away his ashes, eying me askance. "I have noticed your friend about," he said, "and even if you had not
told me, I should have known he was in love. After he has
left his adored, his face wears for the rest of the day the expression with which he has risen from her feet, and more than
once I have felt like touching his elbow, as you would that of
a man who has inadvertently come into a drawing-room in
his overshoes. You say he has offered our friend everything;
but, my dear fellow, he has not everything to offer her. He

evidently is as amiable as the morning, but the lady has no taste for daylight."

"I assure you Pickering is a very interesting fellow," I said.

"Ah, there it is! Has he not some story or other? Isn't he an orphan, or a natural child, or consumptive, or contingent heir to great estates? She will read his little story to the end, and close the book very tenderly and smooth down the cover; and then, when he least expects it, she will toss it into the dusty limbo of her other romances. She will let him dangle, but she will let him drop!"

"Upon my word," I cried with heat, "if she does, she will be a very unprincipled little creature!"

Niedermeyer shrugged his shoulders. "I never said she was a saint!"

Shrewd as I felt Niedermeyer to be, I was not prepared to take his simple word for this event, and in the evening I received a communication which fortified my doubts. It was a note from Pickering, and it ran as follows—

"MY DEAR FRIEND,—I have every hope of being happy, but I am to go to Wiesbaden to learn my fate. Madame Blumenthal goes thither this afternoon to spend a few days, and she allows me to accompany her. Give me your good wishes; you shall hear of the result.   E.P."

One of the diversions of Homburg for new-comers is to dine in rotation at the different *tables d'hôte*. It so happened that, a couple of days later, Niedermeyer took pot-luck at my hotel, and secured a seat beside my own. As we took our places I found a letter on my plate, and, as it was postmarked Wiesbaden, I lost no time in opening it. It contained but three lines—

"I am happy—I am accepted—an hour ago. I can hardly believe it's your poor friend   E.P."

I placed the note before Niedermeyer; not exactly in triumph, but with the alacrity of all felicitous confutation. He looked at it much longer than was needful to read it, stroking down his beard gravely, and I felt it was not so easy to confute a pupil of the school of Metternich. At last, folding the note and handing it back, "Has your friend mentioned Madame Blumenthal's errand at Wiesbaden?" he asked.

"You look very wise. I give it up!" said I.

"She is gone there to make the major follow her. He went by the next train."

"And has the major, on his side, dropped you a line?"

"He is not a letter-writer."

"Well," said I, pocketing my letter, "with this document in my hand I am bound to reserve my judgment. We will have a bottle of Johannisberg, and drink to the triumph of virtue."

For a whole week more I heard nothing from Pickering—somewhat to my surprise, and, as the days went by, not a little to my discomposure. I had expected that his bliss would continue to overflow in brief bulletins, and his silence was possibly an indication that it had been clouded. At last I wrote to his hotel at Wiesbaden, but received no answer; whereupon, as my next resource, I repaired to his former lodging at Homburg, where I thought it possible he had left property which he would sooner or later send for. There I learned that he had indeed just telegraphed from Cologne for his luggage. To Cologne I immediately despatched a line of inquiry as to his prosperity and the cause of his silence. The next day I received three words in answer—a simple uncommented request that I would come to him. I lost no time, and reached him in the course of a few hours. It was dark when I arrived, and the city was sheeted in a cold autumnal rain. Pickering had stumbled, with an indifference which was itself a symptom of distress, on a certain musty old Mainzerhof, and I found him sitting over a smouldering fire in a vast dingy chamber which looked as if it had grown gray with watching the *ennui* of ten generations of travellers. Looking at him, as he rose on my entrance, I saw that he was in extreme tribulation. He was pale and haggard; his face was five years older. Now, at least, in all conscience, he had tasted of the cup of life! I was anxious to know what had turned it so suddenly to bitterness; but I spared him all importunate curiosity, and let him take his time. I accepted tacitly his tacit confession of distress, and we made for a while a feeble effort to discuss the picturesqueness of Cologne. At last he rose and stood a long time looking into the fire, while I slowly paced the length of the dusky room.

"Well!" he said as I came back; "I wanted knowledge, and I certainly know something I didn't a month ago." And herewith, calmly and succinctly enough, as if dismay had worn itself out, he related the history of the foregoing days. He touched lightly on details; he evidently never was to gush as freely again as he had done during the prosperity of his suit. He had been accepted one evening, as explicitly as his imagination could desire, and had gone forth in his rapture and roamed about till nearly morning in the gardens of the Conversationhouse, taking the stars and the perfumes of the summer night into his confidence. "It is worth it all, almost," he said, "to have been wound up for an hour to that celestial pitch. No man, I am sure, can ever know it but once." The next morning he had repaired to Madame Blumenthal's lodging and had been met, to his amazement, by a naked refusal to see him. He had strode about for a couple of hours—in another mood—and then had returned to the charge. The servant handed him a three-cornered note; it contained these words: "Leave me alone to-day; I will give you ten minutes to-morrow evening." Of the next thirty-six hours he could give no coherent account, but at the appointed time Madame Blumenthal had received him. Almost before she spoke there had come to him a sense of the depth of his folly in supposing he knew her. "One has heard all one's days," he said, "of people removing the mask; it's one of the stock phrases of romance. Well, there she stood with her mask in her hand. Her face," he went on gravely, after a pause—"her face was horrible!" . . . . "I give you ten minutes," she had said, pointing to the clock. "Make your scene, tear your hair, brandish your dagger!" And she had sat down and folded her arms. "It's not a joke," she cried, "it's dead earnest; let us have it over. You are dismissed—have you nothing to say?" He had stammered some frantic demand for an explanation; and she had risen and come near him, looking at him from head to feet, very pale, and evidently more excited than she wished him to see. "I have done with you!" she said with a smile; "you ought to have done with me! It has all been delightful, but there are excellent reasons why it should come to an end." "You have been playing a part, then," he had gasped out; "you never cared for me?" "Yes; till I knew you;

till I saw how far you would go. But now the story's finished; we have reached the *dénoûment*. We will close the book and be good friends." "To see how far I would go?" he had repeated. "You led me on, meaning all the while to do *this*?" "I led you on, if you will. I received your visits, in season and out! Sometimes they were very entertaining; sometimes they bored me fearfully. But you were such a very curious case of—what shall I call it?—of sincerity, that I determined to take good and bad together. I wanted to make you commit yourself unmistakably. I should have preferred not to bring you to this place; but that too was necessary. Of course I can't marry you; I can do better. So can you, for that matter; thank your fate for it. You have thought wonders of me for a month, but your good-humour wouldn't last. I am too old and too wise; you are too young and too foolish. It seems to me that I have been very good to you; I have entertained you to the top of your bent, and, except perhaps that I am a little brusque just now, you have nothing to complain of. I would have let you down more gently if I could have taken another month to it; but circumstances have forced my hand. Abuse me, curse me, if you like. I will make every allowance!" Pickering listened to all this intently enough to perceive that, as if by some sudden natural cataclysm, the ground had broken away at his feet, and that he must recoil. He turned away in dumb amazement. "I don't know how I seemed to be taking it," he said, "but she seemed really to desire—I don't know why—something in the way of reproach and vituperation. But I couldn't, in that way, have uttered a syllable. I was sickened; I wanted to get away into the air—to shake her off and come to my senses. 'Have you nothing, nothing, nothing to say?' she cried, as if she were disappointed, while I stood with my hand on the door. 'Haven't I treated you to talk enough?' I believed I answered. 'You will write to me then, when you get home?' 'I think not,' said I. 'Six months hence, I fancy, you will come and see me!' 'Never!' said I. 'That's a confession of stupidity, she answered. 'It means that, even on reflection, you will never understand the philosophy of my conduct.' The word 'philosophy' seemed so strange that I verily believe I smiled. 'I have given you all that you gave me,' she went on. 'Your passion was an affair of the head.' 'I only wish you had told me sooner that you considered it so!' I exclaimed. And I went my way. The next day I came down the Rhine. I sat all day on the boat, not knowing where I was going, where to get off. I was in a kind of ague of terror; it seemed to me I had seen something infernal. At last I saw the cathedral towers here looming over the city. They seemed to say something to me, and when the boat stopped, I came ashore. I have been here a week. I have not slept at night—and yet it has been a week of rest!"

It seemed to me that he was in a fair way to recover, and that his own philosophy, if left to take its time, was adequate to the occasion. After his story was once told I referred to his grievance but once—that evening, later, as we were about to separate for the night. "Suffer me to say that there was some truth in *her* account of your relations," I said. "You were using her intellectually, and all the while, without your knowing it, she was using you. It was diamond cut diamond. Her needs were the more superficial and she got tired of the game first." He frowned and turned uneasily away, but without contradicting me. I waited a few moments, to see if he would remember, before we parted, that he had a claim to make upon me. But he seemed to have forgotten it.

The next day we strolled about the picturesque old city, and of course, before long, went into the cathedral. Pickering said little; he seemed intent upon his own thoughts. He sat down beside a pillar near a chapel, in front of a gorgeous window, and, leaving him to his meditations, I wandered through the church. When I came back I saw he had something to say. But before he had spoken I laid my hand on his shoulder and looked at him with a significant smile. He slowly bent his head and dropped his eyes, with a mixture of assent and humility. I drew forth from where it had lain untouched for a month the letter he had given me to keep, placed it silently on his knee, and left him to deal with it alone.

Half an hour later I returned to the same place, but he had gone, and one of the sacristans, hovering about and seeing me looking for Pickering, said he thought he had left the church. I found him in his gloomy chamber at the inn, pacing slowly up and down. I should doubtless have been at a loss to say just what effect I expected the letter from Smyrna to produce; but his actual aspect surprised me. He was flushed, excited, a trifle irritated.

"Evidently," I said, "you have read your letter."

"It is proper I should tell you what is in it," he answered. "When I gave it to you a month ago, I did my friends injustice."

"You called it a 'summons,' I remember."

"I was a great fool! It's a release!"

"From your engagement?"

"From everything! The letter, of course, is from Mr. Vernor. He desires to let me know at the earliest moment that his daughter, informed for the first time a week before of what had been expected of her, positively refuses to be bound by the contract or to assent to my being bound. She had been given a week to reflect and had spent it in inconsolable tears. She had resisted every form of persuasion; from compulsion, writes Mr. Vernor, he naturally shrinks. The young lady considers the arrangement 'horrible.' After accepting her duties cut and dried all her life, she pretends at last to have a taste of her own. I confess I am surprised; I had been given to believe that she was stupidly submissive and would remain so to the end of the chapter. Not a bit of it. She has insisted on my being formally dismissed, and her father intimates that in case of noncompliance she threatens him with an attack of brain-fever. Mr. Vernor condoles with me handsomely, and lets me know that the young lady's attitude has been a great shock to his nerves. He adds that he will not aggravate such regret as I may do him the honour to entertain, by any allusions to his daughter's charms and to the magnitude of my loss, and he concludes with the hope that, for the comfort of all concerned, I may already have amused my fancy with other 'views.' He reminds me in a postscript that, in spite of this painful occurrence, the son of his most valued friend will always be a welcome visitor at his house. I am free, he observes; I have my life before me; he recommends an extensive course of travel. Should my wanderings lead me to the East, he hopes that no false embarrassment will deter me from presenting myself at Smyrna. He can promise me at least a friendly reception. It's a very polite letter."

Polite as the letter was, Pickering seemed to find no great

exhilaration in having this famous burden so handsomely
lifted from his spirit. He began to brood over his liberation
in a manner which you might have deemed proper to a renewed sense of bondage. "Bad news," he had called his letter
originally; and yet, now that its contents proved to be in flat
contradiction to his foreboding, there was no impulsive voice
to reverse the formula and declare the news was good. The
wings of impulse in the poor fellow had of late been terribly
clipped. It was an obvious reflection, of course, that if he had
not been so stiffly certain of the matter a month before, and
had gone through the form of breaking Mr. Vernor's seal, he
might have escaped the purgatory of Madame Blumenthal's
sub-acid blandishments. But I left him to moralise in private;
I had no desire, as the phrase is, to rub it in. My thoughts,
moreover, were following another train; I was saying to myself
that if to those gentle graces of which her young visage had
offered to my fancy the blooming promise, Miss Vernor added
in this striking measure the capacity for magnanimous action,
the amendment to my friend's career had been less happy than
the rough draught. Presently, turning about, I saw him looking at the young lady's photograph. "Of course, now," he
said, "I have no right to keep it!" And before I could ask for
another glimpse of it, he had thrust it into the fire.

"I am sorry to be saying it just now," I observed after a
while, "but I shouldn't wonder if Miss Vernor were a charming creature."

"Go and find out," he answered gloomily. "The coast is
clear. My part is to forget her," he presently added. "It ought
not to be hard. But don't you think," he went on suddenly,
"that for a poor fellow who asked nothing of fortune but leave
to sit down in a quiet corner, it has been rather a cruel pushing
about?"

Cruel indeed, I declared, and he certainly had the right to
demand a clean page on the book of fate, and a fresh start.
Mr. Vernor's advice was sound; he should amuse himself with
a long journey. If it would be any comfort to him, I would
go with him on his way. Pickering assented without enthusiasm; he had the embarrassed look of a man who, having gone
to some cost to make a good appearance in a drawing-room,
should find the door suddenly slammed in his face. We started

on our journey, however, and little by little his enthusiasm returned. He was too capable of enjoying fine things to remain permanently irresponsive, and after a fortnight spent among pictures and monuments and antiquities, I felt that I was seeing him for the first time in his best and healthiest mood. He had had a fever and then he had had a chill; the pendulum had swung right and left in a manner rather trying to the machine; but now, at last, it was working back to an even, natural beat. He recovered in a measure the generous eloquence with which he had fanned his flame at Homburg, and talked about things with something of the same passionate freshness. One day when I was laid up at the inn at Bruges with a lame foot, he came home and treated me to a rhapsody about a certain meek-faced virgin of Hans Memling, which seemed to me sounder sense than his compliments to Madame Blumenthal. He had his dull days and his sombre moods—hours of irresistible retrospect; but I let them come and go without remonstrance, because I fancied they always left him a trifle more alert and resolute. One evening however, he sat hanging his head in so doleful a fashion that I took the bull by the horns and told him he had by this time surely paid his debt to penitence, and that he owed it to himself to banish that woman for ever from his thoughts.

He looked up, staring; and then with a deep blush—"That woman?" he said. "I was not thinking of Madame Blumenthal!"

After this I gave another construction to his melancholy. Taking him with his hopes and fears, at the end of six weeks of active observation and keen sensation, Pickering was as fine a fellow as need be. We made our way down to Italy and spent a fortnight at Venice. There something happened which I had been confidently expecting; I had said to myself that it was merely a question of time. We had passed the day at Torcello, and came floating back in the glow of the sunset, with measured oar-strokes. "I am well on the way," Pickering said; "I think I will go!"

We had not spoken for an hour, and I naturally asked him, Where? His answer was delayed by our getting into the Piazzetta. I stepped ashore first and then turned to help him.

As he took my hand, he met my eyes, consciously, and it came.
"To Smyrna!"

A couple of days later he started. I had risked the conjecture
that Miss Vernor was a charming creature, and six months
afterwards he wrote me that I was right.

Benvolio

ONCE UPON A TIME (as if he had lived in a fairy-tale) there was a very interesting young man. This is not a fairy-tale, and yet our young man was in some respects as pretty a fellow as any fairy prince. I call him interesting because his type of character is one I have always found it profitable to observe. If you fail to consider him so, I shall be willing to confess that the fault is mine and not his; I shall have told my story with too little skill.

His name was Benvolio; that is, it was not; but we shall call him so for the sake both of convenience and of picturesqueness. He was about to enter upon the third decade of our mortal span; he had a little property, and he followed no regular profession. His personal appearance was in the highest degree prepossessing. Having said this, it were perhaps well that I should let you—you especially, madam—suppose that he exactly corresponded to your ideal of manly beauty; but I am bound to explain definitely wherein it was that he resembled a fairy prince, and I need furthermore to make a record of certain little peculiarities and anomalies in which it is probable that your brilliant conception would be deficient. Benvolio was slim and fair, with clustering locks, remarkably fine eyes, and such a frank, expressive smile that on the journey through life it was almost as serviceable to its owner as the magic key, or the enchanted ring, or the wishing-cap, or any other bauble of necromantic properties. Unfortunately this charming smile was not always at his command, and its place was sometimes occupied by a very perverse and dusky frown, which rendered the young man no service whatever—not even that of frightening people; for though it expressed extreme irritation and impatience, it was characterized by the brevity of contempt, and the only revenge upon disagreeable things and offensive people that it seemed to express a desire for on Benvolio's part was that of forgetting and ignoring them with the utmost possible celerity. It never made any one tremble, though now and then it perhaps made irritable people murmur an imprecation or two. You might have

supposed from Benvolio's manner, when he was in good humour (which was the greater part of the time), from his brilliant, intelligent glance, from his easy, irresponsible step, and
in especial from the sweet, clear, lingering, caressing tone of
his voice—the voice as it were of a man whose fortune has
been made for him, and who assumes, a trifle egotistically, that
the rest of the world is equally at leisure to share with him
the sweets of life, to pluck the wayside flowers, and chase the
butterflies afield—you might have supposed, I say, from all
this luxurious assurance of demeanour, that our hero really
had the wishing-cap sitting invisible on his handsome brow,
or was obliged only to close his knuckles together a moment
to exert an effective pressure upon the magic ring. The young
man, I have said, was a mixture of inconsistencies; I may say
more exactly that he was a tissue of contradictions. He did
possess the magic ring, in a certain fashion; he possessed in
other words the poetic imagination. Everything that fancy
could do for him was done in perfection. It gave him immense
satisfactions; it transfigured the world; it made very common
objects sometimes seem radiantly beautiful, and it converted
beautiful ones into infinite sources of intoxication. Benvolio
had what is called the poetic temperament. It is rather out of
fashion to describe a man in these terms; but I believe, in spite
of much evidence to the contrary, that there are poets still;
and if we may call a spade a spade, why should we not call
such a person as Benvolio a poet?

These contradictions that I speak of ran through his whole
nature, and they were perfectly apparent in his habits, in his
manners, in his conversation, and even in his physiognomy. It
was as if the souls of two very different men had been placed
together to make the voyage of life in the same boat, and had
agreed for convenience' sake to take the helm in alternation.
The helm, with Benvolio, was always the imagination; but in
his different moods it worked very differently. To an acute
observer his face itself would have betrayed these variations;
and it is certain that his dress, his talk, his way of spending
his time, one day and another, abundantly indicated them.
Sometimes he looked very young—rosy, radiant, blooming,
younger than his years. Then suddenly, as the light struck his
head in a particular manner, you would see that his golden

locks contained a surprising number of silver threads; and with
your attention quickened by this discovery, you would proceed to detect something grave and discreet in his smile—
something vague and ghostly, like the dim adumbration of the
darker half of the lunar disk. You might have met Benvolio,
in certain states of mind, dressed like a man of the highest
fashion—wearing his hat on his ear, a rose in his button-hole,
a wonderful intaglio or an antique Syracusan coin, by way of
a pin, in his cravat. Then, on the morrow, you would have
espied him braving the sunshine in a rusty scholar's coat, with
his hat pulled over his brow—a costume wholly at odds with
flowers and gems. It was all a matter of fancy; but his fancy
was a weather-cock, and faced east or west as the wind blew.
His conversation matched his coat and breeches; he talked one
day the talk of the town; he chattered, he gossipped, he asked
questions and told stories; you would have said that he was a
charming fellow for a dinner-party or the pauses of a cotillon.
The next he either talked philosophy or politics, or said nothing at all; he was absent and indifferent; he was thinking his
own thoughts; he had a book in his pocket, and evidently he
was composing one in his head. At home he lived in two
chambers. One was an immense room, hung with pictures,
lined with books, draped with rugs and tapestries, decorated
with a multitude of ingenious devices (for of all these things
he was very fond); the other, his sleeping-room, was almost
as bare as a monastic cell. It had a meagre little strip of carpet
on the floor, and a dozen well-thumbed volumes of classic
poets and sages on the mantelshelf. On the wall hung three
or four coarsely-engraved portraits of the most exemplary of
these worthies; these were the only ornaments. But the room
had the charm of a great window, in a deep embrasure, looking out upon a tangled, silent, moss-grown garden, and in the
embrasure stood the little ink-blotted table at which Benvolio
did most of his poetic scribbling. The windows of his sump-
tuous sitting-room commanded a wide public square, where
people were always passing and lounging, where military music used to play on vernal nights, and half the life of the great
town went forward. At the risk of your thinking our hero a
sad idler, I will say that he spent an inordinate amount of time
in gazing out of these windows (in either direction) with his

elbows on the sill. The garden did not belong to the house which he inhabited, but to a neighbouring one, and the proprietor, a graceless old miser, was very chary of permits to visit his domain. But Benvolio's fancy used to wander through the alleys without stirring the long arms of the untended plants, and to bend over the heavy-headed flowers without leaving a footprint on their beds. It was here that his happiest thoughts came to him—that inspiration (as we may say, speaking of a man of the poetic temperament), descended upon him in silence, and for certain divine, appreciable moments stood poised along the course of his scratching quill. It was not, however, that he had not spent some very charming hours in the larger, richer apartment. He used to receive his friends there—sometimes in great numbers, sometimes at boisterous, many-voiced suppers, which lasted far into the night. When these entertainments were over he never made a direct transition to his little scholar's cell. He went out and wandered for an hour through the dark, sleeping streets of the town, ridding himself of the fumes of wine, and feeling not at all tipsy, but intensely, portentously sober. More than once, when he had come back and prepared to go to bed, he saw the first faint glow of dawn trembling upward over the tree-tops of his garden. His friends, coming to see him, often found the greater room empty, and advancing, rapped at the door of his chamber. But he frequently kept quiet, not desiring in the least to see them, knowing exactly what they were going to say, and not thinking it worth hearing. Then, hearing them stride away, and the outer door close behind them, he would come forth and take a turn in his slippers, over his Persian carpets, and glance out of the window and see his defeated visitant stand scratching his chin in the sunny square. After this he would laugh lightly to himself—as is said to be the habit of the scribbling tribe in moments of production.

Although he had many relatives he enjoyed extreme liberty. His family was so large, his brothers and sisters were so numerous, that he could absent himself and be little missed. Sometimes he used this privilege freely; he tired of people whom he had seen very often, and he had seen, of course, a great deal of his family. At other moments he was extremely domestic; he suddenly found solitude depressing, and it

seemed to him that if one sought society as a refuge, one
needed to be on familiar terms with it, and that with no one
was familiarity so natural as among people who had grown up
at a common fireside. Nevertheless it frequently occurred to
him—for sooner or later everything occurred to him—that he
was too independent and irresponsible; that he would be happier if he had a little golden ball and chain tied to his ankle.
His curiosity about all things—life and love and art and
truth—was great, and his theory was to satisfy it as freely as
might be; but as the years went by this pursuit of impartial
science appeared to produce a singular result. He became conscious of an intellectual condition similar to that of a palate
which has lost its relish. To a man with a disordered appetite
all things taste alike, and so it seemed to Benvolio that the
gustatory faculty of his mind was losing its keenness. It had
still its savoury moments, its feasts and its holidays; but, on
the whole, the spectacle of human life was growing flat and
stale. This is simply a wordy way of expressing that comprehensive fact—Benvolio was *blasé*. He knew it, he knew it be-
times, and he regretted it acutely. He believed that the mind
can keep its freshness to the last, and that it is only fools that
are overbored. There was a way of never being bored, and the
wise man's duty was to find it out. One of its rudiments, he
believed, was that one grows tired of one's self sooner than
of anything else in the world. Idleness, every one admitted,
was the greatest of follies; but idleness was subtle, and exacted
tribute under a hundred plausible disguises. One was often
idle when one seemed to be ardently occupied; one was always idle when one's occupation had not a high aim. One was
idle therefore when one was working simply for one's self.
Curiosity for curiosity's sake, art for art's sake, these were
essentially broken-winded steeds. Ennui was at the end of
everything that did not multiply our relations with life. To
multiply his relations, therefore, Benvolio reflected, should be
the wise man's aim. Poor Benvolio had to reflect on this, because, as I say, he was a poet and not a man of action. A fine
fellow of the latter stamp would have solved the problem
without knowing it, and bequeathed to his fellow men not
frigid formulas but vivid examples. But Benvolio had often
said to himself that he was born to imagine great things—not

to do them; and he had said this by no means sadly, for on
the whole he was very well content with his portion. Imagine
them he determined he would, and on a magnificent scale.
He would multiply his labours at least, and they should be
very serious ones. He would cultivate great ideas, he would
enunciate great truths, he would write immortal verses. In all
this there was a large amount of talent and a liberal share of
ambition. I will not say that Benvolio was a man of genius; it
may seem to make the distinction too cheap; but he was at
any rate a man with an intellectual passion; and if, being near
him, you had been able to listen intently enough, he would,
like the great people of his craft, have seemed to emit something of that vague magical murmur—the voice of the infinite—which lurks in the involutions of a sea-shell. He himself,
by the way, had once made use of this little simile, and had
written a poem in which it was melodiously set forth that the
poetic minds scattered about the world correspond to the little shells one picks up on the beach, all resonant with the echo
of ocean. The whole thing was of course rounded off with
the sands of time, the waves of history, and other harmonious
conceits.

II.

But (as you are naturally expecting to hear), Benvolio knew
perfectly well that there is one relation with life which is a
better antidote to ennui than any other—the relation established with a charming woman. Benvolio was of course in
love. Who was his mistress, you ask (I flatter myself with some
impatience), and was she pretty, was she kind, was he successful? Hereby hangs my tale, which I must relate in due
form.

Benvolio's mistress was a lady whom (as I cannot tell you
her real name) it will be quite in keeping to speak of as the
Countess. The Countess was a young widow, who had some
time since divested herself of her mourning weeds—which
indeed she had never worn but very lightly. She was rich,
extremely pretty, and free to do as she listed. She was passionately fond of pleasure and admiration, and they gushed
forth at her feet in unceasing streams. Her beauty was not of

the conventional type, but it was dazzlingly brilliant; few faces
were more expressive, more fascinating. Hers was never the
same for two days together; it reflected her momentary circumstances with extraordinary vividness, and in knowing her
you had the advantage of knowing a dozen different women.
She was clever and accomplished, and had the credit of being
perfectly amiable; indeed it was difficult to imagine a person
combining a greater number of the precious gifts of nature
and fortune. She represented felicity, gaiety, success; she was
made to charm, to play a part, to exert a sway. She lived in a
great house, behind high verdure-muffled walls, where other
Countesses, in other years, had played a part no less brilliant.
It was an antiquated quarter, into which the tide of commerce
had lately begun to roll heavily; but the turbid wave of trade
broke in vain against the Countess's enclosure, and if in her
garden and her drawing-room you heard the deep uproar of
the city, it was only as a vague undertone to sweeter
things—to music, and witty talk, and tender colloquy. There
was something very striking in this little oasis of luxury and
privacy, in the midst of common toil and traffic.

Benvolio was a great deal at this lady's house; he rarely
desired better entertainment. I spoke just now of privacy; but
privacy was not what he found there, nor what he wished to
find. He went there when he wished to learn with the least
trouble what was going on in the world; for the talk of the
people the Countess generally had about her was an epitome
of the gossip, the rumours, the interests, the hopes and fears,
of polite society. She was a thoroughly liberal hostess; all she
asked was to be entertained; if you would contribute to the
common fund of amusement, of discussion, you were a welcome guest. Sooner or later, among your fellow-guests, you
encountered every one of consequence. There were frivolous
people and wise people; people whose fortune was in their
pockets and people whose fortune was in their brains; people
deeply concerned in public affairs and people concerned only
with the fit of their garments or with the effect upon the
company of the announcement of their names. Benvolio, with
his taste for a large and various social spectacle, appreciated
all this; but he was best pleased, as a general thing, when he
found the Countess alone. This was often his fortune, for the

simple reason that when the Countess expected him she invariably caused herself to be refused to every one else. This is
almost an answer to your inquiry whether Benvolio was successful in his suit. As yet, strictly speaking, there was no suit;
Benvolio had never made love to the Countess. This sounds
very strange, but it is nevertheless true. He was in love with
her; he thought her the most charming creature conceivable;
he spent hours with her alone by her own orders; he had had
opportunity—he had been up to his neck in opportunity—
and yet he had never said to her, as would have seemed so
natural, "Dear Countess, I beseech you to be my wife." If
you are surprised, I may also confide to you that the Countess
was; and surprise under the circumstances very easily became
displeasure. It is by no means certain that if Benvolio had
made the little speech we have just imagined, the Countess
would have fallen into his arms, confessed to an answering
flame, and rung in *finis* to our tale, with the wedding-bells.
But she nevertheless expected him in civility to pay her this
supreme compliment. Her answer would be—what it might
be; but his silence was a permanent offence. Every man,
roughly speaking, had asked the Countess to marry him, and
every man had been told that she was much obliged, but had
not been thinking of changing her condition. But here, with
the one man who failed to ask her, she was perpetually thinking of it, and this negative quality in Benvolio was more present to her mind, gave her more to think about, than all the
positiveness of her other suitors. The truth was she liked
Benvolio extremely, and his independence rendered him excellent service. The Countess had a very lively fancy, and she
had fingered, nimbly enough, the volume of the young man's
merits. She was by nature a trifle cold; she rarely lost her head;
she measured each step as she took it; she had had little fancies
and incipient passions; but on the whole she had thought
much more about love than felt it. She had often tried to form
an image of the sort of man it would be well for her to love
—for so it was she expressed it. She had succeeded but indifferently, and her imagination had never found a pair of wings
until the day she met Benvolio. Then it seemed to her that
her quest was ended—her prize gained. This nervous, ardent,
deep-eyed youth struck her as the harmonious counterpart of

her own facile personality. This conviction rested with the Countess on a fine sense of propriety which it would be vain to attempt to analyze; he was different from herself and from the other men who surrounded her, and she valued him as a specimen of a rare and distinguished type. In the old days she would have appointed him to be her minstrel or her jester—it is to be feared that poor Benvolio would have figured rather dismally in the latter capacity; and at present a woman who was in her own right a considerable social figure, might give such a man a place in her train as an illustrious husband. I don't know how good a judge the Countess was of such matters, but she believed that the world would hear of Benvolio. She had beauty, ancestry, money, luxury, but she had not genius; and if genius was to be had, why not secure it, and complete the list? This is doubtless a rather coarse statement of the Countess's argument; but you have it thrown in gratis, as it were; for all I am bound to tell you is that this charming young woman took a fancy to this clever young man, and that she used to cry sometimes for a quarter of a minute when she imagined he was indifferent to her. Her tears were wasted, because he really cared for her—more even than she would have imagined if she had taken a favourable view of the case. But Benvolio, I cannot too much repeat, was an exceedingly complex character, and there was many a lapse in the logic of his conduct. The Countess charmed him, excited him, interested him; he did her abundant justice—more than justice; but at the end of all he felt that she failed to satisfy him. If a man could have half a dozen wives—and Benvolio had once maintained, poetically, that he ought to have—the Countess would do very well for one of them—possibly even for the best of them. But she would not serve for all seasons and all moods; she needed a complement, an alternative—what the French call a *repoussoir*. One day he was going to see her, knowing that he was expected. There was to be a number of other people—in fact, a very brilliant assembly; but Benvolio knew that a certain touch of the hand, a certain glance of the eye, a certain caress of the voice, would be reserved for him alone. Happy Benvolio, you will say, to be going about the world with such charming secrets as this locked up in his young heart! Happy Benvolio indeed; but mark how he trifled with his happiness. He went to the Countess's gate, but he went no further; he stopped, stood there a moment, frowning intensely, and biting the finger of his glove; then suddenly he turned and strode away in the opposite direction. He walked and walked and left the town behind him. He went his way till he reached the country, and here he bent his steps toward a little wood which he knew very well, and whither indeed, on a spring afternoon, when she had taken a fancy to play at shepherd and shepherdess, he had once come with the Countess. He flung himself on the grass, on the edge of the wood —not in the same place where he had lain at the Countess's feet, pulling sonnets out of his pocket and reading them one by one; a little stream flowed beside him; opposite, the sun was declining; the distant city lay before him, lifting its towers and chimneys against the reddening western sky. The twilight fell and deepened and the stars came out. Benvolio lay there thinking that he preferred them to the Countess's wax candles. He went back to town in a farmer's wagon, talking with the honest rustic who drove it.

Very much in this way, when he had been on the point of knocking at the gate of the Countess's heart and asking ardently to be admitted, he had paused, stood frowning, and then turned short and rambled away into solitude. She never knew how near, two or three times, he had come. Two or three times she had accused him of being rude, and this was nothing but the backward swing of the pendulum. One day it seemed to her that he was altogether too vexatious, and she reproached herself with her good nature. She had made herself too cheap; such conduct was beneath her dignity; she would take another tone. She closed her door to him, and bade her people say, whenever he came, that she was engaged. At first Benvolio only wondered. Oddly enough, he was not what is commonly called sensitive; he never supposed you meant to offend him; not being at all impertinent himself, he was not on the watch for impertinence in others. Only, when he fairly caught you in the act he was immensely disgusted. Therefore, as I say, he simply wondered what had suddenly made the Countess so busy; then he remembered certain other charming persons whom he knew, and went to see how the world wagged with them. But they rendered the Countess

eminent service; she gained by comparison, and Benvolio began to miss her. All that other charming women were who
led the life of the world (as it is called) the Countess was in
a superior, in a perfect degree; she was the ripest fruit of a
high civilization; her companions and rivals, beside her, had
but a pallid bloom, an acrid savour. Benvolio had a relish in
all things for the best, and he found himself breathing sighs
under the Countess's darkened windows. He wrote to her,
asking why in the world she treated him so cruelly, and then
she knew that her charm was working. She was careful not to
answer his letter, and to see that he was refused at her gate as
inexorably as ever. It is an ill wind that blows nobody good,
and Benvolio, one night after his dismissal, wandered about
the moonlit streets till nearly morning, composing the finest
verses he had ever produced. The subscribers to the magazine
to which he sent them were at least the gainers. But unlike
many poets, Benvolio did not on this occasion bury his passion in his poem; or if he did, its ghost was stalking abroad
the very next night. He went again to the Countess's gate,
and again it was closed in his face. So, after a very moderate
amount of hesitation, he bravely (and with a dexterity which
surprised him), scaled her garden wall and dropped down in
the moonshine, upon her lawn. I don't know whether she was
expecting him, but if she had been, the matter could not have
been better arranged. She was sitting in a little niche of shrubbery, with no protector but a microscopic lap-dog. She pretended to be scandalised at his audacity, but his audacity
carried the hour. "This time certainly," thought the Countess,
"he will make his declaration. He didn't jump that wall, at
the risk of his neck, simply to ask me for a cup of tea." Not
a bit of it; Benvolio was devoted, but he was not more explicit
than before. He declared that this was the happiest hour of
his life; that there was a charming air of romance in his position; that, honestly, he thanked the Countess for having
made him desperate; that he would never come to see her
again but by the garden wall; that something, to-night—what
was it?—was vastly becoming to her; that he devoutly hoped
she would receive no one else; that his admiration for her was
unbounded; that the stars, finally, had a curious pink light!
He looked at her, through the flower-scented dusk, with ad-

miring eyes; but he looked at the stars as well; he threw back his head and folded his arms, and let the conversation flag while he examined the firmament. He observed also the long shafts of light proceeding from the windows of the house, as they fell upon the lawn and played among the shrubbery. The Countess had always thought him a singular man, but to-night she thought him more singular than ever. She became satirical, and the point of her satire was that he was after all but a dull fellow; that his admiration was a poor compliment; that he would do well to turn his attention to astronomy! In answer to this he came perhaps (to the Countess's sense) as near as he had ever come to making a declaration.

"Dear lady," he said, "you don't begin to know how much I admire you!"

She left her place at this, and walked about her lawn, looking at him askance while he talked, trailing her embroidered robe over the grass and fingering the folded petals of her flowers. He made a sort of sentimental profession of faith; he assured her that she represented his ideal of a certain sort of woman. This last phrase made her pause a moment and stare at him wide-eyed. "Oh, I mean the finest sort," he cried— "the sort that exerts the widest sway! You represent the world and everything that the world can give, and you represent them at their best—in their most generous, most graceful, most inspiring form. If a man were a revolutionist, you would reconcile him to society. You are a divine embodiment of all the amenities, the refinements, the complexities of life! You are the flower of urbanity, of culture, of tradition! You are the product of so many influences that it widens one's horizon to know you; of you too it is true that to admire you is a liberal education! Your charm is irresistible; I assure you I don't resist it!"

Compliments agreed with the Countess, as we may say; they not only made her happier, but they made her better. It became a matter of conscience with her to deserve them. These were magnificent ones, and she was by no means indifferent to them. Her cheek faintly flushed, her eyes vaguely glowed, and though her beauty, in the literal sense, was questionable, all that Benvolio said of her had never seemed more true. He said more in the same strain, and she listened without interrupting him. But at last she suddenly became impatient; it seemed to her that this was after all a tolerably inexpensive sort of wooing. But she did not betray her impatience with any petulance; she simply shook her finger a moment, to enjoin silence, and then she said, in a voice of extreme gentleness—"You have too much imagination!" He answered that, to do her perfect justice, he had too little. To this she replied that it was not of her any longer he was talking; he had left her far behind. He was spinning fancies about some highly subtilized figment of his brain. The best answer to this, it seemed to Benvolio, was to seize her hand and kiss it. I don't know what the Countess thought of this form of argument; I incline to think it both pleased and vexed her; it was at once too much and too little. She snatched her hand away and went rapidly into the house. Although Benvolio immediately followed her, he was unable to overtake her; she had retired into impenetrable seclusion. A short time afterwards she left town and went for the summer to an estate which she possessed in a distant part of the country.

III.

Benvolio was extremely fond of the country, but he remained in town after all his friends had departed. Many of them made him promise that he would come and see them. He promised, or half promised, but when he reflected that in almost every case he would find a house full of fellow-guests, to whose pursuits he would have to conform, and that if he rambled away with a valued duodecimo in his pocket to spend the morning alone in the woods, he would be denounced as a marplot and a selfish brute, he felt no great desire to pay visits. He had, as we know, his moods of expansion and of contraction; he had been tolerably inflated for many months past, and now he had begun to take in sail. And then I suspect the foolish fellow had no money to travel withal. He had lately put all his available funds into the purchase of a picture—an estimable work of the Venetian school, which had been suddenly thrown into the market. It was offered for a moderate sum, and Benvolio, who was one of the first to see it, secured it, and hung it triumphantly in his room. It had all the classic

Venetian glow, and he used to lie on his divan by the hour, gazing at it. It had, indeed, a peculiar property, of which I have known no other example. Most pictures that are remarkable for their colour (especially if they have been painted for a couple of centuries), need a flood of sunshine on the canvas to bring it out. But this remarkable work seemed to have a hidden radiance of its own, which showed brightest when the room was half darkened. When Benvolio wished especially to enjoy his treasure he dropped his Venetian blinds, and the picture bloomed out into the cool dusk with enchanting effect. It represented, in a fantastic way, the story of Perseus and Andromeda—the beautiful naked maiden chained to a rock, on which, with picturesque incongruity, a wild fig-tree was growing; the green Adriatic tumbling at her feet, and a splendid brown-limbed youth in a curious helmet hovering near her on a winged horse. The journey his fancy made as he lay and looked at his picture Benvolio preferred to any journey he might make by the public conveyances.

But he resorted for entertainment, as he had often done before, to the windows overlooking the old garden behind his house. As the summer deepened, of course the charm of the garden increased. It grew more tangled and bosky and mossy, and sent forth sweeter and heavier odours into the neighbouring air. It was a perfect solitude; Benvolio had never seen a visitor there. One day, therefore, at this time, it puzzled him most agreeably to perceive a young girl sitting under one of the trees. She sat there a long time, and though she was at a distance, he managed, by looking long enough, to make out that she was pretty. She was dressed in black, and when she left her place her step had a kind of nun-like gentleness and demureness. Although she was alone, there was something timid and tentative in her movements. She wandered away and disappeared from sight, save that here and there he saw her white parasol gleaming in the gaps of the foliage. Then she came back to her seat under the great tree, and remained there for some time, arranging in her lap certain flowers that she had gathered. Then she rose again and vanished, and Benvolio waited in vain for her return. She had evidently gone into the house. The next day he saw her again, and the next, and the next. On these occasions she had a book in her hand, and

she sat in her former place a long time, and read it with an
air of great attention. Now and then she raised her head and
glanced toward the house, as if to keep something in sight
which divided her care; and once or twice she laid down her
book and tripped away to her hidden duties with a lighter
step than she had shown the first day. Benvolio formed a theory that she had an invalid parent, or a relation of some kind,
who was unable to walk, and had been moved into a window
overlooking the garden. She always took up her book again
when she came back, and bent her pretty head over it with
charming earnestness. Benvolio had already discovered that
her head was pretty. He fancied it resembled a certain exquisite little head on a Greek silver coin which lay, with several
others, in an agate cup on his table. You see he had also already taken to fancying, and I offer this as the excuse for his
staring at his modest neighbour by the hour. But he was not
during these hours idle, because he was—I can't say falling in
love with her; he knew her too little for that, and besides, he
was in love with the Countess—but because he was at any rate
cudgelling his brains about her. Who was she? what was she?
why had he never seen her before? The house in which she
apparently lived was in another street from Benvolio's own,
but he went out of his way on purpose to look at it. It was
an ancient grizzled, sad-faced structure, with grated windows
on the ground floor; it looked like a convent or a prison. Over
a wall, beside it, there tumbled into the street some stray ten-
drils of a wild creeper from Benvolio's garden. Suddenly
Benvolio began to suspect that the book the young girl in the
garden was reading was none other than a volume of his own,
put forth some six months before. His volume had a white
cover and so had this; white covers are rather rare, and there
was nothing impossible either in this young lady's reading his
book or in her finding it interesting. Very many other women
had done the same. Benvolio's neighbour had a pencil in her
pocket, which she every now and then drew forth, to make
with it a little mark on her page. This quiet gesture gave the
young man an exquisite pleasure.

I am ashamed to say how much time he spent, for a week,
at his window. Every day the young girl came into the garden.
At last there occurred a rainy day—a long, warm summer's

rain—and she staid within doors. He missed her quite acutely,
and wondered, half-smiling, half-frowning, that her absence
should make such a difference for him. He actually depended
upon her. He was ignorant of her name; he knew neither the
colour of her eyes nor the shade of her hair, nor the sound of
her voice; it was very likely that if he were to meet her face
to face, elsewhere, he would not recognise her. But she interested him; he liked her; he found her little indefinite, black-
dressed figure sympathetic. He used to find the Countess
sympathetic, and certainly the Countess was as unlike this
quiet garden-nymph as she could very well be and be yet a
charming woman. Benvolio's sympathies, as we know, were
large. After the rain the young girl came out again, and now
she had another book, having apparently finished Benvolio's.
He was gratified to observe that she bestowed upon this one
a much more wandering attention. Sometimes she let it drop
listlessly at her side, and seemed to lose herself in maidenly
reverie. Was she thinking how much more beautiful Benvolio's verses were than others of the day? Was she perhaps repeating them to herself? It charmed Benvolio to suppose she
might be; for he was not spoiled in this respect. The Countess
knew none of his poetry by heart; she was nothing of a reader.
She had his book on her table, but he once noticed that half
the leaves were uncut.

After a couple of days of sunshine the rain came back again,
to our hero's infinite annoyance, and this time it lasted several
days. The garden lay dripping and desolate; its charm had
quite departed. These days passed gloomily for Benvolio; he
decided that rainy weather, in summer, in town, was intolerable. He began to think of the Countess again—he was sure
that over her broad lands the summer sun was shining. He
saw them, in envious fancy, studded with joyous Watteau-
groups, feasting and making music under the shade of ancestral beeches. What a charming life! he thought—what
brilliant, enchanted, memorable days! He had said the very
reverse of all this, as you remember, three weeks before. I
don't know that he had ever devoted a formula to the idea
that men of imagination are not bound to be consistent, but
he certainly conformed to its spirit. We are not however, by
any means at the end of his inconsistencies. He immediately

wrote a letter to the Countess, asking her if he might pay her a visit.

Shortly after he had sent his letter the weather mended, and he went out for a walk. The sun was near setting; the streets were all ruddy and golden with its light, and the scattered rain-clouds, broken into a thousand little particles, were flecking the sky like a shower of opals and amethysts. Benvolio stopped, as he sauntered along, to gossip a while with his friend the bookseller. The bookseller was a foreigner and a man of taste; his shop was in the arcade of the great square. When Benvolio went in he was serving a lady, and the lady was dressed in black. Benvolio just now found it natural to notice a lady who was dressed in black, and the fact that this lady's face was averted made observation at once more easy and more fruitless. But at last her errand was finished; she had been ordering several books, and the bookseller was writing down their names. Then she turned round, and Benvolio saw her face. He stood staring at her most inconsiderately, for he felt an immediate certainty that she was the bookish damsel of the garden. She gave a glance round the shop, at the books on the walls, at the prints and busts, the apparatus of learning, in various forms, that it contained, and then, with the soundless, half-furtive step which Benvolio now knew so well, she took her departure. Benvolio seized the startled bookseller by the two hands and besieged him with questions. The bookseller, however, was able to answer but few of them. The young girl had been in his shop but once before, and had simply left an address, without any name. It was the address of which Benvolio had assured himself. The books she had ordered were all learned works—disquisitions on philosophy, on history, on the natural sciences, matters, all of them, in which she seemed an expert. For some of the volumes that she had just bespoken the bookseller was to send to foreign countries; the others were to be despatched that evening to the address which the young girl had left. As Benvolio stood there the old bibliophile gathered these latter together, and while he was so engaged he uttered a little cry of distress: one of the volumes of a set was missing. The work was a rare one, and it would be hard to repair the loss. Benvolio on the instant had an inspiration; he demanded leave of his friend to act as messenger: he himself would carry the books, as if he came from the shop, and he would explain the absence of the lost volume, and the bookseller's views about replacing it, far better than one of the hirelings. He asked leave, I say, but he did not wait till it was given; he snatched up the pile of books and strode triumphantly away!

IV.

As there was no name on the parcel, Benvolio, on reaching the old gray house over the wall of whose court an adventurous tendril stretched its long arm into the street, found himself wondering in what terms he should ask to have speech of the person for whom the books were intended. At any hazard he was determined not to retreat until he had caught a glimpse of the interior and its inhabitants; for this was the same man, you must remember, who had scaled the moonlit wall of the Countess's garden. An old serving woman in a quaint cap answered his summons, and stood blinking out at the fading daylight from a little wrinkled white face, as if she had never been compelled to take so direct a look at it before. He informed her that he had come from the bookseller's, and that he had been charged with a personal message for the venerable gentleman who had bespoken the parcel. Might he crave license to speak with him? This obsequious phrase was an improvisation of the moment—he had shaped it on the chance. But Benvolio had an indefinable conviction that it would fit the case; the only thing that surprised him was the quiet complaisance of the old woman.

"If it's on a bookish errand you come, sir," she said, with a little wheezy sigh, "I suppose I only do my duty in admitting you!"

She led him into the house, through various dusky chambers, and at last ushered him into an apartment of which the side opposite to the door was occupied by a broad, low casement. Through its small old panes there came a green dim light—the light of the low western sun shining through the wet trees of the famous garden. Everything else was ancient and brown; the walls were covered with tiers upon tiers of books. Near the window, in the still twilight, sat two persons, one of whom rose as Benvolio came in. This was the young girl of the garden—the young girl who had been an hour since at the bookseller's. The other was an old man, who turned his head, but otherwise sat motionless.

Both his movement and his stillness immediately announced to Benvolio's quick perception that he was blind. In his quality of poet Benvolio was inventive; a brain that is constantly tapped for rhymes is tolerably alert. In a few moments, therefore, he had given a vigorous push to the wheel of fortune. Various things had happened. He had made a soft, respectful speech, he hardly knew about what; and the old man had told him he had a delectable voice—a voice that seemed to belong rather to a person of education than to a tradesman's porter. Benvolio confessed to having picked up an education, and the old man had thereupon bidden the young girl offer him a seat. Benvolio chose his seat where he could see her, as she sat at the low-browed casement. The bookseller in the square thought it likely Benvolio would come back that evening and give him an account of his errand, and before he closed his shop he looked up and down the street, to see whether the young man was approaching. Benvolio came, but the shop was closed. This he never noticed, however; he walked three times round all the arcades, without noticing it. He was thinking of something else. He had sat all the evening with the blind old scholar and his daughter, and he was thinking intently, ardently of them. When I say of them, of course I mean of the daughter.

A few days afterwards he got a note from the Countess, saying it would give her pleasure to receive his visit. He immediately wrote to her that, with a thousand regrets, he found himself urgently occupied in town and must beg leave to defer his departure for a day or two. The regrets were perfectly sincere, but the plea was none the less valid. Benvolio had become deeply interested in his tranquil neighbours, and, for the moment, a certain way the young girl had of looking at him—fixing her eyes, first, with a little vague, half-absent smile, on an imaginary point above his head, and then slowly dropping them till they met his own—was quite sufficient to make him happy. He had called once more on her father, and once more, and yet once more, and he had a vivid prevision

that he should often call again. He had been in the garden
and found its mild mouldiness even more delightful on a
nearer view. He had pulled off his very ill-fitting mask, and
let his neighbours know that his trade was not to carry parcels,
but to scribble verses. The old man had never heard of his
verses; he read nothing that had been published later than the
sixth century; and nowadays he could read only with his
daughter's eyes. Benvolio had seen the little white volume on
the table, and assured himself it was his own; and he noted
the fact that in spite of its well-thumbed air, the young girl
had never given her father a hint of its contents. I said just
now that several things had happened in the first half hour of
Benvolio's first visit. One of them was that this modest maiden
fell in love with our young man. What happened when she
learned that he was the author of the little white volume, I
hardly know how to express; her innocent passion began to
throb and flutter. Benvolio possessed an old quarto volume
bound in Russia leather, about which there clung an agreeable
pungent odour. In this old quarto he kept a sort of diary—if
that can be called a diary in which a whole year had sometimes
been allowed to pass without an entry. On the other hand,
there were some interminable records of a single day. Turning
it over you would have chanced, not infrequently, upon the
name of the Countess; and at this time you would have observed on every page some mention of "the Professor" and
of a certain person named Scholastica. Scholastica, you will
immediately guess, was the Professor's daughter. Probably this
was not her own name, but it was the name by which Benvolio
preferred to know her, and we need not be more exact than
he. By this time of course he knew a great deal about her, and
about her venerable sire. The Professor, before the loss of his
eyesight and his health, had been one of the stateliest pillars
of the University. He was now an old man; he had married
late in life. When his infirmities came upon him he gave up
his chair and his classes and buried himself in his library. He
made his daughter his reader and his secretary, and his prodigious memory assisted her clear young voice and her
softly-moving pen. He was held in great honour in the
scholastic world; learned men came from afar to consult the
blind sage and to appeal to his wisdom as to the ultimate law.

The University settled a pension upon him, and he dwelt in a dusky corner, among the academic shades. The pension was small, but the old scholar and the young girl lived with conventual simplicity. It so happened, however, that he had a brother, or rather a half-brother, who was not a bookish man, save as regarded his ledger and daybook. This personage had made money in trade, and had retired, wifeless and childless, into the old gray house attached to Benvolio's garden. He had the reputation of a skinflint, a curmudgeon, a bloodless old miser who spent his days in shuffling about his mouldy mansion, making his pockets jingle, and his nights in lifting his money-bags out of trapdoors and counting over his hoard. He was nothing but a chilling shadow, an evil name, a pretext for a curse; no one had ever seen him, much less crossed his threshold. But it seemed that he had a soft spot in his heart. He wrote one day to his brother, whom he had not seen for years, that the rumour had come to him that he was blind, infirm, and poor; that he himself had a large house with a garden behind it; and that if the Professor were not too proud, he was welcome to come and lodge there. The Professor had come, in this way, a few weeks before, and though it would seem that to a sightless old ascetic all lodgings might be the same, he took a great satisfaction in his new abode. His daughter found it a paradise, compared with their two narrow chambers under the old gable of the University, where, amid the constant coming and going of students, a young girl was compelled to lead a cloistered life.

Benvolio had assigned as his motive for intrusion, when he had been obliged to acknowledge his real character, an irresistible desire to ask the old man's opinion on certain knotty points of philosophy. This was a pardonable fiction, for the event, at any rate, justified it. Benvolio, when he was fairly launched in a philosophical discussion, was capable of forgetting that there was anything in the world but metaphysics; he revelled in transcendent abstractions and became unconscious of all concrete things—even of that most brilliant of concrete things, the Countess. He longed to embark on a voyage of discovery on the great sea of pure reason. He knew that from such voyages the deep-browed adventurer rarely returns; but if he were to find an El Dorado of thought, why should he

regret the dusky world of fact? Benvolio had high colloquies
with the Professor, who was a devout Neo-Platonist, and
whose venerable wit had spun to subtler tenuity the ethereal
speculations of the Alexandrian school. Benvolio at this season
declared that study and science were the only game in life
worth the candle, and wondered how he could ever for an
instant have cared for more vulgar exercises. He turned off a
little poem in the style of Milton's *Penseroso*, which, if it had
not quite the merit of that famous effusion, was at least the
young man's own happiest performance. When Benvolio liked
a thing he liked it as a whole—it appealed to all his senses.
He relished its accidents, its accessories, its material envelope.
In the satisfaction he took in his visits to the Professor it
would have been hard to say where the charm of philosophy
began or ended. If it began with a glimpse of the old man's
mild, sightless blue eyes, sitting fixed beneath his shaggy white
brows like patches of pale winter sky under a high-piled cloud,
it hardly ended before it reached the little black bow on
Scholastica's slipper; and certainly it had taken a comprehensive sweep in the interval. There was nothing in his friends
that had not a charm, an interest, a character, for his appreciative mind. Their seclusion, their stillness, their super-simple
notions of the world and the world's ways, the faint, musty
perfume of the University which hovered about them, their
brown old apartment, impenetrable to the rumours of the
town—all these things were part of his entertainment. Then
the essence of it perhaps was that in this silent, simple life the
intellectual key, if you touched it, was so finely resonant. In
the way of thought there was nothing into which his friends
were not initiated—nothing they could not understand. The
mellow light of their low-browed room, streaked with the
moted rays that slanted past the dusky book-shelves, was the
atmosphere of intelligence. All this made them, humble folk
as they were, not so simple as they at first appeared. They,
too, in their own fashion, knew the world; they were not people to be patronized; to visit them was not a condescension,
but a privilege.

In the Professor this was not surprising. He had passed fifty
years in arduous study, and it was proper to his character and
his office that he should be erudite and venerable. But his

devoted little daughter seemed to Benvolio at first almost grotesquely wise. She was an anomaly, a prodigy, a charming
monstrosity. Charming, at any rate, she was, and as pretty, I
must lose no more time in saying, as had seemed likely to
Benvolio at his window. And yet, even on a nearer view, her
prettiness shone forth slowly. It was as if it had been covered
with a series of film-like veils, which had to be successively
drawn aside. And then it was such a homely, shrinking, subtle
prettiness, that Benvolio, in the private record I have mentioned, never thought of calling it by the arrogant name of
beauty. He called it by no name at all; he contented himself
with enjoying it—with looking into the young girl's mild gray
eyes and saying things, on purpose, that caused her candid
smile to deepen until (like the broadening ripple of a lake) it
reached a particular dimple in her left cheek. This was its max-
imum; no smile could do more, and Benvolio desired nothing
better. Yet I cannot say he was in love with the young girl; he
only liked her. But he liked her, no doubt, as a man likes a
thing but once in his life. As he knew her better, the oddity
of her great learning quite faded away; it seemed delightfully
natural, and he only wondered why there were not more
women of the same pattern. Scholastica had imbibed the wine
of science instead of her mother's milk. Her mother had died
in her infancy, leaving her cradled in an old folio, three-
quarters opened, like a wide V. Her father had been her nurse,
her playmate, her teacher, her life-long companion, her only
friend. He taught her the Greek alphabet before she knew her
own, and fed her with crumbs from his scholastic revels. She
had taken submissively what was given her, and, without
knowing it, she grew up a little handmaid of science.

Benvolio perceived that she was not in the least a woman
of genius. The passion for knowledge, of its own motion,
would never have carried her far. But she had a perfect understanding—a mind as clear and still and natural as a woodland pool, giving back an exact and definite image of
everything that was presented to it. And then she was so
teachable, so diligent, so indefatigable. Slender and meagre as
she was, and rather pale too, with being much within doors,
she was never tired, she never had a headache, she never
closed her book or laid down a pen with a sigh. Benvolio said

to himself that she was exquisitely constituted for helping a man. What a work he might do on summer mornings and winter nights, with that brightly demure little creature at his side, transcribing, recollecting, sympathising! He wondered how much she cared for these things herself; whether a woman could care for them without being dry and harsh. It was in a great measure for information on this point that he used to question her eyes with the frequency that I have mentioned. But they never gave him a perfectly direct answer, and this was why he came and came again. They seemed to him to say, "If you could lead a student's life for my sake, I could be a life-long household scribe for yours." Was it divine philosophy that made Scholastica charming, or was it she that made philosophy divine? I cannot relate everything that came to pass between these young people, and I must leave a great deal to your imagination. The summer waned, and when the autumn afternoons began to grow vague, the quiet couple in the old gray house had expanded to a talkative trio. For Benvolio the days had passed very fast; the trio had talked of so many things. He had spent many an hour in the garden with the young girl, strolling in the weedy paths, or resting on a moss-grown bench. She was a delightful listener, because she not only attended, but she followed. Benvolio had known women to fix very beautiful eyes upon him, and watch with an air of ecstasy the movement of his lips, and yet had found them three minutes afterwards quite incapable of saying what he was talking about. Scholastica gazed at him, but she understood him too.

v.

You will say that my description of Benvolio has done him injustice, and that, far from being the sentimental weathercock I have depicted, he is proving himself a model of constancy. But mark the sequel! It was at this moment precisely, that, one morning, having gone to bed the night before singing pæans to divine philosophy, he woke up with a headache, and in the worst of humours with abstract science. He remembered Scholastica telling him that she never had headaches, and the memory quite annoyed him. He suddenly found himself thinking of her as a neat little mechanical toy, wound up to turn pages and write a pretty hand, but with neither a head nor a heart that was capable of human ailments. He fell asleep again, and in one of those brief but vivid dreams that sometimes occur in the morning hours, he had a brilliant vision of the Countess. *She* was human beyond a doubt, and duly familiar with headaches and heartaches. He felt an irresistible desire to see her and to tell her that he adored her. This satisfaction was not unattainable, and before the day was over he was well on his way toward enjoying it. He left town and made his pilgrimage to her estate, where he found her holding her usual court and leading a merry life. He had meant to stay with her a week; he staid two months—the most entertaining months he had ever known. I cannot pretend of course to enumerate the diversions of this fortunate circle, or to say just how Benvolio spent every hour of his time. But if the summer had passed quickly with him, the autumn moved with a tread as light. He thought once in a while of Scholastica and her father—once in a while, I say, when present occupations suffered his thoughts to wander. This was not often, for the Countess had always, as the phrase is, a hundred arrows in her quiver. You see, the negative, with Benvolio, always implied as distinct a positive, and his excuse for being inconstant on one side was that he was at such a time very assiduous on another. He developed at this period a talent as yet untried and unsuspected; he proved himself capable of writing brilliant dramatic poetry. The long autumn evenings, in a great country house, were a natural occasion for the much-abused pastime known as private theatricals. The Countess had a theatre, and abundant material for a troupe of amateur players; all that was lacking was a play exactly adapted to her resources. She proposed to Benvolio to write one; the idea took his fancy; he shut himself up in the library, and in a week produced a masterpiece. He had found the subject, one day when he was pulling over the Countess's books, in an old MS. chronicle written by the chaplain of one of her late husband's ancestors. It was the germ of an admirable drama, and Benvolio greatly enjoyed his attempt to make a work of art of it. All his genius, all his imagination went into it. This was the proper mission of his faculties, he cried to himself—the study of warm human passions, the painting of rich dramatic pictures, not the dry chopping of logic. His play was acted with brilliant success, the Countess herself representing the heroine. Benvolio had never seen her don the buskin, and had no idea of her aptitude for the stage; but she was inimitable, she was a natural artist. What gives charm to life, Benvolio hereupon said to himself, is the element of the unexpected; and this one finds only in women of the Countess's type. And I should do wrong to imply that he here made an invidious comparison, for he did not even think of Scholastica. His play was repeated several times, and people were invited to see it from all the country round. There was a great bivouac of servants in the castle-court; in the cold November nights a bonfire was lighted to keep the servants warm. It was a great triumph for Benvolio, and he frankly enjoyed it. He knew he enjoyed it, and how great a triumph it was, and he felt every disposition to drain the cup to the last drop. He relished his own elation, and found himself excellent company. He began immediately an-other drama—a comedy this time—and he was greatly inter-ested to observe that when his work was on the stocks he found himself regarding all the people about him as types and available figures. Everything he saw or heard was grist to his mill; everything presented itself as possible material. Life on these terms became really very interesting, and for several nights the laurels of Molière kept Benvolio awake.

Delightful as this was, however, it could not last for ever. When the winter nights had begun, the Countess returned to town, and Benvolio came back with her, his unfinished com-edy in his pocket. During much of the journey he was silent and abstracted, and the Countess supposed he was thinking of how he should make the most of that capital situation in his third act. The Countess's perspicacity was just sufficient to carry her so far—to lead her, in other words, into plausible mistakes. Benvolio was really wondering what in the name of mystery had suddenly become of his inspiration, and why the witticisms in his play and his comedy had begun to seem as mechanical as the cracking of the post-boy's whip. He looked out at the scrubby fields, the rusty woods, the sullen sky, and asked himself whether *that* was the world to which it had been but yesterday his high ambition to hold up the mirror. The

Countess's *dame de compagnie* sat opposite to him in the carriage. Yesterday he thought her, with her pale, discreet face,
and her eager movements that pretended to be indifferent, a
finished specimen of an entertaining genus. To-day he could
only say that if there was a whole genus it was a thousand
pities, for the poor lady struck him as miserably false and ser-
vile. The real seemed hideous; he felt homesick for his dear
familiar rooms between the garden and the square, and he
longed to get into them and bolt his door and bury himself
in his old arm-chair and cultivate idealism for evermore. The
first thing he actually did on getting into them was to go to
the window and look out into the garden. It had greatly
changed in his absence, and the old maimed statues, which all
the summer had been comfortably muffled in verdure, were
now, by an odd contradiction of propriety, standing white and
naked in the cold. I don't exactly know how soon it was that
Benvolio went back to see his neighbours. It was after no great
interval, and yet it was not immediately. He had a bad conscience, and he was wondering what he should say to them.
It seemed to him now (though he had not thought of it
sooner), that they might accuse him of neglecting them. He
had appealed to their friendship, he had professed the highest
esteem for them, and then he had turned his back on them
without farewell, and without a word of explanation. He had
not written to them; in truth during his sojourn with the
Countess, it would not have been hard for him to persuade
himself that they were people he had only dreamed about, or
read about, at most, in some old volume of memoirs. People
of their value, he could now imagine them saying, were not
to be taken up and dropped for a fancy; and if friendship was
not to be friendship as they themselves understood it, it was
better that he should forget them at once and for ever. It is
perhaps too much to affirm that he imagined them saying all
this; they were too mild and civil, too unused to acting in self-
defence. But they might easily receive him in a way that would
imply a delicate resentment. Benvolio felt profaned, dishonoured, almost contaminated; so that perhaps when he did at
last return to his friends, it was because that was the simplest
way to be purified. How did they receive him? I told you a
good way back that Scholastica was in love with him, and you

may arrange the scene in any manner that best accords with this circumstance. Her forgiveness, of course, when once that chord was touched, was proportionate to her displeasure. But Benvolio took refuge both from his own compunction and from the young girl's reproaches, in whatever form these were conveyed, in making a full confession of what he was pleased to call his frivolity. As he walked through the naked garden with Scholastica, kicking the wrinkled leaves, he told her the whole story of his sojourn with the Countess. The young girl listened with bright intentness, as she would have listened to some thrilling passage in a romance; but she neither sighed, nor looked wistful, nor seemed to envy the Countess or to repine at her own ignorance of the great world. It was all too remote for comparison; it was not, for Scholastica, among the things that might have been. Benvolio talked to her very freely about the Countess. If she liked it, he found on his side that it eased his mind; and as he said nothing that the Countess would not have been flattered by, there was no harm done. Although, however, Benvolio uttered nothing but praise of this distinguished lady, he was very frank in saying that she and her way of life always left him at the end in a worse humour than when they found him. They were very well in their way, he said, but their way was not his way—it only seemed so at moments. For him, he was convinced, the only real felicity was in the pleasures of study! Scholastica answered that it gave her high satisfaction to hear this, for it was her father's belief that Benvolio had a great aptitude for philosophical research, and that it was a sacred duty to cultivate so rare a faculty.

"And what is your belief?" Benvolio asked, remembering that the young girl knew several of his poems by heart.

Her answer was very simple. "I believe you are a poet."

"And a poet oughtn't to run the risk of turning pedant?"

"No," she answered; "a poet ought to run all risks—even that one which for a poet is perhaps most cruel. But he ought to escape them all!"

Benvolio took great satisfaction in hearing that the Professor deemed that he had in him the making of a philosopher, and it gave an impetus to the zeal with which he returned to work.

VI.

Of course even the most zealous student cannot work always, and often, after a very philosophic day, Benvolio spent with the Countess a very sentimental evening. It is my duty as a veracious historian not to conceal the fact that he discoursed to the Countess about Scholastica. He gave such a puzzling description of her that the Countess declared that she must be a delightfully quaint creature and that it would be vastly amusing to know her. She hardly supposed Benvolio was in love with this little bookworm in petticoats, but to make sure—if that might be called making sure—she deliberately asked him. He said No; he hardly saw how he could be, since he was in love with the Countess herself! For a while this answer satisfied her, but as the winter went by she began to wonder whether there were not such a thing as a man being in love with two women at once. During many months that followed, Benvolio led a kind of double life. Sometimes it charmed him and gave him an inspiring sense of personal power. He haunted the domicile of his gentle neighbours, and drank deep of the garnered wisdom of the ages; and he made appearances as frequent in the Countess's drawing-room, where he played his part with magnificent zest and ardour. It was a life of alternation and contrast, and it really demanded a vigorous and elastic temperament. Sometimes his own seemed to him quite inadequate to the occasion—he felt fevered, bewildered, exhausted. But when it came to the point of choosing one thing or the other, it was impossible to give up either his worldly habits or his studious aspirations. Benvolio raged inwardly at the cruel limitations of the human mind, and declared it was a great outrage that a man should not be personally able to do everything he could imagine doing. I hardly know how she contrived it, but the Countess was at this time a more engaging woman than she had ever been. Her beauty acquired an ampler and richer cast, and she had a manner of looking at you as she slowly turned away with a vague reproachfulness that was at the same time an encouragement, which had lighted a hopeless flame in many a youthful breast. Benvolio one day felt in the mood for finishing his comedy, and the Countess and her friends acted it. Its success was no less brilliant than that of its predecessor, and the manager of the theatre immediately demanded the privilege of producing it. You will hardly believe me, however, when I tell you that on the night that his comedy was introduced to the public, its eccentric author sat discussing the absolute and the relative with the Professor and his daughter. Benvolio had all winter been observing that Scholastica never looked so pretty as when she sat, of a winter's night, plying a quiet needle in the mellow circle of a certain antique brass lamp. On the night in question he happened to fall a-thinking of this picture, and he tramped out across the snow for the express purpose of looking at it. It was sweeter even than his memory promised, and it banished every thought of his theatrical honours from his head. Scholastica gave him some tea, and her tea, for mysterious reasons, was delicious; better, strange to say, than that of the Countess, who, however, it must be added, recovered her ground in coffee. The Professor's parsimonious brother owned a ship which made voyages to China and brought him goodly chests of the incomparable plant. He sold the cargo for great sums, but he kept a chest for himself. It was always the best one, and he had at this time carefully measured out a part of his annual dole, made it into a little parcel, and presented it to Scholastica. This is the secret history of Benvolio's fragrant cups. While he was drinking them on the night I speak of—I am ashamed to say how many he drank —his name, at the theatre, was being tossed across the footlights to a brilliant, clamorous multitude, who hailed him as the redeemer of the national stage. But I am not sure that he even told his friends that his play was being acted. Indeed, this was hardly possible, for I meant to say just now that he had forgotten it.

It is very certain, however, that he enjoyed the criticisms the next day in the newspapers. Radiant and jubilant, he went to see the Countess, with half a dozen of them in his pocket. He found her looking terribly dark. She had been at the theatre, prepared to revel in his triumph—to place on his head with her own hand, as it were, the laurel awarded by the public; and his absence had seemed to her a sort of personal slight. Yet his triumph had nevertheless given her an exceeding pleasure, for it had been the seal of her secret hopes of him.

Decidedly he was to be a great man, and this was not the moment for letting him go! At the same time there was something noble in his indifference, his want of eagerness, his finding it so easy to forget his honours. It was only an intellectual Crœsus, the Countess said to herself, who could afford to keep so loose an account with fame. But she insisted on knowing where he had been, and he told her he had been discussing philosophy and tea with the Professor.

"And was not the daughter there?" the Countess demanded.

"Most sensibly!" he cried. And then he added in a moment—"I don't know whether I ever told you, but she's almost as pretty as you."

The Countess resented the compliment to Scholastica much more than she enjoyed the compliment to herself. She felt an extreme curiosity to see this inky-fingered syren, and as she seldom failed, sooner or later, to compass her desires, she succeeded at last in catching a glimpse of her innocent rival. To do so she was obliged to set a great deal of machinery in motion. She induced Benvolio to give a lunch, in his rooms, to some ladies who professed a desire to see his works of art, and of whom she constituted herself the chaperon. She took care that he threw open a certain vestibule that looked into the garden, and here, at the window, she spent much of her time. There was but a chance that Scholastica would come forth into the garden, but it was a chance worth staking something upon. The Countess gave to it time and temper, and she was finally rewarded. Scholastica came out. The poor girl strolled about for half an hour, in profound unconsciousness that the Countess's fine eyes were devouring her. The impression she made was singular. The Countess found her both pretty and ugly: she did not admire her herself, but she understood that Benvolio might. For herself, personally, she detested her, and when Scholastica went in and she turned away from the window, her first movement was to pass before a mirror, which showed her something that, impartially considered, seemed to her a thousand times more beautiful. The Countess made no comments, and took good care Benvolio did not suspect the trick she had played him. There was something more she promised herself to do, and she impatiently awaited her opportunity.

In the middle of the winter she announced to him that she was going to spend ten days in the country; she had received the most attractive accounts of the state of things on her domain. There had been great snow-falls, and the sleighing was magnificent; the lakes and streams were solidly frozen, there was an unclouded moon, and the resident gentry were skating, half the night, by torch-light. The Countess was passionately fond both of sleighing and skating, and she found this picture irresistible. And then she was charitable, and observed that it would be a kindness to the poor resident gentry, whose usual pleasures were of a frugal sort, to throw open her house and give a ball or two, with the village fiddlers. Perhaps even they might organize a bear-hunt—an entertainment at which, if properly conducted, a lady might be present as spectator. The Countess told Benvolio all this one day as he sat with her in her boudoir, in the fire-light, during the hour that precedes dinner. She had said more than once that he must de-camp—that she must go and dress; but neither of them had moved. She did not invite him to go with her to the country; she only watched him as he sat gazing with a frown at the fire-light—the crackling blaze of the great logs which had been cut in the Countess's bear-haunted forests. At last she rose impatiently, and fairly turned him out. After he had gone she stood for a moment looking at the fire, with the tip of her foot on the fender. She had not to wait long; he came back within the minute—came back and begged her leave to go with her to the country—to skate with her in the crystal moonlight and dance with her to the sound of the village violins. It hardly matters in what terms his request was granted; the notable point is that he made it. He was her only companion, and when they were established in the castle the hospitality extended to the resident gentry was less abundant than had been promised. Benvolio, however, did not complain of the absence of it, because, for the week or so, he was passionately in love with his hostess. They took long sleigh-rides and drank deep of the poetry of winter. The blue shadows on the snow, the cold amber lights in the west, the leafless twigs against the snow-charged sky, all gave them extraordinary pleasure. The nights were even better, when the great silver stars, before the moonrise, glittered on the polished ice, and the young Countess and her lover, firmly joining hands, launched themselves into motion and into the darkness and went skimming for miles with their winged steps. On their return, before the great chimney-place in the old library, they lingered a while and drank little cups of wine heated with spices. It was perhaps here, cup in hand—this point is uncertain—that Benvolio broke through the last bond of his reserve, and told the Countess that he loved her, in a manner to satisfy her. To be his in all solemnity, his only and his for ever—this he explicitly, passionately, imperiously demanded of her. After this she gave her ball to her country neighbours, and Benvolio danced, to a boisterous, swinging measure, with a dozen ruddy beauties dressed in the fashions of the year before last. The Countess danced with the lusty male counterparts of these damsels, but she found plenty of chances to watch Benvolio. Toward the end of the evening she saw him looking grave and bored, with very much such a frown in his forehead as when he had sat staring at the fire that last day in her boudoir. She said to herself for the hundredth time that he was the strangest of mortals.

On their return to the city she had frequent occasions to say it again. He looked at moments as if he had repented of his bargain—as if it did not at all suit him that his being the Countess's only lover should involve her being his only mistress. She deemed now that she had acquired the right to make him give an account of his time, and he did not conceal the fact that the first thing he had done on reaching town was to go to see his eccentric neighbours. She treated him hereupon to a passionate outburst of jealousy; called Scholastica a dozen harsh names—a little dingy blue-stocking, a little underhand, hypocritical Puritan; demanded he should promise never to speak to her again, and summoned him to make a choice once for all. Would he belong to her, or to that odious little schoolmistress? It must be one thing or the other; he must take her or leave her; it was impossible she should have a lover who was so little to be depended upon. The Countess did not say this made her unhappy, but she repeated a dozen times that it made her ridiculous. Benvolio turned very pale; she had never seen him so before; a great struggle was evidently taking place within him. A terrible scene was the consequence. He broke out into reproaches and imprecations; he accused the Countess of being his bad angel, of making him neglect his best faculties, mutilate his genius, squander his life; and yet he confessed that he was committed to her, that she fascinated him beyond resistance, and that, at any sacrifice, he must still be her slave. This confession gave the Countess uncommon satisfaction, and made up in a measure for the unflattering remarks that accompanied it. She on her side confessed—what she had always been too proud to acknowledge hitherto—that she cared vastly for him, and that she had waited for long months for him to say something of this kind. They parted on terms which it would be hard to define—full of mutual resentment and devotion, at once adoring and hating each other. All this was deep and stirring emotion, and Benvolio, as an artist, always in one way or another found his profit in emotion, even when it lacerated or suffocated him. There was, moreover, a sort of elation in having burnt his ships behind him, and vowed to seek his fortune, his intellectual fortune, in the tumult of life and action. He did no work; his power of work, for the time at least, was paralyzed. Sometimes this frightened him; it seemed as if his genius were dead, his career cut short; at other moments his faith soared supreme; he heard, in broken murmurs, the voice of the muse, and said to himself that he was only resting, waiting, storing up knowledge. Before long he felt tolerably tranquil again; ideas began to come to him, and the world to seem entertaining. He demanded of the Countess that, without further delay, their union should be solemnized. But the Countess, at that interview I have just related, had, in spite of her high spirit, received a great fright. Benvolio, stalking up and down with clenched hands and angry eyes, had seemed to her a terrible man to marry; and though she was conscious of a strong will of her own, as well as of robust nerves, she had shuddered at the thought that such scenes might often occur. She had hitherto seen little but the mild and genial, or at most the joyous and fantastic side of her friend's disposition; but it now appeared that there was another side to be

taken into account, and that if Benvolio had talked of sacrifices, these were not all to be made by him. They say the world
likes its master—that a horse of high spirit likes being well
ridden. This may be true in the long run; but the Countess,
who was essentially a woman of the world, was not yet prepared to pay our young man the tribute of her luxurious liberty. She admired him more, now that she was afraid of him,
but at the same time she liked him a trifle less. She answered
that marriage was a very serious matter; that they had lately
had a taste of each other's tempers; that they had better wait
a while longer; that she had made up her mind to travel for
a year, and that she strongly recommended him to come with
her, for travelling was notoriously an excellent test of friendship.

VII.

She went to Italy, and Benvolio went with her; but before he
went he paid a visit to his other mistress. He flattered himself
that he had burned his ships behind him, but the fire was still
visibly smouldering. It is true, nevertheless, that he passed a
very strange half-hour with Scholastica and her father. The
young girl had greatly changed; she barely greeted him; she
looked at him coldly. He had no idea her face could wear that
look; it vexed him to find it there. He had not been to see
her for many weeks, and he now came to tell her that he was
going away for a year; it is true these were not conciliatory
facts. But she had taught him to think that she possessed in
perfection the art of trustful resignation, of unprotesting,
cheerful patience—virtues that sat so gracefully on her bended
brow that the thought of their being at any rate supremely
becoming took the edge from his remorse at making them
necessary. But now Scholastica looked older as well as sadder,
and decidedly not so pretty. Her figure was meagre, her movements were angular, her charming eye was dull. After the first
minute he avoided this charming eye; it made him uncomfortable. Her voice she scarcely allowed him to hear. The
Professor, as usual, was serene and frigid, impartial and transcendental. There was a chill in the air, a shadow between
them. Benvolio went so far as to wonder that he had ever

found a great attraction in the young girl, and his present disillusionment gave him even more anger than pain. He took leave abruptly and coldly, and puzzled his brain for a long time afterward over the mystery of Scholastica's reserve.

The Countess had said that travelling was a test of friendship; in this case friendship (or whatever the passion was to be called) promised for some time to resist the test. Benvolio passed six months of the liveliest felicity. The world has nothing better to offer to a man of sensibility than a first visit to Italy during those years of life when perception is at its keenest, when knowledge has arrived, and yet youth has not departed. He made with the Countess a long, slow progress through the lovely land, from the Alps to the Sicilian sea; and it seemed to him that his imagination, his intellect, his genius, expanded with every breath and rejoiced in every glance. The Countess was in an almost equal ecstasy, and their sympathy was perfect in all points save the lady's somewhat indiscriminate predilection for assemblies and receptions. She had a thousand letters of introduction to deliver, which entailed a vast deal of social exertion. Often, on balmy nights when he would have preferred to meditate among the ruins of the Forum, or to listen to the moonlit ripple of the Adriatic, Benvolio found himself dragged away to kiss the hand of a decayed princess, or to take a pinch from the snuff-box of an epicurean cardinal. But the cardinals, the princesses, the ruins, the warm southern tides which seemed the voice of history itself—these and a thousand other things resolved themselves into an immense pictorial spectacle—the very stuff that inspiration is made of. Everything Benvolio had written before coming to Italy now appeared to him worthless; this was the needful stamp, the consecration of talent. One day, however, his felicity was clouded; by a trifle you will say, possibly; but you must remember that in men of Benvolio's disposition primary impulses are almost always produced by small accidents. The Countess, speaking of the tone of voice of some one they had met, happened to say that it reminded her of the voice of that queer little woman at home—the daughter of the blind professor. Was this pure inadvertence, or was it malicious design? Benvolio never knew, though he immediately demanded of her, in surprise, when and where she had heard Scholastica's voice. His whole attention was aroused; the Countess perceived it, and for a moment she hesitated. Then she bravely replied that she had seen the young girl in the musty old book-room where she spent her dreary life. At these words, uttered in a profoundly mocking tone, Benvolio had an extraordinary sensation. He was walking with the Countess in the garden of a palace, and they had just approached the low balustrade of a terrace which commanded a magnificent view. On one side were violet Apennines, dotted here and there with a gleaming castle or convent; on the other stood the great palace through whose galleries the two had just been strolling, with its walls incrusted with medallions and its cornice charged with statues. But Benvolio's heart began to beat; the tears sprang to his eyes; the perfect landscape around him faded away and turned to blankness, and there rose before him, distinctly, vividly present, the old brown room that looked into the dull northern garden, tenanted by the quiet figures he had once told himself that he loved. He had a choking sensation and a sudden overwhelming desire to return to his own country.

The Countess would say nothing more than that the fancy had taken her one day to go and see Scholastica. "I suppose I may go where I please!" she cried in the tone of the great lady who is accustomed to believe that her glance confers honour wherever it falls. "I am sure I did her no harm. She's a good little creature, and it's not her fault if she's so ridiculously plain." Benvolio looked at her intently, but he saw that he should learn nothing from her that she did not choose to tell. As he stood there he was amazed to find how natural, or at least how easy, it was to disbelieve her. She had been with the young girl; that accounted for anything; it accounted abundantly for Scholastica's painful constraint. What had the Countess said and done? what infernal trick had she played upon the poor girl's simplicity? He helplessly wondered, but he felt that she could be trusted to hit her mark. She had done him the honour to be jealous, and in order to alienate Scholastica she had invented some ingenious calumny against himself. He felt sick and angry, and for a week he treated his companion with grim indifference. The charm was broken, the cup of pleasure was drained. This remained no secret to the Countess, who was furious at the mistake she had made. At last she abruptly told Benvolio that the test had failed; they must separate; he would gratify her by taking his leave. He asked no second permission, but bade her farewell in the midst of her little retinue, and went journeying out of Italy with no other company than his thick-swarming memories and projects.

The first thing he did on reaching home was to repair to the Professor's abode. The old man's chair, for the first time, was empty, and Scholastica was not in the room. He went out into the garden, where, after wandering hither and thither, he found the young girl seated in a dusky arbour. She was dressed, as usual, in black; but her head was drooping, her empty hands were folded, and her sweet face was more joyless even than when he had last seen it. If she had been changed then, she was doubly changed now. Benvolio looked round, and as the Professor was nowhere visible, he immediately guessed the cause of her mourning aspect. The good old man had gone to join his immortal brothers, the classic sages, and Scholastica was utterly alone. She seemed frightened at seeing him, but he took her hand, and she let him sit down beside her. "Whatever you were once told that made you think ill of me is detestably false," he said. "I have the tenderest friendship for you, and now more than ever I should like to show it." She slowly gathered courage to meet his eyes; she found them reassuring, and at last, though she never told him in what way her mind had been poisoned, she suffered him to believe that her old confidence had come back. She told him how her father had died, and how, in spite of the philosophic maxims he had bequeathed to her for her consolation, she felt very lonely and helpless. Her uncle had offered her a maintenance, meagre but sufficient; she had the old serving-woman to keep her company, and she meant to live in her present abode and occupy herself with collecting her father's papers and giving them to the world according to a plan for which he had left particular directions. She seemed irresistibly tender and touching, and yet full of dignity and self-support. Benvolio fell in love with her again on the spot, and only abstained from telling her so because he remembered just in time that he had an engagement to be married to the

Countess, and that this understanding had not yet been formally rescinded. He paid Scholastica a long visit, and they went in together and rummaged over her father's books and papers. The old scholar's literary memoranda proved to be extremely valuable; it would be a useful and interesting task to give them to the world. When Scholastica heard Benvolio's high estimate of them her cheek began to glow and her spirit to revive. The present then was secure, she seemed to say to herself, and she would have occupation for many a month. He offered to give her every assistance in his power, and in consequence he came daily to see her. Scholastica lived so much out of the world that she was not obliged to trouble herself about vulgar gossip. Whatever jests were aimed at the young man for his visible devotion to a mysterious charmer, he was very sure that her ear was never wounded by base insinuations. The old serving-woman sat in a corner, nodding over her distaff, and the two friends held long confabulations over yellow manuscripts in which the commentary, it must be confessed, did not always adhere very closely to the text. Six months elapsed, and Benvolio found an ineffable charm in this mild mixture of sentiment and study. He had never in his life been so long of the same mind; it really seemed as if, as the phrase is, the fold were taken for ever—as if he had done with the world and were ready to live henceforth in the closet. He hardly thought of the Countess, and they had no correspondence. She was in Italy, in Greece, in the East, in the Holy Land, in places and situations that taxed the imagination.

One day, in the darkness of the vestibule, after he had left Scholastica, he was arrested by a little old man of sordid aspect, of whom he could make out hardly more than a pair of sharply-glowing eyes and an immense bald head, polished like a ball of ivory. He was a quite terrible little figure in his way, and Benvolio at first was frightened. "Mr. Poet," said the old man, "let me say a single word. I give my niece a maintenance. She may do what she likes. But she forfeits every penny of her allowance and her expectations if she is fool enough to marry a fellow who scribbles rhymes. I am told they are sometimes an hour finding two that will match! Good evening, Mr. Poet!" Benvolio heard a sound like the faint jingle of loose coin in a breeches pocket, and the old man abruptly retreated

into his domiciliary gloom. Benvolio had never seen him before, and he had no wish ever to see him again. He had not
proposed to himself to marry Scholastica, and even if he had,
I am pretty sure he would now have taken the modest view
of the matter and decided that his hand and heart were an
insufficient compensation for the relinquishment of a miser's
fortune. The young girl never spoke of her uncle; he lived
quite alone, apparently, haunting his upper chambers like a
restless ghost, and sending her, by the old serving-woman,
her slender monthly allowance, wrapped up in a piece of old
newspaper. It was shortly after this that the Countess at last
came back. Benvolio had been taking one of those long walks
to which he had always been addicted, and passing through
the public gardens on his way home, he had sat down on a
bench to rest. In a few moments a carriage came rolling by;
in it sat the Countess—beautiful, sombre, solitary. He rose
with a ceremonious salute, and she went her way. But in five
minutes she passed back again, and this time her carriage
stopped. She gave him a single glance, and he got in. For a
week afterward Scholastica vainly awaited him. What had happened? It had happened that though she had proved herself
both false and cruel, the Countess again asserted her charm,
and our precious hero again succumbed to it. But he resumed
his visits to Scholastica after an interval of neglect not long
enough to be unpardonable; the only difference was that now
they were not so frequent.

My story draws to a close, for I am afraid you have already
lost patience with the history of this amiable weathercock.
Another year ran its course, and the Professor's manuscripts
were arranged in great piles and almost ready for the printer.
Benvolio had had a constant hand in the work, and had found
it exceedingly interesting; it involved inquiries and researches
of the most stimulating and profitable kind. Scholastica was
very happy. Her friend was often absent for many days, during
which she knew he was leading the great world's life; but she
had learned that if she patiently waited, the pendulum would
swing back, and he would reappear and bury himself in their
books and papers and talk. And their talk, you may be sure,
was not all technical; they touched on everything that came
into their heads, and Benvolio by no means felt obliged to be

silent about those mundane matters as to which a vow of personal ignorance had been taken for his companion. He took
her into his poetic confidence, and read her everything he had
written since his return from Italy. The more he worked the
more he desired to work; and so, at this time, occupied as he
was with editing the Professor's manuscripts, he had never
been so productive on his own account. He wrote another
drama, on an Italian subject, which was performed with magnificent success; and this production he discussed with
Scholastica scene by scene and speech by speech. He proposed
to her to come and see it acted from a covered box, where
her seclusion would be complete. She seemed for an instant
to feel the force of the temptation; then she shook her head
with a frank smile, and said it was better not. The play was
dedicated to the Countess, who had suggested the subject to
him in Italy, where it had been imparted to her, as a family
anecdote, by one of her old princesses. This easy, fruitful,
complex life might have lasted for ever, but for two most regrettable events. *Might* have lasted I say; you observe I do not
affirm it positively. Scholastica lost her peace of mind; she was
suffering a secret annoyance. She concealed it as far as she
might from her friend, and with some success; for although
he suspected something and questioned her, she persuaded
him that it was his own fancy. In reality it was no fancy at all,
but the very uncomfortable fact that her shabby old uncle, the
miser, was a terrible thorn in her side. He had told Benvolio
that she might do as she liked, but he had recently revoked
this amiable concession. He informed her one day, by means
of an illegible note, scrawled with a blunt pencil, on the back
of an old letter, that her beggarly friend the Poet came to see
her altogether too often; that he was determined she never
should marry a crack-brained rhymester; and that he requested that before the sacrifice became too painful she would
be so good as to dismiss Mr. Benvolio. This was accompanied
by an intimation, more explicit than gracious, that he opened
his money-bags only for those who deferred to his incomparable wisdom. Scholastica was poor, and simple, and lonely;
but she was proud, for all that, with a shrinking and unexpressed pride of her own, and her uncle's charity, proffered
on these terms, became intolerably bitter to her soul. She sent

him word that she thanked him for his past liberality, but she
would no longer be a charge upon him. She said to herself
that she could work; she had a superior education; many
women, she knew, supported themselves. She even found
something inspiring in the idea of going out into the world
of which she knew so little, to seek her fortune. Her great
desire, however, was to keep her situation a secret from
Benvolio, and to prevent his knowing the sacrifice she was
making for him. This it is especially that proves she was proud.
It so happened that circumstances made secrecy possible. I
don't know whether the Countess had always an idea of marrying Benvolio, but her imperious vanity still suffered from
the spectacle of his divided allegiance, and it suggested to her
a truly malignant revenge. A brilliant political mission, to treat
of a special question, was about to be despatched to a neighbouring government, and half a dozen young men of eminence were to be attached to it. The Countess had influence
at Court, and without saying anything to Benvolio, she immediately urged his claim to a post on the ground of his distinguished services to literature. She pulled her wires so
cleverly that in a very short time she had the pleasure of presenting him his appointment on a great sheet of parchment,
from which the royal seal dangled by a blue ribbon. It involved an exile of but a few weeks, and to this with her eye
on the sequel of her project, she was able to resign herself.
Benvolio's imagination took fire at the thought of spending a
month at a foreign court, in the very hotbed of consummate
diplomacy; this was a phase of experience with which he was
as yet unacquainted. He departed, and no sooner had he gone
than the Countess, at a venture, waited upon Scholastica. She
knew the girl was poor, and she believed that in spite of her
homely virtues she would not, if the opportunity were placed
before her in a certain light, prove implacably indisposed to
better her fortunes. She knew nothing of the young girl's contingent expectations from her uncle, and her interference at
this juncture was simply a remarkable coincidence. She laid
before her a proposal from a certain great lady, whose husband, an eminent general, had just been dubbed governor of
an island on the other side of the globe. This lady desired a
preceptress for her children; she had heard of Scholastica's

merit, and she ventured to hope that she might persuade her to accompany her to the Antipodes and reside in her family. The offer was brilliant; to Scholastica it seemed mysteriously and providentially opportune. Nevertheless she hesitated, and demanded time for reflection; without telling herself why, she wished to wait till Benvolio should return. He wrote her two or three letters, full of the echoes of his brilliant actual life, and without a word about the things that were nearer her own experience. The month elapsed, but he was still absent. Scholastica, who was in correspondence with the governor's wife, delayed her decision from week to week. She had sold her father's manuscripts to a publisher, for a very small sum, and gone, meanwhile, to live in a convent. At last the governor's lady demanded her ultimatum. The poor girl scanned the horizon and saw no rescuing friend; Benvolio was still at the court of Illyria! What she saw was the Countess's fine eyes eagerly watching her over the top of her fan. They seemed to contain a horrible menace, and to hold somehow her happiness at their mercy. Her heart sank; she gathered up her few possessions and set sail, with her illustrious protectors, for the Antipodes. Shortly after her departure Benvolio returned. He felt a terrible pang of rage and grief when he learned that she had gone; he went to the Countess, prepared to accuse her of the basest treachery. But she checked his reproaches by arts that she had never gone so far as to use before, and promised him that, if he would trust her, he should never miss that pale-eyed little governess. It can hardly be supposed that he believed her; but he appears to have been guilty of letting himself be persuaded without belief. For some time after this he almost lived with the Countess. He had, with infinite pains, purchased from his neighbour, the miser, the right of occupancy of the late Professor's apartment. This repulsive proprietor, in spite of his constitutional aversion to rhymesters, had not resisted the financial argument, and seemed greatly amazed that a poet should have a dollar to spend. Scholastica had left all things in their old places, but Benvolio, for the present, never went into the room. He turned the key in the door, and kept it in his waistcoat-pocket, where, while he was with the Countess, his fingers fumbled with it. Several months rolled by, and the Countess's promise was not verified. He missed Scholastica wofully, and missed her more as time elapsed. He began at last to go to the old brown room and to try to do some work there. He only half succeeded in a fashion; it seemed dark and empty; doubly empty when he remembered what it might have been. Suddenly he ceased to visit the Countess; a long time passed without her seeing him. She met him at another house, and had some remarkable words with him. She covered him with reproaches that were doubtless deserved, but he made her an answer that caused her to open her eyes and flush, and admit afterward that, for a clever woman, she had been a great fool. "Don't you see," he said, "can't you imagine, that I cared for you only by con-trast? You took the trouble to kill the contrast, and with it you killed everything else. For a constancy I prefer *this!*" And he tapped his poetic brow. He never saw the Countess again.

I rather regret now that I said at the beginning of my story that it was not to be a fairy-tale; otherwise I should be at liberty to relate, with harmonious geniality, that if Benvolio missed Scholastica, he missed the Countess also, and led an extremely fretful and unproductive life, until one day he sailed for the Antipodes and brought Scholastica home. After this he began to produce again; only, many people said that his poetry had become dismally dull. But excuse me; I am writing as if it *were* a fairy-tale!

Crawford's Consistency

WE WERE great friends, and it was natural that he should have let me know with all the promptness of his ardor that his happiness was complete. Ardor is here, perhaps, a misleading word, for Crawford's passion burned with a still and hidden flame; if he had written sonnets to his mistress's eyebrow, he had never declaimed them in public. But he was deeply in love; he had been full of tremulous hopes and fears, and his happiness, for several weeks, had hung by a hair—the extremely fine line that appeared to divide the yea and nay of the young lady's parents. The scale descended at last with their heavily-weighted consent in it, and Crawford gave himself up to tranquil bliss. He came to see me at my office—my name, on the little tin placard beneath my window, was garnished with an M. D., as vivid as new gilding could make it—long before that period of the morning at which my irrepressible buoyancy had succumbed to the teachings of experience (as it usually did about twelve o'clock), and resigned itself to believe that that particular day was not to be distinguished by the advent of the female form that haunted my dreams—the confiding old lady, namely, with a large account at the bank, and a mild, but expensive chronic malady. On that day I quite forgot the paucity of my patients and the vanity of my hopes in my enjoyment of Crawford's contagious felicity. If we had been less united in friendship, I might have envied him; but as it was, with my extreme admiration and affection for him, I felt for half an hour as if I were going to marry the lovely Elizabeth myself. I reflected after he had left me that I was very glad I was not, for lovely as Miss Ingram was, she had always inspired me with a vague mistrust. There was no harm in her, certainly; but there was nothing else either. I don't know to what I compared her—to a blushing rose that had no odor, to a blooming peach that had no taste. All that nature had asked of her was to be the prettiest girl of her time, and this request she obeyed to the letter. But when, of a morning, she had opened wide her beautiful, candid eyes, and half parted her clear, pink lips, and gathered up her splendid golden tresses, her day, as far as her own opportunity was concerned, was at an end; she had put her house in order, and she could fold her arms. She did so invariably, and it was in this attitude that Crawford saw her and fell in love with her. I could heartily congratulate him, for the fact that a blooming statue would make no wife for me, did not in the least discredit his own choice. I was human and erratic; I had an uneven temper and a prosaic soul. I wished to get as much as I gave—to be the planet, in short, and not the satellite. But Crawford had really virtue enough for two—enough of vital fire, of intelligence and devotion. He could afford to marry an inanimate beauty, for he had the wisdom which would supply her shortcomings, and the generosity which would forgive them.

Crawford was a tall man, and not particularly well made. He had, however, what is called a gentlemanly figure, and he had a very fine head—the head of a man of books, a student, a philosopher, such as he really was. He had a dark coloring, thin, fine black hair, a very clear, lucid, dark gray eye, and features of a sort of softly-vigorous outline. It was as if his face had been cast first in a rather rugged and irregular mold, and the image had then been lightly retouched, here and there, by some gentler, more feminine hand. His expression was singular; it was a look which I can best describe as a sort of intelligent innocence—the look of an absent-minded seraph. He knew, if you insisted upon it, about the corruptions of this base world; but, left to himself, he never thought of them. What he did think of, I can hardly tell you: of a great many things, often, in which I was not needed. Of this, long and well as I had known him, I was perfectly conscious. I had never got behind him, as it were; I had never walked all round him. He was reserved, as I am inclined to think that all first rate men are; not capriciously or consciously reserved, but reserved in spite of, and in the midst of, an extreme frankness. For most people he was a clear-visaged, scrupulously polite young man, who, in giving up business so suddenly, had done a thing which required a good deal of charitable explanation, and who was not expected to express any sentiments more personal than a literary opinion re-inforced by the name of some authority, as to whose titles and attributes much vagueness of knowledge was excusable. For me, his literary opinions were the lightest of his sentiments; his good manners, too, I am sure, cost him nothing. Bad manners are the result of irritability, and as Crawford was not irritable he found civility very easy. But if his urbanity was not victory over a morose disposition, it was at least the expression of a very agreeable character. He talked a great deal, though not volubly, stammering a little, and casting about him for his words. When you suggested one, he always accepted it thankfully,— though he sometimes brought in a little later the expression he had been looking for and which had since occurred to him. He had a great deal of gayety, and made jokes and enjoyed them—laughing constantly, with a laugh that was not so much audible as visible. He was extremely deferential to old people, and among the fairer sex, his completest conquests, perhaps, were the ladies of sixty-five and seventy. He had also a great kindness for shabby people, if they were only shabby enough, and I remember seeing him, one summer afternoon, carrying a baby across a crowded part of Broadway, accompanied by its mother,—a bewildered pauper, lately arrived from Europe. Crawford's father had left him a very good property; his income, in New York, in those days, passed for a very easy one. Mr. Crawford was a cotton-broker, and on his son's leaving college, he took him into his business. But shortly after his father's death he sold out his interest in the firm—very quietly, and without asking any one's advice, because, as he told me, he hated buying and selling. There were other things, of course, in the world that he hated too, but this is the only thing of which I remember to have heard him say it. He had a large house, quite to himself (he had lost his mother early, and his brothers were dispersed); he filled it with books and scientific instruments, and passed most of his time in reading and in making awkward experiments. He had the tastes of a scholar, and he consumed a vast number of octavos; but in the way of the natural sciences, his curiosity was greater than his dexterity. I used to laugh at his experiments and, as a thrifty neophyte in medicine, to deprecate his lavish expenditure of precious drugs. Unburdened, independent, master of an all-sufficient fortune, and of the best education that the country could afford, good-looking, gallant, amiable, urbane

—Crawford at seven and twenty might fairly be believed to have drawn the highest prizes in life. And, indeed, except that it was a pity he had not stuck to business, no man heard a word of disparagement either of his merit or of his felicity. On the other hand, too, he was not envied—envied at any rate with any degree of bitterness. We are told that though the world worships success, it hates successful people. Certainly it never hated Crawford. Perhaps he was not regarded in the light of a success, but rather of an ornament, of an agreeable gift to society. The world likes to be pleased, and there was something pleasing in Crawford's general physiognomy and position. They rested the eyes; they were a gratifying change. Perhaps we were even a little proud of having among us so harmonious an embodiment of the amenities of life.

In spite of his bookish tastes and habits, Crawford was not a recluse. I remember his once saying to me that there were some sacrifices that only a man of genius was justified in making to science, and he knew very well that he was not a man of genius. He was not, thank heaven; if he had been, he would have been a much more difficult companion. It was never apparent, indeed, that he was destined to make any great use of his acquisitions. Every one supposed, of course, that he would "write something;" but he never put pen to paper. He liked to bury his nose in books for the hour's pleasure; he had no dangerous *arrière pensée*, and he was simply a very perfect specimen of a class which has fortunately always been numerous—the class of men who contribute to the advancement of learning by zealously opening their ears and religiously closing their lips. He was fond of society, and went out, as the phrase is, a great deal,—the mammas in especial, making him extremely welcome. What the daughters, in general, thought of him, I hardly know; I suspect that the younger ones often preferred worse men. Crawford's merits were rather thrown away upon little girls. To a considerable number of wise virgins, however, he must have been an object of high admiration, and if a good observer had been asked to pick out in the whole town, the most propitious victim to matrimony, he would certainly have designated my friend. There was nothing to be said against him—there was not a shadow in the picture. He himself, indeed, pretended to be in no hurry to marry, and I heard him more than once declare, that he did not know what he should do with a wife, or what a wife would do with him. Of course we often talked of this matter, and I—upon whom the burden of bachelorhood sat heavy—used to say, that in his place, with money to keep a wife, I would change my condition on the morrow. Crawford gave a great many opposing reasons; of course the real one was that he was very happy as he was, and that the most circumspect marriage is always a risk.

"A man should only marry in self-defense," he said, "as Luther became Protestant. He should wait till he is driven to the wall."

Some time passed and our Luther stood firm. I began to despair of ever seeing a pretty Mrs. Crawford offer me a white hand from my friend's fireside, and I had to console myself with the reflection, that some of the finest persons of whom history makes mention, had been celibates, and that a desire to lead a single life is not necessarily a proof of a morose disposition.

"Oh, I give you up," I said at last. "I hoped that if you did not marry for your own sake, you would at least marry for mine. It would make your house so much pleasanter for me. But you have no heart! To avenge myself, I shall myself take a wife on the first opportunity. She shall be as pretty as a picture, and you shall never enter my doors."

"No man should be accounted single till he is dead," said Crawford. "I have been reading Stendhal lately, and learning the philosophy of the *coup de foudre*. It is not impossible that there is a *coup de foudre* waiting for me. All I can say is that it will be lightning from a clear sky."

The lightning fell, in fact, a short time afterward. Crawford saw Miss Ingram, admired her, observed her, and loved her. The impression she produced upon him was indeed a sort of summing up of the impression she produced upon society at large. The circumstances of her education and those under which she made her first appearance in the world, were such as to place her beauty in extraordinary relief. She had been brought up more in the manner of an Italian princess of the middle ages—sequestered from conflicting claims of ward-ship—than as the daughter of a plain American citizen. Up to her eighteenth year, it may be said, mortal eye had scarcely beheld her; she lived behind high walls and triple locks, through which an occasional rumor of her beauty made its way into the world. Mrs. Ingram was a second or third cousin of my mother, but the two ladies, between whom there reigned a scanty sympathy, had never made much of the kinship; I had inherited no claim to intimacy with the family, and Elizabeth was a perfect stranger to me. Her parents had, for economy, gone to live in the country—at Orange—and it was there, in a high-hedged old garden, that her childhood and youth were spent. The first definite mention of her loveliness came to me from old Dr. Beadle, who had been called to attend her in a slight illness. (The Ingrams were poor, but their daughter was their golden goose, and to secure the most expensive medical skill was but an act of common prudence.) Dr. Beadle had a high appreciation of a pretty patient; he, of course, kept it within bounds on the field of action, but he enjoyed expressing it afterward with the freedom of a profound anatomist, to a younger colleague. Elizabeth Ingram, according to this report, was perfect in every particular, and she was being kept in cotton in preparation for her *début* in New York. He talked about her for a quarter of an hour, and concluded with an eloquent pinch of snuff; whereupon I remembered that she was, after a fashion, my cousin, and that pretty cousins are a source of felicity, in this hard world, which no man can afford to neglect. I took a holiday, jumped into the train, and arrived at Orange. There, in a pretty cottage, in a shaded parlor, I found a small, spare woman with a high forehead and a pointed chin, whom I immediately felt to be that Sabrina Ingram, in her occasional allusions to whom my poor mother had expended the very small supply of acerbity with which nature had intrusted her.

"I am told my cousin is extremely beautiful," I said. "I should like so much to see her."

The interview was not prolonged. Mrs. Ingram was frigidly polite; she answered that she was highly honored by my curiosity, but that her daughter had gone to spend the day with a friend ten miles away. On my departure, as I turned to latch the garden gate behind me, I saw dimly through an upper window, the gleam of a golden head, and the orbits of two

gazing eyes. I kissed my hand to the apparition, and agreed
with Dr. Beadle that my cousin was a beauty. But if her image
had been dim, that of her mother had been distinct.

They came up to New York the next winter, took a house,
gave a great party, and presented the young girl to an astonished world. I succeeded in making little of our cousinship,
for Mrs. Ingram did not approve of me, and she gave Elizabeth
instructions in consequence. Elizabeth obeyed them, gave me
the tips of her fingers, and answered me in monosyllables.
Indifference was never more neatly expressed, and I wondered
whether this was mere passive compliance, or whether the girl
had put a grain of her own intelligence into it. She appeared
to have no more intelligence than a snowy-fleeced lamb, but
I fancied that she was, by instinct, a shrewd little politician.
Nevertheless, I forgave her, for my last feeling about her was
one of compassion. She might be as soft as swan's-down, I
said; it could not be a pleasant thing to be her mother's
daughter, all the same. Mrs. Ingram had black bands of hair,
without a white thread, which descended only to the tops of
her ears, and were there spread out very wide, and polished
like metallic plates. She had small, conscious eyes, and the tall
white forehead I have mentioned, which resembled a high
gable beneath a steep roof. Her chin looked like her forehead
reversed, and her lips were perpetually graced with a thin, false
smile. I had seen how little it cost them to tell a categorical
fib. Poor Mr. Ingram was a helpless colossus; an immense man
with a small plump face, a huge back to his neck, and a pair
of sloping shoulders. In talking to you, he generally looked
across at his wife, and it was easy to see that he was mortally
afraid of her.

For this lady's hesitation to bestow her daughter's hand
upon Crawford, there was a sufficiently good reason. He had
money, but he had not money enough. It was a very comfortable match, but it was not a splendid one, and Mrs. Ingram, in putting the young girl forward, had primed herself
with the highest expectations. The marriage was so good that
it was a vast pity it was not a little better. If Crawford's income
had only been twice as large again, Mrs. Ingram would have
pushed Elizabeth into his arms, relaxed in some degree the
consuming eagerness with which she viewed the social field,

and settled down, possibly, to contentment and veracity. That was a bad year in the matrimonial market, for higher offers were not freely made. Elizabeth was greatly admired, but the ideal suitor did not present himself. I suspect that Mrs. Ingram's charms as a mother-in-law had been accurately gauged. Crawford pushed his suit, with low-toned devotion, and he was at last accepted with a good grace. There had been, I think, a certain amount of general indignation at his being kept waiting, and Mrs. Ingram was accused here and there, of not knowing a first-rate man when she saw one. "I never said she was honest," a trenchant critic was heard to observe, "but at least I supposed she was clever." Crawford was not afraid of her; he told me so distinctly. "I defy her to quarrel with me," he said, "and I don't despair of making her like me."

"Like you!" I answered. "That's easily done. The difficulty will be in your liking her."

"Oh, I do better—I admire her," he said. "She knows so perfectly what she wants. It's a rare quality. I shall have a very fine woman for my mother-in-law."

Elizabeth's own preference bore down the scale in Crawford's favor a little, I think; how much I hardly know. She liked him, and thought her mother took little account of her likes (and the young girl was too well-behaved to expect it). Mrs. Ingram reflected probably that her pink and white complexion would last longer if she were married to a man she fancied. At any rate, as I have said, the engagement was at last announced, and Crawford came in person to tell me of it. I had never seen a happier-looking man; and his image, as I beheld it that morning, has lived in my memory all these years, as an embodiment of youthful confidence and deep security. He had said that the art of knowing what one wants was rare, but he apparently possessed it. He had got what he wanted, and the sense of possession was exquisite to him. I see again my shabby little consulting-room, with an oil-cloth on the floor, and a paper, representing seven hundred and forty times (I once counted them) a young woman with a pitcher on her head, on the walls; and in the midst of it I see Crawford standing upright, with his thumbs in the arm-holes of his waistcoat, his head thrown back, and his eyes as radiant as two planets.

"You are too odiously happy," I said. "I should like to give you a dose of something to tone you down."

"If you could give me a sleeping potion," he answered, "I should be greatly obliged to you. Being engaged is all very well, but I want to be married. I should like to sleep through my engagement—to wake up and find myself a husband."

"Is your wedding-day fixed?" I asked.

"The twenty-eighth of April—three months hence. I declined to leave the house last night before it was settled. I offered three weeks, but Elizabeth laughed me to scorn. She says it will take a month to make her wedding-dress. Mrs. Ingram has a list of reasons as long as your arm, and every one of them is excellent; that is the abomination of it. She has a genius for the practical. I mean to profit by it; I shall make her turn my mill-wheel for me. But meanwhile it's an eternity!"

"Don't complain of good things lasting long," said I. "Such eternities are always too short. I have always heard that the three months before marriage are the happiest time of life. I advise you to make the most of these."

"Oh, I am happy, I don't deny it," cried Crawford. "But I propose to be happier yet." And he marched away with the step of a sun-god beginning his daily circuit.

He was happier yet, in the sense that with each succeeding week he became more convinced of the charms of Elizabeth Ingram, and more profoundly attuned to the harmonies of prospective matrimony. I, of course, saw little of him, for he was always in attendance upon his betrothed, at the dwelling of whose parents I was a rare visitor. Whenever I did see him, he seemed to have sunk another six inches further into the mystic depths. He formally swallowed his words when I recalled to him his former brave speeches about the single life.

"All I can say is," he answered, "that I was an immeasurable donkey. Every argument that I formerly used in favor of not marrying, now seems to me to have an exactly opposite application. Every reason that used to seem to me so good for not taking a wife, now seems to me the best reason in the world for taking one. I not to marry, of all men on earth! Why, I am made on purpose for it, and if the thing did not exist, I should have invented it. In fact, I think I *have* invented some little improvements in the institution—of an extremely conservative kind—and when I put them into practice, you shall tell me what you think of them."

This lasted several weeks. The day after Crawford told me of his engagement, I had gone to pay my respects to the two ladies, but they were not at home, and I wrote my compliments on a card. I did not repeat my visit until the engagement had become an old story—some three weeks before the date appointed for the marriage—I had then not seen Crawford in several days. I called in the evening, and was ushered into a small parlor reserved by Mrs. Ingram for familiar visitors. Here I found Crawford's mother-in-law that was to be, seated, with an air of great dignity, on a low chair, with her hands folded rigidly in her lap, and her chin making an acuter angle than ever. Before the fire stood Peter Ingram, with his hands under his coat-tails; as soon as I came in, he fixed his eyes upon his wife. "She has either just been telling, or she is just about to tell, some particularly big fib," I said to myself. Then I expressed my regret at not having found my cousin at home upon my former visit, and hoped it was not too late to offer my felicitations upon Elizabeth's marriage.

For some moments, Mr. Ingram and his wife were silent; after which, Mrs. Ingram said with a little cough, "It *is* too late."

"Really?" said I. "What has happened?"

"Had we better tell him, my dear?" asked Mr. Ingram.

"I didn't mean to receive any one," said Mrs. Ingram. "It was a mistake your coming in."

"I don't offer to go," I answered, "because I suspect that you have some sorrow. I couldn't think of leaving you at such a moment."

Mr. Ingram looked at me with huge amazement. I don't think he detected my irony, but he had a vague impression that I was measuring my wits with his wife. His ponderous attention acted upon me as an incentive, and I continued,

"Crawford has been behaving badly, I suspect?—Oh, the shabby fellow!"

"Oh, not exactly behaving," said Mr. Ingram; "not exactly badly. We can't say that, my dear, eh?"

"It is proper the world should know it," said Mrs. Ingram,

addressing herself to me; "and as I suspect you are a great gossip, the best way to diffuse the information will be to intrust it to you."

"Pray tell me," I said bravely, "and you may depend upon it the world shall have an account of it." By this time I knew what was coming. "Perhaps you hardly need tell me," I went on. "I have guessed your news; it is indeed most shocking. Crawford has broken his engagement!"

Mrs. Ingram started up, surprised into self-betrayal. "Oh, really?" she cried, with a momentary flash of elation. But in an instant she perceived that I had spoken fantastically, and her elation flickered down into keen annoyance. But she faced the situation with characteristic firmness. "We have broken the engagement," she said. "Elizabeth has broken it with our consent."

"You have turned Crawford away?" I cried.

"We have requested him to consider everything at an end."

"Poor Crawford!" I exclaimed with ardor.

At this moment the door was thrown open, and Crawford in person stood on the threshold. He paused an instant, like a falcon hovering; then he darted forward at Mr. Ingram.

"In heaven's name," he cried, "what is the meaning of your letter?"

Mr. Ingram looked frightened and backed majestically away. "Really, sir," he said; "I must beg you to desist from your threats."

Crawford turned to Mrs. Ingram; he was intensely pale and profoundly agitated. "Please tell me," he said, stepping toward her with clasped hands. "I don't understand—I can't take it this way. It's a thunderbolt!"

"We were in hopes you would have the kindness not to make a scene," said Mrs. Ingram. "It is very painful for us, too, but we cannot discuss the matter. I was afraid you would come."

"Afraid I would come!" cried Crawford. "Could you have believed I would not come? Where is Elizabeth?"

"You cannot see her!"

"I cannot see her?"

"It is impossible. It is her wish," said Mrs. Ingram.

Crawford stood staring, his eyes distended with grief, and rage, and helpless wonder. I have never seen a man so thoroughly agitated, but I have also never seen a man exert such an effort at self-control. He sat down; and then, after a moment—"What have I done?" he asked.

Mr. Ingram walked away to the window, and stood closely examining the texture of the drawn curtains. "You have done nothing, my dear Mr. Crawford," said Mrs. Ingram. "We accuse you of nothing. We are very reasonable; I'm sure you can't deny that, whatever you may say. Mr. Ingram explained everything in the letter. We have simply thought better of it. We have decided that we can't part with our child for the present. She is all we have, and she is so very young. We ought never to have consented. But you urged us so, and we were so good-natured. We must keep her with us."

"Is that all you have to say?" asked Crawford.

"It seems to me it is quite enough," said Mrs. Ingram.

Crawford leaned his head on his hands. "I must have done something without knowing it," he said at last. "In heaven's name tell me what it is, and I will do penance and make reparation to the uttermost limit."

Mr. Ingram turned round, rolling his expressionless eyes in quest of virtuous inspiration. "We can't say that you have done anything; that would be going too far. But if you had, we would have forgiven you."

"Where is Elizabeth?" Crawford again demanded.

"In her own apartment," said Mrs. Ingram majestically.

"Will you please to send for her?"

"Really, sir, we must decline to expose our child to this painful scene."

"Your tenderness should have begun farther back. Do you expect me to go away without seeing her?"

"We request that you will."

Crawford turned to me. "Was such a request ever made before?" he asked, in a trembling voice.

"For your own sake," said Mrs. Ingram, "go away without seeing her."

"For my own sake? What do you mean?"

Mrs. Ingram, very pale, and with her thin lips looking like

the blades of a pair of scissors, turned to her husband. "Mr. Ingram," she said, "rescue me from this violence. Speak out—do your duty."

Mr. Ingram advanced with the air and visage of the stage manager of a theater, when he steps forward to announce that the favorite of the public will not be able to play. "Since you drive us so hard, sir, we must tell the painful truth. My poor child would rather have had nothing said about it. The truth is that she has mistaken the character of her affection for you. She has a high esteem for you, but she does not love you."

Crawford stood silent, looking with formidable eyes from the father to the mother. "I must insist upon seeing Elizabeth," he said at last.

Mrs. Ingram gave a toss of her head. "Remember it was your own demand!" she cried, and rustled stiffly out of the room.

We remained silent; Mr. Ingram sat slowly rubbing his knees, and Crawford, pacing up and down, eyed him askance with an intensely troubled frown, as one might eye a person just ascertained to be liable to some repulsive form of dementia. At the end of five minutes, Mrs. Ingram returned, clutching the arm of her daughter, whom she pushed into the room. Then followed the most extraordinary scene of which I have ever been witness.

Crawford strode toward the young girl, and seized her by both hands; she let him take them, and stood looking at him. "Is this horrible news true?" he cried. "What infernal machination is at the bottom of it?"

Elizabeth Ingram appeared neither more nor less composed than on most occasions; the pink and white of her cheeks was as pure as usual, her golden tresses were as artistically braided, and her eyes showed no traces of weeping. Her face was never expressive, and at this moment it indicated neither mortification nor defiance. She met her lover's eyes with the exquisite blue of her own pupils, and she looked as beautiful as an angel. "I am very sorry that we must separate," she said. "But I have mistaken the nature of my affection for you. I have the highest esteem for you, but I do not love you."

I listened to this, and the clear, just faintly trembling, child-like tone in which it was uttered, with absorbing wonder. Was the girl the most consummate of actresses, or had she, literally, no more sensibility than an expensive wax doll? I never discovered, and she has remained to this day, one of the unsolved mysteries of my experience. I incline to believe that she was, morally, absolutely nothing but the hollow reed through which her mother spoke, and that she was really no more cruel now than she had been kind before. But there was something monstrous in her quiet, flute-like utterance of Crawford's damnation.

"Do you say this from your own heart, or have you been instructed to say it? You use the same words your father has just used."

"What can the poor child do better in her trouble than use her father's words?" cried Mrs. Ingram.

"Elizabeth," cried Crawford, "you don't love me?"

"No, Mr. Crawford."

"Why did you ever say so?"

"I never said so."

He stared at her in amazement, and then, after a little—"It is very true," he exclaimed. "You never said so. It was only I who said so."

"Good-bye!" said Elizabeth; and turning away, she glided out of the room.

"I hope you are satisfied, sir," said Mrs. Ingram. "The poor child is before all things sincere."

In calling this scene the most extraordinary that I ever beheld, I had particularly in mind the remarkable attitude of Crawford at this juncture. He effected a change of base, as it were, under the eyes of the enemy—he descended to the depths and rose to the surface again. Horrified, bewildered, outraged, fatally wounded at heart, he took the full measure of his loss, gauged its irreparableness, and, by an amazing effort of the will, while one could count fifty, superficially accepted the situation.

"I have understood nothing!" he said. "Good-night."

He went away, and of course I went with him. Outside the house, in the darkness, he paused and looked around at me.

"What were you doing there?" he asked.

"I had come—rather late in the day—to pay a visit of congratulation. I rather missed it."

"Do you understand—can you imagine?" He had taken his hat off, and he was pressing his hand to his head.

"They have backed out, simply!" I said. "The marriage had never satisfied their ambition—you were not rich enough. Perhaps they have heard of something better."

He stood gazing, lost in thought. "They," I had said; but he, of course, was thinking only of *her*; thinking with inexpressible bitterness. He made no allusion to her, and I never afterward heard him make one. I felt a great compassion for him, but knew not how to help him, nor hardly, even, what to say. It would have done me good to launch some objurgation against the precious little puppet, within doors, but this delicacy forbade. I felt that Crawford's silence covered a fathomless sense of injury; but the injury was terribly real, and I could think of no healing words. He was injured in his love and his pride, his hopes and his honor, his sense of justice and of decency.

"To treat *me* so!" he said at last, in a low tone. "Me! me!—are they blind—are they imbecile? Haven't they seen what I have been to them—what I was going to be?"

"Yes, they are blind brutes!" I cried. "Forget them—don't think of them again. They are not worth it."

He turned away and, in the dark empty street, he leaned his arm on the iron railing that guarded a flight of steps, and dropped his head upon it. I left him standing so a few moments—I could just hear his sobs. Then I passed my arm into his own and walked home with him. Before I left him, he had recovered his outward composure.

After this, so far as one could see, he kept it uninterruptedly. I saw him the next day, and for several days afterward. He looked like a man who had had a heavy blow, and who had yet not been absolutely stunned. He neither raved nor lamented, nor descanted upon his wrong. He seemed to be trying to shuffle it away, to resume his old occupations, and to appeal to the good offices of the arch-healer, Time. He looked very ill—pale, preoccupied, heavy-eyed, but this was an inevitable tribute to his deep disappointment. He gave me no particular opportunity to make consoling speeches, and not being eloquent, I was more inclined to take one by force. Moral and sentimental platitudes always seemed to me partic-

CRAWFORD'S CONSISTENCY 141

ularly flat upon my own lips, and, addressed to Crawford, they would have been fatally so. Nevertheless, I once told him with some warmth, that he was giving signal proof of being a philosopher. He knew that people always end by getting over things, and he was showing himself able to traverse with a stride a great moral waste. He made no rejoinder at the moment, but an hour later, as we were separating, he told me, with some formalism, that he could not take credit for virtues he had not.

"I am not a philosopher," he said; "on the contrary. And I am not getting over it."

His misfortune excited great compassion among all his friends, and I imagine that this sentiment was expressed, in some cases, with well-meaning but injudicious frankness. The Ingrams were universally denounced, and whenever they appeared in public, at this time, were greeted with significant frigidity. Nothing could have better proved the friendly feeling, the really quite tender regard and admiration that were felt for Crawford, than the manner in which every one took up his cause. He knew it, and I heard him exclaim more than once with intense bitterness that he was that abject thing, an "object of sympathy." Some people flattered themselves that they had made the town, socially speaking, too hot to hold Miss Elizabeth and her parents. The Ingrams anticipated by several weeks their projected departure for Newport—they had given out that they were to spend the summer there—and, quitting New York, quite left, like the gentleman in "The School for Scandal," their reputations behind them.

I continued to observe Crawford with interest, and, although I did full justice to his wisdom and self-control, when the summer arrived I was ill at ease about him. He led exactly the life he had led before his engagement, and mingled with society neither more nor less. If he disliked to feel that pitying heads were being shaken over him, or voices lowered in tribute to his misadventure, he made at least no visible effort to ignore these manifestations, and he paid to the full the penalty of being "interesting." But, on the other hand, he showed no disposition to drown his sorrow in violent pleasure, to deafen himself to its echoes. He never alluded to his disappointment, he discharged all the duties of politeness, and questioned people about their own tribulations or satisfactions as deferentially as if he had had no weight upon his heart. Nevertheless, I knew that his wound was rankling—that he had received a dent, and that he would keep it. From this point onward, however, I do not pretend to understand his conduct. I only was witness of it, and I relate what I saw. I do not pretend to speak of his motives.

I had the prospect of leaving town for a couple of months —a friend and fellow-physician in the country having offered me his practice while he took a vacation. Before I went, I made a point of urging Crawford to seek a change of scene—to go abroad, to travel and distract himself.

"To distract myself from what?" he asked, with his usual clear smile.

"From the memory of the vile trick those people played you."

"Do I look, do I behave as if I remembered it?" he demanded with sudden gravity.

"You behave very well, but I suspect that it is at the cost of a greater effort than it is wholesome for a man—quite unassisted—to make."

"I shall stay where I am," said Crawford, "and I shall behave as I have behaved—to the end. I find the effort, so far as there is an effort, extremely wholesome."

"Well, then," said I, "I shall take great satisfaction in hearing that you have fallen in love again. I should be delighted to know that you were well married."

He was silent a while, and then—"It is not impossible," he said. But, before I left him, he laid his hand on my arm, and, after looking at me with great gravity for some time, declared that it would please him extremely that I should never again allude to his late engagement.

The night before I left town, I went to spend half an hour with him. It was the end of June, the weather was hot, and I proposed that instead of sitting indoors, we should take a stroll. In those days, there stood, in the center of the city, a concert-garden, of a somewhat primitive structure, into which a few of the more adventurous representatives of the best society were occasionally seen—under stress of hot weather—to penetrate. It had trees and arbors, and little fountains and small tables, at which ice-creams and juleps were, after hope deferred, dispensed. Its musical attractions fell much below the modern standard, and consisted of three old fiddlers playing stale waltzes, or an itinerant ballad-singer, vocalizing in a language perceived to be foreign, but not further identified, and accompanied by a young woman who performed upon the triangle, and collected tribute at the tables. Most of the frequenters of this establishment were people who wore their gentility lightly, or had none at all to wear; but in compensation (in the latter case), they were generally provided with a substantial sweetheart. We sat down among the rest, and had each a drink with a straw in it, while we listened to a cracked Italian tenor in a velvet jacket and ear-rings. At the end of half an hour, Crawford proposed we should withdraw, whereupon I busied myself with paying for our juleps. There was some delay in making change, during which, my attention wandered; it was some ten minutes before the waiter returned. When at last he restored me my dues, I said to Crawford that I was ready to depart. He was looking another way and did not hear me; I repeated my observation, and then he started a little, looked round, and said that he would like to remain longer. In a moment I perceived the apparent cause of his changing mind. I checked myself just in time from making a joke about it, and yet—as I did so—I said to myself that it was surely not a thing one could take seriously.

Two persons had within a few moments come to occupy a table near our own. One was a weak-eyed young man with a hat poised into artful crookedness upon a great deal of stiffly brushed and much-anointed straw-colored hair, and a harmless scowl of defiance at the world in general from under certain bare visible eyebrows. The defiance was probably prompted by the consciousness of the attractions of the person who accompanied him. This was a woman, still young, and to a certain extent pretty, dressed in a manner which showed that she regarded a visit to a concert-garden as a thing to be taken seriously. Her beauty was of the robust order, her coloring high, her glance unshrinking, and her hands large and red. These last were encased in black lace mittens. She had a small dark eye, of a peculiarly piercing quality, set in her head as flatly as a button-hole in a piece of cotton cloth, and a lower lip which protruded beyond the upper one. She carried her head like a person who pretended to have something in it, and she from time to time surveyed the ample expanse of her corsage with a complacent sense of there being something in that too. She was a large woman, and, when standing upright, must have been much taller than her companion. She had a certain conscious dignity of demeanor, turned out her little finger as she ate her pink ice-cream, and said very little to the young man, who was evidently only her opportunity, and not her ideal. She looked about her, while she consumed her refreshment, with a hard, flat, idle stare, which was not that of an adventuress, but that of a person pretentiously and vulgarly respectable. Crawford, I saw, was observing her narrowly, but his observation was earnestly exercised, and she was not—at first, at least,—aware of it. I wondered, nevertheless, why he was observing her. It was not his habit to stare at strange women, and the charms of this florid damsel were not such as to appeal to his fastidious taste.

"I see you are struck by our lovely neighbor," I said. "Have you ever seen her before?"

"Yes!" he presently answered. "In imagination!"

"One's imagination," I answered, "would seem to be the last place in which to look for such a figure as that. She belongs to the most sordid reality."

"She is very fine in her way," said Crawford. "My image of her was vague; she is far more perfect. It is always interesting to see a supreme representation of any type, whether or no the type be one that we admire. That is the merit of our neighbor. She resumes a certain civilization; she is the last word—the flower."

"The last word of coarseness, and the flower of commonness," I interrupted. "Yes, she certainly has the merit of being unsurpassable, in her own line."

"She is a very powerful specimen," he went on. "She is complete."

"What do you take her to be?"

Crawford did not answer for some time, and I suppose he was not heeding me. But at last he spoke. "She is the daughter of a woman who keeps a third-rate boarding-house in Lexington Avenue. She sits at the foot of the table and pours out bad coffee. She is considered a beauty, in the boarding-house. She makes out the bills—'for three weeks' board,' with *week* spelled *weak*. She has been engaged several times. That young man is one of the boarders, inclined to gallantry. He has invited her to come down here and have ice-cream, and she has consented, though she despises him. Her name is Matilda Jane. The height of her ambition is to be 'fashionable.'"

"Where the deuce did you learn all this?" I asked. "I shouldn't wonder if it were true."

"You may depend upon it that it is very near the truth. The boarding-house may be in the Eighth avenue, and the lady's name may be Araminta; but the general outline that I have given is correct."

We sat awhile longer; Araminta—or Matilda Jane—finished her ice-cream, leaned back in her chair, and fanned herself with a newspaper, which her companion had drawn from his pocket, and she had folded for the purpose. She had by this time, I suppose, perceived Crawford's singular interest in her person, and she appeared inclined to allow him every facility for the gratification of it. She turned herself about, placed her head in attitudes, stroked her glossy tresses, crooked her large little finger more than ever, and gazed with sturdy coquetry at her incongruous admirer. I, who did not admire her, at last, for a second time, proposed an adjournment; but, to my surprise, Crawford simply put out his hand in farewell, and said that he himself would remain. I looked at him hard; it seemed to me that there was a spark of excitement in his eye which I had not seen for many weeks. I made some little joke which might have been taxed with coarseness; but he received it with perfect gravity, and dismissed me with an impatient gesture. I had not walked more than half a block away when I remembered some last word—it has now passed out of my mind—that I wished to say to my friend. It had, I suppose, some importance, for I walked back to repair my omission. I re-entered the garden and returned to the place where we had been sitting. It was vacant; Crawford had moved his chair, and was engaged in conversation with the young woman I have described. His back was turned to me and he was bending over, so that I could not see his face, and that I remained unseen by him. The lady herself was looking at him strangely;

surprise, perplexity, pleasure, doubt as to whether "fashion-able" manners required her to seem elated or offended at Crawford's overture, were mingled on her large, rosy face. Her companion appeared to have decided that his own dignity demanded of him grimly to ignore the intrusion; he had given his hat another cock, shouldered his stick like a musket, and fixed his eyes on the fiddlers. I stopped, embraced the group at a glance, and then quietly turned away and departed.

As a physician—as a physiologist—I had every excuse for taking what are called materialistic views of human conduct; but this little episode led me to make some reflections which, if they were not exactly melancholy, were at least tinged with the irony of the moralist. Men are all alike, I said, and the best is, at bottom, very little more delicate than the worst. If there was a man I should have called delicate, it had been Crawford; but he too was capable of seeking a vulgar com-pensation for an exquisite pain—he also was too weak to be faithful to a memory. Nevertheless I confess I was both amused and re-assured; a limit seemed set to the inward work-ing of his resentment—he was going to take his trouble more easily and naturally. For the next few weeks I heard nothing from him; good friends as we were, we were poor correspon-dents, and as Crawford, moreover, had said about himself— What in the world had he to write about? I came back to town early in September, and on the evening after my return, called upon my friend. The servant who opened the door, and who showed me a new face, told me that Mr. Crawford had gone out an hour before. As I turned away from the house it suddenly occurred to me—I am quite unable to say why— that I might find him at the concert-garden to which we had gone together on the eve of my departure. The night was mild and beautiful, and—though I had not supposed that he had been in the interval a regular *habitué* of those tawdry bow-ers—a certain association of ideas directed my steps. I reached the garden and passed beneath the arch of paper lanterns which formed its glittering portal. The tables were all occu-pied, and I scanned the company in vain for Crawford's fa-miliar face. Suddenly I perceived a countenance which, if less familiar, was, at least, vividly impressed upon my memory. The lady whom Crawford had ingeniously characterized as the daughter of the proprietress of a third-rate boarding-house was in possession of one of the tables where she was enthroned in assured pre-eminence. With a garland of flowers upon her bonnet, an azure-scarf about her shoulders, and her hands flashing with splendid rings, she seemed a substantial proof that the Eighth avenue may, after all, be the road to fortune. As I stood observing her, her eyes met mine, and I saw that they were illumined with a sort of gross, good-humored felicity. I instinctively connected Crawford with her transfiguration, and concluded that he was effectually reconciled to worldly joys. In a moment I saw that she recognized me; after a very brief hesitation she gave me a familiar nod. Upon this hint I approached her.

"You have seen me before," she said. "You have not forgotten me."

"It's impossible to forget you," I answered, gallantly.

"It's a fact that no one ever does forget me?—I suppose I oughtn't to speak to you without being introduced. But wait a moment; there is a gentleman here who will introduce me. He has gone to get some cigars." And she pointed to a gayly bedizened stall on the other side of the garden, before which, in the act of quitting it, his purchase made, I saw Crawford.

Presently he came up to us—he had evidently recognized me from afar. This had given him a few moments. But what, in such a case, were a few moments? He smiled frankly and heartily, and gave my hand an affectionate grasp. I saw, however, that in spite of his smile he was a little pale. He glanced toward the woman at the table, and then, in a clear, serene voice: "You have made acquaintance?" he said.

"Oh, I know him," said the lady; "but I guess he don't know me! Introduce us."

He mentioned my name, ceremoniously, as if he had been presenting me to a duchess. The woman leaned forward and took my hand in her heavily begemmed fingers. "How d'ye do, Doctor?" she said.

Then Crawford paused a moment, looking at me. My eyes rested on his, which, for an instant, were strange and fixed; they seemed to defy me to see anything in them that he wished me not to see. "Allow me to present you," he said at last, in a tone I shall never forget—"allow me to present you to my wife."

I stood staring at him; the woman still grasped my hand. She gave it a violent shake and broke into a loud laugh. "He don't believe it! There's my wedding-ring!" And she thrust out the ample knuckles of her left hand.

A hundred thoughts passed in a flash through my mind, and a dozen exclamations—tragical, ironical, farcical—rose to my lips. But I happily suppressed them all; I simply remained portentously silent, and seated myself mechanically in the chair which Crawford pushed toward me. His face was inscrutable, but in its urbane blankness I found a reflection of the glaring hideousness of his situation. He had committed a monstrous folly. As I sat there, for the next half-hour—it seemed an eternity—I was able to take its full measure. But I was able also to resolve to accept it, to respect it, and to side with poor Crawford, so far as I might, against the consequences of his deed. I remember of that half-hour little beyond a general, rapidly deepening sense of horror. The woman was in a talkative mood; I was the first of her husband's friends upon whom she had as yet been able to lay hands. She gave me much information—as to when they had been married (it was three weeks before), what she had had on, what her husband (she called him "Mr. Crawford") had given her, what she meant to do during the coming winter. "We are going to give a great ball," she said, "the biggest ever seen in New York. It will open the winter, and I shall be introduced to all his friends. They will want to see me, dreadfully, and there will be sure to be a crowd. I don't know whether they will come twice, but they will come once, I'll engage."

She complained of her husband refusing to take her on a wedding-tour—was ever a woman married like that before? "I'm not sure it's a good marriage, without a wedding-tour," she said. "I always thought that to be really man and wife, you had to go to Niagara, or Saratoga, or some such place. But he insists on sticking here in New York; he says he has his reasons. He gave me that to keep me here." And she made one of her rings twinkle.

Crawford listened to this, smiling, unflinching, unwinking.

Before we separated—to say something—I asked Mrs. Craw-ford if she liked music? The fiddlers were scraping away. She turned her empty glass upside down, and with a thump on the table—"I like that!" she cried. It was most horrible. We rose, and Crawford tenderly offered her his arm; I looked at him with a kind of awe.

I went to see him repeatedly, during the ensuing weeks, and did my best to behave as if nothing was altered. In himself, in fact, nothing was altered, and the really masterly manner in which he tacitly assumed that the change in his situation had been in a high degree for the better, might have furnished inspiration to my more bungling efforts. Never had incurably wounded pride forged itself a more consummately impenetra-ble mask; never had bravado achieved so triumphant an imi-tation of sincerity. In his wife's absence, Crawford never alluded to her; but, in her presence, he was an embodiment of deference and attentive civility. His habits underwent little change, and he was punctiliously faithful to his former pur-suits. He studied—or at least he passed hours in his library. What he did—what he was—in solitude, heaven only knows; nothing, I am happy to say, ever revealed it to me. I never asked him a question about his wife; to feign a respectful in-terest in her would have been too monstrous a comedy. She herself, however, more than satisfied my curiosity, and treated me to a bold sketch of her life and adventures. Crawford had hit the nail on the head; she was veritably, at the time he made her acquaintance, residing at a boarding-house, not in the ca-pacity of a boarder. She even told me the terms in which he had made his proposal. There had been no love-making, no nonsense, no flummery. "I have seven thousand dollars a year," he had said—all of a sudden;—"will you please to be-come my wife? You shall have four thousand for your own use." I have no desire to paint the poor woman who imparted to me these facts in blacker colors than she deserves; she was to be pitied certainly, for she had been lifted into a position in which her defects acquired a glaring intensity. She had made no overtures to Crawford; he had come and dragged her out of her friendly obscurity, and placed her unloveliness aloft upon the pedestal of his contrasted good-manners. She had simply taken what was offered her. But for all one's logic, nevertheless, she was a terrible creature. I tried to like her, I tried to find out her points. The best one seemed to be that her jewels and new dresses—her clothes were in atrocious taste—kept her, for the time, in loud good-humor. Might they never be wanting? I shuddered to think of what Crawford would find himself face to face with in case of their failing; —coarseness, vulgarity, ignorance, vanity, and, beneath all, something as hard and arid as dusty bricks. When I had left them, their union always seemed to me a monstrous fable, an evil dream; each time I saw them the miracle was freshly repeated.

People were still in a great measure in the country, and though it had begun to be rumored about that Crawford had taken a very strange wife, there was for some weeks no adequate appreciation of her strangeness. This came, however, with the advance of the autumn and those beautiful October days when all the world was in the streets. Crawford came forth with his terrible bride upon his arm, took every day a long walk, and ran the gauntlet of society's surprise. On Sundays, he marched into church with his incongruous consort, led her up the long aisle to the accompaniment of the opening organ-peals, and handed her solemnly into her pew. Mrs. Crawford's idiosyncrasies were not of the latent and lurking order, and, in the view of her fellow-worshipers of her own sex, surveying her from a distance, were sufficiently summarized in the composition of her bonnets. Many persons probably remember with a good deal of vividness the great festival to which, early in the winter, Crawford convoked all his friends. Not a person invited was absent, for it was a case in which friendliness and curiosity went most comfortably, hand in hand. Every one wished well to Crawford and was anxious to show it, but when they said they wouldn't for the world seem to turn their backs upon the poor fellow, what people really meant was that they would not for the world miss seeing how Mrs. Crawford would behave. The party was very splendid and made an era in New York, in the art of entertainment. Mrs. Crawford behaved very well, and I think people were a good deal disappointed and scandalized at the decency of her demeanor. But she looked deplorably, it was universally agreed, and her native vulgarity came out in the strange bedizenment of her too exuberant person. By the time supper was served, moreover, every one had gleaned an anecdote about her bad grammar, and the low level of her conversation. On all sides, people were putting their heads together, in threes and fours, and tittering over each other's stories. There is nothing like the bad manners of good society, and I, myself, acutely sensitive on Crawford's behalf, found it impossible, by the end of the evening, to endure the growing exhilaration of the assembly. The company had rendered its verdict; namely, that there were the vulgar people one could, at a pinch accept, and the vulgar people one couldn't, and that Mrs. Crawford belonged to the latter class. I was savage with every one who spoke to me. "Yes, she is as bad as you please," I said; "but you are worse!" But I might have spared my resentment, for Crawford, himself, in the midst of all this, was simply sublime. He was the genius of hospitality in person; no one had ever seen him so careless, so free, so charming. When I went to bid him good-night, as I took him by the hand—"You will carry it through!" I said. He looked at me, smiling vaguely, and not showing in the least that he understood me. Then I felt how deeply he was attached to the part he had undertaken to play; he had sacrificed our old good-fellowship to it. Even to me, his oldest friend, he would not raise a corner of the mask.

Mrs. Ingram and Elizabeth were, of course, not at the ball; but they had come back from Newport, bringing an ardent suitor in their train. The event had amply justified Mrs. Ingram's circumspection; she had captured a young Southern planter, whose estates were fabled to cover three-eighths of the State of Alabama. Elizabeth was more beautiful than ever, and the marriage was being hurried forward. Several times, in public, to my knowledge, Elizabeth and her mother, found themselves face to face with Crawford and his wife. What Crawford must have felt when he looked from the exquisite creature he had lost to the full-blown dowdy he had gained, is a matter it is well but to glance at and pass—the more so, as my story approaches its close. One morning, in my consulting-room, I had been giving some advice to a little old gentleman who was as sound as a winter-pippin, but, who used to come and see me once a month to tell me that he felt a hair on his tongue, or, that he had dreamed of a blue-dog, and to ask to be put upon a "diet" in consequence. The basis of a diet, in his view, was a daily pint of port wine. He had retired from business, he belonged to a club, and he used to go about peddling gossip. His wares, like those of most peddlers, were cheap, and usually, for my prescription, I could purchase the whole contents of his tray. On this occasion, as he was leaving me, he remarked that he supposed I had heard the news about our friend Crawford. I said that I had heard nothing. What was the news?

"He has lost every penny of his fortune," said my patient. "He is completely cleaned out." And, then, in answer to my exclamation of dismay, he proceeded to inform me that the New Amsterdam Bank had suspended payment, and would certainly never resume it. All the world knew that Crawford's funds were at the disposal of the bank, and that two or three months before, when things were looking squally, he had come most generously to the rescue. The squall had come, it had proved a hurricane, the bank had capsized, and Crawford's money had gone to the bottom. "It's not a surprise to me," said Mr. Niblett, "I suspected something a year ago. It's true, I am very sharp."

"Do you think any one else suspected anything?" I asked.

"I dare say not; people are so easily hum-bugged. And, then, what could have looked better, above board, than the New Amsterdam?"

"Nevertheless, here and there," I said, "an exceptionally sharp person may have been on the watch."

"Unquestionably—though I am told that they are going on to-day, down town, as if no bank had ever broken before."

"Do you know Mrs. Ingram?" I asked.

"Thoroughly! She is exceptionally sharp, if that is what you mean."

"Do you think it is possible that she foresaw this affair six months ago?"

"Very possible; she always has her nose in Wall street, and she knows more about stocks than the whole board of brokers."

"Well," said I, after a pause, "sharp as she is, I hope she will get nipped, yet!"

"Ah," said my old friend, "you allude to Crawford's affairs? But you shouldn't be a better royalist than the king. He has forgiven her—he has consoled himself. But what will console him now? Is it true his wife was a washerwoman? Perhaps she will not be sorry to know a trade."

I hoped with all my heart that Mr. Niblett's story was an exaggeration, and I repaired that evening to Crawford's house, to learn the real extent of his misfortune. He had seen me coming in, and he met me in the hall and drew me immediately into the library. He looked like a man who had been thrown by a vicious horse, but had picked himself up and resolved to go the rest of the way on foot.

"How bad is it?" I asked.

"I have about a thousand a year left. I shall get some work, and with careful economy we can live."

At this moment I heard a loud voice screaming from the top of the stairs. "Will *she* help you?" I asked.

He hesitated a moment, and then—"No!" he said simply. Immediately, as a commentary upon his answer, the door was thrown open and Mrs. Crawford swept in. I saw in an instant that her good-humor was in permanent eclipse; flushed, disheveled, inflamed, she was a perfect presentation of a vulgar fury. She advanced upon me with a truly formidable weight of wrath.

"Was it you that put him up to it?" she cried. "Was it you that put it into his head to marry me? I'm sure I never thought of him—he isn't the twentieth part of a man! I took him for his money—four thousand a year, clear; I never pretended it was for anything else. To-day, he comes and tells me that it was all a mistake—that we must get on as well as we can on twelve hundred. And he calls himself a gentleman— and so do you, I suppose! There are gentlemen in the State's prison for less. I have been cheated, insulted and ruined; but I'm not a woman you can play that sort of game upon. The money's mine, what is left of it, and he may go and get his fine friends to support him. There ain't a thing in the world he can do—except lie and cheat!"

Crawford, during this horrible explosion, stood with his eyes fixed upon the floor; and I felt that the peculiarly odious part of the scene was that his wife was literally in the right.

She had been bitterly disappointed—she had been practically deceived. Crawford turned to me and put out his hand. "Good-bye," he said. "I must forego the pleasure of receiving you any more in my own house."

"I can't come again?" I exclaimed.

"I will take it as a favor that you should not."

I withdrew with an insupportable sense of helplessness. In the house he was then occupying, he, of course, very soon ceased to live; but for some time I was in ignorance of whither he had betaken himself. He had forbidden me to come and see him, and he was too much occupied in accommodating himself to his change of fortune to find time for making visits. At last I disinterred him in one of the upper streets, near the East River, in a small house of which he occupied but a single floor. I disobeyed him and went in, and as his wife was apparently absent, he allowed me to remain. He had kept his books, or most of them, and arranged a sort of library. He looked ten years older, but he neither made nor suffered me to make, an allusion to himself. He had obtained a place as clerk at a wholesale chemist's, and he received a salary of five hundred dollars. After this, I not infrequently saw him; we used often, on a Sunday, to take a long walk together. On our return we parted at his door; he never asked me to come in. He talked of his reading, of his scientific fancies, of public affairs, of our friends—of everything, except his own troubles. He suffered, of course, most of his purely formal social relations to die out; but if he appeared not to cling to his friends, neither did he seem to avoid them. I remember a clever old lady saying to me at this time, in allusion to her having met him somewhere—"I used always to think Mr. Crawford the most agreeable man in the world, but I think now he has even improved!" One day—we had walked out into the country, and were sitting on a felled log by the road-side, to rest (for in those days New Yorkers could walk out into the country),—I said to him that I had a piece of news to tell him. It was not pleasing, but it was interesting.

"I told you six weeks ago," I said, "that Elizabeth Ingram had been seized with small-pox. She has recovered, and two or three people have seen her. Every ray of her beauty is gone. They say she is hideous."

"I don't believe it!" he said, simply.

"The young man who was to marry her does," I answered. "He has backed out—he has given her up—he has posted back to Alabama."

Crawford looked at me a moment, and then—"The idiot!" he exclaimed.

For myself, I felt the full bitterness of poor Elizabeth's lot; Mrs. Ingram had been "nipped," as I had ventured to express it, in a grimmer fashion than I hoped. Several months afterward, I saw the young girl, shrouded in a thick veil, beneath which I could just distinguish her absolutely blasted face. On either side of her walked her father and mother, each of them showing a visage almost as blighted as her own.

I saw Crawford for a time, as I have said, with a certain frequency; but there began to occur long intervals, during which he plunged into inscrutable gloom. I supposed in a general way, that his wife's temper gave him plenty of occupation at home; but a painful incident—which I need not repeat—at last informed me how much. Mrs. Crawford, it appeared, drank deep; she had resorted to liquor to console herself for her disappointments. During her periods of revelry, her husband was obliged to be in constant attendance upon her, to keep her from exposing herself. She had done so to me, hideously, and it was so that I learned the reason of her husband's fitful absences. After this, I expressed to Crawford my amazement that he should continue to live with her.

"It's very simple," he answered. "I have done her a great wrong, and I have forfeited the right to complain of any she may do to me."

"In heaven's name," I said, "make another fortune and pension her off."

He shook his head. "I shall never make a fortune. My working-power is not of a high value."

One day, not having seen him for several weeks, I went to his house. The door was opened by his wife, in curl-papers and a soiled dressing-gown. After what I can hardly call an exchange of greetings,—for she wasted no politeness upon me,—I asked for news of my friend.

"He's at the New York Hospital," she said.

"What in the world has happened to him?"

"He has broken his leg, and he went there to be taken care of—as if he hadn't a comfortable home of his own! But he's a deep one; that's a hit at me!"

I immediately announced my intention of going to see him, but as I was turning away she stopped me, laying her hand on my arm. She looked at me hard, almost menacingly. "If he tells you," she said, "that it was me that made him break his leg—that I came behind him, and pushed him down the steps of the back-yard, upon the flags, you needn't believe him. I could have done it; I'm strong enough"—and with a vigorous arm she gave a thump upon the door-post. "It would have served him right, too. But it's a lie!"

"He will not tell me," I said. "But you have done so!"

Crawford was in bed, in one of the great, dreary wards of the hospital, looking as a man looks who has been laid up for three weeks with a compound fracture of the knee. I had seen no small amount of physical misery, but I had never seen anything so poignant as the sight of my once brilliant friend in such a place, from such a cause. I told him I would not ask him how his misfortune occurred: I knew! We talked awhile, and at last I said, "Of course you will not go back to her!"

He turned away his head, and at this moment, the nurse came and said that I had made the poor gentleman talk enough.

Of course he did go back to her—at the end of a very long convalescence. His leg was permanently injured; he was obliged to move about very slowly, and what he had called the value of his working-power was not thereby increased. This meant permanent poverty, and all the rest of it. It lasted ten years longer—until 185–, when Mrs. Crawford died of *delirium tremens*. I cannot say that this event restored his equanimity, for the excellent reason that to the eyes of the world —and my own most searching ones—he had never lost it.

The Ghostly Rental

I WAS in my twenty-second year, and I had just left college.
I was at liberty to choose my career, and I chose it with
much promptness. I afterward renounced it, in truth, with
equal ardor, but I have never regretted those two youthful
years of perplexed and excited, but also of agreeable and fruitful experiment. I had a taste for theology, and during my college term I had been an admiring reader of Dr. Channing.
This was theology of a grateful and succulent savor; it seemed
to offer one the rose of faith delightfully stripped of its thorns.
And then (for I rather think this had something to do with
it), I had taken a fancy to the old Divinity School. I have
always had an eye to the back scene in the human drama, and
it seemed to me that I might play my part with a fair chance
of applause (from myself at least), in that detached and tranquil home of mild casuistry, with its respectable avenue on
one side, and its prospect of green fields and contact with
acres of woodland on the other. Cambridge, for the lovers of
woods and fields, has changed for the worse since those days,
and the precinct in question has forfeited much of its mingled
pastoral and scholastic quietude. It was then a College-hall in
the woods—a charming mixture. What it is now has nothing
to do with my story; and I have no doubt that there are still
doctrine-haunted young seniors who, as they stroll near it in
the summer dusk, promise themselves, later, to taste of its fine
leisurely quality. For myself, I was not disappointed. I established myself in a great square, low-browed room, with deep
window-benches; I hung prints from Overbeck and Ary Scheffer on the walls; I arranged my books, with great refinement
of classification, in the alcoves beside the high chimney-shelf,
and I began to read Plotinus and St. Augustine. Among my
companions were two or three men of ability and of good
fellowship, with whom I occasionally brewed a fireside bowl;
and with adventurous reading, deep discourse, potations conscientiously shallow, and long country walks, my initiation
into the clerical mystery progressed agreeably enough.

With one of my comrades I formed an especial friendship,

and we passed a great deal of time together. Unfortunately he had a chronic weakness of one of his knees, which compelled him to lead a very sedentary life, and as I was a methodical pedestrian, this made some difference in our habits. I used often to stretch away for my daily ramble, with no companion but the stick in my hand or the book in my pocket. But in the use of my legs and the sense of unstinted open air, I have always found company enough. I should, perhaps, add that in the enjoyment of a very sharp pair of eyes, I found something of a social pleasure. My eyes and I were on excellent terms; they were indefatigable observers of all wayside incidents, and so long as they were amused I was contented. It is, indeed, owing to their inquisitive habits that I came into possession of this remarkable story. Much of the country about the old College town is pretty now, but it was prettier thirty years ago. That multitudinous eruption of domiciliary pasteboard which now graces the landscape, in the direction of the low, blue Waltham Hills, had not yet taken place; there were no genteel cottages to put the shabby meadows and scrubby orchards to shame—a juxtaposition by which, in later years, neither element of the contrast has gained. Certain crooked cross-roads, then, as I remember them, were more deeply and naturally rural, and the solitary dwellings on the long grassy slopes beside them, under the tall, customary elm that curved its foliage in mid-air like the outward dropping ears of a girdled wheat-sheaf, sat with their shingled hoods well pulled down on their ears, and no prescience whatever of the fashion of French roofs—weather-wrinkled old peasant women, as you might call them, quietly wearing the native coif, and never dreaming of mounting bonnets, and indecently exposing their venerable brows. That winter was what is called an "open" one; there was much cold, but little snow; the roads were firm and free, and I was rarely compelled by the weather to forego my exercise. One gray December afternoon I had sought it in the direction of the adjacent town of Medford, and I was retracing my steps at an even pace, and watching the pale, cold tints—the transparent amber and faded rose-color—which curtained, in wintry fashion, the western sky, and re-minded me of a sceptical smile on the lips of a beautiful woman. I came, as dusk was falling, to a narrow road which

I had never traversed and which I imagined offered me a short cut homeward. I was about three miles away; I was late, and would have been thankful to make them two. I diverged, walked some ten minutes, and then perceived that the road had a very unfrequented air. The wheel-ruts looked old; the stillness seemed peculiarly sensible. And yet down the road stood a house, so that it must in some degree have been a thoroughfare. On one side was a high, natural embankment, on the top of which was perched an apple-orchard, whose tangled boughs made a stretch of coarse black lace-work, hung across the coldly rosy west. In a short time I came to the house, and I immediately found myself interested in it. I stopped in front of it gazing hard, I hardly knew why, but with a vague mixture of curiosity and timidity. It was a house like most of the houses thereabouts, except that it was decidedly a handsome specimen of its class. It stood on a grassy slope, it had its tall, impartially drooping elm beside it, and its old black well-cover at its shoulder. But it was of very large proportions, and it had a striking look of solidity and stoutness of timber. It had lived to a good old age, too, for the wood-work on its door-way and under its eaves, carefully and abundantly carved, referred it to the middle, at the latest, of the last century. All this had once been painted white, but the broad back of time, leaning against the door-posts for a hundred years, had laid bare the grain of the wood. Behind the house stretched an orchard of apple-trees, more gnarled and fantastic than usual, and wearing, in the deepening dusk, a blighted and exhausted aspect. All the windows of the house had rusty shutters, without slats, and these were closely drawn. There was no sign of life about it; it looked blank, bare and vacant, and yet, as I lingered near it, it seemed to have a familiar meaning—an audible eloquence. I have always thought of the impression made upon me at first sight, by that gray colonial dwelling, as a proof that induction may sometimes be near akin to divination; for after all, there was nothing on the face of the matter to warrant the very serious induction that I made. I fell back and crossed the road. The last red light of the sunset disengaged itself, as it was about to vanish, and rested faintly for a moment on the time-silvered front of the old house. It touched, with perfect regularity, the series of small panes in the fan-shaped window above the door, and twinkled there fantastically. Then it died away, and left the place more intensely somber. At this moment, I said to myself with the accent of profound conviction—"The house is simply haunted!"

Somehow, immediately, I believed it, and so long as I was not shut up inside, the idea gave me pleasure. It was implied in the aspect of the house, and it explained it. Half an hour before, if I had been asked, I would have said, as befitted a young man who was explicitly cultivating cheerful views of the supernatural, that there were no such things as haunted houses. But the dwelling before me gave a vivid meaning to the empty words; it had been spiritually blighted.

The longer I looked at it, the intenser seemed the secret that it held. I walked all round it, I tried to peep here and there, through a crevice in the shutters, and I took a puerile satisfaction in laying my hand on the door-knob and gently turning it. If the door had yielded, would I have gone in?— would I have penetrated the dusky stillness? My audacity, fortunately, was not put to the test. The portal was admirably solid, and I was unable even to shake it. At last I turned away, casting many looks behind me. I pursued my way, and, after a longer walk than I had bargained for, reached the high-road. At a certain distance below the point at which the long lane I have mentioned entered it, stood a comfortable, tidy dwelling, which might have offered itself as the model of the house which is in no sense haunted—which has no sinister secrets, and knows nothing but blooming prosperity. Its clean white paint stared placidly through the dusk, and its vine-covered porch had been dressed in straw for the winter. An old, one-horse chaise, freighted with two departing visitors, was leaving the door, and through the undraped windows, I saw the lamp-lit sitting-room, and the table spread with the early "tea," which had been improvised for the comfort of the guests. The mistress of the house had come to the gate with her friends; she lingered there after the chaise had wheeled creakingly away, half to watch them down the road, and half to give me, as I passed in the twilight, a questioning look. She was a comely, quick young woman, with a sharp, dark eye, and I ventured to stop and speak to her.

"That house down that side-road," I said, "about a mile from here—the only one—can you tell me whom it belongs to?"

She stared at me a moment, and, I thought, colored a little. "Our folks never go down that road," she said, briefly.

"But it's a short way to Medford," I answered.

She gave a little toss of her head. "Perhaps it would turn out a long way. At any rate, we don't use it."

This was interesting. A thrifty Yankee household must have good reasons for this scorn of time-saving processes. "But you know the house, at least?" I said.

"Well, I have seen it."

"And to whom does it belong?"

She gave a little laugh and looked away, as if she were aware that, to a stranger, her words might seem to savor of agricultural superstition. "I guess it belongs to them that are in it."

"But is there any one in it? It is completely closed."

"That makes no difference. They never come out, and no one ever goes in." And she turned away.

But I laid my hand on her arm, respectfully. "You mean," I said, "that the house is haunted?"

She drew herself away, colored, raised her finger to her lips, and hurried into the house, where, in a moment, the curtains were dropped over the windows.

For several days, I thought repeatedly of this little adventure, but I took some satisfaction in keeping it to myself. If the house was not haunted, it was useless to expose my imaginative whims, and if it was, it was agreeable to drain the cup of horror without assistance. I determined, of course, to pass that way again; and a week later—it was the last day of the year—I retraced my steps. I approached the house from the opposite direction, and found myself before it at about the same hour as before. The light was failing, the sky low and gray; the wind wailed along the hard, bare ground, and made slow eddies of the frost-blackened leaves. The melancholy mansion stood there, seeming to gather the winter twilight around it, and mask itself in it, inscrutably. I hardly knew on what errand I had come, but I had a vague feeling that if this time the door-knob were to turn and the door to open, I should take my heart in my hands, and let them close behind me. Who were the mysterious tenants to whom the good woman at the corner had alluded? What had been seen or heard—what was related? The door was as stubborn as before, and my impertinent fumblings with the latch caused no upper window to be thrown open, nor any strange, pale face to be thrust out. I ventured even to raise the rusty knocker and give it half-a-dozen raps, but they made a flat, dead sound, and aroused no echo. Familiarity breeds contempt; I don't know what I should have done next, if, in the distance, up the road (the same one I had followed), I had not seen a solitary figure advancing. I was unwilling to be observed hanging about this ill-famed dwelling, and I sought refuge among the dense shadows of a grove of pines near by, where I might peep forth, and yet remain invisible. Presently, the new-comer drew near, and I perceived that he was making straight for the house. He was a little, old man, the most striking feature of whose appearance was a voluminous cloak, of a sort of military cut. He carried a walking-stick, and advanced in a slow, painful, somewhat hobbling fashion, but with an air of extreme resolution. He turned off from the road, and followed the vague wheel-track, and within a few yards of the house he paused. He looked up at it, fixedly and searchingly, as if he were counting the windows, or noting certain familiar marks. Then he took off his hat, and bent over slowly and solemnly, as if he were performing an obeisance. As he stood uncovered, I had a good look at him. He was, as I have said, a diminutive old man, but it would have been hard to decide whether he belonged to this world or to the other. His head reminded me, vaguely, of the portraits of Andrew Jackson. He had a crop of grizzled hair, as stiff as a brush, a lean, pale, smooth-shaven face, and an eye of intense brilliancy, surmounted with thick brows, which had remained perfectly black. His face, as well as his cloak, seemed to belong to an old soldier; he looked like a retired military man of a modest rank; but he struck me as exceeding the classic privilege of even such a personage to be eccentric and grotesque. When he had finished his salute, he advanced to the door, fumbled in the folds of his cloak, which hung down much further in front than behind, and produced a key. This he slowly and carefully inserted into the lock, and then, apparently, he turned it. But the door did not immediately open; first he bent his head, turned his ear, and stood listening, and then he looked up and down the road. Satisfied or re-assured, he applied his aged shoulder to one of the deep-set panels, and pressed a moment. The door yielded—opening into perfect darkness. He stopped again on the threshold, and again removed his hat and made his bow. Then he went in, and carefully closed the door behind him.

Who in the world was he, and what was his errand? He might have been a figure out of one of Hoffman's tales. Was he vision or a reality—an inmate of the house, or a familiar, friendly visitor? What had been the meaning, in either case, of his mystic genuflexions, and how did he propose to proceed, in that inner darkness? I emerged from my retirement, and observed narrowly, several of the windows. In each of them, at an interval, a ray of light became visible in the chink between the two leaves of the shutters. Evidently, he was lighting up; was he going to give a party—a ghostly revel? My curiosity grew intense, but I was quite at a loss how to satisfy it. For a moment I thought of rapping peremptorily at the door; but I dismissed this idea as unmannerly, and calculated to break the spell, if spell there was. I walked round the house and tried, without violence, to open one of the lower windows. It resisted, but I had better fortune, in a moment, with another. There was a risk, certainly, in the trick I was playing— a risk of being seen from within, or (worse) seeing, myself, something that I should repent of seeing. But curiosity, as I say, had become an inspiration, and the risk was highly agreeable. Through the parting of the shutters I looked into a lighted room—a room lighted by two candles in old brass flambeaux, placed upon the mantel-shelf. It was apparently a sort of back parlor, and it had retained all its furniture. This was of a homely, old-fashioned pattern, and consisted of hair-cloth chairs and sofas, spare mahogany tables, and framed samplers hung upon the walls. But although the room was furnished, it had a strangely uninhabited look; the tables and chairs were in rigid positions, and no small, familiar objects were visible. I could not see everything, and I could only guess at the existence, on my right, of a large folding-door. It was apparently open, and the light of the neighboring room

passed through it. I waited for some time, but the room remained empty. At last I became conscious that a large shadow
was projected upon the wall opposite the folding-door—the
shadow, evidently, of a figure in the adjoining room. It was
tall and grotesque, and seemed to represent a person sitting
perfectly motionless, in profile. I thought I recognized the
perpendicular bristles and far-arching nose of my little old
man. There was a strange fixedness in his posture; he appeared
to be seated, and looking intently at something. I watched the
shadow a long time, but it never stirred. At last, however, just
as my patience began to ebb, it moved slowly, rose to the
ceiling, and became indistinct. I don't know what I should
have seen next, but by an irresistible impulse, I closed the
shutter. Was it delicacy?—was it pusillanimity? I can hardly say.
I lingered, nevertheless, near the house, hoping that my friend
would re-appear. I was not disappointed; for he at last
emerged, looking just as when he had gone in, and taking his
leave in the same ceremonious fashion. (The lights, I had already observed, had disappeared from the crevice of each of
the windows.) He faced about before the door, took off his
hat, and made an obsequious bow. As he turned away I had
a hundred minds to speak to him, but I let him depart in
peace. This, I may say, was pure delicacy;—you will answer,
perhaps, that it came too late. It seemed to me that he had a
right to resent my observation; though my own right to exercise it (if ghosts were in the question) struck me as equally
positive. I continued to watch him as he hobbled softly down
the bank, and along the lonely road. Then I musingly retreated in the opposite direction. I was tempted to follow him,
at a distance, to see what became of him; but this, too, seemed
indelicate; and I confess, moreover, that I felt the inclination
to coquet a little, as it were, with my discovery—to pull apart
the petals of the flower one by one.

I continued to smell the flower, from time to time, for its
oddity of perfume had fascinated me. I passed by the house
on the cross-road again, but never encountered the old man
in the cloak, or any other wayfarer. It seemed to keep observers at a distance, and I was careful not to gossip about it: one
inquirer, I said to myself, may edge his way into the secret,
but there is no room for two. At the same time, of course, I

would have been thankful for any chance side-light that might
fall across the matter—though I could not well see whence it
was to come. I hoped to meet the old man in the cloak elsewhere, but as the days passed by without his re-appearing, I
ceased to expect it. And yet I reflected that he probably lived
in that neighborhood, inasmuch as he had made his pilgrimage to the vacant house on foot. If he had come from a distance, he would have been sure to arrive in some old
deep-hooded gig with yellow wheels—a vehicle as venerably
grotesque as himself. One day I took a stroll in Mount Auburn cemetery—an institution at that period in its infancy, and
full of a sylvan charm which it has now completely forfeited.
It contained more maple and birch than willow and cypress,
and the sleepers had ample elbow room. It was not a city of
the dead, but at the most a village, and a meditative pedestrian
might stroll there without too importunate reminder of the
grotesque side of our claims to posthumous consideration. I
had come out to enjoy the first foretaste of Spring—one of
those mild days of late winter, when the torpid earth seems
to draw the first long breath that marks the rupture of the
spell of sleep. The sun was veiled in haze, and yet warm, and
the frost was oozing from its deepest lurking-places. I had
been treading for half an hour the winding ways of the cemetery, when suddenly I perceived a familiar figure seated on a
bench against a southward-facing evergreen hedge. I call the
figure familiar, because I had seen it often in memory and in
fancy; in fact, I had beheld it but once. Its back was turned
to me, but it wore a voluminous cloak, which there was no
mistaking. Here, at last, was my fellow-visitor at the haunted
house, and here was my chance, if I wished to approach him!
I made a circuit, and came toward him from in front. He saw
me, at the end of the alley, and sat motionless, with his hands
on the head of his stick, watching me from under his black
eyebrows as I drew near. At a distance these black eyebrows
looked formidable; they were the only thing I saw in his face.
But on a closer view I was re-assured, simply because I immediately felt that no man could really be as fantastically fierce
as this poor old gentleman looked. His face was a kind of
caricature of martial truculence. I stopped in front of him,
and respectfully asked leave to sit and rest upon his bench.

He granted it with a silent gesture, of much dignity, and I placed myself beside him. In this position I was able, covertly, to observe him. He was quite as much an oddity in the morning sunshine, as he had been in the dubious twilight. The lines in his face were as rigid as if they had been hacked out of a block by a clumsy wood-carver. His eyes were flamboyant, his nose terrific, his mouth implacable. And yet, after awhile, when he slowly turned and looked at me, fixedly, I perceived that in spite of this portentous mask, he was a very mild old man. I was sure he even would have been glad to smile, but, evidently, his facial muscles were too stiff—they had taken a different fold, once for all. I wondered whether he was demented, but I dismissed the idea; the fixed glitter in his eye was not that of insanity. What his face really expressed was deep and simple sadness; his heart perhaps was broken, but his brain was intact. His dress was shabby but neat, and his old blue cloak had known half a century's brushing.

I hastened to make some observation upon the exceptional softness of the day, and he answered me in a gentle, mellow voice, which it was almost startling to hear proceed from such bellicose lips.

"This is a very comfortable place," he presently added.

"I am fond of walking in graveyards," I rejoined deliberately; flattering myself that I had struck a vein that might lead to something.

I was encouraged; he turned and fixed me with his duskily glowing eyes. Then very gravely,—"Walking, yes. Take all your exercise now. Some day you will have to settle down in a graveyard in a fixed position."

"Very true," said I. "But you know there are some people who are said to take exercise even after that day."

He had been looking at me still; at this he looked away.

"You don't understand?" I said, gently.

He continued to gaze straight before him.

"Some people, you know, walk about after death," I went on.

At last he turned, and looked at me more portentously than ever. "You don't believe that," he said simply.

"How do you know I don't?"

"Because you are young and foolish." This was said without

acerbity—even kindly; but in the tone of an old man whose consciousness of his own heavy experience made everything else seem light.

"I am certainly young," I answered; "but I don't think that, on the whole, I am foolish. But say I don't believe in ghosts—most people would be on my side."

"Most people are fools!" said the old man.

I let the question rest, and talked of other things. My companion seemed on his guard, he eyed me defiantly, and made brief answers to my remarks; but I nevertheless gathered an impression that our meeting was an agreeable thing to him, and even a social incident of some importance. He was evidently a lonely creature, and his opportunities for gossip were rare. He had had troubles, and they had detached him from the world, and driven him back upon himself; but the social chord in his antiquated soul was not entirely broken, and I was sure he was gratified to find that it could still feebly resound. At last, he began to ask questions himself; he inquired whether I was a student.

"I am a student of divinity," I answered.

"Of divinity?"

"Of theology. I am studying for the ministry."

At this he eyed me with peculiar intensity—after which his gaze wandered away again. "There are certain things you ought to know, then," he said at last.

"I have a great desire for knowledge," I answered. "What things do you mean?"

He looked at me again awhile, but without heeding my question.

"I like your appearance," he said. "You seem to me a sober lad."

"Oh, I am perfectly sober!" I exclaimed—yet departing for a moment from my soberness.

"I think you are fair-minded," he went on.

"I don't any longer strike you as foolish, then?" I asked.

"I stick to what I said about people who deny the power of departed spirits to return. They *are* fools!" And he rapped fiercely with his staff on the earth.

I hesitated a moment, and then, abruptly, "You have seen a ghost!" I said.

He appeared not at all startled.

"You are right, sir!" he answered with great dignity. "With me it's not a matter of cold theory—I have not had to pry into old books to learn what to believe. *I know!* With these eyes I have beheld the departed spirit standing before me as near as you are!" And his eyes, as he spoke, certainly looked as if they had rested upon strange things.

I was irresistibly impressed—I was touched with credulity.

"And was it very terrible?" I asked.

"I am an old soldier—I am not afraid!"

"When was it?—where was it?" I asked.

He looked at me mistrustfully, and I saw that I was going too fast.

"Excuse me from going into particulars," he said. "I am not at liberty to speak more fully. I have told you so much, because I cannot bear to hear this subject spoken of lightly. Remember in future, that you have seen a very honest old man who told you—on his honor—that he had seen a ghost!" And he got up, as if he thought he had said enough. Reserve, shyness, pride, the fear of being laughed at, the memory, possibly, of former strokes of sarcasm—all this, on one side, had its weight with him; but I suspected that on the other, his tongue was loosened by the garrulity of old age, the sense of solitude, and the need of sympathy—and perhaps, also, by the friendliness which he had been so good as to express toward myself. Evidently it would be unwise to press him, but I hoped to see him again.

"To give greater weight to my words," he added, "let me mention my name—Captain Diamond, sir. I have seen service."

"I hope I may have the pleasure of meeting you again," I said.

"The same to you, sir!" And brandishing his stick portentously—though with the friendliest intentions—he marched stiffly away.

I asked two or three persons—selected with discretion—whether they knew anything about Captain Diamond, but they were quite unable to enlighten me. At last, suddenly, I smote my forehead, and, dubbing myself a dolt, remembered that I was neglecting a source of information to which I had never applied in vain. The excellent person at whose table I habitually dined, and who dispensed hospitality to students at so much a week, had a sister as good as herself, and of conversational powers more varied. This sister, who was known as Miss Deborah, was an old maid in all the force of the term. She was deformed, and she never went out of the house; she sat all day at the window, between a bird-cage and a flower-pot, stitching small linen articles—mysterious bands and frills. She wielded, I was assured, an exquisite needle, and her work was highly prized. In spite of her deformity and her confinement, she had a little, fresh, round face, and an imperturbable serenity of spirit. She had also a very quick little wit of her own, she was extremely observant, and she had a high relish for a friendly chat. Nothing pleased her so much as to have you—especially, I think, if you were a young divinity student—move your chair near her sunny window, and settle yourself for twenty minutes' "talk." "Well, sir," she used always to say, "what is the latest monstrosity in Biblical criticism?"—for she used to pretend to be horrified at the rationalistic tendency of the age. But she was an inexorable little philosopher, and I am convinced that she was a keener rationalist than any of us, and that, if she had chosen, she could have propounded questions that would have made the boldest of us wince. Her window commanded the whole town—or rather, the whole country. Knowledge came to her as she sat singing, with her little, cracked voice, in her low rocking-chair. She was the first to learn everything, and the last to forget it. She had the town gossip at her fingers' ends, and she knew everything about people she had never seen. When I asked her how she had acquired her learning, she said simply—"Oh, I observe!" "Observe closely enough," she once said, "and it doesn't matter where you are. You may be in a pitch-dark closet. All you want is something to start with; one thing leads to another, and all things are mixed up. Shut me up in a dark closet and I will observe after a while, that some places in it are darker than others. After that (give me time), and I will tell you what the President of the United States is going to have for dinner." Once I paid her a compliment. "Your observation," I said, "is as fine as your needle, and your statements are as true as your stitches."

Of course Miss Deborah had heard of Captain Diamond. He had been much talked about many years before, but he had survived the scandal that attached to his name.

"What was the scandal?" I asked.

"He killed his daughter."

"Killed her?" I cried; "how so?"

"Oh, not with a pistol, or a dagger, or a dose of arsenic! With his tongue. Talk of women's tongues! He cursed her—with some horrible oath—and she died!"

"What had she done?"

"She had received a visit from a young man who loved her, and whom he had forbidden the house."

"The house," I said—"ah yes! The house is out in the country, two or three miles from here, on a lonely cross-road."

Miss Deborah looked sharply at me, as she bit her thread.

"Ah, you know about the house?" she said.

"A little," I answered; "I have seen it. But I want you to tell me more."

But here Miss Deborah betrayed an incommunicativeness which was most unusual.

"You wouldn't call me superstitious, would you?" she asked.

"You?—you are the quintessence of pure reason."

"Well, every thread has its rotten place, and every needle its grain of rust. I would rather not talk about that house."

"You have no idea how you excite my curiosity!" I said.

"I can feel for you. But it would make me very nervous."

"What harm can come to you?" I asked.

"Some harm came to a friend of mine." And Miss Deborah gave a very positive nod.

"What had your friend done?"

"She had told me Captain Diamond's secret, which he had told her with a mighty mystery. She had been an old flame of his, and he took her into his confidence. He bade her tell no one, and assured her that if she did, something dreadful would happen to her."

"And what happened to her?"

"She died."

"Oh, we are all mortal!" I said. "Had she given him a promise?"

"She had not taken it seriously, she had not believed him. She repeated the story to me, and three days afterward, she was taken with inflammation of the lungs. A month afterward, here where I sit now, I was stitching her grave-clothes. Since then, I have never mentioned what she told me."

"Was it very strange?"

"It was strange, but it was ridiculous too. It is a thing to make you shudder and to make you laugh, both. But you can't worry it out of me. I am sure that if I were to tell you, I should immediately break a needle in my finger, and die the next week of lock-jaw."

I retired, and urged Miss Deborah no further; but every two or three days, after dinner, I came and sat down by her rocking-chair. I made no further allusion to Captain Diamond; I sat silent, clipping tape with her scissors. At last, one day, she told me I was looking poorly. I was pale.

"I am dying of curiosity," I said. "I have lost my appetite. I have eaten no dinner."

"Remember Bluebeard's wife!" said Miss Deborah.

"One may as well perish by the sword as by famine!" I answered.

Still she said nothing, and at last I rose with a melo-dramatic sigh and departed. As I reached the door she called me and pointed to the chair I had vacated. "I never was hard-hearted," she said. "Sit down, and if we are to perish, may we at least perish together." And then, in very few words, she communicated what she knew of Captain Diamond's secret. "He was a very high-tempered old man, and though he was very fond of his daughter, his will was law. He had picked out a husband for her, and given her due notice. Her mother was dead, and they lived alone together. The house had been Mrs. Diamond's own marriage portion; the Captain, I believe, hadn't a penny. After his marriage they had come to live there, and he had begun to work the farm. The poor girl's lover was a young man with whiskers from Boston. The Captain came in one evening and found them together; he collared the young man, and hurled a terrible curse at the poor girl. The

young man cried that she was his wife, and he asked her if it
was true. She said, No! Thereupon Captain Diamond, his fury
growing fiercer, repeated his imprecation, ordered her out of
the house, and disowned her forever. She swooned away, but
her father went raging off and left her. Several hours later, he
came back and found the house empty. On the table was a
note from the young man telling him that he had killed his
daughter, repeating the assurance that she was his own wife,
and declaring that he himself claimed the sole right to commit
her remains to earth. He had carried the body away in a gig!
Captain Diamond wrote him a dreadful note in answer, saying
that he didn't believe his daughter was dead, but that, whether
or no, she was dead to him. A week later, in the middle of
the night, he saw her ghost. Then, I suppose, he was convinced. The ghost re-appeared several times, and finally began
regularly to haunt the house. It made the old man very uncomfortable, for little by little his passion had passed away,
and he was given up to grief. He determined at last to leave
the place, and tried to sell it or rent it; but meanwhile the
story had gone abroad, the ghost had been seen by other
persons, the house had a bad name, and it was impossible to
dispose of it. With the farm, it was the old man's only property, and his only means of subsistence; if he could neither
live in it nor rent it he was beggared. But the ghost had no
mercy, as he had had none. He struggled for six months, and
at last he broke down. He put on his old blue cloak and took
up his staff, and prepared to wander away and beg his bread.
Then the ghost relented, and proposed a compromise. 'Leave
the house to me!' it said; 'I have marked it for my own. Go
off and live elsewhere. But to enable you to live, I will be your
tenant, since you can find no other. I will hire the house of
you and pay you a certain rent.' And the ghost named a sum.
The old man consented, and he goes every quarter to collect
his rent!"

I laughed at this recital, but I confess I shuddered too, for
my own observation had exactly confirmed it. Had I not been
witness of one of the Captain's quarterly visits, had I not all
but seen him sit watching his spectral tenant count out the
rent-money, and when he trudged away in the dark, had he
not a little bag of strangely gotten coin hidden in the folds of

his old blue cloak? I imparted none of these reflections to Miss
Deborah, for I was determined that my observations should
have a sequel, and I promised myself the pleasure of treating
her to my story in its full maturity. "Captain Diamond," I
asked, "has no other known means of subsistence?"

"None whatever. He toils not, neither does he spin—his
ghost supports him. A haunted house is valuable property!"

"And in what coin does the ghost pay?"

"In good American gold and silver. It has only this peculiarity—that the pieces are all dated before the young girl's
death. It's a strange mixture of matter and spirit!"

"And does the ghost do things handsomely; is the rent
large?"

"The old man, I believe, lives decently, and has his pipe and
his glass. He took a little house down by the river; the door
is sidewise to the street, and there is a little garden before it.
There he spends his days, and has an old colored woman to
do for him. Some years ago, he used to wander about a good
deal, he was a familiar figure in the town, and most people
knew his legend. But of late he has drawn back into his shell;
he sits over his fire, and curiosity has forgotten him. I suppose
he is falling into his dotage. But I am sure, I trust," said Miss
Deborah in conclusion, "that he won't outlive his faculties or
his powers of locomotion, for, if I remember rightly, it was
part of the bargain that he should come in person to collect
his rent."

We neither of us seemed likely to suffer any especial penalty
for Miss Deborah's indiscretion; I found her, day after day,
singing over her work, neither more nor less active than usual.
For myself, I boldly pursued my observations. I went again,
more than once, to the great graveyard, but I was disappointed in my hope of finding Captain Diamond there. I had
a prospect, however, which afforded me compensation. I
shrewdly inferred that the old man's quarterly pilgrimages
were made upon the last day of the old quarter. My first sight
of him had been on the 31st of December, and it was probable
that he would return to his haunted home on the last day of
March. This was near at hand; at last it arrived. I betook myself late in the afternoon to the old house on the cross-road,
supposing that the hour of twilight was the appointed season.

I was not wrong. I had been hovering about for a short time, feeling very much like a restless ghost myself, when he appeared in the same manner as before, and wearing the same costume. I again concealed myself, and saw him enter the house with the ceremonial which he had used on the former occasion. A light appeared successively in the crevice of each pair of shutters, and I opened the window which had yielded to my importunity before. Again I saw the great shadow on the wall, motionless and solemn. But I saw nothing else. The old man re-appeared at last, made his fantastic salaam before the house, and crept away into the dusk.

One day, more than a month after this, I met him again at Mount Auburn. The air was full of the voice of Spring; the birds had come back and were twittering over their Winter's travels, and a mild west wind was making a thin murmur in the raw verdure. He was seated on a bench in the sun, still muffled in his enormous mantle, and he recognized me as soon as I approached him. He nodded at me as if he were an old Bashaw giving the signal for my decapitation, but it was apparent that he was pleased to see me.

"I have looked for you here more than once," I said. "You don't come often."

"What did you want of me?" he asked.

"I wanted to enjoy your conversation. I did so greatly when I met you here before."

"You found me amusing?"

"Interesting!" I said.

"You didn't think me cracked?"

"Cracked?—My dear sir—!" I protested.

"I'm the sanest man in the country. I know that is what insane people always say; but generally they can't prove it. I can!"

"I believe it," I said. "But I am curious to know how such a thing can be proved."

He was silent awhile.

"I will tell you. I once committed, unintentionally, a great crime. Now I pay the penalty. I give up my life to it. I don't shirk it; I face it squarely, knowing perfectly what it is. I haven't tried to bluff it off; I haven't begged off from it; I haven't run away from it. The penalty is terrible, but I have accepted it. I have been a philosopher!

"If I were a Catholic, I might have turned monk, and spent the rest of my life in fasting and praying. That is no penalty; that is an evasion. I might have blown my brains out—I might have gone mad. I wouldn't do either. I would simply face the music, take the consequences. As I say, they are awful! I take them on certain days, four times a year. So it has been these twenty years; so it will be as long as I last. It's my business; it's my avocation. That's the way I feel about it. I call that reasonable!"

"Admirably so!" I said. "But you fill me with curiosity and with compassion."

"Especially with curiosity," he said, cunningly.

"Why," I answered, "if I know exactly what you suffer I can pity you more."

"I'm much obliged. I don't want your pity; it won't help me. I'll tell you something, but it's not for myself; it's for your own sake." He paused a long time and looked all round him, as if for chance eavesdroppers. I anxiously awaited his revelation, but he disappointed me. "Are you still studying theology?" he asked.

"Oh, yes," I answered, perhaps with a shade of irritation. "It's a thing one can't learn in six months."

"I should think not, so long as you have nothing but your books. Do you know the proverb, 'A grain of experience is worth a pound of precept?' I'm a great theologian."

"Ah, you have had experience," I murmured sympathetically.

"You have read about the immortality of the soul; you have seen Jonathan Edwards and Dr. Hopkins chopping logic over it, and deciding, by chapter and verse, that it is true. But I have seen it with these eyes; I have touched it with these hands!" And the old man held up his rugged old fists and shook them portentously. "That's better!" he went on; "but I have bought it dearly. You had better take it from the books—evidently you always will. You are a very good young man; you will never have a crime on your conscience."

I answered with some juvenile fatuity, that I certainly hoped I had my share of human passions, good young man and prospective Doctor of Divinity as I was.

"Ah, but you have a nice, quiet little temper," he said. "So have I—now! But once I was very brutal—very brutal. You ought to know that such things are. I killed my own child."

"Your own child?"

"I struck her down to the earth and left her to die. They could not hang me, for it was not with my hand I struck her. It was with foul and damnable words. That makes a difference; it's a grand law we live under! Well, sir, I can answer for it that *her* soul is immortal. We have an appointment to meet four times a year, and then I catch it!"

"She has never forgiven you?"

"She has forgiven me as the angels forgive! That's what I can't stand—the soft, quiet way she looks at me. I'd rather she twisted a knife about in my heart—O Lord, Lord, Lord!" and Captain Diamond bowed his head over his stick, and leaned his forehead on his crossed hands.

I was impressed and moved, and his attitude seemed for the moment a check to further questions. Before I ventured to ask him anything more, he slowly rose and pulled his old cloak around him. He was unused to talking about his troubles, and his memories overwhelmed him. "I must go my way," he said; "I must be creeping along."

"I shall perhaps meet you here again," I said.

"Oh, I'm a stiff-jointed old fellow," he answered, "and this is rather far for me to come. I have to reserve myself. I have sat sometimes a month at a time smoking my pipe in my chair. But I should like to see you again." And he stopped and looked at me, terribly and kindly. "Some day, perhaps, I shall be glad to be able to lay my hand on a young, unperverted soul. If a man can make a friend, it is always something gained. What is your name?"

I had in my pocket a small volume of Pascal's "Thoughts," on the fly-leaf of which were written my name and address. I took it out and offered it to my old friend. "Pray keep this little book," I said. "It is one I am very fond of, and it will tell you something about me."

He took it and turned it over slowly, then looking up at me with a scowl of gratitude, "I'm not much of a reader," he said; "but I won't refuse the first present I shall have received since—my troubles; and the last. Thank you, sir!" And with the little book in his hand he took his departure.

I was left to imagine him for some weeks after that sitting solitary in his arm-chair with his pipe. I had not another glimpse of him. But I was awaiting my chance, and on the last day of June, another quarter having elapsed, I deemed that it had come. The evening dusk in June falls late, and I was impatient for its coming. At last, toward the end of a lovely summer's day, I revisited Captain Diamond's property. Everything now was green around it save the blighted orchard in its rear, but its own immitigable grayness and sadness were as striking as when I had first beheld it beneath a December sky. As I drew near it, I saw that I was late for my purpose, for my purpose had simply been to step forward on Captain Diamond's arrival, and bravely ask him to let me go in with him. He had preceded me, and there were lights already in the windows. I was unwilling, of course, to disturb him during his ghostly interview, and I waited till he came forth. The lights disappeared in the course of time; then the door opened and Captain Diamond stole out. That evening he made no bow to the haunted house, for the first object he beheld was his fair-minded young friend planted, modestly but firmly, near the door-step. He stopped short, looking at me, and this time his terrible scowl was in keeping with the situation.

"I knew you were here," I said. "I came on purpose."

He seemed dismayed, and looked round at the house uneasily.

"I beg your pardon if I have ventured too far," I added, "but you know you have encouraged me."

"How did you know I was here?"

"I reasoned it out. You told me half your story, and I guessed the other half. I am a great observer, and I had noticed this house in passing. It seemed to me to have a mystery. When you kindly confided to me that you saw spirits, I was sure that it could only be here that you saw them."

"You are mighty clever," cried the old man. "And what brought you here this evening?"

I was obliged to evade this question.

"Oh, I often come; I like to look at the house—it fascinates me."

He turned and looked up at it himself. "It's nothing to look at outside." He was evidently quite unaware of its peculiar outward appearance, and this odd fact, communicated to me thus in the twilight, and under the very brow of the sinister dwelling, seemed to make his vision of the strange things within more real.

"I have been hoping," I said, "for a chance to see the inside. I thought I might find you here, and that you would let me go in with you. I should like to see what you see."

He seemed confounded by my boldness, but not altogether displeased. He laid his hand on my arm. "Do you know what I see?" he asked.

"How can I know, except as you said the other day, by experience? I want to have the experience. Pray, open the door and take me in."

Captain Diamond's brilliant eyes expanded beneath their dusky brows, and after holding his breath a moment, he indulged in the first and last apology for a laugh by which I was to see his solemn visage contorted. It was profoundly grotesque, but it was perfectly noiseless. "Take you in?" he softly growled. "I wouldn't go in again before my time's up for a thousand times that sum." And he thrust out his hand from the folds of his cloak and exhibited a small agglomeration of coin, knotted into the corner of an old silk pocket-handkerchief. "I stick to my bargain no less, but no more!"

"But you told me the first time I had the pleasure of talking with you that it was not so terrible."

"I don't say it's terrible—now. But it's damned disagreeable!"

This adjective was uttered with a force that made me hesitate and reflect. While I did so, I thought I heard a slight movement of one of the window-shutters above us. I looked up, but everything seemed motionless. Captain Diamond, too, had been thinking; suddenly he turned toward the house. "If you will go in alone," he said, "you are welcome."

"Will you wait for me here?"

"Yes, you will not stop long."

"But the house is pitch dark. When you go you have lights."

He thrust his hand into the depths of his cloak and produced some matches. "Take these," he said. "You will find

two candlesticks with candles on the table in the hall. Light
them, take one in each hand and go ahead."

"Where shall I go?"

"Anywhere—everywhere. You can trust the ghost to find
you."

I will not pretend to deny that by this time my heart was
beating. And yet I imagine I motioned the old man with a
sufficiently dignified gesture to open the door. I had made up
my mind that there was in fact a ghost. I had conceded the
premise. Only I had assured myself that once the mind was
prepared, and the thing was not a surprise, it was possible to
keep cool. Captain Diamond turned the lock, flung open the
door, and bowed low to me as I passed in. I stood in the
darkness, and heard the door close behind me. For some moments, I stirred neither finger nor toe; I stared bravely into
the impenetrable dusk. But I saw nothing and heard nothing,
and at last I struck a match. On the table were two old brass
candlesticks rusty from disuse. I lighted the candles and began
my tour of exploration.

A wide staircase rose in front of me, guarded by an antique
balustrade of that rigidly delicate carving which is found so
often in old New England houses. I postponed ascending it,
and turned into the room on my right. This was an old-fashioned parlor, meagerly furnished, and musty with the absence
of human life. I raised my two lights aloft and saw nothing
but its empty chairs and its blank walls. Behind it was the
room into which I had peeped from without, and which, in
fact, communicated with it, as I had supposed, by folding
doors. Here, too, I found myself confronted by no menacing
specter. I crossed the hall again, and visited the rooms on the
other side; a dining-room in front, where I might have written
my name with my finger in the deep dust of the great square
table; a kitchen behind with its pots and pans eternally cold.
All this was hard and grim, but it was not formidable. I came
back into the hall, and walked to the foot of the staircase,
holding up my candles; to ascend required a fresh effort, and
I was scanning the gloom above. Suddenly, with an inexpressible sensation, I became aware that this gloom was animated;
it seemed to move and gather itself together. Slowly—I say

slowly, for to my tense expectancy the instants appeared ages—it took the shape of a large, definite figure, and this figure advanced and stood at the top of the stairs. I frankly confess that by this time I was conscious of a feeling to which I am in duty bound to apply the vulgar name of fear. I may poetize it and call it Dread, with a capital letter; it was at any rate the feeling that makes a man yield ground. I measured it as it grew, and it seemed perfectly irresistible; for it did not appear to come from within but from without, and to be embodied in the dark image at the head of the staircase. After a fashion I reasoned—I remember reasoning. I said to myself, "I had always thought ghosts were white and transparent; this is a thing of thick shadows, densely opaque." I reminded myself that the occasion was momentous, and that if fear were to overcome me I should gather all possible impressions while my wits remained. I stepped back, foot behind foot, with my eyes still on the figure and placed my candles on the table. I was perfectly conscious that the proper thing was to ascend the stairs resolutely, face to face with the image, but the soles of my shoes seemed suddenly to have been transformed into leaden weights. I had got what I wanted; I was seeing the ghost. I tried to look at the figure distinctly so that I could remember it, and fairly claim, afterward, not to have lost my self-possession. I even asked myself how long it was expected I should stand looking, and how soon I could honorably retire. All this, of course, passed through my mind with extreme rapidity, and it was checked by a further movement on the part of the figure. Two white hands appeared in the dark perpendicular mass, and were slowly raised to what seemed to be the level of the head. Here they were pressed together, over the region of the face, and then they were removed, and the face was disclosed. It was dim, white, strange, in every way ghostly. It looked down at me for an instant, after which one of the hands was raised again, slowly, and waved to and fro before it. There was something very singular in this gesture; it seemed to denote resentment and dismissal, and yet it had a sort of trivial, familiar motion. Familiarity on the part of the haunting Presence had not entered into my calculations, and did not strike me pleasantly. I agreed with Captain Diamond that it was "damned disagreeable." I was pervaded by an intense desire to make an orderly, and, if possible, a graceful retreat. I wished to do it gallantly, and it seemed to me that it would be gallant to blow out my candles. I turned and did so, punctiliously, and then I made my way to the door, groped a moment and opened it. The outer light, almost extinct as it was, entered for a moment, played over the dusty depths of the house and showed me the solid shadow.

Standing on the grass, bent over his stick, under the early glimmering stars, I found Captain Diamond. He looked up at me fixedly for a moment, but asked no questions, and then he went and locked the door. This duty performed, he discharged the other—made his obeisance like the priest before the altar—and then without heeding me further, took his departure.

A few days later, I suspended my studies and went off for the summer's vacation. I was absent for several weeks, during which I had plenty of leisure to analyze my impressions of the supernatural. I took some satisfaction in the reflection that I had not been ignobly terrified; I had not bolted nor swooned—I had proceeded with dignity. Nevertheless, I was certainly more comfortable when I had put thirty miles between me and the scene of my exploit, and I continued for many days to prefer the daylight to the dark. My nerves had been powerfully excited; of this I was particularly conscious when, under the influence of the drowsy air of the sea-side, my excitement began slowly to ebb. As it disappeared, I attempted to take a sternly rational view of my experience. Certainly I had seen *something*—that was not fancy; but what had I seen? I regretted extremely now that I had not been bolder, that I had not gone nearer and inspected the apparition more minutely. But it was very well to talk; I had done as much as any man in the circumstances would have dared; it was indeed a physical impossibility that I should have advanced. Was not this paralyzation of my powers in itself a supernatural influence? Not necessarily, perhaps, for a sham ghost that one accepted might do as much execution as a real ghost. But why had I so easily accepted the sable phantom that waved its hand? Why had it so impressed itself? Unquestionably, true or false, it was a very clever phantom. I greatly preferred that it should have been true—in the first place because I did not

care to have shivered and shaken for nothing, and in the second place because to have seen a well-authenticated goblin is,
as things go, a feather in a quiet man's cap. I tried, therefore,
to let my vision rest and to stop turning it over. But an impulse stronger than my will recurred at intervals and set a
mocking question on my lips. Granted that the apparition was
Captain Diamond's daughter; if it was she it certainly was her
spirit. But was it not her spirit and something more?

The middle of September saw me again established among
the theologic shades, but I made no haste to revisit the
haunted house.

The last of the month approached—the term of another
quarter with poor Captain Diamond—and found me indisposed to disturb his pilgrimage on this occasion; though I
confess that I thought with a good deal of compassion of the
feeble old man trudging away, lonely, in the autumn dusk, on
his extraordinary errand. On the thirtieth of September, at
noonday, I was drowsing over a heavy octavo, when I heard
a feeble rap at my door. I replied with an invitation to enter,
but as this produced no effect I repaired to the door and
opened it. Before me stood an elderly negress with her head
bound in a scarlet turban, and a white handkerchief folded
across her bosom. She looked at me intently and in silence;
she had that air of supreme gravity and decency which aged
persons of her race so often wear. I stood interrogative, and
at last, drawing her hand from her ample pocket, she held up
a little book. It was the copy of Pascal's "Thoughts" that I
had given to Captain Diamond.

"Please, sir," she said, very mildly, "do you know this
book?"

"Perfectly," said I, "my name is on the fly-leaf."

"It is your name—no other?"

"I will write my name if you like, and you can compare
them," I answered.

She was silent a moment and then, with dignity—"It would
be useless, sir," she said, "I can't read. If you will give me
your word that is enough. I come," she went on, "from the
gentleman to whom you gave the book. He told me to carry
it as a token—a token—that is what he called it. He is right
down sick, and he wants to see you."

"Captain Diamond—sick?" I cried. "Is his illness serious?"

"He is very bad—he is all gone."

I expressed my regret and sympathy, and offered to go to him immediately, if his sable messenger would show me the way. She assented deferentially, and in a few moments I was following her along the sunny streets, feeling very much like a personage in the Arabian Nights, led to a postern gate by an Ethiopian slave. My own conductress directed her steps toward the river and stopped at a decent little yellow house in one of the streets that descend to it. She quickly opened the door and led me in, and I very soon found myself in the presence of my old friend. He was in bed, in a darkened room, and evidently in a very feeble state. He lay back on his pillow staring before him, with his bristling hair more erect than ever, and his intensely dark and bright old eyes touched with the glitter of fever. His apartment was humble and scrupulously neat, and I could see that my dusky guide was a faithful servant. Captain Diamond, lying there rigid and pale on his white sheets, resembled some ruggedly carven figure on the lid of a Gothic tomb. He looked at me silently, and my companion withdrew and left us alone.

"Yes, it's you," he said, at last, "it's you, that good young man. There is no mistake, is there?"

"I hope not; I believe I'm a good young man. But I am very sorry you are ill. What can I do for you?"

"I am very bad, very bad; my poor old bones ache so!" and, groaning portentously, he tried to turn toward me.

I questioned him about the nature of his malady and the length of time he had been in bed, but he barely heeded me; he seemed impatient to speak of something else. He grasped my sleeve, pulled me toward him, and whispered quickly:

"You know my time's up!"

"Oh, I trust not," I said, mistaking his meaning. "I shall certainly see you on your legs again."

"God knows!" he cried. "But I don't mean I'm dying; not yet a bit. What I mean is, I'm due at the house. This is rent-day."

"Oh, exactly! But you can't go."

"I can't go. It's awful. I shall lose my money. If I am dying,

I want it all the same. I want to pay the doctor. I want to be buried like a respectable man."

"It is this evening?" I asked.

"This evening at sunset, sharp."

He lay staring at me, and, as I looked at him in return, I suddenly understood his motive in sending for me. Morally, as it came into my thought, I winced. But, I suppose I looked unperturbed, for he continued in the same tone. "I can't lose my money. Some one else must go. I asked Belinda; but she won't hear of it."

"You believe the money will be paid to another person?"

"We can try, at least. I have never failed before and I don't know. But, if you say I'm as sick as a dog, that my old bones ache, that I'm dying, perhaps she'll trust you. She don't want me to starve!"

"You would like me to go in your place, then?"

"You have been there once; you know what it is. Are you afraid?"

I hesitated.

"Give me three minutes to reflect," I said, "and I will tell you." My glance wandered over the room and rested on the various objects that spoke of the threadbare, decent poverty of its occupant. There seemed to be a mute appeal to my pity and my resolution in their cracked and faded sparseness. Meanwhile Captain Diamond continued, feebly:

"I think she'd trust you, as I have trusted you; she'll like your face; she'll see there is no harm in you. It's a hundred and thirty-three dollars, exactly. Be sure you put them into a safe place."

"Yes," I said at last, "I will go, and, so far as it depends upon me, you shall have the money by nine o'clock to-night."

He seemed greatly relieved; he took my hand and faintly pressed it, and soon afterward I withdrew. I tried for the rest of the day not to think of my evening's work, but, of course, I thought of nothing else. I will not deny that I was nervous; I was, in fact, greatly excited, and I spent my time in alternately hoping that the mystery should prove less deep than it appeared, and yet fearing that it might prove too shallow. The hours passed very slowly, but, as the afternoon began to wane,

I started on my mission. On the way, I stopped at Captain Diamond's modest dwelling, to ask how he was doing, and to receive such last instructions as he might desire to lay upon me. The old negress, gravely and inscrutably placid, admitted me, and, in answer to my inquiries, said that the Captain was very low; he had sunk since the morning.

"You must be right smart," she said, "if you want to get back before he drops off."

A glance assured me that she knew of my projected expedition, though, in her own opaque black pupil, there was not a gleam of self-betrayal.

"But why should Captain Diamond drop off?" I asked. "He certainly seems very weak; but I cannot make out that he has any definite disease."

"His disease is old age," she said, sententiously.

"But he is not so old as that; sixty-seven or sixty-eight, at most."

She was silent a moment.

"He's worn out; he's used up; he can't stand it any longer."

"Can I see him a moment?" I asked; upon which she led me again to his room.

He was lying in the same way as when I had left him, except that his eyes were closed. But he seemed very "low," as she had said, and he had very little pulse. Nevertheless, I further learned the doctor had been there in the afternoon and professed himself satisfied. "He don't know what's been going on," said Belinda, curtly.

The old man stirred a little, opened his eyes, and after some time recognized me.

"I'm going, you know," I said. "I'm going for your money. Have you anything more to say?" He raised himself slowly, and with a painful effort, against his pillows; but he seemed hardly to understand me. "The house, you know," I said. "Your daughter."

He rubbed his forehead, slowly, awhile, and at last, his comprehension awoke. "Ah, yes," he murmured, "I trust you. A hundred and thirty-three dollars. In old pieces—all in old pieces." Then he added more vigorously, and with a brightening eye: "Be very respectful—be very polite. If not—if not——" and his voice failed again.

"Oh, I certainly shall be," I said, with a rather forced smile. "But, if not?"

"If not, I shall know it!" he said, very gravely. And with this, his eyes closed and he sunk down again.

I took my departure and pursued my journey with a sufficiently resolute step. When I reached the house, I made a propitiatory bow in front of it, in emulation of Captain Diamond. I had timed my walk so as to be able to enter without delay; night had already fallen. I turned the key, opened the door and shut it behind me. Then I struck a light, and found the two candlesticks I had used before, standing on the tables in the entry. I applied a match to both of them, took them up and went into the parlor. It was empty, and though I waited awhile, it remained empty. I passed then into the other rooms on the same floor, and no dark image rose before me to check my steps. At last, I came out into the hall again, and stood weighing the question of going upstairs. The staircase had been the scene of my discomfiture before, and I approached it with profound mistrust. At the foot, I paused, looking up, with my hand on the balustrade. I was acutely expectant, and my expectation was justified. Slowly, in the darkness above, the black figure that I had seen before took shape. It was not an illusion; it was a figure, and the same. I gave it time to define itself, and watched it stand and look down at me with its hidden face. Then, deliberately, I lifted up my voice and spoke.

"I have come in place of Captain Diamond, at his request," I said. "He is very ill; he is unable to leave his bed. He earnestly begs that you will pay the money to me; I will immediately carry it to him." The figure stood motionless, giving no sign. "Captain Diamond would have come if he were able to move," I added, in a moment, appealingly; "but, he is utterly unable."

At this the figure slowly unveiled its face and showed me a dim, white mask; then it began slowly to descend the stairs. Instinctively I fell back before it, retreating to the door of the front sitting-room. With my eyes still fixed on it, I moved backward across the threshold; then I stopped in the middle of the room and set down my lights. The figure advanced; it seemed to be that of a tall woman, dressed in vaporous black crape. As it drew near, I saw that it had a perfectly human face, though it looked extremely pale and sad. We stood gazing at each other; my agitation had completely vanished; I was only deeply interested.

"Is my father dangerously ill?" said the apparition.

At the sound of its voice—gentle, tremulous, and perfectly human—I started forward; I felt a rebound of excitement. I drew a long breath, I gave a sort of cry, for what I saw before me was not a disembodied spirit, but a beautiful woman, an audacious actress. Instinctively, irresistibly, by the force of reaction against my credulity, I stretched out my hand and seized the long veil that muffled her head. I gave it a violent jerk, dragged it nearly off, and stood staring at a large fair person, of about five-and-thirty. I comprehended her at a glance; her long black dress, her pale, sorrow-worn face, painted to look paler, her very fine eyes,—the color of her father's,—and her sense of outrage at my movement.

"My father, I suppose," she cried, "did not send you here to insult me!" and she turned away rapidly, took up one of the candles and moved toward the door. Here she paused, looked at me again, hesitated, and then drew a purse from her pocket and flung it down on the floor. "There is your money!" she said, majestically.

I stood there, wavering between amazement and shame, and saw her pass out into the hall. Then I picked up the purse. The next moment, I heard a loud shriek and a crash of something dropping, and she came staggering back into the room without her light.

"My father—my father!" she cried; and with parted lips and dilated eyes, she rushed toward me.

"Your father—where?" I demanded.

"In the hall, at the foot of the stairs."

I stepped forward to go out, but she seized my arm.

"He is in white," she cried, "in his shirt. It's not he!"

"Why, your father is in his house, in his bed, extremely ill," I answered.

She looked at me fixedly, with searching eyes.

"Dying?"

"I hope not," I stuttered.

She gave a long moan and covered her face with her hands.

"Oh, heavens, I have seen his ghost!" she cried.

She still held my arm; she seemed too terrified to release it.
"His ghost!" I echoed, wondering.

"It's the punishment of my long folly!" she went on.

"Ah," said I, "it's the punishment of my indiscretion—of
my violence!"

"Take me away, take me away!" she cried, still clinging to
my arm. "Not there"—as I was turning toward the hall and
the front door—"not there, for pity's sake! By this door—the
back entrance." And snatching the other candles from the
table, she led me through the neighboring room into the back
part of the house. Here was a door opening from a sort of
scullery into the orchard. I turned the rusty lock and we
passed out and stood in the cool air, beneath the stars. Here
my companion gathered her black drapery about her, and
stood for a moment, hesitating. I had been infinitely flurried,
but my curiosity touching her was uppermost. Agitated, pale,
picturesque, she looked, in the early evening light, very beautiful.

"You have been playing all these years a most extraordinary
game," I said.

She looked at me somberly, and seemed disinclined to reply.
"I came in perfect good faith," I went on. "The last time—
three months ago—you remember?—you greatly frightened
me."

"Of course it was an extraordinary game," she answered at
last. "But it was the only way."

"Had he not forgiven you?"

"So long as he thought me dead, yes. There have been
things in my life he could not forgive."

I hesitated and then—"And where is your husband?" I
asked.

"I have no husband—I have never had a husband."

She made a gesture which checked further questions, and
moved rapidly away. I walked with her round the house to
the road, and she kept murmuring—"It was he—it was he!"
When we reached the road she stopped, and asked me which
way I was going. I pointed to the road by which I had come,
and she said—"I take the other. You are going to my father's?" she added.

"Directly," I said.

"Will you let me know to-morrow what you have found?"

"With pleasure. But how shall I communicate with you?"

She seemed at a loss, and looked about her. "Write a few words," she said, "and put them under that stone." And she pointed to one of the lava slabs that bordered the old well. I gave her my promise to comply, and she turned away. "I know my road," she said. "Everything is arranged. It's an old story."

She left me with a rapid step, and as she receded into the darkness, resumed, with the dark flowing lines of her drapery, the phantasmal appearance with which she had at first appeared to me. I watched her till she became invisible, and then I took my own leave of the place. I returned to town at a swinging pace, and marched straight to the little yellow house near the river. I took the liberty of entering without a knock, and, encountering no interruption, made my way to Captain Diamond's room. Outside the door, on a low bench, with folded arms, sat the sable Belinda.

"How is he?" I asked.

"He's gone to glory."

"Dead?" I cried.

She rose with a sort of tragic chuckle.

"He's as big a ghost as any of them now!"

I passed into the room and found the old man lying there irredeemably rigid and still. I wrote that evening a few lines which I proposed on the morrow to place beneath the stone, near the well; but my promise was not destined to be executed. I slept that night very ill—it was natural—and in my restlessness left my bed to walk about the room. As I did so I caught sight, in passing my window, of a red glow in the north-western sky. A house was on fire in the country, and evidently burning fast. It lay in the same direction as the scene of my evening's adventures, and as I stood watching the crimson horizon I was startled by a sharp memory. I had blown out the candle which lighted me, with my companion, to the door through which we escaped, but I had not accounted for the other light, which she had carried into the hall and dropped—heaven knew where—in her consternation. The next day I walked out with my folded letter and turned into the familiar cross-road. The haunted house was a mass of charred beams and smoldering ashes; the well cover had been pulled off, in quest of water, by the few neighbors who had had the audacity to contest what they must have regarded as a demon-kindled blaze, the loose stones were completely displaced, and the earth had been trampled into puddles.

Four Meetings

I SAW HER only four times, but I remember them vividly; she made an impression upon me. I thought her very pretty and very interesting—a charming specimen of a type. I am very sorry to hear of her death; and yet, when I think of it, why should I be sorry? The last time I saw her she was certainly not—— But I will describe all our meetings in order.

I.

The first one took place in the country, at a little tea-party, one snowy night. It must have been some seventeen years ago. My friend Latouche, going to spend Christmas with his mother, had persuaded me to go with him, and the good lady had given in our honour the entertainment of which I speak. To me it was really entertaining; I had never been in the depths of New England at that season. It had been snowing all day and the drifts were knee-high. I wondered how the ladies had made their way to the house; but I perceived that at Grimwinter a conversazione offering the attraction of two gentlemen from New York was felt to be worth an effort.

Mrs. Latouche in the course of the evening asked me if I "didn't want to" show the photographs to some of the young ladies. The photographs were in a couple of great portfolios, and had been brought home by her son, who, like myself, was lately returned from Europe. I looked round and was struck with the fact that most of the young ladies were provided with an object of interest more absorbing than the most vivid sun-picture. But there was a person standing alone near the mantel-shelf, and looking round the room with a small, gentle smile which seemed at odds, somehow, with her isolation. I looked at her a moment, and then said, "I should like to show them to that young lady."

"Oh yes," said Mrs. Latouche, "she is just the person. She doesn't care for flirting; I will speak to her."

I rejoined that if she did not care for flirting, she was,

perhaps, not just the person; but Mrs. Latouche had already gone to propose the photographs to her.

"She's delighted," she said, coming back. "She is just the person, so quiet and so bright." And then she told me the young lady was, by name, Miss Caroline Spencer, and with this she introduced me.

Miss Caroline Spencer was not exactly a beauty, but she was a charming little figure. She must have been close upon thirty, but she was made almost like a little girl, and she had the complexion of a child. She had a very pretty head, and her hair was arranged as nearly as possible like the hair of a Greek bust, though indeed it was to be doubted if she had ever seen a Greek bust. She was "artistic," I suspected, so far as Grimwinter allowed such tendencies. She had a soft, surprised eye, and thin lips, with very pretty teeth. Round her neck she wore what ladies call, I believe, a "ruche," fastened with a very small pin in pink coral, and in her hand she carried a fan made of plaited straw and adorned with pink ribbon. She wore a scanty black silk dress. She spoke with a kind of soft precision, showing her white teeth between her narrow but tender-looking lips, and she seemed extremely pleased, even a little fluttered, at the prospect of my demonstrations. These went forward very smoothly, after I had moved the portfolios out of their corner and placed a couple of chairs near a lamp. The photographs were usually things I knew,—large views of Switzerland, Italy, and Spain, landscapes, copies of famous buildings, pictures and statues. I said what I could about them, and my companion, looking at them as I held them up, sat perfectly still, with her straw fan raised to her under-lip. Occasionally, as I laid one of the pictures down, she said very softly, "Have you seen that place?" I usually answered that I had seen it several times (I had been a great traveller), and then I felt that she looked at me askance for a moment with her pretty eyes. I had asked her at the outset whether she had been to Europe; to this she answered, "No, no, no," in a little quick, confidential whisper. But after that, though she never took her eyes off the pictures, she said so little that I was afraid she was bored. Accordingly, after we had finished one portfolio, I offered, if she desired it, to desist. I felt that she was not bored, but her reticence puzzled me and I wished to make her speak. I turned round to look at her, and saw that there was a faint flush in each of her cheeks. She was waving her little fan to and fro. Instead of looking at me she fixed her eyes upon the other portfolio, which was leaning against the table.

"Won't you show me that?" she asked, with a little tremor in her voice. I could almost have believed she was agitated.

"With pleasure," I answered, "if you are not tired."

"No, I am not tired," she affirmed. "I like it—I love it."

And as I took up the other portfolio she laid her hand upon it, rubbing it softly.

"And have you been here too?" she asked.

On my opening the portfolio it appeared that I had been there. One of the first photographs was a large view of the Castle of Chillon, on the Lake of Geneva.

"Here," I said, "I have been many a time. Is it not beautiful?" And I pointed to the perfect reflection of the rugged rocks and pointed towers in the clear, still water. She did not say, "Oh, enchanting!" and push it away to see the next picture. She looked awhile, and then she asked if it was not where Bonivard, about whom Byron wrote, was confined. I assented, and tried to quote some of Byron's verses, but in this attempt I succeeded imperfectly.

She fanned herself a moment and then repeated the lines correctly, in a soft, flat, and yet agreeable voice. By the time she had finished, she was blushing. I complimented her and told her she was perfectly equipped for visiting Switzerland and Italy. She looked at me askance again, to see whether I was serious, and I added, that if she wished to recognise Byron's descriptions she must go abroad speedily: Europe was getting sadly dis-Byronised.

"How soon must I go?" she asked.

"Oh, I will give you ten years."

"I think I can go within ten years," she answered very soberly.

"Well," I said, "you will enjoy it immensely; you will find it very charming." And just then I came upon a photograph of some nook in a foreign city which I had been very fond of, and which recalled tender memories. I discoursed (as I suppose) with a certain eloquence; my companion sat listening, breathless.

"Have you been *very* long in foreign lands?" she asked, some time after I had ceased.

"Many years," I said.

"And have you travelled everywhere?"

"I have travelled a great deal. I am very fond of it; and, happily, I have been able."

Again she gave me her sidelong gaze. "And do you know the foreign languages?"

"After a fashion."

"Is it hard to speak them?"

"I don't believe you would find it hard," I gallantly responded.

"Oh, I shouldn't want to speak—I should only want to listen," she said. Then, after a pause, she added—"They say the French theatre is so beautiful."

"It is the best in the world."

"Did you go there very often?"

"When I was first in Paris I went every night."

"Every night!" And she opened her clear eyes very wide. "That to me is—" and she hesitated a moment—"is very wonderful." A few minutes later she asked—"Which country do you prefer?"

"There is one country I prefer to all others. I think you would do the same."

She looked at me a moment, and then she said softly—"Italy?"

"Italy," I answered softly, too; and for a moment we looked at each other. She looked as pretty as if, instead of showing her photographs, I had been making love to her. To increase the analogy, she glanced away, blushing. There was a silence, which she broke at last by saying—

"That is the place, which—in particular—I thought of going to."

"Oh, that's the place—that's the place!" I said.

She looked at two or three photographs in silence. "They say it is not so dear."

"As some other countries? Yes, that is not the least of its charms."

"But it is all very dear, is it not?"

"Europe, you mean?"

"Going there and travelling. That has been the trouble. I have very little money. I give lessons," said Miss Spencer.

"Of course one must have money," I said, "but one can manage with a moderate amount."

"I think I should manage. I have laid something by, and I am always adding a little to it. It's all for that." She paused a moment, and then went on with a kind of suppressed eagerness, as if telling me the story were a rare, but a possibly impure, satisfaction. "But it has not been only the money; it has been everything. Everything has been against it. I have waited and waited. It has been a mere castle in the air. I am almost afraid to talk about it. Two or three times it has been a little nearer, and then I have talked about it and it has melted away. I have talked about it too much," she said, hypocritically; for I saw that such talking was now a small tremulous ecstasy. "There is a lady who is a great friend of mine; she doesn't want to go; I always talk to her about it. I tire her dreadfully. She told me once she didn't know what would become of me. I should go crazy if I did not go to Europe, and I should certainly go crazy if I did."

"Well," I said, "you have not gone yet and nevertheless you are not crazy."

She looked at me a moment, and said—"I am not so sure. I don't think of anything else. I am always thinking of it. It prevents me from thinking of things that are nearer home— things that I ought to attend to. That is a kind of craziness."

"The cure for it is to go," I said.

"I have a faith that I shall go. I have a cousin in Europe!" she announced.

We turned over some more photographs, and I asked her if she had always lived at Grimwinter.

"Oh, no, sir," said Miss Spencer. "I have spent twenty-three months in Boston."

I answered, jocosely, that in that case foreign lands would probably prove a disappointment to her; but I quite failed to alarm her.

"I know more about them than you might think," she said, with her shy, neat little smile. "I mean by reading; I have read a great deal. I have not only read Byron; I have read histories and guide-books. I know I shall like it!"

"I understand your case," I rejoined. "You have the native American passion—the passion for the picturesque. With us, I think, it is primordial—antecedent to experience. Experience comes and only shows us something we have dreamt of."

"I think that is very true," said Caroline Spencer. "I have dreamt of everything; I shall know it all!"

"I am afraid you have wasted a great deal of time."

"Oh yes, that has been my great wickedness."

The people about us had begun to scatter; they were taking their leave. She got up and put out her hand to me, timidly, but with a peculiar brightness in her eyes.

"I am going back there," I said, as I shook hands with her. "I shall look out for you."

"I will tell you," she answered, "if I am disappointed."

And she went away, looking delicately agitated and moving her little straw fan.

II.

A few months after this I returned to Europe, and some three years elapsed. I had been living in Paris, and, toward the end of October, I went from that city to Havre, to meet my sister and her husband, who had written me that they were about to arrive there. On reaching Havre I found that the steamer was already in; I was nearly two hours late. I repaired directly to the hotel, where my relatives were already established. My sister had gone to bed, exhausted and disabled by her voyage; she was a sadly incompetent sailor, and her sufferings on this occasion had been extreme. She wished, for the moment, for undisturbed rest, and was unable to see me more than five minutes; so it was agreed that we should remain at Havre until the next day. My brother-in-law, who was anxious about his wife, was unwilling to leave her room; but she insisted upon his going out with me to take a walk and recover his land-legs. The early autumn day was warm and charming, and our stroll through the bright-coloured, busy streets of the old French sea-port was sufficiently entertaining. We walked along the sunny, noisy quays and then turned into a wide, pleasant

street which lay half in sun and half in shade—a French provincial street, that looked like an old water-colour drawing:
tall, gray, steep-roofed, red-gabled, many-storied houses;
green shutters on windows and old scroll-work above them;
flower-pots in balconies and white-capped women in doorways. We walked in the shade; all this stretched away on the
sunny side of the street and made a picture. We looked at it
as we passed along; then, suddenly, my brother-in-law
stopped—pressing my arm and staring. I followed his gaze
and saw that we had paused just before coming to a café,
where, under an awning, several tables and chairs were disposed upon the pavement. The windows were open behind;
half-a-dozen plants in tubs were ranged beside the door; the
pavement was besprinkled with clean bran. It was a nice little,
quiet, old-fashioned café; inside, in the comparative dusk, I
saw a stout, handsome woman, with pink ribbons in her cap,
perched up with a mirror behind her back, smiling at some
one who was out of sight. All this, however, I perceived
afterwards; what I first observed was a lady sitting alone,
outside, at one of the little marble-topped tables. My brother-
in-law had stopped to look at her. There was something on
the little table, but she was leaning back quietly, with her
hands folded, looking down the street, away from us. I saw
her only in something less than profile; nevertheless, I instantly felt that I had seen her before.

"The little lady of the steamer!" exclaimed my brother-in-
law.

"Was she on your steamer?" I asked.

"From morning till night. She was never sick. She used to
sit perpetually at the side of the vessel with her hands crossed
that way, looking at the eastward horizon."

"Are you going to speak to her?"

"I don't know her. I never made acquaintance with her. I
was too seedy. But I used to watch her and—I don't know
why—to be interested in her. She's a dear little Yankee
woman. I have an idea she is a school-mistress taking a holiday—for which her scholars have made up a purse."

She turned her face a little more into profile, looking at the
steep, gray house-fronts opposite to her. Then I said—"I shall
speak to her myself."

"I wouldn't; she is very shy," said my brother-in-law.

"My dear fellow, I know her. I once showed her photographs at a tea-party."

And I went up to her. She turned and looked at me, and I saw she was in fact Miss Caroline Spencer. But she was not so quick to recognise me; she looked startled. I pushed a chair to the table and sat down.

"Well," I said, "I hope you are not disappointed!"

She stared, blushing a little; then she gave a small jump which betrayed recognition.

"It was you who showed me the photographs—at Grimwinter!"

"Yes, it was I. This happens very charmingly, for I feel as if it were for me to give you a formal reception here—an official welcome. I talked to you so much about Europe."

"You didn't say too much. I am so happy!" she softly exclaimed.

Very happy she looked. There was no sign of her being older; she was as gravely, decently, demurely pretty as before. If she had seemed before a thin-stemmed, mild-hued flower of Puritanism, it may be imagined whether in her present situation this delicate bloom was less apparent. Beside her an old gentleman was drinking absinthe: behind her the *dame de comptoir* in the pink ribbons was calling "Alcibiade! Alcibiade!" to the long-aproned waiter. I explained to Miss Spencer that my companion had lately been her ship-mate, and my brother-in-law came up and was introduced to her. But she looked at him as if she had never seen him before, and I remembered that he had told me that her eyes were always fixed upon the eastward horizon. She had evidently not noticed him, and, still timidly smiling, she made no attempt whatever to pretend that she had. I staid with her at the café door, and he went back to the hotel and to his wife. I said to Miss Spencer that this meeting of ours in the first hour of her landing was really very strange, but that I was delighted to be there and receive her first impressions.

"Oh, I can't tell you," she said; "I feel as if I were in a dream. I have been sitting here for an hour, and I don't want to move. Everything is so picturesque. I don't know whether the coffee has intoxicated me; it's so delicious."

"Really," said I, "if you are so pleased with this poor prosaic Havre, you will have no admiration left for better things.
Don't spend your admiration all the first day; remember it's
your intellectual letter of credit. Remember all the beautiful
places and things that are waiting for you; remember that
lovely Italy!"

"I'm not afraid of running short," she said gayly, still looking at the opposite houses. "I could sit here all day, saying
to myself that here I am at last. It's so dark, and old, and
different."

"By the way," I inquired, "how come you to be sitting
here? Have you not gone to one of the inns?" For I was half
amused, half alarmed at the good conscience with which this
delicately pretty woman had stationed herself in conspicuous
isolation on the edge of the sidewalk.

"My cousin brought me here," she answered. "You know
I told you I had a cousin in Europe. He met me at the steamer
this morning."

"It was hardly worth his while to meet you if he was to
desert you so soon."

"Oh, he has only left me for half-an-hour," said Miss Spencer. "He has gone to get my money."

"Where is your money?"

She gave a little laugh. "It makes me feel very fine to tell
you! It is in some circular notes."

"And where are your circular notes?"

"In my cousin's pocket."

This statement was very serenely uttered, but—I can hardly
say why—it gave me a sensible chill. At the moment I should
have been utterly unable to give the reason of this sensation,
for I knew nothing of Miss Spencer's cousin. Since he was her
cousin, the presumption was in his favour. But I felt suddenly
uncomfortable at the thought that, half-an-hour after her
landing, her scanty funds should have passed into his hands.

"Is he to travel with you?" I asked.

"Only as far as Paris. He is an art-student in Paris. I wrote
to him that I was coming, but I never expected him to come
off to the ship. I supposed he would only just meet me at the
train in Paris. It is very kind of him. But he *is* very kind—and
very bright."

I instantly became conscious of an extreme curiosity to see this bright cousin who was an art-student.

"He is gone to the banker's?" I asked.

"Yes, to the banker's. He took me to an hotel—such a queer, quaint, delicious little place, with a court in the middle, and a gallery all round, and a lovely landlady, in such a beautifully fluted cap, and such a perfectly fitting dress! After a while we came out to walk to the banker's, for I haven't got any French money. But I was very dizzy from the motion of the vessel, and I thought I had better sit down. He found this place for me here, and he went off to the banker's himself. I am to wait here till he comes back."

It may seem very fantastic, but it passed through my mind that he would never come back. I settled myself in my chair beside Miss Spencer and determined to await the event. She was extremely observant; there was something touching in it. She noticed everything that the movement of the street brought before us—the peculiarities of costume, the shapes of vehicles, the big Norman horses, the fat priests, the shaven poodles. We talked of these things, and there was something charming in her freshness of perception and the way her book-nourished fancy recognised and welcomed everything.

"And when your cousin comes back what are you going to do?" I asked.

She hesitated a moment. "We don't quite know."

"When do you go to Paris? If you go by the four o'clock train I may have the pleasure of making the journey with you."

"I don't think we shall do that. My cousin thinks I had better stay here a few days."

"Oh!" said I; and for five minutes said nothing more. I was wondering what her cousin was, in vulgar parlance, "up to." I looked up and down the street, but saw nothing that looked like a bright American art-student. At last I took the liberty of observing that Havre was hardly a place to choose as one of the aesthetic stations of a European tour. It was a place of convenience, nothing more; a place of transit, through which transit should be rapid. I recommended her to go to Paris by the afternoon train, and meanwhile to amuse herself by driving to the ancient fortress at the mouth of the harbour—that picturesque, circular structure which bore the name of Francis the First and looked like a small castle of St. Angelo. (It has lately been demolished.)

She listened with much interest; then for a moment she looked grave.

"My cousin told me that when he returned he should have something particular to say to me, and that we could do nothing or decide nothing until I should have heard it. But I will make him tell me quickly, and then we will go to the ancient fortress. There is no hurry to get to Paris; there is plenty of time."

She smiled with her softly severe little lips as she spoke those last words. But I, looking at her with a purpose, saw just a tiny gleam of apprehension in her eye.

"Don't tell me," I said, "that this wretched man is going to give you bad news!"

"I suspect it is a little bad, but I don't believe it is very bad. At any rate, I must listen to it."

I looked at her again an instant. "You didn't come to Europe to listen," I said. "You came to see!" But now I was sure her cousin would come back; since he had something disagreeable to say to her, he certainly would turn up. We sat a while longer, and I asked her about her plans of travel. She had them on her fingers' ends, and she told over the names with a kind of solemn distinctness: from Paris to Dijon and to Avignon, from Avignon to Marseilles and the Cornice road; thence to Genoa, to Spezia, to Pisa, to Florence, to Rome. It apparently had never occurred to her that there could be the least incommodity in her travelling alone; and since she was unprovided with a companion I of course scrupulously abstained from disturbing her sense of security.

At last her cousin came back. I saw him turn towards us out of a side-street, and from the moment my eyes rested upon him I felt that this was the bright American art-student. He wore a slouch hat and a rusty black velvet jacket, such as I had often encountered in the Rue Bonaparte. His shirt-collar revealed a large section of a throat which, at a distance, was not strikingly statuesque. He was tall and lean; he had red hair and freckles. So much I had time to observe while he approached the café, staring at me with natural surprise from under his umbrageous coiffure. When he came up to us I immediately introduced myself to him as an old acquaintance of Miss Spencer. He looked at me hard with a pair of little red eyes, then he made me a solemn bow in the French fashion, with his sombrero.

"You were not on the ship?" he said.

"No, I was not on the ship. I have been in Europe these three years."

He bowed once more, solemnly, and motioned me to be seated again. I sat down, but it was only for the purpose of observing him an instant—I saw it was time I should return to my sister. Miss Spencer's cousin was a queer fellow. Nature had not shaped him for a Raphaelesque or Byronic attire, and his velvet doublet and naked throat were not in harmony with his facial attributes. His hair was cropped close to his head; his ears were large and ill-adjusted to the same. He had a lackadaisical carriage and a sentimental droop which were peculiarly at variance with his keen, strange-coloured eyes. Perhaps I was prejudiced, but I thought his eyes treacherous. He said nothing for some time; he leaned his hands on his cane and looked up and down the street. Then at last, slowly lifting his cane and pointing with it, "That's a very nice bit," he remarked, softly. He had his head on one side, and his little eyes were half closed. I followed the direction of his stick; the object it indicated was a red cloth hung out of an old window. "Nice bit of colour," he continued; and without moving his head he transferred his half-closed gaze to me. "Composes well," he pursued. "Make a nice thing." He spoke in a hard, vulgar voice.

"I see you have a great deal of eye," I replied. "Your cousin tells me you are studying art." He looked at me in the same way without answering, and I went on with deliberate urbanity—"I suppose you are at the studio of one of those great men."

Still he looked at me, and then he said softly—"Gérôme."

"Do you like it?" I asked.

"Do you understand French?" he said.

"Some kinds," I answered.

He kept his little eyes on me; then he said—"J'adore la peinture!"

"Oh, I understand that kind!" I rejoined. Miss Spencer laid
her hand upon her cousin's arm with a little pleased and fluttered movement; it was delightful to be among people who
were on such easy terms with foreign tongues. I got up to
take leave, and asked Miss Spencer where, in Paris, I might
have the honour of waiting upon her. To what hotel would
she go?

She turned to her cousin inquiringly and he honoured me
again with his little languid leer. "Do you know the Hôtel
des Princes?"

"I know where it is."

"I shall take her there."

"I congratulate you," I said to Caroline Spencer. "I believe
it is the best inn in the world; and in case I should still have
a moment to call upon you here, where are you lodged?"

"Oh, it's such a pretty name," said Miss Spencer, gleefully.
"À la Belle Normande."

As I left them her cousin gave me a great flourish with his
picturesque hat.

III.

My sister, as it proved, was not sufficiently restored to leave
Havre by the afternoon train; so that, as the autumn dusk
began to fall, I found myself at liberty to call at the sign of
the Fair Norman. I must confess that I had spent much of the
interval in wondering what the disagreeable thing was that my
charming friend's disagreeable cousin had been telling her.
The "Belle Normande" was a modest inn in a shady by-street,
where it gave me satisfaction to think Miss Spencer must have
encountered local colour in abundance. There was a crooked
little court, where much of the hospitality of the house was
carried on; there was a stair-case climbing to bedrooms on the
outer side of the wall; there was a small trickling fountain with
a stucco statuette in the midst of it; there was a little boy in
a white cap and apron cleaning copper vessels at a conspicuous
kitchen door; there was a chattering landlady, neatly laced,
arranging apricots and grapes into an artistic pyramid upon a
pink plate. I looked about, and on a green bench outside of
an open door labelled *Salle à Manger*, I perceived Caroline

Spencer. No sooner had I looked at her than I saw that something had happened since the morning. She was leaning back on her bench, her hands were clasped in her lap, and her eyes were fixed upon the landlady, at the other side of the court, manipulating her apricots.

But I saw she was not thinking of apricots. She was staring absently, thoughtfully; as I came near her I perceived that she had been crying. I sat down on the bench beside her before she saw me; then, when she had done so, she simply turned round, without surprise, and rested her sad eyes upon me. Something very bad indeed had happened; she was completely changed.

I immediately charged her with it. "Your cousin has been giving you bad news; you are in great distress."

For a moment she said nothing, and I supposed that she was afraid to speak, lest her tears should come back. But presently I perceived that in the short time that had elapsed since my leaving her in the morning she had shed them all, and that she was now softly stoical—intensely composed.

"My poor cousin is in distress," she said at last. "His news was bad." Then, after a brief hesitation—"He was in terrible want of money."

"In want of yours, you mean?"

"Of any that he could get—honestly. Mine was the only money."

"And he has taken yours?"

She hesitated again a moment, but her glance, meanwhile, was pleading. "I gave him what I had."

I have always remembered the accent of those words as the most angelic bit of human utterance I had ever listened to; but then, almost with a sense of personal outrage, I jumped up. "Good heavens!" I said, "do you call that getting it honestly?"

I had gone too far; she blushed deeply. "We will not speak of it," she said.

"We *must* speak of it," I answered, sitting down again. "I am your friend; it seems to me you need one. What is the matter with your cousin?"

"He is in debt."

"No doubt! But what is the special fitness of your paying his debts?"

"He has told me all his story; I am very sorry for him."

"So am I! But I hope he will give you back your money."

"Certainly he will; as soon as he can."

"When will that be?"

"When he has finished his great picture."

"My dear young lady, confound his great picture! Where is this desperate cousin?"

She certainly hesitated now. Then—"At his dinner," she answered.

I turned about and looked through the open door into the *salle à manger*. There, alone at the end of a long table, I perceived the object of Miss Spencer's compassion—the bright young art-student. He was dining too attentively to notice me at first; but in the act of setting down a well-emptied wine-glass he caught sight of my observant attitude. He paused in his repast, and, with his head on one side and his meagre jaws slowly moving, fixedly returned my gaze. Then the landlady came lightly brushing by with her pyramid of apricots.

"And that nice little plate of fruit is for him?" I exclaimed.

Miss Spencer glanced at it tenderly. "They do that so prettily!" she murmured.

I felt helpless and irritated. "Come now, really," I said; "do you approve of that long strong fellow accepting your funds?" She looked away from me; I was evidently giving her pain. The case was hopeless; the long strong fellow had "interested" her.

"Excuse me if I speak of him so unceremoniously," I said. "But you are really too generous, and he is not quite delicate enough. He made his debts himself—he ought to pay them himself."

"He has been foolish," she answered; "I know that. He has told me everything. We had a long talk this morning; the poor fellow threw himself upon my charity. He has signed notes to a large amount."

"The more fool he!"

"He is in extreme distress; and it is not only himself. It is his poor wife."

"Ah, he has a poor wife?"

"I didn't know it—but he confessed everything. He married two years since, secretly."

"Why secretly?"

Caroline Spencer glanced about her, as if she feared listeners. Then softly, in a little impressive tone—"She was a Countess!"

"Are you very sure of that?"

"She has written me a most beautiful letter."

"Asking you for money, eh?"

"Asking me for confidence and sympathy," said Miss Spencer. "She has been disinherited by her father. My cousin told me the story and she tells it in her own way, in the letter. It is like an old romance. Her father opposed the marriage and when he discovered that she had secretly disobeyed him he cruelly cast her off. It is really most romantic. They are the oldest family in Provence."

I looked and listened, in wonder. It really seemed that the poor woman was enjoying the "romance" of having a discarded Countess-cousin, out of Provence, so deeply as almost to lose the sense of what the forfeiture of her money meant for her.

"My dear young lady," I said, "you don't want to be ruined for picturesqueness' sake?"

"I shall not be ruined. I shall come back before long to stay with them. The Countess insists upon that."

"Come back! You are going home, then?"

She sat for a moment with her eyes lowered, then with an heroic suppression of a faint tremor of the voice—"I have no money for travelling!" she answered.

"You gave it *all* up?"

"I have kept enough to take me home."

I gave an angry groan, and at this juncture Miss Spencer's cousin, the fortunate possessor of her sacred savings and of the hand of the Provençal Countess, emerged from the little dining-room. He stood on the threshold for an instant, removing the stone from a plump apricot which he had brought away from the table; then he put the apricot into his mouth, and while he let it sojourn there, gratefully, stood looking at us, with his long legs apart and his hands dropped into the

pockets of his velvet jacket. My companion got up, giving him
a thin glance which I caught in its passage, and which expressed a strange commixture of resignation and fascination—a sort of perverted exaltation. Ugly, vulgar, pretentious,
dishonest as I thought the creature, he had appealed successfully to her eager and tender imagination. I was deeply disgusted, but I had no warrant to interfere, and at any rate I
felt that it would be vain.

The young man waved his hand with a pictorial gesture.
"Nice old court," he observed. "Nice mellow old place.
Good tone in that brick. Nice crooked old stair-case."

Decidedly, I couldn't stand it; without responding I gave
my hand to Caroline Spencer. She looked at me an instant
with her little white face and expanded eyes, and as she
showed her pretty teeth I suppose she meant to smile.

"Don't be sorry for me," she said, "I am very sure I shall
see something of this dear old Europe yet."

I told her that I would not bid her good-bye—I should
find a moment to come back the next morning. Her cousin,
who had put on his sombrero again, flourished it off at me
by way of a bow—upon which I took my departure.

The next morning I came back to the inn, where I met in
the court the landlady, more loosely laced than in the evening.
On my asking for Miss Spencer,—"*Partie*, monsieur," said
the hostess. "She went away last night at ten o'clock, with
her—her—not her husband, eh?—in fine her *Monsieur*. They
went down to the American ship." I turned away; the poor
girl had been about thirteen hours in Europe.

IV.

I myself, more fortunate, was there some five years longer.
During this period I lost my friend Latouche, who died of a
malarious fever during a tour in the Levant. One of the first
things I did on my return was to go up to Grimwinter to pay
a consolatory visit to his poor mother. I found her in deep
affliction, and I sat with her the whole of the morning that
followed my arrival (I had come in late at night), listening to
her tearful descant and singing the praises of my friend. We
talked of nothing else, and our conversation terminated only

with the arrival of a quick little woman who drove herself up to the door in a "carry-all," and whom I saw toss the reins upon the horse's back with the briskness of a startled sleeper throwing back the bed-clothes. She jumped out of the carry-all and she jumped into the room. She proved to be the minister's wife and the great town-gossip, and she had evidently, in the latter capacity, a choice morsel to communicate. I was as sure of this as I was that poor Mrs. Latouche was not absolutely too bereaved to listen to her. It seemed to me discreet to retire; I said I believed I would go and take a walk before dinner.

"And, by the way," I added, "if you will tell me where my old friend Miss Spencer lives I will walk to her house."

The minister's wife immediately responded. Miss Spencer lived in the fourth house beyond the Baptist church; the Baptist church was the one on the right, with that queer green thing over the door; they called it a portico, but it looked more like an old-fashioned bedstead.

"Yes, do go and see poor Caroline," said Mrs. Latouche. "It will refresh her to see a strange face."

"I should think she had had enough of strange faces!" cried the minister's wife.

"I mean, to see a visitor," said Mrs. Latouche, amending her phrase.

"I should think she had had enough of visitors!" her companion rejoined. "But *you* don't mean to stay ten years," she added, glancing at me.

"Has she a visitor of that sort?" I inquired, perplexed.

"You will see the sort!" said the minister's wife. "She's easily seen; she generally sits in the front yard. Only take care what you say to her, and be very sure you are polite."

"Ah, she is so sensitive?"

The minister's wife jumped up and dropped me a curtsey—a most ironical curtsey.

"That's what she is, if you please. She's a Countess!"

And pronouncing this word with the most scathing accent, the little woman seemed fairly to laugh in the Countess's face. I stood a moment, staring, wondering, remembering.

"Oh, I shall be very polite!" I cried; and grasping my hat and stick, I went on my way.

I found Miss Spencer's residence without difficulty. The Baptist church was easily identified, and the small dwelling near it, of a rusty white, with a large central chimney-stack and a Virginia creeper, seemed naturally and properly the abode of a frugal old maid with a taste for the picturesque. As I approached I slackened my pace, for I had heard that some one was always sitting in the front yard, and I wished to reconnoitre. I looked cautiously over the low white fence which separated the small garden-space from the unpaved street; but I descried nothing in the shape of a Countess. A small straight path led up to the crooked door-step, and on either side of it was a little grass-plot, fringed with currant-bushes. In the middle of the grass, on either side, was a large quince-tree, full of antiquity and contortions, and beneath one of the quince-trees were placed a small table and a couple of chairs. On the table lay a piece of unfinished embroidery and two or three books in bright-coloured paper covers. I went in at the gate and paused half-way along the path, scanning the place for some farther token of its occupant, before whom—I could hardly have said why—I hesitated abruptly to present myself. Then I saw that the poor little house was very shabby. I felt a sudden doubt of my right to intrude; for curiosity had been my motive, and curiosity here seemed singularly indelicate. While I hesitated, a figure appeared in the open door-way and stood there looking at me. I immediately recognised Caroline Spencer, but she looked at me as if she had never seen me before. Gently, but gravely and timidly, I advanced to the door-step, and then I said, with an attempt at friendly badinage—

"I waited for you over there to come back, but you never came."

"Waited where, sir?" she asked softly, and her light-coloured eyes expanded more than before.

She was much older; she looked tired and wasted.

"Well," I said, "I waited at Havre."

She stared; then she recognised me. She smiled and blushed and clasped her two hands together. "I remember you now," she said. "I remember that day." But she stood there, neither coming out nor asking me to come in. She was embarrassed.

I, too, felt a little awkward. I poked my stick into the path. "I kept looking out for you, year after year," I said.

"You mean in Europe?" murmured Miss Spencer.

"In Europe, of course! Here, apparently, you are easy enough to find."

She leaned her hand against the unpainted door-post, and her head fell a little to one side. She looked at me for a moment without speaking, and I thought I recognised the expression that one sees in women's eyes when tears are rising. Suddenly she stepped out upon the cracked slab of stone before the threshold and closed the door behind her. Then she began to smile intently, and I saw that her teeth were as pretty as ever. But there had been tears too.

"Have you been there ever since?" she asked, almost in a whisper.

"Until three weeks ago. And you—you never came back?"

Still looking at me with her fixed smile, she put her hand behind her and opened the door again. "I am not very polite," she said. "Won't you come in?"

"I am afraid I incommode you."

"Oh no!" she answered, smiling more than ever. And she pushed back the door, with a sign that I should enter.

I went in, following her. She led the way to a small room on the left of the narrow hall, which I supposed to be her parlour, though it was at the back of the house, and we passed the closed door of another apartment which apparently enjoyed a view of the quince-trees. This one looked out upon a small wood-shed and two clucking hens. But I thought it very pretty, until I saw that its elegance was of the most frugal kind; after which, presently, I thought it prettier still, for I had never seen faded chintz and old mezzotint engravings, framed in varnished autumn leaves, disposed in so graceful a fashion. Miss Spencer sat down on a very small portion of the sofa, with her hands tightly clasped in her lap. She looked ten years older, and it would have sounded very perverse now to speak of her as pretty. But I thought her so; or at least I thought her touching. She was peculiarly agitated. I tried to appear not to notice it; but suddenly, in the most inconsequent fashion—it was an irresistible memory of our little friendship at

Havre—I said to her—"I do incommode you. You are distressed."

She raised her two hands to her face, and for a moment kept it buried in them. Then, taking them away——"It's because you remind me . . . . ." she said.

"I remind you, you mean, of that miserable day at Havre?"

She shook her head. "It was not miserable. It was delightful."

"I never was so shocked as when, on going back to your inn the next morning, I found you had set sail again."

She was silent a moment; and then she said——"Please let us not speak of that."

"Did you come straight back here?" I asked.

"I was back here just thirty days after I had gone away."

"And here you have remained ever since?"

"Oh yes!" she said gently.

"When are you going to Europe again?"

This question seemed brutal; but there was something that irritated me in the softness of her resignation, and I wished to extort from her some expression of impatience.

She fixed her eyes for a moment upon a small sun-spot on the carpet; then she got up and lowered the window-blind a little, to obliterate it. Presently, in the same mild voice, answering my question, she said—"Never!"

"I hope your cousin repaid you your money."

"I don't care for it now," she said, looking away from me.

"You don't care for your money?"

"For going to Europe."

"Do you mean that you would not go if you could?"

"I can't—I can't," said Caroline Spencer. "It is all over; I never think of it."

"He never repaid you, then!" I exclaimed.

"Please—please," she began.

But she stopped; she was looking toward the door. There had been a rustling and a sound of steps in the hall.

I also looked toward the door, which was open, and now admitted another person—a lady who paused just within the threshold. Behind her came a young man. The lady looked at me with a good deal of fixedness—long enough for my glance

to receive a vivid impression of herself. Then she turned to
Caroline Spencer, and, with a smile and a strong foreign accent——

"Excuse my interruption!" she said. "I knew not you had
company—the gentleman came in so quietly."

With this, she directed her eyes toward me again.

She was very strange; yet my first feeling was that I had
seen her before. Then I perceived that I had only seen ladies
who were very much like her. But I had seen them very far
away from Grimwinter, and it was an odd sensation to be
seeing her here. Whither was it the sight of her seemed to
transport me? To some dusky landing before a shabby Parisian
quatrième —to an open door revealing a greasy ante-chamber,
and to Madame leaning over the banisters while she holds a
faded dressing-gown together and bawls down to the portress
to bring up her coffee. Miss Spencer's visitor was a very large
woman, of middle age, with a plump, dead-white face and
hair drawn back *à la chinoise*. She had a small, penetrating
eye, and what is called in French an agreeable smile. She wore
an old pink cashmere dressing-gown, covered with white embroideries, and, like the figure in my momentary vision, she
was holding it together in front with a bare and rounded arm
and a plump and deeply-dimpled hand.

"It is only to spick about my *café*," she said to Miss Spencer
with her agreeable smile. "I should like it served in the garden
under the leetle tree."

The young man behind her had now stepped into the
room, and he also stood looking at me. He was a pretty-faced
little fellow, with an air of provincial foppishness—a tiny
Adonis of Grimwinter. He had a small, pointed nose, a small,
pointed chin, and, as I observed, the most diminutive feet.
He looked at me foolishly, with his mouth open.

"You shall have your coffee," said Miss Spencer, who had
a faint red spot in each of her cheeks.

"It is well!" said the lady in the dressing-gown. "Find your
bouk," she added, turning to the young man.

He looked vaguely round the room. "My grammar, d'ye
mean?" he asked, with a helpless intonation.

But the large lady was looking at me curiously, and gathering in her dressing-gown with her white arm.

"Find your bouk, my friend," she repeated.

"My poetry, d'ye mean?" said the young man, also gazing at me again.

"Never mind your bouk," said his companion. "To-day we will talk. We will make some conversation. But we must not interrupt. Come," and she turned away. "Under the leetle tree," she added, for the benefit of Miss Spencer.

Then she gave me a sort of salutation, and a "Monsieur!"—with which she swept away again, followed by the young man.

Caroline Spencer stood there with her eyes fixed upon the ground.

"Who is that?" I asked.

"The Countess, my cousin."

"And who is the young man?"

"Her pupil, Mr. Mixter."

This description of the relation between the two persons who had just left the room made me break into a little laugh. Miss Spencer looked at me gravely.

"She gives French lessons; she has lost her fortune."

"I see," I said. "She is determined to be a burden to no one. That is very proper."

Miss Spencer looked down on the ground again. "I must go and get the coffee," she said.

"Has the lady many pupils?" I asked.

"She has only Mr. Mixter. She gives all her time to him."

At this I could not laugh, though I smelt provocation. Miss Spencer was too grave. "He pays very well," she presently added, with simplicity. "He is very rich. He is very kind. He takes the Countess to drive." And she was turning away.

"You are going for the Countess's coffee?" I said.

"If you will excuse me a few moments."

"Is there no one else to do it?"

She looked at me with the softest serenity. "I keep no servants."

"Can she not wait upon herself?"

"She is not used to that."

"I see," said I, as gently as possible. "But before you go, tell me this: who is this lady?"

"I told you about her before—that day. She is the wife of my cousin, whom you saw."

"The lady who was disowned by her family in consequence of her marriage?"

"Yes; they have never seen her again. They have cast her off."

"And where is her husband?"

"He is dead."

"And where is your money?"

The poor girl flinched, there was something too methodical in my questions. "I don't know," she said wearily.

But I continued a moment. "On her husband's death this lady came over here?"

"Yes, she arrived one day."

"How long ago?"

"Two years."

"She has been here ever since?"

"Every moment."

"How does she like it?"

"Not at all."

"And how do *you* like it?"

Miss Spencer laid her face in her two hands an instant, as she had done ten minutes before. Then, quickly, she went to get the Countess's coffee.

I remained alone in the little parlour; I wanted to see more—to learn more. At the end of five minutes the young man whom Miss Spencer had described as the Countess's pupil came in. He stood looking at me for a moment with parted lips. I saw he was a very rudimentary young man.

"She wants to know if you won't come out there?" he observed at last.

"Who wants to know?"

"The Countess. That French lady."

"She has asked you to bring me?"

"Yes, sir," said the young man feebly, looking at my six feet of stature.

I went out with him, and we found the Countess sitting under one of the little quince-trees in front of the house. She was drawing a needle through the piece of embroidery which she had taken from the small table. She pointed graciously to the chair beside her and I seated myself. Mr. Mixter glanced about him, and then sat down in the grass at her feet. He gazed upward, looking with parted lips from the Countess to me.

"I am sure you speak French," said the Countess, fixing her brilliant little eyes upon me.

"I do, madam, after a fashion," I answered, in the lady's own tongue.

"Voilà!" she cried most expressively. "I knew it so soon as I looked at you. You have been in my poor dear country."

"A long time."

"You know Paris?"

"Thoroughly, madam." And with a certain conscious purpose I let my eyes meet her own.

She presently, hereupon, moved her own and glanced down at Mr. Mixter. "What are we talking about?" she demanded of her attentive pupil.

He pulled his knees up, plucked at the grass with his hand, stared, blushed a little. "You are talking French," said Mr. Mixter.

"La belle découverte!" said the Countess.

"Here are ten months," she explained to me, "that I am giving him lessons. Don't put yourself out not to say he's a fool; he won't understand you."

"I hope your other pupils are more gratifying," I remarked.

"I have no others. They don't know what French is in this place; they don't want to know. You may therefore imagine the pleasure it is to me to meet a person who speaks it like yourself." I replied that my own pleasure was not less, and she went on drawing her stitches through her embroidery, with her little finger curled out. Every few moments she put her eyes close to her work, near-sightedly. I thought her a very disagreeable person; she was coarse, affected, dishonest, and no more a Countess than I was a caliph. "Talk to me of Paris," she went on. "The very name of it gives me an emotion! How long since you were there?"

"Two months ago."

"Happy man! Tell me something about it. What were they doing? Oh, for an hour of the boulevard!"

"They were doing about what they are always doing—amusing themselves a good deal."

"At the theatres, eh?" sighed the Countess. "At the *cafés-concerts*—at the little tables in front of the doors? *Quelle existence!* You know I am a Parisienne, monsieur," she added, "—to my finger-tips."

"Miss Spencer was mistaken, then," I ventured to rejoin, "in telling me that you are a Provençale."

She stared a moment, then she put her nose to her embroidery, which had a dingy, desultory aspect. "Ah, I am a Provençale by birth; but I am a Parisienne by—inclination."

"And by experience, I suppose?" I said.

She questioned me a moment with her hard little eyes. "Oh, experience! I could talk of experience if I wished. I never expected, for example, that experience had *this* in store for me." And she pointed with her bare elbow, and with a jerk of her head, at everything that surrounded her—at the little white house, the quince-tree, the rickety paling, even at Mr. Mixter.

"You are in exile!" I said smiling.

"You may imagine what it is! These two years that I have been here I have passed hours—hours! One gets used to things, and sometimes I think I have got used to this. But there are some things that are always beginning over again. For example, my coffee."

"Do you always have coffee at this hour?" I inquired.

She tossed back her head and measured me.

"At what hour would you prefer me to have it? I must have my little cup after breakfast."

"Ah, you breakfast at this hour?"

"At mid-day—*comme cela se fait*. Here they breakfast at a quarter past seven! That 'quarter past' is charming!"

"But you were telling me about your coffee," I observed, sympathetically.

"My *cousine* can't believe in it; she can't understand it. She's an excellent girl; but that little cup of black coffee, with a drop of cognac, served at this hour—they exceed her comprehension. So I have to break the ice every day, and it takes the coffee the time you see to arrive. And when it arrives, monsieur! If I don't offer you any of it you must not take it ill. It will be because I know you have drunk it on the boulevard."

I resented extremely this scornful treatment of poor Caroline Spencer's humble hospitality; but I said nothing, in order to say nothing uncivil. I only looked on Mr. Mixter, who had clasped his arms round his knees and was watching my companion's demonstrative graces in solemn fascination. She presently saw that I was observing him; she glanced at me with a little bold explanatory smile. "You know, he adores me," she murmured, putting her nose into her tapestry again. I expressed the promptest credence and she went on. "He dreams of becoming my lover! Yes, it's his dream. He has read a French novel; it took him six months. But ever since that he has thought himself the hero, and me the heroine!"

Mr. Mixter had evidently not an idea that he was being talked about; he was too preoccupied with the ecstasy of contemplation. At this moment Caroline Spencer came out of the house, bearing a coffee-pot on a little tray. I noticed that on her way from the door to the table she gave me a single quick, vaguely appealing glance. I wondered what it signified; I felt that it signified a sort of half-frightened longing to know what, as a man of the world who had been in France, I thought of the Countess. It made me extremely uncomfortable. I could not tell her that the Countess was very possibly the runaway wife of a little hair-dresser. I tried suddenly, on the contrary, to show a high consideration for her. But I got up; I couldn't stay longer. It vexed me to see Caroline Spencer standing there like a waiting-maid.

"You expect to remain some time at Grimwinter?" I said to the Countess.

She gave a terrible shrug.

"Who knows? Perhaps for years. When one is in misery! * * * *Chère belle*," she added, turning to Miss Spencer, "you have forgotten the cognac!"

I detained Caroline Spencer as, after looking a moment in silence at the little table, she was turning away to procure this missing delicacy. I silently gave her my hand in farewell. She looked very tired, but there was a strange hint of prospective patience in her severely mild little face. I thought she was rather glad I was going. Mr. Mixter had risen to his feet and was pouring out the Countess's coffee. As I went back past the Baptist church I reflected that poor Miss Spencer had been right in her presentiment that she should still see something of that dear old Europe.

Rose-Agathe

I HAD INVITED the excellent fellow to dinner, and had begun to wonder, the stroke of half-past six having sounded, why he did not present himself. At last I stepped out upon the balcony and looked along the street in the direction from which, presumably, he would approach. A Parisian thoroughfare is always an entertaining spectacle, and I had still much of a stranger's alertness of attention. Before long, therefore, I quite forgot my unpunctual guest in my relish of the multifarious animation of the brilliant city. It was a perfect evening, toward the end of April; there was a charming golden glow on the opposite house-tops, which looked toward the west; there was a sort of vernal odour in the street, mingling with the emanations of the restaurant across the way, whose door now always stood open; with the delightful aroma of the chocolate-shop which occupied the ground floor of the house in whose *entresol* I was lodged; and, as I fancied, with certain luscious perfumes hovering about the brilliantly-polished window of the hairdresser's establishment, adjacent to the restaurant. It had above it the sign, "Anatole, Coiffeur;" these artists, in Paris, being known only by their Christian name. Then there was a woman in a minutely-fluted cap, selling violets in a little handcart which she gently pushed along over the smooth asphalte, and which, as she passed, left a sensible trace in the thick, mild air. All this made a thoroughly Parisian mixture, and I envied Sanguinetti the privilege of spending his life in a city in which even the humblest of one's senses is the medium of poetic impressions. There was poetry in the warm, succulent exhalations of the opposite restaurant, where, among the lighted lamps, I could see the little tables glittering with their glass and silver, the tenderly-brown rolls nestling in the petals of the folded napkins, the waiters, in their snowy aprons, standing in the various attitudes of imminent eagerness, the agreeable *dame de comptoir*, sitting idle for the moment and rubbing her plump white hands. To a person so inordinately fond of chocolate as myself—there was literally a pretty little box, half-emptied of large soft globules

of the compound, standing at that moment on my table—
there was of course something very agreeable in the faint upward gusts of the establishment in my rez-de-chaussée. Presently, too, it appeared to me that the savours peculiar to the
hairdressing-shop had assumed an extraordinary intensity, and
that my right-hand nostril was exposed to the titillation of a
new influence. It was as if a bottle of the finest hair-oil had
suddenly been uncorked. Glancing that way again, I perceived
the source of this rich effluvium. The hairdresser's door was
open, and a person whom I supposed to be his wife had come
to inhale upon the threshold the lighter atmosphere of the
street. She stood there for some moments, looking up and
down, and I had time to see that she was very pretty. She
wore a plain black silk dress, and one needed to know no more
of millinery than most men to observe that it was admirably
fitted to a charming figure. She had a little knot of pink ribbon
at her throat and a bunch of violets in her rounded bosom.
Her face seemed to me at once beautiful and lively—two merits that are not always united; for smiles, I have observed, are
infrequent with women who are either very ugly or very
pretty. Her light-brown hair was, naturally enough, dressed
with consummate art, and the character of her beauty being
suggestive of purity and gentleness, she looked (her black silk
dress apart) like a Madonna who should have been *coiffée* by
M. Anatole. What a delightful person for a barber's wife, I
thought; and I saw her sitting in the little front shop, at the
desk, and taking the money with a gracious smile from the
gentlemen who had been having their whiskers trimmed in
the inner sanctuary. I touched my own whiskers, and straightway decided that they needed trimming. In a few moments
this lovely woman stepped out upon the pavement, and
strolled along, in front of the shop-window, on a little tour
of inspection. She stood there a moment, looking at the brilliant array of brightly-capped flacons, of ivory toilet-imple-
ments, of detached human tresses disposed in every variety of
fashionable convolution: she inclined her head to one side and
gently stroked her chin. I was able to perceive that even with
her back turned she was hardly less pretty than when seen in
front—her back had, as they say, so much *chic*. The inclination
of her head denoted contentment, even complacency; and in-

deed, well it might, for the window was most artistically arranged. Its principal glory was conferred by two waxen heads of lovely ladies, such as are usually seen in hairdressers' windows; and these wig-wearing puppets, which maintained a constant rotary movement, seemed to be a triumph of the modeller's art. One of the revolving ladies was dark, and the other fair, and each tossed back her head and thrust out her waxen bosom and parted her rosy lips in the most stylish manner conceivable. Several persons, passing by, had stopped to admire them. In a few moments a second inmate came to the door of the shop, and said a word to the barber's pretty wife. This was not the barber himself, but a young woman apparently employed in the shop. She was a nice-looking young woman enough, but she had by no means the beauty of her companion, who, to my regret, on hearing her voice, instantly went in.

After this I fell to watching something else, I forget what: I had quite forgotten Sanguinetti. I think I was looking at a gentleman and lady who had come into the restaurant and placed themselves near the great sheet of plate-glass which separated the interior from the street. The lady, who had the most wonderfully arched eyebrows, was evidently ordering the dinner, and I was struck with the profusion of its items. At last she began to eat her soup, with her little finger very much curled out, and then my gaze wandered toward the hairdresser's window again. This circumstance reminded me that I was really very good-natured to be waiting so placidly for that dilatory Sanguinetti. There he stood in front of the coiffeur's, staring as intently and serenely into the window as if he had the whole evening before him. I waited a few moments, to give him a chance to move on, but he remained there, gaping like a rustic at a fair. What in the world was he looking at? Had he spied something that could play a part in his collection? For Sanguinetti was a collector, and had a room full of old crockery and uncomfortable chairs. But he cared for nothing that was not a hundred years old, and the pretty things in the hairdresser's window all bore the stamp of the latest Parisian manufacture—were part and parcel of that modern rubbish which he so cordially despised. What then had so forcibly arrested his attention? Was the poor fellow thinking of buying a new chignon, or a solitary pendent curl, for the object of his affections? This could hardly be, for to my almost certain knowledge his affections had no object save the faded crockery and the angular chairs I have mentioned. I had, indeed, more than once thought it a pity that he should not interest himself in some attractive little woman; for he might end by marrying her, and that would be a blessing, inasmuch as she would probably take measures for his being punctual when he was asked out to dinner. I tapped on the edge of the little railing which served as my window-guard, but the noise of the street prevented this admonition from reaching his ear. He was decidedly quite too absorbed. Then I ventured to hiss at him in the manner of the Latin races— a mode of address to which I have always had a lively aversion, but which, it must be confessed, proceeding from Latin lips, reaches its destination in cases in which a nobler volume of sound will stop half way. Still, like the warrior's widow in Tennyson's song, he neither spake nor moved. But here, suddenly, I comprehended the motive of his immobility: he was looking of course at the barber's beautiful wife, the pretty woman with the face of a Madonna and the coiffure of a Parisienne, whom I myself had just found so charming. This was really an excuse, and I felt disposed to allow him a few moments' grace. There was evidently an unobstructed space behind the window, through which this attractive person could be perceived as she sat at her desk in some attitude of graceful diligence—adding up the items of a fine lady's little indebtedness for rouge-pots and rice-powder, or braiding ever so neatly the long tresses of a *fausse natte* of the fashionable colour. I promised myself to look out for this point of visual access the very first time I should pass.

I gave my tarrying guest another five minutes' grace, during which the lamps were lighted in the hairdresser's shop. The window now became extremely brilliant; the ivory brushes and the little silver mirrors glittered and flashed, the coloured cosmetics in the little toilet-bottles acquired an almost appetising radiance, and the beautiful waxen ladies, tossing back their heads more than ever from their dazzling busts, seemed to sniff up the agreeable atmosphere. Of course the hairdresser's wife had become even more vividly visible, and so, evidently, Sanguinetti was finding out. He moved no more than if he himself had been a barber's block. This was all very well, but now, seriously, I was hungry, and I felt extremely disposed to fling a flower-pot at him: I had an array of these ornaments in the balcony. Just then my servant came into the room, and beckoning to this functionary I pointed out to him the gentleman at the barber's window, and bade him go down into the street and interrupt Mr. Sanguinetti's contemplations. He departed, descended, and I presently saw him cross the way. Just as he drew near my friend, however, the latter turned round, abruptly, and looked at his watch. Then, with an obvious sense of alarm, he moved quickly forward; but he had not gone five steps before he paused again and cast back a supreme glance at the object of his admiration. He raised his hand to his lips, and, upon my word, he looked as if he were kissing it. My servant now accosted him with a bow, and motioned toward my balcony; but Sanguinetti, without looking up, simply passed quickly across to my door. He might well be shy about looking up—kissing his hand in the street to pretty *dames de comptoir*: for a modest little man, who was supposed to care for nothing but bric-à-brac, and not to be in the least what is called "enterprising" with women, this was certainly a very smart jump. And the hairdresser's wife? Had she, on her side, been kissing her finger-tips to him? I thought it very possible, and remembered that I had always heard that Paris is the city of gallantry.

Sanguinetti came in, blushing a good deal, and saying that he was extremely sorry to have kept me waiting.

"Oh," I answered, "I understand it very well. I have been watching you from my window for the last quarter of an hour."

He smiled a little, blushing still. "Though I have lived in Paris for fifteen years," he said, "you know I always look at the shops. One never knows what one may pick up."

"You have a taste for picking up pretty faces," I rejoined. "That is certainly a very pretty one at the hairdresser's."

Poor Sanguinetti was really very modest; my "chaff" discomposed him, and he began to fidget and protest.

"Oh," I went on, "your choice does great honour to your taste. She's a very lovely creature; I admire her myself."

He looked at me a moment, with his soup-spoon poised. He was always a little afraid of me; he was sure I thought him a very flimsy fellow, with his passion for cracked teacups and scraps of old brocade. But now he seemed a trifle reassured; he would talk a little if he dared. "You know there are two of them," he said, "but one is much more beautiful than the other."

"Precisely," I answered—"the fair one."

"My dear friend," murmured my guest, "she is the most beautiful object I ever beheld."

"That, perhaps, is going a little too far. But she is uncommonly handsome."

"She is quite perfect," Sanguinetti declared, finishing his soup. And presently he added, "Shall I tell you what she looks like?"

"Like a fashionable angel," I said.

"Yes," he answered, smiling, "or like a Madonna who should have had her hair dressed—over there."

"My dear fellow," I exclaimed, "that is just the comparison I hit upon a while ago!"

"That proves the truth of it. It is a real Madonna type."

"A little Parisianised about the corners of the mouth," I rejoined.

"Possibly," said Sanguinetti. "But the mouth is her loveliest feature."

"Could you see her well?" I inquired, as I helped him to a sweetbread.

"Beautifully—especially after the gas was lighted."

"Had you never noticed her before?"

"Never, strangely enough. But though, as I say, I am very fond of shop-windows, I confess to always having had a great prejudice against those of the hairdressers."

"You see how wrong you were."

"No, not in general; this is an exception. The women are usually hideous. They have the most impossible complexions; they are always fearfully sallow. There is one of them in my street, three doors from my own house: you would say she was made of——" And he paused a moment for his comparison. "You would say she was made of tallow."

We finished our sweetbreads, and, I think, talked of something else, my companion presently drawing from his pocket and exhibiting with some elation a little purchase in the antiquarian line which he had made that morning. It was a small coffee-cup, of the Sèvres manufacture and of the period of Louis XV, very delicately painted over with nosegays and garlands. I was far from being competent in such matters, but Sanguinetti assured me that it bore a certain little earmark which made it a precious acquisition. And he put it back into its little red morocco case, and fell a-musing while his eyes wandered toward the window. He was fond of old gimcracks and bibelots, of every order and epoch, but he had, I knew, a special tenderness for the productions of the baser period of the French monarchy. His collection of snuff-boxes and flowered screens was highly remarkable—might, I suppose, have been called celebrated. In spite of his foreign name he was a genuine compatriot of my own, and indeed our acquaintance had begun with our being, as very small boys, at school together. There was a tradition that Sanguinetti's grandfather had been an Italian image-vendor, in the days when those gentlemen might have claimed in America to be the only representatives of a care for the fine arts. In the early part of the century they were also less numerous than they have since become and it was believed that the founder of the transatlantic stock of the Sanguinettis had, by virtue of his fine Italian eyes, his slouched hat, his earrings, his persuasive eloquence, his foreign idioms and his little tray of plaster effigies and busts, been deemed a personage of sufficient importance to win the heart and hand of the daughter of a well-to-do attorney in the State of Vermont. This lady had brought her husband a property which he invested in some less brittle department of the Italian trade, and, prospering as people, alas! prospered in those good old days, bequeathed, much augmented, to the father of my guest. My companion, who had several sisters, was brought up like a little gentleman, and showed symptoms even at the earliest age of his mania for refuse furniture. At school he used to collect old slate-pencils and match-boxes; I suppose he inherited the taste from his grandfather, who had perambulated the country with a tray covered with the most useless ornaments (like a magnified chess-board) upon his head. When he was twenty years old Sanguinetti lost his father and got his share of the patrimony, with which he immediately came to Europe, where he had lived these many years. When I first saw him, on coming to Paris, I asked him if he meant never to go back to New York, and I very well remember his answer. "My dear fellow" (in a very mournful tone), "what *can* you get there? The things are all second-rate, and during the Louis Quinze period, you know, our poor dear country was really—really——" And he shook his head very slowly and expressively.

I answered that there were (as I had been told) very good spinning-wheels and kitchen-settles, but he rejoined that he cared only for things that were truly elegant. He was a most simple-minded and amiable little bachelor, and would have done anything possible to oblige a friend, but he made no secret of his conviction that "pretty things" were the only objects in the world worth troubling one's self about. He was very near-sighted, and was always putting up his glass to look at something on your chimney-piece or your side-table. He had a lingering, solemn way of talking about the height of Madame de Pompadour's heels and the different shapes of old Dutch candlesticks; and though many of his country-people thought him tremendously "affected," he always seemed to me the least pretentious of men. He never read the newspapers for their politics, and didn't pretend to: he read them only for their lists of auction-sales. I had a great kindness for him; he seemed to me such a pure-minded mortal, sitting there in his innocent company of Dresden shepherdesses and beauties whose smiles were stippled on the lids of snuff-boxes. There is always something agreeable in a man who is a perfect example of a type, and Sanguinetti was all of one piece. He was the perfect authority on pretty things.

He kept looking at the window, as I have said, and it required no great shrewdness to guess that his thoughts had stepped out of it and were hovering in front of the hair-dresser's *étalage*. I was inclined to humour his enthusiasm, for it amused me to see a man who had hitherto found a pink-faced lady on a china plate a sufficiently substantial object of invocation led captive by a charmer who would, as the phrase is, have something to say for herself.

"Shouldn't you have liked to have a closer view of her?" I asked, with a sympathetic smile.

He glanced at me and blushed again. "That lovely creature?"

"That lovely creature. Shouldn't you have liked to get nearer?"

"Indeed I should. That sheet of plate-glass is a great vexation."

"But why didn't you make a pretext for going into the shop? You might have bought a toothbrush."

"I don't know that I should have gained much," said Sanguinetti, simply.

"You would have seen her move; her movement is charming."

"Her movement is—the poetry of motion. But I could see that outside."

"My dear fellow, you are not enterprising enough," I urged. "In your place I should get a footing in the shop."

He fixed his clear little near-sighted eyes upon me. "Yes, yes," he said, "it would certainly be delightful to be able to sit there and watch her: it would be more comfortable than standing outside."

"Rather, my dear boy. But sitting there and watching her? You go rather far."

"I suppose I should be a little in the way. But every now and then she would turn her face toward me. And I don't know but that she is as pretty behind as before," he added.

"You make an observation that I made myself. She has so much *chic*."

Sanguinetti kissed his finger-tips with a movement that he had learned of his long Parisian sojourn. "The poetry of *chic*! But I shall go further," he presently pursued. "I don't despair, I don't despair." And he paused, with his hands in his pockets, tilting himself back in his seat.

"You don't despair of what?"

"Of making her my own."

I burst out laughing. "Your own, my dear fellow! You are more enterprising than I thought. But what do you mean? I don't suppose that, under the circumstances, you can marry her?"

"No: under the circumstances, unfortunately, I can't. But I can have her always there."

"Always where?"

"At home, in my salon. It's just the place for her."

"Ah, my good friend," I rejoined, laughing, but slightly scandalised, "that's a matter of opinion."

"It's a matter of taste. I think it would suit her."

A matter of taste, indeed, this question of common morality! Sanguinetti was more Parisianised than I had supposed, and I reflected that Paris was certainly a very dangerous place, since it had got the better of his inveterate propriety. But I was not too much shocked to be still a good deal amused.

"Of course I shall not go too fast," he went on. "I shall not be too abrupt."

"Pray don't."

"I shall approach the matter gradually. I shall go into the shop several times, to buy certain things. First a pot of cold cream, then a piece of soap, then a bottle of glycerine. I shall go into a great many ecstasies and express no end of admiration. Meanwhile, she will slowly move around, and every now and then she will look at me. And so, little by little, I will come to the great point."

"Perhaps you will not be listened to."

"I will make a very handsome offer."

"What sort of an offer do you mean?"

"I am ashamed to tell you: you will call it throwing away money."

An offer of money! He was really very crude. Should I too come to this, if I continued to live in Paris? "Oh," I said, "if you think that money simply will do it——"

"Why, you don't suppose that I expect to have her for nothing?" He was actually cynical, and I remained silent. "But I shall not be happy again—at least for a long time"—he went on, "unless I succeed. I have always dreamed of just such a woman as that; and now at last, when I behold her perfect image and embodiment, why, I simply can't do without her." He was evidently very sincere.

"You are simply in love," I said.

He looked at me a moment, and blushed. "Yes, I honestly believe I am. It's very absurd."

"From some point of view or other, infatuations are always absurd," I said; and I decided that the matter was none of my business.

We talked of other things for an hour, but before he took leave of me Sanguinetti reverted to the beautiful being at the hairdresser's. "I am sure you will think me a great donkey," he said, "for taking that—that creature so seriously;" and he nodded in the direction of the other side of the street.

"I was always taught, in our country, that it is one's duty to take things seriously!"

I made a point, of course, the next day, of stopping at the hairdresser's window for the purpose of obtaining another glimpse of the remarkable woman who had made such an impression upon my friend. I found, in fact, that there was a large aperture in the back of the window through which it was very possible to see what was going on in a considerable part of the shop. Just then, however, the object of Sangui-netti's admiration was not within the range of vision of a passer-by, and I waited some time without her appearing. At last, having invented something to buy, I entered the aromatic precinct. To my vexation, the attendant who came forward to serve me was not the charming woman whom I had seen the evening before on the pavement, but the young person of inferior attractions who had come to the door to call her. This young person also wore a black silk dress and had a very neat figure; she was beautifully *coiffée* and very polite. But she was a very different affair from Sanguinetti's friend, and I rather grudged the five francs that I paid her for the little bottle of lavender-water that I didn't want. What should I do with a bottle of lavender-water? I would give it to Sanguinetti. I lin-gered in the shop under half-a-dozen pretexts, but still saw no sign of its lovelier inmate. The other young woman stood smiling and rubbing her hands, answering my questions and giving explanations with high-pitched urbanity. At last I took up my little bottle and laid my hand upon the door-knob. At that moment a velvet curtain was raised at the back of the shop, and the hairdresser's wife presented herself. She stood there a moment, with the curtain lifted, looking out and smil-ing; on her beautiful head was poised a crisp little morning-cap. Yes, she was lovely, and I really understood Sanguinetti's sudden passion. But I could not remain staring at her, and, as I had exhausted my expedients, I was obliged to withdraw. I took a position in front of the shop, however, and presently she approached the window. She looked into it to see if it was in proper order. She was still smiling—she seemed always to be smiling—but she gave no sign of seeing me, and I felt that if there had been a dozen men standing there she would have worn that same sweetly unconscious mask. She glanced about her a moment, and then, extending a small, fair, dainty hand, she gave a touch to the back hair of one of the waxen ladies —the right-hand one, the blonde.

A couple of hours later, rising from breakfast, I repaired to my little balcony, from which post of observation I instantly espied a figure stationed at the hairdresser's window. If I had not recognised it otherwise, the attentive, absorbed droop of its head would at once have proved it to be Sanguinetti. "Why does he not go inside?" I asked myself. "He can't look at her properly out there." At this conclusion he appeared himself to have arrived, for he suddenly straightened himself up and entered the establishment. He remained within a long time. I grew tired of waiting for him to reappear, and went back to my arm-chair to finish reading the *Débats*. I had just accomplished this somewhat arduous feat when I heard the lame tinkle of my door-bell, a few moments after which Sanguinetti was ushered in.

He really looked love-sick; he was pale and heavy-eyed. "My too-susceptible friend," I said, "you are very far gone."

"Yes," he answered; "I am really in love. It is too ridiculous. Please don't tell any one."

"I shall certainly tell no one," I declared. "But it does not seem to me exactly ridiculous."

He gave me a grateful stare. "Ah, if you don't find it so, *tant mieux.*"

"Unadvisable, rather; that's what I should call it."

He gave me another stare. "You think I can't afford it?"

"It is not so much that."

"You think it won't look well? I will arrange it so that the harshest critic will be disarmed. This morning she is in great beauty," he added, the next moment.

"Yes, I have had a glimpse of her myself," I said. "And you have been in the shop?"

"I have spent half-an-hour there. I thought it best to go straight to the point."

"What did you say?"

"I said the simple truth—that I have an intense desire to possess her."

"And the hairdresser's wife—how did she take it?"

"She seemed a good deal amused."

"Amused, simply? Nothing more?"

"I think she was a little flattered."

"I hope so."

"Yes," my companion rejoined, "for, after all, her own exquisite taste is half the business." To this proposition I cordially assented, and Sanguinetti went on: "But, after all, too, the dear creature won't lose that in coming to me. I shall make arrangements to have her hair dressed regularly."

"I see that you mean to do things *en prince*. Who is it that dresses her hair?"

"The coiffeur himself."

"The husband?"

"Exactly. They say he is the best in Paris."

"The best husband?" I asked.

"My dear fellow, be serious—the best coiffeur."

"It will certainly be very obliging of him."

"Of course," said Sanguinetti, "I shall pay him for his visits, as—if—as if——" And he paused a moment.

"As if what?"

"As if she were one of his fine ladies. His wife tells me that he goes to all the duchesses."

"Of course that will be something," I replied. "But still——"

"You mean that I live so far away? I know that, but I will give him his cab-fare."

I looked at him, and—I couldn't help it—I began to laugh. I had never seen such a strange mixture of passion and reason.

"Ah," he exclaimed, blushing, "you *do* think it ridiculous!"

"Yes," I said, "coming to this point, I confess it makes me laugh."

"I don't care," Sanguinetti declared, with amiable dogged-
ness; "I mean to keep her to myself."

Just at this time my attention was much taken up by the
arrival in Paris of some relatives who had no great talent for
assimilating their habits to foreign customs, and who carried
me about in their train as cicerone and interpreter. For three
or four weeks I was constantly in their company, and I saw
much less of Sanguinetti than I had done before. He used to
appear, however, at odd moments, in my rooms, being, as may
be imagined, very often in the neighbourhood. I always asked
him for the latest tidings of his audacious flame, which had
begun to blaze in a manner that made him perfectly indifferent to the judgment of others. The poor fellow was sincerely
in love.

"Je suis tout à ma passion," he would say when I asked him
the news. "Until that matter is settled I can think of nothing
else. I have always been so when I have wanted a thing intensely. It has become a monomania, a fixed idea; and naturally this case is not an exception." He was always going into
the shop. "We talk it over," he said. "She can't make up her
mind."

"I can imagine the difficulty," I answered.

"She says it's a great change."

"I can also imagine that."

"I never see the husband," said Sanguinetti. "He is always
away with his duchesses. But she talks it over with him. At
first he wouldn't listen to it."

"Naturally!"

"He said it would be an irreparable loss. But I am in hopes
he will come round. He can get on very well with the other."

"The other?—the little dark one? She is not nearly so
pretty."

"Of course not. But she isn't bad in her way. I really think,"
said Sanguinetti, "that he will come round. If he does not we
will do without his consent, and take the consequences. He
will not be sorry, after all, to have the money."

You may be sure that I felt plenty of surprise at the business-
like tone in which Sanguinetti discussed this unscrupulous
project of becoming the "possessor" of another man's wife.
There was certainly no hypocrisy about it; he had quite passed

beyond the stage at which it is deemed needful to throw a sop to propriety. But I said to myself that this was doubtless the Parisian tone, and that, since it had made its mark upon so perfect a little model of social orthodoxy as my estimable friend, nothing was more possible than that I too should become equally perverted. Whenever, after this, Sanguinetti came in he had something to say at first about the lovely creature across the way. "Have you noticed her this morning?" he would demand. "She is really enchanting. I thought of asking leave to kiss her."

"I wonder you should ask leave," I answered. "I should suppose you would do it without leave, and count upon being forgiven."

"I am afraid of hurting her," he said. "And then if I should be seen from the street, it would look rather absurd."

I could only say that he seemed to me a very odd mixture of perversity and discretion, but he went on without heeding my comments: "You may laugh at the idea, but, upon my word, to me she is different every day; she has never the same expression. Sometimes she's a little melancholy—sometimes she's in high spirits."

"I should say she was always smiling."

"Superficially, yes," said Sanguinetti. "That's all the vulgar see. But there's something beneath it—the most delicious little pensive look. At bottom she's sad. She's weary of her position there, it's so public.—Yesterday she was very pale," he would say at another time; "I'm sure she wants rest. That constant movement can't be good for her. It's true she moves very slowly."

"Yes," said I, "she seemed to me to move very slowly."

"And so beautifully! Still, with me," Sanguinetti went on, "she shall be perfectly quiet; I will see how that suits her."

"I should think she would need a little exercise," I objected.

He stared a moment, and then accused me, as he often did, of "making game" of him. "There is something in your tone in saying that," he remarked; but he shortly afterward forgot my sarcastic tendencies, and came to announce to me a change in the lady's coiffure. "Have you noticed that she has her hair dressed differently? I don't know that I like it; it covers up her forehead. But it's beautifully done, it's entirely new, and you will see that it will set the fashion for all Paris."

"Do they take the fashion from her?" I asked.

"Always. All the knowing people keep a note of her successive coiffures."

"And when you have carried her off, what will the knowing people do?"

"They will go by the other, the dark one—Mademoiselle Clémentine."

"Is that her name? And the name of your sweetheart?"

Sanguinetti looked at me an instant, with his usual helplessly mistrustful little blush, and then he answered, "Rose-Agathe."

When I asked him how his suit was prospering, he usually replied that he believed it to be merely a question of time. "We keep talking it over, and in that way, at any rate, I can see her. The poor woman can't get used to the idea."

"I should think not."

"She says it would change everything—that the shop would be a different place without her. She is so well known, so universally admired. I tell her that it will not be impossible to get a clever substitute; and she answers that, clever as the substitute may be, she will never have the peculiar charm of Rose-Agathe."

"Ah! she herself is aware then of this peculiar charm?"

"Perfectly, and it delights her to have me talk about it."

A part of the charm's peculiarity, I reflected, was that it was not spoiled by the absence of modesty; yet I also remembered the coiffeur's handsome wife had looked extremely *pudique*. Sanguinetti, however, appeared bent upon ministering to her vanity; I learned that he was making her presents. "I have given her a pair of earrings," he announced, "and she is wearing them now. Do notice them as you pass. They are great big amethysts, and are extremely becoming."

I looked out for our beautiful friend the next time I left the house, but she was not visible through the hairdresser's window. Her plainer companion was waiting upon a fine lady, presumably one of the duchesses, while Madame Anatole herself, I supposed, was posturing before one of the mirrors in the inner apartment, with Sanguinetti's big amethysts in her ears.

One day he told me that he had determined to buy her a *parure*, and he greatly wished I would come and help him to choose it. I called him an extravagant dog, but I good-naturedly consented to accompany him to the jeweller's. He led me to the Palais-Royal, and there, somewhat to my surprise, introduced me into one of those dazzling little shops which wear upon their front in neat gilt letters the candid announcement, "Imitation." Here you may purchase any number of glittering gems for the most inconsiderable sum, and indulge at a moderate expense a pardonable taste for splendour. And the splendour is most effective, the glitter of the counterfeit jewels most natural. It is only the sentiment of the thing, you say to yourself, that prevents you from making all your purchases of jewelry in one of these convenient establishments; though, indeed, as their proprietors very aptly remark, fifty thousand francs more (for instance) is a good deal to pay for sentiment. Of this expensive superstition, however, I should have expected Sanguinetti to be guilty.

"You are not going to get a real set?" I asked.

He seemed a little annoyed. "Wouldn't you in that case blow me up for my extravagance?"

"It is highly probable. And yet a present of false jewelry! The handsomer it is, you know, the more ridiculous it is."

"I have thought of that," said my friend, "and I confess I am rather ashamed of myself. I should like to give her a real set. But, you see, I want diamonds and sapphires, and a real set such as I desire would cost about a hundred thousand francs. That's a good deal for—for——" And he paused a moment.

"For a barber's wife," I said to myself.

"Besides," my companion added, "she won't know the difference." I thought he rather underestimated her intelligence: a pretty Parisienne was, by instinct, a judge of parures. I remembered, however, that he had rarely spoken of this lady's intellectual qualities; he had dwelt exclusively upon her beauty and sweetness. So I stood by him while he purchased for two hundred francs a gorgeous necklace, and a coronet of the stones of Golconda. His passion was an odd affair altogether, and an oddity the more or the less hardly mattered. He remarked, moreover, that he had at home a curious collection of artificial gems, and that these things would be an interesting addition to his stock. "I shall make her wear them all," he exclaimed; and I wondered how she would like it.

He told me afterwards that his offering had been most gratefully received, that she was now wearing the wonderful necklace, and that she looked lovelier than ever.

That evening, however, I stopped before the shop to catch a glimpse, if possible, of the barber's lady thus splendidly adorned. I had seldom been fortunate enough to espy her, and on this occasion I turned away disappointed. Just as I was doing so I perceived something which suggested that she was making a fool of my amiable friend. On the radiant bosom of one of the great waxen dolls in her window glittered a necklace of brilliants which bore a striking resemblance to the article I had helped Sanguinetti to select. She had made over her lover's tribute to this rosy effigy, to whom, it must be confessed, it was very becoming.

Yet, for all this, I was out in my calculation. A week later Sanguinetti came into my rooms with a radiant countenance, and announced to me the consummation of his dream. "She is mine! she is mine! mine only!" he cried, dropping into a chair.

"She has left the shop?" I demanded.

"Last night—at eleven o'clock. We went off in a cab."

"You have her at home?"

"For ever and ever!" he exclaimed, ecstatically.

"My dear fellow, my compliments!"

"It was not an easy matter," he went on. "But I held her in my arms."

I renewed my congratulations, and said I hoped she was happy; and he declared that she had an expression of pure bliss. There was something in her eyes. He added that I must immediately come and see her; he was impatient to present me. Nothing, I answered, would give me greater pleasure, but meanwhile what did the husband say?

"He grumbles a bit, but I gave him five hundred francs."

"You have got off easily," I said; and I promised that at my first moment of leisure I would call upon my friend's new companion. I saw him three or four times before this moment arrived, and he assured me that she had made a happy man of him. "Whenever I have greatly wanted a thing, waited for it, and at last got it, I have always been in bliss for a month afterwards," he said. "But I think that this time my pleasure will really last."

"It will last as long, I hope, as she herself does!"

"I am sure it will. This is the sort of thing—yes, smile away—in which I get my happiness."

"Vous n'êtes pas difficile," I rejoined.

"Of course she's perishable," he added in a moment.

"Ah!" said I, "you must take good care of her."

And a day or two later, on his coming for me, I went with him to his apartment. His rooms were charming, and lined from ceiling to floor with the "pretty things" of the occupant—tapestries and bronzes, terra-cotta medallions and precious specimens of porcelain. There were cabinets and tables charged with similar treasures; the place was a perfect little museum. Sanguinetti led me through two or three rooms, and then stopped near a window, close to which, half hidden by the curtain, stood a lady, with her head turned away from us, looking out. In spite of our approach she stood motionless until my friend went up to her and with a gallant, affectionate movement placed his arm round her waist. Hereupon she slowly turned and gazed at me with a beautiful brilliant face and large quiet eyes.

"It is a pity she creaks," said my companion as I was making my bow. And then, as I made it, I perceived with amazement—and amusement—the cause of her creaking. She existed only from the waist upward, and the skirt of her dress was a very neat pedestal covered with red velvet. Sanguinetti gave another loving twist, and she slowly revolved again, making a little gentle squeal. She exhibited the back of her head, with its beautifully braided tresses resting upon her sloping waxen shoulders. She was the right-hand effigy of the coiffeur's window—the blonde! Her movement, as Sanguinetti had claimed, was particularly commendable, and of all his pretty things she was certainly the prettiest.

Daisy Miller: A Study

A<small>T THE LITTLE TOWN</small> of Vevey, in Switzerland, there is a particularly comfortable hotel. There are, indeed, many hotels; for the entertainment of tourists is the business of the place, which, as many travellers will remember, is seated upon the edge of a remarkably blue lake—a lake that it behoves every tourist to visit. The shore of the lake presents an unbroken array of establishments of this order, of every category, from the "grand hotel" of the newest fashion, with a chalk-white front, a hundred balconies, and a dozen flags flying from its roof, to the little Swiss *pension* of an elder day, with its name inscribed in German-looking lettering upon a pink or yellow wall, and an awkward summer-house in the angle of the garden. One of the hotels at Vevey, however, is famous, even classical, being distinguished from many of its upstart neighbours by an air both of luxury and of maturity. In this region, in the month of June, American travellers are extremely numerous; it may be said, indeed, that Vevey assumes at this period some of the characteristics of an American watering-place. There are sights and sounds which evoke a vision, an echo, of Newport and Saratoga. There is a flitting hither and thither of "stylish" young girls, a rustling of muslin flounces, a rattle of dance-music in the morning hours, a sound of high-pitched voices at all times. You receive an impression of these things at the excellent inn of the "Trois Couronnes," and are transported in fancy to the Ocean House or to Congress Hall. But at the "Trois Couronnes," it must be added, there are other features that are much at variance with these suggestions: neat German waiters, who look like secretaries of legation; Russian princesses sitting in the garden; little Polish boys walking about, held by the hand, with their governors; a view of the snowy crest of the Dent du Midi and the picturesque towers of the Castle of Chillon.

I hardly know whether it was the analogies or the differences that were uppermost in the mind of a young American, who, two or three years ago, sat in the garden of the "Trois Couronnes," looking about him, rather idly, at some of the graceful objects I have mentioned. It was a beautiful summer morning, and in whatever fashion the young American looked at things, they must have seemed to him charming. He had come from Geneva the day before, by the little steamer, to see his aunt, who was staying at the hotel—Geneva having been for a long time his place of residence. But his aunt had a headache—his aunt had almost always a headache—and now she was shut up in her room, smelling camphor, so that he was at liberty to wander about. He was some seven-and-twenty years of age; when his friends spoke of him, they usually said that he was at Geneva, "studying." When his enemies spoke of him they said—but, after all, he had no enemies; he was an extremely amiable fellow, and universally liked. What I should say is, simply, that when certain persons spoke of him they affirmed that the reason of his spending so much time at Geneva was that he was extremely devoted to a lady who lived there—a foreign lady—a person older than himself. Very few Americans—indeed I think none—had ever seen this lady, about whom there were some singular stories. But Winterbourne had an old attachment for the little metropolis of Calvinism; he had been put to school there as a boy, and he had afterwards gone to college there—circumstances which had led to his forming a great many youthful friendships. Many of these he had kept, and they were a source of great satisfaction to him.

After knocking at his aunt's door and learning that she was indisposed, he had taken a walk about the town, and then he had come in to his breakfast. He had now finished his breakfast, but he was drinking a small cup of coffee, which had been served to him on a little table in the garden by one of the waiters who looked like an *attaché*. At last he finished his coffee and lit a cigarette. Presently a small boy came walking along the path—an urchin of nine or ten. The child, who was diminutive for his years, had an aged expression of countenance, a pale complexion, and sharp little features. He was dressed in knickerbockers, with red stockings, which displayed his poor little spindleshanks; he also wore a brilliant red cravat. He carried in his hand a long alpenstock, the sharp point of which he thrust into everything that he approached—the flower-beds, the garden-benches, the trains of the ladies' dresses. In front of Winterbourne he paused, looking at him with a pair of bright, penetrating little eyes.

"Will you give me a lump of sugar?" he asked, in a sharp, hard little voice—a voice immature, and yet, somehow, not young.

Winterbourne glanced at the small table near him, on which his coffee-service rested, and saw that several morsels of sugar remained. "Yes, you may take one," he answered; "but I don't think sugar is good for little boys."

This little boy stepped forward and carefully selected three of the coveted fragments, two of which he buried in the pocket of his knickerbockers, depositing the other as promptly in another place. He poked his alpenstock, lance-fashion, into Winterbourne's bench, and tried to crack the lump of sugar with his teeth.

"Oh, blazes; it's har-r-d!" he exclaimed, pronouncing the adjective in a peculiar manner.

Winterbourne had immediately perceived that he might have the honour of claiming him as a fellow-countryman. "Take care you don't hurt your teeth," he said, paternally.

"I haven't got any teeth to hurt. They have all come out. I have only got seven teeth. My mother counted them last night, and one came out right afterwards. She said she'd slap me if any more came out. I can't help it. It's this old Europe. It's the climate that makes them come out. In America they didn't come out. It's these hotels."

Winterbourne was much amused. "If you eat three lumps of sugar, your mother will certainly slap you," he said.

"She's got to give me some candy, then," rejoined his young interlocutor. "I can't get any candy here—any American candy. American candy's the best candy."

"And are American little boys the best little boys?" asked Winterbourne.

"I don't know. I'm an American boy," said the child.

"I see you are one of the best!" laughed Winterbourne.

"Are you an American man?" pursued this vivacious infant. And then, on Winterbourne's affirmative reply—"American men are the best," he declared.

His companion thanked him for the compliment; and the child, who had now got astride of his alpenstock, stood looking about him, while he attacked a second lump of sugar. Winterbourne wondered if he himself had been like this in his infancy, for he had been brought to Europe at about this age.

"Here comes my sister!" cried the child, in a moment. "She's an American girl."

Winterbourne looked along the path and saw a beautiful young lady advancing. "American girls are the best girls," he said, cheerfully, to his young companion.

"My sister ain't the best!" the child declared. "She's always blowing at me."

"I imagine that is your fault, not hers," said Winterbourne. The young lady meanwhile had drawn near. She was dressed in white muslin, with a hundred frills and flounces, and knots of pale-coloured ribbon. She was bare-headed; but she balanced in her hand a large parasol, with a deep border of embroidery; and she was strikingly, admirably pretty. "How pretty they are!" thought Winterbourne, straightening himself in his seat, as if he were prepared to rise.

The young lady paused in front of his bench, near the parapet of the garden, which overlooked the lake. The little boy had now converted his alpenstock into a vaulting-pole, by the aid of which he was springing about in the gravel, and kicking it up not a little.

"Randolph," said the young lady, "what *are* you doing?"

"I'm going up the Alps," replied Randolph. "This is the way!" And he gave another little jump, scattering the pebbles about Winterbourne's ears.

"That's the way they come down," said Winterbourne.

"He's an American man!" cried Randolph, in his little hard voice.

The young lady gave no heed to this announcement, but looked straight at her brother. "Well, I guess you had better be quiet," she simply observed.

It seemed to Winterbourne that he had been in a manner presented. He got up and stepped slowly towards the young girl, throwing away his cigarette. "This little boy and I have made acquaintance," he said, with great civility. In Geneva, as he had been perfectly aware, a young man was not at liberty to speak to a young unmarried lady except under certain rarely-occurring conditions; but here at Vevey, what conditions could be better than these?—a pretty American girl coming and standing in front of you in a garden. This pretty American girl, however, on hearing Winterbourne's observation, simply glanced at him; she then turned her head and looked over the parapet, at the lake and the opposite mountains. He wondered whether he had gone too far; but he decided that he must advance farther, rather than retreat. While he was thinking of something else to say, the young lady turned to the little boy again.

"I should like to know where you got that pole," she said.

"I bought it!" responded Randolph.

"You don't mean to say you're going to take it to Italy!"

"Yes, I am going to take it to Italy!" the child declared.

The young girl glanced over the front of her dress, and smoothed out a knot or two of ribbon. Then she rested her eyes upon the prospect again. "Well, I guess you had better leave it somewhere," she said, after a moment.

"Are you going to Italy?" Winterbourne inquired, in a tone of great respect.

The young lady glanced at him again.

"Yes, sir," she replied. And she said nothing more.

"Are you—a—going over the Simplon?" Winterbourne pursued, a little embarrassed.

"I don't know," she said. "I suppose it's some mountain. Randolph, what mountain are we going over?"

"Going where?" the child demanded.

"To Italy," Winterbourne explained.

"I don't know," said Randolph. "I don't want to go to Italy. I want to go to America."

"Oh, Italy is a beautiful place!" rejoined the young man.

"Can you get candy there?" Randolph loudly inquired.

"I hope not," said his sister. "I guess you have had enough candy, and mother thinks so too."

"I haven't had any for ever so long—for a hundred weeks!" cried the boy, still jumping about.

The young lady inspected her flounces and smoothed her ribbons again; and Winterbourne presently risked an obser-vation upon the beauty of the view. He was ceasing to be embarrassed, for he had begun to perceive that she was not in the least embarrassed herself. There had not been the slightest alteration in her charming complexion; she was evidently neither offended nor fluttered. If she looked another way when he spoke to her, and seemed not particularly to hear him, this was simply her habit, her manner. Yet, as he talked a little more, and pointed out some of the objects of interest in the view, with which she appeared quite unacquainted, she gradually gave him more of the benefit of her glance; and then he saw that this glance was perfectly direct and unshrinking. It was not, however, what would have been called an immodest glance, for the young girl's eyes were singularly honest and fresh. They were wonderfully pretty eyes; and, indeed, Winterbourne had not seen for a long time anything prettier than his fair countrywoman's various features —her complexion, her nose, her ears, her teeth. He had a great relish for feminine beauty; he was addicted to observing and analysing it; and as regards this young lady's face he made several observations. It was not at all insipid, but it was not exactly expressive; and though it was eminently delicate Winterbourne mentally accused it—very forgivingly—of a want of finish. He thought it very possible that Master Randolph's sister was a coquette; he was sure she had a spirit of her own; but in her bright, sweet, superficial little visage there was no mockery, no irony. Before long it became obvious that she was much disposed towards conversation. She told him that they were going to Rome for the winter—she and her mother and Randolph. She asked him if he was a "real American;" she wouldn't have taken him for one; he seemed more like a German—this was said after a little hesitation, especially when he spoke. Winterbourne, laughing, answered that he had met Germans who spoke like Americans; but that he had not, so far as he remembered, met an American who spoke like a German. Then he asked her if she would not be more comfortable in sitting upon the bench which he had just quitted. She answered that she liked standing up and walking about; but she presently sat down. She told him she was from New York State—"if you know where that is." Winterbourne learned more about her by catching hold of her small, slippery brother and making him stand a few minutes by his side.

"Tell me your name, my boy," he said.

"Randolph C. Miller," said the boy, sharply. "And I'll tell you her name;" and he levelled his alpenstock at his sister.

"You had better wait till you are asked!" said this young lady, calmly.

"I should like very much to know your name," said Winterbourne.

"Her name is Daisy Miller!" cried the child. "But that isn't her real name; that isn't her name on her cards."

"It's a pity you haven't got one of my cards!" said Miss Miller.

"Her real name is Annie P. Miller," the boy went on.

"Ask him *his* name," said his sister, indicating Winterbourne.

But on this point Randolph seemed perfectly indifferent; he continued to supply information with regard to his own family. "My father's name is Ezra B. Miller," he announced. "My father ain't in Europe; my father's in a better place than Europe."

Winterbourne imagined for a moment that this was the manner in which the child had been taught to intimate that Mr. Miller had been removed to the sphere of celestial rewards. But Randolph immediately added, "My father's in Schenectady. He's got a big business. My father's rich, you bet."

"Well!" ejaculated Miss Miller, lowering her parasol and looking at the embroidered border. Winterbourne presently released the child, who departed, dragging his alpenstock along the path. "He doesn't like Europe," said the young girl. "He wants to go back."

"To Schenectady, you mean?"

"Yes; he wants to go right home. He hasn't got any boys here. There is one boy here, but he always goes round with a teacher; they won't let him play."

"And your brother hasn't any teacher?" Winterbourne inquired.

"Mother thought of getting him one, to travel round with us. There was a lady told her of a very good teacher; an American lady—perhaps you know her—Mrs. Sanders. I think she came from Boston. She told her of this teacher, and we thought of getting him to travel round with us. But Randolph said he didn't want a teacher travelling round with us. He said he wouldn't have lessons when he was in the cars. And we *are* in the cars about half the time. There was an English lady we met in the cars—I think her name was Miss Featherstone; perhaps you know her. She wanted to know why I didn't give Randolph lessons—give him 'instruction,' she called it. I guess he could give me more instruction than I could give him. He's very smart.''

"Yes," said Winterbourne; "he seems very smart."

"Mother's going to get a teacher for him as soon as we get to Italy. Can you get good teachers in Italy?"

"Very good, I should think," said Winterbourne.

"Or else she's going to find some school. He ought to learn some more. He's only nine. He's going to college." And in this way Miss Miller continued to converse upon the affairs of her family, and upon other topics. She sat there with her extremely pretty hands, ornamented with very brilliant rings, folded in her lap, and with her pretty eyes now resting upon those of Winterbourne, now wandering over the garden, the people who passed by, and the beautiful view. She talked to Winterbourne as if she had known him a long time. He found it very pleasant. It was many years since he had heard a young girl talk so much. It might have been said of this unknown young lady, who had come and sat down beside him upon a bench, that she chattered. She was very quiet, she sat in a charming tranquil attitude; but her lips and her eyes were constantly moving. She had a soft, slender, agreeable voice, and her tone was decidedly sociable. She gave Winterbourne a history of her movements and intentions, and those of her mother and brother, in Europe, and enumerated, in particular, the various hotels at which they had stopped. "That English lady in the cars," she said—"Miss Featherstone—asked me if we didn't all live in hotels in America. I told her I had never been in so many hotels in my life as since I came to Europe. I have never seen so many—it's nothing but hotels." But Miss Miller did not make this remark with a querulous accent; she appeared to be in the best humour with everything. She declared that the hotels were very good, when once you got used to their ways, and that Europe was perfectly sweet. She was not disappointed—not a bit. Perhaps it was because she had heard so much about it before. She had ever so many intimate friends that had been there ever so many times. And then she had had ever so many dresses and things from Paris. Whenever she put on a Paris dress she felt as if she were in Europe.

"It was a kind of a wishing-cap," said Winterbourne.

"Yes," said Miss Miller, without examining this analogy; "it always made me wish I was here. But I needn't have done that for dresses. I am sure they send all the pretty ones to America; you see the most frightful things here. The only thing I don't like," she proceeded, "is the society. There isn't any society; or, if there is, I don't know where it keeps itself. Do you? I suppose there is some society somewhere, but I haven't seen anything of it. I'm very fond of society, and I have always had a great deal of it. I don't mean only in Schenectady, but in New York. I used to go to New York every winter. In New York I had lots of society. Last winter I had seventeen dinners given me; and three of them were by gentlemen," added Daisy Miller. "I have more friends in New York than in Schenectady—more gentlemen friends; and more young lady friends too," she resumed in a moment. She paused again for an instant; she was looking at Winterbourne with all her prettiness in her lively eyes and in her light, slightly monotonous smile. "I have always had," she said, "a great deal of gentlemen's society."

Poor Winterbourne was amused, perplexed, and decidedly charmed. He had never yet heard a young girl express herself in just this fashion; never, at least, save in cases where to say such things seemed a kind of demonstrative evidence of a certain laxity of deportment. And yet was he to accuse Miss Daisy Miller of actual or potential *inconduite*, as they said at Geneva? He felt that he had lived at Geneva so long that he had lost a good deal; he had become dishabituated to the American tone. Never, indeed, since he had grown old enough to appreciate things, had he encountered a young American girl of so pronounced a type as this. Certainly she was very charming; but how deucedly sociable! Was she simply a pretty girl from New York State—were they all like that, the pretty girls who had a good deal of gentlemen's society? Or was she also a designing, an audacious, an unscrupulous young person? Winterbourne had lost his instinct in this matter, and his reason could not help him. Miss Daisy Miller looked extremely innocent. Some people had told him that, after all, American girls were exceedingly innocent; and others had told him that, after all, they were not. He was inclined to think Miss Daisy Miller was a flirt—a pretty American flirt. He had never, as yet, had any relations with young ladies of this category. He had known, here in Europe, two or three women—persons older than Miss Daisy Miller, and provided, for respectability's sake, with husbands—who were great coquettes—dangerous, terrible women, with whom one's relations were liable to take a serious turn. But this young girl was not a coquette in that sense; she was very unsophisticated; she was only a pretty American flirt. Winterbourne was almost grateful for having found the formula that applied to Miss Daisy Miller. He leaned back in his seat; he remarked to himself that she had the most charming nose he had ever seen; he wondered what were the regular conditions and limitations of one's intercourse with a pretty American flirt. It presently became apparent that he was on the way to learn.

"Have you been to that old castle?" asked the young girl, pointing with her parasol to the far-gleaming walls of the Château de Chillon.

"Yes, formerly, more than once," said Winterbourne. "You too, I suppose, have seen it?"

"No; we haven't been there. I want to go there dreadfully. Of course I mean to go there. I wouldn't go away from here without having seen that old castle."

"It's a very pretty excursion," said Winterbourne, "and very easy to make. You can drive, you know, or you can go by the little steamer."

"You can go in the cars," said Miss Miller.

"Yes; you can go in the cars," Winterbourne assented.

"Our courier says they take you right up to the castle," the young girl continued. "We were going last week; but my mother gave out. She suffers dreadfully from dyspepsia. She said she couldn't go. Randolph wouldn't go either; he says he doesn't think much of old castles. But I guess we'll go this week, if we can get Randolph."

"Your brother is not interested in ancient monuments?" Winterbourne inquired, smiling.

"He says he don't care much about old castles. He's only nine. He wants to stay at the hotel. Mother's afraid to leave him alone, and the courier won't stay with him; so we haven't been to many places. But it will be too bad if we don't go up there." And Miss Miller pointed again at the Château de Chillon.

"I should think it might be arranged," said Winterbourne. "Couldn't you get some one to stay—for the afternoon—with Randolph?"

Miss Miller looked at him a moment; and then, very placidly—"I wish *you* would stay with him!" she said.

Winterbourne hesitated a moment. "I would much rather go to Chillon with you."

"With me?" asked the young girl, with the same placidity.

She didn't rise, blushing, as a young girl at Geneva would have done; and yet Winterbourne, conscious that he had been very bold, thought it possible she was offended. "With your mother," he answered very respectfully.

But it seemed that both his audacity and his respect were lost upon Miss Daisy Miller. "I guess my mother won't go, after all," she said. "She don't like to ride round in the afternoon. But did you really mean what you said just now; that you would like to go up there?"

"Most earnestly," Winterbourne declared.

"Then we may arrange it. If mother will stay with Randolph, I guess Eugenio will."

"Eugenio?" the young man inquired.

"Eugenio's our courier. He doesn't like to stay with Randolph; he's the most fastidious man I ever saw. But he's a splendid courier. I guess he'll stay at home with Randolph if mother does, and then we can go to the castle."

Winterbourne reflected for an instant as lucidly as possible—"we" could only mean Miss Daisy Miller and himself. This programme seemed almost too agreeable for credence; he felt as if he ought to kiss the young lady's hand. Possibly he would have done so—and quite spoiled the project; but at this moment another person—presumably Eugenio—appeared. A tall, handsome man, with superb whiskers, wearing a velvet morning-coat and a brilliant watch-chain, approached Miss Miller, looking sharply at her companion. "Oh, Eugenio!" said Miss Miller, with the friendliest accent.

Eugenio had looked at Winterbourne from head to foot; he now bowed gravely to the young lady. "I have the honour to inform mademoiselle that luncheon is upon the table."

Miss Miller slowly rose. "See here, Eugenio," she said. "I'm going to that old castle, any way."

"To the Château de Chillon, mademoiselle?" the courier inquired. "Mademoiselle has made arrangements?" he added, in a tone which struck Winterbourne as very impertinent.

Eugenio's tone apparently threw, even to Miss Miller's own apprehension, a slightly ironical light upon the young girl's situation. She turned to Winterbourne, blushing a little—a very little. "You won't back out?" she said.

"I shall not be happy till we go!" he protested.

"And you are staying in this hotel?" she went on. "And you are really an American?"

The courier stood looking at Winterbourne, offensively. The young man, at least, thought his manner of looking an offence to Miss Miller; it conveyed an imputation that she "picked up" acquaintances. "I shall have the honour of pre-senting to you a person who will tell you all about me," he said smiling, and referring to his aunt.

"Oh, well, we'll go some day," said Miss Miller. And she gave him a smile and turned away. She put up her parasol and walked back to the inn beside Eugenio. Winterbourne stood looking after her; and as she moved away, drawing her muslin furbelows over the gravel, said to himself that she had the *tournure* of a princess.

II.

He had, however, engaged to do more than proved feasible, in promising to present his aunt, Mrs. Costello, to Miss Daisy Miller. As soon as the former lady had got better of her head-ache he waited upon her in her apartment; and, after the proper inquiries in regard to her health, he asked her if she had observed, in the hotel, an American family—a mamma, a daughter, and a little boy.

"And a courier?" said Mrs. Costello. "Oh, yes, I have observed them. Seen them—heard them—and kept out of their way." Mrs. Costello was a widow with a fortune; a person of much distinction, who frequently intimated that, if she were not so dreadfully liable to sick-headaches, she would probably have left a deeper impress upon her time. She had a long pale face, a high nose, and a great deal of very striking white hair, which she wore in large puffs and *rouleaux* over the top of her head. She had two sons married in New York, and another who was now in Europe. This young man was amusing himself at Homburg, and, though he was on his travels, was rarely perceived to visit any particular city at the moment selected by his mother for her own appearance there. Her nephew, who had come up to Vevey expressly to see her, was therefore more attentive than those who, as she said, were nearer to her. He had imbibed at Geneva the idea that one must always be attentive to one's aunt. Mrs. Costello had not seen him for many years, and she was greatly pleased with him, manifesting her approbation by initiating him into many of the secrets of that social sway which, as she gave him to understand, she exerted in the American capital. She admitted that she was very exclusive; but, if he were acquainted with New York, he would see that one had to be. And her picture of the minutely hierarchical constitution of the society of that city, which she presented to him in many different lights, was, to Winterbourne's imagination, almost oppressively striking.

He immediately perceived, from her tone, that Miss Daisy Miller's place in the social scale was low. "I am afraid you don't approve of them," he said.

"They are very common," Mrs. Costello declared. "They are the sort of Americans that one does one's duty by not—not accepting."

"Ah, you don't accept them?" said the young man.

"I can't, my dear Frederick. I would if I could, but I can't."

"The young girl is very pretty," said Winterbourne, in a moment.

"Of course she's pretty. But she is very common."

"I see what you mean, of course," said Winterbourne, after another pause.

"She has that charming look that they all have," his aunt

resumed. "I can't think where they pick it up; and she dresses in perfection—no, you don't know how well she dresses. I can't think where they get their taste."

"But, my dear aunt, she is not, after all, a Comanche savage."

"She is a young lady," said Mrs. Costello, "who has an intimacy with her mamma's courier."

"An intimacy with the courier?" the young man demanded.

"Oh, the mother is just as bad! They treat the courier like a familiar friend—like a gentleman. I shouldn't wonder if he dines with them. Very likely they have never seen a man with such good manners, such fine clothes, so like a gentleman. He probably corresponds to the young lady's idea of a Count. He sits with them in the garden, in the evening. I think he smokes."

Winterbourne listened with interest to these disclosures; they helped him to make up his mind about Miss Daisy. Evidently she was rather wild. "Well," he said, "I am not a courier, and yet she was very charming to me."

"You had better have said at first," said Mrs. Costello with dignity, "that you had made her acquaintance."

"We simply met in the garden, and we talked a bit."

"*Tout bonnement!* And pray what did you say?"

"I said I should take the liberty of introducing her to my admirable aunt."

"I am much obliged to you."

"It was to guarantee my respectability," said Winterbourne.

"And pray who is to guarantee hers?"

"Ah, you are cruel!" said the young man. "She's a very nice girl."

"You don't say that as if you believed it," Mrs. Costello observed.

"She is completely uncultivated," Winterbourne went on. "But she is wonderfully pretty, and, in short, she is very nice. To prove that I believe it, I am going to take her to the Château de Chillon."

"You two are going off there together? I should say it proved just the contrary. How long had you known her, may I ask, when this interesting project was formed? You haven't been twenty-four hours in the house."

"I had known her half-an-hour!" said Winterbourne, smiling.

"Dear me!" cried Mrs. Costello. "What a dreadful girl!"

Her nephew was silent for some moments. "You really think, then," he began, earnestly, and with a desire for trustworthy information—"you really think that——" But he paused again.

"Think what, sir?" said his aunt.

"That she is the sort of young lady who expects a man—sooner or later—to carry her off?"

"I haven't the least idea what such young ladies expect a man to do. But I really think that you had better not meddle with little American girls that are uncultivated, as you call them. You have lived too long out of the country. You will be sure to make some great mistake. You are too innocent."

"My dear aunt, I am not so innocent," said Winterbourne, smiling and curling his moustache.

"You are too guilty, then!"

Winterbourne continued to curl his moustache, meditatively. "You won't let the poor girl know you then?" he asked at last.

"Is it literally true that she is going to the Château de Chillon with you?"

"I think that she fully intends it."

"Then, my dear Frederick," said Mrs. Costello, "I must decline the honour of her acquaintance. I am an old woman, but I am not too old—thank Heaven—to be shocked!"

"But don't they all do these things—the young girls in America?" Winterbourne inquired.

Mrs. Costello stared a moment. "I should like to see my granddaughters do them!" she declared, grimly.

This seemed to throw some light upon the matter, for Winterbourne remembered to have heard that his pretty cousins in New York were "tremendous flirts." If, therefore, Miss Daisy Miller exceeded the liberal license allowed to these young ladies, it was probable that anything might be expected of her. Winterbourne was impatient to see her again, and he was vexed with himself that, by instinct, he should not appreciate her justly.

Though he was impatient to see her, he hardly knew what

he should say to her about his aunt's refusal to become acquainted with her; but he discovered, promptly enough, that
with Miss Daisy Miller there was no great need of walking on
tiptoe. He found her that evening in the garden, wandering
about in the warm starlight, like an indolent sylph, and swinging to and fro the largest fan he had ever beheld. It was ten
o'clock. He had dined with his aunt, had been sitting with
her since dinner, and had just taken leave of her till the morrow. Miss Daisy Miller seemed very glad to see him; she declared it was the longest evening she had ever passed.

"Have you been all alone?" he asked.

"I have been walking round with mother. But mother gets
tired walking round," she answered.

"Has she gone to bed?"

"No; she doesn't like to go to bed," said the young girl.
"She doesn't sleep—not three hours. She says she doesn't
know how she lives. She's dreadfully nervous. I guess she
sleeps more than she thinks. She's gone somewhere after
Randolph; she wants to try to get him to go to bed. He
doesn't like to go to bed."

"Let us hope she will persuade him," observed Winterbourne.

"She will talk to him all she can; but he doesn't like her to
talk to him," said Miss Daisy, opening her fan. "She's going
to try to get Eugenio to talk to him. But he isn't afraid of
Eugenio. Eugenio's a splendid courier, but he can't make
much impression on Randolph! I don't believe he'll go to bed
before eleven." It appeared that Randolph's vigil was in fact
triumphantly prolonged, for Winterbourne strolled about
with the young girl for some time without meeting her
mother. "I have been looking round for that lady you want
to introduce me to," his companion resumed. "She's your
aunt." Then, on Winterbourne's admitting the fact, and expressing some curiosity as to how she had learned it, she said
she had heard all about Mrs. Costello from the chambermaid.
She was very quiet and very *comme il faut*; she wore white
puffs; she spoke to no one, and she never dined at the *table
d'hôte*. Every two days she had a headache. "I think that's a
lovely description, headache and all!" said Miss Daisy, chattering along in her thin, gay voice. "I want to know her ever

so much. I know just what *your* aunt would be; I know I
should like her. She would be very exclusive. I like a lady to
be exclusive; I'm dying to be exclusive myself. Well, we *are*
exclusive, mother and I. We don't speak to every one—or they
don't speak to us. I suppose it's about the same thing. Any
way, I shall be ever so glad to know your aunt."

Winterbourne was embarrassed. "She would be most
happy," he said; "but I am afraid those headaches will interfere."

The young girl looked at him through the dusk. "But I
suppose she doesn't have a headache every day," she said,
sympathetically.

Winterbourne was silent a moment. "She tells me she
does," he answered at last—not knowing what to say.

Miss Daisy Miller stopped and stood looking at him. Her
prettiness was still visible in the darkness; she was opening and
closing her enormous fan. "She doesn't want to know me!"
she said, suddenly. "Why don't you say so? You needn't be
afraid. I'm not afraid!" And she gave a little laugh.

Winterbourne fancied there was a tremor in her voice; he
was touched, shocked, mortified by it. "My dear young lady,"
he protested, "she knows no one. It's her wretched health."

The young girl walked on a few steps, laughing still. "You
needn't be afraid," she repeated. "Why should she want to
know me?" Then she paused again; she was close to the parapet of the garden, and in front of her was the starlit lake.
There was a vague sheen upon its surface, and in the distance
were dimly-seen mountain forms. Daisy Miller looked out
upon the mysterious prospect, and then she gave another little
laugh. "Gracious! she *is* exclusive!" she said. Winterbourne
wondered whether she was seriously wounded, and for a moment almost wished that her sense of injury might be such as
to make it becoming in him to attempt to reassure and comfort her. He had a pleasant sense that she would be very ap-
proachable for consolatory purposes. He felt then, for the
instant, quite ready to sacrifice his aunt, conversationally; to
admit that she was a proud, rude woman, and to declare that
they needn't mind her. But before he had time to commit
himself to this perilous mixture of gallantry and impiety, the
young lady, resuming her walk, gave an exclamation in quite

another tone. "Well; here's mother! I guess she hasn't got Randolph to go to bed." The figure of a lady appeared, at a distance, very indistinct in the darkness, and advancing with a slow and wavering movement. Suddenly it seemed to pause.

"Are you sure it is your mother? Can you distinguish her in this thick dusk?" Winterbourne asked.

"Well!" cried Miss Daisy Miller, with a laugh, "I guess I know my own mother. And when she has got on my shawl, too! She is always wearing my things."

The lady in question, ceasing to advance, hovered vaguely about the spot at which she had checked her steps.

"I am afraid your mother doesn't see you," said Winterbourne. "Or perhaps," he added—thinking, with Miss Miller, the joke permissible—"perhaps she feels guilty about your shawl."

"Oh, it's a fearful old thing!" the young girl replied, serenely. "I told her she could wear it. She won't come here, because she sees you."

"Ah, then," said Winterbourne, "I had better leave you."

"Oh no; come on!" urged Miss Daisy Miller.

"I'm afraid your mother doesn't approve of my walking with you."

Miss Miller gave him a serious glance. "It isn't for me; it's for you—that is, it's for *her*. Well; I don't know who it's for! But mother doesn't like any of my gentlemen friends. She's right down timid. She always makes a fuss if I introduce a gentleman. But I *do* introduce them—almost always. If I didn't introduce my gentlemen friends to mother," the young girl added, in her little soft, flat monotone, "I shouldn't think I was natural."

"To introduce me," said Winterbourne, "you must know my name." And he proceeded to pronounce it.

"Oh, dear; I can't say all that!" said his companion, with a laugh. But by this time they had come up to Mrs. Miller, who, as they drew near, walked to the parapet of the garden and leaned upon it, looking intently at the lake and turning her back upon them. "Mother!" said the young girl, in a tone of decision. Upon this the elder lady turned round. "Mr. Winterbourne," said Miss Daisy Miller, introducing the young man very frankly and prettily. "Common" she was, as

Mrs. Costello had pronounced her; yet it was a wonder to Winterbourne that, with her commonness, she had a singularly delicate grace.

Her mother was a small, spare, light person, with a wandering eye, a very exiguous nose, and a large forehead, decorated with a certain amount of thin, much-frizzled hair. Like her daughter, Mrs. Miller was dressed with extreme elegance; she had enormous diamonds in her ears. So far as Winterbourne could observe, she gave him no greeting—she certainly was not looking at him. Daisy was near her, pulling her shawl straight. "What are you doing, poking round here?" this young lady inquired; but by no means with that harshness of accent which her choice of words may imply.

"I don't know," said her mother, turning towards the lake again.

"I shouldn't think you'd want that shawl!" Daisy exclaimed.

"Well—I do!" her mother answered, with a little laugh.

"Did you get Randolph to go to bed?" asked the young girl.

"No; I couldn't induce him," said Mrs. Miller, very gently. "He wants to talk to the waiter. He likes to talk to that waiter."

"I was telling Mr. Winterbourne," the young girl went on; and to the young man's ear her tone might have indicated that she had been uttering his name all her life.

"Oh, yes!" said Winterbourne; "I have the pleasure of knowing your son."

Randolph's mamma was silent; she turned her attention to the lake. But at last she spoke. "Well, I don't see how he lives!"

"Anyhow, it isn't so bad as it was at Dover," said Daisy Miller.

"And what occurred at Dover?" Winterbourne asked.

"He wouldn't go to bed at all. I guess he sat up all night —in the public parlour. He wasn't in bed at twelve o'clock: I know that."

"It was half-past twelve," declared Mrs. Miller, with mild emphasis.

"Does he sleep much during the day?" Winterbourne demanded.

"I guess he doesn't sleep much," Daisy rejoined.

"I wish he would!" said her mother. "It seems as if he couldn't."

"I think he's real tiresome," Daisy pursued.

Then, for some moments, there was silence. "Well, Daisy Miller," said the elder lady, presently, "I shouldn't think you'd want to talk against your own brother!"

"Well, he *is* tiresome, mother," said Daisy, quite without the asperity of a retort.

"He's only nine," urged Mrs. Miller.

"Well, he wouldn't go to that castle," said the young girl. "I'm going there with Mr. Winterbourne."

To this announcement, very placidly made, Daisy's mamma offered no response. Winterbourne took for granted that she deeply disapproved of the projected excursion; but he said to himself that she was a simple, easily-managed person, and that a few deferential protestations would take the edge from her displeasure. "Yes," he began; "your daughter has kindly allowed me the honour of being her guide."

Mrs. Miller's wandering eyes attached themselves, with a sort of appealing air, to Daisy, who, however, strolled a few steps farther, gently humming to herself. "I presume you will go in the cars," said her mother.

"Yes; or in the boat," said Winterbourne.

"Well, of course, I don't know," Mrs. Miller rejoined. "I have never been to that castle."

"It is a pity you shouldn't go," said Winterbourne, beginning to feel reassured as to her opposition. And yet he was quite prepared to find that, as a matter of course, she meant to accompany her daughter.

"We've been thinking ever so much about going," she pursued; "but it seems as if we couldn't. Of course Daisy—she wants to go round. But there's a lady here—I don't know her name—she says she shouldn't think we'd want to go to see castles *here*; she should think we'd want to wait till we got to Italy. It seems as if there would be so many there," continued Mrs. Miller, with an air of increasing confidence. "Of course, we only want to see the principal ones. We visited several in England," she presently added.

"Ah, yes! in England there are beautiful castles," said Winterbourne. "But Chillon, here, is very well worth seeing."

"Well, if Daisy feels up to it——," said Mrs. Miller, in a tone impregnated with a sense of the magnitude of the enterprise. "It seems as if there was nothing she wouldn't undertake."

"Oh, I think she'll enjoy it!" Winterbourne declared. And he desired more and more to make it a certainty that he was to have the privilege of a *tête-à-tête* with the young lady, who was still strolling along in front of them, softly vocalising. "You are not disposed, madam," he inquired, "to undertake it yourself?"

Daisy's mother looked at him, an instant, askance, and then walked forward in silence. Then—"I guess she had better go alone," she said, simply.

Winterbourne observed to himself that this was a very different type of maternity from that of the vigilant matrons who massed themselves in the forefront of social intercourse in the dark old city at the other end of the lake. But his meditations were interrupted by hearing his name very distinctly pronounced by Mrs. Miller's unprotected daughter.

"Mr. Winterbourne!" murmured Daisy.

"Mademoiselle!" said the young man.

"Don't you want to take me out in a boat?"

"At present?" he asked.

"Of course!" said Daisy.

"Well, Annie Miller!" exclaimed her mother.

"I beg you, madam, to let her go," said Winterbourne, ardently; for he had never yet enjoyed the sensation of guiding through the summer starlight a skiff freighted with a fresh and beautiful young girl.

"I shouldn't think she'd want to," said her mother. "I should think she'd rather go indoors."

"I'm sure Mr. Winterbourne wants to take me," Daisy declared. "He's so awfully devoted!"

"I will row you over to Chillon, in the starlight."

"I don't believe it!" said Daisy.

"Well!" ejaculated the elder lady again.

"You haven't spoken to me for half-an-hour," her daughter went on.

"I have been having some very pleasant conversation with your mother," said Winterbourne.

"Well; I want you to take me out in a boat!" Daisy repeated. They had all stopped, and she had turned round and was looking at Winterbourne. Her face wore a charming smile, her pretty eyes were gleaming, she was swinging her great fan about. No; it's impossible to be prettier than that, thought Winterbourne.

"There are half-a-dozen boats moored at that landing-place," he said, pointing to certain steps which descended from the garden to the lake. "If you will do me the honour to accept my arm, we will go and select one of them."

Daisy stood there smiling; she threw back her head and gave a little light laugh. "I like a gentleman to be formal!" she declared.

"I assure you it's a formal offer."

"I was bound I would make you say something," Daisy went on.

"You see it's not very difficult," said Winterbourne. "But I am afraid you are chaffing me."

"I think not, sir," remarked Mrs. Miller, very gently.

"Do, then, let me give you a row," he said to the young girl.

"It's quite lovely, the way you say that!" cried Daisy.

"It will be still more lovely to do it."

"Yes, it would be lovely!" said Daisy. But she made no movement to accompany him; she only stood there laughing.

"I should think you had better find out what time it is," interposed her mother.

"It is eleven o'clock, madam," said a voice, with a foreign accent, out of the neighbouring darkness; and Winterbourne, turning, perceived the florid personage who was in attendance upon the two ladies. He had apparently just approached.

"Oh, Eugenio," said Daisy, "I am going out in a boat!"

Eugenio bowed. "At eleven o'clock, mademoiselle?"

"I am going with Mr. Winterbourne. This very minute."

"Do tell her she can't," said Mrs. Miller to the courier.

"I think you had better not go out in a boat, mademoiselle," Eugenio declared.

Winterbourne wished to Heaven this pretty girl were not so familiar with her courier; but he said nothing.

"I suppose you don't think it's proper!" Daisy exclaimed. "Eugenio doesn't think anything's proper."

"I am at your service," said Winterbourne.

"Does mademoiselle propose to go alone?" asked Eugenio of Mrs. Miller.

"Oh, no; with this gentleman!" answered Daisy's mamma.

The courier looked for a moment at Winterbourne—the latter thought he was smiling—and then, solemnly, with a bow, "As mademoiselle pleases!" he said.

"Oh, I hoped you would make a fuss!" said Daisy. "I don't care to go now."

"I myself shall make a fuss if you don't go," said Winterbourne.

"That's all I want—a little fuss!" And the young girl began to laugh again.

"Mr. Randolph has gone to bed!" the courier announced, frigidly.

"Oh, Daisy; now we can go!" said Mrs. Miller.

Daisy turned away from Winterbourne, looking at him, smiling and fanning herself. "Good night," she said; "I hope you are disappointed, or disgusted, or something!"

He looked at her, taking the hand she offered him. "I am puzzled," he answered.

"Well; I hope it won't keep you awake!" she said, very smartly; and, under the escort of the privileged Eugenio, the two ladies passed towards the house.

Winterbourne stood looking after them; he was indeed puzzled. He lingered beside the lake for a quarter of an hour, turning over the mystery of the young girl's sudden familiarities and caprices. But the only very definite conclusion he came to was that he should enjoy deucedly "going off" with her somewhere.

Two days afterwards he went off with her to the Castle of Chillon. He waited for her in the large hall of the hotel, where the couriers, the servants, the foreign tourists were lounging about and staring. It was not the place he would have chosen, but she had appointed it. She came tripping downstairs, buttoning her long gloves, squeezing her folded parasol against her pretty figure, dressed in the perfection of a soberly elegant travelling-costume. Winterbourne was a man of imagination and, as our ancestors used to say, of sensibility; as he looked at her dress and, on the great staircase, her little rapid, confiding step, he felt as if there were something romantic going forward. He could have believed he was going to elope with her. He passed out with her among all the idle people that were assembled there; they were all looking at her very hard; she had begun to chatter as soon as she joined him. Winterbourne's preference had been that they should be conveyed to Chillon in a carriage; but she expressed a lively wish to go in the little steamer; she declared that she had a passion for steamboats. There was always such a lovely breeze upon the water, and you saw such lots of people. The sail was not long, but Winterbourne's companion found time to say a great many things. To the young man himself their little excursion was so much of an escapade—an adventure—that, even allowing for her habitual sense of freedom, he had some expectation of seeing her regard it in the same way. But it must be confessed that, in this particular, he was disappointed. Daisy Miller was extremely animated, she was in charming spirits; but she was apparently not at all excited; she was not fluttered; she avoided neither his eyes nor those of any one else; she blushed neither when she looked at him nor when she saw that people were looking at her. People continued to look at her a great deal, and Winterbourne took much satisfaction in his pretty companion's distinguished air. He had been a little afraid that she would talk loud, laugh overmuch, and even, perhaps, desire to move about the boat a good deal. But he quite forgot his fears; he sat smiling, with his eyes upon her face, while, without moving from her place, she delivered herself of a great number of original reflections. It was the most charming garrulity he had ever heard. He had assented to the idea that she was "common;" but was she so, after all, or was he simply getting used to her commonness? Her conversation was chiefly of what metaphysicians term the objective cast; but every now and then it took a subjective turn.

"What on *earth* are you so grave about?" she suddenly demanded, fixing her agreeable eyes upon Winterbourne's.

"Am I grave?" he asked. "I had an idea I was grinning from ear to ear."

"You look as if you were taking me to a funeral. If that's a grin, your ears are very near together."

"Should you like me to dance a hornpipe on the deck?"

"Pray do, and I'll carry round your hat. It will pay the expenses of our journey."

"I never was better pleased in my life," murmured Winterbourne.

She looked at him a moment, and then burst into a little laugh. "I like to make you say those things! You're a queer mixture!"

In the castle, after they had landed, the subjective element decidedly prevailed. Daisy tripped about the vaulted chambers, rustled her skirts in the corkscrew staircases, flirted back with a pretty little cry and a shudder from the edge of the *oubliettes*, and turned a singularly well-shaped ear to everything that Winterbourne told her about the place. But he saw that she cared very little for feudal antiquities, and that the dusky traditions of Chillon made but a slight impression upon her. They had the good fortune to have been able to walk about without other companionship than that of the custodian; and Winterbourne arranged with this functionary that they should not be hurried—that they should linger and pause wherever they chose. The custodian interpreted the bargain generously—Winterbourne, on his side, had been generous—and ended by leaving them quite to themselves. Miss Miller's observations were not remarkable for logical consistency; for anything she wanted to say she was sure to find a pretext. She found a great many pretexts in the rugged embrasures of Chillon for asking Winterbourne sudden questions about himself—his family, his previous history, his tastes, his habits, his intentions—and for supplying information upon corresponding points in her own personality. Of her own tastes, habits and intentions Miss Miller was prepared to give the most definite, and indeed the most favourable, account.

"Well; I hope you know enough!" she said to her companion, after he had told her the history of the unhappy Bonivard. "I never saw a man that knew so much!" The history of Bonivard had evidently, as they say, gone into one ear and out of the other. But Daisy went on to say that she wished Winterbourne would travel with them and "go round" with them;

they might know something, in that case. "Don't you want
to come and teach Randolph?" she asked. Winterbourne said
that nothing could possibly please him so much; but that he
had unfortunately other occupations. "Other occupations? I
don't believe it!" said Miss Daisy. "What do you mean? You
are not in business." The young man admitted that he was
not in business; but he had engagements which, even within
a day or two would force him to go back to Geneva. "Oh,
bother!" she said, "I don't believe it!" and she began to talk
about something else. But a few moments later, when he was
pointing out to her the pretty design of an antique fireplace,
she broke out irrelevantly, "You don't mean to say you are
going back to Geneva?"

"It is a melancholy fact that I shall have to return to Geneva
to-morrow."

"Well, Mr. Winterbourne," said Daisy; "I think you're
horrid!"

"Oh, don't say such dreadful things!" said Winterbourne—"just at the last."

"The last!" cried the young girl; "I call it the first. I have
half a mind to leave you here and go straight back to the hotel
alone." And for the next ten minutes she did nothing but call
him horrid. Poor Winterbourne was fairly bewildered; no
young lady had as yet done him the honour to be so agitated
by the announcement of his movements. His companion, after
this, ceased to pay any attention to the curiosities of Chillon
or the beauties of the lake; she opened fire upon the mysterious charmer in Geneva, whom she appeared to have instantly
taken it for granted that he was hurrying back to see. How did
Miss Daisy Miller know that there was a charmer in Geneva?
Winterbourne, who denied the existence of such a person, was
quite unable to discover; and he was divided between amazement at the rapidity of her induction and amusement at the
frankness of her *persiflage*. She seemed to him, in all this, an
extraordinary mixture of innocence and crudity. "Does she
never allow you more than three days at a time?" asked Daisy,
ironically. "Doesn't she give you a vacation in summer?
There's no one so hard worked but they can get leave to go
off somewhere at this season. I suppose, if you stay another
day, she'll come after you in the boat. Do wait over till Friday,

and I will go down to the landing to see her arrive!" Winterbourne began to think he had been wrong to feel disappointed in the temper in which the young lady had embarked. If he had missed the personal accent, the personal accent was now making its appearance. It sounded very distinctly, at last, in her telling him she would stop "teasing" him if he would promise her solemnly to come down to Rome in the winter.

"That's not a difficult promise to make," said Winterbourne. "My aunt has taken an apartment in Rome for the winter, and has already asked me to come and see her."

"I don't want you to come for your aunt," said Daisy; "I want you to come for me." And this was the only allusion that the young man was ever to hear her make to his invidious kinswoman. He declared that, at any rate, he would certainly come. After this Daisy stopped teasing. Winterbourne took a carriage, and they drove back to Vevey in the dusk; the young girl was very quiet.

In the evening Winterbourne mentioned to Mrs. Costello that he had spent the afternoon at Chillon, with Miss Daisy Miller.

"The Americans—of the courier?" asked this lady.

"Ah, happily," said Winterbourne, "the courier stayed at home."

"She went with you all alone?"

"All alone."

Mrs. Costello sniffed a little at her smelling-bottle. "And that," she exclaimed, "is the young person you wanted me to know!"

III.

Winterbourne, who had returned to Geneva the day after his excursion to Chillon, went to Rome towards the end of January. His aunt had been established there for several weeks, and he had received a couple of letters from her. "Those people you were so devoted to last summer at Vevey have turned up here, courier and all," she wrote. "They seem to have made several acquaintances, but the courier continues to be the most *intime*. The young lady, however, is also very intimate with some third-rate Italians, with whom she rackets about in a way that makes much talk. Bring me that pretty novel of Cherbuliez's—'Paule Méré'—and don't come later than the 23rd."

In the natural course of events, Winterbourne, on arriving in Rome, would presently have ascertained Mrs. Miller's address at the American banker's and have gone to pay his compliments to Miss Daisy. "After what happened at Vevey I certainly think I may call upon them," he said to Mrs. Costello.

"If, after what happens—at Vevey and everywhere—you desire to keep up the acquaintance, you are very welcome. Of course a man may know every one. Men are welcome to the privilege!"

"Pray what is it that happens—here, for instance?" Winterbourne demanded.

"The girl goes about alone with her foreigners. As to what happens farther, you must apply elsewhere for information. She has picked up half-a-dozen of the regular Roman fortune-hunters, and she takes them about to people's houses. When she comes to a party she brings with her a gentleman with a good deal of manner and a wonderful moustache."

"And where is the mother?"

"I haven't the least idea. They are very dreadful people."

Winterbourne meditated a moment. "They are very ignorant—very innocent only. Depend upon it they are not bad."

"They are hopelessly vulgar," said Mrs. Costello. "Whether or no being hopelessly vulgar is being 'bad' is a question for the metaphysicians. They are bad enough to dislike, at any rate; and for this short life that is quite enough."

The news that Daisy Miller was surrounded by half-a-dozen wonderful moustaches checked Winterbourne's impulse to go straightway to see her. He had perhaps not definitely flattered himself that he had made an ineffaceable impression upon her heart, but he was annoyed at hearing of a state of affairs so little in harmony with an image that had lately flitted in and out of his own meditations; the image of a very pretty girl looking out of an old Roman window and asking herself urgently when Mr. Winterbourne would arrive. If, however, he determined to wait a little before reminding Miss Miller of his claims to her consideration, he went very soon to call upon two or three other friends. One of these friends was an American lady who had spent several winters at Geneva, where she had placed her children at school. She was a very accomplished woman and she lived in the Via Gregoriana. Winterbourne found her in a little crimson drawing-room, on a third floor; the room was filled with southern sunshine. He had not been there ten minutes when the servant came in, announcing "Madame Mila!" This announcement was presently followed by the entrance of little Randolph Miller, who stopped in the middle of the room and stood staring at Winterbourne. An instant later his pretty sister crossed the threshold; and then, after a considerable interval, Mrs. Miller slowly advanced.

"I know you!" said Randolph.

"I'm sure you know a great many things," exclaimed Winterbourne, taking him by the hand. "How is your education coming on?"

Daisy was exchanging greetings very prettily with her hostess; but when she heard Winterbourne's voice she quickly turned her head. "Well, I declare!" she said.

"I told you I should come, you know," Winterbourne rejoined, smiling.

"Well—I didn't believe it," said Miss Daisy.

"I am much obliged to you," laughed the young man.

"You might have come to see me!" said Daisy.

"I arrived only yesterday."

"I don't believe that!" the young girl declared.

Winterbourne turned with a protesting smile to her mother; but this lady evaded his glance, and seating herself, fixed her eyes upon her son. "We've got a bigger place than this," said Randolph. "It's all gold on the walls."

Mrs. Miller turned uneasily in her chair. "I told you if I were to bring you, you would say something!" she murmured.

"I told *you*!" Randolph exclaimed. "I tell *you*, sir!" he added jocosely, giving Winterbourne a thump on the knee. "It *is* bigger, too!"

Daisy had entered upon a lively conversation with her hostess; Winterbourne judged it becoming to address a few words to her mother. "I hope you have been well since we parted at Vevey," he said.

Mrs. Miller now certainly looked at him—at his chin. "Not very well, sir," she answered.

"She's got the dyspepsia," said Randolph. "I've got it too. Father's got it. I've got it worst!"

This announcement, instead of embarrassing Mrs. Miller, seemed to relieve her. "I suffer from the liver," she said. "I think it's this climate; it's less bracing than Schenectady, especially in the winter season. I don't know whether you know we reside at Schenectady. I was saying to Daisy that I certainly hadn't found any one like Dr. Davis, and I didn't believe I should. Oh, at Schenectady, he stands first; they think everything of him. He has so much to do, and yet there was nothing he wouldn't do for me. He said he never saw anything like my dyspepsia, but he was bound to cure it. I'm sure there was nothing he wouldn't try. He was just going to try something new when we came off. Mr. Miller wanted Daisy to see Europe for herself. But I wrote to Mr. Miller that it seems as if I couldn't get on without Dr. Davis. At Schenectady he stands at the very top; and there's a great deal of sickness there, too. It affects my sleep."

Winterbourne had a good deal of pathological gossip with Dr. Davis's patient, during which Daisy chattered unremittingly to her own companion. The young man asked Mrs. Miller how she was pleased with Rome. "Well, I must say I am disappointed," she answered. "We had heard so much about it; I suppose we had heard too much. But we couldn't help that. We had been led to expect something different."

"Ah, wait a little, and you will become very fond of it," said Winterbourne.

"I hate it worse and worse every day!" cried Randolph.

"You are like the infant Hannibal," said Winterbourne.

"No, I ain't!" Randolph declared, at a venture.

"You are not much like an infant," said his mother. "But we have seen places," she resumed, "that I should put a long way before Rome." And in reply to Winterbourne's interrogation, "There's Zurich," she observed; "I think Zurich is lovely; and we hadn't heard half so much about it."

"The best place we've seen is the City of Richmond!" said Randolph.

"He means the ship," his mother explained. "We crossed

in that ship. Randolph had a good time on the City of Richmond.''

"It's the best place I've seen," the child repeated. "Only it
was turned the wrong way."

"Well, we've got to turn the right way some time," said
Mrs. Miller, with a little laugh. Winterbourne expressed the
hope that her daughter at least found some gratification in
Rome, and she declared that Daisy was quite carried away.
"It's on account of the society—the society's splendid. She
goes round everywhere; she has made a great number of acquaintances. Of course she goes round more than I do. I must
say they have been very sociable; they have taken her right in.
And then she knows a great many gentlemen. Oh, she thinks
there's nothing like Rome. Of course, it's a great deal pleasanter for a young lady if she knows plenty of gentlemen."

By this time Daisy had turned her attention again to Winterbourne. "I've been telling Mrs. Walker how mean you
were!" the young girl announced.

"And what is the evidence you have offered?" asked Winterbourne, rather annoyed at Miss Miller's want of appreciation of the zeal of an admirer who on his way down to Rome
had stopped neither at Bologna nor at Florence, simply because of a certain sentimental impatience. He remembered
that a cynical compatriot had once told him that American
women—the pretty ones, and this gave a largeness to the axiom—were at once the most exacting in the world and the
least endowed with a sense of indebtedness.

"Why, you were awfully mean at Vevey," said Daisy. "You
wouldn't do anything. You wouldn't stay there when I asked
you."

"My dearest young lady," cried Winterbourne, with eloquence, "have I come all the way to Rome to encounter your
reproaches?"

"Just hear him say that!" said Daisy to her hostess, giving
a twist to a bow on this lady's dress. "Did you ever hear
anything so quaint?"

"So quaint, my dear?" murmured Mrs. Walker, in the tone
of a partisan of Winterbourne.

"Well, I don't know," said Daisy, fingering Mrs. Walker's
ribbons. "Mrs. Walker, I want to tell you something."

"Motherr," interposed Randolph, with his rough ends to his words, "I tell you you've got to go. Eugenio 'll raise something!"

"I'm not afraid of Eugenio," said Daisy, with a toss of her head. "Look here, Mrs. Walker," she went on, "you know I'm coming to your party."

"I am delighted to hear it."

"I've got a lovely dress."

"I am very sure of that."

"But I want to ask a favour—permission to bring a friend."

"I shall be happy to see any of your friends," said Mrs. Walker, turning with a smile to Mrs. Miller.

"Oh, they are not my friends," answered Daisy's mamma, smiling shyly, in her own fashion. "I never spoke to them!"

"It's an intimate friend of mine—Mr. Giovanelli," said Daisy, without a tremor in her clear little voice or a shadow on her brilliant little face.

Mrs. Walker was silent a moment, she gave a rapid glance at Winterbourne. "I shall be glad to see Mr. Giovanelli," she then said.

"He's an Italian," Daisy pursued, with the prettiest serenity. "He's a great friend of mine—he's the handsomest man in the world—except Mr. Winterbourne! He knows plenty of Italians, but he wants to know some Americans. He thinks ever so much of Americans. He's tremendously clever. He's perfectly lovely!"

It was settled that this brilliant personage should be brought to Mrs. Walker's party, and then Mrs. Miller prepared to take her leave. "I guess we'll go back to the hotel," she said.

"You may go back to the hotel, mother, but I'm going to take a walk," said Daisy.

"She's going to walk with Mr. Giovanelli," Randolph proclaimed.

"I am going to the Pincio," said Daisy, smiling.

"Alone, my dear—at this hour?" Mrs. Walker asked. The afternoon was drawing to a close—it was the hour for the throng of carriages and of contemplative pedestrians. "I don't think it's safe, my dear," said Mrs. Walker.

"Neither do I," subjoined Mrs. Miller. "You'll get the fever as sure as you live. Remember what Dr. Davis told you!"

"Give her some medicine before she goes," said Randolph.

The company had risen to its feet; Daisy, still showing her pretty teeth, bent over and kissed her hostess. "Mrs. Walker, you are too perfect," she said. "I'm not going alone; I am going to meet a friend."

"Your friend won't keep you from getting the fever," Mrs. Miller observed.

"Is it Mr. Giovanelli?" asked the hostess.

Winterbourne was watching the young girl; at this question his attention quickened. She stood there smiling and smoothing her bonnet-ribbons; she glanced at Winterbourne. Then, while she glanced and smiled, she answered without a shade of hesitation, "Mr. Giovanelli—the beautiful Giovanelli."

"My dear young friend," said Mrs. Walker, taking her hand, pleadingly, "don't walk off to the Pincio at this hour to meet a beautiful Italian."

"Well, he speaks English," said Mrs. Miller.

"Gracious me!" Daisy exclaimed, "I don't want to do anything improper. There's an easy way to settle it." She continued to glance at Winterbourne. "The Pincio is only a hundred yards distant, and if Mr. Winterbourne were as polite as he pretends he would offer to walk with me!"

Winterbourne's politeness hastened to affirm itself, and the young girl gave him gracious leave to accompany her. They passed down-stairs before her mother, and at the door Winterbourne perceived Mrs. Miller's carriage drawn up, with the ornamental courier whose acquaintance he had made at Vevey seated within. "Good-bye, Eugenio!" cried Daisy, "I'm going to take a walk." The distance from the Via Gregoriana to the beautiful garden at the other end of the Pincian Hill is, in fact, rapidly traversed. As the day was splendid, however, and the concourse of vehicles, walkers, and loungers numerous, the young Americans found their progress much delayed. This fact was highly agreeable to Winterbourne, in spite of his consciousness of his singular situation. The slow-moving, idly-gazing Roman crowd bestowed much attention upon the extremely pretty young foreign lady who was passing through it upon his arm; and he wondered what on earth had been in

Daisy's mind when she proposed to expose herself, unattended, to its appreciation. His own mission, to her sense,
apparently, was to consign her to the hands of Mr. Giovanelli;
but Winterbourne, at once annoyed and gratified, resolved
that he would do no such thing.

"Why haven't you been to see me?" asked Daisy. "You
can't get out of that."

"I have had the honour of telling you that I have only just
stepped out of the train."

"You must have stayed in the train a good while after it
stopped!" cried the young girl, with her little laugh. "I suppose you were asleep. You have had time to go to see Mrs.
Walker."

"I knew Mrs. Walker—" Winterbourne began to explain.

"I knew where you knew her. You knew her at Geneva. She
told me so. Well, you knew me at Vevey. That's just as good.
So you ought to have come." She asked him no other question than this; she began to prattle about her own affairs.
"We've got splendid rooms at the hotel; Eugenio says they're
the best rooms in Rome. We are going to stay all winter—if
we don't die of the fever; and I guess we'll stay then. It's a
great deal nicer than I thought; I thought it would be fearfully
quiet; I was sure it would be awfully poky. I was sure we
should be going round all the time with one of those dreadful
old men that explain about the pictures and things. But we
only had about a week of that, and now I'm enjoying myself.
I know ever so many people, and they are all so charming.
The society's extremely select. There are all kinds—English,
and Germans, and Italians. I think I like the English best. I
like their style of conversation. But there are some lovely
Americans. I never saw anything so hospitable. There's something or other every day. There's not much dancing; but I
must say I never thought dancing was everything. I was always
fond of conversation. I guess I shall have plenty at Mrs.
Walker's—her rooms are so small." When they had passed
the gate of the Pincian Gardens, Miss Miller began to wonder
where Mr. Giovanelli might be. "We had better go straight
to that place in front," she said, "where you look at the view."

"I certainly shall not help you to find him," Winterbourne
declared.

"Then I shall find him without you," said Miss Daisy.

"You certainly won't leave me!" cried Winterbourne.

She burst into her little laugh. "Are you afraid you'll get lost—or run over? But there's Giovanelli, leaning against that tree. He's staring at the women in the carriages: did you ever see anything so cool?"

Winterbourne perceived at some distance a little man standing with folded arms, nursing his cane. He had a handsome face, an artfully poised hat, a glass in one eye and a nosegay in his button-hole. Winterbourne looked at him a moment and then said, "Do you mean to speak to that man?"

"Do I mean to speak to him? Why, you don't suppose I mean to communicate by signs?"

"Pray understand, then," said Winterbourne, "that I intend to remain with you."

Daisy stopped and looked at him, without a sign of troubled consciousness in her face; with nothing but the presence of her charming eyes and her happy dimples. "Well, she's a cool one!" thought the young man.

"I don't like the way you say that," said Daisy. "It's too imperious."

"I beg your pardon if I say it wrong. The main point is to give you an idea of my meaning."

The young girl looked at him more gravely, but with eyes that were prettier than ever. "I have never allowed a gentleman to dictate to me, or to interfere with anything I do."

"I think you have made a mistake," said Winterbourne. "You should sometimes listen to a gentleman—the right one."

Daisy began to laugh again. "I do nothing but listen to gentlemen!" she exclaimed. "Tell me if Mr. Giovanelli is the right one?"

The gentleman with the nosegay in his bosom had now perceived our two friends, and was approaching the young girl with obsequious rapidity. He bowed to Winterbourne as well as to the latter's companion; he had a brilliant smile, an intelligent eye; Winterbourne thought him not a bad-looking fellow. But he nevertheless said to Daisy—"No, he's not the right one."

Daisy evidently had a natural talent for performing introductions; she mentioned the name of each of her companions to the other. She strolled along with one of them on each side of her; Mr. Giovanelli, who spoke English very cleverly—Winterbourne afterwards learned that he had practised the idiom upon a great many American heiresses—addressed her a great deal of very polite nonsense; he was extremely urbane, and the young American, who said nothing, reflected upon that profundity of Italian cleverness which enables people to appear more gracious in proportion as they are more acutely disappointed. Giovanelli, of course, had counted upon something more intimate; he had not bargained for a party of three. But he kept his temper in a manner which suggested far-stretching intentions. Winterbourne flattered himself that he had taken his measure. "He is not a gentleman," said the young American; "he is only a clever imitation of one. He is a music-master, or a penny-a-liner, or a third-rate artist. Damn his good looks!" Mr. Giovanelli had certainly a very pretty face; but Winterbourne felt a superior indignation at his own lovely fellow-countrywoman's not knowing the difference between a spurious gentleman and a real one. Giovanelli chattered and jested and made himself wonderfully agreeable. It was true that if he was an imitation the imitation was very skilful. "Nevertheless," Winterbourne said to himself, "a nice girl ought to know!" And then he came back to the question whether this was in fact a nice girl. Would a nice girl—even allowing for her being a little American flirt—make a rendezvous with a presumably low-lived foreigner? The rendezvous in this case, indeed, had been in broad daylight, and in the most crowded corner of Rome; but was it not impossible to regard the choice of these circumstances as a proof of extreme cynicism? Singular though it may seem, Winterbourne was vexed that the young girl, in joining her *amoroso*, should not appear more impatient of his own company, and he was vexed because of his inclination. It was impossible to regard her as a perfectly well-conducted young lady; she was wanting in a certain indispensable delicacy. It would therefore simplify matters greatly to be able to treat her as the object of one of those sentiments which are called by romancers "lawless passions." That she should seem to wish to get rid of him would help him to think more lightly of her, and to be able to think more lightly of her would make her much less perplexing. But Daisy, on this occasion, continued to present herself as an inscrutable combination of audacity and innocence.

She had been walking some quarter of an hour, attended by her two cavaliers, and responding in a tone of very childish gaiety, as it seemed to Winterbourne, to the pretty speeches of Mr. Giovanelli, when a carriage that had detached itself from the revolving train drew up beside the path. At the same moment Winterbourne perceived that his friend Mrs. Walker —the lady whose house he had lately left—was seated in the vehicle and was beckoning to him. Leaving Miss Miller's side, he hastened to obey her summons. Mrs. Walker was flushed; she wore an excited air. "It is really too dreadful," she said. "That girl must not do this sort of thing. She must not walk here with you two men. Fifty people have noticed her."

Winterbourne raised his eyebrows. "I think it's a pity to make too much fuss about it."

"It's a pity to let the girl ruin herself!"

"She is very innocent," said Winterbourne.

"She's very crazy!" cried Mrs. Walker. "Did you ever see anything so imbecile as her mother? After you had all left me, just now, I could not sit still for thinking of it. It seemed too pitiful, not even to attempt to save her. I ordered the carriage and put on my bonnet, and came here as quickly as possible. Thank heaven I have found you!"

"What do you propose to do with us?" asked Winterbourne, smiling.

"To ask her to get in, to drive her about here for half-an-hour, so that the world may see she is not running absolutely wild, and then to take her safely home."

"I don't think it's a very happy thought," said Winterbourne; "but you can try."

Mrs. Walker tried. The young man went in pursuit of Miss Miller, who had simply nodded and smiled at his interlocutrix in the carriage and had gone her way with her own companion. Daisy, on learning that Mrs. Walker wished to speak to her, retraced her steps with a perfect good grace and with Mr. Giovanelli at her side. She declared that she was delighted to have a chance to present this gentleman to Mrs. Walker. She immediately achieved the introduction, and declared that she had never in her life seen anything so lovely as Mrs. Walker's carriage-rug.

"I am glad you admire it," said this lady, smiling sweetly. "Will you get in and let me put it over you?"

"Oh, no, thank you," said Daisy. "I shall admire it much more as I see you driving round with it."

"Do get in and drive with me," said Mrs. Walker.

"That would be charming, but it's so enchanting just as I am!" and Daisy gave a brilliant glance at the gentlemen on either side of her.

"It may be enchanting, dear child, but it is not the custom here," urged Mrs. Walker, leaning forward in her victoria with her hands devoutly clasped.

"Well, it ought to be, then!" said Daisy. "If I didn't walk I should expire."

"You should walk with your mother, dear," cried the lady from Geneva, losing patience.

"With my mother dear!" exclaimed the young girl. Winterbourne saw that she scented interference. "My mother never walked ten steps in her life. And then, you know," she added with a laugh, "I am more than five years old."

"You are old enough to be more reasonable. You are old enough, dear Miss Miller, to be talked about."

Daisy looked at Mrs. Walker, smiling intensely. "Talked about? What do you mean?"

"Come into my carriage and I will tell you."

Daisy turned her quickened glance again from one of the gentlemen beside her to the other. Mr. Giovanelli was bowing to and fro, rubbing down his gloves and laughing very agreeably; Winterbourne thought it a most unpleasant scene. "I don't think I want to know what you mean," said Daisy presently. "I don't think I should like it."

Winterbourne wished that Mrs. Walker would tuck in her carriage-rug and drive away; but this lady did not enjoy being defied, as she afterwards told him. "Should you prefer being thought a very reckless girl?" she demanded.

"Gracious me!" exclaimed Daisy. She looked again at Mr. Giovanelli, then she turned to Winterbourne. There was a little pink flush in her cheek; she was tremendously pretty.

"Does Mr. Winterbourne think," she asked slowly, smiling, throwing back her head and glancing at him from head to foot, "that—to save my reputation—I ought to get into the carriage?"

Winterbourne coloured; for an instant he hesitated greatly. It seemed so strange to hear her speak that way of her "reputation." But he himself, in fact, must speak in accordance with gallantry. The finest gallantry, here, was simply to tell her the truth; and the truth, for Winterbourne, as the few indications I have been able to give have made him known to the reader, was that Daisy Miller should take Mrs. Walker's advice. He looked at her exquisite prettiness; and then he said very gently, "I think you should get into the carriage."

Daisy gave a violent laugh. "I never heard anything so stiff! If this is improper, Mrs. Walker," she pursued, "then I am all improper, and you must give me up. Good-bye; I hope you'll have a lovely ride!" and, with Mr. Giovanelli, who made a triumphantly obsequious salute, she turned away.

Mrs. Walker sat looking after her, and there were tears in Mrs. Walker's eyes. "Get in here, sir," she said to Winterbourne, indicating the place beside her. The young man answered that he felt bound to accompany Miss Miller; whereupon Mrs. Walker declared that if he refused her this favour she would never speak to him again. She was evidently in earnest. Winterbourne overtook Daisy and her companion and, offering the young girl his hand, told her that Mrs. Walker had made an imperious claim upon his society. He expected that in answer she would say something rather free, something to commit herself still farther to that "recklessness" from which Mrs. Walker had so charitably endeavoured to dissuade her. But she only shook his hand, hardly looking at him, while Mr. Giovanelli bade him farewell with a too emphatic flourish of the hat.

Winterbourne was not in the best possible humour as he took his seat in Mrs. Walker's victoria. "That was not clever of you," he said candidly, while the vehicle mingled again with the throng of carriages.

"In such a case," his companion answered, "I don't wish to be clever, I wish to be *earnest*!"

"Well, your earnestness has only offended her and put her off."

"It has happened very well," said Mrs. Walker. "If she is so perfectly determined to compromise herself, the sooner one knows it the better; one can act accordingly."

"I suspect she meant no harm," Winterbourne rejoined.

"So I thought a month ago. But she has been going too far."

"What has she been doing?"

"Everything that is not done here. Flirting with any man she could pick up; sitting in corners with mysterious Italians; dancing all the evening with the same partners; receiving visits at eleven o'clock at night. Her mother goes away when visitors come."

"But her brother," said Winterbourne, laughing, "sits up till midnight."

"He must be edified by what he sees. I'm told that at their hotel every one is talking about her, and that a smile goes round among the servants when a gentleman comes and asks for Miss Miller."

"The servants be hanged!" said Winterbourne angrily. "The poor girl's only fault," he presently added, "is that she is very uncultivated."

"She is naturally indelicate," Mrs. Walker declared. "Take that example this morning. How long had you known her at Vevey?"

"A couple of days."

"Fancy, then, her making it a personal matter that you should have left the place!"

Winterbourne was silent for some moments; then he said, "I suspect, Mrs. Walker, that you and I have lived too long at Geneva!" And he added a request that she should inform him with what particular design she had made him enter her carriage.

"I wished to beg you to cease your relations with Miss Miller—not to flirt with her—to give her no farther opportunity to expose herself—to let her alone, in short."

"I'm afraid I can't do that," said Winterbourne. "I like her extremely."

"All the more reason that you shouldn't help her to make a scandal."

"There shall be nothing scandalous in my attentions to her."

"There certainly will be in the way she takes them. But I have said what I had on my conscience," Mrs. Walker pursued. "If you wish to rejoin the young lady I will put you down. Here, by-the-way, you have a chance."

The carriage was traversing that part of the Pincian Garden which overhangs the wall of Rome and overlooks the beautiful Villa Borghese. It is bordered by a large parapet, near which there are several seats. One of the seats, at a distance, was occupied by a gentleman and a lady, towards whom Mrs. Walker gave a toss of her head. At the same moment these persons rose and walked towards the parapet. Winterbourne had asked the coachman to stop; he now descended from the carriage. His companion looked at him a moment in silence; then, while he raised his hat, she drove majestically away. Winterbourne stood there; he had turned his eyes towards Daisy and her cavalier. They evidently saw no one; they were too deeply occupied with each other. When they reached the low garden-wall they stood a moment looking off at the great flat-topped pine-clusters of the Villa Borghese; then Giovanelli seated himself familiarly upon the broad ledge of the wall. The western sun in the opposite sky sent out a brilliant shaft through a couple of cloud-bars; whereupon Daisy's companion took her parasol out of her hands and opened it. She came a little nearer and he held the parasol over her; then, still holding it, he let it rest upon her shoulder, so that both of their heads were hidden from Winterbourne. This young man lingered a moment, then he began to walk. But he walked —not towards the couple with the parasol; towards the residence of his aunt, Mrs. Costello.

IV.

He flattered himself on the following day that there was no smiling among the servants when he, at least, asked for Mrs. Miller at her hotel. This lady and her daughter, however, were not at home; and on the next day after, repeating his visit,

Winterbourne again had the misfortune not to find them. Mrs. Walker's party took place on the evening of the third day, and in spite of the frigidity of his last interview with the hostess Winterbourne was among the guests. Mrs. Walker was one of those American ladies who, while residing abroad, make a point, in their own phrase, of studying European society; and she had on this occasion collected several specimens of her diversely-born fellow-mortals to serve, as it were, as text-books. When Winterbourne arrived Daisy Miller was not there; but in a few moments he saw her mother come in alone, very shyly and ruefully. Mrs. Miller's hair, above her exposed-looking temples, was more frizzled than ever. As she approached Mrs. Walker, Winterbourne also drew near.

"You see I've come all alone," said poor Mrs. Miller. "I'm so frightened; I don't know what to do; it's the first time I've ever been to a party alone—especially in this country. I wanted to bring Randolph or Eugenio, or some one, but Daisy just pushed me off by myself. I ain't used to going round alone."

"And does not your daughter intend to favour us with her society?" demanded Mrs. Walker, impressively.

"Well, Daisy's all dressed," said Mrs. Miller, with that accent of the dispassionate, if not of the philosophic, historian with which she always recorded the current incidents of her daughter's career. "She got dressed on purpose before dinner. But she's got a friend of hers there; that gentleman—the Italian—that she wanted to bring. They've got going at the piano; it seems as if they couldn't leave off. Mr. Giovanelli sings splendidly. But I guess they'll come before very long," concluded Mrs. Miller hopefully.

"I'm sorry she should come—in that way," said Mrs. Walker.

"Well, I told her that there was no use in her getting dressed before dinner if she was going to wait three hours," responded Daisy's mamma. "I didn't see the use of her putting on such a dress as that to sit round with Mr. Giovanelli."

"This is most horrible!" said Mrs. Walker, turning away and addressing herself to Winterbourne. *Elle s'affiche*. It's her revenge for my having ventured to remonstrate with her. When she comes I shall not speak to her."

Daisy came after eleven o'clock, but she was not, on such

an occasion, a young lady to wait to be spoken to. She rustled forward in radiant loveliness, smiling and chattering, carrying a large bouquet and attended by Mr. Giovanelli. Every one stopped talking, and turned and looked at her. She came straight to Mrs. Walker. "I'm afraid you thought I never was coming, so I sent mother off to tell you. I wanted to make Mr. Giovanelli practise some things before he came; you know he sings beautifully, and I want you to ask him to sing. This is Mr. Giovanelli; you know I introduced him to you; he's got the most lovely voice and he knows the most charming set of songs. I made him go over them this evening, on purpose; we had the greatest time at the hotel." Of all this Daisy delivered herself with the sweetest, brightest audibleness, looking now at her hostess and now round the room, while she gave a series of little pats, round her shoulders, to the edges of her dress. "Is there any one I know?" she asked.

"I think every one knows you!" said Mrs. Walker pregnantly, and she gave a very cursory greeting to Mr. Giovanelli. This gentleman bore himself gallantly. He smiled and bowed and showed his white teeth, he curled his moustaches and rolled his eyes, and performed all the proper functions of a handsome Italian at an evening party. He sang, very prettily, half-a-dozen songs, though Mrs. Walker afterwards declared that she had been quite unable to find out who asked him. It was apparently not Daisy who had given him his orders. Daisy sat at a distance from the piano, and though she had publicly, as it were, professed a high admiration for his singing, talked, not inaudibly, while it was going on.

"It's a pity these rooms are so small; we can't dance," she said to Winterbourne, as if she had seen him five minutes before.

"I am not sorry we can't dance," Winterbourne answered; "I don't dance."

"Of course you don't dance; you're too stiff," said Miss Daisy. "I hope you enjoyed your drive with Mrs. Walker."

"No, I didn't enjoy it; I preferred walking with you."

"We paired off, that was much better," said Daisy. "But did you ever hear anything so cool as Mrs. Walker's wanting me to get into her carriage and drop poor Mr. Giovanelli; and under the pretext that it was proper? People have different

ideas! It would have been most unkind; he had been talking
about that walk for ten days."

"He should not have talked about it at all," said Winterbourne; "he would never have proposed to a young lady of
this country to walk about the streets with him."

"About the streets?" cried Daisy, with her pretty stare.
"Where then would he have proposed to her to walk? The
Pincio is not the streets, either; and I, thank goodness, am
not a young lady of this country. The young ladies of this
country have a dreadfully poky time of it, so far as I can learn;
I don't see why I should change my habits for *them*."

"I am afraid your habits are those of a flirt," said Winterbourne gravely.

"Of course they are," she cried, giving him her little smiling
stare again. "I'm a fearful, frightful flirt! Did you ever hear of
a nice girl that was not? But I suppose you will tell me now
that I am not a nice girl."

"You're a very nice girl, but I wish you would flirt with
me, and me only," said Winterbourne.

"Ah! thank you, thank you very much; you are the last man
I should think of flirting with. As I have had the pleasure of
informing you, you are too stiff."

"You say that too often," said Winterbourne.

Daisy gave a delighted laugh. "If I could have the sweet
hope of making you angry, I would say it again."

"Don't do that; when I am angry I'm stiffer than ever. But
if you won't flirt with me, do cease at least to flirt with your
friend at the piano; they don't understand that sort of thing
here."

"I thought they understood nothing else!" exclaimed
Daisy.

"Not in young unmarried women."

"It seems to me much more proper in young unmarried
women than in old married ones," Daisy declared.

"Well," said Winterbourne, "when you deal with natives
you must go by the custom of the place. Flirting is a purely
American custom; it doesn't exist here. So when you show
yourself in public with Mr. Giovanelli and without your
mother——"

"Gracious! poor mother!" interposed Daisy.

"Though you may be flirting, Mr. Giovanelli is not; he means something else."

"He isn't preaching, at any rate," said Daisy with vivacity. "And if you want very much to know, we are neither of us flirting; we are too good friends for that; we are very intimate friends."

"Ah!" rejoined Winterbourne, "if you are in love with each other it is another affair."

She had allowed him up to this point to talk so frankly that he had no expectation of shocking her by this ejaculation; but she immediately got up, blushing visibly, and leaving him to exclaim mentally that little American flirts were the queerest creatures in the world. "Mr. Giovanelli, at least," she said, giving her interlocutor a single glance, "never says such very disagreeable things to me."

Winterbourne was bewildered; he stood staring. Mr. Giovanelli had finished singing; he left the piano and came over to Daisy. "Won't you come into the other room and have some tea?" he asked, bending before her with his decorative smile.

Daisy turned to Winterbourne, beginning to smile again. He was still more perplexed, for this inconsequent smile made nothing clear, though it seemed to prove, indeed, that she had a sweetness and softness that reverted instinctively to the pardon of offences. "It has never occurred to Mr. Winterbourne to offer me any tea," she said, with her little tormenting manner.

"I have offered you advice," Winterbourne rejoined.

"I prefer weak tea!" cried Daisy, and she went off with the brilliant Giovanelli. She sat with him in the adjoining room, in the embrasure of the window, for the rest of the evening. There was an interesting performance at the piano, but neither of these young people gave heed to it. When Daisy came to take leave of Mrs. Walker, this lady conscientiously repaired the weakness of which she had been guilty at the moment of the young girl's arrival. She turned her back straight upon Miss Miller and left her to depart with what grace she might. Winterbourne was standing near the door; he saw it all. Daisy turned very pale and looked at her mother, but Mrs. Miller was humbly unconscious of any violation of the usual social forms. She appeared, indeed, to have felt an incongruous impulse to draw attention to her own striking observance of them. "Good night, Mrs. Walker," she said; "we've had a beautiful evening. You see if I let Daisy come to parties without me, I don't want her to go away without me." Daisy turned away, looking with a pale, grave face at the circle near the door; Winterbourne saw that, for the first moment, she was too much shocked and puzzled even for indignation. He on his side was greatly touched.

"That was very cruel," he said to Mrs. Walker.

"She never enters my drawing-room again," replied his hostess.

Since Winterbourne was not to meet her in Mrs. Walker's drawing-room, he went as often as possible to Mrs. Miller's hotel. The ladies were rarely at home, but when he found them the devoted Giovanelli was always present. Very often the polished little Roman was in the drawing-room with Daisy alone, Mrs. Miller being apparently constantly of the opinion that discretion is the better part of surveillance. Winterbourne noted, at first with surprise, that Daisy on these occasions was never embarrassed or annoyed by his own entrance; but he very presently began to feel that she had no more surprises for him; the unexpected in her behaviour was the only thing to expect. She showed no displeasure at her *tête-à-tête* with Giovanelli being interrupted; she could chatter as freshly and freely with two gentlemen as with one; there was always in her conversation, the same odd mixture of audacity and puerility. Winterbourne remarked to himself that if she was seriously interested in Giovanelli it was very singular that she should not take more trouble to preserve the sanctity of their interviews, and he liked her the more for her innocent-looking indifference and her apparently inexhaustible good humour. He could hardly have said why, but she seemed to him a girl who would never be jealous. At the risk of exciting a somewhat derisive smile on the reader's part, I may affirm that with regard to the women who had hitherto interested him it very often seemed to Winterbourne among the possibilities that, given certain contingencies, he should be afraid—literally afraid—of these ladies. He had a pleasant sense that he should never be afraid of Daisy Miller. It must be added that this sentiment was not altogether flattering to Daisy; it was part of his conviction, or rather of his apprehension, that she would prove a very light young person.

But she was evidently very much interested in Giovanelli. She looked at him whenever he spoke; she was perpetually telling him to do this and to do that; she was constantly "chaffing" and abusing him. She appeared completely to have forgotten that Winterbourne had said anything to displease her at Mrs. Walker's little party. One Sunday afternoon, having gone to St. Peter's with his aunt, Winterbourne perceived Daisy strolling about the great church in company with the inevitable Giovanelli. Presently he pointed out the young girl and her cavalier to Mrs. Costello. This lady looked at them a moment through her eyeglass, and then she said:

"That's what makes you so pensive in these days, eh?"

"I had not the least idea I was pensive," said the young man.

"You are very much pre-occupied, you are thinking of something."

"And what is it," he asked, "that you accuse me of thinking of?"

"Of that young lady's—Miss Baker's, Miss Chandler's—what's her name?—Miss Miller's intrigue with that little barber's block."

"Do you call it an intrigue," Winterbourne asked—"an affair that goes on with such peculiar publicity?"

"That's their folly," said Mrs. Costello, "it's not their merit."

"No," rejoined Winterbourne, with something of that pensiveness to which his aunt had alluded. "I don't believe that there is anything to be called an intrigue."

"I have heard a dozen people speak of it; they say she is quite carried away by him."

"They are certainly very intimate," said Winterbourne.

Mrs. Costello inspected the young couple again with her optical instrument. "He is very handsome. One easily sees how it is. She thinks him the most elegant man in the world, the finest gentleman. She has never seen anything like him; he is better even than the courier. It was the courier probably who introduced him, and if he succeeds in marrying the young lady, the courier will come in for a magnificent commission."

"I don't believe she thinks of marrying him," said Winterbourne, "and I don't believe he hopes to marry her."

"You may be very sure she thinks of nothing. She goes on from day to day, from hour to hour, as they did in the Golden Age. I can imagine nothing more vulgar. And at the same time," added Mrs. Costello, "depend upon it that she may tell you any moment that she is 'engaged.' "

"I think that is more than Giovanelli expects," said Winterbourne.

"Who is Giovanelli?"

"The little Italian. I have asked questions about him and learned something. He is apparently a perfectly respectable little man. I believe he is in a small way a *cavaliere avvocato*. But he doesn't move in what are called the first circles. I think it is really not absolutely impossible that the courier introduced him. He is evidently immensely charmed with Miss Miller. If she thinks him the finest gentleman in the world, he, on his side, has never found himself in personal contact with such splendour, such opulence, such expensiveness, as this young lady's. And then she must seem to him wonderfully pretty and interesting. I rather doubt whether he dreams of marrying her. That must appear to him too impossible a piece of luck. He has nothing but his handsome face to offer, and there is a substantial Mr. Miller in that mysterious land of dollars. Giovanelli knows that he hasn't a title to offer. If he were only a count or a *marchese*! He must wonder at his luck at the way they have taken him up."

"He accounts for it by his handsome face, and thinks Miss Miller a young lady *qui se passe ses fantaisies*!" said Mrs. Costello.

"It is very true," Winterbourne pursued, "that Daisy and her mamma have not yet risen to that stage of—what shall I call it?—of culture, at which the idea of catching a count or a *marchese* begins. I believe that they are intellectually incapable of that conception."

"Ah! but the *cavaliere* can't believe it," said Mrs. Costello.

Of the observation excited by Daisy's "intrigue," Winterbourne gathered that day at St. Peter's sufficient evidence. A dozen of the American colonists in Rome came to talk with Mrs. Costello, who sat on a little portable stool at the base of one of the great pilasters. The vesper-service was going forward in splendid chants and organ-tones in the adjacent choir, and meanwhile, between Mrs. Costello and her friends, there was a great deal said about poor little Miss Miller's going really "too far." Winterbourne was not pleased with what he heard; but when, coming out upon the great steps of the church, he saw Daisy, who had emerged before him, get into an open cab with her accomplice and roll away through the cynical streets of Rome, he could not deny to himself that she was going very far indeed. He felt very sorry for her—not exactly that he believed that she had completely lost her head, but because it was painful to hear so much that was pretty and undefended and natural assigned to a vulgar place among the categories of disorder. He made an attempt after this to give a hint to Mrs. Miller. He met one day in the Corso a friend—a tourist like himself—who had just come out of the Doria Palace, where he had been walking through the beautiful gallery. His friend talked for a moment about the superb portrait of Innocent X. by Velasquez, which hangs in one of the cabinets of the palace, and then said, "And in the same cabinet, by-the-way, I had the pleasure of contemplating a picture of a different kind—that pretty American girl whom you pointed out to me last week." In answer to Winterbourne's inquiries, his friend narrated that the pretty American girl—prettier than ever—was seated with a companion in the secluded nook in which the great papal portrait is enshrined.

"Who was her companion?" asked Winterbourne.

"A little Italian with a bouquet in his button-hole. The girl is delightfully pretty, but I thought I understood from you the other day that she was a young lady *du meilleur monde*."

"So she is!" answered Winterbourne; and having assured himself that his informant had seen Daisy and her companion but five minutes before, he jumped into a cab and went to call on Mrs. Miller. She was at home; but she apologised to him for receiving him in Daisy's absence.

"She's gone out somewhere with Mr. Giovanelli," said Mrs. Miller. "She's always going round with Mr. Giovanelli."

"I have noticed that they are very intimate," Winterbourne observed.

"Oh! it seems as if they couldn't live without each other!" said Mrs. Miller. "Well, he's a real gentleman, anyhow. I keep telling Daisy she's engaged!"

"And what does Daisy say?"

"Oh, she says she isn't engaged. But she might as well be!" this impartial parent resumed. "She goes on as if she was. But I've made Mr. Giovanelli promise to tell me, if *she* doesn't. I should want to write to Mr. Miller about it—shouldn't you?"

Winterbourne replied that he certainly should; and the state of mind of Daisy's mamma struck him as so unprecedented in the annals of parental vigilance that he gave up as utterly irrelevant the attempt to place her upon her guard.

After this Daisy was never at home, and Winterbourne ceased to meet her at the houses of their common acquaintance, because, as he perceived, these shrewd people had quite made up their minds that she was going too far. They ceased to invite her, and they intimated that they desired to express to observant Europeans the great truth that, though Miss Daisy Miller was a young American lady, her behaviour was not representative—was regarded by her compatriots as abnormal. Winterbourne wondered how she felt about all the cold shoulders that were turned towards her, and sometimes it annoyed him to suspect that she did not feel at all. He said to himself that she was too light and childish, too uncultivated and unreasoning, too provincial, to have reflected upon her ostracism or even to have perceived it. Then at other moments he believed that she carried about in her elegant and irresponsible little organism a defiant, passionate, perfectly observant consciousness of the impression she produced. He asked himself whether Daisy's defiance came from the consciousness of innocence or from her being, essentially, a young person of the reckless class. It must be admitted that holding oneself to a belief in Daisy's "innocence" came to seem to Winterbourne more and more a matter of fine-spun gallantry. As I have already had occasion to relate, he was angry at finding himself reduced to chopping logic about this young lady; he was vexed at his want of instinctive certitude as to how far her eccentricities were generic, national, and how far they were personal. From either view of them he had somehow missed her, and now it was too late. She was "carried away" by Mr. Giovanelli.

A few days after his brief interview with her mother, he encountered her in that beautiful abode of flowering desolation known as the Palace of the Cæsars. The early Roman spring had filled the air with bloom and perfume, and the rugged surface of the Palatine was muffled with tender verdure. Daisy was strolling along the top of one of those great mounds of ruin that are embanked with mossy marble and paved with monumental inscriptions. It seemed to him that Rome had never been so lovely as just then. He stood looking off at the enchanting harmony of line and colour that remotely encircles the city, inhaling the softly humid odours and feeling the freshness of the year and the antiquity of the place reaffirm themselves in mysterious interfusion. It seemed to him also that Daisy had never looked so pretty; but this had been an observation of his whenever he met her. Giovanelli was at her side, and Giovanelli, too, wore an aspect of even unwonted brilliancy.

"Well," said Daisy, "I should think you would be lonesome!"

"Lonesome?" asked Winterbourne.

"You are always going round by yourself. Can't you get any one to walk with you?"

"I am not so fortunate," said Winterbourne, "as your companion."

Giovanelli, from the first, had treated Winterbourne with distinguished politeness; he listened with a deferential air to his remarks; he laughed, punctiliously, at his pleasantries; he seemed disposed to testify to his belief that Winterbourne was a superior young man. He carried himself in no degree like a jealous wooer; he had obviously a great deal of tact; he had no objection to your expecting a little humility of him. It even seemed to Winterbourne at times that Giovanelli would find a certain mental relief in being able to have a private understanding with him—to say to him, as an intelligent man, that, bless you, *he* knew how extraordinary was this young lady, and didn't flatter himself with delusive—or at least *too* delusive—hopes of matrimony and dollars. On this occasion he strolled away from his companion to pluck a sprig of almond blossom, which he carefully arranged in his button-hole.

"I know why you say that," said Daisy, watching Giovanelli. "Because you think I go round too much with *him*!" And she nodded at her attendant.

"Every one thinks so—if you care to know," said Winterbourne.

"Of course I care to know!" Daisy exclaimed seriously. "But I don't believe it. They are only pretending to be shocked. They don't really care a straw what I do. Besides, I don't go round so much."

"I think you will find they do care. They will show it—disagreeably."

Daisy looked at him a moment. "How—disagreeably?"

"Haven't you noticed anything?" Winterbourne asked.

"I have noticed you. But I noticed you were as stiff as an umbrella the first time I saw you."

"You will find I am not so stiff as several others," said Winterbourne, smiling.

"How shall I find it?"

"By going to see the others."

"What will they do to me?"

"They will give you the cold shoulder. Do you know what that means?"

Daisy was looking at him intently; she began to colour. "Do you mean as Mrs. Walker did the other night?"

"Exactly!" said Winterbourne.

She looked away at Giovanelli, who was decorating himself with his almond-blossom. Then looking back at Winterbourne—"I shouldn't think you would let people be so unkind!" she said.

"How can I help it?" he asked.

"I should think you would say something."

"I do say something;" and he paused a moment. "I say that your mother tells me that she believes you are engaged."

"Well, she does," said Daisy very simply.

Winterbourne began to laugh. "And does Randolph believe it?" he asked.

"I guess Randolph doesn't believe anything," said Daisy.

Randolph's scepticism excited Winterbourne to farther hilarity, and he observed that Giovanelli was coming back to them. Daisy, observing it too, addressed herself again to her countryman. "Since you have mentioned it," she said, "I *am* engaged.". . . Winterbourne looked at her; he had stopped laughing. "You don't believe it!" she added.

He was silent a moment; and then, "Yes, I believe it!" he said.

"Oh, no, you don't," she answered. "Well, then—I am not!"

The young girl and her cicerone were on their way to the gate of the enclosure, so that Winterbourne, who had but lately entered, presently took leave of them. A week afterwards he went to dine at a beautiful villa on the Cælian Hill, and, on arriving, dismissed his hired vehicle. The evening was charming, and he promised himself the satisfaction of walking home beneath the Arch of Constantine and past the vaguely-lighted monuments of the Forum. There was a waning moon in the sky, and her radiance was not brilliant, but she was veiled in a thin cloud-curtain which seemed to diffuse and equalise it. When, on his return from the villa (it was eleven o'clock), Winterbourne approached the dusky circle of the Colosseum, it occurred to him, as a lover of the picturesque, that the interior, in the pale moonshine, would be well worth a glance. He turned aside and walked to one of the empty arches, near which, as he observed, an open carriage—one of the little Roman street-cabs—was stationed. Then he passed in among the cavernous shadows of the great structure, and emerged upon the clear and silent arena. The place had never seemed to him more impressive. One-half of the gigantic circus was in deep shade; the other was sleeping in the luminous dusk. As he stood there he began to murmur Byron's famous lines, out of "Manfred;" but before he had finished his quotation he remembered that if nocturnal meditations in the Colosseum are recommended by the poets, they are deprecated by the doctors. The historic atmosphere was there, certainly; but the historic atmosphere, scientifically considered, was no better than a villanous miasma. Winterbourne walked to the middle of the arena, to take a more general glance, intending thereafter to make a hasty retreat. The great cross in the centre was covered with shadow; it was only as he drew near it that he made it out distinctly. Then he saw that two persons were stationed upon the low steps which formed its base. One of these was a woman, seated; her companion was standing in front of her.

Presently the sound of the woman's voice came to him distinctly in the warm night-air. "Well, he looks at us as one of the old lions or tigers may have looked at the Christian martyrs!" These were the words he heard, in the familiar accent of Miss Daisy Miller.

"Let us hope he is not very hungry," responded the ingenious Giovanelli. "He will have to take me first; you will serve for dessert!"

Winterbourne stopped, with a sort of horror; and, it must be added, with a sort of relief. It was as if a sudden illumination had been flashed upon the ambiguity of Daisy's behaviour and the riddle had become easy to read. She was a young lady whom a gentleman need no longer be at pains to respect. He stood there looking at her—looking at her companion, and not reflecting that though he saw them vaguely, he himself must have been more brightly visible. He felt angry with himself that he had bothered so much about the right way of regarding Miss Daisy Miller. Then, as he was going to advance again, he checked himself; not from the fear that he was doing her injustice, but from a sense of the danger of appearing unbecomingly exhilarated by this sudden revulsion from cautious criticism. He turned away towards the entrance of the place; but as he did so he heard Daisy speak again.

"Why, it was Mr. Winterbourne! He saw me—and he cuts me!"

What a clever little reprobate she was, and how smartly she played an injured innocence! But he wouldn't cut her. Winterbourne came forward again, and went towards the great cross. Daisy had got up; Giovanelli lifted his hat. Winterbourne had now begun to think simply of the craziness, from a sanitary point of view, of a delicate young girl lounging away the evening in this nest of malaria. What if she *were* a clever little reprobate? that was no reason for her dying of the *perniciosa*. "How long have you been here?" he asked, almost brutally.

Daisy, lovely in the flattering moonlight, looked at him a moment. Then—"All the evening," she answered gently. . . . "I never saw anything so pretty."

"I am afraid," said Winterbourne, "that you will not think Roman fever very pretty. This is the way people catch it. I wonder," he added, turning to Giovanelli, "that you, a native Roman, should countenance such a terrible indiscretion."

"Ah," said the handsome native, "for myself, I am not afraid."

"Neither am I—for you! I am speaking for this young lady."

Giovanelli lifted his well-shaped eyebrows and showed his brilliant teeth. But he took Winterbourne's rebuke with docility. "I told the Signorina it was a grave indiscretion; but when was the Signorina ever prudent?"

"I never was sick, and I don't mean to be!" the Signorina declared. "I don't look like much, but I'm healthy! I was bound to see the Colosseum by moonlight; I shouldn't have wanted to go home without that; and we have had the most beautiful time, haven't we, Mr. Giovanelli? If there has been any danger, Eugenio can give me some pills. He has got some splendid pills."

"I should advise you," said Winterbourne, "to drive home as fast as possible and take one!"

"What you say is very wise," Giovanelli rejoined. "I will go and make sure the carriage is at hand." And he went forward rapidly.

Daisy followed with Winterbourne. He kept looking at her; she seemed not in the least embarrassed. Winterbourne said nothing; Daisy chattered about the beauty of the place. "Well, I *have* seen the Colosseum by moonlight!" she exclaimed. "That's one good thing." Then, noticing Winterbourne's silence, she asked him why he didn't speak. He made no answer; he only began to laugh. They passed under one of the dark archways; Giovanelli was in front with the carriage. Here Daisy stopped a moment, looking at the young American. "*Did* you believe I was engaged the other day?" she asked.

"It doesn't matter what I believed the other day," said Winterbourne, still laughing.

"Well, what do you believe now?"

"I believe that it makes very little difference whether you are engaged or not!"

He felt the young girl's pretty eyes fixed upon him through the thick gloom of the archway; she was apparently going to answer. But Giovanelli hurried her forward. "Quick, quick," he said; "if we get in by midnight we are quite safe."

Daisy took her seat in the carriage, and the fortunate Italian placed himself beside her. "Don't forget Eugenio's pills!" said Winterbourne, as he lifted his hat.

"I don't care," said Daisy, in a little strange tone, "whether I have Roman fever or not!" Upon this the cab-driver cracked his whip, and they rolled away over the desultory patches of the antique pavement.

Winterbourne—to do him justice, as it were—mentioned to no one that he had encountered Miss Miller, at midnight, in the Colosseum with a gentleman; but nevertheless, a couple of days later, the fact of her having been there under these circumstances was known to every member of the little American circle, and commented accordingly. Winterbourne reflected that they had of course known it at the hotel, and that, after Daisy's return, there had been an exchange of jokes between the porter and the cab-driver. But the young man was conscious at the same moment that it had ceased to be a matter of serious regret to him that the little American flirt should be "talked about" by low-minded menials. These people, a day or two later, had serious information to give: the little American flirt was alarmingly ill. Winterbourne, when the rumour came to him, immediately went to the hotel for more news. He found that two or three charitable friends had preceded him, and that they were being entertained in Mrs. Miller's salon by Randolph.

"It's going round at night," said Randolph—"that's what made her sick. She's always going round at night. I shouldn't think she'd want to—it's so plaguey dark. You can't see anything here at night, except when there's a moon. In America there's always a moon!" Mrs. Miller was invisible; she was now, at least, giving her daughter the advantage of her society. It was evident that Daisy was dangerously ill.

Winterbourne went often to ask for news of her, and once he saw Mrs. Miller, who, though deeply alarmed, was—rather to his surprise—perfectly composed, and, as it appeared, a most efficient and judicious nurse. She talked a good deal about Dr. Davis, but Winterbourne paid her the compliment of saying to himself that she was not, after all, such a monstrous goose. "Daisy spoke of you the other day," she said to him. "Half the time she doesn't know what she's saying, but that time I think she did. She gave me a message; she told me to tell you. She told me to tell you that she never was engaged to that handsome Italian. I am sure I am very glad; Mr. Giovanelli hasn't been near us since she was taken ill. I thought he was so much of a gentleman; but I don't call that very polite! A lady told me that he was afraid I was angry with him for taking Daisy round at night. Well, so I am; but I suppose he knows I'm a lady. I would scorn to scold him. Any way, she says she's not engaged. I don't know why she wanted you to know; but she said to me three times—'Mind you tell Mr. Winterbourne.' And then she told me to ask if you remembered the time you went to that castle, in Switzerland. But I said I wouldn't give any such messages as that. Only, if she is not engaged, I'm sure I'm glad to know it."

But, as Winterbourne had said, it mattered very little. A week after this the poor girl died; it had been a terrible case of the fever. Daisy's grave was in the little Protestant cemetery, in an angle of the wall of imperial Rome, beneath the cypresses and the thick spring-flowers. Winterbourne stood there beside it, with a number of other mourners; a number larger than the scandal excited by the young lady's career would have led you to expect. Near him stood Giovanelli, who came nearer still before Winterbourne turned away. Giovanelli was very pale; on this occasion he had no flower in his button-hole; he seemed to wish to say something. At last he said, "She was the most beautiful young lady I ever saw, and the most amiable." And then he added in a moment, "And she was the most innocent."

Winterbourne looked at him, and presently repeated his words, "And the most innocent?"

"The most innocent!"

Winterbourne felt sore and angry. "Why the devil," he asked, "did you take her to that fatal place?"

Mr. Giovanelli's urbanity was apparently imperturbable. He

looked on the ground a moment, and then he said, "For myself, I had no fear; and she wanted to go."

"That was no reason!" Winterbourne declared.

The subtle Roman again dropped his eyes. "If she had lived,
I should have got nothing. She would never have married me,
I am sure."

"She would never have married you?"

"For a moment I hoped so. But no. I am sure."

Winterbourne listened to him; he stood staring at the raw
protuberance among the April daisies. When he turned away
again Mr. Giovanelli, with his light slow step, had retired.

Winterbourne almost immediately left Rome; but the following summer he again met his aunt, Mrs. Costello, at Vevey.
Mrs. Costello was fond of Vevey. In the interval Winterbourne
had often thought of Daisy Miller and her mystifying manners. One day he spoke of her to his aunt—said it was on his
conscience that he had done her injustice.

"I am sure I don't know," said Mrs. Costello. "How did
your injustice affect her?"

"She sent me a message before her death which I didn't
understand at the time. But I have understood it since. She
would have appreciated one's esteem."

"Is that a modest way," asked Mrs. Costello, "of saying
that she would have reciprocated one's affection?"

Winterbourne offered no answer to this question; but he
presently said, "You were right in that remark that you made
last summer. I was booked to make a mistake. I have lived
too long in foreign parts."

Nevertheless, he went back to live at Geneva, whence there
continue to come the most contradictory accounts of his motives of sojourn: a report that he is "studying" hard—an intimation that he is much interested in a very clever foreign
lady.

Longstaff's Marriage

FORTY YEARS AGO that traditional and anecdotical liberty of young American women which is notoriously the envy and despair of their foreign sisters, was not so firmly established as at the present hour; yet it was sufficiently recognised to make it no scandal that so pretty a girl as Diana Belfield should start for the grand tour of Europe under no more imposing protection than that of her cousin and intimate friend, Miss Agatha Josling. She had, from the European point of view, beauty enough to make her enterprise perilous—the beauty foreshadowed in her name, which might have been given in prevision of her tall, light figure, her nobly poised head weighted with a coronal of auburn braids, her frank quick glance, and her rapid gliding step. She used often to walk about with a big dog, who had the habit of bounding at her side and tossing his head against her outstretched hand; and she had, moreover, a trick of carrying her long parasol, always folded, for she was not afraid of the sunshine, across her shoulder, in the fashion of a soldier's musket on a march. Thus equipped, she looked wonderfully like that charming antique statue of the goddess of the chase which we encounter in various replicas in half the museums of the world. You half expected to see a sandal-shod foot peep out beneath her fluttering robe. It was with this tread of the wakeful huntress that she stepped upon the old sailing-vessel which was to bear her to foreign lands. Behind her, with a great many shawls and satchels, came her little kinswoman, with quite another *démarche*. Agatha Josling was not a beauty, but she was the most judicious and most devoted of companions. These two persons had been united by the death of Diana's mother, when the latter young lady took possession of her patrimony. The first use she made of her inheritance was to divide it with Agatha, who had not a penny of her own; the next was to purchase a letter of credit upon a European banker. The cousins had contracted a classical friendship—they had determined to be all in all to each other, like the Ladies of Llangollen. Only, though their friendship was exclusive, their Llangollen

296

was to be comprehensive. They would tread the pavements of historic cities and wander through the aisles of Gothic cathedrals, wind on tinkling mules through mountain gorges and sit among dark-eyed peasants on the shores of blue lakes. It may seem singular that a beautiful girl with a pretty fortune should have been left to seek the supreme satisfaction of life in friendship tempered by sight-seeing; but Diana herself considered this pastime no beggarly alternative. Though she never told it herself, her biographer may do so; she had had, in vulgar parlance, a hundred offers. To say that she had declined them is to say too little; they had filled her with contempt. They had come from honourable and amiable men, and it was not her suitors in themselves that she contemned; it was simply the idea of marrying. She found it insupportable; a fact which completes her analogy with the mythic divinity to whom I have likened her. She was passionately single, fiercely virginal; and in the straight-glancing grey eye which provoked men to admire, there was a certain silvery ray which forbade them to hope. The fabled Diana took a fancy to a beautiful shepherd, but the real one had not yet found, sleeping or waking, her Endymion.

Thanks to this defensive eyebeam, the dangerous side of our heroine's enterprise was slow to define itself; thanks, too, to the exquisite propriety of her companion. Agatha Josling had an almost Quakerish purity and dignity; a bristling dragon could not have been a better safeguard than this glossy, grey-breasted dove. Money, too, is a protection, and Diana had money enough to purchase privacy. She travelled largely, and saw all the churches and pictures, the castles and cottages, included in the list which had been drawn up by the two friends in evening talks, at home, between two wax candles. In the evening they used to read aloud to each other from *Corinne* and *Childe Harold*, and they kept a diary in common, at which they "collaborated," like French playwrights, and which was studded with quotations from the authors I have mentioned. This lasted a year, at the end of which they found themselves a trifle weary. A snug posting-carriage was a delightful habitation, but looking at miles of pictures was very fatiguing to the back. Buying souvenirs and trinkets under foreign arcades was a most absorbing occupation; but inns were dreadfully apt to be draughty, and bottles of hot water, for application to the feet, had a disagreeable way of growing lukewarm. For these and other reasons our heroines determined to take a winter's rest, and for this purpose they betook themselves to the charming town of Nice, which was then but in the infancy of its fame. It was simply one of the hundred hamlets of the Riviera—a place where the blue waves broke on an almost empty strand and the olive-trees sprouted at the doors of the inns. In those days Nice was Italian, and the "Promenade des Anglais" existed only in an embryonic form. Exist, however, it did, practically, and British invalids, in moderate numbers, might have been seen taking the January sunshine beneath London umbrellas before the many-twinkling sea. Our young Americans quietly took their place in this harmless society. They drove along the coast, through the strange, dark, huddled fishing-villages, and they rode on donkeys among the bosky hills. They painted in water-colours and hired a piano; they subscribed to the circulating library, and took lessons in the language of Silvio Pellico from an old lady with very fine eyes, who wore an enormous brooch of cracked malachite, and gave herself out as the widow of a Roman exile.

They used to go and sit by the sea, each provided with a volume from the circulating library; but they never did much with their books. The sunshine made the page too dazzling, and the people who strolled up and down before them were more entertaining than the ladies and gentlemen in the novels. They looked at them constantly from under their umbrellas; they learned to know them all by sight. Many of their fellow-visitors were invalids—mild, slow-moving consumptives. But for the fact that women enjoy the exercise of pity, I should have said that these pale promenaders were a saddening spectacle. In several of them, however, our friends took a personal interest; they watched them from day to day; they noticed their changing colour; they had their ideas about who was getting better and who was getting worse. They did little, however, in the way of making acquaintances—partly because pulmonary sufferers are no great talkers, and partly because this was also Diana's disposition. She said to her friend that they had not come to Europe to pay morning-calls; they had left their best bonnets and card-cases behind them. At the bottom of her reserve was the apprehension that she should be "admired;" which was not fatuity, but simply an induction from an embarrassing experience. She had seen in Europe, for the first time, certain horrid men—polished adventurers with offensive looks and mercenary thoughts; and she had a wholesome fear that one of these gentlemen might approach her through some accidental breach in her reserve. Agatha Josling, who had neither in reminiscence nor in prospect the same reasons for turning her graceful back, would have been glad to extend the circle of their acquaintance, and would even have consented to put on her best bonnet for the purpose. But she had to content herself with an occasional murmur of small-talk, on a bench before the sea, with two or three English ladies of the botanising class; jovial little spinsters who wore stout boots, gauntlets, and "uglies," and in pursuit of wayside flowers scrambled into places where the first-mentioned articles were uncompromisingly visible. For the rest, Agatha contented herself with spinning suppositions about the people she never spoke to. She framed a great deal of hypothetic gossip, invented theories and explanations—generally of the most charitable quality. Her companion took no part in these harmless devisings, except to listen to them with an indolent smile. She seldom honoured her fellow-mortals with finding apologies for them, and if they wished her to read their history they must write it out in the largest letters.

There was one person at Nice upon whose biography, if it had been laid before her in this fashion, she probably would have bestowed a certain amount of attention. Agatha had noticed the gentleman first; or Agatha, at least, had first spoken of him. He was young and he looked interesting; Agatha had indulged in a good deal of wondering as to whether or no he belonged to the invalid category. She preferred to believe that one of his lungs was "affected;" it certainly made him more interesting. He used to stroll about by himself and sit for a long time in the sun, with a book peeping out of his pocket. This book he never opened; he was always staring at the sea. I say always, but my phrase demands an immediate modification; he looked at the sea whenever he was not looking at Diana Belfield. He was tall and fair, slight, and, as Agatha

Josling said, aristocratic-looking. He dressed with a certain careless elegance which Agatha deemed picturesque; she declared one day that he reminded her of a love-sick prince. She learned eventually from one of the botanising spinsters that he was not a prince, that he was simply an English gentleman, Mr. Reginald Longstaff. There remained the possibility that he was love-sick; but this point could not be so easily settled. Agatha's informant had assured her, however, that if they were not princes, the Longstaffs, who came from a part of the country in which she had visited, and owned great estates there, had a pedigree which many princes might envy. It was one of the oldest and the best of English names; they were one of the innumerable untitled country families who held their heads as high as the highest. This poor Mr. Longstaff was a beautiful specimen of a young English gentleman; he looked so gentle, yet so brave; so modest, yet so cultivated! The ladies spoke of him habitually as "poor" Mr. Longstaff, for they now took for granted that there was something the matter with him. At last Agatha Josling discovered what it was and made a solemn proclamation of the same. The matter with poor Mr. Longstaff was simply that he was in love with Diana! It was certainly natural to suppose he was in love with some one, and, as Agatha said, it could not possibly be with herself. Mr. Longstaff was pale and slightly dishevelled; he never spoke to any one; he was evidently pre-occupied, and his mild, candid face was a sufficient proof that the weight on his heart was not a bad conscience. What could it be, then, but an unrequited passion? It was, however, equally pertinent to inquire why Mr. Longstaff took no steps to bring about a requital.

"Why in the world does he not ask to be introduced to you?" Agatha Josling demanded of her companion.

Diana replied, quite without eagerness, that it was plainly because he had nothing to say to her; and she declared with a trifle more emphasis, that she was incapable of proposing to him a topic of conversation. She added that she thought they had gossipped enough about the poor man, and that if by any chance he should have the bad taste to speak to them, she would certainly go away and leave him alone with Miss Josling. It is true, however, that at an earlier period, she had let fall the remark that he was quite the most "distinguished" person at Nice; and afterwards, though she was never the first to allude to him, she had more than once let her companion pursue the theme for some time without reminding her of its futility. The one person to whom Mr. Longstaff was observed to speak was an elderly man of foreign aspect who approached him occasionally in the most deferential manner, and whom Agatha Josling supposed to be his servant. This individual was apparently an Italian; he had an obsequious attitude, a pair of grizzled whiskers, an insinuating smile. He seemed to come to Mr. Longstaff for orders; presently he went away to execute them, and Agatha noticed that on retiring he always managed to pass in front of her companion, on whom he fixed his respectful but penetrating gaze. "He knows the secret," she always said, with gentle jocoseness; "he knows what is the matter with his master and he wants to see whether he approves of you. Old servants never want their masters to marry, and I think this worthy man is rather afraid of you. At any rate, the way he stares at you tells the whole story."

"Every one stares at me!" said Diana, wearily. "A cat may look at a king."

As the weeks went by, Agatha Josling quite made up her mind that Mr. Longstaff's complaint was pulmonary. The poor young man's invalid character was now quite apparent; he could hardly hold up his head or drag one foot after the other; his servant was always near him to give him an arm or to hand him an extra overcoat. No one indeed knew with certainty that he was consumptive; but Agatha agreed with the lady who had given the information about his pedigree, that this fact was in itself extremely suspicious; for, as the little Englishwoman forcibly remarked, unless he were ill, why should he make such a mystery of it? Consumption declaring itself in a young man of family and fortune was particularly sad; such people often had diplomatic reasons for pretending to enjoy excellent health. It kept the legacy-hunters, and the hungry next-of-kin from worrying them to death. Agatha observed that this poor gentleman's last hours seemed likely to be only too lonely. She felt very much like offering to nurse him; for, being no relation, he could not accuse her of mercenary motives. From time to time he got up from the bench where he habitually sat, and strolled slowly past the two friends. Every time that he came near them Agatha had a singular feeling—a conviction that now he was really going to speak to them. He would speak with the gravest courtesy— she could not fancy him speaking otherwise. He began, at a distance, by fixing his grave, soft eyes on Diana, and as he advanced you would have said that he was coming straight up to her with some tremulous compliment. But as he drew nearer, his intentness seemed to falter; he strolled more slowly, he looked away at the sea, and he passed in front of her without having the courage to let his eyes rest upon her. Then he passed back again in the same fashion, sank down upon his bench, fatigued apparently by his aimless stroll, and fell into a melancholy reverie. To enumerate these accidents is to attribute to his behaviour a certain aggressiveness which it was far from possessing; there was something scrupulous and subdued in his manner which made it perfectly discreet, and it may be affirmed that not a single idler on the sunny shore suspected his speechless "attentions."

"I wonder why it doesn't annoy us more that he should look at us so much," said Agatha Josling, one day.

"That who should look at us?" asked Diana, not at all affectedly.

Agatha fixed her eyes for a moment on her friend, and then said gently—

"Mr. Longstaff. Now, don't say, 'Who is Mr. Longstaff?'" she added.

"I have yet to learn, really," said Diana, "that the person you appear to mean does look at us. I have never caught him in the act."

"That is because whenever you turn your eyes towards him he looks away. He is afraid to meet them. But I see him."

These words were exchanged one day as the two friends sat as usual before the twinkling sea; and, beyond them, as usual, lounged Reginald Longstaff. Diana bent her head faintly forward and glanced towards him. He was looking full at her and their eyes met, apparently for the first time. Diana dropped her own upon her book again, and then, after a silence of some moments, "It does annoy me," she said. Presently she added that she would go home and write a letter, and, though she had never taken a step in Europe without having Agatha by her side, Miss Josling now allowed her to depart unattended. "You won't mind going alone?" Agatha had asked. "It is but three minutes, you know."

Diana replied that she preferred to go alone, and she moved away, with her parasol over her shoulder.

Agatha Josling had a particular reason for this variation from their maidenly custom. She felt a sudden conviction that if she were left alone, Mr. Longstaff would come and speak to her and say something very important, and she accommodated herself to this conviction without the sense of doing anything immodest. There was something solemn about it; it was a sort of presentiment; but it did not frighten her; it only made her feel very kind and appreciative. It is true that when at the end of ten minutes (they had seemed rather long), she saw the young man rise from his seat and slowly come towards her, she was conscious of a certain trepidation. Mr. Longstaff drew near; at last, he was close to her; he stopped and stood looking at her. She had averted her head, so as not to appear to expect him; but now she looked round again, and he very gravely lifted his hat.

"May I take the liberty of sitting down?" he asked.

Agatha bowed in silence, and, to make room for him, moved a certain blue shawl of Diana's, which was lying on the bench. He slowly sank into the place and then said very gently—

"I have ventured to speak to you, because I have something particular to say." His voice trembled and he was extremely pale. His eyes, which Agatha thought very handsome, had a remarkable expression.

"I am afraid you are ill," she said, with great kindness. "I have often noticed you and pitied you."

"I thought you did, a little," the young man answered. "That is why I made up my mind to speak to you."

"You are getting worse," said Agatha, softly.

"Yes, I am getting worse; I am dying. I am perfectly conscious of it; I have no illusions. I am weaker every day; I shall last but a few weeks." This was said very simply; sadly, but not lugubriously.

But Agatha felt almost awe-stricken; there stirred in her

heart a delicate sense of sisterhood with this beautiful young man who sat there and talked so submissively of death.

"Can nothing be done?" she said.

He shook his head and smiled a little. "Nothing but to try and get what pleasure I can from this little remnant of life."

Though he smiled she felt that he was very serious; that he was, indeed, deeply agitated, and trying to master his emotion.

"I am afraid you get very little pleasure," Agatha rejoined. "You seem entirely alone."

"I am entirely alone. I have no family—no near relations. I am absolutely alone."

Agatha rested her eyes on him compassionately, and then—

"You ought to have spoken to *us*," she said.

He sat looking at her; he had taken off his hat; he was slowly passing his hand over his forehead. "You see I do—at last!"

"You wanted to before?"

"Very often."

"I thought so!" said Agatha, with a candour which was in itself a dignity.

"But I couldn't," said Mr. Longstaff. "I never saw you alone."

Before she knew it Agatha was blushing a little; for, to the ear, simply, his words implied that it was to her only he would have addressed himself for the pleasure he had coveted. But the next instant she had become conscious that what he meant was simply that he admired her companion so much that he was afraid of her, and that, daring to speak to herself, he thought her a much less formidable and less interesting personage. Her blush immediately faded; for there was no resentment to keep the colour in her cheek; and there was no resentment still when she perceived that, though her neighbour was looking straight at her, with his inspired, expanded eyes, he was thinking too much of Diana to have noticed this little play of confusion.

"Yes, it's very true," she said. "It is the first time my friend has left me."

"She is very beautiful," said Mr. Longstaff.

"Very beautiful—and as good as she is beautiful."

"Yes, yes," he rejoined, solemnly. "I am sure of that. I *know* it!"

"I know it even better than you," said Agatha, smiling a little.

"Then you will have all the more patience with what I want to say to you. It is very strange; it will make you think, at first, that I am perhaps out of my mind. But I am not; I am thoroughly reasonable. You will see." Then he paused a moment; his voice had begun to tremble again.

"I know what you are going to say," said Agatha, very gently. "You are in love with my friend."

Mr. Longstaff gave her a look of devoted gratitude; he lifted up the edge of the blue shawl, which he had often seen Diana wear, and pressed it to his lips.

"I am extremely grateful!" he exclaimed. "You don't think me crazy, then?"

"If you are crazy, there have been a great many madmen!" said Agatha.

"Of course there have been a great many. I have said that to myself, and it has helped me. They have gained nothing but the pleasure of their love, and I therefore, in gaining nothing and having nothing, am not worse off than the rest. But they had more than I, didn't they? You see I have had absolutely nothing—not even a glance," he went on. "I have never even seen her look at me. I have not only never spoken to her, but I have never been near enough to speak to her. This is all I have ever had—to lay my hand on something she has worn; and yet for the past month I have thought of her night and day. Sitting over there, a hundred rods away, simply because she was sitting in this place, in the same sunshine, looking out on the same sea: that was happiness enough for me. I am dying, but for the last five weeks that has kept me alive. It was for that I got up every day and came out here; but for that, I should have stayed at home and never have got up again. I have never sought to be presented to her, because I didn't wish to trouble her for nothing. It seemed to me it would be an impertinence to tell her of my admiration. I have nothing to offer her—I am but the shadow of a living man, and if I were to say to her, 'Madam, I love you,' she could only answer, 'Well, sir, what then?' Nothing—nothing! To speak to her of what I felt seemed only to open the lid of a grave in her face. It was more delicate not to do that; so I kept my distance and said nothing. Even this, as I say, has been a happiness, but it has been a happiness that has tired me out. This is the last of it. I must give up and make an end!" And he stopped, panting a little, and apparently exhausted with his eloquence.

Agatha had always heard of love at first sight; she had read of it in poems and romances, but she had never been so near to it as this. It seemed to her wonderfully beautiful, and she believed in it devoutly. It made Mr. Longstaff brilliantly interesting; it cast a glory over the details of his face and person and the pleading inflections of his voice. The little English ladies had been right; he was certainly a perfect gentleman. She could trust him.

"Perhaps if you stay at home a while you will get better," she said, soothingly.

Her tone seemed to him such an indication that she accepted the propriety and naturalness of his passion that he put out his hand, and for an instant laid it on her own.

"I knew you were reasonable—I knew I could talk to you. But I shall not get well. All the great doctors say so, and I believe them. If the passionate desire to get well for a particular purpose could work a miracle and cure a mortal disease, I should have seen the miracle two months ago. To get well and have a right to speak to your friend—that was my passionate desire. But I am worse than ever; I am very weak, and I shall not be able to come out any more. It seemed to me to-day that I should never see you again, and yet I wanted so much to be able to tell you this! It made me very unhappy. What a wonderful chance it is that she went away! I must be grateful; if Heaven doesn't grant my great prayers it grants my small ones. I beg you to render me this service. Tell her what I have told you. Not now—not till I am gone. Don't trouble her with it while I am in life. Please promise me that. But when I am dead it will seem less importunate, because then you can speak of me in the past. It will be like a story. My servant will come and tell you. Then please say to her— 'You were his last thought, and it was his last wish that you should know it.' " He slowly got up and put out his hand; his servant, who had been standing at a distance, came forward with obsequious solemnity, as if it were part of his duty to adapt his deportment to the tone of his master's conversation. Agatha Josling took the young man's hand, and he stood and looked at her a moment longer. She too had risen to her feet; she was much impressed.

"You won't tell her until *after*——?" he said pleadingly. She shook her head. "And then you *will* tell her, faithfully?" She nodded, he pressed her hand, and then, having raised his hat, he took his servant's arm, and slowly moved away.

Agatha kept her word; she said nothing to Diana about her interview. The young Americans came out and sat upon the shore the next day, and the next, and the next, and Agatha watched intently for Mr. Longstaff's re-appearance. But she watched in vain; day after day he was absent, and his absence confirmed his sad prediction. She thought all this a wonderful thing to happen to a woman, and as she glanced askance at her beautiful companion, she was almost irritated at seeing her sit there so careless and serene, while a poor young man was dying, as one might say, of love for her. At moments she wondered whether, in spite of her promise, it were not her Christian duty to tell Diana his story, and give her the chance to go to him. But it occurred to Agatha, who knew very well that her companion had a certain stately pride in which she herself was deficient, that even if she were told of his condition Diana might decline to do anything; and this she felt to be a very painful thing to see. Besides, she had promised, and she always kept her promises. But her thoughts were constantly with Mr. Longstaff and the romance of the affair. This made her melancholy, and she talked much less than usual. Suddenly she was aroused from a reverie by hearing Diana express a careless curiosity as to what had become of the solitary young man who used to sit on the neighbouring bench and do them the honour to stare at them.

For almost the first time in her life, Agatha Josling deliberately dissembled.

"He has either gone away, or he has taken to his bed. I am sure he is dying, alone, in some wretched mercenary lodging."

"I prefer to believe something more cheerful," said Diana. "I believe he is gone to Paris and is eating a beautiful dinner at a great restaurant."

Agatha for a moment said nothing; and then—

"I don't think you care what becomes of him," she ventured to observe.

"My dear child, why should I care?" Diana demanded.

And Agatha Josling was forced to admit that there really was no particular reason. But the event contradicted her. Three days afterwards she took a long drive with her friend, from which they returned only as dusk was closing in. As they descended from the carriage at the door of their lodging she observed a figure standing in the street, slightly apart, which even in the early darkness had an air of familiarity. A second glance assured her that Mr. Longstaff's servant was hovering there in the hope of catching her attention. She immediately determined to give him a liberal measure of it. Diana left the vehicle and passed into the house, while the coachman fortunately asked for orders for the morrow. Agatha briefly gave such as were necessary, and then, before going in, turned to the hovering figure. It approached on tiptoe, hat in hand, and shaking its head very sadly. The old man wore an air of animated affliction which indicated that Mr. Longstaff was a generous master, and he proceeded to address Miss Josling in that macaronic French which is usually at the command of Italian domestics who have seen the world.

"I stole away from my dear gentleman's bedside on purpose to have ten words with you. The old woman at the fruit-stall opposite told me that you had gone to drive, so I waited; but it seemed to me a thousand years till you returned!"

"But you have not left your master alone?" said Agatha.

"He has two Sisters of Charity—heaven reward them! They watch with him night and day. He is very low, *pauvre cher homme!*" And the old man looked at the little lady with that clear, human, sympathetic glance with which Italians of all classes bridge over the social gulf. Agatha felt that he knew his master's secret, and that she might discuss it with him freely.

"Is he dying?" she asked.

"That's the question, dear lady! He is very low. The doctors have given him up; but the doctors don't know his malady. They have felt his dear body all over, they have sounded his lungs, and looked at his tongue and counted his pulse; they know what he eats and drinks—it's soon told! But they haven't seen his *mind*, dear lady. I have; and so far I am a better doctor than they. I know his secret—I know that he loves the beautiful girl above!" and the old man pointed to the upper windows of the house.

"Has your master taken you into his confidence?" Agatha demanded.

He hesitated a moment; then shaking his head a little and laying his hand on his heart—

"Ah, dear lady," he said, "the point is whether I have taken him into mine. I have not, I confess; he is too far gone. But I have determined to be his doctor and to try a remedy the others have never thought of. Will you help me?"

"If I can," said Agatha. "What is your remedy?"

The old man pointed to the upper windows of the house again.

"Your lovely friend! Bring her to his bedside."

"If he is dying," said Agatha, "how would that help him?"

"He is dying for want of it. That's my idea at least, and I think it's worth trying. If a young man loves a beautiful woman, and having never so much as touched the tip of her glove, falls into a mortal illness and wastes away, it requires no great wit to see that his illness doesn't come from his having indulged himself too grossly. It comes rather from the opposite cause! If he sinks when she's away, perhaps he will come up when she's there. At any rate, that's my theory; and any theory is good that will save a dying man. Let the young lady come and stand a moment by his bed, and lay her hand upon his. We shall see what happens. If he gets well, it's worth while; if he doesn't, there is no harm done. A young lady risks nothing in going to see a poor gentleman who lies in a stupor between two holy women."

Agatha was much impressed with this picturesque reasoning, but she answered that it was quite impossible that her beautiful friend should go upon this pious errand without a special invitation from Mr. Longstaff. Even should he beg Diana to come to him, Agatha was by no means sure her companion would go; but it was very certain she would not take such an extraordinary step at the mere suggestion of a servant.

"But you, dear lady, have the happiness not to be a servant," the old man rejoined. "Let the suggestion be yours."

"From me it could come with no force, for what am I supposed to know about your poor master?"

"You have not told your friend what my dear master told you the other day?"

Agatha answered this question by another question.

"Did he tell you what he had told me?"

The old man tapped his forehead an instant and smiled.

"A good servant, you know, dear lady, needs never to be told things! If you have not repeated my master's words to the signorina, I beg you very earnestly to do so. I am afraid she is rather cold."

Agatha glanced a moment at the upper windows, and then she gave a silent nod. She wondered greatly to find herself discussing Diana's character with this aged menial; but the situation was so strange and romantic that one's old landmarks of propriety were quite obliterated, and it seemed natural that an Italian *valet de chambre* should be as frank and familiar as a servant in an old-fashioned comedy.

"If it is necessary that my dear master shall send for the young lady," Mr. Longstaff's domestic resumed, "I think I can promise you that he will. Let me urge you, meanwhile, to talk to her. If she is cold, warm her up! Prepare her to find him very interesting. If you could see him, poor gentleman, lying there as still and handsome as if he were his own monument in a *campo santo*, I think he would interest you."

This seemed to Agatha a very touching image, but it occurred to her that her interview with Mr. Longstaff's representative, now unduly prolonged, was assuming a nocturnal character. She abruptly brought it to a close, after having assured her interlocutor that she would reflect upon what he had told her; and she rejoined her companion in the deepest agitation. Late that evening her agitation broke out. She went into Diana's room, where she found this young lady standing white-robed before her mirror, with her auburn tresses rippling down to her knees; and then, taking her two hands, she told the story of the young Englishman's passion, told of his coming to talk to her that day that Diana had left her alone on the bench by the sea, and of his venerable valet having, a couple of hours before, sought speech of her on the same subject. Diana listened, at first with a rosy flush, and then with a cold, an almost cruel, frown.

"Take pity upon him," said Agatha Josling—"take pity upon him and go and see him."

"I don't understand," said her companion, "and it seems to me very disagreeable. What is Mr. Longstaff to me?" But before they separated, Agatha had persuaded her to say that if a message really should come from the young man's death-bed, she would not refuse him the light of her presence.

The message really came, brought of course by the invalid's zealous chamberlain. He re-appeared on the morrow, announcing that his master humbly begged for the honour of ten minutes' conversation with the two ladies. They consented to follow him, and he led the way to Mr. Longstaff's apartments. Diana still wore her irritated brow, but it made her look more than ever like the easily-startled goddess of the chase. Under the old man's guidance they passed through a low green door in a yellow wall, across a tangled garden full of orange-trees and winter roses, and into a white-wainscoted saloon, where they were presently left alone before a great classic Empire clock, perched upon a frigid southern chimney-place. They waited, however, but a few moments; the door of an adjoining room opened, and the Sisters of Charity, in white-winged hoods and with their hands thrust into the loose sleeves of the opposite arm, came forth and stood with down-cast eyes on either side of the threshold. Then the old servant appeared between them, and beckoned to the two young girls to advance. The latter complied with a certain hesitation, and he led them into the chamber of the dying man. Here, pointing to the bed, he silently left them and withdrew; not closing, however, the door of communication of the saloon, where he took up his station with the Sisters of Charity.

Diana and her companion stood together in the middle of the darker room, waiting for an invitation to approach their summoner. He lay in his bed, propped up on pillows, with his arms outside the counterpane. For a moment he simply gazed at them; he was as white as the sheet that covered him, and he certainly looked like a dying man. But he had the strength to bend forward and to speak in a soft, distinct voice.

"Would you be so kind as to come nearer?" said Mr. Longstaff.

Agatha Josling gently pushed her friend forward, but she followed her to the bedside. Diana stood there, her frown had melted away; and the young man sank back upon his pillows and looked at her. A faint colour came into his face, and he clasped his two hands together on his breast. For some moments he simply gazed at the beautiful girl before him. It was an awkward situation for her, and Agatha expected her at any moment to turn away in disgust. But, slowly, her look of proud compulsion, of mechanical compliance, was exchanged for something more patient and pitying. The young Englishman's face expressed a kind of spiritual ecstasy which, it was impossible not to feel, gave a peculiar sanctity to the occasion.

"It was very generous of you to come," he said at last. "I hardly ventured to hope you would. I suppose you know—I suppose your friend, who listened to me so kindly, has told you?"

"Yes, she knows," murmured Agatha—"she knows."

"I did not intend you should know until after my death," he went on; "but"—and he paused a moment and shook his clasped hands together—"I couldn't wait! And when I felt that I couldn't wait, a new idea, a new desire, came into my mind." He was silent again for an instant, still looking with worshipful entreaty at Diana. The colour in his face deepened. "It is something that you may do for me. You will think it a most extraordinary request; but, in my position, a man grows bold. Dear lady, will you marry me?"

"Oh, dear!" cried Agatha Josling, just audibly. Her companion said nothing—her attitude seemed to say that in this remarkable situation one thing was no more surprising than another. But she paid Mr. Longstaff's proposal the respect of slowly seating herself in a chair which had been placed near his bed; here she rested in maidenly majesty, with her eyes fixed on the ground.

"It will help me to die happy, since die I must!" the young

man continued. "It will enable me to do something for you—the only thing I can do. I have property—lands, houses, a great many beautiful things—things I have loved and am very sorry to be leaving behind me. Lying here helpless and hopeless through so many days, the thought has come to me of what a bliss it would be to know that they should rest in your hands. If you were my wife, they would rest there safely. You might be spared much annoyance; and it is not only that. It is a fancy I have beyond that. It would be the feeling of it! I am fond of life. I don't want to die; but since I must die, it would be a happiness to have got just this out of life—this joining of our hands before a priest. You could go away then. For you it would make no change—it would be no burden. But I should have a few hours in which to lie and think of my happiness."

There was something in the young man's tone so simple and sincere, so tender and urgent, that Agatha Josling was touched to tears. She turned away to hide them, and went on tiptoe to the window, where she silently let them flow. Diana apparently was not unmoved. She raised her eyes and let them rest kindly on those of Mr. Longstaff, who continued softly to urge his proposal. "It would be a great charity," he said, "a great condescension; and it can produce no consequence to you that you could regret. It can only give you a larger liberty. You know very little about me, but I have a feeling that, so far as belief goes, you can believe me, and that is all I ask of you. I don't ask you to love me—that takes time. It is something I can't pretend to. It is only to consent to the form, the ceremony. I have seen the English clergyman; he says he will perform it. He will tell you, besides, all about me—that I am an English gentleman, and that the name I offer you is one of the best in the world."

It was strange to hear a dying man lie there and argue his point so reasonably and consistently; but now, apparently, his argument was finished. There was a deep silence, and Agatha thought it would be discreet on her own part to retire. She moved quietly into the adjoining room, where the two Sisters of Charity still stood with their hands in their sleeves, and the old Italian valet was taking snuff with a melancholy gesture, like a baffled diplomatist. Agatha turned her back to these people, and, approaching a window again, stood looking out into the garden upon the orange-trees and the winter roses. It seemed to her that she had been listening to the most beautiful, most romantic, and most eloquent of declarations. How could Diana be insensible to it? She earnestly hoped her companion would consent to the solemn and interesting ceremony proposed by Mr. Longstaff, and though her delicacy had prompted her to withdraw, it permitted her to listen eagerly to what Diana should say. Then (as she heard nothing) it was eclipsed by the desire to go back and whisper, with a sympathetic kiss, a word of counsel. She glanced round again at the Sisters of Charity, who appeared to have perceived that the moment was a critical one. One of them detached herself, and, as Agatha returned, followed her a few steps into the room. Diana had got up from her chair. She was looking about her uneasily—she grasped at Agatha's hand. Reginald Longstaff lay there with his wasted face and his brilliant eyes, looking at them both. Agatha took her friend's two hands in both her own.

"It is very little to do, dearest," she murmured, "and it will make him very happy."

The young man appeared to have heard her, and he repeated her words in a tone of intense entreaty.

"It is very little to do, dearest!"

Diana looked round at him an instant. Then, for an instant, she covered her face with her two hands. Removing them, but holding them still against her cheeks, she looked at her companion with eyes that Agatha always remembered—eyes through which a thin gleam of mockery flashed from the seriousness of her face.

"Suppose, after all, he should not die?" she murmured.

Longstaff heard it; he gave a long, soft moan, and turned away. The Sister immediately approached his bed, on the other side, dropped on her knees and bent over him, while he leaned his head against the great white cape upon which her crucifix was displayed. Diana stood a moment longer, looking at him; then, gathering her shawl together with a great dignity, she slowly walked out of the room. Agatha could do nothing but follow her. The old Italian, holding the door open for them to pass out, made them an exaggerated obeisance.

In the garden Diana paused, with a flush in her cheek, and said—

"If he could die with it, he could die without it!" But beyond the garden gate, in the empty sunny street, she suddenly burst into tears.

Agatha made no reproaches, no comments; but her companion, during the rest of the day, spoke of Mr. Longstaff several times with an almost passionate indignation. She pronounced his conduct indelicate, egotistic, impertinent; she declared that the scene had been revolting. Agatha, for the moment, remained silent, but the next day she attempted to make some vague apology for the poor young man. Then Diana, with passionate emphasis, begged her to be so good as never to mention his name again; and she added that this disgusting incident had put her completely out of humour with Nice, from which place they would immediately take their departure. This they did without delay; they began to travel again. Agatha heard no more of Reginald Longstaff; the English ladies who had been her original source of information with regard to him had now left Nice; otherwise she would have written to them for news. That is, she would have thought of writing to them; I suspect that, on the whole, she would have denied herself this satisfaction, on the ground of loyalty to her friend. Agatha, at any rate, could only drop a tear, at solitary hours, upon the young man's unanswered prayer and early death. It must be confessed, however, that sometimes, as the weeks elapsed, a certain faint displeasure mingled itself with her sympathy—a wish that, roughly speaking, poor Mr. Longstaff had left them alone. Since that strange interview at his bedside things had not gone well; the charm of their earlier wanderings seemed broken. Agatha said to herself that, really, if she were superstitious, she might fancy that Diana's conduct on this occasion had brought them under an evil spell. It was no superstition, certainly, to think that this young lady had lost a certain generous mildness of temper. She was impatient, absent-minded, indifferent, capricious. She expressed unaccountable opinions and proposed unnatural plans. It is true that disagreeable things were constantly happening to them—things which would have taxed the most unruffled spirit. Their post-horses broke down, their postilions were impertinent, their luggage went astray, their servants betrayed them. The heavens themselves seemed to join in the conspiracy, and for days together were dark and ungenerous, treating them only to wailing winds and watery clouds. It was, in a large measure, in the light of after years that Agatha judged this period; but even at the time she felt it to be depressing, uncomfortable, unnatural. Diana apparently shared her opinion of it, though she never openly avowed it. She took refuge in a kind of haughty silence, and whenever a new disaster came to her knowledge, she simply greeted it with a bitter smile—a smile which Agatha always interpreted as an ironical reflection on poor fantastic, obtrusive Mr. Longstaff, who, through some mysterious action upon the machinery of nature, had turned the tide of their fortunes. At the end of the summer, suddenly, Diana proposed they should go home, speaking of it in the tone of a person who gives up a hopeless struggle. Agatha assented, and the two ladies returned to America, much to the relief of Miss Josling, who had an uncomfortable sense that there was something unexpressed and unregulated between them, which gave their intercourse a resemblance to a sultry morning. But at home they separated very tenderly, for Agatha had to go into the country and devote herself to her nearer kinsfolk. These good people, after her long absence, were exacting, so that for two years she saw nothing of her late companion.

She often, however, heard from her, and Diana figured in the town-talk that was occasionally wafted to her rural home. She sometimes figured strangely—as a rattling coquette who carried on flirtations by the hundred and broke hearts by the dozen. This had not been Diana's former character, and Agatha found matter for meditation in the change. But the young lady's own letters said little of her admirers and displayed no trophies. They came very fitfully—sometimes at the rate of a dozen a month and sometimes not at all; but they were usually of a serious and abstract cast and contained the author's opinions upon life, death, religion, immortality. Mistress of her actions and of a pretty fortune, it might have been expected that news would come in trustworthy form of Diana's having at last accepted one of her rumoured lovers. Such news in fact came, and it was apparently trustworthy, inasmuch as it pro-

ceeded from the young lady herself. She wrote to Agatha that
she was to be married, and Agatha immediately congratulated
her upon her happiness. Then Diana wrote back that though
she was to be married she was not at all happy; and she shortly
afterwards added that she was neither happy nor to be married. She had broken off her projected union and her felicity
was smaller than ever. Poor Agatha was sorely perplexed, and
she found it a comfort that a month after this her friend
should have sent her a peremptory summons to come to her.
She immediately obeyed.

Arriving, after a long journey, at the dwelling of her young
hostess, she saw Diana at the further end of the drawing-
room, with her back turned, looking out of the window. She
was evidently watching for Agatha, but Miss Josling had come
in, by accident, through a private entrance which was not visible from the window. She gently approached her friend and
then Diana turned. She had her two hands laid upon her
cheeks, and her eyes were sad; her face and attitude suggested
something that Agatha had seen before and kept the memory
of. While she kissed her Agatha remembered that it was just
so she had stood for that last moment before poor Mr.
Longstaff.

"Will you come abroad with me again?" Diana asked. "I
am very ill."

"Dearest, what is the matter?" said Agatha.

"I don't know; I believe I am dying. They tell me this place
is bad for me; that I must have another climate; that I must
move about. Will you take care of me? I shall be very easy to
take care of now."

Agatha, for all answer, embraced her afresh, and as soon
after this as possible the two friends embarked again for Europe. Miss Josling had thrown herself the more freely into this
scheme, as her companion's appearance seemed a striking confirmation of her words. Not, indeed, that she looked as if she
were dying; but in the two years that had elapsed since their
separation she had wasted and faded. She looked more than
two years older, and the brilliancy of her beauty was dimmed.
She was pale and languid, and she moved more slowly than
when she seemed a goddess treading the forest leaves. The
beautiful statue had grown human and taken on some of the

imperfections of humanity. And yet the doctors by no means affirmed that she had a mortal malady, and when one of them was asked by an inquisitive matron why he had recommended this young lady to cross the seas, he replied with a smile that it was a principle in his system to prescribe the remedies that his patients greatly desired.

At present the fair travellers had no misadventures. The broken charm had renewed itself; the heavens smiled upon them, and their postilions treated them like princesses. Diana, too, had completely recovered her native serenity; she was the gentlest, the most docile, the most reasonable of women. She was silent and subdued, as was natural in an invalid; though in one important particular her demeanour was certainly at variance with the idea of debility. She had much more taste for motion than for rest, and constant change of place became the law of her days. She wished to see all the places that she had not seen before, and all the old ones over again.

"If I am really dying," she said, smiling softly, "I must leave my farewell cards everywhere." So she passed her days in a great open carriage, leaning back in it and looking, right and left, at everything she passed. On her former journey to Europe she had seen but little of England, and now she determined to visit the whole of this famous island. She rolled for weeks through the beautiful English landscape, past meadows and hedgerows, over the avenues of great estates and under the walls of castles and abbeys. For the English parks and manors, the "Halls" and "Courts," she had an especial admiration, and into the grounds of such as were open to appreciative tourists she made a point of penetrating. Here she stayed her carriage beneath the oaks and beeches, and sat for an hour at a time listening to nightingales and watching browsing deer. She never failed to visit a residence that lay on her road, and as soon as she arrived at a town she inquired punctiliously whether there were any fine country-seats in the neighbourhood. In this delightful fashion she spent a whole summer. Through the autumn she continued to wander restlessly; she visited, on the Continent, a hundred watering-places, and travellers' resorts. The beginning of the winter found her in Rome, where she confessed to being very tired and prepared to seek repose.

"I am weary, weary," she said to her companion. "I didn't know how weary I was. I feel like sinking down in this City of Rest, and resting here for ever."

She took a lodging in an old palace, where her chamber was hung with ancient tapestries, and her drawing-room decorated with the arms of a pope. Here, giving way to her fatigue, she ceased to wander. The only thing she did was to go every day to St. Peter's. She went nowhere else. She sat at her window all day with a big book in her lap, which she never read, looking out into a Roman garden at a fountain plashing into a weedy alcove, and half a dozen nymphs in mottled marble. Sometimes she told her companion that she was happier this way than she had ever been—in this way, and in going to St. Peter's. In the great church she often spent the whole afternoon. She had a servant behind her, carrying a stool; he placed her stool against a marble pilaster, and she sat there for a long time, looking up into the airy hollow of the dome and over the vast, peopled pavement. She noticed every one who passed her; but Agatha, lingering beside her, felt less at liberty, she hardly knew why, to make remarks about the people around them than she had felt when they sat upon the shore at Nice.

One day Agatha left her and strolled about the church by herself. The ecclesiastical life of Rome had not shrunken to its present smallness, and in one corner or another of St. Peter's there was always some occasion of worship. Agatha found plenty of entertainment, and was absent for half an hour. When she came back she found her companion's place deserted, and she sat down on the empty stool to await her re-appearance. Some time elapsed, and then she wandered away in quest of her. She found her at last, near one of the side-altars; but she was not alone. A gentleman stood before her whom she appeared just to have encountered. Her face was very pale, and its expression led Agatha to look straightway at the stranger. Then she saw he was no stranger; he was Reginald Longstaff! He, too, evidently had been much startled, but he was already recovering himself. He stood very gravely an instant longer; then he silently bowed to the two ladies and turned away.

Agatha felt at first as if she had seen a ghost; but the

impression was immediately corrected by the fact that Mr. Longstaff's aspect was very much less ghostly than it had been in life. He looked like a strong man; he held himself upright, and had a handsome colour. What Agatha saw in Diana's face was not surprise; it was a pale radiance which she waited a moment to give a name to. Diana put out her hand and laid it in her arm, and her touch helped Agatha to know what it was that her face expressed. Then she felt too that this knowledge itself was not a surprise; she seemed to have been waiting for it. She looked at her friend again, and Diana was beautiful. Diana blushed and became more beautiful yet. Agatha led her back to her seat near the marble pilaster.

"So you were right," Agatha said presently. "He would, after all, have got well!"

Diana would not sit down; she motioned to her servant to bring away the stool, and continued to move towards the door. She said nothing until she stood without, in the great square, between the colonnades and fountains. Then she spoke.

"I am right now, but I was wrong then. He got well because I refused him. I gave him a hurt that cured him."

That evening, beneath the Roman lamps in the great drawing-room of the arms of the pope, a remarkable conversation took place between the two friends. Diana wept and hid her face; but her tears and her shame were gratuitous. Agatha felt, as I have said, that she had already guessed all the unexplained, and it was needless for her companion to tell her that three weeks after she had refused Reginald Longstaff she insanely loved him. It was needless that Diana should confess that his image had never been out of her mind, that she believed he was still among the living, and that she had come back to Europe with a desperate hope of meeting him. It was in this hope that she had wandered from town to town and looked at every one who passed her; and it was in this hope that she had lingered in so many English parks. She knew her love was very strange; she could only say it had consumed her. It had all come upon her afterwards—in retrospect, in meditation. Or rather, she supposed, it had been there always, since she first saw him, and the revulsion from displeasure to pity, after she left his bedside, had brought it out. And with it came the faith that he had indeed got well, both of his malady and of his own passion. This was her punishment! And then she spoke with a divine simplicity which Agatha, weeping a little too, wished that, if this belief of Diana's were true, the young man might have heard. "I am so glad he is well and strong. And that he looks so handsome and so good!" And she presently added, "Of course he has got well only to hate me. He wishes never to see me again. Very good. I have had my wish; I have seen him once more. That was what I wanted, and I can die content."

It seemed in fact as if she were going to die. She went no more to St. Peter's, and exposed herself to no more encounters with Mr. Longstaff. She sat at her window and looked out at the freckled dryads and the cypresses, or wandered about her quarter of the palace with a vaguely smiling resignation. Agatha watched her with a sadness that was less submissive. This too was something that she had heard of, that she had read of in poetry and fable, but that she had never supposed she should see—her companion was dying of love! Agatha thought of many things and made up her mind upon several. The first of these latter was to send for the doctor. This personage came, and Diana let him look at her through his spectacles and hold her white wrist. He announced that she was ill, and she smiled and said she knew it; and then he gave her a little phial of gold-coloured fluid, which he bade her to drink. He recommended her to remain in Rome, as the climate exactly suited her complaint. Agatha's second desire was to see Mr. Longstaff, who had appealed to her, she reflected, in the day of his own tribulation, and whom she therefore had a right to approach at present. She found it impossible to believe, too, that the passion which led him to take that extraordinary step at Nice, was extinct; such passions as that never died. If he had made no further attempt to see Diana, it was because he believed that she was still as cold as when she turned away from his death-bed. It must be added, moreover, that Agatha felt a lawful curiosity to learn how from that death-bed he had risen again into blooming manhood. This last point there was no theory to explain.

Agatha went to St. Peter's, feeling sure that sooner or later she should encounter him there. At the end of a week she perceived him, and seeing her, he immediately came and spoke to her. As Diana had said, he was now extremely handsome, and he looked particularly good. He was a quiet, blooming, gallant young English gentleman. He seemed much embarrassed, but his manner to Agatha expressed the highest consideration.

"You must think me a dreadful impostor," he said, very gravely. "But I *was* dying—or I believed I was."

"And by what miracle did you recover?"

He was silent a moment, and then he said—

"I suppose it was by the miracle of wounded pride!" She noticed that he asked nothing about Diana; and presently she felt that he knew she was thinking of this. "The strangest part of it," he added, "was, that when my strength came back to me, what had gone before had become as a simple dream. And what happened to me here the other day," he went on, "failed to make it a reality again!"

Agatha looked at him a moment in silence, and saw again that he was handsome and kind; and then dropping a sigh over the wonderful mystery of things, she turned sadly away. That evening, Diana said to her—

"I know that you have seen him!"

Agatha came to her and kissed her.

"And I am nothing to him now?"

"My own dearest—" murmured Agatha.

Diana had drunk the little phial of gold-coloured liquid; but after this, she ceased to wander about the palace; she never left her room. The old doctor was with her constantly now, and he continued to say that the air of Rome was very good for her complaint. Agatha watched her in helpless sadness; she saw her fading and sinking, and yet she was unable to comfort her. She tried once to comfort her by saying hard things about Mr. Longstaff, by pointing out that he had not been honourable; rising herein to a sublime hypocrisy, for on that last occasion at St. Peter's the poor girl had felt that she herself admired him as much as ever—that the timid little flame which was kindled at Nice was beginning to shoot up again. Agatha saw nothing but his good looks and his kind manner.

"What did he want—what did he mean, after all?" she pretended to murmur, leaning over Diana's sofa. "Why should he have been wounded at what you said? It would have been part of the bargain that he should not get well. Did he mean to take an unfair advantage—to make you his wife under false pretences? When you put your finger on the weak spot, why should he resent it? No, it was not honourable."

Diana smiled sadly; she had no false shame now, and she spoke of this thing as if it concerned another person.

"He would have counted on my forgiving him!" she said. A little while after this, she began to sink more rapidly. Then she called her friend to her, and said simply, "Send for him!" And as Agatha looked perplexed and distressed, she added, "I know he is still in Rome."

Agatha at first was at a loss where to find him, but among the benefits of the papal dispensation was the fact that the pontifical police could instantly help you to lay your hand upon any sojourner in the Eternal City. Mr. Longstaff had a passport in detention by the government, and this document formed a basis of instruction to the servant whom Agatha sent to interrogate the authorities. The servant came back with the news that he had seen the distinguished stranger, who would wait upon the ladies at the hour they proposed. When this hour came and Mr. Longstaff was announced, Diana said to her companion that she must remain with her. It was an afternoon in spring; the high windows into the ancient garden were open, and the room was adorned with great sheaves and stacks of the abundant Roman flowers. Diana sat in a deep arm-chair.

It was certainly a difficult position for Reginald Longstaff. He stopped on the threshold and looked a while at the woman to whom he had made his extraordinary offer; then, pale and agitated, he advanced rapidly towards her. He was evidently shocked at the state in which he found her; he took her hand, and, bending over it, raised it to his lips. She fixed her eyes on him a little, and she smiled a little.

"It is I who am dying, now," she said. "And now I want to ask something of *you*—to ask what you asked of me."

He stared, and a deep flush of colour came into his face; he hesitated for an appreciable moment. Then lowering his head with a movement of assent he kissed her hand again.

"Come back to-morrow," she said; "that is all I ask of you."

He looked at her again for a while in silence; then he abruptly turned and left her. She sent for the English clergyman and told him that she was a dying woman, and that she wished the marriage service to be read beside her couch. The clergyman, too, looked at her in much surprise; but he consented to humour so tenderly romantic a whim and made an appointment for the afternoon of the morrow. Diana was very tranquil. She sat motionless, with her hands clasped and her eyes closed. Agatha wandered about, arranging and rearranging the flowers. On the morrow she encountered Mr. Longstaff in one of the outer rooms: he had come before his time. She made this objection to his being admitted; but he answered that he knew he was early and had come with intention; he wished to spend the intervening hour with his prospective bride. So he went in and sat down by her couch again, and Agatha, leaving them alone, never knew what passed between them. At the end of the hour the clergyman arrived, and read the marriage service to them, pronouncing the nuptial blessing, while Agatha stood by as witness. Mr. Longstaff went through all this with a solemn, inscrutable face, and Agatha, observing him, said to herself that one must at least do him the justice to admit that he was performing punctiliously what honour demanded. When the clergyman had gone he asked Diana when he might see her again.

"Never!" she said, with her strange smile. And she added—"I shall not live long now."

He kissed her face, but he was obliged to leave her. He gave Agatha an anxious look as if he wished to say something to her, but she preferred not to listen to him. After this Diana sank rapidly. The next day Reginald Longstaff came back and insisted upon seeing Agatha.

"Why should she die?" he asked. "I want her to live."

"Have you forgiven her?" said Agatha.

"She saved me!" he cried.

Diana consented to see him once more; there were two doctors in attendance now, and they also had consented. He knelt down beside her bed and asked her to live. But she feebly shook her head.

"It would be wrong of me," she said.

Later, when he came back once more, Agatha told him she was gone. He stood wondering, with tears in his eyes.

"I don't understand," he said. "Did she love me or not?"

"She loved you," said Agatha, "more than she believed you could now love her; and it seemed to her that, when she had had her moment of happiness, to leave you at liberty was the tenderest way she could show it!"

An International Episode

FOUR YEARS AGO—in 1874—two young Englishmen had occasion to go to the United States. They crossed the ocean at midsummer, and, arriving in New York on the first day of August, were much struck with the fervid temperature of that city. Disembarking upon the wharf, they climbed into one of those huge high-hung coaches which convey passengers to the hotels, and with a great deal of bouncing and bumping, took their course through Broadway. The midsummer aspect of New York is not perhaps the most favourable one; still, it is not without its picturesque and even brilliant side. Nothing could well resemble less a typical English street than the interminable avenue, rich in incongruities, through which our two travellers advanced—looking out on each side of them at the comfortable animation of the sidewalks, the high-coloured, heterogeneous architecture, the huge white marble facades, glittering in the strong, crude light and bedizened with gilded lettering, the multifarious awnings, banners and streamers, the extraordinary number of omnibuses, horse-cars and other democratic vehicles, the vendors of cooling fluids, the white trousers and big straw-hats of the policemen, the tripping gait of the modish young persons on the pavement, the general brightness, newness, juvenility, both of people and things. The young men had exchanged few observations; but in crossing Union Square, in front of the monument to Washington—in the very shadow, indeed, projected by the image of the *pater patriæ*—one of them remarked to the other, "It seems a rum-looking place."

"Ah, very odd, very odd," said the other, who was the clever man of the two.

"Pity it's so beastly hot," resumed the first speaker, after a pause.

"You know we are in a low latitude," said his friend.

"I daresay," remarked the other.

"I wonder," said the second speaker, presently, "if they can give one a bath."

"I daresay not," rejoined the other.

"Oh, I say!" cried his comrade.

This animated discussion was checked by their arrival at the hotel, which had been recommended to them by an American gentleman whose acquaintance they made—with whom, indeed, they became very intimate—on the steamer, and who had proposed to accompany them to the inn and introduce them, in a friendly way, to the proprietor. This plan, however, had been defeated by their friend's finding that his "partner" was awaiting him on the wharf, and that his commercial associate desired him instantly to come and give his attention to certain telegrams received from St. Louis. But the two Englishmen, with nothing but their national prestige and personal graces to recommend them, were very well received at the hotel, which had an air of capacious hospitality. They found that a bath was not unattainable, and were indeed struck with the facilities for prolonged and reiterated immersion with which their apartment was supplied. After bathing a good deal—more indeed than they had ever done before on a single occasion—they made their way into the dining-room of the hotel, which was a spacious restaurant, with a fountain in the middle, a great many tall plants in ornamental tubs, and an array of French waiters. The first dinner on land, after a sea-voyage, is under any circumstances a delightful occasion, and there was something particularly agreeable in the circumstances in which our young Englishmen found themselves. They were extremely good-natured young men; they were more observant than they appeared; in a sort of inarticulate, accidentally dissimulative fashion, they were highly appreciative. This was perhaps especially the case with the elder, who was also, as I have said, the man of talent. They sat down at a little table which was a very different affair from the great clattering see-saw in the saloon of the steamer. The wide doors and windows of the restaurant stood open, beneath large awnings, to a wide pavement, where there were other plants in tubs, and rows of spreading trees, and beyond which there was a large shady square, without any palings and with marble-paved walks. And above the vivid verdure rose other façades of white marble and of pale chocolate-coloured stone, squaring themselves against the deep blue sky. Here, outside, in the light and the shade and the heat, there was a great tinkling of the bells of innumerable street-cars, and a constant strolling and shuffling and rustling of many pedestrians, a large proportion of whom were young women in Pompadour-looking dresses. Within, the place was cool and vaguely-lighted; with the plash of water, the odour of flowers and the flitting of French waiters, as I have said, upon soundless carpets.

"It's rather like Paris, you know," said the younger of our two travellers.

"It's like Paris—only more so," his companion rejoined.

"I suppose it's the French waiters," said the first speaker. "Why don't they have French waiters in London?"

"Fancy a French waiter at a club," said his friend.

The young Englishman stared a little, as if he could not fancy it. "In Paris I'm very apt to dine at a place where there's an English waiter. Don't you know, what's-his-name's, close to the thingumbob? They always set an English waiter at me. I suppose they think I can't speak French."

"No, more you can." And the elder of the young Englishmen unfolded his napkin.

His companion took no notice whatever of this declaration. "I say," he resumed, in a moment, "I suppose we must learn to speak American. I suppose we must take lessons."

"I can't understand them," said the clever man.

"What the deuce is *he* saying?" asked his comrade, appealing from the French waiter.

"He is recommending some soft-shell crabs," said the clever man.

And so, in desultory observation of the idiosyncrasies of the new society in which they found themselves, the young Englishmen proceeded to dine—going in largely, as the phrase is, for cooling draughts and dishes, of which their attendant offered them a very long list. After dinner they went out and slowly walked about the neighbouring streets. The early dusk of waning summer was coming on, but the heat was still very great. The pavements were hot even to the stout boot-soles of the British travellers, and the trees along the kerb-stone emitted strange exotic odours. The young men wandered through the adjoining square—that queer place without palings, and with marble walks arranged in black and white

lozenges. There were a great many benches, crowded with
shabby-looking people, and the travellers remarked, very
justly, that it was not much like Belgrave Square. On one side
was an enormous hotel, lifting up into the hot darkness an
immense array of open, brightly-lighted windows. At the base
of this populous structure was an eternal jangle of horse-cars,
and all round it, in the upper dusk, was a sinister hum of
mosquitoes. The ground-floor of the hotel seemed to be a
huge transparent cage, flinging a wide glare of gaslight into
the street, of which it formed a sort of public adjunct, absorbing and emitting the passers-by promiscuously. The
young Englishmen went in with every one else, from curiosity,
and saw a couple of hundred men sitting on divans along a
great marble-paved corridor, with their legs stretched out, together with several dozen more standing in a *queue*, as at the
ticket-office of a railway station, before a brilliantly-illumi-
nated counter, of vast extent. These latter persons, who carried portmanteaux in their hands, had a dejected, exhausted
look; their garments were not very fresh, and they seemed to
be rendering some mysterious tribute to a magnificent young
man with a waxed moustache and a shirt front adorned with
diamond buttons, who every now and then dropped an absent
glance over their multitudinous patience. They were American
citizens doing homage to an hotel-clerk.

"I'm glad he didn't tell us to go there," said one of our
Englishmen, alluding to their friend on the steamer, who had
told them so many things. They walked up the Fifth Avenue,
where, for instance, he had told them that all the first families
lived. But the first families were out of town, and our young
travellers had only the satisfaction of seeing some of the second—or perhaps even the third—taking the evening air upon
balconies and high flights of doorsteps, in the streets which
radiate from the more ornamental thoroughfare. They went a
little way down one of these side-streets, and they saw young
ladies in white dresses—charming-looking persons—seated in
graceful attitudes on the chocolate-coloured steps. In one or
two places these young ladies were conversing across the street
with other young ladies seated in similar postures and cos-
tumes in front of the opposite houses, and in the warm night
air their colloquial tones sounded strange in the ears of the

young Englishmen. One of our friends, nevertheless—the younger one—intimated that he felt a disposition to intercept a few of these soft familiarities; but his companion observed, pertinently enough, that he had better be careful. "We must not begin with making mistakes," said his companion.

"But he told us, you know—he told us," urged the young man, alluding again to the friend on the steamer.

"Never mind what he told us!" answered his comrade, who, if he had greater talents, was also apparently more of a moralist.

By bed-time—in their impatience to taste of a terrestrial couch again our seafarers went to bed early—it was still insufferably hot, and the buzz of the mosquitoes at the open windows might have passed for an audible crepitation of the temperature. "We can't stand this, you know," the young Englishmen said to each other; and they tossed about all night more boisterously than they had tossed upon the Atlantic billows. On the morrow, their first thought was that they would re-embark that day for England; and then it occurred to them that they might find an asylum nearer at hand. The cave of Æolus became their ideal of comfort, and they wondered where the Americans went when they wished to cool off. They had not the least idea, and they determined to apply for information to Mr. J. L. Westgate. This was the name inscribed in a bold hand on the back of a letter carefully preserved in the pocket-book of our junior traveller. Beneath the address, in the left-hand corner of the envelope, were the words, "Introducing Lord Lambeth and Percy Beaumont, Esq." The letter had been given to the two Englishmen by a good friend of theirs in London, who had been in America two years previously and had singled out Mr. J. L. Westgate from the many friends he had left there as the consignee, as it were, of his compatriots. "He is a capital fellow," the Englishman in London had said, "and he has got an awfully pretty wife. He's tremendously hospitable—he will do everything in the world for you; and as he knows every one over there, it is quite needless I should give you any other introduction. He will make you see every one; trust to him for putting you into circulation. He has got a tremendously pretty wife." It was natural that in the hour of tribulation Lord Lambeth and Mr.

Percy Beaumont should have bethought themselves of a gentleman whose attractions had been thus vividly depicted; all the more so that he lived in the Fifth Avenue and that the Fifth Avenue, as they had ascertained the night before, was contiguous to their hotel. "Ten to one he'll be out of town," said Percy Beaumont; "but we can at least find out where he has gone, and we can immediately start in pursuit. He can't possibly have gone to a hotter place, you know."

"Oh, there's only one hotter place," said Lord Lambeth, "and I hope he hasn't gone there."

They strolled along the shady side of the street to the number indicated upon the precious letter. The house presented an imposing chocolate-coloured expanse, relieved by facings and window-cornices of florid sculpture, and by a couple of dusty rose-trees, which clambered over the balconies and the portico. This last-mentioned feature was approached by a monumental flight of steps.

"Rather better than a London house," said Lord Lambeth, looking down from this altitude, after they had rung the bell.

"It depends upon what London house you mean," replied his companion. "You have a tremendous chance to get wet between the house-door and your carriage."

"Well," said Lord Lambeth, glancing at the burning heavens, "I 'guess' it doesn't rain so much here!"

The door was opened by a long negro in a white jacket, who grinned familiarly when Lord Lambeth asked for Mr. Westgate.

"He ain't at home, sir; he's down town at his o'fice."

"Oh, at his office?" said the visitors. "And when will he be at home?"

"Well, sir, when he goes out dis way in de mo'ning, he ain't liable to come home all day."

This was discouraging; but the address of Mr. Westgate's office was freely imparted by the intelligent black, and was taken down by Percy Beaumont in his pocket-book. The two gentlemen then returned, languidly, to their hotel, and sent for a hackney-coach and in this commodious vehicle they rolled comfortably down town. They measured the whole length of Broadway again, and found it a path of fire; and then, deflecting to the left, they were deposited by their

conductor before a fresh, light, ornamental structure, ten stories high, in a street crowded with keen-faced, light-limbed
young men, who were running about very quickly and stopping each other eagerly at corners and in doorways. Passing
into this brilliant building, they were introduced by one of the
keen-faced young men—he was a charming fellow, in wonderful cream-coloured garments and a hat with a blue ribbon,
who had evidently perceived them to be aliens and helpless—to a very snug hydraulic elevator, in which they took
their place with many other persons, and which, shooting upward in its vertical socket, presently projected them into the
seventh horizontal compartment of the edifice. Here, after
brief delay, they found themselves face to face with the friend
of their friend in London. His office was composed of several
different rooms, and they waited very silently in one of these
after they had sent in their letter and their cards. The letter
was not one which it would take Mr. Westgate very long to
read, but he came out to speak to them more instantly than
they could have expected; he had evidently jumped up from
his work. He was a tall, lean personage, and was dressed all
in fresh white linen; he had a thin, sharp, familiar face, with
an expression that was at one and the same time sociable and
business-like, a quick, intelligent eye, and a large brown moustache, which concealed his mouth and made his chin, beneath
it, look small. Lord Lambeth thought he looked tremendously
clever.

"How do you do, Lord Lambeth—how do you do, sir?"
he said, holding the open letter in his hand. "I'm very glad
to see you—I hope you're very well. You had better come in
here—I think it's cooler;" and he led the way into another
room, where there were law-books and papers, and windows
wide open beneath striped awnings. Just opposite one of the
windows, on a line with his eyes, Lord Lambeth observed the
weather-vane of a church steeple. The uproar of the street
sounded infinitely far below, and Lord Lambeth felt very high
in the air. "I say it's cooler," pursued their host, "but everything is relative. How do you stand the heat?"

"I can't say we like it," said Lord Lambeth; "but Beaumont
likes it better than I."

"Well, it won't last," Mr. Westgate very cheerfully declared;

"nothing unpleasant lasts over here. It was very hot when Captain Littledale was here; he did nothing but drink sherry-cobblers. He expresses some doubt in his letter whether I shall remember him—as if I didn't remember making six sherry-cobblers for him one day, in about twenty minutes. I hope you left him well; two years having elapsed since then."

"Oh, yes, he's all right," said Lord Lambeth.

"I am always very glad to see your countrymen," Mr. Westgate pursued. "I thought it would be time some of you should be coming along. A friend of mine was saying to me only a day or two ago, 'It's time for the water-melons and the Englishmen.' "

"The Englishmen and the water-melons just now are about the same thing," Percy Beaumont observed, wiping his dripping forehead.

"Ah, well, we'll put you on ice, as we do the melons. You must go down to Newport."

"We'll go anywhere!" said Lord Lambeth.

"Yes, you want to go to Newport—that's what you want to do," Mr. Westgate affirmed. "But let's see—when did you get here?"

"Only yesterday," said Percy Beaumont.

"Ah, yes, by the 'Russia.' Where are you staying?"

"At the 'Hanover,' I think they call it."

"Pretty comfortable?" inquired Mr. Westgate.

"It seems a capital place, but I can't say we like the gnats," said Lord Lambeth.

Mr. Westgate stared and laughed. "Oh, no, of course you don't like the gnats. We shall expect you to like a good many things over here, but we shan't insist upon your liking the gnats; though certainly you'll admit that, as gnats, they are fine, eh? But you oughtn't to remain in the city."

"So we think," said Lord Lambeth. "If you would kindly suggest something——"

"Suggest something, my dear sir?"—and Mr. Westgate looked at him, narrowing his eyelids. "Open your mouth and shut your eyes! Leave it to me, and I'll put you through. It's a matter of national pride with me that all Englishmen should have a good time; and, as I have had considerable practice, I have learned to minister to their wants. I find they generally want the right thing. So just please to consider yourselves my property; and if any one should try to appropriate you, please to say, 'Hands off; too late for the market.' But let's see," continued the American, in his slow, humorous voice, with a distinctness of utterance which appeared to his visitors to be part of a facetious intention—a strangely leisurely, speculative voice for a man evidently so busy and, as they felt, so professional—"let's see; are you going to make something of a stay, Lord Lambeth?"

"Oh dear no," said the young Englishman; "my cousin was coming over on some business, so I just came across, at an hour's notice, for the lark."

"Is it your first visit to the United States?"

"Oh dear, yes."

"I was obliged to come on some business," said Percy Beaumont, "and I brought Lambeth with me."

"And *you* have been here before, sir?"

"Never—never."

"I thought, from your referring to business——" said Mr. Westgate.

"Oh, you see I'm by way of being a barrister," Percy Beaumont answered. "I know some people that think of bringing a suit against one of your railways, and they asked me to come over and take measures accordingly."

Mr. Westgate gave one of his slow, keen looks again. "What's your railroad?" he asked.

"The Tennessee Central."

The American tilted back his chair a little, and poised it an instant. "Well, I'm sorry you want to attack one of our institutions," he said, smiling. "But I guess you had better enjoy yourself *first*!"

"I'm certainly rather afraid I can't work in this weather," the young barrister confessed.

"Leave that to the natives," said Mr. Westgate. "Leave the Tennessee Central to me, Mr. Beaumont. Some day we'll talk it over, and I guess I can make it square. But I didn't know you Englishmen ever did any work, in the upper classes."

"Oh, we do a lot of work; don't we, Lambeth?" asked Percy Beaumont.

"I must certainly be at home by the 19th of September," said the younger Englishman, irrelevantly, but gently.

"For the shooting, eh? or is it the hunting—or the fishing?" inquired his entertainer.

"Oh, I must be in Scotland," said Lord Lambeth, blushing a little.

"Well then," rejoined Mr. Westgate, "you had better amuse yourself first, also. You must go down and see Mrs. Westgate."

"We should be so happy—if you would kindly tell us the train," said Percy Beaumont.

"It isn't a train—it's a boat."

"Oh, I see. And what is the name of—a—the—a—town?"

"It isn't a town," said Mr. Westgate, laughing. "It's a—well, what shall I call it? It's a watering-place. In short, it's Newport. You'll see what it is. It's cool; that's the principal thing. You will greatly oblige me by going down there and putting yourself into the hands of Mrs. Westgate. It isn't per-haps for me to say it; but you couldn't be in better hands. Also in those of her sister, who is staying with her. She is very fond of Englishmen. She thinks there is nothing like them."

"Mrs. Westgate or—a—her sister?" asked Percy Beaumont, modestly, yet in the tone of an inquiring traveller.

"Oh, I mean my wife," said Mr. Westgate. "I don't suppose my sister-in-law knows much about them. She has always led a very quiet life; she has lived in Boston."

Percy Beaumont listened with interest. "That, I believe," he said, "is the most—a—intellectual town?"

"I believe it is very intellectual. I don't go there much," responded his host.

"I say, we ought to go there," said Lord Lambeth to his companion.

"Oh, Lord Lambeth, wait till the great heat is over!" Mr. Westgate interposed. "Boston in this weather would be very trying; it's not the temperature for intellectual exertion. At Boston, you know, you have to pass an examination at the city limits; and when you come away they give you a kind of degree."

Lord Lambeth stared, blushing a little; and Percy Beaumont stared a little also—but only with his fine natural complexion; glancing aside after a moment to see that his companion was not looking too credulous, for he had heard a great deal about American humour. "I daresay it is very jolly," said the younger gentleman.

"I daresay it is," said Mr. Westgate. "Only I must impress upon you that at present—to-morrow morning, at an early hour—you will be expected at Newport. We have a house there; half the people in New York go there for the summer. I am not sure that at this very moment my wife can take you in; she has got a lot of people staying with her; I don't know who they all are; only she may have no room. But you can begin with the hotel, and meanwhile you can live at my house. In that way—simply sleeping at the hotel—you will find it tolerable. For the rest, you must make yourself at home at my place. You mustn't be shy, you know; if you are only here for a month that will be a great waste of time. Mrs. Westgate won't neglect you, and you had better not try to resist her. I know something about that. I expect you'll find some pretty girls on the premises. I shall write to my wife by this afternoon's mail, and to-morrow she and Miss Alden will look out for you. Just walk right in and make yourself comfortable. Your steamer leaves from this part of the city, and I will immediately send out and get you a cabin. Then, at half-past four o'clock, just call for me here, and I will go with you and put you on board. It's a big boat; you might get lost. A few days hence, at the end of the week, I will come down to Newport and see how you are getting on."

The two young Englishmen inaugurated the policy of not resisting Mrs. Westgate by submitting, with great docility and thankfulness, to her husband. He was evidently a very good fellow, and he made an impression upon his visitors; his hospitality seemed to recommend itself, consciously—with a friendly wink, as it were—as if it hinted, judicially, that you could not possibly make a better bargain. Lord Lambeth and his cousin left their entertainer to his labours and returned to their hotel, where they spent three or four hours in their respective shower-baths. Percy Beaumont had suggested that they ought to see something of the town; but "Oh, damn the town!" his noble kinsman had rejoined. They returned to Mr. Westgate's office in a carriage, with their luggage, very punctually; but it must be reluctantly recorded that, this time, he kept them waiting so long that they felt themselves missing the steamer and were deterred only by an amiable modesty from dispensing with his attendance and starting on a hasty scramble to the wharf. But when at last he appeared, and the carriage plunged into the purlieus of Broadway, they jolted and jostled to such good purpose that they reached the huge white vessel while the bell for departure was still ringing and the absorption of passengers still active. It was indeed, as Mr. Westgate had said, a big boat, and his leadership in the innumerable and interminable corridors and cabins, with which he seemed perfectly acquainted, and of which any one and every one appeared to have the *entrée*, was very grateful to the slightly bewildered voyagers. He showed them their state-room—a spacious apartment, embellished with gas-lamps, mirrors *en pied* and sculptured furniture—and then, long after they had been intimately convinced that the steamer was in motion and launched upon the unknown stream that they were about to navigate, he bade them a sociable farewell.

"Well, good-bye, Lord Lambeth," he said. "Good-bye, Mr. Percy Beaumont; I hope you'll have a good time. Just let them do what they want with you. I'll come down by-and-by and look after you."

II.

The young Englishmen emerged from their cabin and amused themselves with wandering about the immense labyrinthine steamer, which struck them as an extraordinary mixture of a ship and an hotel. It was densely crowded with passengers, the larger number of whom appeared to be ladies and very young children; and in the big saloons, ornamented in white and gold, which followed each other in surprising succession, beneath the swinging gas-lights and among the small side-passages where the negro domestics of both sexes assembled with an air of philosophic leisure, every one was moving to and fro and exchanging loud and familiar observations. Eventually, at the instance of a discriminating black, our young men went and had some "supper," in a wonderful place arranged like a theatre, where, in a gilded gallery upon which little boxes appeared to open, a large orchestra was playing operatic selections, and, below, people were handing about bills of fare, as if they had been programmes. All this was sufficiently curious; but the agreeable thing, later, was to sit out on one of the great white decks of the steamer, in the warm, breezy darkness, and, in the vague starlight, to make out the line of low, mysterious coast. The young Englishmen tried American cigars—those of Mr. Westgate—and talked together as they usually talked, with many odd silences, lapses of logic and incongruities of transition; like people who have grown old together and learned to supply each other's missing phrases; or, more especially, like people thoroughly conscious of a common point of view, so that a style of conversation superficially lacking in finish might suffice for a reference to a fund of associations in the light of which everything was all right.

"We really seem to be going out to sea," Percy Beaumont observed. "Upon my word, we are going back to England. He has shipped us off again. I call that 'real mean.'"

"I suppose it's all right," said Lord Lambeth. "I want to see those pretty girls at Newport. You know he told us the place was an island; and aren't all islands in the sea?"

"Well," resumed the elder traveller after a while, "if his house is as good as his cigars, we shall do very well."

"He seems a very good fellow," said Lord Lambeth, as if this idea had just occurred to him.

"I say, we had better remain at the inn," rejoined his companion, presently. "I don't think I like the way he spoke of his house. I don't like stopping in the house with such a tremendous lot of women."

"Oh, I don't mind," said Lord Lambeth. And then they smoked awhile in silence. "Fancy his thinking we do no work in England!" the young man resumed.

"I daresay he didn't really think so," said Percy Beaumont.

"Well, I guess they don't know much about England over here!" declared Lord Lambeth, humorously. And then there was another long pause. "He was devilish civil," observed the young nobleman.

"Nothing, certainly, could have been more civil," rejoined his companion.

"Littledale said his wife was great fun," said Lord Lambeth.

"Whose wife—Littledale's?"

"This American's—Mrs. Westgate. What's his name? J. L."

Beaumont was silent a moment. "What was fun to Little-dale," he said at last, rather sententiously, "may be death to us."

"What do you mean by that?" asked his kinsman. "I am as good a man as Littledale."

"My dear boy, I hope you won't begin to flirt," said Percy Beaumont.

"I don't care. I daresay I shan't begin."

"With a married woman, if she's bent upon it, it's all very well," Beaumont expounded. "But our friend mentioned a young lady—a sister, a sister-in-law. For God's sake, don't get entangled with her."

"How do you mean, entangled?"

"Depend upon it she will try to hook you."

"Oh, bother!" said Lord Lambeth.

"American girls are very clever," urged his companion.

"So much the better," the young man declared.

"I fancy they are always up to some game of that sort," Beaumont continued.

"They can't be worse than they are in England," said Lord Lambeth, judicially.

"Ah, but in England," replied Beaumont, "you have got your natural protectors. You have got your mother and sisters."

"My mother and sisters—" began the young nobleman, with a certain energy. But he stopped in time, puffing at his cigar.

"Your mother spoke to me about it, with tears in her eyes," said Percy Beaumont. "She said she felt very nervous. I promised to keep you out of mischief."

"You had better take care of yourself," said the object of maternal and ducal solicitude.

"Ah," rejoined the young barrister, "I haven't the expectation of a hundred thousand a year—not to mention other attractions."

"Well," said Lord Lambeth, "don't cry out before you're hurt!"

It was certainly very much cooler at Newport, where our

travellers found themselves assigned to a couple of diminutive bed-rooms in a far-away angle of an immense hotel. They had gone ashore in the early summer twilight, and had very promptly put themselves to bed; thanks to which circumstance and to their having, during the previous hours, in their commodious cabin, slept the sleep of youth and health, they began to feel, towards eleven o'clock, very alert and inquisitive. They looked out of their windows across a row of small green fields, bordered with low stone dykes, of rude construction, and saw a deep blue ocean lying beneath a deep blue sky and flecked now and then with scintillating patches of foam. A strong, fresh breeze came in through the curtainless casements and prompted our young men to observe, generously, that it didn't seem half a bad climate. They made other observations after they had emerged from their rooms in pursuit of breakfast—a meal of which they partook in a huge bare hall, where a hundred negroes, in white jackets, were shuffling about upon an uncarpeted floor; where the flies were superabundant and the tables and dishes covered over with a strange, voluminous integument of coarse blue gauze; and where several little boys and girls, who had risen late, were seated in fastidious solitude at the morning repast. These young persons had not the morning paper before them, but they were engaged in languid perusal of the bill of fare.

This latter document was a great puzzle to our friends, who, on reflecting that its bewildering categories had relation to breakfast alone, had an uneasy prevision of an encyclopædic dinner-list. They found a great deal of entertainment at the hotel, an enormous wooden structure, for the erection of which it seemed to them that the virgin forests of the West must have been terribly deflowered. It was perforated from end to end with immense bare corridors, through which a strong draught was blowing—bearing along wonderful figures of ladies in white morning-dresses and clouds of Valenciennes lace, who seemed to float down the long vistas with expanded furbelows, like angels spreading their wings. In front was a gigantic verandah, upon which an army might have encamped—a vast wooden terrace, with a roof as lofty as the nave of a cathedral. Here our young Englishmen enjoyed, as they supposed, a glimpse of American society, which was distributed over the measureless expanse in a variety of sedentary attitudes, and appeared to consist largely of pretty young girls, dressed as if for a *fête champêtre*, swaying to and fro in rocking-chairs, fanning themselves with large straw fans, and enjoying an enviable exemption from social cares. Lord Lambeth had a theory, which it might be interesting to trace to its origin, that it would be not only agreeable, but easily possible, to enter into relations with one of these young ladies; and his companion found occasion to check the young nobleman's colloquial impulses.

"You had better take care," said Percy Beaumont, "or you will have an offended father or brother pulling out a bowie-knife."

"I assure you it is all right," Lord Lambeth replied. "You know the Americans come to these big hotels to make acquaintances."

"I know nothing about it, and neither do you," said his kinsman, who, like a clever man, had begun to perceive that the observation of American society demanded a readjustment of one's standard.

"Hang it, then, let's find out!" cried Lord Lambeth with some impatience. "You know, I don't want to miss anything."

"We will find out," said Percy Beaumont, very reasonably. "We will go and see Mrs. Westgate and make all the proper inquiries."

And so the two inquiring Englishmen, who had this lady's address inscribed in her husband's hand upon a card, descended from the verandah of the big hotel and took their way, according to direction, along a large straight road, past a series of fresh-looking villas, embosomed in shrubs and flowers and enclosed in an ingenious variety of wooden palings. The morning was brilliant and cool, the villas were smart and snug, and the walk of the young travellers was very entertaining. Everything looked as if it had received a coat of fresh paint the day before—the red roofs, the green shutters, the clean, bright browns and buffs of the house-fronts. The flower-beds on the little lawns seemed to sparkle in the radiant air, and the gravel in the short carriage-sweeps to flash and twinkle. Along the road came a hundred little basket-phaetons, in which, almost always, a couple of ladies were

sitting—ladies in white dresses and long white gloves, holding
the reins and looking at the two Englishmen, whose nationality was not elusive, through thick blue veils, tied tightly
about their faces as if to guard their complexions. At last the
young men came within sight of the sea again, and then, having interrogated a gardener over the paling of a villa, they
turned into an open gate. Here they found themselves face to
face with the ocean and with a very picturesque structure,
resembling a magnified *chalet*, which was perched upon a
green embankment just above it. The house had a verandah
of extraordinary width all around it, and a great many doors
and windows standing open to the verandah. These various
apertures had, in common, such an accessible, hospitable air,
such a breezy flutter, within, of light curtains, such expansive
thresholds and reassuring interiors, that our friends hardly
knew which was the regular entrance, and, after hesitating a
moment, presented themselves at one of the windows. The
room within was dark, but in a moment a graceful figure
vaguely shaped itself in the rich-looking gloom, and a lady
came to meet them. Then they saw that she had been seated
at a table, writing, and that she had heard them and had got
up. She stepped out into the light; she wore a frank, charming
smile, with which she held out her hand to Percy Beaumont.

"Oh, you must be Lord Lambeth and Mr. Beaumont," she
said. "I have heard from my husband that you would come.
I am extremely glad to see you." And she shook hands with
each of her visitors. Her visitors were a little shy, but they had
very good manners; they responded with smiles and exclamations, and they apologised for not knowing the front door.
The lady rejoined, with vivacity, that when she wanted to see
people very much she did not insist upon those distinctions,
and that Mr. Westgate had written to her of his English friends
in terms that made her really anxious. "He said you were so
terribly prostrated," said Mrs. Westgate.

"Oh, you mean by the heat?" replied Percy Beaumont.
"We were rather knocked up, but we feel wonderfully better.
We had such a jolly—a—voyage down here. It's so very good
of you to mind."

"Yes, it's so very kind of you," murmured Lord Lambeth.
Mrs. Westgate stood smiling; she was extremely pretty.

"Well, I did mind," she said; "and I thought of sending for you this morning, to the Ocean House. I am very glad you are better, and I am charmed you have arrived. You must come round to the other side of the piazza." And she led the way, with a light, smooth step, looking back at the young men and smiling.

The other side of the piazza was, as Lord Lambeth presently remarked, a very jolly place. It was of the most liberal proportions, and with its awnings, its fanciful chairs, its cushions and rugs, its view of the ocean, close at hand, tumbling along the base of the low cliffs whose level tops intervened in lawn-like smoothness, it formed a charming complement to the drawing-room. As such it was in course of use at the present moment; it was occupied by a social circle. There were several ladies and two or three gentlemen, to whom Mrs. Westgate proceeded to introduce the distinguished strangers. She mentioned a great many names, very freely and distinctly; the young Englishmen, shuffling about and bowing, were rather bewildered. But at last they were provided with chairs—low wicker chairs, gilded and tied with a great many ribbons—and one of the ladies (a very young person, with a little snub nose and several dimples) offered Percy Beaumont a fan. The fan was also adorned with pink love-knots; but Percy Beaumont declined it, although he was very hot. Presently, however, it became cooler; the breeze from the sea was delicious, the view was charming, and the people sitting there looked exceedingly fresh and comfortable. Several of the ladies seemed to be young girls, and the gentlemen were slim, fair youths, such as our friends had seen the day before in New York. The ladies were working upon bands of tapestry, and one of the young men had an open book in his lap. Beaumont afterwards learned from one of the ladies that this young man had been reading aloud—that he was from Boston and was very fond of reading aloud. Beaumont said it was a great pity that they had interrupted him; he should like so much (from all he had heard) to hear a Bostonian read. Couldn't the young man be induced to go on?

"Oh no," said his informant, very freely; "he wouldn't be able to get the young ladies to attend to him now."

There was something very friendly, Beaumont perceived, in

the attitude of the company; they looked at the young Englishmen with an air of animated sympathy and interest; they
smiled, brightly and unanimously, at everything either of the
visitors said. Lord Lambeth and his companion felt that they
were being made very welcome. Mrs. Westgate seated herself
between them, and, talking a great deal to each, they had
occasion to observe that she was as pretty as their friend Littledale had promised. She was thirty years old, with the eyes
and the smile of a girl of seventeen, and she was extremely
light and graceful, elegant, exquisite. Mrs. Westgate was extremely spontaneous. She was very frank and demonstrative,
and appeared always—while she looked at you delightedly
with her beautiful young eyes—to be making sudden confessions and concessions, after momentary hesitations.

"We shall expect to see a great deal of you," she said to
Lord Lambeth, with a kind of joyous earnestness. "We are
very fond of Englishmen here; that is, there are a great many
we have been fond of. After a day or two you must come and
stay with us; we hope you will stay a long time. Newport's a
very nice place when you come really to know it, when you
know plenty of people. Of course, you and Mr. Beaumont will
have no difficulty about that. Englishmen are very well received here; there are almost always two or three of them
about. I think they always like it, and I must say I should
think they would. They receive ever so much attention. I must
say I think they sometimes get spoiled; but I am sure you and
Mr. Beaumont are proof against that. My husband tells me
you are a friend of Captain Littledale; he was such a charming
man. He made himself most agreeable here, and I am sure I
wonder he didn't stay. It couldn't have been pleasanter for
him in his own country. Though I suppose it is very pleasant
in England, for English people. I don't know myself; I have
been there very little. I have been a great deal abroad, but I
am always on the Continent. I must say I'm extremely fond
of Paris; you know we Americans always are; we go there
when we die. Did you ever hear that before? that was said by
a great wit. I mean the good Americans; but we are all good;
you'll see that for yourself. All I know of England is London,
and all I know of London is that place—on that little corner,
you know, where you buy jackets—jackets with that coarse

braid and those big buttons. They make very good jackets in London, I will do you the justice to say that. And some people like the hats; but about the hats I was always a heretic; I always got my hats in Paris. You can't wear an English hat—at least, I never could—unless you dress your hair *à l'Anglaise*; and I must say that is a talent I never possessed. In Paris they will make things to suit your peculiarities; but in England I think you like much more to have—how shall I say it?—one thing for everybody. I mean as regards dress. I don't know about other things; but I have always supposed that in other things everything was different. I mean according to the people— according to the classes, and all that. I am afraid you will think that I don't take a very favourable view; but you know you can't take a very favourable view in Dover Street, in the month of November. That has always been my fate. Do you know Jones's Hotel, in Dover Street? That's all I know of England. Of course, every one admits that the English hotels are your weak point. There was always the most frightful fog; I couldn't see to try my things on. When I got over to Amer- ica—into the light—I usually found they were twice too big. The next time I mean to go in the season; I think I shall go next year. I want very much to take my sister; she has never been to England. I don't know whether you know what I mean by saying that the Englishmen who come here some- times get spoiled. I mean that they take things as a matter of course—things that are done for them. Now, naturally, they are only a matter of course when the Englishmen are very nice. But, of course, they are almost always very nice. Of course, this isn't nearly such an interesting country as En- gland; there are not nearly so many things to see, and we haven't your country life. I have never seen anything of your country life; when I am in Europe I am always on the Con- tinent. But I have heard a great deal about it; I know that when you are among yourselves in the country you have the most beautiful time. Of course, we have nothing of that sort, we have nothing on that scale. I don't apologise, Lord Lam- beth; some Americans are always apologising; you must have noticed that. We have the reputation of always boasting and bragging and waving the American flag; but I must say that what strikes me is that we are perpetually making excuses and trying to smooth things over. The American flag has quite gone out of fashion; it's very carefully folded up, like an old tablecloth. Why should we apologise? The English never apologise—do they? No, I must say I never apologise. You must take us as we come—with all our imperfections on our heads. Of course we haven't your country life, and your old ruins, and your great estates, and your leisure-class, and all that. But if we haven't, I should think you might find it a pleasant change—I think any country is pleasant where they have pleasant manners. Captain Littledale told me he had never seen such pleasant manners as at Newport; and he had been a great deal in European society. Hadn't he been in the diplomatic service? He told me the dream of his life was to get appointed to a diplomatic post in Washington. But he doesn't seem to have succeeded. I suppose that in England promotion—and all that sort of thing—is fearfully slow. With us, you know, it's a great deal too fast. You see I admit our drawbacks. But I must confess I think Newport is an ideal place. I don't know anything like it anywhere. Captain Littledale told me he didn't know anything like it anywhere. It's entirely different from most watering-places; it's a most charming life. I must say I think that when one goes to a foreign country, one ought to enjoy the differences. Of course there are differences; otherwise what did one come abroad for? Look for your pleasure in the differences, Lord Lambeth; that's the way to do it; and then I am sure you will find American society—at least Newport society—most charming and most interesting. I wish very much my husband were here; but he's dreadfully confined to New York. I suppose you think that is very strange —for a gentleman. But you see we haven't any leisure-class."

Mrs. Westgate's discourse, delivered in a soft, sweet voice, flowed on like a miniature torrent and was interrupted by a hundred little smiles, glances, and gestures, which might have figured the irregularities and obstructions of such a stream. Lord Lambeth listened to her with, it must be confessed, a rather ineffectual attention, although he indulged in a good many little murmurs and ejaculations of assent and deprecation. He had no great faculty for apprehending generalisations. There were some three or four indeed which, in the play of his own intelligence, he had originated, and which had seemed convenient at the moment; but at the present time he could hardly have been said to follow Mrs. Westgate as she darted gracefully about in the sea of speculation. Fortunately she asked for no especial rejoinder, for she looked about at the rest of the company as well, and smiled at Percy Beaumont, on the other side of her, as if he too must understand her and agree with her. He was rather more successful than his companion; for besides being, as we know, cleverer, his attention was not vaguely distracted by close vicinity to a remarkably interesting young girl, with dark hair and blue eyes. This was the case with Lord Lambeth, to whom it occurred after a while that the young girl with blue eyes and dark hair was the pretty sister of whom Mrs. Westgate had spoken. She presently turned to him with a remark which established her identity.

"It's a great pity you couldn't have brought my brother-in-law with you. It's a great shame he should be in New York in these days."

"Oh yes; it's so very hot," said Lord Lambeth.

"It must be dreadful," said the young girl.

"I daresay he is very busy," Lord Lambeth observed.

"The gentlemen in America work too much," the young girl went on.

"Oh, do they? I daresay they like it," said her interlocutor.

"I don't like it. One never sees them."

"Don't you, really?" asked Lord Lambeth. "I shouldn't have fancied that."

"Have you come to study American manners?" asked the young girl.

"Oh, I don't know. I just came over for a lark. I haven't got long." Here there was a pause, and Lord Lambeth began again. "But Mr. Westgate will come down here, will not he?"

"I certainly hope he will. He must help to entertain you and Mr. Beaumont."

Lord Lambeth looked at her a little with his handsome brown eyes. "Do you suppose he would have come down with us, if we had urged him?"

Mr. Westgate's sister-in-law was silent a moment, and then—"I daresay he would," she answered.

"Really!" said the young Englishman. "He was immensely civil to Beaumont and me," he added.

"He is a dear good fellow," the young lady rejoined. "And he is a perfect husband. But all Americans are that," she continued, smiling.

"Really!" Lord Lambeth exclaimed again; and wondered whether all American ladies had such a passion for generalising as these two.

III.

He sat there a good while: there was a great deal of talk; it was all very friendly and lively and jolly. Every one present, sooner or later, said something to him, and seemed to make a particular point of addressing him by name. Two or three other persons came in, and there was a shifting of seats and changing of places; the gentlemen all entered into intimate conversation with the two Englishmen, made them urgent offers of hospitality and hoped they might frequently be of service to them. They were afraid Lord Lambeth and Mr. Beaumont were not very comfortable at their hotel—that it was not, as one of them said, "so private as those dear little English inns of yours." This last gentleman went on to say that unfortunately, as yet, perhaps, privacy was not quite so easily obtained in America as might be desired; still, he continued, you could generally get it by paying for it; in fact you could get everything in America nowadays by paying for it. American life was certainly growing a great deal more private; it was growing very much like England. Everything at Newport, for instance, was thoroughly private; Lord Lambeth would probably be struck with that. It was also represented to the strangers that it mattered very little whether their hotel was agreeable, as every one would want them to make visits; they would stay with other people, and, in any case, they would be a great deal at Mrs. Westgate's. They would find that very charming; it was the pleasantest house in Newport. It was a pity Mr. Westgate was always away; he was a man of the highest ability—very acute, very acute. He worked like a horse and he left his wife—well, to do about as she liked. He liked her to enjoy herself, and she seemed to know how. She was extremely brilliant, and a splendid talker. Some people preferred her sister; but Miss Alden was very different; she was in a different style altogether. Some people even thought her prettier, and, certainly, she was not so sharp. She was more in the Boston style; she had lived a great deal in Boston and she was very highly educated. Boston girls, it was intimated, were more like English young ladies.

Lord Lambeth had presently a chance to test the truth of this proposition; for on the company rising in compliance with a suggestion from their hostess that they should walk down to the rocks and look at the sea, the young Englishman again found himself, as they strolled across the grass, in proximity to Mrs. Westgate's sister. Though she was but a girl of twenty, she appeared to feel the obligation to exert an active hospitality; and this was perhaps the more to be noticed as she seemed by nature a reserved and retiring person, and had little of her sister's fraternising quality. She was perhaps rather too thin, and she was a little pale; but as she moved slowly over the grass, with her arms hanging at her sides, looking gravely for a moment at the sea and then brightly, for all her gravity, at him, Lord Lambeth thought her at least as pretty as Mrs. Westgate, and reflected that if this was the Boston style the Boston style was very charming. He thought she looked very clever; he could imagine that she was highly educated; but at the same time she seemed gentle and graceful. For all her cleverness, however, he felt that she had to think a little what to say; she didn't say the first thing that came into her head; he had come from a different part of the world and from a different society, and she was trying to adapt her conversation. The others were scattering themselves near the rocks; Mrs. Westgate had charge of Percy Beaumont.

"Very jolly place, isn't it?" said Lord Lambeth. "It's a very jolly place to sit."

"Very charming," said the young girl; "I often sit here; there are all kinds of cosy corners—as if they had been made on purpose."

"Ah! I suppose you have had some of them made," said the young man.

Miss Alden looked at him a moment. "Oh no, we have had nothing made. It's pure nature."

"I should think you would have a few little benches—rustic seats and that sort of thing. It might be so jolly to sit here, you know," Lord Lambeth went on.

"I am afraid we haven't so many of those things as you," said the young girl, thoughtfully.

"I daresay you go in for pure nature as you were saying. Nature, over here, must be so grand, you know." And Lord Lambeth looked about him.

The little coast-line hereabouts was very pretty, but it was not at all grand; and Miss Alden appeared to rise to a perception of this fact. "I am afraid it seems to you very rough," she said. "It's not like the coast scenery in Kingsley's novels."

"Ah, the novels always overdo it, you know," Lord Lambeth rejoined. "You must not go by the novels."

They were wandering about a little on the rocks, and they stopped and looked down into a narrow chasm where the rising tide made a curious bellowing sound. It was loud enough to prevent their hearing each other, and they stood there for some moments in silence. The young girl looked at her companion, observing him attentively but covertly, as women, even when very young, know how to do. Lord Lambeth repaid observation; tall, straight and strong, he was handsome as certain young Englishmen, and certain young Englishmen almost alone, are handsome; with a perfect finish of feature and a look of intellectual repose and gentle good temper which seemed somehow to be consequent upon his well-cut nose and chin. And to speak of Lord Lambeth's expression of intellectual repose is not simply a civil way of saying that he looked stupid. He was evidently not a young man of an irritable imagination; he was not, as he would himself have said, tremendously clever; but, though there was a kind of appealing dulness in his eye, he looked thoroughly reasonable and competent, and his appearance proclaimed that to be a nobleman, an athlete, and an excellent fellow, was a sufficiently brilliant combination of qualities. The young girl beside him, it may be attested without farther delay, thought him the handsomest young man she had ever seen; and Bessie Alden's imagination, unlike that of her companion, was irritable. He, however, was also making up his mind that she was uncommonly pretty.

"I daresay it's very gay here—that you have lots of balls and parties," he said; for, if he was not tremendously clever, he rather prided himself on having, with women, a sufficiency of conversation.

"Oh yes, there is a great deal going on," Bessie Alden replied. "There are not so many balls, but there are a good many other things. You will see for yourself; we live rather in the midst of it."

"It's very kind of you to say that. But I thought you Americans were always dancing."

"I suppose we dance a good deal; but I have never seen much of it. We don't do it much, at any rate, in summer. And I am sure," said Bessie Alden, "that we don't have so many balls as you have in England."

"Really!" exclaimed Lord Lambeth. "Ah, in England it all depends, you know."

"You will not think much of our gaieties," said the young girl, looking at him with a little mixture of interrogation and decision which was peculiar to her. The interrogation seemed earnest and the decision seemed arch; but the mixture, at any rate, was charming. "Those things, with us, are much less splendid than in England."

"I fancy you don't mean that," said Lord Lambeth, laughing.

"I assure you I mean everything I say," the young girl declared. "Certainly, from what I have read about English society, it is very different."

"Ah, well, you know," said her companion, "those things are often described by fellows who know nothing about them. You mustn't mind what you read."

"Oh, I *shall* mind what I read!" Bessie Alden rejoined. "When I read Thackeray and George Eliot, how can I help minding them?"

"Ah, well, Thackeray—and George Eliot," said the young nobleman; "I haven't read much of them."

"Don't you suppose they know about society?" asked Bessie Alden.

"Oh, I daresay they know; they were so very clever. But those fashionable novels," said Lord Lambeth, "they are awful rot, you know."

His companion looked at him a moment with her dark blue eyes, and then she looked down into the chasm where the water was tumbling about. "Do you mean Mrs. Gore, for instance?" she said presently, raising her eyes.

"I am afraid I haven't read that either," was the young man's rejoinder, laughing a little and blushing. "I am afraid you'll think I am not very intellectual."

"Reading Mrs. Gore is no proof of intellect. But I like reading everything about English life—even poor books. I am so curious about it."

"Aren't ladies always curious?" asked the young man, jestingly.

But Bessie Alden appeared to desire to answer his question seriously. "I don't think so—I don't think we are enough so—that we care about many things. So it's all the more of a compliment," she added, "that I should want to know so much about England."

The logic here seemed a little close; but Lord Lambeth, conscious of a compliment, found his natural modesty just at hand. "I am sure you know a great deal more than I do."

"I really think I know a great deal—for a person who has never been there."

"Have you really never been there?" cried Lord Lambeth. "Fancy!"

"Never—except in imagination," said the young girl.

"Fancy!" repeated her companion. "But I daresay you'll go soon, won't you?"

"It's the dream of my life!" declared Bessie Alden, smiling.

"But your sister seems to know a tremendous lot about London," Lord Lambeth went on.

The young girl was silent a moment. "My sister and I are two very different persons," she presently said. "She has been a great deal in Europe. She has been in England several times. She has known a great many English people."

"But you must have known some, too," said Lord Lambeth.

"I don't think that I have ever spoken to one before. You are the first Englishman that—to my knowledge—I have ever talked with."

Bessie Alden made this statement with a certain gravity—

almost, as it seemed to Lord Lambeth, an impressiveness. Attempts at impressiveness always made him feel awkward, and he now began to laugh and swing his stick. "Ah, you would have been sure to know!" he said. And then he added, after an instant—"I'm sorry I am not a better specimen."

The young girl looked away; but she smiled, laying aside her impressiveness. "You must remember that you are only a beginning," she said. Then she retraced her steps, leading the way back to the lawn, where they saw Mrs. Westgate come towards them with Percy Beaumont still at her side. "Perhaps I shall go to England next year," Miss Alden continued; "I want to, immensely. My sister is going to Europe, and she has asked me to go with her. If we go, I shall make her stay as long as possible in London."

"Ah, you must come in July," said Lord Lambeth. "That's the time when there is most going on."

"I don't think I can wait till July," the young girl rejoined. "By the first of May I shall be very impatient." They had gone farther, and Mrs. Westgate and her companion were near them. "Kitty," said Miss Alden, "I have given out that we are going to London next May. So please to conduct yourself accordingly."

Percy Beaumont wore a somewhat animated—even a slightly irritated—air. He was by no means so handsome a man as his cousin, although in his cousin's absence he might have passed for a striking specimen of the tall, muscular, fair-bearded, clear-eyed Englishman. Just now Beaumont's clear eyes, which were small and of a pale grey colour, had a rather troubled light, and, after glancing at Bessie Alden while she spoke, he rested them upon his kinsman. Mrs. Westgate meanwhile, with her superfluously pretty gaze, looked at every one alike.

"You had better wait till the time comes," she said to her sister. "Perhaps next May you won't care so much about London. Mr. Beaumont and I," she went on, smiling at her companion, "have had a tremendous discussion. We don't agree about anything. It's perfectly delightful."

"Oh, I say, Percy!" exclaimed Lord Lambeth.

"I disagree," said Beaumont, stroking down his black hair, "even to the point of not thinking it delightful."

"Oh, I say!" cried Lord Lambeth again.

"I don't see anything delightful in my disagreeing with Mrs. Westgate," said Percy Beaumont.

"Well, I do!" Mrs. Westgate declared; and she turned to her sister. "You know you have to go to town. The phaeton is there. You had better take Lord Lambeth."

At this point Percy Beaumont certainly looked straight at his kinsman; he tried to catch his eye. But Lord Lambeth would not look at him; his own eyes were better occupied. "I shall be very happy," cried Bessie Alden. "I am only going to some shops. But I will drive you about and show you the place."

"An American woman who respects herself," said Mrs. Westgate, turning to Beaumont with her bright expository air, "must buy something every day of her life. If she cannot do it herself, she must send out some member of her family for the purpose. So Bessie goes forth to fulfil my mission."

The young girl had walked away, with Lord Lambeth by her side, to whom she was talking still; and Percy Beaumont watched them as they passed towards the house. "She fulfils her own mission," he presently said; "that of being a very attractive young lady."

"I don't know that I should say very attractive," Mrs. Westgate rejoined. "She is not so much that as she is charming when you really know her. She is very shy."

"Oh indeed?" said Percy Beaumont.

"Extremely shy," Mrs. Westgate repeated. "But she is a dear good girl; she is a charming species of girl. She is not in the least a flirt; that isn't at all her line; she doesn't know the alphabet of that sort of thing. She is very simple—very serious. She has lived a great deal in Boston, with another sister of mine—the eldest of us—who married a Bostonian. She is very cultivated, not at all like me—I am not in the least cultivated. She has studied immensely and read everything; she is what they call in Boston 'thoughtful.'"

"A rum sort of girl for Lambeth to get hold of!" his lordship's kinsman privately reflected.

"I really believe," Mrs. Westgate continued, "that the most charming girl in the world is a Boston superstructure upon a New York *fonds*; or perhaps a New York superstructure upon a Boston *fonds*. At any rate it's the mixture," said Mrs. Westgate, who continued to give Percy Beaumont a great deal of information.

Lord Lambeth got into a little basket-phaeton with Bessie Alden, and she drove him down the long avenue, whose extent he had measured on foot a couple of hours before, into the ancient town, as it was called in that part of the world, of Newport. The ancient town was a curious affair—a collection of fresh-looking little wooden houses, painted white, scattered over a hill-side and clustered about a long, straight street, paved with enormous cobble-stones. There were plenty of shops—a large proportion of which appeared to be those of fruit-vendors, with piles of huge water-melons and pumpkins stacked in front of them; and, drawn up before the shops, or bumping about on the cobble-stones, were innumerable other basket-phaetons freighted with ladies of high fashion, who greeted each other from vehicle to vehicle and conversed on the edge of the pavement in a manner that struck Lord Lambeth as demonstrative—with a great many "Oh, my dears," and little quick exclamations and caresses. His companion went into seventeen shops—he amused himself with counting them—and accumulated, at the bottom of the phaeton, a pile of bundles that hardly left the young Englishman a place for his feet. As she had no groom nor footman, he sat in the phaeton to hold the ponies; where, although he was not a particularly acute observer, he saw much to entertain him—especially the ladies just mentioned, who wandered up and down with the appearance of a kind of aimless intentness, as if they were looking for something to buy, and who, tripping in and out of their vehicles, displayed remarkably pretty feet. It all seemed to Lord Lambeth very odd, and bright, and gay. Of course, before they got back to the villa, he had had a great deal of desultory conversation with Bessie Alden.

The young Englishmen spent the whole of that day and the whole of many successive days in what the French call the *intimité* of their new friends. They agreed that it was extremely jolly—that they had never known anything more agreeable. It is not proposed to narrate minutely the incidents of their sojourn on this charming shore; though if it were convenient I might present a record of impressions none the less delectable that they were not exhaustively analysed. Many of them still linger in the minds of our travellers, attended by a train of harmonious images—images of brilliant mornings on lawns and piazzas that overlooked the sea; of innumerable pretty girls; of infinite lounging and talking and laughing and flirting and lunching and dining; of universal friendliness and frankness; of occasions on which they knew every one and everything and had an extraordinary sense of ease; of drives and rides in the late afternoon, over gleaming beaches, on long sea-roads, beneath a sky lighted up by marvellous sunsets; of tea-tables, on the return, informal, irregular, agreeable; of evenings at open windows or on the perpetual verandahs, in the summer starlight, above the warm Atlantic. The young Englishmen were introduced to everybody, entertained by everybody, intimate with everybody. At the end of three days they had removed their luggage from the hotel, and had gone to stay with Mrs. Westgate—a step to which Percy Beaumont at first offered some conscientious opposition. I call his opposition conscientious because it was founded upon some talk that he had had, on the second day, with Bessie Alden. He had indeed had a good deal of talk with her, for she was not literally always in conversation with Lord Lambeth. He had meditated upon Mrs. Westgate's account of her sister and he discovered, for himself, that the young lady was clever and appeared to have read a great deal. She seemed very nice, though he could not make out that, as Mrs. Westgate had said, she was shy. If she was shy she carried it off very well.

"Mr. Beaumont," she had said, "please tell me something about Lord Lambeth's family. How would you say it in England?—his position."

"His position?" Percy Beaumont repeated.

"His rank—or whatever you call it. Unfortunately we haven't got a 'Peerage,' like the people in Thackeray."

"That's a great pity," said Beaumont. "You would find it all set forth there so much better than I can do it."

"He is a great noble, then?"

"Oh yes, he is a great noble."

"Is he a peer?"

"Almost."

"And has he any other title than Lord Lambeth?"

"His title is the Marquis of Lambeth," said Beaumont; and then he was silent; Bessie Alden appeared to be looking at him with interest. "He is the son of the Duke of Bayswater," he added, presently.

"The eldest son?"

"The only son."

"And are his parents living?"

"Oh yes; if his father were not living he would be a duke."

"So that when his father dies," pursued Bessie Alden, with more simplicity than might have been expected in a clever girl, "he will become Duke of Bayswater?"

"Of course," said Percy Beaumont. "But his father is in excellent health."

"And his mother?"

Beaumont smiled a little. "The Duchess is uncommonly robust."

"And has he any sisters?"

"Yes, there are two."

"And what are they called?"

"One of them is married. She is the Countess of Pimlico."

"And the other?"

"The other is unmarried; she is plain Lady Julia."

Bessie Alden looked at him a moment. "Is she very plain?"

Beaumont began to laugh again. "You would not find her so handsome as her brother," he said; and it was after this that he attempted to dissuade the heir of the Duke of Bayswater from accepting Mrs. Westgate's invitation. "Depend upon it," he said, "that girl means to try for you."

"It seems to me you are doing your best to make a fool of me," the modest young nobleman answered.

"She has been asking me," said Beaumont, "all about your people and your possessions."

"I am sure it is very good of her!" Lord Lambeth rejoined.

"Well, then," observed his companion, "if you go, you go with your eyes open."

"Damn my eyes!" exclaimed Lord Lambeth. "If one is to be a dozen times a day at the house, it is a great deal more convenient to sleep there. I am sick of travelling up and down this beastly Avenue."

Since he had determined to go, Percy Beaumont would of course have been very sorry to allow him to go alone; he was a man of conscience, and he remembered his promise to the Duchess. It was obviously the memory of this promise that made him say to his companion a couple of days later that he rather wondered he should be so fond of that girl.

"In the first place, how do you know how fond I am of her?" asked Lord Lambeth. "And in the second place, why shouldn't I be fond of her?"

"I shouldn't think she would be in your line."

"What do you call my 'line'? You don't set her down as 'fast'?"

"Exactly so. Mrs. Westgate tells me that there is no such thing as the 'fast girl' in America; that it's an English invention, and that the term has no meaning here."

"All the better. It's an animal I detest."

"You prefer a blue-stocking."

"Is that what you call Miss Alden?"

"Her sister tells me," said Percy Beaumont, "that she is tremendously literary."

"I don't know anything about that. She is certainly very clever."

"Well," said Beaumont, "I should have supposed you would have found that sort of thing awfully slow."

"In point of fact," Lord Lambeth rejoined, "I find it uncommonly lively."

After this, Percy Beaumont held his tongue; but on August 10th he wrote to the Duchess of Bayswater. He was, as I have said, a man of conscience, and he had a strong, incorruptible sense of the proprieties of life. His kinsman, meanwhile, was having a great deal of talk with Bessie Alden—on the red searocks beyond the lawn; in the course of long island rides, with a slow return in the glowing twilight; on the deep verandah, late in the evening. Lord Lambeth, who had stayed at many houses, had never stayed at a house in which it was possible for a young man to converse so frequently with a young lady. This young lady no longer applied to Percy Beaumont for information concerning his lordship. She addressed herself directly to the young nobleman. She asked him a great many questions, some of which bored him a little; for he took no pleasure in talking about himself.

"Lord Lambeth," said Bessie Alden, "are you an hereditary legislator?"

"Oh, I say," cried Lord Lambeth, "don't make me call myself such names as that."

"But you are a member of Parliament," said the young girl.

"I don't like the sound of that either."

"Doesn't your father sit in the House of Lords?" Bessie Alden went on.

"Very seldom," said Lord Lambeth.

"Is it an important position?" she asked.

"Oh dear no," said Lord Lambeth.

"I should think it would be very grand," said Bessie Alden, "to possess simply by an accident of birth the right to make laws for a great nation."

"Ah, but one doesn't make laws. It's a great humbug."

"I don't believe that," the young girl declared. "It must be a great privilege, and I should think that if one thought of it in the right way—from a high point of view—it would be very inspiring."

"The less one thinks of it the better," Lord Lambeth affirmed.

"I think it's tremendous," said Bessie Alden; and on another occasion she asked him if he had any tenantry. Hereupon it was that, as I have said, he was a little bored.

"Do you want to buy up their leases?" he asked.

"Well—have you got any livings?" she demanded.

"Oh, I say!" he cried. "Have you got a clergyman that is looking out?" But she made him tell her that he had a Castle; he confessed to but one. It was the place in which he had been born and brought up, and, as he had an old-time liking for it, he was beguiled into describing it a little and saying it was really very jolly. Bessie Alden listened with great interest, and declared that she would give the world to see such a place. Whereupon—"It would be awfully kind of you to come and stay there," said Lord Lambeth. He took a vague satisfaction in the circumstance that Percy Beaumont had not heard him make the remark I have just recorded.

Mr. Westgate, all this time, had not, as they said at New-port, "come on." His wife more than once announced that she expected him on the morrow; but on the morrow she wandered about a little, with a telegram in her jewelled fingers, declaring it was very tiresome that his business detained him in New York; that he could only hope the Englishmen were having a good time. "I must say," said Mrs. Westgate, "that it is no thanks to him if you are!" And she went on to explain, while she continued that slow-paced promenade which enabled her well-adjusted skirts to display themselves so advantageously, that unfortunately in America there was no leisure-class. It was Lord Lambeth's theory, freely propounded when the young men were together, that Percy Beaumont was having a very good time with Mrs. Westgate, and that under the pretext of meeting for the purpose of animated discussion, they were indulging in practices that imparted a shade of hypocrisy to the lady's regret for her husband's absence.

"I assure you we are always discussing and differing," said Percy Beaumont. "She is awfully argumentative. American ladies certainly don't mind contradicting you. Upon my word I don't think I was ever treated so by a woman before. She's so devilish positive."

Mrs. Westgate's positive quality, however, evidently had its attractions; for Beaumont was constantly at his hostess's side. He detached himself one day to the extent of going to New York to talk over the Tennessee Central with Mr. Westgate; but he was absent only forty-eight hours, during which, with Mr. Westgate's assistance, he completely settled this piece of business. "They certainly do things quickly in New York," he observed to his cousin; and he added that Mr. Westgate had seemed very uneasy lest his wife should miss her visitor—he had been in such an awful hurry to send him back to her. "I'm afraid you'll never come up to an American husband—if that's what the wives expect," he said to Lord Lambeth.

Mrs. Westgate, however, was not to enjoy much longer the entertainment with which an indulgent husband had desired to keep her provided. On August 21st Lord Lambeth received a telegram from his mother, requesting him to return immediately to England; his father had been taken ill, and it was his filial duty to come to him.

The young Englishman was visibly annoyed. "What the deuce does it mean?" he asked of his kinsman. "What am I to do?"

Percy Beaumont was annoyed as well; he had deemed it his duty, as I have narrated, to write to the Duchess, but he had not expected that this distinguished woman would act so promptly upon his hint. "It means," he said, "that your father is laid up. I don't suppose it's anything serious; but you have no option. Take the first steamer; but don't be alarmed."

Lord Lambeth made his farewells; but the few last words that he exchanged with Bessie Alden are the only ones that have a place in our record. "Of course I needn't assure you," he said, "that if you should come to England next year, I expect to be the first person that you inform of it."

Bessie Alden looked at him a little and she smiled. "Oh, if we come to London," she answered, "I should think you would hear of it."

Percy Beaumont returned with his cousin, and his sense of duty compelled him, one windless afternoon, in mid-Atlantic, to say to Lord Lambeth that he suspected that the Duchess's telegram was in part the result of something he himself had written to her. "I wrote to her—as I explicitly notified you I had promised to do—that you were extremely interested in a little American girl."

Lord Lambeth was extremely angry, and he indulged for some moments in the simple language of resentment. But I have said that he was a reasonable young man, and I can give no better proof of it than the fact that he remarked to his companion at the end of half-an-hour—"You were quite right after all. I am very much interested in her. Only, to be fair," he added, "you should have told my mother also that she is not—seriously—interested in me."

Percy Beaumont gave a little laugh. "There is nothing so charming as modesty in a young man in your position. That speech is a capital proof that you are sweet on her."

"She is not interested—she is not!" Lord Lambeth repeated.

"My dear fellow," said his companion, "you are very far gone."

IV.

In point of fact, as Percy Beaumont would have said, Mrs. Westgate disembarked on the 18th of May on the British coast. She was accompanied by her sister, but she was not attended by any other member of her family. To the deprivation of her husband's society Mrs. Westgate was, however, habituated; she had made half-a-dozen journeys to Europe without him, and she now accounted for his absence, to interrogative friends on this side of the Atlantic, by allusion to the regrettable but conspicuous fact that in America there was no leisure-class. The two ladies came up to London and alighted at Jones's Hotel, where Mrs. Westgate, who had made on former occasions the most agreeable impression at this establishment, received an obsequious greeting. Bessie Alden had felt much excited about coming to England; she had expected the "associations" would be very charming, that it would be an infinite pleasure to rest her eyes upon the things she had read about in the poets and historians. She was very fond of the poets and historians, of the picturesque, of the past, of retrospect, of mementoes and reverberations of greatness; so that on coming into the great English world, where strangeness and familiarity would go hand in hand, she was prepared for a multitude of fresh emotions. They began very promptly—these tender, fluttering sensations; they began with the sight of the beautiful English landscape, whose dark richness was quickened and brightened by the season; with the carpeted fields and flowering hedge-rows, as she looked at them from the window of the train; with the spires of the rural churches, peeping above the rook-haunted tree-tops; with the oak-studded parks, the ancient homes, the cloudy light, the speech, the manners, the thousand differences. Mrs. Westgate's impressions had of course much less novelty and keenness, and she gave but a wandering attention to her sister's ejaculations and rhapsodies.

"You know my enjoyment of England is not so intellectual as Bessie's," she said to several of her friends in the course of her visit to this country. "And yet if it is not intellectual, I can't say it is physical. I don't think I can quite say what it is, my enjoyment of England." When once it was settled that the two ladies should come abroad and should spend a few weeks in England on their way to the Continent, they of course exchanged a good many allusions to their London acquaintance.

"It will certainly be much nicer having friends there," Bessie Alden had said one day, as she sat on the sunny deck of the steamer, at her sister's feet, on a large blue rug.

"Whom do you mean by friends?" Mrs. Westgate asked.

"All those English gentlemen whom you have known and entertained. Captain Littledale, for instance. And Lord Lambeth and Mr. Beaumont," added Bessie Alden.

"Do you expect them to give us a very grand reception?"

Bessie reflected a moment; she was addicted, as we know, to reflection. "Well, yes."

"My poor sweet child!" murmured her sister.

"What have I said that is so silly?" asked Bessie.

"You are a little too simple; just a little. It is very becoming, but it pleases people at your expense."

"I am certainly too simple to understand you," said Bessie.

"Shall I tell you a story?" asked her sister.

"If you would be so good. That is what they do to amuse simple people."

Mrs. Westgate consulted her memory, while her companion sat gazing at the shining sea. "Did you ever hear of the Duke of Green-Erin?"

"I think not," said Bessie.

"Well, it's no matter," her sister went on.

"It's a proof of my simplicity."

"My story is meant to illustrate that of some other people," said Mrs. Westgate. "The Duke of Green-Erin is what they call in England a great swell; and some five years ago he came to America. He spent most of his time in New York, and in New York he spent his days and his nights at the Butterworths'. You have heard at least of the Butterworths. *Bien*. They did everything in the world for him—they turned themselves inside out. They gave him a dozen dinner-parties and balls, and were the means of his being invited to fifty more. At first he used to come into Mrs. Butterworth's box at the opera in a tweed travelling-suit; but some one stopped that. At any rate, he had a beautiful time, and they parted the best friends in the world. Two years elapse, and the Butterworths come abroad and go to London. The first thing they see in all the papers—in England those things are in the most prominent place—is that the Duke of Green-Erin has arrived in town for the Season. They wait a little, and then Mr. Butterworth—as polite as ever—goes and leaves a card. They wait a little more; the visit is not returned; they wait three weeks—*silence de mort*—the Duke gives no sign. The Butterworths see a lot of other people, put down the Duke of Green-Erin as a rude, ungrateful man, and forget all about him. One fine day they go to Ascot Races, and there they meet him face to face. He stares a moment and then comes up to Mr. Butterworth, taking something from his pocket-book—something which proves to be a bank-note. 'I'm glad to see you, Mr. Butterworth,' he says, 'so that I can pay you that ten pounds I lost to you in New York. I saw the other day you remembered our bet; here are the ten pounds, Mr. Butterworth. Good-bye, Mr. Butterworth.' And off he goes, and that's the last they see of the Duke of Green-Erin."

"Is that your story?" asked Bessie Alden.

"Don't you think it's interesting?" her sister replied.

"I don't believe it," said the young girl.

"Ah!" cried Mrs. Westgate, "you are not so simple after all. Believe it or not as you please; there is no smoke without fire."

"Is that the way," asked Bessie after a moment, "that you expect your friends to treat you?"

"I defy them to treat me very ill, because I shall not give them the opportunity. With the best will in the world, in that case, they can't be very disobliging."

Bessie Alden was silent a moment. "I don't see what makes you talk that way," she said. "The English are a great people."

"Exactly; and that is just the way they have grown great—by dropping you when you have ceased to be useful. People say they are not clever; but I think they are very clever."

"You know you have liked them—all the Englishmen you have seen," said Bessie.

"They have liked me," her sister rejoined; "it would be more correct to say that. And of course one likes that."

Bessie Alden resumed for some moments her studies in sea-green. "Well," she said, "whether they like me or not, I mean to like them. And happily," she added, "Lord Lambeth does not owe me ten pounds."

During the first few days after their arrival at Jones's Hotel our charming Americans were much occupied with what they would have called looking about them. They found occasion to make a large number of purchases, and their opportunities for conversation were such only as were offered by the deferential London shopmen. Bessie Alden, even in driving from the station, took an immense fancy to the British metropolis, and, at the risk of exhibiting her as a young woman of vulgar tastes, it must be recorded that for a considerable period she desired no higher pleasure than to drive about the crowded streets in a Hansom cab. To her attentive eyes they were full of a strange picturesque life, and it is at least beneath the dignity of our historic muse to enumerate the trivial objects and incidents which this simple young lady from Boston found so entertaining. It may be freely mentioned, however, that whenever, after a round of visits in Bond Street and Regent Street, she was about to return with her sister to Jones's Hotel, she made an earnest request that they should be driven home by way of Westminster Abbey. She had begun by asking whether it would not be possible to take the Tower on the way to their lodgings; but it happened that at a more primitive stage of her culture Mrs. Westgate had paid a visit to this venerable monument, which she spoke of ever afterwards, vaguely, as a dreadful disappointment; so that she expressed the liveliest disapproval of any attempt to combine historical researches with the purchase of hair-brushes and note-paper. The most she would consent to do in this line was to spend half-an-hour at Madame Tussaud's, where she saw several dusty wax effigies of members of the Royal Family. She told Bessie that if she wished to go to the Tower she must get some one else to take her. Bessie expressed hereupon an earnest disposition to go alone; but upon this proposal as well Mrs. Westgate sprinkled cold water.

"Remember," she said, "that you are not in your innocent little Boston. It is not a question of walking up and down Beacon Street." Then she went on to explain that there were two classes of American girls in Europe—those that walked about alone and those that did not. "You happen to belong, my dear," she said to her sister, "to the class that does not."

"It is only," answered Bessie, laughing, "because you happen to prevent me." And she devoted much private meditation to this question of effecting a visit to the Tower of London.

Suddenly it seemed as if the problem might be solved; the two ladies at Jones's Hotel received a visit from Willie Woodley. Such was the social appellation of a young American who had sailed from New York a few days after their own departure, and who, having the privilege of intimacy with them in that city, had lost no time, on his arrival in London, in coming to pay them his respects. He had, in fact, gone to see them directly after going to see his tailor; than which there can be no greater exhibition of promptitude on the part of a young American who has just alighted at the Charing Cross Hotel. He was a slim, pale youth, of the most amiable disposition, famous for the skill with which he led the "German" in New York. Indeed, by the young ladies who habitually figured in this fashionable frolic he was believed to be "the best dancer in the world;" it was in these terms that he was always spoken of, and that his identity was indicated. He was the gentlest, softest young man it was possible to meet; he was beautifully dressed—"in the English style"—and he knew an immense deal about London. He had been at Newport during the previous summer, at the time of our young Englishmen's visit, and he took extreme pleasure in the society of Bessie Alden, whom he always addressed as "Miss Bessie." She immediately arranged with him, in the presence of her sister, that he should conduct her to the scene of Lady Jane Grey's execution.

"You may do as you please," said Mrs. Westgate. "Only—if you desire the information—it is not the custom here for young ladies to knock about London with young men."

"Miss Bessie has waltzed with me so often," observed Willie Woodley; "she can surely go out with me in a Hansom."

"I consider waltzing," said Mrs. Westgate, "the most innocent pleasure of our time."

"It's a compliment to our time!" exclaimed the young man, with a little laugh, in spite of himself.

"I don't see why I should regard what is done here," said Bessie Alden. "Why should I suffer the restrictions of a society of which I enjoy none of the privileges?"

"That's very good—very good," murmured Willie Woodley.

"Oh, go to the Tower, and feel the axe, if you like!" said Mrs. Westgate. "I consent to your going with Mr. Woodley; but I should not let you go with an Englishman."

"Miss Bessie wouldn't care to go with an Englishman!" Mr. Woodley declared, with a faint asperity that was, perhaps, not unnatural in a young man who, dressing in the manner that I have indicated, and knowing a great deal, as I have said, about London, saw no reason for drawing these sharp distinctions. He agreed upon a day with Miss Bessie—a day of that same week.

An ingenious mind might, perhaps, trace a connection between the young girl's allusion to her destitution of social privileges and a question she asked on the morrow as she sat with her sister at lunch.

"Don't you mean to write to—to any one?" said Bessie.

"I wrote this morning to Captain Littledale," Mrs. Westgate replied.

"But Mr. Woodley said that Captain Littledale had gone to India."

"He said he thought he had heard so; he knew nothing about it."

For a moment Bessie Alden said nothing more; then, at last, "And don't you intend to write to—to Mr. Beaumont?" she inquired.

"You mean to Lord Lambeth," said her sister.

"I said Mr. Beaumont because he was so good a friend of yours."

Mrs. Westgate looked at the young girl with sisterly candour. "I don't care two straws for Mr. Beaumont."

"You were certainly very nice to him."

"I am nice to every one," said Mrs. Westgate, simply.

"To every one but me," rejoined Bessie, smiling.

Her sister continued to look at her; then, at last, "Are you in love with Lord Lambeth?" she asked.

The young girl stared a moment, and the question was apparently too humorous even to make her blush. "Not that I know of," she answered.

"Because if you are," Mrs. Westgate went on, "I shall certainly not send for him."

"That proves what I said," declared Bessie, smiling—"that you are not nice to me."

"It would be a poor service, my dear child," said her sister.

"In what sense? There is nothing against Lord Lambeth, that I know of."

Mrs. Westgate was silent a moment. "You *are* in love with him, then?"

Bessie stared again; but this time she blushed a little. "Ah! if you won't be serious," she answered, "we will not mention him again."

For some moments Lord Lambeth was not mentioned again, and it was Mrs. Westgate who, at the end of this period, reverted to him. "Of course I will let him know we are here; because I think he would be hurt—justly enough—if we should go away without seeing him. It is fair to give him a chance to come and thank me for the kindness we showed him. But I don't want to seem eager."

"Neither do I," said Bessie, with a little laugh.

"Though I confess," added her sister, "that I am curious to see how he will behave."

"He behaved very well at Newport."

"Newport is not London. At Newport he could do as he liked; but here, it is another affair. He has to have an eye to consequences."

"If he had more freedom, then, at Newport," argued Bessie, "it is the more to his credit that he behaved well; and if he has to be so careful here, it is possible he will behave even better."

"Better—better," repeated her sister. "My dear child, what is your point of view?"

"How do you mean—my point of view?"

"Don't you care for Lord Lambeth—a little?"

This time Bessie Alden was displeased; she slowly got up

from table, turning her face away from her sister. "You will oblige me by not talking so," she said.

Mrs. Westgate sat watching her for some moments as she moved slowly about the room and went and stood at the window. "I will write to him this afternoon," she said at last.

"Do as you please!" Bessie answered; and presently she turned round. "I am not afraid to say that I like Lord Lambeth. I like him very much."

"He is not clever," Mrs. Westgate declared.

"Well, there have been clever people whom I have disliked," said Bessie Alden; "so that I suppose I may like a stupid one. Besides, Lord Lambeth is not stupid."

"Not so stupid as he looks!" exclaimed her sister, smiling.

"If I were in love with Lord Lambeth, as you said just now, it would be bad policy on your part to abuse him."

"My dear child, don't give me lessons in policy!" cried Mrs. Westgate. "The policy I mean to follow is very deep."

The young girl began to walk about the room again; then she stopped before her sister. "I have never heard in the course of five minutes," she said, "so many hints and innuendoes. I wish you would tell me in plain English what you mean."

"I mean that you may be much annoyed."

"That is still only a hint," said Bessie.

Her sister looked at her, hesitating an instant. "It will be said of you that you have come after Lord Lambeth—that you followed him."

Bessie Alden threw back her pretty head like a startled hind, and a look flashed into her face that made Mrs. Westgate rise from her chair. "Who says such things as that?" she demanded.

"People here."

"I don't believe it," said Bessie.

"You have a very convenient faculty of doubt. But my policy will be, as I say, very deep. I shall leave you to find out this kind of thing for yourself."

Bessie fixed her eyes upon her sister, and Mrs. Westgate thought for a moment there were tears in them. "Do they talk that way here?" she asked.

"You will see. I shall leave you alone."

"Don't leave me alone," said Bessie Alden. "Take me away."

"No; I want to see what you make of it," her sister continued.

"I don't understand."

"You will understand after Lord Lambeth has come," said Mrs. Westgate, with a little laugh.

The two ladies had arranged that on this afternoon Willie Woodley should go with them to Hyde Park, where Bessie Alden expected to derive much entertainment from sitting on a little green chair, under the great trees, beside Rotten Row. The want of a suitable escort had hitherto rendered this pleasure inaccessible; but no escort, now, for such an expedition, could have been more suitable than their devoted young countryman, whose mission in life, it might almost be said, was to find chairs for ladies, and who appeared on the stroke of half-past five with a white camellia in his button-hole.

"I have written to Lord Lambeth, my dear," said Mrs. Westgate to her sister, on coming into the room where Bessie Alden, drawing on her long grey gloves, was entertaining their visitor.

Bessie said nothing, but Willie Woodley exclaimed that his lordship was in town; he had seen his name in the *Morning Post*.

"Do you read the *Morning Post*?" asked Mrs. Westgate.

"Oh yes; it's great fun," Willie Woodley affirmed.

"I want so to see it," said Bessie, "there is so much about it in Thackeray."

"I will send it to you every morning," said Willie Woodley.

He found them what Bessie Alden thought excellent places, under the great trees, beside the famous avenue whose humours had been made familiar to the young girl's childhood by the pictures in *Punch*. The day was bright and warm, and the crowd of riders and spectators and the great procession of carriages were proportionately dense and brilliant. The scene bore the stamp of the London Season at its height, and Bessie Alden found more entertainment in it than she was able to express to her companions. She sat silent, under her parasol, and her imagination, according to its wont, let itself loose into the great changing assemblage of striking and suggestive

figures. They stirred up a host of old impressions and preconceptions, and she found herself fitting a history to this person
and a theory to that, and making a place for them all in her
little private museum of types. But if she said little, her sister
on one side and Willie Woodley on the other expressed themselves in lively alternation.

"Look at that green dress with blue flounces," said Mrs.
Westgate. *"Quelle toilette!"*

"That's the Marquis of Blackborough," said the young
man—"the one in the white coat. I heard him speak the other
night in the House of Lords; it was something about ramrods;
he called them *wamwods*. He's an awful swell."

"Did you ever see anything like the way they are pinned
back?" Mrs. Westgate resumed. "They never know where to
stop."

"They do nothing but stop," said Willie Woodley. "It prevents them from walking. Here comes a great celebrity—Lady
Beatrice Bellevue. She's awfully fast; see what little steps she
takes."

"Well, my dear," Mrs. Westgate pursued, "I hope you are
getting some ideas for your *couturière*?"

"I am getting plenty of ideas," said Bessie, "but I don't
know that my *couturière* would appreciate them."

Willie Woodley presently perceived a friend on horseback,
who drove up beside the barrier of the Row and beckoned to
him. He went forward and the crowd of pedestrians closed
about him, so that for some ten minutes he was hidden from
sight. At last he reappeared, bringing a gentleman with
him—a gentleman whom Bessie at first supposed to be his
friend dismounted. But at a second glance she found herself
looking at Lord Lambeth, who was shaking hands with her
sister.

"I found him over there," said Willie Woodley, "and I told
him you were here."

And then Lord Lambeth, touching his hat a little, shook
hands with Bessie. "Fancy your being here!" he said. He was
blushing and smiling; he looked very handsome, and he had
a kind of splendour that he had not had in America. Bessie
Alden's imagination, as we know, was just then in exercise; so
that the tall young Englishman, as he stood there looking

down at her, had the benefit of it. "He is handsomer and more splendid than anything I have ever seen," she said to herself. And then she remembered that he was a Marquis, and she thought he looked like a Marquis.

"Really, you know," he cried, "you ought to have let a man know you were here!"

"I wrote to you an hour ago," said Mrs. Westgate.

"Doesn't all the world know it?" asked Bessie, smiling.

"I assure you I didn't know it!" cried Lord Lambeth. "Upon my honour I hadn't heard of it. Ask Woodley now; had I, Woodley?"

"Well, I think you are rather a humbug," said Willie Woodley.

"You don't believe that—do you, Miss Alden?" asked his lordship. "You don't believe I'm a humbug, eh?"

"No," said Bessie, "I don't."

"You are too tall to stand up, Lord Lambeth," Mrs. Westgate observed. "You are only tolerable when you sit down. Be so good as to get a chair."

He found a chair and placed it sidewise, close to the two ladies. "If I hadn't met Woodley I should never have found you," he went on. "Should I, Woodley?"

"Well, I guess not," said the young American.

"Not even with my letter?" asked Mrs. Westgate.

"Ah, well, I haven't got your letter yet; I suppose I shall get it this evening. It was awfully kind of you to write."

"So I said to Bessie," observed Mrs. Westgate.

"Did she say so, Miss Alden?" Lord Lambeth inquired. "I daresay you have been here a month."

"We have been here three," said Mrs. Westgate.

"Have you been here three months?" the young man asked again of Bessie.

"It seems a long time," Bessie answered.

"I say, after that you had better not call me a humbug!" cried Lord Lambeth. "I have only been in town three weeks; but you must have been hiding away. I haven't seen you anywhere."

"Where should you have seen us—where should we have gone?" asked Mrs. Westgate.

"You should have gone to Hurlingham," said Willie Woodley.

"No, let Lord Lambeth tell us," Mrs. Westgate insisted.

"There are plenty of places to go to," said Lord Lambeth—"each one stupider than the other. I mean people's houses; they send you cards."

"No one has sent us cards," said Bessie.

"We are very quiet," her sister declared. "We are here as travellers."

"We have been to Madame Tussaud's," Bessie pursued.

"Oh, I say!" cried Lord Lambeth.

"We thought we should find your image there," said Mrs. Westgate—"yours and Mr. Beaumont's."

"In the Chamber of Horrors?" laughed the young man.

"It did duty very well for a party," said Mrs. Westgate. "All the women were *décolletées*, and many of the figures looked as if they could speak if they tried."

"Upon my word," Lord Lambeth rejoined, "you see people at London parties that look as if they couldn't speak if they tried."

"Do you think Mr. Woodley could find us Mr. Beaumont?" asked Mrs. Westgate.

Lord Lambeth stared and looked round him. "I daresay he could. Beaumont often comes here. Don't you think you could find him, Woodley? Make a dive into the crowd."

"Thank you; I have had enough diving," said Willie Woodley. "I will wait till Mr. Beaumont comes to the surface."

"I will bring him to see you," said Lord Lambeth; "where are you staying?"

"You will find the address in my letter—Jones's Hotel."

"Oh, one of those places just out of Piccadilly? Beastly hole, isn't it?" Lord Lambeth inquired.

"I believe it's the best hotel in London," said Mrs. Westgate.

"But they give you awful rubbish to eat, don't they?" his lordship went on.

"Yes," said Mrs. Westgate.

"I always feel so sorry for the people that come up to town and go to live in those places," continued the young man. "They eat nothing but poison."

"Oh, I say!" cried Willie Woodley.

"Well, how do you like London, Miss Alden?" Lord Lambeth asked, unperturbed by this ejaculation.

"I think it's grand," said Bessie Alden.

"My sister likes it, in spite of the 'poison'!" Mrs. Westgate exclaimed.

"I hope you are going to stay a long time."

"As long as I can," said Bessie.

"And where is Mr. Westgate?" asked Lord Lambeth of this gentleman's wife.

"He's where he always is—in that tiresome New York."

"He must be tremendously clever," said the young man.

"I suppose he is," said Mrs. Westgate.

Lord Lambeth sat for nearly an hour with his American friends; but it is not our purpose to relate their conversation in full. He addressed a great many remarks to Bessie Alden, and finally turned towards her altogether, while Willie Woodley entertained Mrs. Westgate. Bessie herself said very little; she was on her guard, thinking of what her sister had said to her at lunch. Little by little, however, she interested herself in Lord Lambeth again, as she had done at Newport; only it seemed to her that here he might become more interesting. He would be an unconscious part of the antiquity, the impressiveness, the picturesqueness of England; and poor Bessie Alden, like many a Yankee maiden, was terribly at the mercy of picturesqueness.

"I have often wished I were at Newport again," said the young man. "Those days I spent at your sister's were awfully jolly."

"We enjoyed them very much; I hope your father is better."

"Oh dear, yes. When I got to England, he was out grouse-shooting. It was what you call in America a gigantic fraud. My mother had got nervous. My three weeks at Newport seemed like a happy dream."

"America certainly is very different from England," said Bessie.

"I hope you like England better, eh?" Lord Lambeth rejoined, almost persuasively.

"No Englishman can ask that seriously of a person of another country."

Her companion looked at her for a moment. "You mean it's a matter of course?"

"If I were English," said Bessie, "it would certainly seem to me a matter of course that every one should be a good patriot."

"Oh dear, yes; patriotism is everything," said Lord Lambeth, not quite following, but very contented. "Now, what are you going to do here?"

"On Thursday I am going to the Tower."

"The Tower?"

"The Tower of London. Did you never hear of it?"

"Oh yes, I have been there," said Lord Lambeth. "I was taken there by my governess, when I was six years old. It's a rum idea, your going there."

"Do give me a few more rum ideas," said Bessie. "I want to see everything of that sort. I am going to Hampton Court, and to Windsor, and to the Dulwich Gallery."

Lord Lambeth seemed greatly amused. "I wonder you don't go to the Rosherville Gardens."

"Are they interesting?" asked Bessie.

"Oh, wonderful!"

"Are they very old? That's all I care for," said Bessie.

"They are tremendously old; they are all falling to ruins."

"I think there is nothing so charming as an old ruinous garden," said the young girl. "We must certainly go there."

Lord Lambeth broke out into merriment. "I say, Woodley," he cried, "here's Miss Alden wants to go to the Rosherville Gardens!"

Willie Woodley looked a little blank; he was caught in the fact of ignorance of an apparently conspicuous feature of London life. But in a moment he turned it off. "Very well," he said, "I'll write for a permit."

Lord Lambeth's exhilaration increased. "'Gad, I believe you Americans would go anywhere!" he cried.

"We wish to go to Parliament," said Bessie. "That's one of the first things."

"Oh, it would bore you to death!" cried the young man.

"We wish to hear you speak."

"I never speak—except to young ladies," said Lord Lambeth, smiling.

Bessie Alden looked at him awhile; smiling, too, in the shadow of her parasol. "You are very strange," she murmured. "I don't think I approve of you."

"Ah, now, don't be severe, Miss Alden!" said Lord Lambeth, smiling still more. "Please don't be severe. I want you to like me—awfully."

"To like you awfully? You must not laugh at me, then, when I make mistakes. I consider it my right—as a free-born American—to make as many mistakes as I choose."

"Upon my word, I didn't laugh at you," said Lord Lambeth.

"And not only that," Bessie went on; "but I hold that all my mistakes shall be set down to my credit. You must think the better of me for them."

"I can't think better of you than I do," the young man declared.

Bessie Alden looked at him a moment again. "You certainly speak very well to young ladies. But why don't you address the House?—isn't that what they call it?"

"Because I have nothing to say," said Lord Lambeth.

"Haven't you a great position?" asked Bessie Alden.

He looked a moment at the back of his glove. "I'll set that down," he said, "as one of your mistakes—to your credit." And, as if he disliked talking about his position, he changed the subject. "I wish you would let me go with you to the Tower, and to Hampton Court, and to all those other places."

"We shall be most happy," said Bessie.

"And of course I shall be delighted to show you the Houses of Parliament—some day that suits you. There are a lot of things I want to do for you. I want you to have a good time. And I should like very much to present some of my friends to you, if it wouldn't bore you. Then it would be awfully kind of you to come down to Branches."

"We are much obliged to you, Lord Lambeth," said Bessie. "What is Branches?"

"It's a house in the country. I think you might like it."

Willie Woodley and Mrs. Westgate, at this moment, were sitting in silence, and the young man's ear caught these last words of Lord Lambeth's. "He's inviting Miss Bessie to one of his castles," he murmured to his companion.

Mrs. Westgate, foreseeing what she mentally called "complications," immediately got up; and the two ladies, taking leave of Lord Lambeth, returned, under Mr. Woodley's conduct, to Jones's Hotel.

V.

Lord Lambeth came to see them on the morrow, bringing Percy Beaumont with him—the latter having instantly declared his intention of neglecting none of the usual offices of civility. This declaration, however, when his kinsman informed him of the advent of their American friends, had been preceded by another remark.

"Here they are, then, and you are in for it."

"What am I in for?" demanded Lord Lambeth.

"I will let your mother give it a name. With all respect to whom," added Percy Beaumont, "I must decline on this occasion to do any more police duty. Her Grace must look after you herself."

"I will give her a chance," said her Grace's son, a trifle grimly. "I shall make her go and see them."

"She won't do it, my boy."

"We'll see if she doesn't," said Lord Lambeth.

But if Percy Beaumont took a sombre view of the arrival of the two ladies at Jones's Hotel, he was sufficiently a man of the world to offer them a smiling countenance. He fell into animated conversation—conversation, at least, that was animated on her side—with Mrs. Westgate, while his companion made himself agreeable to the younger lady. Mrs. Westgate began confessing and protesting, declaring and expounding.

"I must say London is a great deal brighter and prettier just now than it was when I was here last—in the month of November. There is evidently a great deal going on, and you seem to have a good many flowers. I have no doubt it is very charming for all you people, and that you amuse yourselves immensely. It is very good of you to let Bessie and me come and sit and look at you. I suppose you will think I am very satirical, but I must confess that that's the feeling I have in London."

"I am afraid I don't quite understand to what feeling you allude," said Percy Beaumont.

"The feeling that it's all very well for you English people. Everything is beautifully arranged for you."

"It seems to me it is very well for some Americans, sometimes," rejoined Beaumont.

"For some of them, yes—if they like to be patronised. But I must say I don't like to be patronised. I may be very eccentric and undisciplined and unreasonable; but I confess I never was fond of patronage. I like to associate with people on the same terms as I do in my own country; that's a peculiar taste that I have. But here people seem to expect something else—Heaven knows what! I am afraid you will think I am very ungrateful, for I certainly have received a great deal of attention. The last time I was here, a lady sent me a message that I was at liberty to come and see her."

"Dear me, I hope you didn't go," observed Percy Beaumont.

"You are deliciously *naïf*, I must say that for you!" Mrs. Westgate exclaimed. "It must be a great advantage to you here in London. I suppose that if I myself had a little more *naïveté*, I should enjoy it more. I should be content to sit on a chair in the Park, and see the people pass, and be told that this is the Duchess of Suffolk, and that is the Lord Chamberlain, and that I must be thankful for the privilege of beholding them. I daresay it is very wicked and critical of me to ask for anything else. But I was always critical, and I freely confess to the sin of being fastidious. I am told there is some remarkably superior second-rate society provided here for strangers. *Merci!* I don't want any superior second-rate society. I want the society that I have been accustomed to."

"I hope you don't call Lambeth and me second-rate," Beaumont interposed.

"Oh, I am accustomed to you!" said Mrs. Westgate. "Do you know that you English sometimes make the most wonderful speeches? The first time I came to London, I went out to dine—as I told you, I have received a great deal of attention. After dinner, in the drawing-room, I had some conversation with an old lady; I assure you I had. I forget what we talked about; but she presently said, in allusion to something we were discussing, 'Oh, you know, the aristocracy do so-and-so; but in one's own class of life it is very different.' In one's own class of life! What is a poor unprotected American woman to do in a country where she is liable to have that sort of thing said to her?"

"You seem to get hold of some very queer old ladies; I compliment you on your acquaintance!" Percy Beaumont exclaimed. "If you are trying to bring me to admit that London is an odious place, you'll not succeed. I'm extremely fond of it, and I think it the jolliest place in the world."

"*Pour vous autres.* I never said the contrary," Mrs. Westgate retorted. I make use of this expression because both interlocutors had begun to raise their voices. Percy Beaumont naturally did not like to hear his country abused, and Mrs. Westgate, no less naturally, did not like a stubborn debater.

"Hallo!" said Lord Lambeth; "what are they up to now?" And he came away from the window, where he had been standing with Bessie Alden.

"I quite agree with a very clever country-woman of mine," Mrs. Westgate continued, with charming ardour, though with imperfect relevancy. She smiled at the two gentlemen for a moment with terrible brightness, as if to toss at their feet—upon their native heath—the gauntlet of defiance. "For me, there are only two social positions worth speaking of—that of an American lady and that of the Emperor of Russia."

"And what do you do with the American gentlemen?" asked Lord Lambeth.

"She leaves them in America!" said Percy Beaumont.

On the departure of their visitors, Bessie Alden told her sister that Lord Lambeth would come the next day, to go with them to the Tower, and that he had kindly offered to bring his "trap," and drive them thither. Mrs. Westgate listened in silence to this communication, and for some time afterwards she said nothing. But at last, "If you had not requested me the other day not to mention it," she began, "there is something I should venture to ask you." Bessie frowned a little; her dark blue eyes were more dark than blue. But her sister went on. "As it is, I will take the risk. You are not in love with Lord Lambeth: I believe it, perfectly. Very good. But is there, by chance, any danger of your becoming so? It's a very

simple question; don't take offence. I have a particular reason," said Mrs. Westgate, "for wanting to know."

Bessie Alden for some moments said nothing; she only
looked displeased. "No; there is no danger," she answered at
last, curtly.

"Then I should like to frighten them," declared Mrs. Westgate, clasping her jewelled hands.

"To frighten whom?"

"All these people; Lord Lambeth's family and friends."

"How should you frighten them?" asked the young girl.

"It wouldn't be I—it would be you. It would frighten them
to think that you should absorb his lordship's young affections."

Bessie Alden, with her clear eyes still overshadowed by her
dark brows, continued to interrogate. "Why should that
frighten them?"

Mrs. Westgate poised her answer with a smile before deliv-
ering it. "Because they think you are not good enough. You
are a charming girl, beautiful and amiable, intelligent and
clever, and as *bien-élevée* as it is possible to be; but you are
not a fit match for Lord Lambeth."

Bessie Alden was immensely disgusted. "Where do you get
such extraordinary ideas?" she asked. "You have said some
such strange things lately. My dear Kitty, where do you collect
them?"

Kitty was evidently enamoured of her idea. "Yes, it would
put them on pins and needles, and it wouldn't hurt you. Mr.
Beaumont is already most uneasy; I could soon see that."

The young girl meditated a moment. "Do you mean that
they spy upon him—that they interfere with him?"

"I don't know what power they have to interfere, but I
know that a British mamma may worry her son's life out."

It has been intimated that, as regards certain disagreeable
things, Bessie Alden had a fund of scepticism. She abstained
on the present occasion from expressing disbelief, for she
wished not to irritate her sister. But she said to herself that
Kitty had been misinformed—that this was a traveller's tale.
Though she was a girl of a lively imagination, there could in
the nature of things be, to her sense, no reality in the idea of

her belonging to a vulgar category. What she said aloud was—"I must say that in that case I am very sorry for Lord Lambeth."

Mrs. Westgate, more and more exhilarated by her scheme, was smiling at her again. "If I could only believe it was safe!" she exclaimed. "When you begin to pity him, I, on my side, am afraid."

"Afraid of what?"

"Of your pitying him too much."

Bessie Alden turned away impatiently; but at the end of a minute she turned back. "What if I should pity him too much?" she asked.

Mrs. Westgate hereupon turned away, but after a moment's reflection she also faced her sister again. "It would come, after all, to the same thing," she said.

Lord Lambeth came the next day with his trap, and the two ladies, attended by Willie Woodley, placed themselves under his guidance and were conveyed eastward, through some of the duskier portions of the metropolis, to the great turreted donjon which overlooks the London shipping. They all descended from their vehicle and entered the famous enclosure; and they secured the services of a venerable beefeater, who, though there were many other claimants for legendary information, made a fine exclusive party of them and marched them through courts and corridors, through armouries and prisons. He delivered his usual peripatetic discourse, and they stopped and stared, and peeped and stooped, according to the official admonitions. Bessie Alden asked the old man in the crimson doublet a great many questions; she thought it a most fascinating place. Lord Lambeth was in high good-humour; he was constantly laughing; he enjoyed what he would have called the lark. Willie Woodley kept looking at the ceilings and tapping the walls with the knuckle of a pearl-grey glove; and Mrs. Westgate, asking at frequent intervals to be allowed to sit down and wait till they came back, was as frequently informed that they would never come back. To a great many of Bessie's questions—chiefly on collateral points of English history—the ancient warder was naturally unable to reply; whereupon she always appealed to Lord Lambeth. But his lordship was very ignorant. He declared that he knew nothing about that sort of thing, and he seemed greatly diverted at being treated as an authority.

"You can't expect every one to know as much as you," he said.

"I should expect you to know a great deal more," declared Bessie Alden.

"Women always know more than men about names and dates, and that sort of thing," Lord Lambeth rejoined. "There was Lady Jane Grey we have just been hearing about, who went in for Latin and Greek and all the learning of her age."

"*You* have no right to be ignorant, at all events," said Bessie.

"Why haven't I as good a right as any one else?"

"Because you have lived in the midst of all these things."

"What things do you mean? Axes and blocks and thumb-screws?"

"All these historical things. You belong to an historical family."

"Bessie is really too historical," said Mrs. Westgate, catching a word of this dialogue.

"Yes, you are too historical," said Lord Lambeth, laughing, but thankful for a formula. "Upon my honour, you are too historical!"

He went with the ladies a couple of days later to Hampton Court, Willie Woodley being also of the party. The afternoon was charming, the famous horse-chestnuts were in blossom, and Lord Lambeth, who quite entered into the spirit of the cockney excursionist, declared that it was a jolly old place. Bessie Alden was in ecstasies; she went about murmuring and exclaiming.

"It's too lovely," said the young girl, "it's too enchanting; it's too exactly what it ought to be!"

At Hampton Court the little flocks of visitors are not provided with an official bellwether, but are left to browse at discretion upon the local antiquities. It happened in this manner that, in default of another informant, Bessie Alden, who on doubtful questions was able to suggest a great many alternatives, found herself again applying for intellectual assistance to Lord Lambeth. But he again assured her that he was utterly helpless in such matters—that his education had been sadly neglected.

"And I am sorry it makes you unhappy," he added in a moment.

"You are very disappointing, Lord Lambeth," she said.

"Ah, now, don't say that!" he cried. "That's the worst thing you could possibly say."

"No," she rejoined; "it is not so bad as to say that I had expected nothing of you."

"I don't know. Give me a notion of the sort of thing you expected."

"Well," said Bessie Alden, "that you would be more what I should like to be—what I should try to be—in your place."

"Ah, my place!" exclaimed Lord Lambeth; "you are always talking about my place."

The young girl looked at him; he thought she coloured a little; and for a moment she made no rejoinder.

"Does it strike you that I am always talking about your place?" she asked.

"I am sure you do it a great honour," he said, fearing he had been uncivil.

"I have often thought about it," she went on after a moment. "I have often thought about your being an hereditary legislator. An hereditary legislator ought to know a great many things."

"Not if he doesn't legislate."

"But you will legislate; it's absurd your saying you won't. You are very much looked up to here—I am assured of that."

"I don't know that I ever noticed it."

"It is because you are used to it, then. You ought to fill the place."

"How do you mean, to fill it?" asked Lord Lambeth.

"You ought to be very clever and brilliant, and to know almost everything."

Lord Lambeth looked at her a moment. "Shall I tell you something?" he asked. "A young man in my position, as you call it——"

"I didn't invent the term," interposed Bessie Alden. "I have seen it in a great many books."

"Hang it, you are always at your books! A fellow in my position, then, does very well, whatever he does. That's about what I mean to say."

"Well, if your own people are content with you," said Bessie Alden, laughing, "it is not for me to complain. But I shall always think that, properly, you should have a great mind—a great character."

"Ah, that's very theoretic!" Lord Lambeth declared. "Depend upon it, that's a Yankee prejudice."

"Happy the country," said Bessie Alden, "where even people's prejudices are so elevated!"

"Well, after all," observed Lord Lambeth, "I don't know that I am such a fool as you are trying to make me out."

"I said nothing so rude as that; but I must repeat that you are disappointing."

"My dear Miss Alden," exclaimed the young man, "I am the best fellow in the world!"

"Ah, if it were not for that!" said Bessie Alden, with a smile.

Mrs. Westgate had a good many more friends in London than she pretended, and before long she had renewed acquaintance with most of them. Their hospitality was extreme, so that, one thing leading to another, she began, as the phrase is, to go out. Bessie Alden, in this way, saw something of what she found it a great satisfaction to call to herself English society. She went to balls and danced, she went to dinners and talked, she went to concerts and listened (at concerts Bessie always listened), she went to exhibitions and wondered. Her enjoyment was keen and her curiosity insatiable, and, grateful in general for all her opportunities, she especially prized the privilege of meeting certain celebrated persons—authors and artists, philosophers and statesmen—of whose renown she had been a humble and distant beholder, and who now, as a part of the habitual furniture of London drawing-rooms, struck her as stars fallen from the firmament and become palpable —revealing also, sometimes, on contact, qualities not to have been predicted of bodies sidereal. Bessie, who knew so many of her contemporaries by reputation, had a good many personal disappointments; but, on the other hand, she had innumerable satisfactions and enthusiasms, and she communicated the emotions of either class to a dear friend, of her own sex, in Boston, with whom she was in voluminous correspondence. Some of her reflections, indeed, she attempted to impart to Lord Lambeth, who came almost every day to Jones's Hotel, and whom Mrs. Westgate admitted to be really devoted. Captain Littledale, it appeared, had gone to India; and of several others of Mrs. Westgate's ex-pensioners—gentlemen who, as she said, had made, in New York, a club-house of her drawing-room—no tidings were to be obtained; but Lord Lambeth was certainly attentive enough to make up for the accidental absences, the short memories, all the other irregularities, of every one else. He drove them in the Park, he took them to visit private collections of pictures, and having a house of his own, invited them to dinner. Mrs. Westgate, following the fashion of many of her compatriots, caused herself and her sister to be presented at the English Court by her diplomatic representative—for it was in this manner that she alluded to the American Minister to England, inquiring what on earth he was put there for, if not to make the proper arrangements for one's going to a Drawing Room.

Lord Lambeth declared that he hated Drawing Rooms, but he participated in the ceremony on the day on which the two ladies at Jones's Hotel repaired to Buckingham Palace in a remarkable coach which his lordship had sent to fetch them. He had on a gorgeous uniform, and Bessie Alden was particularly struck with his appearance—especially when on her asking him, rather foolishly as she felt, if he were a loyal subject, he replied that he was a loyal subject to *her*. This declaration was emphasised by his dancing with her at a royal ball to which the two ladies afterwards went, and was not impaired by the fact that she thought he danced very ill. He seemed to her wonderfully kind; she asked herself, with growing vivacity, why he should be so kind. It was his disposition—that seemed the natural answer. She had told her sister that she liked him very much, and now that she liked him more she wondered why. She liked him for his disposition; to this question as well that seemed the natural answer. When once the impressions of London life began to crowd thickly upon her she completely forgot her sister's warning about the cynicism of public opinion. It had given her great pain at the moment; but there was no particular reason why she should remember it; it corresponded too little with any sensible reality; and it was disagreeable to Bessie to remember disagreeable things. So she was not haunted with the sense of a vulgar imputation. She was not in love with Lord Lambeth—she assured herself of that. It will immediately be observed that when such assurances become necessary the state of a young lady's affections is already ambiguous; and indeed Bessie Alden made no attempt to dissimulate—to herself, of course—a certain tenderness that she felt for the young nobleman. She said to herself that she liked the type to which he belonged—the simple, candid, manly, healthy English temperament. She spoke to herself of him as women speak of young men they like—alluded to his bravery (which she had never in the least seen tested), to his honesty and gentlemanliness; and was not silent upon the subject of his good looks. She was perfectly conscious, moreover, that she liked to think of his more adventitious merits—that her imagination was excited and gratified by the sight of a handsome young man endowed with such large opportunities—opportunities she hardly knew for what, but, as she supposed, for doing great things—for setting an example, for exerting an influence, for conferring happiness, for encouraging the arts. She had a kind of ideal of conduct for a young man who should find himself in this magnificent position, and she tried to adapt it to Lord Lambeth's deportment, as you might attempt to fit a silhouette in cut paper upon a shadow projected upon a wall. But Bessie Alden's silhouette refused to coincide with his lordship's image; and this want of harmony sometimes vexed her more than she thought reasonable. When he was absent it was of course less striking—then he seemed to her a sufficiently graceful combination of high responsibilities and amiable qualities. But when he sat there within sight, laughing and talking with his customary good humour and simplicity, she measured it more accurately, and she felt acutely that if Lord Lambeth's position was heroic, there was but little of the hero in the young man himself. Then her imagination wandered away from him— very far away; for it was an incontestable fact that at such moments he seemed distinctly dull. I am afraid that while Bessie's imagination was thus invidiously roaming, she cannot have been herself a very lively companion; but it may well have been that these occasional fits of indifference seemed to Lord Lambeth a part of the young girl's personal charm. It had been a part of this charm from the first that he felt that she judged him and measured him more freely and irresponsibly —more at her ease and her leisure, as it were—than several young ladies with whom he had been on the whole about as intimate. To feel this, and yet to feel that she also liked him, was very agreeable to Lord Lambeth. He fancied he had compassed that gratification so desirable to young men of title and fortune—being liked for himself. It is true that a cynical counsellor might have whispered to him, "Liked for yourself? Yes; but not so very much!" He had, at any rate, the constant hope of being liked more.

It may seem, perhaps, a trifle singular—but it is nevertheless true—that Bessie Alden, when he struck her as dull, devoted some time, on grounds of conscience, to trying to like him more. I say on grounds of conscience, because she felt that he had been extremely "nice" to her sister, and because she reflected that it was no more than fair that she should think as well of him as he thought of her. This effort was possibly sometimes not so successful as it might have been, for the result of it was occasionally a vague irritation, which expressed itself in hostile criticism of several British institutions. Bessie Alden went to some entertainments at which she met Lord Lambeth; but she went to others at which his lordship was neither actually nor potentially present; and it was chiefly on these latter occasions that she encountered those literary and artistic celebrities of whom mention has been made. After a while she reduced the matter to a principle. If Lord Lambeth should appear anywhere, it was a symbol that there would be no poets and philosophers; and in consequence—for it was almost a strict consequence—she used to enumerate to the young man these objects of her admiration.

"You seem to be awfully fond of that sort of people," said Lord Lambeth one day, as if the idea had just occurred to him.

"They are the people in England I am most curious to see," Bessie Alden replied.

"I suppose that's because you have read so much," said Lord Lambeth, gallantly.

"I have not read so much. It is because we think so much of them at home."

"Oh, I see!" observed the young nobleman. "In Boston."

"Not only in Boston; everywhere," said Bessie. "We hold them in great honour; they go to the best dinner-parties."

"I dare say you are right. I can't say I know many of them."

"It's a pity you don't," Bessie Alden declared. "It would do you good."

"I dare say it would," said Lord Lambeth, very humbly. "But I must say I don't like the looks of some of them."

"Neither do I—of some of them. But there are all kinds, and many of them are charming."

"I have talked with two or three of them," the young man went on, "and I thought they had a kind of fawning manner."

"Why should they fawn?" Bessie Alden demanded.

"I'm sure I don't know. Why, indeed?"

"Perhaps you only thought so," said Bessie.

"Well, of course," rejoined her companion, "that's a kind of thing that can't be proved."

"In America they don't fawn," said Bessie.

"Ah! well, then, they must be better company."

Bessie was silent a moment. "That is one of the things I don't like about England," she said; "your keeping the distinguished people apart."

"How do you mean, apart?"

"Why, letting them come only to certain places. You never see them."

Lord Lambeth looked at her a moment. "What people do you mean?"

"The eminent people—the authors and artists—the clever people."

"Oh, there are other eminent people besides those!" said Lord Lambeth.

"Well, you certainly keep them apart," repeated the young girl.

"And there are other clever people," added Lord Lambeth, simply.

Bessie Alden looked at him, and she gave a light laugh. "Not many," she said.

On another occasion—just after a dinner-party—she told him that there was something else in England she did not like.

"Oh, I say!" he cried; "haven't you abused us enough?"

"I have never abused you at all," said Bessie; "but I don't like your *precedence*."

"It isn't my precedence!" Lord Lambeth declared, laughing.

"Yes, it is yours—just exactly yours; and I think it's odious," said Bessie.

"I never saw such a young lady for discussing things! Has some one had the impudence to go before you?" asked his lordship.

"It is not the going before me that I object to," said Bessie; "it is their thinking that they have a right to do it—a right that I should recognise."

"I never saw such a young lady as you are for not 'recognising.' I have no doubt the thing is beastly, but it saves a lot of trouble."

"It makes a lot of trouble. It's horrid!" said Bessie.

"But how would you have the first people go?" asked Lord Lambeth. "They can't go last."

"Whom do you mean by the first people?"

"Ah, if you mean to question first principles!" said Lord Lambeth.

"If those are your first principles, no wonder some of your arrangements are horrid," observed Bessie Alden, with a very pretty ferocity. "I am a young girl, so of course I go last; but imagine what Kitty must feel on being informed that she is not at liberty to budge until certain other ladies have passed out!"

"Oh, I say, she is not 'informed'!" cried Lord Lambeth. "No one would do such a thing as that."

"She is made to feel it," the young girl insisted—"as if they were afraid she would make a rush for the door. No, you have a lovely country," said Bessie Alden, "but your precedence is horrid."

"I certainly shouldn't think your sister would like it," rejoined Lord Lambeth, with even exaggerated gravity. But Bessie Alden could induce him to enter no formal protest against this repulsive custom, which he seemed to think an extreme convenience.

VI.

Percy Beaumont all this time had been a very much less frequent visitor at Jones's Hotel than his noble kinsman; he had in fact called but twice upon the two American ladies. Lord Lambeth, who often saw him, reproached him with his neglect, and declared that although Mrs. Westgate had said nothing about it, he was sure that she was secretly wounded by it. "She suffers too much to speak," said Lord Lambeth.

"That's all gammon," said Percy Beaumont; "there's a limit to what people can suffer!" And, though sending no apologies to Jones's Hotel, he undertook in a manner to explain his absence. "You are always there," he said; "and that's reason enough for my not going."

"I don't see why. There is enough for both of us."

"I don't care to be a witness of your—your reckless passion," said Percy Beaumont.

Lord Lambeth looked at him with a cold eye, and for a moment said nothing. "It's not so obvious as you might suppose," he rejoined, dryly, "considering what a demonstrative beggar I am."

"I don't want to know anything about it—nothing whatever," said Beaumont. "Your mother asks me every time she sees me whether I believe you are really lost—and Lady Pimlico does the same. I prefer to be able to answer that I know nothing about it—that I never go there. I stay away for consistency's sake. As I said the other day, they must look after you themselves."

"You are devilish considerate," said Lord Lambeth. "They never question me."

"They are afraid of you. They are afraid of irritating you and making you worse. So they go to work very cautiously, and, somewhere or other, they get their information. They know a great deal about you. They know that you have been with those ladies to the dome of St. Paul's and—where was the other place?—to the Thames Tunnel."

"If all their knowledge is as accurate as that, it must be very valuable," said Lord Lambeth.

"Well, at any rate, they know that you have been visiting the 'sights of the metropolis.' They think—very naturally, as it seems to me—that when you take to visiting the sights of the metropolis with a little American girl, there is serious cause for alarm." Lord Lambeth responded to this intimation by scornful laughter, and his companion continued, after a pause: "I said just now I didn't want to know anything about the affair; but I will confess that I am curious to learn whether you propose to marry Miss Bessie Alden."

On this point Lord Lambeth gave his interlocutor no immediate satisfaction; he was musing, with a frown. "By Jove," he said, "they go rather too far. They *shall* find me dangerous—I promise them."

Percy Beaumont began to laugh. "You don't redeem your promises. You said the other day you would make your mother call."

Lord Lambeth continued to meditate. "I asked her to call," he said, simply.

"And she declined?"

"Yes, but she shall do it yet."

"Upon my word," said Percy Beaumont, "if she gets much more frightened I believe she will." Lord Lambeth looked at him, and he went on. "She will go to the girl herself."

"How do you mean, she will go to her?"

"She will beg her off, or she will bribe her. She will take strong measures."

Lord Lambeth turned away in silence, and his companion watched him take twenty steps and then slowly return. "I have invited Mrs. Westgate and Miss Alden to Branches," he said, "and this evening I shall name a day."

"And shall you invite your mother and your sisters to meet them?"

"Explicitly!"

"That will set the Duchess off," said Percy Beaumont. "I suspect she will come."

"She may do as she pleases."

Beaumont looked at Lord Lambeth. "You do really propose to marry the little sister, then?"

"I like the way you talk about it!" cried the young man. "She won't gobble me down; don't be afraid."

"She won't leave you on your knees," said Percy Beaumont. "What *is* the inducement?"

"You talk about proposing—wait till I have proposed," Lord Lambeth went on.

"That's right, my dear fellow; think about it," said Percy Beaumont.

"She's a charming girl," pursued his lordship.

"Of course she's a charming girl. I don't know a girl more charming, intrinsically. But there are other charming girls nearer home."

"I like her spirit," observed Lord Lambeth, almost as if he were trying to torment his cousin.

"What's the peculiarity of her spirit?"

"She's not afraid, and she says things out, and she thinks herself as good as any one. She is the only girl I have ever seen that was not dying to marry me."

"How do you know that, if you haven't asked her?"

"I don't know how; but I know it."

"I am sure she asked me questions enough about your property and your titles," said Beaumont.

"She has asked me questions, too; no end of them," Lord Lambeth admitted. "But she asked for information, don't you know."

"Information? Ay, I'll warrant she wanted it. Depend upon it that she is dying to marry you just as much and just as little as all the rest of them."

"I shouldn't like her to refuse me—I shouldn't like that."

"If the thing would be so disagreeable, then, both to you and to her, in Heaven's name leave it alone," said Percy Beaumont.

Mrs. Westgate, on her side, had plenty to say to her sister about the rarity of Mr. Beaumont's visits and the non-appearance of the Duchess of Bayswater. She professed, however, to derive more satisfaction from this latter circumstance than she could have done from the most lavish attentions on the part of this great lady. "It is most marked," she said, "most marked. It is a delicious proof that we have made them miserable. The day we dined with Lord Lambeth I was really sorry for the poor fellow." It will have been gathered that the entertainment offered by Lord Lambeth to his American friends had not been graced by the presence of his anxious mother. He had invited several choice spirits to meet them; but the ladies of his immediate family were to Mrs. Westgate's sense—a sense, possibly, morbidly acute—conspicuous by their absence.

"I don't want to express myself in a manner that you dislike," said Bessie Alden; "but I don't know why you should have so many theories about Lord Lambeth's poor mother. You know a great many young men in New York without knowing their mothers."

Mrs. Westgate looked at her sister, and then turned away. "My dear Bessie, you are superb!" she said.

"One thing is certain," the young girl continued. "If I believed I were a cause of annoyance—however unwitting—to Lord Lambeth's family, I should insist——"

"Insist upon my leaving England," said Mrs. Westgate.

"No, not that. I want to go to the National Gallery again; I want to see Stratford-on-Avon and Canterbury Cathedral. But I should insist upon his coming to see us no more."

"That would be very modest and very pretty of you—but you wouldn't do it now."

"Why do you say 'now'?" asked Bessie Alden. "Have I ceased to be modest?"

"You care for him too much. A month ago, when you said you didn't, I believe it was quite true. But at present, my dear child," said Mrs. Westgate, "you wouldn't find it quite so simple a matter never to see Lord Lambeth again. I have seen it coming on."

"You are mistaken," said Bessie. "You don't understand."

"My dear child, don't be perverse," rejoined her sister.

"I know him better, certainly, if you mean that," said Bessie. "And I like him very much. But I don't like him enough to make trouble for him with his family. However, I don't believe in that."

"I like the way you say 'however!'" Mrs. Westgate exclaimed. "Come, you would not marry him?"

"Oh no," said the young girl.

Mrs. Westgate, for a moment, seemed vexed. "Why not, pray?" she demanded.

"Because I don't care to," said Bessie Alden.

The morning after Lord Lambeth had had, with Percy Beaumont, that exchange of ideas which has just been narrated, the ladies at Jones's Hotel received from his lordship a written invitation to pay their projected visit to Branches Castle on the following Tuesday. "I think I have made up a very pleasant party," the young nobleman said. "Several people whom you know, and my mother and sisters, who have so long been regrettably prevented from making your acquaintance." Bessie Alden lost no time in calling her sister's attention to the injustice she had done the Duchess of Bayswater, whose hostility was now proved to be a vain illusion.

"Wait till you see if she comes," said Mrs. Westgate. "And if she is to meet us at her son's house the obligation was all the greater for her to call upon us."

Bessie had not to wait long, and it appeared that Lord Lambeth's mother now accepted Mrs. Westgate's view of her duties. On the morrow, early in the afternoon, two cards were brought to the apartment of the American ladies—one of them bearing the name of the Duchess of Bayswater and the other that of the Countess of Pimlico. Mrs. Westgate glanced at the clock. "It is not yet four," she said; "they have come early; they wish to see us. We will receive them." And she gave orders that her visitors should be admitted. A few moments later they were introduced, and there was a solemn exchange of amenities. The Duchess was a large lady, with a fine fresh colour; the Countess of Pimlico was very pretty and elegant.

The Duchess looked about her as she sat down—looked not especially at Mrs. Westgate. "I dare say my son has told you that I have been wanting to come and see you," she observed.

"You are very kind," said Mrs. Westgate, vaguely—her conscience not allowing her to assent to this proposition—and indeed not permitting her to enunciate her own with any appreciable emphasis.

"He says you were so kind to him in America," said the Duchess.

"We are very glad," Mrs. Westgate replied, "to have been able to make him a little more—a little less—a little more comfortable."

"I think he stayed at your house," remarked the Duchess of Bayswater, looking at Bessie Alden.

"A very short time," said Mrs. Westgate.

"Oh!" said the Duchess; and she continued to look at Bessie, who was engaged in conversation with her daughter.

"Do you like London?" Lady Pimlico had asked of Bessie, after looking at her a good deal—at her face and her hands, her dress and her hair.

"Very much indeed," said Bessie.

"Do you like this hotel?"

"It is very comfortable," said Bessie.

"Do you like stopping at hotels?" inquired Lady Pimlico, after a pause.

"I am very fond of travelling," Bessie answered, "and I suppose hotels are a necessary part of it. But they are not the part I am fondest of."

"Oh, I hate travelling!" said the Countess of Pimlico, and transferred her attention to Mrs. Westgate.

"My son tells me you are going to Branches," the Duchess presently resumed.

"Lord Lambeth has been so good as to ask us," said Mrs. Westgate, who perceived that her visitor had now begun to look at her, and who had her customary happy consciousness of a distinguished appearance. The only mitigation of her felicity on this point was that, having inspected her visitor's own costume, she said to herself, "She won't know how well I am dressed!"

"He has asked me to go, but I am not sure I shall be able," murmured the Duchess.

"He had offered us the p—— the prospect of meeting you," said Mrs. Westgate.

"I hate the country at this season," responded the Duchess.

Mrs. Westgate gave a little shrug. "I think it is pleasanter than London."

But the Duchess's eyes were absent again; she was looking very fixedly at Bessie. In a moment she slowly rose, walked to a chair that stood empty at the young girl's right hand, and silently seated herself. As she was a majestic, voluminous woman, this little transaction had, inevitably, an air of somewhat impressive intention. It diffused a certain awkwardness, which Lady Pimlico, as a sympathetic daughter, perhaps desired to rectify in turning to Mrs. Westgate.

"I dare say you go out a great deal," she observed.

"No, very little. We are strangers, and we didn't come here for society."

"I see," said Lady Pimlico. "It's rather nice in town just now."

"It's charming," said Mrs. Westgate. "But we only go to see a few people—whom we like."

"Of course one can't like every one," said Lady Pimlico.

"It depends upon one's society," Mrs. Westgate rejoined.

The Duchess, meanwhile, had addressed herself to Bessie. "My son tells me the young ladies in America are so clever."

"I am glad they made so good an impression on him," said Bessie, smiling.

The Duchess was not smiling; her large fresh face was very tranquil. "He is very susceptible," she said. "He thinks every one clever, and sometimes they are."

"Sometimes," Bessie assented, smiling still.

The Duchess looked at her a little and then went on— "Lambeth is very susceptible, but he is very volatile, too."

"Volatile?" asked Bessie.

"He is very inconstant. It won't do to depend on him."

"Ah!" said Bessie; "I don't recognise that description. We have depended on him greatly—my sister and I—and he has never disappointed us."

"He will disappoint you yet," said the Duchess.

Bessie gave a little laugh, as if she were amused at the Duchess's persistency. "I suppose it will depend on what we expect of him."

"The less you expect the better," Lord Lambeth's mother declared.

"Well," said Bessie, "we expect nothing unreasonable."

The Duchess, for a moment, was silent, though she appeared to have more to say. "Lambeth says he has seen so much of you," she presently began.

"He has been to see us very often—he has been very kind," said Bessie Alden.

"I dare say you are used to that. I am told there is a great deal of that in America."

"A great deal of kindness?" the young girl inquired, smiling.

"Is that what you call it? I know you have different expressions."

"We certainly don't always understand each other," said Mrs. Westgate, the termination of whose interview with Lady Pimlico allowed her to give her attention to their elder visitor.

"I am speaking of the young men calling so much upon the young ladies," the Duchess explained.

"But surely in England," said Mrs. Westgate, "the young ladies don't call upon the young men?"

"Some of them do—almost!" Lady Pimlico declared. "When the young men are a great *parti*."

"Bessie, you must make a note of that," said Mrs. Westgate. "My sister," she added, "is a model traveller. She writes down all the curious facts she hears, in a little book she keeps for the purpose."

The Duchess was a little flushed; she looked all about the room, while her daughter turned to Bessie. "My brother told us you were wonderfully clever," said Lady Pimlico.

"He should have said my sister," Bessie answered—"when she says such things as that."

"Shall you be long at Branches?" the Duchess asked, abruptly, of the young girl.

"Lord Lambeth has asked us for three days," said Bessie.

"I shall go," the Duchess declared, "and my daughter too."

"That will be charming!" Bessie rejoined.

"Delightful!" murmured Mrs. Westgate.

"I shall expect to see a deal of you," the Duchess continued. "When I go to Branches I monopolise my son's guests."

"They must be most happy," said Mrs. Westgate, very graciously.

"I want immensely to see it—to see the Castle," said Bessie to the Duchess. "I have never seen one—in England at least; and you know we have none in America."

"Ah! you are fond of castles?" inquired her Grace.

"Immensely!" replied the young girl. "It has been the dream of my life to live in one."

The Duchess looked at her a moment, as if she hardly knew how to take this assurance, which, from her Grace's point of view, was either very artless or very audacious. "Well," she said, rising, "I will show you Branches myself." And upon this the two great ladies took their departure.

"What did they mean by it?" asked Mrs. Westgate, when they were gone.

"They meant to be polite," said Bessie, "because we are going to meet them."

"It is too late to be polite," Mrs. Westgate replied, almost grimly. "They meant to overawe us by their fine manners and their grandeur, and to make you *lâcher prise*."

"*Lâcher prise*? What strange things you say!" murmured Bessie Alden.

"They meant to snub us, so that we shouldn't dare to go to Branches," Mrs. Westgate continued.

"On the contrary," said Bessie, "the Duchess offered to show me the place herself."

"Yes, you may depend upon it she won't let you out of her sight. She will show you the place from morning till night."

"You have a theory for everything," said Bessie.

"And you apparently have none for anything."

"I saw no attempt to 'overawe' us," said the young girl. "Their manners were not fine."

"They were not even good!" Mrs. Westgate declared.

Bessie was silent awhile, but in a few moments she observed that she had a very good theory. "They came to look at me!" she said, as if this had been a very ingenious hypothesis. Mrs. Westgate did it justice; she greeted it with a smile and pronounced it most brilliant; while in reality she felt that the young girl's scepticism, or her charity, or, as she had sometimes called it, appropriately, her idealism, was proof against irony. Bessie, however, remained meditative all the rest of that day and well on into the morrow.

On the morrow, before lunch, Mrs. Westgate had occasion to go out for an hour, and left her sister writing a letter. When she came back she met Lord Lambeth at the door of the hotel, coming away. She thought he looked slightly embarrassed; he was certainly very grave. "I am sorry to have missed you. Won't you come back?" she asked.

"No," said the young man, "I can't. I have seen your sister. I can never come back." Then he looked at her a moment, and took her hand. "Good-bye, Mrs. Westgate," he said. "You have been very kind to me." And with what she thought a strange, sad look in his handsome young face, he turned away.

She went in and she found Bessie still writing her letter; that is, Mrs. Westgate perceived she was sitting at the table with the pen in her hand and not writing. "Lord Lambeth has been here," said the elder lady at last.

Then Bessie got up and showed her a pale, serious face. She bent this face upon her sister for some time, confessing silently and, a little, pleading. "I told him," she said at last, "that we could not go to Branches."

Mrs. Westgate displayed just a spark of irritation. "He might have waited," she said with a smile, "till one had seen the Castle." Later, an hour afterwards, she said, "Dear Bessie, I wish you might have accepted him."

"I couldn't," said Bessie, gently.

"He is a dear good fellow," said Mrs. Westgate.

"I couldn't," Bessie repeated.

"If it is only," her sister added, "because those women will think that they succeeded—that they paralysed us!"

Bessie Alden turned away; but presently she added, "They were interesting; I should have liked to see them again."

"So should I!" cried Mrs. Westgate, significantly.

"And I should have liked to see the Castle," said Bessie. "But now we must leave England," she added.

Her sister looked at her. "You will not wait to go to the National Gallery?"

"Not now."

"Nor to Canterbury Cathedral?"

Bessie reflected a moment. "We can stop there on our way to Paris," she said.

Lord Lambeth did not tell Percy Beaumont that the contingency he was not prepared at all to like had occurred; but Percy Beaumont, on hearing that the two ladies had left

London, wondered with some intensity what had happened; wondered, that is, until the Duchess of Bayswater came, a little, to his assistance. The two ladies went to Paris, and Mrs. Westgate beguiled the journey to that city by repeating several times, "That's what I regret; they will think they petrified us." But Bessie Alden seemed to regret nothing.

The Pension Beaurepas

I WAS not rich—on the contrary; and I had been told the Pension Beaurepas was cheap. I had, moreover, been told that a boarding-house is a capital place for the study of human nature. I had a fancy for a literary career, and a friend of mine had said to me, "If you mean to write you ought to go and live in a boarding-house; there is no other such place to pick up material." I had read something of this kind in a letter addressed by Stendhal to his sister: "I have a passionate desire to know human nature, and have a great mind to live in a boarding-house, where people cannot conceal their real characters." I was an admirer of *La Chartreuse de Parme*, and it appeared to me that one could not do better than follow in the footsteps of its author. I remembered, too, the magnificent boarding-house in Balzac's Père Goriot,—the *"pension bourgeoise des deux sexes et autres,"* kept by Madame Vauquer, *née* De Conflans. Magnificent, I mean, as a piece of portraiture; the establishment, as an establishment, was certainly sordid enough, and I hoped for better things from the Pension Beaurepas. This institution was one of the most esteemed in Geneva, and, standing in a little garden of its own, not far from the lake, had a very homely, comfortable, sociable aspect. The regular entrance was, as one might say, at the back, which looked upon the street, or rather upon a little *place*, adorned like every place in Geneva, great or small, with a fountain. This fact was not prepossessing, for on crossing the threshold you found yourself more or less in the kitchen, encompassed with culinary odours. This, however, was no great matter, for at the Pension Beaurepas there was no attempt at gentility or at concealment of the domestic machinery. The latter was of a very simple sort. Madame Beaurepas was an excellent little old woman—she was very far advanced in life, and had been keeping a pension for forty years—whose only faults were that she was slightly deaf, that she was fond of a surreptitious pinch of snuff, and that, at the age of seventy-three, she wore flowers in her cap. There was a tradition in the house that she was not so deaf as she pretended; that she feigned this infirmity in order to possess herself of the secrets of her lodgers. But I never subscribed to this theory; I am convinced that Madame Beaurepas had outlived the period of indiscreet curiosity. She was a philosopher, on a matter-of-fact basis; she had been having lodgers for forty years, and all that she asked of them was that they should pay their bills, make use of the door-mat, and fold their napkins. She cared very little for their secrets. "J'en ai vus de toutes les couleurs," she said to me. She had quite ceased to care for individuals; she cared only for types, for categories. Her large observation had made her acquainted with a great number, and her mind was a complete collection of "heads." She flattered herself that she knew at a glance where to pigeon-hole a new-comer, and if she made any mistakes her deportment never betrayed them. I think that, as regards individuals, she had neither likes nor dislikes; but she was capable of expressing esteem or contempt for a species. She had her own ways, I suppose, of manifesting her approval, but her manner of indicating the reverse was simple and unvarying. "Je trouve que c'est déplacé!"—this exhausted her view of the matter. If one of her inmates had put arsenic into the *pot-au-feu*, I believe Madame Beaurepas would have contented herself with remarking that the proceeding was out of place. The line of misconduct to which she most objected was an undue assumption of gentility; she had no patience with boarders who gave themselves airs. "When people come *chez moi*, it is not to cut a figure in the world; I have never had that illusion," I remember hearing her say; "and when you pay seven francs a day, *tout compris*, it comprises everything but the right to look down upon the others. But there are people who, the less they pay, the more they take themselves *au sérieux*. My most difficult boarders have always been those who have had the little rooms."

Madame Beaurepas had a niece, a young woman of some forty odd years; and the two ladies, with the assistance of a couple of thick-waisted, red-armed peasant women, kept the house going. If on your exits and entrances you peeped into the kitchen, it made very little difference; for Célestine, the cook, had no pretension to be an invisible functionary or to deal in occult methods. She was always at your service, with a grateful grin: she blacked your boots; she trudged off to fetch a cab; she would have carried your baggage, if you had allowed her, on her broad little back. She was always tramping in and out, between her kitchen and the fountain in the place, where it often seemed to me that a large part of the preparation for our dinner went forward—the wringing out of towels and table-cloths, the washing of potatoes and cabbages, the scouring of saucepans and cleansing of water-bottles. You enjoyed, from the door-step, a perpetual back view of Célestine and of her large, loose, woollen ankles, as she craned, from the waist, over into the fountain and dabbled in her various utensils. This sounds as if life went on in a very make-shift fashion at the Pension Beaurepas—as if the tone of the establishment were sordid. But such was not at all the case. We were simply very *bourgeois*; we practised the good old Genevese principle of not sacrificing to appearances. This is an excellent principle—when you have the reality. We had the reality at the Pension Beaurepas: we had it in the shape of soft, short beds, equipped with fluffy *duvets*; of admirable coffee, served to us in the morning by Célestine in person, as we lay recumbent on these downy couches; of copious, wholesome, succulent dinners, conformable to the best provincial traditions. For myself, I thought the Pension Beaurepas picturesque, and this, with me, at that time was a great word. I was young and ingenuous; I had just come from America. I wished to perfect myself in the French tongue, and I innocently believed that it flourished by Lake Leman. I used to go to lectures at the Academy, and come home with a violent appetite. I always enjoyed my morning walk across the long bridge (there was only one, just there, in those days) which spans the deep blue out-gush of the lake, and up the dark, steep streets of the old Calvinistic city. The garden faced this way, toward the lake and the old town; and this was the pleasantest approach to the house. There was a high wall, with a double gate in the middle, flanked by a couple of ancient massive posts; the big rusty *grille* contained some old-fashioned iron-work. The garden was rather mouldy and weedy, tangled and untended; but it contained a little thin-flowing fountain, several green benches, a rickety little table of the same complexion, and three orange-trees, in tubs, which were deposited as effectively as possible in front of the windows of the *salon*.

II.

As commonly happens in boarding-houses, the rustle of petticoats was, at the Pension Beaurepas, the most familiar form
of the human tread. There was the usual allotment of economical widows and old maids, and to maintain the balance
of the sexes there were only an old Frenchman and a young
American. It hardly made the matter easier that the old
Frenchman came from Lausanne. He was a native of that estimable town, but he had once spent six months in Paris, he
had tasted of the tree of knowledge; he had got beyond Lausanne, whose resources he pronounced inadequate. Lausanne,
as he said *"manquait d'agréments."* When obliged, for reasons
which he never specified, to bring his residence in Paris to a
close, he had fallen back on Geneva; he had broken his fall at
the Pension Beaurepas. Geneva was, after all, more like Paris,
and at a Genevese boarding-house there was sure to be plenty
of Americans with whom one could talk about the French
metropolis. M. Pigeonneau was a little lean man, with a large,
narrow nose, who sat a great deal in the garden, reading with
the aid of a large magnifying glass a volume from the *cabinet
de lecture.*

One day, a fortnight after my arrival at the Pension Beaurepas, I came back rather earlier than usual from my academic
session; it wanted half an hour of the midday breakfast. I went
into the salon with the design of possessing myself of the day's
Galignani before one of the little English old maids should
have removed it to her virginal bower—a privilege to which
Madame Beaurepas frequently alluded as one of the attractions of the establishment. In the salon I found a new-comer,
a tall gentleman in a high black hat, whom I immediately
recognised as a compatriot. I had often seen him, or his equivalent, in the hotel-parlours of my native land. He apparently
supposed himself to be at the present moment in a hotel-
parlour; his hat was on his head, or, rather, half off it—pushed
back from his forehead, and rather suspended than poised. He
stood before a table on which old newspapers were scattered,
one of which he had taken up and, with his eye-glass on his
nose, was holding out at arm's length. It was that honourable
but extremely diminutive sheet, the *Journal de Genève*, a news-

paper of about the size of a pocket-handkerchief. As I drew near, looking for my *Galignani*, the tall gentleman gave me, over the top of his eye-glass, a somewhat solemn stare. Presently however, before I had time to lay my hand on the object of my search, he silently offered me the *Journal de Genève.*

"It appears," he said, "to be the paper of the country."

"Yes," I answered, "I believe it's the best,"

He gazed at it again, still holding it at arm's-length, as if it had been a looking-glass. "Well," he said, "I suppose it's natural a small country should have small papers. You could wrap it up, mountains and all, in one of our dailies!"

I found my *Galignani* and went off with it into the garden, where I seated myself on a bench in the shade. Presently I saw the tall gentleman in the hat appear in one of the open windows of the salon, and stand there with his hands in his pockets and his legs a little apart. He looked very much bored, and—I don't know why—I immediately began to feel sorry for him. He was not at all a picturesque personage; he looked like a jaded, faded man of business. But after a little he came into the garden and began to stroll about; and then his restless, unoccupied carriage, and the vague, unacquainted manner in which his eyes wandered over the place seemed to make it proper that, as an older resident, I should exercise a certain hospitality. I said something to him, and he came and sat down beside me on my bench, clasping one of his long knees in his hands.

"When is it this big breakfast of theirs comes off?" he inquired. "That's what I call it—the little breakfast and the big breakfast. I never thought I should live to see the time when I should care to eat two breakfasts. But a man's glad to do anything, over here."

"For myself," I observed, "I find plenty to do."

He turned his head and glanced at me with a dry, deliberate, kind-looking eye. "You're getting used to the life, are you?"

"I like the life very much," I answered, laughing.

"How long have you tried it?"

"Do you mean in this place?"

"Well, I mean anywhere. It seems to me pretty much the same all over."

"I have been in this house only a fortnight," I said.

"Well, what should you say, from what you have seen?" my companion asked.

"Oh," said I, "you can see all there is immediately. It's very simple."

"Sweet simplicity, eh? I'm afraid my two ladies will find it too simple."

"Everything is very good," I went on. "And Madame Beaurepas is a charming old woman. And then it's very cheap."

"Cheap, is it?" my friend repeated meditatively.

"Doesn't it strike you so?" I asked. I thought it very possible he had not inquired the terms. But he appeared not to have heard me; he sat there, clasping his knee and blinking, in a contemplative manner, at the sunshine.

"Are you from the United States, sir?" he presently demanded, turning his head again.

"Yes, sir," I replied; and I mentioned the place of my nativity.

"I presumed," he said, "that you were American or English. I'm from the United States myself; from New York City. Many of our people here?"

"Not so many as, I believe, there have sometimes been. There are two or three ladies."

"Well," my interlocutor declared, "I am very fond of ladies' society. I think when its superior there's nothing comes up to it. I've got two ladies here myself; I must make you acquainted with them."

I rejoined that I should be delighted, and I inquired of my friend whether he had been long in Europe.

"Well, it seems precious long," he said, "but my time's not up yet. We have been here fourteen weeks and a half."

"Are you travelling for pleasure?" I asked.

My companion turned his head again and looked at me—looked at me so long in silence that I at last also turned and met his eyes.

"No, sir," he said presently. "No, sir," he repeated, after a considerable interval.

"Excuse me," said I, for there was something so solemn in his tone that I feared I had been indiscreet.

He took no notice of my ejaculation; he simply continued to look at me. "I'm travelling," he said, at last, "to please the doctors. They seemed to think they would like it."

"Ah, they sent you abroad for your health?"

"They sent me abroad because they were so confoundedly muddled they didn't know what else to do."

"That's often the best thing," I ventured to remark.

"It was a confession of weakness; they wanted me to stop plaguing them. They didn't know enough to cure me, and that's the way they thought they would get round it. I wanted to be cured—I didn't want to be transported. I hadn't done any harm."

I assented to the general proposition of the inefficiency of doctors, and asked my companion if he had been seriously ill.

"I didn't sleep," he said, after some delay.

"Ah, that's very annoying. I suppose you were over-worked."

"I didn't eat; I took no interest in my food."

"Well, I hope you both eat and sleep now," I said.

"I couldn't hold a pen," my neighbour went on. "I couldn't sit still. I couldn't walk from my house to the cars—and it's only a little way. I lost my interest in business."

"You needed a holiday," I observed.

"That's what the doctors said. It wasn't so very smart of them. I had been paying strict attention to business for twenty-three years."

"In all that time you have never had a holiday?" I exclaimed, with horror.

My companion waited a little. "Sundays," he said at last.

"No wonder, then, you were out of sorts."

"Well, sir," said my friend, "I shouldn't have been where I was three years ago if I had spent my time travelling round Europe. I was in a very advantageous position. I did a very large business. I was considerably interested in lumber." He paused, turned his head, and looked at me a moment. "Have you any business interests yourself?" I answered that I had none, and he went on again, slowly, softly, deliberately. "Well, sir, perhaps you are not aware that business in the United States is not what it was a short time since. Business interests are very insecure. There seems to be a general falling-off.

Different parties offer different explanations of the fact, but so far as I am aware none of their observations have set things going again." I ingeniously intimated that if business was dull, the time was good for coming away; whereupon my neighbour threw back his head and stretched his legs a while. "Well, sir, that's one view of the matter certainly. There's something to be said for that. These things should be looked at all round. That's the ground my wife took. That's the ground," he added in a moment "that a lady would naturally take;" and he gave a little dry laugh.

"You think it's slightly illogical," I remarked.

"Well, sir, the ground I took was that the worse a man's business is, the more it requires looking after. I shouldn't want to go out to take a walk—not even to go to church—if my house was on fire. My firm is not doing the business it was; it's like a sick child, it requires nursing. What I wanted the doctors to do was to fix me up, so that I could go on at home. I'd have taken anything they'd have given me, and as many times a day. I wanted to be right there; I had my reasons; I have them still. But I came off, all the same," said my friend, with a melancholy smile.

I was a great deal younger than he, but there was something so simple and communicative in his tone, so expressive of a desire to fraternise, and so exempt from any theory of human differences, that I quite forgot his seniority, and found myself offering him paternal advice. "Don't think about all that," said I. "Simply enjoy yourself, amuse yourself, get well. Travel about and see Europe. At the end of a year, by the time you are ready to go home, things will have improved over there, and you will be quite well and happy."

My friend laid his hand on my knee; he looked at me for some moments, and I thought he was going to say, "You are very young!" But he said presently, "*You* have got used to Europe any way!"

III.

At breakfast I encountered his ladies—his wife and daughter. They were placed, however, at a distance from me, and it was not until the *pensionnaires* had dispersed, and some of them, according to custom, had come out into the garden, that he had an opportunity of making me acquainted with them.

"Will you allow me to introduce you to my daughter?" he said, moved apparently by a paternal inclination to provide this young lady with social diversion. She was standing with her mother, in one of the paths, looking about with no great complacency, as I imagined, at the homely characteristics of the place, and old M. Pigeonneau was hovering near, hesitating apparently between the desire to be urbane and the absence of a pretext. "Mrs. Ruck—Miss Sophy Ruck," said my friend, leading me up.

Mrs. Ruck was a large, plump, light coloured person, with a smooth fair face, a somnolent eye, and an elaborate coiffure. Miss Sophy was a girl of one and twenty, very small and very pretty—what I suppose would have been called a lively brunette. Both of these ladies were attired in black silk dresses, very much trimmed; they had an air of the highest elegance.

"Do you think highly of this pension?" inquired Mrs. Ruck, after a few preliminaries.

"It's a little rough, but it seems to me comfortable," I answered.

"Does it take a high rank in Geneva?" Mrs. Ruck pursued.

"I imagine it enjoys a very fair fame," I said, smiling.

"I should never dream of comparing it to a New York boarding-house," said Mrs. Ruck.

"It's quite a different style," her daughter observed. Miss Ruck had folded her arms; she was holding her elbows with a pair of white little hands, and she was tapping the ground with a pretty little foot.

"We hardly expected to come to a pension," said Mrs. Ruck. "But we thought we would try; we had heard so much about Swiss pensions. I was saying to Mr. Ruck that I wondered whether this was a favourable specimen. I was afraid we might have made a mistake."

"We knew some people who had been here; they thought everything of Madame Beaurepas," said Miss Sophy. "They said she was a real friend."

"Mr. and Mrs. Parker—perhaps you have heard her speak of them," Mrs. Ruck pursued.

"Madame Beaurepas has had a great many Americans; she is very fond of Americans," I replied.

"Well, I must say I should think she would be, if she compares them with some others."

"Mother is always comparing," observed Miss Ruck.

"Of course I am always comparing," rejoined the elder lady. "I never had a chance till now; I never knew my privileges. Give me an American!" And Mrs. Ruck indulged in a little laugh.

"Well, I must say there are some things I like over here," said Miss Sophy, with courage. And indeed I could see that she was a young woman of great decision.

"You like the shops—that's what you like," her father affirmed.

The young lady addressed herself to me, without heeding this remark. "I suppose you feel quite at home here."

"Oh, he likes it; he has got used to the life!" exclaimed Mr. Ruck.

"I wish you'd teach Mr. Ruck," said his wife. "It seems as if he couldn't get used to anything."

"I'm used to you, my dear," the husband retorted, giving me a humorous look.

"He's intensely restless," continued Mrs. Ruck. "That's what made me want to come to a pension. I thought he would settle down more."

"I don't think I *am* used to you, after all," said her husband.

In view of a possible exchange of conjugal repartee I took refuge in conversation with Miss Ruck, who seemed perfectly able to play her part in any colloquy. I learned from this young lady that, with her parents, after visiting the British islands, she had been spending a month in Paris, and that she thought she should have died when she left that city. "I hung out of the carriage, when we left the hotel," said Miss Ruck, "I assure you I did. And mother did, too."

"Out of the other window, I hope," said I.

"Yes, one out of each window," she replied, promptly. "Father had hard work, I can tell you. We hadn't half-finished; there were ever so many places we wanted to go to."

"Your father insisted on coming away?"

"Yes; after we had been there about a month he said he had enough. He's fearfully restless; he's very much out of health. Mother and I said to him that if he was restless in Paris he needn't hope for peace anywhere. We don't mean to leave him alone till he takes us back." There was an air of keen resolution in Miss Ruck's pretty face, of lucid apprehension of desirable ends, which made me, as she pronounced these words, direct a glance of covert compassion toward her poor recalcitrant father. He had walked away a little with his wife, and I saw only his back and his stooping, patient-looking shoulders, whose air of acute resignation was thrown into relief by the voluminous tranquillity of Mrs. Ruck. "He will have to take us back in September, any way," the young girl pursued; "he will have to take us back to get some things we have ordered."

"Have you ordered a great many things?" I asked, jocosely.

"Well, I guess we have ordered *some*. Of course we wanted to take advantage of being in Paris—ladies always do. We have left the principal things till we go back. Of course that is the principal interest, for ladies. Mother said she should feel so shabby, if she just passed through. We have promised all the people to be back in September, and I never broke a promise yet. So Mr. Ruck has got to make his plans accordingly."

"And what are his plans?"

"I don't know; he doesn't seem able to make any. His great idea was to get to Geneva; but now that he has got here he doesn't seem to care. It's the effect of ill health. He used to be so bright; but now he is quite subdued. It's about time he should improve, any way. We went out last night to look at the jewellers' windows—in that street behind the hotel. I had always heard of those jewellers' windows. We saw some lovely things, but it didn't seem to rouse father. He'll get tired of Geneva sooner than he did of Paris."

"Ah," said I, "there are finer things here than the jewellers' windows. We are very near some of the most beautiful scenery in Europe."

"I suppose you mean the mountains. Well, we have seen plenty of mountains at home. We used to go to the mountains every summer. We are familiar enough with the mountains. Aren't we, mother?" the young lady demanded, appealing to Mrs. Ruck, who, with her husband, had drawn near again.

"Aren't we what?" inquired the elder lady.

"Aren't we familiar with the mountains?"

"Well, I hope so," said Mrs. Ruck.

Mr. Ruck, with his hands in his pockets, gave me a sociable wink. "There's nothing much you can tell them!" he said.

The two ladies stood face to face a few moments, surveying each other's garments. "Don't you want to go out?" the young girl at last inquired of her mother.

"Well, I think we had better; we have got to go up to that place."

"To what place?" asked Mr. Ruck.

"To that jeweller's—to that big one."

"They all seemed big enough; they were too big!" And Mr. Ruck gave me another wink.

"That one where we saw the blue cross," said his daughter.

"Oh, come, what do you want of that blue cross?" poor Mr. Ruck demanded.

"She wants to hang it on a black velvet ribbon and tie it round her neck," said his wife.

"A black velvet ribbon? No, I thank you!" cried the young lady. "Do you suppose I would wear that cross on a black velvet ribbon? On a nice little gold chain, if you please—a little narrow gold chain, like an old-fashioned watch-chain. That's the proper thing for that blue cross. I know the sort of chain I mean; I'm going to look for one. When I want a thing," said Miss Ruck, with decision, "I can generally find it."

"Look here, Sophy," her father urged, "you don't want that blue cross."

"I do want it—I happen to want it." And Sophy glanced at me with a little laugh.

Her laugh, which in itself was pretty, suggested that there were various relations in which one might stand to Miss Ruck; but I think I was conscious of a certain satisfaction in not occupying the paternal one. "Don't worry the poor child," said her mother.

"Come on, mother," said Miss Ruck.

"We are going to look about a little," explained the elder lady to me, by way of taking leave.

"I know what that means," remarked Mr. Ruck, as his companions moved away. He stood looking at them a moment, while he raised his hand to his head, behind, and stood rubbing it a little, with a movement that displaced his hat. (I may remark in parenthesis that I never saw a hat more easily displaced than Mr. Ruck's.) I supposed he was going to say something querulous, but I was mistaken. Mr. Ruck was unhappy, but he was very good-natured. "Well, they want to pick up something," he said. "That's the principal interest, for ladies."

IV.

Mr. Ruck distinguished me, as the French say. He honoured me with his esteem, and, as the days elapsed, with a large portion of his confidence. Sometimes he bored me a little, for the tone of his conversation was not cheerful, tending as it did almost exclusively to a melancholy dirge over the financial prostration of our common country. "No, sir, business in the United States is not what it once was," he found occasion to remark several times a day. "There's not the same spring—there's not the same hopeful feeling. You can see it in all departments." He used to sit by the hour in the little garden of the pension, with a roll of American newspapers in his lap and his high hat pushed back, swinging one of his long legs and reading the *New York Herald*. He paid a daily visit to the American banker's, on the other side of the Rhône, and remained there a long time, turning over the old papers on the green velvet table in the middle of the Salon des Étrangers and fraternising with chance compatriots. But in spite of these diversions his time hung heavily upon his hands. I used sometimes to propose to him to take a walk; but he had a mortal horror of pedestrianism, and regarded my own taste for it as a morbid form of activity. "You'll kill yourself, if you don't look out," he said, "walking all over the country. I don't want to walk round that way; I ain't a postman!" Briefly speaking, Mr. Ruck had few resources. His wife and daughter, on the other hand, it was to be supposed, were possessed of a good many that could not be apparent to an unobtrusive young man. They also sat a great deal in the garden or in the salon, side by side, with folded hands, contemplating material objects, and were remarkably independent of most of the usual feminine aids to idleness—light literature, tapestry, the use of the piano. They were, however, much fonder of locomotion than their companion, and I often met them in the Rue du Rhône and on the quays, loitering in front of the jewellers' windows. They might have had a cavalier in the person of old M. Pigeonneau, who possessed a high appreciation of their charms, but who, owing to the absence of a common idiom, was deprived of the pleasures of intimacy. He knew no English, and Mrs. Ruck and her daughter had, as it seemed, an incurable mistrust of the beautiful tongue which, as the old man endeavoured to impress upon them, was preeminently the language of conversation.

"They have a *tournure de princesse*—a *distinction supreme*," he said to me. "One is surprised to find them in a little pension, at seven francs a day."

"Oh, they don't come for economy," I answered. "They must be rich."

"They don't come for my *beaux yeux*—for mine," said M. Pigeonneau, sadly. "Perhaps it's for yours, young man. Je vous recommande la mère."

I reflected a moment. "They came on account of Mr. Ruck—because at hotels he's so restless."

M. Pigeonneau gave me a knowing nod. "Of course he is, with such a wife as that!—a *femme superbe*. Madame Ruck is preserved in perfection—a miraculous *fraîcheur*. I like those large, fair, quiet women; they are often, *dans l'intimité*, the most agreeable. I'll warrant you that at heart Madame Ruck is a finished coquette."

"I rather doubt it," I said.

"You suppose her cold? Ne vous y fiez pas!"

"It is a matter in which I have nothing at stake."

"You young Americans are droll," said M. Pigeonneau; "you never have anything at stake! But the little one, for example; I'll warrant you she's not cold. She is admirably made."

"She is very pretty."

" 'She is very pretty!' Vous dites cela d'un ton! When you pay compliments to Mademoiselle Ruck, I hope that's not the way you do it."

"I don't pay compliments to Mademoiselle Ruck."

"Ah, decidedly," said M. Pigeonneau, "you young Americans are droll!"

I should have suspected that these two ladies would not especially commend themselves to Madame Beaurepas; that as a *maîtresse de salon*, which she in some degree aspired to be, she would have found them wanting in a certain flexibility of deportment. But I should have gone quite wrong; Madame Beaurepas had no fault at all to find with her new pensionnaires. "I have no observation whatever to make about them," she said to me one evening. "I see nothing in those ladies which is at all *déplacé*. They don't complain of anything; they don't meddle; they take what's given them; they leave me tranquil. The Americans are often like that. Often, but not always," Madame Beaurepas pursued. "We are to have a specimen tomorrow of a very different sort."

"An American?" I inquired.

"Two *Américaines*—a mother and a daughter. There are Americans and Americans: when you are *difficiles*, you are more so than any one, and when you have pretensions—ah, *par exemple*, it's serious. I foresee that with this little lady everything will be serious, beginning with her *café au lait*. She has been staying at the Pension Chamousset—my *concurrent*, you know, farther up the street; but she is coming away because the coffee is bad. She holds to her coffee, it appears. I don't know what liquid Madame Chamousset may have invented, but we will do the best we can for her. Only, I know she will make me *des histoires* about something else. She will demand a new lamp for the salon; *vous allez voir cela*. She wishes to pay but eleven francs a day for herself and her daughter, *tout compris*; and for their eleven francs they expect to be lodged like princesses. But she is very 'ladylike'—isn't that what you call it in English? Oh, *pour cela*, she is ladylike!"

I caught a glimpse on the morrow of this ladylike person, who was arriving at her new residence as I came in from a walk. She had come in a cab, with her daughter and her luggage; and, with an air of perfect softness and serenity, she was disputing the fare as she stood among her boxes, on the steps. She addressed her cabman in a very English accent, but with extreme precision and correctness. "I wish to be perfectly reasonable, but I don't wish to encourage you in exorbitant demands. With a franc and a half you are sufficiently paid. It is not the custom at Geneva to give a *pour-boire* for so short a drive. I have made inquiries, and I find it is not the custom, even in the best families. I am a stranger, yes, but I always adopt the custom of the native families. I think it my duty toward the natives."

"But I am a native, too, *moi!*" said the cabman, with an angry laugh.

"You seem to me to speak with a German accent," continued the lady. "You are probably from Basel. A franc and a half is sufficient. I see you have left behind the little red bag which I asked you to hold between your knees; you will please to go back to the other house and get it. Very well, if you are impolite I will make a complaint of you to-morrow at the administration. Aurora, you will find a pencil in the outer pocket of my embroidered satchel; please to write down his number,—87; do you see it distinctly?—in case we should forget it."

The young lady addressed as "Aurora"—a slight, fair girl, holding a large parcel of umbrellas—stood at hand while this allocution went forward, but she apparently gave no heed to it. She stood looking about her, in a listless manner, at the front of the house, at the corridor, at Célestine tucking up her apron in the door-way, at me as I passed in amid the disseminated luggage; her mother's parsimonious attitude seeming to produce in Miss Aurora neither sympathy nor embarrassment. At dinner the two ladies were placed on the same side of the table as myself, below Mrs. Ruck and her daughter, my own position being on the right of Mr. Ruck. I had therefore little observation of Mrs. Church—such I learned to be her name—but I occasionally heard her soft, distinct voice.

"White wine, if you please; we prefer white wine. There is none on the table? Then you will please to get some, and to remember to place a bottle of it always here, between my daughter and myself."

"That lady seems to know what she wants," said Mr. Ruck,

"and she speaks so I can understand her. I can't understand every one, over here. I should like to make that lady's acquaintance. Perhaps she knows what *I* want, too; it seems hard to find out. But I don't want any of their sour white wine; that's one of the things I don't want. I expect she'll be an addition to the pension."

Mr. Ruck made the acquaintance of Mrs. Church that evening in the parlour, being presented to her by his wife, who presumed on the rights conferred upon herself by the mutual proximity, at table, of the two ladies. I suspected that in Mrs. Church's view Mrs. Ruck presumed too far. The fugitive from the Pension Chamousset, as M. Pigeonneau called her, was a little fresh, plump, comely woman, looking less than her age, with a round, bright, serious face. She was very simply and frugally dressed, not at all in the manner of Mr. Ruck's companions, and she had an air of quiet distinction which was an excellent defensive weapon. She exhibited a polite disposition to listen to what Mr. Ruck might have to say, but her manner was equivalent to an intimation that what she valued least in boarding-house life was its social opportunities. She had placed herself near a lamp, after carefully screwing it and turning it up, and she had opened in her lap, with the assistance of a large embroidered marker, an octavo volume, which I perceived to be in German. To Mrs. Ruck and her daughter she was evidently a puzzle, with her economical attire and her expensive culture. The two younger ladies, however, had begun to fraternise very freely, and Miss Ruck presently went wandering out of the room with her arm round the waist of Miss Church. It was a very warm evening; the long windows of the salon stood wide open into the garden, and, inspired by the balmy darkness, M. Pigeonneau and Mademoiselle Beaurepas, a most obliging little woman, who lisped and always wore a huge cravat, declared they would organise a *fête de nuit*. They engaged in this undertaking, and the fête developed itself, consisting of half a dozen red paper lanterns, hung about on the trees, and of several glasses of *sirop*, carried on a tray by the stout-armed Célestine. As the festival deepened to its climax I went out into the garden, where M. Pigeonneau was master of ceremonies.

"But where are those charming young ladies," he cried,

"Miss Ruck and the new-comer, *l'aimable transfuge*? Their absence has been remarked, and they are wanting to the brilliancy of the occasion. *Voyez* I have selected a glass of syrup—a generous glass—for Mademoiselle Ruck, and I advise you, my young friend, if you wish to make a good impression, to put aside one which you may offer to the other young lady. What is her name? Miss Church. I see; it's a singular name. There is a church in which I would willingly worship!"

Mr. Ruck presently came out of the salon, having concluded his interview with Mrs. Church. Through the open window I saw the latter lady sitting under the lamp with her German octavo, while Mrs. Ruck, established, empty-handed, in an arm-chair near her, gazed at her with an air of fascination.

"Well, I told you she would know what I want," said Mr. Ruck. "She says I want to go up to Appenzell, wherever that is; that I want to drink whey and live in a high latitude—what did she call it?—a high altitude. She seemed to think we ought to leave for Appenzell to-morrow; she'd got it all fixed. She says this ain't a high enough lat—a high enough altitude. And she says I mustn't go too high, either; that would be just as bad; she seems to know just the right figure. She says she'll give me a list of the hotels where we must stop, on the way to Appenzell. I asked her if she didn't want to go with us, but she says she'd rather sit still and read. I expect she's a big reader."

The daughter of this accomplished woman now reappeared, in company with Miss Ruck, with whom she had been strolling through the outlying parts of the garden.

"Well," said Miss Ruck, glancing at the red paper lanterns, "are they trying to stick the flower-pots into the trees?"

"It's an illumination in honour of our arrival," the other young girl rejoined. "It's a triumph over Madame Chamousset."

"Meanwhile, at the Pension Chamousset," I ventured to suggest, "they have put out their lights; they are sitting in darkness, lamenting your departure."

She looked at me, smiling; she was standing in the light that came from the house. M. Pigeonneau, meanwhile, who had been awaiting his chance, advanced to Miss Ruck with his glass of syrup. "I have kept it for you, mademoiselle," he said; "I have jealously guarded it. It is very delicious!"

Miss Ruck looked at him and his syrup, without making any motion to take the glass. "Well, I guess it's sour," she said in a moment; and she gave a little shake of her head.

M. Pigeonneau stood staring, with his syrup in his hand; then he slowly turned away. He looked about at the rest of us, as if to appeal from Miss Ruck's insensibility, and went to deposit his rejected tribute on a bench.

"Won't you give it to me?" asked Miss Church, in faultless French. "J'adore le sirop, moi."

M. Pigeonneau came back with alacrity, and presented the glass with a very low bow. "I adore good manners," murmured the old man.

This incident caused me to look at Miss Church with quickened interest. She was not strikingly pretty, but in her charming, irregular face there was something brilliant and ardent. Like her mother, she was very simply dressed.

"She wants to go to America, and her mother won't let her," said Miss Sophy to me, explaining her companion's situation.

"I am very sorry—for America," I answered, laughing.

"Well, I don't want to say anything against your mother, but I think it's shameful," Miss Ruck pursued.

"Mamma has very good reasons; she will tell you them all."

"Well, I'm sure I don't want to hear them," said Miss Ruck. "You have got a right to go to your own country; every one has a right to go to their own country."

"Mamma is not very patriotic," said Aurora Church, smiling.

"Well, I call that dreadful," her companion declared. "I have heard that there are some Americans like that, but I never believed it."

"There are all sorts of Americans," I said, laughing.

"Aurora's one of the right sort," rejoined Miss Ruck, who had apparently become very intimate with her new friend.

"Are you very patriotic?" I asked of the young girl.

"She's right down homesick," said Miss Sophy; "she's dying to go. If I were you my mother would have to take me."

"Mamma is going to take me to Dresden."

"Well, I declare I never heard of anything so dreadful!" cried Miss Ruck. "It's like something in a story."

"I never heard there was anything very dreadful in Dresden," I interposed.

Miss Ruck looked at me a moment. "Well, I don't believe *you* are a good American," she replied, "and I never supposed you were. You had better go in there and talk to Mrs. Church."

"Dresden is really very nice, isn't it?" I asked of her companion.

"It isn't nice if you happen to prefer New York," said Miss Sophy. "Miss Church prefers New York. Tell him you are dying to see New York; it will make him angry," she went on.

"I have no desire to make him angry," said Aurora, smiling.

"It is only Miss Ruck who can do that," I rejoined. "Have you been a long time in Europe?"

"Always."

"I call that wicked!" Miss Sophy declared.

"You might be in a worse place," I continued. "I find Europe very interesting."

Miss Ruck gave a little laugh. "I was saying that you wanted to pass for a European."

"Yes, I want to pass for a Dalmatian."

Miss Ruck looked at me a moment. "Well, you had better not come home," she said. "No one will speak to you."

"Were you born in these countries?" I asked of her companion.

"Oh, no; I came to Europe when I was a small child. But I remember America a little, and it seems delightful."

"Wait till you see it again. It's just too lovely," said Miss Sophy.

"It's the grandest country in the world," I added.

Miss Ruck began to toss her head. "Come away, my dear," she said. "If there's a creature I despise it's a man that tries to say funny things about his own country."

"Don't you think one can be tired of Europe?" Aurora asked, lingering.

"Possibly—after many years."

"Father was tired of it after three weeks," said Miss Ruck.

"I have been here sixteen years," her friend went on, look-ing at me with a charming intentness, as if she had a purpose in speaking. "It used to be for my education. I don't know what it's for now."

"She's beautifully educated," said Miss Ruck. "She knows four languages."

"I am not very sure that I know English."

"You should go to Boston!" cried Miss Sophy. "They speak splendidly in Boston."

"C'est mon rêve," said Aurora, still looking at me.

"Have you been all over Europe," I asked—"in all the dif-ferent countries?"

She hesitated a moment. "Everywhere that there's a *pen-sion*. Mamma is devoted to *pensions*. We have lived, at one time or another, in every *pension* in Europe."

"Well, I should think you had seen about enough," said Miss Ruck.

"It's a delightful way of seeing Europe," Aurora rejoined, with her brilliant smile. "You may imagine how it has attached me to the different countries. I have such charming souvenirs! There is a *pension* awaiting us now at Dresden,—eight francs a day, without wine. That's rather dear. Mamma means to make them give us wine. Mamma is a great authority on *pen-sions*; she is known, that way, all over Europe. Last winter we were in Italy, and she discovered one at Piacenza,—four francs a day. We made economies."

"Your mother doesn't seem to mingle much," observed Miss Ruck, glancing through the window at the scholastic attitude of Mrs. Church.

"No, she doesn't mingle, except in the native society. Though she lives in *pensions*, she detests them."

"Why does she live in them, then?" asked Miss Sophy, rather resentfully.

"Oh, because we are so poor; it's the cheapest way to live. We have tried having a cook, but the cook always steals. Mamma used to set me to watch her; that's the way I passed my *jeunesse*—my *belle jeunesse*. We are frightfully poor," the young girl went on, with the same strange frankness—a cu-rious mixture of girlish grace and conscious cynicism. "Nous

n'avons pas le sou. That's one of the reasons we don't go
back to America; mamma says we can't afford to live there."

"Well, any one can see that you're an American girl," Miss
Ruck remarked, in a consolatory manner. "I can tell an American girl a mile off. You've got the American style."

"I'm afraid I haven't the American *toilette*," said Aurora,
looking at the other's superior splendour.

"Well, your dress was cut in France; any one can see that."

"Yes," said Aurora, with a laugh, "my dress was cut in
France—at Avranches."

"Well, you've got a lovely figure, any way," pursued her
companion.

"Ah," said the young girl, "at Avranches, too, my figure
was admired." And she looked at me askance, with a certain
coquetry. But I was an innocent youth, and I only looked back
at her, wondering. She was a great deal nicer than Miss Ruck,
and yet Miss Ruck would not have said that. "I try to be like
an American girl," she continued; "I do my best, though
mamma doesn't at all encourage it. I am very patriotic. I try
to copy them, though mamma has brought me up *à la française*; that is, as much as one can in *pensions*. For instance, I
have never been out of the house without mamma; oh, never,
never. But sometimes I despair; American girls are so wonderfully frank. I can't be frank, like that. I am always afraid.
But I do what I can, as you see. Excusez du peu!"

I thought this young lady at least as outspoken as most of
her unexpatriated sisters; there was something almost comical
in her despondency. But she had by no means caught, as it
seemed to me, the American tone. Whatever her tone was,
however, it had a fascination; there was something dainty
about it, and yet it was decidedly audacious.

The young ladies began to stroll about the garden again,
and I enjoyed their society until M. Pigeonneau's festival came
to an end.

V.

Mr. Ruck did not take his departure for Appenzell on the
morrow, in spite of the eagerness to witness such an event
which he had attributed to Mrs. Church. He continued, on

the contrary, for many days after, to hang about the garden, to wander up to the banker's and back again, to engage in desultory conversation with his fellow-boarders, and to endeavour to assuage his constitutional restlessness by perusal of the American journals. But on the morrow I had the honour of making Mrs. Church's acquaintance. She came into the salon, after the midday breakfast, with her German octavo under her arm, and she appealed to me for assistance in selecting a quiet corner.

"Would you very kindly," she said, "move that large fauteuil a little more this way? Not the largest; the one with the little cushion. The fauteuils here are very insufficient; I must ask Madame Beaurepas for another. Thank you; a little more to the left, please; that will do. Are you particularly engaged?" she inquired, after she had seated herself. "If not, I should like to have some conversation with you. It is some time since I have met a young American of your—what shall I call it?—your affiliations. I have learned your name from Madame Beaurepas; I think I used to know some of your people. I don't know what has become of all my friends. I used to have a charming little circle at home, but now I meet no one I know. Don't you think there is a great difference between the people one meets and the people one would like to meet? Fortunately, sometimes," added my interlocutress graciously, "it's quite the same. I suppose you are a specimen, a favourable specimen," she went on, "of young America. Tell me, now, what is young America thinking of in these days of ours? What are its feelings, its opinions, its aspirations? What is its *ideal*?" I had seated myself near Mrs. Church, and she had pointed this interrogation with the gaze of her bright little eyes. I felt it embarrassing to be treated as a favourable specimen of young America, and to be expected to answer for the great republic. Observing my hesitation, Mrs. Church clasped her hands on the open page of her book and gave an intense, melancholy smile. "*Has* it an ideal?" she softly asked. "Well, we must talk of this," she went on, without insisting. "Speak, for the present, for yourself simply. Have you come to Europe with any special design?"

"Nothing to boast of," I said. "I am studying a little."

"Ah, I am glad to hear that. You are gathering up a little

European culture; that's what we lack, you know, at home. No individual can do much, of course. But you must not be discouraged; every little counts."

"I see that you, at least, are doing your part," I rejoined gallantly, dropping my eyes on my companion's learned volume.

"Yes, I frankly admit that I am fond of study. There is no one, after all, like the Germans. That is, for facts. For opinions I by no means always go with them. I form my opinions myself. I am sorry to say, however," Mrs. Church continued, "that I can hardly pretend to diffuse my acquisitions. I am afraid I am sadly selfish; I do little to irrigate the soil. I belong—I frankly confess it—to the class of absentees."

"I had the pleasure, last evening," I said, "of making the acquaintance of your daughter. She told me you had been a long time in Europe."

Mrs. Church smiled benignantly. "Can one ever be too long? We shall never leave it."

"Your daughter won't like that," I said, smiling too.

"Has she been taking you into her confidence? She is a more sensible young lady than she sometimes appears. I have taken great pains with her; she is really—I may be permitted to say it—superbly educated."

"She seemed to me a very charming girl," I rejoined. "And I learned that she speaks four languages."

"It is not only that," said Mrs. Church, in a tone which suggested that this might be a very superficial species of culture. "She has made what we call *de fortes études*—such as I suppose you are making now. She is familiar with the results of modern science; she keeps pace with the new historical school."

"Ah," said I, "she has gone much farther than I!"

"You doubtless think I exaggerate, and you force me, therefore, to mention the fact that I am able to speak of such matters with a certain intelligence."

"That is very evident," I said. "But your daughter thinks you ought to take her home." I began to fear, as soon as I had uttered these words, that they savoured of treachery to the young lady, but I was reassured by seeing that they pro-

duced on her mother's placid countenance no symptom whatever of irritation.

"My daughter has her little theories," Mrs. Church observed; "she has, I may say, her illusions. And what wonder!
What would youth be without its illusions? Aurora has a theory that she would be happier in New York, in Boston, in
Philadelphia, than in one of the charming old cities in which
our lot is cast. But she is mistaken, that is all. We must allow
our children their illusions, must we not? But we must watch
over them."

Although she herself seemed proof against discomposure,
I found something vaguely irritating in her soft, sweet positiveness.

"American cities," I said, "are the paradise of young girls."

"Do you mean," asked Mrs. Church, "that the young girls
who come from those places are angels?"

"Yes," I said, resolutely.

"This young lady—what is her odd name?—with whom my
daughter has formed a somewhat precipitate acquaintance: is
Miss Ruck an angel? But I won't force you to say anything
uncivil. It would be too cruel to make a single exception."

"Well," said I, "at any rate, in America young girls have an
easier lot. They have much more liberty."

My companion laid her hand for an instant on my arm. "My
dear young friend, I know America, I know the conditions of
life there, so well. There is perhaps no subject on which I have
reflected more than on our national idiosyncrasies."

"I am afraid you don't approve of them," said I, a little
brutally.

Brutal indeed my proposition was, and Mrs. Church was
not prepared to assent to it in this rough shape. She dropped
her eyes on her book, with an air of acute meditation. Then,
raising them, "We are very crude," she softly observed—"we
are very crude." Lest even this delicately-uttered statement
should seem to savour of the vice that she deprecated, she
went on to explain. "There are two classes of minds, you
know—those that hold back, and those that push forward. My
daughter and I are not pushers; we move with little steps. We
like the old, trodden paths; we like the old, old world."

"Ah," said I, "you know what you like; there is a great virtue in that."

"Yes, we like Europe; we prefer it. We like the opportunities of Europe; we like the *rest*. There is so much in that, you know. The world seems to me to be hurrying, pressing forward so fiercely, without knowing where it is going. 'Whither?' I often ask, in my little quiet way. But I have yet to learn that any one can tell me."

"You're a great conservative," I observed, while I wondered whether I myself could answer this inquiry.

Mrs. Church gave me a smile which was equivalent to a confession. "I wish to retain a *little*—just a little. Surely, we have done so much, we might rest a while; we might pause. That is all my feeling—just to stop a little, to wait! I have seen so many changes. I wish to draw in, to draw in—to hold back, to hold back."

"You shouldn't hold your daughter back!" I answered, laughing and getting up. I got up, not by way of terminating our interview, for I perceived Mrs. Church's exposition of her views to be by no means complete, but in order to offer a chair to Miss Aurora, who at this moment drew near. She thanked me and remained standing, but without at first, as I noticed, meeting her mother's eye.

"You have been engaged with your new acquaintance, my dear?" this lady inquired.

"Yes, mamma dear," said the young girl, gently.

"Do you find her very edifying?"

Aurora was silent a moment; then she looked at her mother. "I don't know, mamma; she is very fresh."

I ventured to indulge in a respectful laugh. "Your mother has another word for that. But I must not," I added, "be crude."

"Ah, vous m'en voulez?" inquired Mrs. Church. "And yet I can't pretend I said it in jest. I feel it too much. We have been having a little social discussion," she said to her daughter. "There is still so much to be said. And I wish," she continued, turning to me, "that I could give you our point of view. Don't you wish, Aurora, that we could give him our point of view?"

"Yes, mamma," said Aurora.

"We consider ourselves very fortunate in our point of view, don't we dearest?" mamma demanded.

"Very fortunate, indeed, mamma."

"You see we have acquired an insight into European life," the elder lady pursued. "We have our place at many a European fireside. We find so much to esteem—so much to enjoy. Do we not, my daughter?"

"So very much, mamma," the young girl went on, with a sort of inscrutable submissiveness. I wondered at it; it offered so strange a contrast to the mocking freedom of her tone the night before; but while I wondered I was careful not to let my perplexity take precedence of my good manners.

"I don't know what you ladies may have found at European firesides," I said, "but there can be very little doubt what you have left there."

Mrs. Church got up, to acknowledge my compliment. "We have spent some charming hours. And that reminds me that we have just now such an occasion in prospect. We are to call upon some Genevese friends—the family of the Pasteur Galopin. They are to go with us to the old library at the Hôtel de Ville, where there are some very interesting documents of the period of the Reformation; we are promised a glimpse of some manuscripts of poor Servetus, the antagonist and victim, you know, of Calvin. Here, of course, one can only speak of Calvin under one's breath, but some day, when we are more private," and Mrs. Church looked round the room, "I will give you my view of him. I think it has a touch of originality. Aurora is familiar with, are you not, my daughter, familiar with my view of Calvin?"

"Yes, mamma," said Aurora, with docility, while the two ladies went to prepare for their visit to the Pasteur Galopin.

VI.

"She has demanded a new lamp; I told you she would!" This communication was made me by Madame Beaurepas a couple of days later. "And she has asked for a new *tapis de lit*, and she has requested me to provide Célestine with a pair of light shoes. I told her that, as a general thing, cooks are not shod with satin. That poor Célestine!"

"Mrs. Church may be exacting," I said, "but she is a clever little woman."

"A lady who pays but five francs and a half shouldn't be too clever. C'est déplacé. I don't like the type."

"What type do you call Mrs. Church's?"

"Mon Dieu," said Madame Beaurepas, "c'est une de ces mamans comme vous en avez, qui promènent leur fille."

"She is trying to marry her daughter? I don't think she's of that sort."

But Madame Beaurepas shrewdly held to her idea. "She is trying it in her own way; she does it very quietly. She doesn't want an American; she wants a foreigner. And she wants a *mari sérieux*. But she is travelling over Europe in search of one. She would like a magistrate."

"A magistrate?"

"A *gros bonnet* of some kind; a professor or a deputy."

"I am very sorry for the poor girl," I said, laughing.

"You needn't pity her too much; she's a sly thing."

"Ah, for that, no!" I exclaimed. "She's a charming girl."

Madame Beaurepas gave an elderly grin. "She has hooked you, eh? But the mother won't have you."

I developed my idea, without heeding this insinuation. "She's a charming girl, but she is a little odd. It's a necessity of her position. She is less submissive to her mother than she has to pretend to be. That's in self-defence; it's to make her life possible."

"She wishes to get away from her mother," continued Madame Beaurepas. "She wishes to *courir les champs*."

"She wishes to go to America, her native country."

"Precisely. And she will certainly go."

"I hope so!" I rejoined.

"Some fine morning—or evening—she will go off with a young man; probably with a young American."

"Allons donc!" said I, with disgust.

"That will be quite America enough," pursued my cynical hostess. "I have kept a boarding-house for forty years. I have seen that type."

"Have such things as that happened *chez vous*?" I asked.

"Everything has happened *chez moi*. But nothing has happened more than once. Therefore this won't happen here. It will be at the next place they go to, or the next. Besides, here there is no young American *pour la partie*—none except you, monsieur. You are susceptible, but you are too reasonable."

"It's lucky for you I am reasonable," I answered. "It's thanks to that fact that you escape a scolding!"

One morning, about this time, instead of coming back to breakfast at the *pension*, after my lectures at the Academy, I went to partake of this meal with a fellow-student, at an ancient eating-house in the collegiate quarter. On separating from my friend, I took my way along that charming public walk known in Geneva as the Treille, a shady terrace, of immense elevation, overhanging a portion of the lower town. There are spreading trees and well-worn benches, and over the tiles and chimneys of the *ville basse* there is a view of the snow-crested Alps. On the other side, as you turn your back to the view, the promenade is overlooked by a row of tall, sober-faced *hôtels*, the dwellings of the local aristocracy. I was very fond of the place, and often resorted to it to stimulate my sense of the picturesque. Presently, as I lingered there on this occasion, I became aware that a gentleman was seated not far from where I stood, with his back to the Alpine chain, which this morning was brilliant and distinct, and a newspaper, unfolded, in his lap. He was not reading, however; he was staring before him in gloomy contemplation. I don't know whether I recognised first the newspaper or its proprietor; one, in either case, would have helped me to identify the other. One was the *New York Herald*; the other, of course, was Mr. Ruck. As I drew nearer, he transferred his eyes from the stony, high-featured masks of the gray old houses on the other side of the terrace, and I knew by the expression of his face just how he had been feeling about these distinguished abodes. He had made up his mind that their proprietors were a dusky, narrow-minded, unsociable company; plunging their roots into a superfluous past. I endeavoured, therefore, as I sat down beside him, to suggest something more impersonal.

"That's a beautiful view of the Alps," I observed.

"Yes," said Mr. Ruck, without moving, "I've examined it. Fine thing, in its way—fine thing. Beauties of nature—that sort of thing. We came up on purpose to look at it."

"Your ladies, then, have been with you?"

"Yes; they are just walking round. They're awfully restless. They keep saying I'm restless, but I'm as quiet as a sleeping child to them. It takes," he added in a moment, drily, "the form of shopping."

"Are they shopping now?"

"Well, if they ain't, they're trying to. They told me to sit here a while, and they'd just walk round. I generally know what that means. But that's the principal interest for ladies," he added, retracting his irony. "We thought we'd come up here and see the cathedral; Mrs. Church seemed to think it a dead loss that we shouldn't see the cathedral, especially as we hadn't seen many yet. And I had to come up to the banker's any way. Well, we certainly saw the cathedral. I don't know as we are any the better for it, and I don't know as I should know it again. But we saw it, any way. I don't know as I should want to go there regularly; but I suppose it will give us, in conversation, a kind of hold on Mrs. Church, eh? I guess we want something of that kind. Well," Mr. Ruck continued, "I stepped in at the banker's to see if there wasn't something, and they handed me out a Herald."

"I hope the Herald is full of good news," I said.

"Can't say it is. D—d bad news."

"Political," I inquired, "or commercial?"

"Oh, hang politics! It's business, sir. There ain't any business. It's all gone to,"—and Mr. Ruck became profane. "Nine failures in one day. What do you say to that?"

"I hope they haven't injured you," I said.

"Well, they haven't helped me much. So many houses on fire, that's all. If they happen to take place in your own street, they don't increase the value of your property. When mine catches, I suppose they'll write and tell me—one of these days, when they've got nothing else to do. I didn't get a blessed letter this morning; I suppose they think I'm having such a good time over here it's a pity to disturb me. If I could attend to business for about half an hour, I'd find out something. But I can't, and it's no use talking. The state of my health was never so unsatisfactory as it was about five o'clock this morning."

"I am very sorry to hear that," I said, "and I recommend you strongly not to think of business."

"I don't," Mr. Ruck replied. "I'm thinking of cathedrals; I'm thinking of the beauties of nature. Come," he went on, turning round on the bench and leaning his elbow on the parapet, "I'll think of those mountains over there; they *are* pretty, certainly. Can't you get over there?"

"Over where?"

"Over to those hills. Don't they run a train right up?"

"You can go to Chamouni," I said. "You can go to Grindelwald and Zermatt and fifty other places. You can't go by rail, but you can drive."

"All right, we'll drive—and not in a one-horse concern, either. Yes, Chamouni is one of the places we put down. I hope there are a few nice shops in Chamouni." Mr. Ruck spoke with a certain quickened emphasis, and in a tone more explicitly humorous than he commonly employed. I thought he was excited, and yet he had not the appearance of excitement. He looked like a man who has simply taken, in the face of disaster, a sudden, somewhat imaginative, resolution not to "worry." He presently twisted himself about on his bench again and began to watch for his companions. "Well, they *are* walking round," he resumed; "I guess they've hit on something, somewhere. And they've got a carriage waiting outside of that archway, too. They seem to do a big business in archways here, don't they. They like to have a carriage to carry home the things—those ladies of mine. Then they're sure they've got them." The ladies, after this, to do them justice, were not very long in appearing. They came toward us, from under the archway to which Mr. Ruck had somewhat invidiously alluded, slowly and with a rather exhausted step and expression. My companion looked at them a moment, as they advanced. "They're tired," he said softly. "When they're tired, like that, it's very expensive."

"Well," said Mrs. Ruck, "I'm glad you've had some company." Her husband looked at her, in silence, through narrowed eyelids, and I suspected that this gracious observation on the lady's part was prompted by a restless conscience.

Miss Sophy glanced at me with her little straightforward air of defiance. "It would have been more proper if *we* had had the company. Why didn't you come after us, instead of sitting there?" she asked of Mr. Ruck's companion.

"I was told by your father," I explained, "that you were engaged in sacred rites." Miss Ruck was not gracious, though I doubt whether it was because her conscience was better than her mother's.

"Well, for a gentleman there is nothing so sacred as ladies' society," replied Miss Ruck, in the manner of a person accustomed to giving neat retorts.

"I suppose you refer to the cathedral," said her mother. "Well, I must say, we didn't go back there. I don't know what it may be of a Sunday, but it gave me a chill."

"We discovered the loveliest little lace-shop," observed the young girl, with a serenity that was superior to bravado.

Her father looked at her a while; then turned about again, leaning on the parapet, and gazed away at the "hills."

"Well, it was certainly cheap," said Mrs. Ruck, also contemplating the Alps.

"We are going to Chamouni," said her husband. "You haven't any occasion for lace at Chamouni."

"Well, I'm glad to hear you have decided to go somewhere," rejoined his wife. "I don't want to be a fixture at a boarding-house."

"You can wear lace anywhere," said Miss Ruck, "if you put it on right. That's the great thing, with lace. I don't think they know how to wear lace in Europe. I know how I mean to wear mine; but I mean to keep it till I get home."

Her father transferred his melancholy gaze to her elaborately-appointed little person; there was a great deal of very new-looking detail in Miss Ruck's appearance. Then, in a tone of voice quite out of consonance with his facial despondency, "Have you purchased a great deal?" he inquired.

"I have purchased enough for you to make a fuss about."

"He can't make a fuss about that," said Mrs. Ruck.

"Well, you'll see!" declared the young girl with a little sharp laugh.

But her father went on, in the same tone: "Have you got it in your pocket? Why don't you put it on—why don't you hang it round you?"

"I'll hang it round *you*, if you don't look out!" cried Miss Sophy.

"Don't you want to show it to this gentleman?" Mr. Ruck continued.

"Mercy, how you do talk about that lace!" said his wife.

"Well, I want to be lively. There's every reason for it; we're going to Chamouni."

"You're restless; that's what's the matter with you." And Mrs. Ruck got up.

"No, I ain't," said her husband. "I never felt so quiet; I feel as peaceful as a little child."

Mrs. Ruck, who had no sense whatever of humour, looked at her daughter and at me. "Well, I hope you'll improve," she said.

"Send in the bills," Mr. Ruck went on, rising to his feet. "Don't hesitate, Sophy. I don't care what you do now. In for a penny, in for a pound."

Miss Ruck joined her mother, with a little toss of her head, and we followed the ladies to the carriage. "In your place," said Miss Sophy to her father, "I wouldn't talk so much about pennies and pounds before strangers."

Poor Mr. Ruck appeared to feel the force of this observation, which, in the consciousness of a man who had never been "mean," could hardly fail to strike a responsive chord. He coloured a little, and he was silent; his companions got into their vehicle, the front seat of which was adorned with a large parcel. Mr. Ruck gave the parcel a little poke with his umbrella, and then, turning to me with a rather grimly penitential smile, "After all," he said, "for the ladies that's the principal interest."

VII.

Old M. Pigeonneau had more than once proposed to me to take a walk, but I had hitherto been unable to respond to so alluring an invitation. It befell, however, one afternoon, that I perceived him going forth upon a desultory stroll, with a certain lonesomeness of demeanour that attracted my sympathy. I hastily overtook him, and passed my hand into his venerable arm, a proceeding which produced in the good old

man so jovial a sense of comradeship that he ardently proposed we should bend our steps to the English Garden; no
locality less festive was worthy of the occasion. To the English
Garden, accordingly, we went; it lay beyond the bridge, beside
the lake. It was very pretty and very animated; there was a
band playing in the middle, and a considerable number of
persons sitting under the small trees, on benches and little
chairs, or strolling beside the blue water. We joined the stroll-
ers, we observed our companions, and conversed on obvious
topics. Some of these last, of course, were the pretty women
who embellished the scene, and who, in the light of M. Pigeonneau's comprehensive criticism, appeared surprisingly numerous. He seemed bent upon our making up our minds as
to which was the prettiest, and as this was an innocent game
I consented to play at it.

Suddenly M. Pigeonneau stopped, pressing my arm with
the liveliest emotion. "La voilà, la voilà, the prettiest!" he
quickly murmured, "coming toward us, in a blue dress, with
the other." It was at the other I was looking, for the other,
to my surprise, was our interesting fellow-pensioner, the
daughter of a vigilant mother. M. Pigeonneau, meanwhile,
had redoubled his exclamations; he had recognised Miss
Sophy Ruck. "Oh, la belle rencontre, nos aimables convives;
the prettiest girl in the world, in effect!"

We immediately greeted and joined the young ladies, who,
like ourselves, were walking arm in arm and enjoying the
scene.

"I was citing you with admiration to my friend, even before
I had recognised you," said M. Pigeonneau to Miss Ruck.

"I don't believe in French compliments," remarked this
young lady, presenting her back to the smiling old man.

"Are you and Miss Ruck walking alone?" I asked of her
companion. "You had better accept of M. Pigeonneau's gallant protection, and of mine."

Aurora Church had taken her hand out of Miss Ruck's arm;
she looked at me, smiling, with her head a little inclined,
while, upon her shoulder, she made her open parasol revolve.
"Which is most improper,—to walk alone or to walk with
gentlemen? I wish to do what is most improper."

"What mysterious logic governs your conduct?" I inquired.

"He thinks you can't understand him when he talks like that," said Miss Ruck. "But I do understand you, always!"

"So I have always ventured to hope, my dear Miss Ruck."

"Well, if I didn't, it wouldn't be much loss," rejoined this young lady.

"Allons, en marche!" cried M. Pigeonneau, smiling still, and undiscouraged by her inhumanity. "Let us make together the tour of the garden." And he imposed his society upon Miss Ruck with a respectful, elderly grace which was evidently unable to see anything in her reluctance but modesty, and was sublimely conscious of a mission to place modesty at its ease. This ill-assorted couple walked in front, while Aurora Church and I strolled along together.

"I am sure this is more improper," said my companion; "this is delightfully improper. I don't say that as a compliment to you," she added. "I would say it to any man, no matter how stupid."

"Oh, I am very stupid," I answered, "but this doesn't seem to me wrong."

"Not for you, no; only for me. There is nothing that a man can do that is wrong, is there? *En morale*, you know, I mean. Ah, yes, he can steal; but I think there is nothing else, is there?"

"I don't know. One doesn't know those things until after one has done them. Then one is enlightened."

"And you mean that you have never been enlightened? You make yourself out very good."

"That is better than making one's self out bad, as you do."

The young girl glanced at me a moment, and then, with her charming smile, "That's one of the consequences of a false position."

"Is your position false?" I inquired, smiling too at this large formula.

"Distinctly so."

"In what way?"

"Oh, in every way. For instance, I have to pretend to be a *jeune fille*. I am not a jeune fille; no American girl is a jeune fille; an American girl is an intelligent, responsible creature. I have to pretend to be very innocent, but I am not very innocent."

"You don't pretend to be very innocent; you pretend to be—what shall I call it?—very wise."

"That's no pretence. I am wise."

"You are not an American girl," I ventured to observe.

My companion almost stopped, looking at me; there was a little flush in her cheek. "Voilà!" she said. "There's my false position. I want to be an American girl, and I'm not."

"Do you want me to tell you?" I went on. "An American girl wouldn't talk as you are talking now."

"Please tell me," said Aurora Church, with expressive eagerness. "How would she talk?"

"I can't tell you all the things an American girl would say, but I think I can tell you the things she wouldn't say. She wouldn't reason out her conduct, as you seem to me to do."

Aurora gave me the most flattering attention. "I see. She would be simpler. To do very simple things that are not at all simple—that is the American girl!"

I permitted myself a small explosion of hilarity. "I don't know whether you are a French girl, or what you are," I said, "but you are very witty."

"Ah, you mean that I strike false notes!" cried Aurora Church, sadly. "That's just what I want to avoid. I wish you would always tell me."

The conversational union between Miss Ruck and her neighbour, in front of us, had evidently not become a close one. The young lady suddenly turned round to us with a question: "Don't you want some ice cream?"

"*She* doesn't strike false notes," I murmured.

There was a kind of pavilion or kiosk, which served as a café, and at which the delicacies procurable at such an establishment were dispensed. Miss Ruck pointed to the little green tables and chairs which were set out on the gravel; M. Pigeonneau, fluttering with a sense of dissipation, seconded the proposal, and we presently sat down and gave our order to a nimble attendant. I managed again to place myself next to Aurora Church; our companions were on the other side of the table.

My neighbour was delighted with our situation. "This is best of all," she said. "I never believed I should come to a café with two strange men! Now, you can't persuade me this isn't wrong."

"To make it wrong we ought to see your mother coming down that path."

"Ah, my mother makes everything wrong," said the young girl, attacking with a little spoon in the shape of a spade the apex of a pink ice. And then she returned to her idea of a moment before: "You must promise to tell me—to warn me in some way—whenever I strike a false note. You must give a little cough, like that—ahem!"

"You will keep me very busy, and people will think I am in a consumption."

"*Voyons,*" she continued, "why have you never talked to me more? Is that a false note? Why haven't you been 'attentive?' That's what American girls call it; that's what Miss Ruck calls it."

I assured myself that our companions were out of ear-shot, and that Miss Ruck was much occupied with a large vanilla cream. "Because you are always entwined with that young lady. There is no getting near you."

Aurora looked at her friend while the latter devoted herself to her ice. "You wonder why I like her so much, I suppose. So does mamma; elle s'y perd. I don't like her particularly; je n'en suis pas folle. But she gives me information; she tells me about America. Mamma has always tried to prevent my knowing anything about it, and I am all the more curious. And then Miss Ruck is very fresh."

"I may not be so fresh as Miss Ruck," I said, "but in future, when you want information, I recommend you to come to me for it."

"Our friend offers to take me to America; she invites me to go back with her, to stay with her. You couldn't do that, could you?" And the young girl looked at me a moment. "*Bon*, a false note! I can see it by your face; you remind me of a *maître de piano.*"

"You overdo the character—the poor American girl," I said. "Are you going to stay with that delightful family?"

"I will go and stay with any one that will take me or ask me. It's a real *nostalgie*. She says that in New York—in Thirty-Seventh Street—I should have the most lovely time."

"I have no doubt you would enjoy it."

"Absolute liberty to begin with."

"It seems to me you have a certain liberty here," I rejoined.

"Ah, *this*? Oh, I shall pay for this. I shall be punished by mamma, and I shall be lectured by Madame Galopin."

"The wife of the pasteur?"

"His *digne épouse*. Madame Galopin, for mamma, is the incarnation of European opinion. That's what vexes me with mamma, her thinking so much of people like Madame Galopin. Going to see Madame Galopin—mamma calls that being in European society. European society! I'm so sick of that expression; I have heard it since I was six years old. Who is Madame Galopin—who thinks anything of her here? She is nobody; she is perfectly third-rate. If I like America better than mamma, I also know Europe better."

"But your mother, certainly," I objected, a trifle timidly, for my young lady was excited, and had a charming little passion in her eye—"your mother has a great many social relations all over the continent."

"She thinks so, but half the people don't care for us. They are not so good as we, and they know it—I'll do them that justice—and they wonder why we should care for them. When we are polite to them, they think the less of us; there are plenty of people like that. Mamma thinks so much of them simply because they are foreigners. If I could tell you all the dull, stupid, second-rate people I have had to talk to, for no better reason than that they were *de leur pays*!—Germans, French, Italians, Turks, everything. When I complain, mamma always says that at any rate it's practice in the language. And she makes so much of the English, too; I don't know what that's practice in."

Before I had time to suggest an hypothesis, as regards this latter point, I saw something that made me rise, with a certain solemnity, from my chair. This was nothing less than the neat little figure of Mrs. Church—a perfect model of the *femme comme il faut*—approaching our table with an impatient step, and followed most unexpectedly in her advance by the preeminent form of Mr. Ruck. She had evidently come in quest of her daughter, and if she had commanded this gentleman's attendance, it had been on no softer ground than that of his

unenvied paternity to her guilty child's accomplice. My movement had given the alarm, and Aurora Church and M. Pigeonneau got up; Miss Ruck alone did not, in the local phrase,
derange herself. Mrs. Church, beneath her modest little bonnet, looked very serious, but not at all fluttered; she came
straight to her daughter, who received her with a smile, and
then she looked all round at the rest of us, very fixedly and
tranquilly, without bowing. I must do both these ladies the
justice to mention that neither of them made the least little
"scene."

"I have come for you, dearest," said the mother.

"Yes, dear mamma."

"Come for you—come for you," Mrs. Church repeated,
looking down at the relics of our little feast. "I was obliged
to ask Mr. Ruck's assistance. I was puzzled; I thought a long
time."

"Well, Mrs. Church, I was glad to see you puzzled once in
your life!" said Mr. Ruck, with friendly jocosity. "But you
came pretty straight for all that. I had hard work to keep up
with you."

"We will take a cab, Aurora," Mrs. Church went on, without heeding this pleasantry—"a closed one. Come, my daughter."

"Yes, dear mamma." The young girl was blushing, yet she
was still smiling; she looked round at us all, and, as her eyes
met mine, I thought she was beautiful. "Good-bye," she said
to us. "I have had a *lovely time*."

"We must not linger," said her mother; "it is five o'clock.
We are to dine, you know, with Madame Galopin."

"I had quite forgotten," Aurora declared. "That will be
charming."

"Do you want me to assist you to carry her back, ma'am?"
asked Mr. Ruck.

Mrs. Church hesitated a moment, with her serene little
gaze. "Do you prefer, then, to leave your daughter to finish
the evening with these gentlemen?"

Mr. Ruck pushed back his hat and scratched the top of his
head. "Well, I don't know. How would you like that, Sophy?"

"Well, I never!" exclaimed Sophy, as Mrs. Church marched
off with her daughter.

VIII.

I had half expected that Mrs. Church would make me feel the weight of her disapproval of my own share in that little act of revelry in the English Garden. But she maintained her claim to being a highly reasonable woman—I could not but admire the justice of this pretension—by recognising my irresponsibility. I had taken her daughter as I found her, which was, according to Mrs. Church's view, in a very equivocal position. The natural instinct of a young man, in such a situation, is not to protest but to profit; and it was clear to Mrs. Church that I had had nothing to do with Miss Aurora's appearing in public under the insufficient chaperonage of Miss Ruck. Besides, she liked to converse, and she apparently did me the honour to believe that of all the members of the Pension Beaurepas I had the most cultivated understanding. I found her in the salon a couple of evenings after the incident I have just narrated, and I approached her with a view of making my peace with her, if this should prove necessary. But Mrs. Church was as gracious as I could have desired; she put her marker into her book, and folded her plump little hands on the cover. She made no specific allusion to the English Garden; she embarked, rather, upon those general considerations in which her refined intellect was so much at home.

"Always at your studies, Mrs. Church," I ventured to observe.

"Que voulez-vous? To say studies is to say too much; one doesn't study in the parlour of a boarding-house. But I do what I can; I have always done what I can. That is all I have ever claimed."

"No one can do more, and you seem to have done a great deal."

"Do you know my secret?" she asked, with an air of brightening confidence. And she paused a moment before she imparted her secret—"To care only for the *best*! To do the best, to know the best—to have, to desire, to recognise, only the best. That's what I have always done, in my quiet little way. I have gone through Europe on my devoted little errand, seeking, seeing, heeding, only the best. And it has not been for myself alone; it has been for my daughter. My daughter has had the best. We are not rich, but I can say that."

"She has had you, madam," I rejoined finely.

"Certainly, such as I am, I have been devoted. We have got something everywhere; a little here, a little there. That's the real secret—to get something everywhere; you always can if you *are* devoted. Sometimes it has been a little music, sometimes a little deeper insight into the history of art; every little counts you know. Sometimes it has been just a glimpse, a view, a lovely landscape, an impression. We have always been on the look-out. Sometimes it has been a valued friendship, a delightful social tie."

"Here comes the 'European society,' the poor daughter's bugbear," I said to myself. "Certainly," I remarked aloud—I admit, rather perversely—"if you have lived a great deal in *pensions*, you must have got acquainted with lots of people."

Mrs. Church dropped her eyes a moment; and then, with considerable gravity, "I think the European pension system in many respects remarkable, and in some satisfactory. But of the friendships that we have formed, few have been contracted in establishments of this kind."

"I am sorry to hear that!" I said, laughing.

"I don't say it for you, though I might say it for some others. We have been interested in European *homes*."

"Oh, I see!"

"We have the *entrée* of the old Genevese society. I like its tone. I prefer it to that of Mr. Ruck," added Mrs. Church, calmly; "to that of Mrs. Ruck and Miss Ruck—of Miss Ruck, especially."

"Ah, the poor Rucks haven't any tone at all," I said. "Don't take them more seriously than they take themselves."

"Tell me this," my companion rejoined, "are they fair examples?"

"Examples of what?"

"Of our American tendencies."

" 'Tendencies' is a big word, dear lady; tendencies are difficult to calculate. And you shouldn't abuse those good Rucks, who have been very kind to your daughter. They have invited her to go and stay with them in Thirty-Seventh Street."

"Aurora has told me. It might be very serious."

"It might be very droll," I said.

"To me," declared Mrs. Church, "it is simply terrible. I think we shall have to leave the Pension Beaurepas. I shall go back to Madame Chamousset."

"On account of the Rucks?" I asked.

"Pray, why don't they go themselves? I have given them some excellent addresses—written down the very hours of the trains. They were going to Appenzell; I thought it was arranged."

"They talk of Chamouni now," I said; "but they are very helpless and undecided."

"I will give them some Chamouni addresses. Mrs. Ruck will send a *chaise à porteurs*; I will give her the name of a man who lets them lower than you get them at the hotels. After that they *must* go."

"Well, I doubt," I observed, "whether Mr. Ruck will ever really be seen on the Mer de Glace—in a high hat. He's not like you; he doesn't value his European privileges. He takes no interest. He regrets Wall Street, acutely. As his wife says, he is very restless, but he has no curiosity about Chamouni. So you must not depend too much on the effect of your addresses."

"Is it a frequent type?" asked Mrs. Church, with an air of self-control.

"I am afraid so. Mr. Ruck is a broken-down man of business. He is broken-down in health, and I suspect he is broken down in fortune. He has spent his whole life in buying and selling; he knows how to do nothing else. His wife and daughter have spent their lives, not in selling, but in buying; and they, on their side, know how to do nothing else. To get something in a shop that they can put on their backs—that is their one idea; they haven't another in their heads. Of course they spend no end of money, and they do it with an implacable persistence, with a mixture of audacity and of cunning. They do it in his teeth and they do it behind his back; the mother protects the daughter, and the daughter eggs on the mother. Between them they are bleeding him to death."

"Ah, what a picture!" murmured Mrs. Church. "I am afraid they are very—uncultivated."

"I share your fears. They are perfectly ignorant; they have no resources. The vision of fine clothes occupies their whole imagination. They have not an idea—even a worse one—to compete with it. Poor Mr. Ruck, who is extremely good-natured and soft, seems to me a really tragic figure. He is getting bad news every day from home; his business is going to the dogs. He is unable to stop it; he has to stand and watch his fortunes ebb. He has been used to doing things in a big way, and he feels 'mean' if he makes a fuss about bills. So the ladies keep sending them in."

"But haven't they common sense? Don't they know they are ruining themselves?"

"They don't believe it. The duty of an American husband and father is to keep them going. If he asks them how, that's his own affair. So, by way of not being mean, of being a good American husband and father, poor Ruck stands staring at bankruptcy."

Mrs. Church looked at me a moment, in quickened meditation. "Why, if Aurora were to go to stay with them, she might not even be properly fed!"

"I don't, on the whole, recommend," I said, laughing, "that your daughter should pay a visit to Thirty-Seventh Street."

"Why should I be subjected to such trials—so sadly *éprouvée*? Why should a daughter of mine like that dreadful girl?"

"*Does* she like her?"

"Pray, do you mean," asked my companion, softly, "that Aurora is a hypocrite?"

I hesitated a moment. "A little, since you ask me. I think you have forced her to be."

Mrs. Church answered this possibly presumptuous charge with a tranquil, candid exultation. "I never force my daughter!"

"She is nevertheless in a false position," I rejoined. "She hungers and thirsts to go back to her own country; she wants to 'come' out in New York, which is certainly, socially speaking, the El Dorado of young ladies. She likes any one, for the moment, who will talk to her of that, and serve as a connecting-link with her native shores. Miss Ruck performs this agreeable office."

"Your idea is, then, that if she were to go with Miss Ruck to America she would drop her afterwards."

I complimented Mrs. Church upon her logical mind, but I repudiated this cynical supposition. "I can't imagine her—when it should come to the point—embarking with the famille Ruck. But I wish she might go, nevertheless."

Mrs. Church shook her head serenely, and smiled at my inappropriate zeal. "I trust my poor child may never be guilty of so fatal a mistake. She is completely in error; she is wholly unadapted to the peculiar conditions of American life. It would not please her. She would not sympathise. My daughter's ideal is not the ideal of the class of young women to which Miss Ruck belongs. I fear they are very numerous; they give the tone—they give the tone."

"It is you that are mistaken," I said; "go home for six months and see."

"I have not, unfortunately, the means to make costly experiments. My daughter has had great advantages—rare advantages—and I should be very sorry to believe that *au fond* she does not appreciate them. One thing is certain: I must remove her from this pernicious influence. We must part company with this deplorable family. If Mr. Ruck and his ladies cannot be induced to go to Chamouni—a journey that no traveller with the smallest self-respect would omit—my daughter and I shall be obliged to retire. We shall go to Dresden."

"To Dresden?"

"The capital of Saxony. I had arranged to go there for the autumn, but it will be simpler to go immediately. There are several works in the gallery with which my daughter has not, I think, sufficiently familiarised herself; it is especially strong in the seventeenth century schools."

As my companion offered me this information I perceived Mr. Ruck come lounging in, with his hands in his pockets, and his elbows making acute angles. He had his usual anomalous appearance of both seeking and avoiding society, and he wandered obliquely toward Mrs. Church, whose last words he had overheard. "The seventeenth century schools," he said, slowly, as if he were weighing some very small object in a very large pair of scales. "Now, do you suppose they *had* schools at that period?"

Mrs. Church rose with a good deal of precision, making no answer to this incongruous jest. She clasped her large volume to her neat little bosom, and she fixed a gentle, serious eye upon Mr. Ruck.

"I had a letter this morning from Chamouni," she said.

"Well," replied Mr. Ruck, "I suppose you've got friends all over."

"I have friends at Chamouni, but they are leaving. To their great regret." I had got up, too; I listened to this statement, and I wondered. I am almost ashamed to mention the subject of my agitation. I asked myself whether this was a sudden improvisation, consecrated by maternal devotion; but this point has never been elucidated. "They are giving up some charming rooms; perhaps you would like them. I would suggest your telegraphing. The weather is glorious," continued Mrs. Church, "and the highest peaks are now perceived with extraordinary distinctness."

Mr. Ruck listened, as he always listened, respectfully. "Well," he said, "I don't know as I want to go up Mount Blank. That's the principal attraction, isn't it?"

"There are many others. I thought I would offer you an —an exceptional opportunity."

"Well," said Mr. Ruck, "you're right down friendly. But I seem to have more opportunities than I know what to do with. I don't seem able to take hold."

"It only needs a little decision," remarked Mrs. Church, with an air which was an admirable example of this virtue. "I wish you good-night, sir." And she moved noiselessly away.

Mr. Ruck, with his long legs apart, stood staring after her; then he transferred his perfectly quiet eyes to me. "Does she own a hotel over there?" he asked. "Has she got any stock in Mount Blank?"

IX.

The next day Madame Beaurepas handed me, with her own elderly fingers, a missive, which proved to be a telegram. After glancing at it, I informed her that it was apparently a signal for my departure; my brother had arrived in England, and proposed to me to meet him there; he had come on business and was to spend but three weeks in Europe. "But my house empties itself!" cried the old woman. "The famille Ruck talks of leaving me, and Madame Church *nous fait la révérence*."

"Mrs. Church is going away?"

"She is packing her trunk; she is a very extraordinary person. Do you know what she asked me this morning? To invent some combination by which the famille Ruck should move away. I informed her that I was not an inventor. That poor famille Ruck! 'Oblige me by getting rid of them,' said Madame Church, as she would have asked Célestine to remove a dish of cabbage. She speaks as if the world were made for Madame Church. I intimated to her that if she objected to the company there was a very simple remedy; and at present *elle fait ses paquets*."

"She really asked you to get the Rucks out of the house?"

"She asked me to tell them that their rooms had been let, three months ago, to another family. She has an *aplomb*!"

Mrs. Church's aplomb caused me considerable diversion; I am not sure that it was not, in some degree, to laugh over it at my leisure that I went out into the garden that evening to smoke a cigar. The night was dark and not particularly balmy, and most of my fellow-pensioners, after dinner, had remained in-doors. A long straight walk conducted from the door of the house to the ancient grille that I have described, and I stood here for some time, looking through the iron bars at the silent empty street. The prospect was not entertaining, and I presently turned away. At this moment I saw, in the distance, the door of the house open and throw a shaft of lamplight into the darkness. Into the lamplight there stepped the figure of a female, who presently closed the door behind her. She disappeared in the dusk of the garden, and I had seen her but for an instant, but I remained under the impression that Aurora Church, on the eve of her departure, had come out for a meditative stroll.

I lingered near the gate, keeping the red tip of my cigar turned toward the house, and before long a young lady emerged from among the shadows of the trees and encountered the light of a lamp that stood just outside the gate. It was in fact Aurora Church, but she seemed more bent upon conversation than upon meditation. She stood a moment looking at me, and then she said,—

"Ought I to retire—to return to the house?"

"If you ought, I should be very sorry to tell you so," I answered.

"But we are all alone; there is no one else in the garden."

"It is not the first time that I have been alone with a young lady. I am not at all terrified."

"Ah, but I?" said the young girl. "I have never been alone"—then, quickly, she interrupted herself. "Good, there's another false note!"

"Yes, I am obliged to admit that one is very false."

She stood looking at me. "I am going away to-morrow; after that there will be no one to tell me."

"That will matter little," I presently replied. "Telling you will do no good."

"Ah, why do you say that?" murmured Aurora Church.

I said it partly because it was true; but I said it for other reasons, as well, which it was hard to define. Standing there bare-headed, in the night air, in the vague light, this young lady looked extremely interesting; and the interest of her appearance was not diminished by a suspicion on my own part that she had come into the garden knowing me to be there. I thought her a charming girl, and I felt very sorry for her; but as I looked at her, the terms in which Madame Beaurepas had ventured to characterise her recurred to me with a certain force. I had professed a contempt for them at the time, but it now came into my head that perhaps this unfortunately situated, this insidiously mutinous, young creature was looking out for a preserver. She was certainly not a girl to throw herself at a man's head, but it was possible that in her intense—her almost morbid—desire to put into effect an ideal which was perhaps after all charged with as many fallacies as her mother affirmed, she might do something reckless and irregular—something in which a sympathetic compatriot, as yet unknown, would find his profit. The image, unshaped though it was, of this sympathetic compatriot filled me with a sort of envy. For some moments I was silent, conscious of these things, and then I answered her question. "Because some things—some differences—are felt, not learned. To you liberty is not natural; you are like a person who has bought a repeater, and, in his satisfaction, is constantly making it sound. To a real American girl her liberty is a very vulgarly-ticking old clock."

"Ah, you mean, then," said the poor girl, "that my mother has ruined me?"

"Ruined you?"

"She has so perverted my mind that when I try to be natural I am necessarily immodest."

"That again is a false note," I said, laughing.

She turned away. "I think you are cruel."

"By no means," I declared; "because, for my own taste, I prefer you as—as——"

I hesitated, and she turned back. "As what?"

"As you are."

She looked at me a while again, and then she said, in a little reasoning voice that reminded me of her mother's, only that it was conscious and studied, "I was not aware that I am under any particular obligation to please you!" And then she gave a clear laugh, quite at variance with her voice.

"Oh, there is no obligation," I said, "but one has preferences. I am very sorry you are going away."

"What does it matter to you? You are going yourself."

"As I am going in a different direction, that makes all the greater separation."

She answered nothing; she stood looking through the bars of the tall gate at the empty, dusky street. "This grille is like a cage," she said at last.

"Fortunately, it is a cage that will open." And I laid my hand on the lock.

"Don't open it," and she pressed the gate back. "If you should open it I would go out—and never return."

"Where should you go?"

"To America."

"Straight away?"

"Somehow or other. I would go to the American consul. I would beg him to give me money—to help me."

I received this assertion without a smile; I was not in a

smiling humour. On the contrary, I felt singularly excited, and I kept my hand on the lock of the gate. I believed (or I thought I believed) what my companion said, and I had—absurd as it may appear—an irritated vision of her throwing herself upon consular sympathy. It seemed to me, for a moment, that to pass out of that gate with this yearning, straining young creature would be to pass into some mysterious felicity. If I were only a hero of romance, I would offer, myself, to take her to America.

In a moment more, perhaps, I should have persuaded myself that I was one, but at this juncture I heard a sound that was not romantic. It proved to be the very realistic tread of Célestine, the cook, who stood grinning at us as we turned about from our colloquy.

"I ask *bien pardon*," said Célestine. "The mother of mademoiselle desires that mademoiselle should come in immediately. M. le Pasteur Galopin has come to make his adieux to *ces dames*."

Aurora gave me only one glance, but it was a touching one. Then she slowly departed with Célestine.

The next morning, on coming into the garden, I found that Mrs. Church and her daughter had departed. I was informed of this fact by old M. Pigeonneau, who sat there under a tree, having his coffee at a little green table.

"I have nothing to envy you," he said; "I had the last glimpse of that charming Miss Aurora."

"I had a very late glimpse," I answered, "and it was all I could possibly desire."

"I have always noticed," rejoined M. Pigeonneau, "that your desires are more moderate than mine. Que voulez-vous? I am of the old school. Je crois que la race se perd. I regret the departure of that young girl: she had an enchanting smile. Ce sera une femme d'esprit. For the mother, I can console myself. I am not sure that *she* was a femme d'esprit, though she wished to pass for one. Round, rosy, *potelée*, she yet had not the temperament of her appearance; she was a *femme austère*. I have often noticed that contradiction in American ladies. You see a plump little woman, with a speaking eye and the contour and complexion of a ripe peach, and if you venture to conduct yourself in the smallest degree in accordance with these *indices*, you discover a species of Methodist—of what do you call it?—of Quakeress. On the other hand, you encounter a tall, lean, angular person, without colour, without grace, all elbows and knees, and you find it's a nature of the tropics! The women of duty look like coquettes, and the others look like alpenstocks! However, we have still the handsome Madame Ruck—a real *femme de Rubens, celle-là.* It is very true that to talk to her one must know the Flemish tongue!"

I had determined, in accordance with my brother's telegram, to go away in the afternoon; so that, having various duties to perform, I left M. Pigeonneau to his international comparisons. Among other things, I went in the course of the morning to the banker's, to draw money for my journey, and there I found Mr. Ruck, with a pile of crumpled letters in his lap, his chair tipped back and his eyes gloomily fixed on the fringe of the green plush table-cloth. I timidly expressed the hope that he had got better news from home; whereupon he gave me a look in which, considering his provocation, the absence of irritation was conspicuous.

He took up his letters in his large hand, and crushing them together held it out to me. "That epistolary matter," he said, "is worth about five cents. But I guess," he added, rising, "I have taken it in by this time." When I had drawn my money, I asked him to come and breakfast with me at the little *brasserie*, much favoured by students, to which I used to resort in the old town. "I couldn't eat, sir," he said, "I couldn't eat. Bad news takes away the appetite. But I guess I'll go with you, so that I needn't go to table down there at the pension. The old woman down there is always accusing me of turning up my nose at her food. Well, I guess I shan't turn up my nose at anything now."

We went to the little brasserie, where poor Mr. Ruck made the lightest possible breakfast. But if he ate very little, he talked a great deal; he talked about business, going into a hundred details in which I was quite unable to follow him. His talk was not angry nor bitter; it was a long, meditative, melancholy monologue; if it had been a trifle less incoherent I should almost have called it philosophic. I was very sorry for him; I wanted to do something for him, but the only thing

I could do was, when we had breakfasted, to see him safely
back to the Pension Beaurepas. We went across the Treille
and down the Corraterie, out of which we turned into the
Rue du Rhône. In this latter street, as all the world knows,
are many of those brilliant jewellers' shops for which Geneva
is famous. I always admired their glittering windows, and
never passed them without a lingering glance. Even on this
occasion, preoccupied as I was with my impending departure
and with my companion's troubles, I suffered my eyes to wander along the precious tiers that flashed and twinkled behind
the huge, clear plates of glass. Thanks to this inveterate habit,
I made a discovery. In the largest and most brilliant of these
establishments I perceived two ladies, seated before the
counter with an air of absorption which sufficiently proclaimed their identity. I hoped my companion would not see
them, but as we came abreast of the door, a little beyond, we
found it open to the warm summer air. Mr. Ruck happened
to glance in, and he immediately recognised his wife and
daughter. He slowly stopped, looking at them; I wondered
what he would do. The salesman was holding up a bracelet
before them, on its velvet cushion, and flashing it about in an
irresistible manner.

Mr. Ruck said nothing, but he presently went in, and I did
the same.

"It will be an opportunity," I remarked, as cheerfully as
possible, "for me to bid good-bye to the ladies."

They turned round when Mr. Ruck came in, and looked at
him without confusion. "Well, you had better go home to
breakfast," remarked his wife. Miss Sophy made no remark,
but she took the bracelet from the attendant and gazed at it
very fixedly. Mr. Ruck seated himself on an empty stool and
looked round the shop.

"Well, you have been here before," said his wife; "you were
here the first day we came."

Miss Ruck extended the precious object in her hands towards me. "Don't you think that sweet?" she inquired.

I looked at it a moment. "No, I think it's ugly."

She glanced at me a moment, incredulous. "Well, I don't
believe you have any taste."

"Why, sir, it's just lovely," said Mrs. Ruck.

"You'll see it some day on me, any way," her daughter declared.

"No, he won't," said Mr. Ruck quietly.

"It will be his own fault, then," Miss Sophy observed.

"Well, if we are going to Chamouni we want to get something here," said Mrs. Ruck. "We may not have another chance."

Mr. Ruck was still looking round the shop, whistling in a very low tone. "We ain't going to Chamouni. We are going to New York city, straight."

"Well, I'm glad to hear that," said Mrs. Ruck. "Don't you suppose we want to take something home?"

"If we are going straight back I must have that bracelet," her daughter declared. "Only I don't want a velvet case; I want a satin case."

"I must bid you good-bye," I said to the ladies. "I am leaving Geneva in an hour or two."

"Take a good look at that bracelet, so you'll know it when you see it," said Miss Sophy.

"She's bound to have something," remarked her mother, almost proudly.

Mr. Ruck was still vaguely inspecting the shop; he was still whistling a little. "I am afraid he is not at all well," I said, softly, to his wife.

She twisted her head a little, and glanced at him.

"Well, I wish he'd improve!" she exclaimed.

"A satin case, and a nice one!" said Miss Ruck to the shop-man.

I bade Mr. Ruck good-bye. "Don't wait for me," he said, sitting there on his stool, and not meeting my eye. "I've got to see this thing through."

I went back to the Pension Beaurepas, and when, an hour later, I left it with my luggage, the family had not returned.

The Diary of a Man of Fifty

FLORENCE, *April 5th, 1874*—They told me I should find
Italy greatly changed; and in seven and twenty years there
is room for changes. But to me everything is so perfectly the
same that I seem to be living my youth over again; all the
forgotten impressions of that enchanting time come back to
me. At the moment they were powerful enough; but they
afterwards faded away. What in the world became of them?
What ever becomes of such things, in the long intervals of
consciousness? Where do they hide themselves away? in what
unvisited cupboards and crannies of our being do they preserve themselves? They are like the lines of a letter written in
sympathetic ink; hold the letter to the fire for a while and the
grateful warmth brings out the invisible words. It is the
warmth of this yellow sun of Florence that has been restoring
the text of my own young romance; the thing has been lying
before me to-day as a clear, fresh page. There have been moments during the last ten years when I have felt so portentously old, so fagged and finished, that I should have taken
as a very bad joke any intimation that this present sense of
juvenility was still in store for me. It won't last, at any rate;
so I had better make the best of it. But I confess it surprises
me. I have led too serious a life; but that perhaps, after all,
preserves one's youth. At all events, I have travelled too far,
I have worked too hard, I have lived in brutal climates and
associated with tiresome people. When a man has reached his
fifty-second year without being, materially, the worse for
wear—when he has fair health, a fair fortune, a tidy conscience
and a complete exemption from embarrassing relatives—I
suppose he is bound, in delicacy, to write himself happy. But
I confess I shirk this obligation. I have not been miserable; I
won't go so far as to say that—or at least as to write it. But
happiness—positive happiness—would have been something
different. I don't know that it would have been better, by all
measurements—that it would have left me better off at the
present time. But it certainly would have made this difference
—that I should not have been reduced, in pursuit of pleasant

images, to disinter a buried episode of more than a quarter of a century ago. I should have found entertainment more— what shall I call it?—more contemporaneous. I should have had a wife and children, and I should not be in the way of making, as the French say, infidelities to the present. Of course it's a great gain to have had an escape, not to have committed an act of thumping folly; and I suppose that, whatever serious step one might have taken at twenty-five, after a struggle, and with a violent effort, and however one's conduct might appear to be justified by events, there would always remain a certain element of regret; a certain sense of loss lurking in the sense of gain; a tendency to wonder, rather wishfully, what *might* have been. What might have been, in this case, would, without doubt, have been very sad, and what has been has been very cheerful and comfortable; but there are nevertheless two or three questions I might ask myself. Why, for instance, have I never married—why have I never been able to care for any woman as I cared for that one? Ah, why are the mountains blue and why is the sunshine warm? Happiness mitigated by impertinent conjectures—that's about my ticket.

6th.—I knew it wouldn't last; it's already passing away. But I have spent a delightful day; I have been strolling all over the place. Everything reminds me of something else, and yet of itself at the same time; my imagination makes a great circuit and comes back to the starting-point. There is that well-remembered odour of spring in the air, and the flowers, as they used to be, are gathered into great sheaves and stacks, all along the rugged base of the Strozzi Palace. I wandered for an hour in the Boboli Gardens; we went there several times together. I remember all those days individually; they seem to me as yesterday. I found the corner where she always chose to sit—the bench of sun-warmed marble, in front of the screen of ilex, with that exuberant statue of Pomona just be-side it. The place is exactly the same, except that poor Pomona has lost one of her tapering fingers. I sat there for half-an-hour, and it was strange how near to me she seemed. The place was perfectly empty—that is, it was filled with *her*. I closed my eyes and listened; I could almost hear the rustle of her dress on the gravel. Why do we make such an ado about death? What is it after all but a sort of refinement of life? She died ten years ago, and yet, as I sat there in the sunny stillness, she was a palpable, audible presence. I went afterwards into the gallery of the palace, and wandered for an hour from room to room. The same great pictures hung in the same places and the same dark frescoes arched above them. Twice, of old, I went there with her; she had a great understanding of art. She understood all sorts of things. Before the Madonna of the Chair I stood a long time. The face is not a particle like hers, and yet it reminded me of her. But everything does that. We stood and looked at it together once for half-an-hour; I remember perfectly what she said.

8th.—Yesterday I felt blue—blue and bored; and when I got up this morning I had half a mind to leave Florence. But I went out into the street, beside the Arno, and looked up and down—looked at the yellow river and the violet hills, and then decided to remain—or rather, I decided nothing. I simply stood gazing at the beauty of Florence, and before I had gazed my fill I was in good-humour again, and it was too late to start for Rome. I strolled along the quay, where something presently happened that rewarded me for staying. I stopped in front of a little jeweller's shop, where a great many objects in mosaic were exposed in the window; I stood there for some minutes—I don't know why, for I have no taste for mosaic. In a moment a little girl came and stood beside me—a little girl with a frowsy Italian head, carrying a basket. I turned away, but, as I turned, my eyes happened to fall on her basket. It was covered with a napkin, and on the napkin was pinned a piece of paper, inscribed with an address. This address caught my glance—there was a name on it I knew. It was very legibly written—evidently by a scribe who had made up in zeal what was lacking in skill. *Contessa Salvi-Scarabelli, Via Ghibellina*—so ran the superscription; I looked at it for some moments; it caused me a sudden emotion. Presently the little girl, becoming aware of my attention, glanced up at me, wondering, with a pair of timid brown eyes.

"Are you carrying your basket to the Countess Salvi?" I asked.

The child stared at me. "To the Countess Scarabelli."

"Do you know the Countess?"

"Know her?" murmured the child, with an air of small dismay.

"I mean, have you seen her?"

"Yes, I have seen her." And then, in a moment, with a sudden soft smile—*"E bella!"* said the little girl. She was beautiful herself as she said it.

"Precisely; and is she fair or dark?"

The child kept gazing at me. *"Bionda—bionda,"* she answered, looking about into the golden sunshine for a comparison.

"And is she young?"

"She is not young—like me. But she is not old like—like—"

"Like me, eh? And is she married?"

The little girl began to look wise. "I have never seen the Signor Conte."

"And she lives in Via Ghibellina?"

"Sicuro. In a beautiful palace."

I had one more question to ask, and I pointed it with certain copper coins. "Tell me a little—is she good?"

The child inspected a moment the contents of her little brown fist. "It's you who are good," she answered.

"Ah, but the Countess?" I repeated.

My informant lowered her big brown eyes, with an air of conscientious meditation that was inexpressibly quaint. "To me she appears so," she said at last, looking up.

"Ah, then she must be so," I said, "because, for your age, you are very intelligent." And having delivered myself of this compliment I walked away and left the little girl counting her *soldi.*

I walked back to the hotel, wondering how I could learn something about the Contessa Salvi-Scarabelli. In the doorway I found the innkeeper, and near him stood a young man whom I immediately perceived to be a compatriot and with whom, apparently, he had been in conversation.

"I wonder whether you can give me a piece of information," I said to the landlord. "Do you know anything about the Count Salvi-Scarabelli?"

The landlord looked down at his boots, then slowly raised

his shoulders, with a melancholy smile. "I have many regrets, dear sir——"

"You don't know the name?"

"I know the name, assuredly. But I don't know the gentleman."

I saw that my question had attracted the attention of the young Englishman, who looked at me with a good deal of earnestness. He was apparently satisfied with what he saw, for he presently decided to speak.

"The Count Scarabelli is dead," he said, very gravely.

I looked at him a moment; he was a pleasing young fellow. "And his widow lives," I observed, "in Via Ghibellina?"

"I daresay that is the name of the street." He was a handsome young Englishman, but he was also an awkward one; he wondered who I was and what I wanted, and he did me the honour to perceive that, as regards these points, my appearance was reassuring. But he hesitated, very properly, to talk with a perfect stranger about a lady whom he knew, and he had not the art to conceal his hesitation. I instantly felt it to be singular that though he regarded me as a perfect stranger, I had not the same feeling about him. Whether it was that I had seen him before, or simply that I was struck with his agreeable young face—at any rate, I felt myself as they say here, in sympathy with him. If I have seen him before I don't remember the occasion, and neither, apparently, does he; I suppose it's only a part of the feeling I have had the last three days about everything. It was this feeling that made me suddenly act as if I had known him a long time.

"Do you know the Countess Salvi?" I asked.

He looked at me a little, and then, without resenting the freedom of my question—"The Countess Scarabelli you mean," he said.

"Yes," I answered; "she's the daughter."

"The daughter is a little girl."

"She must be grown up now. She must be—let me see—close upon thirty."

My young Englishman began to smile. "Of whom are you speaking?"

"I was speaking of the daughter," I said, understanding his smile. "But I was thinking of the mother."

"Of the mother?"

"Of a person I knew twenty-seven years ago—the most charming woman I have ever known. She was the Countess Salvi—she lived in a wonderful old house in Via Ghibellina."

"A wonderful old house!" my young Englishman repeated.

"She had a little girl," I went on; "and the little girl was very fair, like her mother; and the mother and daughter had the same name—Bianca." I stopped and looked at my companion, and he blushed a little. "And Bianca Salvi," I continued, "was the most charming woman in the world." He blushed a little more, and I laid my hand on his shoulder. "Do you know why I tell you this? Because you remind me of what I was when I knew her—when I loved her." My poor young Englishman gazed at me with a sort of embarrassed and fascinated stare, and still I went on. "I say that's the reason I told you this—but you'll think it a strange reason. You remind me of my younger self. You needn't resent that—I was a charming young fellow. The Countess Salvi thought so. Her daughter thinks the same of you."

Instantly, instinctively he raised his hand to my arm. "Truly?"

"Ah, you are wonderfully like me!" I said, laughing. "That was just my state of mind. I wanted tremendously to please her." He dropped his hand and looked away, smiling, but with an air of ingenuous confusion which quickened my interest in him. "You don't know what to make of me," I pursued. "You don't know why a stranger should suddenly address you in this way and pretend to read your thoughts. Doubtless you think me a little cracked. Perhaps I am eccentric; but it's not so bad as that. I have lived about the world a great deal, following my profession, which is that of a soldier. I have been in India, in Africa, in Canada, and I have lived a good deal alone. That inclines people, I think, to sudden bursts of confidence. A week ago I came into Italy, where I spent six months when I was your age. I came straight to Florence—I was eager to see it again, on account of associations. They have been crowding upon me ever so thickly. I have taken the liberty of giving you a hint of them." The young man inclined himself a little, in silence, as if he had been struck with a sudden respect. He stood and looked away for a moment at the river and the mountains. "It's very beautiful," I said.

"Oh, it's enchanting," he murmured.

"That's the way I used to talk. But that's nothing to you."

He glanced at me again. "On the contrary, I like to hear."

"Well, then, let us take a walk. If you too are staying at this inn, we are fellow-travellers. We will walk down the Arno to the Cascine. There are several things I should like to ask of you."

My young Englishman assented with an air of almost filial confidence, and we strolled for an hour beside the river and through the shady alleys of that lovely wilderness. We had a great deal of talk: it's not only myself, it's my whole situation over again.

"Are you very fond of Italy?" I asked.

He hesitated a moment. "One can't express that."

"Just so; I couldn't express it. I used to try—I used to write verses. On the subject of Italy I was very ridiculous."

"So am I ridiculous," said my companion.

"No, my dear boy," I answered, "we are not ridiculous; we are two very reasonable, superior people."

"The first time one comes—as I have done—it's a revelation."

"Oh, I remember well; one never forgets it. It's an introduction to beauty."

"And it must be a great pleasure," said my young friend, "to come back."

"Yes, fortunately the beauty is always here. What form of it," I asked, "do you prefer?"

My companion looked a little mystified; and at last he said, "I am very fond of the pictures."

"So was I. And among the pictures, which do you like best?"

"Oh, a great many."

"So did I; but I had certain favourites."

Again the young man hesitated a little, and then he confessed that the group of painters he preferred on the whole to all others was that of the early Florentines.

I was so struck with this that I stopped short. "That was

exactly my taste!" And then I passed my hand into his arm and we went our way again.

We sat down on an old stone bench in the Cascine, and a solemn blank-eyed Hermes, with wrinkles accentuated by the dust of ages, stood above us and listened to our talk.

"The Countess Salvi died ten years ago," I said.

My companion admitted that he had heard her daughter say so.

"After I knew her she married again," I added. "The Count Salvi died before I knew her—a couple of years after their marriage."

"Yes, I have heard that."

"And what else have you heard?"

My companion stared at me; he had evidently heard nothing.

"She was a very interesting woman—there are a great many things to be said about her. Later, perhaps, I will tell you. Has the daughter the same charm?"

"You forget," said my young man, smiling, "that I have never seen the mother."

"Very true. I keep confounding. But the daughter—how long have you known her?"

"Only since I have been here. A very short time."

"A week?"

For a moment he said nothing. "A month."

"That's just the answer I should have made. A week, a month—it was all the same to me."

"I think it is more than a month," said the young man.

"It's probably six. How did you make her acquaintance?"

"By a letter—an introduction given me by a friend in England."

"The analogy is complete," I said. "But the friend who gave me my letter to Madame de Salvi died many years ago. He, too, admired her greatly. I don't know why it never came into my mind that her daughter might be living in Florence. Somehow I took for granted it was all over. I never thought of the little girl; I never heard what had become of her. I walked past the palace yesterday and saw that it was occupied; but I took for granted it had changed hands."

"The Countess Scarabelli," said my friend, "brought it to her husband as her marriage-portion."

"I hope he appreciated it! There is a fountain in the court, and there is a charming old garden beyond it. The Countess's sitting-room looks into that garden. The staircase is of white marble, and there is a medallion by Luca della Robbia set into the wall at the place where it makes a bend. Before you come into the drawing-room you stand a moment in a great vaulted place hung round with faded tapestry, paved with bare tiles, and furnished only with three chairs. In the drawing-room, above the fire-place, is a superb Andrea del Sarto. The furniture is covered with pale sea-green."

My companion listened to all this.

"The Andrea del Sarto is there; it's magnificent. But the furniture is in pale red."

"Ah, they have changed it then—in twenty-seven years."

"And there's a portrait of Madame de Salvi," continued my friend.

I was silent a moment. "I should like to see that."

He too was silent. Then he asked, "Why don't you go and see it? If you knew the mother so well, why don't you call upon the daughter?"

"From what you tell me I am afraid."

"What have I told you to make you afraid?"

I looked a little at his ingenuous countenance. "The mother was a very dangerous woman."

The young Englishman began to blush again. "The daughter is not," he said.

"Are you very sure?"

He didn't say he was sure, but he presently inquired in what way the Countess Salvi had been dangerous.

"You must not ask me that," I answered; "for, after all, I desire to remember only what was good in her." And as we walked back I begged him to render me the service of mentioning my name to his friend, and of saying that I had known her mother well and that I asked permission to come and see her.

9th.—I have seen that poor boy half-a-dozen times again, and a most amiable young fellow he is. He continues to represent to me, in the most extraordinary manner, my own young identity; the correspondence is perfect at all points, save that he is a better boy than I. He is evidently acutely

interested in his Countess, and leads quite the same life with
her that I led with Madame de Salvi. He goes to see her every
evening and stays half the night; these Florentines keep the
most extraordinary hours. I remember, towards 3 A.M., Madame de Salvi used to turn me out. "Come, come," she
would say, "it's time to go. If you were to stay later people
might talk." I don't know at what time he comes home, but
I suppose his evening seems as short as mine did. To-day he
brought me a message from his Contessa—a very gracious
little speech. She remembered often to have heard her mother
speak of me—she called me her English friend. All her
mother's friends were dear to her, and she begged I would
do her the honour to come and see her. She is always at home
of an evening. Poor young Stanmer (he is of the Devonshire
Stanmers—a great property) reported this speech verbatim,
and of course it can't in the least signify to him that a poor
grizzled, battered soldier, old enough to be his father, should
come to call upon his *inammorata*. But I remember how it
used to matter to me when other men came; that's a point of
difference. However, it's only because I'm so old. At twenty-
five I shouldn't have been afraid of myself at fifty-two.
Camerino was thirty-four—and then the others! She was always at home in the evening, and they all used to come. They
were old Florentine names. But she used to let me stay after
them all; she thought an old English name as good. What a
transcendent coquette! . . . But *basta così*, as she used to say.
I meant to go to-night to Casa Salvi, but I couldn't bring
myself to the point. I don't know what I'm afraid of; I used
to be in a hurry enough to go there once. I suppose I am
afraid of the very look of the place—of the old rooms, the old
walls. I shall go to-morrow night. I am afraid of the very
echoes.

10th.—She has the most extraordinary resemblance to her
mother. When I went in I was tremendously startled; I stood
staring at her. I have just come home; it is past midnight; I
have been all the evening at Casa Salvi. It is very warm—my
window is open—I can look out on the river, gliding past in
the starlight. So, of old, when I came home, I used to stand and
look out. There are the same cypresses on the opposite hills.
   Poor young Stanmer was there, and three or four other

admirers; they all got up when I came in. I think I had been talked about, and there was some curiosity. But why should I have been talked about? They were all youngish men—none of them of my time. She is a wonderful likeness of her mother; I couldn't get over it. Beautiful like her mother, and yet with the same faults in her face; but with her mother's perfect head and brow and sympathetic, almost pitying eyes. Her face has just that peculiarity of her mother's, which, of all human countenances that I have ever known, was the one that passed most quickly and completely from the expression of gaiety to that of repose. Repose, in her face, always suggested sadness; and while you were watching it with a kind of awe, and wondering of what tragic secret it was the token, it kindled, on the instant, into a radiant Italian smile. The Countess Scarabelli's smiles to-night, however, were almost uninterrupted. She greeted me—divinely, as her mother used to do; and young Stanmer sat in the corner of the sofa—as I used to do— and watched her while she talked. She is thin and very fair, and was dressed in light, vaporous black: that completes the resemblance. The house, the rooms, are almost absolutely the same; there may be changes of detail, but they don't modify the general effect. There are the same precious pictures on the walls of the salon—the same great dusky fresco in the concave ceiling. The daughter is not rich, I suppose, any more than the mother. The furniture is worn and faded, and I was admitted by a solitary servant who carried a twinkling taper before me up the great dark marble staircase.

"I have often heard of you," said the Countess, as I sat down near her; "my mother often spoke of you."

"Often?" I answered. "I am surprised at that."

"Why are you surprised? Were you not good friends?"

"Yes, for a certain time—very good friends. But I was sure she had forgotten me."

"She never forgot," said the Countess, looking at me intently and smiling. "She was not like that."

"She was not like most other women in any way," I declared.

"Ah, she was charming," cried the Countess, rattling open her fan. "I have always been very curious to see you. I have received an impression of you."

"A good one, I hope."

She looked at me, laughing, and not answering this: it was just her mother's trick.

" 'My Englishman,' she used to call you—*'il mio Inglese.'*"

"I hope she spoke of me kindly," I insisted.

The Countess, still laughing, gave a little shrug, balancing her hand to and fro. "So-so; I always supposed you had had a quarrel. You don't mind my being frank like this—eh?"

"I delight in it; it reminds me of your mother."

"Every one tells me that. But I am not clever like her. You will see for yourself."

"That speech," I said, "completes the resemblance. She was always pretending she was not clever, and in reality——"

"In reality she was an angel, eh? To escape from dangerous comparisons I will admit then that I am clever. That will make a difference. But let us talk of you. You are very—how shall I say it?—very eccentric."

"Is that what your mother told you?"

"To tell the truth, she spoke of you as a great original. But aren't all Englishmen eccentric? All except that one!" and the Countess pointed to poor Stanmer, in his corner of the sofa.

"Oh, I know just what he is," I said.

"He's as quiet as a lamb—he's like all the world," cried the Countess.

"Like all the world—yes. He is in love with you."

She looked at me with sudden gravity. "I don't object to your saying that for all the world—but I do for him."

"Well," I went on, "he is peculiar in this: he is rather afraid of you."

Instantly she began to smile; she turned her face toward Stanmer. He had seen that we were talking about him; he coloured and got up—then came toward us.

"I like men who are afraid of nothing," said our hostess.

"I know what you want," I said to Stanmer. "You want to know what the Signora Contessa says about you."

Stanmer looked straight into her face, very gravely. "I don't care a straw what she says."

"You are almost a match for the Signora Contessa," I answered. "She declares she doesn't care a pin's head what you think."

"I recognise the Countess's style!" Stanmer exclaimed, turning away.

"One would think," said the Countess, "that you were trying to make a quarrel between us."

I watched him move away to another part of the great saloon; he stood in front of the Andrea del Sarto, looking up at it. But he was not seeing it; he was listening to what we might say. I often stood there in just that way. "He can't quarrel with you, any more than I could have quarrelled with your mother."

"Ah, but you did. Something painful passed between you."

"Yes, it was painful, but it was not a quarrel. I went away one day and never saw her again. That was all."

The Countess looked at me gravely. "What do you call it when a man does that?"

"It depends upon the case."

"Sometimes," said the Countess in French, "it's a *lâcheté*."

"Yes, and sometimes, it's an act of wisdom."

"And sometimes," rejoined the Countess, "it's a mistake."

I shook my head. "For me it was no mistake."

She began to laugh again. "Caro Signore, you're a great original. What had my poor mother done to you?"

I looked at our young Englishman, who still had his back turned to us and was staring up at the picture. "I will tell you some other time," I said.

"I shall certainly remind you; I am very curious to know." Then she opened and shut her fan two or three times, still looking at me. What eyes they have! "Tell me a little," she went on, "if I may ask without indiscretion. Are you married?"

"No, Signora Contessa."

"Isn't that at least a mistake?"

"Do I look very unhappy?"

She dropped her head a little to one side. "For an Englishman—no!"

"Ah," said I, laughing, "you are quite as clever as your mother."

"And they tell me that you are a great soldier," she continued; "you have lived in India. It was very kind of you, so far away, to have remembered our poor dear Italy."

"One always remembers Italy; the distance makes no difference. I remembered it well the day I heard of your mother's death!"

"Ah, that was a sorrow!" said the Countess. "There's not a day that I don't weep for her. But *che vuole*? She's a saint in paradise."

"*Sicuro,*" I answered; and I looked some time at the ground. "But tell me about yourself, dear lady," I asked at last, raising my eyes. "You have also had the sorrow of losing your husband."

"I am a poor widow, as you see. *Che vuole*? My husband died after three years of marriage."

I waited for her to remark that the late Count Scarabelli was also a saint in paradise, but I waited in vain.

"That was like your distinguished father," I said.

"Yes, he too died young. I can't be said to have known him; I was but of the age of my own little girl. But I weep for him all the more."

Again I was silent for a moment.

"It was in India too," I said presently, "that I heard of your mother's second marriage."

The Countess raised her eyebrows.

"In India, then, one hears of everything! Did that news please you?"

"Well, since you ask me—no."

"I understand that," said the Countess, looking at her open fan. "I shall not marry again like that."

"That's what your mother said to me," I ventured to observe.

She was not offended, but she rose from her seat and stood looking at me a moment. Then—

"You should not have gone away!" she exclaimed.

I stayed for another hour; it is a very pleasant house. Two or three of the men who were sitting there seemed very civil and intelligent; one of them was a major of engineers, who offered me a profusion of information upon the new organisation of the Italian army. While he talked, however, I was observing our hostess, who was talking with the others; very little, I noticed, with her young Inglese. She is altogether charming—full of frankness and freedom, of that inimitable *disinvoltura* which in an Englishwoman would be vulgar, and which in her is simply the perfection of apparent spontaneity. But for all her spontaneity she's as subtle as a needlepoint, and knows tremendously well what she is about. If she is not a consummate coquette. . . . . What had she in her head when she said that I should not have gone away?—Poor little Stanmer didn't go away. I left him there at midnight.

12th.—I found him to-day sitting in the church of Santa Croce, into which I wandered to escape from the heat of the sun.

In the nave it was cool and dim; he was staring at the blaze of candles on the great altar, and thinking, I am sure, of his incomparable Countess. I sat down beside him, and after a while, as if to avoid the appearance of eagerness, he asked me how I had enjoyed my visit to Casa Salvi, and what I thought of the *padrona*.

"I think half a dozen things," I said; "but I can only tell you one now. She's an enchantress. You shall hear the rest when we have left the church."

"An enchantress?" repeated Stanmer, looking at me askance.

He is a very simple youth, but who am I to blame him?

"A charmer," I said; "a fascinatress!"

He turned away, staring at the altar-candles.

"An artist—an actress," I went on, rather brutally.

He gave me another glance.

"I think you are telling me all," he said.

"No, no, there is more." And we sat a long time in silence.

At last he proposed that we should go out; and we passed in the street, where the shadows had begun to stretch themselves.

"I don't know what you mean by her being an actress," he said, as we turned homeward.

"I suppose not. Neither should I have known, if any one had said that to me."

"You are thinking about the mother," said Stanmer. "Why are you always bringing *her* in?"

"My dear boy, the analogy is so great; it forces itself upon me."

He stopped, and stood looking at me with his modest,

perplexed young face. I thought he was going to exclaim—
"The analogy be hanged!"—but he said after a moment—

"Well, what does it prove?"

"I can't say it proves anything; but it suggests a great many things."

"Be so good as to mention a few," he said, as we walked on.

"You are not sure of her yourself," I began.

"Never mind that—go on with your analogy."

"That's a part of it. You *are* very much in love with her."

"That's a part of it too, I suppose?"

"Yes, as I have told you before. You are in love with her, and yet you can't make her out; that's just where I was with regard to Madame de Salvi."

"And she too was an enchantress, an actress, an artist, and all the rest of it?"

"She was the most perfect coquette I ever knew, and the most dangerous, because the most finished."

"What you mean, then, is that her daughter is a finished coquette?"

"I rather think so."

Stanmer walked along for some moments in silence.

"Seeing that you suppose me to be a—a great admirer of the Countess," he said at last, "I am rather surprised at the freedom with which you speak of her."

I confessed that I was surprised at it myself. "But it's on account of the interest I take in you."

"I am immensely obliged to you!" said the poor boy.

"Ah, of course you don't like it. That is, you like my interest—I don't see how you can help liking that; but you don't like my freedom. That's natural enough; but, my dear young friend, I want only to help you. If a man had said to me—so many years ago—what I am saying to you, I should certainly also, at first, have thought him a great brute. But, after a little, I should have been grateful—I should have felt that he was helping me."

"You seem to have been very well able to help yourself," said Stanmer. "You tell me you made your escape."

"Yes, but it was at the cost of infinite perplexity—of what I may call keen suffering. I should like to save you all that."

"I can only repeat—it is really very kind of you."

"Don't repeat it too often, or I shall begin to think you don't mean it."

"Well," said Stanmer, "I think this, at any rate—that you take an extraordinary responsibility in trying to put a man out of conceit of a woman who, as he believes, may make him very happy."

I grasped his arm, and we stopped, going on with our talk like a couple of Florentines.

"Do you wish to marry her?"

He looked away, without meeting my eyes. "It's a great responsibility," he repeated.

"Before Heaven," I said, "I would have married the mother! You are exactly in my situation."

"Don't you think you rather overdo the analogy?" asked poor Stanmer.

"A little more, a little less—it doesn't matter. I believe you are in my shoes. But of course if you prefer it I will beg a thousand pardons and leave them to carry you where they will."

He had been looking away, but now he slowly turned his face and met my eyes. "You have gone too far to retreat; what is it you know about her?"

"About this one—nothing. But about the other——"

"I care nothing about the other!"

"My dear fellow," I said, "they are mother and daughter —they are as like as two of Andrea's Madonnas."

"If they resemble each other, then, you were simply mistaken in the mother."

I took his arm and we walked on again; there seemed no adequate reply to such a charge. "Your state of mind brings back my own so completely," I said presently. "You admire her—you adore her, and yet, secretly, you mistrust her. You are enchanted with her personal charm, her grace, her wit, her everything; and yet in your private heart you are afraid of her."

"Afraid of her?"

"Your mistrust keeps rising to the surface; you can't rid yourself of the suspicion that at the bottom of all things she is hard and cruel, and you would be immensely relieved if some one should persuade you that your suspicion is right."

Stanmer made no direct reply to this; but before we reached the hotel he said—"What did you ever know about the mother?"

"It's a terrible story," I answered.

He looked at me askance. "What did she do?"

"Come to my rooms this evening and I will tell you."

He declared he would, but he never came. Exactly the way I should have acted!

14th.—I went again, last evening, to Casa Salvi, where I found the same little circle, with the addition of a couple of ladies. Stanmer was there, trying hard to talk to one of them, but making, I am sure, a very poor business of it. The Countess—well, the Countess was admirable. She greeted me like a friend of ten years, toward whom familiarity should not have engendered a want of ceremony; she made me sit near her, and she asked me a dozen questions about my health and my occupations.

"I live in the past," I said. "I go into the galleries, into the old palaces and the churches. To-day I spent an hour in Michael Angelo's chapel, at San Lorenzo."

"Ah, yes, that's the past," said the Countess. "Those things are very old."

"Twenty-seven years old," I answered.

"Twenty-seven? *Altro!*"

"I mean my own past," I said. "I went to a great many of those places with your mother."

"Ah, the pictures are beautiful," murmured the Countess, glancing at Stanmer.

"Have you lately looked at any of them?" I asked. "Have you gone to the galleries with *him*?"

She hesitated a moment, smiling. "It seems to me that your question is a little impertinent. But I think you are like that."

"A little impertinent? Never. As I say, your mother did me the honour, more than once, to accompany me to the Uffizzi."

"My mother must have been very kind to you."

"So it seemed to me at the time."

"At the time, only?"

"Well, if you prefer, so it seems to me now."

"Eh," said the Countess, "she made sacrifices."

"To what, cara Signora? She was perfectly free. Your lamented father was dead—and she had not yet contracted her second marriage."

"If she was intending to marry again, it was all the more reason she should have been careful."

I looked at her a moment; she met my eyes gravely, over the top of her fan. "Are *you* very careful?" I said.

She dropped her fan with a certain violence. "Ah, yes, you are impertinent!"

"Ah, no," I said. "Remember that I am old enough to be your father; that I knew you when you were three years old. I may surely ask such questions. But you are right; one must do your mother justice. She was certainly thinking of her second marriage."

"You have not forgiven her that!" said the Countess, very gravely.

"Have you?" I asked, more lightly.

"I don't judge my mother. That is a mortal sin. My stepfather was very kind to me."

"I remember him," I said; "I saw him a great many times—your mother already received him."

My hostess sat with lowered eyes, saying nothing; but she presently looked up.

"She was very unhappy with my father."

"That I can easily believe. And your stepfather—is he still living?"

"He died—before my mother."

"Did he fight any more duels?"

"He was killed in a duel," said the Countess, discreetly.

It seems almost monstrous, especially as I can give no reason for it—but this announcement, instead of shocking me, caused me to feel a strange exhilaration. Most assuredly, after all these years, I bear the poor man no resentment. Of course I controlled my manner, and simply remarked to the Countess that as his fault had been, so was his punishment. I think, however, that the feeling of which I speak was at the bottom of my saying to her that I hoped that, unlike her mother's, her own brief married life had been happy.

"If it was not," she said, "I have forgotten it now."—I wonder if the late Count Scarabelli was also killed in a duel, and if his adversary . . . . Is it on the books that his adversary, as well, shall perish by the pistol? Which of those gentlemen is he, I wonder? Is it reserved for poor little Stanmer to put a bullet into him? No; poor little Stanmer, I trust, will do as I did. And yet, unfortunately for him, that woman is consummately plausible. She was wonderfully nice last evening; she was really irresistible. Such frankness and freedom, and yet something so soft and womanly; such graceful gaiety, so much of the brightness, without any of the stiffness, of good breeding, and over it all something so picturesquely simple and southern. She is a perfect Italian. But she comes honestly by it. After the talk I have just jotted down she changed her place, and the conversation for half-an-hour was general. Stanmer indeed said very little; partly, I suppose, because he is shy of talking a foreign tongue. Was I like that—was I so constantly silent? I suspect I was when I was perplexed, and Heaven knows that very often my perplexity was extreme. Before I went away I had a few more words *tête-à-tête* with the Countess.

"I hope you are not leaving Florence yet," she said; "you will stay a while longer?"

I answered that I came only for a week, and that my week was over.

"I stay on from day to day, I am so much interested."

"Eh, it's the beautiful moment. I'm glad our city pleases you!"

"Florence pleases me—and I take a paternal interest in our young friend," I added, glancing at Stanmer. "I have become very fond of him."

"Bel tipo inglese," said my hostess. "And he is very intelligent; he has a beautiful mind."

She stood there resting her smile and her clear, expressive eyes upon me.

"I don't like to praise him too much," I rejoined, "lest I should appear to praise myself; he reminds me so much of what I was at his age. If your beautiful mother were to come to life for an hour she would see the resemblance."

She gave me a little amused stare.

"And yet you don't look at all like him!"

"Ah, you didn't know me when I was twenty-five. I was very handsome! And, moreover, it isn't that, it's the mental resemblance. I was ingenuous, candid, trusting, like him."

"Trusting? I remember my mother once telling me that you were the most suspicious and jealous of men!"

"I fell into a suspicious mood, but I was, fundamentally, not in the least addicted to thinking evil. I couldn't easily imagine any harm of any one."

"And so you mean that Mr. Stanmer is in a suspicious mood?"

"Well, I mean that his situation is the same as mine."

The Countess gave me one of her serious looks.

"Come," she said, "what was it—this famous situation of yours? I have heard you mention it before."

"Your mother might have told you, since she occasionally did me the honour to speak of me."

"All my mother ever told me was that you were a sad puzzle to her."

At this, of course, I laughed out—I laugh still as I write it.

"Well, then, that was my situation—I was a sad puzzle to a very clever woman."

"And you mean, therefore, that I am a puzzle to poor Mr. Stanmer?"

"He is racking his brains to make you out. Remember it was you who said he was intelligent."

She looked round at him, and as fortune would have it, his appearance at that moment quite confirmed my assertion. He was lounging back in his chair with an air of indolence rather too marked for a drawing-room, and staring at the ceiling with the expression of a man who has just been asked a conundrum. Madame Scarabelli seemed struck with his attitude.

"Don't you see," I said, "he can't read the riddle?"

"You yourself," she answered, "said he was incapable of thinking evil. I should be sorry to have him think any evil of *me*."

And she looked straight at me—seriously, appealingly—with her beautiful candid brow.

I inclined myself, smiling, in a manner which might have meant—

"How could that be possible?"

"I have a great esteem for him," she went on; "I want him to think well of me. If I am a puzzle to him, do me a little service. Explain me to him."

"Explain you, dear lady?"

"You are older and wiser than he. Make him understand me."

She looked deep into my eyes for a moment, and then she turned away.

26th.—I have written nothing for a good many days, but meanwhile I have been half a dozen times to Casa Salvi. I have seen a good deal also of my young friend—had a good many walks and talks with him. I have proposed to him to come with me to Venice for a fortnight, but he won't listen to the idea of leaving Florence. He is very happy in spite of his doubts, and I confess that in the perception of his happiness I have lived over again my own. This is so much the case that when, the other day, he at last made up his mind to ask me to tell him the wrong that Madame de Salvi had done me, I rather checked his curiosity. I told him that if he was bent upon knowing I would satisfy him, but that it seemed a pity, just now, to indulge in painful imagery.

"But I thought you wanted so much to put me out of conceit of our friend."

"I admit I am inconsistent, but there are various reasons for it. In the first place—it's obvious—I am open to the charge of playing a double game. I profess an admiration for the Countess Scarabelli, for I accept her hospitality, and at the same time I attempt to poison your mind; isn't that the proper expression? I can't exactly make up my mind to that, though my admiration for the Countess and my desire to prevent you from taking a foolish step are equally sincere. And then, in the second place you seem to me on the whole so happy! One hesitates to destroy an illusion, no matter how pernicious, that is so delightful while it lasts. These are the rare moments of life. To be young and ardent, in the midst of an Italian spring, and to believe in the moral perfection of a beautiful woman—what an admirable situation! Float with the current; I'll stand on the brink and watch you."

"Your real reason is that you feel you have no case against

the poor lady," said Stanmer. "You admire her as much as I do."

"I just admitted that I admired her. I never said she was a vulgar flirt; her mother was an absolutely scientific one. Heaven knows I admired that! It's a nice point, however, how much one is bound in honour not to warn a young friend against a dangerous woman because one also has relations of civility with the lady."

"In such a case," said Stanmer, "I would break off my relations."

I looked at him, and I think I laughed.

"Are you jealous of me, by chance?"

He shook his head emphatically.

"Not in the least; I like to see you there, because your conduct contradicts your words."

"I have always said that the Countess is fascinating."

"Otherwise," said Stanmer, "in the case you speak of I would give the lady notice."

"Give her notice?"

"Mention to her that you regard her with suspicion, and that you propose to do your best to rescue a simple-minded youth from her wiles. That would be more loyal." And he began to laugh again.

It is not the first time he has laughed at me; but I have never minded it, because I have always understood it.

"Is that what you recommend me to say to the Countess?" I asked.

"Recommend you!" he exclaimed, laughing again; "I recommend nothing. I may be the victim to be rescued, but I am at least not a partner to the conspiracy. Besides," he added in a moment, "the Countess knows your state of mind."

"Has she told you so?"

Stanmer hesitated.

"She has begged me to listen to everything you may say against her. She declares that she has a good conscience."

"Ah," said I, "she's an accomplished woman!"

And it is indeed very clever of her to take that tone. Stanmer afterwards assured me explicitly that he has never given her a hint of the liberties I have taken in conversation with—what shall I call it?—with her moral nature; she has guessed them for herself. She must hate me intensely, and yet her manner has always been so charming to me! She is truly an accomplished woman!

May 4th.—I have stayed away from Casa Salvi for a week, but I have lingered on in Florence, under a mixture of impulses. I have had it on my conscience not to go near the Countess again—and yet from the moment she is aware of the way I feel about her, it is open war. There need be no scruples on either side. She is as free to use every possible art to entangle poor Stanmer more closely as I am to clip her fine-spun meshes. Under the circumstances, however, we naturally shouldn't meet very cordially. But as regards her meshes, why, after all, should I clip them? It would really be very interesting to see Stanmer swallowed up. I should like to see how he would agree with her after she had devoured him—(to what vulgar imagery, by the way, does curiosity reduce a man!) Let him finish the story in his own way, as I finished it in mine. It is the same story; but why, a quarter of a century later, should it have the same *dénoûment*? Let him make his own *dénoûment*.

5th.—Hang it, however, I don't want the poor boy to be miserable.

6th.—Ah, but did my *dénoûment* then prove such a happy one?

7th.—He came to my room late last night; he was much excited.

"What was it she did to you?" he asked.

I answered him first with another question. "Have you quarrelled with the Countess?"

But he only repeated his own. "What was it she did to you?"

"Sit down and I'll tell you." And he sat there beside the candle, staring at me. "There was a man always there—Count Camerino."

"The man she married?"

"The man she married. I was very much in love with her, and yet I didn't trust her. I was sure that she lied; I believed that she could be cruel. Nevertheless, at moments, she had a charm which made it pure pedantry to be conscious of her faults; and while these moments lasted I would have done anything for her. Unfortunately, they didn't last long. But you know what I mean; am I not describing the Scarabelli?"

"The Countess Scarabelli never lied!" cried Stanmer.

"That's just what I would have said to any one who should have made the insinuation! But I suppose you are not asking me the question you put to me just now from dispassionate curiosity."

"A man may want to know!" said the innocent fellow.

I couldn't help laughing out. "This, at any rate, is my story. Camerino was always there; he was a sort of fixture in the house. If I had moments of dislike for the divine Bianca, I had no moments of liking for him. And yet he was a very agreeable fellow, very civil, very intelligent, not in the least disposed to make a quarrel with me. The trouble of course was simply that I was jealous of him. I don't know, however, on what ground I could have quarrelled with him, for I had no definite rights. I can't say what I expected—I can't say what, as the matter stood, I was prepared to do. With my name and my prospects, I might perfectly have offered her my hand. I am not sure that she would have accepted it—I am by no means clear that she wanted that. But she wanted, wanted keenly, to attach me to her; she wanted to have me about. I should have been capable of giving up everything—England, my career, my family—simply to devote myself to her, to live near her and see her every day."

"Why didn't you do it, then?" asked Stanmer.

"Why don't you?"

"To be a proper rejoinder to my question," he said, rather neatly, "yours should be asked twenty-five years hence."

"It remains perfectly true that at a given moment I was capable of doing as I say. That was what she wanted—a rich, susceptible, credulous, convenient young Englishman established near her *en permanence*. And yet," I added, "I must do her complete justice. I honestly believe she was fond of me." At this Stanmer got up and walked to the window; he stood looking out a moment, and then he turned round. "You know she was older than I," I went on. "Madame Scarabelli is older than you. One day in the garden, her mother

asked me in an angry tone why I disliked Camerino; for I had
been at no pains to conceal my feeling about him, and something had just happened to bring it out. 'I dislike him,' I said,
'because you like him so much.' 'I assure you I don't like
him,' she answered. 'He has all the appearance of being your
lover,' I retorted. It was a brutal speech, certainly, but any
other man in my place would have made it. She took it very
strangely; she turned pale, but she was not indignant. 'How
can he be my lover after what he has done?' she asked. 'What
has he done?' She hesitated a good while, then she said: 'He
killed my husband.' 'Good heavens!' I cried, 'and you receive
him?' Do you know what she said? She said, *'Che vuole?'*"

"Is that all?" asked Stanmer.

"No; she went on to say that Camerino had killed Count
Salvi in a duel, and she admitted that her husband's jealousy
had been the occasion of it. The Count, it appeared, was a
monster of jealousy—he had led her a dreadful life. He himself, meanwhile, had been anything but irreproachable; he had
done a mortal injury to a man of whom he pretended to be
a friend, and this affair had become notorious. The gentleman
in question had demanded satisfaction for his outraged honour; but for some reason or other (the Countess, to do her
justice, did not tell me that her husband was a coward), he
had not as yet obtained it. The duel with Camerino had come
on first; in an access of jealous fury the Count had struck
Camerino in the face; and this outrage, I know not how justly,
was deemed expiable before the other. By an extraordinary
arrangement (the Italians have certainly no sense of fair play),
the other man was allowed to be Camerino's second. The duel
was fought with swords, and the Count received a wound of
which, though at first it was not expected to be fatal, he died
on the following day. The matter was hushed up as much as
possible for the sake of the Countess's good name, and so
successfully that it was presently observed that, among the
public, the other gentleman had the credit of having put his
blade through M. de Salvi. This gentleman took a fancy not
to contradict the impression, and it was allowed to subsist. So
long as *he* consented, it was of course in Camerino's interest
not to contradict it, as it left him much more free to keep up
his intimacy with the Countess."

Stanmer had listened to all this with extreme attention. "Why didn't *she* contradict it?"

I shrugged my shoulders. "I am bound to believe it was for the same reason. I was horrified, at any rate, by the whole story. I was extremely shocked at the Countess's want of dignity in continuing to see the man by whose hand her husband had fallen."

"The husband had been a great brute, and it was not known," said Stanmer.

"Its not being known made no difference. And as for Salvi having been a brute, that is but a way of saying that his wife, and the man whom his wife subsequently married, didn't like him."

Stanmer looked extremely meditative; his eyes were fixed on mine. "Yes, that marriage is hard to get over. It was not becoming."

"Ah," said I, "what a long breath I drew when I heard of it! I remember the place and the hour. It was at a hill-station in India, seven years after I had left Florence. The post brought me some English papers, and in one of them was a letter from Italy, with a lot of so-called 'fashionable intelligence.' There, among various scandals in high-life, and other delectable items, I read that the Countess Bianca Salvi, famous for some years as the presiding genius of the most agreeable *salon* in Florence, was about to bestow her hand upon Count Camerino, a distinguished Bolognese. Ah, my dear boy, it was a tremendous escape! I had been ready to marry the woman who was capable of that! But my instinct had warned me, and I had trusted my instinct."

" 'Instinct's everything,' as Falstaff says!" And Stanmer began to laugh. "Did you tell Madame de Salvi that your instinct was against her?"

"No; I told her that she frightened me, shocked me, horrified me."

"That's about the same thing. And what did she say?"

"She asked me what I would have? I called her friendship with Camerino a scandal, and she answered that her husband had been a brute. Besides, no one knew it; therefore it was no scandal. Just *your* argument! I retorted that this was odious reasoning, and that she had no moral sense. We had a passionate argument, and I declared I would never see her again. In the heat of my displeasure I left Florence, and I kept my vow. I never saw her again."

"You couldn't have been much in love with her," said Stanmer.

"I was not—three months after."

"If you had been you would have come back—three days after."

"So doubtless it seems to you. All I can say is that it was the great effort of my life. Being a military man, I have had on various occasions to face the enemy. But it was not then I needed my resolution; it was when I left Florence in a post-chaise."

Stanmer turned about the room two or three times, and then he said: "I don't understand! I don't understand why she should have told you that Camerino had killed her husband. It could only damage her."

"She was afraid it would damage her more that I should think he was her lover. She wished to say the thing that would most effectually persuade me that he was not her lover—that he could never be. And then she wished to get the credit of being very frank."

"Good heavens, how you must have analysed her!" cried my companion, staring.

"There is nothing so analytic as disillusionment. But there it is. She married Camerino."

"Yes, I don't like that," said Stanmer. He was silent a while, and then he added—"Perhaps she wouldn't have done so if you had remained."

He has a little innocent way! "Very likely she would have dispensed with the ceremony," I answered dryly.

"Upon my word," he said, "you *have* analysed her!"

"You ought to be grateful to me. I have done for you what you seem unable to do for yourself."

"I don't see any Camerino in my case," he said.

"Perhaps among those gentlemen I can find one for you."

"Thank you," he cried; "I'll take care of that myself!" And he went away—satisfied, I hope.

10th.—He's an obstinate little wretch; it irritates me to see him sticking to it. Perhaps he is looking for his Camerino. I shall leave him at any rate to his fate; it is growing insupportably hot.

11th.—I went this evening to bid farewell to the Scarabelli. There was no one there; she was alone in her great dusky drawing-room, which was lighted only by a couple of candles, with the immense windows open over the garden. She was dressed in white; she was deucedly pretty. She asked me of course why I had been so long without coming.

"I think you say that only for form," I answered. "I imagine you know."

"*Chè!* what have I done?"

"Nothing at all. You are too wise for that."

She looked at me a while. "I think you are a little crazy."

"Ah no, I am only too sane. I have too much reason rather than too little."

"You have at any rate what we call a fixed idea."

"There is no harm in that so long as it's a good one."

"But yours is abominable!" she exclaimed with a laugh.

"Of course you can't like me or my ideas. All things considered, you have treated me with wonderful kindness, and I thank you and kiss your hands. I leave Florence to-morrow."

"I won't say I'm sorry!" she said, laughing again. "But I am very glad to have seen you. I always wondered about you. You are a curiosity."

"Yes, you must find me so. A man who can resist your charms! The fact is, I can't. This evening you are enchanting; and it is the first time I have been alone with you."

She gave no heed to this; she turned away. But in a moment she came back, and stood looking at me, and her beautiful solemn eyes seemed to shine in the dimness of the room.

"How *could* you treat my mother so?" she asked.

"Treat her so?"

"How could you desert the most charming woman in the world?"

"It was not a case of desertion; and if it had been it seems to me she was consoled."

At this moment there was the sound of a step in the antechamber, and I saw that the Countess perceived it to be Stanmer's.

"That wouldn't have happened," she murmured. "My poor mother needed a protector."

Stanmer came in, interrupting our talk, and looking at me, I thought, with a little air of bravado. He must think me indeed a tiresome, meddlesome bore; and upon my word, turning it all over, I wonder at his docility. After all, he's five-and-twenty—and yet, I *must* add, it *does* irritate me—the way he sticks! He was followed in a moment by two or three of the regular Italians, and I made my visit short.

"Good-bye, Countess," I said; and she gave me her hand in silence. "Do *you* need a protector?" I added, softly.

She looked at me from head to foot, and then, almost angrily—

"Yes, Signore."

But, to deprecate her anger, I kept her hand an instant, and then bent my venerable head and kissed it. I think I appeased her.

BOLOGNA, *14th.*—I left Florence on the 11th, and have been here these three days. Delightful old Italian town—but it lacks the charm of my Florentine secret.

I wrote that last entry five days ago, late at night, after coming back from Casa Salvi. I afterwards fell asleep in my chair; the night was half over when I woke up. Instead of going to bed, I stood a long time at the window, looking out at the river. It was a warm, still night, and the first faint streaks of sunrise were in the sky. Presently I heard a slow footstep beneath my window, and looking down, made out by the aid of a street-lamp that Stanmer was but just coming home. I called to him to come to my rooms, and, after an interval, he made his appearance.

"I want to bid you good-bye," I said; "I shall depart in the morning. Don't go to the trouble of saying you are sorry. Of course you are not; I must have bullied you immensely."

He made no attempt to say he was sorry, but he said he was very glad to have made my acquaintance.

"Your conversation," he said, with his little innocent air, "has been very suggestive."

"Have you found Camerino?" I asked, smiling.

"I have given up the search."

"Well," I said, "some day when you find that you have made a great mistake, remember I told you so."

He looked for a minute as if he were trying to anticipate that day by the exercise of his reason.

"Has it ever occurred to you that *you* may have made a great mistake?"

"Oh yes; everything occurs to one sooner or later."

That's what I said to him; but I didn't say that the question, pointed by his candid young countenance, had, for the moment, a greater force than it had ever had before.

And then he asked me whether, as things had turned out, I myself had been so especially happy.

PARIS, *December 17th.*—A note from young Stanmer, whom I saw in Florence—a remarkable little note, dated Rome, and worth transcribing.

"My Dear General,—I have it at heart to tell you that I was married a week ago to the Countess Salvi-Scarabelli. You talked me into a great muddle; but a month after that it was all very clear. Things that involve a risk are like the Christian faith; they must be seen from the inside.—Yours ever, E. S.

"P.S.—A fig for analogies unless you can find an analogy for my happiness!"

His happiness makes him very clever. I hope it will last!—I mean his cleverness, not his happiness.

LONDON, *April 19th, 1877.*—Last night, at Lady H——'s, I met Edmund Stanmer, who married Bianca Salvi's daughter. I heard the other day that they had come to England. A handsome young fellow, with a fresh contented face. He reminded me of Florence, which I didn't pretend to forget; but it was rather awkward, for I remember I used to disparage that woman to him. I had a complete theory about her. But he didn't seem at all stiff; on the contrary, he appeared to enjoy our encounter. I asked him if his wife were there. I had to do that.

"Oh, yes, she's in one of the other rooms. Come and make her acquaintance; I want you to know her."

"You forget that I do know her."

"Oh, no, you don't; you never did." And he gave a little significant laugh.

I didn't feel like facing the *ci-devant* Scarabelli at that moment; so I said that I was leaving the house, but that I would do myself the honour of calling upon his wife. We talked for a minute of something else, and then, suddenly, breaking off and looking at me, he laid his hand on my arm. I must do him the justice to say that he looks felicitous.

"Depend upon it, you were wrong!" he said.

"My dear young friend," I answered, "imagine the alacrity with which I concede it."

Something else again was spoken of, but in an instant he repeated his movement.

"Depend upon it you were wrong."

"I am sure the Countess has forgiven me," I said, "and in that case you ought to bear no grudge. As I have had the honour to say, I will call upon her immediately."

"I was not alluding to my wife," he answered. "I was thinking of your own story."

"My own story?"

"So many years ago. Was it not rather a mistake?"

I looked at him a moment; he's positively rosy.

"That's not a question to solve in a London crush."

And I turned away.

22nd.—I haven't yet called on the *ci-devant*; I am afraid of finding her at home. And that boy's words have been thrumming in my ears—"Depend upon it you were wrong. Wasn't it rather a mistake?" *Was* I wrong—*was* it a mistake? Was I too cautious—too suspicious—too logical? Was it really a protector she needed—a man who might have helped her? Would it have been for his benefit to believe in her and was her fault only that I had forsaken her? Was the poor woman very unhappy? God forgive me, how the questions come crowding in! If I marred her happiness, I certainly didn't make my own. And I might have made it—eh? That's a charming discovery for a man of my age!

A Bundle of Letters

From MISS MIRANDA HOPE, *in Paris, to* MRS. ABRAHAM C. HOPE, *at Bangor, Maine.*

September 5th, 1879.

MY DEAR MOTHER—

I have kept you posted as far as Tuesday week last, and, although my letter will not have reached you yet, I will begin another, before my news accumulates too much. I am glad you show my letters round in the family, for I like them all to know what I am doing, and I can't write to every one, though I try to answer all reasonable expectations. But there are a great many unreasonable ones, as I suppose you know—not yours, dear mother, for I am bound to say that you never required of me more than was natural. You see you are reaping your reward: I write to you before I write to any one else.

There is one thing, I hope—that you don't show any of my letters to William Platt. If he wants to see any of my letters, he knows the right way to go to work. I wouldn't have him see one of these letters, written for circulation in the family, for anything in the world. If he wants one for himself, he has got to write to me first. Let him write to me first, and then I will see about answering him. You can show him this if you like; but if you show him anything more, I will never write to you again.

I told you in my last about my farewell to England, my crossing the channel, and my first impressions of Paris. I have thought a great deal about that lovely England since I left it, and all the famous historic scenes I visited; but I have come to the conclusion that it is not a country in which I should care to reside. The position of woman does not seem to me at all satisfactory, and that is a point, you know, on which I feel very strongly. It seems to me that in England they play a very faded-out part, and those with whom I conversed had a kind of depressed and humiliated tone; a little dull, tame look, as if they were used to being snubbed and bullied, which made me want to give them a good shaking. There are a great many

485

people—and a great many things, too—over here that I should like to perform that operation upon. I should like to shake the starch out of some of them, and the dust out of the others. I know fifty girls in Bangor that come much more up to my notion of the stand a truly noble woman should take, than those young ladies in England. But they had a most lovely way of speaking (in England), and the men are *remarkably handsome*. (You can show this to William Platt, if you like.)

I gave you my first impressions of Paris, which quite came up to my expectations, much as I had heard and read about it. The objects of interest are extremely numerous, and the climate is remarkably cheerful and sunny. I should say the position of woman here was considerably higher, though by no means coming up to the American standard. The manners of the people are in some respects extremely peculiar, and I feel at last that I am indeed in *foreign parts*. It is, however, a truly elegant city (very superior to New York), and I have spent a great deal of time in visiting the various monuments and palaces. I won't give you an account of all my wanderings, though I have been most indefatigable; for I am keeping, as I told you before, a most *exhaustive* journal, which I will allow you the *privilege* of reading on my return to Bangor. I am getting on remarkably well, and I must say I am sometimes surprised at my universal good fortune. It only shows what a little energy and common-sense will accomplish. I have discovered none of these objections to a young lady travelling in Europe by herself, of which we heard so much before I left, and I don't expect I ever shall, for I certainly don't mean to look for them. I know what I want and I always manage to get it.

I have received a great deal of politeness—some of it really most pressing, and I have experienced no drawbacks whatever. I have made a great many pleasant acquaintances in travelling round (both ladies and gentlemen), and had a great many most interesting talks. I have collected a great deal of information, for which I refer you to my journal. I assure you my journal is going to be a splendid thing. I do just exactly as I do in Bangor, and I find I do perfectly right; and at any rate, I don't care if I don't. I didn't come to Europe to lead a merely conventional life; I could do that at Bangor. You know I never *would* do it at Bangor, so it isn't likely I am going to make myself miserable over here. So long as I accomplish what I desire, and make my money hold out, I shall regard the thing as a success. Sometimes I feel rather lonely, especially in the evening; but I generally manage to interest myself in something or in some one. In the evening I usually read up about the objects of interest I have visited during the day, or I post up my journal. Sometimes I go to the theatre; or else I play the piano in the public parlour. The public parlour at the hotel isn't much; but the piano is better than that fearful old thing at the Sebago House. Sometimes I go downstairs and talk to the lady who keeps the books—a French lady, who is remarkably polite. She is very pretty, and always wears a black dress, with the most beautiful fit; she speaks a little English; she tells me she had to learn it in order to converse with the Americans who come in such numbers to this hotel. She has given me a great deal of information about the position of woman in France, and much of it is very encouraging. But she has told me at the same time some things that I should not like to write to you (I am hesitating even about putting them into my journal), especially if my letters are to be handed round in the family. I assure you they appear to talk about things here that we never think of mentioning at Bangor, or even of thinking about. She seems to think she can tell me everything, because I told her I was travelling for general culture. Well, I *do* want to know so much that it seems sometimes as if I wanted to know everything; and yet there are some things that I think I don't want to know. But, as a general thing, everything is intensely interesting; I don't mean only everything that this French lady tells me, but everything I see and hear for myself. I feel really as if I should gain all I desire.

I meet a great many Americans, who, as a general thing, I must say, are not as polite to me as the people over here. The people over here—especially the gentlemen—are much more what I should call *attentive*. I don't know whether Americans are more *sincere*; I haven't yet made up my mind about that. The only drawback I experience is when Americans sometimes express surprise that I should be travelling round alone; so you see it doesn't come from Europeans. I always have my answer ready: "For general culture, to acquire the languages, and to see Europe for myself;" and that generally seems to satisfy them. Dear mother, my money holds out very well, and it *is* real interesting.

II.

From the Same to the Same.

September 16th.

Since I last wrote to you I have left that hotel, and come to live in a French family. It's a kind of boarding-house combined with a kind of school; only it's not like an American boarding-house, nor like an American school either. There are four or five people here that have come to learn the language—not to take lessons, but to have an opportunity for conversation. I was very glad to come to such a place, for I had begun to realise that I was not making much progress with the French. It seemed to me that I should feel ashamed to have spent two months in Paris, and not to have acquired more insight into the language. I had always heard so much of French conversation, and I found I was having no more opportunity to practise it than if I had remained at Bangor. In fact, I used to hear a great deal more at Bangor, from those French Canadians that came down to cut the ice, than I saw I should ever hear at that hotel. The lady that kept the books seemed to want so much to talk to me in English (for the sake of practice, too, I suppose), that I couldn't bear to let her know I didn't like it. The chambermaid was Irish, and all the waiters were German, so that I never heard a word of French spoken. I suppose you might hear a great deal in the shops; only, as I don't buy anything—I prefer to spend my money for purposes of culture—I don't have that advantage.

I have been thinking some of taking a teacher, but I am well acquainted with the grammar already, and teachers always keep you bothering over the verbs. I was a good deal troubled, for I felt as if I didn't want to go away without having, at least, got a general idea of French conversation. The theatre gives you a good deal of insight, and, as I told you in my last, I go a good deal to places of amusement. I find no difficulty

whatever in going to such places alone, and am always treated
with the politeness which, as I told you before, I encounter
everywhere. I see plenty of other ladies alone (mostly French),
and they generally seem to be enjoying themselves as much
as I. But, at the theatre, every one talks so fast that I can
scarcely make out what they say; and, besides, there are a great
many vulgar expressions which it is unnecessary to learn. But
it was the theatre, nevertheless, that put me on the track. The
very next day after I wrote to you last, I went to the Palais
Royal, which is one of the principal theatres in Paris. It is very
small, but it is very celebrated, and in my guide-book it is
marked with *two stars*, which is a sign of importance attached
only to *first-class* objects of interest. But after I had been there
half an hour I found I couldn't understand a single word of
the play, they gabbled it off so fast, and they made use of such
peculiar expressions. I felt a good deal disappointed and troubled—I was afraid I shouldn't gain all I had come for. But
while I was thinking it over—thinking what I *should* do—I
heard two gentlemen talking behind me. It was between the
acts, and I couldn't help listening to what they said. They
were talking English, but I guess they were Americans.

"Well," said one of them, "it all depends on what you are
after. I'm after French; that's what I'm after."

"Well," said the other, "I'm after Art."

"Well," said the first, "I'm after Art too; but I'm after
French most."

Then, dear mother, I am sorry to say the second one swore
a little. He said, "Oh, damn French!"

"No, I won't damn French," said his friend. "I'll acquire
it—that's what I'll do with it. I'll go right into a family."

"What family'll you go into?"

"Into some French family. That's the only way to do—to
go to some place where you can talk. If you're after Art, you
want to stick to the galleries; you want to go right through
the Louvre, room by room; you want to take a room a day,
or something of that sort. But, if you want to acquire French,
the thing is to look out for a family. There are lots of French
families here that take you to board and teach you. My second
cousin—that young lady I told you about—she got in with a
crowd like that, and they booked her right up in three

months. They just took her right in and they talked to her. That's what they do to you; they set you right down and they talk *at* you. You've got to understand them; you can't help yourself. That family my cousin was with has moved away somewhere, or I should try and get in with them. They were very smart people, that family; after she left, my cousin corresponded with them in French. But I mean to find some other crowd, if it takes a lot of trouble!"

I listened to all this with great interest, and when he spoke about his cousin I was on the point of turning around to ask him the address of the family that she was with; but the next moment he said they had moved away; so I sat still. The other gentleman, however, didn't seem to be affected in the same way as I was.

"Well," he said, "you may follow up that if you like; I mean to follow up the pictures. I don't believe there is ever going to be any considerable demand in the United States for French; but I can promise you that in about ten years there'll be a big demand for Art! And it won't be temporary either."

That remark may be very true, but I don't care anything about the demand; I want to know French for its own sake. I don't want to think I have been all this while without having gained an insight. . . . The very next day, I asked the lady who kept the books at the hotel whether she knew of any family that could take me to board and give me the benefit of their conversation. She instantly threw up her hands, with several little shrill cries (in their French way, you know), and told me that her dearest friend kept a regular place of that kind. If she had known I was looking out for such a place she would have told me before; she had not spoken of it herself, because she didn't wish to injure the hotel by being the cause of my going away. She told me this was a charming family, who had often received American ladies (and others as well) who wished to follow up the language, and she was sure I should be delighted with them. So she gave me their address, and offered to go with me to introduce me. But I was in such a hurry that I went off by myself, and I had no trouble in finding these good people. They were delighted to receive me, and I was very much pleased with what I saw of them. They seemed to have plenty of conversation, and there will be no trouble about that.

I came here to stay about three days ago, and by this time I have seen a great deal of them. The price of board struck me as rather high; but I must remember that a quantity of conversation is thrown in. I have a very pretty little room— without any carpet, but with seven mirrors, two clocks, and five curtains. I was rather disappointed after I arrived to find that there are several other Americans here for the same purpose as myself. At least there are three Americans and two English people; and also a German gentleman. I am afraid, therefore, our conversation will be rather mixed, but I have not yet time to judge. I try to talk with Madame de Maisonrouge all I can (she is the lady of the house, and the *real* family consists only of herself and her two daughters). They are all most elegant, interesting women, and I am sure we shall become intimate friends. I will write you more about them in my next. Tell William Platt I don't care what he does.

III.

From MISS VIOLET RAY, *in Paris,*
to MISS AGNES RICH, *in New York.*

September 21st.

We had hardly got here when father received a telegram saying he would have to come right back to New York. It was for something about his business—I don't know exactly what; you know I never understand those things, never want to. We had just got settled at the hotel, in some charming rooms, and mother and I, as you may imagine, were greatly annoyed. Father is extremely fussy, as you know, and his first idea, as soon as he found he should have to go back, was that we should go back with him. He declared he would never leave us in Paris alone, and that we must return and come out again. I don't know what he thought would happen to us; I suppose he thought we should be too extravagant. It's father's theory that we are always running up bills, whereas a little observation would show him that we wear the same old *rags* FOR

MONTHS. But father has no observation; he has nothing but
theories. Mother and I, however, have, fortunately, a great
deal of *practice*, and we succeeded in making him understand
that we wouldn't budge from Paris, and that we would rather
be chopped into small pieces than cross that dreadful ocean
again. So, at last, he decided to go back alone, and to leave
us here for three months. But, to show you how fussy he is,
he refused to let us stay at the hotel, and insisted that we
should go into a *family*. I don't know what put such an idea
into his head, unless it was some advertisement that he saw
in one of the American papers that are published here.

There are families here who receive American and English
people to live with them, under the pretence of teaching them
French. You may imagine what people they are—I mean the
families themselves. But the Americans who choose this peculiar manner of seeing Paris must be actually just as bad.
Mother and I were horrified, and declared that *main force*
should not remove us from the hotel. But father has a way of
arriving at his ends which is more efficient than violence. He
worries and fusses; he "nags," as we used to say at school;
and, when mother and I are quite worn out, his triumph is
assured. Mother is usually worn out more easily than I, and
she ends by siding with father; so that, at last, when they
combine their forces against poor little me, I have to succumb.
You should have heard the way father went on about this
"family" plan; he talked to every one he saw about it; he used
to go round to the banker's and talk to the people there—
the people in the post-office; he used to try and exchange
ideas about it with the waiters at the hotel. He said it would
be more safe, more respectable, more economical; that I
should perfect my French; that mother would learn how a
French household is conducted; that he should feel more easy,
and five hundred reasons more. They were none of them
good, but that made no difference. It's all humbug, his talking
about economy, when every one knows that business in America has completely recovered, that the prostration is all over,
and that *immense fortunes* are being made. We have been
economising for the last five years, and I supposed we came
abroad to reap the benefits of it.

As for my French, it is quite as perfect as I want it to be.

(I assure you I am often surprised at my own fluency, and, when I get a little more practice in the genders and the idioms, I shall do very well in this respect.) To make a long story short, however, father carried his point, as usual; mother basely deserted me at the last moment, and, after holding out alone for three days, I told them to do with me what they pleased! Father lost three steamers in succession by remaining in Paris to argue with me. You know he is like the schoolmaster in Goldsmith's "Deserted Village"—"e'en though vanquished, he would argue still." He and mother went to look at some seventeen families (they had got the addresses somewhere), while I retired to my sofa, and would have nothing to do with it. At last they made arrangements, and I was transported to the establishment from which I now write you. I write you from the bosom of a Parisian ménage—from the depths of a second-rate boarding-house.

Father only left Paris after he had seen us what he calls comfortably settled here, and had informed Madame de Maisonrouge (the mistress of the establishment—the head of the "family") that he wished my French pronunciation especially attended to. The pronunciation, as it happens, is just what I am most at home in; if he had said my genders or my idioms there would have been some sense. But poor father has no tact, and this defect is especially marked since he has been in Europe. He will be absent, however, for three months, and mother and I shall breathe more freely; the situation will be less intense. I must confess that we breathe more freely than I expected, in this place, where we have been for about a week. I was sure, before we came, that it would prove to be an establishment of the *lowest description*; but I must say that, in this respect, I am agreeably disappointed. The French are so clever that they know even how to manage a place of this kind. Of course it is very disagreeable to live with strangers, but as, after all, if I were not staying with Madame de Maisonrouge I should not be living in the Faubourg St.-Germain, I don't know that from the point of view of exclusiveness it is any great loss to be here.

Our rooms are very prettily arranged, and the table is remarkably good. Mamma thinks the whole thing—the place and the people, the manners and customs—very amusing; but mamma is very easily amused. As for me, you know, all that I ask is to be let alone, and not to have people's society *forced upon me.* I have never wanted for society of my own choosing, and, so long as I retain possession of my faculties, I don't suppose I ever shall. As I said, however, the place is very well managed, and I succeed in doing as I please, which, you know, is my most cherished pursuit. Madame de Maisonrouge has a great deal of tact—much more than poor father. She is what they call here a *belle femme,* which means that she is a tall, ugly woman, with style. She dresses very well, and has a great deal of talk; but, though she is a very good imitation of a lady, I never see her behind the dinner-table, in the evening, smiling and bowing, as the people come in, and looking all the while at the dishes and the servants, without thinking of a *dame de comptoir* blooming in a corner of a shop or a restaurant. I am sure that, in spite of her fine name, she was once a *dame de comptoir.* I am also sure that, in spite of her smiles and the pretty things she says to every one, she hates us all, and would like to murder us. She is a hard, clever Frenchwoman, who would like to amuse herself and enjoy her Paris, and she must be bored to death at passing all her time in the midst of stupid English people who mumble broken French at her. Some day she will poison the soup or the *vin rouge*; but I hope that will not be until after mother and I shall have left her. She has two daughters, who, except that one is decidedly pretty, are meagre imitations of herself.

The "family," for the rest, consists altogether of our beloved compatriots, and of still more beloved Englanders. There is an Englishman here, with his sister, and they seem to be rather nice people. He is remarkably handsome, but excessively affected and patronising, especially to us Americans; and I hope to have a chance of biting his head off before long. The sister is very pretty, and, apparently, very nice; but, in costume, she is Britannia incarnate. There is a very pleasant little Frenchman—when they are nice they are charming—and a German doctor, a big, blond man, who looks like a great white bull; and two Americans, besides mother and me. One of them is a young man from Boston,—an æsthetic young man, who talks about its being "a real Corot day," etc., and a young woman—a girl, a female, I don't know what to call her—from Vermont, or Minnesota, or some such place. This young woman is the most extraordinary specimen of artless Yankeeism that I ever encountered; she is really too horrible. I have been three times to Clémentine about your underskirt, etc.

IV.

From LOUIS LEVERETT, *in Paris, to* HARVARD TREMONT, *in Boston.*

September 25th.

MY DEAR HARVARD—
I have carried out my plan, of which I gave you a hint in my last, and I only regret that I should not have done it before. It is human nature, after all, that is the most interesting thing in the world, and it only reveals itself to the truly earnest seeker. There is a want of earnestness in that life of hotels and railroad trains, which so many of our countrymen are content to lead in this strange Old World, and I was distressed to find how far I, myself, had been led along the dusty, beaten track. I had, however, constantly wanted to turn aside into more unfrequented ways; to plunge beneath the surface and see what I should discover. But the opportunity had always been missing; somehow, I never meet those opportunities that we hear about and read about—the things that happen to people in novels and biographies. And yet I am always on the watch to take advantage of any opening that may present itself; I am always looking out for experiences, for sensations—I might almost say for adventures.

The great thing is to *live*, you know—to feel, to be conscious of one's possibilities; not to pass through life mechanically and insensibly, like a letter through the post-office. There are times, my dear Harvard, when I feel as if I were really capable of everything—*capable de tout*, as they say here —of the greatest excesses as well as the greatest heroism. Oh, to be able to say that one has lived—*qu'on a vécu*, as they say here—that idea exercises an indefinable attraction for me. You will, perhaps, reply, it is easy to say it; but the thing is to make people believe you! And, then, I don't want any second-hand, spurious sensations; I want the knowledge that leaves a trace —that leaves strange scars and stains and reveries behind it! But I am afraid I shock you, perhaps even frighten you.

If you repeat my remarks to any of the West Cedar Street circle, be sure you tone them down as your discretion will suggest. For yourself, you will know that I have always had an intense desire to see something of *real French life*. You are acquainted with my great sympathy with the French; with my natural tendency to enter into the French way of looking at life. I sympathise with the artistic temperament; I remember you used sometimes to hint to me that you thought my own temperament too artistic. I don't think that in Boston there is any real sympathy with the artistic temperament; we tend to make everything a matter of right and wrong. And in Boston one can't *live—on ne peut pas vivre*, as they say here. I don't mean one can't reside—for a great many people manage that; but one can't live, æsthetically—I may almost venture to say, sensuously. This is why I have always been so much drawn to the French, who are so æsthetic, so sensuous. I am so sorry that Théophile Gautier has passed away; I should have liked so much to go and see him, and tell him all that I owe him. He was living when I was here before; but, you know, at that time I was travelling with the Johnsons, who are not æsthetic, and who used to make me feel rather ashamed of my artistic temperament. If I had gone to see the great apostle of beauty, I should have had to go clandestinely—*en cachette*, as they say here; and that is not my nature; I like to do everything frankly, freely, *naïvement, au grand jour*. That is the great thing—to be free, to be frank, to be *naïf*. Doesn't Matthew Arnold say that somewhere—or is it Swinburne, or Pater?

When I was with the Johnsons everything was superficial; and, as regards life, everything was brought down to the question of right and wrong. They were too didactic; art should never be didactic; and what is life but an art? Pater has said that so well, somewhere. With the Johnsons I am afraid I lost many opportunities; the tone was gray and cottony, I might almost say woolly. But now, as I tell you, I have determined to take right hold for myself; to look right into European life, and judge it without Johnsonian prejudices. I have taken up my residence in a French family, in a real Parisian house. You see I have the courage of my opinions; I don't shrink from carrying out my theory that the great thing is to *live*.

You know I have always been intensely interested in Balzac, who never shrank from the reality, and whose almost *lurid* pictures of Parisian life have often haunted me in my wanderings through the old wicked-looking streets on the other side of the river. I am only sorry that my new friends—my French family—do not live in the old city—*au cœur du vieux Paris*, as they say here. They live only in the Boulevard Haussman, which is less picturesque; but in spite of this they have a great deal of the Balzac tone. Madame de Maisonrouge belongs to one of the oldest and proudest families in France; but she has had reverses which have compelled her to open an establishment in which a limited number of travellers, who are weary of the beaten track, who have the sense of local colour—she explains it herself, she expresses it so well—in short, to open a sort of boarding-house. I don't see why I should not, after all, use that expression, for it is the correlative of the term *pension bourgeoise*, employed by Balzac in the *Père Goriot*. Do you remember the *pension bourgeoise* of Madame Vauquer *née* de Conflans? But this establishment is not at all like that: and indeed it is not at all *bourgeois*; there is something distinguished, something aristocratic, about it. The Pension Vauquer was dark, brown, sordid, *graisseuse*; but this is in quite a different tone, with high clear, lightly-draped windows, tender, subtle, almost morbid, colours, and furniture in elegant, studied, reed-like lines. Madame de Maisonrouge reminds me of Madame Hulot—do you remember "la belle Madame Hulot?"—in *Les Parents Pauvres*. She has a great charm; a little artificial, a little fatigued, with a little suggestion of hidden things in her life; but I have always been sensitive to the charm of fatigue, of duplicity.

I am rather disappointed, I confess, in the society I find here; it is not so local, so characteristic, as I could have desired. Indeed, to tell the truth, it is not local at all; but, on the other hand, it is cosmopolitan, and there is a great advantage in that. We are French, we are English, we are American, we are German; and, I believe, there are some Russians and Hungarians expected. I am much interested in the study of national types; in comparing, contrasting, seizing the strong

points, the weak points, the point of view of each. It is interesting to shift one's point of view—to enter into strange,
exotic ways of looking at life.

The American types here are not, I am sorry to say, so interesting as they might be, and, excepting myself, are exclusively feminine. We are *thin*, my dear Harvard; we are pale,
we are sharp. There is something meagre about us; our line
is wanting in roundness, our composition in richness. We lack
temperament; we don't know how to live; *nous ne savons pas
vivre*, as they say here. The American temperament is represented (putting myself aside, and I often think that my temperament is not at all American) by a young girl and her
mother, and another young girl without her mother—without
her mother or any attendant or appendage whatever. These
young girls are rather curious types; they have a certain interest, they have a certain grace, but they are disappointing too;
they don't go far; they don't keep all they promise; they don't
satisfy the imagination. They are cold, slim, sexless; the physique is not generous, not abundant; it is only the drapery,
the skirts and furbelows (that is, I mean in the young lady
who has her mother) that are abundant. They are very different: one of them all elegance, all expensiveness, with an air of
high fashion, from New York; the other a plain, pure, clear-
eyed, straight-waisted, straight-stepping maiden from the
heart of New England. And yet they are very much alike
too—more alike than they would care to think themselves; for
they eye each other with cold, mistrustful, deprecating looks.
They are both specimens of the emancipated young American
girl—practical, positive, passionless, subtle, and knowing, as
you please, either too much or too little. And yet, as I say,
they have a certain stamp, a certain grace; I like to talk with
them, to study them.

The fair New Yorker is, sometimes, very amusing; she asks
me if every one in Boston talks like me—if every one is as
"intellectual" as your poor correspondent. She is for ever
throwing Boston up at me; I can't get rid of Boston. The
other one rubs it into me too; but in a different way; she
seems to feel about it as a good Mahommedan feels toward
Mecca, and regards it as a kind of focus of light for the whole

human race. Poor little Boston, what nonsense is talked in thy name! But this New England maiden is, in her way, a strange type: she is travelling all over Europe alone—"to see it," she says, "for herself." For herself! What can that stiff, slim self of hers do with such sights, such visions! She looks at everything, goes everywhere, passes her way, with her clear, quiet eyes wide open; skirting the edge of obscene abysses without suspecting them; pushing through brambles without tearing her robe; exciting, without knowing it, the most injurious suspicions; and always holding her course, passionless, stainless, fearless, charmless! It is a little figure in which, after all, if you can get the right point of view, there is something rather striking.

By way of contrast, there is a lovely English girl, with eyes as shy as violets, and a voice as sweet! She has a sweet Gainsborough head, and a great Gainsborough hat, with a mighty plume in front of it, which makes a shadow over her quiet English eyes. Then she has a sage-green robe, "mystic, wonderful," all embroidered with subtle devices and flowers, and birds of tender tint; very straight and tight in front, and adorned behind, along the spine, with large, strange, iridescent buttons. The revival of taste, of the sense of beauty, in England, interests me deeply; what is there in a simple row of spinal buttons to make one dream—to *donner à rêver*, as they say here? I think that a great æsthetic renascence is at hand, and that a great light will be kindled in England, for all the world to see. There are spirits there that I should like to commune with; I think they would understand me.

This gracious English maiden, with her clinging robes, her amulets and girdles, with something quaint and angular in her step, her carriage something mediæval and Gothic, in the details of her person and dress, this lovely Evelyn Vane (isn't it a beautiful name?) is deeply, delightfully picturesque. She is much a woman—*elle est bien femme*, as they say here; simpler, softer, rounder, richer than the young girls I spoke of just now. Not much talk—a great, sweet silence. Then the violet eye—the very eye itself seems to blush; the great shadowy hat, making the brow so quiet; the strange, clinging, clutching, pictured raiment! As I say, it is a very gracious, tender type.

She has her brother with her, who is a beautiful, fair-haired, gray-eyed young Englishman. He is purely objective; and he, too, is very plastic.

v.

From MIRANDA HOPE *to her* MOTHER.

September 26th.

You must not be frightened at not hearing from me oftener; it is not because I am in any trouble, but because I am getting on so well. If I were in any trouble I don't think I should write to you; I should just keep quiet and see it through myself. But that is not the case at present; and, if I don't write to you, it is because I am so deeply interested over here that I don't seem to find time. It was a real providence that brought me to this house, where, in spite of all obstacles, I am able to do much good work. I wonder how I find the time for all I do; but when I think that I have only got a year in Europe, I feel as if I wouldn't sacrifice a single hour.

The obstacles I refer to are the disadvantages I have in learning French, there being so many persons around me speaking English, and that, as you may say, in the very bosom of a French family. It seems as if you heard English everywhere; but I certainly didn't expect to find it in a place like this. I am not discouraged, however, and I talk French all I can, even with the other English boarders. Then I have a lesson every day from Miss Maisonrouge (the elder daughter of the lady of the house), and French conversation every evening in the *salon*, from eight to eleven, with Madame herself, and some friends of hers that often come in. Her cousin, Mr. Verdier, a young French gentleman, is fortunately staying with her, and I make a point of talking with him as much as possible. I have *extra private lessons* from him, and I often go out to walk with him. Some night, soon, he is to accompany me to the opera. We have also a most interesting plan of visiting all the galleries in Paris together. Like most of the French, he converses with great fluency, and I feel as if I should really gain from him. He is remarkably handsome, and extremely polite—paying a great many compliments, which, I am afraid,

are not always *sincere*. When I return to Bangor I will tell you
some of the things he has said to me. I think you will consider
them extremely curious, and very beautiful *in their way*.

The conversation in the parlour (from eight to eleven) is
often remarkably brilliant, and I often wish that you, or some
of the Bangor folks, could be there to enjoy it. Even though
you couldn't understand it I think you would like to hear the
way they go on; they seem to express so much. I sometimes
think that at Bangor they don't express enough (but it seems
as if over there, there was less to express). It seems as if, at
Bangor, there were things that folks never *tried* to say; but
here, I have learned from studying French that you have no
idea what you *can* say, before you try. At Bangor they seem
to give it up beforehand; they don't make any effort. (I don't
say this in the least for William Platt, *in particular*.)

I am sure I don't know what they will think of me when I
get back. It seems as if, over here, I had learned to come out
with everything. I suppose they will think I am not sincere;
but isn't it more sincere to come out with things than to
conceal them? I have become very good friends with every
one in the house—that is (you see, I *am* sincere), with *almost*
every one. It is the most interesting circle I ever was in.
There's a girl here, an American, that I don't like so much as
the rest; but that is only because she won't let me. I should
like to like her, ever so much, because she is most lovely and
most attractive; but she doesn't seem to want to know me or
to like me. She comes from New York, and she is remarkably
pretty, with beautiful eyes and the most delicate features; she
is also remarkably elegant—in this respect would bear comparison with any one I have seen over here. But it seems as if
she didn't want to recognise me, or associate with me; as if
she wanted to make a difference between us. It is like people
they call "haughty" in books. I have never seen any one like
that before—any one that wanted to make a difference; and
at first I was right down interested, she seemed to me so like
a proud young lady in a novel. I kept saying to myself all day,
"haughty, haughty," and I wished she would keep on so. But
she did keep on; she kept on too long; and then I began to
feel hurt. I couldn't think what I have done, and I can't think
yet. It's as if she had got some idea about me, or had heard

some one say something. If some girls should behave like that I shouldn't make any account of it; but this one is so refined, and looks as if she might be so interesting if I once got to know her, that I think about it a good deal. I am bound to find out what her reason is—for of course she has got some reason; I am right down curious to know.

I went up to her to ask her the day before yesterday; I thought that was the best way. I told her I wanted to know her better, and would like to come and see her in her room—they tell me she has got a lovely room—and that if she had heard anything against me, perhaps she would tell me when I came. But she was more distant than ever, and she just turned it off; said that she had never heard me mentioned, and that her room was too small to receive visitors. I suppose she spoke the truth, but I am sure she has got some reason, all the same. She has got some idea, and I am bound to find out before I go, if I have to ask everybody in the house. I *am* right down curious. I wonder if she doesn't think me refined—or if she had ever heard anything against Bangor? I can't think it is that. Don't you remember when Clara Barnard went to visit in New York, three years ago, how much attention she received? And you know Clara *is* Bangor, to the soles of her shoes. Ask William Platt—so long as he isn't a native—if he doesn't consider Clara Barnard refined.

Apropos, as they say here, of refinement, there is another American in the house—a gentleman from Boston—who is just crowded with it. His name is Mr. Louis Leverett (such a beautiful name, I think), and he is about thirty years old. He is rather small, and he looks pretty sick; he suffers from some affection of the liver. But his conversation is remarkably interesting, and I delight to listen to him—he has such beautiful ideas. I feel as if it were hardly right, not being in French; but, fortunately, he uses a great many French expressions. It's in a different style from the conversation of Mr. Verdier—not so complimentary, but more intellectual. He is intensely fond of pictures, and has given me a great many ideas about them which I should never have gained without him; I shouldn't have known where to look for such ideas. He thinks everything of pictures; he thinks we don't make near enough of them. They seem to make a good deal of them here; but I couldn't help telling him the other day that in Bangor I really don't think we do.

If I had any money to spend I would buy some and take them back, to hang up. Mr. Leverett says it would do them good—not the pictures, but the Bangor folks. He thinks everything of the French, too, and says we don't make nearly enough of *them*. I couldn't help telling him the other day that at any rate they make enough of themselves. But it is very interesting to hear him go on about the French, and it is so much gain to me, so long as that is what I came for. I talk to him as much as I dare about Boston, but I do feel as if this were right down wrong—a stolen pleasure.

I can get all the Boston culture I want when I go back, if I carry out my plan, my happy vision, of going there to reside. I ought to direct all my efforts to European culture now, and keep Boston to finish off. But it seems as if I couldn't help taking a peep now and then, in advance—with a Bostonian. I don't know when I may meet one again; but if there are many others like Mr. Leverett there, I shall be certain not to want when I carry out my dream. He is just as full of culture as he can live. But it seems strange how many different sorts there are.

There are two of the English who I suppose are very cultivated too; but it doesn't seem as if I could enter into theirs so easily, though I try all I can. I do love their way of speaking, and sometimes I feel almost as if it would be right to give up trying to learn French, and just try to learn to speak our own tongue as these English speak it. It isn't the things they say so much, though these are often rather curious, but it is in the way they pronounce, and the sweetness of their voice. It seems as if they must *try* a good deal to talk like that; but these English that are here don't seem to try at all, either to speak or do anything else. They are a young lady and her brother. I believe they belong to some noble family. I have had a good deal of intercourse with them, because I have felt more free to talk to them than to the Americans—on account of the language. It seems as if in talking with them I was almost learning a new one.

I never supposed, when I left Bangor, that I was coming to Europe to learn *English*! If I do learn it, I don't think you will understand me when I get back, and I don't think you'll like it much. I should be a good deal criticised if I spoke like that at Bangor. However, I verily believe Bangor is the most critical place on earth; I have seen nothing like it over here. Tell them all I have come to the conclusion that they are *a great deal too fastidious.* But I was speaking about this English young lady and her brother. I wish I could put them before you. She is lovely to look at; she seems so modest and retiring. In spite of this, however, she dresses in a way that attracts great attention, as I couldn't help noticing when one day I went out to walk with her. She was ever so much looked at; but she didn't seem to notice it, until at last I couldn't help calling attention to it. Mr. Leverett thinks everything of it; he calls it the "costume of the future." I should call it rather the costume of the past—you know the English have such an attachment to the past. I said this the other day to Madame de Maisonrouge—that Miss Vane dressed in the costume of the past. *De l'an passé, vous voulez dire?* said Madame, with her little French laugh (you can get William Platt to translate this, he used to tell me he knew so much French).

You know I told you, in writing some time ago, that I had tried to get some insight into the position of woman in England, and, being here with Miss Vane, it has seemed to me to be a good opportunity to get a little more. I have asked her a great deal about it; but she doesn't seem able to give me much information. The first time I asked her she told me the position of a lady depended upon the rank of her father, her eldest brother, her husband, etc. She told me her own position was very good, because her father was some relation—I forget what—to a lord. She thinks everything of this; and that proves to me that the position of woman in her country cannot be satisfactory; because, if it were, it wouldn't depend upon that of your relations, even your nearest. I don't know much about lords, and it does try my patience (though she is just as sweet as she can live) to hear her talk as if it were a matter of course that I should.

I feel as if it were right to ask her as often as I can if she doesn't consider every one equal; but she always says she doesn't, and she confesses that she doesn't think she is equal to "Lady Something-or-other," who is the wife of that rela-

tion of her father. I try and persuade her all I can that she is;
but it seems as if she didn't want to be persuaded; and when
I ask her if Lady So-and-so is of the same opinion (that Miss
Vane isn't her equal), she looks so soft and pretty with her
eyes, and says, "Of course she is!" When I tell her that this
is right down bad for Lady So-and-so, it seems as if she
wouldn't believe me, and the only answer she will make is
that Lady So-and-so is "extremely nice." I don't believe she
is nice at all; if she were nice, she wouldn't have such ideas as
that. I tell Miss Vane that at Bangor we think such ideas vulgar; but then she looks as though she had never heard of
Bangor. I often want to shake her, though she *is* so sweet. If
she isn't angry with the people who make her feel that way, I
am angry for her. I am angry with her brother, too, for she
is evidently very much afraid of him, and this gives me some
further insight into the subject. She thinks everything of her
brother, and thinks it natural that she should be afraid of him,
not only physically (for this *is* natural as he is enormously tall
and strong, and has very big fists), but morally and intellectually. She seems unable, however, to take in any argument,
and she makes me realise what I have often heard—that if you
are timid nothing will reason you out of it.

Mr. Vane, also (the brother), seems to have the same prejudices, and when I tell him, as I often think it right to do,
that his sister is not his subordinate, even if she does think so,
but his equal, and, perhaps in some respects his superior, and
that if my brother, in Bangor, were to treat me as he treats
this poor young girl, who has not spirit enough to see the
question in its true light, there would be an indignation-meet-
ing of the citizens, to protest against such an outrage to the
sanctity of womanhood—when I tell him all this, at breakfast
or dinner, he bursts out laughing so loud that all the plates
clatter on the table.

But at such a time as this there is always one person who
seems interested in what I say—a German gentleman, a professor, who sits next to me at dinner, and whom I must tell
you more about another time. He is very learned, and has a
great desire for information; he appreciates a great many of
my remarks, and, after dinner, in the salon, he often comes to
me to ask me questions about them. I have to think a little,

sometimes, to know what I did say, or what I do think. He takes you right up where you left off, and he is almost as fond of discussing things as William Platt is. He is splendidly edu-cated, in the German style, and he told me the other day that he was an "intellectual broom." Well, if he is, he sweeps clean; I told him that. After he has been talking to me I feel as if I hadn't got a speck of dust left in my mind anywhere. It's a most delightful feeling. He says he's an observer; and I am sure there is plenty over here to observe. But I have told you enough for to-day. I don't know how much longer I shall stay here; I am getting on so fast that it sometimes seems as if I shouldn't need all the time I have laid out. I suppose your cold weather has promptly begun, as usual; it sometimes makes me envy you. The fall weather here is very dull and damp, and I feel very much as if I should like to be braced up.

VI.

From MISS EVELYN VANE, *in Paris, to the* LADY
AUGUSTA FLEMING, *at Brighton.*

Paris, September 30th.

DEAR LADY AUGUSTA—

I am afraid I shall not be able to come to you on January 7th, as you kindly proposed at Homburg. I am so very, very sorry; it is a great disappointment to me. But I have just heard that it has been settled that mamma and the children are coming abroad for a part of the winter, and mamma wishes me to go with them to Hyères, where Georgina has been ordered for her lungs. She has not been at all well these three months, and now that the damp weather has begun she is very poorly indeed; so that last week papa decided to have a consultation, and he and mamma went with her up to town and saw some three or four doctors. They all of them ordered the south of France, but they didn't agree about the place; so that mamma herself decided for Hyères, because it is the most economical. I believe it is very dull, but I hope it will do Georgina good. I am afraid, however, that nothing will do her good until she consents to take more care of herself; I am afraid she is very wild and wilful, and mamma tells me that all this month it has taken papa's positive orders to make her stop in-doors. She is very cross (mamma writes me) about coming abroad, and doesn't seem at all to mind the expense that papa has been put to,—talks very ill-naturedly about losing the hunting, etc. She expected to begin to hunt in December, and wants to know whether anybody keeps hounds at Hyères. Fancy a girl wanting to follow the hounds when her lungs are so bad! But I dare say that when she gets there she will be glad enough to keep quiet, as they say that the heat is intense. It may cure Georgina, but I am sure it will make the rest of us very ill.

Mamma, however, is only going to bring Mary and Gus and Fred and Adelaide abroad with her; the others will remain at Kingscote until February (about the 3d), when they will go to Eastbourne for a month with Miss Turnover, the new governess, who has turned out such a very nice person. She is going to take Miss Travers, who has been with us so long, but who is only qualified for the younger children, to Hyères, and I believe some of the Kingscote servants. She has perfect confidence in Miss T.; it is only a pity she has such an odd name. Mamma thought of asking her if she would mind taking another when she came; but papa thought she might object. Lady Battledown makes all her governesses take the same name; she gives £5 more a year for the purpose. I forget what it is she calls them; I think it's Johnson (which to me always suggests a lady's maid). Governesses shouldn't have too pretty a name; they shouldn't have a nicer name than the family.

I suppose you heard from the Desmonds that I did not go back to England with them. When it began to be talked about that Georgina should be taken abroad, mamma wrote to me that I had better stop in Paris for a month with Harold, so that she could pick me up on their way to Hyères. It saves the expense of my journey to Kingscote and back, and gives me the opportunity to "finish" a little, in French.

You know Harold came here six weeks ago, to get up his French for those dreadful examinations that he has to pass so soon. He came to live with some French people that take in young men (and others) for this purpose; it's a kind of coaching place, only kept by women. Mamma had heard it was very nice; so she wrote to me that I was to come and stop here with Harold. The Desmonds brought me and made the arrangement, or the bargain, or whatever you call it. Poor Harold was naturally not at all pleased; but he has been very kind, and has treated me like an angel. He is getting on beautifully with his French; for though I don't think the place is so good as papa supposed, yet Harold is so immensely clever that he can scarcely help learning. I am afraid I learn much less, but, fortunately, I have not to pass an examination—except if mamma takes it into her head to examine me. But she will have so much to think of with Georgina that I hope this won't occur to her. If it does, I shall be, as Harold says, in a dreadful funk.

This is not such a nice place for a girl as for a young man, and the Desmonds thought it *exceedingly odd* that mamma should wish me to come here. As Mrs. Desmond said, it is because she is so very unconventional. But you know Paris is so very amusing, and if only Harold remains good-natured about it, I shall be content to wait for the caravan (that's what he calls mamma and the children). The person who keeps the establishment, or whatever they call it, is rather odd, and *exceedingly foreign*; but she is wonderfully civil, and is perpetually sending to my door to see if I want anything. The servants are not at all like English servants, and come bursting in, the footman (they have only one) and the maids alike, at all sorts of hours, in the *most sudden way*. Then when one rings, it is half an hour before they come. All this is very uncomfortable, and I daresay it will be worse at Hyères. There, however, fortunately, we shall have our own people.

There are some very odd Americans here, who keep throwing Harold into fits of laughter. One is a dreadful little man who is always sitting over the fire, and talking about the colour of the sky. I don't believe he ever saw the sky except through the window-pane. The other day he took hold of my frock (that green one you thought so nice at Homburg) and told me that it reminded him of the texture of the Devonshire turf. And then he talked for half an hour about the Devonshire turf, which I thought such a very extraordinary subject. Harold says he is mad. It is very strange to be living in this way, with people one doesn't know. I mean that one doesn't know as one knows them in England.

The other Americans (beside the madman) are two girls, about my own age, one of whom is rather nice. She has a mother; but the mother is always sitting in her bed-room, which seems so very odd. I should like mamma to ask them to Kingscote, but I am afraid mamma wouldn't like the mother, who is rather vulgar. The other girl is rather vulgar too, and is travelling about quite alone. I think she is a kind of schoolmistress; but the other girl (I mean the nicer one, with the mother) tells me she is more respectable than she seems. She has, however, the most extraordinary opinions— wishes to do away with the aristocracy, thinks it wrong that Arthur should have Kingscote when papa dies, etc. I don't see what it signifies to her that poor Arthur should come into the property, which will be so delightful—except for papa dying. But Harold says she is mad. He chaffs her tremendously about her radicalism, and he is so immensely clever that she can't answer him, though she is rather clever, too.

There is also a Frenchman, a nephew, or cousin, or some-thing, of the person of the house, who is extremely nasty; and a German professor, or doctor, who eats with his knife and is a great bore. I am so very sorry about giving up my visit. I am afraid you will never ask me again.

VII.

From Léon Verdier *in Paris, to* Prosper Gobain, *at Lille.*

September 28th.

My Dear Prosper—
It is a long time since I have given you of my news, and I don't know what puts it into my head to-night to recall myself to your affectionate memory. I suppose it is that when we are happy the mind reverts instinctively to those with whom for-merly we shared our exaltations and depressions, and *je t'en ai trop dit, dans le bon temps, mon gros Prosper*, and you always listened to me too imperturbably, with your pipe in your mouth, your waistcoat unbuttoned, for me not to feel that I can count upon your sympathy to-day. *Nous en sommes nous flanquées, des confidences*—in those happy days when my first

thought in seeing an adventure *poindre à l'horizon* was of the pleasure I should have in relating it to the great Prosper. As I tell thee, I am happy; decidedly, I am happy, and from this affirmation I fancy you can construct the rest. Shall I help thee a little? Take three adorable girls . . . three, my good Prosper—the mystic number—neither more nor less. Take them and place thy insatiable little Léon in the midst of them! Is the situation sufficiently indicated, and do you apprehend the motives of my felicity?

You expected, perhaps, I was going to tell you that I had made my fortune, or that the Uncle Blondeau had at last decided to return into the breast of nature, after having constituted me his universal legatee. But I needn't remind you that women are always for something in the happiness of him who writes to thee—for something in his happiness, and for a good deal more in his misery. But don't let me talk of misery now; time enough when it comes; *ces demoiselles* have gone to join the serried ranks of their amiable predecessors. Excuse me— I comprehend your impatience. I will tell you of whom *ces demoiselles* consist.

You have heard me speak of my *cousine* de Maisonrouge, that *grande belle femme*, who, after having married, *en secondes noces*—there had been, to tell the truth, some irregularity about her first union—a venerable relic of the old noblesse of Poitou, was left, by the death of her husband, complicated by the indulgence of expensive tastes on an income of 17,000 francs, on the pavement of Paris, with two little demons of daughters to bring up in the path of virtue. She managed to bring them up; my little cousins are rigidly virtuous. If you ask me how she managed it, I can't tell you; it's no business of mine, and, *à fortiori*, none of yours. She is now fifty years old (she confesses to thirty-seven), and her daughters, whom she has never been able to marry, are respectively twenty-seven and twenty-three (they confess to twenty and to seventeen). Three years ago she had the thrice-blessed idea of opening a sort of *pension* for the entertainment and instruction of the blundering barbarians who come to Paris in the hope of picking up a few stray particles of the language of Voltaire—or of Zola. The idea *lui a porté bonheur*; the shop does a very good business. Until within a few months ago it was carried on by my cousins alone; but lately the need of a few extensions and embellishments has caused itself to be felt. My cousin has undertaken them, regardless of expense; she has asked me to come and stay with her—board and lodging gratis—and keep an eye on the grammatical eccentricities of her *pensionnaires*. I am the extension, my good Prosper; I am the embellishment! I live for nothing, and I straighten up the accent of the prettiest English lips. The English lips are not all pretty, heaven knows, but enough of them are so to make it a gaining bargain for me.

Just now, as I told you, I am in daily conversation with three separate pairs. The owner of one of them has private lessons; she pays extra. My cousin doesn't give me a sou of the money; but I make bold, nevertheless, to say that my trouble is remunerated. But I am well, very well, with the proprietors of the two other pairs. One of them is a little Anglaise, of about twenty—a little *figure de keepsake*; the most adorable miss that you ever, or at least that I ever, beheld. She is decorated all over with beads and bracelets and embroidered dandelions; but her principal decoration consists of the softest little gray eyes in the world, which rest upon you with a profundity of confidence—a confidence that I really feel some compunction in betraying. She has a tint as white as this sheet of paper, except just in the middle of each cheek, where it passes into the purest and most transparent, most liquid, carmine. Occasionally this rosy fluid overflows into the rest of her face— by which I mean that she blushes—as softly as the mark of your breath on the window-pane.

Like every Anglaise, she is rather pinched and prim in public; but it is very easy to see that when no one is looking *elle ne demande qu'à se laisser aller!* Whenever she wants it I am always there, and I have given her to understand that she can count upon me. I have every reason to believe that she appreciates the assurance, though I am bound in honesty to confess that with her the situation is a little less advanced than with the others. *Que voulez-vous?* The English are heavy, and the Anglaises move slowly, that's all. The movement, however, is perceptible, and once this fact is established I can let the pottage simmer. I can give her time to arrive, for I am over-well occupied with her *concurrentes*. *Celles-ci* don't keep me waiting, *par exemple*!

These young ladies are Americans, and you know that it is the national character to move fast. "All right—go ahead!" (I am learning a great deal of English, or, rather, a great deal of American.) They go ahead at a rate that sometimes makes it difficult for me to keep up. One of them is prettier than the other; but this latter (the one that takes the private lessons) is really *une fille prodigieuse. Ah, par exemple, elle brûle ses vaisseux celle-là!* She threw herself into my arms the very first day, and I almost owed her a grudge for having deprived me of that pleasure of gradation, of carrying the defences, one by one, which is almost as great as that of entering the place.

Would you believe that at the end of exactly twelve minutes she gave me a rendezvous? It is true it was in the Galerie d'Apollon, at the Louvre; but that was respectable for a beginning, and since then we have had them by the dozen; I have ceased to keep the account. *Non, c'est une fille qui me dépasse.*

The little one (she has a mother somewhere, out of sight, shut up in a closet or a trunk) is a good deal prettier, and, perhaps, on that account *elle y met plus de façons*. She doesn't knock about Paris with me by the hour; she contents herself with long interviews in the *petit salon*, with the curtains half-drawn, beginning at about three o'clock, when every one is *à la promenade*. She is admirable, this little one; a little too thin, the bones rather accentuated, but the detail, on the whole, most satisfactory. And you can say anything to her. She takes the trouble to appear not to understand, but her conduct, half an hour afterwards, reassures you completely—oh, completely!

However, it is the tall one, the one of the private lessons, that is the most remarkable. These private lessons, my good Prosper, are the most brilliant invention of the age, and a real stroke of genius on the part of Miss Miranda! They also take place in the *petit salon*, but with the doors tightly closed, and with explicit directions to every one in the house that we are not to be disturbed. And we are not, my good Prosper; we are not! Not a sound, not a shadow, interrupts our felicity.

My *cousine* is really admirable; the shop deserves to succeed. Miss Miranda is tall and rather flat; she is too pale; she hasn't the adorable *rougeurs* of the little Anglaise. But she has bright, keen, inquisitive eyes, superb teeth, a nose modelled by a sculptor, and a way of holding up her head and looking every one in the face, which is the most finished piece of impertinence I ever beheld. She is making the *tour du monde*, entirely alone, without even a soubrette to carry the ensign, for the purpose of seeing for herself *à quoi s'en tenir sur les hommes et les choses*—on *les hommes* particularly. *Dis donc*, Prosper, it must be a *drôle de pays* over there, where young persons animated by this ardent curiosity are manufactured! If we should turn the tables, some day, thou and I, and go over and see it for ourselves. It is as well that we should go and find them *chez elles*, as that they should come out here after us. *Dis donc, mon gros Prosper.* . . .

VIII.

From Dr. Rudolf Staub, *in Paris, to* Dr. Julius Hirsch, *at Göttingen.*

My Dear Brother in Science—
I resume my hasty notes, of which I sent you the first instalment some weeks ago. I mentioned then that I intended to leave my hotel, not finding it sufficiently local and national. It was kept by a Pomeranian, and the waiters, without exception, were from the Fatherland. I fancied myself at Berlin, Unter den Linden, and I reflected that, having taken the serious step of visiting the headquarters of the Gallic genius, I should try and project myself, as much as possible, into the circumstances which are in part the consequence and in part the cause of its irrepressible activity. It seemed to me that there could be no well-grounded knowledge without this preliminary operation of placing myself in relations, as slightly as possible modified by elements proceeding from a different combination of causes, with the spontaneous home-life of the country.

I accordingly engaged a room in the house of a lady of pure French extraction and education, who supplements the shortcomings of an income insufficient to the ever-growing demands of the Parisian system of sense-gratification, by providing food and lodging for a limited number of distinguished strangers. I should have preferred to have my room alone in the house, and to take my meals in a brewery, of very good appearance, which I speedily discovered in the same street; but this arrangement, though very lucidly proposed by myself, was not acceptable to the mistress of the establishment (a woman with a mathematical head), and I have consoled myself for the extra expense by fixing my thoughts upon the opportunity that conformity to the customs of the house gives me of studying the table-manners of my companions, and of observing the French nature at a peculiarly physiological moment, the moment when the satisfaction of the *taste*, which is the governing quality in its composition, produces a kind of exhalation, an intellectual transpiration, which, though light and perhaps invisible to a superficial spectator, is nevertheless appreciable by a properly adjusted instrument.

I have adjusted my instrument very satisfactorily (I mean the one I carry in my good, square German head), and I am not afraid of losing a single drop of this valuable fluid, as it condenses itself upon the plate of my observation. A prepared surface is what I need, and I have prepared my surface.

Unfortunately here, also, I find the individual native in the minority. There are only four French persons in the house—the individuals concerned in its management, three of whom are women, and one a man. This preponderance of the feminine element is, however, in itself characteristic, as I need not remind you what an abnormally-developed part this sex has played in French history. The remaining figure is apparently that of a man, but I hesitate to classify him so superficially. He appears to me less human than simian, and whenever I hear him talk I seem to myself to have paused in the street to listen to the shrill clatter of a hand-organ, to which the gambols of a hairy *homunculus* form an accompaniment.

I mentioned to you before that my expectation of rough usage, in consequence of my German nationality, had proved completely unfounded. No one seems to know or to care what my nationality is, and I am treated, on the contrary, with the civility which is the portion of every traveller who pays the bill without scanning the items too narrowly. This, I confess, has been something of a surprise to me, and I have not yet made up my mind as to the fundamental cause of the anomaly. My determination to take up my abode in a French interior was largely dictated by the supposition that I should be substantially disagreeable to its inmates. I wished to observe the different forms taken by the irritation that I should naturally produce; for it is under the influence of irritation that the French character most completely expresses itself. My presence, however, does not appear to operate as a stimulus, and in this respect I am materially disappointed. They treat me as they treat every one else; whereas, in order to be treated differently, I was resigned in advance to be treated worse. I have not, as I say, fully explained to myself this logical contradiction; but this is the explanation to which I tend. The French are so exclusively occupied with the idea of themselves, that in spite of the very definite image the German personality presented to them by the war of 1870, they have at present no distinct apprehension of its existence. They are not very sure that there are any Germans; they have already forgotten the convincing proofs of the fact that were presented to them nine years ago. A German was something disagreeable, which they determined to keep out of their conception of things. I therefore think that we are wrong to govern ourselves upon the hypothesis of the *revanche*; the French nature is too shallow for that large and powerful plant to bloom in it.

The English-speaking specimens, too, I have not been willing to neglect the opportunity to examine; and among these I have paid special attention to the American varieties, of which I find here several singular examples. The two most remarkable are a young man who presents all the characteristics of a period of national decadence; reminding me strongly of some diminutive Hellenised Roman of the third century. He is an illustration of the period of culture in which the faculty of appreciation has obtained such a preponderance over that of production that the latter sinks into a kind of rank sterility, and the mental condition becomes analogous to that of a malarious bog. I learn from him that there is an immense number of Americans exactly resembling him, and that the city of Boston, indeed, is almost exclusively composed

of them. (He communicated this fact very proudly, as if it
were greatly to the credit of his native country; little perceiving the truly sinister impression it made upon me.)

What strikes one in it is that it is a phenomenon to the best
of my knowledge—and you know what my knowledge is—
unprecedented and unique in the history of mankind; the arrival of a nation at an ultimate stage of evolution without
having passed through the mediate one; the passage of the
fruit, in other words, from crudity to rottenness, without the
interposition of a period of useful (and ornamental) ripeness.
With the Americans, indeed, the crudity and the rottenness
are identical and simultaneous; it is impossible to say, as in the
conversation of this deplorable young man, which is one and
which is the other; they are inextricably mingled. I prefer the
talk of the French *homunculus*; it is at least more amusing.

It is interesting in this manner to perceive, so largely developed, the germs of extinction in the so-called powerful
Anglo-Saxon family. I find them in almost as recognisable a
form in a young woman from the State of Maine, in the province of New England, with whom I have had a good deal of
conversation. She differs somewhat from the young man I just
mentioned, in that the faculty of production, of action, is, in
her, less inanimate; she has more of the freshness and vigour
that we suppose to belong to a young civilisation. But unfortunately she produces nothing but evil, and her tastes and
habits are similarly those of a Roman lady of the lower
Empire. She makes no secret of them, and has, in fact, elab-
orated a complete system of licentious behaviour. As the opportunities she finds in her own country do not satisfy her,
she has come to Europe "to try" as she says, "for herself." It
is the doctrine of universal experience professed with a cynicism that is really most extraordinary, and which, presenting
itself in a young woman of considerable education, appears to
me to be the judgment of a society.

Another observation which pushes me to the same induction—that of the premature vitiation of the American popu-
lation—is the attitude of the Americans whom I have before
me with regard to each other. There is another young lady
here, who is less abnormally developed than the one I have
just described, but who yet bears the stamp of this peculiar

combination of incompleteness and effeteness. These three persons look with the greatest mistrust and aversion upon each other; and each has repeatedly taken me apart and assured me, secretly, that he or she only is the real, the genuine, the typical American. A type that has lost itself before it has been fixed—what can you look for from this?

Add to this that there are two young Englanders in the house, who hate all the Americans in a lump, making between them none of the distinctions and favourable comparisons which they insist upon, and you will, I think, hold me warranted in believing that, between precipitate decay and internecine enmities, the English-speaking family is destined to consume itself, and that with its decline the prospect of general pervasiveness, to which I alluded above, will brighten for the deep-lunged children of the Fatherland!

IX.

MIRANDA HOPE *to her* MOTHER.

October 22d.

DEAR MOTHER—

I am off in a day or two to visit some new country; I haven't yet decided which. I have satisfied myself with regard to France, and obtained a good knowledge of the language. I have enjoyed my visit to Madame de Maisonrouge deeply, and feel as if I were leaving a circle of real friends. Everything has gone on beautifully up to the end, and every one has been as kind and attentive as if I were their own sister, especially Mr. Verdier, the French gentleman, from whom I have gained more than I ever expected (in six weeks), and with whom I have promised to *correspond*. So you can imagine me dashing off the most correct French letters; and, if you don't believe it, I will keep the rough draft to show you when I go back.

The German gentleman is also more interesting, the more you know him; it seems sometimes as if I could fairly drink in his ideas. I have found out why the young lady from New York doesn't like me! It is because I said one day at dinner that I *admired* to go to the Louvre. Well, when I first came, it seemed as if I *did* admire everything!

Tell William Platt his letter has come. I knew he would have to write, and I was bound I would make him! I haven't decided what country I will visit yet; it seems as if there were so many to choose from. But I shall take care to pick out a good one, and to meet plenty of fresh experiences.

Dearest mother, my money holds out, and it *is* most interesting!

The Point of View

I

FROM MISS AURORA CHURCH, AT SEA, TO
MISS WHITESIDE, IN PARIS

. . . My dear child, the bromide of sodium (if that's what you call it) proved perfectly useless. I don't mean that it did me no good, but that I never had occasion to take the bottle out of my bag. It might have done wonders for me if I had needed it; but I didn't, simply because I have been a wonder myself. Will you believe that I have spent the whole voyage on deck, in the most animated conversation and exercise? Twelve times round the deck make a mile, I believe; and by this measurement I have been walking twenty miles a day. And down to every meal, if you please, where I have displayed the appetite of a fish-wife. Of course the weather has been lovely; so there's no great merit. The wicked old Atlantic has been as blue as the sapphire in my only ring (a rather good one), and as smooth as the slippery floor of Madame Galopin's dining-room. We have been for the last three hours in sight of land, and we are soon to enter the Bay of New York, which is said to be exquisitely beautiful. But of course you recall it, though they say that everything changes so fast over here. I find I don't remember anything, for my recollections of our voyage to Europe, so many years ago, are exceedingly dim; I only have a painful impression that mamma shut me up for an hour every day in the state-room, and made me learn by heart some religious poem. I was only five years old, and I believe that as a child I was extremely timid; on the other hand, mamma, as you know, was dreadfully severe. She is severe to this day; only I have become indifferent; I have been so pinched and pushed—morally speaking, *bien entendu*. It is true, however, that there are children of five on the vessel to-day who have been extremely conspicuous—ranging all over the ship, and always under one's feet. Of course they are little compatriots, which means that they are little barbarians. I don't mean that all our compatriots are barbarous; they seem to improve, somehow, after their first communion. I don't know whether

it's that ceremony that improves them, especially as so few of
them go in for it; but the women are certainly nicer than the
little girls; I mean, of course, in proportion, you know. You
warned me not to generalise, and you see I have already begun, before we have arrived. But I suppose there is no harm
in it so long as it is favourable. Isn't it favourable when I say
that I have had the most lovely time? I have never had so
much liberty in my life, and I have been out alone, as you
may say, every day of the voyage. If it is a foretaste of what is
to come, I shall take to that very kindly. When I say that I
have been out alone, I mean that we have always been two.
But we two were alone, so to speak, and it was not like always
having mamma, or Madame Galopin, or some lady in the *pension*, or the temporary cook. Mamma has been very poorly;
she is so very well on land, it's a wonder to see her at all taken
down. She says, however, that it isn't the being at sea; it's, on
the contrary, approaching the land. She is not in a hurry to
arrive; she says that great disillusions await us. I didn't know
that she had any illusions—she's so stern, so philosophic. She
is very serious; she sits for hours in perfect silence, with her
eyes fixed on the horizon. I heard her say yesterday to an
English gentleman—a very odd Mr. Antrobus, the only person with whom she converses—that she was afraid she
shouldn't like her native land, and that she shouldn't like not
liking it. But this is a mistake—she will like that immensely (I
mean not liking it). If it should prove at all agreeable, mamma
will be furious, for that will go against her system. You know
all about mamma's system; I have explained that so often. It
goes against her system that we should come back at all; that
was *my* system—I have had at last to invent one! She consented to come only because she saw that, having no *dot*, I
should never marry in Europe; and I pretended to be immensely pre-occupied with this idea, in order to make her
start. In reality *cela m'est parfaitement égal*. I am only afraid
I shall like it too much (I don't mean marriage, of course, but
one's native land). Say what you will, it's a charming thing to
go out alone, and I have given notice to mamma that I mean
to be always *en course*. When I tell her that, she looks at me
in the same silence; her eye dilates, and then she slowly closes
it. It's as if the sea were affecting her a little, though it's so

beautifully calm. I ask her if she will try my bromide, which is there in my bag; but she motions me off, and I begin to walk again, tapping my little boot-soles upon the smooth clean deck. This allusion to my boot-soles, by the way, is not prompted by vanity; but it's a fact that at sea one's feet and one's shoes assume the most extraordinary importance, so that we should take the precaution to have nice ones. They are all you seem to see as the people walk about the deck; you get to know them intimately, and to dislike some of them so much. I am afraid you will think that I have already broken loose; and for aught I know, I am writing as a *demoiselle bien-elevée* should not write. I don't know whether it's the American air; if it is, all I can say is that the American air is very charming. It makes me impatient and restless, and I sit scribbling here because I am so eager to arrive, and the time passes better if I occupy myself. I am in the saloon, where we have our meals, and opposite to me is a big round port-hole, wide open, to let in the smell of the land. Every now and then I rise a little and look through it, to see whether we are arriving. I mean in the Bay, you know, for we shall not come up to the city till dark. I don't want to lose the Bay; it appears that it's so wonderful. I don't exactly understand what it contains, except some beautiful islands; but I suppose you will know all about that. It is easy to see that these are the last hours, for all the people about me are writing letters to put into the post as soon as we come up to the dock. I believe they are dreadful at the custom-house, and you will remember how many new things you persuaded mamma that (with my pre-occupation of marriage) I should take to this country, where even the prettiest girls are expected not to go unadorned. We ruined ourselves in Paris (that is part of mamma's solemnity); *mais au moins je serai belle!* Moreover, I believe that mamma is prepared to say or to do anything that may be necessary for escaping from their odious duties; as she very justly remarks, she can't afford to be ruined twice. I don't know how one approaches these terrible *douaniers*, but I mean to invent something very charming. I mean to say, " *Voyons, Messieurs*, a young girl like me, brought up in the strictest foreign traditions, kept always in the background by a very superior mother—*la voilà*; you can see for yourself!—what is

it possible that she should attempt to smuggle in? Nothing
but a few simple relics of her convent!" I won't tell them that
my convent was called the *Magasin du Bon Marché*. Mamma
began to scold me three days ago for insisting on so many
trunks, and the truth is that, between us, we have not fewer
than seven. For relics, that's a good many! We are all writing
very long letters—or at least we are writing a great number.
There is no news of the Bay as yet. Mr. Antrobus, mamma's
friend, opposite to me, is beginning on his ninth. He is an
Honourable, and a Member of Parliament; he has written,
during the voyage, about a hundred letters, and he seems
greatly alarmed at the number of stamps he will have to buy
when he arrives. He is full of information; but he has not
enough, for he asks as many questions as mamma when she
goes to hire apartments. He is going to "look into" various
things; he speaks as if they had a little hole for the purpose.
He walks almost as much as I, and he has very big shoes. He
asks questions even of me, and I tell him again and again that
I know nothing about America. But it makes no difference;
he always begins again, and, indeed, it is not strange that he
should find my ignorance incredible. "Now, how would it be
in one of your South-Western States?"—that's his favourite
way of opening conversation. Fancy me giving an account of
the South-Western States! I tell him he had better ask
mamma—a little to tease that lady, who knows no more about
such places than I. Mr. Antrobus is very big and black; he
speaks with a sort of brogue; he has a wife and ten children;
he is not very romantic. But he has lots of letters to people
là-bas (I forget that we are just arriving), and mamma, who
takes an interest in him in spite of his views (which are dreadfully advanced, and not at all like mamma's own), has promised to give him the *entrée* to the best society. I don't know
what she knows about the best society over here to-day, for
we have not kept up our connections at all, and no one will
know (or, I am afraid, care) anything about us. She has an
idea that we shall be immensely recognised; but really, except
the poor little Rucks, who are bankrupt, and, I am told, in
no society at all, I don't know on whom we can count. *C'est
égal*. Mamma has an idea that, whether or not we appreciate
America ourselves, we shall at least be universally appreciated.

It's true that we have begun to be, a little; you would see that by the way that Mr. Cockerel and Mr. Louis Leverett are always inviting me to walk. Both of these gentlemen, who are Americans, have asked leave to call upon me in New York, and I have said, *Mon Dieu, oui*, if it's the custom of the country. Of course I have not dared to tell this to mamma, who flatters herself that we have brought with us in our trunks a complete set of customs of our own, and that we shall only have to shake them out a little and put them on when we arrive. If only the two gentlemen I just spoke of don't call at the same time, I don't think I shall be too much frightened. If they do, on the other hand, I won't answer for it. They have a particular aversion to each other, and they are ready to fight about poor little me. I am only the pretext, however; for, as Mr. Leverett says, it's really the opposition of temperaments. I hope they won't cut each other's throats, for I am not crazy about either of them. They are very well for the deck of a ship, but I shouldn't care about them in a *salon*; they are not at all distinguished. They think they are, but they are not; at least Mr. Louis Leverett does; Mr. Cockerel doesn't appear to care so much. They are extremely different (with their opposed temperaments), and each very amusing for a while; but I should get dreadfully tired of passing my life with either. Neither has proposed that, as yet; but it is evidently what they are coming to. It will be in a great measure to spite each other, for I think that *au fond* they don't quite believe in me. If they don't, it's the only point on which they agree. They hate each other awfully; they take such different views. That is, Mr. Cockerel hates Mr. Leverett—he calls him a sickly little ass; he says that his opinions are half affectation, and the other half dyspepsia. Mr. Leverett speaks of Mr. Cockerel as a "strident savage," but he declares he finds him most diverting. He says there is nothing in which we can't find a certain entertainment, if we only look at it in the right way, and that we have no business with either hating or loving; we ought only to strive to understand. To understand is to forgive, he says. That is very pretty, but I don't like the suppression of our affections, though I have no desire to fix mine upon Mr. Leverett. He is very artistic, and talks like an article in some review. He has lived a great deal in Paris, and Mr.

Cockerel says that is what has made him such an idiot. That is not complimentary to you, dear Louisa, and still less to your brilliant brother; for Mr. Cockerel explains that he means it (the bad effect of Paris) chiefly of the men. In fact, he means the bad effect of Europe altogether. This, however, is compromising to mamma; and I am afraid there is no doubt that (from what I have told him) he thinks mamma also an idiot. (I am not responsible, you know—I have always wanted to go home.) If mamma knew him, which she doesn't, for she always closes her eyes when I pass on his arm, she would think him disgusting. Mr. Leverett, however, tells me he is nothing to what we shall see yet. He is from Philadelphia (Mr. Cockerel); he insists that we shall go and see Philadelphia, but mamma says she saw it in 1855, and it was then *affreux*. Mr. Cockerel says that mamma is evidently not familiar with the march of improvement in this country; he speaks of 1855 as if it were a hundred years ago. Mamma says she knows it goes only too fast—it goes so fast that it has time to do nothing well; and then Mr. Cockerel, who, to do him justice, is perfectly good-natured, remarks that she had better wait till she has been ashore and seen the improvements. Mamma rejoins that she sees them from here, the improvements, and that they give her a sinking of the heart. (This little exchange of ideas is carried on through me; they have never spoken to each other.) Mr. Cockerel, as I say, is extremely good-natured, and he carries out what I have heard said about the men in America being very considerate of the women. They evidently listen to them a great deal; they don't contradict them, but it seems to me that this is rather negative. There is very little gallantry in not contradicting one; and it strikes me that there are some things the men don't express. There are others on the ship whom I've noticed. It's as if they were all one's brothers or one's cousins. But I promised you not to generalise, and perhaps there will be more expression when we arrive. Mr. Cockerel returns to America, after a general tour, with a renewed conviction that this is the only country. I left him on deck an hour ago looking at the coast-line with an opera-glass, and saying it was the prettiest thing he had seen in all his tour. When I remarked that the coast seemed rather low, he said it would be all the easier to get ashore; Mr. Leverett doesn't seem in a hurry to get ashore; he is sitting within sight of me in a corner of the saloon—writing letters, I suppose, but looking, from the way he bites his pen and rolls his eyes about, as if he were composing a sonnet and waiting for a rhyme. Perhaps the sonnet is addressed to me; but I forget that he suppresses the affections! The only person in whom mamma takes much interest is the great French critic, M. Lejaune, whom we have the honour to carry with us. We have read a few of his works, though mamma disapproves of his tendencies and thinks him a dreadful materialist. We have read them for the style; you know he is one of the new Academicians. He is a Frenchman like any other, except that he is rather more quiet; and he has a gray mustache and the ribbon of the Legion of Honour. He is the first French writer of distinction who has been to America since De Tocqueville; the French, in such matters, are not very enterprising. Also, he has the air of wondering what he is doing *dans cette galère*. He has come with his *beau-frère*, who is an engineer, and is looking after some mines, and he talks with scarcely any one else, as he speaks no English, and appears to take for granted that no one speaks French. Mamma would be delighted to assure him of the contrary; she has never conversed with an Academician. She always makes a little vague inclination, with a smile, when he passes her, and he answers with a most respectful bow; but it goes no farther, to mamma's disappointment. He is always with the *beau-frère*, a rather untidy, fat, bearded man,—decorated, too, always smoking and looking at the feet of the ladies, whom mamma (though she has very good feet) has not the courage to *aborder*. I believe M. Lejaune is going to write a book about America, and Mr. Leverett says it will be terrible. Mr. Leverett has made his acquaintance, and says M. Lejaune will put him into his book; he says the movement of the French intellect is superb. As a general thing, he doesn't care for Academicians, but he thinks M. Lejaune is an exception, he is so living, so personal. I asked Mr. Cockerel what he thought of M. Lejaune's plan of writing a book, and he answered that he didn't see what it mattered to him that a Frenchman the more should make a monkey of himself. I asked him why he hadn't written a book about Europe, and he said that, in the first place, Europe isn't worth writing about, and, in the second, if he said what he thought, people would think it was a joke. He said they are very superstitious about Europe over here; he wants people in America to behave as if Europe didn't exist. I told this to Mr. Leverett, and he answered that if Europe didn't exist America wouldn't, for Europe keeps us alive by buying our corn. He said, also, that the trouble with America in the future will be that she will produce things in such enormous quantities that there won't be enough people in the rest of the world to buy them, and that we shall be left with our productions—most of them very hideous—on our hands. I asked him if he thought corn a hideous production, and he replied that there is nothing more unbeautiful than too much food. I think that to feed the world too well, however, that will be, after all, a *beau rôle*. Of course I don't understand these things, and I don't believe Mr. Leverett does; but Mr. Cockerel seems to know what he is talking about, and he says that America is complete in herself. I don't know exactly what he means, but he speaks as if human affairs had somehow moved over to this side of the world. It may be a very good place for them, and Heaven knows I am extremely tired of Europe, which mamma has always insisted so on my appreciating; but I don't think I like the idea of our being so completely cut off. Mr. Cockerel says it is not we that are cut off, but Europe, and he seems to think that Europe has deserved it somehow. That may be; our life over there was sometimes extremely tiresome, though mamma says it is now that our real fatigues will begin. I like to abuse those dreadful old countries myself, but I am not sure that I am pleased when others do the same. We had some rather pretty moments there, after all; and at Piacenza we certainly lived on four francs a day. Mamma is already in a terrible state of mind about the expenses here; she is frightened by what people on the ship (the few that she has spoken to) have told her. There is one comfort, at any rate—we have spent so much money in coming here that we shall have none left to get away. I am scribbling along, as you see, to occupy me till we get news of the islands. Here comes Mr. Cockerel to bring it. Yes, they are in sight; he tells me that they are lovelier than ever, and that I must come right up right away. I suppose you will think that I am already beginning to use the language of the country. It is certain that at the end of a month I shall speak nothing else. I have picked up every dialect, wherever we have travelled; you have heard my Platt-Deutsch and my Neapolitan. But, *voyons un peu* the Bay! I have just called to Mr. Leverett to remind him of the islands. "The islands—the islands? Ah, my dear young lady, I have seen Capri, I have seen Ischia!" Well, so have I, but that doesn't prevent . . . (*A little later.*)—I have seen the islands; they are rather queer.

II.

MRS. CHURCH, IN NEW YORK, TO MADAME GALOPIN, AT GENEVA.

October 17, 1880.

If I felt far away from you in the middle of that deplorable Atlantic, *chère* Madame, how do I feel now, in the heart of this extraordinary city? We have arrived,—we have arrived, dear friend; but I don't know whether to tell you that I consider that an advantage. If we had been given our choice of coming safely to land or going down to the bottom of the sea, I should doubtless have chosen the former course; for I hold, with your noble husband, and in opposition to the general tendency of modern thought, that our lives are not our own to dispose of, but a sacred trust from a higher power, by whom we shall be held responsible. Nevertheless, if I had foreseen more vividly some of the impressions that awaited me here, I am not sure that, for my daughter at least, I should not have preferred on the spot to hand in our account. Should I not have been less (rather than more) guilty in presuming to dispose of *her* destiny, than of my own? There is a nice point for dear M. Galopin to settle—one of those points which I have heard him discuss in the pulpit with such elevation. We are safe, however, as I say; by which I mean that we are physically safe. We have taken up the thread of our familiar pension-life, but under strikingly different conditions. We have found a refuge in a boarding-house which has been highly recommended to me, and where the arrangements partake of that barbarous magnificence which in this country is the only alternative from primitive rudeness. The terms, per

week, are as magnificent as all the rest. The landlady wears
diamond ear-rings; and the drawing-rooms are decorated with
marble statues. I should indeed be sorry to let you know how
I have allowed myself to be *rançonnée*; and I should be still
more sorry that it should come to the ears of any of my good
friends in Geneva, who know me less well than you and might
judge me more harshly. There is no wine given for dinner,
and I have vainly requested the person who conducts the establishment to garnish her table more liberally. She says I may
have all the wine I want if I will order it at the merchant's,
and settle the matter with him. But I have never, as you know,
consented to regard our modest allowance of *eau rougie* as an
extra; indeed, I remember that it is largely to your excellent
advice that I have owed my habit of being firm on this point.
There are, however, greater difficulties than the question of
what we shall drink for dinner, *chère* Madame. Still, I have
never lost courage, and I shall not lose courage now. At the
worst, we can re-embark again, and seek repose and refreshment on the shores of your beautiful lake. (There is absolutely
no scenery here!) We shall not, perhaps, in that case have
achieved what we desired, but we shall at least have made an
honourable retreat. What we desire—I know it is just this that
puzzles you, dear friend; I don't think you ever really comprehended my motives in taking this formidable step, though
you were good enough, and your magnanimous husband was
good enough, to press my hand at parting in a way that
seemed to say that you would still be with me, even if I was
wrong. To be very brief, I wished to put an end to the rec-
lamations of my daughter. Many Americans had assured her
that she was wasting her youth in those historic lands which
it was her privilege to see so intimately, and this unfortunate
conviction had taken possession of her. "Let me at least see
for myself," she used to say; "if I should dislike it over there
as much as you promise me, so much the better for you. In
that case we will come back and make a new arrangement at
Stuttgart." The experiment is a terribly expensive one; but
you know that my devotion never has shrunk from an ordeal.
There is another point, moreover, which, from a mother to a
mother, it would be affectation not to touch upon. I remember the just satisfaction with which you announced to me the

betrothal of your charming Cécile. You know with what earnest care my Aurora has been educated,—how thoroughly she is acquainted with the principal results of modern research. We have always studied together; we have always enjoyed together. It will perhaps surprise you to hear that she makes these very advantages a reproach to me,—represents them as an injury to herself. "In this country," she says, "the gentlemen have not those accomplishments; they care nothing for the results of modern research; and it will not help a young person to be sought in marriage that she can give an account of the last German theory of Pessimism." That is possible; and I have never concealed from her that it was not for this country that I had educated her. If she marries in the United States it is, of course, my intention that my son-in-law shall accompany us to Europe. But, when she calls my attention more and more to these facts, I feel that we are moving in a different world. This is more and more the country of the many; the few find less and less place for them; and the individual—well, the individual has quite ceased to be recognised. He is recognised as a voter, but he is not recognised as a gentleman—still less as a lady. My daughter and I, of course, can only pretend to constitute a *few*! You know that I have never for a moment remitted my pretensions as an individual, though, among the agitations of pension-life, I have sometimes needed all my energy to uphold them. "Oh, yes, I may be poor," I have had occasion to say, "I may be unprotected, I may be reserved, I may occupy a small apartment in the *quatrième*, and be unable to scatter unscrupulous bribes among the domestics; but at least I am a *person*, with personal rights." In this country the people have rights, but the person has none. You would have perceived that if you had come with me to make arrangements at this establishment. The very fine lady who condescends to preside over it kept me waiting twenty minutes, and then came sailing in without a word of apology. I had sat very silent, with my eyes on the clock; Aurora amused herself with a false admiration of the room,— a wonderful drawing-room, with magenta curtains, frescoed walls, and photographs of the landlady's friends—as if one cared anything about her friends! When this exalted personage came in, she simply remarked that she had just been trying

on a dress—that it took so long to get a skirt to hang. "It
seems to take very long indeed!" I answered. "But I hope the
skirt is right at last. You might have sent for us to come up
and look at it!" She evidently didn't understand, and when I
asked her to show us her rooms, she handed us over to a
negro as *dégingandé* as herself. While we looked at them I
heard her sit down to the piano in the drawing-room; she
began to sing an air from a comic opera. I began to fear we
had gone quite astray; I didn't know in what house we could
be, and was only reassured by seeing a Bible in every room.
When we came down our musical hostess expressed no hope
that the rooms had pleased us, and seemed quite indifferent
to our taking them. She would not consent, moreover, to the
least diminution, and was inflexible, as I told you, on the subject of wine. When I pushed this point, she was so good as
to observe that she didn't keep a *cabaret*. One is not in the
least considered; there is no respect for one's privacy, for one's
preferences, for one's reserves. The familiarity is without limits, and I have already made a dozen acquaintances, of whom
I know, and wish to know, nothing. Aurora tells me that she
is the "belle of the boarding-house." It appears that this is a
great distinction. It brings me back to my poor child and her
prospects. She takes a very critical view of them herself: she
tells me that I have given her a false education, and that no
one will marry her to-day. No American will marry her, because she is too much of a foreigner, and no foreigner will
marry her because she is too much of an American. I remind
her that scarcely a day passes that a foreigner, usually of distinction, doesn't select an American bride, and she answers
me that in these cases the young lady is not married for her
fine eyes. Not always, I reply; and then she declares that she
would marry no foreigner who should not be one of the first
of the first. You will say, doubtless, that she should content
herself with advantages that have not been deemed insufficient
for Cécile; but I will not repeat to you the remark she made
when I once made use of this argument. You will doubtless
be surprised to hear that I have ceased to argue; but it is time
I should tell you that I have at last agreed to let her act for
herself. She is to live for three months *à l'Américaine*, and I

am to be a mere spectator. You will feel with me that this is a cruel position for a *cœur de mère*. I count the days till our three months are over, and I know that you will join with me in my prayers. Aurora walks the streets alone. She goes out in the tramway; a *voiture de place* costs five francs for the least little *course*. (I beseech you not to let it be known that I have sometimes had the weakness . . .) My daughter is sometimes accompanied by a gentleman—by a dozen gentlemen; she remains out for hours, and her conduct excites no surprise in this establishment. I know but too well the emotions it will excite in your quiet home. If you betray us, *chère* Madame, we are lost; and why, after all, should any one know of these things in Geneva? Aurora pretends that she has been able to persuade herself that she doesn't care who knows them; but there is a strange expression in her face, which proves that her conscience is not at rest. I watch her, I let her go, but I sit with my hands clasped. There is a peculiar custom in this country—I shouldn't know how to express it in Genevese—it is called "being attentive," and young girls are the object of the attention. It has not necessarily anything to do with projects of marriage—though it is the privilege only of the unmarried, and though, at the same time (fortunately, and this may surprise you) it has no relation to other projects. It is simply an invention by which young persons of the two sexes pass their time together. How shall I muster courage to tell you that Aurora is now engaged in this *délassement*, in company with several gentlemen? Though it has no relation to marriage, it happily does not exclude it, and marriages have been known to take place in consequence (or in spite) of it. It is true that even in this country a young lady may marry but one husband at a time, whereas she may receive at once the attentions of several gentlemen, who are equally entitled "admirers." My daughter, then, has admirers to an indefinite number. You will think I am joking, perhaps, when I tell you that I am unable to be exact—I who was formerly *l'exactitude même*. Two of these gentlemen are, to a certain extent, old friends, having been passengers on the steamer which carried us so far from you. One of them, still young, is typical of the American character, but a respectable person, and a lawyer in

considerable practice. Every one in this country follows a profession; but it must be admitted that the professions are more
highly remunerated than *chez vous*. Mr. Cockerel, even while
I write you, is in complete possession of my daughter. He
called for her an hour ago in a "boghey,"—a strange, unsafe,
rickety vehicle, mounted on enormous wheels, which holds
two persons very near together; and I watched her from the
window take her place at his side. Then he whirled her away,
behind two little horses with terribly thin legs; the whole equipage—and most of all her being in it—was in the most questionable taste. But she will return, and she will return very
much as she went. It is the same when she goes down to Mr.
Louis Leverett, who has no vehicle, and who merely comes
and sits with her in the front *salon*. He has lived a great deal
in Europe, and is very fond of the arts, and though I am not
sure I agree with him in his views of the relation of art to life
and life to art, and in his interpretation of some of the great
works that Aurora and I have studied together, he seems to
me a sufficiently serious and intelligent young man. I do not
regard him as intrinsically dangerous; but on the other hand,
he offers absolutely no guarantees. I have no means whatever
of ascertaining his pecuniary situation. There is a vagueness
on these points which is extremely embarrassing, and it never
occurs to young men to offer you a reference. In Geneva I
should not be at a loss; I should come to you, *chère* Madame,
with my little inquiry, and what you should not be able to tell
me would not be worth knowing. But no one in New York
can give me the smallest information about the *état de fortune*
of Mr. Louis Leverett. It is true that he is a native of Boston,
where most of his friends reside; I cannot, however, go to the
expense of a journey to Boston simply to learn, perhaps, that
Mr. Leverett (the young Louis) has an income of five thousand francs. As I say, however, he does not strike me as dangerous. When Aurora comes back to me, after having passed
an hour with the young Louis, she says that he has described
to her his emotions on visiting the home of Shelley, or discussed some of the differences between the Boston Temperament and that of the Italians of the Renaissance. You will not
enter into these *rapprochements*, and I can't blame you. But
you won't betray me, *chère* Madame?

III.

FROM MISS STURDY, AT NEWPORT, TO
MRS. DRAPER, IN FLORENCE.

September 30.

I promised to tell you how I like it, but the truth is, I have
gone to and fro so often that I have ceased to like and dislike.
Nothing strikes me as unexpected; I expect everything in its
order. Then, too, you know, I am not a critic; I have no talent
for keen analysis, as the magazines say; I don't go into the
reasons of things. It is true I have been for a longer time than
usual on the wrong side of the water, and I admit that I feel
a little out of training for American life. They are breaking me
in very fast, however. I don't mean that they bully me; I absolutely decline to be bullied. I say what I think, because I
believe that I have, on the whole, the advantage of knowing
what I think—when I think anything—which is half the battle.
Sometimes, indeed, I think nothing at all. They don't like that
over here; they like you to have impressions. That they like
these impressions to be favourable appears to me perfectly
natural; I don't make a crime to them of that; it seems to me,
on the contrary, a very amiable quality. When individuals have
it, we call them sympathetic; I don't see why we shouldn't
give nations the same benefit. But there are things I haven't
the least desire to have an opinion about. The privilege of
indifference is the dearest one we possess, and I hold that
intelligent people are known by the way they exercise it. Life
is full of rubbish, and we have at least our share of it over
here. When you wake up in the morning you find that during
the night a cartload has been deposited in your front garden.
I decline, however, to have any of it in my premises; there are
thousands of things I want to know nothing about. I have
outlived the necessity of being hypocritical; I have nothing to
gain and everything to lose. When one is fifty years old—
single, stout, and red in the face—one has outlived a good
many necessities. They tell me over here that my increase of
weight is extremely marked, and though they don't tell me
that I am coarse, I am sure they think me so. There is very
little coarseness here—not quite enough, I think—though

there is plenty of vulgarity, which is a very different thing. On the whole, the country is becoming much more agreeable. It isn't that the people are charming, for that they always were (the best of them, I mean, for it isn't true of the others), but that places and things as well have acquired the art of pleasing. The houses are extremely good, and they look so extraordinarily fresh and clean. European interiors, in comparison, seem musty and gritty. We have a great deal of taste; I shouldn't wonder if we should end by inventing something pretty; we only need a little time. Of course, as yet, it's all imitation, except, by the way, these piazzas. I am sitting on one now; I am writing to you with my portfolio on my knees. This broad light *loggia* surrounds the house with a movement as free as the expanded wings of a bird, and the wandering airs come up from the deep sea, which murmurs on the rocks at the end of the lawn. Newport is more charming even than you remember it; like everything else over here, it has improved. It is very exquisite to-day; it is, indeed, I think, in all the world, the only exquisite watering-place, for I detest the whole genus. The crowd has left it now, which makes it all the better, though plenty of talkers remain in these large, light, luxurious houses, which are planted with a kind of Dutch definiteness all over the green carpet of the cliff. This carpet is very neatly laid and wonderfully well swept, and the sea, just at hand, is capable of prodigies of blue. Here and there a pretty woman strolls over one of the lawns, which all touch each other, you know, without hedges or fences; the light looks intense as it plays upon her brilliant dress; her large parasol shines like a silver dome. The long lines of the far shores are soft and pure, though they are places that one hasn't the least desire to visit. Altogether the effect is very delicate, and anything that is delicate counts immensely over here; for delicacy, I think, is as rare as coarseness. I am talking to you of the sea, however, without having told you a word of my voyage. It was very comfortable and amusing; I should like to take another next month. You know I am almost offensively well at sea—that I breast the weather and brave the storm. We had no storm fortunately, and I had brought with me a supply of light literature; so I passed nine days on deck in my sea-chair, with my heels up, reading Tauchnitz novels.

There was a great lot of people, but no one in particular, save some fifty American girls. You know all about the American girl, however, having been one yourself. They are, on the whole, very nice, but fifty is too many; there are always too many. There was an inquiring Briton, a radical M.P., by name Mr. Antrobus, who entertained me as much as any one else. He is an excellent man; I even asked him to come down here and spend a couple of days. He looked rather frightened, till I told him he shouldn't be alone with me, that the house was my brother's, and that I gave the invitation in his name. He came a week ago; he goes everywhere; we have heard of him in a dozen places. The English are very simple, or at least they seem so over here. Their old measurements and comparisons desert them; they don't know whether it's all a joke, or whether it's too serious by half. We are quicker than they, though we talk so much more slowly. We think fast, and yet we talk as deliberately as if we were speaking a foreign language. They toss off their sentences with an air of easy familiarity with the tongue, and yet they misunderstand two-thirds of what people say to them. Perhaps, after all, it is only *our* thoughts they think slowly; they think their own often to a lively tune enough. Mr. Antrobus arrived here at eight o'clock in the morning; I don't know how he managed it; it appears to be his favourite hour; wherever we have heard of him he has come in with the dawn. In England he would arrive at 5.30 P.M. He asks innumerable questions, but they are easy to answer, for he has a sweet credulity. He made me rather ashamed; he is a better American than so many of us; he takes us more seriously than we take ourselves. He seems to think that an oligarchy of wealth is growing up here, and he advised me to be on my guard against it. I don't know exactly what I can do, but I promised him to look out. He is fearfully energetic; the energy of the people here is nothing to that of the inquiring Briton. If we should devote half the energy to building up our institutions that they devote to obtaining information about them, we should have a very satisfactory country. Mr. Antrobus seemed to think very well of us, which surprised me, on the whole, because, say what one will, it's not so agreeable as England. It's very horrid that this should be; and it's delightful, when one thinks of it, that some things

in England are, after all, so disagreeable. At the same time,
Mr. Antrobus appeared to be a good deal pre-occupied with
our dangers. I don't understand, quite, what they are; they
seem to me so few, on a Newport piazza, on this bright, still
day. But, after all, what one sees on a Newport piazza is not
America; it's the back of Europe! I don't mean to say that I
haven't noticed any dangers since my return; there are two or
three that seem to me very serious, but they are not those
that Mr. Antrobus means. One, for instance, is that we shall
cease to speak the English language, which I prefer so much
to any other. It's less and less spoken; American is crowding
it out. All the children speak American, and as a child's language it's dreadfully rough. It's exclusively in use in the
schools; all the magazines and newspapers are in American.
Of course, a people of fifty millions, who have invented a new
civilisation, have a right to a language of their own; that's
what they tell me, and I can't quarrel with it. But I wish they
had made it as pretty as the mother-tongue, from which, after
all, it is more or less derived. We ought to have invented
something as noble as our country. They tell me it's more
expressive, and yet some admirable things have been said in
the Queen's English. There can be no question of the Queen
over here, of course, and American no doubt is the music of
the future. Poor dear future, how "expressive" you'll be! For
women and children, as I say, it strikes one as very rough; and
moreover, they don't speak it well, their own though it be.
My little nephews, when I first came home, had not gone back
to school, and it distressed me to see that, though they are
charming children, they had the vocal inflections of little
news-boys. My niece is sixteen years old; she has the sweetest
nature possible; she is extremely well-bred, and is dressed to
perfection. She chatters from morning till night; but it isn't a
pleasant sound! These little persons are in the opposite case
from so many English girls, who know how to speak, but
don't know how to talk. My niece knows how to talk, but
doesn't know how to speak. *A propos* of the young people,
that is our other danger; the young people are eating us
up,—there is nothing in America but the young people. The
country is made for the rising generation; life is arranged for

them; they are the destruction of society. People talk of them, consider them, defer to them, bow down to them. They are always present, and whenever they are present there is an end to everything else. They are often very pretty; and physically, they are wonderfully looked after; they are scoured and brushed, they wear hygienic clothes, they go every week to the dentist's. But the little boys kick your shins, and the little girls offer to slap your face! There is an immense literature entirely addressed to them, in which the kicking of shins and the slapping of faces is much recommended. As a woman of fifty, I protest. I insist on being judged by my peers. It's too late, however, for several millions of little feet are actively engaged in stamping out conversation, and I don't see how they can long fail to keep it under. The future is theirs; maturity will evidently be at an increasing discount. Longfellow wrote a charming little poem called "The Children's Hour," but he ought to have called it "The Children's Century." And by children, of course, I don't mean simple infants; I mean everything of less than twenty. The social importance of the young American increases steadily up to that age, and then it suddenly stops. The young girls, of course, are more important than the lads; but the lads are very important too. I am struck with the way they are known and talked about; they are little celebrities; they have reputations and pretentions; they are taken very seriously. As for the young girls, as I said just now, there are too many. You will say, perhaps, that I am jealous of them, with my fifty years and my red face. I don't think so, because I don't suffer; my red face doesn't frighten people away, and I always find plenty of talkers. The young girls themselves, I believe, like me very much; and as for me, I delight in the young girls. They are often very pretty; not so pretty as people say in the magazines, but pretty enough. The magazines rather overdo that; they make a mistake. I have seen no great beauties, but the level of prettiness is high, and occasionally one sees a woman completely handsome. (As a general thing, a pretty person here means a person with a pretty face. The figure is rarely mentioned, though there are several good ones.) The level of prettiness is high, but the level of conversation is low; that's one of the signs of its being

a young ladies' country. There are a good many things young
ladies can't talk about; but think of all the things they can,
when they are as clever as most of these. Perhaps one ought
to content one's self with that measure, but it's difficult if one
has lived for a while by a larger one. This one is decidedly
narrow; I stretch it sometimes till it cracks. Then it is that
they call me coarse, which I undoubtedly am, thank Heaven!
People's talk is of course much more *châtiée* over here than
in Europe; I am struck with that wherever I go. There are
certain things that are never said at all, certain allusions that
are never made. There are no light stories, no *propos risqués*.
I don't know exactly what people talk about, for the supply
of scandal is small, and it's poor in quality. They don't seem,
however, to lack topics. The young girls are always there; they
keep the gates of conversation; very little passes that is not
innocent. I find we do very well without wickedness; and, for
myself, as I take my ease, I don't miss my liberties. You remember what I thought of the tone of your table in Florence,
and how surprised you were when I asked you why you allowed such things. You said they were like the courses of the
seasons; one couldn't prevent them; also that to change the
tone of your table you would have to change so many other
things. Of course, in your house one never saw a young girl;
I was the only spinster, and no one was afraid of me! Of
course, too, if talk is more innocent in this country, manners
are so, to begin with. The liberty of the young people is the
strongest proof of it. The young girls are let loose in the
world, and the world gets more good of it than *ces demoiselles*
get harm. In your world—excuse me, but you know what I
mean—this wouldn't do at all. Your world is a sad affair, and
the young ladies would encounter all sorts of horrors. Over
here, considering the way they knock about, they remain wonderfully simple, and the reason is that society protects them
instead of setting them traps. There is almost no gallantry, as
you understand it; the flirtations are child's play. People have
no time for making love; the men, in particular, are extremely
busy. I am told that sort of thing consumes hours; I have
never had any time for it myself. If the leisure class should
increase here considerably, there may possibly be a change;
but I doubt it, for the women seem to me in all essentials

exceedingly reserved. Great superficial frankness, but an extreme dread of complications. The men strike me as very good fellows. I think that at bottom they are better than the women, who are very subtle, but rather hard. They are not so nice to the men as the men are to them; I mean, of course, in proportion, you know. But women are not so nice as men, "anyhow," as they say here. The men, of course, are professional, commercial; there are very few gentlemen pure and simple. This personage needs to be very well done, however, to be of great utility; and I suppose you won't pretend that he is always well done in your countries. When he's not, the less of him the better. It's very much the same, however, with the system on which the young girls in this country are brought up. (You see, I have to come back to the young girls.) When it succeeds, they are the most charming possible; when it doesn't, the failure is disastrous. If a girl is a very nice girl, the American method brings her to great completeness— makes all her graces flower; but if she isn't nice, it makes her exceedingly disagreeable—elaborately and fatally perverts her. In a word, the American girl is rarely negative, and when she isn't a great success she is a great warning. In nineteen cases out of twenty, among the people who know how to live—I won't say what *their* proportion is—the results are highly satisfactory. The girls are not shy, but I don't know why they should be, for there is really nothing here to be afraid of. Manners are very gentle, very humane; the democratic system deprives people of weapons that every one doesn't equally possess. No one is formidable; no one is on stilts; no one has great pretensions or any recognised right to be arrogant. I think there is not much wickedness, and there is certainly less cruelty than with you. Every one can sit; no one is kept standing. One is much less liable to be snubbed, which you will say is a pity. I think it is to a certain extent; but, on the other hand, folly is less fatuous, in form, than in your countries; and as people generally have fewer revenges to take, there is less need of their being stamped on in advance. The general good nature, the social equality, deprive them of triumphs on the one hand, and of grievances on the other. There is extremely little impertinence; there is almost none. You will say I am describing a terrible society,—a society without great figures

or great social prizes. You have hit it, my dear; there are no
great figures. (The great prize, of course, in Europe, is the
opportunity to be a great figure.) You would miss these things
a good deal,—you who delight to contemplate greatness; and
my advice to you, of course, is never to come back. You would
miss the small people even more than the great; every one is
middle-sized, and you can never have that momentary sense
of tallness which is so agreeable in Europe. There are no brilliant types; the most important people seem to lack dignity.
They are very *bourgeois*; they make little jokes; on occasion
they make puns; they have no form; they are too good-
natured. The men have no style; the women, who are fidgety
and talk too much, have it only in their *coiffure*, where they
have it superabundantly. But I console myself with the greater
bonhomie. Have you ever arrived at an English country-house
in the dusk of a winter's day? Have you ever made a call in
London, when you knew nobody but the hostess? People here
are more expressive, more demonstrative; and it is a pleasure,
when one comes back (if one happens, like me, to be no one
in particular), to feel one's social value rise. They attend to
you more; they have you on their mind; they talk to you; they
listen to you. That is, the men do; the women listen very
little—not enough. They interrupt; they talk too much; one
feels their presence too much as a sound. I imagine it is partly
because their wits are quick, and they think of a good many
things to say; not that they always say such wonders. Perfect
repose, after all, is not *all* self-control; it is also partly stupidity.
American women, however, make too many vague exclama-
tions—say too many indefinite things. In short, they have a
great deal of nature. On the whole, I find very little affectation, though we shall probably have more as we improve. As
yet, people haven't the assurance that carries those things off;
they know too much about each other. The trouble is that
over here we have all been brought up together. You will think
this a picture of a dreadfully insipid society; but I hasten to
add that it's not all so tame as that. I have been speaking of
the people that one meets socially; and these are the smallest
part of American life. The others—those one meets on a basis
of mere convenience—are much more exciting; they keep

one's temper in healthy exercise. I mean the people in the shops, and on the railroads; the servants, the hackmen, the labourers, every one of whom you buy anything or have occasion to make an inquiry. With them you need all your best manners, for you must always have enough for two. If you think we are *too* democratic, taste a little of American life in these walks, and you will be reassured. This is the region of inequality, and you will find plenty of people to make your courtesy to. You see it from below—the weight of inequality is on your own back. You asked me to tell you about prices; they are simply dreadful.

IV.

FROM THE HONOURABLE EDWARD
ANTROBUS, M.P., IN BOSTON, TO THE
HONOURABLE MRS. ANTROBUS,

October 17.

MY DEAR SUSAN—I sent you a post-card on the 13th and a native newspaper yesterday; I really have had no time to write. I sent you the newspaper partly because it contained a report—extremely incorrect—of some remarks I made at the meeting of the Association of the Teachers of New England; partly because it is so curious that I thought it would interest you and the children. I cut out some portions which I didn't think it would be well for the children to see; the parts remaining contain the most striking features. Please point out to the children the peculiar orthography, which probably will be adopted in England by the time they are grown up; the amusing oddities of expression, etc. Some of them are intentional; you will have heard of the celebrated American humour, etc. (remind me, by the way, on my return to Thistleton, to give you a few examples of it); others are unconscious, and are perhaps on that account the more diverting. Point out to the children the difference (in so far as you are sure that you yourself perceive it). You must excuse me if these lines are not very legible; I am writing them by the light of a railway lamp, which rattles above my left ear; it being

only at odd moments that I can find time to look into everything that I wish to. You will say that this is a very odd moment, indeed, when I tell you that I am in bed in a
sleeping-car. I occupy the upper berth (I will explain to you
the arrangement when I return), while the lower forms the
couch—the jolts are fearful—of an unknown female. You will
be very anxious for my explanation; but I assure you that it
is the custom of the country. I myself am assured that a lady
may travel in this manner all over the Union (the Union of
States) without a loss of consideration. In case of her occupying the upper berth I presume it would be different; but I
must make inquiries on this point. Whether it be the fact that
a mysterious being of another sex has retired to rest behind
the same curtains, or whether it be the swing of the train,
which rushes through the air with very much the same movement as the tail of a kite, the situation is, at any rate, so anomalous that I am unable to sleep. A ventilator is open just over
my head, and a lively draught, mingled with a drizzle of cin-
ders, pours in through this ingenious orifice. (I will describe
to you its form on my return.) If I had occupied the lower
berth I should have had a whole window to myself, and by
drawing back the blind (a safe proceeding at the dead of
night), I should have been able, by the light of an extraordinary brilliant moon, to see a little better what I write. The
question occurs to me, however,—Would the lady below me
in that case have ascended to the upper berth? (You know my
old taste for contingent inquiries.) I incline to think (from
what I have seen) that she would simply have requested me
to evacuate my own couch. (The ladies in this country ask for
anything they want.) In this case, I suppose, I should have
had an extensive view of the country, which, from what I saw
of it before I turned in (while the lady beneath me was going
to bed), offered a rather ragged expanse, dotted with little
white wooden houses, which looked in the moonshine like
pasteboard boxes. I have been unable to ascertain as precisely
as I should wish by whom these modest residences are occupied; for they are too small to be the homes of country gentlemen, there is no peasantry here, and (in New England, for
all the corn comes from the far West) there are no yeomen
nor farmers. The information that one receives in this country

is apt to be rather conflicting, but I am determined to sift the mystery to the bottom. I have already noted down a multitude of facts bearing upon the points that interest me most—the operation of the school-boards, the co-education of the sexes, the elevation of the tone of the lower classes, the participation of the latter in political life. Political life, indeed, is almost wholly confined to the lower middle class, and the upper section of the lower class. In some of the large towns, indeed, the lowest order of all participates considerably—a very interesting phase, to which I shall give more attention. It is very gratifying to see the taste for public affairs pervading so many social strata; but the indifference of the gentry is a fact not to be lightly considered. It may be objected, indeed, that there are no gentry; and it is very true that I have not yet encountered a character of the type of Lord Bottomley,—a type which I am free to confess I should be sorry to see disappear from our English system, if system it may be called, where so much is the growth of blind and incoherent forces. It is nevertheless obvious that an idle and luxurious class exists in this country, and that it is less exempt than in our own from the reproach of preferring inglorious ease to the furtherance of liberal ideas. It is rapidly increasing, and I am not sure that the indefinite growth of the dilettante spirit, in connection with large and lavishly-expended wealth, is an unmixed good, even in a society in which freedom of development has obtained so many interesting triumphs. The fact that this body is not represented in the governing class, is perhaps as much the result of the jealousy with which it is viewed by the more earnest workers as of its own—I dare not, perhaps, apply a harsher term than—levity. Such, at least, is the impression I have gathered in the Middle States and in New England; in the South-west, the North-west, and the far West, it will doubtless be liable to correction. These divisions are probably new to you; but they are the general denomination of large and flourishing communities, with which I hope to make myself at least superficially acquainted. The fatigue of traversing, as I habitually do, three or four hundred miles at a bound, is, of course, considerable; but there is usually much to inquire into by the way. The conductors of the trains, with whom I freely converse, are often men of vigorous and original minds, and even of some social eminence. One of them, a few days ago, gave me a letter of introduction to his brother-in-law, who is president of a Western University. Don't have any fear, therefore, that I am not in the best society! The arrangements for travelling are, as a general thing, extremely ingenious, as you will probably have inferred from what I told you above; but it must at the same time be conceded that some of them are more ingenious than happy. Some of the facilities, with regard to luggage, the transmission of parcels, etc., are doubtless very useful when explained, but I have not yet succeeded in mastering the intricacies. There are, on the other hand, no cabs and no porters, and I have calculated that I have myself carried my *impedimenta*—which, you know, are somewhat numerous, and from which I cannot bear to be separated—some seventy or eighty miles. I have sometimes thought it was a great mistake not to bring Plummeridge; he would have been useful on such occasions. On the other hand, the startling question would have presented itself—Who would have carried Plummeridge's portmanteau? He would have been useful, indeed, for brushing and packing my clothes, and getting me my tub; I travel with a large tin one—there are none to be obtained at the inns—and the transport of this receptacle often presents the most insoluble difficulties. It is often, too, an object of considerable embarrassment in arriving at private houses, where the servants have less reserve of manner than in England; and to tell you the truth, I am by no means certain at the present moment that the tub has been placed in the train with me. "On board" the train is the consecrated phrase here; it is an allusion to the tossing and pitching of the concatenation of cars, so similar to that of a vessel in a storm. As I was about to inquire, however, Who would get Plummeridge *his* tub, and attend to his little comforts? We could not very well make our appearance, on coming to stay with people, with *two* of the utensils I have named; though, as regards a single one, I have had the courage, as I may say, of a life-long habit. It would hardly be expected that we should both use the same; though there have been occasions in my travels, as to which I see no way of blinking the fact, that Plummeridge would have had to sit down to dinner with me.

Such a contingency would completely have unnerved him; and, on the whole, it was doubtless the wiser part to leave him respectfully touching his hat on the tender in the Mersey. No one touches his hat over here, and though it is doubtless the sign of a more advanced social order, I confess that when I see poor Plummeridge again, this familiar little gesture—familiar, I mean, only in the sense of being often seen—will give me a measurable satisfaction. You will see from what I tell you that democracy is not a mere word in this country, and I could give you many more instances of its universal reign. This, however, is what we come here to look at, and, in so far as there seems to be proper occasion, to admire; though I am by no means sure that we can hope to establish within an appreciable time a corresponding change in the somewhat rigid fabric of English manners. I am not even prepared to affirm that such a change is desirable; you know this is one of the points on which I do not as yet see my way to going as far as Lord B——. I have always held that there is a certain social ideal of inequality as well as of equality, and if I have found the people of this country, as a general thing, quite equal to each other, I am not sure that I am prepared to go so far as to say that, as a whole, they are equal to—excuse that dreadful blot! The movement of the train and the precarious nature of the light—it is close to my nose, and most offensive—would, I flatter myself, long since have got the better of a less resolute diarist! What I was not prepared for was the very considerable body of aristocratic feeling that lurks beneath this republican simplicity. I have on several occasions been made the confidant of these romantic but delusive vagaries, of which the stronghold appears to be the Empire City, —a slang name for New York. I was assured in many quarters that that locality, at least, is ripe for a monarchy, and if one of the Queen's sons would come and talk it over, he would meet with the highest encouragement. This information was given me in strict confidence, with closed doors, as it were; it reminded me a good deal of the dreams of the old Jacobites, when they whispered their messages to the king across the water. I doubt, however, whether these less excusable visionaries will be able to secure the services of a Pretender, for

I fear that in such a case he would encounter a still more fatal Culloden. I have given a good deal of time, as I told you, to the educational system, and have visited no fewer than one hundred and forty-three schools and colleges. It is extraordinary, the number of persons who are being educated in this country; and yet, at the same time, the tone of the people is less scholarly than one might expect. A lady, a few days since, described to me her daughter as being always "on the go," which I take to be a jocular way of saying that the young lady was very fond of paying visits. Another person, the wife of a United States senator, informed me that if I should go to Washington in January, I should be quite "in the swim." I inquired the meaning of the phrase, but her explanation made it rather more than less ambiguous. To say that I am on the go describes very accurately my own situation. I went yesterday to the Pognanuc High School, to hear fifty-seven boys and girls recite in unison a most remarkable ode to the American flag, and shortly afterward attended a ladies' lunch, at which some eighty or ninety of the sex were present. There was only one individual in trousers—his trousers, by the way, though he brought a dozen pair, are getting rather seedy. The men in America do not partake of this meal, at which ladies assemble in large numbers to discuss religious, political, and social topics. These immense female symposia (at which every delicacy is provided) are one of the most striking features of American life, and would seem to prove that men are not so indispensable in the scheme of creation as they sometimes suppose. I have been admitted on the footing of an Englishman—"just to show you some of our bright women," the hostess yesterday remarked. ("Bright" here has the meaning of *intellectual.*) I perceived, indeed, a great many intellectual foreheads. These curious collations are organised according to age. I have also been present as an inquiring stranger at several "girls' lunches," from which married ladies are rigidly excluded, but where the fair revellers are equally numerous and equally bright. There is a good deal I should like to tell you about my study of the educational question, but my position is somewhat cramped, and I must dismiss it briefly. My leading impression is that the children in this country are better educated than the adults. The position of a child is, on the whole, one of great distinction. There is a popular ballad of which the refrain, if I am not mistaken, is "Make me a child again, just for to-night!" and which seems to express the sentiment of regret for lost privileges. At all events they are a powerful and independent class, and have organs, of immense circulation, in the press. They are often extremely "bright." I have talked with a great many teachers, most of them lady-teachers, as they are called in this country. The phrase does not mean teachers of ladies, as you might suppose, but applies to the sex of the instructress, who often has large classes of young men under her control. I was lately introduced to a young woman of twenty-three, who occupies the chair of Moral Philosophy and Belles-Lettres in a Western college, and who told me with the utmost frankness that she was adored by the undergraduates. This young woman was the daughter of a petty trader in one of the South-western States, and had studied at Amanda College, in Missourah, an institution at which young people of the two sexes pursue their education together. She was very pretty and modest, and expressed a great desire to see something of English country life, in consequence of which I made her promise to come down to Thistleton in the event of her crossing the Atlantic. She is not the least like Gwendolen or Charlotte, and I am not prepared to say how they would get on with her; the boys would probably do better. Still, I think her acquaintance would be of value to Miss Bumpus, and the two might pass their time very pleasantly in the school-room. I grant you freely that those I have seen here are much less comfortable than the school-room at Thistleton. Has Charlotte, by the way, designed any more texts for the walls? I have been extremely interested in my visit to Philadelphia, where I saw several thousand little red houses with white steps, occupied by intelligent artizans, and arranged (in streets) on the rectangular system. Improved cooking-stoves, rosewood pianos, gas, and hot water, æsthetic furniture, and complete sets of the British Essayists. A tramway through every street; every block of equal length; blocks and houses scientifically lettered and numbered. There is absolutely no loss of time, and no need of looking for anything, or, indeed, *at* anything. The mind always on one's object; it is very delightful.

V.

November.

The scales have turned, my sympathetic Harvard, and the beam that has lifted you up has dropped me again on this terribly hard spot. I am extremely sorry to have missed you in London, but I received your little note, and took due heed of your injunction to let you know how I got on. I don't get on at all, my dear Harvard—I am consumed with the love of the farther shore. I have been so long away that I have dropped out of my place in this little Boston world, and the shallow tides of New England life have closed over it. I am a stranger here, and I find it hard to believe that I ever was a native. It is very hard, very cold, very vacant. I think of your warm, rich Paris; I think of the Boulevard St. Michel on the mild spring evenings. I see the little corner by the window (of the Café de la Jeunesse)—where I used to sit; the doors are open, the soft deep breath of the great city comes in. It is brilliant, yet there is a kind of tone, of body, in the brightness; the mighty murmur of the ripest civilisation in the world comes in; the dear old *peuple de Paris*, the most interesting people in the world, pass by. I have a little book in my pocket; it is exquisitely printed, a modern Elzevir. It is a lyric cry from the heart of young France, and is full of the sentiment of form. There is no form here, dear Harvard; I had no idea how little form there was. I don't know what I shall do; I feel so un-draped, so uncurtained, so uncushioned; I feel as if I were sitting in the centre of a mighty "reflector." A terrible crude glare is over everything; the earth looks peeled and excoriated; the raw heavens seem to bleed with the quick hard light. I have not got back my rooms in West Cedar Street; they are occupied by a mesmeric healer. I am staying at an hotel, and it is very dreadful. Nothing for one's self; nothing for one's preferences and habits. No one to receive you when you arrive; you push in through a crowd, you edge up to a counter; you write your name in a horrible book, where every one may come and stare at it and finger it. A man behind the counter stares at you in silence; his stare seems to say to you, "What the devil do *you* want?" But after this stare he never looks at you again. He tosses down a key at you; he presses a bell; a savage Irishman arrives. "Take him away," he seems to say to the Irishman; but it is all done in silence; there is no answer to your own speech,—"What is to be done with me, please?" "Wait and you will see," the awful silence seems to say. There is a great crowd around you, but there is also a great stillness; every now and then you hear some one expectorate. There are a thousand people in this huge and hideous structure; they feed together in a big white-walled room. It is lighted by a thousand gas-jets, and heated by cast-iron screens, which vomit forth torrents of scorching air. The temperature is terrible; the atmosphere is more so; the furious light and heat seem to intensify the dreadful definiteness. When things are so ugly, they should not be so definite; and they are terribly ugly here. There is no mystery in the corners; there is no light and shade in the types. The people are haggard and joyless; they look as if they had no passions, no tastes, no senses. They sit feeding in silence, in the dry hard light; occasionally I hear the high firm note of a child. The servants are black and familiar; their faces shine as they shuffle about; there are blue tones in their dark masks. They have no manners; they address you, but they don't answer you; they plant themselves at your elbow (it rubs their clothes as you eat), and watch you as if your proceedings were strange. They deluge you with iced water; it's the only thing they will bring you; if you look round to summon them, they have gone for more. If you read the newspaper—which I don't, gracious Heaven! I can't— they hang over your shoulder and peruse it also. I always fold it up and present it to them; the newspapers here are indeed for an African taste. There are long corridors defended by gusts of hot air; down the middle swoops a pale little girl on parlour skates. "Get out of my way!" she shrieks as she passes; she has ribbons in her hair and frills on her dress; she makes the tour of the immense hotel. I think of Puck, who put a girdle round the earth in forty minutes, and wonder what he said as he flitted by. A black waiter marches past me, bearing a tray, which he thrusts into my spine as he goes. It is laden with large white jugs; they tinkle as he moves, and I recognise the unconsoling fluid. We are dying of iced water, of hot air, of gas. I sit in my room thinking of these things—this room of mine which is a chamber of pain. The walls are white and bare, they shine in the rays of a horrible chandelier of imitation bronze, which depends from the middle of the ceiling. It flings a patch of shadow on a small table covered with white marble, of which the genial surface supports at the present moment the sheet of paper on which I address you; and when I go to bed (I like to read in bed, Harvard) it becomes an object of mockery and torment. It dangles at inaccessible heights; it stares me in the face; it flings the light upon the covers of my book, but not upon the page—the little French Elzevir that I love so well. I rise and put out the gas, and then my room becomes even lighter than before. Then a crude illumination from the hall, from the neighbouring room, pours through the glass openings that surmount the two doors of my apartment. It covers my bed, where I toss and groan; it beats in through my closed lids; it is accompanied by the most vulgar, though the most human, sounds. I spring up to call for some help, some remedy; but there is no bell, and I feel desolate and weak. There is only a strange orifice in the wall, through which the traveller in distress may transmit his appeal. I fill it with incoherent sounds, and sounds more incoherent yet come back to me. I gather at last their meaning; they appear to constitute a somewhat stern inquiry. A hollow impersonal voice wishes to know what I want, and the very question paralyses me. I want everything—yet I want nothing—nothing this hard impersonality can give! I want my little corner of Paris; I want the rich, the deep, the dark Old World; I want to be out of this horrible place. Yet I can't confide all this to that mechanical tube; it would be of no use; a mocking laugh would come up from the office. Fancy appealing in these sacred, these intimate moments, to an "office"; fancy calling out into indifferent space for a candle, for a curtain! I pay incalculable sums in this dreadful house, and yet I haven't a servant to wait upon me. I fling myself back on my couch, and for a long time afterward the orifice in the wall emits strange murmurs and rumblings. It seems unsatisfied, indignant; it is evidently scolding me for my vagueness. My vagueness, indeed, dear Harvard! I loathe their horrible arrangements; isn't that definite enough? You asked me to tell you whom I see, and what I think of my friends. I haven't very many; I don't feel at all *en rapport*. The people are very good, very serious, very devoted to their work; but there is a terrible absence of variety of type. Every one is Mr. Jones, Mr. Brown; and every one looks like Mr. Jones and Mr. Brown. They are thin; they are diluted in the great tepid bath of Democracy! They lack completeness of identity; they are quite without modelling. No, they are not beautiful, my poor Harvard; it must be whispered that they are not beautiful. You may say that they are as beautiful as the French, as the Germans; but I can't agree with you there. The French, the Germans, have the greatest beauty of all—the beauty of their ugliness—the beauty of the strange, the grotesque. These people are not even ugly; they are only plain. Many of the girls are pretty; but to be only pretty is (to my sense) to be plain. Yet I have had some talk. I have seen a woman. She was on the steamer, and I afterward saw her in New York—a peculiar type, a real personality; a great deal of modelling, a great deal of colour, and yet a great deal of mystery. She was not, however, of this country; she was a compound of far-off things. But she was looking for something here—like me. We found each other, and for a moment that was enough. I have lost her now; I am sorry, because she liked to listen to me. She has passed away; I shall not see her again. She liked to listen to me; she almost understood!

VI.

FROM M. GUSTAVE LEJAUNE, OF THE
FRENCH ACADEMY, TO M. ADOLPHE
BOUCHE, IN PARIS.

Washington, October 5.

I give you my little notes; you must make allowances for haste, for bad inns, for the perpetual scramble, for ill-humour. Everywhere the same impression—the platitude of unbalanced democracy intensified by the platitude of the spirit of commerce. Everything on an immense scale—everything illustrated by millions of examples. My brother-in-law is always

busy; he has appointments, inspections, interviews, disputes.
The people, it appears, are incredibly sharp in conversation,
in argument; they wait for you in silence at the corner of the
road, and then they suddenly discharge their revolver. If you
fall, they empty your pockets; the only chance is to shoot them
first. With that, no amenities, no preliminaries, no manners,
no care for the appearance. I wander about while my brother
is occupied; I lounge along the streets; I stop at the corners;
I look into the shops; *je regarde passer les femmes*. It's an easy
country to see; one sees everything there is; the civilisation is
skin deep; you don't have to dig. This positive, practical,
pushing *bourgeoisie* is always about its business; it lives in the
street, in the hotel, in the train; one is always in a crowd—
there are seventy-five people in the tramway. They sit in your
lap; they stand on your toes; when they wish to pass they
simply push you. Everything in silence; they know that silence
is golden, and they have the worship of gold. When the conductor wishes your fare he gives you a poke, very serious,
without a word. As for the types—but there is only one—they
are all variations of the same—the *commis-voyageur* minus the
gaiety. The women are often pretty; you meet the young ones
in the streets, in the trains, in search of a husband. They look
at you frankly, coldly, judicially, to see if you will serve; but
they don't want what you might think (*du moins on me
l'assure*); they only want the husband. A Frenchman may mistake; he needs to be sure he is right, and I always make sure.
They begin at fifteen; the mother sends them out; it lasts all
day (with an interval for dinner at a pastry-cook's); sometimes
it goes on for ten years. If they haven't found the husband
then, they give it up; they make place for the *cadettes*, as the
number of women is enormous. No *salons*, no society, no conversation; people don't receive at home; the young girls have
to look for the husband where they can. It is no disgrace not
to find him—several have never done so. They continue to go
about unmarried—from the force of habit, from the love of
movement, without hopes, without regret—no imagination,
no sensibility, no desire for the convent. We have made several
journeys—few of less than three hundred miles. Enormous
trains, enormous *waggons*, with beds and lavatories, and negroes who brush you with a big broom, as if they were

grooming a horse. A bounding movement, a roaring noise, a crowd of people who look horribly tired, a boy who passes up and down throwing pamphlets and sweetmeats into your lap—that is an American journey. There are windows in the *waggons*—enormous, like everything else; but there is nothing to see. The country is a void—no features, no objects, no details, nothing to show you that you are in one place more than another. *Aussi*, you are not in one place, you are everywhere, anywhere; the train goes a hundred miles an hour. The cities are all the same; little houses ten feet high, or else big ones two hundred; tramways, telegraph-poles, enormous signs, holes in the pavement, oceans of mud, *commis-voyageurs*, young ladies looking for the husband. On the other hand, no beggars and no *cocottes*—none, at least, that you see. A colossal mediocrity, except (my brother-in-law tells me) in the machinery, which is magnificent. Naturally, no architecture (they make houses of wood and of iron), no art, no literature, no theatre. I have opened some of the books; *mais ils ne se laissent pas lire*. No form, no matter, no style, no general ideas! they seem to be written for children and young ladies. The most successful (those that they praise most) are the facetious; they sell in thousands of editions. I have looked into some of the most *vantés*; but you need to be forewarned, to know that they are amusing; *des plaisanteries de croque-mort*. They have a novelist with pretensions to literature, who writes about the chase for the husband and the adventures of the rich Americans in our corrupt old Europe, where their primæval candour puts the Europeans to shame. *C'est proprement écrit*; but it's terribly pale. What isn't pale is the newspapers—enormous, like everything else (fifty columns of advertisements), and full of the *commérages* of a continent. And such a tone, *grand Dieu!* The amenities, the personalities, the recriminations, are like so many *coups de revolver*. Headings six inches tall; correspondences from places one never heard of; telegrams from Europe about Sarah Bernhardt; little paragraphs about nothing at all; the *menu* of the neighbour's dinner; articles on the European situation *à pouffer de rire*; all the *tripotage* of local politics. The *reportage* is incredible; I am chased up and down by the interviewers. The matrimonial infelicities of M. and Madame X. (they give the name), *tout au long*, with every detail—not in six lines, discreetly veiled, with an art of insinuation, as with us; but with all the facts (or the fictions), the letters, the dates, the places, the hours. I open a paper at hazard, and I find *au beau milieu, à propos* of nothing, the announcement—"Miss Susan Green has the longest nose in Western New York." Miss Susan Green (*je me renseigne*) is a celebrated authoress; and the Americans have the reputation of spoiling their women. They spoil them *à coups de poing*. We have seen few interiors (no one speaks French); but if the newspapers give an idea of the domestic *mœurs*, the *mœurs* must be curious. The passport is abolished, but they have printed my *signalement* in these sheets,—perhaps for the young ladies who look for the husband. We went one night to the theatre; the piece was French (they are the only ones), but the acting was American—too American; we came out in the middle. The want of taste is incredible. An Englishman whom I met tells me that even the language corrupts itself from day to day; an Englishman ceases to understand. It encourages me to find that I am not the only one. There are things every day that one can't describe. Such is Washington, where we arrived this morning, coming from Philadelphia. My brother-in-law wishes to see the Bureau of Patents, and on our arrival he went to look at his machines, while I walked about the streets and visited the Capitol! The human machine is what interests me most. I don't even care for the political—for that's what they call their Government here—"the machine." It operates very roughly, and some day, evidently, it will explode. It is true that you would never suspect that they have a government; this is the principal seat, but, save for three or four big buildings, most of them *affreux*, it looks like a settlement of negroes. No movement, no officials, no authority, no embodiment of the state. Enormous streets, *comme toujours*, lined with little red houses where nothing ever passes but the tramway. The Capitol—a vast structure, false classic, white marble, iron and stucco, which has *assez grand air*—must be seen to be appreciated. The goddess of liberty on the top, dressed in a bear's skin; their liberty over here is the liberty of bears. You go into the Capitol as you would into a railway station; you walk about as you would in the Palais Royal. No functionaries, no door-keepers, no

officers, no uniforms, no badges, no restrictions, no authority—nothing but a crowd of shabby people circulating in a
labyrinth of spittoons. We are too much governed, perhaps,
in France; but at least we have a certain incarnation of the
national conscience, of the national dignity. The dignity is absent here, and I am told that the conscience is an abyss.
"L'état c'est moi" even—I like that better than the spittoons.
These implements are architectural, monumental; they are the
only monuments. *En somme*, the country is interesting, now
that we too have the Republic; it is the biggest illustration,
the biggest warning. It is the last word of democracy, and that
word is—flatness. It is very big, very rich, and perfectly ugly.
A Frenchman couldn't live here; for life with us, after all, at
the worst is a sort of appreciation. Here, there is nothing to
appreciate. As for the people, they are the English *minus* the
conventions. You can fancy what remains. The women, *pourtant*, are sometimes rather well turned. There was one at Philadelphia—I made her acquaintance by accident—whom it is
probable I shall see again. She is not looking for the husband;
she has already got one. It was at the hotel; I think the husband doesn't matter. A Frenchman, as I have said, may
mistake, and he needs to be sure he is right. *Aussi*, I always
make sure!

VII.

FROM MARCELLUS COCKEREL, IN
WASHINGTON, TO MRS. COOLER, NÉE
COCKEREL, AT OAKLAND, CALIFORNIA.

October 25.

I ought to have written to you long before this, for I have
had your last excellent letter for four months in my hands.
The first half of that time I was still in Europe; the last I have
spent on my native soil. I think, therefore, my silence is owing
to the fact that over there I was too miserable to write, and
that here I have been too happy. I got back the 1st of September—you will have seen it in the papers. Delightful country,
where one sees everything in the papers—the big, familiar,
vulgar, good-natured, delightful papers, none of which has

any reputation to keep up for anything but getting the news! I really think that has had as much to do as anything else with my satisfaction at getting home—the difference in what they call the "tone of the press." In Europe it's too dreary—the sapience, the solemnity, the false respectability, the verbosity, the long disquisitions on superannuated subjects. Here the newspapers are like the railroad trains, which carry everything that comes to the station, and have only the religion of punctuality. As a woman, however, you probably detest them; you think they are (the great word) vulgar. I admitted it just now, and I am very happy to have an early opportunity to announce to you that that idea has quite ceased to have any terrors for me. There are some conceptions to which the female mind can never rise. Vulgarity is a stupid, superficial, question-begging accusation, which has become to-day the easiest refuge of mediocrity. Better than anything else, it saves people the trouble of thinking, and anything which does that, succeeds. You must know that in these last three years in Europe I have become terribly vulgar myself; that's one service my travels have rendered me. By three years in Europe I mean three years in foreign parts altogether, for I spent several months of that time in Japan, India, and the rest of the East. Do you remember when you bade me good-bye in San Francisco, the night before I embarked for Yokohama? You foretold that I should take such a fancy to foreign life that America would never see me more, and that if *you* should wish to see me (an event you were good enough to regard as possible), you would have to make a rendezvous in Paris or in Rome. I think we made one (which you never kept), but I shall never make another for those cities. It was in Paris, however, that I got your letter; I remember the moment as well as if it were (to my honour) much more recent. You must know that, among many places I dislike, Paris carries the palm. I am bored to death there; it's the home of every humbug. The life is full of that false comfort which is worse than discomfort, and the small, fat, irritable people, give me the shivers. I had been making these reflections even more devoutly than usual one very tiresome evening toward the beginning of last summer, when, as I re-entered my hotel at ten o'clock, the little reptile of a portress handed me your gracious lines. I was in a villainous humour.

I had been having an over-dressed dinner in a stuffy restaurant, and had gone from there to a suffocating theatre, where, by way of amusement, I saw a play in which blood and lies were the least of the horrors. The theatres over there are insupportable; the atmosphere is pestilential. People sit with their elbows in your sides; they squeeze past you every half-hour. It was one of my bad moments; I have a great many in Europe. The conventional perfunctory play, all in falsetto, which I seemed to have seen a thousand times; the horrible faces of the people; the pushing, bullying *ouvreuse*, with her false politeness, and her real rapacity, drove me out of the place at the end of an hour; and, as it was too early to go home, I sat down before a *café* on the Boulevard, where they served me a glass of sour, watery beer. There on the Boulevard, in the summer night, life itself was even uglier than the play, and it wouldn't do for me to tell you what I saw. Besides, I was sick of the Boulevard, with its eternal grimace, and the deadly sameness of the *article de Paris*, which pretends to be so various—the shop-windows a wilderness of rubbish, and the passers-by a procession of manikins. Suddenly it came over me that I was supposed to be amusing myself—my face was a yard long—and that you probably at that moment were saying to your husband: "He stays away so long! What a good time he must be having!" The idea was the first thing that had made me smile for a month; I got up and walked home, reflecting, as I went, that I was "seeing Europe," and that, after all, one *must* see Europe. It was because I had been convinced of this that I came out, and it is because the operation has been brought to a close that I have been so happy for the last eight weeks. I was very conscientious about it, and, though your letter that night made me abominably homesick, I held out to the end, knowing it to be once for all. I sha'n't trouble Europe again; I shall see America for the rest of my days. My long delay has had the advantage that now, at least, I can give you my impressions—I don't mean of Europe; impressions of Europe are easy to get—but of this country, as it strikes the re-instated exile. Very likely you'll think them queer; but keep my letter, and twenty years hence they will be quite commonplace. They won't even be vulgar. It was very deliberate, my going round the world. I knew that one ought to see for one's

self, and that I should have eternity, so to speak, to rest. I
travelled energetically; I went everywhere and saw everything;
took as many letters as possible, and made as many acquaintances. In short, I held my nose to the grindstone. The upshot
of it all is that I have got rid of a superstition. We have so
many, that one the less—perhaps the biggest of all—makes a
real difference in one's comfort. The superstition in question—of course you have it—is that there is no salvation but
through Europe. Our salvation is here, if we have eyes to see
it, and the salvation of Europe into the bargain; that is, if
Europe is to be saved, which I rather doubt. Of course you'll
call me a bird of freedom, a braggart, a waver of the stars and
stripes; but I'm in the delightful position of not minding in
the least what any one calls me. I haven't a mission; I don't
want to preach; I have simply arrived at a state of mind; I have
got Europe off my back. You have no idea how it simplifies
things, and how jolly it makes me feel. Now I can live; now
I can talk. If we wretched Americans could only say once for
all, "Oh, Europe be hanged!" we should attend much better
to our proper business. We have simply to live our life, and
the rest will look after itself. You will probably inquire what
it is that I like better over here, and I will answer that it's
simply—life. Disagreeables for disagreeables, I prefer our own.
The way I have been bored and bullied in foreign parts, and
the way I have had to say I found it pleasant! For a good
while this appeared to be a sort of congenital obligation, but
one fine day it occurred to me that there was no obligation
at all, and that it would ease me immensely to admit to myself
that (for me, at least) all those things had no importance. I
mean the things they rub into you in Europe; the tiresome
international topics, the petty politics, the stupid social customs, the baby-house scenery. The vastness and freshness of
this American world, the great scale and great pace of our
development, the good sense and good nature of the people,
console me for there being no cathedrals and no Titians. I
hear nothing about Prince Bismarck and Gambetta, about the
Emperor William and the Czar of Russia, about Lord Bea-
consfield and the Prince of Wales. I used to get so tired of
their Mumbo-Jumbo of a Bismarck, of his secrets and surprises, his mysterious intentions and oracular words. They

revile us for our party politics; but what are all the European
jealousies and rivalries, their armaments and their wars, their
rapacities and their mutual lies, but the intensity of the spirit
of party? what question, what interest, what idea, what need
of mankind, is involved in any of these things? Their big, pompous armies, drawn up in great silly rows, their gold lace, their
salaams, their hierarchies, seem a pastime for children; there's
a sense of humour and of reality over here that laughs at all
that. Yes, we are nearer the reality—we are nearer what they
will all have to come to. The questions of the future are social
questions, which the Bismarcks and Beaconsfields are very
much afraid to see settled; and the sight of a row of supercil-
ious potentates holding their peoples like their personal property, and bristling all over, to make a mutual impression, with
feathers and sabres, strikes us as a mixture of the grotesque
and the abominable. What do we care for the mutual impressions of potentates who amuse themselves with sitting on
people? Those things are their own affair, and they ought to
be shut up in a dark room to have it out together. Once one
feels, over here, that the great questions of the future are social questions, that a mighty tide is sweeping the world to
democracy, and that this country is the biggest stage on which
the drama can be enacted, the fashionable European topics
seem petty and parochial. They talk about things that we have
settled ages ago, and the solemnity with which they propound
to you their little domestic embarrassments makes a heavy
draft on one's good nature. In England they were talking
about the Hares and Rabbits Bill, about the extension of the
County Franchise, about the Dissenters' Burials, about the
Deceased Wife's Sister, about the abolition of the House of
Lords, about heaven knows what ridiculous little measure for
the propping-up of their ridiculous little country. And they
call *us* provincial! It is hard to sit and look respectable while
people discuss the utility of the House of Lords, and the
beauty of a State Church, and it's only in a dowdy musty
civilisation that you'll find them doing such things. The lightness and clearness of the social air, that's the great relief in
these parts. The gentility of bishops, the propriety of parsons,
even the impressiveness of a restored cathedral, give less of a
charm to life than that. I used to be furious with the bishops

and parsons, with the humbuggery of the whole affair, which every one was conscious of, but which people agreed not to expose, because they would be compromised all round. The convenience of life over here, the quick and simple arrangements, the absence of the spirit of routine, are a blessed change from the stupid stiffness with which I struggled for two long years. There were people with swords and cockades, who used to order me about; for the simplest operation of life I had to kootoo to some bloated official. When it was a question of my doing a little differently from others, the bloated official gasped as if I had given him a blow on the stomach; he needed to take a week to think of it. On the other hand, it's impossible to take an American by surprise; he is ashamed to confess that he has not the wit to do a thing that another man has had the wit to think of. Besides being as good as his neighbour, he must therefore be as clever—which is an affliction only to people who are afraid he may be cleverer. If this general efficiency and spontaneity of the people—the union of the sense of freedom with the love of knowledge—isn't the very essence of a high civilisation, I don't know what a high civilisation is. I felt this greater ease on my first railroad journey—felt the blessing of sitting in a train where I could move about, where I could stretch my legs, and come and go, where I had a seat and a window to myself, where there were chairs, and tables, and food, and drink. The villainous little boxes on the European trains, in which you are stuck down in a corner, with doubled-up knees, opposite to a row of people—often most offensive types, who stare at you for ten hours on end—these were part of my two years' ordeal. The large free way of doing things here is everywhere a pleasure. In London, at my hotel, they used to come to me on Saturday to make me order my Sunday's dinner, and when I asked for a sheet of paper, they put it into the bill. The meagreness, the stinginess, the perpetual expectation of a sixpence, used to exasperate me. Of course, I saw a great many people who were pleasant; but as I am writing to you, and not to one of them, I may say that they were dreadfully apt to be dull. The imagination among the people I see here is more flexible; and then they have the advantage of a larger horizon. It's not bounded on the north by the British aristocracy, and on the south by the *scrutin de liste*. (I mix up the countries a little, but they are not worth the keeping apart.) The absence of little conventional measurements, of little cut-and-dried judgments, is an immense refreshment. We are more analytic, more discriminating, more familiar with realities. As for manners, there are bad manners everywhere, but an aristocracy is bad manners organised. (I don't mean that they may not be polite among themselves, but they are rude to every one else.) The sight of all these growing millions simply minding their business, is impressive to me,—more so than all the gilt buttons and padded chests of the Old World; and there is a certain powerful type of "practical" American (you'll find him chiefly in the West) who doesn't brag as I do (I'm not practical), but who quietly feels that he has the Future in his vitals—a type that strikes me more than any I met in your favourite countries. Of course you'll come back to the cathedrals and Titians, but there's a thought that helps one to do without them—the thought that though there's an immense deal of plainness, there's little misery, little squalor, little degradation. There is no regular wife-beating class, and there are none of the stultified peasants of whom it takes so many to make a European noble. The people here are more conscious of things; they invent, they act, they answer for themselves; they are not (I speak of social matters) tied up by authority and precedent. We shall have all the Titians by and by, and we shall move over a few cathedrals. You had better stay here if you want to have the best. Of course, I am a roaring Yankee; but you'll call me that if I say the least, so I may as well take my ease, and say the most. Washington's a most entertaining place; and here at least, at the seat of government, one isn't overgoverned. In fact, there's no government at all to speak of; it seems too good to be true. The first day I was here I went to the Capitol, and it took me ever so long to figure to myself that I had as good a right there as any one else—that the whole magnificent pile (it *is* magnificent, by the way) was in fact my own. In Europe one doesn't rise to such conceptions, and my spirit had been broken in Europe. The doors were gaping wide—I walked all about; there were no door-keepers, no officers, nor flunkeys—not even a policeman to be seen. It seemed strange not to see a uniform, if only as a patch of colour. But this isn't government by livery. The absence of these things is odd at first; you seem to miss something, to fancy the machine has stopped. It hasn't, though; it only works without fire and smoke. At the end of three days this simple negative impression—the fact is, that there are no soldiers nor spies, nothing but plain black coats—begins to affect the imagination, becomes vivid, majestic, symbolic. It ends by being more impressive than the biggest review I saw in Germany. Of course, I'm a roaring Yankee; but one has to take a big brush to copy a big model. The future is here, of course; but it isn't only that—the present is here as well. You will complain that I don't give you any personal news; but I am more modest for myself than for my country. I spent a month in New York, and while I was there I saw a good deal of a rather interesting girl who came over with me in the steamer, and whom for a day or two I thought I should like to marry. But I shouldn't. She has been spoiled by Europe!

VIII.

FROM MISS AURORA CHURCH, IN NEW YORK, TO MISS WHITESIDE, IN PARIS.

January 9.

I told you (after we landed) about my agreement with mamma—that I was to have my liberty for three months, and if at the end of this time I shouldn't have made a good use of it, I was to give it back to her. Well, the time is up to-day, and I am very much afraid I haven't made a good use of it. In fact, I haven't made any use of it at all—I haven't got married, for that is what mamma meant by our little bargain. She has been trying to marry me in Europe, for years, without a *dot*, and as she has never (to the best of my knowledge) even come near it, she thought at last that, if she were to leave it to me, I might do better. I couldn't certainly do worse. Well, my dear, I have done very badly—that is, I haven't done at all. I haven't even tried. I had an idea that this affair came of itself over here; but it hasn't come to me. I won't say I am disappointed, for I haven't, on the whole, seen any one I should like to marry. When you marry people over here, they expect you to love them, and I haven't seen any one I should like to love. I don't know what the reason is, but they are none of them what I have thought of. It may be that I have thought of the impossible; and yet I have seen people in Europe whom I should have liked to marry. It is true, they were almost always married to some one else. What I *am* disappointed in is simply having to give back my liberty. I don't wish particularly to be married; and I do wish to do as I like—as I have been doing for the last month. All the same, I am sorry for poor mamma, as nothing has happened that she wished to happen. To begin with, we are not appreciated, not even by the Rucks, who have disappeared, in the strange way in which people over here seem to vanish from the world. We have made no sensation; my new dresses count for nothing (they all have better ones); our philological and historical studies don't show. We have been told we might do better in Boston; but, on the other hand, mamma hears that in Boston the people only marry their cousins. Then mamma is out of sorts because the country is exceedingly dear and we have spent all our money. Moreover, I have neither eloped, nor been insulted, nor been talked about, nor—so far as I know—deteriorated in manners or character; so that mamma is wrong in all her previsions. I think she would have rather liked me to be insulted. But I have been insulted as little as I have been adored. They don't adore you over here; they only make you think they are going to. Do you remember the two gentlemen who were on the ship, and who, after we arrived here, came to see me *à tour de rôle*? At first I never dreamed they were making love to me, though mamma was sure it must be that; then, as it went on a good while, I thought perhaps it *was* that; and I ended by seeing that it wasn't anything! It was simply conversation; they are very fond of conversation over here. Mr. Leverett and Mr. Cockerel disappeared one fine day, without the smallest pretension to having broken my heart, I am sure, though it only depended on me to think they had! All the gentlemen are like that; you can't tell what they mean; everything is very confused; society appears to consist of a sort of innocent jilting. I think, on the whole, I *am* a little disappointed—I don't mean about one's not marrying; I mean about the life generally. It seems so

different at first, that you expect it will be very exciting; and
then you find that, after all, when you have walked out for a
week or two by yourself, and driven out with a gentleman in
a buggy, that's about all there is of it, as they say here. Mamma
is very angry at not finding more to dislike; she admitted yesterday that, once once has got a little settled, the country has
not even the merit of being hateful. This has evidently something to do with her suddenly proposing three days ago that
we should go to the West. Imagine my surprise at such an
idea coming from mamma! The people in the pension—who,
as usual, wish immensely to get rid of her—have talked to her
about the West, and she has taken it up with a kind of desperation. You see, we must do something; we can't simply
remain here. We are rapidly being ruined, and we are not—
so to speak—getting married. Perhaps it will be easier in the
West; at any rate, it will be cheaper, and the country will have
the advantage of being more hateful. It is a question between
that and returning to Europe, and for the moment mamma
is balancing. I say nothing: I am really indifferent; perhaps I
shall marry a pioneer. I am just thinking how I shall give back
my liberty. It really won't be possible; I haven't got it any
more; I have given it away to others. Mamma may recover it,
if she can, from *them*! She comes in at this moment to say
that we must push farther—she has decided for the West.
Wonderful mamma! It appears that my real chance is for a
pioneer—they have sometimes millions. But, fancy us in the
West!

The Siege of London

THAT SOLEMN PIECE of upholstery, the curtain of the Comédie Française, had fallen upon the first act of the piece, and our two Americans had taken advantage of the interval to pass out of the huge hot theatre, in company with the other occupants of the stalls. But they were among the first to return, and they beguiled the rest of the intermission with looking at the house, which had lately been cleansed of its historic cobwebs, and ornamented with frescoes illustrative of the classic drama. In the month of September the audience at the Théâtre Français is comparatively thin, and on this occasion the drama—*L'Aventurière* of Emile Augier—had no pretensions to novelty. Many of the boxes were empty, others were occupied by persons of provincial or nomadic appearance. The boxes are far from the stage, near which our spectators were placed; but even at a distance Rupert Waterville was able to appreciate certain details. He was fond of appreciating details, and when he went to the theatre he looked about him a good deal, making use of a dainty but remarkably powerful glass. He knew that such a course was wanting in true distinction, and that it was indelicate to level at a lady an instrument which was often only less injurious in effect than a double-barrelled pistol; but he was always very curious, and he was sure, in any case, that at that moment, at that antiquated play—so he was pleased to qualify the masterpiece of an Academician—he would not be observed by any one he knew. Standing up, therefore, with his back to the stage, he made the circuit of the boxes, while several other persons, near him, performed the same operation with even greater coolness.

"Not a single pretty woman," he remarked at last to his friend; an observation which Littlemore, sitting in his place and staring with a bored expression at the new-looking curtain, received in perfect silence. He rarely indulged in these optical excursions; he had been a great deal in Paris, and had ceased to care about it, or wonder about it, much; he fancied that the French capital could have no more surprises for him, though it had had a good many in former days. Waterville was

still in the stage of surprise; he suddenly expressed this emotion. "By Jove!" he exclaimed; "I beg your pardon—I beg
her pardon—there is, after all, a woman that may be called"
—he paused a little, inspecting her—"a kind of beauty!"

"What kind?" Littlemore asked, vaguely.

"An unusual kind—an indescribable kind." Littlemore was
not heeding his answer, but he presently heard himself
appealed to. "I say, I wish very much you would do me a
favour."

"I did you a favour in coming here," said Littlemore. "It's
insufferably hot, and the play is like a dinner that has been
dressed by the kitchen-maid. The actors are all *doublures.*"

"It's simply to answer me this: is *she* respectable, now?"
Waterville rejoined, inattentive to his friend's epigram.

Littlemore gave a groan, without turning his head. "You
are always wanting to know if they are respectable. What on
earth can it matter?"

"I have made such mistakes—I have lost all confidence,"
said poor Waterville, to whom European civilisation had not
ceased to be a novelty, and who during the last six months
had found himself confronted with problems long unsuspected. Whenever he encountered a very nice-looking woman,
he was sure to discover that she belonged to the class represented by the heroine of M. Augier's drama; and whenever
his attention rested upon a person of a florid style of attraction, there was the strongest probability that she would turn
out to be a countess. The countesses looked so superficial,
and the others looked so exclusive. Now Littlemore distinguished at a glance; he never made mistakes.

"Simply for looking at them, it doesn't matter, I suppose,"
said Waterville, ingenuously, answering his companion's rather
cynical inquiry.

"You stare at them all alike," Littlemore went on, still without moving; "except indeed when I tell you that they are not
respectable—then your attention acquires a fixedness!"

"If your judgment is against this lady, I promise never to
look at her again. I mean the one in the third box from the
passage, in white, with the red flowers," he added, as Littlemore slowly rose and stood beside him. "The young man is

leaning forward. It is the young man that makes me doubt of her. Will you have the glass?"

Littlemore looked about him without concentration. "No, I thank you, my eyes are good enough. The young man's a very good young man," he added in a moment.

"Very indeed; but he's several years younger than she. Wait till she turns her head."

She turned it very soon—she apparently had been speaking to the *ouvreuse*, at the door of the box—and presented her face to the public—a fair, well-drawn face, with smiling eyes, smiling lips, ornamented over the brow with delicate rings of black hair and, in each ear, with the sparkle of a diamond sufficiently large to be seen across the Théâtre Français. Littlemore looked at her; then, abruptly, he gave an exclamation. "Give me the glass!"

"Do you know her?" his companion asked, as he directed the little instrument.

Littlemore made no answer; he only looked in silence; then he handed back the glass. "No, she's not respectable," he said. And he dropped into his seat again. As Waterville remained standing, he added, "Please sit down; I think she saw me."

"Don't you want her to see you?" asked Waterville the interrogator, taking his seat.

Littlemore hesitated. "I don't want to spoil her game." By this time the *entr'acte* was at an end; the curtain rose again.

It had been Waterville's idea that they should go to the theatre. Littlemore, who was always for not doing a thing, had recommended that, the evening being lovely, they should simply sit and smoke at the door of the Grand Café, in a decent part of the Boulevard. Nevertheless, Rupert Waterville enjoyed the second act even less than he had done the first, which he thought heavy. He began to wonder whether his companion would wish to stay to the end; a useless line of speculation, for now that he had got to the theatre, Littlemore's objection to doing things would certainly keep him from going. Waterville also wondered what he knew about the lady in the box. Once or twice he glanced at his friend, and then he saw that Littlemore was not following the play.

He was thinking of something else; he was thinking of that woman. When the curtain fell again he sat in his place, making way for his neighbours, as usual, to edge past him, grinding his knees—his legs were long—with their own protuberances. When the two men were alone in the stalls, Littlemore said: "I think I should like to see her again, after all." He spoke as if Waterville might have known all about her. Waterville was conscious of not doing so, but as there was evidently a good deal to know, he felt that he should lose nothing by being a little discreet. So, for the moment, he asked no questions; he only said—

"Well, here's the glass."

Littlemore gave him a glance of good-natured compassion. "I don't mean that I want to stare at her with that beastly thing. I mean—to see her—as I used to see her."

"How did you use to see her?" asked Waterville, bidding farewell to discretion.

"On the back piazza, at San Diego." And as his interlocutor, in receipt of this information, only stared, he went on —"Come out where we can breathe, and I'll tell you more."

They made their way to the low and narrow door, more worthy of a rabbit-hutch than of a great theatre, by which you pass from the stalls of the Comédie to the lobby, and as Littlemore went first, his ingenuous friend behind him could see that he glanced up at the box in the occupants of which they were interested. The more interesting of these had her back to the house; she was apparently just leaving the box, after her companion; but as she had not put on her mantle it was evident that they were not quitting the theatre. Littlemore's pursuit of fresh air did not lead him into the street; he had passed his arm into Waterville's, and when they reached that fine frigid staircase which ascends to the Foyer, he began silently to mount it. Littlemore was averse to active pleasures, but his friend reflected that now at least he had launched himself—he was going to look for the lady whom, with a monosyllable, he appeared to have classified. The young man resigned himself for the moment to asking no questions, and the two strolled together into the shining saloon where Houdon's admirable statue of Voltaire, reflected in a dozen mirrors, is gaped at by visitors obviously less acute than the genius

expressed in those living features. Waterville knew that Voltaire was very witty; he had read *Candide*, and had already
had several opportunities of appreciating the statue. The Foyer
was not crowded; only a dozen groups were scattered over
the polished floor, several others having passed out to the balcony which overhangs the square of the Palais Royal. The
windows were open, the brilliant lights of Paris made the dull
summer evening look like an anniversary or a revolution; a
murmur of voices seemed to come up from the streets, and
even in the Foyer one heard the slow click of the horses, and
the rumble of the crookedly-driven fiacres on the hard smooth
asphalt. A lady and a gentleman, with their backs to our
friends, stood before the image of Voltaire; the lady was
dressed in white, including a white bonnet. Littlemore felt, as
so many persons feel in that spot, that the scene was conspic-
uously Parisian, and he gave a mysterious laugh.

"It seems comical to see her here! The last time was in New
Mexico."

"In New Mexico?"

"At San Diego."

"Oh, on the back piazza," said Waterville, putting things
together. He had not been aware of the position of San Diego,
for if, on the occasion of his lately being appointed to a subordinate diplomatic post in London, he had been paying a
good deal of attention to European geography, he had rather
neglected that of his own country.

They had not spoken loud, and they were not standing near
her; but suddenly, as if she had heard them, the lady in white
turned round. Her eye caught Waterville's first, and in that
glance he saw that if she had heard them it was not because
they were audible but because she had extraordinary quickness
of ear. There was no recognition in it—there was none, at
first, even when it rested lightly upon George Littlemore. But
recognition flashed out a moment later, accompanied with a
delicate increase of colour and a quick extension of her apparently constant smile. She had turned completely round; she
stood there in sudden friendliness, with parted lips, with a
hand, gloved to the elbow, almost imperiously offered. She
was even prettier than at a distance. "Well, I declare!" she
exclaimed; so loud that every one in the room appeared to

feel personally addressed. Waterville was surprised; he had not been prepared, even after the mention of the back piazza, to find her an American. Her companion turned round as she spoke; he was a fresh, lean young man, in evening dress; he kept his hands in his pockets; Waterville imagined that he, at any rate, was not an American. He looked very grave—for such a fair festive young man—and gave Waterville and Littlemore, though his height was not superior to theirs, a narrow, vertical glance. Then he turned back to the statue of Voltaire, as if it had been, after all, among his premonitions that the lady he was attending would recognise people he didn't know, and didn't even, perhaps, care to know. This possibly confirmed slightly Littlemore's assertion that she was not respectable. The young man was, at least; consummately so. "Where in the world did you drop from?" the lady inquired.

"I have been here some time," Littlemore said, going forward, rather deliberately, to shake hands with her. He smiled a little, but he was more serious than she; he kept his eye on her own as if she had been just a trifle dangerous; it was the manner in which a duly discreet person would have approached some glossy, graceful animal which had an occasional trick of biting.

"Here in Paris, do you mean?"

"No; here and there—in Europe generally."

"Well, it's queer I haven't met you."

"Better late than never!" said Littlemore. His smile was a little fixed.

"Well, you look very natural," the lady went on.

"So do you—or very charming—it's the same thing," Littlemore answered, laughing, and evidently wishing to be easy. It was as if, face to face, and after a considerable lapse of time, he had found her more imposing than he expected when, in the stalls below, he determined to come and meet her. As he spoke, the young man who was with her gave up his inspection of Voltaire and faced about, listlessly, without looking either at Littlemore or at Waterville.

"I want to introduce you to my friend," she went on. "Sir Arthur Demesne—Mr. Littlemore. Mr. Littlemore—Sir Arthur

Demesne. Sir Arthur Demesne is an Englishman—Mr. Little-more is a countryman of mine, an old friend. I haven't seen him for years. For how long? Don't let's count!—I wonder you knew me," she continued, addressing Littlemore. "I'm fearfully changed." All this was said in a clear, gay tone, which was the more audible as she spoke with a kind of caressing slowness. The two men, to do honour to her introduction, silently exchanged a glance; the Englishman perhaps coloured a little. He was very conscious of his companion. "I haven't introduced you to many people yet," she remarked.

"Oh, I don't mind," said Sir Arthur Demesne.

"Well, it's queer to see you!" she exclaimed, looking still at Littlemore. "You have changed, too—I can see that."

"Not where you are concerned."

"That's what I want to find out. Why don't you introduce your friend? I see he's dying to know me!"

Littlemore proceeded to this ceremony; but he reduced it to its simplest elements, merely glancing at Rupert Waterville, and murmuring his name.

"You don't tell him *my* name," the lady cried, while Waterville made her a formal salutation. "I hope you haven't forgotten it!"

Littlemore gave her a glance which was intended to be more penetrating than what he had hitherto permitted himself; if it had been put into words it would have said, "Ah, but *which* name?"

She answered the unspoken question, putting out her hand, as she had done to Littlemore, "Happy to make your acquaintance, Mr. Waterville. I'm Mrs. Headway—perhaps you've heard of me. If you've ever been in America you must have heard of me. Not so much in New York, but in the Western cities. You *are* an American? Well, then, we are all compatriots—except Sir Arthur Demesne. Let me introduce you to Sir Arthur. Sir Arthur Demesne, Mr. Waterville—Mr. Waterville, Sir Arthur Demesne. Sir Arthur Demesne is a member of Parliament; don't he look young?" She waited for no answer to this question, but suddenly asked another, as she moved her bracelets back over her long, loose gloves. "Well, Mr. Littlemore, what are you thinking of?"

He was thinking that he must indeed have forgotten her name, for the one that she had pronounced awakened no association. But he could hardly tell her that.

"I'm thinking of San Diego."

"The back piazza, at my sister's? Oh, don't; it was too horrid. She has left now. I believe every one has left."

Sir Arthur Demesne drew out his watch with the air of a man who could take no part in these domestic reminiscences; he appeared to combine a generic self-possession with a degree of individual shyness. He said something about its being time they should go back to their seats, but Mrs. Headway paid no attention to the remark. Waterville wished her to linger; he felt in looking at her as if he had been looking at a charming picture. Her low-growing hair, with its fine dense undulations, was of a shade of blackness that has now become rare; her complexion had the bloom of a white flower; her profile, when she turned her head, was as pure and fine as the outline of a cameo.

"You know this is the first theatre," she said to Waterville, as if she wished to be sociable. "And this is Voltaire, the celebrated writer."

"I'm devoted to the Comédie Française," Waterville answered, smiling.

"Dreadfully bad house; we didn't hear a word," said Sir Arthur.

"Ah, yes, the boxes!" murmured Waterville.

"I'm rather disappointed," Mrs. Headway went on. "But I want to see what becomes of that woman."

"Doña Clorinde? Oh, I suppose they'll shoot her; they generally shoot the women, in French plays," Littlemore said.

"It will remind me of San Diego!" cried Mrs. Headway.

"Ah, at San Diego the women did the shooting."

"They don't seem to have killed you!" Mrs. Headway rejoined, archly.

"No, but I am riddled with wounds."

"Well, this is very remarkable," the lady went on, turning to Houdon's statue. "It's beautifully modelled."

"You are perhaps reading M. de Voltaire," Littlemore suggested.

"No; but I've purchased his works."

"They are not proper reading for ladies," said the young Englishman, severely, offering his arm to Mrs. Headway.

"Ah, you might have told me before I had bought them!" she exclaimed, in exaggerated dismay.

"I couldn't imagine you would buy a hundred and fifty volumes."

"A hundred and fifty? I have only bought two."

"Perhaps two won't hurt you!" said Littlemore with a smile.

She darted him a reproachful ray. "I know what you mean,—that I'm too bad already! Well, bad as I am, you must come and see me." And she threw him the name of her hotel, as she walked away with her Englishman. Waterville looked after the latter with a certain interest; he had heard of him in London, and had seen his portrait in *Vanity Fair*.

It was not yet time to go down, in spite of this gentleman's saying so, and Littlemore and his friend passed out on the balcony of the Foyer. "Headway—Headway? Where the deuce did she get that name?" Littlemore asked, as they looked down into the animated dusk.

"From her husband, I suppose," Waterville suggested.

"From her husband? From which? The last was named Beck."

"How many has she had?" Waterville inquired, anxious to hear how it was that Mrs. Headway was not respectable.

"I haven't the least idea. But it wouldn't be difficult to find out, as I believe they are all living. She was Mrs. Beck—Nancy Beck—when I knew her."

"Nancy Beck!" cried Waterville, aghast. He was thinking of her delicate profile, like that of a pretty Roman empress. There was a great deal to be explained.

Littlemore explained it in a few words before they returned to their places, admitting indeed that he was not yet able to elucidate her present situation. She was a memory of his Western days; he had seen her last some six years before. He had known her very well, and in several places; the circle of her activity was chiefly the South-West. This activity was of a vague character, except in the sense that it was exclusively social. She was supposed to have a husband, one Philadelphus Beck, the editor of a Democratic newspaper, the *Dakotah*

Sentinel; but Littlemore had never seen him—the pair were living apart—and it was the impression at San Diego that matrimony, for Mr. and Mrs. Beck, was about played out. He remembered now to have heard afterwards that she was getting a divorce. She got divorces very easily, she was so taking in court. She had got one or two before from a man whose name he had forgotten, and there was a legend that even these were not the first. She had been exceedingly divorced! When he first met her in California she called herself Mrs. Grenville, which he had been given to understand was not an appellation acquired in matrimony, but her parental name, resumed after the dissolution of an unfortunate union. She had had these episodes—her unions were all unfortunate—and had borne half a dozen names. She was a charming woman, especially for New Mexico; but she had been divorced too often—it was a tax on one's credulity; she must have repudiated more husbands than she had married.

At San Diego she was staying with her sister, whose actual spouse (she, too, had been divorced), the principal man of the place, kept a bank (with the aid of a six-shooter), and who had never suffered Nancy to want for a home during her unattached periods. Nancy had begun very young; she must be about thirty-seven to-day. That was all he meant by her not being respectable. The chronology was rather mixed; her sister at least had once told him that there was one winter when she didn't know herself *who* was Nancy's husband. She had gone in mainly for editors—she esteemed the journalistic profession. They must all have been dreadful ruffians, for her own amiability was manifest. It was well known that whatever she had done she had done in self-defence. In fine, she had done things; that was the main point now! She was very pretty, good-natured, and clever, and quite the best company in those parts. She was a genuine product of the far West—a flower of the Pacific slope; ignorant, audacious, crude, but full of pluck and spirit, of natural intelligence, and of a certain intermittent, haphazard good taste. She used to say that she only wanted a chance—apparently she had found it now. At one time, without her, he didn't see how he could have put up with the life. He had started a cattle-ranch, to which San Diego was the nearest town, and he used to ride over to see her. Sometimes he stayed there for a week; then he went to see her every evening. It was horribly hot; they used to sit on the back piazza. She was always as attractive, and very nearly as well-dressed, as they had just beheld her. As far as appearance went, she might have been transplanted at an hour's notice from that dusty old settlement to the city by the Seine.

"Some of those Western women are wonderful," Littlemore said. "Like her, they only want a chance."

He had not been in love with her—there never was anything of that sort between them. There might have been, of course; but as it happened, there was not. Headway apparently was the successor of Beck; perhaps there had been others between. She was in no sort of "society;" she only had a local reputation ("the elegant and accomplished Mrs. Beck," the newspapers called her—the other editors, to whom she wasn't married), though, indeed, in that spacious civilisation the locality was large. She knew nothing of the East, and to the best of his belief at that period had never seen New York. Various things might have happened in those six years, however; no doubt she had "come up." The West was sending us everything (Littlemore spoke as a New Yorker); no doubt it would send us at last our brilliant women. This little woman used to look quite over the head of New York; even in those days she thought and talked of Paris, which there was no prospect of her knowing; that was the way she had got on in New Mexico. She had had her ambition, her presentiments; she had known she was meant for better things. Even at San Diego she had prefigured her little Sir Arthur; every now and then a wandering Englishman came within her range. They were not all baronets and M.P.'s, but they were usually a change from the editors. What she was doing with her present acquisition he was curious to see. She was certainly—if he had any capacity for that state of mind, which was not too apparent—making him happy. She looked very splendid; Headway had probably made a "pile," an achievement not to be imputed to any of the others. She didn't accept money—he was sure she didn't accept money.

On their way back to their seats Littlemore, whose tone had been humorous, but with that strain of the pensive which is inseparable from retrospect, suddenly broke into audible laughter.

"The modelling of a statue and the works of Voltaire!" he exclaimed, recurring to two or three things she had said. "It's comical to hear her attempt those flights, for in New Mexico she knew nothing about modelling."

"She didn't strike me as affected," Waterville rejoined, feeling a vague impulse to take a considerate view of her.

"Oh, no; she's only—as she says—fearfully changed."

They were in their places before the play went on again, and they both gave another glance at Mrs. Headway's box. She leaned back, slowly fanning herself, and evidently watching Littlemore, as if she had been waiting to see him come in. Sir Arthur Demesne sat beside her, rather gloomily, resting a round, pink chin upon a high stiff collar; neither of them seemed to speak.

"Are you sure she makes him happy?" Waterville asked.

"Yes—that's the way those people show it."

"But does she go about alone with him that way? Where's her husband?"

"I suppose she has divorced him."

"And does she want to marry the baronet?" Waterville asked, as if his companion were omniscient.

It amused Littlemore for the moment to appear so. "He wants to marry her, I guess."

"And be divorced, like the others?"

"Oh no; this time she has got what she wants," said Littlemore, as the curtain rose.

He suffered three days to elapse before he called at the Hôtel Meurice, which she had designated, and we may occupy this interval in adding a few words to the story we have taken from his lips. George Littlemore's residence in the far West had been of the usual tentative sort—he had gone there to replenish a pocket depleted by youthful extravagance. His first attempts had failed; the days were passing away when a fortune was to be picked up even by a young man who might be supposed to have inherited from an honourable father, lately removed, some of those fine abilities, mainly dedicated to the importation of tea, to which the elder Mr. Littlemore was indebted for the power of leaving his son well off. Littlemore had dissipated his patrimony, and he was not quick to discover his talents, which, consisting chiefly of an unlimited faculty for smoking and horse-breaking, appeared to lie in the direction of none of the professions called liberal. He had been sent to Harvard to have his aptitudes cultivated, but here they took such a form that repression had been found more necessary than stimulus—repression embodied in an occasional sojourn in one of the lovely villages of the Connecticut valley. Rustication saved him, perhaps, in the sense that it detached him; it destroyed his ambitions, which had been foolish. At the age of thirty Littlemore had mastered none of the useful arts, unless we include in the number the great art of indifference. He was roused from his indifference by a stroke of good luck. To oblige a friend who was even in more pressing need of cash than himself, he had purchased for a moderate sum (the proceeds of a successful game of poker) a share in a silver mine, which the disposer, with unusual candour, admitted to be destitute of metal. Littlemore looked into his mine and recognised the truth of the contention, which, however, was demolished some two years later by a sudden revival of curiosity on the part of one of the other shareholders. This gentleman, convinced that a silver mine without silver is as rare as an effect without a cause, discovered the sparkle of the precious element deep down in the reason of things. The discovery was agreeable to Littlemore, and was the beginning of a fortune which, through several dull years and in many rough places, he had repeatedly despaired of, and which a man whose purpose was never very keen did not perhaps altogether deserve. It was before he saw himself successful that he had made the acquaintance of the lady now established at the Hôtel Meurice. To-day he owned the largest share in his mine, which remained perversely productive, and which enabled him to buy, among other things, in Montana, a cattle-ranch of much finer proportions than the dry acres near San Diego. Ranches and mines encourage security, and the consciousness of not having to watch the sources of his income too anxiously (an obligation which for a man of his disposition spoils everything) now added itself to his usual coolness. It was not that this same coolness had not been considerably tried. To take only one—the principal—instance: he had lost his wife after only a twelvemonth of marriage, some three years before the date at which we meet him. He was more than forty when he encountered and wooed a young girl of twenty-three, who, like himself, had consulted all the probabilities in expecting a succession of happy years. She left him a small daughter, now entrusted to the care of his only sister, the wife of an English squire and mistress of a dull park in Hampshire. This lady, Mrs. Dolphin by name, had captivated her landowner during a journey in which Mr. Dolphin had promised himself to examine the institutions of the United States. The institution on which he reported most favourably was the pretty girls of the larger towns, and he returned to New York a year or two later to marry Miss Littlemore, who, unlike her brother, had not wasted her patrimony. Her sister-in-law, married many years later, and coming to Europe on this occasion, had died in London—where she flattered herself the doctors were infallible—a week after the birth of her little girl; and poor Littlemore, though relinquishing his child for the moment, remained in these disappointing countries to be within call of the Hampshire nursery. He was rather a noticeable man, especially since his hair and moustache had turned white. Tall and strong, with a good figure and a bad carriage, he looked capable but indolent, and was usually supposed to have an importance of which he was far from being conscious. His eye was at once keen and quiet, his smile dim and dilatory, but exceedingly genuine. His principal occupation to-day was doing nothing, and he did it with a sort of artistic perfection. This faculty excited real envy on the part of Rupert Waterville, who was ten years younger than he, and who had too many ambitions and anxieties—none of them very important, but making collectively a considerable incubus—to be able to wait for inspiration. He thought it a great accomplishment, he hoped some day to arrive at it; it made a man so independent; he had his resources within his own breast. Littlemore could sit for a whole evening, without utterance or movement, smoking cigars and looking absently at his finger-nails. As every one knew that he was a good fellow and had made his fortune, this dull behaviour could not well be attributed to stupidity or to moroseness. It seemed to imply a fund of reminiscence, an experience of life which had left him hundreds of things to think about. Waterville felt that if he could make a good use of these present years, and keep a sharp look-out for experience, he too, at forty-five, might have time to look at his finger-nails. He had an idea that such contemplations—not of course in their literal, but in their symbolic intensity—were a sign of a man of the world. Waterville, reckoning possibly without an ungrateful Department of State, had also an idea that he had embraced the diplomatic career. He was the junior of the two Secretaries who render the *personnel* of the United States Legation in London exceptionally numerous, and was at present enjoying his annual leave of absence. It became a diplomatist to be inscrutable, and though he had by no means, as a whole, taken Littlemore as his model—there were much better ones in the diplomatic body in London—he thought he looked inscrutable when of an evening, in Paris, after he had been asked what he would like to do, he replied that he should like to do nothing, and simply sat for an interminable time in front of the Grand Café, on the Boulevard de la Madeleine (he was very fond of cafés), ordering a succession of *demitasses*. It was very rarely that Littlemore cared even to go to the theatre, and the visit to the Comédie Française, which we have described, had been undertaken at Waterville's instance. He had seen *Le Demi-Monde* a few nights before, and had been told that *L'Aventurière* would show him a particular treatment of the same subject—the justice to be meted out to unscrupulous women who attempt to thrust themselves into honourable families. It seemed to him that in both of these cases the ladies had deserved their fate, but he wished it might have been brought about by a little less lying on the part of the representatives of honour. Littlemore and he, without being intimate, were very good friends, and spent much of their time together. As it turned out, Littlemore was very glad he had gone to the theatre, for he found himself much interested in this new incarnation of Nancy Beck.

II.

His delay in going to see her was nevertheless calculated; there were more reasons for it than it is necessary to mention. But when he went, Mrs. Headway was at home, and Littlemore was not surprised to see Sir Arthur Demesne in her sitting-room. There was something in the air which seemed to indicate that this gentleman's visit had already lasted a certain time. Littlemore thought it probable that, given the circumstances, he would now bring it to a close; he must have learned from their hostess that Littlemore was an old and familiar friend. He might of course have definite rights—he had every appearance of it; but the more definite they were the more gracefully he could afford to waive them. Littlemore made these reflections while Sir Arthur Demesne sat there looking at him without giving any sign of departure. Mrs. Headway was very gracious—she had the manner of having known you a hundred years; she scolded Littlemore extravagantly for not having been to see her sooner, but this was only a form of the gracious. By daylight she looked a little faded; but she had an expression which could never fade. She had the best rooms in the hotel, and an air of extreme opulence and prosperity; her courier sat outside, in the ante-chamber, and she evidently knew how to live. She attempted to include Sir Arthur in the conversation, but though the young man remained in his place, he declined to be included. He smiled, in silence; but he was evidently uncomfortable. The conversation, therefore, remained superficial—a quality that, of old, had by no means belonged to Mrs. Headway's interviews with her friends. The Englishman looked at Littlemore with a strange, perverse expression, which Littlemore, at first, with a good deal of private amusement, simply attributed to jealousy.

"My dear Sir Arthur, I wish very much you would go," Mrs. Headway remarked, at the end of a quarter of an hour.

Sir Arthur got up and took his hat. "I thought I should oblige you by staying."

"To defend me against Mr. Littlemore? I've known him since I was a baby—I know the worst he can do." She fixed her charming smile for a moment on her retreating visitor, and she added, with much unexpectedness, "I want to talk to him about my past!"

"That's just what I want to hear," said Sir Arthur, with his hand on the door.

"We are going to talk American; you wouldn't understand us!—He speaks in the English style," she explained, in her little sufficient way, as the baronet, who announced that at all events he would come back in the evening, let himself out.

"He doesn't know about your past?" Littlemore inquired, trying not to make the question sound impertinent.

"Oh, yes; I've told him everything; but he doesn't understand. The English are so peculiar; I think they are rather stupid. He has never heard of a woman being——" But here Mrs. Headway checked herself, while Littlemore filled out the blank. "What are you laughing at? It doesn't matter," she went on; "there are more things in the world than those people have heard of. However, I like them very much; at least I like him. He's such a gentleman; do you know what I mean? Only, he stays too long, and he isn't amusing, I'm very glad to see you, for a change."

"Do you mean I'm not a gentleman?" Littlemore asked.

"No, indeed; you used to be, in New Mexico. I think you were the only one—and I hope you are still. That's why I recognised you the other night; I might have cut you, you know."

"You can still, if you like. It's not too late."

"Oh, no; that's not what I want. I want you to help me."

"To help you?"

Mrs. Headway fixed her eyes for a moment on the door. "Do you suppose that man is there still?"

"That young man—your poor Englishman?"

"No; I mean Max. Max is my courier," said Mrs. Headway, with a certain impressiveness.

"I haven't the least idea. I'll see, if you like."

"No; in that case I should have to give him an order, and I don't know what in the world to ask him to do. He sits there for hours; with my simple habits I afford him no employment. I am afraid I have no imagination."

"The burden of grandeur," said Littlemore.

"Oh yes, I'm very grand. But, on the whole, I like it. I'm only afraid he'll hear. I talk so very loud; that's another thing I am trying to get over."

"Why do you want to be different?"

"Well, because everything else is different," Mrs. Headway rejoined, with a little sigh. "Did you hear that I'd lost my husband?" she went on abruptly.

"Do you mean—a—Mr.——?" and Littlemore paused, with an effect that did not seem to come home to her.

"I mean Mr. Headway," she said, with dignity. "I've been through a good deal since you saw me last: marriage, and death, and trouble, and all sorts of things."

"You had been through a good deal of marriage before that," Littlemore ventured to observe.

She rested her eyes on him with soft brightness, and without a change of colour. "Not so much—not so much——"

"Not so much as might have been thought."

"Not so much as was reported. I forget whether I was married when I saw you last."

"It was one of the reports," said Littlemore. "But I never saw Mr. Beck."

"You didn't lose much; he was a simple *wretch*! I have done certain things in my life which I have never understood; no wonder others can't understand them. But that's all over! Are you sure Max doesn't hear?" she asked, quickly.

"Not at all sure. But if you suspect him of listening at the keyhole, I would send him away."

"I don't think he does that. I am always rushing to the door."

"Then he doesn't hear. I had no idea you had so many secrets. When I parted with you, Mr. Headway was in the future."

"Well, now he's in the past. He was a pleasant man—I can understand my doing that. But he only lived a year. He had neuralgia of the heart; he left me very well off." She mentioned these various facts as if they were quite of the same order.

"I'm glad to hear it; you used to have expensive tastes."

"I have plenty of money," said Mrs. Headway. "Mr. Headway had property at Denver, which has increased immensely in value. After his death I tried New York. But I don't like New York." Littlemore's hostess uttered this last sentence in a tone which was the *résumé* of a social episode. I mean to live in Europe—I like Europe," she announced; and the manner of the announcement had a touch of prophecy, as the other words had had a reverberation of history.

Littlemore was very much struck with all this, and he was greatly entertained with Mrs. Headway. "Are you travelling with that young man?" he inquired, with the coolness of a person who wishes to make his entertainment go as far as possible.

She folded her arms as she leaned back in her chair. "Look here, Mr. Littlemore," she said; "I'm about as good-natured as I used to be in America, but I know a great deal more. Of course I ain't travelling with that young man; he's only a friend."

"He isn't a lover?" asked Littlemore, rather cruelly.

"Do people travel with their lovers? I don't want you to laugh at me—I want you to help me." She fixed her eyes on him with an air of tender remonstrance that might have touched him; she looked so gentle and reasonable. "As I tell you, I have taken a great fancy to this old Europe; I feel as if I should never go back. But I want to see something of the life. I think it would suit me—if I could get started a little. Mr. Littlemore," she added, in a moment—"I may as well be frank, for I ain't at all ashamed. I want to get into society. That's what I'm after!"

Littlemore settled himself in his chair, with the feeling of a man who, knowing that he will have to pull, seeks to obtain a certain leverage. It was in a tone of light jocosity, almost of encouragement, however, that he repeated: "Into society? It seems to me you are in it already, with baronets for your adorers."

"That's just what I want to know!" she said, with a certain eagerness. "Is a baronet much?"

"So they are apt to think. But I know very little about it."

"Ain't you in society yourself?"

"I? Never in the world! Where did you get that idea? I care no more about society than about that copy of the *Figaro*."

Mrs. Headway's countenance assumed for a moment a look of extreme disappointment, and Littlemore could see that, having heard of his silver mine and his cattle ranch, and knowing that he was living in Europe, she had hoped to find him immersed in the world of fashion. But she speedily recovered

herself. "I don't believe a word of it. You know you're a gentlemen—you can't help yourself."

"I may be a gentleman, but I have none of the habits of
one." Littlemore hesitated a moment, and then he added—
"I lived too long in the great South-West."

She flushed quickly; she instantly understood—understood
even more than he had meant to say. But she wished to make
use of him, and it was of more importance that she should
appear forgiving—especially as she had the happy consciousness of being so, than that she should punish a cruel speech.
She could afford, however, to be lightly ironical. "That makes
no difference—a gentleman is always a gentleman."

"Not always," said Littlemore, laughing.

"It's impossible that, through your sister, you shouldn't
know something about European society," said Mrs. Headway.

At the mention of his sister, made with a studied lightness
of reference which he caught as it passed, Littlemore was unable to repress a start. "What in the world have you got to
do with my sister?" he would have liked to say. The introduction of this lady was disagreeable to him; she belonged to
quite another order of ideas, and it was out of the question
that Mrs. Headway should ever make her acquaintance—if this
was what, as that lady would have said—she was "after." But
he took advantage of a side issue. "What do you mean by
European society? One can't talk about that. It's a very vague
phrase."

"Well, I mean English society—I mean the society your
sister lives in—that's what I mean," said Mrs. Headway, who
was quite prepared to be definite. "I mean the people I saw
in London last May—the people I saw at the opera and in the
park, the people who go to the Queen's drawing-rooms.
When I was in London I stayed at that hotel on the corner
of Piccadilly—that looking straight down St. James's Street
—and I spent hours together at the window looking at the
people in the carriages. I had a carriage of my own, and when
I was not at my window I was driving all round. I was all
alone; I saw every one, but I knew no one—I had no one to
tell me. I didn't know Sir Arthur then—I only met him a
month ago at Homburg. He followed me to Paris—that's

how he came to be my guest." Serenely, prosaically, without
any of the inflation of vanity, Mrs. Headway made this last
assertion; it was as if she were used to being followed, or as
if a gentleman one met at Homburg would inevitably follow.
In the same tone she went on: "I attracted a good deal of
attention in London—I could easily see that."

"You'll do that wherever you go," Littlemore said, insuf-
ficiently enough, as he felt.

"I don't want to attract so much; I think it's vulgar," Mrs.
Headway rejoined, with a certain soft sweetness which seemed
to denote the enjoyment of a new idea. She was evidently
open to new ideas.

"Every one was looking at you the other night at the theatre," Littlemore continued. "How can you hope to escape
notice?"

"I don't want to escape notice—people have always looked
at me, and I suppose they always will. But there are different
ways of being looked at, and I know the way I want. I mean
to have it, too!" Mrs. Headway exclaimed. Yes, she was very
definite.

Littlemore sat there, face to face with her, and for some
time he said nothing. He had a mixture of feelings, and the
memory of other places, other hours, was stealing over him.
There had been of old a very considerable absence of inter-
posing surfaces between these two—he had known her as one
knew people only in the great South-West. He had liked her
extremely, in a town where it would have been ridiculous to
be difficult to please. But his sense of this fact was somehow
connected with South-Western conditions; his liking for
Nancy Beck was an emotion of which the proper setting was
a back piazza. She presented herself here on a new basis—she
appeared to desire to be classified afresh. Littlemore said to
himself that this was too much trouble; he had taken her in
that way—he couldn't begin at this time of day to take her in
another way. He asked himself whether she were going to be
a bore. It was not easy to suppose Mrs. Headway capable of
this offence; but she might become tiresome if she were bent
upon being different. It made him rather afraid when she began to talk about European society, about his sister, about
things being vulgar. Littlemore was a very good fellow, and

he had at least the average human love of justice; but there was in his composition an element of the indolent, the sceptical, perhaps even the brutal, which made him desire to preserve the simplicity of their former terms of intercourse. He had no particular desire to see a woman rise again, as the mystic process was called; he didn't believe in women's rising again. He believed in their not going down; thought it perfectly possible and eminently desirable, but held it was much better for society that they should not endeavour, as the French say, to *mêler les genres*. In general, he didn't pretend to say what was good for society—society seemed to him in rather a bad way; but he had a conviction on this particular point. Nancy Beck going in for the great prizes, that spectacle might be entertaining for a simple spectator; but it would be a nuisance, an embarrassment, from the moment anything more than contemplation should be expected of him. He had no wish to be rough, but it might be well to show her that he was not to be humbugged.

"Oh, if there's anything you want you'll have it," he said, in answer to her last remark. "You have always had what you want."

"Well, I want something new this time. Does your sister reside in London?"

"My dear lady, what do you know about my sister?" Littlemore asked. "She's not a woman you would care for."

Mrs. Headway was silent a moment. "You don't respect me!" she exclaimed suddenly, in a loud, almost gay tone of voice. If Littlemore wished, as I say, to preserve the simplicity of their old terms of intercourse, she was apparently willing to humour him.

"Ah, my dear Mrs. Beck . . . !" he cried, vaguely, protestingly, and using her former name quite by accident. At San Diego, he had never thought whether he respected her or not; that never came up.

"That's a proof of it—calling me by that hateful name! Don't you believe I'm married? I haven't been fortunate in my names," she added, pensively.

"You make it very awkward when you say such mad things. My sister lives most of the year in the country; she is very

simple, rather dull, perhaps a trifle narrow-minded. You are
very clever, very lively, and as wide as all creation. That's why
I think you wouldn't like her."

"You ought to be ashamed to run down your sister!" cried
Mrs. Headway. "You told me once—at San Diego—that she
was the nicest woman you knew. I made a note of that, you
see. And you told me she was just my age. So that makes it
rather uncomfortable for you, if you won't introduce me!"
And Littlemore's hostess gave a pitiless laugh. "I'm not in the
least afraid of her being dull. It's very distinguished to be dull.
I'm ever so much too lively."

"You are indeed, ever so much! But nothing is more easy
than to know my sister," said Littlemore, who knew perfectly
that what he said was untrue. And then, as a diversion from
this delicate topic, he suddenly asked, "Are you going to
marry Sir Arthur?"

"Don't you think I've been married about enough?"

"Possibly; but this is a new line, it would be different. An
Englishman—that's a new sensation."

"If I should marry, it would be a European," said Mrs.
Headway calmly.

"Your chance is very good; they are all marrying Americans."

"He would have to be some one fine, the man I should
marry now. I have a good deal to make up for! That's what I
want to know about Sir Arthur; all this time you haven't told
me."

"I have nothing in the world to tell—I have never heard of
him. Hasn't he told you himself?"

"Nothing at all; he is very modest. He doesn't brag, nor
make himself out anything great. That's what I like him for:
I think it's in such good taste. I like good taste!" exclaimed
Mrs. Headway. "But all this time," she added, "you haven't
told me you would help me."

"How can I help you? I'm no one, I have no power."

"You can help me by not preventing me. I want you to
promise not to prevent me." She gave him her fixed, bright
gaze again; her eyes seemed to look far into his.

"Good Lord, how could I prevent you?"

"I'm not sure that you could. But you might try."

"I'm too indolent, and too stupid," said Littlemore jocosely.

"Yes," she replied, musing as she still looked at him. "I think you are too stupid. But I think you are also too kind," she added more graciously. She was almost irresistible when she said such a thing as that.

They talked for a quarter of an hour longer, and at last—as if she had had scruples—she spoke to him of his own marriage, of the death of his wife, matters to which she alluded more felicitously (as he thought) than to some other points. "If you have a little girl you ought to be very happy; that's what I should like to have. Lord, I should make her a nice woman! Not like me—in another style!" When he rose to leave her, she told him that he must come and see her very often; she was to be some weeks longer in Paris; he must bring Mr. Waterville.

"Your English friend won't like that—our coming very often," Littlemore said, as he stood with his hand on the door.

"I don't know what he has got to do with it," she answered, staring.

"Neither do I. Only he must be in love with you."

"That doesn't give him any right. Mercy, if I had had to put myself out for all the men that have been in love with me!"

"Of course you would have had a terrible life! Even doing as you please, you have had rather an agitated one. But your young Englishman's sentiments appear to give him the right to sit there, after one comes in, looking blighted and bored. That might become very tiresome."

"The moment he becomes tiresome I send him away. You can trust me for that."

"Oh," said Littlemore, "it doesn't matter, after all." He remembered that it would be very inconvenient to him to have undisturbed possession of Mrs. Headway.

She came out with him into the antechamber. Mr. Max, the courier, was fortunately not there. She lingered a little; she appeared to have more to say.

"On the contrary, he likes you to come," she remarked in a moment; "he wants to study my friends."

"To study them?"

"He wants to find out about me, and he thinks they may tell him something. Some day he will ask you right out, 'What sort of a woman is she, any way?' "

"Hasn't he found out yet?"

"He doesn't understand me," said Mrs. Headway, surveying the front of her dress. "He has never seen any one like me."

"I should imagine not!"

"So he will ask you, as I say."

"I will tell him you are the most charming woman in Europe."

"That ain't a description! Besides, he knows it. He wants to know if I'm respectable."

"He's very curious!" Littlemore cried, with a laugh.

She grew a little pale; she seemed to be watching his lips. "Mind you tell him," she went on with a smile that brought none of her colour back.

"Respectable? I'll tell him you're adorable!"

Mrs. Headway stood a moment longer. "Ah, you're no use!" she murmured. And she suddenly turned away and passed back into her sitting-room, slowly drawing her far-trailing skirts.

III.

"Elle ne doute de rien!" Littlemore said to himself as he walked away from the hotel; and he repeated the phrase in talking about her to Waterville. "She wants to be right," he added; "but she will never really succeed; she has begun too late, she will never be more than half right. However, she won't know when she's wrong, so it doesn't signify!" And then he proceeded to assert that in some respects she would remain incurable; she had no delicacy; no discretion, no shading; she was a woman who suddenly said to you, "You don't respect me!" As if that were a thing for a woman to say!

"It depends upon what she meant by it." Waterville liked to see the meanings of things.

"The more she meant by it the less she ought to say it!" Littlemore declared.

But he returned to the Hôtel Meurice, and on the next occasion he took Waterville with him. The Secretary of Legation, who had not often been in close quarters with a lady of this ambiguous quality, was prepared to regard Mrs. Headway as a very curious type. He was afraid she might be dangerous; but, on the whole, he felt secure. The object of his devotion at present was his country, or at least the Department of State; he had no intention of being diverted from that allegiance. Besides, he had his ideal of the attractive woman—a person pitched in a very much lower key than this shining, smiling, rustling, chattering daughter of the Territories. The woman he should care for would have repose, a certain love of privacy—she would sometimes let one alone. Mrs. Headway was personal, familiar, intimate; she was always appealing or accusing, demanding explanations and pledges, saying things one had to answer. All this was accompanied with a hundred smiles and radiations and other natural graces, but the general effect of it was slightly fatiguing. She had certainly a great deal of charm, an immense desire to please, and a wonderful collection of dresses and trinkets; but she was eager and preoccupied, and it was impossible that other people should share her eagerness. If she wished to get into society, there was no reason why her bachelor visitors should wish to see her there; for it was the absence of the usual social incumbrances which made her drawing-room attractive. There was no doubt whatever that she was several women in one, and she ought to content herself with that sort of numerical triumph. Littlemore said to Waterville that it was stupid of her to wish to scale the heights; she ought to know how much more she was in her place down below. She appeared vaguely to irritate him; even her fluttering attempts at self-culture— she had become a great critic, and handled many of the productions of the age with a bold, free touch—constituted a vague invocation, an appeal for sympathy which was naturally annoying to a man who disliked the trouble of revising old decisions, consecrated by a certain amount of reminiscence that might be called tender. She had, however, one palpable charm; she was full of surprises. Even Waterville was obliged to confess that an element of the unexpected was not to be excluded from his conception of the woman who should have an ideal repose. Of course there were two kinds of surprises, and only one of them was thoroughly pleasant, though Mrs. Headway dealt impartially in both. She had the sudden delights, the odd exclamations, the queer curiosities of a person who has grown up in a country where everything is new and many things ugly, and who, with a natural turn for the arts and amenities of life, makes a tardy acquaintance with some of the finer usages, the higher pleasures. She was provincial—it was easy to see that she was provincial; that took no great cleverness. But what was Parisian enough—if to be Parisian was the measure of success—was the way she picked up ideas and took a hint from every circumstance. "Only give me time, and I shall know all I have need of," she said to Littlemore, who watched her progress with a mixture of admiration and sadness. She delighted to speak of herself as a poor little barbarian who was trying to pick up a few crumbs of knowledge, and this habit took great effect from her delicate face, her perfect dress, and the brilliancy of her manners.

One of her surprises was, that after that first visit she said no more to Littlemore about Mrs. Dolphin. He did her perhaps the grossest injustice; but he had quite expected her to bring up this lady whenever they met. "If she will only leave Agnes alone, she may do what she will," he said to Waterville, expressing his relief. "My sister would never look at her, and it would be very awkward to have to tell her so." She expected assistance; she made him feel that simply by the way she looked at him; but for the moment she demanded no definite service. She held her tongue, but she waited, and her patience itself was a kind of admonition. In the way of society, it must be confessed, her privileges were meagre, Sir Arthur Demesne and her two compatriots being, so far as the latter could discover, her only visitors. She might have had other friends, but she held her head very high, and liked better to see no one than not to see the best company. It was evident that she flattered herself that she produced the effect of being, not neglected, but fastidious. There were plenty of Americans in Paris, but in this direction she failed to extend her acquaintance; the nice people wouldn't come and see her, and nothing would have induced her to receive the others. She had the most exact conception of the people she wished to see and to

avoid. Littlemore expected every day that she would ask him
why he didn't bring some of his friends, and he had his answer
ready. It was a very poor one, for it consisted simply of a
conventional assurance that he wished to keep her for himself.
She would be sure to retort that this was very "thin," as,
indeed, it was; but the days went by without her calling him
to account. The little American colony in Paris is rich in amiable women, but there were none to whom Littlemore could
make up his mind to say that it would be a favour to him to
call on Mrs. Headway. He shouldn't like them the better for
doing so, and he wished to like those of whom he might ask
a favour. Except, therefore, that he occasionally spoke of her
as a little Western woman, very pretty and rather queer, who
had formerly been a great chum of his, she remained unknown
in the *salons* of the Avenue Gabriel and the streets that encircle
the Arch of Triumph. To ask the men to go and see her,
without asking the ladies, would only accentuate the fact that
he didn't ask the ladies; so he asked no one at all. Besides, it
was true—just a little—that he wished to keep her to himself,
and he was fatuous enough to believe that she cared much
more for him than for her Englishman. Of course, however,
he would never dream of marrying her, whereas the Englishman apparently was immersed in that vision. She hated her
past; she used to announce that very often, talking of it as if
it were an appendage of the same order as a dishonest courier,
or even an inconvenient protrusion of drapery. Therefore, as
Littlemore was part of her past, it might have been supposed
that she would hate him too, and wish to banish him, with
all the images he recalled, from her sight. But she made an
exception in his favour, and if she disliked their old relations
as a chapter of her own history, she seemed still to like them
as a chapter of his. He felt that she clung to him, that she
believed he could help her and in the long run would. It was
to the long run that she appeared little by little to have attuned herself.

She succeeded perfectly in maintaining harmony between
Sir Arthur Demesne and her American visitors, who spent
much less time in her drawing-room. She had easily persuaded
him that there were no grounds for jealousy, and that they
had no wish, as she said, to crowd him out; for it was ridic-

ulous to be jealous of two persons at once, and Rupert Waterville, after he had learned the way to her hospitable apartment, appeared there as often as his friend Littlemore. The two, indeed, usually came together, and they ended by relieving their competitor of a certain sense of responsibility. This amiable and excellent but somewhat limited and slightly pretentious young man, who had not yet made up his mind, was sometimes rather oppressed with the magnitude of his undertaking, and when he was alone with Mrs. Headway the tension of his thoughts occasionally became quite painful. He was very slim and straight, and looked taller than his height; he had the prettiest, silkiest hair, which waved away from a large white forehead, and he was endowed with a nose of the so-called Roman model. He looked younger than his years (in spite of those last two attributes), partly on account of the delicacy of his complexion and the almost childlike candour of his round blue eye. He was diffident and self-conscious; there were certain letters he could not pronounce. At the same time he had the manners of a young man who had been brought up to fill a considerable place in the world, with whom a certain correctness had become a habit, and who, though he might occasionally be a little awkward about small things, would be sure to acquit himself honourably in great ones. He was very simple, and he believed himself very serious; he had the blood of a score of Warwickshire squires in his veins; mingled in the last instance with the somewhat paler fluid which animated the long-necked daughter of a banker who had expected an earl for his son-in-law, but who had consented to regard Sir Baldwin Demesne as the least insufficient of baronets. The boy, the only one, had come into his title at five years of age; his mother, who disappointed her auriferous sire a second time when poor Sir Baldwin broke his neck in the hunting field, watched over him with a tenderness that burned as steadily as a candle shaded by a transparent hand. She never admitted, even to herself, that he was not the cleverest of men; but it took all her own cleverness, which was much greater than his, to maintain this appearance. Fortunately he was not wild, so that he would never marry an actress or a governess, like two or three of the young men who had been at Eton with him. With this ground of nervousness the less, Lady Demesne awaited with an air of confidence his promotion to some high office. He represented in Parliament the Conservative instincts and vote of a red-roofed market town, and sent regularly to his bookseller for all the new publications on economical subjects, for he was determined that his political attitude should have a firm statistical basis. He was not conceited; he was only misinformed—misinformed, I mean, about himself. He thought himself indispensable in the scheme of things—not as an individual, but as an institution. This conviction, however, was too sacred to betray itself by vulgar assumptions. If he was a little man in a big place, he never strutted nor talked loud; he merely felt it as a kind of luxury that he had a large social circumference. It was like sleeping in a big bed; one didn't toss about the more, but one felt a greater freshness.

He had never seen anything like Mrs. Headway; he hardly knew by what standard to measure her. She was not like an English lady—not like those at least with whom he had been accustomed to converse; and yet it was impossible not to see that she had a standard of her own. He suspected that she was provincial, but as he was very much under the charm he compromised matters by saying to himself that she was only foreign. It was of course provincial to be foreign; but this was, after all, a peculiarity which she shared with a great many nice people. He was not wild, and his mother had flattered herself that in this all-important matter he would not be perverse; but it was all the same most unexpected that he should have taken a fancy to an American widow, five years older than himself, who knew no one, and who sometimes didn't appear to understand exactly who he was. Though he disapproved of it, it was precisely her foreignness that pleased him; she seemed to be as little as possible of his own race and creed; there was not a touch of Warwickshire in her composition. She was like an Hungarian or a Pole, with the difference that he could almost understand her language. The unfortunate young man was fascinated, though he had not yet admitted to himself that he was in love. He would be very slow and deliberate in such a position, for he was deeply conscious of its importance. He was a young man who had arranged his life; he had determined to marry at thirty-two. A long line of ancestors was watching him; he hardly knew what they would think of Mrs. Headway. He hardly knew what he thought himself; the only thing he was absolutely sure of was that she made the time pass as it passed in no other pursuit. He was vaguely uneasy; he was by no means sure it was right the time should pass like that. There was nothing to show for it but the fragments of Mrs. Headway's conversation, the peculiarities of her accent, the sallies of her wit, the audacities of her fancy, her mysterious allusions to her past. Of course he knew that she had a past; she was not a young girl, she was a widow—and widows are essentially an expression of an accomplished fact. He was not jealous of her antecedents, but he wished to understand them, and it was here that the difficulty occurred. The subject was illumined with fitful flashes, but it never placed itself before him as a general picture. He asked her a good many questions, but her answers were so startling that, like sudden luminous points, they seemed to intensify the darkness round their edges. She had apparently spent her life in an inferior province of an inferior country; but it didn't follow from this that she herself had been low. She had been a lily among thistles; and there was something romantic in a man in his position taking an interest in such a woman. It pleased Sir Arthur to believe he was romantic; that had been the case with several of his ancestors, who supplied a precedent without which he would perhaps not have ventured to trust himself. He was the victim of perplexities from which a single spark of direct perception would have saved him. He took everything in the literal sense; he had not a grain of humour. He sat there vaguely waiting for something to happen, and not committing himself by rash declarations. If he was in love, it was in his own way, reflectively, inexpressively, obstinately. He was waiting for the formula which would justify his conduct and Mrs. Headway's peculiarities. He hardly knew where it would come from; you might have thought from his manner that he would discover it in one of the elaborate *entrées* that were served to the pair when Mrs. Headway consented to dine with him at Bignon's or the Café Anglais; or in one of the numerous band-boxes that arrived from the Rue de la Paix, and from which she often lifted the lid in the presence of her admirer. There were moments when he got weary of waiting in vain, and at these moments the arrival of her American friends (he often wondered that she had so few) seemed to lift the mystery from his shoulders and give him a chance to rest. This formula—she herself was not yet able to give it, for she was not aware how much ground it was expected to cover. She talked about her past, because she thought it the best thing to do; she had a shrewd conviction that it was better to make a good use of it than to attempt to efface it. To efface it was impossible, though that was what she would have preferred. She had no objection to telling fibs, but now that she was taking a new departure, she wished to tell only those that were necessary. She would have been delighted if it had been possible to tell none at all. A few, however, were indispensable, and we need not attempt to estimate more closely the ingenious re-arrangements of fact with which she entertained and mystified Sir Arthur. She knew, of course, that as a product of fashionable circles she was nowhere, but she might have great success as a child of nature.

IV.

Rupert Waterville, in the midst of intercourse in which every one perhaps had a good many mental reservations, never forgot that he was in a representative position, that he was responsible, official; and he asked himself more than once how far it was permitted to him to countenance Mrs. Headway's pretensions to being an American lady typical even of the newer phases. In his own way he was as puzzled as poor Sir Arthur, and indeed he flattered himself that he was as particular as any Englishman could be. Suppose that, after all this free association, Mrs. Headway should come over to London, and ask at the Legation to be presented to the Queen? It would be so awkward to refuse her—of course they would have to refuse her—that he was very careful about making tacit promises. She might construe anything as a tacit promise—he knew how the smallest gestures of diplomatists were studied and interpreted. It was his effort, therefore, to be really the diplomatist in his relations with this attractive but dangerous woman. The party of four used often to dine together—Sir Arthur pushed his confidence so far—and on these occasions Mrs. Headway, availing herself of one of the privileges of a lady, even at the most expensive restaurant—used to wipe her glasses with her napkin. One evening, when after polishing a goblet she held it up to the light, giving it, with her head on one side, the least glimmer of a wink, he said to himself as he watched her that she looked like a modern bacchante. He noticed at this moment that the baronet was gazing at her too, and he wondered if the same idea had come to him. He often wondered what the baronet thought; he had devoted first and last a good deal of speculation to the baronial class. Littlemore, alone, at this moment, was not observing Mrs. Headway; he never appeared to observe her, though she often observed him. Waterville asked himself among other things why Sir Arthur had not brought his own friends to see her, for Paris during the several weeks that now elapsed was rich in English visitors. He wondered whether she had asked him and he had refused; he would have liked very much to know whether she had asked him. He explained his curiosity to Littlemore, who, however, took very little interest in it. Littlemore said, nevertheless, that he had no doubt she had asked him; she never would be deterred by false delicacy.

"She has been very delicate with you," Waterville replied. "She hasn't been at all pressing of late."

"It is only because she has given me up; she thinks I'm a brute."

"I wonder what she thinks of me," Waterville said, pensively.

"Oh, she counts upon you to introduce her to the Minister. It's lucky for you that our representative here is absent."

"Well," Waterville rejoined, "the Minister has settled two or three difficult questions, and I suppose he can settle this one. I shall do nothing but by the orders of my chief." He was very fond of talking about his chief.

"She does me injustice," Littlemore added in a moment. "I have spoken to several people about her."

"Ah; but what have you told them?"

"That she lives at the Hôtel Meurice; and that she wants to know nice people."

"They are flattered, I suppose, at your thinking them nice, but they don't go," said Waterville.

"I spoke of her to Mrs. Bagshaw, and Mrs. Bagshaw has promised to go."

"Ah," Waterville murmured; "you don't call Mrs. Bagshaw nice! Mrs. Headway won't see her."

"That's exactly what she wants,—to be able to cut some one!"

Waterville had a theory that Sir Arthur was keeping Mrs. Headway as a surprise—he meant perhaps to produce her during the next London season. He presently, however, learned as much about the matter as he could have desired to know. He had once offered to accompany his beautiful compatriot to the Museum of the Luxembourg and tell her a little about the modern French school. She had not examined this collection, in spite of her determination to see everything remarkable (she carried her *Murray* in her lap even when she went to see the great tailor in the Rue de la Paix, to whom, as she said, she had given no end of points); for she usually went to such places with Sir Arthur, and Sir Arthur was indifferent to the modern painters of France. "He says there are much better men in England. I must wait for the Royal Academy, next year. He seems to think one can wait for anything, but I'm not so good at waiting as he. I can't afford to wait—I've waited long enough." So much as this Mrs. Headway said, on the occasion of her arranging with Rupert Waterville that they should some day visit the Luxembourg together. She alluded to the Englishman as if he were her husband or her brother, her natural protector and companion.

"I wonder if she knows how that sounds?" Waterville said to himself. "I don't believe she would do it if she knew how it sounds." And he made the further reflection that when one arrived from San Diego there was no end to the things one had to learn: it took so many things to make a well-bred woman. Clever as she was, Mrs. Headway was right in saying that she couldn't afford to wait. She must learn quickly. She wrote to Waterville one day to propose that they should go to the Museum on the morrow; Sir Arthur's mother was in Paris, on her way to Cannes, where she was to spend the winter. She was only passing through, but she would be there three days, and he would naturally give himself up to her. She appeared to have the properest ideas as to what a gentleman would propose to do for his mother. She herself, therefore, would be free, and she named the hour at which she should expect him to call for her. He was punctual to the appointment, and they drove across the river in the large high-hung barouche in which she constantly rolled about Paris. With Mr. Max on the box—the courier was ornamented with enormous whiskers—this vehicle had an appearance of great respectability, though Sir Arthur assured her—she repeated this to her other friends—that in London, next year, they would do the thing much better for her. It struck her other friends, of course, that the baronet was prepared to be very consistent, and this, on the whole, was what Waterville would have expected of him. Littlemore simply remarked that at San Diego she drove herself about in a rickety buggy, with muddy wheels, and with a mule very often in the shafts. Waterville felt something like excitement as he asked himself whether the baronet's mother would now consent to know her. She must of course be aware that it was a woman who was keeping her son in Paris at a season when English gentlemen were most naturally employed in shooting partridges.

"She is staying at the Hôtel du Rhin, and I have made him feel that he mustn't leave her while she is here," Mrs. Headway said, as they drove up the narrow Rue de Seine. "Her name is Lady Demesne, but her full title is the Honourable Lady Demesne, as she's a Baron's daughter. Her father used to be a banker, but he did something or other for the Government—the Tories, you know, they call them—and so he was raised to the peerage. So you see one *can* be raised! She has a lady with her as a companion." Waterville's neighbour gave him this information with a seriousness that made him smile; he wondered whether she thought he didn't know how a Baron's daughter was addressed. In that she was very provincial; she had a way of exaggerating the value of her intellectual acquisitions, and of assuming that others had been as ignorant as she. He noted, too, that she had ended by suppressing poor Sir Arthur's name altogether, and designating him only by a sort of conjugal pronoun. She had been so much, and so easily, married, that she was full of these misleading references to gentlemen.

V.

They walked through the gallery of the Luxembourg, and except that Mrs. Headway looked at everything at once, and at nothing long enough, talked, as usual, rather too loud, and bestowed too much attention on the bad copies that were being made of several indifferent pictures, she was a very agreeable companion and a grateful recipient of knowledge. She was very quick to understand, and Waterville was sure that before she left the gallery she knew something about the French school. She was quite prepared to compare it critically with London exhibitions of the following year. As Littlemore and he had remarked more than once, she was a very odd mixture. Her conversation, her personality, were full of little joints and seams, all of them very visible, where the old and the new had been pieced together. When they had passed through the different rooms of the palace Mrs. Headway proposed that instead of returning directly they should take a stroll in the adjoining gardens, which she wished very much to see, and was sure she should like. She had quite seized the difference between the old Paris and the new, and felt the force of the romantic associations of the Latin quarter as perfectly as if she had enjoyed all the benefits of modern culture. The autumn sun was warm in the alleys and terraces of the Luxembourg; the masses of foliage above them, clipped and squared, rusty with ruddy patches, shed a thick lace-work over the white sky, which was streaked with the palest blue. The beds of flowers near the palace were of the vividest yellow and red, and the sunlight rested on the smooth gray walls of those parts of its basement that looked south; in front of which, on the long green benches, a row of brown-cheeked nurses, in white caps and white aprons, sat offering nutrition to as many bundles of white drapery. There were other white caps wandering in the broad paths, attended by little brown French children; the small, straw-seated chairs, were piled and stacked in some places and disseminated in others. An old lady in black, with white hair fastened over each of her temples by a large black comb, sat on the edge of a stone bench (too high for her delicate length), motionless, staring straight before her and holding a large door-key; under a tree a priest was reading—you could see his lips move at a distance; a young soldier, dwarfish and red-legged, strolled past with his hands in his pockets, which were very much distended. Waterville sat down with Mrs. Headway on the straw-bottomed chairs, and she presently said, "I like this; it's even better than the pictures in the gallery. It's more of a picture."

"Everything in France is a picture—even things that are ugly," Waterville replied. "Everything makes a subject."

"Well, I like France!" Mrs. Headway went on, with a little incongruous sigh. Then, suddenly, from an impulse even more inconsequent than her sigh, she added, "He asked me to go and see her, but I told him I wouldn't. She may come and see me if she likes." This was so abrupt that Waterville was slightly confounded; but he speedily perceived that she had returned by a short cut to Sir Arthur Demesne and his honourable mother. Waterville liked to know about other people's affairs, but he did not like this taste to be imputed to him; and therefore, though he was curious to see how the old lady, as he called her, would treat his companion, he was rather displeased with the latter for being so confidential. He had never imagined he was so intimate with her as that. Mrs. Headway, however, had a manner of taking intimacy for granted; a manner which Sir Arthur's mother at least would be sure not to like. He pretended to wonder a little what she was talking about, but she scarcely explained. She only went on, through untraceable transitions: "The least she can do is to come. I have been very kind to her son. That's not a reason for my going to her—it's a reason for her coming to me. Besides, if she doesn't like what I've done, she can leave me alone. I want to get into European society, but I want to get in in my own way. I don't want to run after people; I want them to run after me. I guess they will, some day!" Waterville listened to this with his eyes on the ground; he felt himself blushing a little. There was something in Mrs. Headway that shocked and mortified him, and Littlemore had been right in saying that she had a deficiency of shading. She was terribly distinct; her motives, her impulses, her desires, were absolutely glaring. She needed to see, to hear, her own thoughts. Vehement thought, with Mrs. Headway, was inevitably speech, though speech was not always thought, and now she had suddenly become vehement. "If she does once come—then, ah, then, I shall be too perfect with her; I shan't let her go! But she must take the first step. I confess, I hope she'll be nice."

"Perhaps she won't," said Waterville perversely.

"Well, I don't care if she isn't. He has never told me anything about her; never a word about any of his own belongings. If I wished, I might believe he's ashamed of them."

"I don't think it's that."

"I know it isn't. I know what it is. It's just modesty. He doesn't want to brag—he's too much of a gentleman. He doesn't want to dazzle me—he wants me to like him for himself. Well, I do like him," she added in a moment. "But I shall like him still better if he brings his mother. They shall know that in America."

"Do you think it will make an impression in America?" Waterville asked, smiling.

"It will show them that I am visited by the British aristocracy. They won't like that."

"Surely they grudge you no innocent pleasure," Waterville murmured, smiling still.

"They grudged me common politeness—when I was in New York! Did you ever hear how they treated me, when I came on from the West?"

Waterville stared; this episode was quite new to him. His companion had turned towards him; her pretty head was tossed back like a flower in the wind; there was a flush in her cheek, a sharper light in her eye. "Ah! my dear New Yorkers, they're incapable of rudeness!" cried the young man.

"You're one of them, I see. But I don't speak of the men. The men were well enough—though they did allow it."

"Allow what, Mrs. Headway?" Waterville was quite in the dark.

She wouldn't answer at once; her eyes, glittering a little, were fixed upon absent images. "What did you hear about me over there? Don't pretend you heard nothing."

He had heard nothing at all; there had not been a word about Mrs. Headway in New York. He couldn't pretend, and he was obliged to tell her this. "But I have been away," he added, "and in America I didn't go out. There's nothing to go out for in New York—only little boys and girls."

"There are plenty of old women! They decided I was improper. I'm very well known in the West—I'm known from Chicago to San Francisco—if not personally (in all cases), at least by reputation. People can tell you out there. In New York they decided I wasn't good enough. Not good enough for New York! What do you say to that?" And she gave a sweet little laugh. Whether she had struggled with her pride before making this avowal, Waterville never knew. The crudity of the avowal seemed to indicate that she had no pride, and yet there was a spot in her heart which, as he now perceived, was intensely sore, and had suddenly begun to throb. "I took a house for the winter—one of the handsomest houses in the place—but I sat there all alone. They didn't think me proper. Such as you see me here, I wasn't a success! I tell you the truth at whatever cost. Not a decent woman came to see me!"

Waterville was embarrassed; diplomatist as he was, he hardly knew what line to take. He could not see what need there was of her telling him the truth, though the incident appeared to have been most curious, and he was glad to know the facts on the best authority. It was the first he knew of this remarkable woman's having spent a winter in his native city—which was virtually a proof of her having come and gone in complete obscurity. It was vain for him to pretend that he had been a good deal away, for he had been appointed to his post in London only six months before, and Mrs. Headway's social failure preceded that event. In the midst of these reflections he had an inspiration. He attempted neither to explain, to minimise, nor to apologise; he ventured simply to lay his hand for an instant on her own and to exclaim, as tenderly as possible, "I wish *I* had known you were there!"

"I had plenty of men—but men don't count. If they are not a positive help, they're a hindrance, and the more you have, the worse it looks. The women simply turned their backs."

"They were afraid of you—they were jealous," Waterville said.

"It's very good of you to try and explain it away; all I know is, not one of them crossed my threshold. You needn't try and tone it down; I know perfectly how the case stands. In New York, if you please, I was a failure!"

"So much the worse for New York!" cried Waterville, who, as he afterwards said to Littlemore, had got quite worked up.

"And now you know why I want to get into society over here?" She jumped up and stood before him; with a dry hard smile she looked down at him. Her smile itself was an answer to her question; it expressed an urgent desire for revenge. There was an abruptness in her movements which left Waterville quite behind; but as he still sat there, returning her glance, he felt that he at last, in the light of that smile, the flash of that almost fierce question, understood Mrs. Headway.

She turned away, to walk to the gate of the garden, and he went with her, laughing vaguely, uneasily, at her tragic tone. Of course she expected him to help her to her revenge; but his female relations, his mother and his sisters, his innumerable cousins, had been a party to the slight she suffered, and he reflected as he walked along that after all they had been right. They had been right in not going to see a woman who could chatter that way about her social wrongs; whether Mrs. Headway were respectable or not, they had a correct instinct, for at any rate she was vulgar. European society might let her in, but European society would be wrong. New York, Waterville said to himself with a glow of civic pride, was quite capable of taking a higher stand in such a matter than London. They went some distance without speaking; at last he said, expressing honestly the thought which at that moment was uppermost in his mind, "I hate that phrase, 'getting into society.' I don't think one ought to attribute to one's self that sort of ambition. One ought to assume that one is in society—that one *is* society—and to hold that if one has good manners, one has, from the social point of view, achieved the great thing. The rest regards others."

For a moment she appeared not to understand; then she broke out: "Well, I suppose I haven't good manners; at any rate, I'm not satisfied! Of course, I don't talk right—I know that very well. But let me get where I want to first—then I'll look after my expressions. If I once get there, I shall be perfect!" she cried, with a tremor of passion. They reached the gate of the garden and stood a moment outside, opposite to the low arcade of the Odéon, lined with bookstalls, at which

Waterville cast a slightly wistful glance, waiting for Mrs. Headway's carriage, which had drawn up at a short distance. The
whiskered Max had seated himself within, and on the tense
elastic cushions had fallen into a doze. The carriage got into
motion without his awaking; he came to his senses only as it
stopped again. He started up, staring; then, without confusion, he proceeded to descend.

"I have learned it in Italy—they say the *siesta*," he remarked, with an agreeable smile, holding the door open to
Mrs. Headway.

"Well, I should think you had!" this lady replied, laughing
amicably as she got into the vehicle, whither Waterville followed her. It was not a surprise to him to perceive that she
spoiled her courier; she naturally would spoil her courier. But
civilisation begins at home, said Waterville; and the incident
threw an ironical light upon her desire to get into society. It
failed, however, to divert her thoughts from the subject she
was discussing with Waterville, for as Max ascended the box
and the carriage went on its way, she threw out another little
note of defiance. "If once I'm all right over here, I can snap
my fingers at New York! You'll see the faces those women will
make."

Waterville was sure his mother and sisters would make no
faces; but he felt afresh, as the carriage rolled back to the
Hôtel Meurice, that now he understood Mrs. Headway. As
they were about to enter the court of the hotel a closed carriage passed before them, and while a few moments later he
helped his companion to alight, he saw that Sir Arthur Demesne had descended from the other vehicle. Sir Arthur perceived Mrs. Headway, and instantly gave his hand to a lady
seated in the *coupé*. This lady emerged with a certain slow
impressiveness, and as she stood before the door of the hotel
—a woman still young and fair, with a good deal of height,
gentle, tranquil, plainly dressed, yet distinctly imposing—Waterville saw that the baronet had brought his mother to call
upon Nancy Beck. Mrs. Headway's triumph had begun; the
Dowager Lady Demesne had taken the first step. Waterville
wondered whether the ladies in New York, notified by some
magnetic wave, were distorting their features. Mrs. Headway,
quickly conscious of what had happened, was neither too

prompt to appropriate the visit, nor too slow to acknowledge it. She just paused, smiling at Sir Arthur.

"I wish to introduce my mother—she wants very much to know you." He approached Mrs. Headway; the lady had taken his arm. She was at once simple, and circumspect; she had all the resources of an English matron.

Mrs. Headway, without advancing a step, put out her hands as if to draw her visitor quickly closer. "I declare, you're too sweet!" Waterville heard her say.

He was turning away, as his own business was over; but the young Englishman, who had surrendered his mother to the embrace, as it might now almost be called, of their hostess, just checked him with a friendly gesture. "I daresay I shan't see you again—I'm going away."

"Good-bye, then," said Waterville. "You return to England?"

"No; I go to Cannes, with my mother."

"You remain at Cannes?"

"Till Christmas very likely."

The ladies, escorted by Mr. Max, had passed into the hotel, and Waterville presently quitted his interlocutor. He smiled as he walked away, reflecting that this personage had obtained a concession from his mother only at the price of a concession.

The next morning he went to see Littlemore, from whom he had a standing invitation to breakfast, and, who, as usual, was smoking a cigar, and looking through a dozen newspapers. Littlemore had a large apartment, and an accomplished cook; he got up late and wandered about his room all the morning, stopping from time to time to look out of his windows, which overhung the Place de la Madeleine. They had not been seated many minutes at breakfast when Waterville announced that Mrs. Headway was about to be abandoned by Sir Arthur, who was going to Cannes.

"That's no news to me," Littlemore said. "He came last night to bid me good-bye."

"To bid you good-bye? He was very civil all of a sudden."

"He didn't come from civility—he came from curiosity. Having dined here, he had a pretext for calling."

"I hope his curiosity was satisfied," Waterville remarked, in

the manner of a person who could enter into such a sentiment.

Littlemore hesitated. "Well, I suspect not. He sat here some
time, but we talked about everything but what he wanted to
know."

"And what did he want to know?"

"Whether I know anything against Nancy Beck."

Waterville stared. "Did he call her Nancy Beck?"

"We never mentioned her; but I saw what he wanted, and
that he wanted me to lead up to her—only I wouldn't do it."

"Ah, poor man!" Watervale murmured.

"I don't see why you pity him," said Littlemore. "Mrs.
Beck's admirers were never pitied."

"Well, of course he wants to marry her."

"Let him do it, then. I have nothing to say to it."

"He believes there's something in her past that's hard to
swallow."

"Let him leave it alone, then."

"How can he, if he's in love with her?" Waterville asked,
in the tone of a man who could enter into that sentiment too.

"Ah, my dear fellow, he must settle it himself. He has no
right, at any rate, to ask me such a question. There was a
moment, just as he was going, when he had it on his tongue's
end. He stood there in the doorway, he couldn't leave me—
he was going to plump out with it. He looked at me straight,
and I looked straight at him; we remained that way for almost
a minute. Then he decided to hold his tongue, and took himself off."

Waterville listened to this little description with intense interest. "And if he had asked you, what would you have said?"

"What do you think?"

"Well, I suppose you would have said that his question
wasn't fair?"

"That would have been tantamount to admitting the
worst."

"Yes," said Waterville, thoughtfully, "you couldn't do that.
On the other hand, if he had put it to you on your honour,
whether she were a woman to marry, it would have been very
awkward."

"Awkward enough. Fortunately, he has no business to put things to me on my honour. Moreover, nothing has passed between us to give him the right to ask me questions about Mrs. Headway. As she is a great friend of mine, he can't pretend to expect me to give confidential information about her."

"You don't think she's a woman to marry, all the same," Waterville declared. "And if a man were to ask you that, you might knock him down, but it wouldn't be an answer."

"It would have to serve," said Littlemore. He added in a moment, "There are certain cases where it's a man's duty to commit perjury."

Waterville looked grave. "Certain cases?"

"Where a woman's honour is at stake."

"I see what you mean. That's of course if he has been himself concerned——"

"Himself, or another. It doesn't matter."

"I think it does matter. I don't like perjury," said Waterville. "It's a delicate question."

They were interrupted by the arrival of the servant with a second course, and Littlemore gave a laugh as he helped himself. "It would be a joke to see her married to that superior being!"

"It would be a great responsibility."

"Responsibility or not, it would be very amusing."

"Do you mean to assist her, then?"

"Heaven forbid! But I mean to bet on her."

Waterville gave his companion a serious glance; he thought him strangely superficial. The situation, however, was difficult, and he laid down his fork, with a little sigh.

VI.

The Easter holidays that year were unusually genial; mild watery sunshine assisted the progress of the spring. The high, dense hedges, in Warwickshire, were like walls of hawthorn imbedded in banks of primrose, and the finest trees in England, springing out of them with a regularity which suggested conservative principles, began to cover themselves with a kind of green downiness. Rupert Waterville, devoted to his duties and faithful in attendance at the Legation, had had little time to enjoy that rural hospitality which is the great invention of the English people, and the most perfect expression of their character. He had been invited now and then—for in London he commended himself to many people as a very sensible young man—but he had been obliged to decline more proposals than he accepted. It was still, therefore, rather a novelty to him to stay at one of those fine old houses, surrounded with hereditary acres, which from the first of his coming to England he had thought of with such curiosity and such envy. He proposed to himself to see as many of them as possible, but he disliked to do things in a hurry, or when his mind was preoccupied, as it was so apt to be, with what he believed to be business of importance. He kept the country-houses in reserve; he would take them up in their order, after he should have got a little more used to London. Without hesitation, however, he had accepted the invitation to Longlands; it had come to him in a simple and familiar note from Lady Demesne, with whom he had no acquaintance. He knew of her return from Cannes, where she had spent the whole winter, for he had seen it related in a Sunday newspaper; yet it was with a certain surprise that he heard from her in these informal terms. "Dear Mr. Waterville," she wrote, "my son tells me that you will perhaps be able to come down here on the 17th, to spend two or three days. If you can, it will give us much pleasure. We can promise you the society of your charming countrywoman, Mrs. Headway."

He had seen Mrs. Headway; she had written to him a fortnight before from an hotel in Cork Street, to say that she had arrived in London for the season, and should be very glad to see him. He had gone to see her, trembling with the fear that she would break ground about her presentation; but he was agreeably surprised to observe that she neglected this topic. She had spent the winter in Rome, travelling directly from that city to England, with just a little stop in Paris, to buy a few clothes. She had taken much satisfaction in Rome, where she made many friends; she assured him that she knew half the Roman nobility. "They are charming people; they have only one fault, they stay too long," she said. And, in answer to his inquiring glance, "I mean when they come to see you," she explained. "They used to come every evening, and they wanted to stay till the next day. They were all princes and counts. I used to give them cigars, etc. I knew as many people as I wanted," she added, in a moment, discovering perhaps in Waterville's eye the traces of that sympathy with which six months before he had listened to her account of her discomfiture in New York. "There were lots of English; I knew all the English, and I mean to visit them here. The Americans waited to see what the English would do, so as to do the opposite. Thanks to that, I was spared some precious specimens. There are, you know, some fearful ones. Besides, in Rome, society doesn't matter, if you have a feeling for the ruins and the Campagna; I had an immense feeling for the Campagna. I was always mooning round in some damp old temple. It reminded me a good deal of the country round San Diego—if it hadn't been for the temples. I liked to think it all over, when I was driving round; I was always brooding over the past." At this moment, however, Mrs. Headway had dismissed the past; she was prepared to give herself up wholly to the actual. She wished Waterville to advise her as to how she should live—what she should do. Should she stay at a hotel or should she take a house? She guessed she had better take a house, if she could find a nice one. Max wanted to look for one, and she didn't know but she'd let him; he got her such a nice one in Rome. She said nothing about Sir Arthur Demesne, who, it seemed to Waterville, would have been her natural guide and sponsor; he wondered whether her relations with the baronet had come to an end. Waterville had met him a couple of times since the opening of Parliament, and they had exchanged twenty words, none of which, however, had reference to Mrs. Headway. Waterville had been recalled to London just after the incident of which he was witness in the court of the Hôtel Meurice; and all he knew of its consequence was what he had learned from Littlemore, who, on his way back to America, where he had suddenly ascertained that there were reasons for his spending the winter, passed through the British capital. Littlemore had reported that Mrs. Headway was enchanted with Lady Demesne, and had no words to speak of her kindness and sweetness. "She told me she liked to know her son's friends, and I told her I liked to know my friends' mothers," Mrs. Headway had related. "I should be willing to be old if I could be like that," she had added, oblivious for the moment that she could scarcely pretend to belong to a budding generation. The mother and son, at any rate, had retired to Cannes together, and at this moment Littlemore had received letters from home which caused him to start for Arizona. Mrs. Headway had accordingly been left to her own devices, and he was afraid she had bored herself, though Mrs. Bagshaw had called upon her. In November she had travelled to Italy, not by way of Cannes.

"What do you suppose she'll do in Rome?" Waterville had asked; his imagination failing him here, for he had not yet trodden the Seven Hills.

"I haven't the least idea. And I don't care!" Littlemore added in a moment. Before he left London he mentioned to Waterville that Mrs. Headway, on his going to take leave of her in Paris, had made another, and a rather unexpected attack. "About the society business—she said I must really do something—she couldn't go on in that way. And she appealed to me in the name—I don't think I quite know how to say it."

"I should be very glad if you would try," said Waterville, who was constantly reminding himself that Americans in Europe were, after all, in a manner, to a man in his position, as the sheep to the shepherd.

"Well, in the name of the affection that we had formerly entertained for each other."

"The affection?"

"So she was good enough to call it. But I deny it all. If one had to have an affection for every woman one used to sit up 'evenings' with——!" And Littlemore paused, not defining the result of such an obligation. Waterville tried to imagine what it would be; while his friend embarked for New York, without telling him how, after all, he had resisted Mrs. Headway's attack.

At Christmas Waterville knew of Sir Arthur's return to England, and believed that he also knew that the baronet had not gone down to Rome. He had a theory that Lady Demesne was a very clever woman—clever enough to make her son do what she preferred, and yet also make him think it his own choice. She had been politic, accommodating, about going to

see Mrs. Headway; but, having seen her and judged her, she
had determined to break the thing off. She had been sweet
and kind, as Mrs. Headway said, because for the moment that
was easiest; but she had made her last visit on the same occasion as her first. She had been sweet and kind, but she had
set her face as a stone, and if poor Mrs. Headway, arriving in
London for the season, expected to find any vague promises
redeemed, she would taste of the bitterness of shattered
hopes. He had made up his mind that, shepherd as he was,
and Mrs. Headway one of his sheep, it was none of his present
duty to run about after her, especially as she could be trusted
not to stray too far. He saw her a second time, and she still
said nothing about Sir Arthur. Waterville, who always had a
theory, said to himself that she was waiting, that the baronet
had not turned up. She was also getting into a house; the
courier had found her in Chesterfield Street, Mayfair, a little
gem, which was to cost her what jewels cost. After all this,
Waterville was greatly surprised at Lady Demesne's note, and
he went down to Longlands with much the same impatience
with which, in Paris, he would have gone, if he had been able,
to the first night of a new comedy. It seemed to him that,
through a sudden stroke of good fortune, he had received a
billet d'auteur.

It was agreeable to him to arrive at an English country-
house at the close of the day. He liked the drive from the
station in the twilight, the sight of the fields and copses and
cottages, vague and lonely in contrast to his definite, lighted
goal; the sound of the wheels on the long avenue, which
turned and wound repeatedly without bringing him to what
he reached however at last—the wide, gray front, with a glow
in its scattered windows and a sweep of still firmer gravel up
to the door. The front at Longlands, which was of this sober
complexion, had a grand, pompous air; it was attributed to
the genius of Sir Christopher Wren. There were wings which
came forward in a semicircle, with statues placed at intervals
on the cornice; so that in the flattering dusk it looked like an
Italian palace, erected through some magical evocation in an
English park. Waterville had taken a late train, which left him
but twenty minutes to dress for dinner. He prided himself
considerably on the art of dressing both quickly and well; but

this operation left him no time to inquire whether the apartment to which he had been assigned befitted the dignity of a
Secretary of Legation. On emerging from his room he found
there was an ambassador in the house, and this discovery was
a check to uneasy reflections. He tacitly assumed that he
would have had a better room if it had not been for the ambassador, who was of course counted first. The large brilliant
house gave an impression of the last century and of foreign
taste, of light colours, high vaulted ceilings, with pale myth-
ological frescoes, gilded doors, surmounted by old French
panels, faded tapestries and delicate damasks, stores of ancient
china, among which great jars of pink roses were conspicuous.
The people in the house had assembled for dinner in the principal hall, which was animated by a fire of great logs, and the
company was so numerous that Waterville was afraid he was
the last. Lady Demesne gave him a smile and a touch of her
hand; she was very tranquil, and, saying nothing in particular,
treated him as if he had been a constant visitor. Waterville was
not sure whether he liked this or hated it; but these alternatives mattered equally little to his hostess, who looked at her
guests as if to see whether the number were right. The master
of the house was talking to a lady before the fire; when he
caught sight of Waterville across the room, he waved him
"how d'ye do," with an air of being delighted to see him. He
had never had that air in Paris, and Waterville had a chance
to observe, what he had often heard, to how much greater
advantage the English appear in their country-houses. Lady
Demesne turned to him again, with her sweet vague smile,
which looked as if it were the same for everything.

"We are waiting for Mrs. Headway," she said.

"Ah, she has arrived?" Waterville had quite forgotten her.

"She came at half-past five. At six she went to dress. She
has had two hours."

"Let us hope that the results will be proportionate," said
Waterville, smiling.

"Oh, the results; I don't know," Lady Demesne murmured,
without looking at him; and in these simple words Waterville
saw the confirmation of his theory that she was playing a deep
game. He wondered whether he should sit next to Mrs. Headway at dinner, and hoped, with due deference to this lady's

charms, that he should have something more novel. The results of a toilet which she had protracted through two hours were presently visible. She appeared on the staircase which descended to the hall, and which, for three minutes, as she came down rather slowly, facing the people beneath, placed her in considerable relief. Waterville, as he looked at her, felt that this was a moment of importance for her: it was virtually her entrance into English society. Mrs. Headway entered English society very well, with her charming smile upon her lips, and with the trophies of the Rue de la Paix trailing behind her. She made a portentous rustling as she moved. People turned their eyes toward her; there was soon a perceptible diminution of talk, though talk had not been particularly audible. She looked very much alone, and it was rather pretentious of her to come down last, though it was possible that this was simply because, before her glass, she had been unable to please herself. For she evidently felt the importance of the occasion, and Waterville was sure that her heart was beating. She was very valiant, however; she smiled more intensely, and advanced like a woman who was used to being looked at. She had at any rate the support of knowing that she was pretty; for nothing on this occasion was wanting to her prettiness, and the determination to succeed, which might have made her hard, was veiled in the virtuous consciousness that she had neglected nothing. Lady Demesne went forward to meet her; Sir Arthur took no notice of her; and presently Waterville found himself proceeding to dinner with the wife of an ecclesiastic, to whom Lady Demesne had presented him for this purpose, when the hall was almost empty. The rank of this ecclesiastic in the hierarchy he learned early on the morrow; but in the meantime it seemed to him strange, somehow, that in England ecclesiastics should have wives. English life, even at the end of a year, was full of those surprises. The lady, however, was very easily accounted for; she was in no sense a violent exception, and there had been no need of the Reformation to produce her. Her name was Mrs. April; she was wrapped in a large lace shawl; to eat her dinner she removed but one glove, and the other gave Waterville at moments an odd impression that the whole repast, in spite of its great completeness, was something of the picnic order. Mrs. Headway

was opposite, at a little distance; she had been taken in, as
Waterville learned from his neighbour, by a general, a gentleman with a lean aquiline face and a cultivated whisker, and
she had on the other side a smart young man of an identity
less definite. Poor Sir Arthur sat between two ladies much
older than himself, whose names, redolent of history, Waterville had often heard, and had associated with figures more
romantic. Mrs. Headway gave Waterville no greeting; she evidently had not seen him till they were seated at table, when
she simply stared at him with a violence of surprise that for a
moment almost effaced her smile. It was a copious and well-
ordered banquet, but as Waterville looked up and down the
table he wondered whether some of its elements might not
be a little dull. As he made this reflection he became conscious
that he was judging the affair much more from Mrs. Headway's point of view than from his own. He knew no one but
Mrs. April, who, displaying an almost motherly desire to give
him information, told him the names of many of their companions; in return for which he explained to her that he was
not in that set. Mrs. Headway got on in perfection with her
general; Waterville watched her more than he appeared to do,
and saw that the general, who evidently was a cool hand, was
drawing her out. Waterville hoped she would be careful. He
was a man of fancy, in his way, and as he compared her with
the rest of the company he said to himself that she was a very
plucky little woman, and that her present undertaking had a
touch of the heroic. She was alone against many, and her op-
ponents were a very serried phalanx; those who were there
represented a thousand others. They looked so different from
her that to the eye of the imagination she stood very much
on her merits. All those people seemed so completely made
up, so unconscious of effort, so surrounded with things to
rest upon; the men with their clean complexions, their well-
hung chins, their cold, pleasant eyes, their shoulders set back,
their absence of gesture; the women, several very handsome,
half strangled in strings of pearls, with smooth plain tresses,
seeming to look at nothing in particular, supporting silence
as if it were as becoming as candle-light, yet talking a little,
sometimes, in fresh rich voices. They were all wrapped in a
community of ideas, of traditions; they understood each

other's accent, even each other's variations. Mrs. Headway, with all her prettiness, seemed to transcend these variations; she looked foreign, exaggerated; she had too much expression; she might have been engaged for the evening. Waterville remarked, moreover, that English society was always looking out for amusement, and that its transactions were conducted on a cash basis. If Mrs. Headway were amusing enough she would probably succeed, and her fortune—if fortune there was—would not be a hindrance.

In the drawing-room, after dinner, he went up to her, but she gave him no greeting. She only looked at him with an expression he had never seen before—a strange, bold expression of displeasure.

"Why have you come down here?" she asked. "Have you come to watch me?"

Waterville coloured to the roots of his hair. He knew it was terribly little like a diplomatist; but he was unable to control his blushes. Besides, he was shocked, he was angry, and in addition, he was mystified. "I came because I was asked," he said.

"Who asked you?"

"The same person that asked you, I suppose—Lady Demesne."

"She's an old cat!" Mrs. Headway exclaimed, turning away from him.

He turned away from her as well. He didn't know what he had done to deserve such treatment. It was a complete surprise; he had never seen her like that before. She was a very vulgar woman; that was the way people talked, he supposed, at San Diego. He threw himself almost passionately into the conversation of the others, who all seemed to him, possibly a little by contrast, extraordinarily genial and friendly. He had not, however, the consolation of seeing Mrs. Headway punished for her rudeness, for she was not in the least neglected. On the contrary, in the part of the room where she sat the group was denser, and every now and then it was agitated with unanimous laughter. If she should amuse them, he said to himself, she would succeed, and evidently she was amusing them.

VII.

If she was strange, he had not come to the end of her strangeness. The next day was a Sunday, and uncommonly fine; he was down before breakfast, and took a walk in the park, stopping to gaze at the thin-legged deer, scattered like pins on a velvet cushion over some of the remoter slopes, and wandering along the edge of a large sheet of ornamental water, which had a temple, in imitation of that of Vesta, on an island in the middle. He thought at this time no more about Mrs. Headway; he only reflected that these stately objects had for more than a hundred years furnished a background to a great deal of family history. A little more reflection would perhaps have suggested to him that Mrs. Headway was possibly an incident of some importance in the history of a family. Two or three ladies failed to appear at breakfast; Mrs. Headway was one of them.

"She tells me she never leaves her room till noon," he heard Lady Demesne say to the general, her companion of the previous evening, who had asked about her. "She takes three hours to dress."

"She's a monstrous clever woman!" the general exclaimed. "To do it in three hours?"

"No, I mean the way she keeps her wits about her."

"Yes; I think she's very clever," said Lady Demesne, in a tone in which Waterville flattered himself that he saw more meaning than the general could see. There was something in this tall, straight, deliberate woman, who seemed at once benevolent and distant, that Waterville admired. With her delicate surface, her conventional mildness, he could see that she was very strong; she had set her patience upon a height, and she carried it like a diadem. She had very little to say to Waterville, but every now and then she made some inquiry of him that showed she had not forgotten him. Demesne himself was apparently in excellent spirits, though there was nothing bustling in his deportment, and he only went about looking very fresh and fair, as if he took a bath every hour or two, and very secure against the unexpected. Waterville had less conversation with him than with his mother; but the young

man had found occasion to say to him the night before, in
the smoking-room, that he was delighted Waterville had been
able to come, and that if he was fond of real English scenery
there were several things about there he should like very much
to show him.

"You must give me an hour or two before you go, you
know; I really think there are some things you'll like."

Sir Arthur spoke as if Waterville would be very fastidious;
he seemed to wish to attach a vague importance to him. On
the Sunday morning after breakfast he asked Waterville if he
should care to go to church; most of the ladies and several of
the men were going.

"It's just as you please, you know; but it's rather a pretty
walk across the fields, and a curious little church of King
Stephen's time."

Waterville knew what this meant; it was already a picture.
Besides, he liked going to church, especially when he sat in
the Squire's pew, which was sometimes as big as a boudoir.
So he replied that he should be delighted. Then he added,
without explaining his reason—

"Is Mrs. Headway going?"

"I really don't know," said his host, with an abrupt change
of tone—as if Waterville had asked him whether the housekeeper were going.

"The English are awfully queer!" Waterville indulged mentally in this exclamation, to which since his arrival in England
he had had recourse whenever he encountered a gap in the
consistency of things. The church was even a better picture
than Sir Arthur's description of it, and Waterville said to himself that Mrs. Headway had been a great fool not to come.
He knew what she was after; she wished to study English life,
so that she might take possession of it, and to pass in among
a hedge of bobbing rustics, and sit among the monuments of
the old Demesnes, would have told her a great deal about
English life. If she wished to fortify herself for the struggle
she had better come to that old church. When he returned to
Longlands—he had walked back across the meadows with the
canon's wife, who was a vigorous pedestrian—it wanted half
an hour of luncheon, and he was unwilling to go indoors. He
remembered that he had not yet seen the gardens, and he

wandered away in search of them. They were on a scale which enabled him to find them without difficulty, and they looked as if they had been kept up unremittingly for a century or two. He had not advanced very far between their blooming borders when he heard a voice that he recognised, and a moment after, at the turn of an alley, he came upon Mrs. Headway, who was attended by the master of Longlands. She was bareheaded beneath her parasol, which she flung back, stopping short, as she beheld her compatriot.

"Oh, it's Mr. Waterville come to spy me out, as usual!" It was with this remark that she greeted the slightly-embarrassed young man.

"Hallo! you've come home from church," Sir Arthur said, pulling out his watch.

Waterville was struck with his coolness. He admired it; for, after all, he said to himself, it must have been disagreeable to him to be interrupted. He felt a little like a fool, and wished he had kept Mrs. April with him, to give him the air of having come for her sake.

Mrs. Headway looked adorably fresh, in a toilet which Waterville, who had his ideas on such matters, was sure would not be regarded as the proper thing for a Sunday morning in an English country-house: a *négligé* of white flounces and frills, interspersed with yellow ribbons—a garment which Madame de Pompadour might have worn when she received a visit from Louis XV., but would probably not have worn when she went into the world. The sight of this costume gave the finishing touch to Waterville's impression that Mrs. Headway knew, on the whole, what she was about. She would take a line of her own; she would not be too accommodating. She would not come down to breakfast; she would not go to church; she would wear on Sunday mornings little elaborately informal dresses, and look dreadfully un-British and un-Protestant. Perhaps, after all, this was better. She began to talk with a certain volubility.

"Isn't this too lovely? I walked all the way from the house. I'm not much at walking, but the grass in this place is like a parlour. The whole thing is beyond everything. Sir Arthur, you ought to go and look after the Ambassador; it's shameful the way I've kept you. You didn't care about the Ambassador?

You said just now you had scarcely spoken to him, and you must make it up. I never saw such a way of neglecting your guests. Is that the usual style over here? Go and take him out for a ride, or make him play a game of billiards. Mr. Waterville will take me home; besides, I want to scold him for spying on me."

Waterville sharply resented this accusation. "I had no idea you were here," he declared.

"We weren't hiding," said Sir Arthur quietly. "Perhaps you'll see Mrs. Headway back to the house. I think I ought to look after old Davidoff. I believe lunch is at two."

He left them, and Waterville wandered through the gardens with Mrs. Headway. She immediately wished to know if he had come there to look after her; but this inquiry was unaccompanied, to his surprise, with the acrimony she had displayed the night before. He was determined not to let that pass, however; when people had treated him in that way they should not be allowed to forget it.

"Do you suppose I am always thinking of you?" he asked. "You're out of my mind sometimes. I came here to look at the gardens, and if you hadn't spoken to me I should have passed on."

Mrs. Headway was perfectly good-natured; she appeared not even to hear his defence. "He has got two other places," she simply rejoined. "That's just what I wanted to know."

But Waterville would not be turned away from his grievance. That mode of reparation to a person whom you had insulted, which consisted in forgetting that you had done so, was doubtless largely in use in New Mexico; but a person of honour demanded something more. "What did you mean last night by accusing me of having come down here to watch you? You must excuse me if I tell you that I think you were rather rude." The sting of this accusation lay in the fact that there was a certain amount of truth in it; yet for a moment Mrs. Headway, looking very blank, failed to recognise the allusion. "She's a barbarian, after all," thought Waterville. "She thinks a woman may slap a man's face and run away!"

"Oh!" cried Mrs. Headway, suddenly, "I remember, I was angry with you; I didn't expect to see you. But I didn't really care about it at all. Every now and then I am angry, like that, and I work it off on any one that's handy. But it's over in three minutes, and I never think of it again. I was angry last night; I was furious with the old woman."

"With the old woman?"

"With Sir Arthur's mother. She has no business here, any way. In this country, when the husband dies, they're expected to clear out. She has a house of her own, ten miles from here, and she has another in Portman Square; so she's got plenty of places to live. But she sticks—she sticks to him like a plaster. All of a sudden it came over me that she didn't invite me here because she liked me, but because she suspects me. She's afraid we'll make a match, and she thinks I ain't good enough for her son. She must think I'm in a great hurry to get hold of him. I never went after him, he came after me. I should never have thought of anything if it hadn't been for him. He began it last summer at Homburg; he wanted to know why I didn't come to England; he told me I should have great suc-cess. He doesn't know much about it, any way; he hasn't got much gumption. But he's a very nice man, all the same; it's very pleasant to see him surrounded by his——" And Mrs. Headway paused a moment, looking admiringly about her—"Surrounded by all his old heirlooms. I like the old place," she went on; "it's beautifully mounted; I'm quite satisfied with what I've seen. I thought Lady Demesne was very friendly; she left a card on me in London, and very soon after, she wrote to me to ask me here. But I'm very quick; I some-times see things in a flash. I saw something yesterday, when she came to speak to me at dinner-time. She saw I looked pretty, and it made her blue with rage; she hoped I would be ugly. I should like very much to oblige her; but what can one do? Then I saw that she had asked me here only because he insisted. He didn't come to see me when I first arrived—he never came near me for ten days. She managed to prevent him; she got him to make some promise. But he changed his mind after a little, and then he had to do something really polite. He called three days in succession, and he made her come. She's one of those women that resists as long as she can, and then seems to give in, while she's really resisting more than ever. She hates me like poison; I don't know what she thinks I've done. She's very underhand; she's a regular old cat. When I saw you last night at dinner, I thought she had got you here to help her."

"To help her?" Waterville asked.

"To tell her about me. To give her information, that she can make use of against me. You may tell her what you like!"

Waterville was almost breathless with the attention he had given this extraordinary burst of confidence, and now he really felt faint. He stopped short; Mrs. Headway went on a few steps, and then, stopping too, turned and looked at him. "You're the most unspeakable woman!" he exclaimed. She seemed to him indeed a barbarian.

She laughed at him—he felt she was laughing at his expression of face—and her laugh rang through the stately gardens. "What sort of a woman is that?"

"You've got no delicacy," said Waterville, resolutely.

She coloured quickly, though, strange to say, she appeared not to be angry. "No delicacy?" she repeated.

"You ought to keep those things to yourself."

"Oh, I know what you mean; I talk about everything. When I'm excited I've got to talk. But I must do things in my own way. I've got plenty of delicacy, when people are nice to me. Ask Arthur Demesne if I ain't delicate—ask George Littlemore if I ain't. Don't stand there all day; come in to lunch!" And Mrs. Headway resumed her walk, while Rupert Waterville, raising his eyes for a moment, slowly overtook her. "Wait till I get settled; then I'll be delicate," she pursued. "You can't be delicate when you're trying to save your life. It's very well for *you* to talk, with the whole American Legation to back you. Of course I'm excited. I've got hold of this thing, and I don't mean to let go!" Before they reached the house she told him why he had been invited to Longlands at the same time as herself. Waterville would have liked to believe that his personal attractions sufficiently explained the fact; but she took no account of this supposition. Mrs. Headway preferred to think that she lived in an element of ingenious machination, and that most things that happened had reference to herself. Waterville had been asked because he represented, however modestly, the American Legation, and their host had a friendly desire to make it appear that this pretty American visitor, of whom no one knew anything, was under the protection of that establishment. "It would start me better," said Mrs. Headway, serenely. "You can't help yourself—you've helped to start me. If he had known the Minister he would have asked him—or the first secretary. But he don't know them."

They reached the house by the time Mrs. Headway had developed this idea, which gave Waterville a pretext more than sufficient for detaining her in the portico. "Do you mean to say Sir Arthur told you this?" he inquired, almost sternly.

"Told me? Of course not! Do you suppose I would let him take the tone with me that I need any favours? I should like to hear him tell me that I'm in want of assistance!"

"I don't see why he shouldn't—at the pace you go yourself. You say it to every one."

"To every one? I say it to you, and to George Little-more—when I'm nervous. I say it to you because I like you, and to him because I'm afraid of him. I'm not in the least afraid of you, by the way. I'm all alone—I haven't got any one. I must have some comfort, mustn't I? Sir Arthur scolded me for putting you off last night—he noticed it; and that was what made me guess his idea."

"I'm much obliged to him," said Waterville, rather be-wildered.

"So mind you answer for me. Don't you want to give me your arm, to go in?"

"You're a most extraordinary combination," he murmured, as she stood smiling at him.

"Oh, come, don't *you* fall in love with me!" she cried, with a laugh; and, without taking his arm, passed in before him.

That evening, before he went to dress for dinner, Waterville wandered into the library, where he felt sure that he should find some superior bindings. There was no one in the room, and he spent a happy half-hour among the treasures of liter-ature and the triumphs of old morocco. He had a great esteem for good literature; he held that it should have handsome covers. The daylight had begun to wane, but whenever, in the rich-looking dimness, he made out the glimmer of a well-gilded back, he took down the volume and carried it to one of the deep-set windows. He had just finished the inspection of a delightfully fragrant folio, and was about to carry it back to its niche, when he found himself standing face to face with Lady Demesne. He was startled for a moment, for her tall, slim figure, her fair visage, which looked white in the high, brown room, and the air of serious intention with which she presented herself, gave something spectral to her presence. He saw her smile, however, and heard her say, in that tone of hers which was sweet almost to sadness, "Are you looking at our books? I'm afraid they are rather dull."

"Dull? Why, they are as bright as the day they were bound." And he turned the glittering panels of his folio towards her.

"I'm afraid I haven't looked at them for a long time," she murmured, going nearer to the window, where she stood looking out. Beyond the clear pane the park stretched away, with the grayness of evening beginning to hang itself on the great limbs of the oaks. The place appeared cold and empty, and the trees had an air of conscious importance, as if nature herself had been bribed somehow to take the side of country families. Lady Demesne was not an easy person to talk with; she was neither spontaneous nor abundant; she was conscious of herself, conscious of many things. Her very simplicity was conventional, though it was rather a noble convention. You might have pitied her, if you had seen that she lived in constant unrelaxed communion with certain rigid ideals. This made her at times seem tired, like a person who has undertaken too much. She gave an impression of still brightness, which was not at all brilliancy, but a carefully-preserved purity. She said nothing for a moment, and there was an appearance of design in her silence, as if she wished to let him know that she had a certain business with him, without taking the trouble to announce it. She had been accustomed to expect that people would suppose things, and to be saved the trouble of explanations. Waterville made some haphazard remark about the beauty of the evening (in point of fact, the weather had changed for the worse), to which she vouchsafed no reply. Then, presently, she said, with her usual gentleness, "I hoped I should find you here—I wish to ask you something."

"Anything I can tell you—I shall be delighted!" Waterville exclaimed.

She gave him a look, not imperious, almost appealing, which seemed to say—"Please be very simple—very simple indeed." Then she glanced about her, as if there had been other people in the room; she didn't wish to appear closeted with him, or to have come on purpose. There she was, at any rate, and she went on. "When my son told me he should ask you to come down, I was very glad. I mean, of course, that we were delighted——"And she paused a moment. Then she added, simply, "I want to ask you about Mrs. Headway."

"Ah, here it is!" cried Waterville within himself. More superficially, he smiled, as agreeably as possible, and said, "Ah yes, I see!"

"Do you mind my asking you? I hope you don't mind. I haven't any one else to ask."

"Your son knows her much better than I do." Waterville said this without an intention of malice, simply to escape from the difficulties of his situation; but after he had said it, he was almost frightened by its mocking sound.

"I don't think he knows her. She knows him, which is very different. When I ask him about her, he merely tells me she is fascinating. She *is* fascinating," said her ladyship, with inimitable dryness.

"So I think, myself. I like her very much," Waterville rejoined, cheerfully.

"You are in all the better position to speak of her, then."

"To speak well of her," said Waterville, smiling.

"Of course, if you can. I should be delighted to hear you do that. That's what I wish—to hear some good of her."

It might have seemed, after this, that nothing would have remained but for Waterville to launch himself in a panegyric of his mysterious countrywoman; but he was no more to be tempted into that danger than into another. "I can only say I like her," he repeated. "She has been very kind to me."

"Every one seems to like her," said Lady Demesne, with an unstudied effect of pathos. "She is certainly very amusing."

"She is very good-natured; she has lots of good intentions."

"What do you call good intentions?" asked Lady Demesne, very sweetly.

"Well, I mean that she wants to be friendly and pleasant."

"Of course you have to defend her. She's your countrywoman."

"To defend her—I must wait till she's attacked," said Waterville, laughing.

"That's very true. I needn't call your attention to the fact that I am not attacking her. I should never attack a person staying in this house. I only want to know something about her, and if you can't tell me, perhaps at least you can mention some one who will."

"She'll tell you herself. Tell you by the hour!"

"What she has told my son? I shouldn't understand it. My son doesn't understand it. It's very strange. I rather hoped you might explain it."

Waterville was silent a moment. "I'm afraid I can't explain Mrs. Headway," he remarked at last.

"I see you admit she is very peculiar."

Waterville hesitated again. "It's too great a responsibility to answer you." He felt that he was very disobliging; he knew exactly what Lady Demesne wished him to say. He was unprepared to blight the reputation of Mrs. Headway to accommodate Lady Demesne; and yet, with his active little imagination, he could enter perfectly into the feelings of this tender, formal, serious woman, who—it was easy to see—had looked for her own happiness in the cultivation of duty and in extreme constancy to two or three objects of devotion chosen once for all. She must, indeed, have had a vision of things which would represent Mrs. Headway as both displeasing and dangerous. But he presently became aware that she had taken his last words as a concession in which she might find help.

"You know why I ask you these things, then?"

"I think I have an idea," said Waterville, persisting in irrelevant laughter. His laugh sounded foolish in his own ears.

"If you know that, I think you ought to assist me." Her tone changed as she spoke these words; there was a quick tremor in it; he could see it was a confession of distress. Her distress was deep; he immediately felt that it must have been, before she made up her mind to speak to him. He was sorry for her, and determined to be very serious.

"If I could help you I would. But my position is very difficult."

"It's not so difficult as mine!" She was going all lengths; she was really appealing to him. "I don't imagine that you are under any obligation to Mrs. Headway—you seem to me very different," she added.

Waterville was not insensible to any discrimination that told in his favour; but these words gave him a slight shock, as if they had been an attempt at bribery. "I am surprised that you don't like her," he ventured to observe.

Lady Demesne looked out of the window a little. "I don't think you are really surprised, though possibly you try to be. I don't like her, at any rate, and I can't fancy why my son should. She's very pretty, and she appears to be very clever; but I don't trust her. I don't know what has taken possession of him; it is not usual in his family to marry people like that. I don't think she's a lady. The person I should wish for him would be so very different—perhaps you can see what I mean. There's something in her history that we don't understand. My son understands it no better than I. If you could only explain to us, that might be a help. I treat you with great confidence the first time I see you; it's because I don't know where to turn. I am exceedingly anxious."

It was very plain that she was anxious; her manner had become more vehement; her eyes seemed to shine in the thickening dusk. "Are you very sure there is danger?" Waterville asked. "Has he asked her to marry him, and has she consented?"

"If I wait till they settle it all, it will be too late. I have reason to believe that my son is not engaged, but he is terribly entangled. At the same time he is very uneasy, and that may save him yet. He has a great sense of honour. He is not satisfied about her past life; he doesn't know what to think of what we have been told. Even what she admits is so strange. She has been married four or five times—she has been divorced again and again—it seems so extraordinary. She tells him that in America it is different, and I daresay you have not our ideas; but really there is a limit to everything. There must have been some great irregularities—I am afraid some great scandals. It's dreadful to have to accept such things. He has not told me all this; but it's not necessary he should tell me; I know him well enough to guess."

"Does he know that you have spoken to me?" Waterville asked.

"Not in the least. But I must tell you that I shall repeat to him anything that you may say against her."

"I had better say nothing, then. It's very delicate. Mrs. Headway is quite undefended. One may like her or not, of course. I have seen nothing of her that is not perfectly correct."

"And you have heard nothing?"

Waterville remembered Littlemore's assertion that there were cases in which a man was bound in honour to tell an untruth, and he wondered whether this were such a case. Lady Demesne imposed herself, she made him believe in the reality of her grievance, and he saw the gulf that divided her from a pushing little woman who had lived with Western editors. She was right to wish not to be connected with Mrs. Headway. After all, there had been nothing in his relations with that lady to make it incumbent on him to lie for her. He had not sought her acquaintance, she had sought his; she had sent for him to come and see her. And yet he couldn't give her away, as they said in New York; that stuck in his throat. "I am afraid I really can't say anything. And it wouldn't matter. Your son won't give her up because I happen not to like her."

"If he were to believe she has done wrong, he would give her up."

"Well, I have no right to say so," said Waterville.

Lady Demesne turned away; she was much disappointed in him. He was afraid she was going to break out—"Why, then, do you suppose I asked you here?" She quitted her place near the window, and was apparently about to leave the room. But she stopped short. "You know something against her, but you won't say it."

Waterville hugged his folio and looked awkward. "You attribute things to me. I shall never say anything."

"Of course you are perfectly free. There is some one else who knows, I think—another American—a gentleman who was in Paris when my son was there. I have forgotten his name."

"A friend of Mrs. Headway's? I suppose you mean George Littlemore."

"Yes—Mr. Littlemore. He has a sister, whom I have met; I didn't know she was his sister till to-day. Mrs. Headway spoke of her, but I find she doesn't know her. That itself is a proof, I think. Do you think *he* would help me?" Lady Demesne asked, very simply.

"I doubt it, but you can try."

"I wish he had come with you. Do you think he would come?"

"He is in America at this moment, but I believe he soon comes back."

"I shall go to his sister; I will ask her to bring him to see me. She is extremely nice; I think she will understand. Unfortunately there is very little time."

"Don't count too much on Littlemore," said Waterville, gravely.

"You men have no pity."

"Why should we pity you? How can Mrs. Headway hurt such a person as you?"

Lady Demesne hesitated a moment. "It hurts me to hear her voice."

"Her voice is very sweet."

"Possibly. But she's horrible!"

This was too much, it seemed to Waterville; poor Mrs. Headway was extremely open to criticism, and he himself had declared she was a barbarian. Yet she was not horrible. "It's for your son to pity you. If he doesn't, how can you expect it of others?"

"Oh, but he does!" And with a majesty that was more striking even than her logic, Lady Demesne moved towards the door.

Waterville advanced to open it for her, and as she passed out he said, "There's one thing you can do—try to like her!"

She shot him a terrible glance. "That would be worst of all!"

VIII.

George Littlemore arrived in London on the twentieth of May, and one of the first things he did was to go and see Waterville at the Legation, where he made known to him that he had taken for the rest of the season a house at Queen Anne's Gate, so that his sister and her husband, who, under

the pressure of diminished rents, had let their own town residence, might come up and spend a couple of months with
him.

"One of the consequences of your having a house will be
that you will have to entertain Mrs. Headway," Waterville
said.

Littlemore sat there with his hands crossed upon his stick;
he looked at Waterville with an eye that failed to kindle at the
mention of this lady's name. "Has she got into European society?" he asked, rather languidly.

"Very much, I should say. She has a house, and a carriage,
and diamonds, and everything handsome. She seems already
to know a lot of people; they put her name in the *Morning
Post*. She has come up very quickly; she's almost famous.
Every one is asking about her—you'll be plied with questions."

Littlemore listened gravely. "How did she get in?"

"She met a large party at Longlands, and made them all
think her great fun. They must have taken her up; she only
wanted a start."

Littlemore seemed suddenly to be struck with the gro-
tesqueness of this news, to which his first response was a burst
of quick laughter. "To think of Nancy Beck! The people here
are queer people. There's no one they won't go after. They
wouldn't touch her in New York."

"Oh, New York's old-fashioned," said Waterville; and he
announced to his friend that Lady Demesne was very eager
for his arrival, and wanted to make him help her prevent her
son's bringing such a person into the family. Littlemore apparently was not alarmed at her ladyship's projects, and intimated, in the manner of a man who thought them rather
impertinent, that he could trust himself to keep out of her
way. "It isn't a proper marriage, at any rate," Waterville
declared.

"Why not, if he loves her?"

"Oh, if that's all you want!" cried Waterville, with a degree
of cynicism that rather surprised his companion. "Would you
marry her yourself?"

"Certainly, if I were in love with her."

"You took care not to be that."

"Yes, I did—and so Demesne had better have done. But since he's bitten——!" and Littlemore terminated his sentence in a suppressed yawn.

Waterville presently asked him how he would manage, in view of his sister's advent, about asking Mrs. Headway to his house; and he replied that he would manage by simply not asking her. Upon this, Waterville declared that he was very inconsistent; to which Littlemore rejoined that it was very possible. But he asked whether they couldn't talk about something else than Mrs. Headway. He couldn't enter into the young man's interest in her, and was sure to have enough of her later.

Waterville would have been sorry to give a false idea of his interest in Mrs. Headway; for he flattered himself the feeling had definite limits. He had been two or three times to see her; but it was a relief to think that she was now quite independent of him. There had been no revival of that intimate intercourse which occurred during the visit to Longlands. She could dispense with assistance now; she knew herself that she was in the current of success. She pretended to be surprised at her good fortune, especially at its rapidity; but she was really surprised at nothing. She took things as they came, and, being essentially a woman of action, wasted almost as little time in elation as she would have done in despondence. She talked a great deal about Lord Edward and Lady Margaret, and about such other members of the nobility as had shown a desire to cultivate her acquaintance; professing to understand perfectly the sources of a popularity which apparently was destined to increase. "They come to laugh at me," she said; "they come simply to get things to repeat. I can't open my mouth but they burst into fits. It's a settled thing that I'm an American humourist; if I say the simplest things, they begin to roar. I must express myself somehow; and indeed when I hold my tongue they think me funnier than ever. They repeat what I say to a great person, and a great person told some of them the other night that he wanted to hear me for himself. I'll do for him what I do for the others; no better and no worse. I don't know how I do it; I talk the only way I can. They tell me it isn't so much the things I say as the way I say them. Well, they're very easy to please. They don't care for me; it's only to be able to repeat Mrs. Headway's 'last.' Every one wants to have it first; it's a regular race." When she found what was expected of her, she undertook to supply the article in abundance; and the poor little woman really worked hard at her Americanisms. If the taste of London lay that way, she would do her best to gratify it; it was only a pity she hadn't known it before; she would have made more extensive preparations. She thought it a disadvantage, of old, to live in Arizona, in Dakotah, in the newly-admitted States; but now she perceived that, as she phrased it to herself, this was the best thing that ever had happened to her. She tried to remember all the queer stories she had heard out there, and keenly regretted that she had not taken them down in writing; she drummed up the echoes of the Rocky Mountains, and practised the intonations of the Pacific slope. When she saw her audience in convulsions, she said to herself that this was success, and believed that, if she had only come to London five years sooner, she might have married a duke. That would have been even a more absorbing spectacle for the London world than the actual proceedings of Sir Arthur Demesne, who, however, lived sufficiently in the eye of society to justify the rumour that there were bets about town as to the issue of his already protracted courtship. It was food for curiosity to see a young man of his pattern—one of the few "earnest" young men of the Tory side, with an income sufficient for tastes more marked than those by which he was known—make up to a lady several years older than himself, whose fund of Californian slang was even larger than her stock of dollars. Mrs. Headway had got a good many new ideas since her arrival in London, but she also retained several old ones. The chief of these—it was now a year old—was that Sir Arthur Demesne was the most irreproachable young man in the world. There were, of course, a good many things that he was not. He was not amusing; he was not insinuating; he was not of an absolutely irrepressible ardour. She believed he was constant; but he was certainly not eager. With these things, however, Mrs. Headway could perfectly dispense; she had, in particular, quite outlived the need of being amused. She had had a very exciting life, and her vision of happiness at present was to be magnificently bored. The idea of complete and uncriticised respectability filled her soul with satisfaction; her imagination prostrated itself in the presence of this virtue. She was aware that she had achieved it but ill in her own person; but she could now, at least, connect herself with it by sacred ties. She could prove in that way what was her deepest feeling. This was a religious appreciation of Sir Arthur's great quality—his smooth and rounded, his blooming, lily-like exemption from social flaws.

She was at home when Littlemore went to see her, and surrounded by several visitors, to whom she was giving a late cup of tea, and to whom she introduced her compatriot. He stayed till they dispersed, in spite of the manœuvres of a gentleman who evidently desired to outstay him, but who, whatever might have been his happy fortune on former visits, received on this occasion no encouragement from Mrs. Headway. He looked at Littlemore slowly, beginning with his boots and travelling upwards, as if to discover the reason of so unexpected a preference, and then, without a salutation, left him face to face with their hostess.

"I'm curious to see what you'll do for me, now that you've got your sister with you," Mrs. Headway presently remarked, having heard of this circumstance from Rupert Waterville. "I suppose you'll have to do something, you know. I'm sorry for you; but I don't see how you can get off. You might ask me to dine some day when she's dining out. I would come even then, I think, because I want to keep on the right side of you."

"I call that the wrong side," said Littlemore.

"Yes, I see. It's your sister that's on the right side. You're in rather an embarrassing position, ain't you? However, you take those things very quietly. There's something in you that exasperates me. What does your sister think of me? Does she hate me?"

"She knows nothing about you."

"Have you told her nothing?"

"Never a word."

"Hasn't she asked you? That shows that she hates me. She thinks I ain't creditable to America. I know all that. She wants to show people over here that, however they may be taken in by me, she knows much better. But she'll have to ask you about me; she can't go on for ever. Then what'll you say?"

"That you're the most successful woman in Europe."

"Oh, bother!" cried Mrs. Headway, with irritation.

"Haven't you got into European society?"

"Maybe I have, maybe I haven't. It's too soon to see. I can't tell this season. Every one says I've got to wait till next, to see if it's the same. Sometimes they take you up for a few weeks, and then never know you again. You've got to fasten the thing somehow—to drive in a nail."

"You speak as if it were your coffin," said Littlemore.

"Well, it is a kind of coffin. I'm burying my past!"

Littlemore winced at this. He was tired to death of her past. He changed the subject, and made her talk about London, a topic which she treated with a great deal of humour. She entertained him for half an hour, at the expense of most of her new acquaintances and of some of the most venerable features of the great city. He himself looked at England from the outside, as much as it was possible to do; but in the midst of her familiar allusions to people and things known to her only since yesterday, he was struck with the fact that she would never really be initiated. She buzzed over the surface of things like a fly on a window-pane. She liked it immensely; she was flattered, encouraged, excited; she dropped her confident judgments as if she were scattering flowers, and talked about her intentions, her prospects, her wishes. But she knew no more about English life than about the molecular theory. The words in which he had described her of old to Waterville came back to him: *"Elle ne doute de rien!"* Suddenly she jumped up; she was going out to dine, and it was time to dress. "Before you leave I want you to promise me something," she said offhand, but with a look which he had seen before, and which meant that the point was important. "You'll be sure to be questioned about me." And then she paused.

"How do people know I know you?"

"You haven't bragged about it? Is that what you mean? You can be a brute when you try. They do know it, at any rate. Possibly I may have told them. They'll come to you, to ask about me. I mean from Lady Demesne, She's in an awful state—she's so afraid her son'll marry me."

Littlemore was unable to control a laugh. "I'm not, if he hasn't done it yet."

"He can't make up his mind. He likes me so much, yet he thinks I'm not a woman to marry." It was positively grotesque, the detachment with which she spoke of herself.

"He must be a poor creature if he won't marry you as you are," Littlemore said.

This was not a very gallant form of speech; but Mrs. Headway let it pass. She only replied, "Well, he wants to be very careful, and so he ought to be!"

"If he asks too many questions he's not worth marrying."

"I beg your pardon—he's worth marrying whatever he does—he's worth marrying for me. And I want to marry him—that's what I want to do."

"Is he waiting for me to settle it?"

"He's waiting for I don't know what—for some one to come and tell him that I'm the sweetest of the sweet. Then he'll believe it. Some one who has been out there and knows all about me. Of course you're the man, you're created on purpose. Don't you remember how I told you in Paris that he wanted to ask you? He was ashamed, and he gave it up; he tried to forget me. But now it's all on again; only, meanwhile, his mother has been at him. She works at him night and day, like a weasel in a hole, to persuade him that I'm far beneath him. He's very fond of her, and he's very open to influence—I mean from his mother, not from any one else. Except me, of course. Oh, I've influenced him, I've explained everything fifty times over. But some things are rather complicated, don't you know; and he keeps coming back to them. He wants every little speck explained. He won't come to you himself, but his mother will, or she'll send some of her people. I guess she'll send the lawyer—the family solicitor, they call him. She wanted to send him out to America to make inquiries, only she didn't know where to send. Of course I couldn't be expected to give the places, they've got to find them out for themselves. She knows all about you, and she has made the acquaintance of your sister. So you see how much I know. She's waiting for you; she means to catch you. She has an idea she can fix you—make you say what'll meet her views. Then she'll lay it before Sir Arthur. So you'll be so good as to deny everything."

Littlemore listened to this little address attentively, but the conclusion left him staring. "You don't mean that anything I can say will make a difference?"

"Don't be affected! You know it will as well as I."

"You make him out a precious idiot."

"Never mind what I make him out. I want to marry him, that's all. And I appeal to you solemnly. You can save me, as you can lose me. If you lose me, you'll be a coward. And if you say a word against me, I shall be lost."

"Go and dress for dinner, that's your salvation," Littlemore answered, separating from her at the head of the stairs.

IX.

It was very well for him to take that tone; but he felt as he walked home that he should scarcely know what to say to people who were determined, as Mrs. Headway put it, to catch him. She had worked a certain spell; she had succeeded in making him feel responsible. The sight of her success, however, rather hardened his heart; he was irritated by her ascending movement. He dined alone that evening, while his sister and her husband, who had engagements every day for a month, partook of their repast at the expense of some friends. Mrs. Dolphin, however, came home rather early, and immediately sought admittance to the small apartment at the foot of the staircase, which was already spoken of as Littlemore's den. Reginald had gone to a "squash" somewhere, and she had returned without delay, having something particular to say to her brother. She was too impatient even to wait till the next morning. She looked impatient; she was very unlike George Littlemore. "I want you to tell me about Mrs. Headway," she said, while he started slightly at the coincidence of this remark with his own thoughts. He was just making up his mind at last to speak to her. She unfastened her cloak and tossed it over a chair, then pulled off her long tight black gloves, which were not so fine as those Mrs. Headway wore; all this as if she were preparing herself for an important interview. She was a small neat woman, who had once been pretty, with a small thin voice, a sweet quiet manner, and a perfect knowledge of what it was proper to do on every occasion in life. She always did it, and her conception of it was so definite that failure would have left her without excuse. She was usually not taken for an American, but she made a point of being one, because she flattered herself that she was of a type which, in that nationality, borrowed distinction from its rarity. She was by nature a great conservative, and had ended by being a better Tory than her husband. She was thought by some of her old friends to have changed immensely since her marriage. She knew as much about English society as if she had invented it; had a way, usually, of looking as if she were dressed for a ride; had also thin lips and pretty teeth; and was as positive as she was amiable. She told her brother that Mrs. Headway had given out that he was her most intimate friend, and she thought it rather odd he had never spoken of her. He admitted that he had known her a long time, referred to the circumstances in which the acquaintance had sprung up, and added that he had seen her that afternoon. He sat there smoking his cigar and looking at the ceiling, while Mrs. Dolphin delivered herself of a series of questions. Was it true that he liked her so much, was it true he thought her a possible woman to marry, was it not true that her antecedents had been most peculiar?

"I may as well tell you that I have a letter from Lady Demesne," Mrs. Dolphin said. "It came to me just before I went out, and I have it in my pocket."

She drew forth the missive, which she evidently wished to read to him; but he gave her no invitation to do so. He knew that she had come to him to extract a declaration adverse to Mrs. Headway's projects, and however little satisfaction he might take in this lady's upward flight, he hated to be urged and pushed. He had a great esteem for Mrs. Dolphin, who, among other Hampshire notions, had picked up that of the preponderance of the male members of a family, so that she treated him with a consideration which made his having an English sister rather a luxury. Nevertheless he was not very encouraging about Mrs. Headway. He admitted once for all that she had not behaved properly—it wasn't worth while to split hairs about that; but he couldn't see that she was much worse than many other women, and he couldn't get up much feeling about her marrying or not marrying. Moreover, it was none of his business, and he intimated that it was none of Mrs. Dolphin's.

"One surely can't resist the claims of common humanity!" his sister replied; and she added that he was very inconsistent. He didn't respect Mrs. Headway, he knew the most dreadful things about her, he didn't think her fit company for his own flesh and blood. And yet he was willing to let poor Arthur Demesne be taken in by her!

"Perfectly willing!" Littlemore exclaimed. "All I've got to do is not to marry her myself."

"Don't you think we have any responsibilities, any duties?"

"I don't know what you mean. If she can succeed, she's welcome. It's a splendid sight in its way."

"How do you mean splendid?"

"Why, she has run up the tree as if she were a squirrel!"

"It's very true that she has an audacity à toute épreuve. But English society has become scandalously easy. I never saw anything like the people that are taken up. Mrs. Headway has had only to appear to succeed. If they think there's something bad about you they'll be sure to run after you. It's like the decadence of the Roman Empire. You can see to look at Mrs. Headway that she's not a lady. She's pretty, very pretty, but she looks like a dissipated dressmaker. She failed absolutely in New York. I have seen her three times—she apparently goes everywhere. I didn't speak of her—I was wanting to see what you would do. I saw that you meant to do nothing, then this letter decided me. It's written on purpose to be shown to you; it's what she wants you to do. She wrote to me before I came to town, and I went to see her as soon as I arrived. I think it very important. I told her that if she would draw up a little statement I would put it before you as soon as we got settled. She's in real distress. I think you ought to feel for her. You ought to communicate the facts exactly as they stand. A woman has no right to do such things, and come and ask to be accepted. She may make it up with her conscience, but she can't make it up with society. Last night at Lady Dovedale's I was afraid she would know who I was, and come and speak to me. I was so frightened that I went away. If Sir Arthur

wishes to marry her for what she is, of course he's welcome.
But at least he ought to know."

Mrs. Dolphin was not excited nor voluble; she moved from
point to point with a calmness which had all the air of being
used to have reason on its side. She deeply desired, however,
that Mrs. Headway's triumphant career should be checked;
she had sufficiently abused the facilities of things. Herself a
party to an international marriage, Mrs. Dolphin naturally
wished that the class to which she belonged should close its
ranks, and carry its standard high.

"It seems to me that she's quite as good as the little baronet," said Littlemore, lighting another cigar.

"As good? What do you mean? No one has ever breathed
a word against him."

"Very likely. But he's a nonentity, and she at least is some-
body. She's a person, and a very clever one. Besides, she's
quite as good as the women that lots of them have married.
I never heard that the British gentry were so unspotted."

"I know nothing about other cases," Mrs. Dolphin said, "I
only know about this one. It so happens that I have been
brought near to it, and that an appeal has been made to me.
The English are very romantic—the most romantic people in
the world, if that's what you mean. They do the strangest
things, from the force of passion—even those from whom you
would least expect it. They marry their cooks—they marry
their coachmen—and their romances always have the most
miserable end. I'm sure this one would be most wretched.
How can you pretend that such a woman as that is to be
trusted? What I see is a fine old race—one of the oldest and
most honourable in England, people with every tradition of
good conduct and high principle—and a dreadful, disrepu-
table, vulgar, little woman, who hasn't an idea of what such
things are, trying to force her way into it. I hate to see such
things—I want to go to the rescue!"

"I don't—I don't care anything about the fine old race."

"Not from interested motives, of course, any more than I.
But surely, on artistic grounds, on grounds of decency?"

"Mrs. Headway isn't indecent—you go too far. You must
remember that she's an old friend of mine." Littlemore
had become rather stern; Mrs. Dolphin was forgetting the

consideration due, from an English point of view, to brothers.

She forgot it even a little more. "Oh, if you are in love with her, too!" she murmured, turning away.

He made no answer to this, and the words had no sting for him. But at last, to finish the affair, he asked what in the world the old lady wanted him to do. Did she want him to go out into Piccadilly, and announce to the passers-by that there was one winter when even Mrs. Headway's sister didn't know who was her husband?

Mrs. Dolphin answered this inquiry by reading out Lady Demesne's letter, which her brother, as she folded it up again, pronounced one of the most extraordinary letters he had ever heard.

"It's very sad—it's a cry of distress," said Mrs. Dolphin. "The whole meaning of it is that she wishes you would come and see her. She doesn't say so in so many words, but I can read between the lines. Besides, she told me she would give anything to see you. Let me assure you it's your duty to go."

"To go and abuse Nancy Beck?"

"Go and praise her, if you like!" This was very clever of Mrs. Dolphin, but her brother was not so easily caught. He didn't take that view of his duty, and he declined to cross her ladyship's threshold. "Then she'll come and see you," said Mrs. Dolphin, with decision.

"If she does, I'll tell her Nancy's an angel."

"If you can say so conscientiously, she'll be delighted to hear it," Mrs. Dolphin replied, as she gathered up her cloak and gloves.

Meeting Rupert Waterville the next day, as he often did, at the St. George's Club, which offers a much appreciated hospitality to secretaries of legation, and to the natives of the countries they assist in representing, Littlemore let him know that his prophecy had been fulfilled, and that Lady Demesne had been making proposals for an interview. "My sister read me a most remarkable letter from her," he said.

"What sort of a letter?"

"The letter of a woman so scared, that she will do anything. I may be a great brute, but her fright amuses me."

"You're in the position of Olivier de Jalin, in the *Demi-Monde*," Waterville remarked.

"In the *Demi-Monde*?" Littlemore was not quick at catching literary allusions.

"Don't you remember the play we saw in Paris? Or like Don Fabrice in *L'Aventurière*. A bad woman tries to marry an honourable man, who doesn't know how bad she is, and they who do know step in and push her back."

"Yes, I remember. There was a good deal of lying, all round."

"They prevented the marriage, however, which is the great thing."

"The great thing, if you care about it. One of them was the intimate friend of the fellow, the other was his son. Demesne's nothing to me."

"He's a very good fellow," said Waterville.

"Go and tell him, then."

"Play the part of Olivier de Jalin? Oh, I can't. I'm not Olivier. But I wish he would come along. Mrs. Headway oughtn't really to be allowed to pass."

"I wish to heaven they'd let me alone," Littlemore murmured, ruefully, staring for a while out of the window.

"Do you still hold to that theory you propounded in Paris? Are you willing to commit perjury?" Waterville asked.

"Of course I can refuse to answer questions—even that one."

"As I told you before, that will amount to a condemnation."

"It may amount to what it pleases. I think I will go to Paris."

"That will be the same as not answering. But it's quite the best thing you can do. I have been thinking a great deal about it, and it seems to me, from the social point of view, that, as I say, she really oughtn't to pass." Waterville had the air of looking at the thing from a great elevation; his tone, the expression of his face, indicated this lofty flight; the effect of which, as he glanced down at his didactic young friend, Littlemore found peculiarly irritating.

"No, after all, hanged if they shall drive me away!" he

exclaimed abruptly; and walked off, while his companion looked after him.

X.

The morning after this Littlemore received a note from Mrs. Headway—a short and simple note, consisting merely of the words, "I shall be at home this afternoon; will you come and see me at five? I have something particular to say to you." He sent no answer to this inquiry, but he went to the little house in Chesterfield Street at the hour that its mistress had designated.

"I don't believe you know what sort of woman I am!" she exclaimed, as soon as he stood before her.

"Oh, Lord!" Littlemore groaned, dropping into a chair. Then he added, "Don't begin on that sort of thing!"

"I shall begin—that's what I wanted to say. It's very important. You don't know me—you don't understand me. You think you do—but you don't."

"It isn't for the want of your having told me—many, many times!" And Littlemore smiled, though he was bored at the prospect that opened before him. The last word of all was, decidedly, that Mrs. Headway was a nuisance. She didn't deserve to be spared!

She glared at him a little at this; her face was no longer the face that smiled. She looked sharp and violent, almost old; the change was complete. But she gave a little angry laugh. "Yes, I know; men are so stupid. They know nothing about women but what women tell them. And women tell them things on purpose, to see how stupid they can be. I've told you things like that, just for amusement, when it was dull. If you believed them, it was your own fault. But now I am serious, I want you really to know."

"I don't want to know. I know enough."

"How do you mean, you know enough?" she cried, with a flushed face. "What business have you to know anything?" The poor little woman, in her passionate purpose, was not obliged to be consistent, and the loud laugh with which Littlemore greeted this interrogation must have seemed to her unduly harsh. "You shall know what I want you to know, however. You think me a bad woman—you don't respect me; I told you that in Paris. I have done things I don't understand, myself, to-day; that I admit, as fully as you please. But I've completely changed, and I want to change everything. You ought to enter into that; you ought to see what I want. I hate everything that has happened to me before this; I loathe it, I despise it. I went on that way, trying—one thing and another. But now I've got what I want. Do you expect me to go down on my knees to you? I believe I will, I'm so anxious. You can help me—no one else can do a thing—no one can do any-thing—they are only waiting to see if he'll do it. I told you in Paris you could help me, and it's just as true now. Say a good word for me, for God's sake! You haven't lifted your little finger, or I should know it by this time. It will just make the difference. Or if your sister would come and see me, I should be all right. Women are pitiless, pitiless, and you are pitiless too. It isn't that she's anything so great, most of my friends are better than that!—but she's the one woman who *knows*, and people know that she knows. *He* knows that she knows, and he knows she doesn't come. So she kills me—she kills me! I understand perfectly what he wants—I shall do everything, be anything, I shall be the most perfect wife. The old woman will adore me when she knows me—it's too stupid of her not to see. Everything in the past is over; it has all fallen away from me; it's the life of another woman. This was what I wanted; I knew I should find it some day. What could I do in those horrible places? I had to take what I could. But now I've got a nice country. I want you to do me justice; you have never done me justice; that's what I sent for you for."

Littlemore suddenly ceased to be bored; but a variety of feelings had taken the place of a single one. It was impossible not to be touched; she really meant what she said. People don't change their nature; but they change their desires, their ideal, their effort. This incoherent and passionate protestation was an assurance that she was literally panting to be respect-able. But the poor woman, whatever she did, was condemned, as Littlemore had said of old, in Paris, to Waterville, to be only half right. The colour rose to her visitor's face as he listened to this outpouring of anxiety and egotism; she had not managed her early life very well, but there was no need of her going down on her knees. "It's very painful to me to hear all this," he said. "You are under no obligation to say such things to me. You entirely misconceive my attitude—my influence."

"Oh yes, you shirk it—you only wish to shirk it!" she cried, flinging away fiercely the sofa-cushion on which she had been resting.

"Marry whom you please!" Littlemore almost shouted, springing to his feet.

He had hardly spoken when the door was thrown open, and the servant announced Sir Arthur Demesne. The baronet entered with a certain briskness, but he stopped short on seeing that Mrs. Headway had another visitor. Recognising Littlemore, however, he gave a slight exclamation, which might have passed for a greeting. Mrs. Headway, who had risen as he came in, looked with extraordinary earnestness from one of the men to the other; then, like a person who had a sudden inspiration, she clasped her hands together and cried out, "I'm so glad you've met; if I had arranged it, it couldn't be better!"

"If you had arranged it?" said Sir Arthur, crinkling a little his high white forehead, while the conviction rose before Littlemore that she had indeed arranged it.

"I'm going to do something very strange," she went on, and her eye glittered with a light that confirmed her words.

"You're excited, I'm afraid you're ill." Sir Arthur stood there with his hat and his stick; he was evidently much annoyed.

"It's an excellent opportunity; you must forgive me if I take advantage." And she flashed a tender, touching ray at the baronet. "I have wanted this a long time—perhaps you have seen I wanted it. Mr. Littlemore has known me a long, long time; he's an old, old friend. I told you that in Paris, don't you remember? Well, he's my only one, and I want him to speak for me." Her eyes had turned now to Littlemore; they rested upon him with a sweetness that only made the whole proceeding more audacious. She had begun to smile again, though she was visibly trembling. "He's my only one," she continued; "it's a great pity, you ought to have known others. But I'm very much alone, I must make the best of what I

THE SIEGE OF LONDON

have. I want so much that some one else than myself should speak for me. Women usually can ask that service of a relative, or of another woman. I can't; it's a great pity, but it's not my fault, it's my misfortune. None of my people are here; and I'm terribly alone in the world. But Mr. Littlemore will tell you; he will say he has known me for years. He will tell you whether he knows any reason—whether he knows anything against me. He's been wanting the chance; but he thought he couldn't begin himself. You see I treat you as an old friend, dear Mr. Littlemore. I will leave you with Sir Arthur. You will both excuse me." The expression of her face, turned towards Littlemore, as she delivered herself of this singular proposal, had the intentness of a magician who wishes to work a spell. She gave Sir Arthur another smile, and then she swept out of the room.

The two men remained in the extraordinary position that she had created for them; neither of them moved even to open the door for her. She closed it behind her, and for a moment there was a deep, portentous silence. Sir Arthur Desmesne, who was very pale, stared hard at the carpet.

"I am placed in an impossible situation," Littlemore said at last, "and I don't imagine that you accept it any more than I do."

The baronet kept the same attitude; he neither looked up nor answered. Littlemore felt a sudden gush of pity for him. Of course he couldn't accept the situation; but all the same, he was half sick with anxiety to see how this nondescript American, who was both so valuable and so superfluous, so familiar and so inscrutable, would consider Mrs. Headway's challenge.

"Have you any question to ask me?" Littlemore went on.

At this Sir Arthur looked up. Littlemore had seen the look before; he had described it to Waterville after the baronet came to call on him in Paris. There were other things mingled with it now—shame, annoyance, pride; but the great thing, the intense desire to *know* was paramount.

"Good God, how can I tell him?" Littlemore exclaimed to himself.

Sir Arthur's hesitation was probably extremely brief; but Littlemore heard the ticking of the clock while it lasted.

"Certainly, I have no question to ask," the young man said in a voice of cool, almost insolent surprise.

"Good-day, then."

"Good-day."

And Littlemore left Sir Arthur in possession. He expected to find Mrs. Headway at the foot of the staircase; but he quitted the house without interruption.

On the morrow, after lunch, as he was leaving the little mansion at Queen Anne's Gate, the postman handed him a letter. Littlemore opened and read it on the steps of his house, an operation which took but a moment. It ran as follows:—

"DEAR MR. LITTLEMORE—It will interest you to know that I am engaged to be married to Sir Arthur Demesne, and that our marriage is to take place as soon as their stupid old Parliament rises. But it's not to come out for some days, and I am sure that I can trust meanwhile to your complete discretion.

                              "Yours very sincerely,
                                        "NANCY H.

"P.S.—He made me a terrible scene for what I did yesterday, but he came back in the evening and made it up. That's how the thing comes to be settled. He won't tell me what passed between you—he requested me never to allude to the subject. I don't care; I was bound you should speak!"

Littlemore thrust this epistle into his pocket and marched away with it. He had come out to do various things, but he forgot his business for the time, and before he knew it had walked into Hyde Park. He left the carriages and riders to one side of him, and followed the Serpentine into Kensington Gardens, of which he made the complete circuit. He felt annoyed, and more disappointed than he understood—than he would have understood if he had tried. Now that Nancy Beck had succeeded, her success seemed offensive, and he was almost sorry he had not said to Sir Arthur—"Oh, well, she was pretty bad, you know." However, now the thing was settled, at least they would leave him alone. He walked off his irritation, and before he went about the business he had come out for, had ceased to think about Mrs. Headway. He went home at six o'clock, and the servant who admitted him informed him in doing so that Mrs. Dolphin had requested he should be told on his return that she wished to see him in the drawing-room. "It's another trap!" he said to himself, instinctively; but, in spite of this reflection, he went upstairs. On entering the apartment in which Mrs. Dolphin was accustomed to sit, he found that she had a visitor. This visitor, who was apparently on the point of departing, was a tall, elderly woman, and the two ladies stood together in the middle of the room.

"I'm so glad you've come back," said Mrs. Dolphin, without meeting her brother's eye. "I want so much to introduce you to Lady Demesne, and I hoped you would come in. Must you really go—won't you stay a little?" she added, turning to her companion; and without waiting for an answer, went on hastily—"I must leave you a moment—excuse me. I will come back!" Before he knew it, Littlemore found himself alone with Lady Demesne, and he understood that, since he had not been willing to go and see her, she had taken upon herself to make an advance. It had the queerest effect, all the same, to see his sister playing the same tricks as Nancy Beck!

"Ah, she must be in a fidget!" he said to himself as he stood before Lady Demesne. She looked delicate and modest, even timid, as far as a tall, serene woman who carried her head very well could look so; and she was such a different type from Mrs. Headway that his present vision of Nancy's triumph gave her by contrast something of the dignity of the vanquished. It made him feel sorry for her. She lost no time; she went straight to the point. She evidently felt that in the situation in which she had placed herself, her only advantage could consist in being simple and businesslike.

"I'm so glad to see you for a moment. I wish so much to ask you if you can give me any information about a person you know, and about whom I have been in correspondence with Mrs. Dolphin. I mean Mrs. Headway."

"Won't you sit down?" asked Littlemore.

"No, I thank you. I have only a moment."

"May I ask you why you make this inquiry?"

"Of course I must give you my reason. I am afraid my son will marry her."

Littlemore was puzzled for a moment; then he felt sure that she was not yet aware of the fact imparted to him in Mrs.

Headway's note. "You don't like her?" he said, exaggerating in spite of himself the interrogative inflexion.

"Not at all," said Lady Demesne, smiling and looking at him. Her smile was gentle, without rancour; Littlemore thought it almost beautiful.

"What would you like me to say?" he asked.

"Whether you think her respectable."

"What good will that do you? How can it possibly affect the event?"

"It will do me no good, of course, if your opinion is favourable. But if you tell me it is not, I shall be able to say to my son that the one person in London who has known her more than six months thinks her a bad woman."

This epithet, on Lady Demesne's clear lips, evoked no protest from Littlemore. He had suddenly become conscious of the need to utter the simple truth with which he had answered Rupert Waterville's first question at the Théâtre Français. "I don't think Mrs. Headway respectable," he said.

"I was sure you would say that." Lady Demesne seemed to pant a little.

"I can say nothing more—not a word. That's my opinion. I don't think it will help you."

"I think it will. I wished to have it from your own lips. That makes all the difference," said Lady Demesne. "I am exceedingly obliged to you." And she offered him her hand; after which he accompanied her in silence to the door.

He felt no discomfort, no remorse, at what he had said; he only felt relief. Perhaps it was because he believed it would make no difference. It made a difference only in what was at the bottom of all things—his own sense of fitness. He only wished he had remarked to Lady Demesne that Mrs. Headway would probably make her son a capital wife. But that, at least, would make no difference. He requested his sister, who had wondered greatly at the brevity of his interview with Lady Demesne, to spare him all questions on this subject; and Mrs. Dolphin went about for some days in the happy faith that there were to be no dreadful Americans in English society compromising her native land.

Her faith, however, was short-lived. Nothing had made any difference; it was, perhaps, too late. The London world heard in the first days of July, not that Sir Arthur Demesne was to marry Mrs. Headway, but that the pair had been privately, and it was to be hoped, as regards Mrs. Headway, on this occasion indissolubly, united. Lady Demesne gave neither sign nor sound; she only retired to the country.

"I think you might have done differently," said Mrs. Dolphin, very pale, to her brother. "But of course everything will come out now."

"Yes, and make her more the fashion than ever!" Littlemore answered, with cynical laughter. After his little interview with the elder Lady Demesne he did not feel himself at liberty to call again upon the younger; and he never learned—he never even wished to know—whether in the pride of her success she forgave him.

Waterville—it was very strange—was positively scandalised at this success. He held that Mrs. Headway ought never to have been allowed to marry a confiding gentleman; and he used, in speaking to Littlemore, the same words as Mrs. Dolphin. He thought Littlemore might have done differently.

He spoke with such vehemence that Littlemore looked at him hard—hard enough to make him blush.

"Did you want to marry her yourself?" his friend inquired. "My dear fellow, you're in love with her! That's what's the matter with you."

This, however, blushing still more, Waterville indignantly denied. A little later he heard from New York that people were beginning to ask who in the world was Mrs. Headway.

The Impressions of a Cousin

NEW YORK, *April 3, 1873.*—There are moments when I feel
that she has asked too much of me—especially since our
arrival in this country. These three months have not done
much toward making me happy here. I don't know what the
difference is—or rather I do; and I say this only because it's
less trouble. It is no trouble, however, to say that I like New
York less than Rome: that, after all, *is* the difference. And then
there's nothing to sketch! For ten years I have been sketching,
and I really believe I do it very well. But how can I sketch
Fifty-third Street? There are times when I even say to myself,
How can I even inhabit Fifty-third Street? When I turn into
it from the Fifth Avenue the vista seems too hideous: the narrow, impersonal houses, with the dry, hard tone of their
brown-stone, a surface as uninteresting as that of sandpaper;
their steep, stiff stoops, giving you such a climb to the door;
their lumpish balustrades, porticoes, and cornices, turned out
by the hundred and adorned with heavy excrescences—such
an eruption of ornament and such a poverty of effect! I suppose my superior tone would seem very pretentious if anybody
were to read this shameless record of personal emotion; and
I should be asked why an expensive up-town residence is not
as good as a slimy Italian palazzo. My answer, of course, is
that I can sketch the palazzo and can do nothing with the up-
town residence. I can live in it, of course, and be very grateful
for the shelter; but that doesn't count. Putting aside that odious fashion of popping into the "parlours" as soon as you
cross the threshold—no interval, no approach—these places
are wonderfully comfortable. This one of Eunice's is perfectly
arranged; and we have so much space that she has given me
a sitting-room of my own—an immense luxury. Her kindness,
her affection, are the most charming, delicate, natural thing I
ever conceived. I don't know what can have put it into her
head to like me so much; I suppose I should say into her
heart, only I don't like to write about Eunice's heart—that
tender, shrinking, shade-loving, and above all fresh and youthful, organ. There is a certain self-complacency, perhaps, in my

assuming that her generosity is mere affection; for her conscience is so inordinately developed that she attaches the idea
of duty to everything—even to her relations to a poor, plain,
unloved and unlovable third-cousin. Whether she is fond of
me or not, she thinks it right to be fond of me; and the effort
of her life is to do what is right. In matters of duty, in short,
she is a real little artist; and her masterpiece (in that way) is
coming back here to live. She can't like it; her tastes are not
here. If she did like it, I am sure she would never have invented such a phrase as the one of which she delivered herself
the other day—"I think one's life has more dignity in one's
own country." That's a phrase made up after the fact. No one
ever gave up living in Europe because there is a want of dignity in it. Poor Eunice talks of "one's own country" as if she
kept the United States in the back-parlour. I have yet to perceive the dignity of living in Fifty-third Street. This, I suppose,
is very treasonable; but a woman isn't obliged to be patriotic.
I believe I should be a good patriot if I could sketch my native
town. But I can't make a picture of the brown-stone stoops
in the Fifth Avenue, or the platform of the elevated railway in
the Sixth. Eunice has suggested to me that I might find some
subjects in the Park, and I have been there to look for them.
But somehow the blistered *sentiers* of asphalt, the rock-work
caverns, the huge iron bridges spanning little muddy lakes,
the whole crowded, cockneyfied place, making up so many
faces to look pretty, don't appeal to me—haven't, from beginning to end, a discoverable "bit." Besides, it's too cold to
sit on a campstool under this clean-swept sky, whose depths
of blue air do very well, doubtless, for the floor of heaven,
but are quite too far away for the ceiling of earth. The sky
over here seems part of the world at large; in Europe it's part
of the particular place. In summer, I dare say, it will be better;
and it will go hard with me if I don't find somewhere some
leafy lane, some cottage roof, something in some degree mossy
or mellow. Nature here, of course, is very fine, though I am
afraid only in large pieces; and with my little yard-measure (it
used to serve for the Roman Campagna!) I don't know what I
shall be able to do. I must try to rise to the occasion.

The Hudson is beautiful; I remember that well enough; and
Eunice tells me that when we are in *villeggiatura* we shall be

close to the loveliest part of it. Her cottage, or villa, or whatever they call it (Mrs. Ermine, by the way, always speaks of it
as a "country-seat"), is more or less opposite to West Point,
where it makes one of its grandest sweeps. Unfortunately, it
has been let these three years that she has been abroad, and
will not be vacant till the first of June. Mr. Caliph, her trustee,
took upon himself to do that; very impertinently, I think, for
certainly if I had Eunice's fortune I shouldn't let my houses
—I mean, of course, those that are so personal. Least of all
should I let my "country-seat." It's bad enough for people
to appropriate one's sofas and tables, without appropriating
one's flowers and trees and even one's views. There is nothing
so personal as one's horizon,—the horizon that one commands, whatever it is, from one's window. Nobody else has
just that one. Mr. Caliph, by the way, is apparently a person
of the incalculable, irresponsible sort. It would have been natural to suppose that having the greater part of my cousin's
property in his care, he would be in New York to receive her
at the end of a long absence and a boisterous voyage. Common civility would have suggested that, especially as he was
an old friend, or rather a young friend, of both her parents.
It was an odd thing to make him sole trustee; but that was
Cousin Letitia's doing: "she thought it would be so much
easier for Eunice to see only one person." I believe she had
found that effort the limit of her own energy; but she might
have known that Eunice would have given her best attention,
every day, to twenty men of business, if such a duty had been
presented to her. I don't think poor Cousin Letitia knew very
much; Eunice speaks of her much less than she speaks of her
father, whose death would have been the greater sorrow if she
dared to admit to herself that she preferred one of her parents
to the other. The number of things that the poor girl doesn't
dare to admit to herself! One of them, I am sure, is that Mr.
Caliph is acting improperly in spending three months in
Washington, just at the moment when it would be most convenient to her to see him. He has pressing business there, it
seems (he is a good deal of a politician—not that I know what
people do in Washington), and he writes to Eunice every week
or two that he will "finish it up" in ten days more, and then
will be completely at her service; but he never finishes it

up—never arrives. She has not seen him for three years; he
certainly, I think, ought to have come out to her in Europe.
She doesn't know that, and I haven't cared to suggest it, for
she wishes (very naturally) to think him a pearl of trustees.
Fortunately he sends her all the money she needs; and the
other day he sent her his brother, a rather agitated (though
not in the least agitating) youth, who presented himself about
lunch-time—Mr. Caliph having (as he explained) told him
that this was the best hour to call. What does Mr. Caliph know
about it, by the way? It's little enough he has tried! Mr. Adrian
Frank had of course nothing to say about business; he only
came to be agreeable, and to tell us that he had just seen his
brother in Washington—as if that were any comfort! They are
brothers only in the sense that they are children of the same
mother; Mrs. Caliph having accepted consolations in her wid-
owhood and produced this blushing boy, who is ten years
younger than the accomplished Caliph. (I say accomplished
Caliph for the phrase. I haven't the least idea of his accomplishments. Somehow, a man with that name ought to have a
good many.) Mr. Frank, the second husband, is dead as well
as herself, and the young man has a very good fortune. He is
shy and simple, colours immensely and becomes alarmed at
his own silences; but is tall and straight and clear-eyed, and
is, I imagine, a very estimable youth. Eunice says that he is as
different as possible from his step-brother; so that perhaps,
though she doesn't mean it in that way, his step-brother is
not estimable. I shall judge of that for myself, if he ever gives
me a chance.

Young Frank, at any rate, is a gentleman, and in spite of his
blushes has seen a great deal of the world. Perhaps that is what
he is blushing for: there are so many things we humans have
no reason to be proud of. He stayed to lunch, and talked a
little about the far East—Babylon, Palmyra, Ispahan, and that
sort of thing—from which he is lately returned. He also is a
sketcher, though evidently he doesn't show. He asked to see
my things, however; and I produced a few old water-colours,
of other days and other climes, which I have luckily brought
to America—produced them with my usual calm assurance. It
was clear he thought me very clever; so I suspect that in
not showing he himself is rather wise. When I said there was

nothing here to sketch, that rectangular towns won't do, etc., he asked me why I didn't try people. What people? the people in the Fifth Avenue? They are even less pictorial than their houses. I don't perceive that those in the Sixth are any better, or those in the Fourth and Third, or in the Seventh and Eighth. Good heavens! what a nomenclature! The city of New York is like a tall sum in addition, and the streets are like columns of figures. What a place for me to live, who hate arithmetic! I have tried Mrs. Ermine, but that is only because she asked me to: Mrs. Ermine asks for whatever she wants. I don't think she cares for it much, for though it's bad, it's not bad enough to please her. I thought she would be rather easy to do, as her countenance is made up largely of negatives— no colour, no form, no intelligence; I should simply have to leave a sort of brilliant blank. I found, however, there was difficulty in representing an expression which consisted so completely of the absence of that article. With her large, fair, featureless face, unillumined by a ray of meaning, she makes the most incoherent, the most unexpected, remarks. She asked Eunice, the other day, whether she should not bring a few gentlemen to see her—she seemed to know so few, to be so lonely. Then when Eunice thanked her, and said she needn't take that trouble: she was not lonely, and in any case did not desire her solitude to be peopled in that manner—Mrs. Ermine declared blandly that it was all right, but that she supposed this was the great advantage of being an orphan, that you might have gentlemen brought to see you. "I don't like being an orphan, even for that," said Eunice; who indeed does not like it at all, though she will be twenty-one next month, and has had several years to get used to it. Mrs. Ermine is very vulgar, yet she thinks she has high distinction. I am very glad our cousinship is not on the same side. Except that she is an idiot and a bore, however, I think there is no harm in her. Her time is spent in contemplating the surface of things—and for that I don't blame her, for I myself am very fond of the surface. But she doesn't see what she looks at, and in short is very tiresome. That is one of the things poor Eunice won't admit to herself—that Lizzie Ermine will end by boring us to death. Now that both her daughters are married, she has her time quite on her hands; for the sons-in-law, I am sure, can't encourage her visits. She may, however, contrive to be with them as well as here, for, as a poor young husband once said to me, a *belle-mère*, after marriage, is as inevitable as stickiness after eating honey. A fool can do plenty of harm without deep intentions. After all, intentions fail; and what you know an accident by is that it doesn't. Mrs. Ermine doesn't like me; she thinks she ought to be in my shoes—that when Eunice lost her old governess, who had remained with her as "companion," she ought, instead of picking me up in Rome, to have come home and thrown herself upon some form of kinship more cushiony. She is jealous of me, and vexed that I don't give her more opportunities; for I know that she has made up her mind that I ought to be a Bohemian: in that case she could persuade Eunice that I am a very unfit sort of person. I am single, not young, not pretty, not well off, and not very desirous to please; I carry a palette on my thumb, and very often have stains on my apron—though except for those stains I pretend to be immaculately neat. What right have I *not* to be a Bohemian, and not to teach Eunice to make cigarettes? I am convinced Mrs. Ermine is disappointed that I don't smoke. Perhaps, after all, she is right, and that I am too much a creature of habits, of rules. A few people have been good enough to call me an artist; but I am not. I am only, in a small way, a worker. I walk too straight; it's ten years since any one asked me to dance! I wish I could oblige you, Mrs. Ermine, by dipping into Bohemia once in a while. But one can't have the defects of the qualities one doesn't possess. I am not an artist, I am too much of a critic. I suppose a she-critic is a kind of monster; women should only be criticised. That's why I keep it all to myself—myself being this little book. I grew tired of myself some months ago, and locked myself up in a desk. It was a kind of punishment, but it was also a great rest, to stop judging, to stop caring, for a while. Now that I have come out, I suppose I ought to take a vow not to be ill-natured.

As I read over what I have written here, I wonder whether it was worth while to have reopened my journal. Still, why not have the benefit of being thought disagreeable—the

luxury of recorded observation? If one is poor, plain, proud
—and in this very private place I may add, clever—there are
certain necessary revenges!

April 10.—Adrian Frank has been here again, and we rather
like him. (That will do for the first note of a more genial
tone.) His eyes are very blue, and his teeth very white—two
things that always please me. He became rather more communicative, and almost promised to show me his sketches—
in spite of the fact that he is evidently as much as ever struck
with my own ability. Perhaps he has discovered that I am trying to be genial! He wishes to take us to drive—that is, to
take Eunice; for of course I shall go only for propriety. She
doesn't go with young men alone; that element was not included in her education. She said to me yesterday, "The only
man I shall drive alone with will be the one I marry." She
talks so little about marrying that this made an impression on
me. That subject is supposed to be a girl's inevitable topic;
but no young women could occupy themselves with it less
than she and I do. I think I may say that we never mention
it at all. I suppose that if a man were to read this he would
be greatly surprised and not particularly edified. As there is
no danger of any man's reading it, I may add that I always
take tacitly for granted that Eunice will marry. She doesn't in
the least pretend that she won't; and if I am not mistaken she
is capable of the sort of affection that is expected of a good
wife. The longer I live with her the more I see that she is a
dear girl. Now that I know her better, I perceive that she is
perfectly natural. I used to think that she tried too much—
that she watched herself, perhaps, with a little secret admiration. But that was because I couldn't conceive of a girl's motives being so simple. She only wants not to suffer—she is
immensely afraid of that. Therefore, she wishes to be universally tender—to mitigate the general sum of suffering, in the
hope that she herself may come off easily. Poor thing! she
doesn't know that we can diminish the amount of suffering
for others only by taking to ourselves a part of their share.
The amount of that commodity in the world is always the
same; it is only the distribution that varies. We all try to dodge
our portion, and some of us succeed. I find the best way is
not to think about it, and to make little water-colours. Eunice

thinks that the best way is to be very generous, to condemn no one unheard.

A great many things happen that I don't mention here; incidents of social life, I believe they call them. People come to see us, and sometimes they invite us to dinner. We go to certain concerts, many of which are very good. We take a walk every day; and I read to Eunice, and she plays to me. Mrs. Ermine makes her appearance several times a week, and gives us the news of the town—a great deal more of it than we have any use for. She thinks we live in a hole; and she has more than once expressed her conviction that I can do nothing socially for Eunice. As to that, she is perfectly right; I am aware of my social insignificance. But I am equally aware that my cousin has no need of being pushed. I know little of the people and things of this place; but I know enough to see that, whatever they are, the best of them are at her service. Mrs. Ermine thinks it a great pity that Eunice should have come too late in the season to "go out" with her; for after this there are few entertainments at which my protecting presence is not sufficient. Besides, Eunice isn't eager; I often wonder at her indifference. She never thinks of the dances she has missed, nor asks about those at which she still may figure. She isn't sad, and it doesn't amount to melancholy; but she certainly is rather detached. She likes to read, to talk with me, to make music, and to dine out when she supposes there will be "real conversation." She is extremely fond of real conversation; and we flatter ourselves that a good deal of it takes place between us. We talk about life and religion and art and George Eliot; all that, I hope, is sufficiently real. Eunice understands everything, and has a great many opinions; she is quite the modern young woman, though she hasn't modern manners. But all this doesn't explain to me why, as Mrs. Ermine says, she should wish to be so dreadfully quiet. That lady's suspicion to the contrary notwithstanding, it is not I who make her so. I would go with her to a party every night if she should wish it, and send out cards to proclaim that we "receive." But her ambitions are not those of the usual girl; or, at any rate, if she is waiting for what the usual girl waits for, she is waiting very patiently. As I say, I can't quite make out the secret of her patience. However, it is not necessary I should; it was no part of the bargain on which I came to her that we were to conceal nothing from each other. I conceal a great deal from Eunice; at least I hope I do: for instance, how fearfully I am bored. I think I am as patient as she; but then I have certain things to help me—my age, my resignation, my ability, and, I suppose I may add, my conceit. Mrs. Ermine doesn't bring the young men, but she talks about them, and calls them Harry and Freddy. She wants Eunice to marry, though I don't see what she is to gain by it. It is apparently a disinterested love of matrimony—or rather, I should say, a love of weddings. She lives in a world of "engagements," and announces a new one every time she comes in. I never heard of so much marrying in all my life before. Mrs. Ermine is dying to be able to tell people that Eunice is engaged; that distinction should not be wanting to a cousin of hers. Whoever marries her, by the way, will come into a very good fortune. Almost for the first time, three days ago, she told me about her affairs.

She knows less about them than she believes—I could see that; but she knows the great matter; which is, that in the course of her twenty-first year, by the terms of her mother's will she becomes mistress of her property, of which for the last seven years Mr. Caliph has been sole trustee. On that day Mr. Caliph is to make over to her three hundred thousand dollars, which he has been nursing and keeping safe. So much on every occasion seems to be expected of this wonderful man! I call him so because I think it was wonderful of him to have been appointed sole depositary of the property of an orphan by a very anxious, scrupulous, affectionate mother, whose one desire, when she made her will, was to prepare for her child a fruitful majority, and whose acquaintance with him had not been of many years, though her esteem for him was great. He had been a friend—a very good friend—of her husband, who, as he neared his end, asked him to look after his widow. Eunice's father didn't however make him trustee of his little estate; he put that into other hands, and Eunice has a very good account of it. It amounts, unfortunately, but to some fifty thousand dollars. Her mother's proceedings with regard to Mr. Caliph were very feminine—so I may express myself in the privacy of these pages. But I believe all women are very feminine in their relations with Mr. Caliph. "Haroun-al-Raschid" I call him to Eunice; and I suppose he expects to find us in a state of Oriental prostration. She says, however, that he is not the least of a Turk, and that nothing could be kinder or more considerate than he was three years ago, before she went to Europe. He was constantly with her at that time, for many months; and his attentions have evidently made a great impression on her. That sort of thing naturally would, on a girl of seventeen; and I have told her she must be prepared to think him much less brilliant a personage to-day. I don't know what he will think of some of her plans of expenditure,—laying out an Italian garden at the house on the river, founding a cot at the children's hospital, erecting a music-room in the rear of this house. Next winter Eunice proposes to receive; but she wishes to have an originality, in the shape of really good music. She will evidently be rather extravagant, at least at first. Mr. Caliph of course will have no more authority; still, he may advise her as a friend.

April 23.—This afternoon, while Eunice was out, Mr. Frank made his appearance, having had the civility, as I afterwards learned, to ask for me, in spite of the absence of the *padronina*. I told him she was at Mrs. Ermine's, and that Mrs. Ermine was her cousin.

"Then I can say what I should not be able to say if she were here," he said, smiling that singular smile which has the effect of showing his teeth and drawing the lids of his eyes together. If he were a young countryman, one would call it a grin. It is not exactly a grin, but it is very simple.

"And what may that be?" I asked, with encouragement.

He hesitated a little, while I admired his teeth, which I am sure he has no wish to exhibit; and I expected something wonderful. "Considering that she is fair, she is really very pretty," he said at last.

I was rather disappointed, and I went so far as to say to him that he might have made that remark in her presence.

This time his blue eyes remained wide open: "So you really think so?"

" 'Considering that she's fair,' that part of it, perhaps, might have been omitted; but the rest surely would have pleased her."

"Do you really think so?"

"Well, 'really very pretty' is, perhaps, not quite right; it seems to imply a kind of surprise. You might have omitted the 'really.'"

"You want me to omit everything," he said, laughing, as if he thought me wonderfully amusing.

"The gist of the thing would remain, 'You are very pretty;' that would have been unexpected and agreeable."

"I think you are laughing at me!" cried poor Mr. Frank, without bitterness. "I have no right to say that till I know she likes me."

"She does like you; I see no harm in telling you so." He seemed to me so modest, so natural, that I felt as free to say this to him as I would have been to a good child: more, indeed, than to a good child, for a child to whom one would say that would be rather a prig, and Adrian Frank is not a prig. I could see this by the way he answered; it was rather odd.

"It will please my brother to know that!"

"Does he take such an interest in the impressions you make?"

"Oh yes; he wants me to appear well." This was said with the most touching innocence; it was a complete confession of inferiority. It was, perhaps, the tone that made it so; at any rate, Adrian Frank has renounced the hope of ever appearing as well as his brother. I wonder if a man must be really inferior, to be in such a state of mind as that. He must at all events be very fond of his brother, and even, I think, have sacrificed himself a good deal. This young man asked me ever so many questions about my cousin; frankly, simply; as if, when one wanted to know, it was perfectly natural to ask. So it is, I suppose; but why should he want to know? Some of his questions were certainly idle. What can it matter to him whether she has one little dog or three, or whether she is an admirer of the music of the future? "Does she go out much, or does she like a quiet evening at home?" "Does she like living in Europe, and what part of Europe does she prefer?" "Has she many relatives in New York, and does she see a great deal of them?" On all these points I was obliged to give Mr. Frank a certain satisfaction; and after that, I thought I had a right to ask why he wanted to know. He was evidently surprised at being challenged, blushed a good deal, and made me feel for a moment as if I had asked a vulgar question. I saw he had no particular reason; he only wanted to be civil, and that is the way best known to him of expressing an interest. He was confused; but he was not so confused that he took his departure. He sat half an hour longer, and let me make up to him by talking very agreeably for the shock I had administered. I may mention here—for I like to see it in black and white— that I *can* talk very agreeably. He listened with the most flattering attention, showing me his blue eyes and his white teeth in alternation, and laughing largely, as if I had a command of the comical. I am not conscious of that. At last, after I had paused a little, he said to me, apropos of nothing: "Do you think the realistic school are—a—to be admired?" Then I saw that he had already forgotten my earlier check—such was the effect of my geniality—and that he would ask me as many questions about myself as I would let him. I answered him freely, but I answered him as I chose. There are certain things about myself I never shall tell, and the simplest way not to tell is to say the contrary. If people are indiscreet, they must take the consequences. I declared that I held the realistic school in horror; that I found New York the most interesting, the most sympathetic of cities; and that I thought the American girl the finest result of civilisation. I am sure I convinced him that I am a most remarkable woman. He went away before Eunice returned. He is a charming creature—a kind of Yankee Donatello. If I could only be his Miriam, the situation would be almost complete, for Eunice is an excellent Hilda.

April 26.—Mrs. Ermine was in great force to-day; she described all the fine things Eunice can do when she gets her money into her own hands. A set of Mechlin lace, a *rivière* of diamonds which she saw the other day at Tiffany's, a set of Russian sables that she knows of somewhere else, a little English phaeton with a pair of ponies and a tiger, a family of pugs to waddle about in the drawing-room—all these luxuries Mrs. Ermine declares indispensable. "I should like to know that you have them—it would do me real good," she said to Eunice. "I like to see people with handsome things. It would give me more pleasure to know you have that set of Mechlin than to have it myself. I can't help that—it's the way I am made. If other people have handsome things I see them more; and then I do want the good of others—I don't care if you think me vain for saying so. I shan't be happy till I see you in an English phaeton. The groom oughtn't to be more than three feet six. I think you ought to show for what you are."

"How do you mean, for what I am?" Eunice asked.

"Well, for a charming girl, with a very handsome fortune."

"I shall never show any more than I do now."

"I will tell you what you do—you show Miss Condit." And Mrs. Ermine presented me her large, foolish face. "If you don't look out, she'll do you up in Morris papers, and then all the Mechlin lace in the world won't matter!"

"I don't follow you at all—I never follow you," I said, wishing I could have sketched her just as she sat there. She was quite grotesque.

"I would rather go without you," she repeated.

"I think that after I come into my property I shall do just as I do now," said Eunice. "After all, where will the difference be? I have to-day everything I shall ever have. It's more than enough."

"You won't have to ask Mr. Caliph for everything."

"I ask him for nothing now."

"Well, my dear," said Mrs. Ermine, "you don't deserve to be rich."

"I am not rich," Eunice remarked.

"Ah, well, if you want a million!"

"I don't want anything," said Eunice.

That's not exactly true. She does want something, but I don't know what it is.

May 2.—Mr. Caliph is really very delightful. He made his appearance to-day and carried everything before him. When I say he carried everything, I mean he carried me; for Eunice had not my prejudices to get over. When I said to her after he had gone, "Your trustee is a very clever man," she only smiled a little, and turned away in silence. I suppose she was amused with the air of importance with which I announced this discovery. Eunice had made it several years ago, and could not be excited about it. I had an idea that some allusion would be made to the way he has neglected her—some apology at least for his long absence. But he did something better than this. He made no definite apology; he only expressed, in his manner, his look, his voice, a tenderness, a charming benevolence, which included and exceeded all apologies. He looks rather tired and preoccupied; he evidently has a great many irons of his own in the fire, and has been thinking these last weeks of larger questions than the susceptibilities of a little girl in New York who happened several years ago to have an exuberant mother. He is thoroughly genial, and is the best talker I have seen since my return. A totally different type from the young Adrian. He is not in the least handsome—is, indeed, rather ugly; but with a fine, expressive, pictorial ugliness. He is forty years old, large and stout, may even be pronounced fat; and there is something about him that I don't know how to describe except by calling it a certain richness. I have seen Italians who have it, but this is the first American. He talks with his eyes, as well as with his lips, and his features are wonderfully mobile. His smile is quick and delightful; his hands are well-shaped, but distinctly fat; he has a pale complexion and a magnificent brown beard—the beard of Haroun-al-Raschid. I suppose I must write it very small; but I have an intimate conviction that he is a Jew, or of Jewish origin. I see that in his plump, white face, of which the tone would please a painter, and which suggests fatigue but is nevertheless all alive; in his remarkable eye, which is full of old expressions—expressions which linger there from the past, even when they are not active to-day; in his profile, in his anointed beard, in the very rings on his large pointed fingers. There is not a touch of all this in his step-brother; so I suppose the Jewish blood is inherited from his father. I don't think he looks like a gentleman; he is something apart from all that. If he is not a gentleman, he is not in the least a bourgeois— neither is he of the Bohemian type. In short, as I say, he is a Jew; and Jews of the upper class have a style of their own. He is very clever, and I think genuinely kind. Nothing could be more charming than his way of talking to Eunice—a certain paternal interest mingled with an air of respectful gallantry (he gives her good advice, and at the same time pays her compliments); the whole thing being not in the least overdone. I think he found her changed—"more of a person," as Mrs.

Ermine says; I even think he was a little surprised. She seems slightly afraid of him, which rather surprised me—she was, from her own account, so familiar with him of old. He is decidedly florid, and was very polite to me; that was a part of the floridity. He asked if we had seen his step-brother; begged us to be kind to him and to let him come and see us often. He doesn't know many people in New York, and at that age it is everything (I quote Mr. Caliph) for a young fellow to be at his ease with one or two charming women. "Adrian takes a great deal of knowing; is horribly shy; but is most intelligent, and has one of the sweetest natures! I'm very fond of him— he's all I've got. Unfortunately the poor boy is cursed with a competence. In this country there is nothing for such a young fellow to do; he hates business, and has absolutely no talent for it. I shall send him back here the next time I see him." Eunice made no answer to this, and, in fact, had little answer to make to most of Mr. Caliph's remarks, only sitting looking at the floor with a smile. I thought it proper therefore to reply that we had found Mr. Frank very pleasant, and hoped he would soon come again. Then I mentioned that the other day I had had a long visit from him alone; we had talked for an hour, and become excellent friends. Mr. Caliph, as I said this, was leaning forward with his elbow on his knee and his hand uplifted, grasping his thick beard. The other hand, with the elbow out, rested on the other knee; his head was turned toward me, askance. He looked at me a moment with his deep bright eye—the eye of a much older man than he; he might have been posing for a water-colour. If I had painted him, it would have been in a high-peaked cap, and an amber-coloured robe, with a wide girdle of pink silk wound many times round his waist, stuck full of knives with jewelled handles. Our eyes met, and we sat there exchanging a glance. I don't know whether he's vain, but I think he must see I appreciate him; I am sure he understands everything.

"I like you when you say that," he remarked at the end of a minute.

"I am glad to hear you like me!" This sounds horrid and pert as I relate it.

"I don't like every one," said Mr. Caliph.

"Neither do Eunice and I; do we, Eunice?"

"I am afraid we only try to," she answered, smiling her most beautiful smile.

"Try to? Heaven forbid! I protest against that," I cried. I said to Mr. Caliph that Eunice was too good.

"She comes honestly by that. Your mother was an angel, my child," he said to her.

Cousin Letitia was not an angel, but I have mentioned that Mr. Caliph is florid. "You used to be very good to her," Eunice murmured, raising her eyes to him.

He had got up; he was standing there. He bent his head, smiling like an Italian. "You must be the same, my child."

"What can I do?" Eunice asked.

"You can believe in me—you can trust me."

"I do, Mr. Caliph. Try me and see!"

This was unexpectedly gushing, and I instinctively turned away. Behind my back, I don't know what he did to her—I think it possible he kissed her. When you call a girl "my child," I suppose you may kiss her; but that may be only my bold imagination. When I turned round he had taken up his hat and stick, to say nothing of buttoning a very tightly-fitting coat round a very spacious person, and was ready to offer me his hand in farewell.

"I am so glad you are with her. I am so glad she has a companion so accomplished—so capable."

"So capable of what?" I said, laughing; for the speech was absurd, as he knows nothing about my accomplishments.

There is nothing solemn about Mr. Caliph; but he gave me a look which made it appear to me that my levity was in bad taste. Yes, humiliating as it is to write it here, I found myself rebuked by a Jew with fat hands! "Capable of advising her well!" he said softly.

"Ah, don't talk about advice," Eunice exclaimed. "Advice always gives an idea of trouble, and I am very much afraid of trouble."

"You ought to get married," he said, with his smile coming back to him.

Eunice coloured and turned away, and I observed—to say something—that this was just what Mrs. Ermine said.

"Mrs. Ermine? ah, I hear she's a charming woman!" And shortly after that he went away.

That was almost the only weak thing he said—the only thing for mere form, for of course no one can really think her charming; least of all a clever man like that. I don't like Americans to resemble Italians, or Italians to resemble Americans; but putting that aside, Mr. Caliph is very prepossessing. He is wonderfully good company; he will spoil us for other people. He made no allusion to business, and no appointment with Eunice for talking over certain matters that are pending; but I thought of this only half an hour after he had gone. I said nothing to Eunice about it, for she would have noticed the omission herself, and that was enough. The only other point in Mr. Caliph that was open to criticism is his asking Eunice to believe in him—to trust him. Why shouldn't she, pray? If that speech was curious—and, strange to say, it almost appeared so—it was incredibly naïf. But this quality is insupposable of Mr. Caliph; who ever heard of a naïf Jew? After he had gone I was on the point of saying to Eunice, "By the way, why did you never mention that he is a Hebrew? That's an important detail." But an impulse that I am not able to define stopped me, and now I am glad I didn't speak. I don't believe Eunice ever made the discovery, and I don't think she would like it if she did make it. That I should have done so on the instant only proves that I am in the habit of studying the human profile!

May 9.—Mrs. Ermine must have discovered that Mr. Caliph has heard she is charming, for she is perpetually coming in here with the hope of meeting him. She appears to think that he comes every day; for when she misses him, which she has done three times (that is, she arrives just after he goes), she says that if she doesn't catch him on the morrow she will go and call upon him. She is capable of that, I think; and it makes no difference that he is the busiest of men and she the idlest of women. He has been here four times since his first call, and has the air of wishing to make up for the neglect that preceded it. His manner to Eunice is perfect; he continues to call her "my child," but in a superficial, impersonal way, as a Catholic priest might do it. He tells us stories of Washington, describes the people there, and makes us wonder whether we should care for K Street and 14½ Street. As yet, to the best of my knowledge, not a word about Eunice's affairs; he behaves as if he had simply forgotten them. It was, after all, not out of place the other day to ask her to "believe in him;" the faith wouldn't come as a matter of course. On the other hand he is so pleasant that one would believe in him just to oblige him. He has a great deal of trust-business, and a great deal of law-business of every kind. So at least he says; we really know very little about him but what he tells us. When I say "we," of course I speak mainly for myself, as I am perpetually forgetting that he is not so new to Eunice as he is to me. She knows what she knows, but I only know what I see. I have been wondering a good deal what is thought of Mr. Caliph "down-town," as they say here, but without much result, for naturally I can't go down-town and see. The appearance of the thing prevents my asking questions about him; it would be very compromising to Eunice, and make people think that she complains of him—which is so far from being the case. She likes him just as he is, and is apparently quite satisfied. I gather, moreover, that he is thought very brilliant, though a little peculiar, and that he has made a great deal of money. He has a way of his own of doing things, and carries imagination and humour, and a sense of the beautiful, into Wall Street and the Stock Exchange. Mrs. Ermine announced the other day that he is "considered the most fascinating man in New York;" but that is the romantic up-town view of him, and not what I want. His brother has gone out of town for a few days, but he continues to recommend the young Adrian to our hospitality. There is something really touching in his relation to that rather limited young man.

May 11.—Mrs. Ermine is in high spirits; she has met Mr. Caliph—I don't know where—and she quite confirms the up-town view. She thinks him the most fascinating man she has ever seen, and she wonders that we should have said so little about him. He is so handsome, so high-bred; his manners are so perfect; he's a regular old dear. I think, of course ill-naturedly, several degrees less well of him since I have heard Mrs. Ermine's impressions. He is not handsome, he is not high-bred, and his manners are not perfect. They are original, and they are expressive; and if one likes him there is an interest in looking for what he will do and say. But if one should happen to dislike him, one would detest his manners and think them familiar and vulgar. As for breeding, he has about him, indeed, the marks of antiquity of race; yet I don't think Mrs. Ermine would have liked me to say, "Oh yes, all Jews have blood!" Besides, I couldn't before Eunice. Perhaps I consider Eunice too much; perhaps I am betrayed by my old habit of trying to see through millstones; perhaps I interpret things too richly—just as (I know) when I try to paint an old wall I attempt to put in too much "character;" character being in old walls, after all, a finite quantity. At any rate she seems to me rather nervous about Mr. Caliph: that appeared after a little when Mrs. Ermine came back to the subject. She had a great deal to say about the oddity of her never having seen him before, of old, "for after all," as she remarked, "we move in the same society—he moves in the very best." She used to hear Eunice talk about her trustee, but she supposed a trustee must be some horrid old man with a lot of papers in his hand, sitting all day in an office. She never supposed he was a prince in disguise. "We've got a trustee somewhere, only I never see him; my husband does all the business. No wonder he keeps him out of the way if he resembles Mr. Caliph." And then suddenly she said to Eunice, "My dear, why don't you marry him? I should think you would want to." Mrs. Ermine doesn't look through millstones; she contents herself with giving them a poke with her parasol. Eunice coloured, and said she hadn't been asked; she was evidently not pleased with Mrs. Ermine's joke, which was of course as flat as you like. Then she added in a moment—"I should be very sorry to marry Mr. Caliph, even if he were to ask me. I like him, but I don't like him enough for that."

"I should think he would be quite in your style—he's so literary. They say he writes," Mrs. Ermine went on.

"Well, I don't write," Eunice answered, laughing.

"You could if you would try. I'm sure you could make a lovely book." Mrs. Ermine's amiability is immense.

"It's safe for you to say that—you never read."

"I have no time," said Mrs. Ermine, "but I like literary conversation. It saves time, when it comes in that way. Mr. Caliph has ever so much."

"He keeps it for you. With us he is very frivolous," I ventured to observe.

"Well, what you call frivolous! I believe you think the prayer-book frivolous."

"Mr. Caliph will never marry any one," Eunice said, after a moment. "That I am very sure of."

Mrs. Ermine stared; there never is so little expression in her face as when she is surprised. But she soon recovered herself. "Don't you believe that! He will take some quiet little woman, after you have all given him up."

Eunice was sitting at the piano, but had wheeled round on the stool when her cousin came in. She turned back to it and struck a few vague chords, as if she were feeling for something. "Please don't speak that way; I don't like it," she said, as she went on playing.

"I will speak any way you like!" Mrs. Ermine cried, with her vacant laugh.

"I think it very low." For Eunice this was severe. "Girls are not always thinking about marriage. They are not always thinking of people like Mr. Caliph—that way."

"They must have changed then, since my time! Wasn't it so in yours, Miss Condit?" She's so stupid that I don't think she meant to make a point.

"I had no 'time,' Mrs. Ermine. I was born an old maid."

"Well, the old maids are the worst. I don't see why it's low to talk about marriage. It's thought very respectable to marry. You have only to look round you."

"I don't want to look round me; it's not always so beautiful, what you see," Eunice said, with a small laugh and a good deal of perversity, for a young woman so reasonable.

"I guess you read too much," said Mrs. Ermine, getting up and setting her bonnet-ribbons at the mirror.

"I should think he would hate them!" Eunice exclaimed, striking her chords.

"Hate who?" her cousin asked.

"Oh, all the silly girls."

"Who is 'he,' pray?" This ingenious inquiry was mine.

"Oh, the Grand Turk!" said Eunice, with her voice covered by the sound of her piano. Her piano is a great resource.

May 12.—This afternoon, while we were having our tea, the Grand Turk was ushered in, carrying the most wonderful bouquet of Boston roses that seraglio ever produced. (That image, by the way, is rather mixed; but as I write for myself alone, it may stand.) At the end of ten minutes he asked Eunice if he might see her alone—"on a little matter of business." I instantly rose to leave them, but Eunice said that she would rather talk with him in the library; so she led him off to that apartment. I remained in the drawing-room, saying to myself that I had at last discovered the *fin mot* of Mr. Caliph's peculiarities, which is so very simple that I am a great goose not to have perceived it before. He is a man with a system; and his system is simply to keep business and entertainment perfectly distinct. There may be pleasure for him in his figures, but there are no figures in his pleasure—which has hitherto been to call upon Eunice as a man of the world. To-day he was to be the trustee; I could see it in spite of his bouquet, as soon as he came in. The Boston roses didn't contradict that, for the excellent reason that as soon as he had shaken hands with Eunice, who looked at the flowers and not at him, he presented them to Catherine Condit. Eunice then looked at this lady; and as I took the roses I met her eyes, which had a charming light of pleasure. It would be base in me, even in this strictly private record, to suggest that she might possibly have been displeased; but if I cannot say that the expression of her face was lovely without appearing in some degree to point to an ignoble alternative, it is the fault of human nature. Why Mr. Caliph should suddenly think it necessary to offer flowers to Catherine Condit—that is a line of inquiry by itself. As I said some time back, it's a part of his floridity. Besides, any presentation of flowers seems sudden; I don't know why, but it's always rather a *coup de théâtre*. I am writing late at night; they stand on my table, and their fragrance is in the air. I don't say it for the flowers, but no one has ever treated poor Miss Condit with such consistent consideration as Mr. Caliph. Perhaps she is morbid: this is probably the Diary of a Morbid Woman; but in such a matter as that she admires consistency. That little glance of Eunice comes back to me as I write; she is a pure, enchanting soul. Mrs. Ermine came in while she was in the library with Mr. Caliph, and immediately noticed the Boston roses, which effaced all the other flowers in the room.

"Were they sent from her seat?" she asked. Then, before I

could answer, "I am going to have some people to dinner to-day; they would look very well in the middle."

"If you wish me to offer them to you, I really can't; I prize them too much."

"Oh, are they yours? Of course you prize them! I don't suppose you have many."

"These are the first I have ever received—from Mr. Caliph."

"From Mr. Caliph? Did he give them to *you*?" Mrs. Ermine's intonations are not delicate. That *"you"* should be in enormous capitals.

"With his own hand—a quarter of an hour ago." This sounds triumphant, as I write it; but it was no great sensation to triumph over Mrs. Ermine.

She laid down the bouquet, looking almost thoughtful. "He *does* want to marry Eunice," she declared in a moment. This is the region in which, after a flight of fancy, she usually alights. I am sick of the irrepressible verb; just at that moment, however, it was unexpected, and I answered that I didn't understand.

"That's why he gives you flowers," she explained. But the explanation made the matter darker still, and Mrs. Ermine went on: "Isn't there some French proverb about paying one's court to the mother in order to gain the daughter? Eunice is the daughter, and you are the mother."

"And you are the grandmother, I suppose! Do you mean that he wishes me to intercede?"

"I can't imagine why else!" and smiling, with her wide lips, she stared at the flowers.

"At that rate you too will get your bouquet," I said.

"Oh, I have no influence! You ought to do something in return—to offer to paint his portrait."

"I don't offer that, you know; people ask me. Besides, you have spoiled me for common models!"

It strikes me, as I write this, that we had gone rather far—farther than it seemed at the time. We might have gone farther yet, however, if at this moment Eunice had not come back with Mr. Caliph, who appeared to have settled his little matter of business briskly enough. He remained the man of business to the end, and, to Mrs. Ermine's evident disappointment, declined to sit down again. He was in a hurry; he had an engagement.

"Are you going up or down? I have a carriage at the door," she broke in.

"At Fifty-third Street one is usually going down;" and he gave his peculiar smile, which always seems so much beyond the scope of the words it accompanies. "If you will give me a lift I shall be very grateful."

He went off with her, she being much divided between the prospect of driving with him and her loss of the chance to find out what he had been saying to Eunice. She probably believed he had been proposing to her, and I hope he mystified her well in the carriage.

He had not been proposing to Eunice; he had given her a cheque, and made her sign some papers. The cheque was for a thousand dollars, but I have no knowledge of the papers. When I took up my abode with her I made up my mind that the only way to preserve an appearance of disinterestedness was to know nothing whatever of the details of her pecuniary affairs. She has a very good little head of her own, and if she shouldn't understand them herself it would be quite out of my power to help her. I don't know why I should care about *appearing* disinterested, when I have in quite sufficient measure the consciousness of being so; but in point of fact I do, and I value that purity as much as any other. Besides, Mr. Caliph is her supreme adviser, and of course makes everything clear to her. At least I hope he does. I couldn't help saying as much as this to Eunice.

"My dear child, I suppose you understand what you sign. Mr. Caliph ought to be—what shall I call it?—crystalline."

She looked at me with the smile that had come into her face when she saw him give me the flowers. "Oh yes, I think so. If I didn't, it's my own fault. He explains everything so beautifully that it's a pleasure to listen. I always read what I sign."

"Je l'espère bien!" I said, laughing.

She looked a little grave. "The closing up a trust is very complicated."

"Yours is not closed yet? It strikes me as very slow."

"Everything can't be done at once. Besides, he has asked

for a little delay. Part of my affairs, indeed, are now in my own hands; otherwise I shouldn't have to sign."

"Is that a usual request—for delay?"

"Oh yes, perfectly. Besides, I don't want everything in my own control. That is, I want it some day, because I think I ought to accept the responsibilities, as I accept all the pleasures; but I am not in a hurry. This way is so comfortable, and Mr. Caliph takes so much trouble for me."

"I suppose he has a handsome commission," I said, rather crudely.

"He has no commission at all; he would never take one."

"In your place, I would much rather he should take one."

"I have asked him to, but he won't!" Eunice said, looking now extremely grave.

Her gravity indeed was so great that it made me smile. "He is wonderfully generous!"

"He is indeed."

"And is it to be indefinitely delayed—the termination of his trust?"

"Oh no; only a few months, 'till he gets things into shape,' as he says."

"He has had several years for that, hasn't he?"

Eunice turned away; evidently our talk was painful to her. But there was something that vaguely alarmed me in her taking, or at least accepting, the sentimental view of Mr. Caliph's services. "I don't think you are kind, Catherine; you seem to suspect him," she remarked, after a little.

"Suspect him of what?"

"Of not wishing to give up the property."

"My dear Eunice, you put things into terrible words! Seriously, I should never think of suspecting him of anything so silly. What could his wishes count for? Is not the thing regulated by law—by the terms of your mother's will? The trust expires of itself at a certain period, doesn't it? Mr. Caliph, surely, has only to act accordingly."

"It is just what he is doing. But there are more papers necessary, and they will not be ready for a few weeks more."

"Don't have too many papers; they are as bad as too few. And take advice of some one else—say of your cousin Ermine, who is so much more sensible than his wife."

"I want no advice," said Eunice, in a tone which showed me that I had said enough. And presently she went on, "I thought you liked Mr. Caliph."

"So I do, immensely. He gives beautiful flowers."

"Ah, you are horrid!" she murmured.

"Of course I am horrid. That's my business—to be horrid." And I took the liberty of being so again, half an hour later, when she remarked that she must take good care of the cheque Mr. Caliph had brought her, as it would be a good while before she should have another. "Why should it be longer than usual?" I asked. "Is he going to keep your income for himself?"

"I am not to have any till the end of the year—any from the trust, at least. Mr. Caliph has been converting some old houses into shops, so that they will bring more rent. But the alterations have to be paid for—and he takes part of my income to do it."

"And pray what are you to live on meanwhile?"

"I have enough without that; and I have savings."

"It strikes me as a cool proceeding, all the same."

"He wrote to me about it before we came home, and I thought that way was best."

"I don't think he ought to have asked you," I said. "As your trustee, he acts in his discretion."

"You are hard to please," Eunice answered.

That is perfectly true; but I rejoined that I couldn't make out whether he consulted her too much or too little. And I don't know that my failure to make it out in the least matters!

May 13.—Mrs. Ermine turned up to-day at an earlier hour than usual, and I saw as soon as she got into the room that she had something to announce. This time it was not an engagement. "He sent me a bouquet—Boston roses—quite as many as yours! They arrived this morning, before I had finished breakfast." This speech was addressed to me, and Mrs. Ermine looked almost brilliant. Eunice scarcely followed her.

"She is talking about Mr. Caliph," I explained.

Eunice stared a moment; then her face melted into a deep little smile. "He seems to give flowers to every one but to me." I could see that this reflection gave her remarkable pleasure.

"Well, when he gives them, he's thinking of you," said Mrs. Ermine. "He wants to get us on his side."

"On his side?"

"Oh yes; some day he will have need of us!" And Mrs. Ermine tried to look sprightly and insinuating. But she is too utterly *fade*, and I think it is not worth while to talk any more to Eunice just now about her trustee. So, to anticipate Mrs. Ermine, I said to her quickly, but very quietly—

"He sent you flowers simply because you had taken him into your carriage last night. It was an acknowledgment of your great kindness."

She hesitated a moment. "Possibly. We had a charming drive—ever so far down-town." Then, turning to Eunice, she exclaimed, "My dear, you don't know that man till you have had a drive with him!" When does one know Mrs. Ermine? Every day she is a surprise!

May 19.—Adrian Frank has come back to New York, and has been three times at this house—once to dinner, and twice at tea-time. After his brother's strong expression of the hope that we should take an interest in him, Eunice appears to have thought that the least she could do was to ask him to dine. She appears never to have offered this privilege to Mr. Caliph, by the way; I think her view of his cleverness is such that she imagines she knows no one sufficiently brilliant to be invited to meet him. She thought Mrs. Ermine good enough to meet Mr. Frank, and she had also young Woodley—Willie Woodley, as they call him—and Mr. Latrobe. It was not very amusing. Mrs. Ermine made love to Mr. Woodley, who took it serenely; and the dark Latrobe talked to me about the Seventh Regiment—an impossible subject. Mr. Frank made an occasional remark to Eunice, next whom he was placed; but he seemed constrained and frightened, as if he knew that his step-brother had recommended him highly and felt it was impossible to come up to the mark. He is really very modest; it is impossible not to like him. Every now and then he looked at me, with his clear blue eye conscious and expanded, as if to beg me to help him on with Eunice; and then, when I threw in a word, to give their conversation a push, he looked at her in the same way, as if to express the hope that she would not abandon him. There was no danger of this, she only wished to be agreeable to him; but she was nervous and preoccupied, as she always is when she has people to dinner—she is so afraid they may be bored—and I think that half the time she didn't understand what he said. She told me afterwards that she liked him more even than she liked him at first; that he has, in her opinion, better manners, in spite of his shyness, than any of the young men; and that he must have a nice nature to have such a charming face;—all this she told me, and she added that, notwithstanding all this, there is something in Mr. Adrian Frank that makes her uncomfortable. It is perhaps rather heartless, but after this, when he called two days ago, I went out of the room and left them alone together. The truth is, there is something in this tall, fair, vague, inconsequent youth, who would look like a Prussian lieutenant if Prussian lieutenants ever hesitated, and who is such a singular mixture of confusion and candour—there is something about him that is not altogether to my own taste, and that is why I took the liberty of leaving him. Oddly enough, I don't in the least know what it is; I usually know why I dislike people. I don't dislike the blushing Adrian, however—that is, after all, the oddest part. No, the oddest part of it is that I think I have a feeling of pity for him; that is probably why (if it were not my duty sometimes to remain) I should always depart when he comes. I don't like to see the people I pity; to be pitied by me is too low a depth. Why I should lavish my compassion on Mr. Frank of course passes my comprehension. He is young, intelligent, in perfect health, master of a handsome fortune, and favourite brother of Haroun-al-Raschid. Such are the consequences of being a woman of imagination. When, at dinner, I asked Eunice if he had been as interesting as usual, she said she would leave it to me to judge; he had talked altogether about Miss Condit! He thinks her very attractive! Poor fellow, when it is necessary he doesn't hesitate, though I can't imagine why it should be necessary. I think that *au fond* he bores Eunice a little; like many girls of the delicate, sensitive kind, she likes older, more confident men.

May 24.—He has just made me a remarkable communication! This morning I went into the Park in quest of a "bit," with some colours and brushes in a small box, and that wonderfully compressible campstool which I can carry in my pocket. I wandered vaguely enough, for half an hour, through the carefully-arranged scenery, the idea of which appears to be to represent the earth's surface *en raccourci*, and at last discovered a small clump of birches which, with their white stems and their little raw green bristles, were not altogether uninspiring. The place was quiet—there were no nurse-maids nor bicycles; so I took up a position and enjoyed an hour's successful work. At last I heard some one say behind me, "I think I ought to tell you I'm looking!" It was Adrian Frank, who had recognised me at a distance, and, without my hearing him, had walked across the grass to where I sat. This time I couldn't leave him, for I hadn't finished my sketch. He sat down near me, on an artistically-preserved rock, and we ended by having a good deal of talk—in which, however, I did the listening, for I can't express myself in two ways at once. What I listened to was this—that Mr. Caliph wishes his step-brother to "make up" to Eunice, and that the candid Adrian wishes to know what I think of his chances.

"Are you in love with her?" I asked.

"Oh dear, no! If I were in love with her I should go straight in, without—without this sort of thing."

"You mean without asking people's opinion?"

"Well, yes. Without even asking yours."

I told him that he needn't say "even" mine; for mine would not be worth much. His announcement rather startled me at first, but after I had thought of it a little, I found in it a good deal to admire. I have seen so many "arranged" marriages that have been happy, and so many "sympathetic" unions that have been wretched, that the political element doesn't alto-gether shock me. Of course I can't imagine Eunice making a political marriage, and I said to Mr. Frank, very promptly, that she might consent if she could be induced to love him, but would never be governed in her choice by his advantages. I said "advantages" in order to be polite; the singular number would have served all the purpose. His only advantage is his fortune; for he has neither looks, talents, nor position that would dazzle a girl who is herself clever and rich. This, then, is what Mr. Caliph has had in his head all this while—this is what has made him so anxious that we should like his step-brother. I have an idea that I ought to be rather scandalised,

but I feel my pulse and find that I am almost pleased. I don't
mean at the idea of her marrying poor Mr. Frank; I mean at
such an indication that Mr. Caliph takes an interest in her. I
don't know whether it is one of the regular duties of a trustee
to provide the trustful with a husband; perhaps in that case
his merit may be less. I suppose he has said to himself that if
she marries his step-brother she won't marry a worse man. Of
course it is possible that he may not have thought of Eunice
at all, and may simply have wished the guileless Adrian to do
a good thing without regard to Eunice's point of view. I am
afraid that even this idea doesn't shock me. Trying to make
people marry is, under any circumstances, an unscrupulous
game; but the offence is minimised when it is a question of
an honest man marrying an angel. Eunice is the angel, and
the young Adrian has all the air of being honest. It would,
naturally, not be the union of her secret dreams, for the hero
of those pure visions would have to be clever and distinguished. Mr. Frank is neither of these things, but I believe he
is perfectly good. Of course he is weak—to come and take a
wife simply because his brother has told him to—or is he
doing it simply for form, believing that she will never have
him, that he consequently doesn't expose himself, and that he
will therefore have on easy terms, since he seems to value it,
the credit of having obeyed Mr. Caliph? Why he should value
it is a matter between themselves, which I am not obliged to
know. I don't think I care at all for the relations of men between themselves. Their relations with women are bad
enough, but when there is no woman to save it a little—*merci!*
I shouldn't think that the young Adrian would care to subject
himself to a simple refusal, for it is not gratifying to receive
the cold shoulder, even from a woman you don't want to
marry. After all, he may want to marry her; there are all sorts
of reasons in things. I told him I wouldn't undertake to do
anything, and the more I think of it the less I am willing. It
would be a weight off my mind to see her comfortably settled
in life, beyond the possibility of marrying some highly varnished brute—a fate in certain circumstances quite open to
her. She is perfectly capable—with her folded angel's wings
—of bestowing herself upon the baker, upon the fishmonger,
if she were to take a fancy to him. The clever man of her

dreams might beat her or get tired of her; but I am sure that Mr. Frank, if he should pronounce his marriage-vows, would keep them to the letter. From that to pushing her into his arms, however, is a long way. I went so far as to tell him that he had my good wishes; but I made him understand that I can give him no help. He sat for some time poking a hole in the earth with his stick and watching the operation. Then he said, with his wide, exaggerated smile—the one thing in his face that recalls his brother, though it is so different—"I think I should like to try." I felt rather sorry for him, and made him talk of something else; and we separated without his alluding to Eunice, though at the last he looked at me for a moment intently, with something on his lips, which was probably a return to his idea. I stopped him; I told him I always required solitude for my finishing-touches. He thinks me *brusque* and queer, but he went away. I don't know what he means to do; I am curious to see whether he will begin his siege. It can scarcely be said, as yet, to have begun—Eunice, at any rate, is all unconscious.

June 6.—Her unconsciousness is being rapidly dispelled; Mr. Frank has been here every day since I last wrote. He is a singular youth, and I don't make him out; I think there is more in him than I supposed at first. He doesn't bore us, and he has become, to a certain extent, one of the family. I like him very much, and he excites my curiosity. I don't quite see where he expects to come out. I mentioned some time back that Eunice had told me he made her uncomfortable; and now, if that continues, she appears to have resigned herself. He has asked her repeatedly to drive with him, and twice she has consented; he has a very pretty pair of horses, and a vehicle that holds but two persons. I told him I could give him no positive help, but I do leave them together. Of course Eunice has noticed this—it is the only intimation I have given her that I am aware of his intentions. I have constantly expected her to say something, but she has said nothing, and it is possible that Mr. Frank is making an impression. He makes love very reasonably; evidently his idea is to be intensely gradual. Of course it isn't gradual to come every day; but he does very little on any one occasion. That, at least, is my impression; for when I talk of his making love I don't mean that I see it.

When the three of us are together he talks to me quite as much as to her, and there is no difference in his manner from one of us to the other. His shyness is wearing off, and he blushes so much less that I have discovered his natural hue. It has several shades less of crimson than I supposed. I have taken care that he should not see me alone, for I don't wish him to talk to me of what he is doing—I wish to have nothing to say about it. He has looked at me several times in the same way in which he looked just before we parted, that day he found me sketching in the Park; that is, as if he wished to have some special understanding with me. But I don't want a special understanding, and I pretend not to see his looks. I don't exactly see why Eunice doesn't speak to me, and why she expresses no surprise at Mr. Frank's sudden devotion. Perhaps Mr. Caliph has notified her, and she is prepared for everything—prepared even to accept the young Adrian. I have an idea he will be rather taken in if she does. Perhaps the day will come soon when I shall think it well to say: "Take care, take care; you *may* succeed!" He improves on acquaintance; he knows a great many things, and he is a gentleman to his finger-tips. We talk very often about Rome; he has made out every inscription for himself, and has got them all written down in a little book. He brought it the other afternoon and read some of them out to us, and it was more amusing than it may sound. I listen to such things because I can listen to anything about Rome; and Eunice listens possibly because Mr. Caliph has told her to. She appears ready to do anything he tells her; he has been sending her some more papers to sign. He has not been here since the day he gave me the flowers; he went back to Washington shortly after that. She has received several letters from him, accompanying documents that look very legal. She has said nothing to me about them, and since I uttered those words of warning which I noted here at the time, I have asked no questions and offered no criticism. Sometimes I wonder whether I myself had not better speak to Mr. Ermine; it is only the fear of being idiotic and meddlesome that restrains me. It seems to me so odd there should be no one else; Mr. Caliph appears to have everything in his own hands. We are to go down to our "seat," as Mrs. Ermine says, next week. That brilliant woman has left town herself, like many other people, and is staying with one of her daughters. Then she is going to the other, and then she is coming to Eunice, at Cornerville.

II.

June 8.—Late this afternoon—about an hour before dinner—Mr. Frank arrived with what Mrs. Ermine calls his equipage, and asked her to take a short drive with him. At first she declined—said it was too hot, too late, she was too tired; but he seemed very much in earnest and begged her to think better of it. She consented at last, and when she had left the room to arrange herself, he turned to me with a little grin of elation. I saw he was going to say something about his prospects, and I determined, this time, to give him a chance. Besides, I was curious to know how he believed himself to be getting on. To my surprise, he disappointed my curiosity; he only said, with his timid brightness, "I am always so glad when I carry my point."

"Your point? Oh yes. I think I know what you mean."

"It's what I told you that day." He seemed slightly surprised that I should be in doubt as to whether he had really presented himself as a lover.

"Do you mean to ask her to marry you?"

He stared a little, looking graver. "Do you mean to-day?"

"Well, yes, to-day, for instance; you have urged her so to drive."

"I don't think I will do it to-day; it's too soon."

His gravity was natural enough, I suppose; but it had suddenly become so intense that the effect was comical, and I could not help laughing. "Very good; whenever you please."

"Don't you think it's too soon?" he asked.

"Ah, I know nothing about it."

"I have seen her alone only four or five times."

"You must go on as you think best," I said.

"It's hard to tell. My position is very difficult." And then he began to smile again. He is certainly very odd.

It is my fault, I suppose, that I am too impatient of what I don't understand; and I don't understand this odd mixture of calculation and passion, or the singular alternation of Mr.

Frank's confessions and reserves. "I can't enter into your position," I said; "I can't advise you or help you in any way." Even to myself my voice sounded a little hard as I spoke, and he was evidently discomposed by it.

He blushed as usual, and fell to putting on his gloves. "I think a great deal of your opinion, and for several days I have wanted to ask you."

"Yes, I have seen that."

"How have you seen it?"

"By the way you have looked at me."

He hesitated a moment. "Yes, I have looked at you—I know that. There is a great deal in your face to see."

This remark, under the circumstances, struck me as absurd; I began to laugh again. "You speak of it as if it were a collection of curiosities." He looked away now, he wouldn't meet my eye, and I saw that I had made him feel thoroughly uncomfortable. To lead the conversation back into the commonplace, I asked him where he intended to drive.

"It doesn't matter much where we go—it's so pretty everywhere now." He was evidently not thinking of his drive, and suddenly he broke out, "I want to know whether you think she likes me."

"I haven't the least idea. She hasn't told me."

"Do you think she knows that I mean to propose to her?"

"You ought to be able to judge of that better than I."

"I am afraid of taking too much for granted; also of taking her by surprise."

"So that—in her agitation—she might accept you? Is that what you are afraid of?"

"I don't know what makes you say that. I wish her to accept me."

"Are you very sure?"

"Perfectly sure. Why not? She is a charming creature."

"So much the better, then; perhaps she will."

"You don't believe it," he exclaimed, as if it were very clever of him to have discovered that.

"You think too much of what I believe. That has nothing to do with the matter."

"No, I suppose not," said Mr. Frank, apparently wishing very much to agree with me.

"You had better find out as soon as possible from Eunice herself," I added.

"I haven't expected to know—for some time."

"Do you mean for a year or two? She will be ready to tell you before that."

"Oh no—not a year or two; but a few weeks."

"You know you come to the house every day. You ought to explain to her."

"Perhaps I had better not come so often."

"Perhaps not!"

"I like it very much," he said, smiling.

I looked at him a moment; I don't know what he has got in his eyes. "Don't change! You are such a good young man that I don't know what we should do without you." And I left him to wait alone for Eunice.

From my window, above, I saw them leave the door; they make a fair, bright young couple as they sit together. They had not been gone a quarter of an hour when Mr. Caliph's name was brought up to me. He had asked for me—me alone; he begged that I would do him the favour to see him for ten minutes. I don't know why this announcement should have made me nervous; but it did. My heart beat at the prospect of entering into direct relations with Mr. Caliph. He is very clever, much thought of, and talked of; and yet I had vaguely suspected him—of I don't know what! I became conscious of that, and felt the responsibility of it; though I didn't foresee, and indeed don't think I foresee yet, any danger of a collision between us. It is to be noted, moreover, that even a woman who is both plain and conceited must feel a certain agitation at entering the presence of Haroun-al-Raschid. I had begun to dress for dinner, and I kept him waiting till I had taken my usual time to finish. I always take some such revenge as that upon men who make me nervous. He is the sort of man who feels immediately whether a woman is well-dressed or not; but I don't think this reflection really had much to do with my putting on the freshest of my three little French gowns.

He sat there, watch in hand; at least he slipped it into his pocket as I came into the room. He was not pleased at having had to wait, and when I apologised, hypocritically, for having kept him, he answered, with a certain dryness, that he had come to transact an important piece of business in a very short space of time. I wondered what his business could be, and whether he had come to confess to me that he had spent Eunice's money for his own purposes. Did he wish me to use my influence with her not to make a scandal? He didn't look like a man who has come to ask a favour of that kind; but I am sure that if he ever does ask it he will not look at all as he might be expected to look. He was clad in white garments, from head to foot, in recognition of the hot weather, and he had half a dozen roses in his button-hole. This time his flowers were for himself. His white clothes made him look as big as Henry VIII.; but don't tell me he is not a Jew! He's a Jew of the artistic, not of the commercial type; and as I stood there I thought him a very strange person to have as one's trustee. It seemed to me that he would carry such an office into transcendental regions, out of all common jurisdictions; and it was a comfort to me to remember that I have no property to be taken care of. Mr. Caliph kept a pocket-handkerchief, with an enormous monogram, in his large tapering hand, and every other moment he touched his face with it. He evidently suffers from the heat. With all that, *il est bien beau*. His business was not what had at first occurred to me; but I don't know that it was much less strange.

"I knew I should find you alone, because Adrian told me this morning that he meant to come and ask our young friend to drive. I was glad of that; I have been wishing to see you alone, and I didn't know how to manage it."

"You see it's very simple. Didn't you send your brother?" I asked. In another place, to another person, this might have sounded impertinent; but evidently, addressed to Mr. Caliph, things have a special measure, and this I instinctively felt. He will take a great deal, and he will give a great deal.

He looked at me a moment, as if he were trying to measure what I would take. "I see you are going to be a very satisfactory person to talk with," he answered. "That's exactly what I counted on. I want you to help me."

"I thought there was some reason why Mr. Frank should urge Eunice so to go," I went on; refreshed a little, I admit, by these words of commendation. "At first she was unwilling."

"Is she usually unwilling—and does he usually have to be urgent?" he asked, like a man pleased to come straight to the point.

"What does it matter, so long as she consents in the end?" I responded, with a smile that made him smile. There is a singular stimulus, even a sort of excitement, in talking with him; he makes one wish to venture. And this not as women usually venture, because they have a sense of impunity, but, on the contrary, because one has a prevision of penalties—those penalties which give a kind of dignity to sarcasm. He must be a dangerous man to irritate.

"Do you think she will consent, in the end?" he inquired; and though I had now foreseen what he was coming to, I felt that, even with various precautions, which he had plainly decided not to take, there would still have been a certain crudity in it when, a moment later, he put his errand into words. "I want my little brother to marry her, and I want you to help me bring it about." Then he told me that he knew his brother had already spoken to me, but that he believed I had not promised him much countenance. He wished me to think well of the plan; it would be a delightful marriage.

"Delightful for your brother, yes. That's what strikes me most."

"Delightful for him, certainly; but also very pleasant for Eunice, as things go here. Adrian is the best fellow in the world; he's a gentleman; he hasn't a vice or a fault; he is very well educated; and he has twenty thousand a year. A lovely property."

"Not in trust?" I said, looking into Mr. Caliph's extraordinary eyes.

"Oh no; he has full control of it. But he is wonderfully careful."

"He doesn't trouble you with it?"

"Oh, dear, no; why should he? Thank God, I haven't got that on my back. His property comes to him from his father, who had nothing to do with me; didn't even like me, I think. He has capital advisers—presidents of banks, overseers of hospitals, and all that sort of thing. They have put him in the way of some excellent investments."

As I write this, I am surprised at my audacity; but, some-

how, it didn't seem so great at the time, and he gave absolutely no sign of seeing more in what I said than appeared.
He evidently desires the marriage immensely, and he was
thinking only of putting it before me so that I too should
think well of it; for evidently, like his brother, he has the most
exaggerated opinion of my influence with Eunice. On Mr.
Frank's part this doesn't surprise me so much; but I confess
it seems to me odd that a man of Mr. Caliph's acuteness
should make the mistake of taking me for one of those persons
who covet influence and like to pull the wires of other people's
actions. I have a horror of influence, and should never have
consented to come and live with Eunice if I had not seen that
she is at bottom much stronger than I, who am not at all
strong, in spite of my grand airs. Mr. Caliph, I suppose, cannot conceive of a woman in my dependent position being
indifferent to opportunities for working in the dark; but he
ought to leave those vulgar imputations to Mrs. Ermine. He
ought, with his intelligence, to see one as one is; or do I
possibly exaggerate that intelligence? "Do you know I feel as
if you were asking me to take part in a conspiracy?" I made
that announcement with as little delay as possible.

He stared a moment, and then he said that he didn't in the
least repudiate that view of his proposal. He admitted that he
was a conspirator—in an excellent cause. All match-making
was conspiracy. It was impossible that as a superior woman I
should enter into his ideas, and he was sure that I had seen
too much of the world to say anything so *banal* as that the
young people were not in love with each other. That was only
a basis for marriage when better things were lacking. It was
decent, it was fitting, that Eunice should be settled in life; his
conscience would not be at rest about her until he should see
that well arranged. He was not in the least afraid of that word
"arrangement;" a marriage was an eminently practical matter,
and it could not be too much arranged. He confessed that he
took the European view. He thought that a young girl's elders
ought to see that she marries in a way in which certain definite
proprieties are observed. He was sure of his brother; he knew
how faultless Adrian was. He talked for some time, and said
a great deal that I had said to myself the other day, after Mr.
Frank spoke to me; said, in particular, very much what I had

thought, about the beauty of arrangements—that there are far too few among Americans who marry, that we are the people in the world who divorce and separate most, that there would be much less of this sort of thing if young people were helped to choose; if marriages were, as one might say, presented to them. I listened to Mr. Caliph with my best attention, thinking it was odd that, on his lips, certain things which I had phrased to myself in very much the same way should sound so differently. They ought to have sounded better, uttered as they were with the energy, the authority, the lucidity, of a man accustomed to making arguments; but somehow they didn't. I am afraid I am very perverse. I answered—I hardly remember what; but there was a taint of that perversity in it. As he rejoined, I felt that he was growing urgent—very urgent; he has an immense desire that something may be done. I remember saying at last, "What I don't understand is why your brother should wish to marry my cousin. He has told me he is not in love with her. Has your presentation of the idea, as you call it—has that been enough? Is he acting simply at your request?"

I saw that his reply was not perfectly ready, and for a moment those strange eyes of his emitted a ray that I had not seen before. They seemed to say, "Are you really taking liberties with me? Be on your guard; I may be dangerous." But he always smiles. Yes, I think he is dangerous, though I don't know exactly what he could do to me. I believe he would smile at the hangman, if he were condemned to meet him. He is very angry with his brother for having admitted to me that the sentiment he entertains for Eunice is not a passion; as if it would have been possible for him, under my eyes, to pretend that he is in love! I don't think I am afraid of Mr. Caliph; I don't desire to take liberties with him (as his eyes seemed to call it) or with any one; but, decidedly, I am not afraid of him. If it came to protecting Eunice, for instance; to demanding justice—But what extravagances am I writing? He answered, in a moment, with a good deal of dignity, and even a good deal of reason, that his brother has the greatest admiration for my cousin, that he agrees fully and cordially with everything he (Mr. Caliph) has said to him about its being an excellent match, that he wants very much to marry, and wants to marry as a gentleman should. If he is not in love with Eunice, moreover, he is not in love with any one else.

"I hope not!" I said, with a laugh; whereupon Mr. Caliph got up, looking, for him, rather grave.

"I can't imagine why you should suppose that Adrian is not acting freely. I don't know what you imagine my means of coercion to be."

"I don't imagine anything. I think I only wish he had thought of it himself."

"He would never think of anything that is for his good. He is not in the least interested."

"Well, I don't know that it matters, because I don't think Eunice will see it—as we see it."

"Thank you for saying 'we.' Is she in love with some one else?"

"Not that I know of; but she may expect to be, some day. And better than that, she may expect—very justly—some one to be in love with her."

"Oh, in love with her! How you women talk! You all of you want the moon. If she is not content to be thought of as Adrian thinks of her, she is a very silly girl. What will she have more than tenderness? That boy is all tenderness."

"Perhaps he is too tender," I suggested. "I think he is afraid to ask her."

"Yes, I know he is nervous—at the idea of a refusal. But I should like her to refuse him once."

"It is not of that he is afraid—it is of her accepting him."

Mr. Caliph smiled, as if he thought this very ingenious. "You don't understand him. I'm so sorry! I had an idea that—with your knowledge of human nature, your powers of ob-servation—you would have perceived how he is made. In fact, I rather counted on that." He said this with a little tone of injury which might have made me feel terribly inadequate if it had not been accompanied with a glance that seemed to say that, after all, he was generous and he forgave me. "Adrian's is one of those natures that are inflamed by not succeeding. He doesn't give up; he thrives on opposition. If she refuses him three or four times he will adore her!"

"She is sure then to be adored—though I am not sure it

will make a difference with her. I haven't yet seen a sign that she cares for him."

"Why then does she go out to drive with him?" There was nothing brutal in the elation with which Mr. Caliph made this point; still, he looked a little as if he pitied me for exposing myself to a refutation so prompt.

"That proves nothing, I think. I would go to drive with Mr. Frank, if he should ask me, and I should be very much surprised if it were regarded as an intimation that I am ready to marry him."

Mr. Caliph had his hands resting on his thighs, and in this position, bending forward a little, with his smile he said, "Ah, but he doesn't want to marry *you*!"

That was a little brutal, I think; but I should have appeared ridiculous if I had attempted to resent it. I simply answered that I had as yet seen no sign even that Eunice is conscious of Mr. Frank's intentions. I think she is, but I don't think so from anything she has said or done. Mr. Caliph maintains that she is capable of going for six months without betraying herself, all the while quietly considering and making up her mind. It is possible he is right—he has known her longer than I. He is far from wishing to wait for six months, however; and the part I must play is to bring matters to a crisis. I told him that I didn't see why he did not speak to her directly—why he should operate in this roundabout way. Why shouldn't he say to her all that he had said to me—tell her that she would make him very happy by marrying his little brother? He answered that this is impossible, that the nearness of relationship would make it unbecoming; it would look like a kind of nepotism. The thing must appear to come to pass of itself—and I, some-how, must be the author of that appearance! I was too much a woman of the world, too acquainted with life, not to see the force of all this. He had a great deal to say about my being a woman of the world; in one sense it is not all complimen-tary; one would think me some battered old dowager who had married off fifteen daughters. I feel that I am far from all that when Mr. Caliph leaves me so mystified. He has some other reason for wishing these nuptials than love of the two young people, but I am unable to put my hand on it. Like the children at hide-and-seek, however, I think I "burn." I don't like him, I mistrust him; but he is a very charming man. His geniality, his richness, his magnetism, I suppose I should say, are extraordinary; he fascinates me, in spite of my suspicions. The truth is, that in his way he is an artist, and in my little way I am also one; and the artist in me recognises the artist in him, and cannot quite resist the temptation to foregather. What is more than this, the artist in him has recognised the artist in me—it is very good of him—and would like to establish a certain freemasonry. "Let us take together the artistic view of life;" that is simply the meaning of his talking so much about my being a woman of the world. That is all very well; but it seems to me there would be a certain baseness in our being artists together at the expense of poor little Eunice. I should like to know some of Mr. Caliph's secrets, but I don't wish to give him any of mine in return for them. Yet I gave him something before he departed; I hardly know what, and hardly know how he extracted it from me. It was a sort of promise that I would after all speak to Eunice,—"as I should like to have you, you know." He remained there for a quarter of an hour after he got up to go; walking about the room with his hands on his hips; talking, arguing, laughing, holding me with his eyes, his admirable face—as natural, as dramatic, and at the same time as diplomatic, as an Italian. I am pretty sure he was trying to produce a certain effect, to entangle, to magnetise me. Strange to say, Mr. Caliph compromises himself, but he doesn't compromise his brother. He has a private reason, but his brother has nothing to do with his privacies. That was my last word to him.

"The moment I feel sure that I may do something for your brother's happiness—your brother's alone—by pleading his cause with Eunice—that moment I will speak to her. But I can do nothing for yours."

In answer to this, Mr. Caliph said something very unexpected. "I wish I had known you five years ago!"

There are many meanings to that; perhaps he would have liked to put me out of the way. But I could take only the polite meaning. "Our acquaintance could never have begun too soon."

"Yes, I should have liked to know you," he went on, "in

spite of the fact that you are not kind, that you are not just. Have I asked you to do anything for my happiness? My happiness is nothing. I have nothing to do with happiness. I don't deserve it. It is only for my little brother—and for your charming cousin."

I was obliged to admit that he was right; that he had asked nothing for himself. "But I don't want to do anything for you even by accident!" I said—laughing, of course.

This time he was grave. He stood looking at me a moment, then put out his hand. "Yes, I wish I had known you!"

There was something so expressive in his voice, so handsome in his face, so tender and respectful in his manner, as he said this, that for an instant I was really moved, and I was on the point of saying with feeling, "I wish indeed you had!" But that instinct of which I have already spoken checked me—the sense that somehow, as things stand, there can be no *rapprochement* between Mr. Caliph and me that will not involve a certain sacrifice of Eunice. So I only replied, "You seem to me strange, Mr. Caliph. I must tell you that I don't understand you."

He kept my hand, still looking at me, and went on as if he had not heard me. "I am not happy—I am not wise nor good." Then suddenly, in quite a different tone, "For God's sake, let her marry my brother!"

There was a quick passion in these words which made me say, "If it is so pressing as that, you certainly ought to speak to her. Perhaps she'll do it to oblige you!"

We had walked into the hall together, and the last I saw of him he stood in the open doorway, looking back at me with his smile. "Hang the nepotism! I *will* speak to her!"

Cornerville, July 6.—A whole month has passed since I have made an entry; but I have a good excuse for this dreadful gap. Since we have been in the country I have found subjects enough and to spare, and I have been painting so hard that my hand, of an evening, has been glad to rest. This place is very lovely, and the Hudson is as beautiful as the Rhine. There are the words, in black and white, over my signature; I can't do more than that. I have said it a dozen times, in answer to as many challenges, and now I record the opinion with all the solemnity I can give it. May it serve for the rest of the summer! This is an excellent old house, of the style that was thought impressive, in this country, forty years ago. It is painted a cheerful slate-colour, save for a multitude of pilasters and facings which are picked out in the cleanest and freshest white. It has a kind of clumsy gable or apex, on top; a sort of roofed terrace, below, from which you may descend to a lawn dotted with delightful old trees; and between the two, in the second story, a deep verandah, let into the body of the building, and ornamented with white balustrades, considerably carved, and big blue stone jars. Add to this a multitude of green shutters and striped awnings, and a mass of Virginia creepers and wisterias, and fling over it the lavish light of the American summer, and you have a notion of some of the conditions of our *villeggiatura*. The great condition, of course, is the splendid river, lying beneath our rounded headland in vast silvery stretches and growing almost vague on the opposite shore. It is a country of views; you are always peeping down an avenue, or ascending a mound, or going round a corner, to look at one. They are rather too shining, too high-pitched, for my little purposes; all nature seems glazed with light and varnished with freshness. But I manage to scrape something off. Mrs. Ermine is here, as brilliant as her setting; and so, strange to say, is Adrian Frank. Strange, for this reason, that the night before we left town I went into Eunice's room and asked her whether she knew, or rather whether she suspected, what was going on. A sudden impulse came to me; it seemed to me unnatural that in such a situation I should keep anything from her. I don't want to interfere, but I think I want even less to carry too far my aversion to interference, and without pretending to advise Eunice, it was revealed to me that she ought to know that Mr. Caliph had come to see me on purpose to induce me to work upon her. It was not till after he was gone that it occurred to me he had sent his brother in advance, on purpose to get Eunice out of the way, and that this was the reason the young Adrian would take no refusal. He was really in excellent training. It was a very hot night. Eunice was alone in her room, without a lamp; the windows were wide open, and the dusk was clarified by the light of the street. She sat there, among things vaguely visible, in a white wrapper, with her fair hair on her shoulders, and I could see her eyes move toward me when I asked her whether she knew that Mr. Frank wished to marry her. I could see her smile, too, as she answered that she knew he thought he did, but also knew he didn't.

"Of course I have only his word for it," I said.

"Has he told you?"

"Oh yes, and his brother, too."

"His brother?" And Eunice slowly got up.

"It's an idea of Mr. Caliph's as well. Indeed Mr. Caliph may have been the first. He came here to-day, while you were out, to tell me how much he should like to see it come to pass. He has set his heart upon it, and he wished me to engage to do all in my power to bring it about. Of course I can't do anything, can I?"

She had sunk into her chair again as I went on; she sat there looking before her, in the dark. Before she answered me she gathered up her thick hair with her hands, twisted it together, and holding it in place, on top of her head, with one hand, tried to fasten a comb into it with the other. I passed behind her to help her; I could see she was agitated. "Oh no, you can't do anything," she said, after a moment, with a laugh that was not like her usual laughter. "I know all about it; they have told me, of course." Her tone was forced, and I could see that she had not really known all about it—had not known that Mr. Caliph is pushing his brother. I went to the window and looked out a little into the hot, empty street, where the gas lamps showed me, up and down, the hundred high stoops, exactly alike, and as ugly as a bad dream. While I stood there a thought suddenly dropped into my mind, which has lain ever since where it fell. But I don't wish to move it, even to write it here. I stayed with Eunice for ten minutes; I told her everything that Mr. Caliph had said to me. She listened in perfect silence—I could see that she was glad to listen. When I related that he didn't wish to speak to her himself on behalf of his brother, because that would seem indelicate, she broke in, with a certain eagerness, "Yes, that is very natural!"

"And now you can marry Mr. Frank without my help!" I said, when I had done.

She shook her head sadly, though she was smiling again. "It's too late for your help. He has asked me to marry him, and I have told him he can hope for it—never!"

I was surprised to hear he had spoken, and she said nothing about the time or place. It must have been that afternoon, during their drive. I said that I was rather sorry for our poor young friend, he was such a very nice fellow. She agreed that he was remarkably nice, but added that this was not a sufficient reason for her marrying him; and when I said that he would try again, that I had Mr. Caliph's assurance that he would not be easy to get rid of, and that a refusal would only make him persist, she answered that he might try as often as he liked; he was so little disagreeable to her that she would take even that from him. And now, to give him a chance to try again, she has asked him down here to stay, thinking apparently that Mrs. Ermine's presence puts us *en règle* with the proprieties. I should add that she assured me there was no real danger of his trying again; he had told her he meant to, but he had said it only for form. Why should he, since he was not in love with her? It was all an idea of his brother's, and she was much obliged to Mr. Caliph, who took his duties much too seriously and was not in the least bound to provide her with a husband. Mr. Frank and she had agreed to remain friends, as if nothing had happened; and I think she then said something about her intending to ask him to this place. A few days after we got here, at all events, she told me that she had written to him, proposing his coming; whereupon I intimated that I thought it a singular overture to make to a rejected lover whom one didn't wish to encourage. He would take it as encouragement, or at all events Mr. Caliph would. She answered that she didn't care what Mr. Caliph thinks, and that she knew Mr. Frank better than I, and knew therefore that he had absolutely no hope. But she had a particular reason for wishing him to be here. That sounded mysterious, and she couldn't tell me more; but in a month or two I would guess her reason. As she said this she looked at me with a brighter smile than she has had for weeks; for I protest that she is troubled—Eunice is greatly troubled. Nearly a month has elapsed, and I haven't guessed that reason. Here is Adrian Frank, at any rate, as I say; and I can't make out whether he persists or renounces. His manner to Eunice is just the same; he is always polite and always shy, never inattentive and never unmistakable. He has not said a word more to me about his suit. Apart from this he is very sympathetic, and we sit about sketching together in the most fraternal manner. He made to me a day or two since a very pretty remark; viz., that he would rather copy a sketch of mine than try, himself, to do the place from nature. This perhaps does not look so *galant* as I repeat it here; but with the tone and glance with which he said it, it really almost touched me. I was glad, by the way, to hear from Eunice the night before we left town that she doesn't care what Mr. Caliph thinks; only, I should be gladder still if I believed it. I don't, unfortunately; among other reasons, because it doesn't at all agree with that idea which descended upon me with a single jump—from heaven knows where—while I looked out of her window at the stoops. I observe with pleasure, however, that he doesn't send her any more papers to sign. These days pass softly, quickly, but with a curious, an unnatural, stillness. It is as if there were something in the air—a sort of listening hush. That sounds very fantastic, and I suppose such remarks are only to be justified by my having the artistic temperament—that is, if I have it! If I haven't, there is no excuse; unless it be that Eunice is distinctly uneasy, and that it takes the form of a voluntary, exaggerated calm, of which I feel the contact, the tension. She is as quiet as a mouse and yet as restless as a flame. She is neither well nor happy; she doesn't sleep. It is true that I asked Mr. Frank the other day what impression she made on him, and he replied, with a little start, and a smile of alacrity, "Oh, delightful, as usual!"—so that I saw he didn't know what he was talking about. He is tremendously sunburnt, and as red as a tomato. I wish he would look a little less at my daubs and a little more at the woman he wishes to marry. In summer I always suffice to myself, and I am so much interested in my work that if I hope, devoutly, as I do, that nothing is going to happen to Eunice, it is probably quite as much from selfish motives as from others. If anything were to happen to her I should be immensely interrupted. Mrs. Ermine is bored, *par exemple!* She is dying to have a garden-party, at which she can drag a long train over the lawn; but day follows day and this entertainment does not take place. Eunice has promised it, however, for another week, and I believe means to send out invitations immediately. Mrs. Ermine has offered to write them all; she has, after all, *du bon*. But the fatuity of her mis-understandings of everything that surrounds her passes belief. She sees nothing that really occurs, and gazes complacently into the void. Her theory is always that Mr. Caliph is in love with Eunice,—she opened up to me on the subject only yes-terday, because with no one else to talk to but the young Adrian, who dodges her, she doesn't in the least mind that she hates me, and that I think her a goose—that Mr. Caliph is in love with Eunice, but that Eunice, who is queer enough for anything, doesn't like him, so that he has sent down his step-brother to tell stories about the good things he has done, and to win over her mind to a more favourable view. Mrs. Ermine believes in these good things, and appears to think such action on Mr. Caliph's part both politic and dramatic. She has not the smallest suspicion of the real little drama that has been going on under her nose. I wish I had that absence of vision; it would be a great rest. Heaven knows I see more than I want—for instance when I see that my poor little cousin is pinched with pain, and yet that I can't relieve her, can't even advise her. I couldn't do the former even if I would, and she wouldn't let me do the latter even if I could. It seems too pitiful, too incredible, that there should be no one to turn to. Surely, if I go up to town for a day next week, as seems prob-able, I may call upon William Ermine. Whether I *may* or not, I will.

July 11.—She has been getting letters, and they have made her worse. Last night I spoke to her—I asked her to come into my room. I told her that I saw she was in distress; that it was terrible to me to see it; that I was sure that she has some miserable secret. Who was making her suffer this way? No one had the right—not even Mr. Caliph, if Mr. Caliph it was, to whom she appeared to have conceded every right. She broke down completely, burst into tears, confessed that she is troubled about money. Mr. Caliph has again requested a delay as to his handing in his accounts, and has told her that she will have no income for another year. She thinks it strange; she is afraid that everything isn't right. She is not afraid of being poor; she holds that it's vile to concern one's self so much about money. But there is something that breaks her heart in thinking that Mr. Caliph should be in fault. She had always admired him, she had always believed in him, she had always—— What it was, in the third place, that she had always done I didn't learn, for at this point she buried her head still deeper in my lap and sobbed for half an hour. Her grief was melting. I was never more troubled, and this in spite of the fact that I was furious at her strange air of acceptance of a probable calamity. She is afraid that everything isn't right, forsooth! I should think it was not, and should think it hadn't been for heaven knows how long. This is what has been in the air; this is what was hanging over us. But Eunice is simply amazing. She declines to see a lawyer; declines to hold Mr. Caliph accountable; declines to complain, to inquire, to investigate in any way. I am sick, I am terribly perplexed—I don't know what to do. Her tears dried up in an instant as soon as I made the very obvious remark that the beautiful, the mysterious, the captivating Caliph is no better than a common swindler; and she gave me a look which might have frozen me if, when I am angry, I were freezable. She took it *de bien haut*; she intimated to me that if I should ever speak in that way again of Mr. Caliph we must part company for ever. She was distressed; she admitted that she felt injured. I had seen for myself how far that went. But she didn't pretend to judge him. He had been in trouble,—he had told her that; and his trouble was worse than hers, inasmuch as his honour was at stake, and it had to be saved.

"It's charming to hear you speak of his honour," I cried, quite regardless of the threat she had just uttered. "Where was his honour when he violated the most sacred of trusts? Where was his honour when he went off with your fortune? Those are questions, my dear, that the courts will make him answer. He shall make up to you every penny that he has stolen, or my name is not Catherine Condit!"

Eunice gave me another look, which seemed meant to let me know that I had suddenly become in her eyes the most indecent of women; and then she swept out of the room. I immediately sat down and wrote to Mr. Ermine, in order to have my note ready to send up to town at the earliest hour the next morning. I told him that Eunice was in dreadful trouble about her money-matters, and that I believed he would render her a great service, though she herself had no wish to ask it, by coming down to see her at his first convenience. I reflected, of course, as I wrote, that he could do her no good if she should refuse to see him; but I made up for this by saying to myself that I at least should see him, and that he would do me good. I added in my note that Eunice had been despoiled by those who had charge of her property; but I didn't mention Mr. Caliph's name. I was just closing my letter when Eunice came into my room again. I saw in a moment that she was different from anything she had ever been before—or at least had ever seemed. Her excitement, her passion, had gone down; even the traces of her tears had vanished. She was perfectly quiet, but all her softness had left her. She was as solemn and impersonal as the priestess of a cult. As soon as her eyes fell upon my letter she asked me to be so good as to inform her to whom I had been writing. I instantly satisfied her, telling her what I had written; and she asked me to give her the document. "I must let you know that I shall immediately burn it up," she added; and she went on to say that if I should send it to Mr. Ermine she herself would write to him by the same post that he was to heed nothing I had said. I tore up my letter, but I announced to Eunice that I would go up to town and see the person to whom I had addressed it. "That brings us precisely to what I came in to say," she answered; and she proceeded to demand of me a solemn vow that I would never speak to a living soul of what I had learned in regard to her affairs. They were her affairs exclusively, and no business of mine or of any other human being; and she had a perfect right to ask and to expect this promise. She has, indeed—more's the pity; but it was impossible to me to admit just then—indignant and excited as I was—that I recognised the right. I did so at last, however, and I made the promise. It seems strange to me to write it here; but I am pledged by a tremendous vow, taken in this "intimate" spot, in the small hours of the morning, never to lift a finger, never to speak a word, to redress any wrong that Eunice may have received at the hands of her treacherous trustee, to bring it to the knowledge of others, or to invoke

justice, compensation or pity. How she extorted this concession from me is more than I can say: she did so by the force
of her will, which, as I have already had occasion to note, is
far stronger than mine; and by the vividness of her passion,
which is none the less intense because it burns inward and
makes her heart glow while her face remains as clear as an
angel's. She seated herself with folded hands, and declared she
wouldn't leave the room until I had satisfied her. She is in a
state of extraordinary exaltation, and from her own point of
view she was eloquent enough. She returned again and again
to the fact that she did not judge Mr. Caliph; that what he
may have done is between herself and him alone; and that if
she had not been betrayed to speaking of it to me in the first
shock of finding that certain allowances would have to be
made for him, no one need ever have suspected it. She was
now perfectly ready to make those allowances. She was un-
speakably sorry for Mr. Caliph. He had been in urgent need
of money, and he had used hers: pray, whose else would I
have wished him to use? Her money had been an insupportable bore to him from the day it was thrust into his hands.
To make him her trustee had been in the worst possible taste;
he was not the sort of person to make a convenience of, and
it had been odious to take advantage of his good nature. She
had always been ashamed of owing him so much. He had been
perfect in all his relations with her, though he must have hated
her and her wretched little investments from the first. If she
had lost money, it was not his fault; he had lost a great deal
more for himself than he had lost for her. He was the kindest,
the most delightful, the most interesting of men. Eunice
brought out all this with pure defiance; she had never treated
herself before to the luxury of saying it, and it was singular
to think that she found her first pretext, her first boldness, in
the fact that he had ruined her. All this looks almost grotesque
as I write it here; but she imposed it upon me last night with
all the authority of her passionate little person. I agreed, as I
say, that the matter was none of my business; that is now
definite enough. Two other things are equally so. One is that
she is to be plucked like a chicken; the other is that she is in
love with the precious Caliph, and has been so for years! I
didn't dare to write that the other night, after the beautiful

idea had suddenly flowered in my mind; but I don't care what I write now. I am so horribly tongue-tied that I must at least relieve myself here. Of course I wonder now that I never guessed her secret before; especially as I was perpetually hovering on the edge of it. It explains many things, and it is very terrible. In love with a pickpocket! *Merci!* I am glad fate hasn't played me that trick.

July 14.—I can't get over the idea that he is to go scot-free. I grind my teeth at it as I sit at work, and I find myself using the most livid, the most indignant colours. I have had another talk with Eunice, but I don't in the least know what she is to live on. She says she has always her father's property, and that this will be abundant; but that of course she cannot pretend to live as she has lived hitherto. She will have to go abroad again and economise; and she will probably have to sell this place—that is, if she can. "If she can," of course means if there is anything to sell; if it isn't devoured with mortgages. What I want to know is, whether Justice, in such a case as this, will not step in, notwithstanding the silence of the victim. If I could only give her a hint—the angel of the scales and sword—in spite of my detestable promise! I can't find out about Mr. Caliph's impunity, as it is impossible for me to allude to the matter to any one who would be able to tell me. Yes, the more I think of it the more reason I see to rejoice that fate hasn't played me that trick of making me fall in love with a common thief! Suffering keener than my poor little cousin's I cannot possibly imagine, or a power of self-sacrifice more awful. Fancy the situation, when the only thing one can do for the man one loves is to forgive him for stealing! What a delicate attention, what a touching proof of tenderness! This Eunice can do; she has waited all these years to do something. I hope she is pleased with her opportunity. And yet when I say she has forgiven him for stealing, I lose myself in the mystery of her exquisite spirit. Who knows what it is she has forgiven—does she even know herself? She consents to being injured, despoiled, and finds in consenting a kind of rapture. But I notice that she has said no more about Mr. Caliph's honour. That substantive she condemns herself never to hear again without a quiver, for she has condoned something too ignoble. What I further want to know is, what conceivable tone he has taken—whether he has made a clean breast of it, and thrown himself upon her mercy; or whether he has sought refuge in bravado, in prevarication? Not indeed that it matters, save for the spectacle of the thing, which I find rich. I should also like much to know whether everything has gone, whether something may yet be saved. It is safe to say that she doesn't know the worst, and that if he has admitted the case is bad, we may take for granted that it leaves nothing to be desired. Let him alone to do the thing handsomely! I have a right to be violent, for there was a moment when he made me like him, and I feel as if he had cheated me too. Her being in love with him makes it perfect; for of course it was in that that he saw his opportunity to fleece her. I don't pretend to say how he discovered it, for she has watched herself as a culprit watches a judge; but from the moment he guessed it he must have seen that he could do what he liked. It is true that this doesn't agree very well with his plan that she should marry his step-brother; but I prefer to believe it, because it makes him more horrible. And apropos of Adrian Frank, it is very well I like *him* so much (that comes out rather plump, by the way), inasmuch as if I didn't it would be quite open to me to believe that he is in league with Caliph. There has been nothing to prove that he has not said to his step-brother, "Very good; you take all you can get, and I will marry her, and being her husband, hush it up,"—nothing but the expression of his blue eyes. That is very little, when we think that expressions and eyes are a specialty of the family, and haven't prevented Mr. Caliph from being a robber. It is those eyes of his that poor Eunice is in love with, and it is for their sake that she forgives him. But the young Adrian's are totally different, and not nearly so fine, which I think a great point in his favour. Mr. Caliph's are southern eyes, and the young Adrian's are eyes of the north. Moreover, though he is so amiable and obliging, I don't think he is amiable enough to *endosser* his brother's victims to that extent, even to save his brother's honour. He needn't care so much about that honour, since Mr. Caliph's name is not his name. And then, poor fellow, he is too stupid; he is almost as stupid as Mrs. Ermine. The two have sat together directing cards for Eunice's garden-party as placidly as if no one had a sorrow in life. Mrs. Ermine proposed this pastime to Mr. Frank; and as he has nothing in the world to do, it is as good an employment for him as another. But it exasperates me to see him sitting at the big table in the library, opposite to Mrs. E., while they solemnly pile one envelope on top of another. They have already a heap as high as their heads; they must have invited a thousand people. I can't imagine who they all are. It is an extraordinary time for Eunice to be giving a party—the day after she discovers that she is penniless; but of course it isn't Eunice, it's Mrs. Ermine. I said to her yesterday that if she was to change her mode of life— simple enough already, poor thing—she had better begin at once; and that her garden-party under Mrs. Ermine's direction would cost her a thousand dollars. She answered that she must go on, since it had already been talked about; she wished no one to know anything—to suspect anything. This would be her last extravagance, her farewell to society. If such resources were open to us poor heretics, I should suppose she meant to go into a convent. She exasperates me too—every one exasperates me. It is some satisfaction, however, to feel that my exasperation clears up my mind. It is Caliph who is "sold," after all. He would not have invented this alliance for his brother if he had known—if he had faintly suspected— that Eunice was in love with him, inasmuch as in this case he had assured impunity. Fancy his not knowing it—the idiot!

July 20.—They are still directing cards, and Mrs. Ermine has taken the whole thing on her shoulders. She has invited people that Eunice has never heard of—a pretty rabble she will have made of it! She has ordered a band of music from New York, and a new dress for the occasion—something in the last degree *champêtre*. Eunice is perfectly indifferent to what she does; I have discovered that she is thinking only of one thing. Mr. Caliph is coming, and the bliss of that idea fills her mind. The more people the better; she will not have the air of making petty economies to afflict him with the sight of what he has reduced her to!

"This is the way Eunice ought to live," Mrs. Ermine said to me this afternoon, rubbing her hands, after the last invitation had departed. When I say the last, I mean the last till she had remembered another that was highly important, and had floated back into the library to scribble it off. She writes a regular invitation-hand—a vague, sloping, silly hand, that looks as if it had done nothing all its days but write, "Mr. and Mrs. Ermine request the pleasure;" or, "Mr. and Mrs. Ermine are delighted to accept." She told me that she knew Eunice far better than Eunice knew herself, and that her line in life was evidently to "receive." No one better than she would stand in a doorway and put out her hand with a smile; no one would be a more gracious and affable hostess, or make a more generous use of an ample fortune. She is really very trying, Mrs. Ermine, with her ample fortune; she is like a clock striking impossible hours. I think she must have engaged a special train for her guests—a train to pick up people up and down the river. Adrian Frank went to town to-day; he comes back on the 23d, and the festival takes place the next day. The festival,—Heaven help us! Eunice is evidently going to be ill; it's as much as I can do to keep from adding that it serves her right! It's a great relief to me that Mr. Frank has gone; this has ceased to be a place for him. It is ever so long since he has said anything to me about his "prospects." They are charming, his prospects!

July 26.—The garden-party has taken place, and a great deal more besides. I have been too agitated, too fatigued and bewildered, to write anything here; but I can't sleep to-night—I'm too nervous—and it is better to sit and scribble than to toss about. I may as well say at once that the party was very pretty—Mrs. Ermine may have that credit. The day was lovely; the lawn was in capital order; the music was good, and the *buffet* apparently inexhaustible. There was an immense number of people; some of them had come even from Albany—many of them strangers to Eunice, and protegés only of Mrs. Ermine; but they dispersed themselves on the grounds, and I have not heard as yet that they stole the spoons or plucked up the plants. Mrs. Ermine, who was exceedingly *champêtre*—white muslin and corn-flowers—told me that Eunice was "receiving adorably," was in her native element. She evidently inspired great curiosity; that was why every one had come. I don't mean because every one suspects her situation, but because as yet, since her return, she has been little seen and known, and is supposed to be a distinguished figure —clever, beautiful, rich, and a *parti*. I think she satisfied every one; she was voted most interesting, and except that she was deadly pale, she was prettier than any one else. Adrian Frank did not come back on the 23d, and did not arrive for the festival. So much I note without as yet understanding it. His absence from the garden-party, after all his exertions under the orders of Mrs. Ermine, is in need of an explanation. Mr. Caliph could give none, for Mr. Caliph was there. He professed surprise at not finding his brother; said he had not seen him in town, that he had no idea what had become of him. This is probably perfectly false. I am bound to believe that everything he says and does is false; and I have no doubt that they met in New York, and that Adrian told him his reason—whatever it was—for not coming back. I don't know how to relate what took place between Mr. Caliph and me; we had an extraordinary scene—a scene that gave my nerves the shaking from which they have not recovered. He is truly a most amazing personage. He is altogether beyond me; I don't pretend to fathom him. To say that he has no moral sense is nothing. I have seen other people who have had no moral sense; but I have seen no one with that impudence, that cynicism, that remorseless cruelty. We had a tremendous encounter; I thank heaven that strength was given me! When I found myself face to face with him, and it came over me that, blooming there in his diabolical assurance, it was he— he with his smiles, his bows, his gorgeous *boutonnière*, the wonderful air he has of being anointed and gilded—he that had ruined my poor Eunice, who grew whiter than ever as he approached: when I felt all this my blood began to tingle, and if I were only a handsome woman I might believe that my eyes shone like those of an avenging angel. He was as fresh as a day in June, enormous, and more than ever like Haroun-al-Raschid. I asked him to take a walk with me; and just for an instant, before accepting, he looked at me, as the French say, in the white of the eyes. But he pretended to be delighted, and we strolled away together to the path that leads down to the river. It was difficult to get away from the people—they were all over the place; but I made him go so far that at the end of ten minutes we were virtually alone together. It was delicious to see how he hated it. It was then that I asked him what had become of his step-brother, and that he professed, as I have said, the utmost ignorance of Adrian's whereabouts. I hated him; it was odious to me to be so close to him; yet I could have endured this for hours in order to make him feel that I despised him. To make him feel it without saying it— there was an inspiration in that idea; but it is very possible that it made me look more like a demon than like the angel I just mentioned. I told him in a moment, abruptly, that his step-brother would do well to remain away altogether in future; it was a farce his pretending to make my cousin reconsider her answer.

"Why, then, did she ask him to come down here?" He launched this inquiry with confidence.

"Because she thought it would be pleasant to have a man in the house; and Mr. Frank is such a harmless, discreet, accommodating one."

"Why, then, do you object to his coming back?"

He had made me contradict myself a little, and of course he enjoyed that. I was confused—confused by my agitation; and I made the matter worse. I was furious that Eunice had made me promise not to speak, and my anger blinded me, as great anger always does, save in organisations so fine as Mr. Caliph's.

"Because Eunice is in no condition to have company. She is very ill; you can see for yourself."

"Very ill? with a garden-party and a band of music! Why, then, did she invite us all?"

"Because she is a little crazy, I think."

"You are very consistent!" he cried, with a laugh. "I know people who think every one crazy but themselves. I have had occasion to talk business with her several times of late, and I find her mind as clear as a bell."

"I wonder if you will allow me to say that you talk business too much? Let me give you a word of advice: wind up her affairs at once without any more procrastination, and place them in her own hands. She is very nervous; she knows this ought to have been done already. I recommend you strongly to make an end of the matter."

I had no idea I could be so insolent, even in conversation with a swindler. I confess I didn't do it so well as I might, for my voice trembled perceptibly in the midst of my efforts to be calm. He had picked up two or three stones and was tossing them into the river, making them skim the surface for a long distance. He held one poised a moment, turning his eye askance on me; then he let it fly, and it danced for a hundred yards. I wondered whether in what I had just said I broke my vow to Eunice; and it seemed to me that I didn't, inasmuch as I appeared to assume that no irreparable wrong had been done her.

"Do you wish yourself to get control of her property?" Mr. Caliph inquired, after he had made his stone skim. It was magnificently said, far better than anything I could do; and I think I answered it—though it made my heart beat fast—almost with a smile of applause.

"Aren't you afraid?" I asked in a moment, very gently.

"Afraid of what—of you?"

"Afraid of justice—of Eunice's friends?"

"That means you, of course. Yes, I am very much afraid. When was a man not, in the presence of a clever woman?"

"I am clever; but I am not clever enough. If I were, you should have no doubt of it."

He folded his arms as he stood there before me, looking at me in that way I have mentioned more than once—like a genial Mephistopheles. "I must repeat what I have already told you, that I wish I had known you ten years ago!"

"How you must hate me to say that!" I exclaimed. "That's some comfort, just a little—your hating me."

"I can't tell you how it makes me feel to see you so indiscreet," he went on, as if he had not heard me. "Ah, my dear lady, don't meddle—a woman like you! Think of the bad taste of it."

"It's bad if you like; but yours is far worse."

"Mine! What do you know about mine? What do you know about me? See how superficial it makes you." He paused a moment, smiling almost compassionately; and then he said, with an abrupt change of tone and manner, as if our conversation wearied him and he wished to sum up and return to the house, "See that she marries Adrian; that's all you have to do!"

"That's a beautiful idea of yours! You know you don't believe in it yourself!" These words broke from me as he turned away, and we ascended the hill together.

"It's the only thing I believe in," he answered, very gravely.

"What a pity for you that your brother doesn't! For he doesn't—I persist in that!" I said this because it seemed to me just then to be the thing I could think of that would exasperate him most. The event proved I was right.

He stopped short in the path—gave me a very bad look. "Do you want him for yourself? Have *you* been making love to him?"

"Ah, Mr. Caliph, for a man who talks about taste!" I answered.

"Taste be damned!" cried Mr. Caliph, as we went on again.

"That's quite my idea!" He broke into an unexpected laugh, as if I had said something very amusing, and we proceeded in silence to the top of the hill. Then I suddenly said to him, as we emerged upon the lawn, "Aren't you really a little afraid?"

He stopped again, looking toward the house and at the brilliant groups with which the lawn was covered. We had lost the music, but we began to hear it again. "Afraid? of course I am! I'm immensely afraid. It comes over me in such a scene as this. But I don't see what good it does you to know."

"It makes me rather happy." That was a fib; for it didn't, somehow, when he looked and talked in that way. He has an absolutely bottomless power of mockery; and really, absurd as it appears, for that instant I had a feeling that it was quite magnanimous of him not to let me know what he thought of my idiotic attempt to frighten him. He feels strong and safe somehow, somewhere; but I can't discover why he should, inasmuch as he certainly doesn't know Eunice's secret, and it is only her state of mind that gives him impunity. He believes her to be merely credulous; convinced by his specious arguments that everything will be right in a few months; a little nervous, possibly—to justify my account of her—but for the present, at least, completely at his mercy. The present, of course, is only what now concerns him; for the future he has invented Adrian Frank. How he clings to this invention was proved by the last words he said to me before we separated on the lawn; they almost indicate that he has a conscience, and this is so extraordinary—

"She must marry Adrian! She must marry Adrian!"

With this he turned away and went to talk to various people whom he knew. He talked to every one; diffused his genial influence all over the place, and contributed greatly to the brilliancy of the occasion. I hadn't therefore the comfort of feeling that Mrs. Ermine was more of a waterspout than usual, when she said to me afterwards that Mr. Caliph was a man to adore, and that the party would have been quite "ordinary" without him. "I mean in comparison, you know." And then she said to me suddenly, with her blank impertinence: "Why don't you set your cap at him? I should think you would!"

"Is it possible you have not observed my frantic efforts to captivate him?" I answered. "Didn't you notice how I drew him away and made him walk with me by the river? It's too soon to say, but I really think I am gaining ground." For so mild a pleasure it really pays to mystify Mrs. Ermine! I kept away from Eunice till almost every one had gone. I knew that she would look at me in a certain way, and I didn't wish to meet her eyes. I have a bad conscience, for turn it as I would I *had* broken my vow. Mr. Caliph went away without my meeting him again; but I saw that half an hour before he left he strolled to a distance with Eunice. I instantly guessed what his business was; he had made up his mind to present to her directly, and in person, the question of her marrying his step-brother. What a happy inspiration, and what a well-selected occasion! When she came back I saw that she had been crying, though I imagine no one else did. I know the signs of her tears, even when she has checked them as quickly as she must have done to-day. Whatever it was that had passed between them, it diverted her from looking at me, when we were alone together, in that way I was afraid of. Mrs. Ermine is prolific; there is no end to the images that succeed each other in her mind. Late in the evening, after the last carriage had rolled away, we went up the staircase together, and at the top she detained me a moment.

"I have been thinking it over, and I am afraid that there is no chance for you. I have reason to believe that he proposed to-day to Eunice!"

August 19.—Eunice is very ill, as I was sure she would be, after the effort of her horrible festival. She kept going for three days more; then she broke down completely, and for a week now she has been in bed. I have had no time to write, for I have been constantly with her, in alternation with Mrs. Ermine. Mrs. Ermine was about to leave us after the garden-party, but when Eunice gave up she announced that she would stay and take care of her. Eunice tells me that she is a good nurse, except that she talks too much, and of course she gives me a chance to rest. Eunice's condition is strange; she has no fever, but her life seems to have ebbed away. She lies with her eyes shut, perfectly conscious, answering when she is spoken to, but immersed in absolute rest. It is as if she had had some terrible strain or fatigue, and wished to steep herself in oblivion. I am not anxious about her—am much less frightened than Mrs. Ermine or the doctor, for whom she is apparently dying of weakness. I tell the doctor I understand her condition—I have seen her so before. It will last probably a month, and then she will slowly pull herself together. The poor man accepts this theory for want of a better, and evidently depends upon me to see her through, as he says. Mrs. Ermine wishes to send for one of the great men from New York, but I have opposed this idea, and shall continue to oppose it. There is (to my mind) a kind of cruelty in exhibiting the poor girl to more people than are absolutely necessary. The dullest of them would see that she is in love. The seat of her illness is in her mind, in her soul, and no rude hands must touch her there. She herself has protested—she has murmured a prayer that she may be forced to see no one else. "I only want to be left alone—to be left alone." So we leave her alone—that is, we simply watch and wait. She will recover—people don't die of these things; she will live to suffer—to suffer always. I am tired to-night, but Mrs. Ermine is with her, and I shall not be wanted till morning; therefore, before I lie down, I will repair in these remarkable pages a serious omission. I scarcely know why I should have written all this, except that the history of things interests me, and I find that it is even a greater pleasure to write it than to read it. If what I have committed to this little book hitherto has not been profitless, I must make a note of an incident which I think more curious than any of the scenes I have described.

Adrian Frank reappeared the day after the garden-party—late in the afternoon, while I sat in the verandah and watched the sunset and Eunice strolled down to the river with Mrs. Ermine. I had heard no sound of wheels, and there was no evidence of a vehicle or of luggage. He had not come through the house, but walked round it from the front, having apparently been told by one of the servants that we were in the grounds. On seeing me he stopped, hesitated a moment, then came up to the steps, shook hands in silence, seated himself near me and looked at me through the dusk. This was all tolerably mysterious, and it was even more so after he had explained a little. I told him that he was a day after the fair, that he had been considerably missed, and even that he was slightly wanting in respect to Eunice. Since he had absented himself from her party it was not quite delicate to assume that she was ready to receive him at his own time. I don't know what made me so truculent—as if there were any danger of his having really not considered us, or his lacking a good reason. It was simply, I think, that my talk with Mr. Caliph the evening before had made me so much bad blood and left me in a savage mood. Mr. Frank answered that he had not stayed away by accident—he had stayed away on purpose; he had been for several days at Saratoga, and on returning to Cornerville had taken quarters at the inn in the village. He had no intention of presuming further on Eunice's hospitality, and had walked over from the hotel simply to bid us good-evening and give an account of himself.

"My dear Mr. Frank, your account is not clear!" I said, laughing. "What in the world were you doing at Saratoga?" I must add that his humility had completely disarmed me; I was ashamed of the brutality with which I had received him, and convinced afresh that he was the best fellow in the world.

"What was I doing at Saratoga? I was trying hard to forget you!"

This was Mr. Frank's rejoinder; and I give it exactly as he uttered it; or rather, not exactly, inasmuch as I cannot give the tone—the quick, startling tremor of his voice. But those are the words with which he answered my superficially-intended question. I saw in a moment that he meant a great deal by them—I became aware that we were suddenly in deep waters; that *he* was, at least, and that he was trying to draw me into the stream. My surprise was immense, complete; I had absolutely not suspected what he went on to say to me. He said many things—but I needn't write them here. It is not in detail that I see the propriety of narrating this incident; I suppose a woman may be trusted to remember the form of such assurances. Let me simply say that the poor dear young man has an idea that he wants to marry me. For a moment,—just a moment—I thought he was jesting; then I saw, in the twilight, that he was pale with seriousness. He is perfectly sincere. It is strange, but it is real, and, moreover, it is his own affair. For myself, when I have said I was amazed, I have said everything; *en tête-à-tête* with myself I needn't blush and protest. I was not in the least annoyed or alarmed; I was filled with kindness and consideration, and I was extremely interested. He talked to me for a quarter of an hour; it seemed a very long time. I asked him to go away; not to wait till Eunice and Mrs. Ermine should come back. Of course I refused him, by the way.

It was the last thing I was expecting at this time of day, and it gave me a great deal to think of. I lay awake that night; I found I was more agitated than I supposed, and all sorts of visions came and went in my head. I shall not marry the young Adrian: I am bound to say that vision was not one of them; but as I thought over what he had said to me it became more clear, more conceivable. I began now to be a little surprised at my surprise. It appears that I have had the honour to please him from the first; when he began to come to see us it was not for Eunice, it was for me. He made a general confession on this subject. He was afraid of me; he thought me proud, sarcastic, cold, a hundred horrid things; it didn't seem to him possible that we should ever be on a footing of familiarity which would enable him to propose to me. He regarded me, in short, as unattainable, out of the question, and made up his mind to admire me for ever in silence. (In plain English, I suppose he thought I was too old, and he has simply got used to the difference in our years.) But he wished to be near me, to see me, and hear me (I am really writing more details than seem worth while); so that when his step-brother recommended him to try and marry Eunice he jumped at the opportunity to make good his place. This situation reconciled everything. He could oblige his brother, he could pay a high compliment to my cousin, and he could see me every day or two. He was convinced from the first that he was in no danger; he was morally sure that Eunice would never smile upon his suit. He didn't know why, and he doesn't know why yet; it was only an instinct. That suit was avowedly perfunctory; still the young Adrian has been a great comedian. He assured me that if he had proved to be wrong, and Eunice had suddenly accepted him, he would have gone with her to the altar and made her an excellent husband; for he would have acquired in this manner the certainty of seeing for the rest of his life a great deal of me! To think of one's possessing, all unexpected, this miraculous influence! When he came down here, after Eunice had refused him, it was simply for the pleasure of living in the house with me; from that moment there was no comedy—everything was clear and comfortable betwixt him and Eunice. I asked him if he meant by this that she knew of the sentiments he entertained for her companion, and he answered that he had never breathed a word on this subject, and flattered himself that he had kept the thing dark. He had no reason to believe that she guessed his motives, and I may add that I have none either; they are altogether too extraordinary! As I have said, it was simply time, and the privilege of seeing more of me, that had dispelled his hesitation. I didn't reason with him; and though, once I was fairly enlightened, I gave him the most respectful attention, I didn't appear to consider his request too seriously. But I *did* touch upon the fact that I am five or six years older than he: I suppose I needn't mention that it was not in a spirit of coquetry. His rejoinder was very gallant; but it belongs to the class of details. He is really in love—heaven forgive him! but I shall not marry him. How strange are the passions of men!

I saw Mr. Frank the next day; I had given him leave to come back at noon. He joined me in the grounds, where as usual I had set up my easel. I left it to his discretion to call first at the house and explain both his absence and his presence to Eunice and Mrs. Ermine—the latter especially—ignorant as yet of his visit the night before, of which I had not spoken to them. He sat down beside me on a garden-chair and watched me as I went on with my work. For half an hour very few words passed between us; I felt that he was happy to sit there,

to be near me, to see me—strange as it seems! and for myself
there was a certain sweetness in knowing it, though it was the
sweetness of charity, not of elation or triumph. He must have
seen I was only pretending to paint—if he followed my brush,
which I suppose he didn't. My mind was full of a determination I had arrived at after many waverings in the hours of
the night. It had come to me toward morning as a kind of
inspiration. I could never marry him, but was there not some
way in which I could utilise his devotion? At the present moment, only forty-eight hours later, it seems strange, unreal,
almost grotesque; but for ten minutes I thought I saw the
light. As we sat there under the great trees, in the stillness of
the noon, I suddenly turned and said to him—

"I thank you for everything you have told me; it gives me
very nearly all the pleasure you could wish. I believe in you;
I accept every assurance of your devotion. I think that devotion is capable of going very far; and I am going to put it to
a tremendous test, one of the greatest, probably, to which a
man was ever subjected."

He stared, leaning forward, with his hands on his knees.
"Any test—any test——" he murmured.

"Don't give up Eunice, then; make another trial; I wish her
to marry you!"

My words may have sounded like an atrocious joke, but
they represented for me a great deal of hope and cheer. They
brought a deep blush into Adrian Frank's face; he winced a
little, as if he had been struck by a hand whose blow he could
not return, and the tears suddenly started to his eyes. "Oh,
Miss Condit!" he exclaimed.

What I saw before me was bright and definite; his distress
seemed to me no obstacle, and I went on with a serenity of
which I longed to make him perceive the underlying support.
"Of course what I say seems to you like a deliberate insult;
but nothing would induce me to give you pain if it were possible to spare you. But it isn't possible, my dear friend; it isn't
possible. There is pain for you in the best thing I can say to
you; there are situations in life in which we can only accept
our pain. I can never marry you; I shall never marry any one.
I am an old maid, and how can an old maid have a husband?
I will be your friend, your sister, your brother, your mother,

but I will never be your wife. I should like immensely to be your brother, for I don't like the brother you have got, and I think you deserve a better one. I believe, as I tell you, in everything you have said to me—in your affection, your tenderness, your honesty, the full consideration you have given to the whole matter. I am happier and richer for knowing it all; and I can assure you that it gives something to life which life didn't have before. We shall be good friends, dear friends, always, whatever happens. But I can't be your wife—I want you for some one else. You will say I have changed—that I ought to have spoken in this way three months ago. But I haven't changed—it is circumstances that have changed. I see reasons for your marrying my cousin that I didn't see then. I can't say that she will listen to you now, any more than she did then; I don't speak of her; I speak only of you and of myself. I wish you to make another attempt; and I wish you to make it, this time, with my full confidence and support. Moreover, I attach a condition to it—a condition I will tell you presently. Do you think me slightly demented, malignantly perverse, atrociously cruel? If you could see the bottom of my heart you would find something there which, I think, would almost give you joy. To ask you to do something you don't want to do as a substitute for something you desire, and to attach to the hard achievement a condition which will require a good deal of thinking of and will certainly make it harder—you may well believe I have some extraordinary reason for taking such a line as this. For remember, to begin with, that I can never marry you."

"Never—never—never?"

"Never, never, never."

"And what is your extraordinary reason?"

"Simply that I wish Eunice to have your protection, your kindness, your fortune."

"My fortune?"

"She has lost her own. She will be poor."

"Pray, how has she lost it?" the poor fellow asked, beginning to frown, and more and more bewildered.

"I can't tell you that, and you must never ask. But the fact is certain. The greater part of her property has gone; she has known it for some little time."

"For some little time? Why, she never showed any change."

"You never saw it, that was all! You were thinking of me," and I believe I accompanied this remark with a smile—a smile which was most inconsiderate, for it could only mystify him more.

I think at first he scarcely believed me. "What a singular time to choose to give a large party!" he exclaimed, looking at me with eyes quite unlike his old—or rather his young—ones; eyes that, instead of overlooking half the things before them (which was their former habit), tried to see a great deal more in my face, in my words, than was visible on the surface. I don't know what poor Adrian Frank saw—I shall never know all that he saw.

"I agree with you that it was a very singular time," I said. "You don't understand me—you can't—I don't expect you to," I went on. "That is what I mean by devotion, and that is the kind of appeal I make to you: to take me on trust, to act in the dark, to do something simply because I wish it."

He looked at me as if he would fathom the depths of my soul, and my soul had never seemed to myself so deep. "To marry your cousin—that's all?" he said, with a strange little laugh.

"Oh no, it's not all: to be very kind to her as well."

"To give her plenty of money, above all?"

"You make me feel very ridiculous; but I should not make this request of you if you had not a fortune."

"She can have my money without marrying me."

"That's absurd. How could she take your money?"

"How, then, can she take me?"

"That's exactly what I wish to see. I told you with my own lips, weeks ago, that she would only marry a man she should love; and I may seem to contradict myself in taking up now a supposition so different. But, as I tell you, everything has changed."

"You think her capable, in other words, of marrying for money."

"For money? Is your money all there is of you? Is there a better fellow than you—is there a more perfect gentleman?"

He turned away his face at this, leaned it in his hands and groaned. I pitied him, but I wonder now that I shouldn't have pitied him more; that my pity should not have checked me. But I was too full of my idea. "It's like a fate," he murmured; "first my brother, and then you. I can't understand."

"Yes, I know your brother wants it—wants it now more than ever. But I don't care what your brother wants; and my idea is entirely independent of his. I have not the least conviction that you will succeed at first any better than you have done already. But it may be only a question of time, if you will wait and watch, and let me help you. You know you asked me to help you before, and then I wouldn't. But I repeat it again and again, at present everything is changed. Let me wait with you, let me watch with you. If you succeed, you will be very dear to me; if you fail, you will be still more so. You see it's an act of devotion, if there ever was one. I am quite aware that I ask of you something unprecedented and extraordinary. Oh, it may easily be too much for you. I can only put it before you—that's all; and as I say, I can help you. You will both be my children—I shall be near you always. If you can't marry me, perhaps you will make up your mind that this is the next best thing. You know you said that last night, yourself."

He had begun to listen to me a little, as if he were being persuaded. "Of course, I should let her know that I love you."

"She is capable of saying that you can't love me more than she does."

"I don't believe she is capable of saying any such folly. But we shall see."

"Yes; but not to-day, not to-morrow. Not at all for the present. You must wait a great many months."

"I will wait as long as you please."

"And you mustn't say a word to me of the kind you said last night."

"Is that your condition?"

"Oh no; my condition is a very different matter, and very difficult. It will probably spoil everything."

"Please, then, let me hear it at once."

"It is very hard for me to mention it; you must give me time." I turned back to my little easel and began to daub again; but I think my hand trembled, for my heart was beating fast. There was a silence of many moments; I couldn't make up my mind to speak.

"How in the world has she lost her money?" Mr. Frank asked, abruptly, as if the question had just come into his mind. "Hasn't my brother the charge of her affairs?"

"Mr. Caliph is her trustee. I can't tell you how the losses have occurred."

He got up quickly. "Do you mean that they have occurred through *him*?"

I looked up at him, and there was something in his face which made me leave my work and rise also. "I will tell you my condition now," I said. "It is that you should ask no questions—not one!" This was not what I had had in my mind; but I had not courage for more, and this had to serve.

He had turned very pale, and I laid my hand on his arm, while he looked at me as if he wished to wrest my secret out of my eyes. My secret, I call it, by courtesy; God knows I had come terribly near telling it. God will forgive me, but Eunice probably will not. Had I broken my vow, or had I kept it? I asked myself this, and the answer, so far as I read it in Mr. Frank's eyes, was not reassuring. I dreaded his next question; but when it came it was not what I had expected. Something violent took place in his own mind—something I couldn't follow.

"If I do what you ask me, what will be my reward?"

"You will make me very happy."

"And what shall I make your cousin?—God help us!"

"Less wretched than she is to-day."

"Is she 'wretched'?" he asked, frowning as he did before—a most distressing change in his mild mask.

"Ah, when I think that I have to tell you that—that you have never noticed it—I despair!" I exclaimed, with a laugh.

I had laid my hand on his arm, and he placed his right hand upon it, holding it there. He kept it a moment in his grasp, and then he said, "Don't despair!"

"Promise me to wait," I answered. "Everything is in your waiting."

"I promise you!" After which he asked me to kiss him, and I did so, on the lips. It was as if he were starting on a journey—leaving me for a long time.

"Will you come when I send for you?" I asked.

"I adore you!" he said; and he turned quickly away, to leave the place without going near the house. I watched him, and in a moment he was gone. He has not reappeared; and when I found, at lunch, that neither Eunice nor Mrs. Ermine alluded to his visit, I determined to keep the matter to myself. I said nothing about it, and up to the moment Eunice was taken ill—the next evening—he was not mentioned between us. I believe Mrs. Ermine more than once gave herself up to wonder as to his whereabouts, and declared that he had not the perfect manners of his step-brother, who was a religious observer of the *convenances*; but I think I managed to listen without confusion. Nevertheless, I had a bad conscience, and I have it still. It throbs a good deal as I sit there with Eunice in her darkened room. I *have* given her away; I *have* broken my vow. But what I wrote above is not true; she *will* forgive me! I sat at my easel for an hour after Mr. Frank left me, and then suddenly I found that I had cured myself of my folly by giving it out. It was the result of a sudden passion of desire to do something for Eunice. Passion is blind, and when I opened my eyes I saw ten thousand difficulties; that is, I saw one, which contained all the rest. That evening I wrote to Mr. Frank, to his New York address, to tell him that I had had a fit of madness, and that it had passed away; but that I was sorry to say it was not any more possible for me to marry him. I have had no answer to this letter; but what answer can he make to that last declaration? He will continue to adore me. How strange are the passions of men!

New York, November 20.—I have been silent for three months, for good reasons. Eunice was ill for many weeks, but there was never a moment when I was really alarmed about her; I knew she would recover. In the last days of October she was strong enough to be brought up to town, where she had business to transact, and now she is almost herself again. I say almost, advisedly; for she will never be herself,—her old, sweet, trustful self, so far as I am concerned. She has simply not forgiven me! Strange things have happened—things that I don't dare to consider too closely, lest I should not forgive myself. Eunice is in complete possession of her property! Mr. Caliph has made over to her everything—everything that had passed away; everything of which, three months ago, he could give no account whatever. He was with her in the country for a long day before we came up to town (during which I took care not to meet her), and after our return he was in and out of this house repeatedly. I once asked Eunice what he had to say to her, and she answered that he was "explaining." A day or two later she told me that he had given a complete account of her affairs; everything was in order; she had been wrong in what she told me before. Beyond this little statement, however, she did no further penance for the impression she had given of Mr. Caliph's earlier conduct. She doesn't yet know what to think; she only feels that if she has recovered her property there has been some interference; and she traces, or at least imputes, such interference to me. If I have interfered, I have broken my vow; and for this, as I say, the gentle creature can't forgive me. If the passions of men are strange, the passions of women are stranger still! It was sweeter for her to suffer at Mr. Caliph's hands than to receive her simple dues from them. She looks at me askance, and her coldness shows through a conscientious effort not to let me see the change in her feeling. Then she is puzzled and mystified; she can't tell what has happened, or how and why it has happened. She has waked up from her illness into a different world—a world in which Mr. Caliph's accounts were correct after all; in which, with the washing away of his stains, the colour has been quite washed out of his rich physiognomy. She vaguely feels that a sacrifice, a great effort of some kind, has been made for her, whereas her plan of life was to make the sacrifices and efforts herself. Yet she asks me no questions; the property is her right, after all, and I think there are certain things she is afraid to know. But I am more afraid than she, for it comes over me that a great sacrifice has indeed been made. I have not seen Adrian Frank since he parted from me under the trees three months ago. He has gone to Europe, and the day before he left I got a note from him. It contained only these words: "When you send for me I will come. I am waiting, as you told me." It is my belief that up to the moment I spoke of Eunice's loss of money and requested him to ask no questions, he had not definitely suspected his noble kinsman, but that my words kindled a train that lay all ready. He went away then to his shame, to the intolerable weight of it, and to heaven knows what sickening explanations with his step-brother! That gentleman has a still more brilliant bloom; he looks to my mind exactly as people look who have accepted a sacrifice; and he hasn't had another word to say about Eunice's marrying Mr. Adrian Frank. Mrs. Ermine sticks to her idea that Mr. Caliph and Eunice will make a match; but my belief is that Eunice is cured. Oh yes, she is cured! But I have done more than I meant to do, and I have not done it as I meant to do it; and I am very weary, and I shall write no more.

November 27.—Oh yes, Eunice is cured! And that is what she has not forgiven me. Mr. Caliph told her yesterday that Mr. Frank meant to spend the winter in Rome.

December 3.—I have decided to return to Europe, and have written about my apartment in Rome. I shall leave New York, if possible, on the 10th. Eunice tells me she can easily believe I shall be happier there.

December 7.—I *must* note something I had the satisfaction to-day to say to Mr. Caliph. He has not been here for three weeks, but this afternoon he came to call. He is no longer the trustee; he is only the visitor. I was alone in the library, into which he was ushered; and it was ten minutes before Eunice appeared. We had some talk, though my disgust for him is now unspeakable. At first it was of a very perfunctory kind; but suddenly he said, with more than his old impudence, "That was a most extraordinary interview of ours, at Corner-ville!" I was surprised at his saying only this, for I expected him to take his revenge on me by some means or other for having put his brother on the scent of his misdeeds. I can only account for his silence on that subject by the supposition that Mr. Frank has been able to extract from him some pledge that I shall not be molested. He was, however, such an image of unrighteous success that the sight of him filled me with gall, and I tried to think of something which would make him smart.

"I don't know what you have done, nor how you have done it," I said; "but you took a very roundabout way to arrive at certain ends. There was a time when you might have married Eunice."

It was of course nothing new that we were frank with each other, and he only repeated, smiling, "Married Eunice?"

"She was very much in love with you last spring."

"Very much in love with me?"

"Oh, it's over now. Can't you imagine that? She's cured."

He broke into a laugh, but I felt I had startled him.

"You are the most delightful woman!" he cried.

"Think how much simpler it would have been—I mean originally, when things were right, if they ever were right. Don't you see my point? But now it's too late. She has seen you when you were not on show. I assure you she is cured!"

At this moment Eunice came in, and just afterwards I left the room. I am sure it was a revelation, and that I have given him a *mauvais quart d'heure*.

Rome, February 23.—When I came back to this dear place Adrian Frank was not here, and I learned that he had gone to Sicily. A week ago I wrote to him: "You said you would come if I should send for you. I should be glad if you would come now." Last evening he appeared, and I told him that I could no longer endure my suspense in regard to a certain subject. Would he kindly inform me what he had done in New York after he left me under the trees at Cornerville? Of what sacrifice had he been guilty; to what high generosity—terrible to me to think of—had he committed himself? He would tell me very little; but he is almost a poor man. He has just enough income to live in Italy.

May 9.—Mrs. Ermine has taken it into her head to write to me. I have heard from her three times; and in her last letter, received yesterday, she returns to her old refrain that Eunice and Mr. Caliph will soon be united. I don't know what may be going on; but can it be possible that I put it into his head? Truly, I have a felicitous touch!

May 15.—I told Adrian yesterday that I would marry him if ever Eunice should marry Mr. Caliph. It was the first time I had mentioned his step-brother's name to him since the explanation I had attempted to have with him after he came back to Rome; and he evidently didn't like it at all.

In the Tyrol, August.—I sent Mrs. Ermine a little water-colour in return for her last letter, for I can't write to her, and that is easier. She now writes me again, in order to get another water-colour. She speaks of course of Eunice and Mr. Caliph, and for the first time there appears a certain reality in what she says. She complains that Eunice is very slow in coming to the point, and relates that poor Mr. Caliph, who has taken her into his confidence, seems at times almost to despair. Nothing would suit him better of course than to appropriate two fortunes: two are so much better than one. But however much he may have explained, he can hardly have explained everything. Adrian Frank is in Scotland; in writing to him three days ago I had occasion to repeat that I will marry him on the day on which a certain other marriage takes place. In that way I am safe. I shall send another water-colour to Mrs. Ermine. Water-colours or no, Eunice doesn't write to me. It is clear that she hasn't forgiven me! She regards me as perjured; and of course I am. Perhaps she will marry him after all.

Lady Barberina

IT IS well known that there are few sights in the world more brilliant than the main avenues of Hyde Park of a fine afternoon in June. This was quite the opinion of two persons who, on a beautiful day at the beginning of that month, four years ago, had established themselves under the great trees in a couple of iron chairs (the big ones with arms, for which, if I mistake not, you pay twopence), and sat there with the slow procession of the Drive behind them, while their faces were turned to the more vivid agitation of the Row. They were lost in the multitude of observers, and they belonged, superficially, at least, to that class of persons who, wherever they may be, rank rather with the spectators than with the spectacle. They were quiet, simple, elderly, of aspect somewhat neutral; you would have liked them extremely, but you would scarcely have noticed them. Nevertheless, in all that shining host, it is to them, obscure, that we must give our attention. The reader is begged to have confidence; he is not asked to make vain concessions. There was that in the faces of our friends which indicated that they were growing old together, and that they were fond enough of each other's company not to object (if it was a condition) even to that. The reader will have guessed that they were husband and wife; and perhaps while he is about it he will have guessed that they were of that nationality for which Hyde Park at the height of the season is most completely illustrative. They were familiar strangers, as it were; and people at once so initiated and so detached could only be Americans. This reflection, indeed, you would have made only after some delay; for it must be admitted that they carried few patriotic signs on the surface. They had the American turn of mind, but that was very subtle; and to your eye—if your eye had cared about it—they might have been of English, or even of Continental, parentage. It was as if it suited them to be colourless; their colour was all in their talk. They were not in the least verdant; they were gray, rather, of monotonous hue. If they were interested in the riders, the horses, the walkers, the great exhibition of English wealth and health, beauty, luxury and leisure, it was because all this referred itself to other impressions, because they had the key to almost everything that needed an answer—because, in a word, they were able to compare. They had not arrived, they had only returned; and recognition much more than surprise was expressed in their quiet gaze. It may as well be said outright that Dexter Freer and his wife belonged to that class of Americans who are constantly "passing through" London. Possessors of a fortune of which, from any standpoint, the limits were plainly visible, they were unable to command that highest of luxuries—a habitation in their own country. They found it much more possible to economise at Dresden or Florence than at Buffalo or Minneapolis. The economy was as great, and the inspiration was greater. From Dresden, from Florence, moreover, they constantly made excursions which would not have been possible in those other cities; and it is even to be feared that they had some rather expensive methods of saving. They came to London to buy their portmanteaus, their toothbrushes, their writing-paper; they occasionally even crossed the Atlantic to assure themselves that prices over there were still the same. They were eminently a social pair; their interests were mainly personal. Their point of view always was so distinctly human that they passed for being fond of gossip; and they certainly knew a good deal about the affairs of other people. They had friends in every country, in every town; and it was not their fault if people told them their secrets. Dexter Freer was a tall, lean man, with an interested eye, and a nose that rather aspired than drooped, yet was salient withal. He brushed his hair, which was streaked with white, forward over his ears, in those locks which are represented in the portraits of clean-shaven gentlemen who flourished fifty years ago, and wore an old-fashioned neckcloth and gaiters. His wife, a small, plump person, of superficial freshness, with a white face, and hair that was still perfectly black, smiled perpetually, but had never laughed since the death of a son whom she had lost ten years after her marriage. Her husband, on the other hand, who was usually quite grave, indulged on great occasions in resounding mirth. People confided in her less than in him; but that mattered little, as she confided sufficiently in herself. Her dress, which was always black or dark gray, was so harmoniously simple that you could see she was fond of it; it was never smart by accident. She was full of intentions, of the most judicious sort; and though she was perpetually moving about the world she had the air of being perfectly stationary. She was celebrated for the promptitude with which she made her sitting-room at an inn, where she might be spending a night or two, look like an apartment long inhabited. With books, flowers, photographs, draperies, rapidly distributed—she had even a way, for the most part, of having a piano—the place seemed almost hereditary. The pair were just back from America, where they had spent three months, and now were able to face the world with something of the elation which people feel who have been justified in a prevision. They had found their native land quite ruinous.

"There he is again!" said Mr. Freer, following with his eyes a young man who passed along the Row, riding slowly. "That's a beautiful thoroughbred!"

Mrs. Freer asked idle questions only when she wished for time to think. At present she had simply to look and see who it was her husband meant. "The horse is too big," she remarked, in a moment.

"You mean that the rider is too small," her husband rejoined; "he is mounted on his millions."

"Is it really millions?"

"Seven or eight, they tell me."

"How disgusting!" It was in this manner that Mrs. Freer usually spoke of the large fortunes of the day. "I wish he would see us," she added.

"He does see us, but he doesn't like to look at us. He is too conscious; he isn't easy."

"Too conscious of his big horse?"

"Yes, and of his big fortune; he is rather ashamed of it."

"This is an odd place to come, then," said Mrs. Freer.

"I am not sure of that. He will find people here richer than himself, and other big horses in plenty, and that will cheer him up. Perhaps, too, he is looking for that girl."

"The one we heard about? He can't be such a fool."

"He isn't a fool," said Dexter Freer. "If he is thinking of her, he has some good reason."

"I wonder what Mary Lemon would say."

"She would say it was right, if he should do it. She thinks he can do no wrong. He is exceedingly fond of her."

"I shan't be sure of that if he takes home a wife who will despise her."

"Why should the girl despise her? She is a delightful woman."

"The girl will never know it—and if she should, it would make no difference; she will despise everything."

"I don't believe it, my dear; she will like some things very much. Every one will be very nice to her."

"She will despise them all the more. But we are speaking as if it were all arranged; I don't believe in it at all," said Mrs. Freer.

"Well, something of the sort—in this case or in some other—is sure to happen sooner or later," her husband replied, turning round a little toward the part of the delta which is formed, near the entrance to the Park, by the divergence of the two great vistas of the Drive and the Row.

Our friends had turned their backs, as I have said, to the solemn revolution of wheels and the densely-packed mass of spectators who had chosen that part of the show. These spectators were now agitated by a unanimous impulse: the pushing back of chairs, the shuffle of feet, the rustle of garments and the deepening murmur of voices sufficiently expressed it. Royalty was approaching—royalty was passing—royalty had passed. Freer turned his head and his ear a little; but he failed to alter his position further, and his wife took no notice of the flurry. They had seen royalty pass, all over Europe, and they knew that it passed very quickly. Sometimes it came back; sometimes it didn't; for more than once they had seen it pass for the last time. They were veteran tourists, and they knew perfectly when to get up and when to remain seated. Mr. Freer went on with his proposition: "Some young fellow is certain to do it, and one of these girls is certain to take the risk. They must take risks, over here, more and more."

"The girls, I have no doubt, will be glad enough; they have had very little chance as yet. But I don't want Jackson to begin."

"Do you know I rather think I do?" said Dexter Freer; "It will be very amusing."

"For us, perhaps, but not for him; he will repent of it, and be wretched. He is too good for that."

"Wretched, never! He has no capacity for wretchedness; and that's why he can afford to risk it."

"He will have to make great concessions," Mrs. Freer remarked.

"He won't make one."

"I should like to see."

"You admit, then, that it will be amusing, which is all I contend for. But, as you say, we are talking as if it were settled, whereas there is probably nothing in it, after all. The best stories always turn out false. I shall be sorry in this case."

They relapsed into silence, while people passed and repassed them—continuous, successive, mechanical, with strange sequences of faces. They looked at the people, but no one looked at them, though every one was there so admittedly to see what was to be seen. It was all striking, all pictorial, and it made a great composition. The wide, long area of the Row, its red-brown surface dotted with bounding figures, stretched away into the distance and became suffused and misty in the bright, thick air. The deep, dark English verdure that bordered and overhung it, looked rich and old, revived and refreshed though it was by the breath of June. The mild blue of the sky was spotted with great silvery clouds, and the light drizzled down in heavenly shafts over the quieter spaces of the Park, as one saw them beyond the Row. All this, however, was only a background, for the scene was before everything personal; superbly so, and full of the gloss and lustre, the contrasted tones, of a thousand polished surfaces. Certain things were salient, pervasive—the shining flanks of the perfect horses, the twinkle of bits and spurs, the smoothness of fine cloth adjusted to shoulders and limbs, the sheen of hats and boots, the freshness of complexions, the expression of smiling, talking faces, the flash and flutter of rapid gallops. Faces were everywhere, and they were the great effect; above all, the fair faces of women on tall horses, flushed a little under their stiff black hats, with figures stiffened, in spite of much definition of curve, by their tight-fitting habits. Their hard little helmets; their neat, compact heads; their straight necks; their firm, tailor-made armour; their blooming, competent physique, made them look doubly like amazons about to ride a charge. The men, with their eyes before them, with hats of undulating brim, good profiles, high collars, white flowers on their chests, long legs and long feet, had an air more elaborately decorative, as they jolted beside the ladies, always out of step. These were youthful types; but it was not all youth, for many a saddle was surmounted by a richer rotundity; and ruddy faces, with short white whiskers or with matronly chins, looked down comfortably from an equilibrium which was moral and social as well as physical. The walkers differed from the riders only in being on foot, and in looking at the riders more than these looked at them; for they would have done as well in the saddle and ridden as the others ride. The women had tight little bonnets and still tighter little knots of hair; their round chins rested on a close swathing of lace, or, in some cases, of silver chains and circlets. They had flat backs and small waists; they walked slowly, with their elbows out, carrying vast parasols, and turning their heads very little to the right or the left. They were amazons unmounted, quite ready to spring into the saddle. There was a great deal of beauty and a general look of successful development, which came from clear, quiet eyes, and from well-cut lips, on which syllables were liquid and sentences brief. Some of the young men, as well as the women, had the happiest proportions and oval faces, in which line and colour were pure and fresh and the idea of the moment was not very intense.

"They are very good-looking," said Mr. Freer, at the end of ten minutes; "they are the finest whites."

"So long as they remain white they do very well; but when they venture upon colour!" his wife replied. She sat with her eyes on a level with the skirts of the ladies who passed her; and she had been following the progress of a green velvet robe, enriched with ornaments of steel and much gathered up in the hands of its wearer, who, herself apparently in her teens, was accompanied by a young lady draped in scanty pink muslin, embroidered, æsthetically, with flowers that simulated the iris.

"All the same, in a crowd, they are wonderfully well turned out," Dexter Freer went on; "take the men, and women, and horses together. Look at that big fellow on the light chestnut:

what could be more perfect? By the way, it's Lord Canterville," he added in a moment, as if the fact were of some
importance.

Mrs. Freer recognised its importance to the degree of raising her glass to look at Lord Canterville. "How do you know
it's he?" she asked, with her glass still up.

"I heard him say something the night I went to the House
of Lords. It was very few words, but I remember him. A man
who was near me told me who he was."

"He is not so handsome as you," said Mrs. Freer, dropping
her glass.

"Ah, you're too difficult!" her husband murmured. "What
a pity the girl isn't with him," he went on; "we might see
something."

It appeared in a moment that the girl was with him. The
nobleman designated had ridden slowly forward from the
start, but just opposite our friends he pulled up to look behind
him, as if he had been waiting for some one. At the same
moment a gentleman in the Walk engaged his attention, so
that he advanced to the barrier which protects the pedestrians,
and halted there, bending a little from his saddle and talking
with his friend, who leaned against the rail. Lord Canterville
was indeed perfect, as his American admirer had said. Upwards of sixty, and of great stature and great presence, he was
really a splendid apparition. In exquisite preservation, he had
the freshness of middle life, and would have been young to
the eye if the lapse of years were not needed to account for
his considerable girth. He was clad from head to foot in garments of a radiant gray, and his fine florid countenance was
surmounted with a white hat, of which the majestic curves
were a triumph of good form. Over his mighty chest was
spread a beard of the richest growth, and of a colour, in spite
of a few streaks, vaguely grizzled, to which the coat of his
admirable horse appeared to be a perfect match. It left no
opportunity, in his uppermost button-hole, for the customary
gardenia; but this was of comparatively little consequence, as
the vegetation of the beard itself was tropical. Astride his great
steed, with his big fist, gloved in pearl-gray, on his swelling
thigh, his face lighted up with good-humoured indifference,
and all his magnificent surface reflecting the mild sunshine,

he was a very imposing man indeed, and visibly, incontestably, a personage. People almost lingered to look at him as they passed. His halt was brief, however, for he was almost immediately joined by two handsome girls, who were as well turned out, in Dexter Freer's phrase, as himself. They had been detained a moment at the entrance to the Row, and now advanced side by side, their groom close behind them. One was taller and older than the other, and it was apparent at a glance that they were sisters. Between them, with their charming shoulders, contracted waists, and skirts that hung without a wrinkle, like a plate of zinc, they represented in a singularly complete form the pretty English girl in the position in which she is prettiest.

"Of course they are his daughters," said Dexter Freer, as they rode away with Lord Canterville; "and in that case one of them must be Jackson Lemon's sweetheart. Probably the bigger; they said it was the eldest. She is evidently a fine creature."

"She would hate it over there," Mrs. Freer remarked, for all answer to this cluster of inductions.

"You know I don't admit that. But granting she should, it would do her good to have to accommodate herself."

"She wouldn't accommodate herself."

"She looks so confoundedly fortunate, perched up on that saddle," Dexter Freer pursued, without heeding his wife's rejoinder.

"Aren't they supposed to be very poor?"

"Yes, they look it!" And his eyes followed the distinguished trio, as, with the groom, as distinguished in his way as any of them, they started on a canter.

The air was full of sound, but it was low and diffused; and when, near our friends, it became articulate, the words were simple and few.

"It's as good as the circus, isn't it, Mrs. Freer?" These words correspond to that description, but they pierced the air more effectually than any our friends had lately heard. They were uttered by a young man who had stopped short in the path, absorbed by the sight of his compatriots. He was short and stout, he had a round, kind face, and short, stiff-looking hair, which was reproduced in a small bristling beard. He wore

a double-breasted walking-coat, which was not, however, buttoned, and on the summit of his round head was perched a
hat of exceeding smallness, and of the so-called "pot" category. It evidently fitted him, but a hatter himself would not
have known why. His hands were encased in new gloves, of a
dark-brown colour, and they hung with an air of unaccustomed inaction at his sides. He sported neither umbrella nor
stick. He extended one of his hands, almost with eagerness,
to Mrs. Freer, blushing a little as he became aware that he
had been eager.

"Oh, Doctor Feeder!" she said, smiling at him. Then she
repeated to her husband, "Doctor Feeder, my dear!" and her
husband said, "Oh, Doctor, how d'ye do?" I have spoken of
the composition of his appearance; but the items were not
perceived by these two. They saw only one thing, his delightful face, which was both simple and clever, and unreservedly
good. They had lately made the voyage from New York in his
company, and it was plain that he would be very genial at sea.
After he had stood in front of them a moment, a chair beside
Mrs. Freer became vacant, on which he took possession of it,
and sat there telling her what he thought of the Park and how
he liked London. As she knew every one she had known many
of his people at home; and while she listened to him she remembered how large their contribution had been to the virtue
and culture of Cincinnati. Mrs. Freer's social horizon included
even that city; she had been on terms almost familiar with
several families from Ohio, and was acquainted with the position of the Feeders there. This family, very numerous, was
interwoven into an enormous cousinship. She herself was
quite out of such a system, but she could have told you whom
Doctor Feeder's great-grandfather had married. Every one,
indeed, had heard of the good deeds of the descendants of
this worthy, who were generally physicians, excellent ones,
and whose name expressed not inaptly their numerous acts of
charity. Sidney Feeder, who had several cousins of this name
established in the same line at Cincinnati, had transferred himself and his ambition to New York, where his practice, at the
end of three years, had begun to grow. He had studied his
profession at Vienna, and was impregnated with German science; indeed, if he had only worn spectacles, he might per-

fectly, as he sat there watching the riders in Rotten Row as if their proceedings were a successful demonstration, have passed for a young German of distinction. He had come over to London to attend a medical congress which met this year in the British capital; for his interest in the healing art was by no means limited to the cure of his patients; it embraced every form of experiment, and the expression of his honest eyes would almost have reconciled you to vivisection. It was the first time he had come to the Park; for social experiments he had little leisure. Being aware, however, that it was a very typical, and as it were symptomatic, sight, he had conscientiously reserved an afternoon, and had dressed himself carefully for the occasion. "It's quite a brilliant show," he said to Mrs. Freer; "it makes me wish I had a mount." Little as he resembled Lord Canterville, he rode very well.

"Wait till Jackson Lemon passes again, and you can stop him and make him let you take a turn." This was the jocular suggestion of Dexter Freer.

"Why, is he here? I have been looking out for him; I should like to see him."

"Doesn't he go to your medical congress?" asked Mrs. Freer.

"Well, yes, he attends; but he isn't very regular. I guess he goes out a good deal."

"I guess he does," said Mr. Freer; "and if he isn't very regular, I guess he has a good reason. A beautiful reason, a charming reason," he went on, bending forward to look down toward the beginning of the Row. "Dear me, what a lovely reason!"

Doctor Feeder followed the direction of his eyes, and after a moment understood his allusion. Little Jackson Lemon, on his big horse, passed along the avenue again, riding beside one of the young girls who had come that way shortly before in the company of Lord Canterville. His lordship followed, in conversation with the other, his younger daughter. As they advanced, Jackson Lemon turned his eyes toward the multitude under the trees, and it so happened that they rested upon the Dexter Freers. He smiled, and raised his hat with all possible friendliness; and his three companions turned to see to whom he was bowing with so much cordiality. As he settled his hat on his head he espied the young man from Cincinnati, whom he had at first overlooked; whereupon he smiled still more brightly and waved Sidney Feeder an airy salutation with his hand, reining in a little at the same time just for an instant, as if he half expected the Doctor to come and speak to him. Seeing him with strangers, however, Sidney Feeder hung back, staring a little as he rode away.

It is open to us to know that at this moment the young lady by whose side he was riding said to him, familiarly enough: "Who are those people you bowed to?"

"Some old friends of mine—Americans," Jackson Lemon answered.

"Of course they are Americans; there is nothing but Americans nowadays."

"Oh yes, our turn's coming round!" laughed the young man.

"But that doesn't say who they are," his companion continued. "It's so difficult to say who Americans are," she added, before he had time to answer her.

"Dexter Freer and his wife—there is nothing difficult about that; every one knows them."

"I never heard of them," said the English girl.

"Ah, that's your fault. I assure you everybody knows them."

"And does everybody know the little man with the fat face whom you kissed your hand to?"

"I didn't kiss my hand, but I would if I had thought of it. He is a great chum of mine,—a fellow-student at Vienna.

"And what's *his* name?"

"Doctor Feeder."

Jackson Lemon's companion was silent a moment. "Are *all* your friends doctors?" she presently inquired.

"No; some of them are in other businesses."

"Are they all in some business?"

"Most of them; save two or three, like Dexter Freer."

"Dexter Freer? I thought you said Doctor Freer."

The young man gave a laugh. "You heard me wrong. You have got doctors on the brain, Lady Barb."

"I am rather glad," said Lady Barb, giving the rein to her horse, who bounded away.

"Well, yes, she's very handsome, the reason," Doctor Feeder remarked, as he sat under the trees.

"Is he going to marry her?" Mrs. Freer inquired.

"Marry her? I hope not."

"Why do you hope not?"

"Because I know nothing about her. I want to know something about the woman that man marries."

"I suppose you would like him to marry in Cincinnati," Mrs. Freer rejoined lightly.

"Well, I am not particular where it is; but I want to know her first." Doctor Feeder was very sturdy.

"We were in hopes you would know all about it," said Mr. Freer.

"No; I haven't kept up with him there."

"We have heard from a dozen people that he has been always with her for the last month; and that kind of thing, in England, is supposed to mean something. Hasn't he spoken of her when you have seen him?"

"No, he has only talked about the new treatment of spinal meningitis. He is very much interested in spinal meningitis."

"I wonder if he talks about it to Lady Barb," said Mrs. Freer.

"Who is she, any way?" the young man inquired.

"Lady Barberina Clement."

"And who is Lady Barberina Clement?"

"The daughter of Lord Canterville."

"And who is Lord Canterville?"

"Dexter must tell you that," said Mrs. Freer.

And Dexter accordingly told him that the Marquis of Canterville had been in his day a great sporting nobleman and an ornament to English society, and had held more than once a high post in her Majesty's household. Dexter Freer knew all these things—how his lordship had married a daughter of Lord Treherne, a very serious, intelligent and beautiful woman, who had redeemed him from the extravagance of his youth and presented him in rapid succession with a dozen little tenants for the nurseries at Pasterns—this being, as Mr. Freer also knew, the name of the principal seat of the Cantervilles. The Marquis was a Tory, but very liberal for a Tory, and very popular in society at large; good-natured, good-looking, knowing how to be genial and yet remain a *grand seigneur*, clever enough to make an occasional speech, and much associated with the fine old English pursuits, as well as with many of the new improvements—the purification of the Turf, the opening of the museums on Sunday, the propagation of coffee-taverns, the latest ideas on sanitary reform. He disapproved of the extension of the suffrage, but he positively had drainage on the brain. It had been said of him at least once (and I think in print) that he was just the man to convey to the popular mind the impression that the British aristocracy is still a living force. He was not very rich, unfortunately (for a man who had to exemplify such truths), and of his twelve children no less than seven were daughters. Lady Barberina, Jackson Lemon's friend, was the second; the eldest had married Lord Beauchemin. Mr. Freer had caught quite the right pronunciation of this name: he called it Bitumen. Lady Louisa had done very well, for her husband was rich, and she had brought him nothing to speak of; but it was hardly to be expected that the others would do so well. Happily the younger girls were still in the schoolroom; and before they had come up, Lady Canterville, who was a woman of resources, would have worked off the two that were out. It was Lady Agatha's first season; she was not so pretty as her sister, but she was thought to be cleverer. Half a dozen people had spoken to him of Jackson Lemon's being a great deal at the Cantervilles. He was supposed to be enormously rich.

"Well, so he is," said Sidney Feeder, who had listened to Mr. Freer's little recital with attention, with eagerness even, but with an air of imperfect apprehension.

"Yes, but not so rich as they probably think."

"Do they want his money? Is that what they're after?"

"You go straight to the point," Mrs. Freer murmured.

"I haven't the least idea," said her husband. "He is a very nice fellow in himself."

"Yes, but he's a doctor," Mrs. Freer remarked.

"What have they got against that?" asked Sidney Feeder.

"Why, over here, you know, they only call them in to prescribe," said Dexter Freer; "the profession isn't—a—what you'd call aristocratic."

"Well, I don't know it, and I don't know that I want to

know it. How do you mean, aristocratic? What profession is? It would be rather a curious one. Many of the gentlemen at the congress there are quite charming."

"I like doctors very much," said Mrs. Freer; "my father was a doctor. But they don't marry the daughters of marquises."

"I don't believe Jackson wants to marry that one."

"Very possibly not—people are such asses," said Dexter Freer. "But he will have to decide. I wish you would find out, by the way; you can if you will."

"I will ask him—up at the congress; I can do that. I suppose he has got to marry some one," Sidney Feeder added, in a moment, "and she may be a nice girl."

"She is said to be charming."

"Very well, then; it won't hurt him. I must say, however, I am not sure I like all that about her family."

"What I told you? It's all to their honour and glory."

"Are they quite on the square? It's like those people in Thackeray."

"Oh, if Thackeray could have done this!" Mrs. Freer exclaimed, with a good deal of expression.

"You mean all this scene?" asked the young man.

"No; the marriage of a British noblewoman and an American doctor. It would have been a subject for Thackeray."

"You see you do want it, my dear," said Dexter Freer quietly.

"I want it as a story, but I don't want it for Doctor Lemon."

"Does he call himself 'Doctor' still?" Mr. Freer asked of young Feeder.

"I suppose he does; I call him so. Of course he doesn't practise. But once a doctor, always a doctor."

"That's doctrine for Lady Barb!"

Sidney Feeder stared. "Hasn't she got a title too? What would she expect him to be? President of the United States? He's a man of real ability; he might have stood at the head of his profession. When I think of that, I want to swear. What did his father want to go and make all that money for?"

"It must certainly be odd to them to see a 'medical man' with six or eight millions," Mr. Freer observed.

"They use the same term as the Choctaws," said his wife.

"Why, some of their own physicians make immense fortunes," Sidney Feeder declared.

"Couldn't he be made a baronet by the Queen?" This suggestion came from Mrs. Freer.

"Yes, then he would be aristocratic," said the young man. "But I don't see why he should want to marry over here; it seems to me to be going out of his way. However, if he is happy, I don't care. I like him very much; he has got lots of ability. If it hadn't been for his father he would have made a splendid doctor. But, as I say, he takes a great interest in medical science, and I guess he means to promote it all he can—with his fortune. He will always be doing something in the way of research. He thinks we *do* know something, and he is bound we shall know more. I hope she won't prevent him, the young marchioness—is that her rank? And I hope they are really good people. He ought to be very useful. I should want to know a good deal about the family I was going to marry into."

"He looked to me, as he rode there, as if he knew a good deal about the Clements," Dexter Freer said, rising, as his wife suggested that they ought to be going; "and he looked to me pleased with the knowledge. There they come, down on the other side. Will you walk away with us, or will you stay?"

"Stop him and ask him, and then come and tell us—in Jermyn Street." This was Mrs. Freer's parting injunction to Sidney Feeder.

"He ought to come himself—tell him that," her husband added.

"Well, I guess I'll stay," said the young man, as his companions merged themselves in the crowd that now was tending toward the gates. He went and stood by the barrier, and saw Doctor Lemon and his friends pull up at the entrance to the Row, where they apparently prepared to separate. The separation took some time, and Sidney Feeder became interested. Lord Canterville and his younger daughter lingered to talk with two gentlemen, also mounted, who looked a good deal at the legs of Lady Agatha's horse. Jackson Lemon and Lady Barberina were face to face, very near each other; and she, leaning forward a little, stroked the overlapping neck of his glossy bay. At a distance he appeared to be talking, and she to be listening and saying nothing. "Oh yes, he's making love to her," thought Sidney Feeder. Suddenly her father turned away, to leave the Park, and she joined him and disappeared, while Doctor Lemon came up on the left again, as if for a final gallop. He had not gone far before he perceived his *confrère*, who awaited him at the rail; and he repeated the gesture which Lady Barberina had spoken of as a kissing of his hand, though it must be added that, to his friend's eyes, it had not quite that significance. When he reached the point where Feeder stood he pulled up.

"If I had known you were coming here I would have given you a mount," he said. There was not in his person that irradiation of wealth and distinction which made Lord Canterville glow like a picture; but as he sat there with his little legs stuck out, he looked very bright and sharp and happy, wearing in his degree the aspect of one of Fortune's favourites. He had a thin, keen, delicate face, a nose very carefully finished, a rapid eye, a trifle hard in expression, and a small moustache, a good deal cultivated. He was not striking, but he was very positive, and it was easy to see that he was full of purpose.

"How many horses have you got—about forty?" his compatriot inquired, in response to his greeting.

"About five hundred," said Jackson Lemon.

"Did you mount your friends—the three you were riding with?"

"Mount them? They have got the best horses in England."

"Did they sell you this one?" Sidney Feeder continued, in the same humorous strain.

"What do you think of him?" said his friend, not deigning to answer this question.

"He's an awful old screw; I wonder he can carry you."

"Where did you get your hat?" asked Doctor Lemon, in return.

"I got it in New York. What's the matter with it?"

"It's very beautiful; I wish I had bought one like it."

"The head's the thing—not the hat. I don't mean yours, but mine. There is something very deep in your question; I must think it over."

"Don't—don't," said Jackson Lemon; "you will never get to the bottom of it. Are you having a good time?"

"A glorious time. Have you been up to-day?"

"Up among the doctors? No; I have had a lot of things to do."

"We had a very interesting discussion. I made a few remarks."

"You ought to have told me. What were they about?"

"About the intermarriage of races, from the point of view——" And Sidney Feeder paused a moment, occupied with the attempt to scratch the nose of his friend's horse.

"From the point of view of the progeny, I suppose?"

"Not at all; from the point of view of the old friends."

"Damn the old friends!" Doctor Lemon exclaimed, with jocular crudity.

"Is it true that you are going to marry a young marchioness?"

The face of the young man in the saddle became just a trifle rigid, and his firm eyes fixed themselves on Doctor Feeder.

"Who has told you that?"

"Mr. and Mrs. Freer, whom I met just now."

"Mr. and Mrs. Freer be hanged! And who told them?"

"Ever so many people; I don't know who."

"Gad, how things are tattled!" cried Jackson Lemon, with some asperity.

"I can see it's true, by the way you say that."

"Do Freer and his wife believe it?" Jackson Lemon went on impatiently.

"They want you to go and see them: you can judge for yourself."

"I will go and see them, and tell them to mind their business."

"In Jermyn Street; but I forget the number. I am sorry the marchioness isn't American," Sidney Feeder continued.

"If I should marry her, she would be," said his friend. "But I don't see what difference it can make to you."

"Why, she'll look down on the profession; and I don't like that from your wife."

"That will touch me more than you."

"Then it *is* true?" cried Feeder, more seriously, looking up at his friend.

"She won't look down; I will answer for that."

"You won't care; you are out of it all now."

"No, I am not; I mean to do a great deal of work."

"I will believe that when I see it," said Sidney Feeder, who was by no means perfectly incredulous, but who thought it salutary to take that tone. "I am not sure that you have any right to work—you oughtn't to have everything; you ought to leave the field to us. You must pay the penalty of being so rich. You would have been celebrated if you had continued to practise—more celebrated than any one. But you won't be now—you can't be. Some one else will be, in your place."

Jackson Lemon listened to this, but without meeting the eyes of the speaker; not, however, as if he were avoiding them, but as if the long stretch of the Ride, now less and less obstructed, invited him and made his companion's talk a little retarding. Nevertheless, he answered, deliberately and kindly enough: "I hope it will be you;" and he bowed to a lady who rode past.

"Very likely it will. I hope I make you feel badly—that's what I'm trying to do."

"Oh, awfully!" cried Jackson Lemon; "all the more that I am not in the least engaged."

"Well, that's good. Won't you come up to-morrow?" Doctor Feeder went on.

"I'll try, my dear fellow; I can't be sure. By-by!"

"Oh, you're lost anyway!" cried Sidney Feeder, as the other started away.

II.

It was Lady Marmaduke, the wife of Sir Henry Marmaduke, who had introduced Jackson Lemon to Lady Beauchemin; after which Lady Beauchemin had made him acquainted with her mother and sisters. Lady Marmaduke was also transatlantic; she had been for her conjugal baronet the most permanent consequence of a tour in the United States. At present, at the end of ten years, she knew her London as she had never known her New York, so that it had been easy for her to be, as she called herself, Jackson Lemon's social godmother. She had views with regard to his career, and these views fitted into a social scheme which, if our space permitted, I should be glad to lay before the reader in its magnitude. She wished to add an arch or two to the bridge on which she had effected her transit from America, and it was her belief that Jackson Lemon might furnish the materials. This bridge, as yet a somewhat sketchy and rickety structure, she saw (in the future) boldly stretching from one solid pillar to another. It would have to go both ways, for reciprocity was the keynote of Lady Marmaduke's plan. It was her belief that an ultimate fusion was inevitable, and that those who were the first to understand the situation would gain the most. The first time Jackson Lemon had dined with her, he met Lady Beauchemin, who was her intimate friend. Lady Beauchemin was remarkably gracious; she asked him to come and see her as if she really meant it. He presented himself, and in her drawing-room met her mother, who happened to be calling at the same moment. Lady Canterville, not less friendly than her daughter, invited him down to Pasterns for Easter week; and before a month had passed it seemed to him that, though he was not what he would have called intimate at any house in London, the door of the house of Clement opened to him pretty often. This was a considerable good fortune, for it always opened upon a charming picture. The inmates were a blooming and beautiful race, and their interior had an aspect of the ripest comfort. It was not the splendour of New York (as New York had lately begun to appear to the young man), but a splendour in which there was an unpurchasable ingredient of age. He himself had a great deal of money, and money was good, even when it was new; but old money was the best. Even after he learned that Lord Canterville's fortune was more ancient than abundant, it was still the mellowness of the golden element that struck him. It was Lady Beauchemin who had told him that her father was not rich; having told him, besides this, many surprising things—things that were surprising in themselves or surprising on her lips. This struck him afresh later that evening—the day he met Sidney Feeder in the Park. He dined out, in the company of Lady Beauchemin, and afterward, as she was alone—her husband had gone down to listen to a debate—she offered to "take him on." She was going to

several places, and he must be going to some of them. They
compared notes, and it was settled that they should proceed
together to the Trumpingtons', whither, also, it appeared at
eleven o'clock that all the world was going, the approach to
the house being choked for half a mile with carriages. It was
a close, muggy night; Lady Beauchemin's chariot, in its place
in the rank, stood still for long periods. In his corner beside
her, through the open window, Jackson Lemon, rather hot,
rather oppressed, looked out on the moist, greasy pavement,
over which was flung, a considerable distance up and down,
the flare of a public-house. Lady Beauchemin, however, was
not impatient, for she had a purpose in her mind, and now
she could say what she wished.

"Do you really love her?" That was the first thing she said.

"Well, I guess so," Jackson Lemon answered, as if he did
not recognise the obligation to be serious.

Lady Beauchemin looked at him a moment in silence; he
felt her gaze, and turning his eyes, saw her face, partly shad-
owed, with the aid of a streetlamp. She was not so pretty as
Lady Barberina; her countenance had a certain sharpness; her
hair, very light in colour and wonderfully frizzled, almost covered her eyes, the expression of which, however, together with
that of her pointed nose, and the glitter of several diamonds,
emerged from the gloom. "You don't seem to know. I never
saw a man in such an odd state," she presently remarked.

"You push me a little too much; I must have time to think
of it," the young man went on. "You know in my country
they allow us plenty of time." He had several little oddities of
expression, of which he was perfectly conscious, and which he
found convenient, for they protected him in a society in which
a lonely American was rather exposed; they gave him the advantage which corresponded with certain drawbacks. He had
very few natural Americanisms, but the occasional use of one,
discreetly chosen, made him appear simpler than he really was,
and he had his reasons for wishing this result. He was not
simple; he was subtle, circumspect, shrewd, and perfectly
aware that he might make mistakes. There was a danger of his
making a mistake at present—a mistake which would be immensely grave. He was determined only to succeed. It is true
that for a great success he would take a certain risk; but the

risk was to be considered, and he gained time while he mul-
tiplied his guesses and talked about his country.

"You may take ten years if you like," said Lady Beauchemin. "I am in no hurry whatever to make you my brother-
in-law. Only you must remember that you spoke to me first."

"What did I say?"

"You told me that Barberina was the finest girl you had
seen in England."

"Oh, I am willing to stand by that; I like her type."

"I should think you might!"

"I like her very much—with all her peculiarities."

"What do you mean by her peculiarities?"

"Well, she has some peculiar ideas," said Jackson Lemon,
in a tone of the sweetest reasonableness; "and she has a peculiar way of speaking."

"Ah, you can't expect us to speak as well as you!" cried
Lady Beauchemin.

"I don't know why not; you do some things much better."

"We have our own ways, at any rate, and we think them
the best in the world. One of them is not to let a gentleman
devote himself to a girl for three or four months without some
sense of responsibility. If you don't wish to marry my sister
you ought to go away."

"I ought never to have come," said Jackson Lemon.

"I can scarcely agree to that; for I should have lost the
pleasure of knowing you."

"It would have spared you this duty, which you dislike very
much."

"Asking you about your intentions? I don't dislike it at all;
it amuses me extremely."

"Should you like your sister to marry me?" asked Jackson
Lemon, with great simplicity.

If he expected to take Lady Beauchemin by surprise he was
disappointed; for she was perfectly prepared to commit herself. "I should like it very much. I think English and American
society ought to be but one—I mean the best of each—a great
whole."

"Will you allow me to ask whether Lady Marmaduke suggested that to you?"

"We have often talked of it."

"Oh yes, that's her aim."

"Well, it's my aim too. I think there's a great deal to be done."

"And you would like me to do it?"

"To begin it, precisely. Don't you think we ought to see more of each other?—I mean the best in each country."

Jackson Lemon was silent a moment. "I am afraid I haven't any general ideas. If I should marry an English girl it wouldn't be for the good of the species."

"Well, we want to be mixed a little; that I am sure of," Lady Beauchemin said.

"You certainly got that from Lady Marmaduke."

"It's too tiresome, your not consenting to be serious! But my father will make you so," Lady Beauchemin went on. "I may as well let you know that he intends in a day or two to ask you your intentions. That's all I wished to say to you. I think you ought to be prepared."

"I am much obliged to you; Lord Canterville will do quite right."

There was, to Lady Beauchemin, something really unfathomable in this little American doctor, whom she had taken up on grounds of large policy, and who, though he was assumed to have sunk the medical character, was neither handsome nor distinguished, but only immensely rich and quite original, for he was not insignificant. It was unfathomable, to begin with, that a medical man should be so rich, or that so rich a man should be medical; it was even, to an eye which was always gratified by suitability, rather irritating. Jackson Lemon himself could have explained it better than any one else, but this was an explanation that one could scarcely ask for. There were other things; his cool acceptance of certain situations; his general indisposition to explain; his way of taking refuge in jokes which at times had not even the merit of being American; his way, too, of appearing to be a suitor without being an aspirant. Lady Beauchemin, however, was, like Jackson Lemon, prepared to run a certain risk. His reserves made him slippery; but that was only when one pressed. She flattered herself that she could handle people lightly. "My father will be sure to act with perfect tact," she said; "of course, if you shouldn't care to be questioned, you can go out of town." She had the air of really wishing to make everything easy for him.

"I don't want to go out of town; I am enjoying it far too much here," her companion answered. "And wouldn't your father have a right to ask me what I meant by that?"

Lady Beauchemin hesitated; she was slightly perplexed. But in a moment she exclaimed: "He is incapable of saying anything vulgar!"

She had not really answered his inquiry, and he was conscious of that; but he was quite ready to say to her, a little later, as he guided her steps from the brougham to the strip of carpet which, between a somewhat rickety border of striped cloth and a double row of waiting footmen, policemen and dingy amateurs of both sexes, stretched from the curbstone to the portal of the Trumpingtons, "Of course I shall not wait for Lord Canterville to speak to me."

He had been expecting some such announcement as this from Lady Beauchemin, and he judged that her father would do no more than his duty. He knew that he ought to be prepared with an answer to Lord Canterville, and he wondered at himself for not yet having come to the point. Sidney Feeder's question in the Park had made him feel rather pointless; it was the first allusion that had been made to his possible marriage, except on the part of Lady Beauchemin. None of his own people were in London; he was perfectly independent, and even if his mother had been within reach he could not have consulted her on the subject. He loved her dearly, better than any one; but she was not a woman to consult, for she approved of whatever he did: it was her standard. He was careful not to be too serious when he talked with Lady Beauchemin; but he was very serious indeed as he thought over the matter within himself, which he did even among the diversions of the next half-hour, while he squeezed obliquely and slowly through the crush in Mrs. Trumpington's drawing-room. At the end of the half-hour he came away, and at the door he found Lady Beauchemin, from whom he had separated on entering the house, and who, this time with a companion of her own sex, was awaiting her carriage and still "going on." He gave her his arm into the street, and as she stepped into the vehicle she repeated that she wished he would go out of town for a few days.

"Who, then, would tell me what to do?" he asked, for answer, looking at her through the window.

She might tell him what to do, but he felt free, all the same; and he was determined this should continue. To prove it to himself he jumped into a hansom and drove back to Brook Street, to his hotel, instead of proceeding to a bright-windowed house in Portland Place, where he knew that after midnight he should find Lady Canterville and her daughters. There had been a reference to the subject between Lady Barberina and himself during their ride, and she would probably expect him; but it made him taste his liberty not to go, and he liked to taste his liberty. He was aware that to taste it in perfection he ought to go to bed; but he did not go to bed, he did not even take off his hat. He walked up and down his sitting-room, with his head surmounted by this ornament, a good deal tipped back, and his hands in his pockets. There were a good many cards stuck into the frame of the mirror, over his chimney-piece, and every time he passed the place he seemed to see what was written on one of them—the name of the mistress of the house in Portland Place, his own name, and, in the lower left-hand corner, the words: "A small Dance." Of course, now, he must make up his mind; he would make it up the next day: that was what he said to himself as he walked up and down; and according to his decision he would speak to Lord Canterville or he would take the night-express to Paris. It was better meanwhile that he should not see Lady Barberina. It was vivid to him, as he paused occasionally, looking vaguely at that card in the chimney-glass, that he had come pretty far; and he had come so far because he was under the charm—yes, he was in love with Lady Barb. There was no doubt whatever of that; he had a faculty for diagnosis, and he knew perfectly well what was the matter with him. He wasted no time in musing upon the mystery of this passion, in wondering whether he might not have escaped it by a little vigilance at first, or whether it would die out if he should go away. He accepted it frankly, for the sake of the pleasure it gave him—the girl was the delight of his eyes—and confined himself to considering whether such a marriage would square with his general situation. This would not at all necessarily follow from the fact that he was in love; too many other things would come in between. The most important of these was the change, not only of the geographical, but of the social, standpoint for his wife, and a certain readjustment that it would involve in his own relation to things. He was not inclined to readjustments, and there was no reason why he should be; his own position was in most respects so advantageous. But the girl tempted him almost irresistibly, satisfying his imagination both as a lover and as a student of the human organism; she was so blooming, so complete, of a type so rarely encountered in that degree of perfection. Jackson Lemon was not an Anglo-maniac, but he admired the physical conditions of the English—their complexion, their temperament, their tissue; and Lady Barberina struck him, in flexible, virginal form, as a wonderful compendium of these elements. There was something simple and robust in her beauty; it had the quietness of an old Greek statue, without the vulgarity of the modern simper or of contemporary prettiness. Her head was antique; and though her conversation was quite of the present period, Jackson Lemon had said to himself that there was sure to be in her soul a certain primitive sincerity which would match with her facial mould. He saw her as she might be in the future, the beautiful mother of beautiful children, in whom the look of race should be conspicuous. He should like his children to have the look of race, and he was not unaware that he must take his precautions accordingly. A great many people had it in England; and it was a pleasure to him to see it, especially as no one had it so unmistakably as the second daughter of Lord Canterville. It would be a great luxury to call such a woman one's own; nothing could be more evident than that, because it made no difference that she was not strikingly clever. Striking cleverness was not a part of harmonious form and the English complexion; it was associated with the modern simper, which was a result of modern nerves. If Jackson Lemon had wanted a nervous wife, of course he could have found her at home; but this tall, fair girl, whose character, like her figure, appeared mainly to have been formed by riding across country, was differently put together. All the same, would it suit his book, as they said in London,

to marry her and transport her to New York? He came back
to this question; came back to it with a persistency which, had
she been admitted to a view of it, would have tried the patience of Lady Beauchemin. She had been irritated, more than
once, at his appearing to attach himself so exclusively to this
horn of the dilemma—as if it could possibly fail to be a good
thing for a little American doctor to marry the daughter of
an English peer. It would have been more becoming, in her
ladyship's eyes, that he should take that for granted a little
more, and the consent of her ladyship's—of their lady-
ships'—family a little less. They looked at the matter so differently! Jackson Lemon was conscious that if he should marry
Lady Barberina Clement it would be because it suited him,
and not because it suited his possible sisters-in-law. He believed that he acted in all things by his own will—an organ
for which he had the highest respect.

   It would have seemed, however, that on this occasion it was
not working very regularly, for though he had come home to
go to bed, the stroke of half-past twelve saw him jump, not
into his couch, but into a hansom which the whistle of the
porter had summoned to the door of his hotel, and in which
he rattled off to Portland Place. Here he found—in a very
large house—an assembly of three hundred people, and a
band of music concealed in a bower of azaleas. Lady Canterville had not arrived; he wandered through the rooms and
assured himself of that. He also discovered a very good conservatory, where there were banks and pyramids of azaleas.
He watched the top of the staircase, but it was a long time
before he saw what he was looking for, and his impatience at
last was extreme. The reward, however, when it came, was all
that he could have desired. It was a little smile from Lady
Barberina, who stood behind her mother while the latter extended her finger-tips to the hostess. The entrance of this
charming woman, with her beautiful daughters—always a noticeable incident—was effected with a certain brilliancy, and
just now it was agreeable to Jackson Lemon to think that it
concerned him more than any one else in the house. Tall,
dazzling, indifferent, looking about her as if she saw very little, Lady Barberina was certainly a figure round which a young
man's fancy might revolve. She was very quiet and simple, had

little manner and little movement; but her detachment was not a vulgar art. She appeared to efface herself, to wait till, in the natural course, she should be attended to; and in this there was evidently no exaggeration, for she was too proud not to have perfect confidence. Her sister, smaller, slighter, with a little surprised smile, which seemed to say that in her extreme innocence she was yet prepared for anything, having heard, indirectly, such extraordinary things about society, was much more impatient and more expressive, and projected across a threshold the pretty radiance of her eyes and teeth before her mother's name was announced. Lady Canterville was thought by many persons to be very superior to her daughters; she had kept even more beauty than she had given them; and it was a beauty which had been called intellectual. She had extraordinary sweetness, without any definite professions; her manner was mild almost to tenderness; there was even a kind of pity in it. Moreover, her features were perfect, and nothing could be more gently gracious than a way she had of speaking, or rather, of listening, to people, with her head inclined a little to one side. Jackson Lemon liked her very much, and she had certainly been most kind to him. He approached Lady Barberina as soon as he could do so without an appearance of precipitation, and said to her that he hoped very much she would not dance. He was a master of the art which flourishes in New York above every other, and he had guided her through a dozen waltzes with a skill which, as she felt, left absolutely nothing to be desired. But dancing was not his business to-night. She smiled a little at the expression of his hope.

"That is what mamma has brought us here for," she said; "she doesn't like it if we don't dance."

"How does she know whether she likes it or not? You have always danced."

"Once I didn't," said Lady Barberina.

He told her that, at any rate, he would settle it with her mother, and persuaded her to wander with him into the conservatory, where there were coloured lights suspended among the plants, and a vault of verdure overhead. In comparison with the other rooms the conservatory was dusky and remote. But they were not alone; half a dozen other couples were in possession. The gloom was rosy with the slopes of azalea, and suffused with mitigated music, which made it possible to talk without consideration of one's neighbours. Nevertheless, though it was only in looking back on the scene later that Lady Barberina perceived this, these dispersed couples were talking very softly. She did not look at them; it seemed to her that, virtually, she was alone with Jackson Lemon. She said something about conservatories, about the fragrance of the air; for all answer to which he asked her, as he stood there before her, a question by which she might have been exceedingly startled.

"How do people who marry in England ever know each other before marriage? They have no chance."

"I am sure I don't know," said Lady Barberina; "I never was married."

"It's very different in my country. There a man may see much of a girl; he may come and see her, he may be constantly alone with her. I wish you allowed that over here."

Lady Barberina suddenly examined the less ornamental side of her fan, as if it had never occurred to her before to look at it. "It must be so very odd, America," she murmured at last.

"Well, I guess in that matter we are right; over here it's a leap in the dark."

"I am sure I don't know," said the girl. She had folded her fan; she stretched out her arm mechanically and plucked a sprig of azalea.

"I guess it doesn't signify, after all," Jackson Lemon remarked. "They say that love is blind at the best." His keen young face was bent upon hers; his thumbs were in the pockets of his trousers; he smiled a little, showing his fine teeth. She said nothing, but only pulled her azalea to pieces. She was usually so quiet that this small movement looked restless.

"This is the first time I have seen you in the least without a lot of people," he went on.

"Yes, it's very tiresome," she said.

"I have been sick of it; I didn't want to come here to-night."

She had not met his eyes, though she knew they were seeking her own. But now she looked at him a moment. She had never objected to his appearance, and in this respect she had no repugnance to overcome. She liked a man to be tall and handsome, and Jackson Lemon was neither; but when she was sixteen, and as tall herself as she was to be at twenty, she had been in love (for three weeks) with one of her cousins, a little fellow in the Hussars, who was shorter even than the American, shorter consequently than herself. This proved that distinction might be independent of stature—not that she ever reasoned it out. Jackson Lemon's facial spareness, his bright little eye, which seemed always to be measuring things, struck her as original, and she thought them very cutting, which would do very well for a husband of hers. As she made this reflection, of course it never occurred to her that she herself might be cut; she was not a sacrificial lamb. She perceived that his features expressed a mind—a mind that would be rather effective. She would never have taken him for a doctor; though, indeed, when all was said, that was very negative and didn't account for the way he imposed himself.

"Why, then, did you come?" she asked, in answer to his last speech.

"Because it seems to me after all better to see you in this way than not to see you at all; I want to know you better."

"I don't think I ought to stay here," said Lady Barberina, looking round her.

"Don't go till I have told you I love you," murmured the young man.

She made no exclamation, indulged in no start; he could not see even that she changed colour. She took his request with a noble simplicity, with her head erect and her eyes lowered.

"I don't think you have a right to tell me that."

"Why not?" Jackson Lemon demanded. "I wish to claim the right; I wish you to give it to me."

"I can't—I don't know you. You have said it yourself."

"Can't you have a little faith? That will help us to know each other better. It's disgusting, the want of opportunity; even at Pasterns I could scarcely get a walk with you. But I have the greatest faith in you. I feel that I love you, and I couldn't do more than that at the end of six months. I love your beauty—I love you from head to foot. Don't move, please don't move." He lowered his tone; but it went straight

to her ear, and it must be believed that it had a certain eloquence. For himself, after he had heard himself say these
words, all his being was in a glow. It was a luxury to speak to
her of her beauty; it brought him nearer to her than he had
ever been. But the colour had come into her face, and it
seemed to remind him that her beauty was not all. "Everything about you is sweet and noble," he went on; "everything
is dear to me. I am sure you are good. I don't know what
you think of me; I asked Lady Beauchemin to tell me, and
she told me to judge for myself. Well, then, I judge you like
me. Haven't I a right to assume that till the contrary is
proved? May I speak to your father? That's what I want to
know. I have been waiting; but now what should I wait for
longer? I want to be able to tell him that you have given me
some hope. I suppose I ought to speak to him first. I meant
to, to-morrow, but meanwhile, to-night, I thought I would
just put this in. In my country it wouldn't matter particularly.
You must see all that over there for yourself. If you should
tell me not to speak to your father, I wouldn't; I would wait.
But I like better to ask your leave to speak to him than to ask
him to speak to you."

His voice had sunk almost to a whisper; but, though it
trembled, his emotion gave it peculiar intensity. He had the
same attitude, his thumbs in his trousers, his attentive head,
his smile, which was a matter of course; no one would have
imagined what he was saying. She had listened without moving, and at the end she raised her eyes. They rested on his a
moment, and he remembered, a good while later, the look
which passed her lids.

"You may say anything that you please to my father, but I
don't wish to hear any more. You have said too much, considering how little idea you have given me before."

"I was watching you," said Jackson Lemon.

Lady Barberina held her head higher, looking straight at
him. Then, quite seriously, "I don't like to be watched," she
remarked.

"You shouldn't be so beautiful, then. Won't you give me a
word of hope?" he added.

"I have never supposed I should marry a foreigner," said
Lady Barberina.

"Do you call me a foreigner?"

"I think your ideas are very different, and your country is different; you have told me so yourself."

"I should like to show it to you; I would make you like it."

"I am not sure what you would make me do," said Lady Barberina, very honestly.

"Nothing that you don't want."

"I am sure you would try," she declared, with a smile.

"Well," said Jackson Lemon, "after all, I am trying now."

To this she simply replied she must go to her mother, and he was obliged to lead her out of the conservatory. Lady Canterville was not immediately found, so that he had time to murmur as they went, "Now that I have spoken, I am very happy."

"Perhaps you are happy too soon," said the girl.

"Ah, don't say that, Lady Barb."

"Of course I must think of it."

"Of course you must!" said Jackson Lemon. "I will speak to your father to-morrow."

"I can't fancy what he will say."

"How can he dislike me?" the young man asked, in a tone which Lady Beauchemin, if she had heard him, would have been forced to attribute to his general affectation of the jocose. What Lady Beauchemin's sister thought of it is not recorded; but there is perhaps a clue to her opinion in the answer she made him after a moment's silence: "Really, you know, you *are* a foreigner!" With this she turned her back upon him, for she was already in her mother's hands. Jackson Lemon said a few words to Lady Canterville; they were chiefly about its being very hot. She gave him her vague, sweet attention, as if he were saying something ingenious of which she missed the point. He could see that she was thinking of the doings of her daughter Agatha, whose attitude toward the contemporary young man was wanting in the perception of differences—a madness without method; she was evidently not occupied with Lady Barberina, who was more to be trusted. This young woman never met her suitor's eyes again; she let her own rest, rather ostentatiously, upon other objects. At last he was going away without a glance from her. Lady Canterville had asked him to come to lunch on the morrow,

and he had said he would do so if she would promise him he
should see his lordship. "I can't pay you another visit until I
have had some talk with him," he said.

"I don't see why not; but if I speak to him I dare say he
will be at home," she answered.

"It will be worth his while!"

Jackson Lemon left the house reflecting that as he had never
proposed to a girl before he could not be expected to know
how women demean themselves in this emergency. He had
heard, indeed, that Lady Barb had had no end of offers; and
though he thought it probable that the number was exaggerated, as it always is, it was to be supposed that her way of
appearing suddenly to have dropped him was but the usual
behaviour for the occasion.

III.

At her mother's the next day she was absent from luncheon,
and Lady Canterville mentioned to him (he didn't ask) that
she had gone to see a dear old great-aunt, who was also her
godmother, and who lived at Roehampton. Lord Canterville
was not present, but our young man was informed by his
hostess that he had promised her he would come in exactly
at three o'clock. Jackson Lemon lunched with Lady Canterville and the children, who appeared in force at this repast, all
the younger girls being present, and two little boys, the jun-
iors of the two sons who were in their teens. Jackson, who
was very fond of children, and thought these absolutely the
finest in the world—magnificent specimens of a magnificent
brood, such as it would be so satisfactory in future days to
see about his own knee—Jackson felt that he was being
treated as one of the family, but was not frightened by what
he supposed the privilege to imply. Lady Canterville betrayed
no consciousness whatever of his having mooted the question
of becoming her son-in-law, and he believed that her eldest
daughter had not told her of their talk the night before. This
idea gave him pleasure; he liked to think that Lady Barb was
judging him for herself. Perhaps, indeed, she was taking counsel of the old lady at Roehampton: he believed that he was

the sort of lover of whom a godmother would approve. God-
mothers in his mind were mainly associated with fairy-tales
(he had had no baptismal sponsors of his own); and that point
of view would be favourable to a young man with a great deal
of gold who had suddenly arrived from a foreign country—
an apparition, surely, sufficiently elfish. He made up his mind
that he should like Lady Canterville as a mother-in-law; she
would be too well-bred to meddle. Her husband came in at
three o'clock, just after they had left the table, and said to
Jackson Lemon that it was very good in him to have waited.

"I haven't waited," Jackson replied, with his watch in his
hand; "you are punctual to the minute."

I know not how Lord Canterville may have judged his
young friend, but Jackson Lemon had been told more than
once in his life that he was a very good fellow, but rather too
literal. After he had lighted a cigarette in his lordship's "den,"
a large brown apartment on the ground-floor, which partook
at once of the nature of an office and of that of a harness-
room (it could not have been called in any degree a library),
he went straight to the point in these terms: "Well now, Lord
Canterville, I feel as if I ought to let you know without more
delay that I am in love with Lady Barb, and that I should like
to marry her." So he spoke, puffing his cigarette, with his
conscious but unextenuating eye fixed on his host.

No man, as I have intimated, bore better being looked at
than this noble personage; he seemed to bloom in the envious
warmth of human contemplation, and never appeared so faultless as when he was most exposed. "My dear fellow, my dear
fellow," he murmured, almost in disparagement, stroking his
ambrosial beard from before the empty fireplace. He lifted his
eyebrows, but he looked perfectly good-natured.

"Are you surprised, sir?" Jackson Lemon asked.

"Why, I suppose any one is surprised at a man wanting one
of his children. He sometimes feels the weight of that sort of
thing so much, you know. He wonders what the devil another
man wants of them." And Lord Canterville laughed pleasantly
out of the copious fringe of his lips.

"I only want one of them," said Jackson Lemon, laughing
too, but with a lighter organ.

"Polygamy would be rather good for the parents. However, Louisa told me the other night that she thought you were looking the way you speak of."

"Yes, I told Lady Beauchemin that I love Lady Barb, and she seemed to think it was natural."

"Oh yes, I suppose there's no want of nature in it! But, my dear fellow, I really don't know what to say."

"Of course you'll have to think of it." Jackson Lemon, in saying this, felt that he was making the most liberal concession to the point of view of his interlocutor; being perfectly aware that in his own country it was not left much to the parents to think of.

"I shall have to talk it over with my wife."

"Lady Canterville has been very kind to me; I hope she will continue."

"My dear fellow, we are excellent friends. No one could appreciate you more than Lady Canterville. Of course we can only consider such a question on the—a—the highest grounds. You would never want to marry without knowing, as it were, exactly what you are doing. I, on my side, naturally, you know, am bound to do the best I can for my own child. At the same time, of course, we don't want to spend our time in—a—walking round the horse. We want to keep to the main line." It was settled between them after a little that the main line was that Jackson Lemon knew to a certainty the state of his affections and was in a position to pretend to the hand of a young lady who, Lord Canterville might say—of course, you know, without any swagger—had a right to expect to do well, as the women call it.

"I should think she had," Jackson Lemon said; "she's a beautiful type."

Lord Canterville stared a moment. "She is a clever, well-grown girl, and she takes her fences like a grasshopper. Does she know all this, by the way?" he added.

"Oh yes, I told her last night."

Again Lord Canterville had the air, unusual with him, of returning his companion's scrutiny. "I am not sure that you ought to have done that, you know."

"I couldn't have spoken to you first—I couldn't," said Jackson Lemon. "I meant to, but it stuck in my crop."

"They don't in your country, I guess," his lordship returned, smiling.

"Well, not as a general thing; however, I find it very pleasant to discuss with you now." And in truth it was very pleasant. Nothing could be easier, friendlier, more informal, than Lord Canterville's manner, which implied all sorts of equality, especially that of age and fortune, and made Jackson Lemon feel at the end of three minutes almost as if he too were a beautifully preserved and somewhat straitened nobleman of sixty, with the views of a man of the world about his own marriage. The young American perceived that Lord Canterville waived the point of his having spoken first to the girl herself, and saw in this indulgence a just concession to the ardour of young affection. For Lord Canterville seemed perfectly to appreciate the sentimental side—at least so far as it was embodied in his visitor—when he said, without deprecation: "Did she give you any encouragement?"

"Well, she didn't box my ears. She told me that she would think of it, but that I must speak to you. But, naturally, I shouldn't have said what I did to her if I hadn't made up my mind during the last fortnight that I am not disagreeable to her."

"Ah, my dear young man, women are odd cattle!" Lord Canterville exclaimed, rather unexpectedly. "But of course you know all that," he added in an instant; "you take the general risk."

"I am perfectly willing to take the general risk; the particular risk is small."

"Well, upon my honour I don't really know my girls. You see a man's time, in England, is tremendously taken up; but I dare say it's the same in your country. Their mother knows them—I think I had better send for their mother. If you don't mind I'll just suggest that she join us here."

"I'm rather afraid of you both together, but if it will settle it any quicker——" said Jackson Lemon. Lord Canterville rang the bell, and, when a servant appeared, despatched him with a message to her ladyship. While they were waiting, the young man remembered that it was in his power to give a more definite account of his pecuniary basis. He had simply said before that he was abundantly able to marry; he shrank from putting himself forward as a billionaire. He had a fine taste, and he wished to appeal to Lord Canterville primarily as a gentleman. But now that he had to make a double impression, he bethought himself of his millions, for millions were always impressive. "I think it only fair to let you know that my fortune is really very considerable," he remarked.

"Yes, I dare say you are beastly rich," said Lord Canterville.

"I have about seven millions."

"Seven millions?"

"I count in dollars; upwards of a million and a half sterling."

Lord Canterville looked at him from head to foot, with an air of cheerful resignation to a form of grossness which threatened to become common. Then he said, with a touch of that inconsequence of which he had already given a glimpse: "What the deuce, then, possessed you to turn doctor?"

Jackson Lemon coloured a little, hesitated, and then replied, quickly: "Because I had the talent for it."

"Of course, I don't for a moment doubt of your ability; but don't you find it rather a bore?"

"I don't practise much. I am rather ashamed to say that."

"Ah, well, of course, in your country it's different. I dare say you've got a door-plate, eh?"

"Oh yes, and a tin sign tied to the balcony!" said Jackson Lemon, smiling.

"What did your father say to it?"

"To my going into medicine? He said he would be hanged if he'd take any of my doses. He didn't think I should succeed; he wanted me to go into the house."

"Into the House—a——" said Lord Canterville, hesitating a little. "Into your Congress—yes, exactly."

"Ah, no, not so bad as that. Into the store," Jackson Lemon replied, in the candid tone in which he expressed himself when, for reasons of his own, he wished to be perfectly national.

Lord Canterville stared, not venturing, even for the moment, to hazard an interpretation; and before a solution had presented itself Lady Canterville came into the room.

"My dear, I thought we had better see you. Do you know

he wants to marry our second girl?" It was in these simple terms that her husband acquainted her with the question.

Lady Canterville expressed neither surprise nor elation; she simply stood there, smiling, with her head a little inclined to the side, with all her customary graciousness. Her charming eyes rested on those of Jackson Lemon; and though they seemed to show that she had to think a little of so serious a proposition, his own discovered in them none of the coldness of calculation. "Are you talking about Barberina?" she asked in a moment, as if her thoughts had been far away.

Of course they were talking about Barberina, and Jackson Lemon repeated to her ladyship what he had said to the girl's father. He had thought it all over, and his mind was quite made up. Moreover, he had spoken to Lady Barb.

"Did she tell you that, my dear?" asked Lord Canterville, while he lighted another cigar.

She gave no heed to this inquiry, which had been vague and accidental on his lordship's part, but simply said to Jackson Lemon that the thing was very serious, and that they had better sit down for a moment. In an instant he was near her on the sofa on which she had placed herself, still smiling and looking up at her husband with an air of general meditation, in which a sweet compassion for every one concerned was apparent.

"Barberina has told me nothing," she said, after a little.

"That proves she cares for me!" Jackson Lemon exclaimed eagerly.

Lady Canterville looked as if she thought this almost too ingenious, almost professional; but her husband said cheerfully, jovially: "Ah, well, if she cares for you, I don't object."

This was a little ambiguous; but before Jackson Lemon had time to look into it, Lady Canterville asked gently: "Should you expect her to live in America?"

"Oh, yes; that's my home, you know."

"Shouldn't you be living sometimes in England?"

"Oh, yes, we'll come over and see you." The young man was in love, he wanted to marry, he wanted to be genial, and to commend himself to the parents of Lady Barb; at the same time it was in his nature not to accept conditions, save in so far as they exactly suited him, to tie himself, or, as they said in New York, to give himself away. In any transaction he preferred his own terms to those of any one else. Therefore, the moment Lady Canterville gave signs of wishing to extract a promise, he was on his guard.

"She'll find it very different; perhaps she won't like it," her ladyship suggested.

"If she likes me, she'll like my country," said Jackson Lemon, with decision.

"He tells me he has got a plate on his door," Lord Canterville remarked humorously.

"We must talk to her, of course; we must understand how she feels," said his wife, looking more serious than she had done as yet.

"Please don't discourage her, Lady Canterville," the young man begged; "and give me a chance to talk to her a little more myself. You haven't given me much chance, you know."

"We don't offer our daughters to people, Mr. Lemon." Lady Canterville was always gentle, but now she was a little majestic.

"She isn't like some women in London, you know," said Jackson Lemon's host, who seemed to remember that to a discussion of such importance he ought from time to time to contribute a word of wisdom. And Jackson Lemon, certainly, if the idea had been presented to him, would have said that, No, decidedly, Lady Barberina had not been thrown at him.

"Of course not," he declared, in answer to her mother's remark. "But, you know, you mustn't refuse them too much, either; you mustn't make a poor fellow wait too long. I admire her, I love her, more than I can say; I give you my word of honour for that."

"He seems to think that settles it," said Lord Canterville, smiling down at the young American, very indulgently, from his place before the cold chimney-piece.

"Of course that's what we desire, Philip," her ladyship returned, very nobly.

"Lady Barb believes it; I am sure she does!" Jackson Lemon exclaimed. "Why should I pretend to be in love with her if I am not?"

Lady Canterville received this inquiry in silence, and her

husband, with just the least air in the world of repressed impatience, began to walk up and down the room. He was a man of many engagements, and he had been closeted for more than a quarter of an hour with the young American doctor. "Do you imagine you should come often to England?" Lady Canterville demanded, with a certain abruptness, returning to that important point.

"I'm afraid I can't tell you that; of course we shall do whatever seems best." He was prepared to suppose they should cross the Atlantic every summer: that prospect was by no means displeasing to him; but he was not prepared to give any such pledge to Lady Canterville, especially as he did not believe it would really be necessary. It was in his mind, not as an overt pretension, but as a tacit implication, that he should treat with Barberina's parents on a footing of perfect equality; and there would somehow be nothing equal if he should begin to enter into engagements which didn't belong to the essence of the matter. They were to give their daughter, and he was to take her: in this arrangement there would be as much on one side as on the other. But beyond this he had nothing to ask of them; there was nothing he wished them to promise, and his own pledges, therefore, would have no equivalent. Whenever his wife should wish it, she should come over and see her people. Her home was to be in New York; but he was tacitly conscious that on the question of absences he should be very liberal. Nevertheless, there was something in the very grain of his character which forbade that he should commit himself at present in respect to times and dates.

Lady Canterville looked at her husband, but her husband was not attentive; he was taking a peep at his watch. In a moment, however, he threw out a remark to the effect that he thought it a capital thing that the two countries should become more united, and there was nothing that would bring it about better than a few of the best people on both sides pairing off together. The English, indeed, had begun it; a lot of fellows had brought over a lot of pretty girls, and it was quite fair play that the Americans should take their pick. They were all one race, after all; and why shouldn't they make one society—the best on both sides, of course? Jackson Lemon smiled as he recognised Lady Marmaduke's philosophy, and

he was pleased to think that Lady Beauchemin had some influence with her father; for he was sure the old gentleman (as
he mentally designated his host) had got all this from her,
though he expressed himself less happily than the cleverest of
his daughters. Our hero had no objection to make to it, especially if there was anything in it that would really help his
case. But it was not in the least on these high grounds that
he had sought the hand of Lady Barb. He wanted her not in
order that her people and his (the best on both sides!) should
make one society; he wanted her simply because he wanted
her. Lady Canterville smiled; but she seemed to have another
thought.

"I quite appreciate what my husband says; but I don't see
why poor Barb should be the one to begin."

"I dare say she'll like it," said Lord Canterville, as if he
were attempting a short cut. "They say you spoil your women
awfully."

"She's not one of their women yet," her ladyship remarked,
in the sweetest tone in the world; and then she added, without
Jackson Lemon's knowing exactly what she meant, "It seems
so strange."

He was a little irritated; and perhaps these simple words
added to the feeling. There had been no positive opposition
to his suit, and Lord and Lady Canterville were most kind;
but he felt that they held back a little, and though he had not
expected them to throw themselves on his neck, he was rather
disappointed, his pride was touched. Why should they hesitate? He considered himself such a good *parti*. It was not so
much the old gentleman, it was Lady Canterville. As he saw
the old gentleman look, covertly, a second time at his watch,
he could have believed he would have been glad to settle the
matter on the spot. Lady Canterville seemed to wish her
daughter's lover to come forward more, to give certain assurances and guarantees. He felt that he was ready to say or do
anything that was a matter of proper form; but he couldn't
take the tone of trying to purchase her ladyship's consent,
penetrated as he was with the conviction that such a man as
he could be trusted to care for his wife rather more than an
impecunious British peer and *his* wife could be supposed (with
the lights he had acquired in English society) to care even for

the handsomest of a dozen children. It was a mistake on Lady Canterville's part not to recognise that. He humoured her mistake to the extent of saying, just a little drily, "My wife shall certainly have everything she wants."

"He tells me he is disgustingly rich," Lord Canterville added, pausing before their companion with his hands in his pockets.

"I am glad to hear it; but it isn't so much that," she answered, sinking back a little on her sofa. If it was not that, she did not say what it was, though she had looked for a moment as if she were going to. She only raised her eyes to her husband's face, as if to ask for inspiration. I know not whether she found it, but in a moment she said to Jackson Lemon, seeming to imply that it was quite another point: "Do you expect to continue your profession?"

He had no such intention, so far as his profession meant getting up at three o'clock in the morning to assuage the ills of humanity; but here, as before, the touch of such a question instantly stiffened him. "Oh, my profession! I am rather ashamed of that matter. I have neglected my work so much, I don't know what I shall be able to do, once I am really settled at home."

Lady Canterville received these remarks in silence, fixing her eyes again upon her husband's face. But this nobleman was really not helpful; still with his hands in his pockets, save when he needed to remove his cigar from his lips, he went and looked out of the window. "Of course we know you don't practise, and when you're a married man you will have less time even than now. But I should really like to know if they call you Doctor over there."

"Oh yes, universally. We are nearly as fond of titles as your people."

"I don't call that a title."

"It's not so good as duke or marquis, I admit; but we have to take what we have got."

"Oh, bother, what does it signify?" Lord Canterville demanded, from his place at the window. "I used to have a horse named Doctor, and a devilish good one too."

"You may call me bishop, if you like," said Jackson Lemon, laughing.

Lady Canterville looked grave, as if she did not enjoy this pleasantry. "I don't care for any titles," she observed; "I don't see why a gentleman shouldn't be called Mr."

It suddenly appeared to Jackson Lemon that there was something helpless, confused, and even slightly comical, in the position of this noble and amiable lady. The impression made him feel kindly; he too, like Lord Canterville, had begun to long for a short cut. He relaxed a moment, and leaning toward his hostess, with a smile and his hands on his little knees, he said softly, "It seems to me a question of no importance; all I desire is that you should call me your son-in-law."

Lady Canterville gave him her hand, and he pressed it almost affectionately. Then she got up, remarking that before anything was decided she must see her daughter, she must learn from her own lips the state of her feelings. "I don't like at all her not having spoken to me already," she added.

"Where has she gone—to Roehampton? I dare say she has told it all to her godmother," said Lord Canterville.

"She won't have much to tell, poor girl!" Jackson Lemon exclaimed. "I must really insist upon seeing with more freedom the person I wish to marry."

"You shall have all the freedom you want, in two or three days," said Lady Canterville. She smiled with all her sweetness; she appeared to have accepted him, and yet still to be making tacit assumptions. "Are there not certain things to be talked of first?"

"Certain things, dear lady?"

Lady Canterville looked at her husband, and though he was still at his window, this time he felt it in her silence, and had to come away and speak. "Oh, she means settlements, and that kind of thing." This was an allusion which came with a much better grace from him.

Jackson Lemon looked from one of his companions to the other; he coloured a little, and gave a smile that was perhaps a trifle fixed. "Settlements? We don't make them in the United States. You may be sure I shall make a proper provision for my wife."

"My dear fellow, over here—in our class, you know, it's the custom," said Lord Canterville, with a richer brightness in his face at the thought that the discussion was over.

"I have my own ideas," Jackson answered, smiling.

"It seems to me it's a question for the solicitors to discuss," Lady Canterville suggested.

"They may discuss it as much as they please," said Jackson Lemon, with a laugh. He thought he saw his solicitors discussing it! He had indeed his own ideas. He opened the door for Lady Canterville, and the three passed out of the room together, walking into the hall in a silence in which there was just a tinge of awkwardness. A note had been struck which grated and scratched a little. A pair of brilliant footmen, at their approach, rose from a bench to a great altitude, and stood there like sentinels presenting arms. Jackson Lemon stopped, looking for a moment into the interior of his hat, which he had in his hand. Then, raising his keen eyes, he fixed them a moment on those of Lady Canterville, addressing her, instinctively, rather than her husband. "I guess you and Lord Canterville had better leave it to me!"

"We have our traditions, Mr. Lemon," said her ladyship, with nobleness. "I imagine you don't know——" she murmured.

Lord Canterville laid his hand on the young man's shoulder. "My dear boy, those fellows will settle it in three minutes."

"Very likely they will!" said Jackson Lemon. Then he asked of Lady Canterville when he might see Lady Barb.

She hesitated a moment, in her gracious way. "I will write you a note."

One of the tall footmen, at the end of the impressive vista, had opened wide the portals, as if even he were aware of the dignity to which the little visitor had virtually been raised. But Jackson lingered a moment; he was visibly unsatisfied, though apparently so little unconscious that he was unsatisfying. "I don't think you understand me."

"Your ideas are certainly different," said Lady Canterville.

"If the girl understands you, that's enough!" Lord Canterville exclaimed in a jovial, detached, irrelevant way.

"May not *she* write to me?" Jackson asked of her mother. "I certainly must write to her, you know, if you won't let me see her."

"Oh yes, you may write to her, Mr. Lemon."

There was a point for a moment in the look that he gave Lady Canterville, while he said to himself that if it were necessary he would transmit his notes through the old lady at Roehampton. "All right, good-bye; you know what I want, at any rate." Then, as he was going, he turned and added: "You needn't be afraid that I won't bring her over in the hot weather!"

"In the hot weather?" Lady Canterville murmured, with vague visions of the torrid zone, while the young American quitted the house with the sense that he had made great concessions.

His host and hostess passed into a small morning-room, and (Lord Canterville having taken up his hat and stick to go out again) stood there a moment, face to face.

"It's clear enough he wants her," said his lordship, in a summary manner.

"There's something so odd about him," Lady Canterville answered. "Fancy his speaking so about settlements!"

"You had better give him his head; he'll go much quieter."

"He's so obstinate—very obstinate; it's easy to see that. And he seems to think a girl in your daughter's position can be married from one day to the other—with a ring and a new frock—like a housemaid."

"Well, of course, over there, that's the kind of thing. But he seems really to have a most extraordinary fortune; and every one does say their women have *carte blanche*."

"*Carte blanche* is not what Barb wishes; she wishes a settlement. She wants a definite income; she wants to be safe."

Lord Canterville stared a moment. "Has she told you so? I thought you said——" And then he stopped. "I beg your pardon," he added.

Lady Canterville gave no explanation of her inconsistency. She went on to remark that American fortunes were notoriously insecure; one heard of nothing else; they melted away like smoke. It was their duty to their child to demand that something should be fixed.

"He has a million and a half sterling," said Lord Canterville. "I can't make out what he does with it."

"She ought to have something very handsome," his wife remarked.

"Well, my dear, you must settle it: you must consider it; you must send for Hilary. Only take care you don't put him off; it may be a very good opening, you know. There is a great deal to be done out there; I believe in all that," Lord Canterville went on, in the tone of a conscientious parent.

"There is no doubt that he *is* a doctor—in those places," said Lady Canterville, musingly.

"He may be a pedlar for all I care."

"If they should go out, I think Agatha might go with them," her ladyship continued, in the same tone, a little disconnectedly.

"You may send them all out if you like. Good-bye!" And Lord Canterville kissed his wife.

But she detained him a moment, with her hand on his arm. "Don't you think he is very much in love?"

"Oh yes, he's very bad; but he's a clever little beggar."

"She likes him very much," Lady Canterville announced, rather formally, as they separated.

IV.

Jackson Lemon had said to Sidney Feeder in the Park that he would call on Mr. and Mrs. Freer; but three weeks elapsed before he knocked at their door in Jermyn Street. In the meantime he had met them at dinner, and Mrs. Freer had told him that she hoped very much he would find time to come and see her. She had not reproached him, nor shaken her finger at him; and her clemency, which was calculated, and very characteristic of her, touched him so much (for he was in fault; she was one of his mother's oldest and best friends), that he very soon presented himself. It was on a fine Sunday afternoon, rather late, and the region of Jermyn Street looked forsaken and inanimate; the native dulness of the landscape appeared in all its purity. Mrs. Freer, however, was at home, resting on a lodging-house sofa—an angular couch, draped in faded chintz—before she went to dress for dinner. She made the young man very welcome; she told him she had been thinking of him a great deal; she had wished to have a chance to talk with him. He immediately perceived what she had in mind, and then he remembered that Sidney Feeder had told him what it was that Mr. and Mrs. Freer took upon themselves to say. This had provoked him at the time, but he had for-gotten it afterward; partly because he became aware, that same evening, that he did wish to marry the "young marchioness," and partly because since then he had had much greater an-noyances. Yes, the poor young man, so conscious of liberal intentions, of a large way of looking at the future, had had much to irritate and disgust him. He had seen the mistress of his affections but three or four times, and he had received letters from Mr. Hilary, Lord Canterville's solicitor, asking him, in terms the most obsequious, it is true, to designate some gentleman of the law with whom the preliminaries of his marriage to Lady Barberina Clement might be arranged. He had given Mr. Hilary the name of such a functionary, but he had written by the same post to his own solicitor (for whose services in other matters he had had much occasion, Jackson Lemon being distinctly contentious), instructing him that he was at liberty to meet Mr. Hilary, but not at liberty to entertain any proposals as to this odious English idea of a settlement. If marrying Jackson Lemon were not settlement enough, then Lord and Lady Canterville had better alter their point of view. It was quite out of the question that he should alter his. It would perhaps be difficult to explain the strong aversion that he entertained to the introduction into his pro-spective union of this harsh diplomatic element; it was as if they mistrusted him, suspected him; as if his hands were to be tied, so that he could not handle his own fortune as he thought best. It was not the idea of parting with his money that displeased him, for he flattered himself that he had plans of expenditure for his wife beyond even the imagination of her distinguished parents. It struck him even that they were fools not to have perceived that they should make a much better thing of it by leaving him perfectly free. This interven-tion of the solicitor was a nasty little English tradition—totally at variance with the large spirit of American habits—to which he would not submit. It was not his way to submit when he disapproved: why should he change his way on this occasion, when the matter lay so near him? These reflections, and a hundred more, had flowed freely through his mind for several days before he called in Jermyn Street, and they had engen-

dered a lively indignation and a really bitter sense of wrong.
As may be imagined, they had infused a certain awkwardness
into his relations with the house of Canterville, and it may be
said of these relations that they were for the moment virtually
suspended. His first interview with Lady Barb, after his con-
ference with the old couple, as he called her august elders,
had been as tender as he could have desired. Lady Canterville,
at the end of three days, had sent him an invitation—five
words on a card—asking him to dine with them to-morrow,
quite *en famille*. This had been the only formal intimation
that his engagement to Lady Barb was recognised; for even at
the family banquet, which included half a dozen outsiders,
there had been no allusion on the part either of his host or
his hostess to the subject of their conversation in Lord Canterville's den. The only allusion was a wandering ray, once or
twice, in Lady Barberina's eyes. When, however, after dinner,
she strolled away with him into the music-room, which was
lighted and empty, to play for him something out of *Carmen*,
of which he had spoken at table, and when the young couple
were allowed to enjoy for upwards of an hour, unmolested,
the comparative privacy of this rich apartment, he felt that
Lady Canterville definitely counted upon him. She didn't believe in any serious difficulties. Neither did he, then; and that
was why it was a nuisance there should be a vain appearance
of them. The arrangements, he supposed Lady Canterville
would have said, were pending, and indeed they were; for he
had already given orders in Bond Street for the setting of an
extraordinary number of diamonds. Lady Barb, at any rate,
during that hour he spent with her, had had nothing to say
about arrangements; and it had been an hour of pure satisfaction. She had seated herself at the piano and had played
perpetually, in a soft incoherent manner, while he leaned over
the instrument, very close to her, and said everything that
came into his head. She was very bright and serene, and she
looked at him as if she liked him very much.

This was all he expected of her, for it did not belong to the
cast of her beauty to betray a vulgar infatuation. That beauty
was more delightful to him than ever; and there was a softness
about her which seemed to say to him that from this moment
she was quite his own. He felt more than ever the value of

such a possession; it came over him more than ever that it had taken a great social outlay to produce such a mixture. Simple and girlish as she was, and not particularly quick in the give and take of conversation, she seemed to him to have a part of the history of England in her blood; she was a *résumé* of generations of privileged people, and of centuries of rich country-life. Between these two, of course, there was no allusion to the question which had been put into the hands of Mr. Hilary, and the last thing that occurred to Jackson Lemon was that Lady Barb had views as to his settling a fortune upon her before their marriage. It may appear singular, but he had not asked himself whether his money operated upon her in any degree as a bribe; and this was because, instinctively, he felt that such a speculation was idle,—the point was not to be ascertained,—and because he was willing to assume that it was agreeable to her that she should continue to live in luxury. It was eminently agreeable to him that he might enable her to do so. He was acquainted with the mingled character of human motives, and he was glad that he was rich enough to pretend to the hand of a young woman who, for the best of reasons, would be very expensive. After that happy hour in the music-room he had ridden with her twice; but he had not found her otherwise accessible. She had let him know, the second time they rode, that Lady Canterville had directed her to make, for the moment, no further appointment with him; and on his presenting himself, more than once at the house, he had been told that neither the mother nor the daughter was at home; it had been added that Lady Barberina was staying at Roehampton. On giving him that information in the Park, Lady Barb had looked at him with a mute reproach— there was always a certain superior dumbness in her eyes—as if he were exposing her to an annoyance that she ought to be spared; as if he were taking an eccentric line on a question that all well-bred people treated in the conventional way. His induction from this was not that she wished to be secure about his money, but that, like a dutiful English daughter, she received her opinions (on points that were indifferent to her) ready-made from a mamma whose fallibility had never been exposed. He knew by this that his solicitor had answered Mr. Hilary's letter, and that Lady Canterville's coolness was the fruit of this correspondence. The effect of it was not in the least to make him come round, as he phrased it; he had not the smallest intention of doing that. Lady Canterville had spoken of the traditions of her family; but he had no need to go to his family for his own. They resided within himself; anything that he had definitely made up his mind to, acquired in an hour a kind of legendary force. Meanwhile, he was in the detestable position of not knowing whether or no he were engaged. He wrote to Lady Barb to inquire—it being so strange that she should not receive him; and she answered in a very pretty little letter, which had to his mind a sort of bygone quality, an old-fashioned freshness, as if it might have been written in the last century by Clarissa or Amelia: she answered that she did not in the least understand the situation; that, of course, she would never give him up; that her mother had said that there were the best reasons for their not going too fast; that, thank God, she was yet young, and could wait as long as he would; but that she begged he wouldn't write her anything about money-matters, as she could never comprehend them. Jackson felt that he was in no danger whatever of making this last mistake; he only noted how Lady Barb thought it natural that there should be a discussion; and this made it vivid to him afresh that he had got hold of a daughter of the Crusaders. His ingenious mind could appreciate this hereditary assumption perfectly, at the same time that, to light his own footsteps, it remained entirely modern. He believed—or he thought he believed—that in the end he should marry Barberina Clement on his own terms; but in the interval there was a sensible indignity in being challenged and checked. One effect of it, indeed, was to make him desire the girl more keenly. When she was not before his eyes in the flesh, she hovered before him as an image; and this image had reasons of its own for being a radiant picture. There were moments, however, when he wearied of looking at it; it was so impalpable and thankless, and then Jackson Lemon, for the first time in his life, was melancholy. He felt alone in London, and very much out of it, in spite of all the acquaintances he had made, and the bills he had paid; he felt the need of a greater intimacy than any he had formed (save, of course, in the case of Lady Barb). He wanted to vent his disgust, to

relieve himself, from the American point of view. He felt that
in engaging in a contest with the great house of Canterville
he was, after all, rather single. That singleness was, of course,
in a great measure an inspiration; but it pinched him a little
at moments. Then he wished his mother had been in London,
for he used to talk of his affairs a great deal with this delightful
parent, who had a soothing way of advising him in the sense
he liked best. He had even gone so far as to wish he had never
laid eyes on Lady Barb and had fallen in love with some transatlantic maiden of a similar composition. He presently came
back, of course, to the knowledge that in the United States
there was—and there could be—nothing similar to Lady Barb;
for was it not precisely as a product of the English climate
and the British constitution that he valued her? He had relieved himself, from his American point of view, by speaking
his mind to Lady Beauchemin, who confessed that she was
very much vexed with her parents. She agreed with him that
they had made a great mistake; they ought to have left him
free; and she expressed her confidence that that freedom
would be for her family, as it were, like the silence of the sage,
golden. He must excuse them; he must remember that what
was asked of him had been their custom for centuries. She did
not mention her authority as to the origin of customs, but
she assured him that she would say three words to her father
and mother which would make it all right. Jackson answered
that customs were all very well, but that intelligent people
recognised, when they saw it, the right occasion for departing
from them; and with this he awaited the result of Lady Beauchemin's remonstrance. It had not as yet been perceptible,
and it must be said that this charming woman was herself
much bothered. When, on her venturing to say to her mother
that she thought a wrong line had been taken with regard to
her sister's *prétendant*, Lady Canterville had replied that Mr.
Lemon's unwillingness to settle anything was in itself a proof
of what they had feared, the unstable nature of his fortune
(for it was useless to talk—this gracious lady could be very
decided—there could be no serious reason but that one): on
meeting this argument, as I say, Jackson's protectress felt considerably baffled. It was perhaps true, as her mother said, that
if they didn't insist upon proper guarantees Barberina might

be left in a few years with nothing but the stars and stripes (this odd phrase was a quotation from Mr. Lemon) to cover her. Lady Beauchemin tried to reason it out with Lady Marmaduke; but these were complications unforeseen by Lady Marmaduke in her project of an Anglo-American society. She was obliged to confess that Mr. Lemon's fortune could not have the solidity of long-established things; it was a very new fortune indeed. His father had made the greater part of it all in a lump, a few years before his death, in the extraordinary way in which people made money in America; that, of course, was why the son had those singular professional attributes. He had begun to study to be a doctor very young, before his expectations were so great. Then he had found he was very clever, and very fond of it; and he had kept on, because, after all, in America, where there were no country-gentlemen, a young man had to have something to do, don't you know? And Lady Marmaduke, like an enlightened woman, intimated that in such a case she thought it in much better taste not to try to sink anything. "Because, in America, don't you see," she reasoned, "you can't sink it—nothing *will* sink. Everything is floating about—in the newspapers." And she tried to console her friend by remarking that if Mr. Lemon's fortune was precarious, it was at all events so big. That was just the trouble for Lady Beauchemin; it was so big, and yet they were going to lose it. He was as obstinate as a mule; she was sure he would never come round. Lady Marmaduke declared that he would come round; she even offered to bet a dozen pair of *gants de Suède* on it; and she added that this consummation lay quite in the hands of Barberina. Lady Beauchemin promised herself to converse with her sister; for it was not for nothing that she herself had felt the international contagion.

Jackson Lemon, to dissipate his chagrin, had returned to the sessions of the medical congress, where, inevitably, he had fallen into the hands of Sidney Feeder, who enjoyed in this disinterested assembly a high popularity. It was Doctor Feeder's earnest desire that his old friend should share it, which was all the more easy as the medical congress was really, as the young physician observed, a perpetual symposium. Jackson Lemon entertained the whole body—entertained it profusely, and in a manner befitting one of the patrons of science rather than its humbler votaries; but these dissipations only made him forget for a moment that his relations with the house of Canterville were anomalous. His great difficulty punctually came back to him, and Sidney Feeder saw it stamped upon his brow. Jackson Lemon, with his acute inclination to open himself, was on the point, more than once, of taking the sympathetic Sidney into his confidence. His friend gave him easy opportunity; he asked him what it was he was thinking of all the time, and whether the young marchioness had concluded she couldn't swallow a doctor. These forms of speech were displeasing to Jackson Lemon, whose fastidiousness was nothing new; but it was for even deeper reasons that he said to himself that, for such complicated cases as his, there was no assistance in Sidney Feeder. To understand his situation one must know the world; and the child of Cincinnati didn't know the world—at least the world with which his friend was now concerned.

"Is there a hitch in your marriage? Just tell me that," Sidney Feeder had said, taking everything for granted, in a manner which was in itself a proof of great innocence. It is true he had added that he supposed he had no business to ask; but he had been anxious about it ever since hearing from Mr. and Mrs. Freer that the British aristocracy was down on the medical profession. "Do they want you to give it up? Is that what the hitch is about? Don't desert your colours, Jackson. The elimination of pain, the mitigation of misery, constitute surely the noblest profession in the world."

"My dear fellow, you don't know what you are talking about," Jackson observed, for answer to this. "I haven't told any one I was going to be married; still less have I told any one that any one objected to my profession. I should like to see them do it. I have got out of the swim to-day, but I don't regard myself as the sort of person that people object to. And I do expect to do something, yet."

"Come home, then, and do it. And excuse me if I say that the facilities for getting married are much greater over there."

"You don't seem to have found them very great."

"I have never had time. Wait till my next vacation, and you will see."

"The facilities over there are too great. Nothing is good

but what is difficult," said Jackson Lemon, in a tone of artificial sententiousness that quite tormented his interlocutor.

"Well, they have got their backs up, I can see that. I'm glad
you like it. Only if they despise your profession, what will they
say to that of your friends? If they think you are queer, what
would they think of me?" asked Sidney Feeder, the turn of
whose mind was not, as a general thing, in the least sarcastic,
but who was pushed to this sharpness by a conviction that (in
spite of declarations which seemed half an admission and half
a denial) his friend was suffering himself to be bothered for
the sake of a good which might be obtained elsewhere without bother. It had come over him that the bother was of an
unworthy kind.

"My dear fellow, all that is idiotic." That had been Jackson
Lemon's reply; but it expressed but a portion of his thoughts.
The rest was inexpressible, or almost; being connected with a
sentiment of rage at its having struck even so genial a mind
as Sidney Feeder's that, in proposing to marry a daughter of
the highest civilisation, he was going out of his way—departing from his natural line. Was he then so ignoble, so pledged
to inferior things, that when he saw a girl who (putting aside
the fact that she had not genius, which was rare, and which,
though he prized rarity, he didn't want) seemed to him the
most complete feminine nature he had known, he was to think
himself too different, too incongruous, to mate with her? He
would mate with whom he chose; that was the upshot of Jackson Lemon's reflections. Several days elapsed, during which
everybody—even the pure-minded, like Sidney Feeder—
seemed to him very abject.

I relate all this to show why it was that in going to see Mrs.
Freer he was prepared much less to be angry with people who,
like the Dexter Freers, a month before, had given it out that
he was engaged to a peer's daughter, than to resent the insinuation that there were obstacles to such a prospect. He sat
with Mrs. Freer alone for half an hour in the sabbatical stillness of Jermyn Street. Her husband had gone for a walk in
the Park; he always walked in the Park on Sunday. All the
world might have been there, and Jackson and Mrs. Freer in
sole possession of the district of St. James's. This perhaps had
something to do with making him at last rather confidential;

the influences were conciliatory, persuasive. Mrs. Freer was extremely sympathetic; she treated him like a person she had known from the age of ten; asked his leave to continue recumbent; talked a great deal about his mother; and seemed almost for a while to perform the kindly functions of that lady. It had been wise of her from the first not to allude, even indirectly, to his having neglected so long to call; her silence on this point was in the best taste. Jackson Lemon had forgotten that it was a habit with her, and indeed a high accomplishment, never to reproach people with these omissions. You might have left her alone for two years, her greeting was always the same; she was never either too delighted to see you or not delighted enough. After a while, however, he perceived that her silence had been to a certain extent a reference; she appeared to take for granted that he devoted all his hours to a certain young lady. It came over him for a moment that his country people took a great deal for granted; but when Mrs. Freer, rather abruptly, sitting up on her sofa, said to him, half simply, half solemnly, "And now, my dear Jackson, I want you to tell me something!"—he perceived that after all she didn't pretend to know more about the impending matter than he himself did. In the course of a quarter of an hour—so appreciatively she listened—he had told her a good deal about it. It was the first time he had said so much to any one, and the process relieved him even more than he would have supposed. It made certain things clear to him, by bringing them to a point—above all, the fact that he had been wronged. He made no allusion whatever to its being out of the usual way that, as an American doctor, he should sue for the hand of a marquis's daughter; and this reserve was not voluntary, it was quite unconscious. His mind was too full of the offensive conduct of the Cantervilles, and the sordid side of their want of confidence. He could not imagine that while he talked to Mrs. Freer—and it amazed him afterward that he should have chattered so; he could account for it only by the state of his nerves—she should be thinking only of the strangeness of the situation he sketched for her. She thought Americans as good as other people, but she didn't see where, in American life the daughter of a marquis would, as she phrased it, work in. To take a simple instance,—they coursed through Mrs. Freer's mind with extraordinary speed—would she not always expect to go in to dinner first? As a novelty, over there, they might like to see her do it, at first; there might be even a pressure for places for the spectacle. But with the increase of every kind of sophistication that was taking place in America, the humorous view to which she would owe her safety might not continue to be taken; and then where would Lady Barberina be? This was but a small instance; but Mrs. Freer's vivid imagination—much as she lived in Europe, she knew her native land so well—saw a host of others massing themselves behind it. The consequence of all of which was that after listening to him in the most engaging silence, she raised her clasped hands, pressed them against her breast, lowered her voice to a tone of entreaty, and, with her perpetual little smile, uttered three words: "My dear Jackson, don't—don't —don't."

"Don't what?" he asked, staring.

"Don't neglect the chance you have of getting out of it; it would never do."

He knew what she meant by his chance of getting out of it; in his many meditations he had, of course, not overlooked that. The ground the old couple had taken about settlements (and the fact that Lady Beauchemin had not come back to him to tell him, as she promised, that she had moved them, proved how firmly they were rooted) would have offered an all-sufficient pretext to a man who should have repented of his advances. Jackson Lemon knew that; but he knew at the same time that he had not repented. The old couple's want of imagination did not in the least alter the fact that Barberina was, as he had told her father, a beautiful type. Therefore he simply said to Mrs. Freer that he didn't in the least wish to get out of it; he was as much in it as ever, and he intended to remain there. But what did she mean, he inquired in a moment, by her statement that it would never do? Why wouldn't it do? Mrs. Freer replied by another inquiry— Should he really like her to tell him? It wouldn't do, because Lady Barb would not be satisfied with her place at dinner. She would not be content—in a society of commoners—with any but the best; and the best she could not expect (and it was to be supposed that he did not expect her) always to have.

"What do you mean by commoners?" Jackson Lemon demanded, looking very serious.

"I mean you, and me, and my poor husband, and Dr. Feeder," said Mrs. Freer.

"I don't see how there can be commoners where there are not lords. It is the lord that makes the commoner; and *vice versâ*."

"Won't a lady do as well? Lady Barberina—a single English girl—can make a million inferiors."

"She will be, before anything else, my wife; and she will not talk about inferiors any more than I do. I never do; it's very vulgar."

"I don't know what she'll talk about, my dear Jackson, but she will think; and her thoughts won't be pleasant—I mean for others. Do you expect to sink her to your own rank?"

Jackson Lemon's bright little eyes were fixed more brightly than ever upon his hostess. "I don't understand you; and I don't think you understand yourself." This was not absolutely candid, for he did understand Mrs. Freer to a certain extent; it has been related that, before he asked Lady Barb's hand of her parents, there had been moments when he himself was not very sure that the flower of the British aristocracy would flourish in American soil. But an intimation from another person that it was beyond his power to pass off his wife—whether she were the daughter of a peer or of a shoemaker—set all his blood on fire. It quenched on the instant his own perception of difficulties of detail, and made him feel only that he was dishonoured—he, the heir of all the ages—by such insinuations. It was his belief—though he had never before had occasion to put it forward—that his position, one of the best in the world, was one of those positions that make everything possible. He had had the best education the age could offer, for if he had rather wasted his time at Harvard, where he entered very young, he had, as he believed, been tremendously serious at Heidelberg and at Vienna. He had devoted himself to one of the noblest of professions—a profession recognised as such everywhere but in England—and he had inherited a fortune far beyond the expectation of his earlier years, the years when he cultivated habits of work which alone—or rather in combination with talents that he neither

exaggerated nor minimised—would have conduced to distinction. He was one of the most fortunate inhabitants of an
immense, fresh, rich country, a country whose future was admitted to be incalculable, and he moved with perfect ease in
a society in which he was not overshadowed by others. It
seemed to him, therefore, beneath his dignity to wonder
whether he could afford, socially speaking, to marry according
to his taste. Jackson Lemon pretended to be strong; and what
was the use of being strong if you were not prepared to undertake things that timid people might find difficult? It was
his plan to marry the woman he liked, and not to be afraid
of her afterward. The effect of Mrs. Freer's doubt of his success was to represent to him that his own character would not
cover his wife's; she couldn't have made him feel otherwise if
she had told him that he was marrying beneath him, and
would have to ask for indulgence. "I don't believe you know
how much I think that any woman who marries me will be
doing very well," he added, directly.

"I am very sure of that; but it isn't so simple—one's being
an American," Mrs. Freer rejoined, with a little philosophic
sigh.

"It's whatever one chooses to make it."

"Well, you'll make it what no one has done yet, if you take
that young lady to America and make her happy there."

"Do you think it's such a very dreadful place?"

"No, indeed; but she will."

Jackson Lemon got up from his chair, and took up his hat
and stick. He had actually turned a little pale, with the force
of his emotion; it had made him really quiver that his marriage
to Lady Barberina should be looked at as too high a flight.
He stood a moment leaning against the mantelpiece, and very
much tempted to say to Mrs. Freer that she was a vulgar-
minded old woman. But he said something that was really
more to the point: "You forget that she will have her consolations."

"Don't go away, or I shall think I have offended you. You
can't console a wounded marchioness."

"How will she be wounded? People will be charming to
her."

"They will be charming to her—charming to her!" These

words fell from the lips of Dexter Freer, who had opened the
door of the room and stood with the knob in his hand, putting himself into relation to his wife's talk with their visitor.
This was accomplished in an instant. "Of course I know
whom you mean," he said, while he exchanged greetings with
Jackson Lemon. "My wife and I—of course you know we are
great busybodies—have talked of your affair, and we differ
about it completely: she sees only the dangers, and I see the
advantages."

"By the advantages he means the fun for us," Mrs. Freer
remarked, settling her sofa-cushions.

Jackson looked with a certain sharp blankness from one of
these disinterested judges to the other; and even yet they did
not perceive how their misdirected familiarities wrought upon
him. It was hardly more agreeable to him to know that the
husband wished to see Lady Barb in America, than to know
that the wife had a dread of such a vision; for there was that
in Dexter Freer's face which seemed to say that the thing
would take place somehow for the benefit of the spectators.
"I think you both see too much—a great deal too much," he
answered, rather coldly.

"My dear young man, at my age I can take certain liberties," said Dexter Freer. "Do it—I beseech you to do it; it
has never been done before." And then, as if Jackson's glance
had challenged this last assertion, he went on: "Never, I assure
you, this particular thing. Young female members of the British aristocracy have married coachmen and fishmongers, and
all that sort of thing; but they have never married you and
me."

"They certainly haven't married you," said Mrs. Freer.

"I am much obliged to you for your advice." It may be
thought that Jackson Lemon took himself rather seriously;
and indeed I am afraid that if he had not done so there would
have been no occasion for my writing this little history. But
it made him almost sick to hear his engagement spoken of as
a curious and ambiguous phenomenon. He might have his
own ideas about it—one always had about one's engagement;
but the ideas that appeared to have peopled the imagination
of his friends ended by kindling a little hot spot in each of his

cheeks. "I would rather not talk any more about my little plans," he added to Dexter Freer. "I have been saying all sorts of absurd things to Mrs. Freer."

"They have been most interesting," that lady declared. "You have been very stupidly treated."

"May she tell me when you go?" her husband asked of the young man.

"I am going now; she may tell you whatever she likes."

"I am afraid we have displeased you," said Mrs. Freer; "I have said too much what I think. You must excuse me, it's all for your mother."

"It's she whom I want Lady Barberina to see!" Jackson Lemon exclaimed, with the inconsequence of filial affection.

"Deary me!" murmured Mrs. Freer.

"We shall go back to America to see how you get on," her husband said; "and if you succeed, it will be a great precedent."

"Oh, I shall succeed!" And with this he took his departure. He walked away with the quick step of a man labouring under a certain excitement; walked up to Piccadilly and down past Hyde Park Corner. It relieved him to traverse these distances, for he was thinking hard, under the influence of irritation; and locomotion helped him to think. Certain suggestions that had been made him in the last half hour rankled in his mind, all the more that they seemed to have a kind of representative value, to be an echo of the common voice. If his prospects wore that face to Mrs. Freer, they would probably wear it to others; and he felt a sudden need of showing such others that they took a pitiful measure of his position. Jackson Lemon walked and walked till he found himself on the highway of Hammersmith. I have represented him as a young man of much strength of purpose, and I may appear to undermine this plea when I relate that he wrote that evening to his solicitor that Mr. Hilary was to be informed that he would agree to any proposals for settlements that Mr. Hilary should make. Jackson's strength of purpose was shown in his deciding to marry Lady Barberina on any terms. It seemed to him, under the influence of his desire to prove that he was not afraid— so odious was the imputation—that terms of any kind were very superficial things. What was fundamental, and of the essence of the matter, would be to marry Lady Barb and carry everything out.

V.

"On Sundays, now, you might be at home," Jackson Lemon said to his wife in the following month of March, more than six months after his marriage.

"Are the people any nicer on Sundays than they are on other days?" Lady Barberina replied, from the depths of her chair, without looking up from a stiff little book.

He hesitated a single instant before answering: "I don't know whether they are, but I think you might be."

"I am as nice as I know how to be. You must take me as I am. You knew when you married me that I was not an American."

Jackson Lemon stood before the fire, towards which his wife's face was turned and her feet were extended; stood there some time, with his hands behind him and his eyes dropped a little obliquely upon the bent head and richly-draped figure of Lady Barberina. It may be said without delay that he was irritated, and it may be added that he had a double cause. He felt himself to be on the verge of the first crisis that had occurred between himself and his wife—the reader will perceive that it had occurred rather promptly—and he was annoyed at his annoyance. A glimpse of his state of mind before his marriage has been given to the reader, who will remember that at that period Jackson Lemon somehow regarded himself as lifted above possibilities of irritation. When one was strong, one was not irritable; and a union with a kind of goddess would of course be an element of strength. Lady Barb was a goddess still, and Jackson Lemon admired his wife as much as the day he led her to the altar; but I am not sure that he felt so strong.

"How do you know what people are?" he said in a moment. "You have seen so few; you are perpetually denying yourself. If you should leave New York to-morrow you would know wonderfully little about it."

"It's all the same," said Lady Barb; "the people are all exactly alike."

"How can you tell? You never see them."

"Didn't I go out every night for the first two months we were here?"

"It was only to about a dozen houses—always the same; people, moreover, you had already met in London. You have got no general impressions."

"That's just what I have got; I had them before I came. Every one is just the same; they have just the same names—just the same manners."

Again, for an instant, Jackson Lemon hesitated; then he said, in that apparently artless tone of which mention has already been made, and which he sometimes used in London during his wooing: "Don't you like it over here?"

Lady Barb raised her eyes from her book. "Did you expect me to like it?"

"I hoped you would, of course. I think I told you so."

"I don't remember. You said very little about it; you seemed to make a kind of mystery. I knew, of course, you expected me to live here, but I didn't know you expected me to like it."

"You thought I asked of you the sacrifice, as it were."

"I am sure I don't know," said Lady Barb. She got up from her chair and tossed the volume she had been reading into the empty seat. "I recommend you to read that book," she added.

"Is it interesting?"

"It's an American novel."

"I never read novels."

"You had better look at that one; it will show you the kind of people you want me to know."

"I have no doubt it's very vulgar," said Jackson Lemon; "I don't see why you read it."

"What else can I do? I can't always be riding in the Park; I hate the Park," Lady Barb remarked.

"It's quite as good as your own," said her husband.

She glanced at him with a certain quickness, her eyebrows slightly lifted. "Do you mean the park at Pasterns?"

"No; I mean the park in London."

"I don't care about London. One was only in London a few weeks."

"I suppose you miss the country," said Jackson Lemon. It was his idea of life that he should not be afraid of anything, not be afraid, in any situation, of knowing the worst that was to be known about it; and the demon of a courage with which discretion was not properly commingled prompted him to take soundings which were perhaps not absolutely necessary for safety, and yet which revealed unmistakable rocks. It was useless to know about rocks if he couldn't avoid them; the only thing was to trust to the wind.

"I don't know what I miss. I think I miss everything!" This was his wife's answer to his too curious inquiry. It was not peevish, for that is not the tone of a goddess; but it expressed a good deal—a good deal more than Lady Barb, who was rarely eloquent, had expressed before. Nevertheless, though his question had been precipitate, Jackson Lemon said to himself that he might take his time to think over what his wife's little speech contained; he could not help seeing that the future would give him abundant opportunity for that. He was in no hurry to ask himself whether poor Mrs. Freer, in Jermyn Street, might not, after all, have been right in saying that, in regard to marrying the product of an English caste, it was not so simple to be an American doctor—might avail little even, in such a case, to be the heir of all the ages. The transition was complicated, but in his bright mind it was rapid, from the brush of a momentary contact with such ideas to certain considerations which led him to say, after an instant, to his wife, "Should you like to go down into Connecticut?"

"Into Connecticut?"

"That's one of our States; it's about as large as Ireland. I'll take you there if you like."

"What does one do there?"

"We can try and get some hunting."

"You and I alone?"

"Perhaps we can get a party to join us."

"The people in the State?"

"Yes; we might propose it to them."

"The tradespeople in the towns?"

"Very true; they will have to mind their shops," said Jackson Lemon. "But we might hunt alone."

"Are there any foxes?"

"No; but there are a few old cows."

Lady Barb had already perceived that her husband took it into his head once in a while to laugh at her, and she was aware that the present occasion was neither worse nor better than some others. She didn't mind it particularly now, though in England it would have disgusted her; she had the consciousness of virtue—an immense comfort—and flattered herself that she had learned the lesson of an altered standard of fitness; there were, moreover, so many more disagreeable things in America than being laughed at by one's husband. But she pretended to mind it, because it made him stop, and above all it stopped discussion, which with Jackson was so often jocular, and none the less tiresome for that. "I only want to be left alone," she said, in answer—though, indeed, it had not the manner of an answer—to his speech about the cows. With this she wandered away to one of the windows which looked out on the Fifth Avenue. She was very fond of these windows, and she had taken a great fancy to the Fifth Avenue, which, in the high-pitched winter weather, when everything sparkled, was a spectacle full of novelty. It will be seen that she was not wholly unjust to her adoptive country: she found it delightful to look out of the window. This was a pleasure she had enjoyed in London only in the most furtive manner; it was not the kind of thing that girls did in England. Besides, in London, in Hill Street, there was nothing particular to see; but in the Fifth Avenue everything and every one went by, and observation was made consistent with dignity by the masses of brocade and lace in which the windows were draped, which, somehow, would not have been tidy in England, and which made an ambush without concealing the brilliant day. Hundreds of women—the curious women of New York, who were unlike any that Lady Barb had hitherto seen—passed the house every hour, and her ladyship was infinitely entertained and mystified by the sight of their clothes. She spent a good deal more time than she was aware of in this amusement; and if she had been addicted to returning upon herself, or asking herself for an account of her conduct—an inquiry which she did not, indeed, completely neglect, but treated very cursorily—it would have made her smile sadly to think what she appeared mainly to have come to America for, conscious though she was that her tastes were very simple, and that so long as she didn't hunt, it didn't much matter what she did.

Her husband turned about to the fire, giving a push with his foot to a log that had fallen out of its place. Then he said—and the connection with the words she had just uttered was apparent enough—"You really must be at home on Sundays, you know. I used to like that so much in London. All the best women here do it. You had better begin to-day. I am going to see my mother; if I meet any one I will tell them to come."

"Tell them not to talk so much," said Lady Barb, among her lace curtains.

"Ah, my dear," her husband replied, "it isn't every one that has your concision!" And he went and stood behind her in the window, putting his arm round her waist. It was as much of a satisfaction to him as it had been six months before, at the time the solicitors were settling the matter, that this flower of an ancient stem should be worn upon his own breast; he still thought its fragrance a thing quite apart, and it was as clear as day to him that his wife was the handsomest woman in New York. He had begun, after their arrival, by telling her this very often; but the assurance brought no colour to her cheek, no light to her eyes; to be the handsomest woman in New York evidently did not seem to her a position in life. Moreover, the reader may be informed that, oddly enough, Lady Barb did not particularly believe this assertion. There were some very pretty women in New York, and without in the least wishing to be like them—she had seen no woman in America whom she desired to resemble—she envied some of their elements. It is probable that her own finest points were those of which she was most unconscious. But her husband was aware of all of them; nothing could exceed the minuteness of his appreciation of his wife. It was a sign of this that after he had stood behind her a moment he kissed her very tenderly. "Have you any message for my mother?" he asked.

"Please give her my love. And you might take her that book."

"What book?"

"That nasty one I have been reading."

"Oh, bother your books," said Jackson Lemon, with a certain irritation, as he went out of the room.

There had been a good many things in her life in New York that cost Lady Barb an effort; but sending her love to her mother-in-law was not one of these. She liked Mrs. Lemon better than any one she had seen in America; she was the only person who seemed to Lady Barb really simple, as she understood that quality. Many people had struck her as homely and rustic, and many others as pretentious and vulgar; but in Jackson's mother she had found the golden mean of a simplicity which, as she would have said, was really nice. Her sister, Lady Agatha, was even fonder of Mrs. Lemon; but then Lady Agatha had taken the most extraordinary fancy to every one and everything, and talked as if America were the most delightful country in the world. She was having a lovely time (she already spoke the most beautiful American), and had been, during the winter that was just drawing to a close, the most prominent girl in New York. She had gone out at first with her sister; but for some weeks past Lady Barb had let so many occasions pass, that Agatha threw herself into the arms of Mrs. Lemon, who found her extraordinarily quaint and amusing and was delighted to take her into society. Mrs. Lemon, as an old woman, had given up such vanities; but she only wanted a motive, and in her good nature she ordered a dozen new caps and sat smiling against the wall while her little English maid, on polished floors, to the sound of music, cultivated the American step as well as the American tone. There was no trouble, in New York, about going out, and the winter was not half over before the little English maid found herself an accomplished diner, rolling about, without any chaperon at all, to banquets where she could count upon a bouquet at her plate. She had had a great deal of correspondence with her mother on this point, and Lady Canterville at last withdrew her protest, which in the meantime had been perfectly useless. It was ultimately Lady Canterville's feeling that if she had married the handsomest of her daughters to an American doctor, she might let another become a professional *raconteuse* (Agatha had written to her that she was expected to talk so much), strange as such a destiny seemed for a girl of

nineteen. Mrs. Lemon was even a much simpler woman than
Lady Barberina thought her; for she had not noticed that Lady
Agatha danced much oftener with Herman Longstraw than
with any one else. Jackson Lemon, though he went little to
balls, had discovered this truth, and he looked slightly preoccupied when, after he had sat five minutes with his mother
on the Sunday afternoon through which I have invited the
reader to trace so much more than (I am afraid) is easily apparent of the progress of this simple story, he learned that his
sister-in-law was entertaining Mr. Longstraw in the library. He
had called half an hour before, and she had taken him into
the other room to show him the seal of the Cantervilles,
which she had fastened to one of her numerous trinkets (she
was adorned with a hundred bangles and chains), and the
proper exhibition of which required a taper and a stick of wax.
Apparently he was examining it very carefully, for they had
been absent a good while. Mrs. Lemon's simplicity was further
shown by the fact that she had not measured their absence; it
was only when Jackson questioned her that she remembered.

Herman Longstraw was a young Californian who had
turned up in New York the winter before, and who travelled
on his moustache, as they were understood to say in his native
State. This moustache, and some of the accompanying features, were very ornamental; several ladies in New York had
been known to declare that they were as beautiful as a dream.
Taken in connection with his tall stature, his familiar good-
nature, and his remarkable Western vocabulary, they constituted his only social capital; for of the two great divisions, the
rich Californians and the poor Californians, it was well known
to which he belonged. Jackson Lemon looked at him as a
slightly mitigated cowboy, and was somewhat vexed at his dear
mother, though he was aware that she could scarcely figure
to herself what an effect such an accent as that would produce
in the halls of Canterville. He had no desire whatever to play
a trick on the house to which he was allied, and knew perfectly
that Lady Agatha had not been sent to America to become
entangled with a Californian of the wrong denomination. He
had been perfectly willing to bring her; he thought, a little
vindictively, that this would operate as a hint to her parents
as to what he might have been inclined to do if they had not

sent Mr. Hilary after him. Herman Longstraw, according to
the legend, had been a trapper, a squatter, a miner, a pioneer—had been everything that one could be in the romantic
parts of America, and had accumulated masses of experience
before the age of thirty. He had shot bears in the Rockies and
buffaloes on the plains; and it was even believed that he had
brought down animals of a still more dangerous kind, among
the haunts of men. There had been a story that he owned a
cattle-ranch in Arizona; but a later and apparently more authentic version of it, though it represented him as looking
after the cattle, did not depict him as their proprietor. Many
of the stories told about him were false; but there is no doubt
that his moustache, his good-nature and his accent were genuine. He danced very badly; but Lady Agatha had frankly told
several persons that that was nothing new to her; and she liked
(this, however, she did not tell) Mr. Herman Longstraw. What
she enjoyed in America was the revelation of freedom; and
there was no such proof of freedom as conversation with a
gentleman who dressed in skins when he was not in New
York, and who, in his usual pursuits, carried his life (as well
as that of other people) in his hand. A gentleman whom she
had sat next to at a dinner in the early part of her stay in New
York, remarked to her that the United States were the paradise
of women and mechanics; and this had seemed to her at the
time very abstract, for she was not conscious, as yet, of belonging to either class. In England she had been only a girl;
and the principal idea connected with that was simply that,
for one's misfortune, one was not a boy. But presently she
perceived that New York was a paradise; and this helped her
to know that she must be one of the people mentioned in the
axiom of her neighbour—people who could do whatever they
wanted, had a voice in everything, and made their taste and
their ideas felt. She saw that it was great fun to be a woman
in America, and that this was the best way to enjoy the New
York winter—the wonderful, brilliant New York winter, the
queer, long-shaped, glittering city, the heterogeneous hours,
among which you couldn't tell the morning from the afternoon or the night from either of them, the perpetual liberties
and walks, the rushings-out and the droppings-in, the inti-
macies, the endearments, the comicalities, the sleigh-bells, the

cutters, the sunsets on the snow, the ice-parties in the frosty clearness, the bright, hot, velvety houses, the bouquets, the bonbons, the little cakes, the big cakes, the irrepressible inspirations of shopping, the innumerable luncheons and dinners that were offered to youth and innocence, the quantities of chatter of quantities of girls, the perpetual motion of the German, the suppers at restaurants after the play, the way in which life was pervaded by Delmonico and Delmonico by the sense that though one's hunting was lost and this so different, it was almost as good—and in all, through all, a kind of suffusion of bright, loud, friendly sound, which was very local, but very human.

Lady Agatha at present was staying, for a little change, with Mrs. Lemon, and such adventures as that were part of the pleasure of her American season. The house was too close; but physically the girl could bear anything, and it was all she had to complain of; for Mrs. Lemon, as we know, thought her a bonnie little damsel, and had none of those old-world scruples in regard to spoiling young people to which Lady Agatha now perceived that she herself, in the past, had been unduly sacrificed. In her own way—it was not at all her sister's way—she liked to be of importance; and this was assuredly the case when she saw that Mrs. Lemon had apparently nothing in the world to do (after spending a part of the morning with her servants) but invent little distractions (many of them of the edible sort) for her guest. She appeared to have certain friends, but she had no society to speak of, and the people who came into her house came principally to see Lady Agatha. This, as we have seen, was strikingly the case with Herman Longstraw. The whole situation gave Lady Agatha a great feeling of success—success of a new and unexpected kind. Of course, in England, she had been born successful, in a manner, in coming into the world in one of the most beautiful rooms at Pasterns; but her present triumph was achieved more by her own effort (not that she had tried very hard) and by her merit. It was not so much what she said (for she could never say half as much as the girls in New York), as the spirit of enjoyment that played in her fresh young face, with its pointless curves, and shone in her gray English eyes. She enjoyed everything, even the street-cars, of which she made liberal use;

and more than everything she enjoyed Mr. Longstraw and his talk about buffaloes and bears. Mrs. Lemon promised to be very careful, as soon as her son had begun to warn her; and this time she had a certain understanding of what she promised. She thought people ought to make the matches they liked; she had given proof of this in her late behaviour to Jackson, whose own union was, in her opinion, marked with all the arbitrariness of pure love. Nevertheless, she could see that Herman Longstraw would probably be thought rough in England; and it was not simply that he was so inferior to Jackson, for, after all, certain things were not to be expected. Jackson Lemon was not oppressed with his mother-in-law, having taken his precautions against such a danger; but he was aware that he should give Lady Canterville a permanent advantage over him if, while she was in America, her daughter Agatha should attach herself to a mere moustache.

It was not always, as I have hinted, that Mrs. Lemon entered completely into the views of her son, though in form she never failed to subscribe to them devoutly. She had never yet, for instance, apprehended his reason for marrying Lady Barberina Clement. This was a great secret, and Mrs. Lemon was determined that no one should ever know it. For herself, she was sure that, to the end of time, she should not discover Jackson's reason. She could never ask about it, for that of course would betray her. From the first she had told him she was delighted; there being no need of asking for explanations then, as the young lady herself, when she should come to know her, would explain. But the young lady had not yet explained; and after this, evidently, she never would. She was very tall, very handsome, she answered exactly to Mrs. Lemon's prefigurement of the daughter of a lord, and she wore her clothes, which were peculiar, but, to her, remarkably becoming, very well. But she did not elucidate; we know ourselves that there was very little that was explanatory about Lady Barb. So Mrs. Lemon continued to wonder, to ask herself, "Why that one, more than so many others, who would have been more natural?" The choice appeared to her, as I have said, very arbitrary. She found Lady Barb very different from other girls she had known, and this led her almost immediately to feel sorry for her daughter-in-law. She said to herself that Barb was to be pitied if she found her husband's people as peculiar as his mother found *her*, for the result of that would be to make her very lonesome. Lady Agatha was different, because she seemed to keep nothing back; you saw all there was of her, and she was evidently not home-sick. Mrs. Lemon could see that Barberina was ravaged by this last passion and was too proud to show it. She even had a glimpse of the ultimate truth; namely, that Jackson's wife had not the comfort of crying, because that would have amounted to a confession that she had been idiotic enough to believe in advance that, in an American town, in the society of doctors, she should escape such pangs. Mrs. Lemon treated her with the greatest gentleness—all the gentleness that was due to a young woman who was in the unfortunate position of having been married one couldn't tell why. The world, to Mrs. Lemon's view, contained two great departments—that of persons, and that of things; and she believed that you must take an interest either in one or the other. The incomprehensible thing in Lady Barb was that she cared for neither side of the show. Her house apparently inspired her with no curiosity and no enthusiasm, though it had been thought magnificent enough to be described in successive columns of the American newspapers; and she never spoke of her furniture or her domestics, though she had a prodigious supply of such possessions. She was the same with regard to her acquaintance, which was immense, inasmuch as every one in the place had called on her. Mrs. Lemon was the least critical woman in the world; but it had sometimes exasperated her just a little that her daughter-in-law should receive every one in New York in exactly the same way. There were differences, Mrs. Lemon knew, and some of them were of the highest importance; but poor Lady Barb appeared never to suspect them. She accepted every one and everything, and asked no questions. She had no curiosity about her fellow-citizens, and as she never assumed it for a moment, she gave Mrs. Lemon no opportunity to enlighten her. Lady Barb was a person with whom you could do nothing unless she gave you an opening; and nothing would have been more difficult than to enlighten her against her will. Of course she picked up a little knowledge; but she confounded and transposed American attributes in the

most extraordinary way. She had a way of calling every one
Doctor; and Mrs. Lemon could scarcely convince her that this
distinction was too precious to be so freely bestowed. She had
once said to her mother-in-law that in New York there was
nothing to know people by, their names were so very monotonous; and Mrs. Lemon had entered into this enough to
see that there was something that stood out a good deal in
Barberina's own prefix. It is probable that during her short
stay in New York complete justice was not done Lady Barb;
she never got credit, for instance, for repressing her annoyance
at the aridity of the social nomenclature, which seemed to her
hideous. That little speech to her mother was the most reckless sign she gave of it; and there were few things that contributed more to the good conscience she habitually enjoyed,
than her self-control on this particular point.

Jackson Lemon was making some researches, just now,
which took up a great deal of his time; and, for the rest, he
passed his hours abundantly with his wife. For the last three
months, therefore, he had seen his mother scarcely more than
once a week. In spite of researches, in spite of medical soci-
eties, where Jackson, to her knowledge, read papers, Lady
Barb had more of her husband's company than she had
counted upon at the time she married. She had never known
a married pair to be so much together as she and Jackson; he
appeared to expect her to sit with him in the library in the
morning. He had none of the occupations of gentlemen and
noblemen in England, for the element of politics appeared to
be as absent as the hunting. There were politics in Washington, she had been told, and even at Albany, and Jackson had
proposed to introduce her to these cities; but the proposal,
made to her once at dinner before several people, had excited
such cries of horror that it fell dead on the spot. "We don't
want you to see anything of that kind," one of the ladies had
said, and Jackson had appeared to be discouraged—that is if,
in regard to Jackson, one could really tell.

"Pray, what is it you want me to see?" Lady Barb had asked
on this occasion.

"Well, New York; and Boston, if you want to very
much—but not otherwise; and Niagara; and, more than anything, Newport."

Lady Barb was tired of their eternal Newport; she had heard of it a thousand times, and felt already as if she had lived there half her life; she was sure, moreover, that she should hate it. This is perhaps as near as she came to having a lively conviction on any American subject. She asked herself whether she was then to spend her life in the Fifth Avenue, with alternations of a city of villas (she detested villas), and wondered whether that was all the great American country had to offer her. There were times when she thought that she should like the backwoods, and that the Far West might be a resource; for she had analysed her feelings just deep enough to discover that when she had—hesitating a good deal—turned over the question of marrying Jackson Lemon, it was not in the least of American barbarism that she was afraid; her dread was of American civilisation. She believed the little lady I have just quoted was a goose; but that did not make New York any more interesting. It would be reckless to say that she suffered from an overdose of Jackson's company, because she had a view of the fact that he was much her most important social resource. She could talk to him about England; about her own England, and he understood more or less what she wished to say, when she wished to say anything, which was not frequent. There were plenty of other people who talked about England; but with them the range of allusion was always the hotels, of which she knew nothing, and the shops, and the opera, and the photographs: they had a mania for photographs. There were other people who were always wanting her to tell them about Pasterns, and the manner of life there, and the parties; but if there was one thing Lady Barb disliked more than another, it was describing Pasterns. She had always lived with people who knew, of themselves, what such a place would be, without demanding these pictorial efforts, proper only, as she vaguely felt, to persons belonging to the classes whose trade was the arts of expression. Lady Barb, of course, had never gone into it; but she knew that in her own class the business was not to express, but to enjoy; not to represent, but to be represented—though, indeed, this latter liability might convey offence; for it may be noted that even for an aristocrat Jackson Lemon's wife was aristocratic.

Lady Agatha and her visitor came back from the library in

course of time, and Jackson Lemon felt it his duty to be rather cold to Herman Longstraw. It was not clear to him what sort of a husband his sister-in-law would do well to look for in America—if there were to be any question of husbands; but as to this he was not bound to be definite, provided he should rule out Mr. Longstraw. This gentleman, however, was not given to perceive shades of manner; he had little observation, but very great confidence.

"I think you had better come home with me," Jackson said to Lady Agatha; "I guess you have stayed here long enough."

"Don't let him say that, Mrs. Lemon!" the girl cried. "I like being with you so very much."

"I try to make it pleasant," said Mrs. Lemon. "I should really miss you now; but perhaps it's your mother's wish." If it was a question of defending her guest from ineligible suitors, Mrs. Lemon felt, of course, that her son was more competent than she; though she had a lurking kindness for Herman Longstraw, and a vague idea that he was a gallant, genial specimen of young America.

"Oh, mamma wouldn't see any difference!" Lady Agatha exclaimed, looking at Jackson with pleading blue eyes. "Mamma wants me to see every one; you know she does. That's what she sent me to America for; she knew it was not like England. She wouldn't like it if I didn't sometimes stay with people; she always wanted us to stay at other houses. And she knows all about you, Mrs. Lemon, and she likes you immensely. She sent you a message the other day, and I am afraid I forgot to give it you—to thank you for being so kind to me and taking such a lot of trouble. Really she did, but I forgot it. If she wants me to see as much as possible of America, it's much better I should be here than always with Barb —it's much less like one's own country. I mean it's much nicer—for a girl," said Lady Agatha, affectionately, to Mrs. Lemon, who began also to look at Jackson with a kind of tender argumentativeness.

"If you want the genuine thing, you ought to come out on the plains," Mr. Longstraw interposed, with smiling sincerity. "I guess that was your mother's idea. Why don't you all come out?" He had been looking intently at Lady Agatha while the remarks I have just repeated succeeded each other on her lips—looking at her with a kind of fascinated approbation, for all the world as if he had been a slightly slow-witted English gentleman and the girl had been a flower of the West—a flower that knew how to talk. He made no secret of the fact that Lady Agatha's voice was music to him, his ear being much more susceptible than his own inflections would have indicated. To Lady Agatha those inflections were not displeasing, partly because, like Mr. Herman himself, in general, she had not a perception of shades; and partly because it never occurred to her to compare them with any other tones. He seemed to her to speak a foreign language altogether—a romantic dialect, through which the most comical meanings gleamed here and there.

"I should like it above all things," she said, in answer to his last observation.

"The scenery's superior to anything round here," Mr. Longstraw went on.

Mrs. Lemon, as we know, was the softest of women; but, as an old New Yorker, she had no patience with some of the new fashions. Chief among these was the perpetual reference, which had become common only within a few years, to the outlying parts of the country, the States and Territories of which children, in her time, used to learn the names, in their order, at school, but which no one ever thought of going to or talking about. Such places, in Mrs. Lemon's opinion, belonged to the geography-books, or at most to the literature of newspapers, but not to society nor to conversation; and the change—which, so far as it lay in people's talk, she thought at bottom a mere affectation—threatened to make her native land appear vulgar and vague. For this amiable daughter of Manhattan, the normal existence of man, and, still more, of woman, had been "located," as she would have said, between Trinity Church and the beautiful Reservoir at the top of the Fifth Avenue—monuments of which she was personally proud; and if we could look into the deeper parts of her mind, I am afraid we should discover there an impression that both the countries of Europe and the remainder of her own continent were equally far from the centre and the light.

"Well, scenery isn't everything," she remarked, mildly, to Mr. Longstraw; "and if Lady Agatha should wish to see anything of that kind, all she has got to do is to take the boat up the Hudson."

Mrs. Lemon's recognition of this river, I should say, was all that it need have been; she thought that it existed for the purpose of supplying New Yorkers with poetical feelings, helping them to face comfortably occasions like the present, and, in general, meet foreigners with confidence—part of the oddity of foreigners being their conceit about their own places.

"That's a good idea, Lady Agatha; let's take the boat," said Mr. Longstraw. "I've had great times on the boats."

Lady Agatha looked at her cavalier a little with those singular, charming eyes of hers—eyes of which it was impossible to say, at any moment, whether they were the shyest or the frankest in the world; and she was not aware, while this contemplation lasted, that her brother-in-law was observing her. He was thinking of certain things while he did so, of things he had heard about the English; who still, in spite of his having married into a family of that nation, appeared to him very much through the medium of hearsay. They were more passionate than the Americans, and they did things that would never have been expected; though they seemed steadier and less excitable, there was much social evidence to show that they were more impulsive.

"It's so very kind of you to propose that," Lady Agatha said in a moment to Mrs. Lemon. "I think I have never been in a ship—except, of course, coming from England. I am sure mamma would wish me to see the Hudson. We used to go in immensely for boating in England."

"Did you boat in a ship?" Herman Longstraw asked, showing his teeth hilariously, and pulling his moustaches.

"Lots of my mother's people have been in the navy." Lady Agatha perceived vaguely and good-naturedly that she had said something which the odd Americans thought odd, and that she must justify herself. Her standard of oddity was getting dreadfully dislocated.

"I really think you had better come back to us," said Jackson; "your sister is very lonely without you."

"She is much more lonely with me. We are perpetually having differences. Barb is dreadfully vexed because I like

America, instead of—instead of——" And Lady Agatha
paused a moment; for it just occurred to her that this might
be a betrayal.

"Instead of what?" Jackson Lemon inquired.

"Instead of perpetually wanting to go to England, as she
does," she went on, only giving her phrase a little softer turn;
for she felt the next moment that her sister could have nothing
to hide, and must, of course, have the courage of her opinions. "Of course England's best, but I dare say I like to be
bad," said Lady Agatha, artlessly.

"Oh, there's no doubt you are awfully bad!" Mr. Longstraw exclaimed, with joyous eagerness. Of course he could not
know that what she had principally in mind was an exchange
of opinions that had taken place between her sister and herself
just before she came to stay with Mrs. Lemon. This incident,
of which Longstraw was the occasion, might indeed have been
called a discussion, for it had carried them quite into the
realms of the abstract. Lady Barb had said she didn't see how
Agatha could look at such a creature as that—an odious, familiar, vulgar being, who had not about him the rudiments
of a gentleman. Lady Agatha had replied that Mr. Longstraw
was familiar and rough, and that he had a twang, and thought
it amusing to talk of her as "the Princess;" but that he was a
gentleman for all that, and that at any rate he was tremendous
fun. Her sister to this had rejoined that if he was rough and
familiar he couldn't be a gentleman, inasmuch as that was just
what a gentleman meant—a man who was civil, and well-bred,
and well-born. Lady Agatha had argued that this was just
where she differed; that a man might perfectly be a gentleman,
and yet be rough, and even ignorant, so long as he was really
nice. The only thing was that he should be really nice, which
was the case with Mr. Longstraw, who, moreover, was quite
extraordinarily civil—as civil as a man could be. And then
Lady Agatha made the strongest point she had ever made in
her life (she had never been so inspired) in saying that Mr.
Longstraw was rough, perhaps, but not rude—a distinction
altogether wasted on her sister, who declared that she had not
come to America, of all places, to learn what a gentleman was.
The discussion, in short, had been lively. I know not whether
it was the tonic effect on them, too, of the fine winter weather,

or, on the other hand, that of Lady Barb's being bored and having nothing else to do; but Lord Canterville's daughters went into the question with the moral earnestness of a pair of Bostonians. It was part of Lady Agatha's view of her admirer that he, after all, much resembled other tall people, with smiling eyes and moustaches, who had ridden a good deal in rough countries, and whom she had seen in other places. If he was more familiar, he was also more alert; still, the difference was not in himself, but in the way she saw him—the way she saw everybody in America. If she should see the others in the same way, no doubt they would be quite the same; and Lady Agatha sighed a little over the possibilities of life; for this peculiar way, especially regarded in connection with gentlemen, had become very pleasant to her.

She had betrayed her sister more than she thought, even though Jackson Lemon did not particularly show it in the tone in which he said: "Of course she knows that she is going to see your mother in the summer." His tone, rather, was that of irritation at the repetition of a familiar idea.

"Oh, it isn't only mamma," replied Lady Agatha.

"I know she likes a cool house," said Mrs. Lemon, suggestively.

"When she goes, you had better bid her good-bye," the girl went on.

"Of course I shall bid her good-bye," said Mrs. Lemon, to whom, apparently, this remark was addressed.

"I shall never bid you good-bye, Princess," Herman Longstraw interposed. "I can tell you that you never will see the last of me."

"Oh, it doesn't matter about me, for I shall come back; but if Barb once gets to England she will never come back."

"Oh, my dear child," murmured Mrs. Lemon, addressing Lady Agatha, but looking at her son.

Jackson looked at the ceiling, at the floor; above all, he looked very conscious.

"I hope you don't mind my saying that, Jackson dear," Lady Agatha said to him, for she was very fond of her brother-in-law.

"Ah, well, then, she shan't go, then," he remarked, after a moment, with a dry little laugh.

"But you promised mamma, you know," said the girl, with the confidence of her affection.

Jackson looked at her with an eye which expressed none even of his very moderate hilarity. "Your mother, then, must bring her back."

"Get some of your navy people to supply an iron-clad!" cried Mr. Longstraw.

"It would be very pleasant if the Marchioness could come over," said Mrs. Lemon.

"Oh, she would hate it more than poor Barb," Lady Agatha quickly replied. It did not suit her mood at all to see a marchioness inserted into the field of her vision.

"Doesn't she feel interested, from what you have told her?" Herman Longstraw asked of Lady Agatha. But Jackson Lemon did not heed his sister-in-law's answer; he was thinking of something else. He said nothing more, however, about the subject of his thought, and before ten minutes were over he took his departure, having, meanwhile, neglected also to revert to the question of Lady Agatha's bringing her visit to his mother to a close. It was not to speak to him of this (for, as we know, she wished to keep the girl, and somehow could not bring herself to be afraid of Herman Longstraw) that when Jackson took leave she went with him to the door of the house, detaining him a little, while she stood on the steps, as people had always done in New York in her time, though it was another of the new fashions she did not like, not to come out of the parlour. She placed her hand on his arm to keep him on the "stoop," and looked up and down into the brilliant afternoon and the beautiful city—its chocolate-coloured houses, so extraordinarily smooth—in which it seemed to her that even the most fastidious people ought to be glad to live. It was useless to attempt to conceal it; her son's marriage had made a difference, had put up a kind of barrier. It had brought with it a problem much more difficult than his old problem of how to make his mother feel that she was still, as she had been in his childhood, the dispenser of his rewards. The old problem had been easily solved; the new one was a visible preoccupation. Mrs. Lemon felt that her daughter-in-law did not take her seriously; and that was a part of the barrier. Even if Barberina liked her better than any one else, this was mostly because she liked every one else so little. Mrs. Lemon had not a grain of resentment in her nature; and it was not to feed a sense of wrong that she permitted herself to criticise her son's wife. She could not help feeling that his marriage was not altogether fortunate if his wife didn't take his mother seriously. She knew she was not otherwise remarkable than as being his mother; but that position, which was no merit of hers (the merit was all Jackson's, in being her son), seemed to her one which, familiar as Lady Barb appeared to have been in England with positions of various kinds, would naturally strike the girl as a very high one, to be accepted as freely as a fine morning. If she didn't think of his mother as an indivisible part of him, perhaps she didn't think of other things either; and Mrs. Lemon vaguely felt that, remarkable as Jackson was, he was made up of parts, and that it would never do that these parts should depreciate one by one, for there was no knowing what that might end in. She feared that things were rather cold for him at home when he had to explain so much to his wife—explain to her, for instance, all the sources of happiness that were to be found in New York. This struck her as a new kind of problem altogether for a husband. She had never thought of matrimony without a community of feeling in regard to religion and country; one took those great conditions for granted, just as one assumed that one's food was to be cooked; and if Jackson should have to discuss them with his wife, he might, in spite of his great abilities, be carried into regions where he would get entangled and embroiled—from which, even, possibly, he would not come back at all. Mrs. Lemon had a horror of losing him in some way; and this fear was in her eyes as she stood on the steps of her house, and, after she had glanced up and down the street, looked at him a moment in silence. He simply kissed her again, and said she would take cold.

"I am not afraid of that, I have a shawl!" Mrs. Lemon, who was very small and very fair, with pointed features and an elaborate cap, passed her life in a shawl, and owed to this habit her reputation for being an invalid—an idea which she scorned, naturally enough, inasmuch as it was precisely her shawl that (as she believed) kept her from being one. "Is it true Barberina won't come back?" she asked of her son.

"I don't know that we shall ever find out; I don't know that I shall take her to England."

"Didn't you promise, dear?"

"I don't know that I promised; not absolutely."

"But you wouldn't keep her here against her will?" said Mrs. Lemon, inconsequently.

"I guess she'll get used to it," Jackson answered, with a lightness he did not altogether feel.

Mrs. Lemon looked up and down the street again, and gave a little sigh. "What a pity she isn't American!" She did not mean this as a reproach, a hint of what might have been; it was simply embarrassment resolved into speech.

"She couldn't have been American," said Jackson, with decision.

"Couldn't she, dear?" Mrs. Lemon spoke with a kind of respect; she felt that there were imperceptible reasons in this.

"It was just as she is that I wanted her," Jackson added.

"Even if she won't come back?" his mother asked, with a certain wonder.

"Oh, she has got to come back!" Jackson said, going down the steps.

VI.

Lady Barb, after this, did not decline to see her New York acquaintances on Sunday afternoons, though she refused for the present to enter into a project of her husband's, who thought it would be a pleasant thing that she should entertain his friends on the evening of that day. Like all good Americans, Jackson Lemon devoted much consideration to the great question how, in his native land, society should be brought into being. It seemed to him that it would help the good cause, for which so many Americans are ready to lay down their lives, if his wife should, as he jocularly called it, open a saloon. He believed, or he tried to believe, the *salon* now possible in New York, on condition of its being reserved entirely for adults; and in having taken a wife out of a country in which social traditions were rich and ancient, he had done something towards qualifying his own house—so splendidly qualified in all strictly material respects—to be the scene of such an effort. A charming woman, accustomed only to the best in each country, as Lady Beauchemin said, what might she not achieve by being at home (to the elder generation) in an easy, early, inspiring, comprehensive way, on the evening in the week on which worldly engagements were least numerous? He laid this philosophy before Lady Barb, in pursuance of a theory that if she disliked New York on a short acquaintance, she could not fail to like it on a long one. Jackson Lemon believed in the New York mind—not so much, indeed, in its literary, artistic, or political achievements, as in its general quickness and nascent adaptability. He clung to this belief, for it was a very important piece of material in the structure that he was attempting to rear. The New York mind would throw its glamour over Lady Barb if she would only give it a chance; for it was exceedingly bright, entertaining, and sympathetic. If she would only have a *salon*, where this charming organ might expand, and where she might inhale its fragrance in the most convenient and luxurious way, without, as it were, getting up from her chair; if she would only just try this graceful, good-natured experiment (which would make every one like *her* so much, too), he was sure that all the wrinkles in the gilded scroll of his fate would be smoothed out. But Lady Barb did not rise at all to his conception, and had not the least curiosity about the New York mind. She thought it would be extremely disagreeable to have a lot of people tumbling in on Sunday evening without being invited; and altogether her husband's sketch of the Anglo-American saloon seemed to her to suggest familiarity, high-pitched talk (she had already made a remark to him about "screeching women"), and exaggerated laughter. She did not tell him— for this, somehow, it was not in her power to express, and, strangely enough, he never completely guessed it—that she was singularly deficient in any natural, or indeed acquired, understanding of what a saloon might be. She had never seen one, and for the most part she never thought of things she had not seen. She had seen great dinners, and balls, and meets, and runs, and races; she had seen garden-parties, and a lot of people, mainly women (who, however, didn't screech), at dull, stuffy teas, and distinguished companies collected in splendid castles; but all this gave her no idea of a tradition of conversation, of a social agreement that the continuity of talk, its accumulations from season to season, should not be lost. Conversation, in Lady Barb's experience, had never been continuous; in such a case it would surely have been a bore. It had been occasional and fragmentary, a trifle jerky, with allusions that were never explained; it had a dread of detail; it seldom pursued anything very far, or kept hold of it very long.

There was something else that she did not say to her husband in reference to his visions of hospitality, which was, that if she should open a saloon (she had taken up the joke as well, for Lady Barb was eminently good-natured), Mrs. Vanderdecken would straightway open another, and Mrs. Vanderdecken's would be the more successful of the two. This lady, for reasons that Lady Barb had not yet explored, was supposed to be the great personage in New York; there were legends of her husband's family having behind them a fabulous antiquity. When this was alluded to, it was spoken of as something incalculable, and lost in the dimness of time. Mrs. Vanderdecken was young, pretty, clever, absurdly pretentious (Lady Barb thought), and had a wonderfully artistic house. Ambition, also, was expressed in every rustle of her garments; and if she was the first person in America (this had an immense sound), it was plain that she intended to remain so. It was not till after she had been several months in New York that it came over Lady Barb that this brilliant, bristling native had flung down the glove; and when the idea presented itself, lighted up by an incident which I have no space to relate, she simply blushed a little (for Mrs. Vanderdecken), and held her tongue. She had not come to America to bandy words about precedence with such a woman as that. She had ceased to think about it much (of course one thought about it in England); but an instinct of self-preservation led her not to expose herself to occasions on which her claim might be tested. This, at bottom, had much to do with her having, very soon after the first flush of the honours paid her on her arrival, and which seemed to her rather grossly overdone, taken the line of scarcely going out. "They can't keep *that* up!" she had said to herself; and, in short, she would stay at home. She had a feeling that whenever she should go forth she would meet Mrs. Vanderdecken, who would withhold, or deny, or contest something—poor Lady Barb could never imagine what. She did not try to, and gave little thought to all this; for she was not prone to confess to herself fears, especially fears from which terror was absent. But, as I have said, it abode within her as a presentiment that if she should set up a drawing-room in the foreign style (it was curious, in New York, how they tried to be foreign), Mrs. Vanderdecken would be beforehand with her. The continuity of conversation, oh! that idea she would certainly have; there was no one so continuous as Mrs. Vanderdecken. Lady Barb, as I have related, did not give her husband the surprise of telling him of these thoughts, though she had given him some other surprises. He would have been very much astonished, and perhaps, after a bit, a little encouraged, at finding that she was liable to this particular form of irritation.

On the Sunday afternoon she was visible; and on one of these occasions, going into her drawing-room late, he found her entertaining two ladies and a gentleman. The gentleman was Sidney Feeder, and one of the ladies was Mrs. Vanderdecken, whose ostensible relations with Lady Barb were of the most cordial nature. If she intended to crush her (as two or three persons, not conspicuous for a narrow accuracy, gave out that she privately declared), Mrs. Vanderdecken wished at least to study the weak points of the invader, to penetrate herself with the character of the English girl. Lady Barb, indeed, appeared to have a mysterious fascination for the representative of the American patriciate. Mrs. Vanderdecken could not take her eyes off her victim; and whatever might be her estimate of her importance, she at least could not let her alone. "Why does she come to see me?" poor Lady Barb asked herself. "I am sure I don't want to see her; she has done enough for civility long ago." Mrs. Vanderdecken had her own reasons; and one of them was simply the pleasure of looking at the Doctor's wife, as she habitually called the daughter of the Cantervilles. She was not guilty of the folly of depreciating this lady's appearance, and professed an unbounded admiration for it, defending it on many occasions against superficial people who said there were fifty women in New York that were handsomer. Whatever might have been Lady Barb's weak points, they were not the curve of her cheek and chin,

the setting of her head on her throat, or the quietness of her
deep eyes, which were as beautiful as if they had been blank,
like those of antique busts. "The head is enchanting—perfectly enchanting," Mrs. Vanderdecken used to say irrelevantly, as if there were only one head in the place. She always
used to ask about the Doctor; and that was another reason
why she came. She brought up the Doctor at every turn; asked
if he were often called up at night; found it the greatest of
luxuries, in a word, to address Lady Barb as the wife of a
medical man, more or less *au courant* of her husband's patients. The other lady, on this Sunday afternoon, was a certain
little Mrs. Chew, whose clothes looked so new that she had
the air of a walking advertisement issued by a great shop, and
who was always asking Lady Barb about England, which Mrs.
Vanderdecken never did. The latter visitor conversed with
Lady Barb on a purely American basis, with that continuity
(on her own side) of which mention has already been made,
while Mrs. Chew engaged Sidney Feeder on topics equally
local. Lady Barb liked Sidney Feeder; she only hated his name,
which was constantly in her ears during the half-hour the
ladies sat with her, Mrs. Chew having the habit, which annoyed Lady Barb, of repeating perpetually the appellation of
her interlocutor.

Lady Barb's relations with Mrs. Vanderdecken consisted
mainly in wondering, while she talked, what she wanted of
her, and in looking, with her sculptured eyes, at her visitor's
clothes, in which there was always much to examine. "Oh,
Doctor Feeder!" "Now, Doctor Feeder!" "Well, Doctor
Feeder,"—these exclamations, on the lips of Mrs. Chew, were
an undertone in Lady Barb's consciousness. When I say that
she liked her husband's *confrère*, as he used to call himself, I
mean that she smiled at him when he came, and gave him her
hand, and asked him if he would have some tea. There was
nothing nasty (as they said in London) in Lady Barb, and she
would have been incapable of inflicting a deliberate snub upon
a man who had the air of standing up so squarely to any work
that he might have in hand. But she had nothing to say to
Sidney Feeder. He apparently had the art of making her shy,
more shy than usual; for she was always a little so; she discouraged him, discouraged him completely. He was not a man

who wanted drawing out, there was nothing of that in him, he was remarkably copious; but Lady Barb appeared unable to follow him, and half the time, evidently, did not know what he was saying. He tried to adapt his conversation to her needs; but when he spoke of the world, of what was going on in society, she was more at sea even than when he spoke of hospitals and laboratories, and the health of the city, and the progress of science. She appeared, indeed, after her first smile, when he came in, which was always charming, scarcely to see him, looking past him, and above him, and below him, and everywhere but at him, until he got up to go again, when she gave him another smile, as expressive of pleasure and of casual acquaintance as that with which she had greeted his entry; it seemed to imply that they had been having delightful talk for an hour. He wondered what the deuce Jackson Lemon could find interesting in such a woman, and he believed that his perverse, though gifted colleague, was not destined to feel that she illuminated his life. He pitied Jackson, he saw that Lady Barb, in New York, would neither assimilate nor be assimilated; and yet he was afraid to betray his incredulity, thinking it might be depressing to poor Lemon to show him how his marriage—now so dreadfully irrevocable—struck others. Sidney Feeder was a man of a strenuous conscience, and he did his duty overmuch by his old friend and his wife, from the simple fear that he should not do it enough. In order not to appear to neglect them, he called upon Lady Barb heroically, in spite of pressing engagements, week after week, enjoying his virtue himself as little as he made it fruitful for his hostess, who wondered at last what she had done to deserve these visitations. She spoke of them to her husband, who wondered also what poor Sidney had in his head, and yet was unable, of course, to hint to him that he need not think it necessary to come so often. Between Doctor Feeder's wish not to let Jackson see that his marriage had made a difference, and Jackson's hesitation to reveal to Sidney that his standard of friendship was too high, Lady Barb passed a good many of those numerous hours during which she asked herself if she had come to America for that. Very little had ever passed between her and her husband on the subject of Sidney Feeder; for an instinct told her that if they were ever to have scenes, she must choose the occasion well; and this odd person was not an occasion. Jackson had tacitly admitted that his friend Feeder was anything she chose to think him; he was not a man to be guilty, in a discussion, of the disloyalty of damning him with praise that was faint. If Lady Agatha had usually been with her sister, Doctor Feeder would have been better entertained; for the younger of the English visitors prided herself, after several months of New York, on understanding everything that was said, and catching every allusion, it mattered not from what lips it fell. But Lady Agatha was never at home; she had learned how to describe herself perfectly by the time she wrote to her mother that she was always "on the go." None of the innumerable victims of old-world tyranny who have fled to the United States as to a land of freedom, have ever offered more lavish incense to that goddess than this emancipated London *débutante*. She had enrolled herself in an amiable band which was known by the humorous name of "the Tearers"—a dozen young ladies of agreeable appearance, high spirits and good wind, whose most general characteristic was that, when wanted, they were to be sought anywhere in the world but under the roof that was supposed to shelter them. They were never at home; and when Sidney Feeder, as sometimes happened, met Lady Agatha at other houses, she was in the hands of the irrepressible Longstraw. She had come back to her sister, but Mr. Longstraw had followed her to the door. As to passing it, he had received direct discouragement from her brother-in-law; but he could at least hang about and wait for her. It may be confided to the reader, at the risk of diminishing the effect of the only incident which in the course of this very level narrative may startle him, that he never had to wait very long.

When Jackson Lemon came in, his wife's visitors were on the point of leaving her; and he did not ask even Sidney Feeder to remain, for he had something particular to say to Lady Barb.

"I haven't asked you half what I wanted—I have been talking so much to Doctor Feeder," the dressy Mrs. Chew said, holding the hand of her hostess in one of her own, and toying with one of Lady Barb's ribbons with the other.

"I don't think I have anything to tell you; I think I have told people everything," Lady Barb answered, rather wearily.

"You haven't told *me* much!" Mrs. Vanderdecken said, smiling brightly.

"What could one tell you?—you know everything," Jackson Lemon interposed.

"Ah, no; there are some things that are great mysteries for me," the lady returned. "I hope you are coming to me on the 17th," she added, to Lady Barb.

"On the 17th? I think we are going somewhere."

"Do go to Mrs. Vanderdecken's," said Mrs. Chew; "you will see the cream of the cream."

"Oh, gracious!" Mrs. Vanderdecken exclaimed.

"Well, I don't care; she will, won't she, Doctor Feeder?—the very pick of American society." Mrs. Chew stuck to her point.

"Well, I have no doubt Lady Barb will have a good time," said Sidney Feeder. "I'm afraid you miss the bran," he went on, with irrelevant jocosity, to Lady Barb. He always tried the jocose when other elements had failed.

"The bran?" asked Lady Barb, staring.

"Where you used to ride, in the Park."

"My dear fellow, you speak as if it were the circus," Jackson Lemon said, smiling; "I haven't married a mountebank!"

"Well, they put some stuff on the road," Sidney Feeder explained, not holding much to his joke.

"You must miss a great many things," said Mrs. Chew, tenderly.

"I don't see what," Mrs. Vanderdecken remarked, "except the fogs and the Queen. New York is getting more and more like London. It's a pity; you ought to have known us thirty years ago."

"You are the queen, here," said Jackson Lemon; "but I don't know what you know about thirty years ago."

"Do you think she doesn't go back?—she goes back to the last century!" cried Mrs. Chew.

"I dare say I should have liked that," said Lady Barb; "but I can't imagine." And she looked at her husband—a look she often had—as if she vaguely wished him to do something.

He was not called upon, however, to take any violent steps, for Mrs. Chew presently said: "Well, Lady Barberina, good-bye;" and Mrs. Vanderdecken smiled in silence at her hostess, and addressed a farewell, accompanied very audibly with his title, to her host; and Sidney Feeder made a joke about stepping on the trains of the ladies' dresses as he accompanied them to the door. Mrs. Chew had always a great deal to say at the last; she talked till she was in the street, and then she did not cease. But at the end of five minutes Jackson Lemon was alone with his wife; and then he told her a piece of news. He prefaced it, however, by an inquiry as he came back from the hall.

"Where is Agatha, my dear?"

"I haven't the least idea. In the streets somewhere, I suppose."

"I think you ought to know a little more."

"How can I know about things here? I have given her up; I can do nothing with her. I don't care what she does."

"She ought to go back to England," Jackson Lemon said, after a pause.

"She ought never to have come."

"It was not my proposal, God knows!" Jackson answered, rather sharply.

"Mamma could never know what it really is," said his wife.

"No, it has not been as yet what your mother supposed! Herman Longstraw wants to marry her. He has made me a formal proposal. I met him half an hour ago in Madison Avenue, and he asked me to come with him into the Columbia Club. There, in the billiard-room, which to-day is empty, he opened himself—thinking evidently that in laying the matter before me he was behaving with extraordinary propriety. He tells me he is dying of love, and that she is perfectly willing to go and live in Arizona."

"So she is," said Lady Barb. "And what did you tell him?"

"I told him that I was sure it would never do, and that at any rate I could have nothing to say to it. I told him explicitly, in short, what I had told him virtually before. I said that we should send Agatha straight back to England, and that if they have the courage they must themselves broach the question over there."

"When shall you send her back?" asked Lady Barb.

"Immediately; by the very first steamer."

"Alone, like an American girl?"

"Don't be rough, Barb," said Jackson Lemon. "I shall easily find some people; lots of people are sailing now."

"I must take her myself," Lady Barb declared in a moment. "I brought her out, and I must restore her to my mother's hands."

Jackson Lemon had expected this, and he believed he was prepared for it. But when it came he found his preparation was not complete; for he had no answer to make—none, at least, that seemed to him to go to the point. During these last weeks it had come over him, with a quiet, irresistible, unmerciful force, that Mrs. Dexter Freer had been right when she said to him, that Sunday afternoon in Jermyn Street, the summer before, that he would find it was not so simple to be an American. Such an identity was complicated, in just the measure that she had foretold, by the difficulty of domesticating one's wife. The difficulty was not dissipated by his having taken a high tone about it; it pinched him from morning till night, like a misfitting shoe. His high tone had given him courage when he took the great step; but he began to perceive that the highest tone in the world cannot change the nature of things. His ears tingled when he reflected that if the Dexter Freers, whom he had thought alike ignoble in their hopes and their fears, had been by ill-luck spending the winter in New York, they would have found his predicament as entertaining as they could desire. Drop by drop the conviction had entered his mind—the first drop had come in the form of a word from Lady Agatha—that if his wife should return to England she would never again cross the Atlantic to the West. That word from Lady Agatha had been the touch from the outside, at which, often, one's fears crystallise. What she would do, how she would resist—this he was not yet prepared to tell himself; but he felt, every time he looked at her, that this beautiful woman whom he had adored was filled with a dumb, insuperable, ineradicable purpose. He knew that if she should plant herself, no power on earth would move her; and her blooming, antique beauty, and the general loftiness of her breeding, came to seem to him—rapidly—but the magnificent expression of a dense, patient, imperturbable obstinacy. She was not light, she was not supple, and after six months of marriage he had made up his mind that she was not clever; but nevertheless she would elude him. She had married him, she had come into his fortune and his consideration—for who was she, after all? Jackson Lemon was once so angry as to ask himself, reminding himself that in England Lady Claras and Lady Florences were as thick as blackberries—but she would have nothing to do, if she could help it, with his country. She had gone in to dinner first in every house in the place, but this had not satisfied her. It *had* been simple to be an American, in this sense that no one else in New York had made any difficulties; the difficulties had sprung from her peculiar feelings, which were after all what he had married her for, thinking they would be a fine temperamental heritage for his brood. So they would, doubtless, in the coming years, after the brood should have appeared; but meanwhile they interfered with the best heritage of all—the nationality of his possible children. Lady Barb would do nothing violent; he was tolerably certain of that. She would not return to England without his consent; only, when she should return, it would be once for all. His only possible line, then, was not to take her back—a position replete with difficulties, because, of course, he had, in a manner, given his word, while she had given no word at all, beyond the general promise she murmured at the altar. She had been general, but he had been specific; the settlements he had made were a part of that. His difficulties were such as he could not directly face. He must tack in approaching so uncertain a coast. He said to Lady Barb presently that it would be very inconvenient for him to leave New York at that moment: she must remember that their plans had been laid for a later departure. He could not think of letting her make the voyage without him, and, on the other hand, they must pack her sister off without delay. He would therefore make instant inquiry for a chaperon, and he relieved his irritation by expressing considerable disgust at Herman Longstraw.

Lady Barb did not trouble herself to denounce this gentleman; her manner was that of having for a long time expected the worst. She simply remarked dryly, after having listened to her husband for some minutes in silence: "I would as lief she should marry Doctor Feeder!"

The day after this, Jackson Lemon closeted himself for an hour with Lady Agatha, taking great pains to set forth to her the reasons why she should not unite herself with her Californian. Jackson was kind, he was affectionate; he kissed her and put his arm round her waist, he reminded her that he and she were the best of friends, and that she had always been awfully nice to him; therefore he counted upon her. She would break her mother's heart, she would deserve her father's curse, and she would get him, Jackson, into a pickle from which no human power could ever disembroil him. Lady Agatha listened and cried, and returned his kiss very affectionately, and admitted that her father and mother would never consent to such a marriage; and when he told her that he had made arrangements for her to sail for Liverpool (with some charming people) the next day but one, she embraced him again and assured him that she could never thank him enough for all the trouble he had taken about her. He flattered himself that he had convinced, and in some degree comforted her, and reflected with complacency that even should his wife take it into her head, Barberina would never get ready to embark for her native land between a Monday and a Wednesday. The next morning Lady Agatha did not appear at breakfast; but as she usually rose very late, her absence excited no alarm. She had not rung her bell, and she was supposed still to be sleeping. But she had never yet slept later than midday; and as this hour approached her sister went to her room. Lady Barb then discovered that she had left the house at seven o'clock in the morning, and had gone to meet Herman Longstraw at a neighbouring corner. A little note on the table explained it very succinctly, and put beyond the power of Jackson Lemon and his wife to doubt that by the time this news reached them their wayward sister had been united to the man of her preference as closely as the laws of the State of New York could bind her. Her little note set forth that as she knew she should never be permitted to marry him, she had determined to marry him without permission, and that directly after the ceremony, which would be of the simplest kind, they were to take a train for the far West. Our history is concerned

only with the remote consequences of this incident, which
made, of course, a great deal of trouble for Jackson Lemon.
He went to the far West in pursuit of the fugitives, and overtook them in California; but he had not the audacity to propose to them to separate, as it was easy for him to see that
Herman Longstraw was at least as well married as himself.
Lady Agatha was already popular in the new States, where the
history of her elopement, emblazoned in enormous capitals,
was circulated in a thousand newspapers. This question of the
newspapers had been for Jackson Lemon one of the most definite results of his sister-in-law's *coup de tête*. His first thought
had been of the public prints, and his first exclamation a prayer
that they should not get hold of the story. But they did get
hold of it, and they treated the affair with their customary
energy and eloquence. Lady Barb never saw them; but an affectionate friend of the family, travelling at that time in the
United States, made a parcel of some of the leading journals,
and sent them to Lord Canterville. This missive elicited from
her ladyship a letter addressed to Jackson Lemon which shook
the young man's position to the base. The phials of an un-
nameable vulgarity had been opened upon the house of
Canterville, and his mother-in-law demanded that in compensation for the affronts and injuries that were being heaped
upon her family, and bereaved and dishonoured as she was,
she should at least be allowed to look on the face of her other
daughter. "I suppose you will not, for very pity, be deaf to
such a prayer as that," said Lady Barb; and though shrinking
from recording a second act of weakness on the part of a man
who had such pretensions to be strong, I must relate that poor
Jackson, who blushed dreadfully over the newspapers, and felt
afresh, as he read them, the force of Mrs. Freer's terrible axiom
—poor Jackson paid a visit to the office of the Cunarders.
He said to himself afterward that it was the newspapers that
had done it; he could not bear to appear to be on their side;
they made it so hard to deny that the country was vulgar, at
a time when one was in such need of all one's arguments.
Lady Barb, before sailing, definitely refused to mention any
week or month as the date of their pre-arranged return to
New York. Very many weeks and months have elapsed since
then, and she gives no sign of coming back. She will never fix

a date. She is much missed by Mrs. Vanderdecken, who still alludes to her—still says the line of the shoulders was superb; putting the statement, pensively, in the past tense. Lady Beauchemin and Lady Marmaduke are much disconcerted; the international project has not, in their view, received an impetus.

Jackson Lemon has a house in London, and he rides in the park with his wife, who is as beautiful as the day, and a year ago presented him with a little girl, with features that Jackson already scans for the look of race—whether in hope or fear, to-day, is more than my muse has revealed. He has occasional scenes with Lady Barb, during which the look of race is very visible in her own countenance; but they never terminate in a visit to the Cunarders. He is exceedingly restless, and is constantly crossing to the Continent; but he returns with a certain abruptness, for he cannot bear to meet the Dexter Freers, and they seem to pervade the more comfortable parts of Europe. He dodges them in every town. Sidney Feeder feels very badly about him; it is months since Jackson has sent him any "results." The excellent fellow goes very often, in a consolatory spirit, to see Mrs. Lemon; but he has not yet been able to answer her standing question: "Why that girl more than another?" Lady Agatha Longstraw and her husband arrived a year ago in England, and Mr. Longstraw's personality had immense success during the last London season. It is not exactly known what they live on, though it is perfectly known that he is looking for something to do. Meanwhile it is as good as known that Jackson Lemon supports them.

Pandora

IT HAS long been the custom of the North German Lloyd steamers, which convey passengers from Bremen to New York, to anchor for several hours in the pleasant port of Southampton, where their human cargo receives many additions. An intelligent young German, Count Otto Vogelstein, hardly knew, a few years ago, whether to condemn this custom or approve it. He leaned over the bulwarks of the *Donau* as the American passengers crossed the plank—the travellers who embark at Southampton are mainly of that nationality—and curiously, indifferently, vaguely, through the smoke of his cigar, saw them absorbed in the huge capacity of the ship, where he had the agreeable consciousness that his own nest was comfortably made. To watch from a point of vantage the struggles of later comers—of the uninformed, the unprovided, the bewildered—is an occupation not devoid of sweetness, and there was nothing to mitigate the complacency with which our young friend gave himself up to it; nothing, that is, save a natural benevolence which had not yet been extinguished by the consciousness of official greatness. For Count Vogelstein was official, as I think you would have seen from the straightness of his back, the lustre of his light, elegant spectacles, and something discreet and diplomatic in the curve of his moustache, which looked as if it might well contribute to the principal function, as cynics say, of the lips—the concealment of thought. He had been appointed to the secretaryship of the German legation at Washington, and in these first days of the autumn he was going to take possession of his post. He was a model character for such a purpose—serious, civil, ceremonious, stiff, inquisitive, stuffed with knowledge, and convinced that at present the German empire is the country in the world most highly evolved. He was quite aware, however, of the claims of the United States, and that this portion of the globe presented an enormous field for study. The process of inquiry had already begun, in spite of his having as yet spoken to none of his fellow-passengers; for Vogelstein inquired not only with his tongue—he inquired with his eyes (that is, with his spectacles), with his ears, with his nose, with his palate, with all his senses and organs.

He was an excellent young man, and his only fault was that he had not a high sense of humour. He had enough, however, to suspect this deficiency, and he was aware that he was about to visit a highly humorous people. This suspicion gave him a certain mistrust of what might be said of him; and if circumspection is the essence of diplomacy, our young aspirant promised well. His mind contained several millions of facts, packed too closely together for the light breeze of the imagination to draw through the mass. He was impatient to report himself to his superior in Washington, and the loss of time in an English port could only incommode him, inasmuch as the study of English institutions was no part of his mission. But, on the other hand, the day was charming; the blue sea, in Southampton Water, pricked all over with light, had no movement but that of its infinite shimmer. And he was by no means sure that he should be happy in the United States, where doubtless he should find himself soon enough disembarked. He knew that this was not an important question and that happiness was an unscientific term, which he was ashamed to use even in the silence of his thoughts. But lost in the inconsiderate crowd, and feeling himself neither in his own country nor in that to which he was in a manner accredited, he was reduced to his mere personality; so that, for the moment, to fill himself out, he tried to have an opinion on the subject of this delay to which the German steamer was subjected in English waters. It appeared to him that it might be proved to be considerably greater than the occasion demanded.

Count Vogelstein was still young enough in diplomacy to think it necessary to have opinions. He had a good many, indeed, which had been formed without difficulty; they had been received ready-made from a line of ancestors who knew what they liked. This was, of course—and he would have admitted it—an unscientific way of furnishing one's mind. Our young man was a stiff conservative, a Junker of Junkers; he thought modern democracy a temporary phase, and expected to find many arguments against it in the United States. In regard to these things, it was a pleasure to him to feel that, with his complete training, he had been taught thoroughly to

appreciate the nature of evidence. The ship was heavily laden
with German emigrants, whose mission in the United States
differed considerably from Count Otto's. They hung over the
bulwarks, densely grouped; they leaned forward on their elbows for hours, with their shoulders on a level with their ears;
the men in furred caps, smoking long-bowled pipes, the
women with babies hidden in their shawls. Some were yellow
Germans and some were black, and all of them looked greasy
and matted with the sea-damp. They were destined to swell
the current of western democracy, and Count Vogelstein
doubtless said to himself that they would not improve its quality. Their numbers, however, were striking, and I know not
what he thought of the nature of this evidence.

The passengers who came on board at Southampton were
not of the greasy class; they were for the most part American
families who had been spending the summer, or a longer period, in Europe. They had a great deal of luggage, innumerable bags and rugs and hampers and sea-chairs, and were
composed largely of ladies of various ages, a little pale with
anticipation, wrapped in striped shawls and crowned with very
high hats and feathers. They darted to and fro across the
gangway, looking for each other and for their scattered parcels; they separated and reunited, they exclaimed and declared,
they eyed with dismay the occupants of the steerage, who
seemed numerous enough to sink the vessel, and their voices
sounded faint and far as they rose to Vogelstein's ear over the
tarred sides of the ship. He observed that in the new contingent there were many young girls, and he remembered what
a lady in Dresden had once said to him—that America was a
country of girls. He wondered whether he should like that,
and reflected that it would be a question to study, like everything else. He had known in Dresden an American family, in
which there were three daughters who used to skate with the
officers; and some of the ladies now coming on board seemed
to him of that same habit, except that in the Dresden days
feathers were not worn quite so high.

At last the ship began to creak and slowly budge, and the
delay at Southampton came to an end. The gangway was removed, and the vessel indulged in the awkward evolutions
which were to detach her from the land. Count Vogelstein

had finished his cigar, and he spent a long time in walking up and down the upper deck. The charming English coast passed before him, and he felt that this was the last of the old world. The American coast also might be pretty—he hardly knew what one would expect of an American coast; but he was sure it would be different. Differences, however, were half the charm of travel. As yet, indeed, there were very few on the steamer. Most of his fellow-passengers appeared to be of the same persuasion, and that persuasion the least to be mistaken. They were Jews and commercial, to a man. And by this time they had lighted their cigars and put on all manner of seafaring caps, some of them with big ear-lappets, which somehow had the effect of bringing out their peculiar facial type. At last the new voyagers began to emerge from below and to look about them, vaguely, with that suspicious expression of face which is to be perceived in the newly embarked, and which, as directed to the receding land, resembles that of a person who begins to perceive that he is the victim of a trick. Earth and ocean, in such glances, are made the subject of a general objection, and many travellers, in these circumstances, have an air at once duped and superior, which seems to say that they could easily go ashore if they would.

It still wanted two hours of dinner, and, by the time Vogelstein's long legs had measured three or four miles on the deck, he was ready to settle himself in his sea-chair and draw from his pocket a Tauchnitz novel by an American author whose pages, he had been assured, would help to prepare him. On the back of his chair his name was painted in rather large letters, this being a precaution taken at the recommendation of a friend, who had told him that on the American steamers the passengers—especially the ladies—thought nothing of pilfering one's little comforts. His friend had even said that in his place he would have his coronet painted. This cynical adviser had added that the Americans are greatly impressed by a coronet. I know not whether it was scepticism or modesty, but Count Vogelstein had omitted this ensign of his rank; the precious piece of furniture which, on the Atlantic voyage, is depended upon to remain steady among general concussions, was emblazoned simply with his title and name. It happened, however, that the blazonry was huge; the back of the chair was covered with enormous German characters. This time there can be no doubt; it was modesty that caused the secretary of the legation, in placing himself, to turn this portion of his seat outward, away from the eyes of his companions—to present it to the balustrade of the deck. The ship was passing the Needles—the beautiful outermost point of the Isle of Wight. Certain tall white cones of rock rose out of the purple sea; they flushed in the afternoon light, and their vague rosiness gave them a kind of human expression, in face of the cold expanse towards which the ship was turned; they seemed to say farewell, to be the last note of a peopled world. Vogelstein saw them very comfortably from his place, and after a while he turned his eyes to the other quarter, where the sky and sea, between them, managed to make so poor an opposition. Even his American novelist was more amusing than that, and he prepared to return to this author.

In the great curve which it described, however, his glance was arrested by the figure of a young lady who had just ascended to the deck, and who paused at the mouth of the companion-way. In itself this was not an extraordinary phenomenon; but what attracted Vogelstein's attention was the fact that the young person appeared to have fixed her eyes on him. She was slim, brightly dressed, and rather pretty. Vogelstein remembered in a moment that he had noticed her among the people on the wharf at Southampton. She very soon saw that he was looking at her; whereupon she began to move along the deck with a step which seemed to indicate that she was coming straight towards him. Vogelstein had time to wonder whether she could be one of the girls he had known at Dresden; but he presently reflected that they would now be much older than this. It was true they came straight towards one, like that. This young lady, however, was no longer looking at him, and though she passed near him it was now tolerably clear that she had come upstairs simply to take a general survey. She was a quick, handsome, competent girl, and she wished to see what one could think of the ship, of the weather, of the appearance of England from such a position as that; possibly even of one's fellow-passengers. She satisfied herself promptly on these points, and then she looked

about, while she walked, as if she were in search of a missing
object; so that Vogelstein presently saw this was what she really had come up for. She passed near him again, and this time
she almost stopped, with her eyes bent upon him attentively.
He thought her conduct remarkable, even after he had perceived that it was not at his face, with its yellow moustache,
she was looking, but at the chair on which he was seated.
Then those words of his friend came back to him,—the speech
about the people, especially the ladies, on the American
steamers taking to themselves one's little belongings. Especially the ladies, he might well say; for here was one who
apparently wished to pull from under him the very chair he
was sitting on. He was afraid she would ask him for it, so he
pretended to read, without meeting her eye. He was conscious
that she hovered near him, and he was curious to see what
she would do. It seemed to him strange that such a nice-
looking girl (for her appearance was really charming) should
endeavour by acts so flagrant to attract the attention of a secretary of legation. At last it became evident to him that she
was trying to look round a corner, as it were, trying to see
what was written on the back of his chair. "She wants to find
out my name; she wants to see who I am!" This reflection
passed through his mind, and caused him to raise his eyes.
They rested on her own—which for an appreciable moment
she did not withdraw. The latter were brilliant and expressive,
and surmounted a delicate aquiline nose, which, though
pretty, was perhaps just a trifle too hawk-like. It was the oddest coincidence in the world; the story Vogelstein had taken
up treated of a flighty, forward little American girl, who plants
herself in front of a young man in the garden of an hotel. Was
not the conduct of this young lady a testimony to the truthfulness of the tale, and was not Vogelstein himself in the position of the young man in the garden? That young man
ended by speaking to his invader (as she might be called), and
after a very short hesitation Vogelstein followed his example.
"If she wants to know who I am, she is welcome," he said to
himself; and he got out of the chair, seized it by the back,
and, turning it round, exhibited the superscription to the girl.
She coloured slightly, but she smiled and read his name, while
Vogelstein raised his hat.

"I am much obliged to you. That's all right," she remarked, as if the discovery had made her very happy.

It seemed to him indeed all right that he should be Count Otto Vogelstein; this appeared even a rather flippant mode of disposing of the fact. By way of rejoinder, he asked her if she desired his seat.

"I am much obliged to you; of course not. I thought you had one of our chairs, and I didn't like to ask you. It looks exactly like one of ours; not so much now as when you sit in it. Please sit down again. I don't want to trouble you. We have lost one of ours, and I have been looking for it everywhere. They look so much alike; you can't tell till you see the back. Of course I see there will be no mistake about yours," the young lady went on, with a frank smile. "But we have such a small name—you can scarcely see it," she added, with the same friendly intention. "Our name is Day. If you see that on anything, I should be so obliged if you would tell me. It isn't for myself, it's for my mother; she is so dependent on her chair, and that one I am looking for pulls out so beautifully. Now that you sit down again and hide the lower part, it does look just like ours. Well, it must be somewhere. You must excuse me; I am much obliged to you."

This was a long and even confidential speech for a young woman, presumably unmarried, to make to a perfect stranger; but Miss Day acquitted herself of it with perfect simplicity and self-possession. She held up her head and stepped away, and Vogelstein could see that the foot she pressed upon the clean, smooth deck was slender and shapely. He watched her disappear through the trap by which she had ascended, and he felt more than ever like the young man in his American tale. The girl in the present case was older and not so pretty, as he could easily judge, for the image of her smiling eyes and speaking lips still hovered before him. He went back to his book with the feeling that it would give him some information about her. This was rather illogical, but it indicated a certain amount of curiosity on the part of Count Vogelstein. The girl in the book had a mother, it appeared, and so had this young lady; the former had also a brother, and he now remembered that he had noticed a young man on the wharf—a young man in a high hat and a white overcoat—who seemed united to

Miss Day by this natural tie. And there was some one else too, as he gradually recollected, an older man, also in a high hat, but in a black overcoat—in black altogether—who completed the group, and who was presumably the head of the family. These reflections would indicate that Count Vogelstein read his volume of Tauchnitz rather interruptedly. Moreover, they represented a considerable waste of time; for was he not to be afloat in an oblong box, for ten days, with such people, and could it be doubted that he should see a great deal of them?

It may as well be said without delay that he did see a great deal of them. I have depicted with some precision the circumstances under which he made the acquaintance of Miss Day, because the event had a certain importance for this candid Teuton; but I must pass briefly over the incidents that immediately followed it. He wondered what it was open to him, after such an introduction, to do with regard to her, and he determined he would push through his American tale and discover what the hero did. But in a very short time he perceived that Miss Day had nothing in common with the heroine of that work, save a certain local quality and the fact that the male sex was not terrible to her. Her local quality, indeed, he took rather on trust than apprehended for himself. She was a native of a small town in the interior of the American continent; and a lady from New York, who was on the ship, and with whom he had a good deal of conversation, assured him Miss Day was exceedingly provincial. How this lady ascertained the fact did not appear, for Vogelstein observed that she held no communication with the girl. It is true that she threw some light on her processes by remarking to him that certain Americans could tell immediately who other Americans were, leaving him to judge whether or no she herself belonged to the discriminating class. She was a Mrs. Dangerfield, a handsome, confidential, insinuating woman, and Vogelstein's talk with her took a turn that was almost philosophic. She convinced him, rather effectually, that even in a great democracy there are human differences, and that American life was full of social distinctions, of delicate shades, which foreigners are often too stupid to perceive. Did he suppose that every one knew every one else, in the biggest country in the world, and that one was not as free to choose one's company there as in the most monarchical communities? She laughed these ideas to scorn, as Vogelstein tucked her beautiful furred coverlet (they reclined together a great deal in their elongated chairs) well over her feet. How free an American lady was to choose her company she abundantly proved by not knowing any one on the steamer but Count Otto.

He could see for himself that Mr. and Mrs. Day had not her peculiar stamp. They were fat, plain, serious people, who sat side by side on the deck for hours, looking straight before them. Mrs. Day had a white face, large cheeks, and small eyes; her forehead was surrounded with a multitude of little tight black curls, and her lips and cheeks moved as if she had always a lozenge in her mouth. She wore entwined about her head an article which Mrs. Dangerfield spoke of as a "nuby"—a knitted pink scarf which covered her coiffure and encircled her neck, leaving among its convolutions a hole for her perfectly expressionless face. Her hands were folded on her stomach, and in her still, swathed figure her little bead-like eyes, which occasionally changed their direction, alone represented life. Her husband had a stiff gray beard on his chin, and a bare, spacious upper lip, to which constant shaving had imparted a kind of hard glaze. His eyebrows were thick and his nostrils wide, and when he was uncovered, in the saloon, it was visible that his grizzled hair was dense and perpendicular. He might have looked rather grim and truculent, if it had not been for the mild, familiar, accommodating gaze with which his large, light-coloured pupils—the leisurely eyes of a silent man—appeared to consider surrounding objects. He was evidently more friendly than fierce, but he was more diffident than friendly. He liked to look at you, but he would not have pretended to understand you much nor to classify you, and would have been sorry that it should put you under an obligation. He and his wife spoke sometimes, but they seldom talked, and there was something passive and patient about them, as if they were victims of a spell. The spell, however, was evidently pleasant; it was the fascination of prosperity, the confidence of security, which sometimes makes people arrogant, but which had had such a different effect upon this simple, satisfied pair, in which further development of every kind appeared to have been arrested.

Mrs. Dangerfield told Count Vogelstein that every morning, after breakfast, the hour at which he wrote his journal, in his cabin, the old couple were guided upstairs and installed in their customary corner by Pandora. This she had learned to be the name of their elder daughter, and she was immensely amused by her discovery. " Pandora"—that was in the highest degree typical; it placed them in the social scale, if other evidence had been wanting; you could tell that a girl was from the interior—the mysterious interior about which Vogelstein's imagination was now quite excited—when she had such a name as that. This young lady managed the whole family, even a little the small beflounced sister, who, with bold, pretty, innocent eyes, a torrent of fair, silky hair, a crimson fez, such as is worn by male Turks, very much askew on top of it, and a way of galloping and straddling about the ship in any company she could pick up (she had long, thin legs, very short skirts, and stockings of every tint), was going home, in elaborate French clothes, to resume an interrupted education. Pandora overlooked and directed her relatives; Vogelstein could see that for himself, could see that she was very active and decided, that she had in a high degree the sentiment of responsibility, and settled most of the questions that could come up for a family from the interior. The voyage was remarkably fine, and day after day it was possible to sit there under the salt sky and feel one's self rounding the great curves of the globe. The long deck made a white spot in the sharp black circle of the ocean and in the intense sea-light, while the shadow of the smoke-steamers trembled on the familiar floor, the shoes of fellow-passengers, distinctive now, and in some cases irritating, passed and repassed, accompanied, in the air so tremendously "open," that rendered all voices weak and most remarks rather flat, by fragments of opinion on the run of the ship. Vogelstein by this time had finished his little American story, and now definitely judged that Pandora Day was not at all like the heroine. She was of quite another type; much more serious and preoccupied, and not at all keen, as he had supposed, about making the acquaintance of gentlemen. Her speaking to him that first afternoon had been, he was bound to believe, an incident without importance for herself, in spite of her having followed it up the next day by the remark, thrown at him as she passed, with a smile that was almost familiar, "It's all right, sir. I have found that old chair!" After this she had not spoken to him again, and had scarcely looked at him. She read a great deal, and almost always French books, in fresh yellow paper; not the lighter forms of that literature, but a volume of Sainte-Beuve, of Renan, or at the most, in the way of dissipation, of Alfred de Musset. She took frequent exercise, and almost always walked alone, not, apparently, having made many friends on the ship, and being without the resource of her parents, who, as has been related, never budged out of the cosy corner in which she planted them for the day.

Her brother was always in the smoking-room, where Vogelstein observed him, in very tight clothes, his neck encircled with a collar like a palisade. He had a sharp little face, which was not disagreeable; he smoked enormous cigars, and began his drinking early in the day; but his appearance gave no sign of these excesses. As regards euchre and poker and the other distractions of the place, he was guilty of none. He evidently understood such games in perfection, for he used to watch the players, and even at moments impartially advise them; but Vogelstein never saw the cards in his hand. He was referred to as regards disputed points, and his opinion carried the day. He took little part in the conversation, usually much relaxed, that prevailed in the smoking-room, but from time to time he made, in his soft, flat, youthful voice, a remark which everyone paused to listen to, and which was greeted with roars of laughter. Vogelstein, well as he knew English, could rarely catch the joke; but he could see, at least, that these were the most transcendent flights of American humour. The young man, in his way, was very remarkable, for, as Vogelstein heard some one say once, after the laughter had subsided, he was only nineteen. If his sister did not resemble the dreadful little girl in the tale I have so often mentioned, there was, for Vogelstein, at least an analogy between young Mr. Day and a certain small brother—a candy-loving Madison, Hamilton, or Jefferson—who, in the Tauchnitz volume, was attributed to that unfortunate maid. This was what the little Madison would have grown up to at nineteen, and the improvement was greater than might have been expected.

The days were long, but the voyage was short, and it had almost come to an end before Count Vogelstein yielded to an attraction peculiar in its nature and finally irresistible, and, in spite of Mrs. Dangerfield's warnings, sought an opportunity for a little continuous talk with Miss Pandora Day. To mention this sentiment without mentioning sundry other impressions of his voyage, with which it had nothing to do, is perhaps to violate proportion and give a false idea; but to pass it by would be still more unjust. The Germans, as we know, are a transcendental people, and there was at last a vague fascination for Vogelstein in this quick, bright, silent girl, who could smile and turn vocal in an instant, who imparted a sort of originality to the filial character, and whose profile was delicate as she bent it over a volume which she cut as she read, or presented it, in absentminded attitudes, at the side of the ship, to the horizon they had left behind. But he felt it to be a pity, as regards a possible acquaintance with her, that her parents should be heavy little burghers, that her brother should not correspond to Vogelstein's conception of a young man of the upper class, and that her sister should be a Daisy Miller *en herbe*. Repeatedly warned by Mrs. Dangerfield, the young diplomatist was doubly careful as to the relations he might form at the beginning of his sojourn in the United States. Mrs. Dangerfield reminded him, and he had made the observation himself, in other capitals, that the first year, and even the second, is the time for prudence. One is ignorant of proportions and values; one is exposed, lonely, thankful for attention; and one may give one's self away to people who afterwards prove a great encumbrance. Mrs. Dangerfield struck a note which resounded in Vogelstein's imagination. She assured him that if he didn't "look out" he would be falling in love with some American girl with an impossible family. In America, when one fell in love with a girl, there was nothing to be done but marry her, and what should he say, for instance, to finding himself a near relation of Mr. and Mrs. P. W. Day? (These were the initials inscribed on the back of the two chairs of that couple.) Vogelstein felt the peril, for he could immediately think of a dozen men he knew who had married American girls. There appeared now to be a constant danger of marrying the American girl; it was something one had to reckon with, like the rise in prices, the telephone, the discovery of dynamite, the Chassepôt rifle, the socialistic spirit; it was one of the complications of modern life.

It would doubtless be too much to say that Vogelstein was afraid of falling in love with Pandora Day, a young woman who was not strikingly beautiful, and with whom he had talked, in all, but ten minutes. But, as I say, he went so far as to wish that the human belongings of a girl whose independence appeared to have no taint either of fastness, as they said in England, or of subversive opinion, and whose nose was so very well bred, should not be a little more distinguished. There was something almost comical in her attitude toward these belongings; she appeared to regard them as a care, but not as an interest; it was as if they had been entrusted to her honour and she had engaged to convey them safe to a certain point; she was detached and inadvertent; then, suddenly, she remembered, repented, and came back to tuck her parents into their blankets, to alter the position of her mother's umbrella, to tell them something about the run of the ship. These little offices were usually performed deftly, rapidly, with the minimum of words, and when their daughter came near them, Mr. and Mrs. Day closed their eyes placidly, like a pair of household dogs that expect to be scratched. One morning she brought up the captain to present to them. She appeared to have a private and independent acquaintance with this officer, and the introduction to her parents had the air of a sudden inspiration. It was not so much an introduction as an exhibition, as if she were saying to him, "This is what they look like; see how comfortable I make them. Aren't they rather queer little people? But they leave me perfectly free. Oh, I can assure you of that. Besides, you must see it for yourself." Mr. and Mrs. Day looked up at the captain with very little change of countenance; then looked at each other in the same way. He saluted and bent towards them a moment; but Pandora shook her head, she seemed to be answering for them; she made little gestures as if she were explaining to the captain some of their peculiarities, as, for instance, that they wouldn't speak. They closed their eyes at last; she appeared to have a kind of mesmeric influence on them, and Miss Day walked away with the commander of the ship, who treated

her with evident consideration, bowing very low, in spite of
his supreme position, when, presently after, they separated.
Vogelstein could see that she was capable of making an
impression; and the moral of our episode is that in spite of
Mrs. Dangerfield, in spite of the resolutions of his prudence,
in spite of the meagreness of the conversation that had
passed between them, in spite of Mr. and Mrs. Day and the
young man in the smoking-room, she had fixed his attention.

It was the evening after the scene with the captain that he
joined her, awkwardly, abruptly, irresistibly, on the deck,
where she was pacing to and fro alone, the evening being mild
and brilliant and the stars remarkably fine. There were scattered talkers and smokers, and couples, unrecognisable, that
moved quickly through the gloom. The vessel dipped, with
long, regular pulsations; vague and spectral, under the stars,
with its swaying pinnacles spotted here and there with lights,
it seemed to rush through the darkness faster than by day.
Vogelstein had come up to walk, and as the girl brushed past
him he distinguished Pandora's face (with Mrs. Dangerfield
he always spoke of her as Pandora) under the veil that seemed
intended to protect it from the sea-damp. He stopped, turned,
hurried after her, threw away his cigar, and asked her if she
would do him the honour to accept his arm. She declined his
arm, but accepted his company, and he walked with her for
an hour. They had a great deal of talk, and he remembered
afterwards some of the things she said. There was now a certainty of the ship getting into dock the next morning but one,
and this prospect afforded an obvious topic. Some of Miss
Day's expressions struck him as singular; but, of course, as he
knew, his knowledge of English was not nice enough to give
him a perfect measure.

"I am not in a hurry to arrive; I am very happy here," she
said. "I'm afraid I shall have such a time putting my people
through."

"Putting them through?"

"Through the custom-house. We have made so many purchases. Well, I have written to a friend to come down, and
perhaps he can help us. He's very well acquainted with the
head. Once I'm chalked, I don't care. I feel like a kind of

black-board by this time, any way. We found them awful in
Germany."

Vogelstein wondered whether the friend she had written to
was her lover, and if she were betrothed to him, especially
when she alluded to him again as "that gentleman that is
coming down." He asked her about her travels, her impressions, whether she had been long in Europe, and what she
liked best; and she told him that they had gone abroad, she
and her family, for a little fresh experience. Though he found
her very intelligent he suspected she gave this as a reason because he was a German and she had heard that Germans were
fond of culture. He wondered what form of culture Mr. and
Mrs. Day had brought back from Italy, Greece, and Palestine
(they had travelled for two years and been everywhere), especially when their daughter said, "I wanted father and
mother to see the best things. I kept them three hours on the
Acropolis. I guess they won't forget that!" Perhaps it was of
Pheidias and Pericles they were thinking, Vogelstein reflected,
as they sat ruminating in their rugs. Pandora remarked also
that she wanted to show her little sister everything while she
was young; remarkable sights made so much more impression
when the mind was fresh; she had read something of that sort
in Goethe, somewhere. She had wanted to come herself when
she was her sister's age; but her father was in business then,
and they couldn't leave Utica. Vogelstein thought of the little
sister frisking over the Parthenon and the Mount of Olives,
and sharing for two years, the years of the schoolroom, this
extraordinary odyssey of her parents, and wondered whether
Goethe's dictum had been justified in this case. He asked Pandora if Utica were the seat of her family; if it were a pleasant
place; if it would be an interesting city for him, as a stranger,
to see. His companion replied frankly that it was horrid, but
added that all the same she would ask him to "come and visit
us at our home," if it were not that they should probably soon
leave it.

"Ah! You are going to live elsewhere?"

"Well, I am working for New York. I flatter myself I have
loosened them while we have been away. They won't find
Utica the same; that was my idea. I want a big place, and, of
course, Utica——" And the girl broke off, with a little sigh.

"I suppose Utica is small?" Vogelstein suggested.

"Well, no, it's middle-sized. I hate anything middling," said Pandora Day. She gave a light, dry laugh, tossing back her head a little as she made this declaration. And looking at her askance, in the dusk, as she trod the deck that vaguely swayed, he thought there was something in her air and port that carried out such a spirit.

"What is her social position?" he inquired of Mrs. Dangerfield the next day. "I can't make it out at all, it is so contradictory. She strikes me as having so much cultivation and so much spirit. Her appearance, too, is very neat. Yet her parents are little burghers. That is easily seen."

"Oh, social position!" Mrs. Dangerfield exclaimed, nodding two or three times, rather portentously. "What big expressions you use! Do you think everybody in the world has a social position? That is reserved for an infinitely small minority of mankind. You can't have a social position at Utica, any more than you can have an opera-box. Pandora hasn't got any; where should she have found it? Poor girl, it isn't fair of you to ask such questions as that."

"Well," said Vogelstein, "if she is of the lower class, that seems to be very—very——" And he paused a moment, as he often paused in speaking English, looking for his word.

"Very what, Count Vogelstein?"

"Very significant, very representative."

"Oh, dear, she isn't of the lower class," Mrs. Dangerfield murmured, helplessly.

"What is she, then?"

"Well, I'm bound to admit that since I was at home last she is a novelty. A girl like that, with such people—it's a new type."

"I like novelties," said Count Vogelstein, smiling, with an air of considerable resolution. He could not, however, be satisfied with an explanation that only begged the question; and when they disembarked in New York, he felt, even amid the confusion of wharf and the heaps of disembowelled baggage, a certain acuteness of regret at the idea that Pandora and her family were about to vanish into the unknown. He had a consolation, however: it was apparent that for some reason or other—illness or absence from town—the gentleman to whom

she had written had not, as she said, come down. Vogelstein
was glad—he couldn't have told you why—that this sympathetic person had failed her; even though without him Pandora had to engage single-handed with the United States
custom-house. Vogelstein's first impression of the western
world was received on the landing-place of the German steamers, at Jersey City—a huge wooden shed, covering a wooden
wharf which resounded under the feet, palisaded with rough-
hewn, slanting piles, and bestrewn with masses of heterogeneous luggage. At one end, towards the town, was a row of
tall, painted palings, behind which he could distinguish a press
of hackney-coachmen, brandishing their whips and awaiting
their victims, while their voices rose, incessant, with a sharp,
strange sound, at once fierce and familiar. The whole place,
behind the fence, appeared to bristle and resound. Out there
was America, Vogelstein said to himself, and he looked towards it with a sense that he ought to muster resolution. On
the wharf people were rushing about amid their trunks, pulling their things together, trying to unite their scattered parcels. They were heated and angry, or else quite bewildered
and discouraged. The few that had succeeded in collecting
their battered boxes had an air of flushed indifference to the
efforts of their neighbours, not even looking at people with
whom they had been intimate on the steamer. A detachment
of the officers of the customs was in attendance, and energetic
passengers were engaged in attempts to draw them towards
their luggage or to drag heavy pieces towards them. These
functionaries were good-natured and taciturn, except when
occasionally they remarked to a passenger whose open trunk
stared up at them, imploring, that they were afraid the voyage
had had a good deal of sameness. They had a friendly, leisurely, speculative way of performing their office, and if they
perceived a victim's name written on the portmanteau, they
addressed him by it, in a tone of old acquaintance. Vogelstein
found, however, that if they were familiar, they were not indiscreet. He had heard that in America all public functionaries
were the same, that there was not a different *tenue*, as they
said in France, for different positions; and he wondered
whether at Washington the President and ministers, whom he
expected to see, would be like that.

He was diverted from these speculations by the sight of Mr. and Mrs. Day, who were seated side by side upon a trunk, encompassed, apparently, by the accumulations of their tour. Their faces expressed more consciousness of surrounding objects than he had hitherto perceived, and there was an air of placid expansion in the mysterious couple which suggested that this consciousness was agreeable. Mr. and Mrs. Day, as they would have said, were glad to get back. At a little distance, on the edge of the dock, Vogelstein remarked their son, who had found a place where, between the sides of two big ships, he could see the ferry-boats pass; the large, pyramidal, low-laden ferry-boats of American waters. He stood there, patient and considering, with his small neat foot on a coil of rope, his back to everything that had been disembarked, his neck elongated in its polished cylinder, while the fragrance of his big cigar mingled with the odour of the rotting piles, and his little sister, beside him, hugged a huge post and tried to see how far she could crane over the water without falling in. Vogelstein's servant, an Englishman (he had taken him for practice in the language), had gone in pursuit of an examiner; he had got his things together and was waiting to be released, fully expecting that for a person of his importance the ceremony would be brief. Before it began he said a word to young Mr. Day, taking off his hat at the same time to the little girl, whom he had not yet greeted, and who dodged his salute by swinging herself boldly outwards, to the dangerous side of the pier. She was not much "formed" yet, but she was evidently as light as a feather.

"I see you are kept waiting, like me. It is very tiresome," Count Vogelstein said.

The young man answered without looking behind him. "As soon as we begin we shall go straight. My sister has written to a gentleman to come down."

"I have looked for Miss Day to bid her good-bye," Vogelstein went on; "but I don't see her."

"I guess she has gone to meet that gentleman; he's a great friend of hers."

"I presume he's her lover!" the little girl broke out. "She was always writing to him, in Europe."

Her brother puffed his cigar in silence for a moment.

"That was only for this. I'll tell on you," he presently added.

But the younger Miss Day gave no heed to his announcement; she addressed herself to Vogelstein. "This is New York; I like it better than Utica."

Vogelstein had no time to reply, for his servant had arrived with one of the emissaries of the customs; but as he turned away he wondered, in the light of the child's preference, about the towns of the interior. He was very well treated. The officer who took him in hand, and who had a large straw hat and a diamond breastpin, was quite a man of the world, and in reply to the formal declarations of the Count only said, "Well, I guess it's all right; I guess I'll just pass you;" and he distributed, freely, a dozen chalk-marks. The servant had unlocked and unbuckled various pieces, and while he was closing them the officer stood there wiping his forehead and conversing with Vogelstein. "First visit to our country, Count?—quite alone—no ladies? Of course the ladies are what we are after." It was in this manner he expressed himself, while the young diplomatist wondered what he was waiting for, and whether he ought to slip something into his palm. But Vogelstein's visitor left him only a moment in suspense; he presently turned away, with the remark, very quietly uttered, that he hoped the Count would make quite a stay; upon which the young man saw how wrong he should have been to offer him a tip. It was simply the American manner, and it was very amicable, after all. Vogelstein's servant had secured a porter, with a truck, and he was about to leave the place when he saw Pandora Day dart out of the crowd and address herself, with much eagerness, to the functionary who had just liberated him. She had an open letter in her hand, which she gave him to read, and he cast his eyes over it, deliberately, stroking his beard. Then she led him away to where her parents sat upon their luggage. Vogelstein sent off his servant with the porter, and followed Pandora, to whom he really wished to say a word in farewell. The last thing they had said to each other on the ship was that they should meet again on shore. It seemed improbable, however, that the meeting would occur anywhere but just here on the dock; inasmuch as Pandora was decidedly not in society, where Vogelstein would be, of course, and as, if Utica was not—he had her sharp little sister's word for it—as agreeable as what was about him there, he would be hanged if he would go to Utica. He overtook Pandora quickly; she was in the act of introducing the customs-officer to her parents, quite in the same manner in which she had introduced the captain of the steamer. Mr. and Mrs. Day got up and shook hands with him, and they evidently all prepared to have a little talk. "I should like to introduce you to my brother and sister," he heard the girl say; and he saw her look about her for these appendages. He caught her eye as she did so, and advanced, with his hand outstretched, reflecting the while that evidently the Americans, whom he had always heard described as silent and practical, were not unversed in certain social arts. They dawdled and chattered like so many Neapolitans.

"Good-bye, Count Vogelstein," said Pandora, who was a little flushed with her various exertions, but did not look the worse for it. "I hope you'll have a splendid time, and appreciate our country."

"I hope you'll get through all right," Vogelstein answered, smiling and feeling himself already more idiomatic.

"That gentleman is sick that I wrote to," she rejoined; "isn't it too bad? But he sent me down a letter to a friend of his, one of the examiners, and I guess we won't have any trouble. Mr. Lansing, let me make you acquainted with Count Vogelstein," she went on, presenting to her fellow-passenger the wearer of the straw hat and the breast-pin, who shook hands with the young German as if he had never seen him before. Vogelstein's heart rose for an instant to his throat. He thanked his stars that he had not offered a tip to the friend of a gentleman who had often been mentioned to him, and who had been described by a member of Pandora's family as her lover.

"It's a case of ladies this time," Mr. Lansing remarked to Vogelstein, with a smile which seemed to confess, surreptitiously, and as if neither party could be eager, to recognition.

"Well, Mr. Bellamy says you'll do anything for *him*," Pandora said, smiling very sweetly at Mr. Lansing. "We haven't got much; we have been gone only two years."

Mr. Lansing scratched his head a little, behind, with a

movement which sent his straw hat forward in the direction of his nose. "I don't know as I would do anything for him that I wouldn't do for you," he responded, returning the smile of the girl. "I guess you had better open that one." And he gave a little affectionate kick to one of the trunks.

"Oh, mother, isn't he lovely! It's only your sea-things," Pandora cried, stooping over the coffer instantly, with the key in her hand.

"I don't know as I like showing them," Mrs. Day murmured, modestly.

Vogelstein made his German salutation to the company in general, and to Pandora he offered an audible good-bye, which she returned in a bright, friendly voice, but without looking round, as she fumbled at the lock of her trunk.

"We'll try another, if you like," said Mr. Lansing, laughing.

"Oh no, it has got to be this one! Good-bye, Count Vogelstein. I hope you'll judge us correctly!"

The young man went his way and passed the barrier of the dock. Here he was met by his servant, with a face of consternation which led him to ask whether a cab were not forthcoming.

"They call 'em 'acks 'ere, sir," said the man, "and they're beyond everything. He wants thirty shillings to take you to the inn."

Vogelstein hesitated a moment. "Couldn't you find a German?"

"By the way he talks he *is* a German!" said the man; and in a moment Count Vogelstein began his career in America by discussing the tariff of hackney-coaches in the language of the fatherland.

II.

Vogelstein went wherever he was asked, on principle, partly to study American society, and partly because, in Washington, pastimes seemed to him not so numerous that one could afford to neglect occasions. Of course, at the end of two winters he had a good many of various kinds, and his study of American society had yielded considerable fruit. When, however, in April, during the second year of his residence, he presented himself at a large party given by Mrs. Bonnycastle, and of which it was believed that it would be the last serious affair of the season, his being there (and still more his looking very fresh and talkative) was not the consequence of a rule of conduct. He went to Mrs. Bonnycastle's simply because he liked the lady, whose receptions were the pleasantest in Washington, and because if he didn't go there he didn't know what he should do. That absence of alternatives had become rather familiar to him in Washington—there were a great many things he did because if he didn't do them he didn't know what he should do. It must be added that in this case, even if there had been an alternative, he would still have decided to go to Mrs. Bonnycastle's. If her house was not the pleasantest there, it was at least difficult to say which was pleasanter; and the complaint sometimes made of it that it was too limited, that it left out, on the whole, more people than it took in, applied with much less force when it was thrown open for a general party. Towards the end of the social year, in those soft, scented days of the Washington spring, when the air began to show a southern glow, and the little squares and circles (to which the wide, empty avenues converged according to a plan so ingenious, yet so bewildering) to flush with pink blossom and to make one wish to sit on benches—at this period of expansion and condonation Mrs. Bonnycastle, who during the winter had been a good deal on the defensive, relaxed her vigilance a little, became humorously inconsistent, vernally reckless, as it were, and ceased to calculate the consequences of an hospitality which a reference to the back-files—or even to the morning's issue—of newspapers might easily show to be a mistake. But Washington life, to Vogelstein's apprehension, was paved with mistakes; he felt himself to be in a society which was founded on necessary lapses. Little addicted as he was to the sportive view of existence, he had said to himself, at an early stage of his sojourn, that the only way to enjoy the United States would be to burn one's standards and warm one's self at the blaze. Such were the reflections of a theoretic Teuton, who now walked for the most part amid the ashes of his prejudices. Mrs. Bonnycastle had endeavoured more than once to explain to him the principles on which she received certain people and ignored certain others; but it was with difficulty that he entered into her discriminations. She perceived differences where he only saw resemblances, and both the merits and defects of a good many members of Washington society, as that society was interpreted to him by Mrs. Bonnycastle, he was often at a loss to understand. Fortunately she had a fund of good humour which, as I have intimated, was apt to come uppermost with the April blossoms, and which made the people she did not invite to her house almost as amusing to her as those she did. Her husband was not in politics, though politics were much in him; but the couple had taken upon themselves the responsibilities of an active patriotism; they thought it right to live in America, differing therein from a great many of their acquaintance, who only thought it expensive. They had that burdensome heritage of foreign reminiscence with which so many Americans are saddled; but they carried it more easily than most of their country-people, and you knew they had lived in Europe only by their present exultation, never in the least by their regrets. Their regrets, that is, were only for their ever having lived there, as Mrs. Bonnycastle once told the wife of a foreign minister. They solved all their problems successfully, including those of knowing none of the people they did not wish to, and of finding plenty of occupation in a society supposed to be meagrely provided with resources for persons of leisure. When, as the warm weather approached, they opened both the wings of their door, it was because they thought it would entertain them, and not because they were conscious of a pressure. Alfred Bonnycastle, all winter indeed, chafed a little at the definiteness of some of his wife's reserves; he thought that, for Washington, their society was really a little too good. Vogelstein still remembered the puzzled feeling (it had cleared up somewhat now) with which, more than a year before, he had heard Mr. Bonnycastle exclaim one evening, after a dinner in his own house, when every guest but the German secretary, who often sat late with the pair, had departed, "Hang it, there is only a month left; let us have some fun—let us invite the President!"

This was Mrs. Bonnycastle's carnival, and on the occasion to which I began my little chapter by referring, the President had not only been invited but had signified his intention of being present. I hasten to add that this was not the same functionary to whom Alfred Bonnycastle's irreverent allusion had been made. The White House had received a new tenant (the old one, then, was just leaving it), and Otto Vogelstein had had the advantage, during the first eighteen months of his stay in America, of seeing an electoral campaign, a presidential inauguration, and a distribution of spoils. He had been bewildered, during those first weeks, by finding that in the national capital, in the houses that he supposed to be the best, the head of the State was not a coveted guest; for this could be the only explanation of Mr. Bonnycastle's whimsical proposal to invite him, as it were, in carnival. His successor went out a good deal, for a President.

The legislative session was over, but this made little difference in the aspect of Mrs. Bonnycastle's rooms, which, even at the height of the congressional season, could not be said to overflow with the representatives of the people. They were garnished with an occasional senator, whose movements and utterances often appeared to be regarded with a mixture of alarm and indulgence, as if they would be disappointing if they were not rather odd, and yet might be dangerous if they were not carefully watched. Vogelstein had grown to have a kindness for these conscript fathers of invisible families, who had something of the toga in the voluminous folds of their conversation, but were otherwise rather bare and bald, with stony wrinkles in their faces, like busts and statues of ancient lawgivers. There seemed to him something chill and exposed in their being at once so exalted and so naked; there were lonesome glances in their eyes, sometimes, as if in the social world their legislative consciousness longed for the warmth of a few comfortable laws ready-made. Members of the House were very rare, and when Washington was new to Vogelstein he used sometimes to mistake them, in the hall and on the staircases where he met them, for the functionaries engaged for the evening to usher in guests and wait at supper. It was only a little later that he perceived these functionaries were almost always impressive, and had a complexion which served as a livery. At present, however, such misleading figures were much less to be encountered than during the months of winter, and, indeed, they never were to be encountered at Mrs.

Bonnycastle's. At present the social vistas of Washington, like the vast fresh flatness of the lettered and numbered streets, which at this season seemed to Vogelstein more spacious and vague than ever, suggested but a paucity of political phenomena. Count Otto, that evening, knew every one, or almost every one. There were very often inquiring strangers, expecting great things, from New York and Boston, and to them, in the friendly Washington way, the young German was promptly introduced. It was a society in which familiarity reigned, and in which people were liable to meet three times a day, so that their ultimate essence became a matter of importance.

"I have got three new girls," Mrs. Bonnycastle said. "You must talk to them all."

"All at once?" Vogelstein asked, reversing in imagination a position which was not unknown to him. He had often, in Washington, been discoursed to at the same moment by several virginal voices.

"Oh no; you must have something different for each; you can't get off that way. Haven't you discovered that the American girl expects something especially adapted to herself? It's very well in Europe to have a few phrases that will do for any girl. The American girl isn't any girl; she's a remarkable individual in a remarkable genus. But you must keep the best this evening for Miss Day."

"For Miss Day!" Vogelstein exclaimed, staring. "Do you mean Pandora?"

Mrs. Bonnycastle stared a moment, in return; then laughed very hard. "One would think you had been looking for her over the globe! So you know her already, and you call her by her pet name?"

"Oh no, I don't know her; that is, I haven't seen her, nor thought of her, from that day to this. We came to America in the same ship."

"Isn't she an American, then?"

"Oh yes; she lives at Utica, in the interior."

"In the interior of Utica? You can't mean my young woman then, who lives in New York, where she is a great beauty and a great success, and has been immensely admired this winter."

"After all," said Vogelstein, reflecting and a little disap-

pointed, "the name is not so uncommon; it is perhaps another. But has she rather strange eyes, a little yellow, but very
pretty, and a nose a little arched?"

"I can't tell you all that; I haven't seen her. She is staying
with Mrs. Steuben. She only came a day or two ago, and Mrs.
Steuben is to bring her. When she wrote to me to ask leave
she told me what I tell you. They haven't come yet."

Vogelstein felt a quick hope that the subject of this correspondence might indeed be the young lady he had parted
from on the dock at New York, but the indications seemed to
point the other way, and he had no wish to cherish an illusion.
It did not seem to him probable that the energetic girl who
had introduced him to Mr. Lansing would have the entrée of
the best house in Washington; besides, Mrs. Bonnycastle's
guest was described as a beauty and as belonging to the brilliant city.

"What is the social position of Mrs. Steuben?" it occurred
to him to ask in a moment, as he meditated. He had an earnest, artless, literal way of uttering such a question as that;
you could see from it that he was very thorough.

Mrs. Bonnycastle broke into mocking laughter. "I am sure
I don't know! What is your own?" And she left him, to turn
to her other guests, to several of whom she repeated his question. Could they tell her what was the social position of Mrs.
Steuben? There was Count Vogelstein, who wanted to know.
He instantly became aware, of course, that he ought not to
have made such an inquiry. Was not the lady's place in the
scale sufficiently indicated by Mrs. Bonnycastle's acquaintance
with her? Still, there were fine degrees, and he felt a little
unduly snubbed. It was perfectly true, as he told his hostess,
that, with the quick wave of new impressions that had rolled
over him after his arrival in America, the image of Pandora
was almost completely effaced; he had seen a great many
things which were quite as remarkable in their way as the
daughter of the Days. But at the touch of the idea that he
might see her again at any moment she became as vivid in his
mind as if they had parted but the day before; he remembered
the exact shade of the eyes he had described to Mrs. Bonnycastle as yellow; the tone of her voice when, at the last, she
expressed the hope that he would judge America correctly.

Had he judged it correctly? If he were to meet her again she doubtless would try to ascertain. It would be going much too far to say that the idea of such an ordeal was terrible to Otto Vogelstein; but it may at least be said that the thought of meeting Pandora Day made him nervous. The fact is certainly singular, but I shall not take upon myself to explain it; there are some things that even the most philosophic historian is not bound to account for.

He wandered into another room, and there, at the end of five minutes, he was introduced by Mrs. Bonnycastle to one of the young ladies of whom she had spoken. This was a very intelligent girl, who came from Boston, showing much acquaintance with Spielhagen's novels. "Do you like them?" Vogelstein asked, rather vaguely, not taking much interest in the matter, as he read works of fiction only in case of a sea-voyage. The young lady from Boston looked pensive and concentrated; then she answered that she liked some of them, but that there were others she did not like, and she enumerated the works that came under each of these heads. Spielhagen is a voluminous writer, and such a catalogue took some time; at the end of it, moreover, Vogelstein's question was not answered, for he could not have told you whether she liked Spielhagen or not. On the next topic, however, there was no doubt about her feelings. They talked about Washington as people talk only in the place itself, revolving about the subject in widening and narrowing circles, perching successively on its many branches, considering it from every point of view. Vogelstein had been long enough in America to discover that, after half a century of social neglect, Washington had become the fashion, possessed the great advantage of being a new resource in conversation. This was especially the case in the months of spring, when the inhabitants of the commercial cities came so far southward to escape that boisterous interlude. They were all agreed that Washington was fascinating, and none of them were better prepared to talk it over than the Bostonians. Vogelstein originally had been rather out of step with them; he had not seized their point of view, had not known with what they compared this object of their infatuation. But now he knew everything; he had settled down to the pace; there was not a possible phase of the discussion

which could find him at a loss. There was a kind of Hegelian
element in it; in the light of these considerations the American
capital took on the semblance of a monstrous, mystical *Werden*. But they fatigued Vogelstein a little, and it was his preference, as a general thing, not to engage the same evening
with more than one new-comer, one visitor in the freshness
of initiation. This was why Mrs. Bonnycastle's expression of a
wish to introduce him to three young ladies had startled him
a little; he saw a certain process, in which he flattered himself
that he had become proficient, but which was after all tolerably exhausting, repeated for each of the damsels. After separating from his bright Bostonian he rather evaded Mrs.
Bonnycastle, and contented himself with the conversation of
old friends, pitched, for the most part, in a lower and more
sceptical key.

At last he heard it mentioned that the President had arrived,
had been some half-an-hour in the house, and he went in
search of the illustrious guest, whose whereabouts at Washington parties was not indicated by a cluster of courtiers. He
made it a point, whenever he found himself in company with
the President, to pay him his respects; and he had not been
discouraged by the fact that there was no association of ideas
in the eye of the great man as he put out his hand, presiden-
tially, and said, "Happy to see you, sir." Vogelstein felt himself
taken for a mere constituent, possibly for an office-seeker; and
he used to reflect at such moments that the monarchical form
had its merits: it provided a line of heredity for the faculty of
quick recognition. He had now some difficulty in finding the
chief magistrate, and ended by learning that he was in the tea-
room, a small apartment devoted to light refection, near the
entrance of the house. Here Vogelstein presently perceived
him, seated on a sofa, in conversation with a lady. There were
a number of people about the table, eating, drinking, talking;
and the couple on the sofa, which was not near it, but against
the wall, in a kind of recess, looked a little withdrawn, as if
they had sought seclusion and were disposed to profit by the
diverted attention of the others. The President leaned back;
his gloved hands, resting on either knee, made large white
spots. He looked eminent, but he looked relaxed, and the lady
beside him was making him laugh. Vogelstein caught her voice

as he approached—he heard her say, "Well, now, remember; I consider it a promise." She was very prettily dressed, in rose-colour; her hands were clasped in her lap, and her eyes were attached to the presidential profile.

"Well, madam, in that case it's about the fiftieth promise I have given to-day."

It was just as he heard these words, uttered by her companion in reply, that Vogelstein checked himself, turned away, and pretended to be looking for a cup of tea. It was not customary to disturb the President, even simply to shake hands, when he was sitting on a sofa with a lady, and Vogelstein felt it in this case to be less possible than ever to break the rule, for the lady on the sofa was none other than Pandora Day. He had recognised her without her appearing to see him, and even in his momentary look he had perceived that she was now a person to be reckoned with. She had an air of elation, of success; she looked brilliant in her rose-coloured dress; she was extracting promises from the ruler of fifty millions of people. What an odd place to meet her, Vogelstein thought, and how little one could tell, after all, in America, who people were! He didn't wish to speak to her yet; he wished to wait a little, and learn more; but, meanwhile, there was something attractive in the thought that she was just behind him, a few yards off, that if he should turn he might see her again. It was she whom Mrs. Bonnycastle had meant; it was she who was so much admired in New York. Her face was the same, yet Vogelstein had seen in a moment that she was vaguely prettier; he had recognised the arch of her nose, which suggested ambition. He took two ices, which he did not want, in order not to go away. He remembered her *entourage* on the steamer: her father and mother, the silent burghers, so little "of the world," her infant sister, so much of it, her humorous brother, with his tall hat and his influence in the smoking-room. He remembered Mrs. Dangerfield's warnings—yet her perplexities too, and the letter from Mr. Bellamy, and the introduction to Mr. Lansing, and the way Pandora had stooped down on the dirty dock, laughing and talking, mistress of the situation, to open her trunk for the customs. He was pretty sure that she had paid no duties that day; that had been the purpose, of course, of Mr. Bellamy's letter. Was she still in correspondence with this gentleman, and had he recovered from his sickness? All this passed through Vogelstein's mind, and he saw that it was quite in Pandora's line to be mistress of the situation, for there was nothing, evidently, on the present occasion that could call itself her master. He drank his tea, and as he put down his cup he heard the President, behind him, say, "Well, I guess my wife will wonder why I don't come home."

"Why didn't you bring her with you?" Pandora asked.

"Well, she doesn't go out much. Then she has got her sister staying with her—Mrs. Runkle, from Natchez. She's a good deal of an invalid, and my wife doesn't like to leave her."

"She must be a very kind woman," Pandora remarked, sympathetically.

"Well, I guess she isn't spoiled yet."

"I should like very much to come and see her," said Pandora.

"Do come round. Couldn't you come some night?" the President responded.

"Well, I will come some time. And I shall remind you of your promise."

"All right. There's nothing like keeping it up. Well," said the President, "I must bid good-bye to these kind folks."

Vogelstein heard him rise from the sofa, with his companion, and he gave the pair time to pass out of the room before him, which they did with a certain impressive deliberation, people making way for the ruler of fifty millions and looking with a certain curiosity at the striking pink person at his side. When, after a few moments, Vogelstein followed them across the hall, into one of the other rooms, he saw the hostess accompany the President to the door, and two foreign ministers and a judge of the Supreme Court address themselves to Pandora Day. He resisted the impulse to join this circle; if he spoke to her at all he wished to speak to her alone. She continued, nevertheless, to occupy him, and when Mrs. Bonnycastle came back from the hall he immediately approached her with an appeal. "I wish you would tell me something more about that girl—that one, opposite, in pink?"

"The lovely Day—that is what they call her, I believe? I wanted you to talk with her."

"I find she is the one I have met. But she seems to be so different here. I can't make it out."

There was something in his expression which provoked Mrs. Bonnycastle to mirth. "How we do puzzle you Europeans; you look quite bewildered!"

"I am sorry I look so; I try to hide it. But, of course, we are very simple. Let me ask, then, a simple question. Are her parents also in society?"

"Parents in society! D'où tombez-vous? Did you ever hear of a girl—in rose-colour—whose parents were in society?"

"Is she, then, all alone?" Count Vogelstein inquired, with a strain of melancholy in his voice.

Mrs. Bonnycastle stared at him a moment, with her laughter in her face. "You are too pathetic. Don't you know what she is? I supposed, of course, you knew."

"It's exactly what I am asking you."

"Why, she's the new type. It has only come up lately. They have had articles about it in the papers. That's the reason I told Mrs. Steuben to bring her."

"The new type? What new type, Mrs. Bonnycastle?" said Vogelstein, pleadingly, and conscious that all types in America were new.

Her laughter checked her reply for a moment, and by the time she had recovered herself the young lady from Boston, with whom Vogelstein had been talking, stood there to take leave. This, for an American type, was an old one, he was sure; and the process of parting between the guest and her hostess had an ancient elaboration. Vogelstein waited a little; then he turned away and walked up to Pandora Day, whose group of interlocutors had now been reinforced by a gentleman that had held an important place in the cabinet of the late occupant of the presidential chair. Vogelstein had asked Mrs. Bonny-castle if she were "all alone;" but there was nothing in Pandora's present situation that suggested isolation. She was not sufficiently alone for Vogelstein's taste; but he was impatient, and he hoped she would give him a few words to himself. She recognised him without a moment's hesitation, and with the sweetest smile, a smile that matched the tone in which she said, "I was watching you; I wondered whether you were not going to speak to me."

"Miss Day was watching him," one of the foreign ministers exclaimed, "and we flattered ourselves that her attention was all with us!"

"I mean before," said the girl, "while I was talking with the President."

At this the gentlemen began to laugh, and one of them remarked that that was the way the absent were sacrificed, even the great; while another said that he hoped Vogelstein was duly flattered.

"Oh, I was watching the President too," said Pandora. "I have got to watch *him*. He has promised me something."

"It must be the mission to England," the judge of the Supreme Court suggested. "A good position for a lady; they have got a lady at the head, over there."

"I wish they would send you to my country," one of the foreign ministers suggested. "I would immediately get recalled."

"Why, perhaps in your country I wouldn't speak to you! It's only because you are here," the girl returned, with a gay familiarity which with her was evidently but one of the arts of defence. "You'll see what mission it is when it comes out. But I will speak to Count Vogelstein anywhere," she went on. "He is an older friend than any one here. I have known him in difficult days."

"Oh yes, on the ocean," said the young man, smiling. "On the watery waste, in the tempest!"

"Oh, I don't mean that so much; we had a beautiful voyage, and there wasn't any tempest. I mean when I was living in Utica. That's a watery waste, if you like, and a tempest there would have been a pleasant variety."

"Your parents seemed to me so peaceful!" Vogelstein exclaimed, with a vague wish to say something sympathetic.

"Oh, you haven't seen them on shore. At Utica they were very lively. But that is no longer our home. Don't you remember I told you I was working for New York? Well, I worked—I had to work hard. But we have moved."

"And I hope they are happy," said Vogelstein.

"My father and mother? Oh, they will be, in time. I must give them time. They are very young yet; they have years before them. And you have been always in Washington?"

Pandora continued. "I suppose you have found out everything about everything."

"Oh no; there are some things I can't find out."

"Come and see me, and perhaps I can help you. I am very
different from what I was on the ship. I have advanced a great
deal since then."

"Oh, how was Miss Day on the ship?" asked the cabinet
minister of the last administration.

"She was delightful, of course," said Vogelstein.

"He is very flattering; I didn't open my mouth!" Pandora
cried. "Here comes Mrs. Steuben to take me to some other
place. I believe it's a literary party, near the Capitol. Everything seems so separate in Washington. Mrs. Steuben is going
to read a poem. I wish she would read it here; wouldn't it do
as well?"

This lady, arriving, signified to Pandora the necessity of
their moving on. But Miss Day's companions had various
things to say to her before giving her up. She had an answer
for each of them, and it was brought home to Vogelstein, as
he listened, that, as she said, she had advanced a great deal.
Daughter of small burghers as she was, she was really brilliant.
Vogelstein turned away a little, and, while Mrs. Steuben
waited, asked her a question. He had made her, half an hour
before, the subject of that inquiry to which Mrs. Bonnycastle
returned so ambiguous an answer; but this was not because
he had not some direct acquaintance with Mrs. Steuben, as
well as a general idea of the esteem in which she was held.
He had met her in various places, and he had been at her
house. She was the widow of a commodore—a handsome,
mild, soft, swaying woman, whom every one liked, with glossy
bands of black hair and a little ringlet depending behind each
ear. Some one had said that she looked like the Queen in
Hamlet. She had written verses which were admired in the
South, wore a full-length portrait of the commodore on her
bosom, and spoke with the accent of Savannah. She had about
her a positive odour of Washington. It had certainly been very
crude in Vogelstein to question Mrs. Bonnycastle about her
social position.

"Do kindly tell me," he said, lowering his voice, "what is

the type to which that young lady belongs. Mrs. Bonnycastle tells me it's a new one."

Mrs. Steuben for a moment fixed her liquid eyes upon the secretary of legation. She always seemed to be translating the prose of your speech into the finer rhythms with which her own mind was familiar. "Do you think anything is really new?" she asked. "I am very fond of the old; you know that is a weakness of we Southerners." The poor lady, it will be observed, had another weakness as well. "What we often take to be the new is simply the old under some novel form. Were there not remarkable natures in the past? If you doubt it you should visit the South, where the past still lingers."

Vogelstein had been struck before this with Mrs. Steuben's pronunciation of the word by which her native latitudes were designated: transcribing it from her lips, you would have written it (as the nearest approach) the Sooth. But, at present, he scarcely observed this peculiarity; he was wondering, rather, how a woman could be at once so copious and so unsatisfactory. What did he care about the past, or even about the Sooth? He was afraid of starting her again. He looked at her, discouraged and helpless, as bewildered almost as Mrs. Bonnycastle had found him half an hour before; looked also at the commodore, who, on her bosom, seemed to breathe again with his widow's respirations. "Call it an old type, then, if you like," he said in a moment. "All I want to know is *what* type it is! It seems impossible to find out."

"You can find out by the newspapers. They have had articles about it. They write about everything now. But it isn't true about Miss Day. It is one of the first families. Her great-grandfather was in the Revolution." Pandora by this time had given her attention again to Mrs. Steuben. She seemed to signify that she was ready to move on. "Wasn't your great-grandfather in the Revolution?" Mrs. Steuben asked. "I am telling Count Vogelstein about him."

"Why are you asking about my ancestors?" the girl demanded, smiling, of the young German. "Is that the thing that you said just now that you can't find out? Well, if Mrs. Steuben will only be quiet you never will."

Mrs. Steuben shook her head, rather dreamily. "Well, it's

no trouble for a Southerner to be quiet. There's a kind of languor in our blood. Besides, we have to be, to-day. But I have got to show some energy to-night. I have got to get you to the end of Pennsylvania Avenue."

Pandora gave her hand to Count Vogelstein, and asked him if he thought they should meet again. He answered that in Washington people were always meeting, and that at any rate he should not fail to come and see her. Hereupon, just as the two ladies were detaching themselves, Mrs. Steuben remarked that if Count Vogelstein and Miss Day wished to meet again the picnic would be a good chance—the picnic that she was getting up for the following Thursday. It was to consist of about twenty bright people, and they would go down the Potomac to Mount Vernon. Vogelstein answered that, if Mrs. Steuben thought him bright enough, he should be delighted to join the party; and he was told the hour for which the tryst was taken.

He remained at Mrs. Bonnycastle's after every one had gone, and then he informed this lady of his reason for waiting. Would she have mercy on him and let him know, in a single word, before he went to rest—for without it rest would be impossible—what was this famous type to which Pandora Day belonged?

"Gracious, you don't mean to say you have not found out that type yet!" Mrs. Bonnycastle exclaimed, with a return of her hilarity. "What have you been doing all the evening? You Germans may be thorough, but you certainly are not quick!"

It was Alfred Bonnycastle who at last took pity on him. "My dear Vogelstein, she is the latest, freshest fruit of our great American evolution. She is the self-made girl!"

Vogelstein gazed a moment. "The fruit of the great American Revolution? Yes, Mrs. Steuben told me her great-grand-father——" But the rest of his sentence was lost in the explosion of Mrs. Bonnycastle's mirth. He bravely continued his interrogation, however, and, desiring his host's definition to be defined, inquired what the self-made girl might be.

"Sit down, and we'll tell you all about it," Mrs. Bonnycastle said. "I like talking this way after a party's over. You can smoke, if you like, and Alfred will open another window. Well, to begin with, the self-made girl is a new feature. That, how-

ever, you know. In the second place, she isn't self-made at all.
We all help to make her, we take such an interest in her."

"That's only after she is made!" Alfred Bonnycastle broke
in. "But it's Vogelstein that takes an interest. What on earth
has started you up so on the subject of Miss Day?"

Vogelstein explained, as well as he could, that it was merely
the accident of his having crossed the ocean in the steamer
with her; but he felt the inadequacy of this account of the
matter, felt it more than his hosts, who could know neither
how little actual contact he had had with her on the ship, how
much he had been affected by Mrs. Dangerfield's warnings,
nor how much observation at the same time he had lavished
on her. He sat there half an hour, and the warm, dead stillness
of the Washington night—nowhere are the nights so silent—came in at the open windows, mingled with a soft,
sweet, earthy smell—the smell of growing things. Before he
went away he had heard all about the self-made girl, and there
was something in the picture that almost inspired him. She
was possible, doubtless, only in America; American life had
smoothed the way for her. She was not fast nor emancipated
nor crude nor loud, and there was not in her, of necessity at
least, a grain of the stuff of which the adventuress is made.
She was simply very successful, and her success was entirely
personal. She had not been born with the silver spoon of social
opportunity; she had grasped it by honest exertion. You knew
her by many different signs, but chiefly, infallibly, by the appearance of her parents. It was her parents that told the story;
you always saw that her parents could never have made her.
Her attitude with regard to them might vary, in innumerable
ways; the great fact on her own side being that she had lifted
herself from a lower social plane, done it all herself, and done
it by the simple lever of her personality. In this view, of course,
it was to be expected that she should leave the authors of her
being in the shade. Sometimes she had them in her wake, lost
in the bubbles and the foam that showed where she had
passed; sometimes, as Alfred Bonnycastle said, she let them
slide; sometimes she kept them in close confinement;
sometimes she exhibited them to the public in discreet
glimpses, in prearranged attitudes. But the general characteristic of the self-made girl was that, though it was frequently

understood that she was privately devoted to her kindred, she never attempted to impose them on society, and it was striking that she was much better than they. They were almost always solemn and portentous, and they were for the most part of a deathly respectability. She was not necessarily snobbish, unless it was snobbish to want the best. She didn't cringe, she didn't make herself smaller than she was; on the contrary, she took a stand of her own, and attracted things to herself. Naturally, she was possible only in America, only in a country where certain competitions were absent. The natural history of this interesting creature was at last completely exhibited to Vogelstein, who, as he sat there in the animated stillness, with the fragrant wreath of the western world in his nostrils, was convinced of what he had already suspected, that conversation in the United States is much more psychological than elsewhere. Another thing, as he learned, that you knew the self-made girl by was her culture, which was perhaps a little too obvious. She had usually got into society more or less by reading, and her conversation was apt to be garnished with literary allusions, even with sudden quotations. Vogelstein had not had time to observe this element in a developed form in Pandora Day; but Alfred Bonnycastle said that he wouldn't trust her to keep it under in a *tête-à-tête*. It was needless to say that these young persons had always been to Europe; that was usually the first thing they did. By this means they sometimes got into society in foreign lands before they did so at home; it was to be added, on the other hand, that this resource was less and less valuable; for Europe, in the United States, had less and less prestige, and people in the latter country now kept a watch on that roundabout road. All this applied perfectly to Pandora Day—the journey to Europe, the culture (as exemplified in the books she read on the ship), the effacement of the family. The only thing that was exceptional was the rapidity with which she had advanced; for the jump she had taken since he left her in the hands of Mr. Lansing struck Vogelstein, even after he had made all allowance for the abnormal homogeneity of American society, as really considerable. It took all her cleverness to account for it. When she moved her family from Utica, the battle appeared virtually to have been gained.

Vogelstein called on her the next day, and Mrs. Steuben's blackamoor informed him, in the communicative manner of his race, that the ladies had gone out to pay some visits and look at the Capitol. Pandora apparently had not hitherto examined this monument, and the young man wished he had known the evening before of her omission, so that he might have offered to be her initiator. There is too obvious a connection for me to attempt to conceal it between his regret and the fact that in leaving Mrs. Steuben's door he reminded himself that he wanted a good walk, and took his way along Pennsylvania Avenue. His walk had become fairly good by the time he reached the great white edifice which unfolds its repeated colonnades and uplifts its isolated dome at the end of a long vista of saloons and tobacco-shops. He slowly climbed the great steps, hesitating a little, and wondering why he had come there. The superficial reason was obvious enough, but there was a real one behind it which seemed to Vogelstein rather wanting in the solidity that should characterise the motives of an emissary of Prince Bismarck. The superficial reason was a belief that Mrs. Steuben would pay her visit first—it was probably only a question of leaving cards—and bring her young friend to the Capitol at the hour when the yellow afternoon light gives a tone to the blankness of its marble walls. The Capitol was a splendid building, but it was rather wanting in tone. Vogelstein's curiosity about Pandora Day had been much more quickened than checked by the revelations made to him in Mrs. Bonnycastle's drawing-room. It was a relief to see the young lady classified; but he had a desire, of which he had not been conscious before, to judge really to the end how well a girl could make herself. His calculations had been just, and he had wandered about the rotunda for only ten minutes, looking again at the paintings, commemorative of national history, which occupy its panels, and at the simulated sculptures, so touchingly characteristic of early American taste, which adorn its upper reaches, when the charming women he had hoped for presented themselves in charge of a licensed guide. He went to meet them, and did not conceal from them that he had marked them for his own. The encounter was happy on both sides, and he accompanied them through the queer and endless interior, through labyrinths of white, bare passages, into legislative and judicial halls. He thought it a hideous place; he had seen it all before, and he asked himself what he was doing *dans cette galère*. In the lower House there were certain bedaubed walls, in the basest style of imitation, which made him feel faintly sick; there was a lobby adorned with artless prints and photographs of eminent congressmen, which was too serious for a joke and too comical for anything else.

But Pandora was greatly interested; she thought the Capitol very fine; it was easy to criticise the details, but as a whole it was the most impressive building she had ever seen. She was very good company; she had constantly something to say, but she never insisted too much; it was impossible to be less heavy, to drag less, in the business of walking behind a cicerone. Vogelstein could see, too, that she wished to improve her mind; she looked at the historical pictures, at the uncanny statues of local worthies, presented by the different States— they were of different sizes, as if they had been "numbered," in a shop—she asked questions of the conductor, and in the chamber of the Senate requested him to show her the chairs of the gentlemen from New York. She sat down in one of them, though Mrs. Steuben told her *that* senator (she mistook the chair, dropping into another State) was a horrid old thing. Throughout the hour that he spent with her Vogelstein seemed to see how it was that she had made herself. They walked about afterwards on the magnificent terrace that sur-rounds the Capitol, the great marble table on which it stands, and made vague remarks (Pandora's were the most definite) about the yellow sheen of the Potomac, the hazy hills of Virginia, the far-gleaming pediment of Arlington, the raw, confused-looking country. Washington was beneath them, bristling and geometrical; the long lines of its avenues seemed to stretch into national futures. Pandora asked Vogelstein if he had ever been to Athens, and, on his replying in the affir-mative, inquired whether the eminence on which they stood did not give him an idea of the Acropolis in its prime. Vo-gelstein deferred the answer to this question to their next meeting; he was glad (in spite of the question) to make pretexts for seeing her again.

He did so on the morrow; Mrs. Steuben's picnic was still

three days distant. He called on Pandora a second time, and
he met her every evening in the Washington world. It took
very little of this to remind him that he was forgetting both
Mrs. Dangerfield's warnings and the admonitions—long familiar to him—of his own conscience. Was he in peril of love?
Was he to be sacrificed on the altar of the American girl—an
altar at which those other poor fellows had poured out some
of the bluest blood in Germany, and at which he had declared
himself that he would never seriously worship? He decided
that he was not in real danger; that he had taken his precautions too well. It was true that a young person who had succeeded so well for herself might be a great help to her
husband; but Vogelstein, on the whole, preferred that his
success should be his own; it would not be agreeable to him
to have the air of being pushed by his wife. Such a wife as
that would wish to push him; and he could hardly admit to
himself that this was what fate had in reserve for him—to be
propelled in his career by a young lady who would perhaps
attempt to talk to the Kaiser as he had heard her the other
night talk to the President. Would she consent to relinquish
relations with her family, or would she wish still to borrow
plastic relief from that domestic background? That her family
was so impossible was to a certain extent an advantage; for if
they had been a little better the question of a rupture would
have been less easy. Vogelstein turned over these ideas in spite
of his security, or perhaps, indeed, because of it. The security
made them speculative and disinterested. They haunted him
during the excursion to Mount Vernon, which took place according to traditions long established.

Mrs. Steuben's picnickers assembled on the steamer, and
were set afloat on the big brown stream which had already
seemed to Vogelstein to have too much bosom and too little
bank. Here and there, however, he became aware of a shore
where there was something to look at, even though he was
conscious at the same time that he had of old lost great opportunities of idyllic talk in not sitting beside Pandora Day on
the deck of the North German Lloyd. The two turned round
together to contemplate Alexandria, which for Pandora, as she
declared, was a revelation of old Virginia. She told Vogelstein
that she was always hearing about it during the civil war, years

before. Little girl as she had been at the time, she remembered all the names that were on people's lips during those years of reiteration. This historic spot had a certain picturesqueness of decay, a reference to older things, to a dramatic past. The past of Alexandria appeared in the vista of three or four short streets, sloping up a hill and bordered with old brick ware-houses, erected for merchandise that had ceased to come or go. It looked hot and blank and sleepy, down to the shabby waterside where tattered darkies dangled their bare feet from the edge of the rotting wharves. Pandora was even more in-terested in Mount Vernon (when at last its wooded bluff be-gan to command the river) than she had been in the Capitol; and after they had disembarked and ascended to the cele-brated mansion she insisted on going into every room it con-tained. She declared that it had the finest situation in the world, and that it was a shame they didn't give it to the Pres-ident for his villeggiatura. Most of her companions had seen the house often, and were now coupling themselves, in the grounds, according to their sympathies, so that it was easy for Vogelstein to offer the benefit of his own experience to the most inquisitive member of the party. They were not to lunch for another hour, and in the interval Vogelstein wandered about with Pandora. The breath of the Potomac, on the boat, had been a little harsh, but on the softly-curving lawn, be-neath the clustered trees, with the river relegated to a mere shining presence far below and in the distance, the day gave out nothing but its mildness, and the whole scene became noble and genial.

Vogelstein could joke a little on great occasions, and the present one was worthy of his humour. He maintained to his companion that the shallow, painted mansion looked like a false house, a "fly," a structure of daubed canvas, on the stage; but she answered him so well with certain economical palaces she had seen in Germany, where, as she said, there was noth-ing but china stoves and stuffed birds, that he was obliged to admit the home of Washington was after all really *gemüthlich*. What he found so, in fact, was the soft texture of the day, his personal situation, the sweetness of his suspense. For suspense had decidedly become his portion; he was under a charm which made him feel that he was watching his own life and that his susceptibilities were beyond his control. It hung over him that things might take a turn, from one hour to the other, which would make them very different from what they had been yet; and his heart certainly beat a little faster as he wondered what that turn might be. Why did he come to picnics on fragrant April days with American girls who might lead him too far? Would not such girls be glad to marry a Pomeranian count? And would they, after all, talk that way to the Kaiser? If he were to marry one of them he should have to give her some lessons. In their little tour of the house Vogelstein and his companion had had a great many fellow-visitors, who had also arrived by the steamer and who had hitherto not left them an ideal privacy. But the others gradually dispersed; they circled about a kind of showman, who was the authorised guide, a big, slow, genial, familiar man, with a large beard, and a humorous, edifying, patronising tone, which had immense success when he stopped here and there to make his points, to pass his eyes over his listening flock, then fix them quite above it with a meditative look, and bring out some ancient pleasantry as if it were a sudden inspiration. He made a cheerful thing even of a visit to the tomb of the *pater patriæ*. It is enshrined in a kind of grotto in the grounds, and Vogelstein remarked to Pandora that he was a good man for the place, but that he was too familiar.

"Oh, he would have been familiar with Washington," said the girl, with the bright dryness with which she often uttered amusing things.

Vogelstein looked at her a moment, and it came over him, as he smiled, that she herself probably would not have been abashed even by the hero with whom history has taken fewest liberties. "You look as if you could hardly believe that," Pandora went on. "You Germans are always in such awe of great people." And it occurred to Vogelstein that perhaps, after all, Washington would have liked her manner, which was wonderfully fresh and natural. The man with the beard was an ideal cicerone for American shrines; he played upon the curiosity of his little band with the touch of a master, and drew them away to see the classic ice-house where the old lady had been found weeping in the belief that it was Washington's grave. While this monument was under inspection Vogelstein

and Pandora had the house to themselves, and they spent
some time on a pretty terrace, upon which certain windows
of the second floor opened—a little roofless verandah, which
overhung in a manner, obliquely, all the magnificence of the
view—the immense sweep of the river, the artistic plantations,
the last-century garden, with its big box-hedges and remains
of old espaliers. They lingered here for nearly half an hour,
and it was in this spot that Vogelstein enjoyed the only approach to intimate conversation that fate had in store for him
with a young woman in whom he had been unable to persuade himself that he was not interested. It is not necessary,
and it is not possible, that I should reproduce this colloquy;
but I may mention that it began—as they leaned against the
parapet of the terrace and heard the fraternising voice of the
showman wafted up to them from a distance—with his saying
to her, rather abruptly, that he couldn't make out why they
hadn't had more talk together when they crossed the ocean.

"Well, I can, if you can't," said Pandora. "I would have
talked if you had spoken to me. I spoke to you first."

"Yes, I remember that," Vogelstein replied, rather awkwardly.

"You listened too much to Mrs. Dangerfield."

"To Mrs. Dangerfield?"

"That woman you were always sitting with; she told you
not to speak to me. I have seen her in New York; she speaks
to me now herself. She recommended you to have nothing to
do with me."

"Oh, how can you say such dreadful things?" the young
man murmured, blushing very red.

"You know you can't deny it. You were not attracted by
my family. They are charming people when you know them.
I don't have a better time anywhere than I have at home,"
the girl went on, loyally. "But what does it matter? My family
are very happy. They are getting quite used to New York. Mrs.
Dangerfield is a vulgar wretch; next winter she will call on
me."

"You are unlike any girl I have ever seen; I don't understand you," said poor Vogelstein, with the colour still in his
face.

"Well, you never will understand me, probably; but what difference does it make?"

Vogelstein attempted to tell her what difference it made, but I have not space to follow him here. It is known that when the German mind attempts to explain things it does not always reduce them to simplicity, and Pandora was first mystified, then amused, by some of her companion's revelations. At last I think she was a little frightened, for she remarked irrelevantly, with some decision, that lunch would be ready and they ought to join Mrs. Steuben. He walked slowly, on purpose, as they left the house together, for he had a vague feeling that he was losing her.

"And shall you be in Washington many days yet?" he asked her as they went.

"It will all depend. I am expecting some news. What I shall do will be influenced by that."

The way she talked about expecting news made him feel, somehow, that she had a career, that she was active and independent, so that he could scarcely hope to stop her as she passed. It was certainly true that he had never seen any girl like her. It would have occurred to him that the news she was expecting might have reference to the favour she had asked of the President, if he had not already made up his mind, in the calm of meditation, after that talk with the Bonnycastles, that this favour must be a pleasantry. What she had said to him had a discouraging, a somewhat chilling, effect; nevertheless it was not without a certain ardour that he asked of her whether, so long as she stayed in Washington, he might not come and see her.

"You may come as often as you like," she answered, "but you won't care for it long."

"You try to torment me," said Vogelstein.

She hesitated a moment. "I mean that I may have some of my family."

"I shall be delighted to see them once more."

She hesitated again. "There are some you have never seen."

In the afternoon, returning to Washington on the steamer, Count Vogelstein received a warning. It came from Mrs. Bonnycastle, and constituted, oddly enough, the second occasion on which an officious female friend had, on the deck of a vessel, advised him on the subject of Pandora Day.

"There is one thing we forgot to tell you, the other night, about the self-made girl," Mrs. Bonnycastle said. "It is never safe to fix your affections upon her, because she has almost always got an impediment somewhere in the background."

Vogelstein looked at her askance, but he smiled and said, "I should understand your information—for which I am so much obliged—a little better if I knew what you mean by an impediment."

"Oh, I mean she is always engaged to some young man who belongs to her earlier phase."

"Her earlier phase?"

"The time before she had made herself—when she lived at home. A young man from Utica, say. They usually have to wait; he is probably in a store. It's a long engagement."

"Do you mean a betrothal—to be married?"

"I don't mean anything German and transcendental. I mean that peculiarly American institution, a precocious engagement; to be married, of course."

Vogelstein very properly reflected that it was no use his having entered the diplomatic career if he were not able to bear himself as if this interesting generalisation had no particular message for him. He did Mrs. Bonnycastle, moreover, the justice to believe that she would not have taken up the subject so casually if she had suspected that she should make him wince. The whole thing was one of her jokes, and the notification, moreover, was really friendly. "I see, I see," he said in a moment. "The self-made girl has, of course, always had a past. Yes, and the young man in the store—from Utica—is part of her past."

"You express it perfectly," said Mrs. Bonnycastle. "I couldn't say it better myself."

"But, with her present, with her future, I suppose it's all over. How do you say it in America? She lets him slide."

"We don't say it at all!" Mrs. Bonnycastle cried. "She does nothing of the sort; for what do you take her? She sticks to him; that, at least, is what we expect her to do," Mrs. Bonnycastle added, more thoughtfully. "As I tell you, the type is new. We haven't yet had time for complete observations."

"Oh, of course, I hope she sticks to him," Vogelstein declared simply, and with his German accent more apparent, as it always was when he was slightly agitated.

For the rest of the trip he was rather restless. He wandered about the boat, talking little with the returning revellers. Towards the last, as they drew near Washington, and the white dome of the Capitol hung aloft before them, looking as simple as a suspended snowball, he found himself, on the deck, in proximity to Mrs. Steuben. He reproached himself with having rather neglected her during an entertainment for which he was indebted to her bounty, and he sought to repair his omission by a little friendly talk. But the only thing he could think of to say to her was to ask her by chance whether Miss Day were, to her knowledge, engaged.

Mrs. Steuben turned her Southern eyes upon him with a look of almost romantic compassion. "To my knowledge? Why, of course I would know! I should think you would know too. Didn't you know she was engaged? Why, she has been engaged since she was sixteen."

Vogelstein stared at the dome of the Capitol. "To a gentleman from Utica?"

"Yes, a native of her place. She is expecting him soon."

"Oh, I am so glad to hear it," said Vogelstein, who decidedly, for his career, had promise. "And is she going to marry him?"

"Why, what do people get engaged for? I presume they will marry before long."

"But why have they never done so, in so many years?"

"Well, at first she was too young, and then she thought her family ought to see Europe—of course they could see it better with her—and they spent some time there. And then Mr. Bellamy had some business difficulties which made him feel as if he didn't want to marry just then. But he has given up business, and I presume he feels more free. Of course it's rather long, but all the while they have been engaged. It's a true, true love," said Mrs. Steuben, who had a little flute-like way of sounding the adjective.

"Is his name Mr. Bellamy?" Vogelstein asked, with his haunting reminiscence. "D. F. Bellamy, eh? And has he been in a store?"

"I don't know what kind of business it was; it was some kind of business in Utica. I think he had a branch in New York. He is one of the leading gentlemen of Utica, and very highly educated. He is a good deal older than Miss Day. He is a very fine man. He stands very high in Utica. I don't know why you look as if you doubted it."

Vogelstein assured Mrs. Steuben that he doubted nothing, and indeed what she told him struck him as all the more credible, as it seemed to him eminently strange. Bellamy had been the name of the gentleman who, a year and a half before, was to have met Pandora on the arrival of the German steamer; it was in Bellamy's name that she had addressed herself with such effusion to Bellamy's friend, the man in the straw hat, who was to fumble in her mother's old clothes. This was a fact which seemed to Vogelstein to finish the picture of her contradictions; it wanted at present no touch to be complete. Yet even as it hung there before him it continued to fascinate him, and he stared at it, detached from surrounding things and feeling a little as if he had been pitched out of an overturned vehicle, till the boat bumped against one of the outstanding piles of the wharf at which Mrs. Steuben's party was to disembark. There was some delay in getting the steamer adjusted to the dock, during which the passengers stood watching the process, over the side and extracting what entertainment they might from the appearance of the various persons collected to receive it. There were darkies and loafers and hackmen, and also individuals with tufts on their chins, toothpicks in their mouths, their hands in their pockets, rumination in their jaws, and diamond-pins in their shirt-fronts, who looked as if they had sauntered over from Pennsylvania Avenue to while away half an hour, forsaking for that interval their various postures of inclination in the porticos of the hotels and the doorways of the saloons.

"Oh, I am so glad! How sweet of you to come down!" It was a voice close to Vogelstein's shoulder that spoke these words, and the young secretary of legation had no need to turn to see from whom it proceeded. It had been in his ears the greater part of the day, though, as he now perceived, without the fullest richness of expression of which it was capable. Still less was he obliged to turn to discover to whom it was addressed, for the few simple words I have quoted had been flung across the narrowing interval of water, and a gentleman who had stepped to the edge of the dock without Vogelstein's observing him tossed back an immediate reply.

"I got here by the three o'clock train. They told me in K Street where you were, and I thought I would come down and meet you."

"Charming attention!" said Pandora Day, with her friendly laugh; and for some moments she and her interlocutor appeared to continue the conversation only with their eyes. Meanwhile Vogelstein's, also, were not idle. He looked at Pandora's visitor from head to foot, and he was aware that she was quite unconscious of his own nearness. The gentleman before him was tall, good-looking, well-dressed; evidently he would stand well not only at Utica, but, judging from the way he had planted himself on the dock, in any position which circumstances might compel him to take up. He was about forty years old; he had a black moustache and a business-like eye. He waved a gloved hand at Pandora, as if, when she exclaimed, "Gracious, ain't they long!" to urge her to be patient. She was patient for a minute, and then she asked him if he had any news. He looked at her an instant in silence, smiling, after which he drew from his pocket a large letter with an official seal, and shook it jocosely above his head. This was discreetly, covertly done. No one appeared to observe the little interview but Vogelstein. The boat was now touching the wharf, and the space between the pair was inconsiderable.

"Department of State?" Pandora asked, dropping her voice.

"That's what they call it."

"Well, what country?"

"What's your opinion of the Dutch?" the gentleman asked, for an answer.

"Oh, gracious!" cried Pandora.

"Well, are you going to wait for the return trip?" said the gentleman.

Vogelstein turned away, and presently Mrs. Steuben and her companions disembarked together. When this lady entered a carriage with Pandora, the gentleman who had spoken to the girl followed them; the others scattered, and Vogelstein, declining with thanks a "lift" from Mrs. Bonnycastle, walked home alone, in some intensity of meditation. Two days later he saw in a newspaper an announcement that the President had offered the post of Minister to Holland to D. F. Bellamy, of Utica; and in the course of a month he heard from Mrs. Steuben that Pandora's long engagement had terminated at the nuptial altar. He communicated this news to Mrs. Bonny-castle, who had not heard it, with the remark that there was now ground for a new induction as to the self-made girl.

The Author of "Beltraffio"

M UCH as I wished to see him, I had kept my letter of
introduction for three weeks in my pocket-book. I was
nervous and timid about meeting him—conscious of youth
and ignorance, convinced that he was tormented by strangers,
and especially by my country-people, and not exempt from
the suspicion that he had the irritability as well as the brilliancy
of genius. Moreover, the pleasure, if it should occur (for I
could scarcely believe it was really at hand), would be so great
that I wished to think of it in advance, to feel that it was in
my pocket, not to mix it with satisfactions more superficial
and usual. In the little game of new sensations that I was
playing with my ingenuous mind, I wished to keep my visit
to the author of *Beltraffio* as a trump-card. It was three years
after the publication of that fascinating work, which I had read
over five times, and which now, with my riper judgment, I
admire on the whole as much as ever. This will give you about
the date of my first visit (of any duration) to England; for you
will not have forgotten the commotion—I may even say the
scandal—produced by Mark Ambient's masterpiece. It was the
most complete presentation that had yet been made of the
gospel of art; it was a kind of æsthetic war-cry. People had
endeavoured to sail nearer to "truth" in the cut of their
sleeves and the shape of their sideboards; but there had not
as yet been, among English novels, such an example of beauty
of execution and value of subject. Nothing had been done in
that line from the point of view of art for art. This was my
own point of view, I may mention, when I was twenty-five;
whether it is altered now I won't take upon myself to say—
especially as the discerning reader will be able to judge for
himself. I had been in England a twelvemonth before the time
to which I began by alluding, and had learned then that Mr.
Ambient was in distant lands—was making a considerable
tour in the East. So there was nothing to do but to keep my
letter till I should be in London again. It was of little use to
me to hear that his wife had not left England and, with her
little boy, their only child, was spending the period of her

husband's absence—a good many months—at a small place they had down in Surrey. They had a house in London which was let. All this I learned, and also that Mrs. Ambient was charming (my friend, the American poet, from whom I had my introduction, had never seen her, his relations with the great man being only epistolary); but she was not, after all, though she had lived so near the rose, the author of *Beltraffio*, and I did not go down into Surrey to call on her. I went to the Continent, spent the following winter in Italy, and returned to London in May. My visit to Italy opened my eyes to a good many things, but to nothing more than the beauty of certain pages in the works of Mark Ambient. I had every one of his productions in my portmanteau—they are not, as you know, very numerous, but he had preluded to *Beltraffio* by some exquisite things—and I used to read them over in the evening at the inn. I used to say to myself that the man who drew those characters and wrote that style understood what he saw and knew what he was doing. This is my only reason for mentioning my winter in Italy. He had been there much in former years, and he was saturated with what painters call the "feeling" of that classic land. He expressed the charm of the old hill-cities of Tuscany, the look of certain lonely grass-grown places which, in the past, had echoed with life; he understood the great artists, he understood the spirit of the Renaissance, he understood everything. The scene of one of his earlier novels was laid in Rome, the scene of another in Florence, and I moved through these cities in company with the figures whom Mark Ambient had set so firmly upon their feet. This is why I was now so much happier even than before in the prospect of making his acquaintance.

At last, when I had dallied with this privilege long enough, I despatched to him the missive of the American poet. He had already gone out of town; he shrank from the rigour of the London season, and it was his habit to migrate on the first of June. Moreover, I had heard that this year he was hard at work on a new book, into which some of his impressions of the East were to be wrought, so that he desired nothing so much as quiet days. This knowledge, however, did not prevent me—*cet âge est sans pitié*—from sending with my friend's letter a note of my own, in which I asked Mr. Ambient's leave to come down and see him for an hour or two, on a day to be designated by himself. My proposal was accompanied with a very frank expression of my sentiments, and the effect of the whole projectile was to elicit from the great man the kindest possible invitation. He would be delighted to see me, especially if I should turn up on the following Saturday and could remain till the Monday morning. We would take a walk over the Surrey commons, and I should tell him all about the other great man, the one in America. He indicated to me the best train, and it may be imagined whether on the Saturday afternoon I was punctual at Waterloo. He carried his benevolence to the point of coming to meet me at the little station at which I was to alight, and my heart beat very fast as I saw his handsome face, surmounted with a soft wide-awake, and which I knew by a photograph long since enshrined upon my mantelshelf, scanning the carriage-windows as the train rolled up. He recognised me as infallibly as I had recognised him; he appeared to know by instinct how a young American of an æsthetic turn would look when much divided between eagerness and modesty. He took me by the hand, and smiled at me, and said, "You must be—a—*you*, I think!" and asked if I should mind going on foot to his house, which would take but a few minutes. I remember thinking it a piece of extraordinary affability that he should give directions about the conveyance of my bag, and feeling altogether very happy and rosy, in fact quite transported, when he laid his hand on my shoulder as we came out of the station. I surveyed him, askance, as we walked together; I had already—I had indeed instantly—seen that he was a delightful creature. His face is so well known that I needn't describe it; he looked to me at once an English gentleman and a man of genius, and I thought that a happy combination. There was just a little of the Bohemian in his appearance; you would easily have guessed that he belonged to the guild of artists and men of letters. He was addicted to velvet jackets, to cigarettes, to loose shirt-collars, to looking a little dishevelled. His features, which were fine but not perfectly regular, are fairly enough represented in his portraits; but no portrait that I have seen gives any idea of his expression. There were so many things in it, and they chased each other in and out of his face. I have seen people who were grave and gay in quick alternation; but Mark Ambient was grave and gay at one and the same moment. There were other strange oppositions and contradictions in his slightly faded and fatigued countenance. He seemed both young and old, both anxious and indifferent. He had evidently had an active past, which inspired one with curiosity, and yet it was impossible not to be more curious still about his future. He was just enough above middle height to be spoken of as tall, and rather lean and long in the flank. He had the friendliest, frankest manner possible, and yet I could see that he was shy. He was thirty-eight years old at the time *Beltraffio* was published. He asked me about his friend in America, about the length of my stay in England, about the last news in London and the people I had seen there; and I remember looking for the signs of genius in the very form of his questions—and thinking I found it. I liked his voice. There was genius in his house, too, I thought, when we got there; there was imagination in the carpets and curtains, in the pictures and books, in the garden behind it, where certain old brown walls were muffled in creepers that appeared to me to have been copied from a masterpiece of one of the pre-Raphaelites. That was the way many things struck me at that time, in England; as if they were reproductions of something that existed primarily in art or literature. It was not the picture, the poem, the fictive page, that seemed to me a copy; these things were the originals, and the life of happy and distinguished people was fashioned in their image. Mark Ambient called his house a cottage, and I perceived afterwards that he was right; for if it had not been a cottage it must have been a villa, and a villa, in England at least, was not a place in which one could fancy him at home. But it was, to my vision, a cottage glorified and translated; it was a palace of art, on a slightly reduced scale—it was an old English demesne. It nestled under a cluster of magnificent beeches, it had little creaking lattices that opened out of, or into, pendent mats of ivy, and gables, and old red tiles, as well as a general aspect of being painted in water-colours and inhabited by people whose lives would go on in chapters and volumes. The lawn seemed to me of extraordinary extent, the garden-walls of incalculable height, the whole air of the place delightfully still, and private, and proper to itself. "My wife must be somewhere about," Mark Ambient said, as we went in. "We shall find her perhaps; we have got about an hour before dinner. She may be in the garden. I will show you my little place."

We passed through the house, and into the grounds, as I should have called them, which extended into the rear. They covered but three or four acres, but, like the house, they were very old and crooked, and full of traces of long habitation, with inequalities of level and little steps—mossy and cracked were these—which connected the different parts with each other. The limits of the place, cleverly dissimulated, were muffled in the deepest verdure. They made, as I remember, a kind of curtain at the farther end, in one of the folds of which, as it were, we presently perceived, from afar, a little group. "Ah, there she is!" said Mark Ambient; "and she has got the boy." He made this last remark in a tone slightly different from any in which he yet had spoken. I was not fully aware of it at the time, but it lingered in my ear and I afterwards understood it.

"Is it your son?" I inquired, feeling the question not to be brilliant.

"Yes, my only child. He is always in his mother's pocket. She coddles him too much." It came back to me afterwards, too—the manner in which he spoke these words. They were not petulant; they expressed rather a sudden coldness, a kind of mechanical submission. We went a few steps further, and then he stopped short, and called the boy, beckoning to him repeatedly.

"Dolcino, come and see your daddy!" There was something in the way he stood still and waited that made me think he did it for a purpose. Mrs. Ambient had her arm round the child's waist, and he was leaning against her knee; but though he looked up at the sound of his father's voice, she gave no sign of releasing him. A lady, apparently a neighbour, was seated near her, and before them was a garden-table, on which a tea-service had been placed.

Mark Ambient called again, and Dolcino struggled in the maternal embrace, but he was too tightly held, and after two or three fruitless efforts he suddenly turned round and buried his head deep in his mother's lap. There was a certain awkwardness in the scene; I thought it rather odd that Mrs. Ambient should pay so little attention to her husband. But I would not for the world have betrayed my thought, and, to conceal it, I observed that it must be such a pleasant thing to have tea in the garden. "Ah, she won't let him come!" said Mark Ambient, with a sigh; and we went our way till we reached the two ladies. He mentioned my name to his wife, and I noticed that he addressed her as "My dear," very genially, without any trace of resentment at her detention of the child. The quickness of the transition made me vaguely ask myself whether he were henpecked—a shocking conjecture, which I instantly dismissed. Mrs. Ambient was quite such a wife as I should have expected him to have; slim and fair, with a long neck and pretty eyes and an air of great refinement. She was a little cold, and a little shy; but she was very sweet, and she had a certain look of race, justified by my afterwards learning that she was "connected" with two or three great families. I have seen poets married to women of whom it was difficult to conceive that they should gratify the poetic fancy—women with dull faces and glutinous minds, who were none the less, however, excellent wives. But there was no obvious incongruity in Mark Ambient's union. Mrs. Ambient, delicate and quiet, in a white dress, with her beautiful child at her side, was worthy of the author of a work so distinguished as *Beltraffio*. Round her neck she wore a black velvet ribbon, of which the long ends, tied behind, hung down her back, and to which, in front, was attached a miniature portrait of her little boy. Her smooth, shining hair was confined in a net. She gave me a very pleasant greeting, and Dolcino—I thought this little name of endearment delightful—took advantage of her getting up to slip away from her and go to his father, who said nothing to him, but simply seized him and held him high in his arms for a moment, kissing him several times. I had lost no time in observing that the child, who was not more than seven years old, was extraordinarily beautiful. He had the face of an angel—the eyes, the hair, the more than mortal bloom, the smile of innocence. There was something touching, almost alarming, in his beauty, which seemed to be composed of elements too fine and pure for the breath of this world. When I spoke to him, and he came and held out his hand and smiled at me, I felt a sudden pity for him, as if he had been an orphan, or a changeling, or stamped with some social stigma. It was impossible to be, in fact, more exempt from these misfortunes, and yet, as one kissed him, it was hard to keep from murmuring "Poor little devil!" though why one should have applied this epithet to a living cherub is more than I can say. Afterwards, indeed, I knew a little better; I simply discovered that he was too charming to live, wondering at the same time that his parents should not have perceived it, and should not be in proportionate grief and despair. For myself, I had no doubt of his evanescence, having already noticed that there is a kind of charm which is like a death-warrant. The lady who had been sitting with Mrs. Ambient was a jolly, ruddy personage, dressed in velveteen and rather limp feathers, whom I guessed to be the vicar's wife—our hostess did not introduce me—and who immediately began to talk to Ambient about chrysanthemums. This was a safe subject, and yet there was a certain surprise for me in seeing the author of *Beltraffio* even in such superficial communion with the Church of England. His writings implied so much detachment from that institution, expressed a view of life so profane, as it were, so independent, and so little likely, in general, to be thought edifying, that I should have expected to find him an object of horror to vicars and their ladies—of horror repaid on his own part by good-natured but brilliant mockery. This proves how little I knew as yet of the English people and their extraordinary talent for keeping up their forms, as well as of some of the mysteries of Mark Ambient's hearth and home. I found afterwards that he had, in his study, between smiles and cigar-smoke, some wonderful comparisons for his clerical neighbours; but meanwhile the chrysanthemums were a source of harmony, for he and the vicaress were equally fond of them, and I was surprised at the knowledge they exhibited of this interesting plant. The lady's visit, however, had presumably already been long, and she presently got up, saying she must go, and kissed Mrs. Ambient. Mark started to walk with her to the gate of the grounds, holding Dolcino by the hand.

"Stay with me, my darling," Mrs. Ambient said to the boy, who was wandering away with his father.

Mark Ambient paid no attention to the summons, but Dolcino turned round and looked with eyes of shy entreaty at his mother. "Can't I go with papa?"

"Not when I ask you to stay with me."

"But please don't ask me, mamma," said the child, in his little clear, new voice.

"I must ask you when I want you. Come to me, my darling." And Mrs. Ambient, who had seated herself again, held out her long, slender hands.

Her husband stopped, with his back turned to her, but without releasing the child. He was still talking to the vicaress, but this good lady, I think, had lost the thread of her attention. She looked at Mrs. Ambient and at Dolcino, and then she looked at me, smiling very hard, in an extremely fixed, cheerful manner.

"Papa," said the child, "mamma wants me not to go with you."

"He's very tired—he has run about all day. He ought to be quiet till he goes to bed. Otherwise he won't sleep." These declarations fell successively and gravely from Mrs. Ambient's lips.

Her husband, still without turning round, bent over the boy and looked at him in silence. The vicaress gave a genial, irrelevant laugh, and observed that he was a precious little pet. "Let him choose," said Mark Ambient. "My dear little boy, will you go with me or will you stay with your mother?"

"Oh, it's a shame!" cried the vicar's lady, with increased hilarity.

"Papa, I don't think I can choose," the child answered, making his voice very low and confidential. "But I have been a great deal with mamma to-day," he added in a moment.

"And very little with papa! My dear fellow, I think you have chosen!" And Mark Ambient walked off with his son, accompanied by re-echoing but inarticulate comments from my fellow-visitor.

His wife had seated herself again, and her fixed eyes, bent upon the ground, expressed for a few moments so much mute agitation that I felt as if almost any remark from my own lips would be a false note. But Mrs. Ambient quickly recovered herself, and said to me civilly enough that she hoped I didn't mind having had to walk from the station. I reassured her on this point, and she went on, "We have got a thing that might have gone for you, but my husband wouldn't order it."

"That gave me the pleasure of a walk with him," I rejoined.

She was silent a minute, and then she said, "I believe the Americans walk very little."

"Yes, we always run," I answered, laughingly.

She looked at me seriously, and I began to perceive a certain coldness in her pretty eyes. "I suppose your distances are so great."

"Yes; but we break our marches! I can't tell you what a pleasure it is for me to find myself here," I added. "I have the greatest admiration for Mr. Ambient."

"He will like that. He likes being admired."

"He must have a very happy life, then. He has many worshippers."

"Oh yes, I have seen some of them," said Mrs. Ambient, looking away, very far from me, rather as if such a vision were before her at the moment. Something in her tone seemed to indicate that the vision was scarcely edifying, and I guessed very quickly that she was not in sympathy with the author of *Beltraffio.* I thought the fact strange, but, somehow, in the glow of my own enthusiasm, I didn't think it important; it only made me wish to be rather explicit about that enthusiasm.

"For me, you know," I remarked, "he is quite the greatest of living writers."

"Of course I can't judge. Of course he's very clever," said Mrs. Ambient, smiling a little.

"He's magnificent, Mrs. Ambient! There are pages in each of his books that have a perfection that classes them with the greatest things. Therefore, for me to see him in this familiar way—in his habit as he lives—and to find, apparently, the man as delightful as the artist, I can't tell you how much too good to be true it seems, and how great a privilege I think it." I knew that I was gushing, but I couldn't help it, and what I said was a good deal less than what I felt. I was by no means sure that I should dare to say even so much as this to Ambient himself, and there was a kind of rapture in speaking it out to his wife, which was not affected by the fact that, as a wife, she appeared peculiar. She listened to me with her face grave again, and with her lips a little compressed, as if there were no doubt, of course, that her husband was remarkable, but at the same time she had heard all this before and couldn't be expected to be particularly interested in it. There was even in her manner an intimation that I was rather young, and that people usually got over that sort of thing. "I assure you that for me this is a red-letter day," I added.

She made no response, until after a pause, looking round her, she said abruptly, though gently, "We are very much afraid about the fruit this year."

My eyes wandered to the mossy, mottled, garden-walls, where plum-trees and pear-trees, flattened and fastened upon the rusty bricks, looked like crucified figures with many arms. "Doesn't it promise well?" I inquired.

"No, the trees look very dull. We had such late frosts."

Then there was another pause. Mrs. Ambient kept her eyes fixed on the opposite end of the grounds, as if she were watching for her husband's return with the child. "Is Mr. Ambient fond of gardening?" it occurred to me to inquire, irresistibly impelled as I felt myself, moreover, to bring the conversation constantly back to him.

"He is very fond of plums," said his wife.

"Ah, well then, I hope your crop will be better than you fear. It's a lovely old place," I continued. "The whole character of it is that of certain places that he describes. Your house is like one of his pictures."

"It's a pleasant little place. There are hundreds like it."

"Oh, it has got his tone," I said laughing, and insisting on my point the more that Mrs. Ambient appeared to see in my appreciation of her simple establishment a sign of limited experience.

It was evident that I insisted too much. "His tone?" she repeated, with a quick look at me and a slightly heightened colour.

"Surely he has a tone, Mrs. Ambient."

"Oh yes, he has indeed! But I don't in the least consider that I am living in one of his books; I shouldn't care for that, at all," she went on, with a smile which had in some degree the effect of converting my slightly sharp protest into a joke deficient in point. "I am afraid I am not very literary," said Mrs. Ambient. "And I am not artistic."

"I am very sure you are not stupid nor *bornée*," I ventured to reply, with the accompaniment of feeling immediately afterwards that I had been both familiar and patronising. My only consolation was in the reflection that it was she, and not I, who had begun it. She had brought her idiosyncrasies into the discussion.

"Well, whatever I am, I am very different from my husband. If you like him, you won't like me. You needn't say anything. Your liking me isn't in the least necessary."

"Don't defy me!" I exclaimed.

She looked as if she had not heard me, which was the best thing she could do; and we sat some time without further speech. Mrs. Ambient had evidently the enviable English quality of being able to be silent without being restless. But at last she spoke; she asked me if there seemed to be many people in town. I gave her what satisfaction I could on this point, and we talked a little about London and of some pictures it presented at that time of the year. At the end of this I came back, irrepressibly, to Mark Ambient.

"Doesn't he like to be there now? I suppose he doesn't find the proper quiet for his work. I should think his things had been written, for the most part, in a very still place. They suggest a great stillness, following on a kind of tumult—don't you think so? I suppose London is a tremendous place to collect impressions, but a refuge like this, in the country, must be much better for working them up. Does he get many of his impressions in London, do you think?" I proceeded from point to point, in this malign inquiry, simply because my hostess, who probably thought me a very pushing and talkative young man, gave me time; for when I paused—I have not represented my pauses—she simply continued to let her eyes wander, and, with her long fair fingers, played with the medallion on her neck. When I stopped altogether, however, she was obliged to say something, and what she said was that she had not the least idea where her husband got his impressions. This made me think her, for a moment, positively disagreeable; delicate and proper and rather aristocratically dry as she sat there. But I must either have lost the impression a moment later, or been goaded by it to further aggression, for I remember asking her whether Mr. Ambient was in a good vein of work, and when we might look for the appearance of the book on which he was engaged. I have every reason now to know that she thought me an odious person.

She gave a strange, small laugh as she said, "I'm afraid you think I know a great deal more about my husband's work than I do. I haven't the least idea what he is doing," she added presently, in a slightly different, that is, a more explanatory, tone; as if she recognised in some degree the enormity of her confession. "I don't read what he writes!"

She did not succeed (and would not, even had she tried much harder) in making it seem to me anything less than monstrous. I stared at her, and I think I blushed. "Don't you admire his genius? Don't you admire *Beltraffio*?"

She hesitated a moment, and I wondered what she could possibly say. She did not speak—I could see—the first words that rose to her lips; she repeated what she had said a few minutes before. "Oh, of course he's very clever!" And with this she got up; her husband and little boy had reappeared. Mrs. Ambient left me and went to meet them; she stopped and had a few words with her husband, which I did not hear, and which ended in her taking the child by the hand and returning to the house with him. Her husband joined me in a moment, looking, I thought, the least bit conscious and constrained, and said that if I would come in with him he would show me my room. In looking back upon these first moments of my visit to him, I find it important to avoid the error of appearing to have understood his situation from the first, and to have seen in him the signs of things which I learnt only afterwards. This later knowledge throws a backward light, and makes me forget that at least on the occasion of which I am speaking now (I mean that first afternoon), Mark Ambient struck me as a fortunate man. Allowing for this, I think he was rather silent and irresponsive as we walked back to the house—though I remember well the answer he made to a remark of mine in relation to his child.

"That's an extraordinary little boy of yours," I said. "I have never seen such a child."

"Why do you call him extraordinary?"

"He's so beautiful—so fascinating. He's like a little work of art."

He turned quickly, grasping my arm an instant. "Oh, don't call him that, or you'll—you'll——!" And in his hesitation he broke off, suddenly, laughing at my surprise. But immediately afterwards he added, "You will make his little future very difficult."

I declared that I wouldn't for the world take any liberties with his little future—it seemed to me to hang by threads of such delicacy. I should only be highly interested in watching it. "You Americans are very sharp," said Ambient. "You notice more things than we do."

"Ah, if you want visitors who are not struck with you, you shouldn't ask me down here!"

He showed me my room, a little bower of chintz, with open windows where the light was green, and before he left me he said irrelevantly, "As for my little boy, you know, we shall probably kill him between us, before we have done with him!" And he made this assertion as if he really believed it, without any appearance of jest, with his fine, near-sighted, expressive eyes looking straight into mine.

"Do you mean by spoiling him?"

"No—by fighting for him!"

"You had better give him to me to keep for you," I said. "Let me remove the apple of discord."

I laughed, of course, but he had the air of being perfectly serious. "It would be quite the best thing we could do. I should be quite ready to do it."

"I am greatly obliged to you for your confidence."

Mark Ambient lingered there, with his hands in his pockets. I felt, within a few moments, as if I had, morally speaking, taken several steps nearer to him. He looked weary, just as he faced me then, looked preoccupied, and as if there were something one might do for him. I was terribly conscious of the limits of my own ability, but I wondered what such a service might be—feeling at bottom, however, that the only thing I could do for him was to like him. I suppose he guessed this, and was grateful for what was in my mind; for he went on presently, "I haven't the advantage of being an American. But I also notice a little, and I have an idea that—a——" here he smiled and laid his hand on my shoulder, "that even apart from your nationality, you are not destitute of intelligence! I have only known you half an hour, but—a——" And here he hesitated again. "You are very young, after all."

"But you may treat me as if I could understand you!" I said; and before he left me to dress for dinner he had virtually given me a promise that he would.

When I went down into the drawing-room—I was very punctual—I found that neither my hostess nor my host had appeared. A lady rose from a sofa, however, and inclined her head as I rather surprisedly gazed at her. "I dare say you don't know me," she said, with a modern laugh. "I am Mark Ambient's sister." Whereupon I shook hands with her—saluting her very low. Her laugh was modern—by which I mean that it consisted of the vocal agitation which, between people who meet in drawing-rooms, serves as the solvent of social mysteries, the medium of transitions; but her appearance was—what shall I call it?—mediæval. She was pale and angular, with a long, thin face, inhabited by sad, dark eyes, and black hair intertwined with golden fillets and curious chains. She wore a faded velvet robe, which clung to her when she moved, fashioned, as to the neck and sleeves, like the garments of old Venetians and Florentines. She looked pictorial and melancholy, and was so perfect an image of a type which I—in my ignorance—supposed to be extinct, that while she rose before me I was almost as much startled as if I had seen a ghost. I afterwards perceived that Miss Ambient was not incapable of deriving pleasure from the effect she produced, and I think this sentiment had something to do with her sinking again into her seat, with her long, lean, but not ungraceful arms locked together in an archaic manner on her knees, and her mournful eyes addressing themselves to me with an intentness which was an earnest of what they were destined subsequently to inflict upon me. She was a singular, self-conscious, artificial creature, and I never, subsequently, more than half penetrated her motives and mysteries. Of one thing I am sure, however: that they were considerably less extraordinary than her appearance announced. Miss Ambient was a restless, yearning spinster, consumed with the love of Michael-Angelesque attitudes and mystical robes; but I am pretty sure she had not in her nature those depths of unutterable thought which, when you first knew her, seemed to look out from her eyes and to prompt her complicated gestures. Those features, in especial, had a misleading eloquence; they rested upon you with a far-off dimness, an air of obstructed sympathy, which was certainly not always a key to the spirit of their owner; and I suspect that a young lady could not really have been so dejected and disillusioned as Miss Ambient looked, without having committed a crime for which she was consumed with remorse or parted with a hope which she could not sanely have entertained. She had, I believe, the usual allowance of vulgar impulses; she wished to be looked at, she wished to be married, she wished to be thought original. It costs me something to speak in this irreverent manner of Mark Ambient's sister, but I shall have still more disagreeable things to say before I have finished my little anecdote, and moreover—I confess it—I owe the young lady a sort of grudge. Putting aside the curious cast of her face, she had no natural aptitude for an artistic development—she had little real intelligence. But her affectations rubbed off on her brother's renown, and as there were plenty of people who disapproved of him totally, they could easily point to his sister as a person formed by his influence. It was quite possible to regard her as a warning, and she had done him but little good with the world at large. He was the original, and she was the inevitable imitation. I think he was scarcely aware of the impression she produced—beyond having a general idea that she made up very well as a Rossetti; he was used to her, and he was sorry for her—wishing she would marry and observing that she didn't. Doubtless I take her too seriously, for she did me no harm—though I am bound to add that I feel I can only half account for her. She was not so mystical as she looked, but she was a strange, indirect, uncomfortable, embarrassing woman. My story will give the reader at best so very small a knot to untie that I need not hope to excite his curiosity by delaying to remark that Mrs. Ambient hated her sister-in-law. This I only found out afterwards, when I found out some other things. But I mention it at once, for I shall perhaps not seem to count too much on having enlisted the imagination of the reader if I say that he will already have guessed it. Mrs.

Ambient was a person of conscience, and she endeavoured to behave properly to her kinswoman, who spent a month with her twice a year; but it required no great insight to discover that the two ladies were made of a very different paste, and that the usual feminine hypocrisies must have cost them, on either side, much more than the usual effort. Mrs. Ambient, smooth-haired, thin-lipped, perpetually fresh, must have regarded her crumpled and dishevelled visitor as a very stale joke; she herself was not a Rossetti, but a Gainsborough or a Lawrence, and she had in her appearance no elements more romantic than a cold, ladylike candour, and a well-starched muslin dress. It was in a garment, and with an expression, of this kind, that she made her entrance, after I had exchanged a few words with Miss Ambient. Her husband presently followed her, and there being no other company we went to dinner. The impression I received from that repast is present to me still. There were elements of oddity in my companions, but they were vague and latent, and didn't interfere with my delight. It came mainly, of course, from Ambient's talk, which was the most brilliant and interesting I had ever heard. I know not whether he laid himself out to dazzle a rather juvenile pilgrim from over the sea; but it matters little, for it was very easy for him to shine. He was almost better as a talker than as a writer; that is, if the extraordinary finish of his written prose be really, as some people have maintained, a fault. There was such a kindness in him, however, that I have no doubt it gave him ideas to see me sit open-mouthed, as I suppose I did. Not so the two ladies, who not only were very nearly dumb from beginning to the end of the meal, but who had not the air of being struck with such an exhibition of wit and knowledge. Mrs. Ambient, placid and detached, met neither my eye nor her husband's; she attended to her dinner, watched the servants, arranged the puckers in her dress, exchanged at wide intervals a remark with her sister-in-law, and while she slowly rubbed her white hands, between the courses, looked out of the window at the first signs of twilight—the long June day allowing us to dine without candles. Miss Ambient appeared to give little direct heed to her brother's discourse; but, on the other hand, she was much engaged in watching its effect upon me. Her lustreless pupils continued to attach themselves to my countenance, and it was only her air of belonging to another century that kept them from being importunate. She seemed to look at me across the ages, and the interval of time diminished the realism of the performance. It was as if she knew in a general way that her brother must be talking very well, but she herself was so rich in ideas that she had no need to pick them up, and was at liberty to see what would become of a young American when subjected to a high æsthetic temperature. The temperature was æsthetic, certainly, but it was less so than I could have desired, for I was unsuccessful in certain little attempts to make Mark Ambient talk about himself. I tried to put him on the ground of his own writings, but he slipped through my fingers every time and shifted the saddle to one of his contemporaries. He talked about Balzac and Browning, and what was being done in foreign countries, and about his recent tour in the East, and the extraordinary forms of life that one saw in that part of the world. I perceived that he had reasons for not wishing to descant upon literature, and suffered him without protest to deliver himself on certain social topics, which he treated with extraordinary humour and with constant revelations of that power of ironical portraiture of which his books are full. He had a great deal to say about London, as London appears to the observer who doesn't fear the accusation of cynicism, during the high-pressure time—from April to July—of its peculiarities. He flashed his faculty of making the fanciful real and the real fanciful over the perfunctory pleasures and desperate exertions of so many of his compatriots, among whom there were evidently not a few types for which he had little love. London bored him, and he made capital sport of it; his only allusion, that I can remember, to his own work was his saying that he meant some day to write an immense grotesque epic of London society. Miss Ambient's perpetual gaze seemed to say to me, "Do you perceive how artistic we are? frankly now, is it possible to be more artistic than this? You surely won't deny that we are remarkable." I was irritated by her use of the plural pronoun, for she had no right to pair herself with her brother; and moreover, of course, I could not see my way to include Mrs. Ambient. But there was no doubt that (for that matter) they were all remarkable, and, with all allowances, I had never heard anything so artistic. Mark Ambient's conversation seemed to play over the whole field of knowledge and taste; it made me feel that this at last was real talk, that this was distinction, culture, experience.

After the ladies had left us he took me into his study, to smoke, and here I led him on to gossip freely enough about himself. I was bent upon proving to him that I was worthy to listen to him, upon repaying him (for what he had said to me before dinner) by showing him how perfectly I understood. He liked to talk, he liked to defend his ideas (not that I attacked them), he liked a little perhaps—it was a pardonable weakness—to astonish the youthful mind and to feel its admiration and sympathy. I confess that my own youthful mind was considerably astonished at some of his speeches; he startled me and he made me wince. He could not help forgetting, or rather he couldn't know, how little personal contact I had had with the school in which he was master; and he promoted me at a jump, as it were, to the study of its innermost mysteries. My trepidations, however, were delightful; they were just what I had hoped for, and their only fault was that they passed away too quickly, for I found that, as regards most things, I very soon seized Mark Ambient's point of view. It was the point of view of the artist to whom every manifestation of human energy was a thrilling spectacle, and who felt for ever the desire to resolve his experience of life into a literary form. On this matter of the passion for form—the attempt at perfection, the quest for which was to his mind the real search for the holy grail, he said the most interesting, the most inspiring things. He mixed with them a thousand illustrations from his own life, from other lives that he had known, from history and fiction, and, above all, from the annals of the time that was dear to him beyond all periods—the Italian *cinque-cento*. I saw that in his books he had only said half of his thought, and what he had kept back—from motives that I deplored when I learnt them later—was the richer part. It was his fortune to shock a great many people, but there was not a grain of bravado in his pages (I have always maintained it, though often contradicted), and at bottom the poor fellow, an artist to his finger-tips, and regarding a failure of completeness as a crime, had an extreme dread of scandal. There are

people who regret that having gone so far he did not go further; but I regret nothing (putting aside two or three of the
motives I just mentioned), for he arrived at perfection, and I
don't see how you can go beyond that. The hours I spent in
his study—this first one and the few that followed it; they were
not, after all, so numerous—seem to glow, as I look back on
them, with a tone which is partly that of the brown old room,
rich, under the shaded candlelight where we sat and smoked,
with the dusky, delicate bindings of valuable books; partly that
of his voice, of which I still catch the echo, charged with the
images that came at his command. When we went back to the
drawing-room we found Miss Ambient alone in possession of
it; and she informed us that her sister-in-law had a quarter of
an hour before been called by the nurse to see Dolcino, who
appeared to be a little feverish.

"Feverish! how in the world does he come to be feverish?"
Ambient asked. "He was perfectly well this afternoon."

"Beatrice says you walked him about too much—you almost killed him."

"Beatrice must be very happy—she has an opportunity to
triumph!" Mark Ambient said, with a laugh of which the bitterness was just perceptible.

"Surely not if the child is ill," I ventured to remark, by way
of pleading for Mrs. Ambient.

"My dear fellow, you are not married—you don't know the
nature of wives!" my host exclaimed.

"Possibly not; but I know the nature of mothers."

"Beatrice is perfect as a mother," said Miss Ambient, with
a tremendous sigh and her fingers interlaced on her embroidered knees.

"I shall go up and see the child," her brother went on.
"Do you suppose he's asleep?"

"Beatrice won't let you see him, Mark," said the young
lady, looking at me, though she addressed our companion.

"Do you call that being perfect as a mother?" Ambient
inquired.

"Yes, from her point of view."

"Damn her point of view!" cried the author of *Beltraffio*.
And he left the room; after which we heard him ascend the
stairs.

I sat there for some ten minutes with Miss Ambient, and we, naturally, had some conversation, which was begun, I think, by my asking her what the point of view of her sister-in-law could be.

"Oh, it's so very odd," she said. "But we are so very odd, altogether. Don't you find us so? We have lived so much abroad. Have you people like us in America?"

"You are not all alike, surely; so that I don't think I understand your question. We have no one like your brother—I may go so far as that."

"You have probably more persons like his wife," said Miss Ambient, smiling.

"I can tell you that better when you have told me about her point of view."

"Oh yes—oh yes. Well, she doesn't like his ideas. She doesn't like them for the little boy. She thinks them undesirable."

Being quite fresh from the contemplation of some of Mark Ambient's *arcana*, I was particularly in a position to appreciate this announcement. But the effect of it was to make me (after staring a moment) burst into laughter, which I instantly checked when I remembered that there was a sick child above.

"What has that infant to do with ideas?" I asked. "Surely, he can't tell one from another. Has he read his father's novels?"

"He's very precocious and very sensitive, and his mother thinks she can't begin to guard him too early." Miss Ambient's head drooped a little to one side, and her eyes fixed themselves on futurity. Then, suddenly, there was a strange alteration in her face; she gave a smile that was more joyless than her gravity—a conscious, insincere smile, and added, "When one has children, it's a great responsibility—what one writes."

"Children are terrible critics," I answered. "I am rather glad I haven't got any."

"Do you also write then? And in the same style as my brother? And do you like that style? And do people appreciate it in America? I don't write, but I think I feel." To these and various other inquiries and remarks the young lady treated me, till we heard her brother's step in the hall again and Mark

Ambient reappeared. He looked flushed and serious, and I supposed that he had seen something to alarm him in the condition of his child. His sister apparently had another idea; she gazed at him a moment as if he were a burning ship on the horizon, and simply murmured—"Poor old Mark!"

"I hope you are not anxious," I said.

"No, but I am disappointed. She won't let me in. She has locked the door, and I'm afraid to make a noise." I suppose there might have been something ridiculous in a confession of this kind, but I liked my new friend so much that for me it didn't detract from his dignity. "She tells me—from behind the door—that she will let me know if he is worse."

"It's very good of her," said Miss Ambient.

I had exchanged a glance with Mark in which it is possible that he read that my pity for him was untinged with contempt—though I know not why he should have cared; and as, presently, his sister got up and took her bedroom candlestick, he proposed that we should go back to his study. We sat there till after midnight; he put himself into his slippers, into an old velvet jacket, lighted an ancient pipe, and talked considerably less than he had done before. There were longish pauses in our communion, but they only made me feel that we had advanced in intimacy. They helped me, too, to understand my friend's personal situation, and to perceive that it was by no means the happiest possible. When his face was quiet, it was vaguely troubled; it seemed to me to show that for him, too, life was a struggle, as it has been for many other men of genius. At last I prepared to leave him, and then, to my ineffable joy, he gave me some of the sheets of his forthcoming book—it was not finished, but he had indulged in the luxury, so dear to writers of deliberation, of having it "set up," from chapter to chapter, as he advanced—he gave me, I say, the early pages, the *prémices*, as the French have it, of this new fruit of his imagination, to take to my room and look over at my leisure. I was just quitting him when the door of his study was noiselessly pushed open, and Mrs. Ambient stood before us. She looked at us a moment, with her candle in her hand, and then she said to her husband that as she supposed he had not gone to bed she had come down to tell him that Dolcino was more quiet and would probably be

better in the morning. Mark Ambient made no reply; he simply slipped past her, in the doorway, as if he were afraid she
would seize him in his passage, and bounded upstairs, to
judge for himself of his child's condition. Mrs. Ambient
looked slightly discomfited, and for a moment I thought she
was going to give chase to her husband. But she resigned
herself, with a sigh, while her eyes wandered over the lamp-
lit room, where various books, at which I had been looking,
were pulled out of their places on the shelves, and the fumes
of tobacco seemed to hang in mid-air. I bade her good-night,
and then, without intention, by a kind of fatality, the perversity which had already made me insist unduly on talking with
her about her husband's achievements, I alluded to the precious proof-sheets with which Ambient had entrusted me, and
which I was nursing there under my arm. "It is the opening
chapters of his new book," I said. "Fancy my satisfaction at
being allowed to carry them to my room!"

She turned away, leaving me to take my candlestick from
the table in the hall; but before we separated, thinking it apparently a good occasion to let me know once for all—since
I was beginning, it would seem, to be quite "thick" with my
host—that there was no fitness in my appealing to her for
sympathy in such a case; before we separated, I say, she remarked to me, with her quick, round, well-bred utterance, "I
daresay you attribute to me ideas that I haven't got. I don't
take that sort of interest in my husband's proof-sheets. I consider his writings most objectionable!"

II.

I had some curious conversation the next morning with Miss
Ambient, whom I found strolling in the garden before breakfast. The whole place looked as fresh and trim, amid the twit-
ter of the birds, as if, an hour before, the housemaids had
been turned into it with their dustpans and feather-brushes. I
almost hesitated to light a cigarette, and was doubly startled
when, in the act of doing so, I suddenly perceived the sister
of my host, who had, in any case, something of the oddity of
an apparition, standing before me. She might have been posing for her photograph. Her sad-coloured robe arranged itself

in serpentine folds at her feet; her hands locked themselves listlessly together in front; and her chin rested upon a *cinque-cento* ruff. The first thing I did, after bidding her good morning, was to ask her for news of her little nephew—to express the hope that she had heard he was better. She was able to gratify this hope, and spoke as if we might expect to see him during the day. We walked through the shrubberies together, and she gave me a great deal of information about her brother's *ménage*, which offered me an opportunity to mention to her that his wife had told me, the night before, that she thought his productions objectionable.

"She doesn't usually come out with that so soon!" Miss Ambient exclaimed, in answer to this piece of gossip.

"Poor lady, she saw that I am a fanatic."

"Yes, she won't like you for that. But you mustn't mind, if the rest of us like you! Beatrice thinks a work of art ought to have a 'purpose.' But she's a charming woman—don't you think her charming?—she's such a type of the lady."

"She's very beautiful," I answered; while I reflected that though it was true, apparently, that Mark Ambient was mismated, it was also perceptible that his sister was perfidious. She told me that her brother and his wife had no other difference but this one, that she thought his writings immoral and his influence pernicious. It was a fixed idea; she was afraid of these things for the child. I answered that it was not a trifle—a woman's regarding her husband's mind as a well of corruption; and she looked quite struck with the novelty of my remark. "But there hasn't been any of the sort of trouble that there so often is among married people," she said. "I suppose you can judge for yourself that Beatrice isn't at all—well, whatever they call it when a woman misbehaves herself. And Mark doesn't make love to other people, either. I assure you he doesn't! All the same, of course, from her point of view, you know, she has a dread of my brother's influence on the child—on the formation of his character, of his principles. It is as if it were a subtle poison, or a contagion, or something that would rub off on Dolcino when his father kisses him or holds him on his knee. If she could, she would prevent Mark from ever touching him. Every one knows it; visitors see it for themselves; so there is no harm in my telling

you. Isn't it excessively odd? It comes from Beatrice's being
so religious, and so tremendously moral, and all that. And
then, of course, we mustn't forget," my companion added,
unexpectedly, "that some of Mark's ideas are—well, really—
rather queer!"

I reflected, as we went into the house, where we found
Ambient unfolding the *Observer* at the breakfast-table, that
none of them were probably quite so queer as his sister. Mrs.
Ambient did not appear at breakfast, being rather tired with
her ministrations, during the night, to Dolcino. Her husband
mentioned, however, that she was hoping to go to church. I
afterwards learned that she did go, but I may as well announce
without delay that he and I did not accompany her. It was
while the church-bell was murmuring in the distance that the
author of *Beltraffio* led me forth for the ramble he had spoken
of in his note. I will not attempt to say where we went, or to
describe what we saw. We kept to the fields and copses and
commons, and breathed the same sweet air as the nibbling
donkeys and the browsing sheep, whose woolliness seemed to
me, in those early days of my acquaintance with English objects, but a part of the general texture of the small, dense
landscape, which looked as if the harvest were gathered by the
shears. Everything was full of expression for Mark Ambient's
visitor—from the big, bandy-legged geese, whose whiteness
was a "note," amid all the tones of green, as they wandered
beside a neat little oval pool, the foreground of a thatched
and white-washed inn, with a grassy approach and a pictorial
sign—from these humble wayside animals to the crests of high
woods which let a gable or a pinnacle peep here and there,
and looked, even at a distance, like trees of good company,
conscious of an individual profile. I admired the hedgerows,
I plucked the faint-hued heather, and I was for ever stopping
to say how charming I thought the thread-like footpaths
across the fields, which wandered, in a diagonal of finer grain,
from one smooth stile to another. Mark Ambient was abundantly good-natured, and was as much entertained with my
observations as I was with the literary allusions of the landscape. We sat and smoked upon stiles, broaching paradoxes in
the decent English air; we took short cuts across a park or
two, where the bracken was deep, and my companion nodded

to the old woman at the gate; we skirted rank covers, which rustled here and there as we passed, and we stretched ourselves at last on a heathery hillside where, if the sun was not too hot, neither was the earth too cold, and where the country lay beneath us in a rich blue mist. Of course I had already told Ambient what I thought of his new novel, having the previous night read every word of the opening chapters before I went to bed.

"I am not without hope of being able to make it my best," he said, as I went back to the subject, while we turned up our heels to the sky. "At least the people who dislike my prose —and there are a great many of them, I believe—will dislike this work most." This was the first time I had heard him allude to the people who couldn't read him—a class which is supposed always to sit heavy upon the consciousness of the man of letters. A man organised for literature, as Mark Ambient was, must certainly have had the normal proportion of sensitiveness, of irritability; the artistic *ego*, capable in some cases of such monstrous development, must have been, in his composition, sufficiently erect and definite. I will not therefore go so far as to say that he never thought of his detractors, or that he had any illusions with regard to the number of his admirers (he could never so far have deceived himself as to believe he was popular); but I may at least affirm that adverse criticism, as I had occasion to perceive later, ruffled him visibly but little, that he had an air of thinking it quite natural he should be offensive to many minds, and that he very seldom talked about the newspapers—which, by the way, were always very stupid in regard to the author of *Beltraffio*. Of course he may have thought about them—the newspapers—night and day; the only point I wish to make is that he didn't show it; while, at the same time, he didn't strike one as a man who was on his guard. I may add that, as regards his hope of making the work on which he was then engaged the best of his books, it was only partly carried out. That place belongs, incontestably, to *Beltraffio*, in spite of the beauty of certain parts of its successor. I am pretty sure, however, that he had, at the moment of which I speak, no sense of failure; he was in love with his idea, which was indeed magnificent, and though for him, as (I suppose) for every artist, the act of execution had in it as much torment as joy, he saw his work growing a little every day and filling out the largest plan he had yet conceived. "I want to be truer than I have ever been," he said, settling himself on his back, with his hands clasped behind his head; "I want to give an impression of life itself. No, you may say what you will, I have always arranged things too much, always smoothed them down and rounded them off and tucked them in—done everything to them that life doesn't do. I have been a slave to the old superstitions."

"You a slave, my dear Mark Ambient? You have the freest imagination of our day!"

"All the more shame to me to have done some of the things I have! The reconciliation of the two women in *Ginistrella*, for instance—which could never really have taken place. That sort of thing is ignoble; I blush when I think of it! This new affair must be a golden vessel, filled with the purest distillation of the actual; and oh, how it bothers me, the shaping of the vase—the hammering of the metal! I have to hammer it so fine, so smooth; I don't do more than an inch or two a day. And all the while I have to be so careful not to let a drop of the liquor escape! When I see the kind of things that Life does, I despair of ever catching her peculiar trick. She has an impudence, Life! If one risked a fiftieth part of the effects she risks! It takes ever so long to believe it. You don't know yet, my dear fellow. It isn't till one has been watching Life for forty years that one finds out half of what she's up to! Therefore one's earlier things must inevitably contain a mass of rot. And with what one sees, on one side, with its tongue in its cheek, defying one to be real enough, and on the other the *bonnes gens* rolling up their eyes at one's cynicism, the situation has elements of the ludicrous which the artist himself is doubtless in a position to appreciate better than any one else. Of course one mustn't bother about the *bonnes gens*," Mark Ambient went on, while my thoughts reverted to his ladylike wife, as interpreted by his remarkable sister.

"To sink your shaft deep, and polish the plate through which people look into it—that's what your work consists of," I remember remarking.

"Ah, polishing one's plate—that is the torment of execution!" he exclaimed, jerking himself up and sitting forward. "The effort to arrive at a surface—if you think a surface necessary—some people don't, happily for them! My dear fellow, if you could see the surface I dream of—as compared with the one with which I have to content myself. Life is really too short for art—one hasn't time to make one's shell ideally hard. Firm and bright—firm and bright!—the devilish thing has a way, sometimes, of being bright without being firm. When I rap it with my knuckles it doesn't give the right sound. There are horrible little flabby spots where I have taken the second-best word, because I couldn't for the life of me think of the best. If you knew how stupid I am sometimes! They look to me now like pimples and ulcers on the brow of beauty!"

"That's very bad—very bad," I said, as gravely as I could.

"Very bad? It's the highest social offence I know; it ought—it absolutely ought—I'm quite serious—to be capital. If I knew I should be hanged else, I should manage to find the best word. The people who couldn't—some of them don't know it when they see it—would shut their inkstands, and we shouldn't be deluged by this flood of rubbish!"

I will not attempt to repeat everything that passed between us or to explain just how it was that, every moment I spent in his company, Mark Ambient revealed to me more and more that he looked at all things from the standpoint of the artist, felt all life as literary material. There are people who will tell me that this is a poor way of feeling it, and I am not concerned to defend my statement—having space merely to remark that there is something to be said for any interest which makes a man feel so much. If Mark Ambient did really, as I suggested above, have imaginative contact with "all life," I, for my part, envy him his *arrière-pensée*. At any rate it was through the receipt of this impression of him that by the time we returned I had acquired the feeling of intimacy I have noted. Before we got up for the homeward stretch he alluded to his wife's having once—or perhaps more than once—asked him whether he should like Dolcino to read *Beltraffio*. I think he was unconscious at the moment of all that this conveyed to me—as well, doubtless, of my extreme curiosity to hear what he had replied. He had said that he hoped very much Dolcino

892   THE AUTHOR OF "BELTRAFFIO"

would read all his works—when he was twenty; he should like him to know what his father had done. Before twenty it would be useless—he wouldn't understand them.

"And meanwhile do you propose to hide them—to lock them up in a drawer?" Mrs. Ambient had inquired.

"Oh no; we must simply tell him that they are not intended for small boys. If you bring him up properly, after that he won't touch them."

To this Mrs. Ambient had made answer that it would be very awkward when he was about fifteen, and I asked her husband if it was his opinion in general, then, that young people should not read novels.

"Good ones—certainly not!" said my companion. I suppose I had had other views, for I remember saying that, for myself, I was not sure it was bad for them—if the novels were "good" enough. "Bad for *them*, I don't say so much!" Ambient exclaimed. "But very bad, I am afraid, for the novel." That oblique, accidental allusion to his wife's attitude was followed by a franker style of reference as we walked home. "The difference between us is simply the opposition between two distinct ways of looking at the world, which have never succeeded in getting on together, or making any kind of common ménage, since the beginning of time. They have borne all sorts of names, and my wife would tell you it's the difference between Christian and Pagan. I may be a pagan, but I don't like the name—it sounds sectarian. She thinks me, at any rate, no better than an ancient Greek. It's the difference between making the most of life and making the least—so that you'll get another better one in some other time and place. Will it be a sin to make the most of that one too, I wonder? and shall we have to be bribed off in the future state, as well as in the present? Perhaps I care too much for beauty—I don't know; I delight in it, I adore it, I think of it continually, I try to produce it, to reproduce it. My wife holds that we shouldn't think too much about it. She's always afraid of that—always on her guard. I don't know what she has got on her back! And she's so pretty, too, herself! Don't you think she's lovely? She was, at any rate, when I married her. At that time I wasn't aware of that difference I speak of—I thought it all came to the same thing: in the end, as they say. Well, perhaps it will in the end. I don't know what the end will be. Moreover, I care for seeing things as they are; that's the way I try to show them in my novels. But you mustn't talk to Mrs. Ambient about things as they are. She has a mortal dread of things as they are."

"She's afraid of them for Dolcino," I said: surprised a moment afterwards at being in a position—thanks to Miss Ambient—to be so explanatory; and surprised even now that Mark shouldn't have shown visibly that he wondered what the deuce I knew about it. But he didn't; he simply exclaimed, with a tenderness that touched me—

"Ah, nothing shall ever hurt *him*!" He told me more about his wife before we arrived at the gate of his house, and if it be thought that he was querulous, I am afraid I must admit that he had some of the foibles as well as the gifts of the artistic temperament; adding, however, instantly, that hitherto, to the best of my belief, he had very rarely complained. "She thinks me immoral—that's the long and short of it," he said, as we paused outside a moment, and his hand rested on one of the bars of his gate; while his conscious, expressive, perceptive eyes—the eyes of a foreigner, I had begun to account them, much more than of the usual Englishman—viewing me now evidently as quite a familiar friend, took part in the declaration. "It's very strange, when one thinks it all over, and there's a grand comicality in it which I should like to bring out. She is a very nice woman, extraordinarily well behaved, upright, and clever, and with a tremendous lot of good sense about a good many matters. Yet her conception of a novel—she has explained it to me once or twice, and she doesn't do it badly, as exposition—is a thing so false that it makes me blush. It is a thing so hollow, so dishonest, so lying, in which life is so blinked and blinded, so dodged and disfigured, that it makes my ears burn. It's two different ways of looking at the whole affair," he repeated, pushing open the gate. "And they are irreconcilable!" he added with a sigh. We went forward to the house, but on the walk, half way to the door, he stopped, and said to me, "If you are going into this kind of thing, there's a fact you should know beforehand; it may save you some disappointment. There's a hatred of art —there's a hatred of literature!" I looked up at the charming house, with its genial colour and crookedness, and I answered with a smile that those evil passions might exist, but that I should never have expected to find them there. "Oh, it doesn't matter, after all," he said, laughing; which I was glad to hear, for I was reproaching myself with having excited him.

If I had, his excitement soon passed off, for at lunch he was delightful; strangely delightful, considering that the difference between himself and his wife was, as he had said, irreconcilable. He had the art, by his manner, by his smile, by his natural kindliness, of reducing the importance of it in the common concerns of life, and Mrs. Ambient, I must add, lent herself to this transaction with a very good grace. I watched her, at table, for further illustrations of that fixed idea of which Miss Ambient had spoken to me; for in the light of the united revelations of her sister-in-law and her husband, she had come to seem to me a very singular personage. I am obliged to say that the signs of a fanatical temperament were not more striking in my hostess than before; it was only after a while that her air of incorruptible conformity, her tapering, monosyllabic correctness, began to appear to be themselves a cold, thin flame. Certainly, at first, she looked like a woman with as few passions as possible; but if she had a passion at all, it would be that of Philistinism. She might have been, for there are guardian-spirits, I suppose, of all great principles—the angel of propriety. Mark Ambient, apparently, ten years before, had simply perceived that she was an angel, without asking himself of what. He had been quite right in calling my attention to her beauty. In looking for the reason why he should have married her, I saw, more than before, that she was, physically speaking, a wonderfully cultivated human plant—that she must have given him many ideas and images. It was impossible to be more pencilled, more garden-like, more delicately tinted and petalled.

If I had had it in my heart to think Ambient a little of a hypocrite for appearing to forget at table everything he had said to me during our walk, I should instantly have cancelled such a judgment on reflecting that the good news his wife was able to give him about their little boy was reason enough for his sudden air of happiness. It may have come partly, too, from a certain remorse at having complained to me of the fair lady who sat there—a desire to show me that he was after all not so miserable. Dolcino continued to be much better, and he had been promised he should come down stairs after he had had his dinner. As soon as we had risen from our own meal Ambient slipped away, evidently for the purpose of going to his child; and no sooner had I observed this than I became aware that his wife had simultaneously vanished. It happened that Miss Ambient and I, both at the same moment, saw the tail of her dress whisk out of a doorway—which led the young lady to smile at me, as if I now knew all the secrets of the place. I passed with her into the garden, and we sat down on a dear old bench which rested against the west wall of the house. It was a perfect spot for the middle period of a Sunday in June, and its felicity seemed to come partly from an antique sun-dial which, rising in front of us and forming the centre of a small, intricate parterre, measured the moments ever so slowly, and made them safe for leisure and talk. The garden bloomed in the suffused afternoon, the tall beeches stood still for an example, and, behind and above us, a rose-tree of many seasons, clinging to the faded grain of the brick, expressed the whole character of the scene in a familiar, exquisite smell. It seemed to me a place for genius to have every sanction, and not to encounter challenges and checks. Miss Ambient asked me if I had enjoyed my walk with her brother, and whether we had talked of many things.

"Well, of most things," I said, smiling, though I remembered that we had not talked of Miss Ambient.

"And don't you think some of his theories are very peculiar?"

"Oh, I guess I agree with them all." I was very particular, for Miss Ambient's entertainment, to guess.

"Do you think art is everything?" she inquired in a moment.

"In art, of course I do!"

"And do you think beauty is everything?"

"I don't know about its being everything. But it's very delightful."

"Of course it is difficult for a woman to know how far to go," said my companion. "I adore everything that gives a charm to life. I am intensely sensitive to form. But sometimes I draw back—don't you see what I mean?—I don't quite see where I shall be landed. I only want to be quiet, after all," Miss Ambient continued, in a tone of stifled yearning which seemed to indicate that she had not yet arrived at her desire. "And one must be good, at any rate, must not one?" she inquired, with a cadence apparently intended for an assurance that my answer would settle this recondite question for her. It was difficult for me to make it very original, and I am afraid I repaid her confidence with an unblushing platitude. I re-member, moreover, appending to it an inquiry, equally des-titute of freshness, and still more wanting perhaps in tact, as to whether she did not mean to go to church, as that was an obvious way of being good. She replied that she had per-formed this duty in the morning, and that for her, on Sunday afternoon, supreme virtue consisted in answering the week's letters. Then suddenly, without transition, she said to me, "It's quite a mistake about Dolcino being better. I have seen him, and he's not at all right."

"Surely his mother would know, wouldn't she?" I sug-gested.

She appeared for a moment to be counting the leaves on one of the great beeches. "As regards most matters, one can easily say what, in a given situation, my sister-in-law would do. But as regards this one, there are strange elements at work."

"Strange elements? Do you mean in the constitution of the child?"

"No, I mean in my sister-in-law's feelings."

"Elements of affection, of course; elements of anxiety. Why do you call them strange?"

She repeated my words. "Elements of affection, elements of anxiety. She is very anxious."

Miss Ambient made me vaguely uneasy—she almost fright-ened me, and I wished she would go and write her letters. "His father will have seen him now," I said, "and if he is not satisfied he will send for the doctor."

"The doctor ought to have been here this morning. He lives only two miles away."

I reflected that all this was very possibly only a part of the general tragedy of Miss Ambient's view of things; but I asked her why she hadn't urged such a necessity upon her sister-in-law. She answered me with a smile of extraordinary significance, and told me that I must have very little idea of what her relations with Beatrice were; but I must do her the justice to add that she went on to make herself a little more comprehensible by saying that it was quite reason enough for her sister not to be alarmed that Mark would be sure to be. He was always nervous about the child, and as they were predestined by nature to take opposite views, the only thing for Beatrice was to cultivate a false optimism. If Mark were not there, she would not be at all easy. I remembered what he had said to me about their dealings with Dolcino—that between them they would put an end to him; but I did not repeat this to Miss Ambient: the less so that just then her brother emerged from the house, carrying his child in his arms. Close behind him moved his wife, grave and pale; the boy's face was turned over Ambient's shoulder, towards his mother. We got up to receive the group, and as they came near us Dolcino turned round. I caught, on his enchanting little countenance, a smile of recognition, and for the moment would have been quite content with it. Miss Ambient, however, received another impression, and I make haste to say that her quick sensibility, in which there was something maternal, argues that in spite of her affectations there was a strain of kindness in her. "It won't do at all—it won't do at all," she said to me under her breath. "I shall speak to Mark about the doctor."

The child was rather white, but the main difference I saw in him was that he was even more beautiful than the day before. He had been dressed in his festal garments—a velvet suit and a crimson sash—and he looked like a little invalid prince, too young to know condescension, and smiling familiarly on his subjects.

"Put him down, Mark, he's not comfortable," Mrs. Ambient said.

"Should you like to stand on your feet, my boy?" his father asked.

"Oh yes; I'm remarkably well," said the child.

Mark placed him on the ground; he had shining, pointed

slippers, with enormous bows. "Are you happy now, Mr. Ambient?"

"Oh yes, I am particularly happy," Dolcino replied. The words were scarcely out of his mouth when his mother caught him up, and in a moment, holding him on her knees, she took her place on the bench where Miss Ambient and I had been sitting. This young lady said something to her brother, in consequence of which the two wandered away into the garden together. I remained with Mrs. Ambient; but as a servant had brought out a couple of chairs I was not obliged to seat myself beside her. Our conversation was not animated, and I, for my part, felt there would be a kind of hypocrisy in my trying to make myself agreeable to Mrs. Ambient. I didn't dislike her—I rather admired her; but I was aware that I differed from her inexpressibly. Then I suspected, what I afterwards definitely knew and have already intimated, that the poor lady had taken a dislike to me; and this of course was not encouraging. She thought me an obtrusive and even depraved young man, whom a perverse Providence had dropped upon their quiet lawn to flatter her husband's worst tendencies. She did me the honour to say to Miss Ambient, who repeated the speech, that she didn't know when she had seen her husband take such a fancy to a visitor; and she measured, apparently, my evil influence by Mark's appreciation of my society. I had a consciousness, not yet acute, but quite sufficient, of all this; but I must say that if it chilled my flow of small-talk, it didn't prevent me from thinking that the beautiful mother and beautiful child, interlaced there against their background of roses, made a picture such as I perhaps should not soon see again. I was free, I supposed, to go into the house and write letters, to sit in the drawing-room, to repair to my own apartment and take a nap; but the only use I made of my freedom was to linger still in my chair and say to myself that the light hand of Sir Joshua might have painted Mark Ambient's wife and son. I found myself looking perpetually at Dolcino, and Dolcino looked back at me, and that was enough to detain me. When he looked at me he smiled, and I felt it was an absolute impossibility to abandon a child who was smiling at one like that. His eyes never wandered; they attached themselves to mine, as if among all the small incipient things of his nature there was a desire to say something to me. If I could have taken him upon my own knee he perhaps would have managed to say it; but it would have been far too delicate a matter to ask his mother to give him up, and it has remained a constant regret for me that on that Sunday afternoon I did not, even for a moment, hold Dolcino in my arms. He had said that he felt remarkably well, and that he was especially happy; but though he may have been happy, with his charming head pillowed on his mother's breast and his little crimson silk legs depending from her lap, I did not think he looked well. He made no attempt to walk about; he was content to swing his legs softly and strike one as languid and angelic.

Mark came back to us with his sister; and Miss Ambient, making some remark about having to attend to her correspondence, passed into the house. Mark came and stood in front of his wife, looking down at the child, who immediately took hold of his hand, keeping it while he remained. "I think Allingham ought to see him," Ambient said; "I think I will walk over and fetch him."

"That's Gwendolen's idea, I suppose," Mrs. Ambient replied, very sweetly.

"It's not such an out-of-the-way idea, when one's child is ill."

"I'm not ill, papa; I'm much better now," Dolcino remarked.

"Is that the truth, or are you only saying it to be agreeable? You have a great idea of being agreeable, you know."

The boy seemed to meditate on this distinction, this imputation, for a moment; then his exaggerated eyes, which had wandered, caught my own as I watched him. "Do *you* think me agreeable?" he inquired, with the candour of his age and with a smile that made his father turn round to me, laughing, and ask, mutely, with a glance, "Isn't he adorable?"

"Then why don't you hop about, if you feel so lusty?" Ambient went on, while the boy swung his hand.

"Because mamma is holding me close!"

"Oh yes; I know how mamma holds you when I come near!" Ambient exclaimed, looking at his wife.

She turned her charming eyes up to him, without deprecation or concession, and after a moment she said, "You can go for Allingham if you like. I think myself it would be better. You ought to drive."

"She says that to get me away," Ambient remarked to me, laughing; after which he started for the doctor's.

I remained there with Mrs. Ambient, though our conversation had more pauses than speeches. The boy's little fixed white face seemed, as before, to plead with me to stay, and after a while it produced still another effect, a very curious one, which I shall find it difficult to express. Of course I expose myself to the charge of attempting to give fantastic reasons for an act which may have been simply the fruit of a native want of discretion; and indeed the traceable consequences of that perversity were too lamentable to leave me any desire to trifle with the question. All I can say is that I acted in perfect good faith, and that Dolcino's friendly little gaze gradually kindled the spark of my inspiration. What helped it to glow were the other influences—the silent, suggestive garden-nook, the perfect opportunity (if it was not an opportunity for that, it was an opportunity for nothing), and the plea that I speak of, which issued from the child's eyes and seemed to make him say, "The mother that bore me and that presses me here to her bosom—sympathetic little organism that I am—has really the kind of sensibility which she has been represented to you as lacking; if you only look for it patiently and respectfully. How is it possible that she shouldn't have it? how is it possible that *I* should have so much of it (for I am quite full of it, dear strange gentleman), if it were not also in some degree in her? I am my father's child, but I am also my mother's, and I am sorry for the difference between them!" So it shaped itself before me, the vision of reconciling Mrs. Ambient with her husband, of putting an end to their great disagreement. The project was absurd, of course, for had I not had his word for it—spoken with all the bitterness of experience—that the gulf that divided them was well-nigh bottomless? Nevertheless, a quarter of an hour after Mark had left us, I said to his wife that I couldn't get over what she told me the night before about her thinking her husband's writings "objectionable." I had been so very sorry to hear it, had thought of it constantly, and wondered whether it were not possible to make her change her mind. Mrs.

Ambient gave me rather a cold stare—she seemed to be recommending me to mind my own business. I wish I had taken this mute counsel, but I did not. I went on to remark that it seemed an immense pity so much that was beautiful should be lost upon her.

"Nothing is lost upon me," said Mrs. Ambient. "I know they are very beautiful."

"Don't you like papa's books?" Dolcino asked, addressing his mother, but still looking at me. Then he added to me, "Won't you read them to me, American gentleman?"

"I would rather tell you some stories of my own," I said. "I know some that are very interesting."

"When will you tell them—to-morrow?"

"To-morrow, with pleasure, if that suits you."

Mrs. Ambient was silent at this. Her husband, during our walk, had asked me to remain another day; my promise to her son was an implication that I had consented; and it is not probable that the prospect was agreeable to her. This ought, doubtless, to have made me more careful as to what I said next; but all I can say is that it didn't. I presently observed that just after leaving her, the evening before, and after hearing her apply to her husband's writings the epithet I had already quoted, I had, on going up to my room, sat down to the perusal of those sheets of his new book which he had been so good as to lend me. I had sat entranced till nearly three in the morning—I had read them twice over. "You say you haven't looked at them. I think it's such a pity you shouldn't. Do let me beg you to take them up. They are so very remarkable. I'm sure they will convert you. They place him in—really—such a dazzling light. All that is best in him is there. I have no doubt it's a great liberty, my saying all this; but excuse me, and *do* read them!"

"Do read them, mamma!" Dolcino repeated. "Do read them!"

She bent her head and closed his lips with a kiss. "Of course I know he has worked immensely over them," she said; and after this she made no remark, but sat there looking thoughtful, with her eyes on the ground. The tone of these last words was such as to leave me no spirit for further aggression, and after expressing a fear that her husband had not found the doctor at home, I got up and took a turn about the grounds. When I came back ten minutes later, she was still in her place, watching her boy, who had fallen asleep in her lap. As I drew near she put her finger to her lips, and a moment afterwards she rose, holding the child, and murmured something about its being better that he should go up stairs. I offered to carry him, and held out my hands to take him; but she thanked me and turned away, with the child seated on her arm, his head on her shoulder. "I am very strong," she said, as she passed into the house, and her slim, flexible figure bent backwards with the filial weight. So I never touched Dolcino.

I betook myself to Ambient's study, delighted to have a quiet hour to look over his books by myself. The windows were open into the garden, the sunny stillness, the mild light of the English summer, filled the room, without quite chasing away the rich, dusky air which was a part of its charm, and which abode in the serried shelves where old morocco exhaled the fragrance of curious learning, and in the brighter intervals where medals and prints and miniatures were suspended upon a surface of faded stuff. The place had both colour and quiet; I thought it a perfect room for work, and went so far as to say to myself that if it were mine, to sit and scribble in, there was no knowing but that I might learn to write as well as the author of *Beltraffio*. This distinguished man did not turn up, and I rummaged freely among his treasures. At last I took down a book that detained me a while, and seated myself in a fine old leather chair, by the window, to turn it over. I had been occupied in this way for half an hour—a good part of the afternoon had waned—when I became conscious of another presence in the room, and, looking up from my quarto, saw that Mrs. Ambient, having pushed open the door in the same noiseless way that marked—or disguised—her entrance the night before, had advanced across the threshold. On seeing me she stopped; she had not, I think, expected to find me. But her hesitation was only of a moment; she came straight to her husband's writing-table, as if she were looking for something. I got up and asked her if I could help her. She glanced about an instant, and then put her hand upon a roll of papers which I recognised, as I had placed it in that spot in the morning, on coming down from my room.

"Is this the new book?" she asked, holding it up.

"The very sheets, with precious annotations."

"I mean to take your advice." And she tucked the little bundle under her arm. I congratulated her cordially, and ventured to make of my triumph, as I presumed to call it, a subject of pleasantry. But she was perfectly grave, and turned away from me, as she had presented herself, without a smile; after which I settled down to my quarto again, with the reflection that Mrs. Ambient was a queer woman. My triumph, too, suddenly seemed to me rather vain. A woman who couldn't smile in the right place would never understand Mark Ambient. He came in at last in person, having brought the doctor back with him. "He was away from home," Mark said, "and I went after him—to where he was supposed to be. He had left the place, and I followed him to two or three others, which accounts for my delay." He was now with Mrs. Ambient, looking at the child, and was to see Mark again before leaving the house. My host noticed, at the end of ten minutes, that the proof-sheets of his new book had been removed from the table, and when I told him, in reply to his question as to what I knew about them, that Mrs. Ambient had carried them off to read, he turned almost pale for an instant with surprise. "What has suddenly made her so curious?" he exclaimed; and I was obliged to tell him that I was at the bottom of the mystery. I had had it on my conscience to assure her that she really ought to know of what her husband was capable. "Of what I am capable? *Elle ne s'en doute que trop!*" said Ambient, with a laugh; but he took my meddling very good-naturedly, and contented himself with adding that he was very much afraid she would burn up the sheets, with his emendations, of which he had no duplicate. The doctor paid a long visit in the nursery, and before he came down I retired to my own quarters, where I remained till dinner-time. On entering the drawing-room at this hour I found Miss Ambient in possession, as she had been the evening before.

"I was right about Dolcino," she said as soon as she saw me, with a strange little air of triumph. "He is really very ill."

"Very ill! Why, when I last saw him, at four o'clock, he was in fairly good form."

"There has been a change for the worse—very sudden and

rapid—and when the doctor got here he found diphtheritic symptoms. He ought to have been called, as I knew, in the morning, and the child oughtn't to have been brought into the garden."

"My dear lady, he was very happy there," I answered, much appalled.

"He would be happy anywhere. I have no doubt he is happy now, with his poor little throat in a state——" She dropped her voice as her brother came in, and Mark let us know that, as a matter of course, Mrs. Ambient would not appear. It was true that Dolcino had developed diphtheritic symptoms, but he was quiet for the present, and his mother was earnestly watching him. She was a perfect nurse, Mark said, and the doctor was coming back at ten o'clock. Our dinner was not very gay; Ambient was anxious and alarmed, and his sister irritated me by her constant tacit assumption, conveyed in the very way she nibbled her bread and sipped her wine, of having "told me so." I had had no disposition to deny anything she told me, and I could not see that her satisfaction in being justified by the event made poor Dolcino's throat any better. The truth is that, as the sequel proved, Miss Ambient had some of the qualities of the sibyl, and had therefore, perhaps, a right to the sibylline contortions. Her brother was so preoccupied that I felt my presence to be an indiscretion, and was sorry I had promised to remain over the morrow. I said to Mark that, evidently, I had better leave them in the morning; to which he replied that, on the contrary, if he was to pass the next days in the fidgets my company would be an extreme relief to him. The fidgets had already begun for him, poor fellow, and as we sat in his study with our cigars, after dinner, he wandered to the door whenever he heard the sound of the doctor's wheels. Miss Ambient, who shared this apartment with us, gave me at such moments significant glances; she had gone up stairs before rejoining us, to ask after the child. His mother and his nurse gave a tolerable account of him; but Miss Ambient found his fever high and his symptoms very grave. The doctor came at ten o'clock, and I went to bed after hearing from Mark that he saw no present cause for alarm. He had made every provision for the night, and was to return early in the morning.

I quitted my room at eight o'clock the next day, and as I came down stairs saw, through the open door of the house, Mrs. Ambient standing at the front gate of the grounds, in colloquy with the physician. She wore a white dressing-gown, but her shining hair was carefully tucked away in its net, and in the freshness of the morning, after a night of watching, she looked as much "the type of the lady" as her sister-in-law had described her. Her appearance, I suppose, ought to have re-assured me; but I was still nervous and uneasy, so that I shrank from meeting her with the necessary question about Dolcino. None the less, however, was I impatient to learn how the morning found him; and, as Mrs. Ambient had not seen me, I passed into the grounds by a roundabout way, and, stopping at a further gate, hailed the doctor just as he was driving away. Mrs. Ambient had returned to the house before he got into his gig.

"Excuse me—but, as a friend of the family, I should like very much to hear about the little boy."

The doctor, who was a stout, sharp man, looked at me from head to foot, and then he said, "I'm sorry to say I haven't seen him."

"Haven't seen him?"

"Mrs. Ambient came down to meet me as I alighted, and told me that he was sleeping so soundly, after a restless night, that she didn't wish him disturbed. I assured her I wouldn't disturb him, but she said he was quite safe now and she could look after him herself.

"Thank you very much. Are you coming back?"

"No, sir; I'll be hanged if I come back!" exclaimed Dr. Allingham, who was evidently very angry. And he started his horse again with the whip.

I wandered back into the garden, and five minutes later Miss Ambient came forth from the house to greet me. She explained that breakfast would not be served for some time, and that she wished to catch the doctor before he went away. I informed her that this functionary had come and departed, and I repeated to her what he had told me about his dismissal. This made Miss Ambient very serious—very serious indeed—and she sank into a bench, with dilated eyes, hugging her elbows with crossed arms. She indulged in many ejaculations,

she confessed that she was infinitely perplexed, and she finally
told me what her own last news of her nephew had been. She
had sat up very late—after me, after Mark—and before going
to bed had knocked at the door of the child's room, which
was opened to her by the nurse. This good woman had admitted her, and she had found Dolcino quiet, but flushed and
"unnatural," with his mother sitting beside his bed. "She held
his hand in one of hers," said Miss Ambient, "and in the
other—what do you think?—the proof-sheets of Mark's new
book! She was reading them there, intently: did you ever hear
of anything so extraordinary? Such a very odd time to be reading an author whom she never could abide!" In her agitation
Miss Ambient was guilty of this vulgarism of speech, and I
was so impressed by her narrative that it was only in recalling
her words later that I noticed the lapse. Mrs. Ambient had
looked up from her reading with her finger on her lips—I
recognised the gesture she had addressed to me in the afternoon—and, though the nurse was about to go to rest, had
not encouraged her sister-in-law to relieve her of any part of
her vigil. But certainly, then, Dolcino's condition was far from
reassuring—his poor little breathing was most painful; and
what change could have taken place in him in those few hours
that would justify Beatrice in denying the physician access to
him? This was the moral of Miss Ambient's anecdote—the
moral for herself at least. The moral for me, rather, was that
it *was* a very singular time for Mrs. Ambient to be going into
a novelist she had never appreciated and who had simply happened to be recommended to her by a young American she
disliked. I thought of her sitting there in the sick-chamber in
the still hours of the night, after the nurse had left her, turning
over those pages of genius and wrestling with their magical
influence.

I must relate very briefly the circumstances of the rest of
my visit to Mark Ambient—it lasted but a few hours
longer—and devote but three words to my later acquaintance
with him. That lasted five years—till his death—and was full
of interest, of satisfaction, and, I may add, of sadness. The
main thing to be said with regard to it is, that I had a secret
from him. I believe he never suspected it, though of this I am
not absolutely sure. If he did, the line he had taken, the line

of absolute negation of the matter to himself, shows an immense effort of the will. I may tell my secret now, giving it for what it is worth, now that Mark Ambient has gone, that he has begun to be alluded to as one of the famous early dead, and that his wife does not survive him; now, too, that Miss Ambient, whom I also saw at intervals during the years that followed, has, with her embroideries and her attitudes, her necromantic glances and strange intuitions, retired to a Sisterhood, where, as I am told, she is deeply immured and quite lost to the world.

Mark came into breakfast after his sister and I had for some time been seated there. He shook hands with me in silence, kissed his sister, opened his letters and newspapers, and pretended to drink his coffee. But I could see that these movements were mechanical, and I was little surprised when, suddenly he pushed away everything that was before him, and with his head in his hands and his elbows on the table, sat staring strangely at the cloth.

"What is the matter *fratello mio*?" Miss Ambient inquired, peeping from behind the urn.

He answered nothing, but got up with a certain violence and strode to the window. We rose to our feet, his sister and I, by a common impulse, exchanging a glance of some alarm, while he stared for a moment into the garden. "In heaven's name, what has got possession of Beatrice?" he cried at last, turning round with an almost haggard face. And he looked from one of us to the other; the appeal was addressed to me as well as to his sister.

Miss Ambient gave a shrug. "My poor Mark, Beatrice is always—Beatrice!"

"She has locked herself up with the boy—bolted and barred the door—she refuses to let me come near him!" Ambient went on.

"She refused to let the doctor see him an hour ago!" Miss Ambient remarked, with intention, as they say on the stage.

"Refused to let the doctor see him? By heaven, I'll smash in the door!" And Mark brought his fist down upon the table, so that all the breakfast-service rang.

I begged Miss Ambient to go up and try to have speech of her sister-in-law, and I drew Mark out into the garden.

"You're exceedingly nervous, and Mrs. Ambient is probably right," I said to him. "Women know—women should be supreme in such a situation. Trust a mother—a devoted mother, my dear friend!" With such words as these I tried to soothe and comfort him, and, marvellous to relate, I succeeded, with the help of many cigarettes, in making him walk about the garden and talk, or listen at least to my own ingenious chatter, for nearly an hour. At the end of this time Miss Ambient returned to us, with a very rapid step, holding her hand to her heart.

"Go for the doctor, Mark; go for the doctor this moment!"

"Is he dying—has she killed him?" poor Ambient cried, flinging away his cigarette.

"I don't know what she has done! But she's frightened, and now she wants the doctor."

"He told me he would be hanged if he came back," I felt myself obliged to announce.

"Precisely—therefore Mark himself must go for him, and not a messenger. You must see him and tell him it's to save your child. The trap has been ordered—it's ready."

"To save him? I'll save him, please God!" Ambient cried, bounding with his great strides across the lawn.

As soon as he had gone I felt that I ought to have volunteered in his place, and I said as much to Miss Ambient; but she checked me by grasping my arm quickly, while we heard the wheels of the dog-cart rattle away from the gate. "He's off—he's off—and now I can think! To get him away—while I think—while I think!"

"While you think of what, Miss Ambient?"

"Of the unspeakable thing that has happened under this roof!"

Her manner was habitually that of such a prophetess of ill that my first impulse was to believe I must allow here for a great exaggeration. But in a moment I saw that her emotion was real. "Dolcino *is* dying then—he is dead?"

"It's too late to save him. His mother has let him die! I tell you that, because you are sympathetic, because you have imagination," Miss Ambient was good enough to add, interrupting my expression of horror. "That's why you had the idea of making her read Mark's new book!"

"What has that to do with it? I don't understand you—your accusation is monstrous."

"I see it all—I'm not stupid," Miss Ambient went on, heedless of the harshness of my tone. "It was the book that finished her—it was that decided her!"

"Decided her? Do you mean she has murdered her child?" I demanded, trembling at my own words.

"She sacrificed him—she determined to do nothing to make him live. Why else did she lock herself up—why else did she turn away the doctor? The book gave her a horror, she determined to rescue him—to prevent him from ever being touched. He had a crisis at two o'clock in the morning. I know this from the nurse, who had left her then, but whom, for a short time, she called back. Dolcino got much worse, but she insisted on the nurse's going back to bed, and after that she was alone with him for hours."

"Do you pretend that she has no pity—that she's insane?"

"She held him in her arms—she pressed him to her breast, not to see him; but she gave him no remedies—she did nothing the doctor ordered. Everything is there, untouched. She has had the honesty not even to throw the drugs away!"

I dropped upon the nearest bench, overcome with wonder and agitation: quite as much at Miss Ambient's terrible lucidity as at the charge she made against her sister-in-law. There was an amazing coherency in her story, and it was dreadful to me to see myself figuring in it as so proximate a cause. "You are a very strange woman, and you say strange things."

"You think it necessary to protest—but you are quite ready to believe me. You have received an impression of my sister-in-law, you have guessed of what she is capable."

I do not feel bound to say what concession on this point I made to Miss Ambient, who went on to relate to me that within the last half-hour Beatrice had had a revulsion; that she was tremendously frightened at what she had done; that her fright itself betrayed her; and that she would now give heaven and earth to save the child. "Let us hope she will!" I said, looking at my watch and trying to time poor Ambient; whereupon my companion repeated, in a singular tone, "Let us hope so!" When I asked her if she herself could do nothing, and whether she ought not to be with her sister-in-law, she replied, "You had better go and judge; she is like a wounded tigress!" I never saw Mrs. Ambient till six months after this, and therefore cannot pretend to have verified the comparison. At the latter period she was again the type of the lady. "She'll be nicer to him after this," I remember Miss Ambient saying, in response to some quick outburst (on my part) of compassion for her brother. Although I had been in the house but thirty-six hours this young lady had treated me with extraordinary confidence, and there was therefore a certain demand which, as an intimate, I might make of her. I extracted from her a pledge that she would never say to her brother what she had just said to me; she would leave him to form his own theory of his wife's conduct. She agreed with me that there was misery enough in the house without her contributing a new anguish, and that Mrs. Ambient's proceedings might be explained, to her husband's mind, by the extravagance of a jealous devotion. Poor Mark came back with the doctor much sooner than we could have hoped, but we knew, five minutes afterward, that they arrived too late. Poor little Dolcino was more exquisitely beautiful in death than he had been in life. Mrs. Ambient's grief was frantic; she lost her head and said strange things. As for Mark's—but I will not speak of that. *Basta*, as he used to say. Miss Ambient kept her secret—I have already had occasion to say that she had her good points—but it rankled in her conscience like a guilty participation, and, I imagine, had something to do with her retiring ultimately to a Sisterhood. And, *à propos* of consciences, the reader is now in a position to judge of my compunction for my effort to convert Mrs. Ambient. I ought to mention that the death of her child in some degree converted her. When the new book came out—it was long delayed—she read it over as a whole, and her husband told me that a few months before her death—she failed rapidly after losing her son, sank into a consumption, and faded away at Mentone—during those few supreme weeks she even dipped into *Beltraffio*.

CHRONOLOGY

NOTE ON THE TEXTS

NOTES

Chronology

1843   Born April 15 at 21 Washington Place, New York City, the second child (after William, born January 11, 1842, N.Y.C.) of Henry James of Albany and Mary Robertson Walsh of New York. Father lives on inheritance of $10,000 a year, his share of litigated $3,000,000 fortune of his Albany father, William James, an Irish immigrant who came to the U.S. immediately after the Revolution.

1843–45   Accompanied by mother's sister, Catharine Walsh, and servants, the James parents take infant children to England and later to France. Reside at Windsor, where father has nervous collapse ("vastation") and experiences spiritual illumination. He becomes a Swedenborgian (May 1844), devoting his time to lecturing and religious-philosophical writings. James later claimed his earliest memory was a glimpse, during his second year, of the Place Vendôme in Paris with its Napoleonic column.

1845–47   Family returns to New York. Garth Wilkinson James (Wilky) born July 21, 1845. Family moves to Albany at 50 N. Pearl St., a few doors from grandmother Catharine Barber James. Robertson James (Bob or Rob) born August 29, 1846.

1847–55   Family moves to a large house at 58 W. 14th St., New York. Alice James born August 7, 1848. Relatives and father's friends and acquaintances—Horace Greeley, George Ripley, Charles Anderson Dana, William Cullen Bryant, Bronson Alcott, and Ralph Waldo Emerson ("I knew he was great, greater than any of our friends")—are frequent visitors. Thackeray calls during his lecture tour on the English humorists. Summers at New Brighton on Staten Island and Fort Hamilton on Long Island's south shore. On steamboat to Fort Hamilton August 1850, hears Washington Irving tell his father of Margaret Fuller's drowning in shipwreck off Fire Island. Frequently visits Barnum's American Museum on free days. Taken to art shows and theaters; writes and draws stage scenes. Described by father as "a devourer of libraries." Taught in assorted private schools and by tutors in lower Broadway and Greenwich Village. But father claims in 1848 that American schooling fails to provide "sensuous education" for his children and plans to take them to Europe.

1855–58   Family (with Aunt Kate) sails for Liverpool, June 27. James is intermittently sick with malarial fever as they travel to Paris, Lyon, and Geneva. After Swiss summer, leaves for London where Robert Thomson (later Robert Louis Stevenson's tutor) is engaged. Early summer 1856, family moves to Paris. Another tutor engaged and children attend experimental Fourierist school. Acquires fluency in French. Family goes to Boulogne-sur-mer in summer, where James contracts typhoid. Spends late October in Paris, but American crash of 1857 returns family to Boulogne where they can live more cheaply. Attends public school (fellow classmate is Coquelin, the future French actor).

1858–59   Family returns to America and settles in Newport, Rhode Island. Goes boating, fishing, and riding. Attends the Reverend W. C. Leverett's Berkeley Institute, and forms friendship with classmate Thomas Sergeant Perry. Takes long walks and sketches with the painter John La Farge.

1859–60   Father, still dissatisfied with American education, returns family to Geneva in October. James attends a pre-engineering school, Institution Rochette, because parents, with "a flattering misconception of my aptitudes," feel he might benefit from less reading and more mathematics. After a few months withdraws from all classes except French, German, and Latin, and joins William as a special student at the Academy (later the University of Geneva) where he attends lectures on literary subjects. Studies German in Bonn during summer 1860.

1860–62   Family returns to Newport in September where William studies with William Morris Hunt, and James sits in on his classes. La Farge introduces him to works of Balzac, Merimée, Musset, and Browning. Wilky and Bob attend Frank Sanborn's experimental school in Concord with children of Hawthorne and Emerson and John Brown's daughter. Early in 1861, orphaned Temple cousins come to live in Newport. Develops close friendship with cousin

Mary (Minnie) Temple. Goes on a week's walking tour in July in New Hampshire with Perry. William abandons art in autumn 1861 and enters Lawrence Scientific School at Harvard. James suffers back injury in a stable fire while serving as a volunteer fireman. Reads Hawthorne ("an American could be an artist, one of the finest").

1862–63   Enters Harvard Law School (Dane Hall). Wilky enlists in the Massachusetts 44th Regiment, and later in Colonel Robert Gould Shaw's 54th, one of the first black regiments. Summer 1863, Bob joins the Massachusetts 55th, another black regiment, under Colonel Hollowell. James withdraws from law studies to try writing. Sends unsigned stories to magazines. Wilky is badly wounded and brought home to Newport in August.

1864   Family moves from Newport to 13 Ashburton Place, Boston. First tale, "A Tragedy of Error" (unsigned), published in *Continental Monthly* (Feb. 1864). Stays in Northampton, Massachusetts, early August–November. Begins writing book reviews for *North American Review* and forms friendship with its editor, Charles Eliot Norton, and his family, including his sister Grace (with whom he maintains a long-lasting correspondence). Wilky returns to his regiment.

1865   First signed tale, "The Story of a Year," published in *Atlantic Monthly* (March 1865). Begins to write reviews for the newly founded *Nation* and publishes anonymously in it during next fifteen years. William sails on a scientific expedition with Louis Agassiz to the Amazon. During summer James vacations in the White Mountains with Minnie Temple and her family; joined by Oliver Wendell Holmes Jr. and John Chipman Gray, both recently demobilized. Father subsidizes plantation for Wilky and Bob in Florida with black hired workers. (The idealistic but impractical venture fails in 1870.)

1866–68   Continues to publish reviews and tales in Boston and New York journals. William returns from Brazil and resumes medical education. James has recurrence of back ailment and spends summer in Swampscott, Massachusetts. Begins friendship with William Dean Howells. Family moves to 20 Quincy St., Cambridge. William, suffering from nervous ailments, goes to Germany in spring 1867. "Poor Richard," James's longest story to date, published in *Atlantic Monthly* (June–Aug. 1867). William begins intermittent criticism of Henry's story-telling and style (which will continue throughout their careers). Momentary meeting with Charles Dickens at Norton's house. Vacations in Jefferson, New Hampshire, summer 1868. William returns from Europe.

1869–70   Sails in February for European tour. Visits English towns and cathedrals. Through Nortons meets Leslie Stephen, William Morris, Dante Gabriel Rossetti, Edward Burne-Jones, John Ruskin, Charles Darwin, and George Eliot (the "one marvel" of his stay in London). Goes to Paris in May, then travels in Switzerland in summer and hikes into Italy in autumn, where he stays in Milan, Venice (Sept.), Florence, and Rome (Oct. 30–Dec. 28). Returns to England to drink the waters at Malvern health spa in Worcestershire because of digestive troubles. Stays in Paris en route and has first experience of Comédie Française. Learns that his beloved cousin, Minnie Temple, has died of tuberculosis.

1870–72   Returns to Cambridge in May. Travels to Rhode Island, Vermont, and New York to write travel sketches for *The Nation*. Spends a few days with Emerson in Concord. Meets Bret Harte at Howells' home April 1871. *Watch and Ward*, his first novel, published in *Atlantic Monthly* (Aug.–Dec. 1871). Serves as occasional art reviewer for the *Atlantic* January–March 1872.

1872–74   Accompanies Aunt Kate and sister Alice on tour of England, France, Switzerland, Italy, Austria, and Germany from May through October. Writes travel sketches for *The Nation*. Spends autumn in Paris, becoming friends with James Russell Lowell. Escorts Emerson through the Louvre. (Later, on Emerson's return from Egypt, will show him the Vatican.) Goes to Florence in December and from there to Rome, where he becomes friends with actress Fanny Kemble, her daughter Sarah Butler Wister, and William Wetmore Story and his family. In Italy sees old family friend Francis Boott and his daughter Elizabeth (Lizzie), expatriates who have lived for many years in Florentine villa on Bellosguardo. Takes up horseback riding on the Campagna. Encounters Matthew Arnold in April 1873 at Story's. Moves from Rome hotel to rooms of his own. Continues writing and now earns enough to support himself. Leaves Rome in June, spends summer in Bad Homburg. In October goes to Florence, where William joins him. They also visit Rome, William returning to America in March. In Baden-Baden June–August and returns to America September 4, with *Roderick Hudson* all but finished.

1875   *Roderick Hudson* serialized in *Atlantic Monthly* from January (published by Osgood at the end of the year). First book, *A Passionate Pilgrim and Other Tales*, published January 31. Tries living and writing in New York, in rooms at 111 E. 25th Street. Earns $200 a month from novel installments and continued reviewing, but finds New York too expensive. *Transatlantic Sketches*, published in April, sells almost 1,000 copies in three months. In Cambridge in July decides to return to Europe; arranges with John Hay, assistant to the publisher, to write Paris letters for the *New York Tribune*.

1875–76 Arriving in Paris in November, he takes rooms at 29 Rue de Luxembourg (since renamed Cambon). Becomes friend of Ivan Turgenev and is introduced by him to Gustave Flaubert's Sunday parties. Meets Edmond de Goncourt, Émile Zola, G. Charpentier (the publisher), Catulle Mendès, Alphonse Daudet, Guy de Maupassant, Ernest Renan, Gustave Doré. Makes friends with Charles Sanders Peirce, who is in Paris. Reviews (unfavorably) the early Impressionists at the Durand-Ruel gallery. By midsummer has received $400 for *Tribune* pieces, but editor asks for more Parisian gossip and James resigns. Travels in France during July, visiting Normandy and the Midi, and in September crosses to San Sebastian, Spain, to see a bullfight ("I thought the bull, in any case, a finer fellow than any of his tormentors"). Moves to London in December, taking rooms at 3 Bolton Street, Piccadilly, where he will live for the next decade.

1877   *The American* published. Meets Robert Browning and George du Maurier. Leaves London in midsummer for visit to Paris and then goes to Italy. In Rome rides again in Campagna and hears of an episode that inspires "Daisy

Miller." Back in England, spends Christmas at Stratford
with Fanny Kemble.

1878   Publishes first book in England, *French Poets and Novelists*
          (Macmillan). Appearance of "Daisy Miller" in *Cornhill
          Magazine*, edited by Leslie Stephen, is international suc-
          cess, but by publishing it abroad loses American copyright
          and story is pirated in U.S. *Cornhill* also prints "An Inter-
          national Episode." *The Europeans* is serialized in *Atlantic*.
          Now a celebrity, he dines out often, visits country houses,
          gains weight, takes long walks, fences, and does weight-
          lifting to reduce. Elected to Reform Club. Meets Tenny-
          son, George Meredith, and James McNeill Whistler. Wil-
          liam marries Alice Howe Gibbens.

1879   Immersed in London society (". . . dined out during the
          past winter 107 times!"). Meets Edmund Gosse and
          Robert Louis Stevenson, who will later become his close
          friends. Sees much of Henry Adams and his wife, Marian
          (Clover), in London and later in Paris. Takes rooms in
          Paris, September–December. *Confidence* is serialized in
          Scribner's and published by Chatto & Windus. *Hawthorne*
          appears in Macmillan's "English Men of Letters" series.

1880–81   Stays in Florence March–May to work on *The Portrait of
          a Lady*. Meets Constance Fenimore Woolson, American
          novelist and grandniece of James Fenimore Cooper. Re-
          turns to Bolton Street in June, where William visits him.
          Washington Square serialized in *Cornhill Magazine* and
          published in U.S. by Harper & Brothers (Dec. 1880). *The
          Portrait of a Lady* serialized in *Macmillan's Magazine* (Oct.
          1880–Nov. 1881) and *Atlantic Monthly*, published by Mac-
          millan and Houghton, Mifflin (Nov. 1881). Publication
          both in United States and in England yields him the then-
          large income of $500 a month, though book sales are dis-
          appointing. Leaves London in February for Paris, the
          south of France, the Italian Riviera, and Venice, and re-
          turns home in July. Sister Alice comes to London with
          her friend Katharine Loring. James goes to Scotland in
          September.

1881–83   In November revisits America after absence of six years.
          Lionized in New York. Returns to Quincy Street for
          Christmas and sees ailing brother Wilky for the first time

in ten years. In January visits Washington and the Henry
Adamses and meets President Chester A. Arthur. Summoned to Cambridge by mother's death January 29 ("the
sweetest, gentlest, most beneficent human being I have
ever known"). All four brothers are together for the first
time in fifteen years at her funeral. Alice and father move
from Cambridge to Boston. Prepares a stage version of
"Daisy Miller" and returns to England in May. William,
now a Harvard professor, comes to Europe in September.
Proposed by Leslie Stephen, James becomes member,
without the usual red tape, of the Atheneum Club. Travels
in France in October to write *A Little Tour in France*
(published 1884) and has last visit with Turgenev, who is
dying. Returns to England in December and learns of
father's illness. Sails for America but Henry James Sr. dies
December 18, 1882, before his arrival. Made executor of
father's will. Visits brothers Wilky and Bob in Milwaukee
in January. Quarrels with William over division of property—James wants to restore Wilky's share. Macmillan
publishes a collected pocket edition of James's novels and
tales in fourteen volumes. *Siege of London* and *Portraits of
Places* published. Returns to Bolton Street in September.
Wilky dies in November. Constance Fenimore Woolson
comes to London for the winter.

1884–86   Goes to Paris in February and visits Daudet, Zola, and
Goncourt. Again impressed with their intense concern
with "art, form, manner" but calls them "mandarins."
Misses Turgenev, who had died a few months before.
Meets John Singer Sargent and persuades him to settle in
London. Returns to Bolton Street. Sargent introduces him
to young Paul Bourget. During country visits encounters many British political and social figures, including W. E. Gladstone, John Bright, and Charles Dilke.
Alice, suffering from nervous ailment, arrives in England
for visit in November but is too ill to travel and settles
near her brother. *Tales of Three Cities* ("The Impressions
of a Cousin," "Lady Barberina," "A New England Winter") and "The Art of Fiction" published 1884. Alice goes
to Bournemouth in late January. James joins her in May
and becomes an intimate of Robert Louis Stevenson, who
resides nearby. Spends August at Dover and is visited by
Paul Bourget. Stays in Paris for the next two months.
Moves into a flat at 34 De Vere Gardens in Kensington

early in March 1886. Alice takes rooms in London. *The Bostonians* serialized in *Century* (Feb. 1885–Feb. 1886; published 1886), *The Princess Casamassima* serialized in *Atlantic Monthly* (Sept. 1885–Oct. 1886; published 1886).

1886–87   Leaves for Italy in December for extended stay, mainly in Florence and Venice. Sees much of Constance Fenimore Woolson and stays in her villa. Writes "The Aspern Papers" and other tales. Returns to De Vere Gardens in July and begins work on *The Tragic Muse*. Pays several country visits. Dines out less often ("I know it all—all that one sees by 'going out'—today, as if I had made it. But if I had, I would have made it better!").

1888   *The Reverberator*, *The Aspern Papers*, *Louisa Pallant*, *The Modern Warning*, and *Partial Portraits* published. Elizabeth Boott Duveneck dies. Robert Louis Stevenson leaves for the South Seas. Engages fencing teacher to combat "symptoms of a portentous corpulence." Goes abroad in October to Geneva (where he visits Woolson), Genoa, Monte Carlo, and Paris.

1889–90   Catharine Walsh (Aunt Kate) dies March 1889. William comes to England to visit Alice in August. James goes to Dover in September and then to Paris for five weeks. Writes account of Robert Browning's funeral in Westminster Abbey. Dramatizes *The American* for the Compton Comedy Company. Meets and becomes close friends with American journalist William Morton Fullerton and young American publisher Wolcott Balestier. Goes to Italy for the summer, staying in Venice and Florence, and takes a brief walking tour in Tuscany with W. W. Baldwin, an American physician practicing in Florence. Miss Woolson moves to Cheltenham, England, to be near James. *Atlantic Monthly* rejects his story "The Pupil," but it appears in England. Writes series of drawing-room comedies for theater. Meets Rudyard Kipling. *The Tragic Muse* serialized in *Atlantic Monthly* (Jan. 1889–May 1890; published 1890). *A London Life* (including "The Patagonia," "The Liar," "Mrs. Temperly") published 1889.

1891   *The American* produced at Southport is a success during road tour. After residence in Leamington, Alice returns to London, cared for by Katharine Loring. Doctors discover she has breast cancer. James circulates comedies (*Mrs. Vibert*, later called *Tenants*, and *Mrs. Jasper*, later named *Disengaged*) among theater managers who are cool to his work. Unimpressed at first by Ibsen, writes an appreciative review after seeing a performance of *Hedda Gabler* with Elizabeth Robins, a young Kentucky actress; persuades her to take the part of Mme. de Cintré in the London production of *The American*. Recuperates from flu in Ireland. James Russell Lowell dies. *The American* opens in London, September 26, and runs for seventy nights. Wolcott Balestier dies, and James attends his funeral in Dresden in December.

1892   Alice James dies March 6. James travels to Siena to be near the Paul Bourgets, and Venice, June–July, to visit the Daniel Curtises, then to Lausanne to meet William and his family, who have come abroad for sabbatical. Attends funeral of Tennyson at Westminster Abbey. Augustin Daly agrees to produce *Mrs. Jasper*. *The American* continues to be performed on the road by the Compton Company. *The Lesson of the Master* (with a collection of stories including "The Marriages," "The Pupil," "Brooksmith," "The Solution," and "Sir Edmund Orme") published.

1893   Fanny Kemble dies in January. Continues to write unproduced plays. In March goes to Paris for two months. Sends Edward Compton first act and scenario for *Guy Domville*. Meets William and family in Lucerne and stays a month, returning to London in June. Spends July completing *Guy Domville* in Ramsgate. George Alexander, actor-manager, agrees to produce the play. Daly stages first reading of *Mrs. Jasper*, and James withdraws it, calling the rehearsal a mockery. *The Real Thing and Other Tales* (including "The Wheel of Time," "Lord Beaupré," "The Visit") published.

1894   Constance Fenimore Woolson dies in Venice, January. Shocked and upset, James prepares to attend funeral in Rome but changes his mind on learning she is a suicide. Goes to Venice in April to help her family settle her affairs. Receives one of four copies, privately printed by Miss Loring, of Alice's diary. Finds it impressive but is concerned that so much gossip he told Alice in private has been included (later burns his copy). Robert Louis Ste-

venson dies in the South Pacific. *Guy Domville* goes into
rehearsal. *Theatricals: Two Comedies* and *Theatricals: Second
Series* published.

1895   *Guy Domville* opens January 5 at St. James's Theatre. At
play's end James is greeted by a fifteen-minute roar of
boos, catcalls, and applause. Horrified and depressed, abandons the theater. Play earns him $1,300 after five-week run.
Feels he can salvage something useful from playwriting for
his fiction ("a key that, working in the same *general* way
fits the complicated chambers of *both* the dramatic and the
narrative lock"). Writes scenario for *The Spoils of Poynton*.
Visits Lord Wolseley and Lord Houghton in Ireland. In
the summer goes to Torquay in Devonshire and stays until
November while electricity is being installed in De Vere
Gardens flat. Friendship with W. E. Norris, who resides
at Torquay. Writes a one-act play ("Mrs. Gracedew") at
request of Ellen Terry. *Terminations* (containing "The
Death of the Lion," "The Coxon Fund," "The Middle
Years," "The Altar of the Dead") published.

1896–97   Finishes *The Spoils of Poynton* (serialized in *Atlantic
Monthly* April–Oct. 1896 as *The Old Things*; published
1897). *Embarrassments* ("The Figure in the Carpet,"
"Glasses," "The Next Time," "The Way It Came") published. Takes a house on Point Hill, Playden, opposite the
old town of Rye, Sussex, August–September. Ford Madox Hueffer (later Ford Madox Ford) visits him. Converts
play *The Other House* into novel and works on *What
Maisie Knew* (published Sept. 1897). George du Maurier
dies early in October. Because of increasing pain in wrist,
hires stenographer William MacAlpine in February and
then purchases a typewriter; soon begins direct dictation
to MacAlpine at the machine. Invites Joseph Conrad to
lunch at De Vere Gardens and begins their friendship.
Goes to Bournemouth in July. Serves on jury in London
before going to Dunwich, Suffolk, to spend time with
Temple-Emmet cousins. In late September 1897 signs a
twenty-one-year lease for Lamb House in Rye for £70 a
year ($350). Takes on extra work to pay for setting up his
house—the life of William Wetmore Story ($1,250 ad-
vance) and will furnish an "American Letter" for new
magazine *Literature* (precursor of *Times Literary Supple-
ment*) for $200 a month. Howells visits.

1898   "The Turn of the Screw" (serialized in *Collier's* Jan.–April;
            published with "Covering End" under the title *The Two
            Magics*) proves his most popular work since "Daisy
            Miller." Sleeps in Lamb House for first time June 28. Soon
            after is visited by William's son, Henry James Jr. (Harry),
            followed by a stream of visitors: future Justice Oliver
            Wendell Holmes, Mrs. J. T. Fields, Sarah Orne Jewett, the
            Paul Bourgets, the Edward Warrens, the Daniel Curtises,
            the Edmund Gosses, and Howard Sturgis. His witty
            friend Jonathan Sturges, a young, crippled New Yorker,
            stays for two months during autumn. *In the Cage* pub-
            lished. Meets neighbors Stephen Crane and H. G. Wells.

1899   Finishes *The Awkward Age* and plans trip to the Conti-
            nent. Fire in Lamb House delays departure. To Paris in
            March and then visits the Paul Bourgets at Hyères. Stays
            with the Curtises in their Venice palazzo, where he meets
            and becomes friends with Jessie Allen. In Rome meets
            young American-Norwegian sculptor Hendrik C. Ander-
            sen; buys one of his busts. Returns to England in July and
            Andersen comes for three days in August. William, his
            wife, Alice, and daughter, Peggy, arrive at Lamb House
            in October. First meeting of brothers in six years. William
            now has confirmed heart condition. James B. Pinker be-
            comes literary agent and for first time James's professional
            relations are systematically organized; he reviews copy-
            rights, finds new publishers, and obtains better prices for
            work ("the germ of a new career"). Purchases Lamb
            House for $10,000 with an easy mortgage.

1900   Unhappy at whiteness of beard which he has worn since
            the Civil War, he shaves it off. Alternates between Rye
            and London. Works on *The Sacred Fount*. Works on and
            then sets aside *The Sense of the Past* (never finished). Be-
            gins *The Ambassadors*. *The Soft Side*, a collection of twelve
            tales, published. Niece Peggy comes to Lamb House for
            Christmas.

1901   Obtains permanent room at the Reform Club for London
            visits and spends eight weeks in town. Sees funeral of
            Queen Victoria. Decides to employ a typist, Mary Weld,
            to replace the more expensive overqualified shorthand ste-
            nographer, MacAlpine. Completes *The Ambassadors* and
            begins *The Wings of the Dove*. *The Sacred Fount* published.

Has meeting with George Gissing. William James, much improved, returns home after two years in Europe. Young Cambridge admirer Percy Lubbock visits. Discharges his alcoholic servants of sixteen years (the Smiths). Mrs. Paddington is new housekeeper.

1902   In London for the winter but gout and stomach disorder force him home earlier. Finishes *The Wings of the Dove* (published in August). William James Jr. (Billy) visits in October and becomes a favorite nephew. Writes "The Beast in the Jungle" and "The Birthplace."

1903   *The Ambassadors, The Better Sort* (a collection of eleven tales), and *William Wetmore Story and His Friends* published. After another spell in town, returns to Lamb House in May and begins work on *The Golden Bowl*. Meets and establishes close friendship with Dudley Jocelyn Persse, a nephew of Lady Gregory. First meeting with Edith Wharton in December.

1904–05 Completes *The Golden Bowl* (published Nov. 1904). Rents Lamb House for six months, and sails in August for America after twenty-year absence. Sees new Manhattan skyline from New Jersey on arrival and stays with Colonel George Harvey, president of Harper's, in Jersey shore house with Mark Twain as fellow guest. Goes to William's country house at Chocorua in the White Mountains, New Hampshire. Re-explores Cambridge, Boston, Salem, Newport, and Concord, where he visits brother Bob. In October stays with Edith Wharton in the Berkshires and motors with her through Massachusetts and New York. Later visits New York, Philadelphia (where he delivers lecture "The Lesson of Balzac"), and then Washington, D.C., as a guest in Henry Adams' house. Meets (and is critical of) President Theodore Roosevelt. Returns to Philadelphia to lecture at Bryn Mawr. Travels to Richmond, Charleston, Jacksonville, Palm Beach, and St. Augustine. Then lectures in St. Louis, Chicago, South Bend, Indianapolis, Los Angeles (with a short vacation at Coronado Beach near San Diego), San Francisco, Portland, and Seattle. Returns to explore New York City ("the terrible town"), May–June. Lectures on "The Question of Our Speech" at Bryn Mawr commencement. Elected to newly founded American Academy of Arts and Letters

(William declines). Returns to England in July; lectures had more than covered expenses of his trip. Begins revision of novels for the New York Edition.

1906–08   Writes "The Jolly Corner" and *The American Scene* (published 1907). Writes eighteen prefaces for the New York Edition (twenty-four volumes published 1907–09). Visits Paris and Edith Wharton in spring 1907 and motors with her in Midi. Travels to Italy for the last time, visiting Hendrik Andersen in Rome, and goes on to Florence and Venice. Engages Theodora Bosanquet as his typist in autumn. Again visits Edith Wharton in Paris, spring 1908. William comes to England to give a series of lectures at Oxford and receives an honorary Doctor of Science degree. James goes to Edinburgh in March to see a tryout by the Forbes-Robertsons of his play *The High Bid*, a rewrite in three acts of the one-act play originally written for Ellen Terry (revised earlier as the story "Covering End"). Play gets only five special matinees in London. Shocked by slim royalties from sales of the New York Edition.

1909   Growing acquaintance with young writers and artists of Bloomsbury, including Virginia and Vanessa Stephen and others. Meets and befriends young Hugh Walpole in February. Goes to Cambridge in June as guest of admiring dons and undergraduates and meets John Maynard Keynes. Feels unwell and sees doctors about what he believes may be heart trouble. They reassure him. Late in year burns forty years of his letters and papers at Rye. Suffers severe attacks of gout. *Italian Hours* published.

1910   Very ill in January ("food-loathing") and spends much time in bed. Nephew Harry comes to be with him in February. In March is examined by Sir William Osler, who finds nothing physically wrong. James begins to realize that he has had "a sort of nervous breakdown." William, in spite of now severe heart trouble, and his wife, Alice, come to England to give him support. Brothers and Alice go to Bad Nauheim for cure, then travel to Zurich, Lucerne, and Geneva, where they learn Robertson (Bob) James has died in America of heart attack. James's health begins to improve but William is failing. Sails with William and Alice for America in August. William dies at Chocorua soon after arrival, and James remains with the family for the winter. *The Finer Grain* and *The Outcry* published.

1911   Honorary degree from Harvard in spring. Visits with Howells and Grace Norton. Sails for England July 30. On return to Lamb House, decides he will be too lonely there and starts search for a London flat. Theodora Bosanquet obtains two work rooms adjoining her flat in Chelsea and he begins autobiography, *A Small Boy and Others*. Continues to reside at the Reform Club.

1912   Delivers "The Novel in *The Ring and the Book*," on the 100th anniversary of Browning's birth, to the Royal Society of Literature. Honorary Doctor of Letters from Oxford University June 26. Spends summer at Lamb House. Sees much of Edith Wharton ("the Firebird"), who spends summer in England. (She secretly arranges to have Scribner's put $8,000 into James's account.) Takes 21 Carlyle Mansions, in Cheyne Walk, Chelsea, as London quarters. Writes a long admiring letter for William Dean Howells' seventy-fifth birthday. Meets André Gide. Contracts bad case of shingles and is ill four months, much of the time not able to leave bed.

1913   Moves into Cheyne Walk flat. Two hundred and seventy friends and admirers subscribe for seventieth birthday portrait by Sargent and present also a silver-gilt Charles II porringer and dish ("golden bowl"). Sargent turns over his payment to young sculptor Derwent Wood, who does a bust of James. Autobiography *A Small Boy and Others* published. Goes with niece Peggy to Lamb House for the summer.

1914   *Notes of a Son and Brother* published. Works on "The Ivory Tower." Returns to Lamb House in July. Niece Peggy joins him. Horrified by the war ("this crash of our civilisation," "a nightmare from which there is no waking"). In London in September participates in Belgian Relief, visits wounded in St. Bartholomew's and other hospitals; feels less "finished and useless and doddering" and recalls Walt Whitman and his Civil War hospital visits. Accepts chairmanship of American Volunteer Motor Ambulance Corps in France. *Notes on Novelists* (essays on Balzac, Flaubert, Zola) published.

1915–16   Continues work with the wounded and war relief. Has
           occasional lunches with Prime Minister Asquith and fam-
           ily, and meets Winston Churchill and other war leaders.
           Discovers that he is considered an alien and has to report
           to police before going to coastal Rye. Decides to become
           a British national and asks Asquith to be one of his spon-
           sors. Receives Certificate of Naturalization on July 26.
           H. G. Wells satirizes him in *Boon* ("leviathan retrieving
           pebbles") and James, in the correspondence that follows,
           writes: "Art *makes* life, makes interest, makes importance."
           Burns more papers and photographs at Lamb House in
           autumn. Has a stroke December 2 in his flat, followed by
           another two days later. Develops pneumonia and during
           delirium gives his last confused dictation (dealing with the
           Napoleonic legend) to Theodora Bosanquet, who types it
           on the familiar typewriter. Mrs. William James arrives De-
           cember 13 to care for him. On New Year's Day, George V
           confers the Order of Merit. Dies February 28. Funeral ser-
           vices held at the Chelsea Old Church. The body is cre-
           mated and the ashes are buried in Cambridge Cemetery
           family plot.

Note on the Texts

This volume, one of five collecting the complete stories of Henry James, presents in the approximate chronological order of their composition 19 stories that were first published between 1874 and 1884. All of these stories were published in periodicals and, with three exceptions, were later collected, with revisions, in book form. During this period James published with different firms in England and America. The majority of stories in this volume appeared in book form in America first and then were further revised from the American book versions for English publication; in certain cases, James seems to have submitted the periodical versions of the stories to two separate processes of revision for English and American publication. James, living in England during most of this period, monitored and supervised the publication of the English versions of the stories more closely than the American versions. The English editions therefore contain James' latest revisions to the stories in the period immediately following their composition, and, except for the three stories not collected by James, the texts printed here are taken from their first English book editions.

The following list gives the first periodical, first American, and first English book publications of the stories printed in this volume. (James later included 10 of the stories in the 1907–9 New York Edition of his collected works: "Four Meetings," "Daisy Miller: A Study," "An International Episode," "The Pension Beaurepas," "A Bundle of Letters," "The Point of View," "The Siege of London," "Lady Barberina," "Pandora," and "The Author of 'Beltraffio.' ")

"Professor Fargo." *Galaxy*, August 1874. Never collected by James in his lifetime; the *Galaxy* text is printed here.

"Eugene Pickering." *Atlantic Monthly*, October–November 1874. Collected in *A Passionate Pilgrim and Other Tales* (Boston: James R. Osgood, 1875), and *Madonna of the Future and Other Tales* (2 vols. London: Macmillan, 1879).

"Benvolio." *Galaxy*, August 1875. Collected in *Madonna of the Future and Other Tales* (2 vols. London: Macmillan, 1879). No American book publication during James' lifetime.

"Crawford's Consistency." *Scribner's Monthly*, August 1876. Never collected by James in his lifetime; the *Scribner's Monthly* text is printed here.

"The Ghostly Rental." *Scribner's Monthly*, September 1876. Never collected by James in his lifetime; the *Scribner's Monthly* text is printed here.

"Four Meetings." *Scribner's Monthly*, November 1877. Collected in *Daisy Miller: A Study, An International Episode, Four Meetings* (London: Macmillan, 1879), and *The Author of Beltraffio* (Boston: James R. Osgood, 1885).

"Rose-Agathe." *Lippincott's Magazine*, May 1878, with the title "Theodolinde." No American book publication during James' lifetime. Collected in *Stories Revived*, Vol. 2. (London: Macmillan, 1885).

"Daisy Miller: A Study." *Cornhill Magazine*, June and July 1878. Published separately as *Daisy Miller* (New York: Harper and Brothers, 1879). Collected in *Daisy Miller: A Study, An International Episode, Four Meetings* (London: Macmillan, 1879).

"Longstaff's Marriage." *Scribner's Monthly*, August 1878. Collected in *Madonna of the Future and Other Tales.* (2 vols. London: Macmillan, 1879). No American book publication during James' lifetime.

"An International Episode." *Cornhill Magazine*, December 1878 and January 1879. Published separately as *An International Episode.* (New York: Harper and Brothers, 1879). Collected in *Daisy Miller: A Study, An International Episode, Four Meetings.* (2 vols. London: Macmillan, 1879).

"The Pension Beaurepas." *Atlantic Monthly*, April 1879. Collected in *Washington Square, The Pension Beaurepas, A Bundle of Letters* (2 vols. London: Macmillan, 1881), and in *The Siege of London, The Pension Beaurepas, and The Point of View* (Boston: J.R. Osgood, 1883.)

"The Diary of a Man of Fifty." *Harper's New Monthly Magazine* (New York), July 1879, and *Macmillan's Magazine* (London), July 1879. Collected in *Madonna of the Future and Other Tales* (2 vols. London: Macmillan, 1879), and in *The Diary of a Man of Fifty and A Bundle of Letters* (New York: Harper and Brothers, 1880).

"A Bundle of Letters." *Parisian*, December 18, 1879. Collected in *The Diary of a Man of Fifty and A Bundle of Letters* (New York: Harper and Brothers, 1880), and in *Washington Square, The Pension Beaurepas, A Bundle of Letters* (2 vols. London: Macmillan, 1881).

"The Point of View." *Century Magazine*, December 1882. Collected in *The Siege of London, The Pension Beaurepas, and The Point of View* (Boston: James R. Osgood, 1883), and in *An International Episode, The Pension Beaurepas, The Point of View* (London: Macmillan, 1883).

"The Siege of London." *Century Magazine*, January–February 1883. Collected in *The Siege of London, The Pension Beaurepas, and The Point of View* (Boston: James R. Osgood, 1883), and in *The Siege of London, Madame De Mauves.* (London: Macmillan, 1883).

NOTE ON THE TEXTS

"The Impressions of a Cousin." *Century Magazine*, November–December 1883. Collected in *Tales of Three Cities* (Boston: James R. Osgood, 1884); and in *Tales of Three Cities* (London: Macmillan, 1884).

"Lady Barberina." *Century Magazine*, May–July 1884. Collected in *Tales of Three Cities* (Boston: James R. Osgood, 1884), and in *Tales of Three Cities* (London: Macmillan, 1884).

"Pandora." *New York Sun*, June 1 and 8, 1884. Collected in *The Author of Beltraffio* (Boston: James R. Osgood, 1885), and in *Stories Revived*, Vol. 1 (London: Macmillan, 1885).

"The Author of 'Beltraffio.'" *English Illustrated Magazine* June–July 1884. Collected in *The Author of Beltraffio* (Boston: James R. Osgood, 1885), and in *Stories Revived*, Vol. 1 (London: Macmillan, 1885).

This volume presents the texts of the printings chosen for inclusion here but does not attempt to reproduce features of their typographic design. Spelling, punctuation, and capitalization often are expressive features, and they are not altered, even when inconsistent or irregular. The following is a list of typographical errors corrected, cited by page and line number: 10.25, admisson; 11.28, thump; 26.20, "Whatever; 45.20, than; 50.1, 'steep; 92.36, to night; 171.1, Had; 171.14 "I; 174.35, I will; 174.40, philosopher!'"; 178.21, agglommeration; 184.24, sparseness,; 189.8, Everything; 215.24, wont; 251.7, courier?; 272.29, one?; 298.2, aplication; 308.3, restaurant.; 368.27, we; 374.5, "poison'; 378.31, to.; 393.38, however!'; 424.36, 'That; 457.11, fellow,; 490.32, way; 493.28, have him; 497.29, *Barents*; 499.24, *donnor*; 502.7, yesday; 517.16, XI.; 530.39, *l Américaine*; 540.2, (the; 543.10, phrase; 576.9, changed.; 620.14–15 accompanied; 628.27, she; 651.20, Fifty; 680.30, we; 702.25, *July 10*; 704.25, *bontonnière*; 746.25, up to the; 747.25. conspicious; 752.21, his; 754.2, I; 758.32, Ah; 763.23, silence;; 766.12, "His.

Notes

In the notes below, the reference numbers denote page and line of this volume (the line count includes titles and headings). No note is made for material included in standard desk-reference books such as Webster's *Collegiate, Biographical,* and *Geographical* dictionaries. Quotations from Shakespeare are keyed to *The Riverside Shakespeare,* ed. G. Blakemore Evans (Boston: Houghton Mifflin, 1974). For further background than is provided in the notes, see *Henry James Letters,* ed. Leon Edel (Cambridge: The Bellknap Press of Harvard University Press, Vol. I—1843–1875 [1974]; Vol. II—1875–1883 [1975]; Vol III—1883–1895 [1980]; Vol. IV—1895–1916 [1984]) and *The Complete Notebooks of Henry James,* ed. Leon Edel and Lyall H. Powers (New York and Oxford: Oxford University Press, 1987).

2.34   *fioriture*]   Flourishes.

6.22   La Mancha]   Home province of Don Quixote.

11.15   Mignon]   In Goethe's novel *Wilhelm Meisters Lehrjahr* (1795–96), daughter (by his own sister) of a mysterious old harper, who besides being incestuous is a pyromaniac and suicidal.

15.14   *tendresse*]   Affection.

36.4   Kursaal]   Main building of a health spa.

38.15   a Bettina, a Rahel]   Bettina von Arnim (1785–1859), best known for her publication of a free adaptation of Goethe's letters; Varnhagen von Ense, neé Rahel Levin (1771–1833), a central figure of a literary salon in Berlin.

44.16   *laisser-aller*]   Indulgence, laxity.

48.9–10   copperplate hand]   Stylized calligraphy, as for etchings on copper.

50.38–39   Oberkellner]   Headwaiter; here, concierge.

54.37]   *Historisches Trauerspiel*]   Historical tragedy.

60.25   Gräfin]   Countess.

61.3–4   conversion of Lola Montez]   The story of Lola Montez's repentance for her notorious life and of her "conversion" to evangelical Episcopalian religion had been published in 1867 by the Reverend Francis Lister in *Lola Montez: The Story of a Penitent.*

931

68.17   *Revue des Deux Mondes*] Bi-monthly review of arts and politics founded in 1829 and widely read in the 1870's.

103.8   Milton's *Penseroso*] Pastoral lyric composed around 1631, celebrating sober contemplative pleasures in contrast with those described in the companion poem "L'Allegro."

108.1   *dame de compagnie*] Lady's companion.

129.25   *arrière pensée*] Ulterior motive.

130.28   *coup de foudre*] Bolt of lightning, thunderclap: i.e., love at first sight.

141.27–28   like the gentleman . . . behind them] Cf. Sir Peter Surface's speech in Sheridan's *The School for Scandal*, Act Two, Scene Two: "I leave my character behind me."

157.28–29   Overbeck and Ary Scheffer] J. F. Overbeck (1789–1869), German artist of the so-called "Nazarene" group in Rome that wished to return religious painting to the style of Raphael. Ary Scheffer (1795–1858), Dutch painter who worked in France and was known for his paintings of historical, biblical, and literary scenes.

173.6.   He toils not, neither does he spin] Cf. Matthew 6:28–29.

193.19–20   where Bonivard . . . was confined] François Bonnivard was imprisoned (1530–35) in the castle of Chillon for actions on behalf of Genevan independence from Savoy. Byron's poem, "The Prisoner of Chillon" (1816), made the castle a popular tourist destination.

198.23–24   *dame de comptoir*] Barmaid.

201.2   castle of St. Angelo] Monumental circular structure overlooking the Tiber in Rome, originally built as the Emperor Hadrian's tomb in A.D. 135.

202.39–40   J'adore la peinture!] I adore painting!

203.38   *Salle à Manger*] Dining room.

212.13   *quatrième*] Apartment on the fifth floor.

215.21   *La belle découverte!*] A beautiful discovery!

216.4–5   *Quelle existence!*] What a way to live!

216.31   *comme cela se fait*] As one does.

220.3   rez-de-chaussée] Ground floor.

222.17–18   warrior's widow . . . moved] Tennyson, *The Princess* (1847): "Home they brought her warrior dead. / She nor swoon'd, nor utter'd cry: / All her maidens, watching, said, / "She must weep or she will die."

222.29   *fausse natte*]   False hairpiece.

226.36   *étalage*]   Display window.

230.22   *Débats*]   *Le Journal des Débats*, founded in 1789 and revived in 1814 after the Napoleonic interval, offered liberal reportage of the actions of the National Assembly.

230.33   *tant mieux*]   So much the better.

231.18   *en prince*]   In princely style.

232.15   Je suis tout à ma passion]   I'm entirely taken up with my passion.

234.29   *pudique*]   Modest.

235.4   *parure*]   Set of jewels.

237.11   Vous n'êtes pas difficile]   You're easy.

238.26–27   Ocean House . . . Congress Hall]   Principal hotels at, respectively, Newport, Rhode Island, and Saratoga Springs, New York.

238.33   Castle of Chillon]   See note 193.19–20.

246.32   *inconduite*]   Loose behavior.

249.30   *tournure*]   Figure.

250.8   *rouleaux*]   Rolls.

251.23   *Tout bonnement!*]   Quite simply so!

262.36   Bonivard]   See note 193.19–20.

273.32   *amoroso*]   Boyfriend.

279.37   *Elle s'affiche*]   She shows herself off.

285.13   *cavaliere avvocato*]   Gentleman lawyer.

285.29   *qui se passe ses fantaisies!*]   Who allows herself fantasies!

286.31   *du meilleur monde*]   Of the best society.

290.33   Byron's . . . "Manfred;"]   Cf. Manfred, *A Dramatic Poem* (1817), III.iv.8–41.

291.38–39   *perniciosa*]   Malaria.

294.23   Protestant cemetery]   Burial place of non-Catholic foreigners where the body of Keats and the ashes of Shelley are interred.

296.21   statue . . . chase]   The statue known as the Diana of Ephesus, which was taken from Italy to France in the seventeenth century and has been displayed at the Louvre since 1802.

296.27–28   *démarche*]   Gait.

296.36   Ladies of Llangollen]   Lady Eleanor Butler and the Honorable Sarah Pousonby, eccentric disciples of Rousseau who lived on an estate at Plas Newydd in Wales.

297.33   *Corinne*]   *Corinne; or, Italy* (1807), novel by Mme. de Staël.

297.33   *Childe Harold*]   Byron's *Childe Harold's Pilgrimage* (1812–18).

299.15   "uglies"]   Shades attached to the front of ladies' bonnets.

308.33–34   *pauvre cher homme!*]   Poor dear man!

310.30   *campo santo*]   Holy ground; a cemetery.

326.25   Union Square . . . monument to Washington]   A heroic bronze equestrian statue by Henry Kirke Brown erected in 1856.

326.27   *pater patriæ*]   Father of his country.

337.15   mirrors *en pied*]   Standing mirrors.

341.3   *fête champêtre*]   Country feast, picnic.

344.36–37   said by a great wit]   The Bostonian Thomas Gold Appleton (1812–84) originated the remark that "good Americans, when they die, go to Paris." It was later quoted by Oliver Wendell Holmes in *The Autocrat of the Breakfast Table* (1858) and by Oscar Wilde in *Lady Windermere's Fan* (1892).

350.12   coast scenery in Kingsley's novels]   The novels of Charles Kingsley (1819–75) contain descriptions of the Cornwall and Devonshire coasts.

352.8   Mrs. Gore]   Mrs. Catherine Grace (Moody) Gore (1799–1861) published about seventy novels and plays.

354.40   *fonds*]   Base (with the financial suggestion of "funds").

357.40   beastly Avenue]   Belmont Avenue, the main drive in Newport.

364.8   *silence de mort*]   Silence of death.

370.11   Rotten Row]   Riding path in Hyde Park in central London.

370.33   *Punch*]   Weekly illustrated comic periodical founded in 1841.

371.8   *Quelle toilette!*]   What an outfit!

379.11   *Pour vous autres*]   For you others.

380.20   *bien-élevée*]   Well brought up.

397.17   *parti*]   Match.

398.15   *lâcher prise*]   Let go.

401.12–14   *La Chartreuse de Parme* . . . its author]   *La Chartreuse de Parma (The Charterhouse of Parma)*, 1839 novel by Stendhal.

401.15–16   *pension bourgeoise des deux sexes et autres*]   Bourgeois boarding-house for the two sexes and others.

402.7–8   J'en ai vus de toutes les couleurs]   I've seen all kinds.

402.19   Je trouve que c'est déplacé!]   I find it inappropriate!

402.28   *tout compris*]   Everything included.

402.31   *au sérieux*]   Very seriously.

404.12   *manquait d'agréments*]   Lacked attractions.

404.20–21   *cabinet de lecture*]   Reading room.

414.17   *tournure de princesse*]   Bearing of a princess.

414.22   *beaux yeux*]   Beautiful eyes.

414.23–24   Je vous recommande la mère]   I recommend the mother to you.

414.29   *fraîcheur*]   Freshness.

414.30   *dans l'intimité*]   In private.

414.34   Ne vous y fiez pas!]   Don't be so sure!

415.1   Vous dites cela d'un ton!]   You say that in quite a tone!

415.24   *par exemple*]   My word.

415.31   make me *des histoires*]   Give me some trouble.

415.32   *vous allez voir cela*]   Just wait and see.

415.36   *pour cela*]   For all that.

418.3   *Voyez*]   Look.

421.11   C'est mon rêve]   It's my dream.

421.38   *jeunesse*—my *belle jeunesse*]   Youth—my lovely youth.

421.40–422.1   Nous n'avons pas le sou]   We haven't got a penny.

422.25   Excusez du peu!]   Pardon how little it is!

424.28   *de fortes études*]   Studies of high quality.

426.33   vous m'en voulez?]   Do you hold it against me?

427.35   *tapis de lit*]   Bedcover.

428.6–7   Mon Dieu . . . fille]   My God, she's one of those mamas of yours who parade their daughters.

428.13   *mari sérieux*]   Important husband.

428.16   *gros bonnet*]   Bigwig.

428.28   *courir les champs*]   Run wild.

428.34   Allons donc!]   Come now!

429.2   *pour la partie*]   For the role.

429.14   *ville basse*]   Lower town.

434.23   la belle rencontre, nos aimables convives]   What a lovely meeting, our pleasant cohabitants.

435.21   *En morale*]   Morally speaking.

437.13   *Voyons*]   Let's see.

437.23   elle s'y perd]   She's at a loss.

437.23–24   je n'en suis pas folle]   I'm not crazy about her.

437.35   *maître de piano*]   Piano teacher.

438.7   *digne épouse*]   Worthy spouse.

438.27   *de leur pays*]   Of their country.

440.26   *Que voulez-vous?*]   What can I say?

442.14   *chaise à porteurs*]   Sedan chairs.

443.24–25   *éprouvée*]   Tested.

446.6   *nous fait la révérence*]   Is leaving us (bowing out).

446.17   *elle fait ses paquets*]   She is packing her bags.

449.31   Je crois que la race se perd]   I believe the breed is disappearing.

449.33   Ce sera une femme d'esprit]   She will become a spirited woman.

449.35   *potelée*]   Plump.

455.8–9   Madonna of the Chair]   *Madonna della Seggiola* by Raphael.

456.9   *Bionda*]   Fair.

456.19   *Sicuro*]   That's right.

462.26   *basta così*]   That's enough.

465.17   *lâcheté*]   Act of cowardice.

466.5   *che vuole?*]   What can you do?

467.1   *disinvoltura*]   Ease of manner, offhandedness.

467.16   *padrona*]   Mistress of the house.

470.22   Michael Angelo's chapel, at San Lorenzo]   The so-called "New Sacristy" at the church of San Lorenzo, designed as the Medici funerary chapel. Michelangelo's first architectural work, it was begun in 1520 and left unfinished.

470.26   *Altro!*]   Quite wrong!

472.32   *Bel tipo inglese*]   A beautiful English type.

479.30   'Instinct's everything,' as Falstaff says!]   Cf. *1 Henry IV*, IV.iv. 271–73.

484.1   *ci-devant*]   Ex-noble.

493.9   "Deserted Village"]   *The Deserted Village* (1770) by Oliver Goldsmith; line 205 is slightly misquoted: "For e'en though vanquished, he could argue still."

497.24   *graisseuse*]   Greasy.

504.18   *De l'an passé, vous voulez dire?*]   Of last year, do you mean?

509.32–33 *je t'en . . . mon gros Prosper*]   I told you too much of them, in the good old days, my dear Prosper.

509.36–37 *Nous en sommes nous flanqueés, des confidences*]   Did we ever pelt each other with secrets.

510.1   *poindre à l'horizon*]   Dawns on the horizon.

510.22–23 *en secondes noces*]   For the second time.

510.39   *lui a porté bonheur*]   Brought her happiness.

511.31–32 *elle ne demande qu'à se laisser aller!*]   She only asks to be allowed to let herself go!

512.2   *concurrentes*]   Competitors.

512.2–3   *Celles-ci . . . par exemple!*]   These . . . that's for sure!

512.10–11 *par exemple, elle brûle ses vaisseux, celle-la!*]   Well, well, she's burning her ships, that one!

512.19–20 *c'est une fille qui me dépasse*]   She's a girl who's beyond me.

512.23   *elle y met plus de façons*]   She puts on greater airs.

513.3   *rougeurs*]   Blushes.

513.7   *tour de monde*]   Tour of the world.

513.9–10   *à quoi s'en tenir sur les hommes et les choses*]   What's what about men and things.

513.10   *Dis donc*]   Look here.

513.11   *drôle de pays*]   Strange sort of country.

516.26–27 lower Empire]   Greek-influenced area of southern Italy and Sicily.

519.31   *bien entendu*]   Of course.

520.34   *cela m'est parfaitement égal*] It's all the same to me.

520.38   *en course*] On the go.

521.32   *mais au moins je serai belle!*] But at least I'll be beautiful!

523.26   *au fond*] Deep down.

524.14   *affreux*] Frightful.

525.17   *dans cette galère*] "In such surroundings," a usage derived from a line in Molière's play *Les Fourberies de Scapin* (1671) in which a father, hearing that his son has been kidnapped in a Turkish vessel, asks why he was *in that galley* in the first place.

525.18   *beau-frère*] Brother-in-law.

525.29   *aborder*] Approach.

527.4   *voyons un peu*] Let's take a peek at.

528.4   *rançonnée*] Fleeced.

528.12   *eau rougie*] Water mixed with red wine.

530.6   *dégingandé*] Gangling.

531.2   *cœur de mère*] A mother's heart.

531.5   *voiture de place*] Hackney carriage.

531.26   *délassement*] Relaxation.

531.35–36   *l'exactitude même*] Exactitude itself.

532.28   *état de fortune*] Comparisons.

534.40   Tauchnitz novels] A series of cheap reprints of works by British and American novelists issued in Leipzig, Germany, beginning in 1841.

538.8   *châtiée*] Purified, chaste.

538.11   *propos risqués*] Risque topics.

545.39   Pretender] After the deposition of the Stuarts from the throne of England in 1688, the "pretender" to the kingship was in exile on the Continent.

547.1   popular ballad] "Rock Me to Sleep," by Elizabeth Akers Allen (1860), begins: "Backward, turn backward, O Time, in your flight, / Make me a child again just for to-night!" The actual refrain is "Rock me to sleep, mother,—rock me to sleep!"

549.36–37   Puck . . . minutes] Cf. Shakespeare's *A Midsummer Night's Dream*, II.1.175–76.

552.9   *je regarde passer les femmes*] I watch the women pass by.

552.20   *commis-voyageur*] Traveling salesman.

552.24–25   *du moins on me l'assure*] At least that's what I'm assured.

552.30   *cadettes*] Younger ones.

553.8   *Aussi*] Also.

553.18–19   *mais ils ne se laissent pas lire*] But they are unreadable.

553.23   *vantés*] Celebrated.

553.24   *des plaisanteries de croque-mort*] Mortuary humor.

553.28–29   *C'est proprement écrit*] It's properly written.

553.31   *commérages*] Gossip.

553.37   *à pouffer de rire*] To make you burst out laughing.

553.38   *tripotage*] Underhanded actions.

554.1   *tout au long*] At full length.

554.4   *au beau milieu*] Right in the middle.

554.7   *je me renseigne*] I inform myself.

554.9   *à coups de poing*] With punches.

554.12   *signalement*] Description.

554.33   *comme toujours*] As always.

554.36   *assez grand air*] A rather grand air.

555.7   *"L'état c'est moi"*] "I am the state," claim attributed to Louis XIV of France.

555.16–17   *pourtant*] Even so.

557.10   *ouvreuse*] Usher.

561.1   *scrutin de liste*] Voting ballot.

563.28   *à tour de rôle*] In turn.

566.12   *doublures*] From the second cast.

579.23   *Le Demi-Monde*] Comedy by Alexandre Dumas *fils*, first performed in 1855.

583.35   *Figaro*] Parisian daily filled with society gossip and celebrated for its wit.

586.10   *mêler les genres*] Mix up the genres.

589.25   *Elle ne doute de rien!*] She has no doubts!

598.15   *Murray*] One of a series of popular travel-guides to the Continent published by John Murray in London beginning in 1820.

612.23   *billet d'auteur*]   Author's free pass.

636.27   a "squash"]   A party.

638.18   *à toute épreuve*]   That never fails.

651.23   *sentiers*]   Paths.

651.40   *villeggiatura*]   Vacationing in the country towns and villas.

655.4   *belle-mère*]   Mother-in-law.

658.40–659.1   "Haroun-al-Raschid"]   A Caliph of Baghdad (786–809) who is recalled by Tennyson in a lyric of Oriental fantasy, "Recollections of the Arabian Nights" (1830), as a ruler in a sensuously ideal time and place.

661.27–28   Yankee . . . Hilda]   In Hawthorne's romance *The Marble Faun* (1860), three expatriate artists in Rome get involved with an young Italian nobleman named Donatello, whom they identify with an antique marble statue of a faun. Miriam is a darkly mysterious woman adored by Donatello; Hilda is a woman of virginal purity from New England. "Almost complete" points to the absence of a counterpart to the book's fourth major character, Hilda's suitor, Kenyon.

662.12   Morris papers]   Referring to the highly colored and heavily patterned wallpaper designed by William Morris (1834–96), contrasting with the Mechlin lace from Belgium, the pattern of which is defined only by flat thread.

670.7   *fin mot*]   The key.

672.36   Je l'espère bien]   I hope so very much.

675.6   *fade*]   Insipid.

675.29–30   Seventh Regiment]   Known as the "silk stocking regiment," the Seventh had been organized in 1847 from earlier military groups; in 1879 it had opened a huge new armory on Park Avenue; lavish interior decorations had been unveiled in 1881.

676.34–35   *au fond*]   At bottom.

677.3   *en raccourci*]   In miniature.

694.16   *en règle*]   In line.

696.4   *du bon*]   Some good in her.

697.21–22   *de bien haut*]   Full force.

701.34   *endosser*]   Take on.

703.40   *parti*]   Someone of consequence.

718.10   *convenances*]   Proprieties.

721.11   *mauvais quart d'heure*]   A bad quarter of an hour.

735.4–5   purification of the Turf]   Horse-racing scandals of the time had even involved detectives of Scotland Yard.

771.13   Clarissa or Amelia]   Heroines of the novels *Clarissa Harlowe* (1747–48) by Samuel Richardson, and *Amelia* (1751) by Henry Fielding.

772.33   *prétendant*]   Suitor.

773.28   *gants de Suède*]   Suede gloves (Swedish leather).

787.37–38   *raconteuse*]   Female storyteller.

814.11   *coup de tête*]   Impulse.

827.20–21   Daisy Miller *en herbe*]   Referring to James' own character (see the novella in the present collection); *"en herbe"* means "unripe."

832.37   *tenue*]   Dress, manner.

839.23   conscript fathers]   Ancient Roman senators.

842.13   Spielhagen's]   Friedrich Spielhagen (1829–1911), German writer who wrote sixteen novels between 1857 and 1900.

843.3–4   *Werden*]   Becoming.

846.9   D'où tombez-vous?]   Wherever are you from?

854.30   far-gleaming pediment of Arlington]   The pediment of the Custis-Lee Mansion, built in 1802–18 in the Greek revival style on a bluff overlooking the Potomac in Arlington, Virginia.

866.39   *cet âge est sans pitié*]   That age is pitiless.

868.21   pre-Raphaelites]   A society of English painters founded in 1848 to revive the style of early Italian painting practiced before Raphael. Dante Gabriel Rosetti, mentioned below, was a major figure in the movement.

869.29   Dolcino]   Sweet little one.

875.3   *bornée*]   Narrow-minded.

877.25   apple of discord]   In Greco-Roman myth, the goddess Discord, not being invited to a wedding, tossed an apple labeled "For the Fairest" among the guests. Venus, Juno, and Minerva claimed it; the shepherd Paris awarded the apple to Venus, a decision that led indirectly to the Trojan War.

890.33   *bonnes gens*]   Good people.

898.34   Sir Joshua]   The painter Joshua Reynolds.

903.27   *Elle ne s'en doute que trop!*]   She's only too suspicious of it!

Library of Congress Cataloging-in-Publication Data

James, Henry, 1843–1916.
  [Short stories. Selections]
  Complete stories, 1874–1884 / Henry James.
    p. cm. — (Library of America ; 106)
  ISBN 1–883011–63–9
  I. Title. II. Series.
PS2112 1999b
813′.4—dc21   98–19252
                                      CIP

THE LIBRARY OF AMERICA SERIES

This book is set in 10 point Linotron Galliard,
a face designed for photocomposition by Matthew Carter
and based on the sixteenth-century face Granjon. The paper is
acid-free Ecusta Nyalite and meets the requirements for permanence
of the American National Standards Institute. The binding
material is Brillianta, a woven rayon cloth made by
Van Heek-Scholco Textielfabrieken, Holland.
The composition is by The Clarinda
Company. Printing and binding by
R.R.Donnelley & Sons Company.
Designed by Bruce Campbell.

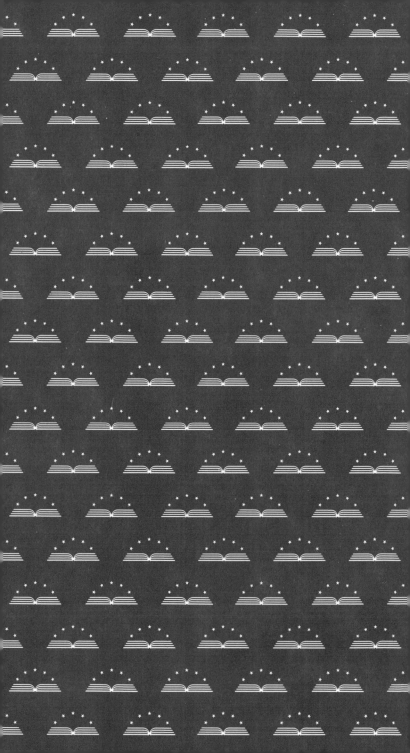